Social Stratification:
Class, Race, and Gender in Sociological Perspective

Social Stratification

Class, Race, and Gender in Sociological Perspective
2nd edition

edited by
David B. Grusky
Cornell University

Westview
PRESS

A Member of the Perseus Books Group

*For my parents and
in memory of my grandparents*

Copyright © 2001 by Westview Press, A Member of the Perseus Books Group

Published in 2001 in the United States of America by Westview Press, 5500 Central Avenue, Boulder, Colorado 80301-2877, and in the United Kingdom by Westview Press, 12 Hid's Copse Road, Cumnor Hill, Oxford OX2 9JJ

Find us on the World Wide Web at www.westviewpress.com

A CIP catalog in publication record is available for this title from the Library of Congress
ISBN-10 0-8133-6654-2
ISBN-13 978-0-8133-6654-8

The paper used in this publication meets the requirements of the American National Standard for Permanence of Paper for Printed Library Materials Z39.48–1984.

EBA   06   07   08   09   20   19   18   17   16   15   14   13   12   11   10   9   8   7

Contents

Part I   Introduction

Part II   Forms and Sources of Stratification

The Functions of Stratification

The Dysfunctions of Stratification

Concluding Commentary to Part Two

Part III   The Structure of Contemporary Stratification

Theories of Class

Marx and Post-Marxists

Weber and Post-Weberians

Part V   The Consequences of Stratification

Part VII   The Future of Stratification

Study Guide

This book is designed to be used in conjunction with study materials that are available at http://www.inequality.com. In the various pages of this site, readers will not only find materials that are explicitly devised for readers of *Social Stratification* (e.g., study questions, supplementary readings), but also a wealth of additional information more broadly relevant to issues of inequality and poverty. This site further reports on ongoing activities of the Center for the Study of Inequality at Cornell University and provides links to related centers as well. The materials provided in this site will of course be frequently revised to reflect changes in the field as well as reactions to the book by professors, students, and other readers.

In using this book, some professors may prefer to treat it as a stand-alone text, whereas others may instead treat it as a source of supplementary readings that are assigned in conjunction with other texts. Although most of the chapters are reprints of past and present classics in the field, many are newly commissioned pieces that provide students with the conceptual background and introductory commentary that a stand-alone text requires. The lead chapter was formulated with this didactic objective explicitly in mind, while the concluding chapters for each of the six substantive parts of the book provide further commentary on the main subfields of stratification research and the analytic orientations underlying them. In all cases, the contributing authors were permitted to write with their own "voice," and the present book thus departs from conventional texts that seek to represent fields of research in (putatively) objective or balanced fashion.

In assembling this text, every effort was made to select articles that were both path-breaking *and* readable, yet on occasion it proved necessary to compromise on one of these two objectives. The following chapters, in particular, rest on concepts or methods that might be challenging to some undergraduate students:

Karl Marx, "Alienation and Social Classes"
Edward Shils, "Deference"
David L. Featherman & Robert M. Hauser, "A Refined Model of Occupational Mobility"
David B. Grusky & Robert M. Hauser, "Comparative Mobility Revisited: Models of Convergence and Divergence in 16 Countries"
Richard Breen & John H. Goldthorpe, "Explaining Educational Differentials: Towards a Formal Rational Action Theory"
John Allen Logan, "Rational Choice and the TSL Model of Occupational Opportunity"
Charles Hirschman & C. Matthew Snipp, "The State of the American Dream: Race and Ethnic Socioeconomic Inequality in the United States, 1970–1990"
David B. Grusky & Maria Charles, "Is There a Worldwide Sex Segregation Regime?"
Margaret Mooney Marini & Pi-Ling Fan, "The Gender Gap in Earnings at Career Entry"
Barbara Stanek Kilbourne, Paula England, George Farkas, Kurt Beron, & Dorothea Weir, "Returns to Skill, Compensating Differentials, and Gender Bias: Effects of Occupational Characteristics on the Wages of White Women and Men"

Although the foregoing chapters present materials that should be mastered by all advanced students (both graduates and undergraduates), they can be safely excised for the purposes of a purely introductory course. The remaining readings were selected so as to ensure that introductory students will still be acquainted with the most important concepts, findings, and debates in the field.

D.B.G.

Preface and Acknowledgments

The standard rationale for publishing an anthology is that new concepts, theories, and findings have been accumulating so rapidly that some sort of organizing or synthesizing effort is needed. Indeed, given the frequency with which rhetoric of this kind appears in the prefaces of anthologies, the skeptical consumer of sociology might reasonably ask whether such a wide array of subfields and specialties can possibly be flourishing at once. In this context, there is something to be said for passing over the usual partisan rhetoric and providing, as much as possible, a more dispassionate reading of the current standing of stratification research. If, for example, one uses publication rates as an arbiter of disciplinary standing, the available evidence suggests that the position of stratification research has remained quite stable in recent decades (almost eerily so), with issues of inequality and mobility playing a featured role in roughly 25 percent of all articles published in major sociology journals since the 1960s (see Figure 1 in Mary Diane Burton and David B. Grusky, 1992, "A Quantitative History of Comparative Stratification Research," *Contemporary Sociology* 21, pp. 623–631). The appropriate conclusion is not that some sort of "take-off period" is still underway, but rather that stratification research is firmly institutionalized and has successfully consolidated its standing as one of the dominant approaches within sociology.

In the six years following the publication of the first edition of *Social Stratification*, the field has made substantial progress on a number of fronts, perhaps most obviously in the areas of race, ethnicity, and gender. Although it may be unfashionable to represent intellectual change as "progress," in the present case this characterization may have some merit, at least in the naive sense that much new evidence has accumulated and many old theories and hypotheses have been supplanted. This rapid change has made it necessary to revise the first edition substantially. To be sure, virtually all of the so-called classics appearing in the first edition were retained, but a great many contemporary pieces were replaced with yet newer selections that provided important extensions, revisions, and even rebuttals of prior research. The second edition is therefore half-new; that is, of the 95 selections appearing in the second edition, 36 are fresh additions that cannot be found in the first edition, while another 10 are revised versions of pieces that appeared in the first edition. These new selections address issues such as the functions of postmodern inequality (Part II); the class structure of post-communist societies (Part III); the usefulness of neo-Marxian and post-Marxian concepts of exploitation (Part III); the rationale for abandoning or overhauling conventional socioeconomic scales of inequality (Part III); the effects of social capital and networks on finding jobs and "getting ahead" (Part IV); the amount of persistent poverty in advanced industrialism and the plausibility of the "welfare trap" hypothesis (Part IV); the viability of rational action and related choice-based models of mobility and attainment (Part IV); the alleged decoupling of individual attitudes, behaviors, and lifestyles from objective class situations (Part V); the structure of recent trends in racial and ethnic inequality (Part VI); the life chances of second-generation immigrants who either assimilate or remain ensconced in their ethnic enclaves (Part VI); the contribution of spatial segregation to maintaining racial inequality (Part VI); the rise of a dual racial hierarchy in which the black–nonblack distinction intensifies even as inequality among nonblacks lessens (Part VI); the extent to which occupational segregation can explain the gender gap in wages (Part VI); the empirical case for policies of "comparable worth" that seek to eliminate wage discrimination against female-dominated occupations (Part VI); the sources and causes of recent increases in income inequality (Part VII); and the likely future of social inequality and mobility under postindustrialism or postmodernity (Part VII).

As this listing suggests, the research literature has become so large and complex that the task of reducing it to manageable form poses difficulties of all kinds, not the least of which is simply defining defensible boundaries for a field that at times seems indistinguishable from sociology at large. In carrying out this task, it was clearly useful to start off with some "priors" about the subfields and types of contributions that should be featured, yet much of the organizational structure of the first and second editions emerged more gradually in the course of sifting through the literature. As a result, one might view the prefatory comments that follow as a dissonance reduction exercise in which the goal is to infer, after the fact, the larger logic that presumably guided the project. The six organizing principles listed below should be interpreted accordingly:

1. In assembling this collection, the first and foremost objective was to represent the diversity of research traditions on offer, while at the same time giving precedence to those traditions that have so far borne the greatest fruit. As is often the case, the pool of disciplinary knowledge has developed in uneven and ramshackle fashion, so much so that any attempt to cover all subjects equally would grossly misrepresent the current strengths and weaknesses of contemporary stratification research.

2. This sensitivity to disciplinary fashion reveals itself, for example, in the relatively large number of selections addressing and discussing issues of race, ethnicity, and gender. These subfields rose to prominence in the 1970s and continue to be popular even after a quarter-century of intensive and productive research. If the concepts of class, status, and power formed the "holy trinity" of postwar stratification theorizing, then the (partly overlapping) concepts of class, race, and gender are playing analogous roles now.

3. The second disciplinary development of interest is the emergence of stratification analysis as the preferred forum for introducing and marketing new methods. Although the study of stratification has become increasingly technical in method, most of the articles selected for this anthology are nonetheless accessible to introductory sociology students and other novices who are committed to careful study and dissection of the texts (see the Study Guide for details).

4. The readers of this volume will thus be disproportionately exposed to contemporary approaches to analyzing stratification systems. However, given that most stratification research has a strongly cumulative character, there is didactic value in incorporating earlier sociological classics as well as some of the "near-classics" that were written well after the foundational contributions of Karl Marx or Max Weber. The latter body of intervening work is often ignored by editors of anthologies, thereby perpetuating (in some small way) the view that all sociological research can or should be stamped with an exclusively Marxian or Weberian imprimatur.

5. In most anthologies, the classics so chosen make the research literature appear more coherent and cumulative than it truly is, as the natural tendency is to emphasize those aspects of the sociological past that seem to best anticipate or motivate current disciplinary interests. The novice reader may be left, then, with the impression that all past sociological work leads directly and inevitably to current disciplinary interests. This form of academic teleology will likely always be popular, yet in the present case some innoculation against it was secured by commissioning a series of concluding essays that locate the selections within a broader historical and substantive context.

6. The final, and most difficult, task faced by editors of anthologies is to chart an optimal course between the Scylla of overly aggressive excerpting and the Charybdis of excessive editorial timidity. By the usual stan-

dards of anthologies, the course charted here was very much an average one, as the objective was to eliminate all inessential material while still preserving the analytic integrity of the contributions. To be sure, some of our readers and contributors would no doubt oppose *all* excerpting, yet the high cost of implementing such a radical stance would be a substantial reduction in the number of articles that could be reproduced.

The editing rules adopted throughout this anthology were in most cases conventional. For example, brackets were used to mark off a passage that was inserted for the purpose of clarifying meaning, whereas ellipses were used whenever a passage appearing in the original contribution was excised altogether. The latter convention was violated, however, if the excised text was merely a footnote or a minor reference to a table or passage (e.g., "see table 1") that was itself excerpted out. When necessary, tables and footnotes were renumbered without so indicating in the text, and all articles that were cited in excised passages were likewise omitted, without indication, from the list of references appearing at the end of each chapter. The spelling, grammar, and stylistic conventions of the original contributions were otherwise preserved. In this respect, the reader should be forewarned that some of the terms appearing in the original contributions would now be regarded as inappropriate (e.g., "Negro"), whereas others have passed out of common usage and will possibly be unfamiliar. Although a strong argument could clearly be made for eliminating all language that is no longer acceptable, this type of sanitizing would not only exceed usual editorial license but would also generate a final text that contained inconsistent, and possibly confusing, temporal cues. At the end of the book, a special section can be found that details the more controversial editing decisions that in some circumstances had to be made, such as omitting tables, resequencing paragraphs, and smoothing out transitional prose between adjacent sections

(see "Supplementary Information on Sources and Excerpting").

The truism that scholarly research is a collective enterprise probably holds for this book more so than others. Among the various functions that an anthology fills, one of more obvious ones is to define and celebrate what a field has achieved, and in so doing to pay tribute to those who made such achievement possible. I am duly grateful, therefore, to the dozens of scholars who allowed their work to be reproduced for this anthology or who agreed to write one of the commissioned essays that glue the various sections of it together. This book provides a well-deserved occasion to recognize the many successes of a field that is perhaps better known for its contentiousness and controversy.

The task of fashioning a book out of such a large and diverse field rested, in large part, on the careful labor of dedicated graduate research assistants. In assembling the first edition, I relied extensively on Karen Aschaffenburg and Ivan K. Fukumoto to locate and review hundreds of possible selections, while Mariko Lin Chang provided invaluable help in constructing the subject index and proofing the galleys. The same functions were filled admirably by Matthew Di Carlo, Gabriela Galescu, and Devah Pager in assembling the second edition. I have also profited from the advice and suggestions of the following scholars: James N. Baron, Monica Boyd, Mary C. Brinton, Mary Diane Burton, Phillip A. Butcher, Maria Charles, Paul J. DiMaggio, Thomas A. DiPrete, Mitchell Duneier, Paula England, Mariah Evans, John H. Goldthorpe, Oscar Grusky, Robert M. Hauser, Jerald R. Herting, Leonard J. Hochberg, Michael Hout, Jonathan Kelley, Harold R. Kerbo, Gerhard E. Lenski, Robert D. Mare, John W. Meyer, Martina Morris, Victor Nee, Trond Petersen, Barbara F. Reskin, Manuela Romero, Rachel A. Rosenfeld, Aage B. Sørensen, Jesper B. Sørensen, Eve B. Spangler, Kenneth I. Spenner, Iván Szelényi, Marta Tienda, Nancy B. Tuma, Kim A. Weeden, Raymond S. Wong, and Morris Zelditch Jr. The seven anonymous reviewers of the first edition also provided constructive criticisms that were most helpful in assembling the second edition. If this book proves to be at all useful, it is in large part because my friends and colleagues guided me in fruitful directions.

The selections reproduced here have all been pre-tested in graduate and undergraduate stratification classes at the University of Chicago, Stanford University, and Cornell University. I am indebted to the many students in these classes who shared their reactions to the selections and thereby shaped the final product more than they may appreciate or realize. The students attending my first stratification class at Cornell University require special mention in this regard, as they were unusually dedicated in commenting on the selections appearing in the first edition and suggesting useful revisions and excisions.

The funding for this project came from the usual assortment of public and private sources. The first draft of my introductory essay was completed while I was on fellowship leave funded by the National Science Foundation through the Center for Advanced Study in the Behavioral Sciences (NSF BNS–8700864). The honoraria for some of the commissioned essays were paid from Stanford University and Cornell University research funds, while the monies for research assistance were provided by the Presidential Young Investigator Program of the National Science Foundation (NSF SES–8858467), the Stanford Center for the Study of Families, Children, and Youth, and my Stanford University and Cornell University research funds. Although I am most grateful for the monies that these organizations so generously provided, they are of course in no way responsible for the views and opinions expressed herein.

It is fitting to conclude by singling out those contributions that make the concept of altruism seem all the more necessary. I would like to give special thanks to Stanley Lieberson for his active assistance in assembling selections for the second edition and to Andrew Day, Thomas Kulesa, Michelle Mallin, David McBride, Adina Popescu, and Leo Wiegman of Westview Press for their advice and support throughout the ordeal that publishing a book inevitably becomes. At the latter stages of the production process, Jennifer Ballentine dealt with impossible deadlines with improbable calm, and Jill Rothenberg of Westview Press was likewise a steadying influence whose wise counsel averted many potential disasters. I am most appreciative, finally, of the grace with which Szonja Szelényi shouldered the triple burden of being a wife and mother, an academic, and an in-house scholarly advisor to her husband. This book bears her imprint in innumerable ways.

D.B.G.

Part I
Introduction

DAVID B. GRUSKY

The Past, Present, and Future
of Social Inequality

In advanced industrial societies, much rhetoric and social policy have been directed against economic and social inequality, yet despite such efforts the brute facts of poverty and massive inequality are still everywhere with us. The human condition has so far been a fundamentally unequal one; indeed, all known societies have been characterized by inequalities of some kind, with the most privileged individuals or families enjoying a disproportionate share of power, prestige, and other valued resources. The task of contemporary stratification research is to describe the contours and distribution of inequality and to explain its persistence despite modern egalitarian or anti-stratification values.

The term *stratification system* refers to the complex of social institutions that generate observed inequalities of this sort. The key components of such systems are (1) the institutional processes that define certain types of goods as valuable and desirable, (2) the rules of allocation that distribute these goods across various positions or occupations in the division of labor (e.g., doctor, farmer, "housewife"), and (3) the mobility mechanisms that link individuals to occupations and thereby generate unequal control over valued resources. It follows that inequality is produced by two types of matching processes: The social roles in society are first matched to "reward packages" of unequal value, and individual members of society are then allocated to the positions so defined and rewarded.[1] In all societies, there is a constant flux of occupational incumbents as newcomers enter the labor force and replace dying, retiring, or out-

migrating workers, yet the positions themselves and the reward packages attached to them typically change only gradually. As Schumpeter (1953, 171) puts it, the occupational structure can be seen as "a hotel . . . which is always occupied, but always by different persons."

The contents of these reward packages may well differ across modern societies, but the range of variability appears not to be great. We have listed in Table 1 the various goods and assets that have been socially valued in past or present societies (for related listings, see Kerbo 2000, 43–44; Rothman 1999, 2–4; Gilbert 1998, 11–14; Duncan 1968, 686–90; Runciman 1968; Svalastoga 1965, 70).[2] In constructing this table, we have followed the usual objective of including all those goods that are valuable in their own right (i.e., consumption goods) while excluding any "second-order goods" (i.e., investments) that are deemed valuable only insofar as they provide access to other intrinsically desirable goods. The resulting list nonetheless includes resources and assets that serve some investment functions. For example, most economists regard schooling as an investment that generates future streams of income (see Becker 1975), and some sociologists likewise regard cultural resources (e.g., Bourdieu 1977) or social networks (e.g., Coleman 1990) as forms of capital that can be parlayed into educational credentials and other goods.[3] Although most of the assets listed in Table 1 are clearly convertible in this fashion, they are not necessarily regarded as investments by the individuals involved. In fact, many valuable

TABLE 1
Types of Assets, Resources, and Valued Goods Underlying Stratification Systems

Asset Group	Selected Examples	Relevant Scholars
1. Economic	Ownership of land, farms, factories, professional practices, businesses, liquid assets, humans (i.e., slaves), labor power (e.g., serfs)	Karl Marx; Erik Wright
2. Political	Household authority (e.g., head of household); workplace authority (e.g., manager); party and societal authority (e.g., legislator); charismatic leader	Max Weber; Ralf Dahrendorf
3. Cultural	High-status consumption practices; "good manners"; privileged lifestyle	Pierre Bourdieu; Paul DiMaggio
4. Social	Access to high-status social networks, social ties, associations and clubs, union memberships	W. Lloyd Warner; James Coleman
5. Honorific	Prestige; "good reputation"; fame; deference and derogation; ethnic and religious purity	Edward Shils; Donald Treiman
6. Civil	Rights of property, contract, franchise, and membership in elective assemblies; freedom of association and speech	T. H. Marshall; Rogers Brubaker
7. Human	Skills; expertise; on-the-job training; experience; formal education; knowledge	Kaare Svalastoga; Gary Becker

assets can be secured at birth or through childhood socialization (e.g., the "good manners" of the aristocracy), and they are therefore acquired without the beneficiaries explicitly weighing the costs of acquisition against the benefits of future returns.[4]

The implicit claim underlying Table 1 is that the listed assets exhaust all possible consumption goods and, as such, constitute the raw materials of stratification systems. Given the complexity of modern reward systems, one might expect stratification scholars to adopt a multidimensional approach, with the objective being to describe and explain the *multivariate distribution* of goods. Although some scholars have indeed advocated a multidimensional approach of this sort (e.g., Halaby and Weakliem 1993; Landecker 1981), most have instead opted to characterize stratification systems in terms of discrete classes or strata whose members are endowed with similar levels or types of assets. In the most extreme versions of this approach, the resulting classes are assumed to be real entities that pre-exist the distribution of assets, and many

scholars therefore refer to the "effects" of class location on the assets that their incumbents control (see the following section for details).

The goal of stratification research has thus been reduced to describing the structure of these social classes and specifying the processes by which they are generated and maintained. The following types of questions are central to the field:

- *Forms and sources of stratification:* What are the major forms of inequality in human history? Can the ubiquity of inequality be attributed to individual differences in talent or ability? Is some form of inequality an inevitable feature of human life?
- *The structure of contemporary stratification:* What are the principal "fault lines" or social cleavages that define the contemporary class structure? Have these cleavages strengthened or weakened with the transition to modernity and postmodernity?

- *Generating stratification:* How frequently do individuals move into new classes, occupations, or income groups? Is there a permanent "underclass?" To what extent are occupational outcomes determined by such forces as intelligence, effort, schooling, aspirations, social contacts, and individual luck?

- *The consequences of stratification:* How are the lifestyles, attitudes, and behaviors of individuals shaped by their class locations? Are there identifiable "class cultures" in past and present societies?

- *Ascriptive processes:* What types of social processes and state policies serve to maintain or alter racial, ethnic, and sex discrimination in labor markets? Have these forms of discrimination weakened or strengthened with the transition to modernity and postmodernity?

- *The future of stratification:* Will stratification systems take on completely new and distinctive forms in the future? How unequal will these systems be? Is the concept of social class still useful in describing postmodern forms of stratification? Are stratification systems gradually shedding their distinctive features and converging toward some common (i.e., "postmodern") regime?

The foregoing questions all adopt a critical orientation to human stratification systems that is distinctively modern in its underpinnings. For the greater part of human history, the existing stratification order was regarded as an immutable feature of society, and the implicit objective of commentators was to explain or justify this order in terms of religious or quasi-religious doctrines (see Bottomore 1965; Tawney 1931). It was only with the Enlightenment that a critical "rhetoric of equality" emerged in opposition to the civil and legal advantages of the aristocracy and other privileged status groupings. After these advantages were largely eliminated in the eighteenth and nineteenth centuries, the same egalitarian ideal was extended and recast to encompass not merely civil assets (e.g., voting rights) but also economic assets in the form of land, property, and the means of production. In its most radical form, this economic egalitarianism led to Marxist interpretations of human history, and it ultimately provided the intellectual underpinnings for socialist stratification systems. Although much of stratification theory has been formulated in reaction and opposition to these early forms of Marxist scholarship,[5] the field nonetheless shares with Marxism a distinctively modern (i.e., Enlightenment) orientation based on the premise that individuals are "ultimately morally equal" (see Meyer 2001; see also Tawney 1931). This premise implies that issues of inequality are critical in evaluating the legitimacy of stratification systems.

The purpose of the present volume is to acquaint readers with some of these modern theories and analyses. As has frequently been noted (e.g., Grusky and Takata 1992), the field of stratification covers an exceedingly diverse terrain, and we shall therefore delimit our review by first defining some core stratification concepts and then focusing on the six classes of empirical questions previously identified. The readings presented after this introductory essay are likewise organized around the same set of empirical questions.

Basic Concepts and Simplifying Strategies

The stratification literature has developed its own vocabulary to describe the distribution of assets, goods, and resources listed in Table 1. The key concepts of this literature can be defined as follows:

1. The degree of *inequality* in a given reward or asset depends, of course, on its dispersion or concentration across the individuals in the population. Although many scholars seek to characterize the overall level of societal inequality with a single parameter, such attempts will obviously be compromised insofar as some types of rewards are distributed more

equally than others. This complexity clearly arises in the case of modern stratification systems; for example, the recent emergence of "citizenship rights" implies that civil goods are now widely dispersed across all citizens, whereas economic and political goods continue to be disproportionately controlled by a relatively small elite (see, e.g., Marshall 1981).

2. The *rigidity* of a stratification system is indexed by the continuity (over time) in the social standing of its members. The stratification system is said to be highly rigid, for example, if the current wealth, power, or prestige of individuals can be accurately predicted on the basis of their prior statuses or those of their parents. It should again be emphasized that the amount of rigidity (or "social closure") in any given society will typically vary across the different types of resources and assets listed in Table 1.

3. The stratification system rests on *ascriptive processes* to the extent that traits present at birth (e.g., sex, race, ethnicity, parental wealth, nationality) influence the subsequent social standing of individuals. If ascriptive processes of this sort are in operation, it is possible (but by no means guaranteed) that the underlying traits themselves will become bases for group formation and collective action (e.g., race riots, feminist movements). In modern societies, ascription of all kinds is usually seen as undesirable or discriminatory, and much governmental policy is therefore directed toward fashioning a stratification system in which individuals acquire resources solely by virtue of their achievements.[6]

4. The degree of *status crystallization* is indexed by the correlations among the assets in Table 1. If these correlations are strong, the same individuals (i.e., the "upper class") will consistently appear at the top of all status hierarchies, while other individuals (i.e., the "lower

class") will consistently appear at the bottom of the stratification system. By contrast, various types of status inconsistencies (e.g., a poorly educated millionaire) will emerge in stratification systems with weakly correlated hierarchies, and it is correspondingly difficult in such systems to define a unitary set of classes that have predictive power with respect to all resources.

The foregoing discussion suggests, then, that stratification systems are complex and multidimensional. However, many scholars are quick to argue that this complexity is mere "surface appearance," with the implication being that stratification systems can in fact be adequately understood with a smaller and simpler set of principles. We shall proceed by reviewing three simplifying assumptions that have proved to be especially popular.

Reductionism

The prevailing approach is to claim that only one of the "asset groups" in Table 1 is truly fundamental in understanding the structure, sources, or evolution of societal stratification.[7] There are nearly as many claims of this sort as there are dimensions in Table 1. To be sure, Marx is most commonly criticized (with some justification) for placing "almost exclusive emphasis on economic factors as determinants of social class" (Lipset 1968, 300), but in fact much of what passes for stratification theorizing amounts to reductionism of one form or another. Among non-Marxist scholars, inequalities in honor or power are frequently regarded as the most fundamental sources of class formation, whereas the distribution of economic assets is seen as purely secondary (or "epiphenomenal"). For example, Dahrendorf (1959, 172) argues that "differential authority in associations is the ultimate 'cause' of the formation of conflict groups" (see also Lenski 1966), and Shils (1968, 130) suggests that "without the intervention of considerations of deference position the . . . inequalities in the distribution of any particular facility or reward would not be grouped into a relatively small number of vaguely bounded strata." These extreme forms of reductionism have been less popular of late; indeed, even neo-Marxian scholars now typically recognize several stratification dimensions, with the social classes of interest then being defined as particular combinations of scores on the selected variables (e.g., Wright 1997; see also Bourdieu 1984). The contributions in Part III of this volume were selected, in part, to acquaint readers with these various claims and the arguments on which they are based.

Synthesizing Approaches

There is an equally long tradition of research based on synthetic measures that simultaneously tap a wide range of assets and resources. As noted above, many of the rewards in Table 1 (e.g., income) are principally allocated through the jobs or social roles that individuals occupy, and one can therefore measure the standing of individuals by classifying them in terms of their social positions. In this context, Parkin (1971, 18) has referred to the occupational structure as the "backbone of the entire reward system of modern Western society," and Hauser and Featherman (1977, 4) argue that studies "framed in terms of occupational mobility . . . yield information simultaneously (albeit, indirectly) on status power, economic power, and political power" (see also Duncan 1968, 689–90; Parsons 1954, 326–29). The most recent representatives of this position, Grusky and Sørensen (1998), have argued that detailed occupations are not only the main conduits through which valued goods are disbursed but are also deeply institutionalized categories that are salient to workers, constitute meaningful social communities and reference groups, and provide enduring bases of collective action (see also Grusky and Sørensen 2001). Although occupations continue, then, to be the preferred measure within this tradition, other scholars have pursued the same synthesizing objective by simply asking community members to locate their peers in a hierarchy of social classes (e.g., Warner 1949). Under the latter approach, a synthetic classification is no longer secured by ranking and sorting occupations in terms of the bundles of rewards attached to them, but rather by passing the raw data of inequality through the fulcrum of individual judgment.[8]

Classification Exercises

Regardless of whether a reductionist or synthesizing approach is taken, most scholars adopt the final simplifying step of defining a relatively small number of discrete classes.[9] For example, Parkin (1971, 25) argues for six occupational classes with the principal "cleavage falling between the manual and non-manual categories," whereas Dahrendorf (1959, 170) argues for a two-class solution with a "clear line drawn between those who participate in the exercise [of authority] . . . and those who are subject to the authoritative commands of others."[10] Although close variants of the Parkin scheme continue to be used, the emerging convention among quantitative stratification scholars is to apply either the 12-category neo-Marxian scheme fashioned by Wright (1997; 1989; 1985) or the 11-category neo-Weberian scheme devised by Erikson and Goldthorpe (2001; 1992). At the same time, new classification schemes continue to be regularly proposed, with the impetus for such efforts typically being the continuing expansion of the service sector (e.g., Esping-Andersen 1999; 1993) or the associated growth of contingent work relations (e.g., Perrucci and Wysong 1999). The question that necessarily arises for all contemporary schemes is whether the constituent categories are purely nominal entities or are truly meaningful to the individuals involved. If the categories are intended to be meaningful, one would expect class members not only to be aware of their membership (i.e., "class awareness") but also to identify with their class (i.e., "class identification") and occasionally act on its behalf (i.e., "class action").[11] There is no shortage of debate about the conditions under which classes of this (real) sort are generated.

The simplifying devices listed here are discussed in greater detail in our review of contemporary models of class and status groupings (see "The Structure of Modern Stratification"). However, rather than turning directly to the analysis of contemporary systems, we first set the stage by outlining a highly stylized and compressed history of the stratification forms that appear in premodern, modern, and postmodern periods.

Forms of Stratification

The starting point for any comparative analysis of social inequality is the purely descriptive task of classifying various types of stratification systems. The staple of modern classification efforts has been the tripartite distinction among class, caste, and estate (e.g., Tumin 1985; Svalastoga 1965), but there is also a long and illustrious tradition of Marxian typological work that introduces the additional categories of primitive communism, slave society, and socialism (see Wright 1985; Marx [1939] 1971). As shown in Table 2, these conventional approaches are largely (but not entirely) complementary, and it is therefore possible to fashion a hybrid classification that incorporates most of the standard distinctions (for related work, see Kerbo 2000; Rossides 1996; Runciman 1974).

The typology presented here relies heavily on some of the simplifying devices discussed earlier. For each of the stratification forms listed in Table 2, we have assumed not only that certain types of assets tend to emerge as the dominant stratifying forces (see column 2), but also that the asset groups so identified constitute the major axis around which social classes or status groupings are organized (see column 3). If the latter assumptions hold, the rigidity of stratification systems can be indexed by the amount of class persistence (see column 5), and the degree of crystallization can be indexed by the correlation between class membership and each of the assets listed in Table 1 (see column 6).[12] The final column in Table 2 rests on the further assumption that stratification systems have (reasonably) coherent ideologies that legitimate the rules and criteria by which individuals are allocated to positions in the class structure (see column 7). In most cases, ideologies of this kind are largely conservative in their effects, but they can sometimes serve as forces for change as well as stability. For example, if the facts of labor market processes are inconsistent with the prevailing ideology (e.g., racial discrimination in advanced industrial societies), then various sorts of ameliorative action might be anticipated (e.g., affirmative action programs).

The stratification forms represented in Table 2 should thus be seen as ideal types rather than as viable descriptions of real systems existing in the past or present. In constructing these categories, our intention is not to make empirical claims about how existing systems operate in practice, but rather to capture (and distill) the accumulated wisdom about how these systems might operate in their purest form. These ideal-typical models can nonetheless assist us in understanding empirical systems. Indeed, insofar as societies evolve through the gradual "overlaying" of new stratification forms on older (and partly superseded) ones, it becomes possible to interpret contemporary systems as a complex mixture of several of the ideal types presented in Table 2 (see Schumpeter 1951).

The first panel in this table pertains to the "primitive" tribal systems that dominated human society from the very beginning of human evolution until the Neolithic revolution of some 10,000 years ago. The characterizations of columns 2–7 necessarily conceal much variability; as Anderson (1974, 549) puts it, "merely in the night of our ignorance [do] all alien shapes take on the same hue." These variable features of tribal societies are clearly of interest, but for our purposes the important similarities are that (1) the total size of the distributable surplus was in all cases quite limited, and (2) this cap on the surplus placed corresponding limits on the

TABLE 2
Basic Parameters of Stratification for Eight Ideal-Typical Systems

System (1)	Principal Assets (2)	Major Strata or Classes (3)	Inequality (4)	Rigidity (5)	Crystalliza-tion (6)	Justifying Ideology (7)
A. Hunting and gathering society						
1. Tribalism	Human (hunting and magic skills)	Chiefs, shamans, and other tribe members	Low	Low	High	Meritocratic selection
B. Horticultural and agrarian society						
2. Asiatic mode	Political (i.e., incumbency of state office)	Office-holders and peasants	High	Medium	High	Tradition and religious doctrine
3. Feudalism	Economic (land and labor power)	Nobility, clergy, and commoners	High	Medium-High	High	Tradition and Roman Catholic doctrine
4. Slavery	Economic (human property)	Slave owners, slaves, "free men"	High	Medium-High	High	Doctrine of natural and social inferior-ity (of slaves)
5. Caste society	Honorific and cultural (ethnic purity and "pure" lifestyles)	Castes and subcastes	High	High	High	Tradition and Hindu religious doctrine
C. Industrial society						
6. Class system	Economic (means of production)	Capitalists and workers	Medium-High	Medium	High	Classical liberalism
7. State socialism	Political (party and workplace authority)	Managers and managed	Low-Medium	Low-Medium	High	Marxism and Leninism
8. "Advanced" industrialism	Human (i.e., education, expertise)	Skill-based occupational groupings	Medium	Low-Medium	Medium	Classical liberalism

overall level of economic inequality (but not necessarily on other forms of inequality). It should also be noted that customs such as gift exchange, food sharing, and the like were commonly practiced in tribal societies and had obvious redistributive effects. In fact, some observers (e.g., Marx [1939] 1971) treated these societies as examples of "primitive communism," because the means of production (e.g., tools, land) were owned collectively and other types of property typically were distributed evenly among tribal members. This is not to suggest that a perfect equality prevailed; after all, the more powerful medicine men (i.e., shamans) often secured a disproportionate share of resources,

and the tribal chief could exert considerable influence on the political decisions of the day. However, these residual forms of power and privilege were never directly inherited, nor were they typically allocated in accord with well-defined ascriptive traits (e.g., racial traits).[13] It was only by demonstrating superior skills in hunting, magic, or leadership that tribal members could secure political office or acquire status and prestige (see Kerbo 2000; Nolan and Lenski 1998; Lenski 1966). Although meritocratic forms of allocation are often seen as prototypically modern, in fact they were present in incipient form at the very earliest stages of societal development.

With the emergence of agrarian forms of production, the economic surplus became large enough to support more complex systems of stratification. Among Marxist theorists (e.g., Godelier 1978; Chesneaux 1964), the "Asiatic mode" is often treated as an intermediate formation in the transition to advanced agrarian society (e.g., feudalism), and we have therefore led off our typology with the Asiatic case (see line B2).[14] In doing so, we should emphasize that the explicit evolutionary theories of Godelier (1978) and others have not been well received, yet many scholars still take the fallback position that Asiaticism is an important "analytical, though not chronological, stage" in the development of class society (Hobsbawm 1965, 37; see also Anderson 1974, 486; Mandel 1971, 116–39). The main features of this formation are (1) a large peasant class residing in agricultural villages that are "almost autarkic" (O'Leary 1989, 17); (2) the absence of strong legal institutions recognizing private property rights; (3) a state elite that extracts surplus agricultural production through rents or taxes and expends it on "defense, opulent living, and the construction of public works" (Shaw 1978, 127);[15] and (4) a constant flux in elite personnel due to "wars of dynastic succession and wars of conquest by nomadic warrior tribes" (O'Leary 1989, 18; for more extensive reviews, see Brook 1989; Krader 1975).

Beyond this skeletal outline, all else is open to dispute. There are long-standing debates, for example, about how widespread the Asiatic mode was (see Mandel 1971, 124–28) and about the appropriateness of reducing all forms of Asian development to a "uniform residual category" (Anderson 1974, 548–49). These issues are clearly worth pursuing, but for our purposes it suffices to note that the Asiatic mode provides a conventional example of how a "dictatorship of officialdom" can flourish in the absence of private property and a well-developed proprietary class (Gouldner 1980, 327–28). By this reading of Asiaticism, the parallel with modern socialism looms large (at least in some quarters), so much so that various scholars have suggested that Marx downplayed the Asian case for fear of exposing it as a "parable for socialism" (see Gouldner 1980, 324–52; see also Wittfogel 1981).

Whereas the institution of private property was underdeveloped in the East, the ruling class under Western feudalism was, by contrast, very much a propertied one.[16] The distinctive feature of feudalism was that the nobility not only owned large estates or manors but also held legal title to the labor power of its serfs (see line B3).[17] If a serf fled to the city, this was considered a form of theft: The serf was stealing that portion of his or her labor power owned by the lord (Wright 1985, 78). Under this interpretation, the statuses of serf and slave differ only in degree, and slavery thereby constitutes the "limiting case" in which workers lose all control over their own labor power (see line B4). At the same time, it would obviously be a mistake to reify this distinction, given that the history of agrarian Europe reveals "almost infinite gradations of subordination" (Bloch 1961, 256) that confuse and blur the conventional dividing lines between slavery, serfdom, and freedom (see Finley 1960 on the complex gradations of Greek slavery; see also Patterson 1982, 21–27). The slavery of Roman society provides the best example of complete subordination (Sio 1965), whereas some of the slaves of the early feudal period were bestowed with rights of real consequence (e.g., the right to sell surplus product), and some of the (nominally) free men were in fact obliged to provide rents or services to the manorial lord (Bloch 1961, 255–74).[18] The social classes that emerged under European agrarianism were thus structured in quite diverse ways. In all cases, we nonetheless find that property ownership was firmly established and that the life chances of individuals were defined, in large part, by their control over property in its differing forms. Unlike the ideal-typical Asiatic case, the nation-state was largely peripheral to the feudal stratification system, because the means of production (i.e., land, labor) were controlled by a proprietary class that emerged quite independently of the state.[19]

The historical record makes it clear that agrarian stratification systems were not always based on strictly hereditary forms of social closure (see panel B, column 5). The case of European feudalism is especially instructive in this regard, because it suggests that stratification systems often become more rigid as the underlying institutional forms mature and take shape (see Kelley 1981; Hechter and Brustein 1980; Mosca 1939). Although it is well-known that the era of classical feudalism (i.e., post-twelfth century) was characterized by a "rigid stratification of social classes" (Bloch 1961, 325),[20] there was greater permeability during the period prior to the institutionalization of the manorial system and the associated transformation of the nobility into a legal class. In this transitional period, access to the nobility was not yet legally restricted to the offspring of nobility, nor was marriage across classes or estates formally prohibited (see Bloch 1961, 320–31, for further details). The case of ancient Greece provides a complementary example of a (relatively) open agrarian society. As Finley (1960) and others have noted, the condition of slavery was indeed heritable under Greek law, yet manumission (i.e., the freeing of slaves) was so common that the slave class had to be constantly replenished with new captives secured through war or piracy. The possibility of servitude was thus something that "no man, woman, or child, regardless of status or wealth, could be sure to escape" (Finley 1960, 161). At the same time, hereditary forms of closure were more fully developed in some slave systems, most notably the American one. As Sio (1965, 303) notes, slavery in the antebullum South was "hereditary, endogamous, and permanent," with the annual manumission rate apparently as low as 0.04 percent by 1850 (see Patterson 1982, 273). The slave societies of Jamaica, South Africa, and rural Iraq were likewise based on largely permanent slave populations (see Rodriguez and Patterson 1999; Patterson 1982).

The most extreme examples of hereditary closure are of course found in caste societies (see line B5). In some respects, American slav-

ery might be seen as having "caste-like features" (see Berreman 1981), but Hindu India clearly provides the defining case of caste organization.[21] The Indian caste system is based on (1) a hierarchy of status groupings (i.e., castes) that are ranked by ethnic purity, wealth, and access to goods or services, (2) a corresponding set of "closure rules" that restrict all forms of inter-caste marriage or mobility and thereby make caste membership both hereditary and permanent; (3) a high degree of physical and occupational segregation enforced by elaborate rules and rituals governing intercaste contact; and (4) a justifying ideology (i.e., Hinduism) that induces the population to regard such extreme forms of inequality as legitimate and appropriate (Smaje 2000; Bayly 1999; Sharma 1999; Sharma 1997; Jalali 1992; Brass 1985; 1983; Berreman 1981; Dumont 1970; Srinivas 1962; Leach 1960). What makes this system so distinctive, then, is not merely its well-developed closure rules but also the fundamentally honorific (and noneconomic) character of the underlying social hierarchy. As indicated in Table 2, the castes of India are ranked on a continuum of ethnic and ritual purity, with the highest positions in the system reserved for castes that prohibit behaviors that are seen as dishonorable or "polluting." Under some circumstances, castes that acquired political and economic power eventually advanced in the status hierarchy, yet they typically did so only after mimicking the behaviors and lifestyles of higher castes (Srinivas 1962).

The defining feature of the industrial era (see panel C) has been the emergence of egalitarian ideologies and the consequent "delegitimation" of the extreme forms of stratification found in caste, feudal, and slave systems. This can be seen, for example, in the European revolutions of the eighteenth and nineteenth centuries that pitted the egalitarian ideals of the Enlightenment against the privileges of rank and the political power of the nobility. In the end, these struggles eliminated the last residue of feudal privilege, but they also made new types of inequality and stratification possible. Under the class system that ultimately emerged (see line C6), the estates of the feudal era were replaced by purely economic groups (i.e., "classes"), and closure rules based on heredity were likewise supplanted by (formally) meritocratic processes. The resulting classes were neither legal entities nor closed status groupings, and the associated class-based inequalities could therefore be represented and justified as the natural outcome of competition among individuals with differing abilities, motivation, or moral character (i.e., "classical liberalism"). As indicated in line C6 of Table 2, the class structure of early industrialism had a clear "economic base" (Kerbo 1991, 23), so much so that Marx ([1894] 1972) defined classes in terms of their relationship to the means of economic production. The precise contours of the industrial class structure are nonetheless a matter of continuing debate (see "The Structure of Contemporary Stratification"); for example, a simple Marxian model focuses on the cleavage between capitalists and workers, whereas more elaborate Marxian and neo-Marxian models identify additional intervening or "contradictory" classes (e.g., Wright 1997; 1985), and yet other (non-Marxian) approaches represent the class structure as a continuous gradation of "monetary wealth and income" (Mayer and Buckley 1970, 15).[22]

Whatever the relative merits of these models might be, the ideology underlying the socialist revolutions of the nineteenth and twentieth centuries was of course explicitly Marxist. The intellectual heritage of these revolutions and their legitimating ideologies can again be traced to the Enlightenment, but the rhetoric of equality that emerged in this period was now directed against the economic power of the capitalist class rather than the status and honorific privileges of the nobility. The evidence from Eastern Europe and elsewhere suggests that these egalitarian ideals were only partially realized (e.g., Lenski 2000; Szelényi 1998; Connor 1991). In the immediate postrevolutionary period, factories and farms were indeed collectivized or social-

ized, and various fiscal and economic reforms were instituted for the express purpose of reducing income inequality and wage differentials among manual and nonmanual workers (Parkin 1971, 137–59; Giddens 1973, 226–30). Although these egalitarian policies were subsequently weakened through the reform efforts of Stalin and others, inequality on the scale of prerevolutionary society was never reestablished among rank-and-file workers (cf. Lenski 2001). There nonetheless remained substantial inequalities in power and authority; most notably, the socialization of productive forces did not have the intended effect of empowering workers, as the capitalist class was replaced by a "new class" of party officials and managers who continued to control the means of production and to allocate the resulting social surplus (see Eyal, Szelényi, and Townsley 2001). This class has been variously identified with intellectuals or intelligentsia (e.g., Gouldner 1979), bureaucrats or managers (e.g., Rizzi 1985), and party officials or appointees (e.g., Djilas 1965). Regardless of the formulation adopted, the presumption is that the working class ultimately lost out in contemporary socialist revolutions, just as it did in the so-called bourgeois revolutions of the eighteenth and nineteenth centuries.

Whereas the means of production were socialized in the revolutions of Eastern Europe and the former Soviet Union, the capitalist class remained largely intact throughout the process of industrialization in the West. However, the propertied class may ultimately be weakened by ongoing structural changes, with the most important of these being (1) the rise of a service economy and the growing power of the "service class" (Esping-Andersen 1999; 1993; Goldthorpe 1982; Ehrenreich and Ehrenreich 1979), (2) the increasing centrality of theoretical knowledge in the transition to a new "information age" (Castells 1999; Bell 1973), and (3) the consequent emergence of technical expertise, educational degrees, and training certificates as "new forms of property" (Berg 1973, 183; Gouldner 1979). The foregoing developments all suggest that human and cultural capital are replacing economic capital as the principal stratifying forces in advanced industrial society (see line C8). By this formulation, a dominant class of cultural elites may be emerging in the West, much as the transition to state socialism (allegedly) generated a new class of intellectuals in the East.

This is not to suggest that all theorists of advanced industrialism posit a grand divide between the cultural elite and an undifferentiated working mass. In fact, some commentators (e.g., Dahrendorf 1959, 48–57) have argued that skill-based cleavages are crystallizing throughout the occupational structure, with the result being a finely differentiated class system made up of discrete occupations (Grusky and Sørensen 1998) or a continuous gradation of socioeconomic status (e.g., Parsons 1970; see also Grusky and Van Rompaey 1992). In nearly all models of advanced industrial society, it is further assumed that education is the principal mechanism by which individuals are sorted into such classes, and educational institutions thus serve in this context to "license" human capital and convert it to cultural currency.[23] The rise of mass education is sometimes represented as a rigidifying force (e.g., Bourdieu and Passeron 1977), but the prevailing view is that the transition to advanced industrialism has equalized life chances and produced a more open society (see line C8, column 5).[24]

As postmodernism gains adherents, it has become fashionable to argue that such conventional representations of advanced industrialism, both in their Marxian and non-Marxian form, have become less useful in understanding contemporary stratification and its developmental tendencies (e.g., Pakulski and Waters 1996; Bradley 1996; Crook, Pakulski, and Waters 1992; Beck 1992; Bauman 1992). Although the postmodern literature is notoriously fragmented, the variants of postmodernism that are relevant for our purposes invariably proceed from the assumption that class identities, ideologies, and organization are attenuating and that "new theories, perhaps more cultural than structural, [are] in

order" (Davis 1982, 585). In the parlance of Table 2, the core claim is that postmodern stratification involves a radical decline in status crystallization, as participation in particular life-styles or communities is no longer class-determined and increasingly becomes a "function of individual taste, choice, and commitment" (Crook, Pakulski, and Waters 1992, 222).[25]

This line of argument has not yet been subjected to convincing empirical test and may well prove to be premature (for critiques, see Marshall 1997; Hout, Brooks, and Manza 1993). However, even if lifestyles and life chances are truly "decoupling" from economic class, this ought not be misunderstood as a more general decline in stratification per se. The brute facts of inequality will of course still be with us even if social classes of the conventional form are weakening. As is well-known, some forms of inequality have increased in recent years (see Levy 1998; Danziger and Gottschalk 1993; 1995), and others clearly show no signs of disappearing or withering away.

Sources of Stratification

The preceding sketch makes it clear that a wide range of stratification systems emerged over the course of human history. The question that arises, then, is whether some form of stratification or inequality is an inevitable feature of human society. In taking on this question, one turns naturally to the functionalist theory of Davis and Moore (1945, 242), as it addresses explicitly "the universal necessity which calls forth stratification in any system" (see also Davis 1953; Moore 1963a; 1963b). The starting point for any functionalist approach is the premise that all societies must devise some means to motivate the best workers to fill the most important and difficult occupations. This "motivational problem" might be addressed in a variety of ways, but perhaps the simplest solution is to construct a hierarchy of rewards (e.g., prestige, property, power) that privileges the incumbents of functionally significant positions. As noted by Davis and Moore (1945, 243), this amounts to setting up a system of institutionalized inequality (i.e., a "stratification system"), with the occupational structure serving as a conduit through which unequal rewards and perquisites are allocated. The stratification system may be seen, therefore, as an "unconsciously evolved device by which societies insure that the important positions are conscientiously filled by the most qualified persons" (Davis and Moore 1945, 243).

The Davis-Moore hypothesis has of course come under criticism from several quarters (see Huaco 1966 for an early review). The prevailing view, at least among postwar commentators, is that the original hypothesis cannot adequately account for inequalities in "stabilized societies where statuses are ascribed" (Wesolowski 1962, 31; Tumin 1953). Indeed, whenever the vacancies in the occupational structure are allocated on purely hereditary grounds, one cannot reasonably argue that the reward system is serving its putative function of matching qualified workers to important positions. What must be recognized, however, is that a purely hereditary system is rarely achieved in practice; in fact, even in caste societies of the most rigid sort, one typically finds that talented and qualified individuals have some opportunities for upward mobility. With the Davis-Moore formulation (1945), this slow trickle of mobility is regarded as essential to the functioning of the social system, so much so that elaborate systems of inequality have evidently been devised to ensure that the trickle continues (see Davis 1948, 369–70, for additional and related comments). Although the Davis-Moore hypothesis can therefore be used to explain stratification in societies with *some* mobility, the original hypothesis is clearly untenable insofar as there is complete closure.

The functionalist approach has been further criticized for neglecting the "power element" in stratification systems (Wrong 1959, 774). It has long been argued that Davis and Moore failed "to observe that incumbents [of functionally important positions] have the

power not only to insist on payment of expected rewards but to demand even larger ones" (Wrong 1959, 774; see also Dahrendorf 1968). The stratification system thus becomes "self-reproducing" (see Collins 1975) insofar as incumbents of important positions use their power to preserve or extend their privileges. By this argument, the distribution of rewards reflects not only the latent needs of the larger society but also the balance of power among competing groups and their members. The emerging neo-Marxian literature on exploitative "rents" is directly relevant to such anti-functionalist formulations, because it identifies the conditions under which workers enjoy economic returns that are greater than training costs (e.g., schooling, wages foregone) and hence in excess of the functionally necessary wage. The standard rent-generating tactic among modern workers is to create artificial labor shortages; that is, excess returns can be secured by restricting opportunities for training or credentialing, as doing so prevents additional rent-seeking workers from entering the field and driving wages down to the level found elsewhere (Sørensen 2001; 1996; Roemer 1988; Wright 1985). These excess returns therefore arise because occupational incumbents can use their positional power to limit the supply of competing labor.

It bears emphasizing that the foregoing position operates outside a functionalist account but is not necessarily inconsistent with it. Under a Davis-Moore formulation, the latent function of inequality is to guarantee that labor is allocated efficiently, but Davis and Moore (1945) acknowledge that excess inequality may also arise for other reasons and through other processes. The extreme forms of stratification found in existing societies may thus exceed the "minimum . . . necessary to maintain a complex division of labor" (Wrong 1959, 774). There are of course substantial cross-national differences in the extent and patterning of inequality that are best explained in historical and institutional terms (Fischer et al. 1996). Most notably, there is much institutional variability in the conditions under which rent-generating closure is allowed, especially those forms of closure involving manual labor (i.e., unionization). As argued by Esping-Andersen (1999; 1990), countries also "choose" different ways of allocating production between the market and the state, with market-based regimes typically involving higher levels of inequality. The American system, for example, is highly unequal not merely because union-based closure has historically been suppressed, but also because state-sponsored redistributive programs are poorly developed and market forces are relied on to allocate services that in other countries are provided universally (e.g., healthcare).

Obversely, the egalitarian policies of state socialism demonstrate that substantial reductions in inequality are achievable through state-mandated reform, especially during the early periods of radical institutional restructuring (see Kelley 1981). It is nonetheless possible that such reform was pressed too far and that "many of the internal, systemic problems of Marxist societies were the result of inadequate motivational arrangements" (Lenski 2001). As Lenski (2001) notes, the socialist commitment to wage leveling made it difficult to recruit and motivate highly skilled workers, and the "visible hand" of the socialist economy could never be calibrated to mimic adequately the natural incentive of capitalist profit-taking. These results lead Lenski (2001) to the neo-functionalist conclusion that "successful incentive systems involve . . . motivating the best qualified people to seek the most important positions." It remains to be seen whether this negative reading of the socialist "experiments in destratification" (Lenski 1978) will generate a new round of functionalist theorizing and debate.

The Structure of Contemporary Stratification

The history of stratification theory is in large part a history of debates about the contours of class, status, and prestige hierarchies in advanced industrial societies. These debates might appear to be nothing more than academic infighting, but the participants treat them with high seriousness as a "necessary prelude to the conduct of political strategy" (Parkin 1979, 16). For example, considerable energy has been devoted to identifying the correct dividing line between the working class and the bourgeoisie, because the task of locating the oppressed class is seen as a prerequisite to devising a political strategy that might appeal to it. It goes without saying that political and intellectual goals are often conflated in such mapmaking efforts, and the assorted debates in this subfield are thus infused with more than the usual amount of scholarly contention. These debates are complex and wide-ranging, but it suffices for our purposes to distinguish the following five schools of thought (see Wright 1997 for a more detailed review).

Marxists and Post-Marxists

The debates within the Marxist and neo-Marxist camps have been especially contentious, not only because of the foregoing political motivations, but also because the discussion of class within *Capital* (Marx [1894] 1972) is too fragmentary and unsystematic to adjudicate between various competing interpretations. At the end of the third volume of *Capital,* the now-famous fragment on "the classes" (Marx [1894] 1972, 862–63) breaks off just when Marx appeared ready to advance a formal definition of the term, thus providing precisely the ambiguity needed to sustain decades of debate. It is clear, nonetheless, that his abstract model of capitalism was resolutely dichotomous, with the conflict between capitalists and workers constituting the driving force behind further social development. This simple two-class model should be viewed as an ideal type designed to capture the developmental tendencies of capitalism; indeed, whenever Marx carried out concrete analyses of existing capitalist systems, he acknowledged that the class structure was complicated by the persistence of transitional classes (e.g., landowners), quasi-class groupings (e.g., peasants), and class fragments (e.g., the lumpen proletariat). It was only with the progressive maturation of capitalism that Marx expected these complications to disappear as the "centrifugal forces of class struggle and crisis flung all *dritte Personen* [third persons] to one camp or the other" (Parkin 1979, 16).

The recent history of modern capitalism reveals that the class structure has not evolved in such a precise and tidy fashion. As Dahrendorf (1959) points out, the old middle class of artisans and shopkeepers has indeed declined in relative size, yet a new middle class of managers, professionals, and nonmanual workers has expanded to occupy the newly vacated space (see also Wright 1997; Steinmetz and Wright 1989). The last 50 years of neo-Marxist theorizing can be seen as the intellectual fallout from this development, with some commentators seeking to minimize its implications, and others putting forward a revised mapping of the class structure that accommodates the new middle class in explicit terms. Within the former camp, the principal tendency is to claim that the lower sectors of the new middle class are in the process of being proletarianized, because "capital subjects [nonmanual labor] . . . to the forms of rationalization characteristic of the capitalist mode of production" (Braverman 1974, 408; see Spenner 1995 for a review of the "deskilling" literature). This line of reasoning suggests that the working class may gradually expand in relative size and therefore regain its earlier power. In an updated version of this argument, Aronowitz and DiFazio (1994, 16) also describe the "proletarianization of work at every level below the [very] top," but they further suggest that such proletarianization proceeds by eliminating labor as well as deskilling it. The labor-saving forces of technological change thus produce a vast reserve army of unemployed, underemployed, and intermittently employed workers.

At the other end of the continuum, Poulantzas (1974) has argued that most members of the new intermediate stratum fall outside the working class proper, because they are not exploited in the classical Marxian sense (i.e., surplus value is not extracted). The latter approach may have the merit of keeping the working class conceptually pure, but it also reduces the size of this class to "pygmy proportions" (see Parkin 1979, 19) and dashes the hopes of those who would see workers as a viable political force. This result has motivated contemporary scholars to develop class models that fall somewhere between the extremes advocated by Braverman (1974) and Poulantzas (1974). For example, the neo-Marxist model proposed by Wright (1978) generates an American working class that is acceptably large (i.e., approximately 46 percent of the labor force), yet the class mappings in this model still pay tribute to the various cleavages and divisions among workers who sell their labor power. That is, professionals are placed in a distinct "semi-autonomous class" by virtue of their control over the work process, and upper-level supervisors are located in a "managerial class" by virtue of their authority over workers (Wright 1978; see also Wright 1985). The dividing lines proposed in this model rest, then, on concepts (e.g., autonomy, authority relations) that were once purely the province of Weberian or neo-Weberian sociology, leading Parkin (1979, 25) to claim that "inside every neo-Marxist there seems to be a Weberian struggling to get out."[26]

These early class models, which were once quite popular, have now been superseded by various second-generation models that rely more explicitly on the concept of exploitation. As noted previously, Roemer (1988) and others (especially Sørensen 2000; 1996; Wright 1997) have redefined exploitation as the extraction of "rent," where this refers to the excess earnings that are secured by limiting access to positions and thus artificially restricting the supply of qualified labor. If an approach of this sort is adopted, one can then test for skill-based exploitation by calculating whether the cumulated lifetime earnings of skilled labor exceeds that of unskilled labor by an amount larger than the implied training costs (e.g., school tuition, forgone earnings).

In a perfectly competitive market, labor will perforce flow to the most rewarding occupations, thereby equalizing the lifetime earnings of workers and eliminating exploitative returns. However, when opportunities are limited by imposing restrictions on entry (e.g., qualifying exams), the equilibrating flow of labor is disrupted and the potential for exploitation within the labor market emerges. This approach was devised, then, to recognize various dividing lines within the working class and to understand them as the outcome of exploitative processes. There is of course no guarantee that these internal fractures can be overcome; that is, a rent-based model appreciates that workers have potentially differing interests, with more privileged workers presumably oriented toward preserving and extending the institutional mechanisms (e.g., credentialing) that allow them to reap exploitative returns (cf. Wright 1997).

Weberians and Post-Weberians

The rise of the "new middle class" has proven less problematic for scholars working within a Weberian framework. Indeed, the class model advanced by Weber suggests a multiplicity of class cleavages, given that it equates the economic class of workers with their "market situation" in the competition for jobs and valued goods (Weber [1922] 1968, 926–40). Under this formulation, the class of skilled workers is privileged because its incumbents are in high demand on the labor market, and because its economic power can be parlayed into high wages and an advantaged position in commodity markets (Weber [1922] 1968, 927–28). At the same time, the stratification system is further complicated by the existence of "status groupings," which Weber saw as forms of social affiliation that can compete, coexist, or overlap with class-based groupings. Although an economic class is merely an aggregate of individuals in a similar market situation, a status grouping is defined as a community of individuals who share a style of life and interact as status equals (e.g., the nobility, an ethnic caste). In

some circumstances, the boundaries of a status grouping are determined by purely economic criteria, yet Weber ([1922] 1968, 932) notes that "status honor normally stands in sharp opposition to the pretensions of sheer property."

This formulation has been especially popular in the United States. During the postwar decades, American sociologists typically dismissed the Marxist model of class as overly simplistic and one-dimensional, whereas they celebrated the Weberian model as properly distinguishing between the numerous variables that Marx had conflated in his definition of class (see, e.g., Barber 1968). In the most extreme versions of this approach, the dimensions identified by Weber were disaggregated into a multiplicity of stratification variables (e.g., income, education, ethnicity), and the correlations between these variables were then shown to be weak enough to generate various forms of "status inconsistency" (e.g., a poorly educated millionaire). The resulting picture suggested a "pluralistic model" of stratification; that is, the class system was represented as intrinsically multidimensional, with a host of cross-cutting affiliations producing a complex patchwork of internal class cleavages. The multidimensionalists were often accused of providing a "sociological portrait of America as drawn by Norman Rockwell" (Parkin 1979, 604), but it should be kept in mind that some of these theorists also emphasized the seamy side of pluralism. In fact, Lenski (1954) and others (e.g., Lipset 1959) have argued that modern stratification systems might be seen as breeding grounds for personal stress and political radicalism, given that individuals with contradictory statuses may feel relatively deprived and thus support "movements designed to alter the political *status quo*" (Lenski 1966, 88). This line of research ultimately died out in the early-1970s under the force of negative and inconclusive findings (e.g., Jackson and Curtis 1972).

Although postmodernists have not explicitly drawn on classical multidimensionalist accounts, there is nonetheless much similarity, apparently inadvertent, between these two lines of theorizing. Indeed, contemporary postmodernists argue that class-based identities are far from fundamental or "essential," that individuals instead have "multiple and cross-cutting identities" (Crook, Pakulski, and Waters 1992, 222), and that the various contradictions and inconsistencies among these identities can lead to a "decentered self" and consequent stress and disaffection (see Bauman 2000; Bradley 1996; Pakulski and Waters 1996; Beck 1992; 1987). There are of course important points of departure as well; most notably, postmodernists do not regard status affiliations as fixed or exogeneous, instead referring to the active construction of "reflexive biographies that depend on the decisions of the actor" (Beck 1992, 91–101). The resulting "individualization of inequality" (Beck 1992) implies that lifestyles and consumption practices could become decoupled from work identities as well as other status group memberships. Despite these differences, postmodern commentators might well gain from reexamining this older neo-Weberian literature, if only because it addressed the empirical implications of multidimensional theorizing more directly and convincingly.

It would be a mistake to regard the foregoing multidimensionalists as the only intellectual descendants of Weber. In recent years, the standard multidimensionalist interpretation of "Class, Status, and Party" (Weber 1946, 180–95) has fallen into disfavor, and an alternative version of neo-Weberian stratification theory has gradually taken shape. This revised reading of Weber draws on the concept of social closure as defined and discussed in the essay "Open and Closed Relationships" (Weber [1922] 1968, 43–46, 341–48; see also Weber 1947, 424–29). By social closure, Weber was referring to the processes by which groups devise and enforce rules of membership, with the purpose of such rules typically being to "improve the position [of the group] by monopolistic tactics" (Weber [1922] 1968, 43). Although Weber did not directly link this discussion with his other contributions to stratification theory,

subsequent commentators have pointed out that social classes and status groupings are generated by simple exclusionary processes operating at the macrostructural level (e.g., Manza 1992; Murphy 1988; Goldthorpe 1987; Parkin 1979; Giddens 1973).[27] Under modern industrialism, there are no formal sanctions preventing labor from crossing class boundaries, yet various institutional forces (e.g., private property, union shops) are nonetheless quite effective in limiting the amount of class mobility over the life course and between generations. These exclusionary mechanisms not only "maximize claims to rewards and opportunities" among the incumbents of closed classes (Parkin 1979, 44), they also provide the demographic continuity needed to generate distinctive class cultures and to "reproduce common life experience over the generations" (Giddens 1973, 107). As noted by Giddens (1973, 107–12), barriers of this sort are not the only source of "class structuration," yet they clearly play a contributing role in the formation of identifiable classes under modern industrialism.[28] This revisionist interpretation of Weber has reoriented the discipline toward examining the sources and causes of class formation rather than the (potentially) fragmenting effects of cross-cutting affiliations and cleavages.[29]

Durkheim and Post-Durkheimians

Although Marx and Weber are more frequently invoked by contemporary scholars of inequality, the work of Durkheim ([1893] 1933) is also directly relevant to issues of class. In his preface to *The Division of Labor*, Durkheim ([1893] 1933, 28) predicted that interdependent corporate occupations would gradually become "intercalated between the state and the individual," thereby solving the problem of order by regulating industrial conflict and creating local forms of "mechanical solidarity" (i.e., solidarity based on shared norms and values). As the occupational structure differentiates, Durkheim argued that shared values at the societal level would become more abstract and less constraining, while compensating forms of local solidarism would simultaneously emerge at the level of detailed occupations. For Durkheim ([1893] 1933, 27), the modern order is thus characterized by "moral polymorphism," where this refers to the rise of multiple, occupation-specific "centers of moral life" that provide a counterbalance to the threat of class formation on one hand and that of state tyranny on the other (see Grusky 2000).

This line of argumentation may well have contemporary relevance. Indeed, even if class-based organization is an increasingly "spent force" in the postmodern period (e.g., Pakulski and Waters 1996), it is well to bear in mind that occupation-level structuration of the sort emphasized by Durkheim is seemingly alive and well (Grusky and Sørensen 2001; 1998; Barley 1996; Barley and Tolbert 1991; see also Bourdieu 1984). The conversion of work-based distinctions into meaningful social groupings occurs at the disaggregate level because (1) the forces of self-selection operate to bring like-minded workers into the same occupation; (2) the resulting social interaction with coworkers tends to reinforce and elaborate these shared values; (3) the homogenizing effects of informal interaction may be supplemented with explicit training and socialization in the form of apprenticeships, certification programs, and professional schooling; and (4) the incumbents of occupations have common interests that may be pursued, in part, by aligning themselves with their occupation and pursuing collective ends (e.g., closure, certification). The foregoing processes all suggest that social closure coincides with occupational boundaries and generates *gemeinschaftlich* communities at a more disaggregate level than neo-Marxian or neo-Weberian class analysts have appreciated (Weeden 1998; Sørensen and Grusky 1996; Van Maanen and Barley 1984). In effect, a neo-Durkheimian mapping allows for a unification of class and *Stand* that, according to Weber ([1922] 1968), occurs only rarely in the context of conventional aggregate classes.

The neo-Marxian concept of rent can likewise be recast in Durkheimian terms (see Grusky and Sørensen 2001; 1998; Sørensen 2001; 1996). In some neo-Marxian schemes, aggregate "class" categories are formed by grouping together all workers who profit from similar types of exploitation (e.g., Wright 1997), with the apparent claim being that incumbents of these categories will ultimately come to appreciate and act on behalf of their shared interests. If a neo-Durkheimian approach is adopted, such aggregation becomes problematic because it conceals the more detailed level at which social closure and skill-based exploitation occurs. The key point in this context is that the working institutions of closure (i.e., professional associations, craft unions) restrict the supply of labor to occupations rather than aggregate classes. As a result, the fundamental units of exploitation would appear to be occupations themselves, whereas neo-Marxian "classes" are merely heterogeneous aggregations of occupations that have similar capacities for exploitation.

The main empirical question that arises in this context is whether the contemporary world is becoming "Durkheimianized" as local structuration strengthens at the expense of aggregate forms of class organization. The prevailing "postoccupational view" is that contemporary firms are relying increasingly on teamwork, cross-training, and multiactivity jobs that break down conventional skill-based distinctions (e.g., Casey 1995; Baron 1994; Drucker 1993). At the same time, this account is not without its critics, some of whom (especially Barley 1996) suggest that pressures for an occupational logic of organizing may be rising because (1) occupationally organized sectors of the labor force (e.g., professions) are expanding in size, (2) occupationalization is extending into new sectors (e.g., management) that had previously been resistant to such pressures, and (3) the spread of outsourcing replaces firm-based ties and association with occupation-based organization (see also Barley and Bechky 1994; Freidson 1994, 103–4). In this regard, the archetypal organizational form of the future may well be the construction industry, relying as it does on the collaboration of independent experts who guard their occupationally defined bodies of knowledge jealously.

The Ruling Class and Elites

With elite studies, the focus shifts of course to the top of the class structure, with the typical point of departure again being the economic analysis of Marx and various neo-Marxians. The classical elite theorists (Mills 1956; Mosca 1939; Pareto 1935) sought to replace the Marxian model of economic classes with a purely political analysis resting on the distinction between the rulers and the ruled. As Mills (1956, 277) put it, Marx formulated the "short-cut theory that the economic class rules politically," whereas elite theorists contend that the composition of the ruling class reflects the outcome of political struggles that may not necessarily favor economic capital. In their corollary to this thesis, Pareto and Mosca further claim that the movement of history can be understood as a cyclical succession of elites, with the relative size of the governing minority tending to diminish as the political community grows (Mosca 1939, 53). The common end point of all revolutions is therefore the "dominion of an organized minority" (Mosca 1939, 53); indeed, Mosca points out that all historical class struggles have culminated with a new elite taking power, while the lowliest class invariably remains as such (see also Gouldner 1979, 93). Although Marx would have agreed with this oligarchical interpretation of presocialist revolutions, he nonetheless insisted that the socialist revolution would break the pattern and culminate in a dictatorship of the proletariat and ultimately a classless state.[30] The elite theorists were, by contrast, unconvinced that the "iron law of oligarchy" (Michels 1949) could be so conveniently suspended for this final revolution.

As elite theory evolved, this original interest in the long-term dynamics of class systems was largely abandoned, and emphasis shifted to describing the structure and composition of modern elites (cf. Lachmann 1990). The research agenda of contemporary elite theorists is dominated by the following types of questions:

1. Who wields power and influence in contemporary society? Is there an "inner circle" of powerful corporate leaders (Useem 1984), a "governing class" of hereditary political elites (Shils 1982; Mosca 1939), or a more encompassing "power elite" that cuts across political, economic, and military domains (Domhoff 1998; Mills 1956)?

2. How cohesive are the elite groupings so defined? Do they form a unitary "upper class" (Domhoff 1998, 2), or are they divided by conflicting interests and unable to achieve unity (Lerner, Nagai, and Rothman 1996; Keller 1991)?

3. Are certain sectors of the elite especially cohesive or conflictual? Is the business elite, for example, fractured by competition and accordingly weakened in pressing its interests? Or have interlocking directorates and other forms of corporate networking and association unified the business elite (Mizruchi 1996; 1982)? How has the separation of ownership and control affected elite unity (e.g., Fligstein and Brantley 1992)?

4. How much elite mobility is there? Are elites continuously circulating (Shils 1982; Pareto 1935), or have hereditary forms of closure remained largely intact even today (see Baltzell 1991; 1964; 1958)?

5. What are the prerequisites for elite membership? Are elites invariably drawn from prestigious schools (Lerner, Nagai, and Rothman 1996; Useem and Karabel 1986)? Are women and minorities increasingly represented in the economic, political, or cultural elite of advanced industrial societies (Zweigenhaft and Domhoff 1998)?

6. How do elites adapt and react to revolutionary change? Were socialist elites

successful, for example, in converting their discredited political capital into economic or cultural power (see Nee 2001; Eyal, Szelényi, and Townsley 1998; Rona-Tas 1997; 1994; Szelényi and Szelényi 1995)?

There are nearly as many elite theories as there are possible permutations of responses to questions of this sort. If there is any unifying theme to contemporary theorizing, it is merely that subordinate classes lack any meaningful control over the major economic and political decisions of the day (Domhoff 1998). Although it was once fashionable to argue that "ordinary citizens can acquire as much power . . . as their free time, ability, and inclination permit" (Rose 1967, 247), such extreme versions of pluralism have of course now fallen into disrepute.

Gradational Measurements of Social Standing

The foregoing theorists have all proceeded by mapping individuals or families into mutually exclusive and exhaustive categories (e.g., "classes"). As the preceding review indicates, there continues to be much debate about the location of the boundaries separating these categories, yet the shared assumption is that boundaries of some kind are present, if only in latent or incipient form. By contrast, the implicit claim underlying gradational approaches is that such "dividing lines" are largely the construction of overzealous sociologists, and that the underlying structure of modern stratification can, in fact, be more closely approximated with gradational measures of income, status, or prestige (Nisbet 1959; see also Clark and Lipset 1991; cf. Hout, Brooks, and Manza 1993). The standard concepts of class action and consciousness are likewise typically discarded; that is, whereas most categorical models are based on the (realist) assumption that the constituent categories are "structures of interest that pro-

vide the basis for collective action" (Wright 1979, 7), gradational models are usually represented as taxonomic or statistical classifications of purely heuristic interest.[31]

There is no shortage of gradational measures that might be used to characterize the social welfare or reputational ranking of individuals. Although there is some sociological precedent for treating income as an indicator of class (e.g., Mayer and Buckley 1970, 15), most sociologists seem content with a disciplinary division of labor that leaves matters of income to economists. It does not follow that distinctions of income are sociologically uninteresting; after all, if one is truly intent on assessing the "market situation" of workers (Weber [1922] 1968), there is much to recommend a direct measurement of their income and wealth. The preferred approach has nonetheless been to define classes as "groups of persons who are members of effective kinship units which, as units, are approximately equally valued" (Parsons 1954, 77). This formulation was first operationalized in the postwar community studies (e.g., Warner 1949) by constructing broadly defined categories of reputational equals (e.g., "upper-upper class," "upper-middle class").[32] However, when the disciplinary focus shifted to the national stratification system, the measure of choice soon became either (1) prestige scales based on popular evaluations of occupational standing (e.g., Treiman 1977; 1976), or (2) socioeconomic scales constructed as weighted averages of occupational income and education (e.g., Blau and Duncan 1967). The latter scales have served as standard measures of class background for nearly 40 years (for reviews, see Wegener 1992; Grusky and Van Rompaey 1992).

The staying power of prestige and socioeconomic scales is thus impressive in light of the faddishness of most sociological research. This long run may nonetheless be coming to an end; indeed, while a widely supported alternative to socioeconomic scales has yet to appear, the socioeconomic tradition has been subjected to increasing criticism on various fronts. The following four lines of questioning have attracted special attention:

- *Are conventional scales well-suited for the purpose of studying social mobility and socioeconomic attainment?* There is much research suggesting that conventional prestige and socioeconomic scales overstate the fluidity and openness of the stratification system (Hauser and Warren 1997; Rytina 1992; Hauser and Featherman 1977). This finding has motivated various efforts to better represent the "mobility chances" embedded in occupations; for example, Rytina (2000; 1992) has scaled occupations by the mobility trajectories of their incumbents, and Hauser and Warren (1997) have suggested that attainment processes are best captured by indexing occupations in terms of education alone (rather than the usual weighted combination of education and earnings).[33]
- *Is the underlying desirability of jobs adequately indexed by conventional scales?* In a related line of research, some scholars have questioned whether the desirability of jobs can be adequately measured with any occupation-based scale, given that much of the variability in earnings, autonomy, and other relevant job attributes is located within detailed occupational categories rather than between them (see Jencks, Perman, and Rainwater 1988).[34] This criticism implies that new composite indices should be constructed by combining job-level data on all variables relevant to judgments of desirability (e.g., earnings, fringe benefits, promotion opportunities).
- *Can a unidimensional scale capture all job attributes of interest?* The two preceding approaches share with conventional socioeconomic scaling the long-standing objective of "gluing together" various dimensions (e.g., education, income) into a single composite scale of social standing (cf. Hauser and Warren

1997, 251). If this objective is abandoned, one can of course construct any number of scales that separately index such job-level attributes as authority, autonomy, and substantive complexity (Halaby and Weakliem 1993; Kohn and Schooler 1983; see also Bourdieu 1984). This multidimensionalism has appeal because the attributes of interest (e.g., earnings, authority, autonomy) are imperfectly correlated and do not perform identically when modeling different class outcomes.
- *Should occupations necessarily be converted to variables?* The latter approach nonetheless retains the conventional assumption that occupations (or jobs) should be converted to variables and thereby reduced to a vector of quantitative scores. This assumption may well be costly in terms of explanatory power foregone; that is, insofar as distinctive cultures and styles of life emerge within occupations, such reductionist approaches amount to stripping away precisely that symbolic content that presumably generates much variability in attitudes, lifestyles, and consumption practices (Grusky and Sørensen 1998; Aschaffenburg 1995).

These particular lines of criticism may of course never take hold and crystallize into competing traditions. Although socioeconomic scales are hardly optimal for all purposes, the advantages of alternative scales and purpose-specific measurement strategies may not be substantial enough to overcome the forces of inertia and conservatism, especially given the long history and deep legitimacy of conventional approaches.

Generating Stratification

The language of stratification theory makes a sharp distinction between the distribution of social rewards (e.g., the income distribution) and the distribution of opportunities for securing these rewards. As sociologists have frequently noted (e.g., Kluegel and Smith 1986), it is the latter distribution that governs popular judgments about the legitimacy of stratification: The typical American, for example, is quite willing to tolerate substantial inequalities in power, wealth, or prestige provided that the opportunities for securing these social goods are distributed equally across all individuals (Hochschild 1995; 1981). Whatever the wisdom of this popular logic might be, stratification researchers have long sought to explore its factual underpinnings by monitoring and describing the structure of mobility chances.

In most of these analyses, the liberal ideal of an open and class-neutral system is treated as an explicit benchmark, and the usual objective is to expose any inconsistencies between this ideal and the empirical distribution of life chances. This is not to suggest, however, that all mobility scholars necessarily take a positive interest in mobility or regard liberal democracy as "the good society itself in operation" (Lipset 1959, 439). In fact, Lipset and Bendix (1959, 286) emphasize that open stratification systems can lead to high levels of "social and psychic distress," and not merely because the heightened aspirations that such systems engender are so frequently frustrated (Young 1958). The further difficulty that arises is that open stratification systems will typically generate various types of status inconsistency, as upward mobility projects in plural societies are often "partial and incomplete" (Lipset and Bendix 1959, 286) and therefore trap individuals between collectivities with conflicting expectations. The nouveaux riches, for example, are typically unable to parlay their economic mobility into social esteem and acceptance from their new peers, with the result sometimes being personal resentment and consequent "combativeness, frustration, and rootlessness" (Lipset and Bendix 1959, 285). Although the empirical evidence for such inconsistency effects is at best weak (e.g., Davis 1982), the continuing effort to uncover them makes it clear that mobility researchers are motivated by a wider

range of social interests than commentators and critics have often allowed (see Goldthorpe 1987, 1–36, for a relevant review).

The study of social mobility continues, then, to be undergirded by diverse interests and research questions. This diversity complicates the task of reviewing work in the field, but of course broad classes of inquiry can still be distinguished, as indicated below.

Mobility Analysis

The conventional starting point for mobility scholars has been to analyze bivariate "mobility tables" formed by cross-classifying the class origins and destinations of individuals. The tables so constructed can be used to estimate densities of inheritance, to map the social distances between classes and their constituent occupations, and to examine differences across sub-populations in the amount and patterning of fluidity and opportunity (e.g., Sørensen and Grusky 1996; Biblarz and Raftery 1993; Hout 1988; Featherman and Hauser 1978). Moreover, when comparable mobility tables are assembled from several countries, it becomes possible to address classical debates about the underlying contours of cross-national variation in stratification systems (e.g., Ishida, Müller, and Ridge 1995; Erikson and Goldthorpe 1992; Western and Wright 1994; Grusky and Hauser 1984; Lipset and Bendix 1959). This long-standing line of analysis, although still underway, has nonetheless declined of late, perhaps because past research (especially Erikson and Goldthorpe 1992) has been so definitive as to undercut further efforts (cf. Hout and Hauser 1992; Sørensen 1992). In recent years, the focus has thus shifted to studies of income mobility, with the twofold impetus for this development being (1) concerns that poverty may be increasingly difficult to escape and that a permanent underclass may be forming (e.g., Corcoran and Adams 1997), and (2) the obverse hypothesis that growing income inequality may be counterbalanced by increases in the rate of mobility between income groups (e.g., Gottschalk 1997). The bulk of this work has been completed by economists (e.g., Birdsall and Graham 2000), but the issues at stake are eminently sociological and have generated much sociological research as well (e.g., DiPrete and McManus 1996).

The Process of Stratification

It is by now a sociological truism that Blau and Duncan (1967) and their colleagues (e.g., Sewell, Haller, and Portes 1969) revolutionized the field with their formal "path models" of stratification. These models were intended to represent, if only partially, the process by which background advantages could be converted into socioeconomic status through the mediating variables of schooling, aspirations, and parental encouragement. Under formulations of this kind, the main sociological objective was to show that socioeconomic outcomes were structured not only by ability and family origins but also by various intervening variables (e.g., schooling) that were themselves only partly determined by origins and other ascriptive forces. The picture of modern stratification that emerged suggested that market outcomes depend in large part on unmeasured career contingencies (i.e., "individual luck") rather than influences of a more structural sort (Jencks et al. 1972; Blau and Duncan 1967, 174; cf. Hauser, Tsai, and Sewell 1983; Jencks et al. 1979). This line of research, which fell out of favor by the mid-1980s, has been recently reinvigorated as stratification scholars react to the controversial claim (i.e., Herrnstein and Murray 1994) that inherited intelligence is increasingly determinative of stratification outcomes (e.g., Hauser and Huang 1997; Fischer et al. 1996). In a related development, contemporary scholars have also turned their attention to ongoing changes in family structure, given that new non-traditional family arrangements (e.g., female-headed households) may in some cases reduce the influence of biological parents and otherwise complicate the reproduction of class. This new research literature addresses such topics as the effects of family disruption on mobility (e.g., Biblarz and Raftery 1999), the consequences of childhood poverty for early achievement (e.g., Hauser and Sweeney 1997), and the role of mothers in shaping educational aspirations and outcomes (e.g., Kalmijn 1994).

Structural Analysis

The foregoing "attainment models" are frequently criticized for failing to attend to the social structural constraints that operate on the stratification process independently of individual-level traits (e.g., Sørensen and Kalleberg 1981). The structuralist accounts that ultimately emerged from these critiques initially amounted, in most cases, to refurbished versions of dual economy and market segmentation models that were introduced and popularized many decades ago by institutional economists (e.g., Piore 1975; Doeringer and Piore 1971; Averitt 1968; see also Smith 1990). When these models were redeployed by sociologists in the early 1980s, the usual objective was to demonstrate that women and minorities were disadvantaged not merely by virtue of deficient human capital investments (e.g., inadequate schooling and experience) but also by their consignment to secondary labor markets that, on average, paid out lower wages and offered fewer opportunities for promotion or advancement. In recent years, more deeply sociological forms of structuralism have appeared, both in the form of (1) meso-level accounts of the effects of social networks and "social capital" on attainment (e.g., Lin 1999; Burt 1997; Podolny and Baron 1997), and (2) macro-level accounts of the effects of institutional context (e.g., welfare regimes) on mobility processes and outcomes (DiPrete et al. 1997; Fligstein and Byrkjeflot 1996; Kerckhoff 1996; Brinton, Lee, and Parish 1995). Although there is of course a long tradition of comparative mobility research, these new macro-level analyses are distinctive in attempting to theorize more rigorously the institutional sources of cross-national variation.

*   *   *

The history of these research traditions is arguably marked more by statistical and methodological signposts than by substantive ones. Indeed, when reviews of the field are attempted, the tendency is to identify methodological watersheds, such as the emergence of structural equation, log-linear, and event-history models (e.g., Ganzeboom, Treiman, and Ultee 1991). The more recent rise of sequence analysis, which allows researchers to identify the normative ordering of events, may also redefine and reinvigorate the study of careers and attainment (e.g., Han and Moen 1999; Blair-Loy 1999; Stovel, Savage, and Bearman 1996). At the same time, it is often argued that "theory formulation in the field has become excessively narrow" (Ganzeboom, Treiman, and Ultee 1991, 278), and that "little, if any, refinement of major theoretical positions has recently occurred" (Featherman 1981, 364; see also Burton and Grusky 1992, 628). The conventional claim in this regard is that mobility researchers have become entranced by quantitative methods and have accordingly allowed the "methodological tail to [wag] the substantive dog" (Coser 1975, 652). However, the latter argument can no longer be taken exclusively in the (intended) pejorative sense, because new models and methods have often opened up important substantive questions that had previously been overlooked (Burton and Grusky 1992).

It also bears emphasizing that mobility and attainment research has long relied on middle-range theorizing about the forces making for discrimination (e.g., queuing, statistical discrimination); the processes by which educational returns are generated (e.g., credentialing, human capital, signaling); the mechanisms through which class-based advantage is reproduced (e.g., social capital, networks); and the effects of industrialism, capitalism, and socialism on mobility processes (e.g., thesis of industrialism, transition theory). The subfield is thus highly theory driven in the middle range. To be sure, there is no grand theory here that unifies seemingly disparate models and analyses, but this is hardly unusual within the discipline, nor necessarily undesirable. The main contenders, at present, for grand theory status are various forms of rational action analysis that allow middle-range theories to be recast in terms of individual-level incentives and purposive behavior. Indeed, just as the assumption of utility maximization underlies labor economics, so too a theory of purposive behavior might ultimately organize much, albeit not all, of sociological theory on social mobility and attainment. The two "rational action" selections reprinted in this volume (i.e., Breen and Goldthorpe 1997; Logan 1996) reveal the promise (and pitfalls) of this formulation.

The Consequences of Stratification

We have so far taken it for granted that the sociological study of classes and status groupings is more than a purely academic exercise. For Marxist scholars, there is of course a strong macrostructural rationale for class analysis: The defining assumption of Marxism is that human history unfolds through the conflict between classes and the "revolutionary reconstruction of society" (Marx 1948, 9) that such conflict ultimately brings about. In recent years, macrostructural claims of this sort have typically been deemphasized, with many scholars looking outside the locus of production to understand and interpret ongoing social change. Although some macrostructural analyses can still be found (e.g., Portes forthcoming), the motivation for class analysis increasingly rests on the simple empirical observation that class background affects a wide range of individual outcomes (e.g., consumption practices, lifestyles, religious affiliation, voting behavior, mental health and deviance, fertility and mortality, values and attitudes). This analytical approach makes for a topically diverse subfield; in fact, one would be hard pressed to identify any aspect of human experience that has not been linked to class-based variables in some way, thus prompting DiMaggio (2001) to refer to measures of social class as modern-day "crack troops in the war on unexplained variance."

The resulting analyses of "class effects" continue to account for a substantial proportion of contemporary stratification research (see Burton and Grusky 1992). There has long been interest in studying the effects of class origins on schooling, occupation, and earnings (see prior section); by contrast, other topics of study within the field tend to fluctuate more in popularity, as developments in and out of academia influence the types of class effects that sociologists find salient or important. It is currently fashionable to study such topics as (1) the structure of socioeconomic disparities in health outcomes and the sources, causes, and consequences of the widening of some disparities (Williams and Collins 1995; Pappas et al. 1993); (2) the extent to which social class is a subjectively salient identity and structures perceptions of inter-class conflict (Wright 1997; Kelley and Evans 1995; Marshall et al. 1988); (3) the effects of social class on tastes for popular or high culture and the role of these tastes in establishing or reinforcing inter-class boundaries (Bryson 1996; Halle 1996; Peterson and Kern 1996; Lamont 1992; DiMaggio 1992; Bourdieu 1984); (4) the relationship between class and political behavior and the possible weakening of class-based politics as "postmaterialist values" spread and take hold (Evans 1999; Manza and Brooks 1999; Abramson and Inglehart 1995); and (5) the influence of working conditions on self-esteem, intellectual flexibility, and other facets of individual psychological functioning (Kohn et al. 1997; Kohn and Slomczynski 1990).

The relationship between class and these various class outcomes has been framed and conceptualized in diverse ways. We have sought to organize this literature below by distinguishing between such diverse traditions as market research, postmodern analysis, re-

production approaches, and structuration theory (for detailed reviews, see Crompton 1996; Chaney 1996; Gartman 1991).

Market Research

The natural starting point for our review is standard forms of market research (e.g., Michman 1991; Weiss 1988; Mitchell 1983) that operationalize the Weberian concept of status by constructing detailed typologies of modern lifestyles and consumption practices. It should be kept in mind that Weber joined two analytically separable elements in his definition of status; namely, members of a given status group were not only assumed to be honorific equals in the symbolic (or "subjective") sphere, but were also seen as sharing a certain style of life and having similar tastes or preferences in the sphere of consumption (see Giddens 1973, 80, 109). The former feature of status groups can be partly captured by conventional prestige scales, whereas the latter can only be indexed by classifying the actual consumption practices of individuals as revealed by their "cultural possessions, material possessions, and participation in the group activities of the community" (Chapin 1935, 374). This approach has been operationalized either by (1) analyzing market data to define status groups that are distinguished by different lifestyle "profiles" (e.g., "ascetics," "materialists"), or (2) examining the consumption practices of existing status groups that are defined on dimensions other than consumption (e.g., teenagers, fundamentalists). The status groups of interest are in either case analytically distinct from Weberian classes; that is, the standard Weberian formula is to define classes within the domain of *production*, whereas status groups are determined by the "*consumption* of goods as represented by special styles of life" (Weber [1922] 1968, 937; italics in original).

Postmodern Analysis

The postmodern literature on lifestyles and consumption practices provides some of the conceptual underpinnings for market research of the above sort. This is evident, for example, in the characteristic postmodern argument that consumption practices are increasingly individuated and that the Weberian distinction between class and status thus takes on special significance in the contemporary context (e.g., Pakulski and Waters 1996; Beck 1992; Featherstone 1991; Saunders 1987). The relationship between group membership and consumption cannot for postmodernists be read off in some deterministic fashion; indeed, because individuals are presumed to associate with a complex mosaic of status groups (e.g., religious groups, internet chat groups, social movements), it is difficult to know how these combine and are selectively activated to produce (and reflect) individual tastes and practices. The stratification system may be seen, then, as a "status bizarre" (Pakulski and Waters 1996, 157) in which identities are reflexively constructed as individuals select and are shaped by their multiple statuses. Although postmodernists thus share with market researchers a deep skepticism of class-based analyses, the simple consumption-based typologies favored by some market researchers (e.g., Michman 1991) also fall short by failing to represent the fragmentation, volatility, and reflexiveness of postmodern consumption.

Reproduction Theory

The work of Bourdieu (e.g., 1984; 1977) can be read as an explicit effort to rethink the conventional distinction between class and status groupings (for related approaches, see Biernacki 1995; Calhoun, LiPuma, and Postone 1993; Lamont 1992). If one assumes, as does Bourdieu, that classes are highly efficient agents of selection and socialization, then their members will necessarily evince the shared dispositions, tastes, and styles of life that demarcate and define status groupings (see Gartman 1991; Brubaker 1985). Although it is hardly controversial to treat classes as socializing forces (see, e.g., Hyman 1966), Bourdieu takes the more extreme

stance that class-based conditioning "structures the whole experience of subjects" (1979, 2) and thus creates a near-perfect correspondence between the objective conditions of existence and internalized dispositions or tastes.[35] This correspondence is further strengthened because Bourdieu defines class so fluidly; namely, class is represented as the realization of exclusionary processes that create boundaries around workers with homogeneous dispositions, thus implying that classes will *necessarily* overlap with consumption-based status groupings. The key question, then, is whether such boundaries tend to emerge around objective categories (e.g., occupation) that are typically associated with class. For Bourdieu, occupational categories define some of the conditions of existence upon which classes are typically formed, yet other conditions of existence (e.g., race) are also implicated and may generate class formations that are not entirely coterminous with occupation. It follows that class boundaries are not objectively fixed but instead are like a "flame whose edges are in constant movement" (Bourdieu 1987, 13).

Structuration Theory

The foregoing approach is increasingly popular, but there is also continuing support for a middle-ground position that neither treats status groupings in isolation from class (e.g., Pakulski and Waters 1996) nor simply conflates them with class (e.g., Bourdieu 1984). The starting point for this position is the proposition that status and class are related in historically specific and contingent ways. For example, Giddens (1973, 109) adopts the usual assumption that classes are founded in the sphere of production, yet he further maintains that the "structuration" of such classes depends on the degree to which incumbents are unified by shared patterns of consumption and behavior (also see Weber [1922] 1968, 932–38). The twofold conclusion reached by Giddens is that (1) classes become distinguishable formations only insofar as they *overlap* with status groupings, and (2) the degree of overlap should be regarded as an empirical matter rather than something resolvable by conceptual fiat (cf. Bourdieu 1984). This type of formula appears to inform much of the current research on the consequences of class (e.g., Kingston forthcoming; Wright 1997; see also Goldthorpe and Marshall 1992). If contemporary commentators are so often exercised about the strength of "class effects," this is largely because these effects (purportedly) speak to the degree of class structuration and the consequent viability of class analysis in modern society.

*   *   *

The empirical results coming out of these various research programs have been interpreted in conflicting ways. Although some researchers have emphasized the strength and pervasiveness of class effects (e.g., Marshall 1997; Bourdieu 1984; Fussell 1983; Kohn 1980), others have argued that consumption practices are becoming uncoupled from class and that new theories are required to account for the attitudes and lifestyles that individuals adopt (e.g., Kingston forthcoming; Pakulski and Waters 1996). The evidence adduced for the latter view has sometimes been impressionistic in nature. For example, Nisbet (1959) concluded from his analysis of popular literature that early industrial workers could be readily distinguished by class-specific markers (e.g., distinctive dress, speech), whereas their postwar counterparts were increasingly participating in a "mass culture" that offered the same commodities to all classes and produced correspondingly standardized tastes, attitudes, and behaviors (see also Hall 1992; Clark and Lipset 1991, 405; Parkin 1979, 69; Goldthorpe et al. 1969, 1–29). The critical issue, of course, is not merely whether a mass culture of this sort is indeed emerging, but also whether the resulting standardization of lifestyles constitutes convincing evidence of a decline in class-based forms of social organization. As we have noted earlier, some commentators would regard the rise of mass culture as an important force for class destructuration (e.g., Gid-

dens 1973), whereas others have suggested that the "thin veneer of mass culture" (Adorno 1976) only obscures and conceals the more fundamental inequalities upon which classes are based (see also Horkheimer and Adorno 1972).

Ascriptive Processes

The forces of race, ethnicity, and gender have historically been relegated to the sociological sidelines by class theorists of both Marxist and non-Marxist persuasion.[36] In early versions of class analytic theory, status groups were treated as secondary forms of affiliation, whereas class-based ties were seen as more fundamental and decisive determinants of social and political action. This is not to suggest that race and ethnicity were ignored altogether in such treatments; however, when competing forms of communal solidarity were incorporated into conventional class models, they were typically represented as vestiges of traditional loyalties that would wither away under the rationalizing influence of socialism (e.g., Kautsky 1903), industrialism (e.g., Levy 1966), or modernization (e.g., Parsons 1975). Likewise, the forces of gender and patriarchy were of course frequently studied, yet the main objective in doing so was to understand their relationship to class formation and reproduction (see, e.g., Barrett 1980).

The first step in the intellectual breakdown of such approaches was the fashioning of a multidimensional model of stratification. Whereas many class theorists gave theoretical or conceptual priority to the economic dimension of stratification, the early multidimensionalists emphasized that social behavior could only be understood by taking into account all status group memberships (e.g., racial, gender) and the complex ways in which these interacted with one another and with class outcomes. The class analytic approach was further undermined by the apparent reemergence of racial, ethnic, and nationalist conflicts in the late postwar period. Far from withering away under the force of industrialism, the bonds of race and ethnicity seemed to be alive and well: The modern world was witnessing a "sudden increase in tendencies by people in many countries and many circumstances to insist on the significance of their group distinctiveness" (Glazer and Moynihan 1975, 3). This resurgence of status politics continues apace today. Indeed, not only have ethnic and regional solidarities intensified with the decline of conventional class politics in Eastern Europe and elsewhere (see Jowitt 1992), but gender-based affiliations and loyalties have likewise strengthened as feminist movements diffuse throughout much of the modern world.

The latter turn of events has led some commentators to proclaim that ascribed solidarities of race, ethnicity, and gender are replacing the class affiliations of the past and becoming the driving force behind future stratificational change. Although this line of argumentation was initially advanced by early theorists of gender and ethnicity (e.g., Firestone 1972; Glazer and Moynihan 1975), the recent diffusion of postmodernism has infused it with new life (especially Beck 1992, 91–101). These accounts typically rest on some form of zero-sum imagery; for example, Bell (1975) suggests quite explicitly that a trade-off exists between class-based and ethnic forms of solidarity, with the latter strengthening whenever the former weakens (see Hannan 1994, 506; Weber 1946, 193–94). As the conflict between labor and capital is institutionalized, Bell (1975) argues that class-based affiliations typically lose their affective content and that workers must turn to racial, ethnic, or religious ties to provide them with a renewed sense of identification and commitment. It could well be argued that gender politics often fill the same "moral vacuum" that the decline in class politics has allegedly generated (Parkin 1979, 34).

It may be misleading, of course, to treat the competition between ascriptive and class-based forces as a sociological horse race in which one, and only one, of these two principles can ultimately win out. In a pluralist society of the American kind, workers can choose an identity appropriate to the situational context; a modern-day worker might behave as "an industrial laborer in the morning, a black in the afternoon, and an American in the evening" (Parkin 1979, 34). Among recent postmodernists, the "essentialism" of conventional theorizing is rejected even more forcefully, so much so that even ethnicity and gender are no longer simply assumed to be privileged replacement statuses for class. This leads to an unusually long list of competing statuses that can become salient in situationally specific ways. As the British sociologist Saunders (1989, 4–5) puts it, "On holiday in Spain we feel British, waiting for a child outside the school gates we are parents, shopping in Marks and Spencer we are consumers, and answering questions, framed by sociologists with class on the brain, we are working class" (see also Calhoun 1994). The results of Emmison and Western (1990) on contemporary identity formation likewise suggest that manifold statuses are held in reserve and activated in situation-specific terms.

Although this situational model has not been widely adopted in contemporary research, there is renewed interest in understanding the diverse affiliations of individuals and the "multiple oppressions" (see Wright forthcoming) that these affiliations engender. It is now fashionable, for example, to assume that the major status groupings in contemporary stratification systems are defined by the *intersection* of ethnic, gender, or class affiliations (e.g., black working-class women, white middle-class men). The theoretical framework motivating this approach is not well-specified, but the implicit claim seems to be that these subgroupings shape the experiences, lifestyles, and life chances of individuals and thus define the social settings in which interests and subcultures typically emerge (Cotter, Hermsen, and Vanneman 1999; Hill Collins 1990; see also Gordon 1978; Baltzell 1964). The obvious effect of this approach is to invert the traditional post-Weberian perspective on status groupings; that is, whereas orthodox multidimensionalists described the stress experienced by individuals in inconsistent statuses (e.g., poorly educated doctors), these new multidimensionalists emphasize the shared interests and cultures generated within commonly encountered status sets (e.g., black working-class women).

The sociological study of gender, race, and ethnicity has thus burgeoned of late. In organizing this literature, one might usefully distinguish between (1) macro-level research addressing the structure of ascriptive solidarities and their relationship to class formation, and (2) attainment research exploring the effects of race, ethnicity, and gender on individual life chances. At the macro-level, scholars have typically examined such issues as the social processes by which ascriptive categories (e.g., "white," "black") are constructed; the sources and causes of ethnic conflict and solidarity; and the relationship between patriarchy, racism, and class-based forms of organization. The following types of research questions have thus been posed:

- *Awareness and consciousness:* How do conventional racial and ethnic classification schemes come to be accepted and institutionalized (Waters 2000; Cornell 2000)? Under what conditions are racial, ethnic, and gender identities likely to be salient or "activated" (Ridgeway and Smith-Lovin 1999; Ferrante and Brown 1996)?
- *Social conflict:* What generates variability across time and space in ethnic conflict and solidarity? Does modernization produce a "cultural division of labor" (Hechter 1975) that strengthens communal ties by making ethnicity a principal arbiter of life chances? Is ethnic conflict further intensified when ethnic groups compete for the same niche in the occupational structure (Waldinger 1996; Hannan 1994; Olzak 1992; Bonacich 1972)?
- *Class and ascriptive solidarities:* Are class-based solidarities weakened or strengthened by the forces of patriarchy and racism? Does housework serve to

reproduce capitalist relations of production by socializing children into submissive roles and providing male workers with a "haven in a heartless world" (e.g., Lasch 1977; see Baxter and Western forthcoming; Szelényi 2001)? Are capitalists or male majority workers the main beneficiaries of ethnic antagonism and patriarchy (e.g., Tilly 1998; Wright 1997; Hartmann 1981; Reich 1977; Bonacich 1972)?

These macro-level issues, although still of interest, have not taken off in popularity to the extent that attainment issues have. The literature on attainment is unusually rich and diverse; at the same time, there is much faddishness in the particular types of research questions that have been addressed, and the resulting body of work has a correspondingly haphazard and scattered feel (Lieberson 2001). The following questions have nonetheless emerged as (relatively) central ones in the field:

- *Modeling supply and demand:* What types of social forces account for ethnic, racial, and gender differentials in income and other valued resources? Are these differentials attributable to supply-side variability in the human capital that workers bring to the market (Marini and Fan 1997; Polachek and Siebert 1993; Marini and Brinton 1984)? Or are they produced by demand-side forces such as market segmentation, statistical or institutional discrimination, and the (seemingly) irrational tastes and preferences of employers (e.g., Reskin 2000; Nelson and Bridges 1999; Piore 1975; Arrow 1973; Becker 1957)?
- *Valuative discrimination:* Are occupations that rely on stereotypically female skills (e.g., nurturing) "culturally devalued" and hence more poorly remunerated than occupations that are otherwise similar? What types of organizational and cultural forces might

produce such valuative discrimination? Will this discrimination disappear as market forces gradually bring pay in accord with marginal productivity (Nelson and Bridges 1999; Kilbourne et al. 1994; Tam 1997)?

- *Segregation*: What are the causes and consequences of racial, ethnic, and gender segregation in housing and in the workplace? Does segregation arise from discrimination, economic forces, or voluntary choices or "tastes" for separation (Reskin, McBrier, and Kmec 1999; Reskin 1993; Bielby and Baron 1986)? Are ghettoization and other forms of segregation the main sources of African American disadvantage (e.g., Wilson 1999a; Massey and Denton 1993)? Under what conditions, if any, can ethnic or gender segregation (e.g., enclaving, same-sex schools) assist in socioeconomic attainment or assimilation (Waters 1999; Portes and Zhou 1993; Sanders and Nee 1987)?

- *The future of ascriptive inequalities:* What is the future of ethnic, racial, and gender stratification (Ridgeway and Correll 2000; Bielby 2000; Johnson, Rush, and Feagin 2000)? Does the "logic" of industrialism (and the spread of egalitarianism) require universalistic personnel practices and consequent declines in overt discrimination (Sakamoto, Wu, and Tzeng 2000; Hirschman and Snipp 1999; Jackson 1998; Wilson 1980)? Can this logic be reconciled with the persistence of massive segregation by sex and race (e.g., Massey 1996), the loss of manufacturing jobs and the associated rise of a modern ghetto underclass (Wilson 1996; Waldinger 1996), and the emergence of new forms of poverty and hardship among single women and recent immigrants (e.g., Waters 1999; Edin and Lein 1997; Portes 1996)?

- *Social policy:* What types of social policy and intervention are likely to reduce ascriptive inequalities (Johnson, Rush, and Feagin 2000; Nelson and Bridges 1999; Leicht 1999; Reskin 1998; Burstein 1998; 1994; England 1992)? Is there much popular support for affirmative action, comparable worth, and other reform strategies (e.g., Schuman et al. 1998)? Does opposition to such reform reflect deeply internalized racism and sexism (e.g., Kluegel and Bobo 1993)? Could this opposition be overcome by substituting race-based interventions (e.g., affirmative action) with class-based ones (e.g., Wilson 1999b; Kluegel and Bobo 1993)?

The preceding questions make it clear that ethnic, racial, and gender inequalities are often classed together and treated as analytically equivalent forms of ascription. Although Parsons (1951) and others (e.g., Tilly 1998; Mayhew 1970) have indeed emphasized the shared properties of "communal ties," one should bear in mind that such ties can be maintained (or subverted) in very different ways. It has long been argued, for example, that some forms of inequality can be rendered more palatable by the practice of pooling resources (e.g., income) across all family members. As Lieberson (2001) points out, the family operates to bind males and females together in a single unit of consumption, whereas extrafamilial institutions (e.g., schools, labor markets) must be relied on to provide the same integrative functions for ethnic groups. If these functions are left wholly unfilled, one might expect ethnic separatist and nationalist movements to emerge (e.g., Hechter 1975). The same "nationalist" option is obviously less viable for single-sex groups; indeed, barring any revolutionary changes in family structure or kinship relations, it seems unlikely that separatist solutions will ever garner much support among men or women. The latter considerations may account for the absence of a well-developed literature on *overt* conflict between single-sex groups (cf. Firestone 1972; Hartmann 1981).[37]

The Future of Stratification

It is instructive to conclude by briefly reviewing current approaches to understanding the
changing structure of contemporary stratification. As indicated in Figure 1, some commentators have suggested that future forms of
stratification will be defined by structural
changes in the productive system (i.e., structural approaches), whereas others have argued that modernity and postmodernity can
only be understood by looking beyond the
economic system and its putative consequences (i.e., cultural approaches). It will suffice to review these various approaches in cursory fashion because they are based on
theories and models that have been covered
extensively elsewhere in this essay.

The starting point for our discussion is the
now-familiar claim that human and political
capital are replacing economic capital as the
principal stratifying forces in advanced industrial society. In the most extreme versions of
this claim, the old class of moneyed capital is
represented as a dying force, and a new class
of intellectuals (e.g., Gouldner 1979), managers (e.g., Burnham 1962), or party bureaucrats (e.g., Djilas 1965) is assumed to be on
the road to power. There is still much new
class theorizing; however, because such accounts were tailor-made for the socialist case,
the fall of socialism complicates the analysis
and opens up new futures that are potentially
more complex than past theorists had anticipated. By some accounts, the rise of a new
class was effectively aborted by market reform, and transitional societies will ultimately revert to a classical form of capitalism
with its characteristically powerful economic
elite. This scenario need not imply a wholesale circulation of elites during the transitional period; to be sure, the old elite may
well oversee the creation of new entrepreneurs from agents other than itself (e.g.,
Nee 2001), but alternatively it might succeed
in converting its political capital into economic capital and install itself as the new
elite (Walder 1996; Rona-Tas 1997). It is also
possible that post-socialist managers will re-

tain considerable power even as the transition to capitalism unfolds. Under the latter
formulation, Central European elites take a
"historic short cut and move directly to the
most 'advanced' stage of corporate capitalism, never sharing their managerial power
(even temporarily) with a class of individual
owners" (Eyal, Szelényi, and Townsley 1998,
2). This implies, then, an immediate transition in Central Europe to advanced forms
of "capitalism without capitalists" (Eyal,
Szelényi, and Townsley 1998).

There is also much criticism of standard
"new class" interpretations of Western stratification systems. The (orthodox) Marxist
stance is that "news of the demise of the capitalist class is . . . somewhat premature"
(Zeitlin 1982, 216),[38] whereas the contrasting
position taken by Bell (1973) is that neither
the old capitalist class nor the so-called new
class will have unfettered power in the postindustrial future. Although there is widespread
agreement among postindustrial theorists that
human capital is becoming a dominant form
of property, this need not imply that "the
amorphous bloc designated as the knowledge
stratum has sufficient community of interest
to form a class" (Bell 1987, 464). The members of the knowledge stratum have diverse
interests because they are drawn from structurally distinct situses (e.g., military, business,
university) and because their attitudes are further influenced (and thus rendered heterogeneous) by noneconomic forces of various
sorts. The postindustrial vision of Bell (1973)
thus suggests that well-formed classes will be
replaced by the more benign divisions of situs.

As is well-known, Bell (1973) also argues
that human capital (e.g., educational credentials) will become the main determinant of life
chances, if only because job skills are upgraded by the expansion of professional, technical, and service sectors. Although the returns to education are indeed increasing as
predicted (e.g., Grusky and DiPrete 1990), the
occupational structure is evidently not upgrading quite as straightforwardly as Bell
(1973) suggested, and various "pessimistic
versions" of postindustrialism have accord-

FIGURE 1

Possible trajectories of change in advanced stratification systems

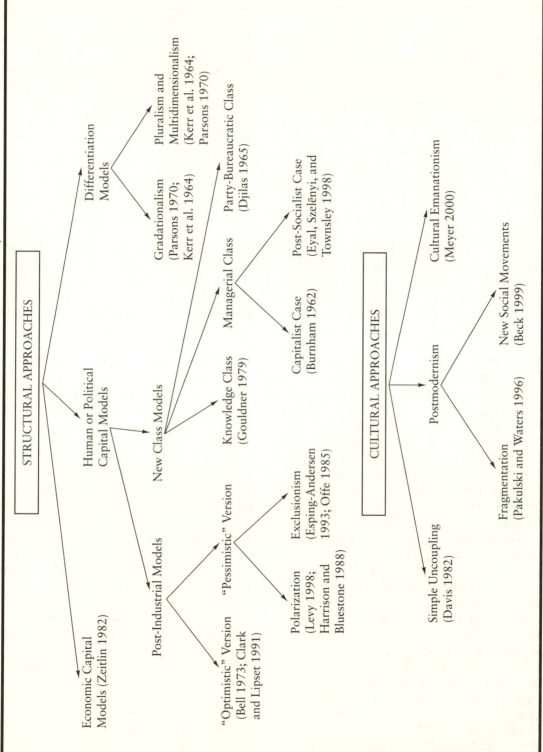

ingly emerged. In the American variant of such pessimism, the main concern is that postindustrialism leads to a "declining middle" and consequent polarization, as manufacturing jobs are either rendered technologically obsolete or exported to less-developed countries where labor costs are lower (e.g., Perrucci and Wysong 1999; Levy 1998; Harrison and Bluestone 1988). These losses are of course compensated by the predicted growth in the service sector, yet the types of service jobs that have emerged are quite often low skill, routinized, and accordingly less desirable than Bell (1973) imagined. In Europe, the same low-skill service jobs are less commonly found, with the resulting occupational structure more closely approximating the highly professionalized world that Bell (1973) envisaged. The European pessimists are nonetheless troubled by the rise of mass unemployment and the associated emergence of "outsider classes" that bear disproportionately the burden of unemployment (Esping-Andersen 1999; Brown and Crompton 1994; see also Aronowitz and DiFazio 1994). In both the European and American cases, the less-skilled classes are therefore losing out in the market, either by virtue of unemployment and exclusion (i.e., Europe) or low pay and poor prospects for advancement (i.e., the United States). The new pessimists thus anticipate a "resurgent proletarian underclass and, in its wake, a menacing set of new class correlates" (Esping-Andersen 1999, 95).

The foregoing variants of structuralism frequently draw on the quasi-functionalist premise that classes are configured around control over dominant assets (e.g., human capital) and that class constellations therefore shift as new types of assets assume increasingly prominent roles in production. The just-so histories that new class theorists tend to advance have a correspondingly zero-sum character in which stratificational change occurs as old forms of capital (e.g., economic capital) are superseded by new forms (e.g., human capital).[39] This framework might be contrasted, then, to stratification theories that treat the emergence of multiple bases of solidarity and affiliation as one of the distinctive features of modernity. For example, Parsons (1970) argues that the oft-cited "separation of ownership from control" (e.g., Berle and Means 1932) is not a unique historical event, but instead is merely one example of the broader tendency for ascriptively fused structures to break down into separate substructures and create a "complex composite of differentiated and articulating . . . units of community" (Parsons 1970, 25). This process of differentiation is further revealed in (1) the emergence of a finely graded hierarchy of specialized occupations (Parsons 1970; Kerr et al. 1964); (2) the spread of professional and voluntary associations that provide additional and competing bases of affiliation and solidarity (e.g., Parsons 1970; Kerr et al. 1964); and (3) the breakdown of the "kinship complex" as evidenced by the declining salience of family ties for careers, marriages, and other stratification outcomes (e.g., Parsons 1970; Featherman and Hauser 1978, 222–32; Treiman 1970; Blau and Duncan 1967, 429–31). The latter tendencies imply that the class standing of modern individuals is becoming "divorced from its historic relation to both kinship and property" (Parsons 1970, 24). As Parsons (1970) argues, the family may have once been the underlying unit of stratification, yet increasingly the class standing of individuals is determined by all the collectivities to which they belong, both familial and otherwise (see also Szelényi 2001). This multidimensionalist approach thus provides the analytic basis for rejecting the conventional family-based model of stratification that Parsons himself earlier espoused (e.g., Parsons 1954).[40]

The driving force behind these accounts is, of course, structural change of the sort conventionally described by such terms as *industrialism* (Kerr et al. 1964), *post-industrialism* (Bell 1973), *post-fordism* (Piore and Sabel 1984), and *differentiation* (Parsons 1970). By contrast, cultural accounts of change tend to deemphasize these forces or to cast them as epiphenomenal, with the focus thus shifting to the independent role of ideologies, social movements, and cultural practices in changing stratification forms. The culturalist tradition encompasses a host of accounts that have not, as yet, been fashioned into a unitary or cohesive whole. The following positions within this tradition might therefore be distinguished:

1. The weakest form of culturalism rests on the straightforward claim that economic interests are no longer decisive determinants of attitudes or lifestyles (e.g., Davis 1982; see Goldthorpe et al. 1969 on the "embourgeoisement" hypothesis). This "uncoupling" of class and culture is not necessarily inconsistent with structuralist models of change; for example, Adorno (1976) has long argued that mass culture only serves to obscure the more fundamental class divisions that underlie all historical change, and other neo-Marxians (e.g., Althusser 1969) have suggested that some forms of ideological convergence are merely transitory and will ultimately wither away as economic interests reassert themselves in the "last instance." The uncoupling thesis can therefore be rendered consistent with assorted versions of structuralism, yet it nonetheless lays the groundwork for theories that are fundamentally anti-structuralist in tone or character.

2. In some variants of postmodernism, the cultural sphere is not merely represented as increasingly autonomous from class, but the underlying dynamics of this sphere are also laid out in detail. The characteristic claim in this regard is that lifestyles, consumption practices, and identities are a complex function of the multiple status affiliations of individuals and the correspondingly "permanent and irreducible pluralism of the cultures" in which they participate (Bauman 1992, 102; see also Pakulski and Waters 1996; Hall 1989). This account cannot of course be reduced to structuralist forms of multidimensionalism (Parsons 1970); after all, most postmodernists argue that status affiliations do not mechanically determine consumption practices, as the latter are subjectively constructed in ways that allow for "respecification and invention of preferences . . . and provide for continuous regeneration" (Pakulski and Waters 1996, 155). It follows that lifestyles and identification are "shifting and unstable" (Pakulski and Waters 1996, 155), "indeterminate at the boundaries" (Crook, Pakulski, and Waters 1992), and accordingly "difficult to predict" (Pakulski and Waters 1996, 155).

3. In more ambitious variants of postmodernism, the focus shifts away from simply mapping the sources of individual-level attitudes or lifestyles, and the older class-analytic objective of understanding macro-level stratificational change is resuscitated. This ambition underlies, for example, all forms of postmodernism that seek to represent "new social movements" (e.g., feminism, ethnic and peace movements, environmentalism) as the vanguard force behind future stratificatory change. As argued by Eyerman (1992) and others (e.g., Touraine 1981), the labor movement can be seen as a fading enterprise rooted in the old conflicts of the workplace and industrial capitalism, whereas new social movements provide a more appealing call for collective action by virtue of their emphasis on issues of lifestyle, personal identity, and normative change. With this formulation, the proletariat is stripped of its privileged status as a universal class, and new social movements emerge as an alternative force "shaping the future of modern societies" (Haferkamp and Smelser 1992, 17). Although no self-respecting postmodernist will offer up a fresh "grand narrative" to replace that of discredited Marxism, new social movements are nonetheless represented within this sub-tradition as a potential source of change, albeit one that plays out in fundamentally unpredictable ways (e.g., Beck 1999).

4. The popularity of modern social movements might be attributed to ongoing structural transformations (e.g., the rise of the new class) rather than to any intrinsic appeal of the egalitarian ideals or values that these movements typically represent. Although structural arguments of this kind continue to be pressed (see, e.g., Eyerman 1992; Brint 1984), the alternative position staked out by Meyer (2001) and others (e.g., Eisenstadt 1992) is that cultural premises such as egalitarianism and functionalism are true generative forces underlying the rise and spread of modern stratification systems (see also Parsons 1970). As Meyer (2001) points out, egalitarian values not only produce a real reduction in some forms of inequality (e.g., civil inequalities), they also generate various societal subterfuges (e.g., differentiation) by which inequality is merely concealed from view rather than eliminated. The recent work of Meyer (2001) provides, then, an extreme example of how classical idealist principles can be deployed to account for modern stratificational change.

The final, and more prosaic, question that might be posed is whether changes of the preceding sort presage a general decline in the field of stratification itself. It could well be argued that Marxian and neo-Marxian models of class will decline in popularity with the rise of postmodern stratification systems and the associated uncoupling of class from lifestyles, consumption patterns, and political behavior (see Clark and Lipset 1991). This line of reasoning is not without merit, but it is worth noting that (1) past predictions of this sort have generated protracted debates that, if anything, have reenergized the field (see, e.g., Nisbet 1959); (2) the massive facts of economic, political, and honorific inequality will still be with us even if narrowly conceived models of class ultimately lose out in such debates; and (3) the continuing diffusion of egalitarian values suggests that all departures from equality, no matter how small, will be the object of considerable interest among sociologists and the lay public alike (see Meyer 2001). In making the latter point, our intent is not merely to note that sociologists may become "ever more ingenious" (Nisbet 1959, 12) in teasing out increasingly small departures from perfect equality, but also to suggest that entirely new forms and sources of inequality will likely be discovered and marketed by sociologists. This orientation has long been in evidence; for example, when the now-famous *Scientific American* studies (e.g., Taylor, Sheatsley, and Greeley 1978) revealed that overt forms of racial and ethnic prejudice were withering away, the dominant reaction within the discipline was to ask whether such apparent change concealed the emergence of more subtle and insidious forms of symbolic racism (see, e.g., Sears, Hensler, and Speer 1979). In similar fashion, when Beller (1982) reported a modest decline in occupational sex segregation, other sociologists were quick to ask whether the models and methods being deployed misrepresented the structure of change (e.g., Charles and Grusky 1995) or whether the classification system being used disguised counteracting trends at the intra-occupational level (e.g., Bielby and Baron 1986). The rise of personal computing and the Internet has likewise led to much fretting about possible class-based inequalities in access to computers (e.g., Nie and Erbring, 2000; Bosah 1998; Luke 1997). The point here is not to suggest that concerns of this kind are in any way misguided, but only to emphasize that modern sociologists are highly sensitized to inequalities and have a special interest in uncovering those "deep structures" of social differentiation (e.g., Baron 1994, 390) that are presumably concealed from ordinary view. This sensitivity to all things unequal bodes well for the future of the field even in the (unlikely) event of a long-term secular movement toward diminishing inequality.

Notes

1. In some stratification systems, the distribution of rewards can be described with a single matching algorithm, because individuals receive rewards directly rather than by virtue of the social positions that they occupy. The limiting case here would be the tribal economies of Melanesia in which "Big Men" (Oliver 1955) secured prestige and power through personal influence rather than through incumbency of any well-defined roles (see also Granovetter 1981, 12–14).

2. It goes without saying that the assets listed in Table 1 are institutionalized in quite diverse ways. For example, some assets are legally recognized by the state or by professional associations (e.g., civil rights, property ownership, educational credentials), others are reserved for incumbents of specified work roles (e.g., workplace authority), and yet others have no formal legal or institutional standing and are revealed probabilistically through patterns of behavior and action (e.g., high-status consumption practices, deference, derogation).

3. It is sometimes claimed that educational credentials are *entirely* investment goods and should therefore be excluded from any listing of the primitive dimensions underlying stratification systems (e.g., Runciman 1968, 33). In evaluating this claim, it is worth noting that an investment rhetoric for schooling became fashionable only quite recently (e.g., Becker 1975), whereas intellectuals and humanists have long viewed education as a simple consumption good.

4. This is not to gainsay the equally important point that parents often encourage their children to acquire such goods because of their putative benefits.

5. The term *stratification* has itself been seen as anti-Marxist by some commentators (e.g., Duncan 1968), because it places emphasis on the vertical ranking of classes rather than the exploitative relations between them. The geological metaphor implied by this term does indeed call attention to issues of hierarchy; nonetheless, whenever it is used in the present essay, the intention is to refer generically to inequality of all forms (including those involving exploitation).

6. Although native ability is by definition established at birth, it is often seen as a legitimate basis for allocating rewards (because it is presumed to be relevant to judgments of merit).

7. The scholars listed in the right-hand column of Table 1 are not necessarily reductionists of this sort.

8. The viability of a synthesizing approach clearly depends on the extent to which the stratification system is crystallized. If the degree of crystallization is low, then one cannot construct a unidimensional scale that is strongly correlated with its constituent parts.

9. There is, of course, an ongoing tradition of research in which the class structure is represented in gradational terms (see, e.g., Blau and Duncan 1967). However, no attempt has been made to construct an exhaustive rank-ordering of individuals based on their control over the resources listed in Table 1, nor is there any available rank-ordering of the thousands of detailed occupational titles that can be found in modern industrial societies (cf. Cain and Treiman 1981; Jencks, Perman, and Rainwater 1988). The approach taken by most gradationalists has been (1) to map individuals into a relatively small number (i.e., approximately 500) of broad occupational categories and (2) to subsequently map these categories into an even smaller number of prestige or socioeconomic scores.

10. According to Dahrendorf (1959, 171–73), the classes so formed are always specific to particular organizational settings, and the social standing of any given individual may therefore differ across the various associations in which he or she participates (e.g., workplace, church, polity). This line of reasoning leads Dahrendorf (1959, 171) to conclude that "if individuals in a given society are ranked according to the sum of their authority positions in all associations, the resulting pattern will not be a dichotomy but rather like scales of stratification according to income or prestige."

11. The class structure can also operate in less obtrusive ways; for example, one might imagine a social system in which classes have demonstrable macro-level consequences (and are therefore "real"), yet their members are not fully aware of these consequences nor of their membership in any particular class.

12. The assumptions embedded in columns 4–6 of Table 2 are clearly far-reaching. Unless a stratification system is perfectly crystallized, its parameters for inequality and rigidity cannot be represented as scalar quantities, nor can the intercorrelations between the multiple stratification dimensions be easily summarized in a single parameter. Moreover, even in stratification systems that are perfectly crystallized, there is no reason to believe that persistence over the lifecourse (i.e., intragenerational persistence) will always vary in tandem with persistence between generations (i.e., intergenerational inheritance). We have nonetheless assumed that each of our ideal-typical stratification systems can be characterized in terms of a single "rigidity parameter" (see column 5).

13. This claim does not hold with respect to gender; that is, men and women were typically assigned to different roles, which led to consequent differences in the distribution of rewards (e.g., see Pfeiffer 1977; Leakey and Lewin 1977).

14. It should again be stressed that our typology by no means exhausts the variability of agrarian stratification forms (see Kerbo 2000 for an extended review).

15. The state elite was charged with constructing and maintaining the massive irrigation systems that made agriculture possible in regions such as China, India, and the Middle East (cf. Anderson 1974, 490–92).

16. This is not to suggest that feudalism could only be found in the West or that the so-called Asiatic mode was limited to the East. Indeed, the social structure of Japan was essentially feudalistic until the mid-nineteenth century (with the rise of the Meiji State), and the Asiatic mode has been discovered in areas as diverse as Africa, pre-Columbian America, and even Mediterranean Europe (see Godelier 1978). The latter "discoveries" were of course predicated on a broad and ahistorical definition of the underlying ideal type. As always, there is a tension between scholars who seek to construct ideal types that are closely tied to historical social systems and those who seek to construct ones that are broader and more encompassing in their coverage.

17. This economic interpretation of feudalism is clearly not favored by all scholars. For example, Bloch (1961, 288–89) argues that the defining feature of feudalism is the monopolization of *authority* by a small group of nobles, with the economic concomitants of this authority (e.g., land ownership) thus being reduced to a position of secondary importance. The "authority classes" that emerge under his specification might be seen as feudal analogues to the social classes that Dahrendorf (1959) posits for the capitalist case.

18. In the so-called secondary stage of feudalism (Bloch 1961), the obligations of serfs and free men became somewhat more formalized and standardized, yet regional variations of various sorts still persisted.

19. It was not until the early fourteenth century that states of the modern sort appeared in Europe (see Hechter and Brustein 1980).

20. In describing this period of classical feudalism, Bloch (1961, 325) noted that "access to the circle of knights . . . was not absolutely closed, [yet] the door was nevertheless only very slightly ajar."

21. The Indian caste system flourished during the agrarian period, yet it persists in attenuated form within modern industrialized India (see Jalali 1992).

22. This is by no means an exhaustive listing of the various approaches that have been taken (see pp. 15–22 for a more detailed review).

23. Although educational institutions clearly play a certifying role, it does not follow that they emerge merely to fill a "functional need" for highly trained workers (see Collins 1979).

24. This issue is addressed in greater detail in Part IV ("Generating Inequality").

25. Although Pakulski and Waters (1996) use the label *postmodern* in their analyses, other scholars have invented such alternative terms as *late modernity, high modernity,* or *reflexive modernization* (Beck 1999; Lash 1999; Giddens 1991), and yet others continue to use *modernity* on the grounds that the changes at issue are mere extensions of those long underway (e.g., Maryanski and Turner 1992). We use the conventional term *postmodern* without intending to disadvantage the analyses of those who prefer other labels.

26. The rise of synthetic approaches makes it increasingly difficult to label scholars in meaningful ways. Although we have avoided standard "litmus test" definitions of what constitutes a true neo-Marxist or neo-Weberian, we have nonetheless found it possible (and useful) to classify scholars broadly in terms of the types of intellectual problems, debates, and literatures they address.

27. This position contrasts directly with the conventional wisdom that "social mobility as such is irrelevant to the problem of the existence of classes" (Dahrendorf 1959, 109; see also Poulantzas 1974, 37; Schumpeter 1951).

28. It should be stressed that Giddens departs from usual neo-Weberian formulations on issues such as "the social and political significance of the new middle class, the importance of bureaucracy as a form of domination, and the character of the state as a focus of political and military power" (Giddens 1980, 297). As indicated in the contents, we have nonetheless reluctantly imposed the neo-Weberian label on Giddens, if only because he follows the lead of Weber in treating the foregoing issues as central to understanding modern industrialism and capitalism (see note 26).

29. There is a close affinity between models of closure and those of exploitation. In comparing these approaches, the principal point of distinction is that neo-Marxians focus on the economic returns and interests that exclusionary practices generate, whereas closure theorists emphasize the common culture, sociocultural cohesiveness, and shared market and life experiences that such practices may produce (see Grusky and Sørensen 1998, 1211).

30. However, insofar as "every new class achieves its hegemony on a broader basis than that of the class ruling previously" (Marx and Engels [1947] 1970, 66), the presocialist revolutions can be interpreted as partial steps toward a classless society.

31. It is frequently argued that Americans have an elective affinity for gradational models of class. In accounting for this affinity, Ossowski (1963) and others (e.g., Lipset and Bendix 1959) have cited the absence of a feudal or aristocratic past in American history and the consequent reluctance of

Americans to recognize differences in status or power with overt forms of deference or derogation.

32. Although some of the research completed by Warner was gradational in character (e.g., Warner 1949, ch. 2), his preferred mapping of the American class structure is based on purely discrete categories.

33. This recommendation holds only for studies of attainment processes. In fact, given that other weightings may be optimal in other research contexts, Hauser and Warren (1997, 251) argue that "the global concept of occupational status is scientifically obsolete."

34. In this context, a "job" is a collection of activities that a worker is expected to perform in exchange for remuneration, whereas an "occupation" refers to an aggregation of jobs that are similar in terms of the activities performed.

35. This is not to suggest that the "subjects" themselves always fully appreciate the class-based sources of their tastes and preferences. As argued by Bourdieu (1977), the conditioning process is typically so seamless and unobtrusive that the sources of individual dispositions are concealed from view, and the "superior" tastes and privileged outcomes of socioeconomic elites are therefore misperceived (and legitimated) as the product of individual merit or worthiness.

36. The defining feature of ethnic groups is that their members "entertain a subjective belief in their common descent because of similarities of physical type or of customs or both, or because of memories of colonization and migration" (Weber [1922] 1968, 389). This definition implies that "races" are particular types of ethnic groups in which putative physical similarities provide the basis for a subjective belief in common descent (see Alba 1992, 575–76 for competing definitions).

37. There is, of course, a large popular literature that represents gender conflict in wholly individualistic terms. This tendency to personalize gender conflicts reflects the simple fact that men and women interact frequently and intimately in family settings.

38. The position that Zeitlin (1982) takes here is directed against the conventional argument that corporate ownership in Western industrialized societies is so diffused across multiple stockholders that effective corporate power has now defaulted to managers.

39. The recent work of Wright (1985) is similarly zero-sum in character. Although Wright emphasizes that multiple forms of capital tend to co-exist in any given historical system, he nonetheless defines the march of history in terms of transitions from one dominant form of capital to another.

40. The importance of distinguishing between the early and mature Parsons on matters of stratification should therefore be stressed. This distinc-tion has not been sufficiently appreciated in recent debates about the appropriateness of treating families as the primitive units of modern stratification analysis (see Szelényi 2001).

References

Abramson, Paul, and Ronald Inglehart. 1995. *Value Change in Global Perspective*. Ann Arbor: University of Michigan Press.

Adorno, Theodore. 1976. *Introduction to the Sociology of Music*. New York: Continuum.

Alba, Richard D. 1992. "Ethnicity." Pages 575–84 in *Encyclopedia of Sociology*, edited by Edgar F. Borgatta and Marie L. Borgatta. New York: Macmillan.

Althusser, Louis. 1969. *For Marx*. London: Verso.

Anderson, Perry. 1974. *Lineages of the Absolutist State*. London: Verso.

Aronowitz, Stanley, and William DiFazio. 1994. *The Jobless Future: Sci-Tech and the Dogma of Work*. Minneapolis: University of Minnesota Press.

Arrow, Kenneth J. 1973. "The Theory of Discrimination." Pages 3–33 in *Discrimination in Labor Markets*, edited by Orley Ashenfelter and Albert Rees. Princeton: Princeton University Press.

Aschaffenburg, Karen E. 1995. "On the Distribution of Cultural Capital: Social Location and Cultural Participation." Ph.D. diss., Department of Sociology, Stanford University.

Averitt, Robert T. 1968. *The Dual Economy: The Dynamics of American Industry Structure*. New York: Norton.

Baltzell, Edward D. 1958. *Philadelphia Gentlemen*. Glencoe, IL: Free Press.

Baltzell, Edward D. 1964. *The Protestant Establishment*. New York: Random House.

Baltzell, Edward D. 1991. *The Protestant Establishment Revisited*. New Brunswick, NJ: Transaction Publishers.

Barber, Bernard. 1968. "Social Stratification." Pages 288–95 in *International Encyclopedia of the Social Sciences*, edited by D. L. Sills. New York: Macmillan.

Barley, Stephen R. 1996. "Technicians in the Workplace: Ethnographic Evidence for Bringing Work into Organization Studies." *Administrative Science Quarterly* 41:404–41.

Barley, Stephen R., and Beth A. Bechky. 1994. "In the Backrooms of Science: The Work of Technicians in Science Labs." *Work and Occupations* 21:85–126.

Barley, Stephen R. and Pamela S. Tolbert. 1991. "Introduction: At the Intersection of Organizations and Occupations." *Research in the Sociology of Organizations* 8:1–13.

Baron, James N. 1994. "Reflections on Recent Generations of Mobility Research." Pages 384–93 in *Social Stratification: Class, Race, and Gender in Sociological Perspective*, edited by David B. Grusky. Boulder, CO: Westview Press.

Barrett, Michèle. 1980. *Women's Oppression Today: Problems in Marxist Feminist Analysis*. London: Verso.

Bauman, Zygmunt. 1992. *Intimations of Postmodernity*. London: Routledge.

Bauman, Zygmunt. 2000. *Liquid Modernity*. Cambridge: Polity Press.

Baumol, William J. 1967. "The Macro-Economics of Unbalanced Growth." *American Economic Review* 57:415–26.

Baxter, Janeen, and Mark Western. Forthcoming. *Reconfigurations of Class and Gender*. Stanford: Stanford University Press.

Bayly, Susan. 1999. *The New Cambridge History of India*. Cambridge: Cambridge University Press.

Beck, Ulrich. 1987. "Beyond Status and Class: Will There be an Individualized Class Society?" In *Modern German Sociology*, edited by Volker Meja, Dieter Misgeld, and Nico Stehr. New York: Columbia University Press.

Beck, Ulrich. 1992. *Risk Society*. London: Sage Publications.

Beck, Ulrich. 1999. *World Risk Society*. Cambridge: Polity Press.

Becker, Gary S. 1957. *The Economics of Discrimination*. Chicago: University of Chicago Press.

Becker, Gary S. 1975. *Human Capital*. Chicago: University of Chicago Press.

Bell, Daniel. 1973. *The Coming of Post-Industrial Society*. New York: Basic Books.

Bell, Daniel. 1975. "Ethnicity and Social Change." Pages 141–74 in *Ethnicity: Theory and Experience*, edited by Nathan Glazer and Daniel P. Moynihan. Cambridge: Harvard University Press.

Bell, Daniel. 1987. "The New Class: A Muddled Concept." Pages 455-68 in *Structured Social Inequality*, 2d ed., edited by Celia S. Heller. New York: Macmillan.

Beller, Andrea H. 1982. "Occupational Segregation by Sex and Race, 1960-81." Pages 11–26 in *Sex Segregation in the Workplace*, edited by Barbara F. Reskin. Washington, DC: National Academy.

Berg, Ivar. 1973. *Education and Jobs: The Great Training Robbery*. Harmondsworth: Penguin Books.

Berle, Adolf, and Gardiner Means. 1932. *The Modern Corporation and Private Property*. New York: Macmillan.

Berreman, Gerald. 1981. *Caste and Other Inequities*. Delhi: Manohar.

Biblarz, Timothy J., and Adrian E. Raftery. 1993. "The Effects of Family Disruption on Social Mobility." *American Sociological Review* 58: 97–109.

Biblarz, Timothy J., and Adrian E. Raftery. 1999. "Family Structure, Educational Attainment, and Socioeconomic Success: Rethinking the 'Pathology of Matriarchy'." *American Journal of Sociology* 105:321–65.

Bielby, William T. 2000. "Minimizing Workplace Gender and Racial Bias." *Contemporary Sociology* 29:120–29.

Bielby, William T., and James N. Baron. 1986. "Men and Women at Work: Sex Segregation and Statistical Discrimination." *American Journal of Sociology* 91:759–99.

Biernacki, Richard. 1995. *The Fabrication of Labor: Germany and Britain, 1640–1914*. Berkeley: University of California Press.

Birdsall, Nancy, and Carol Graham. 2000. *New Markets, New Opportunities? Economic and Social Mobility in a Changing World*. Washington, DC: Brookings Institution Press.

Blair-Loy, Mary. 1999. "Career Patterns of Executive Women in France: An Optimal Matching Analysis." *American Journal of Sociology* 104: 1346–97.

Blau, Peter M., and Otis Dudley Duncan. 1967. *The American Occupational Structure*. New York: Wiley.

Bloch, Marc. 1961. *Feudal Society*. London: Routledge & Kegan Paul.

Bonacich, Edna. 1972. "A Theory of Ethnic Antagonism: The Split Labor Market." *American Sociological Review* 37:547–59.

Bosah, Ebo, ed. 1998. *Cyberghetto or Cybertopia? Race, Class, and Gender on the Internet*. Westport, CT: Praeger.

Bottomore, Thomas B. 1965. *Classes in Modern Society*. London: Allen & Unwin.

Bourdieu, Pierre. 1977. *Outline of a Theory of Practice*. Translated by Richard Nice. New York: Cambridge University Press.

Bourdieu, Pierre. 1979. *Algeria 1960*. Translated by Richard Nice. Cambridge: Cambridge University Press.

Bourdieu, Pierre. 1984. *Distinction. A Social Critique of the Judgement of Taste*. Translated by Richard Nice. Cambridge: Harvard University Press.

Bourdieu, Pierre. 1987. "What Makes a Social Class?" *Berkeley Journal of Sociology* 22:1–18.

Bourdieu, Pierre, and Jean-Claude Passeron. 1977. *Reproduction in Education, Society, and Culture*. Beverly Hills, CA: Sage Publications.

Bradley, Harriet. 1996. *Fractured Identities: Changing Patterns of Inequality*. Cambridge: Polity Press.

Brass, Paul R. 1983. *Caste, Faction, and Party in Indian Politics: Faction and Party*. Vol. 1. Delhi: Chanakya Publications.

Brass, Paul R. 1985. *Caste, Faction, and Party in Indian Politics: Elections Studies.* Vol. 2. Delhi: Chanakya Publications.

Braverman, Harry. 1974. *Labor and Monopoly Capital.* New York and London: Monthly Review Press.

Breen, Richard, and John H. Goldthorpe. 1997. "Explaining Educational Differentials: Towards a Formal Rational Action Theory." *Rationality and Society* 9:275–305.

Brint, Steven. 1984. "New Class and Cumulative Trend Explanations of Liberal Political Attitudes of Professionals." *American Journal of Sociology* 90:30–71.

Brinton, Mary C., Yean-Ju Lee, and William L. Parish. 1995. "Married Women's Employment in Rapidly Industrializing Societies: Examples from East Asia." *American Journal of Sociology* 100:1099–1130.

Brook, Timothy. 1989. *The Asiatic Mode of Production in China.* Armonk, NY: M. E. Sharpe.

Broom, Leonard, and Robert G. Cushing. 1977. "A Modest Test of an Immodest Theory: The Functional Theory of Stratification." *American Sociological Review* 42:157–69.

Brown, Phillip, and Rosemary Crompton, eds. 1994. *Economic Restructuring and Social Exclusion.* London: Taylor & Francis.

Brubaker, Rogers. 1985. "Rethinking Classical Theory: The Sociological Vision of Pierre Bourdieu." *Theory and Society* 14:745–75.

Bryson, Bethany. 1996. "'Anything But Heavy Metal': Symbolic Exclusion and Musical Dislikes." *American Sociological Review* 61:884–99.

Burnham, James. 1962. *The Managerial Revolution.* Bloomington: Indiana University Press.

Burstein, Paul, ed. 1994. *Equal Employment Opportunity: Labor Market Discrimination and Public Policy.* New York: Aldine de Gruyter.

Burstein, Paul. 1998. *Discrimination, Jobs, and Politics: The Struggle for Equal Employment Opportunity in the United States since the New Deal.* Chicago: University of Chicago Press.

Burt, Ronald S. 1997. "The Contingent Value of Social Capital." *Administrative Science Quarterly* 42:339–65.

Burton, Mary D., and David B. Grusky. 1992. "A Quantitative History of Comparative Stratification Research." *Contemporary Sociology* 21:623–31.

Cain, Pamela S., and Donald J. Treiman. 1981. "The Dictionary of Occupational Titles as a Source of Occupational Data." *American Sociological Review* 46:253–78.

Calhoun, Craig, Edward LiPuma, and Moishe Postone, eds. 1993. *Bourdieu: Critical Perspectives.* Chicago: University of Chicago Press.

Calhoun, Craig, ed. 1994. *Social Theory and the Politics of Identity.* Oxford: Blackwell.

Casey, Catherine. 1995. *Work, Self, and Society.* London: Routledge.

Castells, Manuel. 1999. *The Information Age: Economy, Society, and Culture.* Vols. I, II, and III. Oxford: Basil Blackwell.

Chaney, David. 1996. *Lifestyles.* London: Routledge.

Chapin, Francis S. 1935. *Contemporary American Institutions: A Sociological Analysis.* New York: Harper & Row.

Charles, Maria, and David B. Grusky. 1995. "Models for Describing the Underlying Structure of Sex Segregation." *American Journal of Sociology* 100:931–71.

Chesneaux, Jean. 1964. "Le mode de production asiatique: Une nouvelle étape de la discussion." *Eirenc* 3:131–46.

Clark, Terry N., and Seymour M. Lipset. 1991. "Are Social Classes Dying?" *International Sociology* 6:397–410.

Coleman, James S. 1990. *Foundations of Social Theory.* Cambridge: Harvard University Press.

Collins, Randall. 1975. *Conflict Sociology.* New York: Academic Press.

Collins, Randall. 1979. *The Credential Society.* New York: Academic Press.

Connor, Walter D. 1991. *The Accidental Proletariat: Workers, Politics, and Crisis in Gorbachev's Russia.* Princeton: Princeton University Press.

Corcoran, Mary, and Terry Adams. 1997. "Race, Sex, and the Intergenerational Transmission of Poverty." Pages 461–517 in *Consequences of Growing Up Poor*, edited by Greg J. Duncan and Jeanne Brooks-Gunn. New York: Russell Sage Foundation.

Cornell, Stephen. 2000. "That's the Story of Our Life." Pages 41–53 in *We Are a People: Narrative and Multiplicity in Constructing Ethnic Identity*, edited by Paul Spickard and W. Jeffrey Burroughs. Philadelphia: Temple University Press.

Coser, Lewis A. 1975. "Presidential Address: Two Methods in Search of a Substance." *American Sociological Review* 40:691–700.

Cotter, David A., Joan M. Hermsen, and Reeve Vanneman. 1999. "Systems of Gender, Race, and Class Inequality: Multilevel Analyses." *Social Forces* 78:433–60.

Crompton, Rosemary. 1996. *Class and Stratification: An Introduction to Current Debates.* Cambridge: Polity Press.

Crook, Stephen, Jan Pakulski, and Malcolm Waters. 1992. *Postmodernization.* London: Sage Publications.

Cullen, John B., and Shelley M. Novick. 1979. "The Davis-Moore Theory of Stratification: A Further Examination and Extension." *American Journal of Sociology* 84:1424–37.

Dahrendorf, Ralf. 1959. *Class and Class Conflict in Industrial Society*. Stanford: Stanford University Press.

Dahrendorf, Ralf. 1968. *Essays in the Theory of Society*. Stanford: Stanford University Press.

Danziger, Sheldon, and Peter Gottschalk, eds. 1993. *Uneven Tides: Rising Inequality in America*. New York: Russell Sage.

Danziger, Sheldon, and Peter Gottschalk. 1995. *America Unequal*. New York: Russell Sage.

Davis, James. 1982. "Achievement Variables and Class Cultures: Family, Schooling, Job, and Forty-Nine Dependent Variables in the Cumulative GSS." *American Sociological Review* 47:569–86.

Davis, Kingsley. 1948. *Human Society*. New York: Macmillan.

Davis, Kingsley. 1953. "Reply." *American Sociological Review* 18:394–97.

Davis, Kingsley, and Wilbert E. Moore. 1945. "Some Principles of Stratification." *American Sociological Review* 10:242–49.

DiMaggio, Paul. 1992. "Cultural Boundaries and Structural Change: The Extension of the High Culture Model to Theater, Opera, and the Dance, 1900–1940." Pages 21–57 in *Cultivating Differences: Symbolic Boundaries and the Making of Inequality*, edited by Michèle Lamont and Marcel Fournier. Chicago: University of Chicago Press.

DiMaggio, Paul. 2000. "Social Stratification, Life Style, and Social Cognition." Pages 542–552 in *Social Stratification: Class, Race, and Gender in Sociological Perspective*, 2d ed., edited by David B. Grusky. Boulder, CO: Westview Press.

DiPrete, Thomas A., Paul M. de Graaf, Ruud Luijkx, Michael Tåhlin, and Hans-Peter Blossfeld. 1997. "Collectivist versus Individualist Mobility Regimes? Structural Change and Job Mobility in Four Countries." *American Journal of Sociology* 103:318–58.

DiPrete, Thomas A., and Patricia A. McManus. 1996. "Institutions, Technical Change, and Diverging Life Chances: Earnings Mobility in the United States and Germany." *American Journal of Sociology* 102:34–79.

Djilas, Milovan. 1965. *The New Class*. New York: Praeger.

Doeringer, Peter, and Michael Piore. 1971. *Internal Labor Markets and Manpower Analysis*. Lexington, MA: D. C. Heath.

Domhoff, G. William. 1998. *Who Rules America? Power and Politics in the Year 2000*. Mountain View, CA: Mayfield Publishing.

Drucker, Peter. 1993. *Post-Capitalist Society*. New York: Harper.

Dumont, Louis. 1970. *Homo Hierarchicus*. Chicago: University of Chicago Press.

Duncan, Otis Dudley. 1968. "Social Stratification and Mobility: Problems in the Measurement of Trend." Pages 675–719 in *Indicators of Social Change*, edited by Eleanor B. Sheldon and Wilbert E. Moore. New York: Russell Sage Foundation.

Durkheim, Émile. [1893] 1933. *The Division of Labor in Society*. New York: Macmillan.

Edin, Kathryn, and Laura Lein. 1997. *Making Ends Meet: How Single Mothers Survive Welfare and Low-Wage Work*. New York: Russell Sage Foundation.

Ehrenreich, Barbara, and John Ehrenreich. 1979. "The Professional-Managerial Class." Pages 5–45 in *Between Labor and Capital*, edited by Pat Walker. Boston: South End Press.

Eisenstadt, S. N. 1992. "A Reappraisal of Theories of Social Change and Modernization." Pages 412–29 in *Social Change and Modernity*, edited by Hans Haferkamp and Neil J. Smelser. Berkeley: University of California Press.

Emmison, Michael, and Mark Western. 1990. "Social Class and Social Identity: A Comment on Marshall et al." *Sociology* 24:241–53.

England, Paula. 1992. *Comparable Worth: Theories and Evidence*. New York: de Gruyter.

Erikson, Robert, and John H. Goldthorpe. 1992. *The Constant Flux: A Study of Class Mobility in Industrial Societies*. Oxford: Clarendon Press.

Erikson, Robert, and John H. Goldthorpe. 2000. "Trends in Class Mobility: The Post-War European Experience." Pages 344–372 in *Social Stratification: Class, Race, and Gender in Sociological Perspective*, 2d ed., edited by David B. Grusky. Boulder, CO: Westview Press.

Esping-Andersen, Gøsta. 1990. *The Three Worlds of Welfare Capitalism*. Cambridge: Polity Press.

Esping-Andersen, Gøsta. 1993. *Changing Classes: Stratification and Mobility in Post-Industrial Societies*. London: Sage.

Esping-Andersen, Gøsta. 1999. *Social Foundations of Postindustrial Economies*. Oxford: Oxford University Press.

Evans, Geoffrey. 1999. *The End of Class Politics? Class Voting in Comparative Context*. Oxford: Oxford University Press.

Eyal, Gil, Iván Szelényi, and Eleanor Townsley. 1998. *Making Capitalism without Capitalists: The New Ruling Elites in Eastern Europe*. London: Verso.

Eyal, Gil, Iván Szelényi, and Eleanor Townsley. 2000. "Making Capitalism without Capitalists." Pages 852–858 in *Social Stratification: Class, Race, and Gender in Sociological Perspective*, 2d ed., edited by David B. Grusky. Boulder, CO: Westview Press.

Eyerman, Ron. 1992. "Modernity and Social Movements." Pages 37–54 in *Social Change and Modernity*, edited by Hans Haferkamp and Neil J. Smelser. Berkeley: University of California Press.

Featherman, David L. 1981. "Social Stratification and Mobility." *American Behavioral Scientist* 24:364–85.

Featherman, David L., and Robert M. Hauser. 1978. *Opportunity and Change*. New York: Academic Press.

Featherstone, Mike. 1991. *Consumer Culture and Postmodernism*. London: Sage.

Ferrante, Joan, and Prince Brown, Jr. 1996. *The Social Construction of Race and Ethnicity in the United States*. New York: Longman.

Finley, Moses J. 1960. *Slavery in Classical Antiquity*. Cambridge: W. Heffer & Sons.

Firestone, Shulamith. 1972. *The Dialectic of Sex*. New York: Bantam.

Fischer, Claude S., Michael Hout, Martín Sánchez Jankowski, Samuel R. Lucas, Ann Swidler, and Kim Voss. 1996. *Inequality by Design: Cracking the Bell Curve Myth*. Princeton: Princeton University Press.

Fligstein, Neil, and Peter Brantley. 1992. "Bank Control, Owner Control, or Organizational Dynamics: Who Controls the Modern Corporation?" *American Journal of Sociology* 98:280–307.

Fligstein, Neil, and Haldor Byrkjeflot. 1996. "The Logic of Employment Systems." Pages 11–35 in *Social Differentiation and Social Inequality*, edited by James N. Baron, David B. Grusky, and Donald J. Treiman. Boulder, CO: Westview Press.

Freidson, Eliot. 1994. *Professionalism Reborn: Theory, Prophecy, and Policy*. Chicago: University of Chicago Press.

Fussell, Paul. 1983. *Class*. New York: Ballantine.

Ganzeboom, Harry B. G., Donald J. Treiman, and Wout C. Ultee. 1991. "Comparative Intergenerational Stratification Research: Three Generations and Beyond." *Annual Review of Sociology* 17:277–302.

Gartman, David. 1991. "Culture as Class Symbolization or Mass Reification? A Critique of Bourdieu's *Distinction*." *American Journal of Sociology* 97:421–47.

Gershuny, Jonathan. 1983. *Social Innovation and the Division of Labor*. Oxford: Oxford University Press.

Giddens, Anthony. 1973. *The Class Structure of the Advanced Societies*. London: Hutchinson.

Giddens, Anthony. 1980. "Postscript." In *The Class Structure of the Advanced Societies*. London: Hutchinson.

Giddens, Anthony. 1991. *Modernity and Self-Identity: Self and Society in the Late Modern Age*. Stanford: Stanford University Press.

Gilbert, Dennis. 1998. *The American Class Structure in an Age of Growing Inequality*. Belmont, CA: Wadsworth Publishing.

Glazer, Nathan, and Daniel P. Moynihan. 1975. "Introduction." Pages 3–26 in *Ethnicity: The-ory and Experience*, edited by Nathan Glazer and Daniel P. Moynihan. Cambridge: Harvard University Press.

Godelier, Maurice. 1978. "The Concept of the 'Asiatic Mode of Production' and Marxist Models of Social Evolution." Pages 209–57 in *Relations of Production, Marxist Approaches to Economic Anthropology*, edited by D. Seddon. London: Cass.

Goldthorpe, John H. 1982. "On the Service Class: Its Formation and Future." Pages 162–185 in *Social Class and the Division of Labor*, edited by A. Giddens and G. Mackenzie. Cambridge: Cambridge University Press.

Goldthorpe, John H. 1987. *Social Mobility and Class Structure in Modern Britain*. Oxford: Clarendon Press.

Goldthorpe, John H., David Lockwood, Frank Bechhofer, and Jennifer Platt. 1969. *The Affluent Worker in the Class Structure*. London: Cambridge University Press.

Goldthorpe, John H., and Gordon Marshall. 1992. "The Promising Future of Class Analysis: A Response to Recent Critiques." *Sociology* 26:381–400.

Gordon, Milton M. 1978. *Human Nature, Class, and Ethnicity*. New York: Oxford University Press.

Gottschalk, Peter. 1997. "Inequality, Income Growth, and Mobility: The Basic Facts." *Journal of Economic Perspectives* 11:21–40.

Gouldner, Alvin. 1979. *The Future of Intellectuals and the Rise of the New Class*. New York: Seabury.

Gouldner, Alvin. 1980. *The Two Marxisms: Contradictions and Anomalies in the Development of Theory*. New York: Seabury Press.

Granovetter, Mark. 1981. "Toward a Sociological Theory of Income Differences." Pages 11–47 in *Sociological Perspectives on Labor Markets*, edited by Ivar Berg. New York: Academic Press.

Grusky, David B. 2000. "Foundations of Class Analysis: A Durkheimian Perspective." Center for the Study of Inequality Working Paper, Cornell University, Ithaca.

Grusky, David B., and Thomas A. DiPrete. 1990. "Recent Trends in the Process of Stratification." *Demography* 27:617–37.

Grusky, David B., and Robert M. Hauser. 1984. "Comparative Social Mobility Revisited: Models of Convergence and Divergence in 16 Countries." *American Sociological Review* 49:19–38.

Grusky, David B., and Jesper B. Sørensen. 1998. "Can Class Analysis Be Salvaged?" *American Journal of Sociology* 103:1187–1234.

Grusky, David B., and Jesper B. Sørensen. 2001. "Are There Big Social Classes?" Pages 183–194 in *Social Stratification: Class, Race, and Gen-*

der in Sociological Perspective, 2d ed., edited by David B. Grusky. Boulder, CO: Westview Press.

Grusky, David B., and Ann Azumi Takata. 1992. "Social Stratification." Pages 1955–70 in *Encyclopedia of Sociology*, edited by Edgar F. Borgatta and Marie L. Borgatta. New York: Macmillan.

Grusky, David B., and Stephen E. Van Rompaey. 1992. "The Vertical Scaling of Occupations: Some Cautionary Comments and Reflections." *American Journal of Sociology* 97:1712–28.

Haferkamp, Hans, and Neil J. Smelser. 1992. "Introduction." Pages 1–33 in *Social Change and Modernity*, edited by Hans Haferkamp and Neil J. Smelser. Berkeley: University of California Press.

Halaby, Charles N., and David Weakliem. 1993. "Class and Authority in the Earnings Function." *American Sociological Review* 58:16–30.

Hall, Stuart. 1989. "The Meaning of New Times." Pages 116–34 in *New Times: The Changing Face of Politics in the 1990s*, edited by Stuart Hall and Martin Jacques. London: Lawrence & Wishart.

Hall, John R. 1992. "The Capital(s) of Cultures: A Nonholistic Approach to Status Situations, Class, Gender, and Ethnicity." Pages 257–85 in *Cultivating Differences. Symbolic Boundaries and the Making of Inequality*. Chicago: University of Chicago Press.

Halle, David. 1996. *Inside Culture: Art and Class in the American Home*. Chicago: University of Chicago Press.

Han, Shin-Kap, and Phyllis Moen. 1999. "Clocking Out: Temporal Patterning of Retirement." *American Journal of Sociology* 105:191–236.

Hannan, Michael. 1994. "Dynamics of Ethnic Boundaries." Pages 500–8 in *Social Stratification: Class, Race, and Gender in Sociological Perspective*, edited by David B. Grusky. Boulder, CO: Westview Press.

Harrison, Bennett, and Barry Bluestone. 1988. *The Great U-Turn: Corporate Restructuring and the Polarizing of America*. New York: Basic Books.

Hartmann, Heidi. 1981. "The Unhappy Marriage of Marxism and Feminism: Towards a More Progressive Union." Pages 1–41 in *Women and Revolution*, edited by Lydia Sargent. Boston: South End Press.

Hauser, Robert M., and David L. Featherman. 1977. *The Process of Stratification: Trends and Analyses*. New York: Academic Press.

Hauser, Robert M., and Min-Hsiung Huang. 1997. "Verbal Ability and Socioeconomic Success: A Trend Analysis." *Social Science Research* 26:331–76.

Hauser, Robert M., and Megan M. Sweeney. 1997. "Does Poverty in Adolescence Affect the Life Chances of High School Graduates?" Pages 541–95 in *Consequences of Growing Up Poor*, edited by Greg J. Duncan and Jeanne Brooks-Gunn. New York: Russell Sage Foundation.

Hauser, Robert M., and John Robert Warren. 1997. "Socioeconomic Indexes of Occupational Status: A Review, Update, and Critique." Pages 177–298 in *Sociological Methodology, 1997*, edited by Adrian Raftery. Cambridge: Blackwell.

Hauser, Robert M., Shu-Ling Tsai, and William H. Sewell. 1983. "A Model of Stratification with Response Error in Social and Psychological Variables." *Sociology of Education* 56:20–46.

Hechter, Michael. 1975. *Internal Colonialism: The Celtic Fringe in British National Development, 1536–1966*. Berkeley: University of California Press.

Hechter, Michael, and William Brustein. 1980. "Regional Modes of Production and Patterns of State Formation in Western Europe." *American Journal of Sociology* 85:1061–94.

Herrnstein, Richard J., and Charles Murray. 1994. *The Bell Curve: Intelligence and Class Structure in American Life*. New York: Simon & Schuster.

Hill Collins, Patricia. 1990. *Black Feminist Thought: Knowledge, Consciousness, and the Politics of Empowerment*. London: Routledge.

Hirschman, Charles, and C. Matthew Snipp. 1999. "The State of the American Dream: Race and Ethnic Socioeconomic Inequality in the United States, 1970–1990." Pages 89–107 in *A Nation Divided: Diversity, Inequality, and Community in American Society*, edited by Phyllis Moen, Donna Dempster-McClain, and Henry A. Walker. Ithaca: Cornell University Press.

Hobsbawm, Eric J. 1965. "Introduction." Pages 9–65 in *Pre-Capitalist Economic Formations*, translated by Jack Cohen and edited by Eric J. Hobsbawm. New York: International Publishers.

Hochschild, Jennifer L. 1981. *What's Fair? American Beliefs about Distributive Justice*. Cambridge: Harvard University Press.

Hochschild, Jennifer L. 1995. *Facing Up to the American Dream: Race, Class, and the Soul of the Nation*. Princeton: Princeton University Press.

Horkheimer, Max, and Theodor Adorno. 1972. *Dialectic of Enlightenment*. New York: Herder & Herder.

Hout, Michael. 1988. "More Universalism, Less Structural Mobility: The American Occupational Structure in the 1980s." *American Journal of Sociology* 93:1358–1400.

Hout, Michael, and Robert M. Hauser. 1992. "Symmetry and Hierarchy in Social Mobility: A Methodological Analysis of the CASMIN Model of Class Mobility." *European Sociological Review* 8:239–66.

Hout, Michael, Clem Brooks, and Jeff Manza. 1993. "The Persistence of Classes in Post-Industrial Societies." *International Sociology* 8:259–77.

Huaco, George A. 1966. "The Functionalist Theory of Stratification: Two Decades of Controversy." *Inquiry* 9:215–40.

Hyman, Herbert H. 1966. "The Value Systems of Different Classes. A Social Psychological Contribution to the Analysis of Stratification." Pages 488–99 in *Class, Status, and Power*, edited by Reinhard Bendix and Seymour M. Lipset. New York: Free Press.

Ishida, Hiroshi, Walter Müller, and John M. Ridge. 1995. "Class Origin, Class Destination, and Education: A Cross-National Study of Ten Industrial Nations." *American Journal of Sociology* 101:145–93.

Jackson, Elton F., and Richard F. Curtis. 1972. "Effects of Vertical Mobility and Status Inconsistency: A Body of Negative Evidence." *American Sociological Review* 37:701–13.

Jackson, Robert Max. 1998. *Destined for Equality: The Inevitable Rise of Women's Status*. Cambridge: Harvard University Press.

Jalali, Rita. 1992. "Caste and Class." Pages 172–76 in *Encyclopedia of Sociology*, edited by Edgar F. Borgatta and Marie L. Borgatta. New York: Macmillan.

Jencks, Christopher, Susan Bartlett, Mary Corcoran, James Crouse, David Eaglesfield, Gregory Jackson, Kent McClelland, Peter Mueser, Michael Olneck, Joseph Schwartz, Sherry Ward, and Jill Williams. 1979. *Who Gets Ahead? The Determinants of Economic Success in America*. New York: Basic Books.

Jencks, Christopher, Lauri Perman, and Lee Rainwater. 1988. "What Is a Good Job? A New Measure of Labor-Market Success." *American Journal of Sociology* 93:1322–57.

Jencks, Christopher, Marshall Smith, Henry Acland, Mary Jo Bane, David Cohen, Herbert Gintis, Barbara Heyns, and Stephen Michelson. 1972. *Inequality: A Reassessment of the Effect of Family and Schooling in America*. New York: Basic Books.

Johnson, Jacqueline, Sharon Rush, and Joe Feagin. 2000. "Doing Antiracism and Making a Nonracist Society." *Contemporary Sociology* 29:95–110.

Jowitt, Ken. 1992. *New World Disorder: The Leninist Extinction*. Berkeley: University of California Press.

Kalmijn, Matthijs. 1994. "Mother's Occupational Status and Children's Schooling." *American Sociological Review* 59:257–75.

Kautsky, Karl. 1903. *The Social Revolution*. Chicago: C. H. Kerr and Company.

Keller, Suzanne. 1991. *Beyond the Ruling Class: Strategic Elites in Modern Society*. New Brunswick, NJ: Transaction Publishers.

Kelley, Jonathan. 1981. *Revolution and the Rebirth of Inequality*. Berkeley: University of California Press.

Kelley, Jonathan, and M. D. R. Evans. 1995. "Class and Class Conflict in Six Western Nations." *American Sociological Review* 60:157–78.

Kerbo, Harold R. 1991. *Social Stratification and Inequality: Class Conflict in Historical and Comparative Perspective*. New York: McGraw-Hill.

Kerbo, Harold R. 2000. *Social Stratification and Inequality: Class Conflict in Historical, Comparative, and Global Perspective*. New York: McGraw-Hill.

Kerckhoff, Alan C. 1996. *Generating Social Stratification: Toward a New Research Agenda*. Boulder, CO: Westview Press.

Kerr, Clark, John T. Dunlop, Frederick H. Harbison, and Charles A. Myers. 1964. *Industrialism and Industrial Man*. New York: Oxford University Press.

Kilbourne, Barbara Stanek, Paula England, George Farkas, Kurt Beron, and Dorothea Weir. 1994. "Returns to Skill, Compensating Differentials, and Gender Bias: Effects of Occupational Characteristics on the Wages of White Women and Men." *American Journal of Sociology* 100:689–719.

Kingston, Paul W. Forthcoming. *The Classless Society*. Stanford: Stanford University Press.

Kluegel, James R., and Lawrence Bobo. 1993. "Opposition to Race-Targeting: Self-Interest, Stratification Ideology, or Racial Attitudes?" *American Sociological Review* 58:443–64.

Kluegel, James R., and Eliot R. Smith. 1986. *Beliefs About Inequality: Americans' Views of What Is and What Ought to Be*. New York: Aldine de Gruyter.

Kohn, Melvin L. 1980. "Job Complexity and Adult Personality." Pages 193–210 in *Themes of Work and Love in Adulthood*, edited by Neil J. Smelser and Erik H. Erikson. Cambridge: Harvard University Press.

Kohn, Melvin L., and Carmi Schooler (with the collaboration of Joanne Miller, Karen A. Miller, Carrie Schoenbach, and Ronald Schoenberg). 1983. *Work and Personality: An Inquiry into the Impact of Social Stratification*. Norwood, NJ: Ablex.

Kohn, Melvin L., and Kazimierz M. Slomczynski (with the collaboration of Carrie Schoenbach). 1990. *Social Structure and Self-Direction: A Comparative Analysis of the United States and Poland*. Oxford: Blackwell.

Kohn, Melvin L., Kazimierz M. Slomczynski, Krystyna Janicka, Valeri Khmelko, Bogdan W. Mach, Vladimir Paniotto, Wojciech Zaborowski, Roberto Gutierrez, and Cory Heyman. 1997. "Social Structure and Personality Under Conditions of Radical Social Change: A Comparative Analysis of Poland and Ukraine." *American Sociological Review* 62:614–38.

Konrád, George, and Iván Szelényi. 1979. *The Intellectuals on the Road to Class Power*. New York: Harcourt Brace Jovanovich.

Krader, Lawrence. 1975. *The Asiatic Mode of Production: Sources, Development, and Critique in the Writings of Karl Marx*. Assen: Van Gorcum.

Lachmann, Richard. 1990. "Class Formation without Class Struggle: An Elite Conflict Theory of the Transition to Capitalism." *American Sociological Review* 55:398–414.

Lamont, Michèle. 1992. *Money, Morals, and Manners: The Culture of the French and the American Upper-Middle Class*. Chicago: University of Chicago Press.

Landecker, Werner S. 1981. *Class Crystallization*. New Brunswick: Rutgers University Press.

Lasch, Christopher. 1977. *Haven in a Heartless World*. New York: Basic Books.

Lash, Scott. 1999. *Another Modernity, A Different Rationality*. Oxford: Blackwell.

Leach, Edmund R. 1960. *Aspects of Caste in South India, Ceylon, and North-West Pakistan*. Cambridge: Cambridge University Press.

Leakey, Richard, and Roger Lewin. 1977. *Origins*. New York: Dutton.

Leicht, Kevin T., ed. 1999. *The Future of Affirmative Action*. Stamford: JAI Press.

Lenski, Gerhard E. 1954. "Status Crystallization: A Non-Vertical Dimension of Social Status." *American Sociological Review* 19:405–13.

Lenski, Gerhard E. 1966. *Power and Privilege*. New York: McGraw-Hill.

Lenski, Gerhard E. 1978. "Marxist Experiments in Destratification: An Appraisal." *Social Forces* 57:364–83.

Lenski, Gerhard E. 2001. "New Light on Old Issues: The Relevance of 'Really Existing Socialist Societies' for Stratification Theory." Pages 77–84 in *Social Stratification: Class, Race, and Gender in Sociological Perspective*, 2d ed., edited by David B. Grusky. Boulder, CO: Westview Press.

Lerner, Robert, Althea K. Nagai, and Stanley Rothman. 1996. *American Elites*. New Haven: Yale University Press.

Levy, Frank. 1998. *The New Dollars and Dreams: American Incomes and Economic Change*. New York: Russell Sage Foundation.

Levy, Marion, Jr. 1966. *Modernization and the Structure of Societies*. Princeton: Princeton University Press.

Lieberson, Stanley. 2001. "Understanding Ascriptive Stratification: Some Issues and Principles." Pages 580–592 in *Social Stratification: Class, Race, and Gender in Sociological Perspective*, 2d ed., edited by David B. Grusky. Boulder, CO: Westview Press.

Lin, Nan. 1999. "Social Networks and Status Attainment." *Annual Review of Sociology* 25:467–87.

Lipset, Seymour M. 1959. *Political Man: The Social Bases of Politics*. Baltimore: Johns Hopkins University Press.

Lipset, Seymour M. 1968. "Social Class." Pages 296–316 in *International Encyclopedia of the Social Sciences*, edited by D. L. Sills. New York: Macmillan.

Lipset, Seymour M., and Reinhard Bendix. 1959. *Social Mobility in Industrial Society*. Berkeley: University of California Press.

Logan, John Allen. 1996. "Rational Choice and the TSL Model of Occupational Opportunity." *Rationality and Society* 8:207–30.

Luke, Timothy W. 1997. "The Politics of Digital Inequality: Access, Capability, and Distribution in Cyberspace." *New Political Science* 41–42: 121–44.

Mandel, Ernest. 1971. *The Formation of the Economic Thought of Karl Marx*. New York: Monthly Review Press.

Manza, Jeff. 1992. "Classes, Status Groups, and Social Closure: A Critique of Neo-Weberian Social Theory." Pages 275–302 in *Current Perspectives in Social Theory*, edited by Ben Agger. Greenwich, CT: JAI Press.

Manza, Jeff, and Clem Brooks. 1999. *Social Cleavages and Political Change: Voter Alignments and U.S. Party Coalitions*. Oxford: Oxford University Press.

Marini, Margaret M., and Mary C. Brinton. 1984. "Sex Typing in Occupational Socialization." Pages 192–232 in *Sex Segregation in the Workplace*, edited by Barbara Reskin. Washington, DC: National Academy Press.

Marini, Margaret Mooney, and Pi-Ling Fan. 1997. "The Gender Gap in Earnings at Career Entry." *American Sociological Review* 62: 588–604.

Marshall, Gordon, David Rose, Howard Newby, and Carolyn Vogler. 1988. *Social Class in Modern Britain*. London: Unwin Hyman.

Marshall, Gordon. 1997. *Repositioning Class: Social Inequality in Industrial Societies*. London: Sage Publications.

Marshall, Thomas H. 1981. *The Right to Welfare and Other Essays*. New York: Free Press.

Marx, Karl. 1948. *Manifesto of the Communist Party*. New York: International Publishers.

Marx, Karl. [1939] 1971. *The Grundrisse*. New York: Harper & Row.

Marx, Karl. [1894] 1972. *Capital*. 3 vols. London: Lawrence & Wishart.

Marx, Karl, and Frederick Engels. [1947] 1970. *The German Ideology*. Edited by C. J. Arthur. New York: International Publishers.

Maryanski, Alexandra, and Jonathan H. Turner. 1992. *The Social Cage: Human Nature and the Evolution of Society*. Stanford: Stanford University Press.

Massey, Douglas S. 1996. "The Age of Extremes: Concentrated Affluence and Poverty in the Twenty-First Century." *Demography* 33: 395–412.

Massey, Douglas S., and Nancy A. Denton. 1993. *American Apartheid: Segregation and the Making of the Underclass*. Cambridge: Harvard University Press.

Mayer, Kurt B., and Walter Buckley. 1970. *Class and Society*. New York: Random House.

Mayhew, Leon. 1970. "Ascription in Modern Societies." Pages 308–23 in *The Logic of Social Hierarchies*, edited by Edward O. Laumann, Paul M. Siegel, and Robert W. Hodge. Chicago: Markham Publishing.

Meyer, John W. 2001. "The Evolution of Modern Stratification Systems. Pages 881–890 in *Social Stratification: Class, Race, and Gender in Sociological Perspective*, 2d ed., edited by David B. Grusky. Boulder, CO: Westview Press.

Michels, Robert. 1949. *Political Parties*. Translated by Eden Paul and Cedar Paul. Glencoe, IL: Free Press.

Michman, Ronald D. 1991. *Lifestyle Market Segmentation*. New York: Praeger.

Mills, C. Wright. 1956. *The Power Elite*. New York: Oxford University Press.

Mitchell, Arnold. 1983. *The Nine American Lifestyles*. New York: Macmillan.

Mizruchi, Mark S. 1982. *The American Corporate Network, 1904–1974*. Beverly Hills, CA: Sage Publications.

Mizruchi, Mark S. 1996. "What Do Interlocks Do? An Analysis, Critique, and Assessment of Research on Interlocking Directorates." *Annual Review of Sociology* 22:271–98.

Moore, Wilbert E. 1963a. "But Some Are More Equal Than Others." *American Sociological Review* 28:13–28.

Moore, Wilbert E. 1963b. "Rejoinder." *American Sociological Review* 28:27.

Mosca, Gaetano. 1939. *The Ruling Class*. New York: McGraw-Hill.

Murphy, Raymond. 1988. *Social Closure: The Theory of Monopolization and Exclusion*. Oxford: Clarendon Press.

Nee, Victor. 2001. "Postsocialist Transition." Pages 846–852 in *Social Stratification: Class, Race, and Gender in Sociological Perspective*, 2d ed., edited by David Grusky. Boulder, CO: Westview Press.

Nelson, Robert L., and William P. Bridges. 1999. *Legalizing Gender Inequality: Courts, Markets, and Unequal Pay for Women in America*. Cambridge: Cambridge University Press.

Nie, Norman H., and Lutz, Erbring. 2000. *Internet and Society: A Preliminary Report*. Palo Alto, CA: Stanford Institute for the Quantitative Study of Society.

Nisbet, Robert A. 1959. "The Decline and Fall of Social Class." *Pacific Sociological Review* 2:11–17.

Nolan, Patrick, and Gerhard Lenski. 1998. *Human Societies: An Introduction to Macrosociology*. New York: McGraw-Hill.

Offe, Claus. 1985. *Disorganized Capitalism*. Cambridge: MIT Press.

O'Leary, Brendan. 1989. *The Asiatic Mode of Production*. Oxford: Basil Blackwell.

Oliver, Douglas L. 1955. *A Solomon Island Society*. Cambridge: Harvard University Press.

Olzak, Susan. 1992. *The Dynamics of Ethnic Competition and Conflict*. Stanford: Stanford University Press.

Ossowski, Stanislaw. 1963. *Class Structure in the Social Consciousness*. New York: Free Press.

Pakulski, Jan, and Malcolm Waters. 1996. *The Death of Class*. London: Sage Publications.

Pappas, Gregory, Susan Queen, Wilbur Hadden, and Gail Fisher. 1993. "The Increasing Disparity in Mortality Between Socioeconomic Groups in the United States, 1960 and 1986." *The New England Journal of Medicine* 329:103–9.

Pareto, Vilfredo. 1935. *The Mind and Society*. Translated by A. Bongiorno and A. Livingston, edited by A. Livingston. New York: Harcourt, Brace.

Parkin, Frank. 1971. *Class Inequality and Political Order: Social Stratification in Capitalist and Communist Societies*. New York: Praeger.

Parkin, Frank. 1979. *Marxism and Class Theory: A Bourgeois Critique*. New York: Columbia University Press.

Parsons, Talcott. 1951. *The Social System*. Glencoe, IL: Free Press.

Parsons, Talcott. 1954. *Essays in Sociological Theory*. Glencoe, IL: Free Press.

Parsons, Talcott. 1970. "Equality and Inequality in Modern Society, or Social Stratification Revisited." Pages 13–72 in *Social Stratification: Research and Theory for the 1970s*, edited by Edward O. Laumann. Indianapolis: Bobbs-Merrill.

Parsons, Talcott. 1975. "Some Theoretical Considerations on the Nature and Trends of Change of Ethnicity." Pages 53–83 in *Ethnicity: Theory and Experience*, edited by Nathan Glazer and Daniel P. Moynihan. Cambridge: Harvard University Press.

Patterson, Orlando. 1982. *Slavery and Social Death*. Cambridge: Harvard University Press.

Perrucci, Robert, and Earl Wysong. 1999. *The New Class Society*. Lanham, MD: Rowman & Littlefield.

Peterson, Richard A., and Roger M. Kern. 1996. "Changing Highbrow Taste: From Snob to Omnivore." *American Sociological Review* 61:900–7.

Pfeiffer, John. 1977. *The Emergence of Society: A Prehistory of the Establishment*. New York: McGraw-Hill.

Piore, Michael J. 1975. "Notes for a Theory of Labor Market Segmentation." Pages 125–71 in *Labor Market Segmentation*, edited by Richard C. Edwards, Michael Reich, and David M. Gordon. Lexington, MA.: D. C. Heath.

Piore, Michael J., and Charles F. Sabel. 1984. *The Second Industrial Divide*. New York: Basic Books.

Podolny, Joel M., and James N. Baron. 1997. "Resources and Relationships: Social Networks and Mobility in the Workplace." *American Sociological Review* 62:673–93.

Polachek, Solomon W., and W. Stanley Siebert. 1993. *The Economics of Earnings*. Cambridge: Cambridge University Press.

Portes, Alejandro, ed. 1996. *The New Second Generation*. New York: Russell Sage Foundation.

Portes, Alejandro. Forthcoming. "The Resilient Importance of Class: A Nominalist Interpretation." *Political Power and Social Theory*.

Portes, Alejandro, and Min Zhou. 1993. "The New Second Generation: Segmented Assimilation and Its Variants." *The Annals of the American Academy of Political and Social Science* 530:74–96.

Poulantzas, Nicos. 1974. *Classes in Contemporary Capitalism*. London: Verso.

Reich, Michael. 1977. "The Economics of Racism." Pages 184–88 in *Problems in Political Economy: An Urban Perspective*, edited by David M. Gordon. Lexington, MA: D. C. Heath.

Reskin, Barbara F. 1993. "Sex Segregation in the Workplace." *Annual Review of Sociology* 19:241–70.

Reskin, Barbara F. 1998. *The Realities of Affirmative Action in Employment*. Washington, DC: American Sociological Association.

Reskin, Barbara F. 2000. "The Proximate Causes of Employment Discrimination." *Contemporary Sociology* 29:319–28.

Reskin, Barbara F., Debra B. McBrier, and Julie A. Kmec. 1999. "The Determinants and Consequences of Workplace Sex and Race Composition." *Annual Review of Sociology* 25:335–61.

Ridgeway, Cecilia L., and Shelley Correll. 2000. "Limiting Gender Inequality through Interaction: The End(s) of Gender." *Contemporary Sociology* 29:110–20.

Ridgeway, Cecilia L., and Lynn Smith-Lovin. 1999. "The Gender System and Interaction." *Annual Review of Sociology* 25:191–216.

Rizzi, Bruno. 1985. *The Bureaucratization of the World*. London: Tavistock Publications.

Rodriguez, Junius P., and Orlando Patterson. 1999. *Chronology of Slavery*. Santa Barbara, CA: ABC-Clio.

Roemer, John. 1988. *Free to Lose*. Cambridge: Harvard University Press.

Rona-Tas, Ákos. 1994. "The First Shall Be the Last? Entrepreneurship and Communist Cadres in the Transition from Socialism." *American Journal of Sociology* 100:40–69.

Rona-Tas, Ákos. 1997. *The Great Surprise of the Small Transformation: The Demise of Communism and the Rise of the Private Sector in Hungary*. Ann Arbor: University of Michigan Press.

Rose, Arnold. 1967. *The Power Structure*. New York: Oxford University Press.

Rossides, Daniel W. 1996. *Social Stratification: The Interplay of Class, Race, and Gender*. Englewood Cliffs, NJ: Prentice Hall.

Rothman, Robert A. 1999. *Inequality and Stratification*. Upper Saddle River, NJ: Prentice Hall.

Runciman, Walter G. 1968. "Class, Status, and Power?" Pages 25–61 in *Social Stratification*, edited by J. A. Jackson. New York: Cambridge University Press.

Runciman, Walter G. 1974. "Towards a Theory of Social Stratification." Pages 55–81 in *The Social Analysis of Class Structure*, edited by Frank Parkin. London: Tavistock Publications.

Rytina, Steven. 1992. "Scaling Intergenerational Continuity: Is Occupational Inheritance Ascriptive After All?" *American Journal of Sociology* 97:1658–88.

Rytina, Steven. 2000. "Is Occupational Mobility Declining in the United States?" *Social Forces* 78: 1227–76.

Sakamoto, Arthur, Huei-Hsia Wu, and Jessie M. Tzeng. 2000. "The Declining Significance of Race Among American Men During the Latter Half of the Twentieth Century." *Demography* 37: 41–51.

Sanders, Jimy M., and Victor Nee. 1987. "Limits of Ethnic Solidarity in the Enclave Economy." *American Sociological Review* 52:745–67.

Saunders, Peter R. 1987. *Social Theory and the Urban Question*. London: Unwin Hyman.

Saunders, Peter R. 1989. "Left Write in Sociology." *Network* 44:3–4.

Schuman, Howard, Charlotte Steeh, Lawrence Bobo, and Maria Krysan. 1998. *Racial Attitudes in America: Trends and Interpretations.* Cambridge: Harvard University Press.

Schumpeter, Joseph. 1951. *Imperialism and Social Classes.* New York: Augustus M. Kelley.

Schumpeter, Joseph. 1953. *Aufsätze zur Soziologie.* Tübingen: Mohr/Siebeck.

Sears, David O., Carl P. Hensler, and Leslie K. Speer. 1979. "Whites' Opposition to 'Busing': Self-Interest or Symbolic Politics?" *American Political Science Review* 73:369–84.

Sewell, William H., Archibald O. Haller, and Alejandro Portes. 1969. "The Educational and Early Occupational Attainment Process." *American Sociological Review* 34:82–92.

Sharma, Kanhaiyalal. 1997. *Social Stratification in India: Issues and Themes.* Beverly Hills, CA: Sage Publications.

Sharma, Ursula. 1999. *Caste.* Buckingham: Open University Press.

Shaw, William H. 1978. *Marx's Theory of History.* Stanford: Stanford University Press.

Shils, Edward. 1968. "Deference." Pages 104–32 in *Social Stratification*, edited by J. A. Jackson. New York: Cambridge University Press.

Shils, Edward. 1982. "The Political Class in the Age of Mass Society: Collectivistic Liberalism and Social Democracy." Pages 13–32 in *Does Who Governs Matter? Elite Circulation in Contemporary Societies*, edited by Moshe M. Czudnowski. DeKalb: Northern Illinois University Press.

Sio, Arnold A. 1965. "Interpretations of Slavery: The Slave Status in the Americas." *Comparative Studies in Society and History* VII: 289–308.

Smaje, Chris. 2000. *Natural Hierarchies: The Historical Sociology of Race and Caste.* Oxford: Basil Blackwell.

Smith, Michael R. 1990. "What Is New in 'New Structuralist' Analyses of Earnings?" *American Sociological Review* 55:827–41.

Sobel, Michael E. 1981. *Lifestyle and Social Structure: Concepts, Definitions, Analyses.* New York: Academic Press.

Sørensen, Aage B. 1996. "The Structural Basis of Social Inequality." *American Journal of Sociology* 101:1333–65.

Sørensen, Aage B. 2001. "The Basic Concepts of Stratification Research: Class, Status, and Power." Pages 287–300 in *Social Stratification: Class, Race, and Gender in Sociological Perspective*, 2d ed., edited by David Grusky. Boulder, CO: Westview Press.

Sørensen, Aage B., and Arne L. Kalleberg. 1981. "An Outline of a Theory of the Matching of Persons to Jobs." Pages 49–74 in *Sociological Perspectives on Labor Markets*, edited by Ivar Berg. New York: Academic Press.

Sørensen, Jesper B. 1992. "Locating Class Cleavages in Inter-Generational Mobility: Cross-National Commonalities and Variations in Mobility Patterns." *European Sociological Review* 8:267–81.

Sørensen, Jesper B., and David B. Grusky. 1996. "The Structure of Career Mobility in Microscopic Perspective." Pages 83–114 in *Social Differentiation and Social Inequality*, edited by James N. Baron, David B. Grusky, and Donald J. Treiman. Boulder, CO: Westview Press.

Spenner, Kenneth I. 1995. "Technological Change, Skill Requirements, and Education: The Case for Uncertainty." Pages 81–137 in *The New Modern Times: Factors Reshaping the World of Work*, edited by David B. Bills. Albany: State University of New York Press.

Srinivas, Mysore N. 1962. *Caste in Modern India.* London: Asia Publishing House.

Steinmetz, George, and Erik O. Wright. 1989. "The Fall and Rise of the Petty Bourgeoisie: Changing Patterns of Self-Employment in the Postwar United States." *American Journal of Sociology* 94:973–1018.

Stovel, Katherine, Michael Savage, and Peter Bearman. 1996. "Ascription into Achievement: Models of Career Systems at Lloyds Bank, 1890–1970." *American Journal of Sociology* 102:358–99.

Svalastoga, Kaare. 1965. *Social Differentiation.* New York: D. McKay.

Szelényi, Iván, and Szonja Szelényi. 1995. "Circulation and Reproduction of Elites in Post-Communist Transformation." *Theory and Society* 24:615–38.

Szelényi, Szonja. 1998. *Equality by Design: The Grand Experiment in Destratification in Socialist Hungary.* Stanford: Stanford University Press.

Szelényi, Szonja. 2001. "The 'Woman Problem' in Stratification Theory and Research." Pages 681–688 in *Social Stratification: Class, Race, and Gender in Sociological Perspective*, 2d ed., edited by David Grusky. Boulder, CO: Westview Press.

Tam, Tony. 1997. "Sex Segregation and Occupational Gender Inequality in the United States: Devaluation or Specialized Training?" *American Journal of Sociology* 102:1652–92.

Tawney, R. H. 1931. *Equality.* London: Allen & Unwin.

Taylor, D. Garth, Paul B. Sheatsley, and Andrew M. Greeley. 1978. "Attitudes Toward Racial Integration." *Scientific American* 238:42–51.

Tilly, Charles. 1998. *Durable Inequality.* Berkeley: University of California Press.

Touraine, Alain. 1981. *The Voice and the Eye: An Analysis of Social Movements.* Cambridge: Cambridge University Press.

Treiman, Donald J. 1970. "Industrialization and Social Stratification." Pages 207–34 in *Social Stratification: Research and Theory for the 1970s*, edited by Edward O. Laumann. Indianapolis: Bobbs-Merrill.

Treiman, Donald J. 1976. "A Standard Occupational Prestige Scale for Use with Historical Data." *Journal of Interdisciplinary History* 7:283–304.

Treiman, Donald J. 1977. *Occupational Prestige in Comparative Perspective*. New York: Academic Press.

Tumin, Melvin M. 1953. "Some Principles of Stratification: A Critical Analysis." *American Sociological Review* 18:378–94.

Tumin, Melvin M. 1985. *Social Stratification. The Forms and Functions of Inequality*. Englewood Cliffs, NJ: Prentice Hall.

Useem, Michael. 1984. *The Inner Circle*. New York: Oxford University Press.

Useem, Michael, and Jerome Karabel. 1986. "Pathways to Top Corporate Management." *American Sociological Review* 51:184–200.

Van Maanen, John, and Stephen R. Barley. 1984. "Occupational Communities: Culture and Control in Organizations." *Research in Organizational Behavior* 6:287–365.

Walder, Andrew G. 1996. "Markets and Inequality in Transitional Economies: Toward Testable Theories." *American Journal of Sociology* 101:950–92.

Waldinger, Roger. 1996. *Still the Promised City? African-Americans and New Immigrants in Postindustrial New York*. Cambridge: Harvard University Press.

Warner, W. Lloyd. 1949. *Social Class in America*. Chicago: Science Research Associates.

Waters, Mary C. 1999. *Black Identities: West Indian Immigrant Dreams and American Realities*. New York: Russell Sage Foundation.

Waters, Mary C. 2000. "Multiple Ethnicities and Identity in the United States." Pages 23–40 in *We Are a People: Narrative and Multiplicity in Constructing Ethnic Identity*, edited by Paul Spickard and W. Jeffrey Burroughs. Philadelphia: Temple University Press.

Weber, Max. 1946. *From Max Weber: Essays in Sociology*. Edited and translated by Hans Gerth and C. Wright Mills. New York: Oxford University Press.

Weber, Max. 1947. *The Theory of Social and Economic Organization*. Edited by Talcott Parsons. New York: Free Press.

Weber, Max. [1922] 1968. *Economy and Society*. Berkeley: University of California Press.

Weeden, Kim. 1998. "From Borders to Barriers: Strategies of Occupational Closure and the Structure of Occupational Rewards." Unpublished paper, Department of Sociology, Stanford University.

Wegener, Bernd. 1992. "Concepts and Measurement of Prestige." *Annual Review of Sociology* 18:253–80.

Weiss, Michael J. 1988. *The Clustering of America*. New York: Harper & Row.

Wesolowski, Wlodzimierz. 1962. "Some Notes on the Functional Theory of Stratification." *Polish Sociological Bulletin* 3–4:28–38.

Western, Mark, and Erik Olin Wright. 1994. "The Permeability of Class Boundaries to Intergenerational Mobility Among Men in the United States, Canada, Norway, and Sweden." *American Sociological Review* 59:606–29.

Williams, David R., and Chiquita Collins. 1995. "United States Socioeconomic and Racial Differences in Health: Patterns and Explanations." *Annual Review of Sociology* 21: 349–86.

Wilson, William Julius. 1980. *The Declining Significance of Race: Blacks and Changing American Institutions*. 2d ed. Chicago: University of Chicago Press.

Wilson, William Julius. 1996. *When Work Disappears: The World of the New Urban Poor*. New York: Alfred A. Knopf.

Wilson, William Julius. 1999a. "Jobless Poverty: A New Form of Social Dislocation in the Inner-City Ghetto." Pages 133–50 in *A Nation Divided: Diversity, Inequality, and Community in American Society*, edited by Phyllis Moen, Donna Dempster-McClain, and Henry A. Walker. Ithaca: Cornell University Press.

Wilson, William Julius. 1999b. *The Bridge Over the Racial Divide: Rising Inequality and Coalition Politics*. Berkeley: University of California Press.

Wittfogel, Karl A. 1981. *Oriental Despotism: A Comparative Study of Total Power*. New York: Vintage Books.

Wright, Erik O. 1978. *Class, Crisis, and the State*. London: New Left Books.

Wright, Erik O. 1979. *Class Structure and Income Determination*. New York: Academic Press.

Wright, Erik O. 1985. *Classes*. London: Verso.

Wright, Erik O. 1989. *The Debate on Classes*. London: Verso.

Wright, Erik O. 1997. *Class Counts: Comparative Studies in Class Analysis*. Cambridge: Cambridge University Press.

Wright, Erik O. Forthcoming. "A Conceptual Menu for Studying the Interconnections of Class and Gender." In *Reconfigurations of Class and Gender*, edited by Janeen Baxter and Mark Western. Stanford: Stanford University Press.

Wrong, Dennis H. 1959. "The Functional Theory of Stratification: Some Neglected Considerations." *American Sociological Review* 24: 772–82.

Young, Michael. 1958. *The Rise of the Meritocracy*. Harmondsworth: Penguin Books.

Zeitlin, Maurice. 1982. "Corporate Ownership and Control: The Large Corporation and the Capitalist Class." Pages 196–223 in *Classes, Power, and Conflict*, edited by Anthony Giddens and David Held. Berkeley: University of California Press.

Zweigenhaft, Richard L., and G. William Domhoff. 1998. *Diversity in the Power Elite: Have Women and Minorities Reached the Top?* New Haven: Yale University Press.

Part II
Forms and Sources of Stratification

The Functions of Stratification

The Dysfunctions of Stratification

The Functions of Stratification

KINGSLEY DAVIS AND WILBERT E. MOORE

Some Principles of Stratification

In a previous paper some concepts for handling the phenomena of social inequality were presented.[1] In the present paper a further step in stratification theory is undertaken—an attempt to show the relationship between stratification and the rest of the social order.[2] Starting from the proposition that no society is "classless," or unstratified, an effort is made to explain, in functional terms, the universal necessity which calls forth stratification in any social system. Next, an attempt is made to explain the roughly uniform distribution of prestige as between the major types of positions in every society. Since, however, there occur between one society and another great differences in the degree and kind of stratification, some attention is also given to the varieties of social inequality and the variable factors that give rise to them.

Clearly, the present task requires two different lines of analysis—one to understand the universal, the other to understand the variable features of stratification. Naturally each line of inquiry aids the other and is indispensable, and in the treatment that follows the two will be interwoven, although, because of space limitations, the emphasis will be on the universals.

Throughout, it will be necessary to keep in mind one thing—namely, that the discussion

relates to the system of positions, not to the individuals occupying those positions. It is one thing to ask why different positions carry different degrees of prestige, and quite another to ask how certain individuals get into those positions. Although, as the argument will try to show, both questions are related, it is essential to keep them separate in our thinking. Most of the literature on stratification has tried to answer the second question (particularly with regard to the ease or difficulty of mobility between strata) without tackling the first. The first question, however, is logically prior and, in the case of any particular individual or group, factually prior.

The Functional Necessity of Stratification

Curiously the main functional necessity explaining the universal presence of stratification is precisely the requirement faced by any society of placing and motivating individuals in the social structure. As a functioning mechanism a society must somehow distribute its members in social positions and induce them to perform the duties of these positions. It must thus concern itself with motivation at two different levels: to instill in the proper individuals the desire to fill certain positions, and, once in these positions, the desire to perform the duties attached to them. Even

Originally published in 1945. Please see complete source information beginning on page 891.

though the social order may be relatively static in form, there is a continuous process of metabolism as new individuals are born into it, shift with age, and die off. Their absorption into the positional system must somehow be arranged and motivated. This is true whether the system is competitive or non-competitive. A competitive system gives greater importance to the motivation to achieve positions, whereas a non-competitive system gives perhaps greater importance to the motivation to perform the duties of the positions; but in any system both types of motivation are required.

If the duties associated with the various positions were all equally pleasant to the human organism, all equally important to societal survival, and all equally in need of the same ability or talent, it would make no difference who got into which positions, and the problem of social placement would be greatly reduced. But actually it does make a great deal of difference who gets into which positions, not only because some positions are inherently more agreeable than others, but also because some require special talents or training and some are functionally more important than others. Also, it is essential that the duties of the positions be performed with the diligence that their importance requires. Inevitably, then, a society must have, first, some kind of rewards that it can use as inducements, and, second, some way of distributing these rewards differentially according to positions. The rewards and their distribution become a part of the social order, and thus give rise to stratification.

One may ask what kind of rewards a society has at its disposal in distributing its personnel and securing essential services. It has, first of all, the things that contribute to sustenance and comfort. It has, second, the things that contribute to humor and diversion. And it has, finally, the things that contribute to self respect and ego expansion. The last, because of the peculiarly social character of the self, is largely a function of the opinion of others, but it nonetheless ranks in importance with the first two. In any social system all three kinds of rewards must be dispensed differentially according to positions.

In a sense the rewards are "built into" the position. They consist in the "rights" associated with the position, plus what may be called its accompaniments or perquisites. Often the rights, and sometimes the accompaniments, are functionally related to the duties of the position. (Rights as viewed by the incumbent are usually duties as viewed by other members of the community.) However, there may be a host of subsidiary rights and perquisites that are not essential to the function of the position and have only an indirect and symbolic connection with its duties, but which still may be of considerable importance in inducing people to seek the positions and fulfil the essential duties.

If the rights and perquisites of different positions in a society must be unequal, then the society must be stratified, because that is precisely what stratification means. Social inequality is thus an unconsciously evolved device by which societies insure that the most important positions are conscientiously filled by the most qualified persons. Hence every society, no matter how simple or complex, must differentiate persons in terms of both prestige and esteem, and must therefore possess a certain amount of institutionalized inequality.

It does not follow that the amount or type of inequality need be the same in all societies. This is largely a function of factors that will be discussed presently.

The Two Determinants of Positional Rank

Granting the general function that inequality subserves, one can specify the two factors that determine the relative rank of different positions. In general those positions convey the best reward, and hence have the highest rank, which (a) have the greatest importance for the society and (b) require the greatest training or talent. The first factor concerns function and is a matter of relative significance; the second concerns means and is a matter of scarcity.

Differential Functional Importance. Actually a society does not need to reward positions in proportion to their functional importance. It merely needs to give sufficient reward to them to insure that they will be filled competently. In other words, it must see that less essential positions do not compete successfully with more essential ones. If a position is easily filled, it need not be heavily rewarded, even though important. On the other hand, if it is important but hard to fill, the reward must be high enough to get it filled anyway. Functional importance is therefore a necessary but not a sufficient cause of high rank being assigned to a position.[3]

Differential Scarcity of Personnel. Practically all positions, no matter how acquired, require some form of skill or capacity for performance. This is implicit in the very notion of position, which implies that the incumbent must, by virtue of his incumbency, accomplish certain things.

There are, ultimately, only two ways in which a person's qualifications come about: through inherent capacity or through training. Obviously, in concrete activities both are always necessary, but from a practical standpoint the scarcity may lie primarily in one or the other, as well as in both. Some positions require innate talents of such high degree that the persons who fill them are bound to be rare. In many cases, however, talent is fairly abundant in the population but the training process is so long, costly, and elaborate that relatively few can qualify. Modern medicine, for example, is within the mental capacity of most individuals, but a medical education is so burdensome and expensive that virtually none would undertake it if the position of the M.D. did not carry a reward commensurate with the sacrifice.

If the talents required for a position are abundant and the training easy, the method of acquiring the position may have little to do with its duties. There may be, in fact, a virtually accidental relationship. But if the skills required are scarce by reason of the rarity of talent or the costliness of training, the position, if functionally important, must have an attractive power that will draw the necessary skills in competition with other positions. This means, in effect, that the position must be high in the social scale—must command great prestige, high salary, ample leisure, and the like.

How Variations Are to Be Understood. In so far as there is a difference between one system of stratification and another, it is attributable to whatever factors affect the two determinants of differential reward—namely, functional importance and scarcity of personnel. Positions important in one society may not be important in another, because the conditions faced by the societies, or their degree of internal development, may be different. The same conditions, in turn, may affect the question of scarcity; for in some societies the stage of development, or the external situation, may wholly obviate the necessity of certain kinds of skill or talent. Any particular system of stratification, then, can be understood as a product of the special conditions affecting the two aforementioned grounds of differential reward.

Major Societal Functions and Stratification

Religion

The reason why religion is necessary is apparently to be found in the fact that human society achieves its unity primarily through the possession by its members of certain ultimate values and ends in common. Although these values and ends are subjective, they influence behavior, and their integration enables the society to operate as a system. Derived neither from inherited nor from external nature, they have evolved as a part of culture by communication and moral pressure. They must, however, appear to the members of the society to have some reality, and it is the role of religious belief and ritual to supply and reinforce this appearance of reality. Through belief and ritual the common ends and values are connected with an imaginary world symbolized by concrete sacred objects, which world in turn is related in a meaningful way to the facts and trials of the individual's life. Through the worship of the sacred objects and the beings they symbolize, and the acceptance of supernatural prescriptions that are at the same time codes of behavior, a powerful control over human conduct is exercised, guiding it along lines sustaining the institutional structure and conforming to the ultimate ends and values.

If this conception of the role of religion is true, one can understand why in every known society the religious activities tend to be under the charge of particular persons, who tend thereby to enjoy greater rewards than the ordinary societal member. Certain of the rewards and special privileges may attach to only the highest religious functionaries, but others usually apply, if such exists, to the entire sacerdotal class.

Moreover, there is a peculiar relation between the duties of the religious official and the special privileges he enjoys. If the supernatural world governs the destinies of men more ultimately than does the real world, its earthly representative, the person through whom one may communicate with the supernatural, must be a powerful individual. He is a keeper of sacred tradition, a skilled performer of the ritual, and an interpreter of lore and myth. He is in such close contact with the gods that he is viewed as possessing some of their characteristics. He is, in short, a bit sacred, and hence free from some of the more vulgar necessities and controls.

It is no accident, therefore, that religious functionaries have been associated with the very highest positions of power, as in theocratic regimes. Indeed, looking at it from this point of view, one may wonder why it is that they do not get *entire* control over their societies. The factors that prevent this are worthy of note.

In the first place, the amount of technical competence necessary for the performance of religious duties is small. Scientific or artistic capacity is not required. Anyone can set himself up as enjoying an intimate relation with deities, and nobody can successfully dispute him. Therefore, the factor of scarcity of personnel does not operate in the technical sense.

One may assert, on the other hand, that religious ritual is often elaborate and religious lore abstruse, and that priestly ministrations require tact, if not intelligence. This is true, but the technical requirements of the profession are for the most part adventitious, not related to the end in the same way that science is related to air travel. The priest can never be free from competition, since the criteria of whether or not one has genuine contact with the supernatural are never strictly clear. It is this competition that debases the priestly position below what might be expected at first glance. That is why priestly prestige is highest in those societies where membership in the profession is rigidly controlled by the priestly guild itself. That is why, in part at least, elaborate devices are utilized to stress the identification of the person with his office—spectacular costume, abnormal conduct, special diet, segregated residence, celibacy, conspicuous leisure, and the like. In fact, the priest is always in danger of becoming somewhat discredited—as happens in a secularized society—because in a world of stubborn fact, ritual and sacred knowledge alone will not grow crops or build houses. Furthermore, unless he is protected by a professional guild, the priest's identification with the supernatural tends to preclude his acquisition of abundant worldly goods.

As between one society and another it seems that the highest general position awarded the priest occurs in the medieval type of social order. Here there is enough economic production to afford a surplus, which can be used to support a numerous and highly organized priesthood; and yet the populace is unlettered and therefore credulous to a high degree. Perhaps the most extreme example is to be found in the Buddhism of Tibet, but others are encountered in the Catholicism of feudal Europe, the Inca regime of Peru, the Brahminism of India, and the Mayan priesthood of Yucatan. On the other hand, if the society is so crude as to have no surplus and little differentiation, so that every priest must be also a cultivator or hunter, the separation of the priestly status from the others has hardly gone far enough for priestly prestige to mean much. When the priest actually has high prestige under these circumstances, it is because he also performs other important functions (usually political and medical).

In an extremely advanced society built on scientific technology, the priesthood tends to lose status, because sacred tradition and supernaturalism drop into the background. The ultimate values and common ends of the society tend to be expressed in less anthropomorphic ways, by officials who occupy fundamentally political, economic, or educational rather than religious positions. Nevertheless, it is easily possible for intellectuals to exaggerate the degree to which the priesthood in a presumably secular milieu has lost prestige. When the matter is closely examined the urban proletariat, as well as the rural citizenry, proves to be surprisingly god-fearing and priest-ridden. No society has become so completely secularized as to liquidate entirely the belief in transcendental ends and supernatural entities. Even in a secularized society some system must exist for the integration of ultimate values, for their ritualistic expression, and for the emotional adjustments required by disappointment, death, and disaster.

Government

Like religion, government plays a unique and indispensable part in society. But in contrast to religion, which provides integration in terms of sentiments, beliefs, and rituals, it organizes the society in terms of law and authority. Furthermore, it orients the society to the actual rather than the unseen world.

The main functions of government are, internally, the ultimate enforcement of norms, the final arbitration of conflicting interests, and the overall planning and direction of society; and externally, the handling of war and diplomacy. To carry out these functions it acts as the agent of the entire people, enjoys a monopoly of force, and controls all individuals within its territory.

Political action, by definition, implies authority. An official can command because he has authority, and the citizen must obey because he is subject to that authority. For this reason stratification is inherent in the nature of political relationships.

So clear is the power embodied in political position that political inequality is sometimes thought to comprise all inequality. But it can be shown that there are other bases of stratification, that the following controls operate in practice to keep political power from becoming complete: (a) The fact that the actual holders of political office, and especially those determining top policy must necessarily be few in number compared to the total population. (b) The fact that the rulers represent the interest of the group rather than of themselves, and are therefore restricted in their behavior by rules and mores designed to enforce this limitation of interest. (c) The fact that the holder of political office has his authority by virtue of his office and nothing else, and therefore any special knowledge, talent, or capacity he may claim is purely incidental, so that he often has to depend upon others for technical assistance.

In view of these limiting factors, it is not strange that the rulers often have less power and prestige than a literal enumeration of their formal rights would lead one to expect.

Wealth, Property, and Labor

Every position that secures for its incumbent a livelihood is, by definition, economically rewarded. For this reason there is an economic aspect to those positions (e.g. political and religious) the main function of which is not economic. It therefore becomes convenient for the society to use unequal economic returns as a principal means of controlling the entrance of persons into positions and stimulating the performance of their duties. The amount of the economic return therefore becomes one of the main indices of social status.

It should be stressed, however, that a position does not bring power and prestige *because* it draws a high income. Rather, it draws a high income because it is functionally important and the available personnel is for one reason or another scarce. It is therefore superficial and erroneous to regard high income as the cause of a man's power and prestige, just as it is erroneous to think that a man's fever is the cause of his disease.[4]

The economic source of power and prestige is not income primarily, but the ownership of capital goods (including patents, good will, and professional reputation). Such ownership should be distinguished from the possession of consumers' goods, which is an index rather than a cause of social standing. In other words, the ownership of producers' goods is properly speaking, a source of income like other positions, the income itself remaining an index. Even in situations where social values are widely commercialized and earnings are the readiest method of judging social position, income does not confer prestige on a position so much as it induces people to compete for the position. It is true that a man who has a high income as a result of one position may find this money helpful in climbing into another position as well, but this again reflects the effect of his initial, economically advantageous status, which exercises its influence through the medium of money.

In a system of private property in productive enterprise, an income above what an individual spends can give rise to possession of capital wealth. Presumably such possession is a reward for the proper management of one's finances originally and of the productive enterprise later. But as social differentiation becomes highly advanced and yet the institution of inheritance persists, the phenomenon of pure ownership, and reward for pure ownership, emerges. In such a case it is difficult to prove that the position is functionally important or that the scarcity involved is anything other than extrinsic and accidental. It is for this reason, doubtless, that the institution of private property in productive goods becomes more subject to criticism as social develop-ment proceeds toward industrialization. It is only this pure, that is, strictly legal and functionless ownership, however, that is open to attack; for some form of active ownership, whether private or public, is indispensable.

One kind of ownership of production goods consists in rights over the labor of others. The most extremely concentrated and exclusive of such rights are found in slavery, but the essential principle remains in serfdom, peonage, encomienda, and indenture. Naturally this kind of ownership has the greatest significance for stratification, because it necessarily entails an unequal relationship.

But property in capital goods inevitably introduces a compulsive element even into the nominally free contractual relationship. Indeed, in some respects the authority of the contractual employer is greater than that of the feudal landlord, inasmuch as the latter is more limited by traditional reciprocities. Even the classical economics recognized that competitors would fare unequally, but it did not pursue this fact to its necessary conclusion that, however it might be acquired, unequal control of goods and services must give unequal advantage to the parties to a contract.

Technical Knowledge

The function of finding means to single goals, without any concern with the choice between goals, is the exclusively technical sphere. The explanation of why positions requiring great technical skill receive fairly high rewards is easy to see, for it is the simplest case of the rewards being so distributed as to draw talent and motivate training. Why they seldom if ever receive the highest rewards is also clear: the importance of technical knowledge from a societal point of view is never so great as the integration of goals, which takes place on the religious, political, and economic levels. Since the technological level is concerned solely with means, a purely technical position must ultimately be subordinate to other positions that are religious, political, or economic in character.

Nevertheless, the distinction between expert and layman in any social order is fundamental, and cannot be entirely reduced to other terms. Methods of recruitment, as well as of reward, sometimes lead to the erroneous interpretation that technical positions are economically determined. Actually, however, the acquisition of knowledge and skill cannot be accomplished by purchase, although the opportunity to learn may be. The control of the avenues of training may inhere as a sort of property right in certain families or classes, giving them power and prestige in consequence. Such a situation adds an artificial scarcity to the natural scarcity of skills and talents. On the other hand, it is possible for an opposite situation to arise. The rewards of technical position may be so great that a condition of excess supply is created, leading to at least temporary devaluation of the rewards. Thus "unemployment in the learned professions" may result in a debasement of the prestige of those positions. Such adjustments and readjustments are constantly occurring in changing societies; and it is always well to bear in mind that the efficiency of a stratified structure may be affected by the modes of recruitment for positions. The social order itself, however, sets limits to the inflation or deflation of the prestige of experts: an oversupply tends to debase the rewards and discourage recruitment or produce revolution, whereas an under-supply tends to increase the rewards or weaken the society in competition with other societies.

Particular systems of stratification show a wide range with respect to the exact position of technically competent persons. This range is perhaps most evident in the degree of specialization. Extreme division of labor tends to create many specialists without high prestige since the training is short and the required native capacity relatively small. On the other hand it also tends to accentuate the high position of the true experts—scientists, engineers, and administrators—by increasing their authority relative to other functionally important positions. But the idea of a technocratic social order or a government or priesthood of engineers or social scientists neglects the limitations of knowledge and skills as a basis for performing social functions. To the extent that the social structure is truly specialized the prestige of the technical person must also be circumscribed.

Variation in Stratified Systems

The generalized principles of stratification here suggested form a necessary preliminary to a consideration of types of stratified systems, because it is in terms of these principles that the types must be described. This can be seen by trying to delineate types according to certain modes of variation. For instance, some of the most important modes (together with the polar types in terms of them) seem to be as follows:

(a) **The Degree of Specialization.** The degree of specialization affects the fineness and multiplicity of the gradations in power and prestige. It also influences the extent to which particular functions may be emphasized in the invidious system, since a given function cannot receive much emphasis in the hierarchy until it has achieved structural separation from the other functions. Finally, the amount of specialization influences the bases of selection. Polar types: *Specialized, Unspecialized.*

(b) **The Nature of the Functional Emphasis.** In general when emphasis is put on sacred matters, a rigidity is introduced that tends to limit specialization and hence the development of technology. In addition, a brake is placed on social mobility, and on the development of bureaucracy. When the preoccupation with the sacred is withdrawn, leaving greater scope for purely secular preoccupations, a great development, and rise in status, of economic and technological positions seemingly takes place. Curiously, a concomitant rise in political position is not likely, because it has usually been allied with the religious and stands to gain little by the decline of the latter. It is also possible for a society to emphasize family functions—as in relatively undifferentiated societies where high mortality requires high fertility and kinship forms the main basis of social organization. Main types: *Familistic, Authoritarian* (*Theocratic* or sacred, and *Totalitarian* or secular), *Capitalistic*.

(c) The Magnitude of Invidious Differences. What may be called the amount of social distance between positions, taking into account the entire scale, is something that should lend itself to quantitative measurement. Considerable differences apparently exist between different societies in this regard, and also between parts of the same society. Polar types: *Equalitarian, Inequalitarian*.

(d) The Degree of Opportunity. The familiar question of the amount of mobility is different from the question of the comparative equality or inequality of rewards posed above, because the two criteria may vary independently up to a point. For instance, the tremendous divergences in monetary income in the United States are far greater than those found in primitive societies, yet the equality of opportunity to move from one rung to the other in the social scale may also be greater in the United States than in a hereditary tribal kingdom. Polar types: *Mobile* (open), *Immobile* (closed).

(e) The Degree of Stratum Solidarity. Again, the degree of "class solidarity" (or the presence of specific organizations to promote class interests) may vary to some extent independently of the other criteria, and hence is an important principle in classifying systems of stratification. Polar types: *Class organized, Class unorganized*.

External Conditions

What state any particular system of stratification is in with reference to each of these modes of variation depends on two things: (1) its state with reference to the other ranges of variation, and (2) the conditions outside the system of stratification which nevertheless influence that system. Among the latter are the following:

(a) The Stage of Cultural Development. As the cultural heritage grows, increased specialization becomes necessary, which in turn contributes to the enhancement of mobility, a decline of stratum solidarity, and a change of functional emphasis.

(b) Situation with Respect to Other Societies. The presence or absence of open conflict with other societies, of free trade relations or cultural diffusion, all influence the class structure to some extent. A chronic state of warfare tends to place emphasis upon the military functions, especially when the opponents are more or less equal. Free trade, on the other hand, strengthens the hand of the trader at the expense of the warrior and priest. Free movement of ideas generally has an equalitarian effect. Migration and conquest create special circumstances.

(c) Size of the Society. A small society limits the degree to which functional specialization can go, the degree of segregation of different strata, and the magnitude of inequality.

Composite Types

Much of the literature on stratification has attempted to classify concrete systems into a certain number of types. This task is deceptively simple, however, and should come at the end of an analysis of elements and principles, rather than at the beginning. If the preceding discussion has any validity, it indicates that there are a number of modes of variation between different systems, and that any one system is a composite of the society's status with reference to all these modes of variation. The danger of trying to classify whole societies under such rubrics as *caste, feudal,* or *open class* is that one or two criteria are selected and others ignored, the result being an unsatisfactory solution to the problem posed.

The present discussion has been offered as a possible approach to the more systematic classification of composite types.

Notes

1. Kingsley Davis, "A Conceptual Analysis of Stratification," *American Sociological Review.* 7:309–321, June, 1942.

2. The writers regret (and beg indulgence) that the present essay, a condensation of a longer study, covers so much in such short space that adequate evidence and qualification cannot be given and that as a result what is actually very tentative is presented in an unfortunately dogmatic manner.

3. Unfortunately, functional importance is difficult to establish. To use the position's prestige to establish it, as is often unconsciously done, constitutes circular reasoning from our point of view. There are, however, two independent clues: (a) the degree to which a position is functionally unique, there being no other positions that can perform the same function satisfactorily; (b) the degree to which other positions are dependent on the one in question. Both clues are best exemplified in organized systems of positions built around one major function. Thus, in most complex societies the religious, political, economic, and educational functions are handled by distinct structures not easily interchangeable. In addition, each structure possesses many different positions, some clearly dependent on, if not subordinate to, others. In sum, when an institutional nucleus becomes differentiated around one main function, and at the same time organizes a large portion of the population into its relationships, the *key* positions in it are of the highest functional importance. The absence of such specialization does not prove functional unimportance, for the whole society may be relatively unspecialized; but it is safe to assume that the more important functions receive the first and clearest structural differentiation.

4. The symbolic rather than intrinsic role of income in social stratification has been succinctly summarized by Talcott Parsons, "An Analytical Approach to the Theory of Social Stratification," *American Journal of Sociology.* 45:841–862, May, 1940.

The Dysfunctions of Stratification

M E L V I N   M .   T U M I N

Some Principles of Stratification: A Critical Analysis

The fact of social inequality in human society is marked by its ubiquity and its antiquity. Every known society, past and present, distributes its scarce and demanded goods and services unequally. And there are attached to the positions which command unequal amounts of such goods and services certain highly morally-toned evaluations of their importance for the society.

The ubiquity and the antiquity of such inequality has given rise to the assumption that there must be something both inevitable and positively functional about such social arrangements.

Clearly, the truth or falsity of such an assumption is a strategic question for any general theory of social organization. It is therefore most curious that the basic premises and implications of the assumption have only been most casually explored by American sociologists.

The most systematic treatment is to be found in the well-known article by Kingsley Davis and Wilbert Moore, entitled "Some Principles of Stratification."[1] More than twelve years have passed since its publication,

Originally published in 1953. Please see complete source information beginning on page 891.

and though it is one of the very few treatments of stratification on a high level of generalization, it is difficult to locate a single systematic analysis of its reasoning. It will be the principal concern of this paper to present the beginnings of such an analysis.

The central argument advanced by Davis and Moore can be stated in a number of sequential propositions, as follows:

1. Certain positions in any society are functionally more important than others, and require special skills for their performance.
2. Only a limited number of individuals in any society have the talents which can be trained into the skills appropriate to these positions.
3. The conversion of talents into skills involves a training period during which sacrifices of one kind or another are made by those undergoing the training.
4. In order to induce the talented persons to undergo these sacrifices and acquire the training, their future positions must carry an inducement value in the form of differential, i.e., privileged and disproportionate access to the scarce and desired rewards which the society has to offer.[2]
5. These scarce and desired goods consist of the rights and perquisites attached to,

65

or built into, the positions, and can be classified into those things which contribute to (a) sustenance and comfort, (b) humor and diversion, (c) self-respect and ego expansion.

6. This differential access to the basic rewards of the society has as a consequence the differentiation of the prestige and esteem which various strata acquire. This may be said, along with the rights and perquisites, to constitute institutionalized social inequality, i.e., stratification.

7. Therefore, social inequality among different strata in the amounts of scarce and desired goods, and the amounts of prestige and esteem which they receive, is both positively functional and inevitable in any society.

Let us take these propositions and examine them *seriatim*.[3]

(1) Certain positions in any society are more functionally important than others and require special skills for their performance.

The key term here is "functionally important." The functionalist theory of social organization is by no means clear and explicit about this term. The minimum common referent is to something known as the "survival value" of a social structure.[4] This concept immediately involves a number of perplexing questions. Among these are: (a) the issue of minimum vs. maximum survival, and the possible empirical referents which can be given to those terms; (b) whether such a proposition is a useless tautology since any *status quo* at any given moment is nothing more and nothing less than everything present in the *status quo*. In these terms, all acts and structures must be judged positively functional in that they constitute essential portions of the *status quo*; (c) what kind of calculus of functionality exists which will enable us, at this point in our development, to add and subtract long and short range consequences, with their mixed qualities, and arrive at some summative judgment regarding the rating an act or structure should receive on a scale of greater or lesser

functionality? At best, we tend to make primarily intuitive judgments. Often enough, these judgments involve the use of value-laden criteria, or, at least, criteria which are chosen in preference to others not for any sociologically systematic reasons but by reason of certain implicit value preferences.

Thus, to judge that the engineers in a factory are functionally more important to the factory than the unskilled workmen involves a notion regarding the dispensability of the unskilled workmen, or their replaceability, relative to that of the engineers. But this is not a process of choice with infinite time dimensions. For at some point along the line one must face the problem of adequate motivation for *all* workers at all levels of skill in the factory. In the long run, *some* labor force of unskilled workmen is as important and as indispensable to the factory as *some* labor force of engineers. Often enough, the labor force situation is such that this fact is brought home sharply to the entrepreneur in the short run rather than in the long run.

Moreover, the judgment as to the relative indispensability and replaceability of a particular segment of skills in the population involves a prior judgment about the bargaining-power of that segment. But this power is itself a culturally shaped *consequence* of the existing system of rating, rather than something inevitable in the nature of social organization. At least the contrary of this has never been demonstrated, but only assumed.

A generalized theory of social stratification must recognize that the prevailing system of inducements and rewards is only one of many variants in the whole range of possible systems of motivation which, at least theoretically, are capable of working in human society. It is quite conceivable, of course, that a system of norms could be institutionalized in which the idea of threatened withdrawal of services, except under the most extreme circumstances, would be considered as absolute moral anathema. In such a case, the whole notion of relative functionality, as advanced by Davis and Moore, would have to be radically revised.

(2) Only a limited number of individuals in any society have the talents which can be trained into the skills appropriate to these positions (i.e., the more functionally important positions).

The truth of this proposition depends at least in part on the truth of proposition 1 above. It is, therefore, subject to all the limitations indicated above. But for the moment, let us assume the validity of the first proposition and concentrate on the question of the rarity of appropriate talent.

If all that is meant is that in every society there is a *range* of talent, and that some members of any society are by nature more talented than others, no sensible contradiction can be offered, but a question must be raised here regarding the amount of sound knowledge present in any society concerning the presence of talent in the population.

For, in every society there is some demonstrable ignorance regarding the amount of talent present in the population. *And the more rigidly stratified a society is, the less chance does that society have of discovering any new facts about the talents of its members.* Smoothly working and stable systems of stratification, wherever found, tend to build-in obstacles to the further exploration of the range of available talent. This is especially true in those societies where the opportunity to discover talent in any one generation varies with the differential resources of the parent generation. Where, for instance, access to education depends upon the wealth of one's parents, and where wealth is differentially distributed, large segments of the population are likely to be deprived of the chance even to *discover* what are their talents.

Whether or not differential rewards and opportunities are functional in any one generation, it is clear that if those differentials are allowed to be socially inherited by the next generation, then, the stratification system is specifically dysfunctional for the discovery of talents in the next generation. In this fashion, systems of social stratification tend to limit the chances available to maximize the efficiency of discovery, recruitment and training of "functionally important talent."[5]

Additionally, the unequal distribution of rewards in one generation tends to result in the unequal distribution of motivation in the succeeding generation. Since motivation to succeed is clearly an important element in the entire process of education, the unequal distribution of motivation tends to set limits on the possible extensions of the educational system, and hence, upon the efficient recruitment and training of the widest body of skills available in the population.[6]

Lastly, in this context, it may be asserted that there is some noticeable tendency for elites to restrict further access to their privileged positions, once they have sufficient power to enforce such restrictions. This is especially true in a culture where it is possible for an elite to contrive a high demand and a proportionately higher reward for its work by restricting the numbers of the elite available to do the work. The recruitment and training of doctors in modern United States is at least partly a case in point.

Here, then, are three ways, among others which could be cited, in which stratification systems, once operative, tend to reduce the survival value of a society by limiting the search, recruitment and training of functionally important personnel far more sharply than the facts of available talent would appear to justify. It is only when there is genuinely equal access to recruitment and training for all potentially talented persons that differential rewards can conceivably be justified as functional. And stratification systems are apparently *inherently antagonistic* to the development of such full equality of opportunity.

(3) The conversion of talents into skills involves a training period during which sacrifices of one kind or another are made by those undergoing the training.

Davis and Moore introduce here a concept, "sacrifice" which comes closer than any of the rest of their vocabulary of analysis to being a direct reflection of the rationalizations, offered by the more fortunate members of a society, of the rightness of their occupancy of privileged positions. It is the least critically thought-out concept in the repertoire, and can also be shown to be least supported by the actual facts.

In our present society, for example, what are the sacrifices which talented persons undergo in the training period? The possibly serious losses involve the surrender of earning power and the cost of the training. The latter is generally borne by the parents of the talented youth undergoing training, and not by the trainees themselves. But this cost tends to be paid out of income which the parents were able to earn generally by virtue of *their* privileged positions in the hierarchy of stratification. That is to say, the parents' ability to pay for the training of their children is part of the differential *reward* they, the parents, received for their privileged positions in the society. And to charge this sum up against sacrifices made by the youth is falsely to perpetrate a bill or a debt already paid by the society to the parents.

So far as the sacrifice of earning power by the trainees themselves is concerned, the loss may be measured relative to what they might have earned had they gone into the labor market instead of into advanced training for the "important" skills. There are several ways to judge this. One way is to take all the average earnings of age peers who did go into the labor market for a period equal to the average length of the training period. The total income, so calculated, roughly equals an amount which the elite can, on the average, earn back in the first decade of professional work, over and above the earnings of his age peers who are not trained. Ten years is probably the maximum amount needed to equalize the differential.[7] There remains, on the average, twenty years of work during each of which the skilled person then goes on to earn far more than his unskilled age peers. And, what is often forgotten, there is then still another ten or fifteen year period during which the skilled person continues to work and earn when his unskilled age peer is either totally or partially out of the labor market by virtue of the attrition of his strength and capabilities.

One might say that the first ten years of differential pay is perhaps justified, in order to regain for the trained person what he lost during his training period. But it is difficult to imagine what would justify continuing such differential rewards beyond that period.

Another and probably sounder way to measure how much is lost during the training period is to compare the per capita income available to the trainee with the per capita income of the age peer on the untrained labor market during the so-called sacrificial period. If one takes into account the earlier marriage of untrained persons, and the earlier acquisition of family dependents, it is highly dubious that the per capita income of the wage worker is significantly larger than that of the trainee. Even assuming, for the moment, that there is a difference, the amount is by no means sufficient to justify a lifetime of continuing differentials.

What tends to be completely overlooked, in addition, are the psychic and spiritual rewards which are available to the elite trainees by comparison with their age peers in the labor force. There is, first, the much higher prestige enjoyed by the college student and the professional-school student as compared with persons in shops and offices. There is, second, the extremely highly valued privilege of having greater opportunity for self-development. There is, third, all the psychic gain involved in being allowed to delay the assumption of adult responsibilities such as earning a living and supporting a family. There is, fourth, the access to leisure and freedom of a kind not likely to be experienced by the persons already at work.

If these are never taken into account as rewards of the training period it is not because they are not concretely present, but because the emphasis in American concepts of reward is almost exclusively placed on the material returns of positions. The emphases on enjoyment, entertainment, ego enhancement, prestige and esteem are introduced only when the differentials in these which accrue to the skilled positions need to be justified. If these other rewards were taken into account, it would be much more difficult to demonstrate that the training period, as presently operative, is really sacrificial. Indeed, it might turn out to be the case that even at this point in their careers, the elite trainees were being differentially rewarded relative to their age peers in the labor force.

All of the foregoing concerns the quality of the training period under our present system of motivation and rewards. Whatever may turn out to be the factual case about the present system—and the factual case is moot—the more important theoretical question concerns the assumption that the training period under *any* system must be sacrificial.

There seem to be no good theoretical grounds for insisting on this assumption. For, while under any system certain costs will be involved in training persons for skilled positions, these costs could easily be assumed by the society-at-large. Under these circumstances, there would be no need to compensate anyone in terms of differential rewards once the skilled positions were staffed. In short, there would be no need or justification for stratifying social positions on *these* grounds.

(4) In order to induce the talented persons to undergo these sacrifices and acquire the training, their future positions must carry an inducement value in the form of differential, i.e., privileged and disproportionate access to the scarce and desired rewards which the society has to offer.

Let us assume, for the purposes of the discussion, that the training period is sacrificial and the talent is rare in every conceivable human society. There is still the basic problem as to whether the allocation of differential rewards in scarce and desired goods and services is the only or the most efficient way of recruiting the appropriate talent to these positions.

For there are a number of alternative motivational schemes whose efficiency and adequacy ought at least to be considered in this context. What can be said, for instance, on behalf of the motivation which De Man called "joy in work," Veblen termed "instinct for workmanship" and which we latterly have come to identify as "intrinsic work satisfaction?" Or, to what extent could the motivation of "social duty" be institutionalized in

such a fashion that self interest and social interest come closely to coincide? Or, how much prospective confidence can be placed in the possibilities of institutionalizing "social service" as a widespread motivation for seeking one's appropriate position and fulfilling it conscientiously?

Are not these types of motivations, we may ask, likely to prove most appropriate for precisely the "most functionally important positions?" Especially in a mass industrial society, where the vast majority of positions become standardized and routinized, it is the skilled jobs which are likely to retain most of the quality of "intrinsic job satisfaction" and be most readily identifiable as socially serviceable. Is it indeed impossible then to build these motivations into the socialization pattern to which we expose our talented youth?

To deny that such motivations could be institutionalized would be to overclaim our present knowledge. In part, also, such a claim would seem to derive from an assumption that what has not been institutionalized yet in human affairs is incapable of institutionalization. Admittedly, historical experience affords us evidence we cannot afford to ignore. But such evidence cannot legitimately be used to deny absolutely the possibility of heretofore untried alternatives. Social innovation is as important a feature of human societies as social stability.

On the basis of these observations, it seems that Davis and Moore have stated the case much too strongly when they insist that a "functionally important position" which requires skills that are scarce, "must command great prestige, high salary, ample leisure, and the like," if the appropriate talents are to be attracted to the position. Here, clearly, the authors are postulating the unavoidability of very specific types of rewards and, by implication, denying the possibility of others.

(5) These scarce and desired goods consist of rights and perquisites attached to, or built into, the positions and can be classified into those things which contribute to (a) sustenance and comfort; (b) humor and diversion; (c) self respect and ego expansion.

*(6) This differential access to the basic re-
wards of the society has as a consequence the
differentiation of the prestige and esteem
which various strata acquire. This may be
said, along with the rights and perquisites, to
constitute institutionalized social inequality,
i.e., stratification.*

With the classification of the rewards offered
by Davis and Moore there need be little argument. Some question must be raised, however,
as to whether any reward system, built into a
general stratification system, must allocate
equal amounts of all three types of reward in
order to function effectively, or whether one
type of reward may be emphasized to the virtual neglect of others. This raises the further
question regarding which type of emphasis is
likely to prove most effective as a differential
inducer. Nothing in the known facts about human motivation impels us to favor one type of
reward over the other, or to insist that all three
types of reward must be built into the positions
in comparable amounts if the position is to
have an inducement value.

It is well known, of course, that societies
differ considerably in the kinds of rewards
they emphasize in their efforts to maintain a
reasonable balance between responsibility
and reward. There are, for instance, numerous societies in which the conspicuous display
of differential economic advantage is considered extremely bad taste. In short, our present
knowledge commends to us the possibility of
considerable plasticity in the way in which
different types of rewards can be structured
into a functioning society. This is to say, it
cannot yet be demonstrated that it is *unavoidable* that differential prestige and esteem shall
accrue to positions which command differential rewards in power and property.

What does seem to be unavoidable is that
differential prestige shall be given to those in
any society who conform to the normative
order as against those who deviate from that
order in a way judged immoral and detrimental. On the assumption that the continuity of
a society depends on the continuity and stability of its normative order, some such distinction between conformists and deviants
seems inescapable.

It also seems to be unavoidable that in any
society, no matter how literate its tradition,
the older, wiser and more experienced individuals who are charged with the enculturation
and socialization of the young must have
more power than the young, on the assumption that the task of effective socialization demands such differential power.

But this differentiation in prestige between
the conformist and the deviant is by no means
the same distinction as that between strata of
individuals each of which operates *within* the
normative order, and is composed of adults.
The *latter* distinction, in the form of differentiated rewards and prestige between social
strata is what Davis and Moore, and most sociologists, consider the structure of a stratification system. The *former* distinctions have
nothing necessarily to do with the workings
of such a system nor with the efficiency of
motivation and recruitment of functionally
important personnel.

Nor does the differentiation of power between young and old necessarily create differentially valued strata. For no society rates its
young as less morally worthy than its older
persons, no matter how much differential
power the older ones may temporarily enjoy.

*(7) Therefore, social inequality among dif-
ferent strata in the amounts of scarce and desired goods, and the amounts of prestige and
esteem which they receive, is both positively
functional and inevitable in any society.*

If the objections which have heretofore
been raised are taken as reasonable, then it
may be stated that the only items which any
society *must* distribute unequally are the
power and property necessary for the performance of different tasks. If such differential
power and property are viewed by all as
commensurate with the differential responsibilities, and if they are culturally defined as
resources and not as rewards, then, no
differentials in prestige and esteem need
follow.

Historically, the evidence seems to be that
every time power and property are distributed
unequally, no matter what the cultural definition, prestige and esteem differentiations have
tended to result as well. Historically, however,

no systematic effort has ever been made, under propitious circumstances, to develop the tradition that each man is as socially worthy as all other men so long as he performs his appropriate tasks conscientiously. While such a tradition seems utterly utopian, no known facts in psychological or social science have yet demonstrated its impossibility or its dysfunctionality for the continuity of a society. The achievement of a full institutionalization of such a tradition seems far too remote to contemplate. Some successive approximations at such a tradition, however, are not out of the range of prospective social innovation.

What, then, of the "positive functionality" of social stratification? Are there other, negative, functions of institutionalized social inequality which can be identified, if only tentatively? Some such dysfunctions of stratification have already been suggested in the body of this paper. Along with others they may now be stated, in the form of provisional assertions, as follows:

1. Social stratification systems function to limit the possibility of discovery of the full range of talent available in a society. This results from the fact of unequal access to appropriate motivation, channels of recruitment and centers of training.

2. In foreshortening the range of available talent, social stratification systems function to set limits upon the possibility of expanding the productive resources of the society, at least relative to what might be the case under conditions of greater equality of opportunity.

3. Social stratification systems function to provide the elite with the political power necessary to procure acceptance and dominance of an ideology which rationalizes the *status quo*, whatever it may be, as "logical," "natural" and "morally right." In this manner, social stratification systems function as essentially conservative influences in the societies in which they are found.

4. Social stratification systems function to distribute favorable self-images unequally throughout a population. To the extent that such favorable self-images are requisite to the development of the creative potential inherent in men, to that extent stratification systems function to limit the development of this creative potential.

5. To the extent that inequalities in social rewards cannot be made fully acceptable to the less privileged in a society, social stratification systems function to encourage hostility, suspicion and distrust among the various segments of a society and thus to limit the possibilities of extensive social integration.

6. To the extent that the sense of significant membership in a society depends on one's place on the prestige ladder of the society, social stratification systems function to distribute unequally the sense of significant membership in the population.

7. To the extent that loyalty to a society depends on a sense of significant membership in the society, social stratification systems function to distribute loyalty unequally in the population.

8. To the extent that participation and apathy depend upon the sense of significant membership in the society, social stratification systems function to distribute the motivation to participate unequally in a population.

Each of the eight foregoing propositions contains implicit hypotheses regarding the consequences of unequal distribution of rewards in a society in accordance with some notion of the functional importance of various positions. These are empirical hypotheses, subject to test. They are offered here only as exemplary of the kinds of consequences of social stratification which are not often taken into account in dealing with the problem. They should also serve to reinforce the doubt that social inequality is a device which is uniformly functional for the role of guaranteeing that the most important tasks in a society will be performed conscientiously by the most competent persons.

The obviously mixed character of the functions of social inequality should come as no surprise to anyone. If sociology is sophisticated in any sense, it is certainly with regard to its awareness of the mixed nature of any social arrangement, when the observer takes into account long as well as short range consequences and latent as well as manifest dimensions.

Summary

In this paper, an effort has been made to raise questions regarding the inevitability and positive functionality of stratification, or institutionalized social inequality in rewards, allocated in accordance with some notion of the greater and lesser functional importance of various positions. The possible alternative meanings of the concept "functional importance" has been shown to be one difficulty. The question of the scarcity or abundance of available talent has been indicated as a principal source of possible variation. The extent to which the period of training for skilled positions may reasonably be viewed as sacrificial has been called into question. The possibility has been suggested that very different types of motivational schemes might conceivably be made to function. The separability of differentials in power and property considered as resources appropriate to a task from such differentials considered as rewards for the performance of a task has also been suggested. It has also been maintained that differentials in prestige and esteem do not necessarily follow upon differentials in power and property when the latter are considered as appropriate resources rather than rewards. Finally, some negative functions, or dysfunctions, of institutionalized social inequality have been tentatively identified, revealing the mixed character of the outcome of social stratification, and casting doubt on the contention that

Social inequality is thus an unconsciously evolved device by which societies insure that the most important positions are conscientiously filled by the most qualified persons.[8]

Notes

The writer has had the benefit of a most helpful criticism of the main portions of this paper by Professor W. J. Goode of Columbia University. In addition, he has had the opportunity to expose this paper to criticism by the Staff Seminar of the Sociology Section at Princeton. In deference to a possible rejoinder by Professors Moore and Davis, the writer has not revised the paper to meet the criticisms which Moore has already offered personally.

1. *American Sociological Review*, X (April, 1945), pp. 242–249. An earlier article by Kingsley Davis, entitled, "A Conceptual Analysis of Stratification," *American Sociological Review*, VII (June, 1942), pp. 309–321, is devoted primarily to setting forth a vocabulary for stratification analysis. A still earlier article by Talcott Parsons, "An Analytical Approach to the Theory of Social Stratification," *American Journal of Sociology*, XLV (November, 1940), pp. 849–862, approaches the problem in terms of why "differential ranking is considered a really fundamental phenomenon of social systems and what are the respects in which such ranking is important." The principal line of integration asserted by Parsons is with the fact of the normative orientation of any society. Certain crucial lines of connection are left unexplained, however, in this article, and in the Davis and Moore article of 1945 only some of these lines are made explicit.

2. The "scarcity and demand" qualities of goods and services are never explicitly mentioned by Davis and Moore. But it seems to the writer that the argument makes no sense unless the goods and services are so characterized. For if rewards are to function as differential inducements they must not only be differentially distributed but they must be both scarce and demanded as well. Neither the scarcity of an item by itself nor the fact of its being in demand is sufficient to allow it to function as a differential inducement in a system of unequal rewards. Leprosy is scarce and oxygen is highly demanded.

3. The arguments to be advanced here are condensed versions of a much longer analysis entitled, *An Essay on Social Stratification*. Perforce, all the reasoning necessary to support some of the contentions cannot be offered within the space limits of this article.

4. Davis and Moore are explicitly aware of the difficulties involved here and suggest two "independent clues" other than survival value. See footnote 3 on p. 244 of their article.

5. Davis and Moore state this point briefly on p. 248 but do not elaborate it.

6. In the United States, for instance, we are only now becoming aware of the amount of productivity we, as a society, lose by allocating inferior opportunities and rewards, and hence, inferior motivation, to our Negro population. The actual amount of loss is difficult to specify precisely. Some rough estimate can be made, however, on the assumption that there is present in the Negro population about the same range of talent that is found in the White population.

7. These are only very rough estimates, of course, and it is certain that there is considerable income variation within the so-called elite group, so that the proposition holds only relatively more or less.

8. Davis and Moore, *op. cit.*, p. 243.

CLAUDE S. FISCHER, MICHAEL HOUT, MARTÍN SÁNCHEZ JANKOWSKI, SAMUEL R. LUCAS, ANN SWIDLER, AND KIM VOSS

Inequality by Design

Why do some Americans have a lot more than others? Perhaps, inequality follows inevitably from human nature. Some people are born with more talent than others; the first succeed while the others fail in life's competition. Many people accept this explanation, but it will not suffice. Inequality is not fated by nature, nor even by the "invisible hand" of the market; it is a social construction, a result of our historical acts. *Americans have created the extent and type of inequality we have, and Americans maintain it.*

To answer the question of what explains inequality in America, we must divide it in two. First, who gets ahead and who falls behind in the competition for success? Second, what determines how much people get for being ahead or behind? To see more clearly that the two questions are different, think of a ladder that represents the ranking of affluence in a society. Question one asks why this person rather than that person ended up on a higher or lower rung. Question two asks why some societies have tall and narrowing ladders—ladders that have huge distances between top and bottom rungs and that taper off at the top so that there is room for only a few people—while other societies have short and broad ladders—ladders with little distance between top and bottom and with lots of room for many people all the way to the top.

The answer to the question of who ends up where is that people's social environments largely influence what rung of the ladder they end up on.[1] The advantages and disadvantages that people inherit from their parents, the resources that their friends can share with them, the quantity and quality of their schooling, and even the historical era into which they are born boost some up and hold others down. The children of professors, our own children, have substantial head starts over children of, say, factory workers. Young men who graduated from high school in the booming 1950s had greater opportunities than the

Originally published in 1996. Please see complete source information beginning on page 891.

ones who graduated during the Depression. Context matters tremendously.

The answer to the question of why societies vary in their structure of rewards is more political. In significant measure, societies choose the height and breadth of their "ladders." By loosening markets or regulating them, by providing services to all citizens or rationing them according to income, by subsidizing some groups more than others, societies, through their politics, build their ladders. To be sure, historical and external constraints deny full freedom of action, but a substantial freedom of action remains. In a democracy, this means that the inequality Americans have is, in significant measure, the historical result of policy choices Americans—or, at least, Americans' representatives—have made. In the United States, the result is a society that is distinctively *un*equal. Our ladder is, by the standards of affluent democracies and even by the standards of recent American history, unusually extended and narrow—and becoming more so.

To see how policies shape the structure of rewards (i.e., the equality of outcomes), consider these examples: Laws provide the ground rules for the marketplace—rules covering incorporation, patents, wages, working conditions, unionization, security transactions, taxes, and so on. Some laws widen differences in income and earnings among people in the market; others narrow differences. Also, many government programs affect inequality more directly through, for example, tax deductions, food stamps, social security, Medicare, and corporate subsidies.

To see how policies also affect which particular individuals get to the top and which fall to the bottom of our ladder (i.e., the equality of opportunity), consider these examples: The amount of schooling young Americans receive heavily determines the jobs they get and the income they make. In turn, educational policies—what sorts of schools are provided, the way school resources are distributed (usually according to the community in which children live), teaching methods such as tracking, and so on—strongly affect how much schooling

children receive. Similarly, local employment opportunities constrain how well people can do economically. Whether and where governments promote jobs or fail to do so will, in turn, influence who is poised for well-paid employment and who is not.

Claiming that intentional policies have significantly constructed the inequalities we have and that other policies could change those inequalities may seem a novel idea in the current ideological climate. So many voices tell us that inequality is the result of individuals' "natural" talents in a "natural" market. Nature defeats any sentimental efforts by society to reduce inequality, they say; such efforts should therefore be dropped as futile and wasteful. Appeals to nature are common and comforting. As Kenneth Bock wrote in his study of social philosophy, "We have been quick to seek explanations of our problems and failures in what we *are* instead of what we *do*. We seem wedded to the belief that our situation is a consequence of our nature rather than of our historical acts."[2] In this case, appeals to nature are shortsighted.

Arguments from nature are useless for answering the question of what determines the structure of rewards because that question concerns differences in equality *among societies*. Theories of natural inequality cannot tell us why countries with such similar genetic stocks (and economic markets) as the United States, Canada, England, and Sweden can vary so much in the degree of economic inequality their citizens experience. The answer lies in deliberate policies.

Appeals to nature also cannot satisfactorily answer even the first question: Why do some *individuals* get ahead and some fall behind? Certainly, genetic endowment helps. Being tall, slender, good-looking, healthy, male, and white helps in the race for success, and these traits are totally or partly determined genetically. But these traits matter to the degree that society makes them matter—determining how much, for example, good looks or white skin are rewarded. More important yet than these traits are the social milieux in which people grow up and live.

Realizing that intentional policies account for much of our expanding inequality is not only more accurate than theories of natural inequality; it is also more optimistic. We are today more unequal than we have been in seventy years. We are more unequal than any other affluent Western nation. Intentional policies could change those conditions, could reduce and reverse our rush to a polarized society, could bring us closer to the average inequality in the West, could expand both equality of opportunity and equality of result.

Still, the "natural inequality" viewpoint is a popular one. Unequal outcomes, the best-selling *Bell Curve* argues, are the returns from a fair process that sorts people out according to how intelligent they are.[3] But *The Bell Curve*'s explanation of inequality is inadequate. The authors err in assuming that human talents can be reduced to a single, fixed, and essentially innate skill they label intelligence. They err in asserting that this trait largely determines how people end up in life. And they err in imagining that individual competition explains the structure of inequality in society. . . .

Disparities in income and wealth, [other] analysts argue, encourage hard work and saving. The rich, in particular, can invest their capital in production and thus create jobs for all.[4] This was the argument of "supply-side" economics in the 1980s, that rewarding the wealthy—for example, by reducing income taxes on returns from their investments—would stimulate growth to the benefit of all. The 1980s did not work out that way, but the theory is still influential. We *could* force more equal outcomes, these analysts say, but doing so would reduce living standards for all Americans.

Must we have so much inequality for overall growth? The latest economic research concludes *not;* it even suggests that inequality may *retard* economic growth. In a detailed statistical analysis, economists Torsten Persson and Guido Tabellini reported finding that, historically, societies that had more inequality of earnings tended to have lower, not higher, subsequent economic growth. Replications by

other scholars substantiated the finding: More unequal nations grew less quickly than did more equal societies.[5] . . .

This recent research has not demonstrated precisely how greater equality helps economic growth,[6] but we can consider a few possibilities. Increasing resources for those of lower income might, by raising health, educational attainment, and hope, increase people's abilities to be productive and entrepreneurial. Reducing the income of those at the top might reduce unproductive and speculative spending. Take, as a concrete example, the way American corporations are run compared with German and Japanese ones. The American companies are run by largely autonomous managers whose main responsibility is to return short-term profits and high stock prices to shareholders and—because they are often paid in stock options—to themselves as well. Japanese and German managers are more like top employees whose goals largely focus on keeping the company a thriving enterprise. The latter is more conducive to reinvesting profits and thus to long-term growth.[7] Whatever the mechanisms may be, inequality appears to undermine growth. Americans certainly need not feel that they must accept the high levels of inequality we currently endure in order to have a robust economy.

A related concern for Americans is whether "leveling" stifles the drive to get ahead. Americans prefer to encourage Horatio Alger striving and to provide opportunities for everyone. Lincoln once said "that some would be rich shows that others may become rich."[8] Many, if not most, Americans believe that inequality is needed to encourage people to work hard.[9] But, if so, *how much* inequality is needed?

For decades, sociologists have been comparing the patterns of social mobility across societies, asking: In which countries are people most likely to overcome the disadvantages of birth and move up the ladder? In particular, does more or less equality encourage such an "open" society? The answer is that Western societies vary little in the degree to which children's economic successes are constrained by their parents' class positions. America, the most unequal Western society, has somewhat more fluid intergenerational mobility than do other nations, but so does Sweden, the most equal Western society.[10] There is no case for encouraging inequality in this evidence, either.

In sum, the assumption that considerable inequality is needed for, or even encourages, economic growth appears to be false. We do not need to make a morally wrenching choice between more affluence and more equality; we can have both. But even if such a choice were necessary, both sides of the debate, the "altruists" who favor intervention for equalizing and the supposed "realists" who resist it, agree that inequality can be shaped by policy decisions: wittingly or unwittingly, we choose our level of inequality.

Notes

1. We know that in statistical models of individual status attainment much, if not most, of the variance is unaccounted for. Of the explained variance, however, the bulk is due to social environment broadly construed. Also, we believe that much of the residual, unexplained variance is attributable to unmeasured social rather than personal factors.

2. Kenneth Bock, *Human Nature Mythology* (Urbana 1994), p. 9.

3. Richard J. Herrnstein and Charles Murray, *The Bell Curve: Intelligence and Class Structure in American Life* (New York 1994).

4. See, for example, Rich Thomas, "Rising Tide Lifts the Yachts: The Gap Between Rich and Poor Has Widened, but There Are Some Comforting Twists," *Newsweek,* May 1, 1995. See also George Will, "What's Behind Income Disparity," *San Francisco Chronicle,* April 24, 1995.

5. Torsten Persson and Guido Tabellini, "Is Inequality Harmful for Growth?," *American Economic Review* 84, 1994; Roberto Chang, "Income Inequality and Economic Growth: Evidence and Recent Theories," *Economic Review* 79, 1994; George R.G. Clarke, "More Evidence on Income Distribution and Growth," *Journal of Development Economics* 47, 1995. See also Peter H. Lindert, "The Rise of Social Spending," *Explorations in Economic History* 31, 1994.

6. Persson and Tabellini's explanation ("Is Inequality Harmful?") for their results is that in societies with greater earnings inequality, there is less political pressure for government redistribution; such redistribution impairs growth. However, their evidence for the explanation is thin, and Clarke's results ("More Evidence") are inconsistent with that argument. Chang ("Income Inequality") suggests that with more equality, lower-income families could make longer-term investment decisions. In any event, the statistical results suggest that government intervention on behalf of equality in the market, rather than after the market, would be beneficial.

7. See, for example, Michael Porter, *Capital Choices: Changing the Way America Invests in Industry* (Washington 1992).

8. Quoted by Alan Trachtenberg, *The Incorporation of America: Culture and Society in the Gilded Age* (New York 1982), p. 75.

9. See, for example, Lee Rainwater, *What Money Buys: Inequality and the Social Meanings of Income* (New York 1974); James R. Kluegel and E.R. Smith, "Beliefs About Stratification," *Annual Review of Sociology* 7, 1981.

10. Harry B.G. Ganzeboom, Donald J. Treiman, and Wout C. Ultee, "Comparative Intergenerational Stratification Research," *Annual Review of Sociology* 17, 1991.

GERHARD LENSKI

New Light on Old Issues: The Relevance of "Really Existing Socialist Societies" for Stratification Theory

Scholars have long debated the causes, consequences, and legitimacy of systems of social inequality, with some defending them as natural, inevitable, or even divinely ordained, and others challenging them as unnatural, unnecessary, and immoral (Lenski 1966, ch. 1). In the twentieth century, the most important challenges have come from groups and individuals inspired, directly or indirectly, by the work of Marx and his followers.

One does not need to look far in sociology to see the impact of Marx's vision and the controversies it has created. As many have observed, the long-running debate between functionalists and their critics is, in many ways, a debate over the merits of Marxism: Functionalists maintain that economic inequality is both necessary for societies and beneficial for the vast majority of their members, whereas their critics argue that it is neither.

Unfortunately, from the standpoint of our understanding of the causes and consequences of systems of stratification and the merits of Marx's ideas, the debate among sociologists has focused almost entirely on the experience of Western "capitalist" societies.[1] Surprisingly little attention has been devoted to the experience of the former Soviet republics, Poland, East Germany before unification, the once-united Czechoslovakia, Hungary, the former Yugoslavia, Romania,

Bulgaria, Albania, China, Cuba, North Korea, Vietnam, and other societies that were or have been governed for extended periods by dedicated Marxists. Yet, as East European sociologists have often pointed out in recent years, these societies have provided a unique set of laboratories for observing the effects of "really existing socialism."[2] They allow us to observe socialist societies functioning in the real world under real-life conditions. In these societies, we can see what actually happens when private ownership is abolished and the emphasis in a society's system of rewards is shifted from material incentives to moral incentives. Imperfect though these tests have been, they shed valuable new light on the causes and consequences of inequalities in power and privilege.[3] The results have been much too consistent to be ignored or written off as simply a matter of chance, and the consistency is especially impressive when one considers the great cultural diversity of the societies involved.

For many years, Western sociologists could justify their inattention to "really existing socialist societies" because of the difficulties of obtaining reliable data. By the early 1970s, however, a sufficient body of evidence had accumulated, and political conditions in a number of Marxist societies had improved to the point that one could, with some confidence, begin to form a fairly accurate view of a number of important aspects of the new Marxist systems of stratification. On the basis of mate-

---

This is an original article prepared for this book.

rials available at the time, I concluded in an earlier article (Lenski 1978) that these "experiments in destratification" had enjoyed their greatest successes in reducing *economic* inequality: Differentials in wealth and income appeared to be substantially less in societies governed by Marxist elites than in other societies. These successes were offset, however, by two major failures: (1) *Political* inequalities in these societies were enormous, far greater than in any of the Western industrial democracies, and (2) none of these societies had achieved anything remotely resembling the critical transformation in human nature that Marx had predicted would follow the abolition of private property and would lay the foundation for the subsequent evolution of societies from socialism to communism. These failures, I concluded, were due in large measure to a critical flaw in Marxian theory—its unrealistic assumptions about human nature.

Looking back, I believe these conclusions have stood the test of time fairly well. Of course, information that has since emerged and the wisdom of hindsight would lead me to modify and extend them. For example, recent revelations following the overthrow of the Marxist regimes in Eastern Europe indicate that the level of economic inequality in those societies was greater than I was then aware. To cite but three examples: (1) After the overthrow of Todor Zhikov, the Bulgarian public and the rest of the world learned that during his years in power he had acquired no fewer than thirty separate homes for his personal use and that he and other top Communist Party leaders had accumulated millions of dollars in secret foreign bank accounts (Laber 1990); (2) the longtime Communist leader of Romania, Nicolae Ceauçescu, amassed forty villas and twenty palaces for himself and his family and accumulated millions in Swiss bank accounts at a time when the bulk of the population was often living without heat or light (*Washington Post* 1990); and (3) in East Germany, Erich Honecker accumulated millions of dollars in Swiss bank accounts by skimming profits from arms sales to Third World nations, while sharing with other top

Communist Party leaders exclusive private hunting preserves and other luxuries that were denied to, and hidden from, the rest of the population. Although it has long been clear that Communist Party elites enjoyed many privileges that were denied to others (Matthews 1978), the extent of these privileges has proved to be much greater than most had supposed. That these were not merely aberrations of East European Marxism is indicated by non-European examples: In Nicaragua, the villas and much of the other property once owned by Anastasio Somoza and his associates became the personal property of top Sandinista leaders and their families, while in China and Vietnam, Communist Party elites continue to live in closed compounds (similar to those in the former East Germany) where living conditions are carefully hidden from public scrutiny (Salisbury 1992).

At the other extreme, poverty in these societies was more widespread and more serious than Western observers generally realized. Reports by Soviet authorities in the late 1980s indicated that at least 20 percent of the population was living at or below the official poverty level (Fein 1989). Homelessness was also reported to be a problem in Moscow and other Soviet cities, while studies in Hungary at the end of the Communist era found that a quarter of the population was living in poverty (Kamm 1989).

Despite these revelations, it still appears that the level of economic inequality in Marxist societies never equaled the level found in Japan and most of the Western democracies. Wealthy and privileged though the Zhikovs, Ceauçescus, and Honeckers were by comparison with their fellow citizens, the magnitude of their wealth never compared with the great fortunes amassed by leading Western and Japanese businessmen and by oil-rich Middle Eastern leaders. Furthermore, passing wealth on to the next generation has always been much more difficult in Marxist societies than elsewhere, as the unhappy experiences of the Leonid Brezhnev family and others indicate.[4]

A more serious flaw in my earlier assessment was its failure to anticipate the speed and magnitude of the changes that lay ahead. Although I anticipated that the gradual process of political liberalization that began after Stalin's death would continue, and that other changes would occur in response to problems encountered and to the changing needs and growing demands of a better educated population, I cannot pretend to have foreseen the sudden collapse of Communist Party hegemony, the rapid emergence of multiparty systems, or the radical economic changes that have occurred in most of Eastern Europe.

The benefit of hindsight makes clear that the internal, systemic problems of the command economies and one-party polities of Marxist societies were far more serious than most Western observers suspected. In fact, it now appears that the greatest success of Marxist regimes was their ability to dissimulate—a success that was too often achieved because of the readiness of large numbers of Western journalists, scholars, and others to accept glowing reports of socialist successes uncritically (Hollander 1981; Fang 1990). With the revelations that have followed in the wake of the democratic revolutions in Eastern Europe, we now know that the economies of these societies had been stagnating for years and that much of the population had become disaffected and hostile. Worse yet, Marxism and Marxist elites had lost whatever legitimacy they once enjoyed in the minds of many people, especially intellectuals and other opinion leaders and even Party members. (Ironically, this was at a time when Marxism was becoming increasingly fashionable among Western intellectuals.)

These developments have great relevance for our understanding of the causes and consequences of inequality, since it seems that many of the internal, systemic problems of Marxist societies were the result of inadequate motivational arrangements of the sort debated by stratification theorists such as Davis and Moore (1945), Davis (1953), and Tumin (1953). These problems were of two basic types: (1) undermotivation of ordinary workers and (2) misdirected motivation of managers, bureaucrats, and other decision-makers.

The first of these problems was summarized succinctly years ago by East European workers themselves who said, "They pretend to pay us, and we pretend to work" (Dobbs 1981). The rewards for most kinds of work simply did not justify anything more than minimal, perfunctory effort (Shlapentokh 1989, ch. 2). Shoddy workmanship, sullen workers, absenteeism, corruption, and bureaucratic pathologies of various kinds came to typify worker performance in Marxist societies (*The Economist* 1988). These problems are present in every society to some degree, but they became far more prevalent and far more serious in the socialist economies of Marxist societies than in most others. They became so serious, in fact, that they had demoralizing consequences for the vast majority of citizens: endless hours spent in lines queuing for merchandise that was either of poor quality or in short supply, frequent confrontations with surly state employees, unsatisfactory housing, an inadequate health-care system, and more. To add insult to injury, most citizens became aware that a small minority of their fellows was exempted from most of these problems: For them, there were well-stocked stores with better quality merchandise in ample supply and more responsive employees, better housing, better health-care facilities, better schools for their children, second homes, and countless other perks. Worse, this elite preached socialism and the need for sacrifice while enjoying all these special privileges.

To describe the conditions that developed in these societies is to raise the question of why the system failed so badly. What went wrong, and why was the promise of freedom and affluence for the masses never achieved?

For many years, Marxist elites in Eastern Europe and their Western sympathizers explained away these problems on the grounds of *external factors:* the historic backwardness of Eastern Europe, the damage to the Soviet economy caused by the civil war that followed the 1917 revolution, and the hostility of the Western democracies. Although there was much truth to these claims, it has become increasingly clear that *internal, systemic factors* were also a major source of problems for many years. By the late 1980s, this had become obvious even to the leaders of these societies, with many of them becoming advocates of change, and some abandoning Marxism altogether.

Over the years, Marxist societies experimented with a variety of incentive systems, but the egalitarian nature of Marxist ideology always led to substantial limitations on wage differentials for the masses of workers.[5] Over time, however, the severity of these limitations varied as Party elites attempted either to improve the economic performance of their societies or, alternatively, to conform more closely to socialist principles. In a few instances, in an excess of socialist zeal, wage differentials were virtually eliminated: In Czechoslovakia in the early 1960s, for example, wage differences were reduced to the point that engineers and highly skilled workers earned only 5 percent more than unskilled workers. Because of this, large numbers of talented young people dropped out of school, feeling that it was not worth the effort required and the income that would be sacrificed to continue their education. Morale problems also developed among skilled workers, engineers, and other professionals. Within several years, problems had become so acute that authorities were forced to reverse themselves and increase rewards for better educated and more highly skilled workers. A similar crisis developed in the Soviet Union in the early 1930s, forcing Stalin to increase material incentives and wage differentials substantially (Inkeles 1950), and there is growing evidence that the economic crisis in the Soviet Union of the 1980s developed initially in response to a process of wage leveling begun under Brezhnev.

The chief reason for these problems appears to be a basic flaw in Marxist theory. Writing in the nineteenth century, Marx was heir to the eighteenth-century Enlightenment view of human nature—an optimistic view that saw the unattractive aspects of human life as products of corrupting social institutions that could be eliminated by rational social engineering. Whereas the French philosophes blamed the defects in human nature on the influence of church and state, Marx saw private property as the ultimate source of society's ills: If it were abolished, human nature would be transformed. Once socialism was established and the means of production were owned by all, moral incentives could replace material incentives and workers would find work intrinsically rewarding (see also Tumin [1953] on this point). They would work for the sheer joy of working and for the satisfaction of contributing to society's needs, not simply to earn a livelihood.

Unfortunately, the abolition of private property failed to produce the happy transformation in human nature that Marx anticipated. On the contrary, freed from the fear of unemployment and lacking adequate material incentives, worker performance deteriorated and production stagnated or declined in Marxist societies everywhere (Shlapentokh 1989; *The Economist* 1988; Silk 1990; Kamm 1989; Jones 1981; Scammel 1990; Huberman and Sweezy 1967; Zeitlin 1970). The most compelling evidence of this has come from the two Germanys, which shared a common cultural heritage that involved a long tradition of worker pride. Yet by the closing days of the German Democratic Republic, reports of slack work patterns were widespread, and many East German workers were quoted as expressing concern that they would be unable to adapt to the more demanding standards of West German industry. In 1990, at the twenty-eighth Communist Party congress in the Soviet Union, President Mikhail Gorbachev's close associate, Aleksandr Yakovlev, asserted that labor productivity in capitalist South Korea was substantially greater than in socialist North Korea (New York Times News Service 1990). Tatiana Zaslavskaia, a leading Soviet sociologist, found that as many as a third of Soviet workers hated work and were unresponsive to incentives of any kind (Shlapentokh 1987).

But the motivational problems of Marxist societies stemmed from more than faulty assumptions about human nature. They were also due to defective organizational arrangements spawned by the command economies of those societies. Lacking the system of automatic controls inherent in a market economy, economic planners were forced to devise elaborate plans and assign production quotas for the managers of every enterprise. To ensure fulfillment of these quotas, managers were awarded bonuses for meeting or exceeding them and were penalized severely for any shortfall. One unanticipated consequence of this seemingly rational procedure was that managers acquired a strong incentive to stockpile essential resources of every kind—*including labor* (Kostakov 1989; Smith 1976; Greenhouse 1989). Thus, labor resources in these societies came to be used very inefficiently; the result was that workers became cynical about the value of what they were called on to do.

Managers also developed a variety of other unfortunate adaptations to central planning. They learned, for example, that quantity, not quality, was what their bosses, the central planners, cared about (Parkhomovsky 1982).[6] They also learned that production figures could be inflated without much risk because their bosses were also rewarded for good statistics and no one had any interest in seeing if actual performance matched reported performance (G. Medvedev 1989; Z. Medvedev 1990).

Finally, managers learned that there were only minimal rewards for reinvestment and for technological innovation. Lacking pressures from direct economic competition, Party leaders and planners failed to appreciate the importance of continuous modernization of their industrial plant. According to one account, Soviet managers received bonuses of 33 percent for fulfilling production quotas but only 8 percent for fulfilling the plan for new technology (*The Economist* 1988, 11). Thus, because capital investment and technological advance were badly neglected, the command economies of Marxist societies became less and less competitive in world markets.[7]

All of this evidence seems to confirm Davis's (1953) assertion that successful incentive systems involve (1) motivating the best qualified people to seek the most important positions and (2) motivating them to perform to the best of their ability once they are in them. Marxist societies seem to have failed on both counts, using political criteria primarily both to allocate positions and to reward incumbents (Voslensky 1984; Kennedy and Bialecki 1989; Voinovich 1989).

The many malfunctions in the command economies of Marxist societies raise the question of whether they were more or less inevitable consequences of the system itself. This is a question of considerable importance, since command economies are not confined to Marxist societies. The public sector in every society functions as a command economy, and the public sector has been expanding in most societies in recent decades.

Although it is not possible to explore this question in depth here, several observations are in order. First, a substantial majority of the citizens in most of the once socialist societies of Eastern Europe rejected the system when given the chance. Even many Party leaders came to have little faith in central planning and the command economy. As one member of the Soviet Congress of People's Deputies said on the floor of that body, his nation taught the world a valuable lesson by testing, at great cost to itself, what proved to be "an impossible system of economic development" (Zakharov 1990).

Second, there have been remarkable similarities in the performance of command economies in otherwise widely divergent Marxist societies. Most of the pathologies found in Eastern Europe—absenteeism, poor work discipline, low levels of productivity, failure to reinvest in plants and to encourage innovation—have also been reported in China, Cuba, and elsewhere.

Finally, many of these same problems are also evident in the public sector of non-Marxist societies. Government workers and workers in state-owned Western enterprises are widely perceived as less diligent, innovative, enterprising, and responsive than workers in private industry: Negative associations with the term "bureaucrat" are almost as strong in non-Marxist societies as in Marxist ones. In addition, government agencies in these societies are often noted for their inefficient use of human and other resources. Managers in these bureaucracies often find that they are more likely to maximize their own rewards by expanding the size of the work force and other resources under their supervision (regardless of need) than by using these resources efficiently.

Some observers have argued that the massive failures of the socialist economies of Marxist societies in Eastern Europe and elsewhere demonstrate the obvious superiority of capitalism and indicate that the future lies with capitalism. That conclusion, however, seems unwarranted. As noted earlier, even those societies that are usually referred to as "capitalist" have, in reality, very *mixed economies*. To paraphrase Marx, they are societies in which rewards are allocated partly on the basis of *need,* partly on the basis of *work,* and partly on the basis of *property.* In short, they combine elements of communism, socialism, and capitalism and are the product of trial-and-error experimentation guided, in large measure, by a spirit of pragmatism. Mixed economies are systems that recognize the need for material incentives and acknowledge the benefits of economic inequality. But they are also systems that recognize the necessity of allocating a part of the economic product on the basis of need and most on the basis of work.[8] In short, the old view of societies as being either capitalist or socialist seems increasingly irrelevant.

Over time, an ever-increasing number of societies and their leaders have accomplished what scholarly theorists have so notably failed to achieve: They have created a workable synthesis out of seemingly contradictory principles of allocation. One of the urgent tasks for students of inequality in the years ahead will be to catch up with this new social reality and create the kind of theoretical synthesis that does justice to the economic synthesis that has been created in most Western

democracies in recent decades. Too much of stratification theory still resembles the work of the proverbial blind men struggling to describe an elephant.

No real synthesis is likely to emerge, however, so long as students of stratification ignore the crucial body of evidence that has accumulated concerning the effects on motivation and productivity of the massive experiments in destratification conducted in the twentieth century by Marxist elites. In effect, these experiments have provided us with far better evidence than any we have had before of the limits of what is possible in terms of the reduction of differentials in wealth and income. And although these tests cannot be considered definitive, neither can they be written off and ignored as most analysts have done so far.

Notes

I wish to thank Peter Bearman, David Grusky, Michael Kennedy, and Anthony Oberschall for valuable suggestions concerning a prior draft of this paper. They are, of course, in no way responsible for flaws and errors in this final version.

1. I have qualified the label *capitalist* because all Western industrial societies now have mixed economies with substantial state controls over and limitations on the rights of ownership.

2. The terms *really existing socialism* and *really existing socialist societies* were coined by East European sociologists. Although the Marxist-Leninist societies, to which the terms have been applied, represent but one version of socialism, they are especially important for stratification theory because the former leaders of these societies were able to implement the basic socialist principle of abolishing private property far more successfully than socialists in Western Europe ever were.

3. Unfortunately, imperfect tests are a fact of life in the social sciences. If the tests of Marxist theory that are possible in Marxist societies fall short of the scientific ideal, the same is true of almost every test in the social sciences. To deny the relevance of evidence from imperfect tests would be to deny the relevance of most of what has been learned over the years in the social sciences.

4. Shortly after Brezhnev's death, his son-in-law was arrested and sentenced to prison on charges of corruption.

5. The salaries of Party leaders were also kept quite low, but they were compensated generously in a variety of other ways.

6. Quality controls are far more likely when consumers can choose among competing products. When people must use their own money to purchase goods and services, they are not nearly so willing to accept inferior products as when they are using public funds.

7. For example, only 23 percent of Soviet inventions were put to use within two years of their date of patenting, compared to 66 percent of American inventions and 64 percent of West German (*The Economist* 1988).

8. Internal Revenue Service data indicate that approximately 10 percent of U.S. GNP is allocated on the basis of need (public health, welfare, and education expenditures), 70 percent on work (wages and salaries), and 20 percent on property (interest, rents, dividends, capital gains) (Lenski 1984, 202).

References

Davis, Kingsley. 1953. "Reply [to Tumin, 1945]." *American Sociological Review* 18:394–397.

Davis, Kingsley, and Wilbert Moore. 1945. "Some Principles of Stratification." *American Sociological Review* 10:242–249.

Dobbs, Michael. 1981. "'They Pretend to Pay Us, We Pretend to Work,' East Europeans Say." *Washington Post*, April 22.

The Economist. 1988. "The Soviet Economy." April 9, pp. 3–18.

Fang, Lizhi. 1990. "The Chinese Amnesia." *New York Review of Books*, September 27, pp. 30–31.

Fein, Esther. 1989. "Glasnost Is Opening the Door on Poverty." *New York Times*, January 29.

Greenhouse, Steven. 1989. "Can Poland's Dinosaur Evolve?" *New York Times*, November 27.

Hollander, Paul. 1981. *Political Pilgrims: Travels of Western Intellectuals to the Soviet Union, China, and Cuba, 1928–1978.* New York: Oxford University Press.

Huberman, Leo, and Paul Sweezy. 1967. *Socialism in Cuba.* New York: Modern Reader Paperbacks.

Inkeles, Alex. 1950. "Social Stratification and Mobility in the Soviet Union: 1940–1950." *American Sociological Review* 15:465–479.

Jones, T. Anthony. 1981. "Work, Workers, and Modernization in the USSR." *Sociology of Work* 1:249–283.

Kamm, Henry. 1989. "Hungarians Shocked by News of Vast Poverty in Their Midst." *New York Times,* February 6.

Kennedy, Michael, and Ireneusz Bialecki. 1989. "Power and the Logic of Distribution in Poland." *Eastern European Politics and Societies* 3:300–328.

Kostakov, Vladimir. 1989. "Employment: Scarcity or Surplus?" Pp. 159–175 in Anthony Jones and William Moskoff, eds., *Perestroika and the Economy.* Armonk, N.Y.: Sharpe.

Laber, Jeri. 1990. "The Bulgarian Difference." *New York Review of Books,* May 17, pp. 34–36.

Lenski, Gerhard. 1966. *Power and Privilege: A Theory of Social Stratification.* New York: McGraw-Hill.

———. 1978. "Marxist Experiments in Destratification: An Appraisal." *Social Forces* 57:364–383.

———. 1984. "Income Stratification in the United States: Toward a Revised Model of the System." *Research in Social Stratification and Mobility* 3:173–205.

Matthews, Mervyn. 1978. *Privilege in the Soviet Union.* London: Allen & Unwin.

Medvedev, Grigorii. 1989. *Chernobyl'skaia Kronika.* Moscow: Sovremennik. Cited by David Holloway. 1990. "The Catastrophe and After." *New York Review of Books,* July 19, p. 5.

Medvedev, Zhores. 1990. *The Legacy of Chernobyl.* New York: Norton.

New York Times News Service. 1990. "Gorbachev Checks Headstrong Congress." July 8.

Parkhovmosky, Elrad. 1982. "Can't Anybody Here Make Shoes?" *Izvestia.* Reprinted in *World Press Review,* July, p. 36.

Salisbury, Harrison. 1992. *The New Emperors: China in the Era of Mao and Deng.* Boston: Little, Brown.

Scammel, Michael. 1990. "Yugoslavia: The Awakening." *New York Review of Books,* June 28, pp. 42–47.

Shlapentokh, Vladimir. 1987. "Soviet People: Too Rich for Reform." *New York Times,* November 23.

———. 1989. *Public and Private Life of the Soviet People.* New York: Oxford University Press.

Silk, Leonard. 1990. "Soviet Crisis Worse, Economists Declare." *New York Times,* March 15.

Smith, Hedrick. 1976. *The Russians.* New York: Quadrangle.

Tumin, Melvin. 1953. "Some Principles of Stratification: A Critical Analysis." *American Sociological Review* 18:387–394.

Voinovich, Vladimir. 1989. *The Fur Hat*. New York: Harcourt Brace Jovanovich.

Voslensky, Michael. 1984. *Nomenklatura: The Soviet Ruling Class*. Garden City, N.Y.: Doubleday.

Washington Post. 1990. May 6.

Zakharov, Mark. 1990. "A Glimpse in 1990: Politics and Democracy." *Literaturnaya Gazetta* (international ed.), March, p. 5.

Zeitlin, Maurice. 1970. *Revolutionary Politics and the Cuban Working Class*. New York: Harper & Row.

Part III
The Structure of Contemporary Stratification

Theories of Class
Marx and Post-Marxists
Weber and Post-Weberians
Durkheim and Post-Durkheimians
The Ruling Class and Elites

Gradational Status Groupings
Reputation, Deference, and Prestige
Occupational Hierarchies

K A R L   M A R X

Alienation and Social Classes

We shall begin from a *contemporary* economic fact. The worker becomes poorer the more wealth he produces and the more his production increases in power and extent. The worker becomes an ever cheaper commodity the more goods he creates. The *devaluation* of the human world increases in direct relation with the *increase in value* of the world of things. Labour does not only create goods; it also produces itself and the worker as a *commodity,* and indeed in the same proportion as it produces goods.

This fact simply implies that the object produced by labour, its product, now stands opposed to it as an *alien being,* as a *power independent* of the producer. The product of labour is labour which has been embodied in an object and turned into a physical thing; this product is an *objectification* of labour. The performance of work is at the same time its objectification. The performance of work appears in the sphere of political economy as a *vitiation* of the worker, objectification as a *loss* and as *servitude to the object,* and appropriation as *alienation.*

So much does the performance of work appear as vitiation that the worker is vitiated to the point of starvation. So much does objecti-

fication appear as loss of the object that the worker is deprived of the most essential things not only of life but also of work. Labour itself becomes an object which he can acquire only by the greatest effort and with unpredictable interruptions. So much does the appropriation of the object appear as alienation that the more objects the worker produces the fewer he can possess and the more he falls under the domination of his product, of capital.

All these consequences follow from the fact that the worker is related to the *product of his labour* as to an *alien* object. For it is clear on this presupposition that the more the worker expends himself in work the more powerful becomes the world of objects which he creates in face of himself, the poorer he becomes in his inner life, and the less he belongs to himself. It is just the same as in religion. The more of himself man attributes to God the less he has left in himself. The worker puts his life into the object, and his life then belongs no longer to himself but to the object. The greater his activity, therefore, the less he possesses. What is embodied in the product of his labour is no longer his own. The greater this product is, therefore, the more he is diminished. The *alienation* of the worker in his product means not only that his labour becomes an object, assumes an *external* existence, but that it exists independently, *outside himself,* and alien to him, and that it stands opposed to him as an autonomous power.

Originally published from "The Economic and Philosophical Manuscripts" in 1963 and from "The Holy Family: A Critique of Critical Criticism" in 1972 & 1978. Please see complete source information beginning on page 891.

The life which he has given to the object sets itself against him as an alien and hostile force. . . .

So far we have considered the alienation of the worker only from one aspect; namely, *his relationship with the products of his labour.* However, alienation appears not merely in the result but also in the *process* of *production,* within *productive activity* itself. How could the worker stand in an alien relationship to the product of his activity if he did not alienate himself in the act of production itself? The product is indeed only the *résumé* of activity, of production. Consequently, if the product of labour is alienation, production itself must be active alienation—the alienation of activity and the activity of alienation. The alienation of the object of labour merely summarizes the alienation in the work activity itself.

What constitutes the alienation of labour? First, that the work is *external* to the worker, that it is not part of his nature; and that, consequently, he does not fulfil himself in his work but denies himself, has a feeling of misery rather than well-being, does not develop freely his mental and physical energies but is physically exhausted and mentally debased. The worker, therefore, feels himself at home only during his leisure time, whereas at work he feels homeless. His work is not voluntary but imposed, *forced labour.* It is not the satisfaction of a need, but only a *means* for satisfying other needs. Its alien character is clearly shown by the fact that as soon as there is no physical or other compulsion it is avoided like the plague. External labour, labour in which man alienates himself, is a labour of self-sacrifice, of mortification. Finally, the external character of work for the worker is shown by the fact that it is not his own work but work for someone else, that in work he does not belong to himself but to another person.

Just as in religion the spontaneous activity of human fantasy, of the human brain and heart, reacts independently as an alien activity of gods or devils upon the individual, so the activity of the worker is not his own spontaneous activity. It is another's activity and a loss of his own spontaneity.

We arrive at the result that man (the worker) feels himself to be freely active only in his animal functions—eating, drinking and procreating, or at most also in his dwelling and in personal adornment—while in his human functions he is reduced to an animal. The animal becomes human and the human becomes animal.

Eating, drinking and procreating are of course also genuine human functions. But abstractly considered, apart from the environment of human activities, and turned into final and sole ends, they are animal functions.

We have now considered the act of alienation of practical human activity, labour, from two aspects: (1) the relationship of the worker to the *product of labour* as an alien object which dominates him. This relationship is at the same time the relationship to the sensuous external world, to natural objects, as an alien and hostile world; (2) the relationship of labour to the *act of production* within *labour.* This is the relationship of the worker to his own activity as something alien and not belonging to him, activity as suffering (passivity), strength as powerlessness, creation as emasculation, the *personal* physical and mental energy of the worker, his personal life (for what is life but activity?), as an activity which is directed against himself, independent of him and not belonging to him. This is *self-alienation* as against the above-mentioned alienation of the *thing.*

We have now to infer a third characteristic of *alienated labour* from the two we have considered.

Man is a species-being not only in the sense that he makes the community (his own as well as those of other things) his object both practically and theoretically, but also (and this is simply another expression for the same thing) in the sense that he treats himself as the present, living species, as a *universal* and consequently free being.

Species-life, for man as for animals, has its physical basis in the fact that man (like animals) lives from inorganic nature, and since man is more universal than an animal so the range of inorganic nature from which he lives is more universal. Plants, animals, minerals, air, light, etc. constitute, from the theoretical aspect, a part of human consciousness as objects of natural science and art; they are man's spiritual inorganic nature, his intellectual means of life, which he must first prepare for enjoyment and perpetuation. So also, from the practical aspect, they form a part of human life and activity. In practice man lives only from these natural products, whether in the form of food, heating, clothing, housing, etc. The universality of man appears in practice in the universality which makes the whole of nature into his inorganic body: (1) as a direct means of life; and equally (2) as the material object and instrument of his life activity. Nature is the inorganic body of man; that is to say nature, excluding the human body itself. To say that man *lives* from nature means that nature is his *body* with which he must remain in a continuous interchange in order not to die. The statement that the physical and mental life of man, and nature, are interdependent means simply that nature is interdependent with itself, for man is a part of nature.

Since alienated labour: (1) alienates nature from man; and (2) alienates man from himself, from his own active function, his life activity; so it alienates him from the species. It makes *species-life* into a means of individual life. In the first place it alienates species-life and individual life, and secondly, it turns the latter, as an abstraction, into the purpose of the former, also in its abstract and alienated form.

For labour, *life activity, productive life,* now appear to man only as *means* for the satisfaction of a need, the need to maintain his physical existence. Productive life is, however, species-life. It is life creating life. In the type of life activity resides the whole character of a species, its species-character; and free, conscious activity is the species-character of human beings. Life itself appears only as a *means of life.*

The animal is one with its life activity. It does not distinguish the activity from itself. It is *its activity.* But man makes his life activity itself an object of his will and consciousness. He has a conscious life activity. It is not a determination with which he is completely iden-

tified. Conscious life activity distinguishes man from the life activity of animals. Only for this reason is he a species-being. Or rather, he is only a self-conscious being, i.e. his own life is an object for him, because he is a species-being. Only for this reason is his activity free activity. Alienated labour reverses the relationship, in that man because he is a self-conscious being makes his life activity, his *being,* only a means for his *existence.*

The practical construction of an *objective world,* the *manipulation* of inorganic nature, is the confirmation of man as a conscious species-being, i.e. a being who treats the species as his own being or himself as a species-being. Of course, animals also produce. They construct nests, dwellings, as in the case of bees, beavers, ants, etc. But they only produce what is strictly necessary for themselves or their young. They produce only in a single direction, while man produces universally. They produce only under the compulsion of direct physical needs, while man produces when he is free from physical need and only truly produces in freedom from such need. Animals produce only themselves, while man reproduces the whole of nature. The products of animal production belong directly to their physical bodies, while man is free in face of his product. Animals construct only in accordance with the standards and needs of the species to which they belong, while man knows how to produce in accordance with the standards of every species and knows how to apply the appropriate standard to the object. Thus man constructs also in accordance with the laws of beauty.

It is just in his work upon the objective world that man really proves himself as a *species-being.* This production is his active species-life. By means of it nature appears as *his* work and his reality. The object of labour is, therefore, the *objectification of man's species-life;* for he no longer reproduces himself merely intellectually, as in consciousness, but actively and in a real sense, and he sees his own reflection in a world which he has constructed. While, therefore, alienated labour takes away the object of production from man, it also takes away his *species-life,* his real objectivity as a species-being, and changes his advantage over animals into a disadvantage in so far as his inorganic body, nature, is taken from him.

Just as alienated labour transforms free and self-directed activity into a means, so it transforms the species-life of man into a means of physical existence.

Consciousness, which man has from his species, is transformed through alienation so that species-life becomes only a means for him. (3) Thus alienated labour turns the *species-life of man,* and also nature as his mental species-property, into an *alien* being and into a *means* for his *individual existence.* It alienates from man his own body, external nature, his mental life and his *human* life. (4) A direct consequence of the alienation of man from the product of his labour, from his life activity and from his species-life, is that *man* is *alienated* from other *men*. When man confronts himself he also confronts *other* men. What is true of man's relationship to his work, to the product of his work and to himself, is also true of his relationship to other men, to their labour and to the objects of their labour.

In general, the statement that man is alienated from his species-life means that each man is alienated from others, and that each of the others is likewise alienated from human life.

Human alienation, and above all the relation of man to himself, is first realized and expressed in the relationship between each man and other men. Thus in the relationship of alienated labour every man regards other men according to the standards and relationships in which he finds himself placed as a worker.

We began with an economic fact, the alienation of the worker and his production. We have expressed this fact in conceptual terms as *alienated labour,* and in analysing the concept we have merely analysed an economic fact.

Let us now examine further how this concept of alienated labour must express and reveal itself in reality. If the product of labour is alien to me and confronts me as an alien power, to whom does it belong? If my own activity does not belong to me but is an alien,

forced activity, to whom does it belong? To a being *other* than myself. And who is this being? The *gods*? It is apparent in the earliest stages of advanced production, e.g. temple building, etc. in Egypt, India, Mexico, and in the service rendered to gods, that the product belonged to the gods. But the gods alone were never the lords of labour. And no more was *nature*. What a contradiction it would be if the more man subjugates nature by his labour, and the more the marvels of the gods are rendered superfluous by the marvels of industry, the more he should abstain from his joy in producing and his enjoyment of the product for love of these powers.

The *alien* being to whom labour and the product of labour belong, to whose service labour is devoted, and to whose enjoyment the product of labour goes, can only be *man* himself. If the product of labour does not belong to the worker, but confronts him as an alien power, this can only be because it belongs to *a man other than the worker*. If his activity is a torment to him it must be a source of *enjoyment* and pleasure to another. Not the gods, nor nature, but only man himself can be this alien power over men.

Consider the earlier statement that the relation of man to himself is first *realized, objectified,* through his relation to other men. If he is related to the product of his labour, his objectified labour, as to an *alien,* hostile, powerful and independent object, he is related in such a way that another alien, hostile, powerful and independent man is the lord of this object. If he is related to his own activity as to unfree activity, then he is related to it as activity in the service, and under the domination, coercion and yoke, of another man. . . .

Thus, through alienated labour the worker creates the relation of another man, who does not work and is outside the work process, to this labour. The relation of the worker to work also produces the relation of the capitalist (or whatever one likes to call the lord of labour) to work. *Private property* is, therefore, the product, the necessary result, of *alienated labour,* of the external relation of the worker to nature and to himself.

Private property is thus derived from the analysis of the concept of *alienated labour;* that is, alienated man, alienated labour, alienated life, and estranged man.

We have, of course, derived the concept of *alienated labour* (*alienated life*) from political economy, from an analysis of the *movement of private property*. But the analysis of this concept shows that although private property appears to be the basis and cause of alienated labour, it is rather a consequence of the latter, just as the gods are *fundamentally* not the cause but the product of confusions of human reason. At a later stage, however, there is a reciprocal influence.

Only in the final stage of the development of private property is its secret revealed, namely, that it is on one hand the *product* of alienated labour, and on the other hand the *means* by which labour is alienated, *the realization of this alienation.*

The Economic and Philosophical Manuscripts,
pp. 121–131

The possessing class and the proletarian class represent one and the same human self-alienation. But the former feels satisfied and affirmed in this self-alienation, experiences the alienation as a sign *of its own power,* and possesses in it the *appearance* of a human existence. The latter, however, feels destroyed in this alienation, seeing in it its own impotence and the reality of an inhuman existence. To use Hegel's expression, this class is, within depravity, an *indignation* against this depravity, an indignation necessarily aroused in this class by the contradiction between its human *nature* and its life-situation, which is a blatant, outright and all-embracing denial of that very nature.

Within the antagonism as a whole, therefore, private property represents the *conservative* side and the proletariat the *destructive* side. From the former comes action aimed at preserving the antagonism; from the latter, action aimed at its destruction.

The Holy Family: A Critique of Critical Criticism,
pp. 133–134

KARL MARX

Classes in Capitalism and Pre-Capitalism

The history of all hitherto existing society[1] is the history of class struggles.

Freeman and slave, patrician and plebeian, lord and serf, guild-master[2] and journeyman, in a word, oppressor and oppressed, stood in constant opposition to one another, carried on an uninterrupted, now hidden, now open

Originally published in 1963. Please see complete source information beginning on page 891.

fight, a fight that each time ended, either in a revolutionary re-constitution of society at large, or in the common ruin of the contending classes.

In the earlier epochs of history, we find almost everywhere a complicated arrangement of society into various orders, a manifold gradation of social rank. In ancient Rome we have patricians, knights, plebeians, slaves; in the Middle Ages, feudal lords, vassals, guild-masters, journeymen, apprentices, serfs; in

92 III / The Structure of Contemporary Stratification

almost all of these classes, again, subordinate gradations.

The modern bourgeois society that has sprouted from the ruins of feudal society has not done away with class antagonisms. It has but established new classes, new conditions of oppression, new forms of struggle in place of the old ones.

Our epoch, the epoch of the bourgeoisie, possesses, however, this distinctive feature: it has simplified the class antagonisms. Society as a whole is more and more splitting up into two great hostile camps, into two great classes directly facing each other: Bourgeoisie and Proletariat.

From the serfs of the Middle Ages sprang the chartered burghers of the earliest towns. From these burgesses the first elements of the bourgeoisie were developed.

The discovery of America, the rounding of the Cape, opened up fresh ground for the rising bourgeoisie. The East-Indian and Chinese markets, the colonisation of America, trade with the colonies, the increase in the means of exchange and in commodities generally, gave to commerce, to navigation, to industry, an impulse never before known, and thereby, to the revolutionary element in the tottering feudal society, a rapid development.

The feudal system of industry, under which industrial production was monopolised by closed guilds, now no longer sufficed for the growing wants of the new markets. The manufacturing system took its place. The guild-masters were pushed on one side by the manufacturing middle class; division of labour between the different corporate guilds vanished in the face of division of labour in each single workshop.

Meantime the markets kept ever growing, the demand ever rising. Even manufacture no longer sufficed. Thereupon, steam and machinery revolutionised industrial production. The place of manufacture was taken by the giant, Modern Industry, the place of the industrial middle class, by industrial millionaires, the leaders of whole industrial armies, the modern bourgeois.

Modern industry has established the world-market, for which the discovery of America paved the way. This market has given an immense development to commerce, to navigation, to communication by land. This development has, in its turn, reacted on the extension of industry; and in proportion as industry, commerce, navigation, railways extended, in the same proportion the bourgeoisie developed, increased its capital, and pushed into the background every class handed down from the Middle Ages.

We see, therefore, how the modern bourgeoisie is itself the product of a long course of development, of a series of revolutions in the modes of production and of exchange.

Each step in the development of the bourgeoisie was accompanied by a corresponding political advance of that class. An oppressed class under the sway of the feudal nobility, an armed and self-governing association in the mediaeval commune[3]; here independent urban republic (as in Italy and Germany), there taxable "third estate" of the monarchy (as in France), afterwards, in the period of manufacture proper, serving either the semi-feudal or the absolute monarchy as a counterpoise against the nobility, and, in fact, cornerstone of the great monarchies in general, the bourgeoisie has at last, since the establishment of Modern Industry and of the world-market, conquered for itself, in the modern representative State, exclusive political sway. The executive of the modern State is but a committee for managing the common affairs of the whole bourgeoisie.

The bourgeoisie, historically, has played a most revolutionary part. The bourgeoisie, wherever it has got the upper hand, has put an end to all feudal, patriarchal, idyllic relations. It has pitilessly torn asunder the motley feudal ties that bound man to his "natural superiors," and has left remaining no other nexus between man and man than naked self-interest, than callous "cash payment." It has drowned the most heavenly ecstasies of religious fervour, of chivalrous enthusiasm, of philistine sentimentalism, in the icy water of egotistical calculation. It has resolved personal worth into exchange value, and in place of the numberless indefeasible chartered freedoms, has set up that single, unconscionable freedom—Free Trade. In one word, for exploitation, veiled by religious and political illusions, it has substituted naked, shameless, direct, brutal exploitation.

The bourgeoisie has stripped of its halo every occupation hitherto honoured and looked up to with reverent awe. It has converted the physician, the lawyer, the priest, the poet, the man of science, into its paid wage-labourers.

The bourgeoisie has torn away from the family its sentimental veil, and has reduced the family relation to a mere money relation.

The bourgeoisie has disclosed how it came to pass that the brutal display of vigour in the Middle Ages, which Reactionists so much admire, found its fitting complement in the most slothful indolence. It has been the first to show what man's activity can bring about. It has accomplished wonders far surpassing Egyptian pyramids, Roman aqueducts, and Gothic cathedrals; it has conducted expeditions that put in the shade all former Exoduses of nations and crusades.

The bourgeoisie cannot exist without constantly revolutionising the instruments of production, and thereby the relations of production, and with them the whole relations of society. Conservation of the old modes of production in unaltered form, was, on the contrary, the first condition of existence for all earlier industrial classes. Constant revolutionising of production, uninterrupted disturbance of all social conditions, everlasting uncertainty and agitation distinguish the bourgeois epoch from all earlier ones. All fixed, fast-frozen relations, with their train of ancient and venerable prejudices and opinions, are swept away, all new-formed ones become antiquated before they can ossify. All that is solid melts into air, all that is holy is profaned, and man is at last compelled to face with sober senses, his real conditions of life, and his relations with his kind.

The need of a constantly expanding market for its products chases the bourgeoisie over the whole surface of the globe. It must nestle everywhere, settle everywhere, establish connexions everywhere.

The bourgeoisie has through its exploitation of the world-market given a cosmopolitan character to production and consumption in every country. To the great chagrin of Reactionists, it has drawn from under the feet of industry the national ground on which it stood. All old-established national industries have been destroyed or are daily being destroyed. They are dislodged by new industries, whose introduction becomes a life and death question for all civilised nations, by industries that no longer work up indigenous raw material, but raw material drawn from the remotest zones; industries whose products are consumed, not only at home, but in every quarter of the globe. In place of the old wants, satisfied by the productions of the country, we find new wants, requiring for their satisfaction the products of distant lands and climes. In place of the old local and national seclusion and self-sufficiency, we have intercourse in every direction, universal interdependence of nations. And as in material, so also in intellectual production. The intellectual creations of individual nations become common property. National one-sidedness and narrow-mindedness become more and more impossible, and from the numerous national and local literatures, there arises a world literature.

The bourgeoisie, by the rapid improvement of all instruments of production, by the immensely facilitated means of communication, draws all, even the most barbarian, nations into civilisation. The cheap prices of its commodities are the heavy artillery with which it batters down all Chinese walls, with which it forces the barbarians' intensely obstinate hatred of foreigners to capitulate. It compels all nations, on pain of extinction, to adopt the bourgeois mode of production; it compels them to introduce what it calls civilisation into their midst, *i.e.,* to become bourgeois themselves. In one word, it creates a world after its own image.

The bourgeoisie has subjected the country to the rule of the towns. It has created enormous cities, has greatly increased the urban population as compared with the rural, and has thus rescued a considerable part of the population from the idiocy of rural life. Just as it has made the country dependent on the towns, so it has made barbarian and semi-barbarian countries dependent on the civilised ones, nations of peasants on nations of bourgeois, the East on the West.

The bourgeoisie keeps more and more doing away with the scattered state of the population, of the means of production, and of property. It has agglomerated population, centralised means of production, and has concentrated property in a few hands. The necessary consequence of this was political centralisation. Independent, or but loosely connected provinces, with separate interests, laws, governments and systems of taxation, became lumped together into one nation, with one government, one code of laws, one national class-interest, one frontier and one customs-tariff.

The bourgeoisie, during its rule of scarce one hundred years, has created more massive and more colossal productive forces than have all preceding generations together. Subjection of Nature's forces to man, machinery, application of chemistry to industry and agriculture, steam-navigation, railways, electric telegraphs, clearing of whole continents for cultivation, canalisation of rivers, whole populations conjured out of the ground—what earlier century had even a presentiment that such productive forces slumbered in the lap of social labour?

We see then: the means of production and of exchange, on whose foundation the bourgeoisie built itself up, were generated in feudal society. At a certain stage in the development of these means of production and of exchange, the conditions under which feudal society produced and exchanged, the feudal organisation of agriculture and manufacturing industry, in one word, the feudal relations of property became no longer compatible with the already developed productive forces; they became so many fetters. They had to be burst asunder; they were burst asunder.

Into their place stepped free competition, accompanied by a social and political constitution adapted to it, and by the economical and political sway of the bourgeois class.

A similar movement is going on before our own eyes. Modern bourgeois society with its relations of production, of exchange and of property, a society that has conjured up such gigantic means of production and of exchange, is like the sorcerer, who is no longer able to control the powers of the nether world whom he has called up by his spells. For many a decade past the history of industry and commerce is but the history of the revolt of modern productive forces against modern conditions of production, against the property relations that are the conditions for the existence of the bourgeoisie and of its rule. It is enough to mention the commercial crises that by their periodical return put on its trial, each time more threateningly, the existence of the entire bourgeois society. In these crises a great part not only of the existing products, but also of the previously created productive forces, are periodically destroyed. In these crises there breaks out an epidemic that, in all earlier epochs, would have seemed an absurdity—the epidemic of over-production. Society suddenly finds itself put back into a state of momentary barbarism; it appears as if a famine, a universal war of devastation had cut off the supply of every means of subsistence; industry and commerce seem to be destroyed; and why? Because there is too much civilisation, too much means of subsistence, too much industry, too much commerce. The productive forces at the disposal of society no longer tend to further the development of the conditions of bourgeois property; on the contrary, they have become too powerful for these conditions, by which they are fettered, and so soon as they overcome these fetters, they bring disorder into the whole of bourgeois society, endanger the existence of bourgeois property. The conditions of bourgeois society are too narrow to comprise the wealth created by them. And how does the bourgeoisie get over these crises? On the one hand by enforced destruction of a mass of productive forces; on the other, by the conquest of new markets, and by the more thorough exploitation of the old ones. That is to say, by paving the way for more extensive and more destructive crises, and by diminishing the means whereby crises are prevented.

The weapons with which the bourgeoisie felled feudalism to the ground are now turned against the bourgeoisie itself.

But not only has the bourgeoisie forged the weapons that bring death to itself; it has also called into existence the men who are to wield those weapons—the modern working class—the proletarians.

In proportion as the bourgeoisie, *i.e.,* capital, is developed, in the same proportion is the proletariat, the modern working class, developed—a class of labourers, who live only so long as they find work, and who find work only so long as their labour increases capital. These labourers, who must sell themselves piecemeal, are a commodity, like every other article of commerce, and are consequently exposed to all the vicissitudes of competition, to all the fluctuations of the market.

Owing to the extensive use of machinery and to division of labour, the work of the proletarians has lost all individual character, and, consequently, all charm for the workman. He becomes an appendage of the machine, and it is only the most simple, most monotonous, and most easily acquired knack, that is required of him. Hence, the cost of production of a workman is restricted, almost entirely, to the means of subsistence that he requires for his maintenance, and for the propagation of his race. But the price of a commodity, and therefore also of labour, is equal to its cost of production. In proportion, therefore, as the repulsiveness of the work increases, the wage decreases. Nay more, in proportion as the use of machinery and division of labour increases, in the same proportion the burden of toil also increases, whether by prolongation of the working hours, by increase of the work ex-

acted in a given time or by increased speed of the machinery, etc.

Modern industry has converted the little workshop of the patriarchal master into the great factory of the industrial capitalist. Masses of labourers, crowded into the factory, are organised like soldiers. As privates of the industrial army they are placed under the command of a perfect hierarchy of officers and sergeants. Not only are they slaves of the bourgeois class, and of the bourgeois State; they are daily and hourly enslaved by the machine, by the overlooker, and, above all, by the individual bourgeois manufacturer himself. The more openly this despotism proclaims gain to be its end and aim, the more petty, the more hateful and the more embittering it is.

The less the skill and exertion of strength implied in manual labour, in other words, the more modern industry becomes developed, the more is the labour of men superseded by that of women. Differences of age and sex have no longer any distinctive social validity for the working class. All are instruments of labour, more or less expensive to use, according to their age and sex.

No sooner is the exploitation of the labourer by the manufacturer, so far, at an end, and he receives his wages in cash, than he is set upon by the other portions of the bourgeoisie, the landlord, the shopkeeper, the pawnbroker, etc.

The lower strata of the middle class—the small tradespeople, shopkeepers, and retired tradesmen generally, the handicraftsmen and peasants—all these sink gradually into the proletariat, partly because their diminutive capital does not suffice for the scale on which Modern Industry is carried on, and is swamped in the competition with the large capitalists, partly because their specialised skill is rendered worthless by new methods of production. Thus the proletariat is recruited from all classes of the population.

The proletariat goes through various stages of development. With its birth begins its struggle with the bourgeoisie. At first the contest is carried on by individual labourers, then by the workpeople of a factory, then by the operatives of one trade, in one locality, against the individual bourgeois who directly exploits them. They direct their attacks not against the bourgeois conditions of production, but against the instruments of production themselves: they destroy imported wares that compete with their labour, they smash to pieces machinery, they set factories ablaze, they seek to restore by force the vanished status of the workman of the Middle Ages.

At this stage the labourers still form an incoherent mass scattered over the whole country, and broken up by their mutual competition. If anywhere they unite to form more compact bodies, this is not yet the consequence of their own active union, but of the union of the bourgeoisie, which class, in order to attain its own political ends, is compelled to set the whole proletariat in motion, and is moreover yet, for a time, able to do so. At this stage, therefore, the proletarians do not fight their enemies, but the enemies of their enemies, the remnants of absolute monarchy, the landowners, the non-industrial bourgeois, the petty bourgeoisie. Thus the whole historical movement is concentrated in the hands of the bourgeoisie; every victory so obtained is a victory for the bourgeoisie.

But with the development of industry the proletariat not only increases in number; it becomes concentrated in greater masses, its strength grows, and it feels that strength more. The various interests and conditions of life within the ranks of the proletariat are more and more equalised, in proportion as machinery obliterates all distinctions of labour, and nearly everywhere reduces wages to the same low level. The growing competition among the bourgeois, and the resulting commercial crises, make the wages of the workers ever more fluctuating. The unceasing improvement of machinery, ever more rapidly developing, makes their livelihood more and more precarious; the collisions between individual workmen and individual bourgeois take more and more the character of collisions between two classes. Thereupon the workers begin to form combinations (Trades' Unions) against the bourgeois; they club together in order to keep up the rate of wages; they found permanent associations in order to make provision beforehand for these occasional revolts. Here and there the contest breaks out into riots.

Now and then the workers are victorious, but only for a time. The real fruit of their battles lies, not in the immediate result, but in the ever-expanding union of the workers. This union is helped on by the improved means of communication that are created by modern industry and that place the workers of different localities in contact with one another. It was just this contact that was needed to centralise the numerous local struggles, all of the same character, into one national struggle between classes. But every class struggle is a political struggle. And that union, to attain which the burghers of the Middle Ages, with their miserable highways, required centuries, the modern proletarians, thanks to railways, achieve in a few years.

This organisation of the proletarians into a class, and consequently into a political party, is continually being upset again by the competition between the workers themselves. But it ever rises up again, stronger, firmer, mightier. It compels legislative recognition of particular interests of the workers, by taking advantage of the divisions among the bourgeoisie itself. Thus the ten-hours' bill in England was carried.

Altogether collisions between the classes of the old society further, in many ways, the course of development of the proletariat. The bourgeoisie finds itself involved in a constant battle. At first with the aristocracy; later on, with those portions of the bourgeoisie itself, whose interests have become antagonistic to the progress of industry; at all times, with the bourgeoisie of foreign countries. In all these battles it sees itself compelled to appeal to the proletariat, to ask for its help, and thus, to drag it into the political arena. The bourgeoisie itself, therefore, supplies the proletariat with its own elements of political and general education, in other words, it furnishes the proletariat with weapons for fighting the bourgeoisie.

Further, as we have already seen, entire sections of the ruling classes are, by the advance of industry, precipitated into the proletariat, or are at least threatened in their conditions of existence. These also supply the proletariat with fresh elements of enlightenment and progress.

Finally, in times when the class struggle nears the decisive hour, the process of dissolution going on within the ruling class, in fact within the whole range of old society, assumes such a violent, glaring character, that a small section of the ruling class cuts itself adrift, and joins the revolutionary class, the class that holds the future in its hands. Just as, therefore, at an earlier period, a section of the nobility went over to the bourgeoisie, so now a portion of the bourgeoisie goes over to the proletariat, and in particular, a portion of the bourgeois ideologists, who have raised themselves to the level of comprehending theoretically the historical movement as a whole.

Of all the classes that stand face to face with the bourgeoisie today, the proletariat alone is a really revolutionary class. The other classes decay and finally disappear in the face of Modern Industry; the proletariat is its special and essential product.

The lower middle class, the small manufacturer, the shopkeeper, the artisan, the peasant, all these fight against the bourgeoisie, to save from extinction their existence as fractions of the middle class. They are therefore not revolutionary, but conservative. Nay more, they are reactionary, for they try to roll back the wheel of history. If by chance they are revolutionary, they are so only in view of their impending transfer into the proletariat, they thus defend not their present, but their future interests, they desert their own standpoint to place themselves at that of the proletariat.

The "dangerous class," the social scum, that passively rotting mass thrown off by the lowest layers of old society, may, here and there, be swept into the movement by a proletarian revolution, its conditions of life, however, prepare it far more for the part of a bribed tool of reactionary intrigue.

In the conditions of the proletariat, those of old society at large are already virtually swamped. The proletarian is without property; his relation to his wife and children has no longer anything in common with the bourgeois family-relations; modern, industrial labour, modern subjection to capital, the same in England as in France, in America as in Germany, has stripped him of every trace of national character. Law, morality, religion, are to him so many bourgeois prejudices, behind which lurk in ambush just as many bourgeois interests.

All the preceding classes that got the upper hand, sought to fortify their already acquired status by subjecting society at large to their conditions of appropriation. The proletarians cannot become masters of the productive forces of society, except by abolishing their own previous mode of appropriation, and thereby also every other previous mode of appropriation. They have nothing of their own to secure and to fortify; their mission is to destroy all previous securities for, and insurances of, individual property.

All previous historical movements were movements of minorities, or in the interests of minorities. The proletarian movement is the self-conscious, independent movement of the immense majority, in the interests of the immense majority. The proletariat, the lowest stratum of our present society, cannot stir, cannot raise itself up, without the whole superincumbent strata of official society being sprung into the air.

Though not in substance, yet in form, the struggle of the proletariat with the bourgeoisie is at first a national struggle. The proletariat of each country must, of course, first of all settle matters with its own bourgeoisie.

In depicting the most general phases of the development of the proletariat, we traced the more or less veiled civil war, raging within existing society, up to the point where that war breaks out into open revolution, and where the violent overthrow of the bourgeoisie lays the foundation for the sway of the proletariat.

Hitherto, every form of society has been based, as we have already seen, on the antagonism of oppressing and oppressed classes. But in order to oppress a class, certain conditions must be assured to it under which it can, at least, continue its slavish existence. The serf, in the period of serfdom, raised himself to membership in the commune, just as the petty bourgeois, under the yoke of feudal absolutism, managed to develop into a bourgeois. The modern labourer, on the contrary, instead of rising with the progress of industry, sinks deeper and deeper below the conditions of existence of his own class. He becomes a pauper, and pauperism develops more rapidly than population and wealth. And here it becomes evident, that the bourgeoisie is unfit any longer to be the ruling class in society, and to impose its conditions of existence upon society as an overriding law. It is unfit to rule because it is incompetent to assure an existence to its slave within his slavery, because it cannot help letting him sink into such a state, that it has to feed him, instead of being fed by him. Society can no longer live under this bourgeoisie, in other words, its existence is no longer compatible with society.

The essential condition for the existence, and for the sway of the bourgeois class, is the formation and augmentation of capital; the condition for capital is wage-labour. Wage-labour rests exclusively on competition between the labourers. The advance of industry, whose involuntary promoter is the bourgeoisie, replaces the isolation of the labourers, due to competition, by their revolutionary combination, due to association. The development of Modern Industry, therefore, cuts from under its feet the very foundation on which the bourgeoisie produces and appropriates products. What the bourgeoisie, therefore, produces, above all, is its own grave-diggers. Its fall and the victory of the proletariat are equally inevitable.

Notes

1. That is, all *written* history. In 1847, the pre-history of society, the social organisation existing previous to recorded history, was all but unknown. [*Note by Engels to the English edition of 1888.*]

2. Guild-master, that is, a full member of a guild, a master within, not a head of a guild. [*Note by Engels to the English edition of 1888.*]

3. "Commune" was the name taken, in France, by the nascent towns even before they had conquered from their feudal lords and masters local self-government and political rights as the "Third Estate". Generally speaking, for the economical development of the bourgeoisie, England is here taken as the typical country; for its political development, France. [*Note by Engels to the English edition of 1888.*]

This was the name given their urban communities by the townsmen of Italy and France, after they had purchased or wrested their initial rights of self-government from their feudal lords. [*Note by Engels to the German edition of 1890.*]

The Communist Manifesto, pp. 108–119

The first attempts of workers to *associate* among themselves always take place in the form of combinations.

Large-scale industry concentrates in one place a crowd of people unknown to one another. Competition divides their interests. But the maintenance of wages, this common interest which they have against their boss, unites them in a common thought of resistance—*combination*. Thus combination always has a double aim, that of stopping competition among the workers, so that they can carry on general competition with the capitalist. If the first aim of resistance was merely the maintenance of wages, combinations, at first isolated, constitute themselves into groups as the capitalists in their turn unite for the purpose of repression, and in face of always united capital, the maintenance of the association becomes more necessary to them than that of wages. This is so true that English economists are amazed to see the workers sacrifice a good part of their wages in favour of associations, which, in the eyes of these economists, are established solely in favour of wages. In this struggle—a veritable civil war—all the elements necessary for a coming battle unite and develop. Once it has reached this point, association takes on a political character.

Economic conditions had first transformed the mass of the people of the country into workers. The combination of capital has created for this mass a common situation, common interests. This mass is thus already a class as against capital, but not yet for itself. In the struggle, of which we have noted only a few phases, this mass becomes united, and constitutes itself as a class for itself. The interests it defends become class interests. But the struggle of class against class is a political struggle.

In the bourgeoisie we have two phases to distinguish: that in which it constituted itself as a class under the regime of feudalism and absolute monarchy, and that in which, already constituted as a class, it overthrew feudalism and monarchy to make society into a bourgeois society. The first of these phases was the longer and necessitated the greater efforts. This too began by partial combinations against the feudal lords.

Much research has been carried out to trace the different historical phases that the bourgeoisie has passed through, from the commune up to its constitution as a class.

But when it is a question of making a precise study of strikes, combinations and other forms in which the proletarians carry out before our eyes their organization as a class, some are seized with real fear and others display a *transcendental* disdain.

An oppressed class is the vital condition for every society founded on the antagonism of classes. The emancipation of the oppressed class thus implies necessarily the creation of a new society. For the oppressed class to be able to emancipate itself it is necessary that the productive powers already acquired and the existing social relations should no longer be capable of existing side by side. Of all the instruments of production, the greatest productive power is the revolutionary class itself. The organization of revolutionary elements as a class supposes the existence of all the productive forces which could be engendered in the bosom of the old society.

Does this mean that after the fall of the old society there will be a new class domination culminating in a new political power? No.

The condition for the emancipation of the working class is the abolition of every class, just as the condition for the liberation of the third estate, of the bourgeois order, was the abolition of all estates[1] and all orders.

The working class, in the course of its development, will substitute for the old civil society an association which will exclude classes and their antagonism, and there will be no more political power properly so-called, since political power is precisely the official expression of antagonism in civil society.

Meanwhile the antagonism between the proletariat and the bourgeoisie is a struggle of class against class, a struggle which carried to its highest expression is a total revolution. Indeed, is it at all surprising that a society founded on the opposition of classes should culminate in brutal *contradiction,* the shock of body against body, as its final *dénouement?*

Do not say that social movement excludes political movement. There is never a political movement which is not at the same time social.

It is only in an order of things in which there are no more classes and class antagonisms that *social evolutions* will cease to be *political revolutions.* Till then, on the eve of every general reshuffling of society, the last word of social science will always be:

"Le combat ou la mort; la lutte sanguinaire ou le néant. C'est ainsi que la question est invinciblement posée."[2]

Notes

1. Estates here in the historical sense of the estates of feudalism, estates with definite and limited privileges. The revolution of the bourgeoisie abolished the estates and their privileges. Bourgeois society knows only *classes.* It was, therefore, absolutely in contradiction with history to describe the proletariat as the "fourth estate." [*Note by F. Engels to the German edition, 1885.*]

2. "Combat or death; bloody struggle or extinction. It is thus that the question is inexorably put." George Sand, *Jean Ziska*.

The Poverty of Philosophy, pp. 172–175

The small-holding peasants form a vast mass, the members of which live in similar conditions but without entering into manifold relations with one another. Their mode of production isolates them from one another instead of bringing them into mutual intercourse. The isolation is increased by France's bad means of communication and by the poverty of the peasants. Their field of production, the small holding, admits of no division of labour in its cultivation, no application of science and, therefore, no diversity of development, no variety of talent, no wealth of social relationships. Each individual peasant family is almost self-sufficient; it itself directly produces the major part of its consumption and thus acquires its means of life more through exchange with nature than in intercourse with society. A small holding, a peasant and his family; alongside them another small holding, another peasant and another family. A few score of these make up a village, and a few score of villages make up a Department. In this way, the great mass of the French nation is formed by simple addition of homologous magnitudes, much as potatoes in a sack form a sack of potatoes. In so far as millions of families live under economic conditions of existence that separate their mode of life, their interests and their culture from those of the other classes, and put them in hostile opposition to the latter, they form a class. In so far as there is merely a local interconnection among these small-holding peasants, and the identity of their interests begets no community, no national bond and no political organisation among them, they do not form a class. They are consequently incapable of enforcing their class interests in their own name, whether through a parliament or through a convention. They cannot represent themselves, they must be represented. Their representative must at the same time appear as their master, as an authority over them, as an unlimited governmental power that protects them against the other classes and sends them rain and sunshine from above. The political influence of the small-holding peasants, therefore, finds its final expression in the executive power subordinating society to itself.

The Eighteenth Brumaire of Louis Bonaparte,
pp. 478–479

The owners merely of labour-power, owners of capital, and landowners, whose respective sources of income are wages, profit and ground-rent, in other words, wage-labourers, capitalists and landowners, constitute then three big classes of modern society based upon the capitalist mode of production.

In England, modern society is indisputably most highly and classically developed in economic structure. Nevertheless, even here the stratification of classes does not appear in its pure form. Middle and intermediate strata even here obliterate lines of demarcation everywhere (although incomparably less in rural districts than in the cities). However, this is immaterial for our analysis. We have seen that the continual tendency and law of development of the capitalist mode of production is more and more to divorce the means of production from labour, and more and more to concentrate the scattered means of production into large groups, thereby transforming labour into wage-labour and the means of production into capital. And to this tendency, on the other hand, corresponds the independent separation of landed property from capital and labour, or the transformation of all landed property into the form of landed property corresponding to the capitalist mode of production.

The first question to be answered is this: What constitutes a class?—and the reply to this follows naturally from the reply to another question, namely: What makes wage-labourers, capitalists and landlords constitute the three great social classes?

At first glance—the identity of revenues and sources of revenue. There are three great social groups whose members, the individuals forming them, live on wages, profit and ground-rent respectively, on the realisation of their labour-power, their capital, and their landed property.

However, from this standpoint, physicians and officials, e.g., would also constitute two classes, for they belong to two distinct social groups, the members of each of these groups receiving their revenue from one and the same source. The same would also be true of the infinite fragmentation of interest and rank into which the division of social labour splits labourers as well as capitalists and landlords—the latter, e.g., into owners of vineyards, farm owners, owners of forests, mine owners and owners of fisheries.

[Here the manuscript breaks off.]

Capital, Vol. III, pp. 885–886

K A R L   M A R X

Ideology and Class

The ideas of the ruling class are in every epoch the ruling ideas, i.e. the class which is the ruling *material* force of society, is at the same time its ruling *intellectual* force. The class which has the means of material production at its disposal, has control at the same time over the means of mental production, so that thereby, generally speaking, the ideas of those who lack the means of mental production are subject to it. The ruling ideas are nothing more than the ideal expression of the dominant material relationships, the dominant material relationships grasped as ideas; hence of the relationships which make the one class the ruling one, therefore, the ideas of its dominance. The individuals composing the ruling class possess among other things consciousness, and therefore think. Insofar, therefore, as they rule as a class and determine the extent

and compass of an epoch, it is self-evident that they do this in its whole range, hence among other things rule also as thinkers, as producers of ideas, and regulate the production and distribution of the ideas of their age: thus their ideas are the ruling ideas of the epoch. For instance, in an age and in a country where royal power, aristocracy, and bourgeoisie are contending for mastery and where, therefore, mastery is shared, the doctrine of the separation of powers proves to be the dominant idea and is expressed as an "eternal law".

The division of labour manifests itself in the ruling class as the division of mental and material labour, so that inside this class one part appears as the thinkers of the class (its active, conceptive ideologists, who make the perfecting of the illusion of the class about itself their chief source of livelihood), while the others' attitude to these ideas and illusions is more passive and receptive, because they are in reality the active members of this class and have less time to make up illusions and ideas

Originally published in 1970. Please see complete source information beginning on page 891.

about themselves. Within this class this cleavage can even develop into a certain opposition and hostility between the two parts, which, however, in the case of a practical collision, in which the class itself is endangered, automatically comes to nothing, in which case there also vanishes the semblance that the ruling ideas were not the ideas of the ruling class and had a power distinct from the power of this class. The existence of revolutionary ideas in a particular period presupposes the existence of a revolutionary class.

If now in considering the course of history we detach the ideas of the ruling class from the ruling class itself and attribute to them an independent existence, if we confine ourselves to saying that these or those ideas were dominant at a given time, without bothering ourselves about the conditions of production and the producers of these ideas, if we thus ignore the individuals and world conditions which are the source of the ideas, we can say, for instance, that during the time that the aristocracy was dominant, the concepts honour, loyalty, etc. were dominant, during the dominance of the bourgeoisie the concepts freedom, equality, etc. The ruling class itself on the whole imagines this to be so. This conception of history, which is common to all historians, particularly since the eighteenth century, will necessarily come up against the phenomenon that increasingly abstract ideas hold sway, i.e. ideas which increasingly take on the form of universality. For each new class which puts itself in the place of one ruling before it, is compelled, merely in order to carry through its aim, to represent its interest as the common interest of all the members of society, that is, expressed in ideal form: it has to give its ideas the form of universality, and represent them as the only rational, universally valid ones. The class making a revolution appears from the very start, if only because it is opposed to a *class*, not as a class but as the representative of the whole of society; it appears as the whole mass of society

confronting the one ruling class.[1] It can do this because, to start with, its interest really is more connected with the common interest of all other non-ruling classes, because under the pressure of hitherto existing conditions its interest has not yet been able to develop as the particular interest of a particular class. Its victory, therefore, benefits also many individuals of the other classes which are not winning a dominant position, but only insofar as it now puts these individuals in a position to raise themselves into the ruling class. When the French bourgeoisie overthrew the power of the aristocracy, it thereby made it possible for many proletarians to raise themselves above the proletariat, but only insofar as they become bourgeois. Every new class, therefore, achieves its hegemony only on a broader basis than that of the class ruling previously, whereas the opposition of the non-ruling class against the new ruling class later develops all the more sharply and profoundly. Both these things determine the fact that the struggle to be waged against this new ruling class, in its turn, aims at a more decided and radical negation of the previous conditions of society than could all previous classes which sought to rule.

This whole semblance, that the rule of a certain class is only the rule of certain ideas, comes to a natural end, of course, as soon as class rule in general ceases to be the form in which society is organised, that is to say, as soon as it is no longer necessary to represent a particular interest as general or the "general interest" as ruling.

Notes

1. Universality corresponds to (1) the class versus the estate, (2) the competition, world-wide intercourse, etc., (3) the great numerical strength of the ruling class, (4) the illusion of the *common* interests (in the beginning this illusion is true), (5) the delusion of the ideologists and the division of labour. [*Marginal note by Marx.*]

KARL MARX

Value and Surplus Value

What is the common *social substance* of all commodities? It is *Labour*. To produce a commodity a certain amount of labour must be bestowed upon it, or worked up in it. And I say not only *Labour*, but *social Labour*. A man who produces an article for his own immediate use, to consume it himself, creates a *product*, but not a *commodity*. As a self-sustaining producer he has nothing to do with society. But to produce a *commodity*, a man must not only produce an article satisfying some *social* want, but his labour itself must form part and parcel of the total sum of labour expended by society. It must be subordinate to the *Division of Labour within Society*. It is nothing without the other divisions of labour, and on its part is required to *integrate* them.

If we consider *commodities as values*, we consider them exclusively under the single aspect of *realised, fixed,* or, if you like, *crystallised social labour*. In this respect they can *differ* only by representing greater or smaller quantities of labour, as, for example, a greater amount of labour may be worked up in a silken handkerchief than in a brick. But how does one measure *quantities of labour?* By the *time the labour lasts,* in measuring the labour by the hour, the day, etc. Of course, to apply this measure, all sorts of labour are reduced to average or simple labour as their unit.

Originally published in 1969. Please see complete source information beginning on page 891.

We arrive, therefore, at this conclusion. A commodity has a *value,* because it is a *crystallisation of social labour.* The *greatness* of its value, of its *relative* value, depends upon the greater or less amount of that social substance contained in it; that is to say, on the relative mass of labour necessary for its production. The *relative values of commodities* are, therefore, determined by the *respective quantities or amounts of labour, worked up, realised, fixed in them.* The *correlative* quantities of commodities which can be produced in the *same time of labour* are *equal.* Or the value of one commodity is to the value of another commodity as the quantity of labour fixed in the one is to the quantity of labour fixed in the other. . . .

What, then, is the *Value of Labouring Power?*

Like that of every other commodity, its value is determined by the quantity of labour necessary to produce it. The labouring power of a man exists only in his living individuality. A certain mass of necessaries must be consumed by a man to grow up and maintain his life. But the man, like the machine, will wear out, and must be replaced by another man. Beside the mass of necessaries required for *his own* maintenance, he wants another amount of necessaries to bring up a certain quota of children that are to replace him on the labour market and to perpetuate the race of labourers. Moreover, to develop his labouring power, and acquire a given skill, another amount of values must be spent. For our purpose it suffices to consider only *average* labour, the costs of whose education and development are vanishing magnitudes. Still I must seize upon this occasion to state that, as the costs of producing labouring powers of different quality differ, so must differ the values of the labouring powers employed in different trades. The cry for an *equality of wages* rests, therefore, upon a mistake, is an *insane* wish never to be fulfilled. It is an offspring of that false and superficial radicalism that accepts premises and tries to evade conclusions. Upon the basis of the wages system the value of labouring power is settled like that of every other commodity; and as different kinds of labouring power have different values, or require different quantities of labour for their production, they *must* fetch different prices in the labour market. To clamour for *equal or even equitable retribution* on the basis of the wages system is the same as to clamour for *freedom* on the basis of the slavery system. What you think just or equitable is out of the question. The question is: What is necessary and unavoidable with a given system of production?

After what has been said, it will be seen that the *value of labouring power* is determined by the *value of the necessaries* required to produce, develop, maintain, and perpetuate the labouring power.

Now suppose that the average amount of the daily necessaries of a labouring man require *six hours of average labour* for their production. Suppose, moreover, six hours of average labour to be also realised in a quantity of gold equal to 3s. Then 3s. would be the *Price,* or the monetary expression of the *Daily Value* of that man's *Labouring Power.* If he worked daily six hours he would daily produce a value sufficient to buy the average amount of his daily necessaries, or to maintain himself as a labouring man.

But our man is a wages labourer. He must, therefore, sell his labouring power to a capitalist. If he sells it at 3s. daily, or 18s. weekly, he sells it at its value. Suppose him to be a spinner. If he works six hours daily he will add to the cotton a value of 3s. daily. This value, daily added by him, would be an exact equivalent for the wages, or the price of his labouring power, received daily. But in that

case *no surplus value* or *surplus produce* whatever would go to the capitalist. Here, then, we come to the rub.

In buying the labouring power of the workman, and paying its value, the capitalist, like every other purchaser, has acquired the right to consume or use the commodity bought. You consume or use the labouring power of a man by making him work as you consume or use a machine by making it run. By paying the daily or weekly value of the labouring power of the workman, the capitalist has, therefore, acquired the right to use or make that labouring power work during the *whole day or week.* . . .

For the present I want to turn your attention to one decisive point.

The *value* of the labouring power is determined by the quantity of labour necessary to maintain or reproduce it, but the *use* of that labouring power is only limited by the active energies and physical strength of the labourer. The daily or weekly *value* of the labouring power is quite distinct from the daily or weekly exercise of that power, the same as the food a horse wants and the time it can carry the horseman are quite distinct. The quantity of labour by which the *value* of the workman's labouring power is limited forms by no means a limit to the quantity of labour which his labouring power is apt to perform. Take the example of our spinner. We have seen that, to daily reproduce his labouring power, he must daily reproduce a value of three shillings, which he will do by working six hours daily. But this does not disable him from working ten or twelve or more hours a day. But by paying the daily or weekly *value* of the spinner's labouring power, the capitalist has acquired the right of using that labouring power during *the whole day or week.* He will, therefore, make him work say, daily, *twelve* hours. *Over and above* the six hours required to replace his wages, or the value of his labouring power, he will, therefore, have to work *six other hours,* which I shall call hours of *surplus labour,* which surplus labour will realise itself in a *surplus value* and a *surplus produce.* If our spinner, for example, by his daily labour of six hours, added three shillings' value to the cotton, a value forming an exact equivalent to his wages, he will, in twelve hours, add six shillings' worth to the cotton, and produce *a proportional surplus of yarn.* As he has sold his labouring power to the capitalist, the whole value or produce created by him belongs to the capitalist, the owner *pro tem.* of his labouring power. By advancing three shillings, the capitalist will, therefore, realise a value of six shillings, because, advancing a value in which six hours of labour are crystallised, he will receive in return a value in which twelve hours of labour are crystallised. By repeating this same process daily, the capitalist will daily advance three shillings and daily pocket six shillings, one-half of which will go to pay wages anew, and the other half of which will form *surplus value,* for which the capitalist pays no equivalent. It is this *sort of exchange between capital and labour* upon which capitalistic production, or the wages system, is founded, and which must constantly result in reproducing the working man as a working man, and the capitalist as a capitalist.

The rate of surplus value, all other circumstances remaining the same, will depend on the proportion between that part of the working day necessary to reproduce the value of the labouring power and the *surplus time* or *surplus labour* performed for the capitalist. It will, therefore, depend on the *ratio in which the working day is prolonged over and above that extent,* by working which the working man would only reproduce the value of his labouring power, or replace his wages.

RALF DAHRENDORF

Class and Class Conflict in Industrial Society

One of the main questions which the present investigation is supposed to answer is: Do classes and class conflicts belong to that group of phenomena by which only the capitalist type of industrial society is characterized, or is their existence a consequence of industrial production itself, and are they therefore a lasting feature of industrial societies? This question will accompany us throughout the following analysis of changes in the structure of industrial societies since Marx.

Originally published in 1959. Please see complete source information beginning on page 891.

Ownership and Control, or the Decomposition of Capital

Marx was right in seeking the root of social change in capitalist society in the sphere of industrial production, but the direction these changes took turned out to be directly contrary to Marx's expectations. With respect to capital, he had, in his later years, at least a vision of what was going to happen, as his brief and somewhat puzzled analysis of joint-stock companies shows. Joint-stock companies were legally recognized in Germany, England, France, and the United States in the second half of the nineteenth century. Laws often indicate the conclusion of social developments, and indeed early forms of joint-stock companies can be traced back at least to the commercial companies and trade societies of the seventeenth century. But it was in the nineteenth and early twentieth centuries that this type of enterprise first gained wide recognition and expanded into all branches of economic activity. Today, more than two-thirds of all companies in advanced industrial societies are joint-stock companies, and their property exceeds four-fifths of the total property in economic enterprises. The enterprise owned and run by an individual, or even a family, has long ceased to be the dominant pattern of economic organization. . . .

According to the radical view, joint-stock companies involve a complete break with earlier capitalist traditions. By separating what has come to be called ownership and control, they give rise to a new group of managers who are utterly different from their capitalist predecessors. Thus for Marx, the joint-stock company involves a complete alienation of capital "from the real producers, and its opposition as alien property to all individuals really participating in production, from the manager down to the last day-laborer" (1953, Vol. III, p. 478). In other words, by separating ownership and control, the joint-stock company reduces the distance between manager and worker while at the same time removing the owners altogether from the sphere of production and thereby isolating their function as exploiters of others. It is merely a step from this kind of analysis to the thesis that, as Renner has it, the "capitalists without function" yield to the "functionaries without capital," and that this new ruling group of industry bears little resemblance to the old "full capitalists" (1953, pp. 182, 198). Burnham, Geiger, Sering, and others followed Marx (and Renner) in this radical interpretation of the social effects of joint-stock companies.

The conservative view, on the other hand, holds that the consequences of the apparent separation of ownership and control have been vastly overrated. It is argued that in fact owners and controllers, i.e., stockholders and managers, are a fairly homogeneous group. There are often direct connections between

them, and where this is not the case, their outlook is sufficiently similar to justify insisting on the old assumption of a homogeneous class of capitalists opposed to an equally homogeneous class of laborers. This view is not often heard in the West nowadays, although traces of it are evident in the work of C. Wright Mill's (1954, 1956). It may be added that this conservative view is clearly contrary to Marx's own analysis. . . .

There is little reason to follow Marx and describe the condition of separation of ownership and control as a transitional form of historical development. It is no more transitional than any other stage of history, and it has already proven quite a vital pattern of social and economic structure. But I think that we can follow Marx in his radical interpretation of this phenomenon. The separation of ownership and control has replaced one group by two whose positions, roles, and outlooks are far from identical. In taking this view, one does of course agree with Marx against himself. For it follows from this that the homogeneous capitalist class predicted by Marx has in fact not developed. Capital—and thereby capitalism—has dissolved and given way in the economic sphere, to a plurality of partly agreed, partly competing, and partly simply different groups. The effect of this development on class conflict is threefold: first, the replacement of capitalists by managers involves a change in the composition of the groups participating in conflict; second, and as a consequence of this change in recruitment and composition, there is a change in the nature of the issues that cause conflicts, for the interests of the functionaries without capital differ from those of full-blown capitalists, and so therefore do the interests of labor vis-à-vis their new opponents; and third, the decomposition of capital involves a change in the patterns of conflict. One might question whether this new conflict, in which labor is no longer opposed to a homogeneous capitalist class, can still be described as a class conflict at all. In any case, it is different from the division of the whole society into two great and homogeneous hostile camps with which Marx was concerned. While I would follow the radical view of the separation of ownership and control in industry to this point, there is one thing to be said in favor of the conservative view. Changes in the composition of conflict groups, of the issues, and of patterns of conflict do not imply the abolition of conflict or even of the specific conflict between management and labor in industry. Despite the effects of the decomposition of capital on class structure, we have no reason to believe that antagonisms and clashes of interest have now been banned from industrial enterprises.

Skill and Stratification, or the Decomposition of Labor

While Marx had at least a premonition of things to come with respect to capital, he remained unaware of developments affecting the unity and homogeneity of labor. Yet in this respect, too, the sphere of production which loomed so large in Marx's analyses became the starting point of changes that clearly refute his predictions. The working class of today, far from being a homogeneous group of equally unskilled and impoverished people, is in fact a stratum differentiated by numerous subtle and not-so-subtle distinctions. Here, too, history has dissolved one position, or role, and has substituted for it a plurality of roles that are endowed with diverging and often conflicting expectations. . . .

Analysis of industrial conditions suggests quite clearly that within the labor force of advanced industry we have to distinguish at least three skill groups: a growing stratum of highly skilled workmen who increasingly merge with both engineers and white-collar employees, a relatively stable stratum of semiskilled workers with a high degree of diffuse as well as specific industrial experience, and a dwindling stratum of totally unskilled laborers who are characteristically either newcomers to industry (beginners, former agricultural laborers, immigrants) or semi-unemployables. It appears, furthermore, that these three groups differ not only in their level of skill, but also in other attributes and determinants of social status. The semiskilled almost invariably earn a higher wage than the unskilled, whereas the skilled are often salaried and thereby participate in white-collar status. The hierarchy of skill corresponds exactly to the hierarchy of responsibility and delegated authority within the working class. From numerous studies it would seem beyond doubt that it also correlates with the hierarchy of prestige, at the top of which we find the skilled man whose prolonged training, salary, and security convey special status, and at the bottom of which stands the unskilled man who is, according to a recent German investigation into workers' opinions, merely "working" without having an "occupation" proper (see Kluth, 1955, p. 67). Here as elsewhere Marx was evidently mistaken. "Everywhere, the working class differentiates itself more and more, on the one hand into occupational groups, on the other hand into three large categories with different, if not contradictory, interests: the skilled craftsmen, the unskilled laborers, and the semiskilled specialist workers" (Philip, 1955, p. 2).

In trying to assess the consequences of this development, it is well to remember that, for Marx, the increasing uniformity of the working class was an indispensable condition of that intensification of the class struggle which was to lead, eventually, to its climax in a revolution. The underlying argument of what for Marx became a prediction appears quite plausible. For there to be a revolution, the conflicts within a society have to become extremely intense. For conflicts to be intense, one would indeed expect its participants to be highly unified and homogeneous groups. But neither capital nor labor have developed along these lines. Capital has dissolved into at least two, in many ways distinct, elements, and so has labor. The proletarian, the impoverished slave of industry who is indistinguishable from his peers in terms of his work, his skill, his wage, and his prestige, has left the scene. What is more, it appears that by now he has been followed by his less depraved, but equally alienated successor, the worker. In modern industry, "the worker" has become precisely the kind of abstraction which Marx quite justly resented so much. In his place, we find a plurality of status and skill groups whose interests often diverge. Demands of the skilled for security may injure the semiskilled; wage claims of the semiskilled may raise objections by the skilled; and any interest on the part of the unskilled is bound to set their more highly skilled fellow workmen worrying about differentials.

Again, as in the case of capital, it does not follow from the decomposition of labor that there is no bond left that unites most workers—at least for specific goals; nor does it follow that industrial conflict has lost its edge. But here, too, a change of the issues and, above all, of the patterns of conflict is indicated. As with the capitalist class, it has become doubtful whether speaking of the working class still makes much sense. Probably Marx would have agreed that class "is a force that unites into groups people who differ from one another, by overriding the differences between them" (Marshall, 1950, p. 114), but he certainly did not expect the differences to be so great, and the uniting force so precarious as it has turned out to be in the case both of capital and of labor. . . .

The Institutionalization of Class Conflict

A historian might argue that all the tendencies of change here described as changes in the structure of industrial societies since Marx had in fact begun before and in some cases long before Marx died in 1883. . . . There is, however, one line of social development in industrial societies which has both originated and spread since about the time of Marx's death, and which is directly relevant to our problem. Geiger, who has described this change as the "institutionalization of class conflict," says: "The tension between capital and labor is recognized as a principle of the structure of the labor market and has become a legal institution of society. . . . The methods, weapons, and techniques of the class struggle

are recognized—and are thereby brought under control. The struggle evolves according to certain rules of the game. Thereby the class struggle has lost its worst sting, it is converted into a legitimate tension between power factors which balance each other. Capital and labor struggle with each other, conclude compromises, negotiate solutions, and thereby determine wage levels, hours of work, and other conditions of work" (1949, p. 184).

Marx displayed a certain sociological naïveté when he expressed his belief that capitalist society would be entirely unable to cope with the class conflict generated by its structure. In fact, every society is capable of coping with whatever new phenomena arise in it, if only by the simple yet effective inertia which can be described, a little pretentiously, as the process of institutionalization. In the case of class conflict, institutionalization assumed a number of successive and complementary forms. It began with the painful process of recognition of the contending parties as legitimate interest groups. Within industry, a "secondary system of industrial citizenship" (Marshall, 1950, p. 68) enabled both workers and entrepreneurs to associate and defend their interests collectively. Outside industry, the primary system of political citizenship had the same effect. And while, in the stage of organization, conflict may develop a greater visible intensity, organization has at least two side effects which operate in the opposite direction. Organization presupposes the legitimacy of conflict groups, and it thereby removes the permanent and incalculable threat of guerrilla warfare. At the same time, it makes systematic regulations of conflicts possible. Organization is institutionalization, and whereas its manifest function is usually an increasingly articulate and outspoken defense of interests, it invariably has the latent function also of inaugurating routines of conflict which contribute to reducing the violence of clashes of interest. . . .

Nobody can, of course, ever be sure that a given pattern of conflict regulation will always prove successful. There are still strikes, and for all we know they will continue to occur. But it has proved possible for industrial society to get along with the clashes of interest arising from its industrial and political structure—and it has proved possible for interest groups to get along with industrial society. Instead of a battlefield, the scene of group conflict has become a kind of market in which relatively autonomous forces contend according to certain rules of the game, by virtue of which nobody is a permanent winner or loser. This course of development must naturally be bitter for the orthodox and the dogmatic, but theirs is the kind of bitterness which makes liberal minds rejoice. . . .

Power and Authority

One of the central theses of this study consists in the assumption that the differential distribution of authority invariably becomes the determining factor of systematic social conflicts of a type that is germane to class conflicts in the traditional (Marxian) sense of this term. The structural origin of such group conflicts must be sought in the arrangement of social roles endowed with expectations of domination or subjection. Wherever there are such roles, group conflicts of the type in question are to be expected. Differentiation of groups engaged in such conflicts follows the lines of differentiation of roles that are relevant from the point of view of the exercise of authority. Identification of variously equipped authority roles is the first task of conflict analysis;[1] conceptually and empirically all further steps of analysis follow from the investigation of distributions of power and authority.

"Unfortunately, the concept of power is not a settled one in the social sciences, either in political science or in sociology" (Parsons, 1957, p. 139). Max Weber (1947), Pareto (1955), Mosca (1950), later Russell (1938), Bendix (1952), Lasswell (1936), and others have explored some of the dimensions of this category; they have not, however, reached such a degree of consensus as would enable us to employ the categories of power and authority without at least brief conceptual preliminaries. So far as the terms "power" and "authority" and their distinction are concerned, I shall follow in this study the useful and well-considered definitions of Max Weber. For Weber, power is the "probability that one actor within a social relationship will be in a position to carry out his own will despite resistance, regardless of the basis on which this probability rests"; whereas authority (*Herrschaft*) is the "probability that a command with a given specific content will be obeyed by a given group of persons" (1947, p. 28). The important difference between power and authority consists in the fact that whereas power is essentially tied to the personality of individuals, authority is always associated with social positions or roles. The demagogue has power over the masses to whom he speaks or whose actions he controls; but the control of the officer over his men, the manager over his workers, the civil servant over his clientele is authority, because it exists as an expectation independent of the specific person occupying the position of officer, manager, civil servant. It is only another way of putting this difference if we say—as does Max Weber—that while power is merely a factual relation, authority is a legitimate relation of domination and subjection. In this sense, authority can be described as legitimate power.

In the present study we are concerned exclusively with relations of authority, for these alone are part of social structure and therefore permit the systematic derivation of group conflicts from the organization of total societies and associations within them. The significance of such group conflicts rests with the fact that they are not the product of structurally fortuitous relations of power but come forth wherever authority is exercised—and that means in all societies under all historical conditions. (1) Authority relations are always relations of super- and subordination. (2) Where there are authority relations, the superordinate element is socially expected to control, by orders and commands, warnings and prohibitions, the behavior of the subordinate element. (3) Such expectations attach to relatively permanent social positions rather than to the character of individuals; they are in this sense legitimate. (4) By virtue of this fact, they always involve specification of the persons subject to control and of the spheres within which control is permissible. Authority, as distinct from power, is never a relation of generalized control over others. (5) Authority being a legitimate relation, noncompliance with authoritative commands can be sanctioned; it is indeed one of the functions of the legal system (and of course of quasi-legal customs and norms) to support the effective exercise of legitimate authority.

Alongside the term "authority," we shall employ in this study the terms "domination" and "subjection." These will be used synonymously with the rather clumsy expressions "endowed with authority" or "participating in the exercise of authority" (domination), and "deprived of authority" or "excluded from the exercise of authority" (subjection).

It seems desirable for purposes of conflict analysis to specify the relevant unit of social organization in analogy to the concept of social system in the analysis of integration. To speak of specification here is perhaps misleading. "Social system" is a very general concept applicable to all types of organization; and we shall want to employ an equally general concept which differs from that of social system by emphasizing a different aspect of the same organizations. It seems to me that Max Weber's category "imperatively coordinated association" (*Herrschaftsverband*) serves this purpose despite its clumsiness. . . .

Empirically it is not always easy to identify the border line between domination and subjection. Authority has not remained unaffected by the modern process of division of labor. But even here, groups or aggregates can be identified which do not participate in the exercise of authority other than by complying with given commands or prohibitions. Contrary to all criteria of social stratification, authority does not permit the construction of a scale. So-called hierarchies of authority (as displayed, for example, in organization charts) are in fact hierarchies of the "plus-side" of authority, i.e., of the differentiation of domination; but there is, in every association, also a "minus-side" consisting of those who are subjected to authority rather than participate in its exercise.

In two respects this analysis has to be specified, if not supplemented. First, for the individual incumbent of roles, domination in one association does not necessarily involve domination in all others to which he belongs, and subjection, conversely, in one association does not mean subjection in all. The dichotomy of positions of authority holds for specific associations only. In a democratic state, there are both mere voters and incumbents of positions of authority such as cabinet ministers, representatives, and higher civil servants. But this does not mean that the "mere voter" cannot be incumbent of a position of authority in a different context, say, in an industrial enterprise; conversely, a cabinet minister may be, in his church, a mere member, i.e., subject to the authority of others. Although empirically a certain correlation of the authority positions of individuals in different associations seems likely, it is by no means general and is in any case a matter of specific empirical conditions. It is at least possible, if not probable, that if individuals in a given society are ranked according to the sum total of their authority positions in all associations, the resulting pattern will not be a dichotomy but rather like scales of stratification according to income or prestige. For this reason it is necessary to emphasize that in the sociological analysis of group conflict the unit of analysis is always a specific association and the dichotomy of positions within it.

As with respect to the set of roles associated with an individual, total societies, also, do not usually present an unambiguously dichotomic authority structure. There are a large number of imperatively coordinated associations in any given society. Within every one of them we can distinguish the aggregates of those who dominate and those who are subjected. But since domination in industry does not necessarily involve domination in the state, or a church, or other associations, total societies can present the picture of a plurality of competing dominant (and, conversely, subjected) aggregates. This, again, is a problem for the analysis of specific historical societies and must not be confounded with the clearer lines of differentiation within any one association. Within the latter, the distribution of authority always sums up to zero, i.e., there always is a division involving domination and subjection.

I need hardly emphasize that from the point of view of "settling" the concepts of power and authority, the preceding discussion has raised more problems than it has solved. I believe, however, that for the purposes of this study, and of a sociological theory of conflict, little needs to be added to what has been stated here. In order somewhat to substantiate this perhaps rather bold assertion, it seems useful to recapitulate briefly the heuristic purpose and logical status of the considerations of this section.

I have introduced, as a structural determinant of conflict groups, the category of authority as exercised in imperatively coordinated associations. While agreeing with Marx that source and level of income—even socioeconomic status—cannot usefully be conceived as determinants of conflict groups, I have added to this list of erroneous approaches Marx's own in terms of property in the means of production. Authority is both a more general and a more significant social relation. The former has been shown in our critique of Marx; the latter will have to be demonstrated [elsewhere (see Dahrendorf 1959)]. The concept of authority is used, in this context, in a specific sense. It is differentiated from power by what may roughly be referred to as the element of legitimacy; and it has to be understood throughout in the restricted sense of authority as distributed and exercised in imperatively coordinated associations. While its "disruptive" or conflict-generating consequences are not the only aspect of authority, they are the one relevant in terms of the coercion model of society. Within the frame of reference of this model, (1) the distribution of authority in associations is the ultimate "cause" of the formation of conflict groups, and (2) being dichotomous, it is, in any given association, the cause of the formation of two, and only two, conflict groups.

Notes

1. To facilitate communication, I shall employ in this study a number of abbreviations. These must not however be misunderstood. Thus, "conflict analysis" in this context stands for "analysis of group conflicts of the class type, class being understood in the traditional sense." At no point do I want to imply a claim for a generalized theory of social conflict.

Bibliography

Reinhard Bendix. 1952. "Bureaucracy and the Problem of Power." *Reader in Bureaucracy.* Edited by R.K. Merton, A.P. Gray, B. Hockey, and H.C. Selvin. Glencoe.

Ralf Dahrendorf. 1959. *Class and Class Conflict in Industrial Society.* Stanford.

Theodor Geiger. 1949. *Die Klassengesellschaft im Schmelztiegel.* Cologne and Hagen.

Heinz B. Kluth. 1955. "Arbeiterjugend—Begriff und Wirklichkeit," in Helmut Schelsky, ed., *Arbeiterjugend—gestern und heute.* Heidelberg.

Harold Lasswell. 1936. *Politics—Who Gets What, When, and How?* New York.

T.H. Marshall. 1950. *Citizenship and Social Class.* Cambridge.

Karl Marx. 1953. *Das Kapital.* Vols. I, III. New ed. Berlin.

C.W. Mills. 1954. *The New Men of Power.* New York.

C.W. Mills. 1956. *The Power Elite.* New York.

Gaetano Mosca. 1950. *Die herrschende Klasse.* Bern.

Vilfredo Pareto. 1955. *Allgemeine Soziologie.* Translated and edited by C. Brinkmann. Tübingen.

Talcott Parsons. 1957. "The Distribution of Power in American Society," *World Politics* X, No. 1, October.

André Philip. 1955. *La démocratie industrielle.* Paris.

Karl Renner. 1953. *Wandlungen der modernen Gesellschaft: zwei Abhandlungen über die Probleme der Nachkriegszeit.* Vienna.

Bertrand Russell. 1938. *Power: A New Social Analysis.* London.

Paul Sering. 1947. *Jenseits des Kapitalismus.* Nürnberg.

Max Weber. 1947. *Wirtschaft und Gesellschaft* (Grundriss der Sozialökonomik, section III). 4th ed. Tübingen.

ERIK OLIN WRIGHT

Varieties of Marxist Conceptions of Class Structure

The general outlines of the theory of contradictory locations within class relations were first presented in an essay in the *New Left Review* in 1976 and later elaborated in a series of other publications.[1] The basic argument revolves around an analysis of three interconnected dimensions of domination and subordination within production. Each of these dimensions involves a social relation of domination and subordination with respect to some particular resource within production: *money capital,* that is, the flow of investments into production and the direction of the overall accumulation process (accumulation of surplus value); *physical capital,* that is, the actual means of production within the production process; and *labor,* that is, the laboring activity of the direct producers within production. These relations can be characterized as relations of domination and subordination because each relation simultaneously defines those positions that have the capacity to control the particular resource and those that are excluded from such control. The first of these dimensions is often referred to as "real economic ownership"; the second and third together are often referred to as "possession."

In no sense should these three *dimensions* be thought of as three independent *types* of relations. Within capitalist production they are each necessary conditions for the existence of the others; there is no sense in which they can exist autonomously. Nevertheless, while these three dimensions of social relations are intrinsically interdependent, there is still a clear hierarchy of determination among them. The social relations of control over money capital structure, or set limits upon, the relations of control over physical capital, which in turn limit the direct control over labor within production. A rentier capitalist, therefore, who is not directly involved in control over physical capital or labor, nevertheless falls within the capitalist class because of the social relations of control over money capital ("real economic ownership" of the means of production).

The fundamental class relation between labor and capital can be thought of as a polarized, antagonistic relation along all three of these dimensions: The capitalist class occupies the dominant position with respect to the social relations of control over money capital, physical capital, and labor; the working class occupies the subordinate position within each of these dimensions of social relations.

When the class structure is analyzed at the highest level of abstraction—the level of the "pure" capitalist mode of production—these are the only two classes defined by these three dimensions of relations of production. When we move to a lower level of abstraction—the level of what Marxists call the "social formation"—other classes enter the analysis. This occurs for two basic reasons. First, concrete capitalist social formations are never characterized simply by the capitalist mode of production. Various kinds of precapitalist rela-

Originally published in 1980. Please see complete source information beginning on page 891.

tions of production exist side by side with capitalist relations, although typically these are of marginal importance and are socially subordinated in various ways to the capitalist mode of production. Of particular importance in these terms is simple commodity production: the production and sale of goods by self-employed individuals who employ no workers. In terms of the three dimensions of social relations of production discussed above, such "petty bourgeois" class locations involve control over money capital and physical capital but not over labor (since no labor power is employed within production).

The second way in which additional class locations appear when we study class structures within concrete capitalist societies is that the three dimensions of social relations of production need not necessarily coincide perfectly—indeed, there are systemic forces in capitalist development working against their doing so. Such noncorrespondence generates what I have termed "contradictory locations within class relations." Three such contradictory locations are particularly important.

Managers and supervisors occupy a contradictory location between the working class and the capitalist class. Like the working class they are excluded from control over money capital (that is, from basic decisions about allocation of investments and the direction of accumulation), but unlike workers they have a certain degree of control of the physical means of production and over the labor of workers within production. Within the manager-supervisor contradictory location, top managers occupy the position closest to the capitalist class, whereas foremen occupy the location closest to the working class.

Small employers occupy a contradictory location between the petty bourgeoisie and the capitalist class proper. Unlike the petty bourgeoisie, they do employ some labor power and thus are in a relation of exploitation with workers. But unlike the capitalist class, they are themselves directly engaged in production alongside their workers, and they do not employ sufficient quantities of labor power to accumulate large masses of capital.

Semiautonomous employees occupy a contradictory location between the petty bourgeoisie and the working class. Like the working class, they are excluded from any control over money capital and the labor of others, but like the petty bourgeoisie they do have some real control over their immediate physical means of production, over their direct activity within the labor process. These three contradictory locations are schematically represented in the accompanying figure and in a more formal way in table 1.

It should be noted that in table 1 there is more than one position (or "level") within each of the three dimensions of social relations of production. Take, for example, the social relations of control over physical capital, one of the two aspects of "possession" of the means of production. "Full" control in this instance implies that the position is involved in decisions concerning the operation and planning of the entire production process; "partial" control implies participation in decisions concerning specific segments of the production process; "minimal" control implies control over one's immediate means of production within the labor process; "no" control implies complete exclusion from decisions concerning the operation of the means of production. Each of these "levels" of control must be understood in terms of the social relations with other levels; they are not simply points on a scale. Taken together, they make it possible to identify more precisely specific positions within each contradictory location.

It is important to understand the precise sense in which these class locations are "contradictory" locations within class relations. They are not contradictory simply because they cannot be neatly pigeonholed in any of the basic classes. The issue is not one of typological aesthetics. Rather they are contradictory locations because they simultaneously share the relational characteristics of two distinct classes. As a result, they share class interests with two different classes but have interests identical to neither. It is in this sense that they can be viewed as being objectively torn between class locations.

TABLE 1
Formal Criteria for Contradictory Locations Within Class Relations

Class Positions		Dimensions of Social Relations of Production[a]		
		Relations of Economic Ownership	Relations of Possession	
		Control over Money Capital	Control over Physical Capital	Control over Labor
Bourgeoisie	Traditional capitalist	+	+	+
	Top corporate executive	+	+	+
Contradictory class location between the bourgeoisie and the proletariat	Top managers	Partial/minimal	+	+
	Middle managers	Minimal/−	Partial	Partial
	Technocrats	−	Minimal	Minimal
	Foremen/supervisors	−	−	Minimal
Proletariat		−	−	−
Contradictory class location between the proletariat and the petty bourgeoisie	Semiautonomous employees	−	Minimal	−
Petty Bourgeoisie		+	+	−
Contradictory class location between the petty bourgeoisie and the bourgeoisie	Small employers	+	+	Minimal

NOTE: + = Full control; − = no control

[a]Levels of control within each dimension of production relations may be defined, schematically, as follows:

	Relations of Economic Ownership	Relations of Possession	
		Control of Means of Production	Control of Labor
Full control	Control over the overall investment and accumulation process	Control over the entire apparatus of production	Control over the entire supervisory hierarchy
Partial control	Participation in decisions concerning either subunits of the total production process or partial aspects of the entire investment process	Control over one segment of the total production process	Control over one segment of the supervisory hierarchy
Minimal control	Participation in decisions concerning narrow aspects of subunits of production	Control over one's immediate instruments of production; some autonomy in the immediate labor process	Control over the direct producers, over immediate subordinates, but not part of the hierarchy as such
No control	Complete exclusion from participation in investment and accumulation decisions	Negligible control over any aspect of the means of production	No ability to invoke sanctions on other workers

The basic class relations of capitalist society

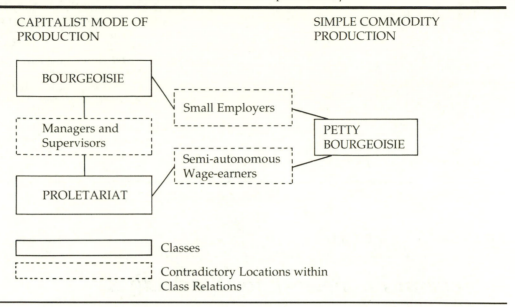

The schema represented in the figure and table 1 is not without its difficulties. While it does provide a fairly comprehensive way of locating positions within the social relations of production, there is a degree of arbitrariness involved in trying to define precisely the boundaries of each of these contradictory locations. On the one hand, at a certain point, supervisors become mere conduits for information from above and lose any capacity for actually controlling the labor of subordinates. Such nominal supervisors should be considered part of the working class. As top managers shade into top executives, on the other hand, and begin to participate in the control of basic investment decisions, then they should be placed within the bourgeoisie proper. Similar problems are encountered in defining the "boundaries" of the semi-autonomous-employee location and the small-employer category.

Furthermore, in the case of semiautonomous employees there is a real ambiguity in the very content of the "autonomy" that defines the contradictory class location. Does the possession of specialized skills or knowl-edge constitute control over the immediate labor process? Does one have to have some control over *what* is produced as well as *how* it is produced? Is the issue autonomy vis-à-vis supervisors per se, or is it autonomy with respect to concrete tasks?

Finally, the schema as represented above only includes positions directly engaged in production. Positions located outside immediate capitalist production—state employees, housewives, pensioners, students, and so forth—are not directly defined by the criteria. Are these positions in some sense "outside" the class structure, or are they situated within class relations through social relations other than production relations? Elsewhere I have offered a provisional solution to this problem.[2]

These and other issues are still in the process of resolution. It may well be that in the course of adequately solving these problems, the basic schema itself will undergo substantial modification. It is precisely through such a process of "theoretical practice," to use the Althusserian expression, that concepts are transformed.

Notes

1. The initial formulation was in Erik Olin Wright, "Class Boundaries in Advanced Capitalist Societies," *New Left Review,* no. 98 (1976), pp. 3–41. This essay was then revised as chap. 2 in *Class, Crisis and the State* (London: New Left Books, 1978). Other discussions of contradictory locations include: idem, "Intellectuals and the Working Class," *The Insurgent Sociologist,* Summer 1978; idem, *Class Structure and Income Determination* (New York: Academic Press, 1979); and idem, "Class, Occupation and Organization," *International Yearbook of Organizational Theory,* vol. 1, ed. David Dunkerley and Grahem Saleman (London: Routledge and Kegan Paul, 1979). For some critical remarks on the analysis of contradictory locations, see Edward S. Greenberg and Thomas F. Mayer, "Review of *Class, Crisis and the State,*" *Kapitalistate,* no. 7 (1979), pp. 167–86; and Barbara Ehrenreich and John Ehrenreich, "Rejoinder," in *Between Capital and Labor,* ed. Pat Walker (Boston: South End Press, 1979), esp. pp. 325, 331–32.

2. See *Class, Crisis and the State,* chap. 2; and idem, "Intellectuals and the Working Class," *The Insurgent Sociologist,* Summer 1978.

ERIK OLIN WRIGHT

A General Framework for the Analysis of Class Structure

The Point of Departure: Neo-Marxist Analyses of Class Structure

At the heart of the recent resurgence of Marxist theorizing on the problem of class has been what might be termed the "embarrassment" of the middle class. For all of their disagreements, all Marxists share a basic commitment to a polarized abstract concept of class relations. Yet, at least at first glance, the concrete class structures of contemporary advanced capitalist societies look anything but polarized. This empirical evidence of a large middle class has provided critics of Marxism with one of their principal arguments against Marxist class theory. In response, a variety of solutions to the problem of the middle class have been proposed in the recent Marxist debates.

Without going into any detail, it is possible to identify four broadly different strategies that Marxists have adopted to deal with the conceptual problem of nonpolarized class positions within a logic of polarized class relations.[1] First, the class structure of advanced capitalist societies really *is* polarized; the "middle class" is strictly an ideological illusion. This position deals with the problem of the middle class by denying the problem itself. Second, the middle class should be viewed as a *segment* of some other class, typically a "new petty bourgeoisie" or "new working class."[2] In this strategy the basic class map of capitalism remains intact, but significant internal differentiations within classes are added to the analysis of class structure. Third, the middle class is really a new class in its own right, completely distinct from either the bourgeoisie, the proletariat, or the petty bourgeoisie. Sometimes this class is given a specific name, such as the Professional Managerial Class,[3] sometimes it is simply called "the New Class."[4] By adding entirely new classes to the class structure, this approach more radically

Originally published in 1984. Please see complete source information beginning on page 891.

alters the class map of capitalism than the class-segment strategy. Fourth, the positions aggregated under the popular rubric "middle class" are not really in *a* class at all. Rather they should be viewed as locations that are simultaneously in more than one class, positions that I have characterized as "contradictory locations within class relations."[5] Managers, for example, should be viewed as simultaneously in the working class (in so far as they are wage laborers dominated by capitalists) and in the capitalist class (in so far as they control the operation of production and the labor of workers). This strategy departs most from the traditional Marxist vision of class structure since the very meaning of a "location" is altered: there is no longer a one-to-one correspondence between structural locations filled by individuals and classes.

I no longer feel that this fourth solution is satisfactory. Specifically, it suffers from two important problems that it shares with most other neo-Marxist conceptualizations of class structure: it tends to shift the analysis of class relations from exploitation to domination; and it implicitly regards socialism—a society within which the working class is the "ruling class"—as the only possible alternative to capitalism.

Domination Versus Exploitation

Throughout the development of the concept of contradictory class locations I have insisted that this was a reformulation of a distinctively Marxist class concept. As part of the rhetoric of such an enterprise, I affirmed the relationship between class and exploitation. Nevertheless, in practice the concept of contradictory locations within class relations rested almost exclusively on relations of *domination* rather than exploitation. Reference to exploitation functioned more as a background concept to the discussion of classes than as a constitutive element of the analysis of class structures. Managers, for example, were basically defined as a contradictory location because they were simultaneously dominators

and dominated. Domination relations were also decisive in defining the class character of "semiautonomous employees"—locations that, I argued, were simultaneously petty bourgeois and proletarian by virtue of their self-direction within the labor process—since "autonomy" defines a condition with respect to domination. This same tendency of substituting domination for exploitation at the core of the concept of class is found in most other neo-Marxist conceptualizations of class structure.

For some people, of course, marginalizing the concept of exploitation is a virtue, not a sin. My own view, however, is that this is a serious weakness. The marginalization of exploitation both undermines claims that classes have "objective" interests and erodes the centrality Marxists have accorded class in social theory.

The concept of domination does not in and of itself imply any specific interest of actors. Parents dominate small children, but this does not imply that they have intrinsically opposed interests to their children. What would make those interests antagonistic is if the relation of parents to children were exploitative as well. Exploitation, unlike domination, intrinsically implies a set of opposing material interests. If we wish to retain some sense in which the interests of individuals as members of classes are not simply whatever interests those individuals subjectively hold, then the shift to a domination-centered concept renders this more difficult.

Domination-centered concepts of class also tend to slide into what can be termed "the multiple oppressions" approach to understanding society. Societies, in this view, are characterized by a plurality of oppressions each rooted in a different form of domination—sexual, racial, national, economic—none of which has any explanatory priority over any other. Class, then, becomes just one of many oppressions, with no particular centrality for social and historical analysis. How important class is in a given society becomes an historically contingent question.

Again, this displacement of class from the center stage may be viewed as an achievement rather than a problem. It may be that class should not occupy a privileged place in social theory. But if one believes, as Marxists traditionally have believed, that only by giving class this central place is it possible to develop a scientific theory of the trajectory of historical development, and in particular, a theory of the real historical alternatives to capitalism, then the domination-centered concept of class risks eroding the theoretical justification for Marxian class analysis itself.

Classes in Postcapitalist Societies

Classical Marxism was absolutely unequivocal about the historical prognosis for capitalism: socialism—and ultimately communism—was the future of capitalist societies. The bearer of that necessary future was the working class. The polarized class structure *within* capitalism between the bourgeoisie and the proletariat thus paralleled the polarized historical alternatives *between* capitalism and socialism.

The actual historical experience of the twentieth century has called into question, although not unambiguously refuted, this historical vision. As I have argued elsewhere, it is necessary to at least entertain the possibility of postcapitalist class structures.[6] The difficulty is that with very few exceptions, the conceptual frameworks adopted by Marxists for analyzing capitalist class relations do not contain adequate criteria for understanding postcapitalist classes.[7] In particular, all of the class categories in my analysis of contradictory locations within class relations were either situated firmly within capitalist relations (bourgeoisie, managers, workers) or in contradictory locations involving basically pre-capitalist relations (semiautonomous employees, the petty bourgeoisie, small employers). There were no elements within this analysis of class relations in capitalist society that could point the direction for the analysis of post-capitalist classes. The result is a tendency for discussions of postcapitalist class structures—the class structures of "actually existing socialism"—to have a very ad hoc character to them.

Given these conceptual problems—the shift from exploitation to domination and the lack of a conceptual basis for analyzing postcapitalist classes—there are really two theoretical alternatives that could be pursued. One possibility is to celebrate the shift to a domination-centered concept and use this new class concept as the basis for analyzing both capitalist and postcapitalist society. This would lead class analysis firmly in the direction of Dahrendorf's analysis of classes as positions within authority relations.[8] A second alternative is to attempt to restore exploitation as the center of class analysis in such a way that it can both accommodate the empirical complexities of the middle class within capitalism and the historical reality of postcapitalist class structures. It is this second course of action that I will pursue in the rest of this paper.

The basis for this reconstruction of an exploitation-centered concept of class comes from the recent work of John Roemer.[9] While Roemer himself has not been particularly concerned with problems of empirical investigation or the elaboration of concrete maps of class structures, nevertheless his work does provide a rich foundation for such endeavors. As I will attempt to show, with suitable modification and extension, his strategy of analysis can provide a rigorous basis for resolving the problems in the concept of contradictory class locations.

Roemer's Account of Class and Exploitation

The Concept of Exploitation

We observe inequalities in the distribution of incomes, the real consumption packages available to individuals, families, groups. The concept of exploitation is a particular way of analyzing such inequalities. To describe an inequality as reflecting exploitation is to make the claim that there exists a particular kind of causal relationship between the incomes of different actors. More concretely, we will say that the rich exploit the poor when two things can be established: that the welfare of the rich causally depends on the deprivations of the poor—the rich are rich *because* the poor are poor; and that the welfare of the rich depends upon the *effort* of the poor—the rich, through one mechanism or another, appropriate part of the fruits of labor of the poor. The first of these criteria by itself defines *economic oppression,* but not exploitation. Unemployed workers, in these terms, are economically oppressed but not exploited. Exploitation implies both economic oppression and appropriation of at least part of the social surplus by the oppressor.

The traditional Marxist concept of exploitation is clearly a special case of this general concept. In Marxian exploitation one class appropriates the surplus labor performed by another class through various mechanisms. The income of the exploiting class comes from the labor performed by the exploited class. There is thus a straightforward causal linkage between the poverty and effort of the exploited and the affluence of the exploiter. The latter benefits at the expense of the former.

Roemer has attempted to elaborate this view of exploitation using two strategies. The first of these involves studying through a series of formal mathematical models the flows of "surplus labor" from one category of actors to another in the course of various exchange relations; the second involves adopting a kind of game-theory approach to specifying different forms of exploitation. Let us briefly examine each of these in turn.

The Labor-Transfer Approach

The analysis of labor transfers is an extension of the traditional Marxist view of exploitation, although Roemer self-consciously does not rely on the labor theory of value in order to explore such labor transfers. The main target of his analysis is the view, commonly held by Marxists, that a necessary condition for the exploitation of labor in a market economy is the institution of wage labor. Roemer demonstrates two basic propositions. First, Roemer demonstrates that exploitation can occur in an economy in which all producers

own their own means of production and in which there is no market in labor power and no credit market (that is, no borrowing). The only things that are traded are products. In such an economy if different producers own different amounts of productive assets such that different producers have to work different numbers of hours to produce the exchange-equivalent of their own subsistence, then free trade among these producers will lead to exploitation of the asset poor by the asset rich. What Roemer shows in this simple economy is not simply that some producers work less than others for the same subsistence, but that the workers who work less are able to do so *because* the less-endowed producers have to work more. The critical proof in this example is that if the asset-poor person simply stopped producing—died—and the asset-rich person took over the asset-poor's assets, then the asset-rich producer would have to work longer hours than before to maintain the same subsistence. There is thus not merely an inequality among the producers in this economy, but exploitation as well.

Second, Roemer demonstrates that there is complete symmetry in the structure of exploitation in a system in which capital hires wage laborers and in a system in which workers rent capital (that is, systems with credit and labor markets). For this analysis, he compares the class structures and patterns of exploitation on the two imaginary islands, "labor-market island" and "credit-market island." On both islands some people own no means of production and other people own varying amounts of the means of production. The distribution of these assets is identical on the two islands. And on both islands people have the same motivations: they all seek to minimize the amount of labor-time they must expend to achieve a common level of subsistence. The two islands differ in only one respect: on the labor-market island people are allowed to sell their labor power, whereas on the credit-market island people are prohibited from selling their labor power but are allowed to borrow, at some interest rate, the means of production. Roemer shows that on each island there is a strict correspondence between class location (derived from ownership of differing amounts of means of production, including no means of production) and exploitation status (having one's surplus labor appropriated by someone else). This is what he terms the "Class-Exploitation Correspondence Principle." He also shows that the two class structures are completely isomorphic: every individual on one island would be in exactly the same exploitation status on the other island.

The upshot of these two propositions (and others that Roemer explores) is the claim that market-based exploitation is strictly a consequence of inequalities in the distribution of the means of production. However, while this may typically play itself out through a labor market, this is only one concrete institutional form for such exploitation: it is not the necessary condition for the exploitation to occur.

The Game-Theory Approach

While the labor-transfer analyses of exploitation were primarily designed to reveal the underlying logic of exploitation in market exchanges, the game-theory approach is used by Roemer to compare different systems of exploitation. The idea is to compare different systems of exploitation by treating the organization of production as a "game" and asking if a coalition of players would be better off if they withdrew from the game under certain specified procedures. Different types of exploitation are defined by the withdrawal rules that would make certain agents better off.

More formally, Roemer argues that a coalition of actors S can be said to be exploited, and another coalition S´ (the complement of S) can be said to be exploiting, if "there is no alternative, which we may conceive of as hypothetically feasible, in which S would be better off than in its present situation, [and if,] under this alternative, the complement to S . . . would be worse off than at present."[10] The counterfactual in these two conditions is meant to convey the sense in which the welfare of S´ is causally dependent upon the deprivation of S.

Roemer uses this strategy to define three kinds of exploitation: feudal exploitation, capitalist exploitation, and what he refers to as socialist exploitation. Let's begin with capitalist exploitation. Workers own no physical assets (means of production) and sell their labor power to capitalists for a wage. Are workers exploited under capitalism? The answer to this question, in the game theoretic formulation, requires posing an alternative game to the game of capitalism within which the two conditions specified above hold. What is the alternative? It is a game within which each worker receives his/her *per capita share of society's total productive assets*. What Roemer demonstrates is that if the coalition of all wage-earners were to leave the game of capitalism with their per capita share of society's assets, then they would be better off than staying in capitalism, and capitalists would be worse off. The "withdrawal rule" in this case—leaving the game with per capita shares of physical assets—then becomes the formal "test" of whether or not a particular social system involves capitalistic exploitation.

In contrast, the withdrawal rule to specify feudal exploitation is leaving the game with one's *personal assets* (rather than one's per capita share of total social assets). This is equivalent to the feudal serf being freed from all obligations based on personal bondage. Peasants would be better off under such circumstances; feudal lords would be worse off.[11]

The concept of the socialist exploitation is the least systematically worked out in Roemer's analysis. The withdrawal rule in this case is leaving the game with one's *per capita share of inalienable assets* (skills). A coalition will be said to be socialistically exploited if it would improve its position by leaving with its per capita skills while its complement would be worse off under such circumstances. This implies that people with high levels of skills in the game receive high income not simply because they have high skills, but because of the differentials in skill levels across actors. The highly skilled would become worse off if the unskilled obtained skills; they thus have an interest in maintaining skill differentials, and this is what underpins the claim that their income reflects exploitation.[12] If a skilled person's income reflected no more than the amount of time and resources it takes to obtain the skill, then there would be no skill-based exploitation. The higher incomes would simply be reimbursement for real costs incurred. The argument behind skill exploitation is that people with scarce skills receive incomes above the costs of producing those skills, a "rent" component to their income; it is this element that constitutes exploitation.

Class and Exploitation

The central message of both of Roemer's strategies for analyzing exploitation is that the material basis of exploitation is inequalities in distributions of productive assets, or what is usually referred to as property relations. On the one hand, inequalities of assets are sufficient to account for transfers of labor surplus; on the other hand, different forms of asset inequality specify different systems of exploitation. Classes are then defined as positions within the social relations of production derived from these relations of exploitation.[13]

These conclusions have led Roemer to challenge directly the tendency of Marxists (like myself) to define class relations primarily in terms of domination relations within production. Of course, exploiting classes dominate exploited classes in the sense of preventing the exploited classes from taking the exploiting class's productive assets. But domination *within* production, Roemer insists, is not a central part of defining class relations as such.

In previous work I have criticized Roemer's position on this issue.[14] I argued that class relations intrinsically involved domination *at the point of production*, not simply in the repressive protection of the property relations as such. I now think that Roemer is correct on this point. That capitalists boss workers around within production is unquestionably an important feature of most historic forms of capitalist production and may play an impor-

tant role in explaining the forms of class organization and class conflict within production. However, the basis of the capital-labor relation should be identified with relations of effective control (that is, real economic ownership) over productive assets as such.

One of the reasons why I resisted Roemer's conceptualization of classes in terms of property relations is that it seemed to blur the difference between Marxist definitions of class and Weberian definitions. Weberian definitions, as I construed them, were "market based" definitions of class, whereas Marxist definitions were "production based." The reputed advantage of the latter was that production was more "fundamental" than exchange, and therefore production-based class concepts had more explanatory power than market-based concepts.

What now seems clear to me is that definitions of classes in terms of property relations should not be identified with strictly market-based definitions. Property-relations accounts of classes do not define classes by income shares, by the results of market transactions, but by the productive assets that classes control, which lead them to adopt certain strategies within exchange relations and which thereby determine the outcomes of those market transactions.

Toward a General Framework of Class Analysis

Extending Roemer's Analysis

The heart of Roemer's analysis is the linkage between the distribution of productive assets of various sorts and exploitation. Different mechanisms of exploitation are defined by different kinds of assets, and different class systems are defined by which of these assets is most important for shaping the patterns of exploitation in the society.

In Roemer's own explicit formulation, only two kinds of assets are formally considered: physical assets (alienable assets in his terminology) and skill assets (inalienable assets).

The distinction between exploitation in feudalism and exploitation in capitalism revolves around the nature of the withdrawal rules with respect to physical assets (withdrawing with one's personal assets to define feudal exploitation versus withdrawing with one's per capita share of assets to define capitalist exploitation). The feudal case, however, can be characterized in a somewhat different way. Labor power is a productive asset.[15] In capitalist societies everyone owns one unit of this asset, namely themselves. In feudalism, on the other hand, ownership rights over labor power are unequally distributed: feudal lords have more than one unit, serfs have less than one unit. To be sure, it is not typical of feudalism for serfs to own no labor power—they are generally not slaves divested of all ownership rights in their own labor power—but they do not have complete effective control over their own persons as productive actors, and this is what it means to "own" one's own labor power assets. The withdrawal rule that defines feudal exploitation can then be specified as leaving the feudal game with one's per capita share of society's assets in labor power, namely one unit. Feudal exploitation is thus exploitation (transfers of labor) that results from inequalities in the distribution of assets in labor power.

Reformulating feudal exploitation in this manner makes the game-theory specification of different exploitations in Roemer's analysis symmetrical: feudal exploitation is based on inequalities generated by ownership of labor-power assets; capitalist exploitation on inequalities generated by ownership of alienable assets; socialist exploitation on inequalities generated by ownership of inalienable assets. And corresponding to each of these exploitation-generating inequalities of assets, there is a specific class relation: lords and serfs in feudalism, bourgeoisie and proletariat in capitalism, experts and workers in socialism.

But how, it might be asked, should "actually existing socialist societies" be theorized within these categories? The anticapitalist revolution in Russia resulted in the virtual elimination of private property in the means of production: individuals cannot own means of production, they cannot inherit them or dispose of them on a market, and so on. And yet it seems unsatisfactory to characterize such societies simply in terms of skill-based exploitation. Experts do not appear to be the "ruling class" in those societies, and the dynamic of the societies does not seem to revolve around skill inequalities as such.

Roemer recognized this problem and introduced what he termed "status exploitation" to deal with it. The exploitation exercised by bureaucrats is the prototypical example. "If these positions," Roemer writes, "required special skills, then one might be justified in calling the differential remuneration to these positions an aspect of socialist [skill-based] exploitation. . . . [However] there is some extra remuneration to holders of those positions which accrues solely by virtue of the position and not by virtue of the skill necessary to carry out the tasks associated with it. These special payments to positions give rise to *status exploitation*."[16]

Roemer's concept of status exploitation is unsatisfactory for two principal reasons. First, it is outside of the logic of the rest of his analysis of exploitation. In each of the other cases, exploitation is rooted in relations to the forces of production. Each of the other forms of exploitation is "materialist" not only because the concept is meant to explain material distribution, but also because it is based on the relation to the material conditions of production. "Status" exploitation has no necessary relationship to production at all. Second, it is hard to rigorously distinguish status exploitation from feudal exploitation. The "lord" receives remuneration strictly because of an incumbency in a position, not because of skills or ownership of capital. Yet, it hardly seems reasonable to consider the logic of exploitation and class in the contemporary Soviet Union and in fourteenth-century feudal Europe as being essentially the same.

The problems with the concept of status exploitation can be solved by analyzing exploitation based on a fourth element in the inventory of productive assets, an asset that can be referred to as "organization." As both Adam Smith and Marx noted, the technical division of labor among producers is itself a source of productivity. The way the production process is organized is a productive resource independent of the expenditure of labor power, the use of means of production, or the skills of the producer. Of course there is an interrelationship between organization and these other assets, just as there is an interdependence between means of production and skills. But organization—the conditions of coordinated cooperation among producers in a complex division of labor—is a productive resource in its own right.

How is this asset distributed in different kinds of societies? In contemporary capitalism, organization assets are generally controlled by managers and capitalists: managers control the organization assets within specific firms under constraints imposed by the ownership of the capital assets by capitalists. Entrepreneurial capitalists directly control both kinds of assets (and probably skill assets as well); pure rentier capitalists ("coupon clippers") only own capital assets. Because of the anarchy of the capitalist market, no set of actors controls the technical division of labor across firms.

In state bureaucratic socialism, organization assets assume a much greater importance. Controlling the technical division of labor—the coordination of productive activities within and across labor processes—becomes a societal task organized at the center. The control over organization assets is no longer simply the task of firm-level managers but extends into the central organs of planning within the state. Exploitation in such societies is thus based on bureaucratic power: the control over organization assets defines the material basis for class relations and exploitation.

This notion of organization assets bears a close relation to the problem of authority and hierarchy. The asset is organization. The activity of using that asset is coordinated decision making over a complex technical division of labor. When that asset is distributed unequally, so some positions have effective control over much more of the asset than others, then the social relation with respect to that asset takes the form of hierarchical authority. Authority, however, is not the asset as such; organization is the asset and is controlled through a hierarchy of authority.

The claim that effective control over organization assets is a basis of exploitation is equivalent to saying that nonmanagers would be better off and managers/bureaucrats worse off if nonmanagers were to withdraw with their per capita share of organization assets (or equivalently, if organizational control were democratized); and that by virtue of effectively controlling organization assets managers/bureaucrats control part or all of the socially produced surplus.[17]

A Typology of Class Structures, Assets, and Exploitation

If we add organization assets to the list in Roemer's analysis, we generate the more complex typology presented in Table 1. Let us briefly look at each row of this table and examine its logic. Feudalism is a class system based on unequal distribution of ownership rights in labor power. What "personal bondage" means is that feudal lords have partial effective economic control over vassals. The empirical manifestation of this unequal distribution of ownership rights over labor power in classical feudalism is the coercive extraction of labor dues from serfs. When corvée labor is commuted to rents in kind and eventually money rents, the feudal character of the exploitation relation is reflected in legal prohibitions on the movement of peasants off the land. The "flight" of a peasant to the city is, in effect, a form of theft: the peasant is stealing part of the labor power owned by the lord. Feudal lords may also have more means of production than serfs, more organizational assets, and more productive skills (although this is unlikely), and thus they may be exploiters with respect to these assets as well. What defines the society as "feudal", however, is the primacy of the distinctively feudal

TABLE 1
Assets, Exploitation, and Classes

Type of class structure	Principal asset that is unequally distributed	Mechanism of exploitation	Classes	Central task of revolutionary transformation
Feudalism	Labor power	Coercive extraction of surplus labor	Lords and serfs	Individual liberty
Capitalism	Means of production	Market exchanges of labor power and commodities	Capitalists and workers	Socializing means of production
State bureaucratic socialism	Organization	Planned appropriation and distribution of surplus based on hierarchy	Managers/ bureaucrats and nonmanagement	Democratization of organizational control
Socialism	Skills	Negotiated redistribution of surplus from workers to experts	Experts and workers	Substantive equality

mechanisms of exploitation. Accordingly, feudal class relations will be the primary structural basis of class struggle.

The bourgeois revolutions radically redistributed productive assets in people: everyone, at least in principle, owns one unit. This is what is meant by "bourgeois freedoms," and in this sense capitalism can be regarded as an historically progressive force. But capitalism raises the second type of exploitation, exploitation based on property relations in means of production, to an unprecedented level.

The typical institutional form of capitalist class relations is capitalists having full ownership rights in the means of production and workers none. Other possibilities, however, have existed historically. Cottage industries in early capitalism involved workers owning some of their means of production, but not having sufficient assets to actually produce commodities without the assistance of merchant capitalists. Such workers were still being capitalistically exploited even though there was no formal labor market with wages. In all capitalist exploitation, the mediating mechanism is market exchanges. Unlike in feudalism, surplus is not directly appropriated from workers in the form of coerced labor. Rather, it is appropriated through market exchanges: workers are paid a wage that covers the costs of production of their labor power; capitalists

receive an income from the sale of the commodities produced by workers. The difference in these quantities constitutes the exploitative surplus appropriated by capitalists.

Anticapitalist revolutions attempt to eliminate the distinctively capitalist form of exploitation, exploitation based on private ownership of the means of production. The nationalization of the principal means of production is, in effect, a radical equalization of ownership of capital: everyone owns one citizen-share. Such revolutions, however, do not eliminate, and indeed may considerably strengthen and deepen, inequalities of effective control over organization assets. Whereas in capitalism the control over organization assets does not extend beyond the firm, in state bureaucratic socialism the coordinated integration of the division of labor extends to the whole society through institutions of central state planning. The mechanism by which this generates exploitative transfers of surplus involves the centrally planned bureaucratic appropriation and distribution of the surplus along hierarchical principles. The corresponding class relation is therefore between managers/bureaucrats—people who control organization assets—and nonmanagers.

The historical task of revolutionary transformation of state bureaucratic socialism revolves around the equalization of effective economic control over organization assets, or, equivalently, the democratization of bureaucratic apparatuses of production. This does not imply total direct democracy, where all decisions of any consequence are directly made in democratic assemblies. There will still inevitably be delegated responsibilities, and there certainly can be representative forms of democratic control. But it does mean that the basic parameters of planning and coordinating social production are made through democratic mechanisms and that incumbency within delegated positions of responsibility does not give incumbents any personal claims on the social surplus. Such equalization, however, would not necessarily affect exploitation based on skills/credentials. Such exploitation would remain a central feature of socialism.

"Skill" in this context is not a trivial concept. The mere possession of enhanced laboring capabilities acquired through training is not sufficient to generate relations of exploitation, since the income of such trained labor may simply reflect the costs of acquiring the training. In such cases there is neither a transfer of surplus, nor would the untrained be better off under the game-theory specification of exploitation. For a skill to be the basis of exploitation, therefore, it has to be in some sense scarce relative to its demand, and there must be a mechanism through which individual owners of scarce skills are able to translate that scarcity into higher incomes.

There are basically three ways that skills can become scarce: first, they may require special *talents* that are naturally scarce in a population; second, access to the training needed to develop the skill may be restricted through various mechanisms, creating an artificial scarcity of trained people; third, a certification system may be established that prohibits uncertified people from being employed to use the skill even if they have it. In all of these cases, the exploitation comes from the skilled/certified individual receiving an income that is above the costs of production of the skills by virtue of the scarcity of the availability of the skill.

In this conceptualization of socialism, a socialist society is essentially a kind of democratic technocracy. Experts control their own skills and knowledge within production, and by virtue of such control are able to appropriate some of the surplus out of production. However, because of the democratization of organization assets, actual planning decisions will not be made under the direct control of experts but will be made through some kind of democratic procedure (this is in effect what democratization of organization assets means: equalizing control over the planning and coordinating of social production). This means that the actual class power of a socialist technocratic exploiting class will be much weaker than the class power of exploiting classes in other class systems. Their ownership rights extend to only a limited part of the social surplus.

This much more limited basis of *domination* implied by skill-based exploitation is consistent with the spirit, if not the letter, of Marx's claim that socialism is the "lower stage" of "communism," since classes are already in a partial state of dissolution in a society with only skill-based exploitation. Communism itself, then, would be understood as a society within which skill-based exploitation itself had "withered away," that is, in which ownership rights in skills had been equalized. This does not mean, it must be stressed, that all individuals would actually *possess* the same skills in communism, any more than eliminating property rights in means of production implies that all individuals would actively use the same amount of physical capital. What is equalized is effective control over skills as a productive resource and claims to differential incomes resulting from differential use of skills.[18] . . .

The Middle Classes and Contradictory Locations

The framework in Table 1 enables us to pose the problem of middle classes in a new way. Two different kinds of nonpolarized class lo-

TABLE 2
Basic Typology of Exploitation and Class

Assets in the means of production

Owners (%)	Nonowners (wage laborers) (%)			

1 Bourgeoisie US 1.8 Sweden 0.7	**4 Expert manager** US 3.9 Sweden 4.4	**7 Semicredentialed manager** US 6.2 Sweden 4.0	**10 Uncredentialed manager** US 2.3 Sweden 2.5	+
2 Small employer US 6.0 Sweden 4.8	**5 Expert supervisor** US 3.7 Sweden 3.8	**8 Semicredentialed supervisor** US 6.8 Sweden 3.2	**11 Uncredentialed supervisor** US 6.9 Sweden 3.1	>0 Organization assets
3 Petty bourgeoisie US 6.9 Sweden 5.4	**6 Expert nonmanager** US 3.4 Sweden 6.8	**9 Semicredentialed worker** US 12.2 Sweden 17.8	**12 Proletarian** US 39.9 Sweden 43.5	−

	+	>0	−
		Skill assets	

United States: N = 1487
Sweden: N = 1179

Note: Distributions are of people working in the labor force, thus excluding unemployed, housewives, pensioners, etc.
Source: Comparative Project on Class Structure and Class Consciousness.

cations can be defined in the logic of this framework:

1. There are class locations that are neither exploiters nor exploited, that is, people who have precisely the per capita level of the relevant asset. A petty bourgeois, self-employed producer with average capital stock, for example, would be neither exploiter nor exploited within capitalist relations. These kinds of positions are what can be called the "traditional" or "old" middle class of a particular kind of class system.

2. Since concrete societies are rarely, if ever, characterized by a single mode of production, the actual class structures of given societies will be characterized by complex patterns of intersecting exploitation relations. There will therefore tend to be some positions that are exploiting along one dimension of exploitation relations and are exploited along another. Highly skilled wage-earners (for example, professionals) in

capitalism are a good example: they are capitalistically exploited because they lack assets in capital, and yet they are skill exploiters. Such positions are what are typically referred to as the "new middle class" of a given system.

Table 2 presents a schematic typology of such complex class locations for capitalism. The typology is divided into two segments: one for owners of the means of production and one for nonowners. Within the wage-earner section of the typology, locations are distinguished by the two subordinate relations of exploitation characteristic of capitalist society—organization assets and skill/credential assets. It is thus possible within this framework to distinguish a whole terrain of class locations in capitalist *society* that are distinct from the polarized classes of the capitalist *mode of production*: expert managers, nonmanagerial experts, nonexpert managers, and so on.[19]

What is the relationship between this heterogeneous exploitation definition of the middle class and my previous conceptualization of such positions as contradictory locations within class relations? There is still a sense in which such positions could be characterized as "contradictory locations," for they will typically hold contradictory interests with respect to the primary forms of class struggle in capitalist society, the struggle between labor and capital. On the one hand, they are like workers, in being excluded from ownership of the means of production. On the other hand, they have interests opposed to workers because of their effective control of organization and skill assets. Within the struggles of capitalism, therefore, these new middle classes do constitute contradictory locations, or more precisely, contradictory locations within exploitation relations.

This conceptualization of the middle classes also suggests that historically the principal forms of contradictory locations will vary depending upon the particular combinations of exploitation relations in a given society. These principal contradictory locations are presented in Table 3. In feudalism, the critical contradictory location is constituted by the bourgeoisie, the rising class of the successor mode of production. Within capitalism, the central contradictory location within exploitation relations is constituted by managers and state bureaucrats. They embody a principle of class organization that is quite distinct from capitalism and that potentially poses an alternative to capitalist relations. This is particularly true for state managers who, unlike corporate managers, are less likely to have their careers tightly integrated with the interests of the capitalist class. Finally, in state bureaucratic socialism, the "intelligentsia" broadly defined constitutes the pivotal contradictory location.

One of the upshots of this reconceptualization of the middle class is that it is no longer axiomatic that the proletariat is the unique, or perhaps even the central, rival to the capitalist class for class power in capitalist society. That classical Marxist assumption depended upon the thesis that there were no other classes within capitalism that could be viewed as the "bearers" of an historical alternative to capi-

TABLE 3
Basic Classes and Contradictory Locations
in Successive Modes of Production

Mode of production	Basic classes	Principal contradictory location
Feudalism	Lords and serfs	Bourgeoisie
Capitalism	Bourgeoisie and proletariat	Managers/bureaucrats
State bureaucratic socialism	Bureaucrats and workers	Intelligentsia/experts

talism. Socialism (as the transition to communism) was the only possible future for capitalism. What Table 3 suggests is that there are other class forces within capitalism that potentially pose an alternative to capitalism. This does not imply that there is any inevitability to the sequence feudalism-capitalism-state bureaucratic socialism-socialism-communism; state bureaucrats are not inevitably destined to be the future ruling class of present-day capitalisms. But it does suggest that the process of class formation and class struggle is considerably more complex and indeterminate than the traditional Marxist story has allowed.

Notes

1. For a more detailed review of these alternatives, see E.O. Wright, "Varieties of Marxist Concepts of Class Structure," *Politics and Society*, vol. 9, no. 3 (1980).

2. The leading proponent of the concept of the "new petty bourgeoisie" is N. Poulantzas, *Classes in Contemporary Capitalism* (London: Verso, 1975). For the new-working-class concept, see S. Mallet, *La Nouvelle Classe Ouvrière* (Paris: Seuil, 1963).

3. B. Ehrenreich and J. Ehrenreich, "The Professional and Managerial Class," *Radical America*, vol. 11, no. 2 (1977).

4. A. Gouldner, *The Future of Intellectuals and the Rise of the New Class* (New York: Seabury Press, 1979); and G. Konrad and I. Szelényi, *Intellectuals on the Road to Class Power* (New York: Harcourt, Brace, Jovanovich, 1979).

5. E.O. Wright, "Class Boundaries in Advanced Capitalist Societies," *New Left Review*, no. 98 (1976); and *Class, Crisis and the State* (London:

New Left Books, 1978). See also G. Carchedi, *The Economic Identification of Social Classes* (London: Routledge and Kegan Paul, 1977).

6. E.O. Wright, "Capitalism's Futures," *Socialist Review*, no. 68 (1983).

7. A partial exception to this can be found in arguments for the existence of a "new class" of intellectuals and/or bureaucrats in capitalist and postcapitalist society. See: A. Gouldner, *The Future of Intellectuals;* and I. Szelényi and W. Martin, *New Class Theory and Beyond* (unpublished book manuscript, Department of Sociology, University of Wisconsin, 1985).

8. R. Dahrendorf, *Class and Class Conflict in Industrial Society* (Palo Alto: Stanford University Press, 1959).

9. Roemer is a Marxist economist engaged in a long-term project of elaborating what he calls the "microfoundations" of Marxist theory. His most important work is entitled *A General Theory of Exploitation and Class* (Cambridge: Harvard University Press, 1982).

10. Roemer, *A General Theory*, pp. 194–95.

11. But note: workers in capitalism are *not* feudalistically exploited; they would be worse off, not better off, if they withdrew from the game of capitalism with only their personal assets. As Roemer argues, the claim by neoclassical theorists that wage earners in capitalism are not exploited is generally equivalent to the claim that they are not feudalistically exploited, that is, that they are not subjected to surplus extraction based on relations of personal bondage. See Roemer, *A General Theory*, p. 206.

12. The asset-exploitation nexus thus depends upon the capacity of asset-holders to deprive others of that asset. The social basis of exploitation, understood in this way, is quite similar to Frank Parkin's characterization of Weber's concept of social closure as "the process by which social collectivities seek to maximize rewards by restricting access to resources and opportunities to a limited circle of eligibles." F. Parkin, *Marxism and Class Theory: A Bourgeois Critique* (New York: Columbia University Press, 1979). While Parkin's central concern is with the kinds of attributes that serve as the basis for closure—race, religion, language—Roemer's is with the nature of the resources (productive assets) over which closure is organized.

13. Roemer's conceptualization of the relationship between class and exploitation is similar in certain aspects to Alvin Gouldner's, although Roemer is unaware of Gouldner's work. Gouldner defines the "New Class" as a *cultural* bourgeoisie defined by its control over "cultural capital," where

"capital" is defined as "any produced object used to make saleable utilities, thus providing its possessor with *incomes,* or claims to incomes defined as legitimate because of their imputed contribution to economic productivity." (*Future of Intellectuals,* p. 21). While Gouldner does not characterize this income allocation process in terms of exploitation, Roemer's exploitation concept would fit comfortably within Gouldner's general approach.

14. E.O. Wright, "The Status of the Political in the Concept of Class Structure," *Politics and Society,* vol. 11, no. 3 (1982).

15. See G.A. Cohen, *Karl Marx's Theory of History: A Defense* (Princeton: Princeton University Press, 1978), pp. 40–41, for a discussion of why labor power should be considered part of the forces of production (that is, a productive asset).

16. Roemer, *A General Theory*, p. 243.

17. This "control of the surplus," it must be noted, is *not* the equivalent of the *actual* personal consumption income of managers and bureaucrats, any more than capitalist profits or feudal rents are the equivalent of the personally consumed income of capitalists and feudal lords. It is historically variable both within and between types of societies what fraction of the surplus effectively controlled by exploiting classes is used for personal consumption and what portion is used for other purposes (feudal military expenditures, capitalist accumulation, organization growth). The claim that managers-bureaucrats would be "worse off" under conditions of a redistribution of organization assets refers to the amount of income they effectively control, which is therefore potentially available for personal appropriation, not simply the amount they personally consume.

18. It may be utopian to imagine a society without skill-based exploitation, or even a society without organization-asset exploitation, particularly if we reject the claim that a future society will ever exist in a state of absolute abundance. In the absence of absolute abundance, all societies will face dilemmas and trade-offs around the problem of distribution of consumption, and such dilemmas may pose intractable incentive problems in the absence of exploitation. For a careful exposition of the problem of utopian fantasies in Marxist theory, see A. Nove, *The Economics of Feasible Socialism* (Hemel Hempstead: George Allen and Unwin, 1983).

19. The labor-force data in this table come from the comparative project on class structure and class consciousness, University of Wisconsin. Details of the coding of categories and the operationalization of variables can be found in E.O. Wright, *Classes* (London: Verso, 1985), appendix 2.

IMMANUEL WALLERSTEIN

Class Conflict in the Capitalist World Economy

What is capitalism as a mode of production? This is not an easy question, and for that reason is not in fact a widely discussed one. It seems to me that there are several elements that combine to constitute the 'model'. Capitalism is the *only* mode of production in which the *maximization* of surplus creation is rewarded *per se*. In every historical system, there has been *some* production for *use,* and *some* production for *exchange,* but only in capitalism are all producers rewarded primarily in terms of the exchange value they produce and penalized to the extent they neglect it. The 'rewards' and 'penalties' are mediated through a structure called the 'market'. It is a structure but not an institution. It is a structure molded by *many* institutions (political, economic, social, even cultural), and it is the principal arena of economic struggle.

Not only is surplus maximized for its own sake, but those who use the surplus to accumulate more capital to produce still more surplus are further rewarded. Thus the pressure is for constant expansion, although the individualistic premise of the system simultaneously renders *constant* expansion impossible.

How does the search for profit operate? It operates by creating legal protections for individual firms (which can range in size from individuals to quite large organizations, including parastatal agencies) to appropriate the

surplus value created by the labor of the primary producers. Were all or most of this surplus value however consumed by the few who owned or controlled the 'firms', we would not have capitalism. This is in fact approximately what had happened in various pre-capitalist systems.

Capitalism involves in addition structures and institutions which reward primarily that subsegment of the owners and controllers who use the surplus value only *in part* for their own consumption, and in another (usually larger) part for further investment. The structure of the market ensures that those who do not accumulate capital (but merely consume surplus value) lose out economically over time to those who do accumulate capital.

We may thereupon designate as the bourgeoisie those who receive a part of the surplus value they do not themselves create and use some of it to accumulate capital. What defines the bourgeois is not a particular profession and not even the legal status of proprietor (although this was historically important) but the fact that the bourgeois obtains, either as an individual or a member of some collectivity, a part of the surplus that he did not create and is in the position to invest (again either individually or as part of a collectivity) some of this surplus in capital goods.

There is a very large gamut of organizational arrangements which can permit this, of which the classic model of the 'free entrepreneur' is only one. Which organizational arrangements prevail at particular moments of time in particular states (for these arrangements are dependent on the legal framework)

Originally published in 1979. Please see complete source information beginning on page 891.

is a function of the state of development of the world-economy as a whole (and the role of a particular state in that world-economy) on the one hand, and the consequent forms of class struggle in the world-economy (and within the particular state) on the other. Hence, like all other social constructs, the 'bourgeoisie' is not a static phenomenon. It is the designation of a class in the process of perpetual re-creation and hence of constant change of form and composition. . . .

The fundamental role of the state as an institution in the capitalist world-economy is to augment the advantage of some against others in the market—that is, to *reduce* the 'freedom' of the market. Everyone is in favor of this, as long as one is the beneficiary of the 'distortion', and everyone opposed to the extent that one loses. It is all a matter of whose ox is being gored.

The modes of augmenting advantage are many. The state can transfer income by taking it from some and giving it to others. The state can restrict access to the market (of commodities or of labor) which favor those who thereby share in the oligopoly or oligopsony. The state can restrain persons from organizing to change the actions of the state. And, of course, the state can act not only within its jurisdiction but beyond it. This may be licit (the rules concerning transit over boundaries) or illicit (interference in the internal affairs of another state). Warfare is of course one of the mechanisms used.

What is crucial to perceive is that the state is a special kind of organization. Its 'sovereignty', a notion of the modern world, is the claim to the monopolization (regulation) of the legitimate use of force within its boundaries, and it is in a relatively strong position to interfere effectively with the flow of factors of production. Obviously also it is possible for particular social groups to alter advantage by altering state boundaries; hence both movements for secession (or autonomy) and movements for annexation (or federation).

It is this realistic ability of states to interfere with the flow of factors of production that provides the political underpinnings of the structural division of labor in the capitalist world-economy as a whole. Normal market considerations may account for recurring initial thrusts to specialization (natural or socio-historical advantages in the production of one or another commodity), but it is the state system which encrusts, enforces, and exaggerates the patterns, and it has regularly required the use of state machinery to revise the pattern of the world-wide division of labor.

Furthermore, the ability of states to interfere with flows becomes differentiated. That is, core states become *stronger* than peripheral states, and use this differential power to maintain a differential degree of interstate freedom of flow. Specifically, core states have historically arranged that world-wide and over time, money and goods have flowed more 'freely' than labor. The reason for doing this is that core states have thereby received the advantages of 'unequal exchange'.

In effect, unequal exchange is simply a part of the world-wide process of the appropriation of surplus. We analyze falsely if we try to take literally the model of *one* proletarian relating to *one* bourgeois. In fact, the surplus value that the producer creates passes through a series of persons and firms. It is therefore the case that *many* bourgeois *share* the surplus value of *one* proletarian. The exact share of different groups in the chain (property owner, merchants, intermediate consumers) is subject to much historical change and is itself a principal analytical variable in the functioning of the capitalist world-economy.

This chain of the transfer of surplus value frequently (often? almost always?) traverses national boundaries and, when it does, state operations intervene to tilt the sharing among bourgeois towards those bourgeois located in core states. This is unequal exchange, a mechanism in the overall process of the appropriation of surplus value.

One of the socio-geographic consequences of this system is the uneven distribution of the bourgeoisie and proletariat in different states, core states containing a higher percentage nationally of bourgeois than peripheral states. In addition, there are systematic differences in *kinds* of bourgeois and proletarians located in the two zones. For example, the percentage of wage-earning proletarians is systematically higher in core states.

Since states are the primary arena of political conflict in a capitalist world-economy, and since the functioning of the world-economy is such that national class composition varies widely, it is easy to perceive why the politics of states differentially located in relation to the world-economy should be so dissimilar. It is also then easy to perceive that using the political machinery of a given state to change the social composition and world-economic function of national production does not *per se* change the capitalist world-system as such.

Obviously, however, these various national thrusts to a change in structural position (which we misleadingly often call 'development') do in fact affect, indeed over the long run do in fact transform, the world-system. But they do so via the intervening variable of their impact on world-wide class consciousness of the proletariat.

Core and periphery then are simply phrases to locate one crucial part of the system of surplus appropriation by the bourgeoisie. To oversimplify, capitalism is a system in which the surplus value of the proletarian is appropriated by the bourgeois. When this proletarian is located in a different country from this bourgeois, one of the mechanisms that has affected the process of appropriation is the manipulation of controlling flows over state boundaries. This results in patterns of 'uneven development' which are *summarized* in the concepts of core, semiperiphery, and periphery. This is an intellectual tool to help analyze the multiple forms of class conflict in the capitalist world-economy.

MAX WEBER

Class, Status, Party

Economically Determined Power and the Social Order

Law exists when there is a probability that an order will be upheld by a specific staff of men who will use physical or psychical compulsion with the intention of obtaining conformity with the order, or of inflicting sanctions for infringement of it.[1] The structure of every legal order directly influences the distribution of power, economic or otherwise, within its respective community. This is true of all legal orders and not only that of the state. In general, we understand by 'power' the chance of a man or of a number of men to realize their own will in a communal action even against the resistance of others who are participating in the action.

'Economically conditioned' power is not, of course, identical with 'power' as such. On the contrary, the emergence of economic power may be the consequence of power existing on other grounds. Man does not strive for power only in order to enrich himself economically. Power, including economic power, may be valued 'for its own sake.' Very frequently the striving for power is also conditioned by the social 'honor' it entails. Not all power, however, entails social honor: The typical American Boss, as well as the typical big speculator,

deliberately relinquishes social honor. Quite generally, 'mere economic' power, and especially 'naked' money power, is by no means a recognized basis of social honor. Nor is power the only basis of social honor. Indeed, social honor, or prestige, may even be the basis of political or economic power, and very frequently has been. Power, as well as honor, may be guaranteed by the legal order, but, at least normally, it is not their primary source. The legal order is rather an additional factor that enhances the chance to hold power or honor; but it cannot always secure them.

The way in which social honor is distributed in a community between typical groups participating in this distribution we may call the 'social order.' The social order and the economic order are, of course, similarly related to the 'legal order.' However, the social and the economic order are not identical. The economic order is for us merely the way in which economic goods and services are distributed and used. The social order is of course conditioned by the economic order to a high degree, and in its turn reacts upon it.

Now: 'classes,' 'status groups,' and 'parties' are phenomena of the distribution of power within a community.

Determination of Class-Situation by Market-Situation

In our terminology, 'classes' are not communities; they merely represent possible, and frequent, bases for communal action. We may

Originally published in 1946 & 1958. Please see complete source information beginning on page 891.

speak of a 'class' when (1) a number of people have in common a specific causal component of their life chances, in so far as (2) this component is represented exclusively by economic interests in the possession of goods and opportunities for income, and (3) is represented under the conditions of the commodity or labor markets. [These points refer to 'class situation,' which we may express more briefly as the typical chance for a supply of goods, external living conditions, and personal life experiences, in so far as this chance is determined by the amount and kind of power, or lack of such, to dispose of goods or skills for the sake of income in a given economic order. The term 'class' refers to any group of people that is found in the same class situation.]

It is the most elemental economic fact that the way in which the disposition over material property is distributed among a plurality of people, meeting competitively in the market for the purpose of exchange, in itself creates specific life chances. According to the law of marginal utility this mode of distribution excludes the non-owners from competing for highly valued goods; it favors the owners and, in fact, gives to them a monopoly to acquire such goods. Other things being equal, this mode of distribution monopolizes the opportunities for profitable deals for all those who, provided with goods, do not necessarily have to exchange them. It increases, at least generally, their power in price wars with those who, being propertyless, have nothing to offer but their services in native form or goods in a form constituted through their own labor, and who above all are compelled to get rid of these products in order barely to subsist. This mode of distribution gives to the propertied a monopoly on the possibility of transferring property from the sphere of use as a 'fortune,' to the sphere of 'capital goods'; that is, it gives them the entrepreneurial function and all chances to share directly or indirectly in returns on capital. All this holds true within the area in which pure market conditions prevail. 'Property' and 'lack of property' are, therefore, the basic categories of all class situations. It does not matter whether these two

categories become effective in price wars or in competitive struggles.

Within these categories, however, class situations are further differentiated: on the one hand, according to the kind of property that is usable for returns; and, on the other hand, according to the kind of services that can be offered in the market. Ownership of domestic buildings; productive establishments; warehouses; stores; agriculturally usable land, large and small holdings—quantitative differences with possibly qualitative consequences—; ownership of mines; cattle; men (slaves); disposition over mobile instruments of production, or capital goods of all sorts, especially money or objects that can be exchanged for money easily and at any time; disposition over products of one's own labor or of others' labor differing according to their various distances from consumability; disposition over transferable monopolies of any kind—all these distinctions differentiate the class situations of the propertied just as does the 'meaning' which they can and do give to the utilization of property, especially to property which has money equivalence. Accordingly, the propertied, for instance, may belong to the class of rentiers or to the class of entrepreneurs.

Those who have no property but who offer services are differentiated just as much according to their kinds of services as according to the way in which they make use of these services, in a continuous or discontinuous relation to a recipient. But always this is the generic connotation of the concept of class: that the kind of chance in the *market* is the decisive moment which presents a common condition for the individual's fate. 'Class situation' is, in this sense, ultimately 'market situation.' The effect of naked possession *per se,* which among cattle breeders gives the nonowning slave or serf into the power of the cattle owner, is only a forerunner of real 'class' formation. However, in the cattle loan and in the naked severity of the law of debts in such communities, for the first time mere 'possession' as such emerges as decisive for the fate of the individual. This is very much in contrast to the agricultural communities based on labor. The creditor-debtor relation becomes the basis of 'class situations' only in those cities where a 'credit market,' however primitive, with rates of interest increasing according to the extent of dearth and a factual monopolization of credits, is developed by a plutocracy. Therewith 'class struggles' begin.

Those men whose fate is not determined by the chance of using goods or services for themselves on the market, e.g. slaves, are not, however, a 'class' in the technical sense of the term. They are, rather, a 'status group.'

Communal Action Flowing from Class Interest

According to our terminology, the factor that creates 'class' is unambiguously economic interest, and indeed, only those interests involved in the existence of the 'market.' Nevertheless, the concept of 'class-interest' is an ambiguous one: even as an empirical concept it is ambiguous as soon as one understands by it something other than the factual direction of interests following with a certain probability from the class situation for a certain 'average' of those people subjected to the class situation. The class situation and other circumstances remaining the same, the direction in which the individual worker, for instance, is likely to pursue his interests may vary widely, according to whether he is constitutionally qualified for the task at hand to a high, to an average, or to a low degree. In the same way, the direction of interests may vary according to whether or not a *communal* action of a larger or smaller portion of those commonly affected by the 'class situation,' or even an association among them, e.g. a 'trade union,' has grown out of the class situation from which the individual may or may not expect promising results. [Communal action refers to that action which is oriented to the feeling of the actors that they belong together. Societal action, on the other hand, is oriented to a rationally motivated adjustment of interests.] The rise of societal or even of communal action from a common

class situation is by no means a universal phenomenon.

The class situation may be restricted in its effects to the generation of essentially *similar* reactions, that is to say, within our terminology, of 'mass actions.' However, it may not have even this result. Furthermore, often merely an amorphous communal action emerges. For example, the 'murmuring' of the workers known in ancient oriental ethics: the moral disapproval of the work-master's conduct, which in its practical significance was probably equivalent to an increasingly typical phenomenon of precisely the latest industrial development, namely, the 'slow down' (the deliberate limiting of work effort) of laborers by virtue of tacit agreement. The degree in which 'communal action' and possibly 'societal action,' emerges from the 'mass actions' of the members of a class is linked to general cultural conditions, especially to those of an intellectual sort. It is also linked to the extent of the contrasts that have already evolved, and is especially linked to the *transparency* of the connections between the causes and the consequences of the 'class situation.' For however different life chances may be, this fact in itself, according to all experience, by no means gives birth to 'class action' (communal action by the members of a class). The fact of being conditioned and the results of the class situation must be distinctly recognizable. For only then the contrast of life chances can be felt not as an absolutely given fact to be accepted, but as a resultant from either (1) the given distribution of property, or (2) the structure of the concrete economic order. It is only then that people may react against the class structure not only through acts of an intermittent and irrational protest, but in the form of rational association. There have been 'class situations' of the first category (1), of a specifically naked and transparent sort, in the urban centers of Antiquity and during the Middle Ages; especially then, when great fortunes were accumulated by factually monopolized trading in industrial products of these localities or in foodstuffs. Furthermore, under certain circumstances, in the rural economy of the most diverse periods, when agriculture was increasingly exploited in a profit-making manner. The most important historical example of the second category (2) is the class situation of the modern 'proletariat.'

Types of 'Class Struggle'

Thus every class may be the carrier of any one of the possibly innumerable forms of 'class action,' but this is not necessarily so: In any case, a class does not in itself constitute a community. To treat 'class' conceptually as having the same value as 'community' leads to distortion. That men in the same class situation regularly react in mass actions to such tangible situations as economic ones in the direction of those interests that are most adequate to their average number is an important and after all simple fact for the understanding of historical events. Above all, this fact must not lead to that kind of pseudo-scientific operation with the concepts of 'class' and 'class interests' so frequently found these days, and which has found its most classic expression in the statement of a talented author, that the individual may be in error concerning his interests but that the 'class' is 'infallible' about its interests. Yet, if classes as such are not communities, nevertheless class situations emerge only on the basis of communalization. The communal action that brings forth class situations, however, is not basically action between members of the identical class; it is an action between members of different classes. Communal actions that directly determine the class situation of the worker and the entrepreneur are: the labor market, the commodities market, and the capitalistic enterprise. But, in its turn, the existence of a capitalistic enterprise presupposes that a very specific communal action exists and that it is specifically structured to protect the possession of goods *per se,* and especially the power of individuals to dispose, in principle freely, over the means of production. The existence of a capitalistic enterprise is preconditioned

by a specific kind of 'legal order.' Each kind of class situation, and above all when it rests upon the power of property *per se,* will become most clearly efficacious when all other determinants of reciprocal relations are, as far as possible, eliminated in their significance. It is in this way that the utilization of the power of property in the market obtains its most sovereign importance.

Now 'status groups' hinder the strict carrying through of the sheer market principle. In the present context they are of interest to us only from this one point of view. Before we briefly consider them, note that not much of a general nature can be said about the more specific kinds of antagonism between 'classes' (in our meaning of the term). The great shift, which has been going on continuously in the past, and up to our times, may be summarized, although at the cost of some precision: the struggle in which class situations are effective has progressively shifted from consumption credit toward, first, competitive struggles in the commodity market and, then, toward price wars on the labor market. The 'class struggles' of antiquity—to the extent that they were genuine class struggles and not struggles between status groups—were initially carried on by indebted peasants, and perhaps also by artisans threatened by debt bondage and struggling against urban creditors. For debt bondage is the normal result of the differentiation of wealth in commercial cities, especially in seaport cities. A similar situation has existed among cattle breeders. Debt relationships as such produced class action up to the time of Cataline. Along with this, and with an increase in provision of grain for the city by transporting it from the outside, the struggle over the means of sustenance emerged. It centered in the first place around the provision of bread and the determination of the price of bread. It lasted throughout antiquity and the entire Middle Ages. The propertyless as such flocked together against those who actually and supposedly were interested in the dearth of bread. This fight spread until it involved all those commodities essential to the way of life and to handicraft production. There were only incipient discussions of wage disputes in antiquity and in the Middle Ages. But they have been slowly increasing up into modern times. In the earlier periods they were completely secondary to slave rebellions as well as to fights in the commodity market.

The propertyless of antiquity and of the Middle Ages protested against monopolies, pre-emption, forestalling, and the withholding of goods from the market in order to raise prices. Today the central issue is the determination of the price of labor.

This transition is represented by the fight for access to the market and for the determination of the price of products. Such fights went on between merchants and workers in the putting-out system of domestic handicraft during the transition to modern times. Since it is quite a general phenomenon we must mention here that the class antagonisms that are conditioned through the market situation are usually most bitter between those who actually and directly participate as opponents in price wars. It is not the rentier, the shareholder, and the banker who suffer the ill will of the worker, but almost exclusively the manufacturer and the business executives who are the direct opponents of workers in price wars. This is so in spite of the fact that it is precisely the cash boxes of the rentier, the share-holder, and the banker into which the more or less 'unearned' gains flow, rather than into the pockets of the manufacturers or of the business executives. This simple state of affairs has very frequently been decisive for the role the class situation has played in the formation of political parties. For example, it has made possible the varieties of patriarchal socialism and the frequent attempts—formerly, at least—of threatened status groups to form alliances with the proletariat against the 'bourgeoisie.'

Status Honor

In contrast to classes, *status groups* are normally communities. They are, however, often of an amorphous kind. In contrast to the purely economically determined 'class situation' we wish to designate as 'status situation' every typical component of the life fate of men that is determined by a specific, positive or negative, social estimation of *honor*. This honor may be connected with any quality shared by a plurality, and, of course, it can be knit to a class situation: class distinctions are linked in the most varied ways with status distinctions. Property as such is not always recognized as a status qualification, but in the long run it is, and with extraordinary regularity. In the subsistence economy of the organized neighborhood, very often the richest man is simply the chieftain. However, this often means only an honorific preference. For example, in the so-called pure modern 'democracy,' that is, one devoid of any expressly ordered status privileges for individuals, it may be that only the families coming under approximately the same tax class dance with one another. This example is reported of certain smaller Swiss cities. But status honor need not necessarily be linked with a 'class situation.' On the contrary, it normally stands in sharp opposition to the pretensions of sheer property.

Both propertied and propertyless people can belong to the same status group, and frequently they do with very tangible consequences. This 'equality' of social esteem may, however, in the long run become quite precarious. The 'equality' of status among the American 'gentlemen,' for instance, is expressed by the fact that outside the subordination determined by the different functions of 'business,' it would be considered strictly repugnant—wherever the old tradition still prevails—if even the richest 'chief,' while playing billiards or cards in his club in the evening, would not treat his 'clerk' as in every sense fully his equal in birthright. It would be repugnant if the American 'chief' would bestow upon his 'clerk' the condescending 'benevolence' marking a distinction of 'position,' which the German chief can never dissever from his attitude. This is one of the most important reasons why in America the German 'clubby-ness' has never been able to attain the attraction that the American clubs have.

Guarantees of Status Stratification

In content, status honor is normally expressed by the fact that above all else a specific *style of life* can be expected from all those who wish to belong to the circle. Linked with this expectation are restrictions on 'social' intercourse (that is, intercourse which is not subservient to economic or any other of business's 'functional' purposes). These restrictions may confine normal marriages to within the status circle and may lead to complete endogamous closure. As soon as there is not a mere individual and socially irrelevant imitation of another style of life, but an agreed-upon communal action of this closing character, the 'status' development is under way.

In its characteristic form, stratification by 'status groups' on the basis of conventional styles of life evolves at the present time in the United States out of the traditional democracy. For example, only the resident of a certain street ('the street') is considered as belonging to 'society,' is qualified for social intercourse, and is visited and invited. Above all, this differentiation evolves in such a way as to make for strict submission to the fashion that is dominant at a given time in society. This submission to fashion also exists among men in America to a degree unknown in Germany. Such submission is considered to be an indication of the fact that a given man *pretends* to qualify as a gentleman. This submission decides, at least *prima facie,* that he will be treated as such. And this recognition becomes just as important for his employment chances in 'swank' establishments, and above all, for social intercourse and marriage with 'esteemed' families, as the qualification for dueling among Germans in the Kaiser's day. As for the rest: certain families resident for a long time, and, of course, correspondingly wealthy, e.g. 'F. F. V., i.e. First Families of Virginia,' or the actual or alleged descendants of the 'Indian Princess' Pocahontas, of the Pil-

grim fathers, or of the Knickerbockers, the members of almost inaccessible sects and all sorts of circles setting themselves apart by means of any other characteristics and badges . . . all these elements usurp 'status' honor. The development of status is essentially a question of stratification resting upon usurpation. Such usurpation is the normal origin of almost all status honor. But the road from this purely conventional situation to legal privilege, positive or negative, is easily traveled as soon as a certain stratification of the social order has in fact been 'lived in' and has achieved stability by virtue of a stable distribution of economic power.

'Ethnic' Segregation and 'Caste'

Where the consequences have been realized to their full extent, the status group evolves into a closed 'caste.' Status distinctions are then guaranteed not merely by conventions and laws, but also by *rituals.* This occurs in such a way that every physical contact with a member of any caste that is considered to be 'lower' by the members of a 'higher' caste is considered as making for a ritualistic impurity and to be a stigma which must be expiated by a religious act. Individual castes develop quite distinct cults and gods.

In general, however, the status structure reaches such extreme consequences only where there are underlying differences which are held to be 'ethnic.' The 'caste' is, indeed, the normal form in which ethnic communities usually live side by side in a 'societalized' manner. These ethnic communities believe in blood relationship and exclude exogamous marriage and social intercourse. Such a caste situation is part of the phenomenon of 'pariah' peoples and is found all over the world. These people form communities, acquire specific occupational traditions of handicrafts or of other arts, and cultivate a belief in their ethnic community. They live in a 'diaspora' strictly segregated from all personal intercourse, except that of an unavoidable sort, and their situation is legally precarious.

Yet, by virtue of their economic indispensability, they are tolerated, indeed, frequently privileged, and they live in interspersed political communities. The Jews are the most impressive historical example.

A 'status' segregation grown into a 'caste' differs in its structure from a mere 'ethnic' segregation: the caste structure transforms the horizontal and unconnected coexistences of ethnically segregated groups into a vertical social system of super- and subordination. Correctly formulated: a comprehensive societalization integrates the ethnically divided communities into specific political and communal action. In their consequences they differ precisely in this way: ethnic coexistences condition a mutual repulsion and disdain but allow each ethnic community to consider its own honor as the highest one; the caste structure brings about a social subordination and an acknowledgment of 'more honor' in favor of the privileged caste and status groups. This is due to the fact that in the caste structure ethnic distinctions as such have become 'functional' distinctions within the political societalization (warriors, priests, artisans that are politically important for war and for building, and so on). But even pariah people who are most despised are usually apt to continue cultivating in some manner that which is equally peculiar to ethnic and to status communities: the belief in their own specific 'honor.' This is the case with the Jews.

Only with the negatively privileged status groups does the 'sense of dignity' take a specific deviation. A sense of dignity is the precipitation in individuals of social honor and of conventional demands which a positively privileged status group raises for the deportment of its members. The sense of dignity that characterizes positively privileged status groups is naturally related to their 'being' which does not transcend itself, that is, it is to their 'beauty and excellence.' Their kingdom is 'of this world.' They live for the present and by exploiting their great past. The sense of dignity of the negatively privileged strata naturally refers to a future lying beyond the present, whether it is of this life or of another. In other words, it must be nurtured by the belief in a providential 'mission' and by a belief in a specific honor before God. The 'chosen people's' dignity is nurtured by a belief either that in the beyond 'the last will be the first,' or that in this life a Messiah will appear to bring forth into the light of the world which has cast them out the hidden honor of the pariah people. This simple state of affairs, and not the 'resentment' which is so strongly emphasized in Nietzsche's much admired construction in the *Genealogy of Morals,* is the source of the religiosity cultivated by pariah status groups. In passing, we may note that resentment may be accurately applied only to a limited extent; for one of Nietzsche's main examples, Buddhism, it is not at all applicable.

Incidentally, the development of status groups from ethnic segregations is by no means the normal phenomenon. On the contrary, since objective 'racial differences' are by no means basic to every subjective sentiment of an ethnic community, the ultimately racial foundation of status structure is rightly and absolutely a question of the concrete individual case. Very frequently a status group is instrumental in the production of a thoroughbred anthropological type. Certainly a status group is to a high degree effective in producing extreme types, for they select personally qualified individuals (e.g. the Knighthood selects those who are fit for warfare, physically and psychically). But selection is far from being the only, or the predominant, way in which status groups are formed: Political membership or class situation has at all times been at least as frequently decisive. And today the class situation is by far the predominant factor, for of course the possibility of a style of life expected for members of a status group is usually conditioned economically.

Status Privileges

For all practical purposes, stratification by status goes hand in hand with a monopolization of ideal and material goods or opportunities, in a manner we have come to know as typical. Besides the specific status honor, which always rests upon distance and exclusiveness, we find all sorts of material monopolies. Such honorific preferences may consist of the privilege of wearing special costumes, of eating special dishes taboo to others, of carrying arms—which is most obvious in its consequences—the right to pursue certain non-professional dilettante artistic practices, e.g. to play certain musical instruments. Of course, material monopolies provide the most effective motives for the exclusiveness of a status group; although, in themselves, they are rarely sufficient, almost always they come into play to some extent. Within a status circle there is the question of intermarriage: the interest of the families in the monopolization of potential bridegrooms is at least of equal importance and is parallel to the interest in the monopolization of daughters. The daughters of the circle must be provided for. With an increased inclosure of the status group, the conventional preferential opportunities for special employment grow into a legal monopoly of special offices for the members. Certain goods become objects for monopolization by status groups. In the typical fashion these include 'entailed estates' and frequently also the possessions of serfs or bondsmen and, finally, special trades. This monopolization occurs positively when the status group is exclusively entitled to own and to manage them; and negatively when, in order to maintain its specific way of life, the status group must *not* own and manage them.

The decisive role of a 'style of life' in status 'honor' means that status groups are the specific bearers of all 'conventions.' In whatever way it may be manifest, all 'stylization' of life either originates in status groups or is at least conserved by them. Even if the principles of status conventions differ greatly, they reveal certain typical traits, especially among those strata which are most privileged. Quite generally, among privileged status groups there is a status disqualification that operates against the performance of common physical labor. This disqualification is now 'setting in' in America against the old tradition of esteem

for labor. Very frequently every rational economic pursuit, and especially 'entrepreneurial activity,' is looked upon as a disqualification of status. Artistic and literary activity is also considered as degrading work as soon as it is exploited for income, or at least when it is connected with hard physical exertion. An example is the sculptor working like a mason in his dusty smock as over against the painter in his salon-like 'studio' and those forms of musical practice that are acceptable to the status group.

Economic Conditions and Effects of Status Stratification

The frequent disqualification of the gainfully employed as such is a direct result of the principle of status stratification peculiar to the social order, and of course, of this principle's opposition to a distribution of power which is regulated exclusively through the market. These two factors operate along with various individual ones, which will be touched upon below.

We have seen above that the market and its processes 'knows no personal distinctions': 'functional' interests dominate it. It knows nothing of 'honor.' The status order means precisely the reverse, viz.: stratification in terms of 'honor' and of styles of life peculiar to status groups as such. If mere economic acquisition and naked economic power still bearing the stigma of its extra-status origin could bestow upon anyone who has won it the same honor as those who are interested in status by virtue of style of life claim for themselves, the status order would be threatened at its very root. This is the more so as, given equality of status honor, property *per se* represents an addition even if it is not overtly acknowledged to be such. Yet if such economic acquisition and power gave the agent any honor at all, his wealth would result in his attaining more honor than those who successfully claim honor by virtue of style of life. Therefore all groups having interests in the status order react with special sharpness precisely against the pretensions of purely economic acquisition. In most cases they react the more vigorously the more they feel themselves threatened. Calderon's respectful treatment of the peasant, for instance, as opposed to Shakespeare's simultaneous and ostensible disdain of the *canaille* illustrates the different way in which a firmly structured status order reacts as compared with a status order that has become economically precarious. This is an example of a state of affairs that recurs everywhere. Precisely because of the rigorous reactions against the claims of property *per se,* the 'parvenu' is never accepted, personally and without reservation, by the privileged status groups, no matter how completely his style of life has been adjusted to theirs. They will only accept his descendants who have been educated in the conventions of their status group and who have never besmirched its honor by their own economic labor.

As to the general *effect* of the status order, only one consequence can be stated, but it is a very important one: the hindrance of the free development of the market occurs first for those goods which status groups directly withheld from free exchange by monopolization. This monopolization may be effected either legally or conventionally. For example, in many Hellenic cities during the epoch of status groups, and also originally in Rome, the inherited estate (as is shown by the old formula for indication against spendthrifts) was monopolized just as were the estates of knights, peasants, priests, and especially the clientele of the craft and merchant guilds. The market is restricted, and the power of naked property *per se,* which gives its stamp to 'class formation,' is pushed into the background. The results of this process can be most varied. Of course, they do not necessarily weaken the contrasts in the economic situation. Frequently they strengthen these contrasts, and in any case, where stratification by status permeates a community as strongly as was the case in all political communities of antiquity and of the Middle Ages, one can never speak of a genuinely free market competition as we understand it today. There are wider effects than this direct exclusion of special goods from the market. From the contrariety between the status order and the purely economic order mentioned above, it follows that in most instances the notion of honor peculiar to status absolutely abhors that which is essential to the market: higgling. Honor abhors higgling among peers and occasionally it taboos higgling for the members of a status group in general. Therefore, everywhere some status groups, and usually the most influential, consider almost any kind of overt participation in economic acquisition as absolutely stigmatizing.

With some over-simplification, one might thus say that 'classes' are stratified according to their relations to the production and acquisition of goods; whereas 'status groups' are stratified according to the principles of their *consumption* of goods as represented by special 'styles of life.'

An 'occupational group' is also a status group. For normally, it successfully claims social honor only by virtue of the special style of life which may be determined by it. The differences between classes and status groups frequently overlap. It is precisely those status communities most strictly segregated in terms of honor (viz. the Indian castes) who today show, although within very rigid limits, a relatively high degree of indifference to pecuniary income. However, the Brahmins seek such income in many different ways.

As to the general economic conditions making for the predominance of stratification by 'status,' only very little can be said. When the bases of the acquisition and distribution of goods are relatively stable, stratification by status is favored. Every technological repercussion and economic transformation threatens stratification by status and pushes the class situation into the foreground. Epochs and countries in which the naked class situation is of predominant significance are regularly the periods of technical and economic transformations. And every slowing down of the shifting of economic stratifications leads, in due course, to the growth of status structures and makes for a resuscitation of the important role of social honor.

Parties

Whereas the genuine place of 'classes' is within the economic order, the place of 'status groups' is within the social order, that is, within the sphere of the distribution of 'honor.' From within these spheres, classes and status groups influence one another and they influence the legal order and are in turn influenced by it. But 'parties' live in a house of 'power.'

Their action is oriented toward the acquisition of social 'power,' that is to say, toward influencing a communal action no matter what its content may be. In principle, parties may exist in a social 'club' as well as in a 'state.' As over against the actions of classes and status groups, for which this is not necessarily the case, the communal actions of 'parties' always mean a societalization. For party actions are always directed toward a goal which is striven for in planned manner. This goal may be a 'cause' (the party may aim at realizing a program for ideal or material purposes), or the goal may be 'personal' (sinecures, power, and from these, honor for the leader and the followers of the party). Usually the party action aims at all these simultaneously. Parties are, therefore, only possible within communities that are societalized, that is, which have some rational order and a staff of persons available who are ready to enforce it. For parties aim precisely at influencing this staff, and if possible, to recruit it from party followers.

In any individual case, parties may represent interests determined through 'class situation' or 'status situation,' and they may recruit their following respectively from one or the other. But they need be neither purely 'class' nor purely 'status' parties. In most cases they are partly class parties and partly status parties, but sometimes they are neither. They may represent ephemeral or enduring

structures. Their means of attaining power may be quite varied, ranging from naked violence of any sort to canvassing for votes with coarse or subtle means: money, social influence, the force of speech, suggestion, clumsy hoax, and so on to the rougher or more artful tactics of obstruction in parliamentary bodies.

The sociological structure of parties differs in a basic way according to the kind of communal action which they struggle to influence. Parties also differ according to whether or not the community is stratified by status or by classes. Above all else, they vary according to the structure of domination within the community. For their leaders normally deal with the conquest of a community. They are, in the general concept which is maintained here, not only products of specially modern forms of domination. We shall also designate as parties the ancient and medieval 'parties,' despite the fact that their structure differs basically from the structure of modern parties. By virtue of these structural differences of domination it is impossible to say anything about the structure of parties without discussing the structural forms of social domination *per se*. Parties, which are always structures struggling for domination, are very frequently organized in a very strict 'authoritarian' fashion. . . .

Concerning 'classes,' 'status groups,' and 'parties,' it must be said in general that they necessarily presuppose a comprehensive societalization, and especially a political framework of communal action, within which they operate. This does not mean that parties would be confined by the frontiers of any individual political community. On the contrary, at all times it has been the order of the day that the societalization (even when it aims at the use of military force in common) reaches beyond the frontiers of politics. This has been the case in the solidarity of interests among the Oligarchs and among the democrats in Hellas, among the Guelfs and among Ghibellines in the Middle Ages, and within the Calvinist party during the period of religious struggles. It has been the case up to the solidarity of the landlords (international congress of agrarian landlords), and has continued among princes (holy alliance, Karlsbad decrees), socialist workers, conservatives (the longing of Prussian conservatives for Russian intervention in 1850). But their aim is not necessarily the establishment of new international political, i.e. *territorial*, dominion. In the main they aim to influence the existing dominion.[2]

Notes

1. *Wirtschaft und Gesellschaft,* part III, chap. 4, pp. 631–40. The first sentence in paragraph one and the several definitions in this chapter which are in brackets do not appear in the original text. They have been taken from other contexts of *Wirtschaft und Gesellschaft.*

2. The posthumously published text breaks off here. We omit an incomplete sketch of types of 'warrior estates.'

M A X   W E B E R

Status Groups and Classes

The Concepts of Class and Class Situation

The term 'class situation'[1] will be applied to the typical probability that a given state of (a) provision with goods, (b) external conditions of life, and (c) subjective satisfaction or frustration will be possessed by an individual or a group. These probabilities define class situation in so far as they are dependent on the kind and extent of control or lack of it which the individual has over goods or services and existing possibilities of their exploitation for the attainment of income or receipts within a given economic order.

A 'class' is any group of persons occupying the same class situation. The following types of classes may be distinguished: (a) A class is a 'property class' when class situation for its members is primarily determined by the dif-

Originally published in 1947. Please see complete source information beginning on page 891.

ferentiation of property holdings; (b) a class is an 'acquisition class' when the class situation of its members is primarily determined by their opportunity for the exploitation of services on the market; (c) the 'social class' structure is composed of the plurality of class situations between which an interchange of individuals on a personal basis or in the course of generations is readily possible and typically observable. On the basis of any of the three types of class situation, associative relationships between those sharing the same class interests, namely, corporate class organizations may develop. This need not, however, necessarily happen. The concepts of class and class situation as such designate only the fact of identity or similarity in the typical situation in which a given individual and many others find their interests defined. In principle control over different combinations of consumer goods, means of production, investments, capital funds or marketable abilities constitute class situations which are different with each variation and combination. Only persons who are completely unskilled, without property and dependent on employment without regular occupation, are in a strictly identical class situation. Transitions from one class situation to another vary greatly in fluidity and in the ease with which an individual can enter the class. Hence the unity of 'social' classes is highly relative and variable.

The Significance of Property Classes

The primary significance of a positively privileged property class lies in the following facts: (i) Its members may be able to monopolize the purchase of high-priced consumer goods. (ii) They may control the opportunities of pursuing a systematic monopoly policy in the sale of economic goods. (iii) They may monopolize opportunities for the accumulation of property through unconsumed surpluses. (iv) They may monopolize opportunities to accumulate capital by saving, hence, the possibility of investing property in loans and the related possibility of control over executive positions in business. (v) They may monopolize the privileges of socially advantageous kinds of education so far as these involve expenditures.

Positively privileged property classes typically live from property income. This may be derived from property rights in human beings, as with slaveowners, in land, in mining property, in fixed equipment such as plant and apparatus, in ships, and as creditors in loan relationships. Loans may consist of domestic animals, grain, or money. Finally they may live on income from securities.

Class interests which are negatively privileged with respect to property belong typically to one of the following types: (a) They are themselves objects of ownership, that is they are unfree. (b) They are 'outcasts,' that is 'proletarians' in the sense meant in Antiquity. (c) They are debtor classes and, (d) the 'poor.'

In between stand the 'middle' classes. This term includes groups who have all sorts of property, or of marketable abilities through training, who are in a position to draw their support from these sources. Some of them may be 'acquisition' classes. Entrepreneurs are in this category by virtue of essentially positive privileges; proletarians, by virtue of

negative privileges. But many types such as peasants, craftsmen, and officials do not fall in this category.

The differentiation of classes on the basis of property alone is not 'dynamic,' that is, it does not necessarily result in class struggles or class revolutions. It is not uncommon for very strongly privileged property classes, such as slaveowners, to exist side by side with such far less privileged groups as peasants or even outcasts without any class struggle. There may even be ties of solidarity between privileged property classes and unfree elements. However, such conflicts as that between land owners and outcast elements or between creditors and debtors, the latter often being a question of urban patricians as opposed to either rural peasants or urban craftsmen, may lead to revolutionary conflict. Even this, however, need not necessarily aim at radical changes in economic organization. It may, on the contrary, be concerned in the first instance only with a redistribution of wealth. These may be called 'property revolutions.'

A classic example of the lack of class antagonism has been the relation of the 'poor white trash,' originally those not owning slaves, to the planters in the Southern States of the United States. The 'poor whites' have often been much more hostile to the Negro than the planters who have frequently had a large element of patriarchal sentiment. The conflict of outcast against the property classes, of creditors and debtors, and of landowners and outcasts are best illustrated in the history of Antiquity.

The Significance of Acquisition and Social Classes

The primary significance of a positively privileged acquisition class is to be found in two directions. On the one hand it is generally possible to go far toward attaining a monopoly of the management of productive enterprises in favour of the members of the class and their business interests. On the other hand, such a class tends to insure the security of its economic position by exercising influence on the economic policy of political bodies and other groups.

The members of positively privileged acquisition classes are typically entrepreneurs. The following are the most important types: merchants, shipowners, industrial and agricultural entrepreneurs, bankers and financiers. Under certain circumstances two other types are also members of such classes, namely, members of the 'liberal' professions with a privileged position by virtue of their abilities or training, and workers with special skills commanding a monopolistic position, regardless of how far they are hereditary or the result of training.

Acquisition classes in a negatively privileged situation are workers of the various principal types. They may be roughly classified as skilled, semi-skilled and unskilled.

In this connexion as well as the above, independent peasants and craftsmen are to be treated as belonging to the 'middle classes.' This category often includes in addition officials, whether they are in public or private employment, the liberal professions, and workers with exceptional monopolistic assets or positions.

Examples of 'social classes' are: (a) The 'working' class as a whole. It approaches this type the more completely mechanized the productive process becomes. (b) The petty bourgeoisie.[2] (c) The 'intelligentsia' without independent property and the persons whose social position is primarily dependent on technical training such as engineers, commercial and other officials, and civil servants. These groups may differ greatly among themselves, in particular according to costs of training. (d) The classes occupying a privileged position through property and education.

The unfinished concluding section of Karl Marx's *Kapital* was evidently intended to deal with the problem of the class unity of the proletariat, which he held existed in spite of the high degree of qualitative differentiation. A decisive factor is the increase in the importance of semi-skilled workers who have been trained in a relatively short time directly on the machines themselves, at the expense of the older type of 'skilled' labour and also of un-

skilled. However, even this type of skill may often have a monopolistic aspect. Weavers are said to attain the highest level of productivity only after five years' experience.

At an earlier period every worker could be said to have been primarily interested in becoming an independent small bourgeois, but the possibility of realizing this goal is becoming progressively smaller. From one generation to another the most readily available path to advancement both for skilled and semi-skilled workers is into the class of technically trained individuals. In the most highly privileged classes, at least over the period of more than one generation, it is coming more and more to be true that money is overwhelmingly decisive. Through the banks and corporate enterprises members of the lower middle class and the salaried groups have certain opportunities to rise into the privileged class.

Organized activity of class groups is favoured by the following circumstances: (a) The possibility of concentrating on opponents where the immediate conflict of interests is vital. Thus workers organize against management and not against security holders who are the ones who really draw income without working. Similarly peasants are not apt to organize against landlords. (b) The existence of a class situation which is typically similar for large masses of people. (c) The technical possibility of being easily brought together. This is particularly true where large numbers work together in a small area, as in the modern factory. (d) Leadership directed to readily understandable goals. Such goals are very generally imposed or at least are interpreted by persons, such as intelligentsia, who do not belong to the class in question.

Status and Status Group

The term of 'status'[3] will be applied to a typically effective claim to positive or negative privilege with respect to social prestige so far as it rests on one or more of the following bases: (a) mode of living, (b) a formal process of education which may consist in empirical or rational training and the acquisition of the corresponding modes of life, or (c) on the prestige of birth, or of an occupation.

The primary practical manifestations of status with respect to social stratification are conubium, commensality, and often monopolistic appropriation of privileged economic opportunities and also prohibition of certain modes of acquisition. Finally, there are conventions or traditions of other types attached to a status.

Status may be based on class situation directly or related to it in complex ways. It is not, however, determined by this alone. Property and managerial positions are not as such sufficient to lend their holder a certain status, though they may well lead to its acquisition. Similarly, poverty is not as such a disqualification for high status though again it may influence it.

Conversely, status may partly or even wholly determine class situation, without, however, being identical with it. The class situation of an officer, a civil servant, and a student as determined by their income may be widely different while their status remains the same, because they adhere to the same mode of life in all relevant respects as a result of their common education.

A 'status group' is a plurality of individuals who, within a larger group, enjoy a particular kind and level of prestige by virtue of their position and possibly also claim certain special monopolies.

The following are the most important sources of the development of distinct status groups: (a) The most important is by the development of a peculiar style of life including, particularly, the type of occupation pursued. (b) The second basis is hereditary charisma arising from the successful claim to a position of prestige by virtue of birth. (c) The third is the appropriation of political or hierocratic authority as a monopoly by socially distinct groups.

The development of hereditary status groups is usually a form of the hereditary appropriation of privileges by an organized group or by individual qualified persons. Every well-established case of appropriation of opportunities and abilities, especially of exercising imperative powers, has a tendency to lead to the development of distinct status groups. Conversely, the development of status groups has a tendency in turn to lead to the monopolistic appropriation of governing powers and of the corresponding economic advantages.

Acquisition classes are favoured by an economic system oriented to market situations, whereas status groups develop and subsist most readily where economic organization is of a monopolistic and liturgical character and where the economic needs of corporate groups are met on a feudal or patrimonial basis. The type of class which is most closely related to a status group is the 'social' class, while the 'acquisition' class is the farthest removed. Property classes often constitute the nucleus of a status group.

Every society where status groups play a prominent part is controlled to a large extent by conventional rules of conduct. It thus creates economically irrational conditions of consumption and hinders the development of free markets by monopolistic appropriation and by restricting free disposal of the individual's own economic ability. This will have to be discussed further elsewhere.

Notes

1. Although Parsons chooses to translate *Klasse* as 'class status' in this context, to do so is potentially confusing because Weber so carefully distinguishes between the concepts of class and status. I have therefore followed the lead of Roth and Wittich (*Economy and Society,* 1968) and opted for the term 'class situation' throughout this essay.—ED.

2. I have again followed Roth and Wittich (*Economy and Society,* 1968) in translating the German term *Kleinbürgertum* as 'petty bourgeoisie,' whereas Parsons opted for the more ambiguous term 'lower middle' class.—ED.

3. For the purposes of consistency with the other selections, I have translated the term *ständische Lage* as 'status' (see Roth and Wittich, *Economy and Society,* 1968), whereas Parsons opted for the terms 'social status,' 'stratifactory status,' and the like.—ED.

MAX WEBER

Open and Closed Relationships

Social Relationships

A social relationship, regardless of whether it is communal or associative in character, will be spoken of as "open" to outsiders if and insofar as its system of order does not deny participation to anyone who wishes to join and is actually in a position to do so. A relationship will, on the other hand, be called "closed" against outsiders so far as, according to its subjective meaning and its binding rules, participation of certain persons is excluded, limited, or subjected to conditions. Whether a relationship is open or closed may be determined traditionally, affectually, or rationally in terms of values or of expediency. It is especially likely to be closed, for rational reasons, in the following type of situation: a social relationship may provide the parties to it with opportunities for the satisfaction of spiritual or material interests, whether absolutely or instrumentally, or whether it is achieved through co-operative action or by a compromise of interests. If the participants expect that the admission of others will lead to an improvement of their situation, an improvement in degree, in kind, in the security or the value of the satisfaction, their interest will be in keeping the relationship open. If, on the other hand, their expectations are of improving their position by monopolistic tactics, their interest is in a closed relationship.

Originally published in 1968. Please see complete source information beginning on page 891.

There are various ways in which it is possible for a closed social relationship to guarantee its monopolized advantages to the parties. (a) Such advantages may be left free to competitive struggle within the group; (b) they may be regulated or rationed in amount and kind, or (c) they may be appropriated by individuals or sub-groups on a permanent basis and become more or less inalienable. The last is a case of closure within, as well as against outsiders. Appropriated advantages will be called "rights." As determined by the relevant order, appropriation may be (1) for the benefit of the members of particular communal or associative groups (for instance, household groups), or (2) for the benefit of individuals. In the latter case, the individual may enjoy his rights on a purely personal basis or in such a way that in case of his death one or more other persons related to the holder of the right by birth (kinship), or by some other social relationship, may inherit the rights in question. Or the rights may pass to one or more individuals specifically designated by the holder. These are cases of hereditary appropriation. Finally, (3) it may be that the holder is more or less fully empowered to alienate his rights by voluntary agreement, either to other specific persons or to anyone he chooses. This is alienable appropriation. A party to a closed social relationship will be called a "member"; in case his participation is regulated in such a way as to guarantee him appropriated advantages, a privileged member (*Rechtsgenosse*). Appropriated rights which are enjoyed by individuals through inheritance or by hereditary groups, whether communal or associative, will be called the "property" of the individual or of groups in question; and, insofar as they are alienable, "free" property.

The apparently gratuitous tediousness involved in the elaborate definition of the above concepts is an example of the fact that we often neglect to think out clearly what seems to be obvious, because it is intuitively familiar.

1. a. Examples of communal relationships, which tend to be closed on a traditional basis, are those in which membership is determined by family relationship.

b. Personal emotional relationships are usually affectually closed. Examples are erotic relationships and, very commonly, relations of personal loyalty.

c. Closure on the basis of value-rational commitment to values is usual in groups sharing a common system of explicit religious belief.

d. Typical cases of rational closure on grounds of expediency are economic associations of a monopolistic or a plutocratic character.

A few examples may be taken at random. Whether a group of people engaged in conversation is open or closed depends on its content. General conversation is apt to be open, as contrasted with intimate conversation or the imparting of official information. Market relationships are in most, or at least in many, cases essentially open. In the case of many relationships, both communal and associative, there is a tendency to shift from a phase of expansion to one of exclusiveness. Examples are the guilds and the democratic city-states of Antiquity and the Middle Ages. At times these groups sought to increase their membership in the interest of improving the security of their position of power by adequate numbers. At other times they restricted their membership to protect the value of their monopolistic position. The same phenomenon is not uncommon in monastic orders and religious sects which have passed from a stage of religious proselytizing to one of restriction in the interest of the maintenance of an ethical standard or for the protection of material interests. There is a similar close relationship between the extension of market relationships in the interest of increased turnover on the one hand, their monopolistic restriction on the other. The promotion of linguistic uniformity is today a natural result of the interests of publishers and writers, as opposed to the earlier, not uncommon, tendency for status groups to maintain linguistic peculiarities or even for secret languages to emerge.

2. Both the extent and the methods of regulation and exclusion in relation to outsiders may vary widely, so that the transition from a state of openness to one of regulation and closure is gradual. Various conditions of participation may be laid down; qualifying tests, a period of probation, requirement of possession of a share which can be purchased under certain conditions, election of new members by ballot, membership or eligibility by birth or by virtue of achievements open to anyone. Finally, in case of closure and the appropriation of rights within the group, participation may be dependent on the acquisition of an appropriated right. There is a wide variety of different degrees of closure and of conditions of participation. Thus regulation and closure are relative concepts. There are all manner of gradual shadings as between an exclusive club, a theatrical audience the members of which have purchased tickets, and a party rally to which the largest possible number has been urged to come; similarly, from a church service open to the general public through the rituals of a limited sect to the mysteries of a secret cult.

3. Similarly, closure within the group may also assume the most varied forms. Thus a caste, a guild, or a group of stock exchange brokers, which is closed to outsiders, may allow to its members a perfectly free competition for all the advantages which the group as a whole monopolizes for itself. Or it may assign every member strictly to the enjoyment of certain advantages, such as claims over customers or particular business opportunities, for life or even on a hereditary basis. This is particularly characteristic of India. Similarly, a closed group of settlers (*Markgenossen-*

schaft) may allow its members free use of the resources of its area or may restrict them rigidly to a plot assigned to each individual household. A closed group of colonists may allow free use of the land or sanction and guarantee permanent appropriation of separate holdings. In such cases all conceivable transitional and intermediate forms can be found. Historically, the closure of eligibility to fiefs, benefices, and offices within the group, and the appropriation on the part of those enjoying them, have occurred in the most varied forms. Similarly, the establishment of rights to and possession of particular jobs on the part of workers may develop all the way from the "closed shop" to a right to a particular job. The first step in this development may be to prohibit the dismissal of a worker without the consent of the workers' representatives. The development of the "works councils" [in Germany after 1918] might be a first step in this direction, though it need not be. . . .

4. The principal motives for closure of a relationship are: (a) The maintenance of quality, which is often combined with the interest in prestige and the consequent opportunities to enjoy honor, and even profit; examples are communities of ascetics, monastic orders, especially, for instance, the Indian mendicant orders, religious sects like the Puritans, organized groups of warriors, of *ministeriales* and other functionaries, organized citizen bodies as in the Greek states, craft guilds; (b) the contraction of advantages in relation to consumption needs (*Nahrungsspielraum*); examples are monopolies of consumption, the most developed form of which is a self-subsistent village community; (c) the growing scarcity of opportunities for acquisition (*Erwerbsspielraum*). This is found in trade monopolies such as guilds, the ancient monopolies of fishing rights, and so on. Usually motive (a) is combined with (b) or (c). . . .

Economic Relationships

One frequent economic determinant [of closure] is the competition for a livelihood—offices, clients and other remunerative opportunities. When the number of competitors increases in relation to the profit span, the participants become interested in curbing competition. Usually one group of competitors takes some externally identifiable characteristic of another group of (actual or potential) competitors—race, language, religion, local or social origin, descent, residence, etc.—as a pretext for attempting their exclusion. It does not matter which characteristic is chosen in the individual case: whatever suggests itself most easily is seized upon. Such group action may provoke a corresponding reaction on the part of those against whom it is directed.

In spite of their continued competition against one another, the jointly acting competitors now form an "interest group" toward outsiders; there is a growing tendency to set up some kind of association with rational regulations; if the monopolistic interests persist, the time comes when the competitors, or another group whom they can influence (for example, a political community), establish a legal order that limits competition through formal monopolies; from then on, certain persons are available as "organs" to protect the monopolistic practices, if need be, with force. In such a case, the interest group has developed into a *"legally privileged group"* (*Rechtsgemeinschaft*) and the participants have become *"privileged members"* (*Rechtsgenossen*). Such closure, as we want to call it, is an ever-recurring process; it is the source of property in land as well as of all guild and other group monopolies.

The tendency toward the monopolization of specific, usually economic opportunities is always the driving force in such cases as: "cooperative organization," which always means closed monopolistic groups, for example, of fishermen taking their name from a certain fishing area; the establishment of an association of engineering graduates, which seeks to secure a legal, or at least factual, monopoly over certain positions; the exclusion of outsiders from sharing in the fields and commons of a village; "patriotic" associations of shop clerks; the *ministeriales,* knights, university graduates and craftsmen of a given region or locality; ex-soldiers entitled to civil service positions—all these groups first engage in some joint action (*Gemeinschaftshandeln*) and later perhaps an explicit association. This monopolization is directed against competitors who share some positive or negative characteristics; its purpose is always the closure of social and economic opportunities to *outsiders.* Its extent may vary widely, especially so far as the group member shares in the apportionment of monopolistic advantages. . . .

This monopolistic tendency takes on specific forms when groups are formed by persons with shared qualities *acquired* through upbringing, apprenticeship and training. These characteristics may be economic qualifications of some kind, the holding of the same or of similar offices, a knightly or ascetic way of life, etc. If in such a case an association results from social action, it tends toward the *guild.* Full members make a vocation out of monopolizing the disposition of spiritual, intellectual, social and economic goods, duties and positions. Only those are admitted to the unrestricted practice of the vocation who (1) have completed a novitiate in order to acquire the proper training, (2) have proven their qualification, and (3) sometimes have passed through further wait-

ing periods and met additional requirements. This development follows a typical pattern in groups ranging from the juvenile student fraternities, through knightly associations and craft-guilds, to the qualifications required of the modern officials and employees. It is true that the interest in guaranteeing an efficient performance may everywhere have some importance; the participants may desire it for idealistic or materialistic reasons in spite of their possibly continuing competition with one another: local craftsmen may desire it for the sake of their business reputation, *ministeriales* and knights of a given association for the sake of their professional reputation and also their own military security, and ascetic groups for fear that the gods and demons may turn their wrath against all members because of faulty manipulations. (For example, in almost all primitive tribes, persons who sang falsely during a ritual dance were originally slain in expiation of such an offense.) But normally this concern for efficient performance recedes behind the interest in limiting the supply of candidates for the benefices and honors of a given occupation. The novitiates, waiting periods, masterpieces and other demands, particularly the expensive entertainment of group members, are more often economic than professional tests of qualification.

M A X   W E B E R

The Rationalization of Education and Training

We cannot here analyze the far-reaching and general cultural effects that the advance of the rational bureaucratic structure of domination, as such, develops quite independently of the areas in which it takes hold. Naturally, bureaucracy promotes a 'rationalist' way of life, but the concept of rationalism allows for widely differing contents. Quite generally, one can only say that the bureaucratization of all domination very strongly furthers the development of 'rational matter-of-factness' and the personality type of the professional expert. This has far-reaching ramifications, but only one important element of the process can be briefly indicated here: its effect upon the nature of training and education.

Educational institutions on the European continent, especially the institutions of higher learning—the universities, as well as technical academies, business colleges, gymnasiums, and other middle schools—are dominated and influenced by the need for the kind of 'education' that produces a system of special examinations and the trained expertness that is increasingly indispensable for modern bureaucracy.

The 'special examination,' in the present sense, was and is found also outside of bureaucratic structures proper; thus, today it is found in the 'free' professions of medicine and law and in the guild-organized trades. Expert examinations are neither indispensable

to nor concomitant phenomena of bureaucratization. The French, English, and American bureaucracies have for a long time foregone such examinations entirely or to a large extent, for training and service in party organizations have made up for them.

'Democracy' also takes an ambivalent stand in the face of specialized examinations, as it does in the face of all the phenomena of bureaucracy—although democracy itself promotes these developments. Special examinations, on the one hand, mean or appear to mean a 'selection' of those who qualify from all social strata rather than a rule by notables. On the other hand, democracy fears that a merit system and educational certificates will result in a privileged 'caste.' Hence, democracy fights against the special-examination system.

The special examination is found even in pre-bureaucratic or semi-bureaucratic epochs. Indeed, the regular and earliest locus of special examinations is among prebendally organized dominions. Expectancies of prebends, first of church prebends—as in the Islamite Orient and in the Occidental Middle Ages—then, as was especially the case in China, secular prebends, are the typical prizes for which people study and are examined. These examinations, however, have in truth only a partially specialized and expert character.

The modern development of full bureaucratization brings the system of rational, specialized, and expert examinations irresistibly to the fore. The civil-service reform gradually imports expert training and specialized examinations into the United States. In all other countries this system also advances, stemming

---

Originally published in 1946 & 1958. Please see complete source information beginning on page 891.

from its main breeding place, Germany. The increasing bureaucratization of administration enhances the importance of the specialized examination in England. In China, the attempt to replace the semi-patrimonial and ancient bureaucracy by a modern bureaucracy brought the expert examination; it took the place of a former and quite differently structured system of examinations. The bureaucratization of capitalism, with its demand for expertly trained technicians, clerks, et cetera, carries such examinations all over the world. Above all, the development is greatly furthered by the social prestige of the educational certificates acquired through such specialized examinations. This is all the more the case as the educational patent is turned to economic advantage. Today, the certificate of education becomes what the test for ancestors has been in the past, at least where the nobility has remained powerful: a prerequisite for equality of birth, a qualification for a canonship, and for state office.

The development of the diploma from universities, and business and engineering colleges, and the universal clamor for the creation of educational certificates in all fields make for the formation of a privileged stratum in bureaus and in offices. Such certificates support their holders' claims for intermarriages with notable families (in business offices people naturally hope for preferment with regard to the chief's daughter), claims to be admitted into the circles that adhere to 'codes of honor,' claims for a 'respectable' remuneration rather than remuneration for work done, claims for assured advancement and old-age insurance, and, above all, claims to monopolize socially and economically advantageous positions. When we hear from all sides the demand for an introduction of regular curricula and special examinations, the reason behind it is, of course, not a suddenly awakened 'thirst for education' but the desire for restricting the supply for these positions and their monopolization by the owners of educational certificates. Today, the 'examination' is the universal means of this monopolization, and therefore examinations irre-

sistibly advance. As the education prerequisite to the acquisition of the educational certificate requires considerable expense and a period of waiting for full remuneration, this striving means a setback for talent (charisma) in favor of property. For the 'intellectual' costs of educational certificates are always low, and with the increasing volume of such certificates, their intellectual costs do not increase, but rather decrease. . . .

Social prestige based upon the advantage of special education and training as such is by no means specific to bureaucracy. On the contrary! But educational prestige in other structures of domination rests upon substantially different foundations.

Expressed in slogan-like fashion, the 'cultivated man,' rather than the 'specialist,' has been the end sought by education and has formed the basis of social esteem in such various systems as the feudal, theocratic, and patrimonial structures of dominion: in the English notable administration, in the old Chinese patrimonial bureaucracy, as well as under the rule of demagogues in the so-called Hellenic democracy.

The term 'cultivated man' is used here in a completely value-neutral sense; it is understood to mean solely that the goal of education consists in the quality of a man's bearing in life which was *considered* 'cultivated,' rather than in a specialized training for expertness. The 'cultivated' personality formed the educational ideal, which was stamped by the structure of domination and by the social condition for membership in the ruling stratum. Such education aimed at a chivalrous or an ascetic type; or, at a literary type, as in China; a gymnastic-humanist type, as in Hellas; or it aimed at a conventional type, as in the case of the Anglo-Saxon gentleman. The qualification of the ruling stratum as such rested upon the possession of 'more' cultural quality (in the absolutely changeable, value-neutral sense in which we use the term here), rather than upon 'more' expert knowledge. Special military, theological, and juridical ability was of course intensely practiced; but the point of gravity in Hellenic, in medieval, as well as in Chinese education, has rested upon educational elements that were entirely different from what was 'useful' in one's specialty.

Behind all the present discussions of the foundations of the educational system, the struggle of the 'specialist type of man' against the older type of 'cultivated man' is

hidden at some decisive point. This fight is determined by the irresistibly expanding bureaucratization of all public and private relations of authority and by the ever-increasing importance of expert and specialized knowledge. This fight intrudes into all intimate cultural questions.

A N T H O N Y   G I D D E N S

The Class Structure of the Advanced Societies

The Weberian Critique

For the most significant developments in the theory of classes since Marx, we have to look to those forms of social thought whose authors, while being directly influenced by Marx's ideas, have attempted at the same time to criticise or to reformulate them. This tendency has been strongest, for a combination of historical and intellectual reasons, in German sociology, where a series of attempts have been made to provide a fruitful critique of Marx—beginning with Max Weber, and continuing through such authors as Geiger, Renner and Dahrendorf.[1] Weber's critique of Marx here has been of particular importance. But, especially in the English-speaking world, the real import of Weber's analysis has frequently been misrepresented. The customary procedure has been to contrast Weber's discussion of 'Class, status and party', a fragment of *Economy and Society*, with the con-

ception of class supposedly taken by Marx, to the detriment of the latter. Marx, so it is argued, treated 'class' as a purely economic phenomenon and, moreover, regarded class conflicts as in some way the 'inevitable' outcome of clashes of material interest. He failed to realise, according to this argument, that the divisions of economic interest which create classes do not necessarily correspond to sentiments of communal identity which constitute differential 'status'. Thus, status, which depends upon subjective evaluation, is a separate 'dimension of stratification' from class, and the two may vary independently. There is yet a third dimension, so the argument continues, which Weber recognised as an independently variable factor in 'stratification', but which Marx treated as directly contingent upon class interests. This is the factor of 'power'.[2]

Evaluation of the validity of this interpretation is difficult because there is no doubt that Weber himself accepted it—or certain elements of it. What is often portrayed in the secondary literature as a critique of 'Marx's conception of class' actually takes a stilted and impoverished form of crude Marxism as its main target of attack. But this sort of determinist Marxism was already current in Germany in

Originally published in 1973. Please see complete source information beginning on page 891.

Weber's lifetime, and since Weber himself set out to question this determinism, the true lines of similarity and difference between his and Marx's analysis of classes are difficult to disentangle.[3] . . .

In the two versions of 'Class, status and party' which have been embodied in *Economy and Society,*[4] Weber provides what is missing in Marx: an explicit discussion of the concept of class. There are two principal respects in which this analysis differs from Marx's 'abstract model' of classes. One is that which is familiar from most secondary accounts—the differentiation of 'class' from 'status' and 'party'. The second, however, as will be argued below, is equally important: this is that, although Weber employs for some purposes a dichotomous model which in certain general respects resembles that of Marx, his viewpoint strongly emphasises a *pluralistic conception of classes*. Thus Weber's distinction between 'ownership classes' (*Besitzklassen*) and 'acquisition classes' (*Erwerbsklassen*) is based upon a fusion of two criteria: 'on the one hand . . . the kind of property that is usable for returns; and, on the other hand . . . the kind of services that can be offered on the market', thus producing a complex typology. The sorts of property which may be used to obtain market returns, although dividing generally into two types—creating ownership (*rentier*) and acquisition (entrepreneurial) classes—are highly variable, and may produce many differential interests within dominant classes:

Ownership of dwellings; workshops; warehouses; stores; agriculturally usable land in large or small-holdings—a quantitative difference with possibly qualitative consequences; ownership of mines; cattle; men (slaves); disposition over mobile instruments of production, or capital goods of all sorts, especially money or objects that can easily be exchanged for money; disposition over products of one's own labour or of others' labour differing according to their various distances from consumability; disposition over transferable monopolies of any kind—all these distinctions differentiate the class situations of the propertied . . . [5]

But the class situations of the propertyless are also differentiated, in relation both to the types and the degree of 'monopolisation' of 'marketable skills' which they possess. Consequently, there are various types of 'middle class' which stand between the 'positively privileged' classes (the propertied) and the 'negatively privileged' classes (those who possess neither property nor marketable skills). While these groupings are all nominally propertyless, those who possess skills which have a definite 'market value' are certainly in a different class situation from those who have nothing to offer but their (unskilled) labour. In acquisition classes—i.e., those associated particularly with the rise of modern capitalism—educational qualifications take on a particular significance in this respect; but the monopolisation of trade skills by manual workers is also important.

Weber insists that a clear-cut distinction must be made between class 'in itself' and class 'for itself': 'class', in his terminology, always refers to market interests, which exist independently of whether men are aware of them. Class is thus an 'objective' characteristic influencing the life-chances of men. But only under certain conditions do those sharing a common class situation become conscious of, and act upon, their mutual economic interests. In making this emphasis, Weber undoubtedly intends to separate his position from that adopted by many Marxists, involving what he calls a 'pseudo-scientific operation' whereby the link between class and class consciousness is treated as direct and immediate.[6] Such a consideration evidently also underlies the emphasis which Weber places upon 'status groups' (*Stände*) as contrasted to classes. The contrast between class and status group, however, is not, as often seems to be assumed, merely, nor perhaps even primarily, a distinction between subjective and objective aspects of differentiation. While class is founded upon differentials of economic interest in market relationships, Weber nowhere denies that, under certain given circumstances, a class may be a subjectively aware 'community'. The importance of status groups—

which are normally 'communities' in this sense—derives from the fact that they are built upon criteria of grouping other than those stemming from market situation. The contrast between classes and status groups is sometimes portrayed by Weber as one between the objective and the subjective; but it is also one between production and consumption. Whereas class expresses relationships involved in production, status groups express those involved in consumption, in the form of specific 'styles of life'.

Status affiliations may cut across the relationships generated in the market, since membership of a status group usually carries with it various sorts of monopolistic privileges. Nonetheless, classes and status groups tend in many cases to be closely linked, through property: possession of property is both a major determinant of class situation and also provides the basis for following a definite 'style of life'. The point of Weber's analysis is not that class and status constitute two 'dimensions of stratification', but that classes and status communities represent two possible, and competing, modes of group formation in relation to the distribution of power in society. Power is *not*, for Weber, a 'third dimension' in some sense comparable to the first two. He is quite explicit about saying that classes, status groups and parties are all 'phenomena of the distribution of power'.[7] The theorem informing Weber's position here is his insistence that power is not to be assimilated to economic domination—again, of course, a standpoint taken in deliberate contrast to that of Marx. The party, oriented towards the acquisition or maintenance of political leadership, represents, like the class and the status group, a major focus of social organisation relevant to the distribution of power in a society. It is, however, only characteristic of the modern rational state. . . .

In his conceptual discussion of class, besides distinguishing the purely economic *Besitzklassen* and *Erwerbsklassen*, Weber also refers to what he calls 'social classes'. A social class, in Weber's sense, is formed of a cluster of class situations which are linked together by virtue of the fact that they involve common mobility chances, either within the career of individuals or across the generations. Thus while a worker may fairly readily move from an unskilled to a semi-skilled manual occupation, and the son of an unskilled worker may become a semi-skilled or perhaps a skilled worker, the chances of either intra- or inter-generational mobility into non-manual occupations are much less. While the conception of the 'social class' remains relatively undeveloped in Weber's writings, it is of particular interest in relation to his model of capitalist development. As Weber himself points out, the notion of 'social class' comes much closer to that of 'status group' than does the conception of purely economic class (although, as with economic class situation, individuals who are in the same social class are not necessarily conscious of the fact). The notion of social class is important because it introduces a unifying theme into the diversity of cross-cutting class relationships which may stem from Weber's identification of 'class situation' with 'market position'. If the latter is applied strictly, it is possible to distinguish an almost endless multiplicity of class situations. But a 'social class' exists only when these class situations cluster together in such a way as to create a common nexus of social interchange between individuals. In capitalism, Weber distinguishes four main social class groupings: the manual working class; the petty bourgeoisie; propertyless white-collar workers: 'technicians, various kinds of white-collar employees, civil servants—possibly with considerable social differences depending on the cost of their training'; and those 'privileged through property and education'.[8] Of these social class groupings, the most significant are the working class, the propertyless 'middle class' and the propertied 'upper class'. Weber agrees with Marx that the category of small property-owners (*Kleinbürgertum*) tends to become progressively more restricted with the increasing maturity of capitalism. The result of this process, however, is not normally that they 'sink into the proletariat', but that they become absorbed into the expanding category of skilled manual or non-manual salaried workers.

To emphasise, therefore, that Weber's 'abstract model' of classes is a pluralistic one is not to hold that he failed to recognise unifying ties between the numerous combinations of class interests made possible by his conception of 'class situation'. But there is no doubt that his viewpoint drastically amends important elements of Marx's picture of the typical trend of development of the capitalist class structure. Even Weber's simplified ('social class') model of capitalism diverges significantly from the Marxian conception, in treating the propertyless 'middle class' as the category which tends to expand most with the advance of capitalism. Moreover, the social classes do not necessarily constitute 'communities', and they may be fragmented by interest divisions deriving from differentials in market position; and finally, as Weber shows in his historical writings, the relationship between class structure and the political sphere is a contingent one. . . .

Rethinking the Theory of Class

The deficiency in Weber's reinterpretation of Marx's view is that it is not sufficiently radical. While Weber recognises the unsatisfactory character of the Marxian standpoint, particularly as regards the undifferentiated category of the 'propertyless', he does not pursue the implications of his own conception far enough. Dahrendorf has suggested that we may stand the Marxian concept of property on its head in terms of its relation to authority;[9] the implications of the Weberian analysis, however, are that the conception of property may be 'inverted' or generalised in a different way, which does not sacrifice the economic foundation of the concept of class. 'Property' refers, not to any characteristics of physical objects as such, but to rights which are associated with them, which in turn confer certain capacities upon the 'owner'. . . . In the market, of course, the significance of capital as private property is that it confers certain

very definite capacities upon its possessor as compared to those who are 'propertyless'—those who do not own their means of production. But we can readily perceive that, even in the Marxian view, the notion of 'propertylessness' is something of a misnomer. For if 'property' is conceived of as a set of capacities of action with reference to the operations of the market, it is evident that the wage-labourer does possess such capacities. The 'property' of the wage-labourer is the labour-power which he brings for sale in entering into the contractual relation. While this fundamentally disadvantages him in the competitive bargaining situation in relation to the owner of capital, this is not simply a one-way power relationship: the 'property' which the wage-labourer possesses is needed by the employer, and he must pay at least some minimal attention to the demands of the worker—providing a basis for the collective withdrawal of labour as a possible sanction. It would be departing too much from usual terminology to refer to capital and to the labour-power of the worker both as 'property'; and, anyway, the point is rather that 'property' (capital) is a particular case of capacity to determine the bargaining outcome, rather than vice versa. So I shall continue to speak below of 'property' (in the means of production) in a conventional sense, and shall use the term 'market capacity' in an inclusive manner *to refer to all forms of relevant attributes which individuals may bring to the bargaining encounter.*

It is an elementary fact that where ownership of property is concentrated in the hands of a minority and in a society in which the mass of the population is employed in industrial production, the vast majority consequently offer their labour for sale on the market. Because of his general emphasis upon 'productive labour', and because of his expectation that it is in the nature of modern technology to reduce productive operations to a homogeneous skill-level, Marx failed to recognise the potential significance of differentiations of market capacity which do not derive directly from the factor of property ownership. Such differentiations, it seems clear, are contingent upon the scarcity value of what the individual 'owns' and is able to offer on the market. As Weber indicates, possession of recognised 'skills'—including educational qualifications—is the major factor influencing market capacity. Differentiations in market capacity may be used, as various recent authors have indicated, to secure economic returns other than income as such. These include, principally, security of employment, prospects of career advancement, and a range of 'fringe benefits', such as pension rights, etc.[10] In the same way as the capacities which individuals bring to the bargaining process may be regarded as a form of 'property' which they exchange on the market, so these material returns may be regarded as forms of 'good' which are obtained through the sale of labour-power.

In the market structure of competitive capitalism, *all* those who participate in the exchange process are in a certain sense in (interest) conflict with one another for access to scarce returns. Conflict of interest may be created by the existence of many sorts of differential market capacities. Moreover, the possible relationships between property and 'propertyless' forms of market capacity are various. Speculative investment in property may, for example, be one of the specific market advantages used by those in certain occupations (thus directors are often able to use 'inside knowledge' to profit from property deals). Marx himself, of course, recognised the existence of persistent conflicts of interest within property-owning groupings: notably, between financial and industrial sectors of the large bourgeoisie, and between large and petty bourgeoisie.

The difficulty of identifying 'class' with common market capacity has already been alluded to with reference to Weber. While Weber's concept of 'market situation' successfully moves away from some of the rigidities of the Marxian scheme, it tends to imply the recognition of a cumbersome plurality of classes. There would appear to be as many 'classes', and as many 'class conflicts', as there

are differing market positions. The problem here, however, is not the recognition of the diversity of the relationships and conflicts created by the capitalist market as such, but that of making the *theoretical transition from such relationships and conflicts to the identification of classes as structured forms*. The unsatisfactory and ill-defined character of the connections between 'class position', the typology of *Besitzklassen* and *Erwerbsklassen,* and 'social classes' in Weber's work has already been mentioned. But the problem is by no means confined to Weber's theoretical scheme. Marx was certainly conscious of the problematic character of the links between class as a latent set of characteristics generated by the capitalist system and class as an historical, dynamic entity, an 'historical actor'. But his contrast between class 'in itself' and class 'for itself' is primarily one distinguishing between class relationships as a cluster of economic connections on the one hand and class consciousness on the other. This emphasis was very much dictated by the nature of Marx's interests, lying as they did above all in understanding and promoting the rise of a revolutionary class consciousness within capitalism. While it would by no means be true to hold that Marx ignored this completely, it can be said that he gave only little attention to the modes in which classes, founded in a set of economic relationships, take on or 'express' themselves in definite social forms.

Nor has the matter been adequately dealt with in the writings of later authors. In fact, one of the leading dilemmas in the theory of class—which figures prominently, for example, in Aron's discussion—is that of identifying the 'reality' of class.[11] Not only has there been some considerable controversy over whether class is a 'real' or 'nominal' category, but many have argued that, since it is difficult or impossible to draw the 'boundaries' between classes with any degree of clarity, we should abandon the notion of class as a useful sociological concept altogether.[12] Only Dahrendorf seems to have attempted to give attention to the problem within the framework of an overall theory of class, and since his identification of class with authority divisions is unacceptable [for reasons outlined elsewhere],[13] his analysis does not help greatly.

The major problems in the theory of class, I shall suggest, do not so much concern the nature and application of the class concept itself, as what, for want of a better word, I shall call the *structuration* of class relationships.[14] Most attempts to revise class theory since Marx have sought to accomplish such a revision primarily by refining, modifying, or substituting an altogether different notion for the Marxian concept of class. While it is useful to follow and develop certain of Weber's insights in this respect, the most important blank spots in the theory of class concern the processes whereby 'economic classes' become 'social classes', and whereby in turn the latter are related to other social forms. As Marx was anxious to stress in criticising the premises of political economy, all economic relationships, and any sort of 'economy', presuppose a set of social ties between producers. In arguing for the necessity of conceptualising the structuration of class relationships, I do not in any way wish to question the legitimacy of this insight, but rather to focus upon *the modes in which* 'economic' relationships become translated into 'non-economic' social structures.

One source of terminological ambiguity and conceptual confusion in the usage of the term 'class' is that it has often been employed to refer both to an economic *category* and to a specifiable cluster of social groupings. Thus Weber uses the term in both of these ways, although he seeks terminologically to indicate the difference between 'class' (as a series of 'class positions') and 'social class'. But in order to insist that the study of class and class conflict must concern itself with the interdependence of economy and society, it is not necessary to identify the term 'class' with the divisions and interests generated by the market as such. Consequently, in the remainder of this [essay], I shall use the term in the sense of Weber's 'social class'—appropriately expli-

cated. While there may be an indefinite multiplicity of cross-cutting interests created by differential market capacities, there are only, in any given society, a limited number of classes.

It will be useful at this juncture to state what class is *not*. First, a class is not a specific 'entity'—that is to say, a bounded social form in the way in which a business firm or a university is—and a class has no publicly sanctioned identity. It is extremely important to stress this, since established linguistic usage often encourages us to apply active verbs to the term 'class'; but the sense in which a class 'acts' in a certain way, or 'perceives' elements in its environment on a par with an individual actor, is highly elliptical, and this sort of verbal usage is to be avoided wherever possible. Similarly, it is perhaps misleading to speak of 'membership' of a class, since this might be held to imply participation in a definite 'group'. This form of expression, however, is difficult to avoid altogether, and I shall not attempt to do so in what follows. Secondly, class has to be distinguished from 'stratum', and class theory from the study of 'stratification' as such. The latter, comprising what Ossowski terms a gradation scheme, involves a criterion or set of criteria in terms of which individuals may be ranked descriptively along a scale.[15] The distinction between class and stratum is again a matter of some significance, and bears directly upon the problem of class 'boundaries'. For the divisions between strata, for analytical purposes, may be drawn very precisely, since they may be set upon a measurement scale—as, for example, with 'income strata'. The divisions between classes are *never* of this sort; nor, moreover, do they lend themselves to easy visualisation, in terms of any ordinal scale of 'higher' and 'lower', as strata do—although this sort of imagery cannot be escaped altogether. Finally we must distinguish clearly between class and elite. Elite theory, as formulated by Pareto and Mosca, developed in part as a conscious and deliberate repudiation of class analysis.[16] In place of the concept of class relationships, the elite theorists substituted the opposition of 'elite' and 'mass'; and in place of the Marxian juxtaposition of class society and classlessness they substituted the idea of the cyclical replacement of elites *in perpetuo*. . . .

The Structuration of Class Relationships

It is useful, initially, to distinguish the *mediate* from the *proximate* structuration of class relationships. By the former term, I refer to the factors which intervene between the existence of certain given market capacities and the formation of classes as identifiable social groupings, that is to say which operate as 'overall' connecting links between the market on the one hand and structured systems of class relationships on the other. In using the latter phrase, I refer to 'localised' factors which condition or shape class formation. The mediate structuration of class relationships is governed above all by the distribution of mobility chances which pertain within a given society. Mobility has sometimes been treated as if it were in large part separable from the determination of class structure. According to Schumpeter's famous example, classes may be conceived of as like conveyances, which may be constantly carrying different 'passengers' without in any way changing their shape. But, compelling though the analogy is at first sight, it does not stand up to closer examination, especially within the framework I am suggesting here.[17] In general, the greater the degree of 'closure' of mobility chances—both intergenerationally and within the career of the individual—the more this facilitates the formation of identifiable classes. For the effect of closure in terms of intergenerational movement is to provide for the *reproduction* of common life experience over the generations; and this homogenisation of experience is reinforced to the degree to which the individual's movement within the labour market is confined to occupations which generate a similar range of material outcomes. In general we may state that the structuration of classes is facilitated *to the degree to which mobility closure exists*

in relation to any specified form of market capacity. There are three sorts of market capacity which can be said to be normally of importance in this respect: ownership of property in the means of production; possession of educational or technical qualifications; and possession of manual labour-power. In so far as it is the case that these tend to be tied to closed patterns of inter- and intragenerational mobility, this yields the foundation of *a basic three-class system* in capitalist society: an 'upper', 'middle', and 'lower' or 'working' class. But as has been indicated previously, it is an intrinsic characteristic of the development of the capitalist market that there exist no legally sanctioned or formally prescribed limitations upon mobility, and hence it must be emphasised that there is certainly never anything even approaching complete closure. In order to account for the emergence of structured classes, we must look in addition at the proximate sources of structuration.

There are three, related, sources of proximate structuration of class relationships: the division of labour within the productive enterprise; the authority relationships within the enterprise; and the influence of what I shall call 'distributive groupings'. I have already suggested that Marx tended to use the notion of 'division of labour' very broadly, to refer both to market relationships and to the allocation of occupational tasks within the productive organisation. Here I shall use the term only in this second, more specific, sense. In capitalism, the division of labour in the enterprise is in principle governed by the promotion of productive efficiency in relation to the maximisation of profit; but while responding to the same exigencies as the capitalist market in general, the influence of the division of labour must be analytically separated as a distinctive source of structuration (and, as will be discussed later, as a significant influence upon class consciousness). The division of labour, it is clear, may be a basis of the fragmentation as well as the consolidation of class relationships. It furthers the formation of classes to the degree to which it creates homogeneous groupings which cluster along the same lines as those which are fostered by mediate structuration. Within the modern industrial order, the most significant influence upon proximate structuration in the division of labour is undoubtedly that of technique. The effect of industrial technique (more recently, however, modified by the introduction of cybernetic systems of control) is to create a decisive separation between the conditions of labour of manual and non-manual workers. 'Machine-minding', in one form or another, regardless of whether it involves a high level of manual skill, tends to create a working environment quite distinct from that of the administrative employee, and one which normally enforces a high degree of physical separation between the two groupings.[18]

This effect of the division of labour thus overlaps closely with the influence of the mediate structuration of class relationships through the differential apportionment of mobility chances; but it is, in turn, potentially heavily reinforced by the typical authority system in the enterprise. In so far as administrative workers participate in the framing, or merely in the enforcement, of authoritative commands, they tend to be separated from manual workers, who are subject to those commands. But the influence of differential authority is also basic as a reinforcing agent of the structuration of class relationships at the 'upper' levels. Ownership of property, in other words, confers certain fundamental capacities of command, maximised within the 'entrepreneurial' enterprise in its classical form. To the extent to which this serves to underlie a division at 'the top', in the control of the organisation (something which is manifestly influenced, but not at all destroyed, if certain of the suppositions advanced by the advocates of the theory of the separation of 'ownership and control' are correct) it supports the differentiation of the 'upper' from the 'middle' class.

The third source of the proximate structuration of class relationships is that originating in the sphere of consumption rather than production. Now according to the traditional interpretations of class structure, including those of Marx and Weber, 'class' is a phenomenon of production: relationships established in consumption are therefore quite distinct from, and secondary to, those formed in the context of productive activity. There is no reason to deviate from this general emphasis. But without dropping the conception that classes are founded ultimately in the economic structure of the capitalist market, it is still possible to regard consumption patterns as a major influence upon class structuration. Weber's notions of 'status' and 'status group', as I previously pointed out, confuse two separable elements: the formation of groupings in consumption, on the one hand, and the formation of types of social differentiation based upon some sort of non-economic value providing a scale of 'honour' or 'prestige' on the other. While the two may often coincide, they do not necessarily do so, and it seems worthwhile to distinguish them terminologically. Thus I shall call *distributive groupings* those relationships involving common patterns of the consumption of economic goods, regardless of whether the individuals involved make any type of conscious evaluation of their honour or prestige relative to others; 'status' refers to the existence of such evaluations, and a 'status group' is, then, any set of social relationships which derives its coherence from their application.[19]

In terms of class structuration, distributive groupings are important in so far as they interrelate with the other sets of factors distinguished above in such a way as to reinforce the typical separations between forms of market capacity. The most significant distributive groupings in this respect are those formed through the tendency towards community or neighbourhood segregation. Such a tendency is not normally based only upon differentials in income, but also upon such factors as access to housing mortgages, etc. The creation of distinctive 'working-class neighbourhoods' and 'middle-class neighbourhoods', for example, is naturally promoted if those in manual labour are by and large denied mortgages for house buying, while those in non-manual occupations experience little difficulty in obtaining such loans. Where industry is located outside of the major urban areas, homogeneous 'working-class communities' frequently develop through the dependence of workers upon housing provided by the company.

In summary, to the extent to which the various bases of mediate and proximate class structuration overlap, classes will exist as distinguishable formations. I wish to say that *the combination of the sources of mediate and proximate structuration distinguished here, creating a threefold class structure, is generic to capitalist society.* But the mode in which these elements are merged to form *a specific class system,* in any given society, differs significantly according to variations in economic and political development. It should be evident that structuration is never an all-or-nothing matter. The problem of the existence of distinct class 'boundaries', therefore, is not one which can be settled *in abstracto*: one of the specific aims of class analysis in relation to empirical societies must necessarily be that of determining how strongly, in any given case, the 'class principle' has become established as a mode of structuration. Moreover, the operation of the 'class principle' may also involve the creation of forms of structuration within the major class divisions. One case in point is that which Marx called the 'petty bourgeoisie'. In terms of the preceding analysis, it is quite easy to see why ownership of small property in the means of production might come to be differentiated both from the upper class and from the ('new') middle class. If it is the case that the chances of mobility, either inter- or intragenerationally, from small to large property ownership are slight, this is likely to isolate the small property-owner from membership of the upper class as such. But the fact that he enjoys directive control of an enterprise, however minute, acts to distinguish him from those who are part of a hierarchy of authority in a larger organisation. On the other hand, the income and other economic returns of the petty bourgeois are likely to be similar to the white-collar worker, and hence they may belong to similar distributive groupings. A second potentially important influence

upon class formation is to be traced to the factor of skill differential within the general category of manual labour. The manual worker who has undergone apprenticeship, or a comparable period of training, possesses a market capacity which sets him apart from the unskilled or semi-skilled worker. This case will be discussed in more detail [elsewhere];[20] it is enough merely to indicate at this point that there are certain factors promoting structuration on the basis of this differentiation in market capacity (e.g., that the chances of intergenerational mobility from skilled manual to white-collar occupations are considerably higher than they are from unskilled and semi-skilled manual occupations).

So far I have spoken of structuration in a purely formal way, as though class could be defined in terms of relationships which have no 'content'. But this obviously will not do: if classes become social realities, this must be manifest in the formation of common patterns of behaviour and attitude. Since Weber's discussion of classes and status groups, the notion of 'style of life' has normally come to be identified as solely pertaining to the mode whereby a status group expresses its claim to distinctiveness. However, in so far as there is marked convergence of the sources of structuration mentioned above, classes will also tend to manifest common styles of life.

An initial distinction can be drawn here between 'class awareness' and 'class consciousness'.[21] We may say that, in so far as class is a structurated phenomenon, there will tend to exist a common awareness and acceptance of similar attitudes and beliefs, linked to a common style of life, among the members of the class. 'Class awareness', as I use the term here, does *not* involve a recognition that these attitudes and beliefs signify a particular class affiliation, or the recognition that there exist other classes, characterised by different attitudes, beliefs, and styles of life; 'class consciousness', by contrast, as I shall use the notion, does imply both of these. The difference between class awareness and class consciousness is a fundamental one, because class awareness may take the form of *a denial of the existence or reality of classes.*[22] Thus the class awareness of the middle class, in so far as it involves beliefs which place a premium upon individual responsibility and achievement, is of this order.

Within ethnically and culturally homogeneous societies, the degree of class structuration will be determined by the interrelationship between the sources of structuration identified previously. But many, if not the majority, of capitalist societies are not homogeneous in these respects. Traditionally, in class theory, racial or religious divisions have been regarded as just so many 'obstacles' to the formation of classes as coherent unities. This may often be so, where these foster types of structuration which deviate from that established by the 'class principle' (as typically was the case in the battles fought by the rearguard of feudalism against the forces promoting the emergence of capitalism). The idea that ethnic or cultural divisions serve to dilute or hinder the formation of classes is also very explicitly built into Weber's separation of (economic) 'class' and 'status group'. But this, in part at least, gains its cogency from the contrast between estate, as a legally constituted category, and class, as an economic category. While it may be agreed, however, that the *bases* of the formation of classes and status groups (in the sense in which I have employed these concepts) are different, nonetheless the tendency to class structuration may receive a considerable impetus *where class coincides with the criteria of status group membership*—in other words, where structuration deriving from economic organisation 'overlaps' with, or, in Dahrendorf's terms, is 'superimposed' upon, that deriving from evaluative categorisations based upon ethnic or cultural differences.[23] Where this is so, status group membership itself becomes a form of market capacity. Such a situation frequently offers the strongest possible source of class structuration, whereby there develop clear-cut differences in attitudes, beliefs and style of life between the classes. Where ethnic differences serve as a 'disqualifying' market capacity, such that those in the category in question are heavily concentrated among the lowest-paid occupations, or are chronically unemployed or semi-employed, we may speak of the existence of an *underclass*.[24]

Notes

1. Theodor Geiger, *Die Klassengesellschaft im Schmeltztiegel* (Cologne 1949); Karl Renner, *Wandlungen der modernen Gesellschaft* (Vienna 1953); Ralf Dahrendorf, *Class and Class Conflict in Industrial Society* (Stanford 1959).

2. For a cogent representation of this view, see W. G. Runciman, 'Class, status and power', in J. A. Jackson, *Social Stratification* (Cambridge 1968).

3. See my *Capitalism and Modern Social Theory* (Cambridge 1971), pp. 185ff. and *passim*.

4. *Economy and Society,* vol. 2 (New York 1968), pp. 926–40, and vol. 1, pp. 302–7.

5. ibid., vol. 2, p. 928.

6. ibid., p. 930.

7. ibid., p. 927.

8. ibid., p. 305.

9. Dahrendorf, *Class and Class Conflict.*

10. See, for example, David Lockwood, *The Blackcoated Worker* (London 1958), pp. 202–4; Frank Parkin, *Class Inequality and Political Order* (London 1971).

11. Raymond Aron, *La lutte des classes* (Paris 1964).

12. See Robert A. Nisbet, 'The decline and fall of social class', *Pacific Sociological Review* 2, 1959.

13. Anthony Giddens, *The Class Structure of the Advanced Societies* (New York 1973), ch. 4.

14. What I call class structuration, Gurvitch calls negatively 'résistance à la pénétration par la société globale'. Georges Gurvitch, *Le concept de classes sociales de Marx à nos jours* (Paris 1954), p. 116 and *passim*.

15. Stanislaw Ossowski, *Class Structure in the Social Consciousness* (London 1963).

16. Vilfredo Pareto, *The Mind and Society* (New York 1935); Gaetano Mosca, *The Ruling Class* (New York 1939).

17. We may, however, agree with Schumpeter that 'The family, not the physical person, is the true unit of class and class theory' (Joseph Schumpeter, *Imperialism, Social Classes,* Cleveland 1961). This is actually completely consistent with the idea that mobility is fundamental to class formation.

18. Lockwood, *The Blackcoated Worker,* op. cit.

19. It might be pointed out that it would easily be possible to break down the notion of status group further: according, for example, to whether the status evaluations in question are made primar-

ily by others outside the group, and rejected by those inside it, etc.

20. Giddens, *The Class Structure of the Advanced Societies.*

21. This is not, of course, the same as Lukács' 'class-conditioned unconsciousness'; but I believe that Lukács is correct in distinguishing qualitatively different 'levels' of class consciousness. Georg Lukács, *History and Class Consciousness* (London 1971), pp. 52ff.

22. cf. Nicos Poulantzas, *Pouvoir politique et classes sociales de l'état capitaliste* (Paris 1970). It is misleading, however, to speak of *classes sans conscience,* as Crozier does. See Michel Crozier, 'Classes sans conscience ou préfiguration de la société sans classes', *Archives européenes de sociolo-*

gie 1, 1960; also 'L'ambiguité de la conscience de classe chez les employés et les petits fonctionnaires', *Cahiers internationaux de sociologie* 28, 1955.

23. Or, to use another terminology, where there is 'overdetermination' (Louis Althusser, *For Marx,* London 1969, pp. 89–128).

24. Marx's *Lumpenproletariat,* according to this usage, is only an underclass when the individuals in question tend to derive from distinctive ethnic backgrounds. Leggett has referred to the underclass as the 'marginal working class', defining this as 'a sub-community of workers who belong to a subordinate ethnic or racial group which is usually proletarianised and highly segregated' (John C. Leggett, *Class, Race, and Labor,* New York 1968, p. 14).

FRANK PARKIN

Marxism and Class Theory: A Bourgeois Critique

The 'Boundary Problem' in Sociology

The persistent attractions of Marxist class theory have almost certainly been boosted by the less than inspiring alternative offered by academic sociology. In so far as there is any sort of tacitly agreed upon model of class among western social theorists it takes the form of the familiar distinction between manual and non-manual labour. No other criterion for identifying the class boundary seems to enjoy such widespread acceptance among those who conduct investigations into family structure, political attitudes, social imagery, life-styles, educational attainment, and similar enquiries that

keep the wheels of empirical sociology endlessly turning. Paradoxically, however, although the manual/non-manual model is felt to be highly serviceable for research purposes, it is not commonly represented as a model of class cleavage and conflict. That is to say, the two main social categories distinguished by sociology for purposes of class analysis are not invested with antagonistic properties comparable to those accorded to proletariat and bourgeoisie in Marxist theory. This would be less cause for comment if proponents of the manual/non-manual model normally construed the social order as a harmonious and integrated whole; but to construe it instead in terms of conflict, dichotomy, and cleavage, as most of these writers now appear to do, seems to reveal an awkward contrast between the empirical model of class and the general conception of capitalist society.

Originally published in 1979. Please see complete source information beginning on page 891.

The strongest case that could be made out for identifying the line between manual and non-manual labour as the focal point of class conflict would be one that treated capitalist society as the industrial firm writ large. It is only within the framework of 'factory despotism' that the blue-collar/white-collar divide closely corresponds to the line of social confrontation over the distribution of spoils and the prerogatives of command. And this is particularly the case in those industrial settings where even the lowest grades of white-collar staff are cast in the role of managerial subalterns physically and emotionally removed from the shop-floor workers. Within the microcosm of capitalism represented by the typical industrial firm, the sociological model of class has something to recommend it as an alternative to one constructed around the rights of property.

The drawback is, however, that social relations within the capitalist *firm* are a less accurate guide to class relations within capitalist *society* than they might once have been. The reason for this is that the post-war expansion of the public sector has given rise to an ever-increasing assortment of non-manual groups in local government and welfare services that cannot in any real sense be thought of as the tail-end of a broad managerial stratum aligned against a manual workforce. Frequently, in fact there is no manual workforce to confront in the occupational settings within which these white-collar groups are employed.[1] And even where teachers, social workers, nurses, local government clerks, lower civil servants, and the like do form part of an organization that includes janitors, orderlies, cleaners, and other workers by hand, they do not usually stand in the same quasi-managerial relationship to them as does the staff employee to the industrial worker in the capitalist firm.

The usual rationale for treating intermediate and lower white-collar groups as a constituent element of a dominant class is that these groups traditionally have identified themselves with the interests of capital and management rather than with the interests of organized labour. But for various reasons this identification is easier to accomplish in the sphere of private industry and commerce than in the public sector. In the latter, as already pointed out, not only is there usually no subordinate manual group physically present to inspire a sense of white-collar status elevation, but also the charms of management are likely to seem less alluring when the chain of command stretches ever upwards and out of sight into the amorphous and unlovely body of the state. Moreover, public sector employees do not have the same opportunities as those in the commercial sector for transferring their special skills and services to different and competing employers; all improvements in pay and conditions must be negotiated with a monopoly employer, and one who is under close budgetary scrutiny. All this makes for a relationship of some tension between white-collar employees and the state *qua* employer, a condition more akin to that found between manual labour and management than between white-collar employees and management in the private sector. Thus, the validity of the manual/non-manual model as a representation of class conflict relies more heavily upon a view of the commercial employee as the prototypical case of the white-collar worker than really is justified, given the enormous growth of public-sector employment.

What this suggests is that manual and non-manual groups can usefully be thought of as entities socially differentiated from each other in terms of life-chances and opportunities, but not as groups standing in a relationship of exploiter and exploited, of dominance and subordination, in the manner presumably required of a genuine conflict model. Expressed differently, the current sociological model does not fulfil even the minimal Weberian claim that the relations between classes are to be understood as 'aspects of the distribution of power'. Instead of a theoretical framework organized around the central ideas of mutual antagonism and the incompatibility of interests we find one organized around the recorded facts of mere social differentiation. . . .

The 'Boundary Problem' in Marxism

The variety of [Marxist] interpretations on offer make it more than usually difficult to speak of 'the' Marxist theory of class. In some respects the range of differences within this camp has tended to blur the simple contrast between Marxist and bourgeois theories; and this is particularly so given the tendency for Marxists to adopt familiar sociological categories under substitute names. The most striking example of this is the tacit acknowledgment of the role of *authority* in the determination of bourgeois status. This arises from the need to find some theoretical principle by which the managerial stratum, in particular, can be assigned to the same class as the owners of capital. Although allusions may occasionally be made to the fact that managers are sometimes shareholders in the companies that employ them, it is clear that this is a contingent feature of managerial status and could not be regarded as theoretically decisive. Managers with and without private company shares do not appear to be different political and ideological animals.

The exercise of discipline over the workforce, on the other hand, is a necessary feature of the managerial role, not a contingent one; and as such it recommends itself as a major criterion of bourgeois class membership. Indeed, for some Marxists managerial authority has in certain respects superseded property ownership as *the* defining attribute of a capitalist class. According to Carchedi, 'the manager, rather than the capitalist rentier, is the central figure, he, rather than the capitalist rentier, is the non-labourer, the non-producer, the exploiter. He, rather than the capitalist rentier, is capital personified.'[2]

Interestingly, by proclaiming that the supervision and control of subordinates is the new hallmark of bourgeois status, Marxist theorists have come surprisingly close to endorsing Dahrendorf's view of the determinate role of authority in establishing the class boundary.[3] Their strict avoidance of this term in favour of some synonym or circumlocution ('mental labour', 'global function of capital', 'labour of superintendence') is perhaps a tacit admission of this embarrassing affinity with Dahrendorf's position. Although none of these writers would accept Dahrendorf's proposition that authority is a general phenomenon that encompasses property, it is nevertheless the case that their treatment of authority relations, however phrased, takes up far more of their analysis than the discussion of property relations.

To make property the centrepiece of class analysis would bring with it the duty of explaining precisely why the apparatus of managerial authority and control was thought to grow out of the institution of private ownership. Presumably it has come to the attention of western Marxists that societies that have done away with property in its private forms nevertheless have their own interesting little ways of seeing to the 'superintendence of labour'. The view that class and authority relations under capitalism are a unique product of private ownership must rest on a belief that these things are ordered in a very different way under the socialist mode of production. The fact that this mode of production figures not at all in any of the class analyses referred to suggests that Marxists are none too happy about drawing the very comparisons that are so essential to their case. After all, supposing it was discovered that factory despotism, the coercive uses of knowledge, and the privileges of mental labour were present not only in societies where the manager was 'capital personified', but also in societies where he was the party personified? Marxists would then be faced with the unwelcome choice of either having to expand the definition of capitalism to embrace socialist society, or of disowning the cherished concepts of private property and surplus extraction upon which their class theory is grounded. The obvious reluctance to engage in the comparative analysis of class under the two ostensibly different modes of production is therefore understandable enough. As for the credibility of Marxist class theory, it would seem that the advent of socialist society is about the worst thing that could have happened to it.

A further difficulty encountered by this theory is the attempt to arrive at some general principles by which to demarcate the established professions from routine white-collar employees, a distinction required by the evident self-identification of the former with the general interests of the bourgeoisie. In place of any general principles, however, resort is had to an eclectic assortment of descriptive indices demonstrating that 'higher' white-collar groups are in various ways simply better off than 'lower' white-collar groups. Braverman, for example, lists advantages such as higher pay, security of employment, and the privileged market position of the professions.[4] In similar vein, Westergaard and Resler suggest drawing a line of class demarcation beneath professional and managerial groups on the grounds that 'they are not dependent on the markets in which they sell their labour in anything like the way that other earners are'.[5] Their incomes 'are determined by market rules and mechanisms over which, in effect, they themselves have considerable influence in their own corners of the market'.[6]

The one notable thing about this kind of analysis is that despite its avowedly Marxist provenance it is indistinguishable from the approach of modern bourgeois social theory. It is, after all, Weber rather than Marx who provides the intellectual framework for understanding class in terms of market opportunities, life-chances, and symbolic rewards. The focus upon income differences and other market factors is difficult to reconcile with the standard Marxist objection to bourgeois sociology that it mistakenly operates on the level of distribution instead of on the level of productive relations. It might also be said that it is from Weber rather than Marx that the postulated link between class position and bureaucratic authority most clearly derives. The fact that these normally alien concepts of authority relations, life-chances, and market rewards have now been comfortably absorbed

by contemporary Marxist theory is a handsome, if unacknowledged, tribute to the virtues of bourgeois sociology. Inside every neo-Marxist there seems to be a Weberian struggling to get out. . . .

Social Closure

By social closure Weber means the process by which social collectivities seek to maximize rewards by restricting access to resources and opportunities to a limited circle of eligibles. This entails the singling out of certain social or physical attributes as the justificatory basis of exclusion. Weber suggests that virtually any group attribute—race, language, social origin, religion—may be seized upon provided it can be used for 'the monopolization of specific, usually economic opportunities'.[7] This monopolization is directed against competitors who share some positive or negative characteristic; its purpose is always the 'closure of social and economic opportunities to *outsiders*'.[8] The nature of these exclusionary practices, and the completeness of social closure, determine the general character of the distributive system.

Surprisingly, Weber's elaboration of the closure theme is not linked in any immediate way with his other main contributions to stratification theory, despite the fact that processes of exclusion can properly be conceived of as an aspect of the distribution of power, which for Weber is practically synonymous with stratification. As a result, the usefulness of the concept for the study of class and similar forms of structured inequality becomes conditional on the acceptance of certain refinements and enlargements upon the original usage.

An initial step in this direction is to extend the notion of closure to encompass other forms of collective social action designed to maximize claims to rewards and opportunities. Closure strategies would thus include not only those of an exclusionary kind, but also those adopted by the excluded themselves as a direct response to their status as outsiders. It is in any case hardly possible to consider the effectiveness of exclusion practices without due reference to the countervailing actions of socially defined ineligibles. As Weber acknowledges: 'Such group action may provoke a corresponding reaction on the part of those against whom it is directed'.[9] In other words, collective efforts to resist a pattern of dominance governed by exclusion principles can properly be regarded as the other half of the social closure equation. This usage is in fact employed by Weber in his discussion of 'community closure' which, as Neuwirth has shown, bears directly upon those forms of collective action mounted by the excluded—that is, 'negatively privileged status groups'.[10]

The distinguishing feature of exclusionary closure is the attempt by one group to secure for itself a privileged position at the expense of some other group through a process of subordination. That is to say, it is a form of collective social action which, intentionally or otherwise, gives rise to a social category of ineligibles or outsiders. Expressed metaphorically, exclusionary closure represents the use of power in a 'downward' direction because it necessarily entails the creation of a group, class, or stratum of legally defined inferiors. Countervailing action by the 'negatively privileged', on the other hand, represents the use of power in an upward direction in the sense that collective attempts by the excluded to win a greater share of resources always threaten to bite into the privileges of legally defined superiors. It is in other words a form of action having usurpation as its goal. *Exclusion* and *usurpation* may therefore be regarded as the two main generic types of social closure, the latter always being a consequence of, and collective response to, the former.[11]

Strategies of exclusion are the predominant mode of closure in all stratified systems. Where the excluded in their turn also succeed in closing off access to remaining rewards and opportunities, so multiplying the number of substrata, the stratification order approaches the furthest point of contrast to the Marxist model of class polarization. The traditional caste system and the stratification of ethnic communities in the United States provide the clearest illustrations of this closure pattern, though similar processes are easily detectable in societies in which class formation is paramount. Strategies of usurpation vary in scale from those designed to bring about marginal redistribution to those aimed at total expropriation. But whatever their intended scale they nearly always contain a potential challenge to the prevailing system of allocation and to the authorized version of distributive justice.

All this indicates the ease with which the language of closure can be translated into the language of power. Modes of closure can be thought of as different means of mobilizing power for the purpose of engaging in distributive struggle. To conceive of power as a built-in attribute of closure is at the very least to dispense with those fruitless searches for its 'location' inspired by Weber's more familiar but completely unhelpful definition in terms of the ubiquitous struggle between contending wills. Moreover, to speak of power in the light of closure principles is quite consistent with the analysis of class relations. Thus, to anticipate the discussion, the familiar distinction between bourgeoisie and proletariat, in its classic as well as in its modern guise, may be conceived of as an expression of conflict between classes defined not specifically in relation to their place in the productive process but in relation to their prevalent modes of closure, exclusion and usurpation, respectively. . . .

In modern capitalist society the two main exclusionary devices by which the bourgeoisie constructs and maintains itself as a class are, first, those surrounding the institutions of property; and, second, academic or professional qualifications and credentials. Each represents a set of legal arrangements for restricting access to rewards and privileges: property ownership is a form of closure designed to prevent general access to the means of production and its fruits; credentialism is a form of closure designed to control and monitor entry to key positions in the division of labour. The two sets of beneficiaries of these state-enforced exclusionary practices may thus be thought of as the core components of the dominant class under modern capitalism. Before taking up the discussion of common class interests fostered by private property and credentials it may be useful to consider each of the two principal closure strategies separately.

It has already been remarked upon how the concept of property has been devalued in the modern sociology of class as a result of the heavy weighting accorded to the division of labour. This has not always been true of bourgeois sociology. Weber was in full accord with Marx in asserting that '"Property" and "lack of property" are . . . the basic characteristics of all class situations'.[12] The post-Weberian tendency to analyse social relations as if the propertyless condition had painlessly arrived is perhaps a natural extension of the use of 'western' or 'industrial' to denote societies formerly referred to as capitalist. The postwar impact of functionalist theory certainly contributed to this tendency, since the proclamation of belief in the ultimate victory of achievement values and the merit system of reward naturally cast doubt on the importance of property as an institution. The inheritance of wealth after all requires notably little expenditure of those talents and efforts that are said to be the only keys to the gates of fortune.

The extent to which property has come to be regarded as something of an embarrassing theoretical anomaly is hinted at in the fact that it receives only the most cursory acknowledgment in Davis and Moore's functionalist manifesto, and even then in the shape of an assertion that 'strictly legal and functionless ownership . . . is open to attack' as capitalism develops.[13] To propose that the imposition of death duties and estate taxes constitutes evidence for an assault upon property rights is somewhat like suggesting that the introduction of divorce laws is evidence of state support for the dissolution of the family.

Property in this scheme of things can only be understood as a case of cultural lag—one of those quaint institutional remnants from an earlier epoch which survives by the grace of social inertia.

Several generations earlier Durkheim had reasoned along similar lines in declaring that property inheritance was 'bound up with archaic concepts and practices that have no part in our present day ethics'.[14] And although he felt it was not bound to disappear on this account he was willing to predict that inherited wealth would 'lose its importance more and more', and if it survived at all it would only be 'in a weakened form'.[15] Durkheim was not of course opposed to private property as such, only its transmission through the family. 'It is obvious that inheritance, by creating inequalities amongst men from birth, that are unrelated to merit or services, invalidates the whole contractual system at its very roots'.[16] Durkheim wanted society made safe for property by removing those legal practices that could not be squared with conceptions of liberal individualism and which therefore threatened to cause as much moral and social disturbance as the 'forced' division of labour.

There was not much likelihood of property itself declining as an institution because it was part of the order of things invested with a sacred character, understood in that special Durkheimian sense of an awesome relationship rooted deeply in the *conscience collective*. Although the sacred character of property arose originally from its communal status, the source of all things holy, the marked evolutionary trend towards the individualization of property would not be accompanied by any decline in its divinity. Personal rights to property were therefore seen by Durkheim as part of that general line of social development by which the individual emerges as a distinct and separate entity from the shadow of the group. The individual affirms himself as such by claiming exclusive rights to things over and above the rights of the collectivity. There is more than an echo here of Hegel's dictum that 'In his property a person exists for the first time as reason'.[17] As Plamenatz comments:

'It makes sense to argue, as Hegel does, that it is partly in the process of coming to own things, and to be recognised as their owners, that human beings learn to behave rationally and responsibly, to lead an ordered life. It is partly in the process of learning to distinguish mine from thine that a child comes to recognise itself as a person, as a bearer of rights and duties, as a member of a community with a place of its own inside it'.[18]

As Plamenatz goes on to say, however plausible as a defence of personal property this may be, as a defence of capitalist property relations it is 'lamentably inadequate'.[19]

The reason for this is that Hegel, like Durkheim, and many contemporary sociologists, never clearly distinguishes between property as rights to personal *possessions* and property as capital. Parsons is only one of many who reduces all forms of property to the status of a possession; this is understood as 'a right or a bundle of rights. In other words it is a set of expectations relative to social behaviour and attitudes.'[20] If property is simply a specific form of possession, or a certain bundle of rights, then everyone in society is a proprietor to some degree. On this reckoning there can be no clear social division between owners and non-owners, only a gradual, descending scale from those with very much to those with very little. This is well in line with Parsons' usual theoretical strategy of asserting the benign quality of any resource by reference to its widespread distribution. The possession of a toothbrush or an oilfield confers similar rights and obligations upon their owners, so that property laws cannot be interpreted as class laws. As Rose and his colleagues have suggested:

'the ideological significance of such a universalistic and disinterested legal interpretation of property in modern capitalist society is two-fold. First, as the law protects and recognises *all* private property, and as virtually all members of the society can claim title to *some* such property, it may be claimed

that all members of society have some vested interest in the *status quo*. From such a perspective, therefore, it can be argued that, far from representing an irreconcilable conflict of interests, the distribution of property in modern capitalist society gives rise to a commensurability of interests, any differences being variations of degree rather than kind. The office developer, the shareholder, the factory-owner, the householder and even the second-hand car owner may thus be represented as sharing fundamentally common interests, if not identities'.[21]

What the sociological definition of property as possessions interestingly fails to ask is why only certain limited forms of possession are legally admissible. It is patently not the case, for example, that workers are permitted to claim legal possession of their jobs; nor can tenants claim rights of possession to their homes, nor welfare claimants enforceable rights to benefits. Possession in all these cases is pre-empted by the conflicting claims of employers, landlords, and the state respectively, which are accorded legal priority. Although the law may treat the rights of ownership in true universalistic fashion it is silent on the manner by which only some 'expectations' are successfully converted to the status of property rights and others not. . . .

The case for restoring the notion of property into the centre of class analysis is that it is the most important single form of social closure common to industrial societies. That is to say, rights of ownership can be understood not as a special case of authority so much as a specific form of exclusion. As Durkheim expresses it, 'the right of property is the right of a given individual to exclude other individual and collective entities from the usage of a given thing'.[22] Property is defined negatively by 'the exclusion it involves rather than the prerogatives it confers'.[23] Durkheim's reference to *individual* rights of exclusion clearly indicates that once again he has possessions in mind, and that, characteristically, he sees no important distinction between objects of personal ownership, and the control of resources resulting in the exercise of power.

It is clearly necessary to distinguish property as possessions from property as capital, since only the latter is germane to the analysis of class systems. Property as capital is, to paraphrase Macpherson, that which 'confers the right to deny men access to the means of life and labour'.[24] This exclusionary right can obviously be vested in a variety of institutional forms, including the capitalist firm, a nationalized industry, or a Soviet enterprise. All these are examples of property that confers legal powers upon a limited few to grant or deny general access to the means of production and the distribution of its fruits. Although personal possessions and capital both entail rights of exclusion, it is only the exclusionary rights embedded in the latter that have important consequences for the life-chances and social condition of the excluded. To speak of property in the context of class analysis is, then, to speak of capital only, and not possessions.

Once property is conceptualized as a form of exclusionary social closure there is no need to become entangled in semantic debates over whether or not workers in socialist states are 'really' exploited. The relevant question is not whether surplus extraction occurs, but whether the state confers rights upon a limited circle of eligibles to deny access to the 'means of life and labour' to the rest of the community. If such exclusionary powers are legally guaranteed and enforced, an exploitative relationship prevails as a matter of definition. It is not of overriding importance to know whether these exclusionary powers are exercised by the formal owners of property or by their appointed agents, since the social consequences of exclusion are not demonstrably different in the two cases. Carchedi and other neo-Marxists may therefore be quite correct in suggesting that 'the manager is capital personified'; but all that needs to be added is first, that this dictum holds good not only for monopoly capitalism, but for *all*, including socialism, systems in which access to property and its benefices is in the legal gift of a select few; and, second, that it squares far more comfortably with the assumptions of bourgeois, or at least Weberian, sociology than with classical Marxist theory.

Of equal importance to the exclusionary rights of property is that set of closure practices sometimes referred to as 'credentialism'—that is, the inflated use of educational certificates as a means of monitoring entry to key positions in the division of labour. Well before the onset of mass higher education, Weber had pointed to the growing use of credentials as a means of effecting exclusionary closure.

'The development of the diploma from universities, and business and engineering colleges, and the universal clamour for the creation of educational certificates in all fields make for the formation of a privileged stratum in bureaus and offices. Such certificates support their holders' claims for intermarriages with notable families . . . , claims to be admitted into the circles that adhere to "codes of honour", claims for a "respectable" remuneration rather than remuneration for work well done, claims for assured advancement and old-age insurance, and, above all, claims to monopolize social and economically advantageous positions. When we hear from all sides the demand for an introduction of regular curricula and special examinations, the reason behind it is, of course, not a suddenly awakened "thirst for education" but the desire for restricting the supply of these positions and their monopolization by the owners of educational certificates. Today the "examination" is the universal means of this monopolization, and therefore examinations irresistibly advance'.[25]

The use of credentials for closure purposes, in the manner elaborated by Weber, has accompanied the attempt by an ever-increasing number of white collar occupations to attain the status of professions. Professionalization itself may be understood as a strategy designed, amongst other things, to limit and control the supply of entrants to an occupation in order to safeguard or enhance its market value. Much of the literature on the professions has tended to stress their differences from workaday occupations, usually accepting the professions' own evaluation of their singularity in creating rigorous codes of technical competence and ethical standards. It is perfectly possible to accept that the monopolization of skills and services does enable the professions to exercise close control over the moral and technical standards of their members, whilst also endorsing Weber's judgment that 'normally this concern for efficient performance recedes behind the interest in limiting the supply of candidates for the benefices and honours of a given occupation'.[26]

It would seem to be the professions' anxiety to control the supply side of labour that accounts, in part at least, for the qualifications epidemic referred to by Dore as the 'diploma disease'.[27] This is the universal tendency among professions to raise the minimum standards of entry as increasing numbers of potential candidates attain the formerly scarce qualifications. The growing reliance upon credentials as a precondition of professional candidature is commonly justified by reference to the greater complexity of the tasks to be performed and the consequent need for more stringent tests of individual capacity. Yet Berg's careful analysis of these claims was able to turn up no evidence to show that variations in the level of formal education were matched by variations in the quality of work performance.[28] Nor was there anything to suggest that professional tasks were in fact becoming more complex such as to justify a more rigorous intellectual screening of potential entrants. Berg's conclusion, in line with Weber's, is that credentials are accorded their present importance largely because they simplify and legitimate the exclusionary process. It is on these grounds, among others, that Jencks suggests that 'the use of credentials or tests scores to exclude "have not" groups from desirable jobs can be viewed in the same light as any other arbitrary form of discrimination'.[29]

Formal qualifications and certificates would appear to be a handy device for ensuring that those who possess 'cultural capital' are given the best opportunity to transmit the benefits of professional status to their own children. Credentials are usually supplied on the basis of tests designed to measure certain class-related qualities and attributes rather than those practical skills and aptitudes that may not so easily be passed on through the family line. It is illuminating in this respect to contrast the white-collar professions with the sporting and entertaining professions. What is especially remarkable about the latter is how relatively few of the children of successful footballers, boxers, baseball and tennis stars, or the celebrities of stage and screen have succeeded in reproducing their parents' elevated status. One reason for this would seem to be that the skills called for in these pursuits are of a kind that must be acquired and cultivated by the individual in the actual course of performance, and which are thus not easily transferred from parent to child. That is, there seems to be no equivalent to cultural capital that can be socially transmitted to the children of those gifted in the performing arts that could give them a head start in the fiercely competitive world of professional sport and show business. Presumably, if the rewards of professional sport could be more or less guaranteed along conventional career or bureaucratic lines serious proposals would eventually be put forward to limit entry to those candidates able to pass qualifying examinations in the theory of sporting science. This would have the desired effect of giving a competitive edge to those endowed with examination abilities over those merely excelling in the activity itself.[30]

The reason why professional sports, and the entertainment professions in general, are likely to be resistant to the 'diploma disease' offers a further instructive comment upon the nature of the white-collar professions. The supreme advantage of occupational closure based upon credentials is that all those in possession of a given qualification are deemed competent to provide the relevant skills and services for the rest of their professional lives. There is no question of retesting abilities at a later stage in the professional career. The professional bodies' careful insistence that members of the lay public are not competent to sit in judgement on professional standards effectively means that a final certificate is a meal ticket for life. In the sporting and entertainment professions, by contrast, the skills and abilities of the performers are kept under continuous open review by the public; those who consume the services are themselves the ultimate arbiters of an individual's competence and hence his market value, as expressed via their aggregate purchasing power. There can be no resort to the umbrella protection of a professional licence when sporting prowess and the ability to entertain are felt to be in decline in the eyes of those who pass collective judgement.

Against this exacting yardstick, then, credentialism stands out as a doubly effective device for protecting the learned professions from the hazards of the marketplace. Not merely does it serve the convenient purpose of monitoring and restricting the supply of labour, but also effectively masks all but the most extreme variations in the level of ability of professional members, thereby shielding the least competent from ruinous economic punishment. The small irony is that credentialist strategies aimed at neutralizing the competitive effects of the market confer most benefit upon that class that is most prone to trumpet the virtues of a free market economy and the sins of collectivism.

The use of systematic restrictions upon occupational entry has not of course been wholly confined to the white-collar professions. Certain skilled manual trades have adopted similar techniques designed to regulate supply, as in the case of the apprenticeship system or certain forms of the closed shop. Some unskilled occupations such as dock work and market-portering have also sought to restrict entry to the kinsmen of those already employed, though this does not normally guarantee control over the actual volume of labour supply. The crucial difference between these attempts at occupational exclusion by manual trades and those adopted by the professions is that the latter generally seek to establish a *legal monopoly* over the provision of services through licensure by the state. Whereas the learned profes-

sions have been remarkably successful in winning for themselves the status of what Weber calls 'legally privileged groups', it has been far less common for the manual trades to secure the blessing of the state for their exclusionary tactics. Indeed, the resort to 'restrictive practices' on the part of organized labour is commonly condemned as a breach of industrial morality that should be curbed rather than sanctified by law. Presumably the fact that governments have usually been reluctant to legislate formally against such practices is not unrelated to the awkwardness that might arise in drawing legal distinctions between these practices and the exclusionary devices of the professions, including the profession of law itself.

A further point of difference between professional closure and restrictive practices by trade unions is that the main purpose behind the latter activity has been the attempt to redress in some small part the disadvantages accruing to labour in its uneven contest with capital. Closure by skilled workers has been a strategy embarked upon in the course of struggle against a superior and highly organized opponent, and not primarily with the conscious intent of reducing the material opportunities of other members of the labour force. Credentialism, on the other hand, cannot be seen as a response to exploitation by powerful employers; the learned or free professions were never directly subordinate to an employing class during the period when they were effecting social closure. Their conflict, concealed beneath the rhetoric of professional ethics was, if anything, with the lay public. It was the struggle to establish a monopoly of certain forms of knowledge and practice and to win legal protection from lay interference. The aim was to ensure that the professional-client relationship was one in which the organized few confronted the disorganized many. Under modern conditions, where many professionals are indirectly in the service of the state and occasionally in conflict with the government of the day over pay and conditions, a somewhat better case could perhaps be made for likening the position of professions to that of craft unions, in so far as both could be said to employ closure for purposes of bargaining with a more powerful agency. But however acrimonious relations may become between professional bodies and the state, it is worth noting that the state rarely if ever threatens to take sanctions against professions in the way that would most seriously damage their interests—namely, by rescinding their legal monopoly.

On all these grounds it is necessary to regard credentialism as a form of exclusionary social closure comparable in its importance for class formation to the institution of property. Both entail the use of exclusionary rules that confer benefits and privileges on the few through denying access to the many, rules that are enshrined in law and upheld by the coercive authority of the state. It follows from this that the dominant class under modern capitalism can be thought of as comprising those who possess or control productive capital and those who possess a legal monopoly of professional services. These groups represent the core body of the dominant or exploiting class by virtue of their exclusionary powers which necessarily have the effect of creating a reciprocal class of social inferiors and subordinates. . . .

Class Reproduction

There is a definite tension between the commitment to closure by way of property and credentials on the part of one generation and the desire to pass on benefits to subsequent generations of kith and kin. It is not in the least necessary to deny that most members of the exclusionary class will strive to put their own advantages to the service of their children, while asserting at the same time that bourgeois forms of closure are not exactly tailor-made for self-recruiting purposes. In fact exclusionary institutions formed under capitalism do not seem to be designed first and foremost to solve the problem of class reproduction through the family line. The kin-

ship link can only be preserved as a result of *adaptation* by the bourgeois family to the demands of institutions designed to serve a different purpose; it does not come about as a natural consequence of the closure rules themselves. In systems based on aristocratic, caste, or racial exclusion, families of the dominant group can expect to pass on their privileged status to their own descendants as a direct result of the closure rules in operation, however socially lethargic those families might be. The bourgeois family, by contrast, cannot rest comfortably on the assumption of automatic class succession; it must make definite social exertions of its own or face the very real prospect of generational decline. In other words, although the typical bourgeois family will certainly be better equipped than most to cope with the closure system on its children's behalf, it must still approach the task more in the manner of a challenge with serious risks attached than as a foregone conclusion. Even when it is successful it must face the prospect of sharing bourgeois status with uncomfortably large numbers of parvenus. What kind of system is this to provoke such anxieties in the breasts of those supposedly in command?

The answer must be that it is a system designed to promote a class formation biased more in the direction of sponsorship and careful selection of successors than of hereditary transmission. Although *both* aims might be held desirable, the first takes ideological precedence over the second, so that succession along kinship lines must be accomplished in conformity with the application of criteria that are ostensibly indifferent to the claims of blood. There is nothing especially bizarre about an arrangement whereby a dominant class relinquishes its children's patrimony in order to ensure that the calibre of its replacements is of the highest possible order. It would only appear strange to those unable to conceive that the attachment to doctrine could ever take precedence over the claims of kinship. As Orwell noted in his discussion of communist party oligarchies:

'The essence of oligarchical rule is not father-to-son inheritance, but the persistence of a certain world-view and a certain way of life, imposed by the dead upon the living. A ruling group is a ruling group so long as it can nominate its successors. The Party is not concerned with perpetuating its blood but with perpetuating itself'.[31]

There are also powerful forces in capitalist society that are more dedicated to the perpetuation of bourgeois values than bourgeois blood. Ideological commitment to the rights of property and the value of credentials may be just as fierce as any faith in Leninist party principles. Each represents a set of ideals that can be held quite irrespective of the consequences upon the family fortunes of their advocates. The party militant's belief in a system of political selection and exclusion that could tell against his own ideologically wayward children has its counterpart in the liberal's belief in the validity of meritocratic criteria that would find against his not too clever offspring. It was perhaps examples of this kind that Weber had in mind when referring to patterns of closure distinguished by a 'rational commitment to values'. The same idea is also more than hinted at in Marx's well-known assertion that the bourgeoisie always puts the interests of the whole class above the interests of any of its individual members. These priorities are not, presumably, reversed whenever the individual members in question happen to be someone's children.

To suggest that predominant forms of closure under modern capitalism are in some tension with the common desire to transmit privileges to one's own is to point up politically significant differences of interpretation of bourgeois ideology. The classical liberal doctrine of individualism contains a powerful rejection of those principles and practices that evaluate men on the basis of group or collectivist criteria. The political driving force of individualist doctrines arose in part from the opposition of the emergent middle classes to aristocratic pretensions and exclusiveness

centred around the notion of descent. The emphasis upon lineage was an obvious hindrance to those who had raised themselves into the ranks of property by way of industry and commerce, but who lacked the pedigree necessary to enter the charmed circles inhabited by those of political power and social honour. Although non-landed wealth could occasionally be cleansed through marriage into the nobility, the new rising class sought to make property respectable in its own right by divorcing it from its associations with particular status groups. Property in all its forms was to become the hallmark of moral worth without reference back, as it were, to the quality of proprietorial blood. In the individualist credo, property thus assumed the same characteristic as money in the marketplace, where the ability to pay overrides all questions as to the actual source of the buyer's cash. . . .

One reason for pressing the distinction between collectivist and individualist criteria underlying all forms of exclusion is to suggest that subordinate classes or strata are likely to differ in their political character according to which of the two sets of criteria is predominant. Looked at in ideal-typical terms, purely collectivist types of exclusion, such as those based on race, religion, ethnicity, and so on, would produce a subordinate group of a communal character—that is, one defined in terms of a total all-encompassing negative status. Blacks under *apartheid* or minority groups herded into religious and racial ghettoes are the familiar modern examples. The polar archetypal case would be that of exclusion based solely on individualist criteria, giving rise to a subordinate group marked by intense social fragmentation and inchoateness. The example here is furnished by the model of a pure meritocracy in which class is virtually replaced by a condition of discrete segmental statuses never quite reaching the point of coalescence. In non-fictional societies, of course, individualist and collectivist criteria are usually applied in some combination or other, so producing stratified systems located at various points between these two extremes. This can be depicted in simplified form as follows:

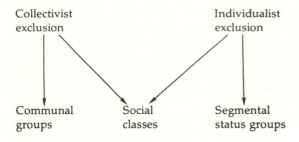

Thus, of the three major types of subordination, classes are presented as a combination of both types of exclusionary criteria. Schematically, a subordinate class could be located towards either of the opposite poles according to the relative weighting of the two sets of criteria. The proletariat of early and mid-nineteenth century Europe, for example, would approximate to the communal pole by virtue of its wholesale exclusion from civil society arising from the treatment of its members as a *de facto* collectivity. The badge of proletarian status carried with it the kinds of stigmata commonly associated with subordinate racial and ethnic groups. It was a total condition which permitted little leeway for the cultivation of those small part-time identities that bring temporary release from the humilities of servile status. Correspondingly, of course, the proletarian condition under communal exclusion offered fertile ground for movements and ideologies which raised large questions about the nature of the political order and its legitimacy, and not merely about the fact of unequal shares.

It is the very hallmark of the communal condition that subordination is experienced through a myriad of direct personal degradations and affronts to human dignity, encouraged by the submersion of the individual into the stereotype of his 'membership' group. It is largely as a result of this that the politics of communal exclusion so frequently stresses the need for subordinate groups to create an alternative moral identity to that fashioned for them by their oppressors. Although the condition of the early proletariat was never completely of a communal kind, it was not so different from that of a despised ethnic group, if only because the visible signs and trappings of status were as unmistakably clear as racial features. Certainly the mixture of horror, fear, and revulsion felt by the upper classes for the great unwashed was not a far remove from the sentiments usually held by dominant racial or ethnic groups towards those whom they simultaneously exploit and despise.

To speak of a gradual shift in the nature of exclusionary rules, from collectivism to individualism, is thus to point to those tendencies making for the progressive erosion of the communal components of proletarian status, otherwise referred to as working-class incorporation into civil society. Although under advanced capitalism labour remains an exploited commodity, the status of the worker does not derive to anything like the same extent from his immersion in a total collective identity and its accompanying rituals of personal degradation. Mills' portrayal of the pattern of 'status cycles' by which the modern urban worker is able to find escape in class anonymity during leisure periods and vacations may be somewhat overdrawn;[32] but there is a real sense in which the absence of clearly visible and unambiguous marks of inferior status has made the enforcement of an all-pervasive deference system almost impossible to sustain outside the immediate work situation. It would now take an unusually sharp eye to detect the social class of Saturday morning shoppers in the High Street, whereas to any earlier generation it would have been the most elementary task. More to the point, even assuming that a lynx-eyed bourgeois could accurately spot a worker in mufti, what real hope could he now entertain of having any claim to deference actually honoured? A system of deference can only operate effectively when the status of strangers can accurately be judged, and the information required for this is difficult to come by without the aid of a collectivist stereotype. In this respect the personal dignity of the modern worker has been enhanced by the evolution towards individualist exclusion, even though his subordination to capital remains a central fact of life.

As class subordination becomes increasingly less communal in character, the political ideals and programmes that flourish among its members tend to become less inspired by visions of a new moral order and the promise of emancipation, and rather more preoccupied with the issues of distributive justice. Those who deplore the apparent flickering of those energies and passions that produced nineteenth-century socialism might care to reflect on the possibility that this has less to do with the iniquities of working-class leadership than with the system of modern exploitation, in which the engines of political resentment are not so lavishly fuelled by the personal degradations arising from wholesale collectivist exclusion. . . .

Conclusion

By way of concluding this part of the discussion, it might be appropriate to offer some general remarks on the explanatory status of the closure model. This model, like any other, recommends the use of a particular sociological vocabulary and an attendant battery of concepts that contain barely disguised moral assumptions about the nature of class society. It is not strictly speaking a 'theory' of class but a way of conceptualizing it that differs from that proposed by other variants of bourgeois sociology or by Marxism. Most of what we conventionally call theories of class are in fact conceptual methods of this kind. They are, for the most part, take-it-or-leave-it moral classifications, not sets of propositions that stand or fall under the impact of evidence. What conceivable social facts could destroy either the Marxist conception of class as an exploitative relationship, or the liberal conception of class as an exchange relationship? Since conceptual models are ways of presenting social reality, it follows that the preference for one presentation over another

entails a personal judgement of some kind about the moral standing of class society.

On this score, the closure model is almost bound to appear defective by liberal and Marxist theorists alike. Liberal theory endorses a contractual view of class, in which the notion of mutual interest and harmony is the essential ingredient. Marxism, on the other hand, assumes not merely the absence of harmony and common class interests, but, more importantly, the presence of irresolvable antagonisms that drive the system to ultimate breakdown. The neo-Weberian position advanced here is that the relation between classes is neither one of harmony and mutual benefit, nor of irresolvable and fatal contradiction. Rather, the relationship is understood as one of mutual antagonism and permanent *tension;* that is, a condition of unrelieved distributive struggle that is not necessarily impossible to 'contain'. Class conflict may be without cease, but it is not inevitably fought to a conclusion. The competing notions of harmony, contradiction, and tension could thus be thought of as the three broad possible ways of conceptualizing the relation between classes, and on which all class models are grounded.

Since class models are not subject to direct empirical assault, the case for advancing the cause of one in preference to another rests partly on the claim that it draws attention to a set of problems and issues that are otherwise obscured. Thus, one of the attractions of the closure model is that it highlights the fact of communal cleavage and its relationship to class, and seeks to analyse both within the same conceptual framework. More generally, it proposes that intra-class relations be treated as conflict phenomena of the same general order as inter-class relations, and not as mere disturbances or complications within a 'pure' class model. Hence the extension of the concept of exploitation to cover both sets of phenomena. There is, in addition, a recommendation that social classes be defined by reference to their mode of collective action rather than to their place in the productive process or the division of labour. The reason for this is that incumbency of position in a formally defined structure does not normally correspond to class alignment where it really counts—at the level of organized political sentiment and conduct. This serious lack of fit between all positional or systemic definitions of class and the actual behaviour of classes in the course of distributive struggle, is not due to any lack othe categories employed. It arises from the initial theoretical decision to discount the significance and effect of variations in the cultural and social make-up of the groups assigned to the categories in question. Models constructed upon such formal, systemic definitions require of their advocates much ingenuity in accounting for the continuous and wholesale discrepancies between class position and class behaviour. A good deal of the intellectual energy of western Marxism has been dissipated in wrestling with this very problem which is of its own conceptual making.

Notes

1. The hospital setting provides, perhaps, the most important exception. Industrial conflicts between medical staff and the manual workers' unions over issues such as 'pay beds' are unusual in having clear-cut ideological, rather than bread-and-butter, causes.
2. Carchedi 1975:48. For Braverman, too, managers and executives are 'part of the class that personifies capital . . .' (1974:405).
3. Dahrendorf 1959.
4. Braverman 1974: Chapter 18.
5. Westergaard and Resler 1975:92.
6. Westergaard and Resler 1975:346.
7. Weber (eds Roth and Wittich) 1968:342.
8. Weber (eds Roth and Wittich) 1968:342.
9. Weber (eds Roth and Wittich) 1968:342.
10. Neuwirth 1969.
11. These arguments were first tentatively sketched out in my 'Strategies of Social Closure in Class Formation' (Parkin 1974). In that publication the two types of closure were referred to as *exclusion* and *solidarism*. This latter term does not, however, satisfactorily describe a mode of collective action standing in direct opposition to exclusion, since solidaristic behaviour can itself be used for blatantly exclusionary ends. That is to say, solidarism does not properly refer to the purposes for which power is employed. The term *usurpation*

more adequately captures the notion of collective action designed to improve the lot of a subordinate group at the expense of a dominant group. Solidarism is simply one means among others to this end.

12. Weber (eds Gerth and Mills) 1948:182.
13. Davis and Moore 1945:247.
14. Durkheim 1957:174.
15. Durkheim 1957:175 and 217.
16. Durkheim 1957:213.
17. Plamenatz 1975:120.
18. Plamenatz 1975:121.
19. Plamenatz 1975:121.
20. Parsons 1951:119. The entry in the index under 'Property' invites the reader to 'see Possessions'.
21. Rose *et al.* 1976:703.
22. Durkheim 1957:142.
23. Durkheim 1957:142.
24. Macpherson 1973.
25. Weber (eds Gerth and Mills) 1948:241–42.
26. Weber (eds Roth and Wittich) 1968:344.
27. Dore 1976.
28. Berg 1973.
29. Jencks 1972:192.
30. It transpires that the idea is not so far-fetched after all. The Council for National Academic Awards has recently approved the syllabus for a BA Degree in Sports Studies. Undergraduates will be instructed in 'the variables influencing performance in sport; a science and its sports application; scientific methods, statistics and computing; and wide practical experience in a number of sports.' *Daily Telegraph*, Monday, 28 August 1978, p. 3.
31. Orwell 1949:215.
32. Mills 1956:257–58.

Bibliography

Berg, I. (1973) *Education and Jobs: The Great Training Robbery*. Harmondsworth: Penguin Books.

Braverman, H. (1974) *Labor and Monopoly Capital*. New York: Monthly Review Press.

Carchedi, G. (1975) On the Economic Identification of the New Middle Class. *Economy and Society* 4 (1).

Dahrendorf, R. (1959) *Class and Class Conflict in Industrial Society*. London: Routledge.

Davis, K. and Moore, W. E. (1945) Some Principles of Stratification. *American Sociological Review* X (2).

Dore, R. (1976) *The Diploma Disease*. London: Allen and Unwin.

Durkheim, E. (1957) *Professional Ethics and Civic Morals*. London: Routledge.

Jencks, C. (1972) *Inequality*. New York: Basic Books.

Macpherson, C. B. (1973) A Political Theory of Property. In *Democratic Theory: Essays in Retrieval*. Oxford University Press.

Mills, C. W. (1956) *White Collar*. New York: Oxford University Press.

Neuwirth, G. (1969) A Weberian Outline of a Theory of Community: Its Application to the 'Dark Ghetto'. *British Journal of Sociology* 20 (2).

Orwell, G. (1949) *Nineteen Eighty-Four*. London: Secker and Warburg.

Parkin, F. (ed.) (1974) *The Social Analysis of Class Structure*. London: Tavistock.

Parsons, T. (1951) *The Social System*. London: Routledge.

Plamenatz, J. (1975) *Karl Marx's Philosophy of Man*. Oxford: Clarendon Press.

Rose, D., Saunders, P., Newby, H., and Bell, C. (1976) Ideologies of Property: A Case Study. *Sociological Review* 24 (4).

Weber, M. (1945) *From Max Weber*. Gerth, H. H. and Mills, C. W. (eds) London: Routledge.

———. (1968) *Economy and Society*. Roth, G. and Wittich, C. (eds) New York: Bedminster Press.

Westergaard, J. and Resler, H. (1975) *Class in a Capitalist Society*. London: Heinemann.

EMILE DURKHEIM

The Division of Labor in Society

In *The Division of Labor in Society,* we emphasise the state of legal and moral anomie in which economic life exists at the present time. In fact, in this particular sphere of activity, professional ethics only exist in a very rudimentary state. There are professional ethics for the lawyer and magistrate, the soldier and professor, the doctor and priest, etc. Yet if we attempted to express in somewhat more precise terms contemporary ideas of what should be the relationship between employer and white-collar worker, between the industrial worker and the factory boss, between industrialists in competition with one another or between industrialists and the public, how imprecise would be the statements that we could formulate! Some vague generalities about the loyalty and commitment that employees of every kind owe to those who employ them, or about the moderation that employers should manifest in exercising their economic superiority, a certain condemnation of any competition that is too blatantly unfair, or of any too glaring exploitation of the consumer: this is almost the sum total of what the ethical consciousness of these professions comprises. Moreover, most of these precepts lack any juridical character. They are backed only by

public opinion and not by the law—and it is well known how indulgent that opinion shows itself to be about the way in which such vague obligations are fulfilled. Those actions most blameworthy are so often excused by success that the boundary between the permissible and the prohibited, between what is just and what is unjust, is no longer fixed in any way, but seems capable of being shifted by individuals in an almost arbitrary fashion. So vague a morality, one so inconsistent, cannot constitute any kind of discipline. The upshot is that this entire sphere of collective life is for the most part removed from the moderating action of any rules.

It is to this state of anomie that must be attributed the continually recurring conflicts and disorders of every kind of which the economic world affords so sorry a spectacle. For, since nothing restrains the forces present from reacting together, or prescribes limits for them that they are obliged to respect, they tend to grow beyond all bounds, each clashing with the other, each warding off and weakening the other. . . .

Political society as a whole, or the state, clearly cannot draw up the system of rules that is now lacking. Economic life, because it is very special and is daily becoming increasingly specialised, lies outside their authority and sphere of action. Activity within a profession can only be effectively regulated through a group close enough to that profession to be thoroughly cognisant of how it functions, capable of perceiving all its needs and following every fluctuation in them. The sole group that meets these conditions is that constituted by

Originally published in 1984. Please see complete source information beginning on page 891.

all those working in the same industry, assembled together and organised in a single body. This is what is termed a corporation, or professional group.

Yet in the economic field the professional group no more exists than does a professional ethic. Since the last century when, *not without reason,* the ancient corporations were dissolved, hardly more than fragmentary and incomplete attempts have been made to reconstitute them on a different basis. Doubtless, individuals who are busy in the same trade are in contact with one another by the very fact that their activities are similar. Competition with one another engenders mutual relationships. But these are in no way regular; depending upon chance meetings, they are very often entirely of an individual nature. One industrialist finds himself in contact with another, but the body of industrialists in some particular speciality do not meet to act in concert. Exceptionally, we do see all members of the same profession come together at a conference to deal with some problem of common interest. But such conferences last only a short while: they do not survive the particular circumstances that gave rise to them. Consequently the collective life for which they provided an opportunity dies more or less entirely with them. . . .

Can we legitimately believe that corporative organisation is called upon to play in contemporary societies a more considerable part? If we deem it indispensable it is not because of the services it might render the economy, but on account of the moral influence it could exercise. What we particularly see in the professional grouping is a moral force capable of curbing individual egoism, nurturing among workers a more envigorated feeling of their common solidarity, and preventing the law of the strongest from being applied too brutally in industrial and commercial relationships. Yet such a grouping is deemed unfit for such a role. Because it springs from temporal interests, it can seemingly only serve utilitarian ends, and the memories that survive of the corporations during the *ancien régime* only confirm this impression. We incline to vizualise them in the future as they were towards the end of their former existence, intent above all on maintaining or increasing their privileges and monopolies. We fail to see how such narrow vocational concerns might have any beneficial effect upon the morality of the corporation or its members.

However, we should refrain from extending to the entire corporative system what may have been true of certain corporations during a very short period in their development. Far from the system having been, because of its very constitution, infected by a kind of moral sickness, during the greater part of its existence it played above all a moral role. This is especially evident with the Roman corporation. 'Among the Romans,' declares Walzing, 'the corporations of artisans were far from having so pronounced a professional character as in the Middle Ages. We come across no regulations concerning methods, no obligatory apprenticeship, and no monopoly. Nor was their purpose to accumulate the capital necessary to exploit an industry.'[1] Doubtless their associating together gave them more power to safeguard the common interest, when the need arose. But this was only one of the useful by-products that the institution engendered. It was not the justification for its existence, nor its main function. Above all else, the corporation was a collegiate religious body. Each one possessed its own particular god, who, when the means were available, was worshipped in a special temple. Just as every family had its *Lar familiaris* and every city its *Genius publicus,* so every collegiate body had its protecting divinity, the *Genius collegii.* Naturally this professional form of worship was not without its festivities, and sacrifices and banquets were celebrated in common together. Moreover, all kinds of circumstances would serve as the occasion for festive gatherings; distribution of food and money was often made at the expense of the community. . . .

The facts cited adequately demonstrate that a professional grouping is not at all incapable of exerting a moral effect. The very important place that religion held in its life highlights very particularly the true nature of its functions, for in such times every religious community constituted a moral environment, just as every kind of moral discipline necessarily tended to take on a religious form. Moreover, this characteristic of corporative organisation is due to the effect of very general causes which we can see at work in different circumstances. Within a political society, as soon as a certain number of individuals find they hold in common ideas, interests, sentiments and occupations which the rest of the population does not share in, it is inevitable that, under the influence of these similarities, they should be attracted to one another. They will seek one another out, enter into relationships and associate together. Thus a restricted group is gradually formed within society as a whole, with its own special features. Once such a group is formed, a moral life evolves within it which naturally bears the distinguishing mark of the special conditions in which it has developed. It is impossible for men to live together and be in regular contact with one another without their acquiring some feeling for the group which they constitute through having united together, without their becoming attached to it, concerning themselves with its interests and taking it into account in their behaviour. And this attachment to something that transcends the individual, this subordination of the particular to the general interest, is the very well-spring of all moral activity. Let this sentiment only crystallise and grow more determinate, let it be translated into well-defined formulas by being applied to the most common circumstances of life, and we see gradually being constituted a corpus of moral rules.

Domestic morality did not arise any differently. Because of the prestige that the family retains in our eyes, if it appears to us to have been and continue to be a school of altruism and abnegation, the highest seat of morality, it is through the very special characteristics it is privileged to possess, ones that could not be found at any level elsewhere. We like to believe that in blood kinship there exists an extraordinarily powerful reason for moral iden-

tification with others. But, as we have often had occasion to show,[2] blood kinship has in no way the extraordinary effectiveness attributed to it. The proof of this is that in a large number of societies relations not linked by the blood tie are very numerous in a family. Thus so-called artificial kinship is entered into very readily and has all the effects of natural kinship. Conversely, very frequently those closely knit by ties of blood are morally and legally strangers to one another. For example, this is true of blood kin in the Roman family. Thus the family does not derive its whole strength from unity of descent. Quite simply, it is a group of individuals who have drawn close to one another within the body politic through a very specially close community of ideas, feelings and interests. Blood kinship was able to make such a concentration of individuals easier, for it naturally tends to have the effect of bringing different consciousnesses together. Yet many other factors have also intervened: physical proximity, solidarity of interest, the need to unite to fight a common danger, or simply to unite, have been causes of a different kind which have made people come together.

Such causes are not peculiar to the family but are to be found, although in different forms, within the corporation. Thus if the former group has played so important a role in the moral history of humanity, why should not also the latter be capable of so doing? Undoubtedly one difference will always exist between them, inasmuch as family members share in common their entire existence, whereas the members of a corporation share only their professional concerns. The family is a kind of complete society whose influence extends to economic activity as well as to that of religion, politics, and science, etc. Everything of any importance that we do, even outside the home, has repercussions upon it and sparks off an appropriate reaction. In one sense the corporation's sphere of influence is more limited. Yet we must not forget the ever more important place that our profession assumes in our lives as work becomes increasingly segmented. . . .

What past experience demonstrates above all is that the organisational framework of the professional group should always be related to that of economic life. It is because this condition was not fulfilled that the system of corporations disappeared. Thus, since the market, from being municipal as it once was, has become national and international, the corporation should assume the same dimensions. Instead of being restricted exclusively to the artisans of one town, it must grow so as to include all the members of one profession scattered over the whole country,[3] for in whatever region they may be, whether they live in town or countryside, they are all linked to one another and share a common life. Since this common life is in certain respects independent of any territorial boundaries, a suitable organism must be created to give expression to this life and to regulate its functions. Because of the dimensions that it assumes, such an organism should necessarily be closely in contact and directly linked with the central organism of the life of the collectivity. Events important enough to affect a whole category of industrial enterprises within a country necessarily have wide repercussions of which the state cannot fail to be aware. This impels it to intervene. Thus for good reason the royal power tended instinctively not to leave large-scale industry outside its ambit as soon as it appeared. It could not fail to take an interest in a form of activity which by its very nature is always liable to affect society as a whole. Yet such regulatory action, although necessary, should not degenerate into utter subordination, as happened in the seventeenth and eighteenth centuries. The two organisms, although in contact with each other, should remain distinct and autonomous; each has functions that it alone can perform. If it falls to political assemblies to lay down the general principles for industrial legislation, they are not capable of diversifying them according to the various types of industry. It is this diversification that is the corporation's proper task.[4] A unitary organisation over a whole country also in no way precludes the formation of secondary organisations which include similar workers in the same region or locality. Their role could be to spell out even more specifically, in accordance with local or regional needs, the regulations for a profession. Thus economic activity could be regulated and demarcated without losing any of its diversity.

Moreover, we must reject the belief that the corporation's sole role should consist in laying down and applying rules. It is undoubtedly true that wherever a group is formed, a moral discipline is also formed. But the institution of that discipline is only one of the numerous ways in which any collective activity manifests itself. A group is not only a moral authority regulating the life of its members, but also a source of life *sui generis*. From it there arises a warmth that quickens or gives fresh life to each individual, which makes him disposed to empathise, causing selfishness to melt away. Thus in the past the family has been responsible for legislating a code of law and morality whose severity has often been carried to an extreme of harshness. But it has also been the environment where, for the first time, men have learnt to appreciate the outpouring of feeling. We have likewise seen how the corporation, both in Rome and during the Middle Ages, created these same needs and sought to satisfy them. The corporations of the future will be assigned even greater and more complex functions, because of their increased scope. Around their purely professional functions will be grouped others which at present are exercised by the communes and private associations. Among these are functions of mutual assistance which, in order to be entirely fulfilled, assume between helpers and helped feelings of solidarity as well as a certain homogeneity of intellect and morals, such as that readily engendered by the exercise of the same profession. Many educational activities (technical education, adult education, etc.) should also, it seems, find in the corporation their natural habitat. The same is also true for a certain type of artistic activity. It would seem in accordance with the nature of things that such a noble form of diversion and recreation should develop alongside the more serious aspects of life, acting as a balancing and restorative influence. In fact we now already see trade unions acting at the same time as friendly societies, and others are setting up communal centres where courses are organised, and concerts and dramatic performances held. Hence the activity of a corporation can take on the most varied forms.

We may even reasonably suppose that the corporation will be called upon to become the foundation, or one of the essential foundations, of our political organisation. We have seen that, although it first began outside the social system, it tended to become more and more closely involved in it as economic life developed. We have therefore every reason to anticipate that, if progress continues on the same lines, the corporation is destined to assume an ever more central and preponderant place in society. It was once the elementary division of communal organisation. Now that the commune, from being the autonomous unit that it once was, has been absorbed into the state just as the municipal market was absorbed into the national market, may we not legitimately think that the corporation should also undergo a corresponding transformation and become the elementary division of the state, the basic political unit? Society, instead of remaining what it is today—a conglomerate of land masses juxtaposed together— would become a vast system of national corporations. The demand is raised in various quarters for electoral colleges to be constituted by professions and not by territorial constituencies. Certainly in this way political assemblies would more accurately reflect the diversity of social interests and their interconnections. They would more exactly epitomise social life as a whole. Yet if we state that the country, in order to become conscious of itself, should be grouped by professions, is not this to acknowledge that the organised profession or the corporation should become the essential organ of public life?

In this way a serious gap in the structure of European societies, and in our own in particular, would be filled. We shall see how, as history unfolds, an organisation based on territorial groupings (village, town, district or province, etc.) becomes progressively weaker. There is no doubt that we each belong to a commune or a *département,* but the ties binding us to them become daily more loose and tenuous. These geographical divisions are in the main artificial, and no longer arouse deep emotions within us. The provincial spirit has vanished beyond recall. 'Parish pump' patriotism has become an anachronism that cannot be restored at will. Strictly local or *département* matters hardly affect or enthrall us either any longer, save in so far as they go hand in hand with matters relating to our profession. Our activity extends much beyond these groups, which are too narrow for it; moreover, much of what happens within them leaves us indifferent. Thus what might be described as the spontaneous collapse of the old social structure has occurred. But this internal organisation cannot disappear without something taking its place. A society made up of an extremely large mass of unorganised individuals, which an overgrown state attempts to limit and restrain, constitutes a veritable sociological monstrosity. For collective activity is always too complex to be capable of finding expression in the one single organ of the state. Moreover, the state is too remote from individuals, its connections with them too superficial and irregular, to be able to penetrate the depths of their consciousness and socialise them from within. This is why, when the state constitutes the sole environment in which men can fit themselves for the business of living in common, they inevitably 'contract out', detaching themselves from one another, and thus society disintegrates to a corresponding extent. A nation cannot be maintained unless, between the state and individuals, a whole range of secondary groups are interposed. These must be close enough to the individual to attract him strongly to their activities and, in so doing, to absorb him into the mainstream of social life. We have just demonstrated how professional groupings are fitted to perform this role, and how indeed everything marks them out for it. Hence we can comprehend how important it is, particularly in the economic sphere, that they should emerge from that inchoate and disorganised state in which they have lain for a century, since professions of this kind today absorb the greater part of the energies of society.[5]

Notes

1. Waltzing, *Etude historique sur les corporations profession chez les Romains,* vol. I, p. 194.
2. Cf. especially *Année sociologique,* vol. I, pp. 313 ff.
3. We need not discuss the international organisation which, because of the international character of the market, would necessarily develop at a level above that of the national organisation. For at present the latter alone can constitute a legal entity. In the present state of European law the former can only result from arrangements freely concluded between national corporations.
4. This specialisation could not occur without the help of elected assemblies charged with representing the corporation. In the present state of industry, these assemblies, as well as those tribunals entrusted with the task of applying the regulations of an occupation, should clearly include representatives of employees and employers, as is already the case with the industrial arbitration tribunals. The proportion of each should correspond to the respective importance attributed by public opinion to these two factors of production. But if it is necessary for both sides to meet on the governing councils of the corporation it is no less indispensable for them to constitute distinct and independent groups at the lower level of corporative organisation, because too often their interests vie with one another and are opposing. To feel that they exist freely, they must be aware of their separate existence. The two bodies so constituted can then appoint their representatives to the common assemblies.
5. Moreover, we do not mean that territorial constitutencies are destined to disappear completely, but only that they will fade into the background. Old institutions never vanish in the face of new ones to such an extent that they leave no trace of themselves. They persist not only by the mere fact of survival, but also because there persists some trace of the needs to which they corresponded. Material proximity will always constitute a link between men. Consequently the political and social organisation based on territory will certainly subsist. But it will no longer enjoy its present predominance, precisely because that link is losing some of its force. What is more, we have shown above that, even at the base of the corporation will still be found geographical divisions. Moreover, between the various corporations from a same locality or region there will necessarily be special relationships of solidarity which will, from time to time, demand an appropriate organisation.

DAVID B. GRUSKY AND JESPER B. SØRENSEN

Are There Big Social Classes?

The study of social class has a volatile history in which waves of creative class analytic scholarship are interspersed with periods of cynicism about the class analytic enterprise. In the present cynical phase, criticisms of both Marxian and non-Marxian class analysis continue to escalate, with many commentators now feeling bold enough to argue that the concept of class is "ceasing to do any useful work for sociology" (Pahl 1989, p. 710; also, Pakulski and Waters 1996; Clark and Lipset 1991). By way of response, the most ardent defenders of class models have simply reaffirmed the class analytic status quo, albeit sometimes with the concession that class-based formulations now apply in rather weakened form (e.g., Wright 1996; Hout, Brooks, and Manza 1993; Goldthorpe and Marshall 1992). The debate between these two camps has proceeded along stylized lines. Indeed, although the literature is well stocked

Originally published in 1998. Please see complete source information beginning on page 891.

with all manner of defense and critique of conventional class analysis, there have been few, if any, truly constructive efforts to refashion class analysis.

Against this intellectual backdrop, we have recently suggested that critics of class analysis have too quickly dismissed the power of class analytic language, whereas defenders of class analysis have not appreciated that such language, for all its power, yields little insight when applied to conventional, highly aggregate social classes (see Grusky and Sørensen 1998; Grusky 1999; Grusky and Weeden forthcoming). This formulation leads to the prescription that class analysis should be ratcheted down to an analytic level where real social groupings (i.e., "occupations") form around functional niches in the division of labor. The great virtue of disaggregating is that the nominal categories of conventional class analysis can be replaced by *Gemeinschaftlich* groupings that are embedded in the very fabric of society and are thereby meaningful not merely to sociologists but to the lay public as well.

The foregoing line of argument is not entirely without precedent. Indeed, whenever sociologists have turned their attention to the professions (e.g., Abbott 1988), the longstanding tendency has been to emphasize the great heterogeneity and sectional divisiveness within this (putative) new class. The recent commentary of Freidson (1986) is illustrative here: "The range of education, income, and prestige of the professional occupations in question . . . [makes] it hard to imagine them sharing a common culture of any significance, a common set of material interests, or a common inclination to act politically in the same fashion and direction" (p. 57). Although this critique is surely of interest, it falls short of our own position insofar as it pertains only to the professional sector and fails to engage more broadly with contemporary anticlass critiques. In similar fashion, stratification scholars are currently quite interested in "unpacking" conventional class categories (Marshall et al. 1988), yet the ultimate objective

has invariably been to argue for some new and preferred form of *reaggregation*.

We would be hard-pressed, then, to locate a direct line of intellectual heritage. If forced to identify a partial and approximate one, the principal inspiration would have to be scholars such as Durkheim ([1893] 1933), Bourdieu (1984), and their intellectual descendants (e.g., Lamont 1992; also, Freidson 1994; Van Maanen and Barley 1984). Under the Durkheimian developmental model, occupational associations come to serve as important intermediaries between the modern state and individual, yet they play a largely integrative role and eschew the more partisan behavior of "maintaining or increasing privileges and monopolies" (Durkheim [1893] 1933, p. 10). Likewise, Bourdieu (1984) has argued that sociologists should "rethink Weber's opposition between class and *Stand*" (p. xii), but his recent empirical work emphasizes the cultural rather than economic implications of occupational closure. This work is nonetheless distinguished by its relatively detailed analyses; that is, Bourdieu resorts to disaggregate data in characterizing the habitus and the lifestyles it generates, because the conditions of existence of conventional aggregate classes are assumed to be unacceptably heterogeneous. In our own analysis, we shall similarly insist on extreme disaggregation, yet we regard the resulting occupations as economic and cultural groupings that constitute precisely that unification of "class and *Stand*" that Bourdieu (1984) so ambitiously sought.

The Case for Disaggregation

The following discussion summarizes the main virtues of disaggregation in understanding patterns of class identification, social closure, collective action, and lifestyles and attitudes. For each of these topics, our summary of the conceptual rationale for disaggregation will be brief, as more comprehensive analyses can be found elsewhere (see Grusky and

Sørensen 1998; Grusky 1999; Grusky and Weeden forthcoming).

Class Identification

We can usefully begin by considering the subjective domain of stratification as revealed in patterns of class identification and awareness. Although some sociologists remain convinced that contemporary identities are strongly shaped by aggregate affiliations (e.g., Marshall et al. 1988), the prevailing post-Marxist position is that conventional classes now have only a weak hold over workers. For example, Emmison and Western (1990) report that only 7 percent of all Australians regard their social class as a "very important" identity, whereas other commentators (e.g., Saunders 1989) have stressed that open-ended queries about class identification tend to yield confused responses, refusals to answer, and even explicit denials that classes exist. This evidence has led many sociologists to conclude that class is now a "passive identity" (Bradley 1996, p. 72) and that the realm of production is no longer the principal locus of identity formation.

We regard such accounts as overreactive to concerns that, although legitimate, surely do not require abandoning class analysis altogether. The Emmison–Western results are again revealing on this point, because they indicate that detailed occupations continue to be one of the main social identities for contemporary workers (see Emmison and Western 1990, pp. 247–48). This result should come as no surprise; after all, occupational categories are deeply embedded in the institutions of advanced industrialism, whereas aggregate classes are highly abstract constructs that are evidently more appealing to academics than to workers, employers, or the state. As Treiman (1977) notes, workers invariably represent their career aspirations in occupational terms, while professional and vocational schools train workers for occupationally defined skills, and employers construct and advertise jobs in terms of corresponding occupational designations. The class analytic fallacy thus amounts to insisting on aggregate categories even when disaggregate ones are more deeply institutionalized and hence subjectively more salient.

Social Closure

If subjectivist models of class were once dominant in sociology (e.g., Warner, Meeker, and Eells 1949), they have now been superseded by analytic approaches that focus on the social processes by which class membership is restricted to qualified eligibles (Freidson 1994, pp. 80–84; Murphy 1988; Collins 1979; Parkin 1979; Weber [1922] 1968). These models emphasize not only the institutionalized means by which closure is secured (e.g., private property, credentials, licenses) but also the efforts of excluded parties to challenge these institutions and the inequality that they maintain. Although closure theory provides, then, a new sociological language for understanding interclass relations, the actual class mappings posited by closure theorists have proven to be standard aggregate fare. The two-class solution proposed, for example, by Parkin (1979, p. 58) features an exclusionary class comprising those who control productive capital and professional services and a subordinate class comprising all those who are excluded from these positions of control.

We might usefully ask whether an aggregate formulation is fundamental to closure theory or merely superfluous adjunct. The latter interpretation strikes us as more plausible; that is, if closure theory could somehow be reinvented without the coloration of class analytic convention, its authors would likely emphasize that the real working institutions of closure (i.e., professional associations, craft unions) are largely local associations "representing the credential-holders themselves" (Murphy 1988, p. 174). These associations establish and enforce local jurisdictional settlements that prevent other occupations from providing competing services. In most cases, the associated closure devices (e.g., licensing, credentialling, apprenticeships) do not govern entry to aggregate classes, but instead serve only to control entry (and exit) at the more detailed occupational level. By contrast, there are no analogous organizations that represent aggregate classes, nor are there jurisdictional settlements or closure devices that are truly aggregate in scope. This conclusion implies that conventional aggregate mappings of "exploitation classes" (e.g., Wright 1985) conceal the highly disaggregate level at which rent is extracted and interests are formed (see Sørensen 1996; 1994). Indeed, given that unions and associations establish local rather than classwide restrictions on labor supply, the "rent" that is thereby generated should create interests principally at the disaggregate level.

Collective Action

For most neo-Marxists, social closure is of interest not because it provides a vehicle for pursuing purely local concerns (i.e., "trade union consciousness"), but rather because it allegedly facilitates the development of classwide interests and grander forms of interclass conflict. The aggregate classes identified by contemporary sociologists have so far shown a decided reluctance to act in accord with such theorizing. This quiescence at the aggregate level has led to considerable neo-Marxian handwringing as well as more radical claims that postmodern interests are increasingly defined and established outside the realm of production (e.g., Laraña, Johnston, and Gusfield 1994). The latter form of postmodernism, popular as it is, overlooks the simple fact that much collective action flows unproblematically out of structurally defined groupings, albeit only when those groupings are defined in less aggregate terms than is conventionally the case. The three principal types of collective action at the level of unit occupations are (a) downwardly directed closure strategies designed to restrict access to occupational positions, (b) lateral competitive struggles between occupational associations

over functional niches in the division of labor, and (c) upwardly directed collective action oriented toward securing occupation-specific benefits (e.g., monopoly protection) from the state and from employers. We thus concur with Krause (1971, p. 87) that "there has historically been more occupation-specific consciousness and action than cross-occupational combination" (also, see Freidson 1994, pp. 75–91).

This is not to suggest that local conflict at the unit occupational level drives the course of human history. To the contrary, local associations typically pursue sectional objectives, and the wider systemic effects of such microlevel conflict are neither obvious nor necessarily profound (cf. Durkheim [1893] 1933). We might conclude, then, that our disaggregate class analysis is an intellectually modest project, but it bears noting that aggregate class analysts have likewise scaled back their ambitions and effectively discarded comprehensive class-based theories of history (e.g., Goldthorpe and Marshall 1992, p. 385).

Class Outcomes

In this sense, the class analytic project is becoming gradually more limited in its objectives, with many contemporary scholars now satisfied to merely document that class membership conditions individual-level outcomes of all kinds (e.g., attitudes, voting behavior, lifestyles). The resulting analyses typically examine either the categorical effects of aggregate classes or the gradational effects of variables that represent the many dimensions (e.g., socioeconomic status, substantive complexity) underlying disaggregate occupations. Although these approaches have yielded new and important results, it is nonetheless troubling that they typically conceal or ignore the *Gemeinschaftlich* character of (some) disaggregate occupations. If modern closure is indeed secured principally at the detailed occupational level, then the reesulting restriction of social interaction will generate and maintain occupational subcultures that are correspondingly disaggregate. These local cultures are initially forged through intensive secondary socialiation of the kind provided in apprenticeships, police and military academies, and graduate and professional schools. As Caplow (1954) noted long ago, many occupations require prolonged training that serves to inculcate explicit codes of behavior, whereas aggregate classes have no comparable influence or authority over secondary patterns of socialization. The occupational habitus is further strengthened insofar as workers choose occupations receptive to their values and employers choose workers with values that are (putatively) compatible with occupational demands. The great failing of conventional analyses of lifestyles, dispositions, and attitudes is that *Gemeinschaftlich* occupations are regarded as nominal categories and are therefore blithely aggregated or dimensionalized.

The moral to our story, then, is that sociologists have searched for structuration at the wrong level of analysis. Ironically, class analysts have sought realist solutions at the aggregate level when only nominal ones were viable, whereas occupational analysts have settled on nominal solutions (e.g., socioeconomic scales) when in fact realist ones were feasible. Among Marxian and non-Marxian scholars alike, the division of labor is typically represented as purely "technical" in character (see, esp., Wright 1980; Abercrombie and Urry 1983, p. 109), even though nominal task-based groupings are often converted into real social collectivities with a shared culture and set of interests. We think that sociological research stands to benefit from taking such local organization more explicitly into account.

Issues of Trend

Although disaggregate structuration has been largely overlooked by contemporary class analysts, it is nonetheless possible that such structuration, strong though it may be, is growing gradually weaker in ways that are consistent with a standard poststructuralist vision. The prevailing view, especially among European commentators, is that the site of production is indeed of diminishing relevance in understanding stratification systems. The virtues of poststructuralism may be "taken for granted among contemporary social and cultural analysts" (Casey 1995, p. 8), but the lack of substantiating evidence for this position is quite striking; and it is accordingly premature to foreclose on all further debate about the principal forces of change.

The available literature on such matters can be readily simplified by classifying theories in terms of the institutional domains that they reference. We shall thus proceed by distinguishing between (a) the types of technical tasks embodied in the division of labor, (b) the organizational settings in which these tasks are carried out, and (c) the associational forms that characteristically develop at the site of production (e.g., trade unions, professional associations). As shall be evident, the foregoing domains do not evolve in isolation from one another, but it is still analytically useful to distinguish between them.

Sociotechnical Change

The current fashion is to approach longstanding debates about sociotechnical change from a post-Fordist perspective (Piore and Sabel 1984). As Amin (1994) notes, post-Fordists suggest that early industrialism brought about much craft deskilling and homogenization, yet this process is alleged to be reversing itself as "Fordist" factories are gradually supplanted by small-scale production, flexible specialization, and a rejuvenated artisanal sector, all of which serve to reintroduce those distinctions of manual labor that Marx ([1894] 1964) promised would ultimately disappear. This account may therefore be seen as a freshened form of postindustrial theory in which the forces of upgrading and reskilling are presumed to play out not merely in the professional, technical, and service categories but in the craft sector as well. In this context, one might expect postmodernists to view post-Fordism with some antipathy, yet in fact these two accounts are often conflated in the literature. For example, the "new times" post-Fordism of Hall (1988) and his colleagues (e.g., Hall and Jacques 1989) becomes virtually indistinguishable from conventional postmodernism, as it emphasizes that sociotechnical changes weaken aggregate solidarities and generate a new stratification order based on "lifestyle, taste, and culture rather than categories of social class" (Hall 1988, p. 24). This account rests on the characteristic postmodernist assumption that an "increasingly fragmented" productive realm (Hall 1988, p. 24) necessarily weakens *all* forms of solidarity within the division of labor.

The pathbreaking work of Piore and Sabel (1984) clearly has merit, but we would necessarily take issue with these more elaborated accounts that attempt to smuggle in post-structuralism under a post-Fordist banner. If one accepts the core post-Fordist claim that flexible specialization breathes new life into artisanal production (e.g., Piore and Sabel 1984), the appropriate implication is not that all production-based solidarities shall wither away but rather that such solidarities are increasingly localistic. In any standard post-Fordist account, the new and emerging forms of craft production are assumed to require worker "solidarity and communitarianism" (Piore and Sabel 1984, p. 278), and the rejuvenated artisanal sector therefore brings early-industrial "craft communities into the twenty-first century on the basis of a newly decentralized production process" (Aronowitz and DiFazio 1994, p. 98). The end result, then, is a manifestly prostructuralist account whereby modern craftworkers are increasingly "bound to an often familial community [that] promotes both greater control and a sense of belonging" (Aronowitz and DiFazio 1994, p. 97).

The same conclusion holds with respect to older sociotechnical models of differentiation (e.g., Parsons 1970; Dahrendorf 1959). When such models were initially formulated, there was little interest in elaborating a positive theory of local structuration, because the principal objective was merely to counter Marxian approaches by calling attention to the class-decomposing effects of differentiation. If a positive theory of local solidarities *were* attempted, it would likely emphasize that (a) the process of differentiation generates local collective action as emergent occupational groupings vie with one another for jurisdiction over new functional niches, and (b) the resulting occupations become meaningful communities not only because of the "mechanical solidarity" spawned by functional similarities (Durkheim [1893] 1933, p. 16) but also because of the affiliative ties forged in the originating jurisdictional struggles (see Abbott 1988).

The above considerations suggest that differentiation creates solidarities that are increasingly localistic. At the same time, one must bear in mind that the newly differentiated occupations are, by virtue of their newness, hampered in developing stereotypical behavioral expectations that can then be enforced by the outside public. The subcultures of these occupations may therefore be less binding; for instance, the occupations of "systems analyst," "day trader," or "Web site designer" may not evoke stereotypical expectations that are as well formed as those characterizing more established occupations, such as professor (absentminded), cook (excitable), or reporter (cynical). In his seminal work, Caplow (1954, pp. 134–35) makes much of this liability of newness, as he regarded the "public stereotype as itself the most important agent for the conditioning of roles." The latter argument fails, however, to appreciate that newness can itself be an asset; indeed, just as religious cults generate solidarity by capitalizing on missionary zeal, so too one suspects that new occupations can impose behavioral expectations on incumbents without these expectations being well known or appreciated by outsiders. Under this formulation, rapid differentiation prevents the public from understanding the increasingly complex mosaic of occupational subcultures and communities, but it may not greatly weaken the hold of these local communities over their members.

Organizational Change

As sociologists so frequently point out, the division of labor is not intrinsic to the structure of tasks, but rather is a social construction that reflects organizational constraints as well as the interests of relevant parties (e.g., Edwards 1979). The rise of industrialism in the eighteenth century can be attributed, for example, to the spread of vertical strategies of coordination that fragmented tasks into increasingly simple jobs and thus rendered them amenable to purely administrative or bureaucratic oversight (Weber [1922] 1968). By contrast, preindustrial craft workers defined and organized the production process themselves, and the division of labor was accordingly controlled by self-regulating occupational experts rather than organizationally empowered administrators (Zabusky and Barley 1996, pp. 188–92). The obvious question that then arises is whether vertical methods of control will continue to encroach on occupationally defined labor as postindustrialism evolves.

This question cannot be as easily answered as some postmodernists seemingly suggest. In fact, one can identify incipient organizational theories on either side of this debate, with the contemporary literature thus encompassing both (a) postoccupational theories describing the gradual withering away of functionally defined positions, and (b) revisionist theories suggesting that a new occupationally oriented logic of production is on the rise. The former literature, which is clearly dominant, rests on the claim that contemporary organizations are relying increasingly on teamwork, cross-training, and multiactivity jobs that break down conventional skill-based distinctions (e.g., Casey 1995). These new polyvalent jobs are created either by combining formerly distinct skills or by appending managerial and coordinative functions to production positions. The resulting story thus privileges the forces of integration over those of differentiation; that is, whereas many early industrial craft occupations (e.g., shoemaker) were dissolved through task simplification, the postindustrial organizations described by

Casey (1995) putatively eliminate occupations through task fusion, elaboration, and complication.

The preceding account, popular though it may be, is not without its critics, some of whom have argued that "pressures for an occupational logic of organizing may in fact be rising" (Barley 1995, p. 40). This revisionist argument rests on the twofold claim that (a) the occupationally organized sectors of the labor force (e.g., professionals) are rapidly expanding in size, and (b) the remaining vertically organized sectors of the labor force (e.g., management) are increasingly differentiating into functional areas and therefore becoming "occupationalized" (Freidson 1994). In developing these claims, Barley (1995) suggests that the seeds of the future have been sown in the burgeoning technical sector, where the work process is dominated by experts who have so far rigorously defended their occupational jurisdictions and have accordingly resisted cross-training, job mergers, and all forms of hierarchy. The resulting "technicist archetype" (Barley 1995) thus rests on the collaboration of experts who control knowledge through extended training within a community of practice. Under the latter formulation, teams and work groups figure no less prominently than in the postoccupationalist archetype (e.g., Casey 1995), but of course the constituent experts now control mutually exclusive bodies of knowledge. The resulting team solidarity may be seen, then, as organic rather than mechanical.

Although most expert teams are presently formed within the confines of firms, one might anticipate that production will increasingly be contracted out to independent workers who are brought together by managers or brokers. The construction industry serves as the conventional exemplar here both because of its extreme occupationalism and characteristic reliance on outsourcing. In fact, the emerging fashion among organizational theorists is to represent the construction industry not as a historical remnant that "God forgot and the industrial revolution overlooked" (Lawrence and Dyer 1983, p. 599), but rather as a heroic survivor that will in the end supersede mass production, thereby shaping the future of work more generally. For our purposes, it suffices to stress that these revisionist theories are inconsistent with those of postoccupationalism, and not merely because they rest explicitly on a well-developed (and intensifying) division of labor. We would further emphasize that the concomitant growth of outsourcing and externalization increases pressures to identify and affiliate with occupations rather than organizations.

Associational Change

The final institutions of interest to us are the various intermediary associations (e.g., trade unions, professional associations) that characteristically develop at the site of production. Within the Marxian framework, the long-standing concern has been that "trade union consciousness" is intrinsically sectional, thus requiring intellectuals and party functionaries to carry out supplementary ideological work that presumably cultivates more encompassing class-based interests (esp. Lenin 1927). This Marxian concern appears now to have been well founded. If the history of guilds, unions, and related production-based associations is reevaluated from the long view, it is evident that true classwide organization emerged for only a brief historical moment and that postmodern forms are reverting back to localism and sectionalism. The widely documented difficulties facing contemporary unions should be interpreted accordingly; namely, despite an evident weakening in the "encompassiveness of union movements" (Visser 1988, p. 167), there is much evidence suggesting that purely local unions and associations have by no means lost their hold over workers (e.g., the American Federation of Teachers). In many countries, centralized bargaining between national unions and employers is indeed on the decline, yet decentralized negotiations have taken their place as "instrumental collectivism, based on sectional self-interest, becomes the order of the day" (Marshall et al. 1988, p. 7). This interpreta-

tion, if borne out, does not speak to destructuration per se but rather to increasing disaggregation and differentiation of associational forms.

The professional sector has given rise to organizational forms that are yet more localistic. As Parkin (1979) points out, professionals eschew all types of interoccupational confederation, whereas they typically seek out sectional associations that can defend jurisdictional claims and thereby protect against incursions by neighboring occupations. In assessing the future of professionalization, one must consider not only the ongoing growth of traditional professional occupations (e.g., lawyer) and the consequent increase in the number of workers who find themselves in classlike groupings, but also the emergence of new high-skill sectors that may allow further occupations to undertake professionalization projects. To be sure, oppositional movements may possibly emerge and stall these closure projects, yet there is relatively little in the contemporary political arena that might now be interpreted as incipient antiprofessionalism. This conclusion serves to emphasize our larger point that the future of local solidarities is more ambiguous than standard poststructuralist formulas allow.

Conclusions

In his celebrated preface to *The Division of Labor*, Durkheim ([1893] 1933, p. 28) predicted that occupational associations would gradually become "intercalated between the state and the individual," thereby providing an organizational counterbalance to the threat of class formation on one hand and state tyranny on the other. This account is ritually rehearsed by Durkheimian scholars but has never been treated as a credible developmental model. As the Marxian project falls out of favor, scholars have therefore settled into some version of Weberianism or postmodernism, neither of which pays much attention to occupation-level structuration. We have outlined above a quasi-Durkheimian third road that refocuses attention on local forms of structuration within the division of labor.

In laying out this case for disaggregation, we have largely ignored cross-national variability in local structuration, but not because we believe such variability to be either trivial or inconsequential. To the contrary, we suspect that convergence theories (e.g., Erikson and Goldthorpe 1992) may be rather less appealing when disaggregate analyses are attempted, because national idiosyncrasies are necessarily concealed through the abstracting and aggregating operations of class analysis. The case of Germany, for example, provides a revealing example of the extent to which local institutional forms can support and sustain disaggregate structuration. As class analysts have long stressed, Germany has a well-developed system of vocational training and apprenticeship, both of which serve to encourage occupation-specific investments and promote professional commitment and craftsmanship (e.g., Blossfeld 1992). In systems of this sort, workers must invest in a single trade early in their careers, and the correspondingly high costs of retraining produce relatively closed occupational groupings.

If the German system reveals, then, the limits of disaggregate structuration, the case of Japan conversely reveals the extent to which such structuration can be institutionally suppressed. The standard characterization of Japan emphasizes such distinguishing features as (a) an educational curriculum that is generalist in orientation rather than functionally differentiated, (b) a vocational training system that cultivates firm-specific *"nenko skills"* (Dore 1973) through teamwork and continuous job rotation, (c) an organizational commitment to "lifetime employment" that further strengthens firm-specific ties at the expense of more purely occupational ones, and (d) a weakly developed system of enterprise unions that cuts across functional specializations and thereby eliminates any residual craft-based loyalties. This conjunction of forces produces a postoccupational system that some commentators might well regard as prototypically postmodern.

Although further cross-national comparisons of the preceding sort would surely be instructive, we think that comparative analysis becomes especially powerful when local and aggregate forms of structuration are considered in tandem. In the past, structuration has been treated as a unidimensional concept, and scholars accordingly sought to characterize countries on a simple continuum representing the extent to which their stratification systems were well formed (cf. Giddens 1973). The two cases discussed above suggest that such practice may not be altogether misleading; after all, Japan is well known for its attenuated class structure as well as its postoccupationalism (Nakane 1970), while Germany likewise combines strong vocationalism with a deeply class-based labor market and political system. We would nonetheless caution against assuming that such cross-level consistency is the norm. In fact, low-level structuration is often assumed to *undermine* the development of class-based organization, with the United States serving as the typical case in point. The scholarly literature on American exceptionalism is obviously wide ranging, but one of the continuing themes is that class formation was inhibited in the American case not so much by simple individualism as by low-level structuration in the form of craft unions and professionalism (e.g., Dahrendorf 1959). The zero-sum imagery underlying such analyses suggests that aggregate and disaggregate structuration may sometimes work at cross-purposes.

It is also worth considering the obverse case in which class-based organization flourishes in the absence of competing local structuration. This is clearly the stuff of textbook Marxism, yet ironically it comes closest to empirical realization within countries, such as Sweden, that opted for the social democratic road quite early. In standard analyses of Swedish exceptionalism (e.g., Therborn 1988), the well-known solidarism of labor is attributed not merely to the historic weakness of guild organization and craft unionism, but also to party negotiating tactics that privileged classwide collective bargaining over purely sectional wage demands. At the same time, the "active labor market" programs embodied in the Rehn-Meidner model (Esping-Andersen 1988, pp. 47–53) provide extensive state assistance for worker retraining and relocation, thereby blurring interoccupational boundaries and further undermining local sectionalism and closure. In this context, unit-level occupations are still defined by functional positions in the Swedish division of labor, but the social trappings (e.g., associations, closure) that usually emerge around such technical distinctions have been partly repressed. Although Sweden appears, then, to be properly characterized by the neo-Marxian formula that "technical features do not entail social features" (Abercrombie and Urry 1983, p. 109), it is unclear whether this form of structuration extends much beyond Sweden and Scandinavia more generally. If it is more widespread than we suspect, then our preferred line of argumentation is admittedly weakened.

The larger conclusion to be drawn is that sociologists in all countries have typically been too quick to fall back on purely nominal categories and the descriptive models that they imply. The longstanding Marxian distinction between *klasse an sich* and *klasse für sich* only reinforces such nominalist tendencies, as it legitimates the claim that conventional aggregate categories, although presently latent or quiescent, may someday become meaningful and activated. This approach is of course peculiarly modern. In characterizing stratification systems of the past, sociologists have typically relied on categories that were embedded in the fabric of society (e.g., estates, castes), thereby rendering them sensible and meaningful to intellectuals and the lay public alike.

The modern analogues to such realist categories are the unit occupational groups that emerge around functional positions in the division of labor. If analyses are ratcheted down to this level, we can construct models that rely on real institutional forces and assume more nearly structural form. The proof of our approach rests, then, on the additional explana-

tory power and understanding that accrues from referencing the real institutional processes that create classes, constrain mobility chances, generate earnings, and define lifestyles. The task of mapping disaggregate stratification is hardly trivial, but the intellectual payoff to so proceeding is likely to be greater than that secured by carrying out yet another study at the aggregate level.

References

Abbott, Andrew. 1988. *The System of Professions: An Essay on the Division of Expert Labor.* Chicago: University of Chicago Press.

Abercrombie, Nicholas, and John Urry. 1983. *Capital, Labour, and the Middle Classes.* London: Allen & Unwin.

Amin, Ash. 1994. "Post-Fordism: Models, Fantasies, and Phantoms of Transition." Pages 1–39 in *Post-Fordism: A Reader,* edited by Ash Amin. Oxford: Blackwell.

Aronowitz, Stanley, and William DiFazio. 1994. *The Jobless Future.* Minneapolis: University of Minnesota Press.

Barley, Stephen R. 1995. "The Technician as an Occupational Archetype: A Case for Bringing Work into Organizational Studies." Working Paper, Stanford University.

Blossfeld, Hans-Peter. 1992. "Is the German Dual System a Model for a Modern Vocational Training System?" *International Journal of Comparative Sociology* 33:168–81.

Bourdieu, Pierre. 1984. *Distinction: A Social Critique of the Judgement of Taste,* translated by Richard Nice. New York: Cambridge University Press.

Bradley, Harriet. 1996. *Fractured Identities: Changing Patterns of Inequality.* Cambridge: Polity Press.

Caplow, Theodore. 1954. *The Sociology of Work.* Minneapolis: University of Minnesota Press.

Casey, Catherine. 1995. *Work, Self, and Society.* London: Routledge.

Clark, Terry N., and Seymour M. Lipset. 1991. "Are Social Classes Dying?" *International Sociology* 6:397–410.

Collins, Randall. 1979. *The Credential Society: An Historical Sociology of Education and Stratification.* New York: Academic Press.

Dahrendorf, Ralf. 1959. *Class and Class Conflict in Industrial Society.* Stanford: Stanford University Press.

Dore, Ronald P. 1973. *British Factory—Japanese Factory.* London: Allen & Unwin.

Durkheim, Emile. [1893] 1933. *The Division of Labor in Society.* New York: Macmillan.

Edwards, Richard. 1979. *Contested Terrain.* New York: Basic Books.

Emmison, Michael, and Mark Western. 1990. "Social Class and Social Identity: A Comment on Marshall et al." *Sociology* 24:241–53.

Erikson, Robert, and John F. Goldthorpe. 1992. *The Constant Flux: A Study of Class Mobility in Industrial Societies.* Oxford: Clarendon Press.

Esping-Andersen, Gösta. 1988. "The Making of a Social Democratic Welfare State." Pages 35–66 in *Creating Social Democracy: A Century of the Social Democratic Labor Party in Sweden,* edited by Klaus Misgeld, Karl Molin, and Klas Amark. University Park, PA: The Pennsylvania State University Press.

Freidson, Eliot. 1994. *Professionalism Reborn: Theory, Prophecy, and Policy.* Chicago: University of Chicago Press.

Freidson, Eliot. 1986. *Professional Powers: A Study of the Institutionalization of Formal Knowledge.* Chicago: University of Chicago Press.

Giddens, Anthony. 1973. *The Class Structure of the Advanced Societies.* London: Hutchinson.

Goldthorpe, John H., and Gordon Marshall. 1992. "The Promising Future of Class Analysis: A Response to Recent Critiques." *Sociology* 26:381–400.

Grusky, David B. 1999. "Foundations of Class Analysis: A Durkheimian Perspective." Working paper, Department of Sociology, Cornell University.

Grusky, David B., and Jesper B. Sørensen. 1998. "Can Class Analysis Be Salvaged?" *American Journal of Sociology* 103:1187–1234.

Grusky, David B., and Kim A. Weeden. Forthcoming. "Decomposition without Death: A Research Agenda for the New Class Analysis." *Social Psychology and Social Stratification,* edited by David B. Bills.

Hall, Stuart. 1988. "Brave New World." *Marxism Today,* October: 24–9.

Hall, Stuart, and Martin Jacques. 1989. *New Times: The Changing Face of Politics in the 1990s.* London: Lawrence and Wishart.

Hout, Michael, Clem Brooks, and Jeff Manza. 1993. "The Persistence of Classes in Postindustrial Societies." *International Sociology* 8: 259–77.

Krause, Elliot A. 1971. *The Sociology of Occupations.* Boston: Little, Brown.

Lamont, Michele. 1992. *Money, Morals, and Manners: The Culture of the French and American Upper-Middle Class.* Chicago: University of Chicago Press.

Laraña, Enrique, Hank Johnston, and Joseph R. Gusfield. 1994. *New Social Movements: From Ideology to Identity.* Philadelphia: Temple University Press.

Lawrence, Paul R., and Davis Dyer. 1983. *Renewing American Industry.* New York: Free Press.

Lenin, Vladimir I. 1927. *Collected Works of V. I. Lenin.* New York: International Publishers.

Marshall, Gordon, David Rose, Howard Newby, and Carolyn Vogler. 1988. *Social Class in Modern Britain.* London: Unwin Hyman.

Marx, Karl. [1894] 1964. *Selected Works: Volume 1.* Moscow: Progress Publishers.

Murphy, Raymond. 1988. *Social Closure: The Theory of Monopolization and Exclusion.* Oxford: Clarendon.

Nakane, Chie. 1970. *Japanese Society.* London: Weidenfeld and Nicolson.

Pahl, R. E. 1989. "Is the Emperor Naked? Some Questions on the Adequacy of Sociological Theory in Urban and Regional Research." *International Journal of Urban and Regional Research* 13:709–20.

Pakulski, Jan, and Malcolm Waters. 1996. *The Death of Class.* London: Sage Publications.

Parkin, Frank. 1979. *Marxism and Class Theory: A Bourgeois Critique.* New York: Columbia University Press.

Parsons, Talcott. 1970. "Equality and Inequality in Modern Society, or Social Stratification Revisited." Pages 13–72 in *Social Stratification: Research and Theory for the 1970s,* edited by Edward O. Laumann. Indianapolis: Bobbs-Merrill Company.

Piore, Michael J., and Charles F. Sabel. 1984. *The Second Industrial Divide: Possibilities for Prosperity.* New York: Basic Books.

Saunders, Peter. 1989. "Left Write in Sociology." *Network* 44:3–4.

Sørensen, Aage B. 1996. "The Structural Basis of Social Inequality." *American Journal of Sociology* 101:1333–65.

Sørensen, Aage B. 1994. "The Basic Concepts of Stratification Research: Class, Status, and Power." Pp. 229–41 in *Social Stratification: Class, Race, and Gender in Sociological Perspective,* edited by David B. Grusky. Boulder, Colo.: Westview.

Therborn, Göran. 1988. "A Unique Chapter in the History of Democracy: The Social Democrats in Sweden." Pages 1–34 in *Creating Social Democracy: A Century of the Social Democratic Labor Party in Sweden,* edited by Klaus Misgeld, Karl Molin, and Klas Amark. University Park, PA: The Pennsylvania State University Press.

Treiman, Donald J. 1977. *Occupational Prestige in Comparative Perspective.* New York: Academic Press.

Van Maanen, John, and Stephen R. Barley. 1984. "Occupational Communities: Culture and Control in Organizations." *Research in Organizational Behavior* 6:287–365.

Visser, Jelle. 1988. "Trade Unionism in Western Europe: Present Situation and Prospects." *Labour and Society* 13:125–82.

Warner, W. Lloyd, Marchia Meeker, and Kenneth Eells. 1949. *Social Class in America*. Chicago: Science Research Associates.

Weber, Max. [1922] 1968. *Economy and Society*. Berkeley: University of California Press.

Wright, Erik O. 1996. "The Continuing Relevance of Class Analysis." *Theory and Society* 25:697–716.

Wright, Erik O. 1985. *Classes*. London: Verso.

Wright, Erik O. 1980. "Class and Occupation." *Theory and Society* 9:177–214.

Zabusky, Stacia E., and Stephen R. Barley. 1996. "Redefining Success: Ethnographic Observations on the Careers of Technicians." Pages 185–214 in *Broken Ladders: Managerial Careers in the New Economy,* edited by Paul Osterman. Oxford: Oxford University Press.

GAETANO MOSCA

The Ruling Class

1. Among the constant facts and tendencies that are to be found in all political organisms, one is so obvious that it is apparent to the most casual eye. In all societies—from societies that are very meagerly developed and have barely attained the dawnings of civilization, down to the most advanced and powerful societies—two classes of people appear—a class that rules and a class that is ruled. The first class, always the less numerous, performs all political functions, monopolizes power and enjoys the advantages that power brings, whereas the second, the more numerous class, is directed and controlled by the first, in a manner that is now more or less legal, now more or less arbitrary and violent, and supplies the first, in appearance at least, with material means of subsistence and with the instrumentalities that are essential to the vitality of the political organism.

In practical life we all recognize the existence of this ruling class (or political class, as we have elsewhere chosen to define it).[1] We all know that, in our own country, whichever it may be, the management of public affairs is in the hands of a minority of influential persons, to which management, willingly or unwillingly, the majority defer. We know that the same thing goes on in neighboring countries,

and in fact we should be put to it to conceive of a real world otherwise organized—a world in which all men would be directly subject to a single person without relationships of superiority or subordination, or in which all men would share equally in the direction of political affairs. If we reason otherwise in theory, that is due partly to inveterate habits that we follow in our thinking and partly to the exaggerated importance that we attach to two political facts that loom far larger in appearance than they are in reality.

The first of these facts—and one has only to open one's eyes to see it—is that in every political organism there is one individual who is chief among the leaders of the ruling class as a whole and stands, as we say, at the helm of the state. That person is not always the person who holds supreme power according to law. At times, alongside of the hereditary king or emperor there is a prime minister or a major-domo who wields an actual power that is greater than the sovereign's. At other times, in place of the elected president the influential politician who has procured the president's election will govern. Under special circumstances there may be, instead of a single person, two or three who discharge the functions of supreme control.

The second fact, too, is readily discernible. Whatever the type of political organization, pressures arising from the discontent of the masses who are governed, from the passions by which they are swayed, exert a certain amount of influence on the policies of the ruling, the political, class.

Originally published in 1939. Please see complete source information beginning on page 891.

But the man who is at the head of the state would certainly not be able to govern without the support of a numerous class to enforce respect for his orders and to have them carried out; and granting that he can make one individual, or indeed many individuals, in the ruling class feel the weight of his power, he certainly cannot be at odds with the class as a whole or do away with it. Even if that were possible, he would at once be forced to create another class, without the support of which action on his part would be completely paralyzed. On the other hand, granting that the discontent of the masses might succeed in deposing a ruling class, inevitably, as we shall later show, there would have to be another organized minority within the masses themselves to discharge the functions of a ruling class. Otherwise all organization, and the whole social structure, would be destroyed.

2. From the point of view of scientific research the real superiority of the concept of the ruling, or political, class lies in the fact that the varying structure of ruling classes has a preponderant importance in determining the political type, and also the level of civilization, of the different peoples. According to a manner of classifying forms of government that is still in vogue, Turkey and Russia were both, up to a few years ago, absolute monarchies, England and Italy were constitutional, or limited, monarchies, and France and the United States were classed as republics. The classification was based on the fact that, in the first two countries mentioned, headship in the state was hereditary and the chief was nominally omnipotent; in the second two, his office is hereditary but his powers and prerogatives are limited; in the last two, he is elected.

That classification is obviously superficial. Absolutisms though they were, there was little in common between the manners in which Russia and Turkey were managed politically, the levels of civilization in the two countries and the organization of their ruling classes being vastly different. On the same basis, the regime in Italy, a monarchy, is much more similar to the regime in France, a republic, than it is to the regime in England, also a

monarchy; and there are important differences between the political organizations of the United States and France, though both countries are republics.

As we have already suggested, ingrained habits of thinking have long stood, as they still stand, in the way of scientific progress in this matter. The classification mentioned above, which divides governments into absolute monarchies, limited monarchies and republics, was devised by Montesquieu and was intended to replace the classical categories of Aristotle, who divided governments into monarchies, aristocracies and democracies. What Aristotle called a democracy was simply an aristocracy of fairly broad membership. Aristotle himself was in a position to observe that in every Greek state, whether aristocratic or democratic, there was always one person or more who had a preponderant influence. Between the day of Polybius and the day of Montesquieu, many writers perfected Aristotle's classification by introducing into it the concept of "mixed" governments. Later on the modern democratic theory, which had its source in Rousseau, took its stand upon the concept that the majority of the citizens in any state can participate, and in fact *ought* to participate, in its political life, and the doctrine of popular sovereignty still holds sway over many minds in spite of the fact that modern scholarship is making it increasingly clear that democratic, monarchical and aristocratic principles function side by side in every political organism. We shall not stop to refute this democratic theory here, since that is the task of this work as a whole. Besides, it would be hard to destroy in a few pages a whole system of ideas that has become firmly rooted in the human mind. As Las Casas aptly wrote in his life of Christopher Columbus, it is often much harder to unlearn than to learn.

3. We think it may be desirable, nevertheless, to reply at this point to an objection which might very readily be made to our point of view. If it is easy to understand that a single individual cannot command a group without finding within the group a minority to support him, it is rather difficult to grant,

as a constant and natural fact, that minorities rule majorities, rather than majorities minorities. But that is one of the points—so numerous in all the other sciences—where the first impression one has of things is contrary to what they are in reality. In reality the dominion of an organized minority, obeying a single impulse, over the unorganized majority is inevitable. The power of any minority is irresistible as against each single individual in the majority, who stands alone before the totality of the organized minority. At the same time, the minority is organized for the very reason that it is a minority. A hundred men acting uniformly in concert, with a common understanding, will triumph over a thousand men who are not in accord and can therefore be dealt with one by one. Meanwhile it will be easier for the former to act in concert and have a mutual understanding simply because they are a hundred and not a thousand. It follows that the larger the political community, the smaller will the proportion of the governing minority to the governed majority be, and the more difficult will it be for the majority to organize for reaction against the minority.

However, in addition to the great advantage accruing to them from the fact of being organized, ruling minorities are usually so constituted that the individuals who make them up are distinguished from the mass of the governed by qualities that give them a certain material, intellectual or even moral superiority; or else they are the heirs of individuals who possessed such qualities. In other words, members of a ruling minority regularly have some attribute, real or apparent, which is highly esteemed and very influential in the society in which they live.

4. In primitive societies that are still in the early stages of organization, military valor is the quality that most readily opens access to the ruling, or political, class. In societies of advanced civilization, war is the exceptional condition. It may be regarded as virtually normal in societies that are in the initial stages of their development; and the individuals who show the greatest ability in war easily gain supremacy over their fellows—the bravest become chiefs. The fact is constant, but the forms it may assume, in one set of circumstances or another, vary considerably.

As a rule the dominance of a warrior class over a peaceful multitude is attributed to a superposition of races, to the conquest of a relatively unwarlike group by an aggressive one. Sometimes that is actually the case—we have examples in India after the Aryan invasions, in the Roman Empire after the Germanic invasions and in Mexico after the Aztec conquest. But more often, under certain social conditions, we note the rise of a warlike ruling class in places where there is absolutely no trace of a foreign conquest. As long as a horde lives exclusively by the chase, all individuals can easily become warriors. There will of course be leaders who will rule over the tribe, but we will not find a warrior class rising to exploit, and at the same time to protect, another class that is devoted to peaceful pursuits. As the tribe emerges from the hunting stage and enters the agricultural and pastoral stage, then, along with an enormous increase in population and a greater stability in the means of exerting social influence, a more or less clean-cut division into two classes will take place, one class being devoted exclusively to agriculture, the other class to war. In this event, it is inevitable that the warrior class should little by little acquire such ascendancy over the other as to be able to oppress it with impunity. . . .

5. Everywhere—in Russia and Poland, in India and medieval Europe—the ruling warrior classes acquire almost exclusive ownership of the land. Land, as we have seen, is the chief source of production and wealth in countries that are not very far advanced in civilization. But as civilization progresses, revenue from land increases proportionately. With the growth of population there is, at least in certain periods, an increase in rent, in the Ricardian sense of the term, largely because great centers of consumption arise— such at all times have been the great capitals and other large cities, ancient and modern. Eventually, if other circumstances permit, a very important social transformation occurs.

Wealth rather than military valor comes to be the characteristic feature of the dominant class: the people who rule are the rich rather than the brave.

The condition that in the main is required for this transformation is that social organization shall have concentrated and become perfected to such an extent that the protection offered by public authority is considerably more effective than the protection offered by private force. In other words, private property must be so well protected by the practical and real efficacy of the laws as to render the power of the proprietor himself superfluous. This comes about through a series of gradual alterations in the social structure whereby a type of political organization, which we shall call the "feudal state," is transformed into an essentially different type, which we shall term the "bureaucratic state." We are to discuss these types at some length hereafter, but we may say at once that the evolution here referred to is as a rule greatly facilitated by progress in pacific manners and customs and by certain moral habits which societies contract as civilization advances.

Once this transformation has taken place, wealth produces political power just as political power has been producing wealth. In a society already somewhat mature—where, therefore, individual power is curbed by the collective power—if the powerful are as a rule the rich, to be rich is to become powerful. And, in truth, when fighting with the mailed fist is prohibited whereas fighting with pounds and pence is sanctioned, the better posts are inevitably won by those who are better supplied with pounds and pence.

There are, to be sure, states of a very high level of civilization which in theory are organized on the basis of moral principles of such a character that they seem to preclude this overbearing assertiveness on the part of wealth. But this is a case—and there are many such—where theoretical principles can have no more than a limited application in real life. In the United States all powers flow directly or indirectly from popular elections, and suffrage is equal for all men and women in all the states of the Union. What is more, democracy prevails not only in institutions but to a certain extent also in morals. The rich ordinarily feel a certain aversion to entering public life, and the poor a certain aversion to choosing the rich for elective office. But that does not prevent a rich man from being more influential than a poor man, since he can use pressure upon the politicians who control public administration. It does not prevent elections from being carried on to the music of clinking dollars. It does not prevent whole legislatures and considerable numbers of national congressmen from feeling the influence of powerful corporations and great financiers.[2] . . .

6. In societies in which religious beliefs are strong and ministers of the faith form a special class a priestly aristocracy almost always arises and gains possession of a more or less important share of the wealth and the political power. Conspicuous examples of that situation would be ancient Egypt (during certain periods), Brahman India and medieval Europe. Oftentimes the priests not only perform religious functions. They possess legal and scientific knowledge and constitute the class of highest intellectual culture. Consciously or unconsciously, priestly hierarchies often show a tendency to monopolize learning and hamper the dissemination of the methods and procedures that make the acquisition of knowledge possible and easy. To that tendency may have been due, in part at least, the painfully slow diffusion of the demotic alphabet in ancient Egypt, though that alphabet was infinitely more simple than the hieroglyphic script. The Druids in Gaul were acquainted with the Greek alphabet but would not permit their rich store of sacred literature to be written down, requiring their pupils to commit it to memory at the cost of untold effort. To the same outlook may be attributed the stubborn and frequent use of dead languages that we find in ancient Chaldea, in India, and in medieval Europe. Sometimes, as was the case in India, lower classes have been explicitly forbidden to acquire knowledge of sacred books.

Specialized knowledge and really scientific culture, purged of any sacred or religious aura, become important political forces only in a highly advanced stage of civilization, and only then do they give access to membership in the ruling class to those who possess them. But in this case too, it is not so much learning in itself that has political value as the practical applications that may be made of learning to the profit of the public or the state. Sometimes all that is required is mere possession of the mechanical processes that are indispensable to the acquisition of a higher culture. This may be due to the fact that on such a basis it is easier to ascertain and measure the skill which a candidate has been able to acquire— it is easier to "mark" or grade him. So in certain periods in ancient Egypt the profession of scribe was a road to public office and power, perhaps because to have learned the hieroglyphic script was proof of long and patient study. In modern China, again, learning the numberless characters in Chinese script has formed the basis of the mandarin's education.[3] In present-day Europe and America the class that applies the findings of modern science to war, public administration, public works and public sanitation holds a fairly important position, both socially and politically, and in our western world, as in ancient Rome, an altogether privileged position is held by lawyers. They know the complicated legislation that arises in all peoples of long-standing civilization, and they become especially powerful if their knowledge of law is coupled with the type of eloquence that chances to have a strong appeal to the taste of their contemporaries.

There are examples in abundance where we see that longstanding practice in directing the military and civil organization of a community creates and develops in the higher reaches of the ruling class a real art of governing which is something better than crude empiricism and better than anything that mere individual experience could suggest. In such circumstances aristocracies of functionaries arise, such as the Roman senate, the Venetian nobility and to a certain extent the English aristocracy. Those bodies all stirred John Stuart Mill to admiration and certainly they all three developed governments that were distinguished for carefully considered policies and for great steadfastness and sagacity in carrying them out. This art of governing is not political science, though it has, at one time or another, anticipated applications of a number of the postulates of political science. However, even if the art of governing has now and again enjoyed prestige with certain classes of persons who have long held possession of political functions, knowledge of it has never served as an ordinary criterion for admitting to public offices persons who were barred from them by social station. The degree of mastery of the art of governing that a person possesses is, moreover, apart from exceptional cases, a very difficult thing to determine if the person has given no practical demonstration that he possesses it.

7. In some countries we find hereditary castes. In such cases the governing class is explicitly restricted to a given number of families, and birth is the one criterion that determines entry into the class or exclusion from it. Examples are exceedingly common. There is practically no country of long-standing civilization that has not had a hereditary aristocracy at one period or another in its history. We find hereditary nobilities during certain periods in China and ancient Egypt, in India, in Greece before the wars with the Medes, in ancient Rome, among the Slavs, among the Latins and Germans of the Middle Ages, in Mexico at the time of the Discovery and in Japan down to a few years ago.

In this connection two preliminary observations are in point. In the first place, all ruling classes tend to become hereditary in fact if not in law. All political forces seem to possess a quality that in physics used to be called the force of inertia. They have a tendency, that is, to remain at the point and in the state in which they find themselves. Wealth and military valor are easily maintained in certain families by moral tradition and by heredity. Qualification for important office—the habit of, and to an extent the capacity for, dealing with affairs of consequence—is much more readily acquired when one has had a certain familiarity with them from childhood. Even when academic degrees, scientific training, special aptitudes as tested by examinations and competitions, open the way to public office, there is no eliminating that special advantage in favor of certain individuals which the French call the advantage of *positions déjà prises*. In actual fact, though examinations and competitions may theoretically be open to all, the majority never have the resources for meeting the expense of long preparation, and many others are without the connections and kinships that set an individual promptly on the right road, enabling him to avoid the gropings and blunders that are inevitable when one enters an unfamiliar environment without any guidance or support.

The democratic principle of election by broadbased suffrage would seem at first glance to be in conflict with the tendency toward stability which, according to our theory, ruling classes show. But it must be noted that candidates who are successful in democratic elections are almost always the ones who possess the political forces above enumerated, which are very often hereditary. In the English, French and Italian parliaments we frequently see the sons, grandsons, brothers, nephews and sons-in-law of members and deputies, ex-members and ex-deputies.

In the second place, when we see a hereditary caste established in a country and monopolizing political power, we may be sure that such a status de jure was preceded by a similar status de facto. Before proclaiming their exclusive and hereditary right to power the families or castes in question must have held the scepter of command in a firm grasp, completely monopolizing all the political forces of that country at that period. Otherwise such a claim on their part would only have aroused the bitterest protests and provoked the bitterest struggles.

Hereditary aristocracies often come to vaunt supernatural origins, or at least origins different from, and superior to, those of the governed classes. Such claims are explained by a highly significant social fact, namely that every governing class tends to justify its actual exercise of power by resting it on some universal moral principle. This same sort of claim has come forward in our time in scientific trappings. A number of writers, developing and amplifying Darwin's theories, contend that upper classes represent a higher level in social evolution and are therefore superior to lower classes by organic structure. Gumplowicz goes to the point of maintaining that the divisions of populations into trade groups and professional classes in modern civilized countries are based on ethnological heterogeneousness.[4]

Now history very definitely shows the special abilities as well as the special defects—both very marked—which have been displayed by aristocracies that have either remained absolutely closed or have made entry into their circles difficult. The ancient Roman patriciate and the English and German nobilities of modern times give a ready idea of the type we refer to. Yet in dealing with this fact, and with the theories that tend to exaggerate its significance, we can always raise the same objection—that the individuals who belong to the aristocracies in question owe their special qualities not so much to the blood that flows in their veins as to their very particular upbringing, which has brought out certain intellectual and moral tendencies in them in preference to others. . . .

8. Finally, if we were to keep to the idea of those who maintain the exclusive influence of the hereditary principle in the formation of ruling classes, we should be carried to a conclusion somewhat like the one to which we were carried by the evolutionary principle: The political history of mankind ought to be much simpler than it is. If the ruling class really belonged to a different race, or if the qualities that fit it for dominion were transmitted primarily by organic heredity, it is difficult to see how, once the class was formed, it could decline and lose its power. The peculiar qualities of a race are exceedingly tenacious. Keeping to the evolutionary theory, acquired capacities in the parents are inborn in their

children and, as generation succeeds generation, are progressively accentuated. The descendants of rulers, therefore, ought to become better and better fitted to rule, and the other classes ought to see their chances of challenging or supplanting them become more and more remote. Now the most commonplace experience suffices to assure one that things do not go in that way at all.

What we see is that as soon as there is a shift in the balance of political forces—when, that is, a need is felt that capacities different from the old should assert themselves in the management of the state, when the old capacities, therefore, lose some of their importance or changes in their distribution occur—then the manner in which the ruling class is constituted changes also. If a new source of wealth develops in a society, if the practical importance of knowledge grows, if an old religion declines or a new one is born, if a new current of ideas spreads, then, simultaneously, far-reaching dislocations occur in the ruling class. One might say, indeed, that the whole history of civilized mankind comes down to a conflict between the tendency of dominant elements to monopolize political power and transmit possession of it by inheritance, and the tendency toward a dislocation of old forces and an insurgence of new forces; and this conflict produces an unending ferment of endosmosis and exosmosis between the upper classes and certain portions of the lower. Ruling classes decline inevitably when they cease to find scope for the capacities through which they rose to power, when they can no longer render the social services which they once rendered, or when their talents and

the services they render lose in importance in the social environment in which they live. So the Roman aristocracy declined when it was no longer the exclusive source of higher officers for the army, of administrators for the commonwealth, of governors for the provinces. So the Venetian aristocracy declined when its nobles ceased to command the galleys and no longer passed the greater part of their lives in sailing the seas and in trading and fighting.

In inorganic nature we have the example of our air, in which a tendency to immobility produced by the force of inertia is continuously in conflict with a tendency to shift about as the result of inequalities in the distribution of heat. The two tendencies, prevailing by turn in various regions on our planet, produce now calm, now wind and storm. In much the same way in human societies there prevails now the tendency that produces closed, stationary, crystallized ruling classes, now the tendency that results in a more or less rapid renovation of ruling classes.

Notes

1. Mosca, *Teorica dei governi e governo parlamentare,* chap. I.
2. Jannet, *Le istituzioni politiche e sociali degli Stati Uniti d'America,* part II, chap. X.
3. This was true up to a few years ago, the examination of a mandarin covering only literary and historical studies—as the Chinese understood such studies, of course.
4. *Der Rassenkampf.* This notion transpires from Gumplowicz's whole volume. It is explicitly formulated in book II, chap. XXXIII.

C. WRIGHT MILLS

The Power Elite

The powers of ordinary men are circumscribed by the everyday worlds in which they live, yet even in these rounds of job, family, and neighborhood they often seem driven by forces they can neither understand nor govern. 'Great changes' are beyond their control, but affect their conduct and outlook none the less. The very framework of modern society confines them to projects not their own, but from every side, such changes now press upon the men and women of the mass society, who accordingly feel that they are without purpose in an epoch in which they are without power.

But not all men are in this sense ordinary. As the means of information and of power are centralized, some men come to occupy positions in American society from which they can look down upon, so to speak, and by their decisions mightily affect, the everyday worlds of ordinary men and women. They are not made by their jobs; they set up and break down jobs for thousands of others; they are not confined by simple family responsibilities; they can escape. They may live in many hotels and houses, but they are bound by no one community. They need not merely 'meet the demands of the day and hour'; in some part, they create these demands, and cause others to meet them. Whether or not they profess their power, their technical and political experience of it far transcends that of the underlying population. What Jacob Burckhardt said

of 'great men,' most Americans might well say of their elite: 'They are all that we are not.'[1]

The power elite is composed of men whose positions enable them to transcend the ordinary environments of ordinary men and women; they are in positions to make decisions having major consequences. Whether they do or do not make such decisions is less important than the fact that they do occupy such pivotal positions: their failure to act, their failure to make decisions, is itself an act that is often of greater consequence than the decisions they do make. For they are in command of the major hierarchies and organizations of modern society. They rule the big corporations. They run the machinery of the state and claim its prerogatives. They direct the military establishment. They occupy the strategic command posts of the social structure, in which are now centered the effective means of the power and the wealth and the celebrity which they enjoy.

The power elite are not solitary rulers. Advisers and consultants, spokesmen and opinion-makers are often the captains of their higher thought and decision. Immediately below the elite are the professional politicians of the middle levels of power, in the Congress and in the pressure groups, as well as among the new and old upper classes of town and city and region. Mingling with them in curious ways are those professional celebrities who live by being continually displayed but are never, so long as they remain celebrities, displayed enough. If such celebrities are not at the head of any dominating hierarchy, they do often have the power to distract the attention of the public or afford sensations to the

---

Originally published in 1956. Please see complete source information beginning on page 891.

masses, or, more directly, to gain the ear of those who do occupy positions of direct power. More or less unattached, as critics of morality and technicians of power, as spokesmen of God and creators of mass sensibility, such celebrities and consultants are part of the immediate scene in which the drama of the elite is enacted. But that drama itself is centered in the command posts of the major institutional hierarchies.

1

The truth about the nature and the power of the elite is not some secret which men of affairs know but will not tell. Such men hold quite various theories about their own roles in the sequence of event and decision. Often they are uncertain about their roles, and even more often they allow their fears and their hopes to affect their assessment of their own power. No matter how great their actual power, they tend to be less acutely aware of it than of the resistances of others to its use. Moreover, most American men of affairs have learned well the rhetoric of public relations, in some cases even to the point of using it when they are alone, and thus coming to believe it. The personal awareness of the actors is only one of the several sources one must examine in order to understand the higher circles. Yet many who believe that there is no elite, or at any rate none of any consequence, rest their argument upon what men of affairs believe about themselves, or at least assert in public.

There is, however, another view: those who feel, even if vaguely, that a compact and powerful elite of great importance does now prevail in America often base that feeling upon the historical trend of our time. They have felt, for example, the domination of the military event, and from this they infer that generals and admirals, as well as other men of decision influenced by them, must be enormously powerful. They hear that the Congress has again abdicated to a handful of men decisions clearly related to the issue of war or peace.

They know that the bomb was dropped over Japan in the name of the United States of America, although they were at no time consulted about the matter. They feel that they live in a time of big decisions; they know that they are not making any. Accordingly, as they consider the present as history, they infer that at its center, making decisions or failing to make them, there must be an elite of power.

On the one hand, those who share this feeling about big historical events assume that there is an elite and that its power is great. On the other hand, those who listen carefully to the reports of men apparently involved in the great decisions often do not believe that there is an elite whose powers are of decisive consequence.

Both views must be taken into account, but neither is adequate. The way to understand the power of the American elite lies neither solely in recognizing the historic scale of events nor in accepting the personal awareness reported by men of apparent decision. Behind such men and behind the events of history, linking the two, are the major institutions of modern society. These hierarchies of state and corporation and army constitute the means of power; as such they are now of a consequence not before equaled in human history—and at their summits, there are now those command posts of modern society which offer us the sociological key to an understanding of the role of the higher circles in America.

Within American society, major national power now resides in the economic, the political, and the military domains. Other institutions seem off to the side of modern history, and, on occasion, duly subordinated to these. No family is as directly powerful in national affairs as any major corporation; no church is as directly powerful in the external biographies of young men in America today as the military establishment; no college is as powerful in the shaping of momentous events as the National Security Council. Religious, educational, and family institutions are not autonomous centers of national power; on the contrary, these decentralized areas are increasingly shaped by the big three, in which developments of decisive and immediate consequence now occur. . . .

Within each of the big three, the typical institutional unit has become enlarged, has become administrative, and, in the power of its decisions, has become centralized. Behind these developments there is a fabulous technology, for as institutions, they have incorporated this technology and guide it, even as it shapes and paces their developments.

The economy—once a great scatter of small productive units in autonomous balance—has become dominated by two or three hundred giant corporations, administratively and politically interrelated, which together hold the keys to economic decisions.

The political order, once a decentralized set of several dozen states with a weak spinal cord, has become a centralized, executive establishment which has taken up into itself many powers previously scattered, and now enters into each and every cranny of the social structure.

The military order, once a slim establishment in a context of distrust fed by state militia, has become the largest and most expensive feature of government, and, although well versed in smiling public relations, now has all the grim and clumsy efficiency of a sprawling bureaucratic domain.

In each of these institutional areas, the means of power at the disposal of decision makers have increased enormously; their central executive powers have been enhanced; within each of them modern administrative routines have been elaborated and tightened up.

As each of these domains becomes enlarged and centralized, the consequences of its activities become greater, and its traffic with the others increases. The decisions of a handful of corporations bear upon military and political as well as upon economic developments around the world. The decisions of the military establishment rest upon and grievously affect political life as well as the very level of economic activity. The decisions made within the political domain determine economic activities and military programs. There is no longer, on the one hand, an economy, and, on the other hand, a political order containing a military establishment unimportant to politics and to money-making. There is a political economy linked, in a thousand ways, with military institutions and decisions. On each side of the world-split running through central Europe and around the Asiatic rimlands, there is an ever-increasing interlocking of economic, military, and political structures.[2] If there is government intervention in the corporate economy, so is there corporate intervention in the governmental process. In the structural sense, this triangle of power is the source of the interlocking directorate that is most important for the historical structure of the present.

The fact of the interlocking is clearly revealed at each of the points of crisis of modern capitalist society—slump, war, and boom. In each, men of decision are led to an awareness of the interdependence of the major institutional orders. In the nineteenth century, when the scale of all institutions was smaller, their liberal integration was achieved in the automatic economy, by an autonomous play of market forces, and in the automatic political domain, by the bargain and the vote. It was then assumed that out of the imbalance and friction that followed the limited decisions then possible a new equilibrium would in due course emerge. That can no longer be assumed, and it is not assumed by the men at the top of each of the three dominant hierarchies.

For given the scope of their consequences, decisions—and indecisions—in any one of these ramify into the others, and hence top decisions tend either to become co-ordinated or to lead to a commanding indecision. It has not always been like this. When numerous small entrepreneurs made up the economy, for example, many of them could fail and the consequences still remain local; political and military authorities did not intervene. But now, given political expectations and military commitments, can they afford to allow key units of the private corporate economy to break down in slump? Increasingly, they do intervene in economic affairs, and as they do so, the controlling decisions in each order are inspected by agents of the other two, and economic, military, and political structures are interlocked.

At the pinnacle of each of the three enlarged and centralized domains, there have arisen those higher circles which make up the economic, the political, and the military elites. At the top of the economy, among the corporate rich, there are the chief executives; at the top of the political order, the members of the political directorate; at the top of the military establishment, the elite of soldier-statesmen clustered in and around the Joint Chiefs of Staff and the upper echelon. As each of these domains has coincided with the others, as decisions tend to become total in their consequence, the leading men in each of the three domains of power—the warlords, the corporation chieftains, the political directorate—tend to come together, to form the power elite of America.

2

The higher circles in and around these command posts are often thought of in terms of what their members possess: they have a greater share than other people of the things and experiences that are most highly valued. From this point of view, the elite are simply those who have the most of what there is to have, which is generally held to include money, power, and prestige—as well as all the ways of life to which these lead.[3] But the elite are not simply those who have the most, for they could not 'have the most' were it not for their positions in the great institutions. For such institutions are the necessary bases of power, of wealth, and of prestige, and at the same time, the chief means of exercising power, of acquiring and retaining wealth, and of cashing in the higher claims for prestige.

By the powerful we mean, of course, those who are able to realize their will, even if others resist it. No one, accordingly, can be truly powerful unless he has access to the command of major institutions, for it is over these institutional means of power that the truly powerful are, in the first instance, powerful. Higher politicians and key officials of government command such institutional power; so do admirals and generals, and so do the major owners and executives of the larger corporations. Not all power, it is true, is anchored in and exercised by means of such institutions, but only within and through them can power be more or less continuous and important. . . .

If we took the one hundred most powerful men in America, the one hundred wealthiest, and the one hundred most celebrated away from the institutional positions they now occupy, away from their resources of men and women and money, away from the media of mass communication that are now focused upon them—then they would be powerless and poor and uncelebrated. For power is not of a man. Wealth does not center in the person of the wealthy. Celebrity is not inherent in any personality. To be celebrated, to be wealthy, to have power requires access to major institutions, for the institutional positions men occupy determine in large part their chances to have and to hold these valued experiences.

3

The people of the higher circles may also be conceived as members of a top social stratum, as a set of groups whose members know one another, see one another socially and at business, and so, in making decisions, take one another into account. The elite, according to this conception, feel themselves to be, and are felt by others to be, the inner circle of 'the upper social classes.'[4] They form a more or less compact social and psychological entity; they have become self-conscious members of a social class. People are either accepted into this class or they are not, and there is a qualitative split, rather than merely a numerical scale, separating them from those who are not elite. They are more or less aware of themselves as a social class and they behave toward one another differently from the way they do toward members of other classes. They accept one another, understand one another, marry one another, tend to work and to think if not together at least alike.

Now, we do not want by our definition to prejudge whether the elite of the command posts are conscious members of such a socially recognized class, or whether considerable proportions of the elite derive from such a clear and distinct class. These are matters to be investigated. Yet in order to be able to recognize what we intend to investigate, we must note something that all biographies and memoirs of the wealthy and the powerful and the eminent make clear: no matter what else they may be, the people of these higher circles are involved in a set of overlapping 'crowds' and intricately connected 'cliques.' There is a kind of mutual attraction among those who 'sit on the same terrace'—although this often becomes clear to them, as well as to others, only at the point at which they feel the need to draw the line; only when, in their common defense, they come to understand what they have in common, and so close their ranks against outsiders.

The idea of such ruling stratum implies that most of its members have similar social origins, that throughout their lives they maintain a network of informal connections, and that to some degree there is an interchangeability of position between the various hierarchies of money and power and celebrity. We must, of course, note at once that if such an elite stratum does exist, its social visibility and its form, for very solid historical reasons, are quite different from those of the noble cousinhoods that once ruled various European nations.

That American society has never passed through a feudal epoch is of decisive importance to the nature of the American elite, as well as to American society as a historic whole. For it means that no nobility or aristocracy, established before the capitalist era, has stood in tense opposition to the higher bourgeoisie. It means that this bourgeoisie has monopolized not only wealth but prestige and power as well. It means that no set of noble families has commanded the top positions and monopolized the values that are generally held in high esteem; and certainly that no set has done so explicitly by inherited right. It means that no high church dignitaries or court nobilities, no entrenched landlords with honorific accouterments, no monopolists of high army posts have opposed the enriched bourgeoisie and in the name of birth and prerogative successfully resisted its self-making.

But this does *not* mean that there are no upper strata in the United States. That they emerged from a 'middle class' that had no recognized aristocratic superiors does not mean they remained middle class when enormous increases in wealth made their own superiority possible. Their origins and their newness may have made the upper strata less visible in America than elsewhere. But in America today there are in fact tiers and ranges of wealth and power of which people in the middle and lower ranks know very little and may not even dream. There are families who, in their well-being, are quite insulated from the economic jolts and lurches felt by the merely prosperous and those farther down the scale. There are also men of power who in quite small groups make decisions of enormous consequence for the underlying population.

The American elite entered modern history as a virtually unopposed bourgeoisie. No national bourgeoisie, before or since, has had such opportunities and advantages. Having no military neighbors, they easily occupied an isolated continent stocked with natural resources and immensely inviting to a willing labor force. A framework of power and an ideology for its justification were already at hand. Against mercantilist restriction, they inherited the principle of *laissez-faire;* against Southern planters, they imposed the principle of industrialism. The Revolutionary War put an end to colonial pretensions to nobility, as loyalists fled the country and many estates were broken up. The Jacksonian upheaval with its status revolution put an end to pretensions to monopoly of descent by the old New England families. The Civil War broke the power, and so in due course the prestige, of the antebellum South's claimants for the higher esteem. The tempo of the whole capitalist development made it impossible for an inherited nobility to develop and endure in America.

No fixed ruling class, anchored in agrarian life and coming to flower in military glory, could contain in America the historic thrust of commerce and industry, or subordinate to itself the capitalist elite—as capitalists were subordinated, for example, in Germany and Japan. Nor could such a ruling class anywhere in the world contain that of the United States when industrialized violence came to decide history. Witness the fate of Germany and Japan in the two world wars of the twentieth century; and indeed the fate of Britain herself and her model ruling class, as New York became the inevitable economic, and Washington the inevitable political capital of the western capitalist world.

4

The elite who occupy the command posts may be seen as the possessors of power and wealth and celebrity; they may be seen as members of the upper stratum of a capitalistic society. They may also be defined in terms of psychological and moral criteria, as certain kinds of selected individuals. So defined, the elite, quite simply, are people of superior character and energy.

The humanist, for example, may conceive of the 'elite' not as a social level or category, but as a scatter of those individuals who attempt to transcend themselves, and accordingly, are more noble, more efficient, made out of better stuff. It does not matter whether they are poor or rich, whether they hold high position or low, whether they are acclaimed or despised; they are elite because of the kind of individuals they are. The rest of the population is mass, which, according to this conception, sluggishly relaxes into uncomfortable mediocrity.[5]

This is the sort of socially unlocated conception which some American writers with conservative yearnings have recently sought to develop. But most moral and psychological conceptions of the elite are much less sophisticated, concerning themselves not with individuals but with the stratum as a whole. Such ideas, in fact, always arise in a society in which some people possess more than do others of what there is to possess. People with advantages are loath to believe that they just happen to be people with advantages. They come readily to define themselves as inherently worthy of what they possess; they come to believe themselves 'naturally' elite; and, in fact, to imagine their possessions and their privileges as natural extensions of their own elite selves. In this sense, the idea of the elite as composed of men and women having a finer moral character is an ideology of the elite as a privileged ruling stratum, and this is true whether the ideology is elite-made or made up for it by others.

In eras of equalitarian rhetoric, the more intelligent or the more articulate among the lower and middle classes, as well as guilty members of the upper, may come to entertain ideas of a counter-elite. In western society, as a matter of fact, there is a long tradition and varied images of the poor, the exploited, and the oppressed as the truly virtuous, the wise, and the blessed. Stemming from Christian tradition, this moral idea of a counter-elite composed of essentially higher types condemned to a lowly station, may be and has been used by the underlying population to justify harsh criticism of ruling elites and to celebrate utopian images of a new elite to come.

The moral conception of the elite, however, is not always merely an ideology of the overprivileged or a counter-ideology of the underprivileged. It is often a fact: having controlled experiences and select privileges, many individuals of the upper stratum do come in due course to approximate the types of character they claim to embody. Even when we give up—as we must—the idea that the elite man or woman is born with an elite character, we need not dismiss the idea that their experiences and trainings develop in them characters of a specific type. . . .

5

These several notions of the elite, when appropriately understood, are intricately bound up with one another, and we shall use them all in this examination of American success. We shall study each of several higher circles as offering candidates for the elite, and we shall do so in terms of the major institutions making up the total society of America; within and between each of these institutions, we shall trace the interrelations of wealth and power and prestige. But our main concern is with the power of those who now occupy the command posts, and with the role which they are enacting in the history of our epoch.

Such an elite may be conceived as omnipotent, and its powers thought of as a great hidden design. Thus, in vulgar Marxism, events and trends are explained by reference to 'the will of the bourgeoisie'; in Nazism, by reference to 'the conspiracy of the Jews'; by the petty right in America today, by reference to 'the hidden force' of Communist spies. According to such notions of the omnipotent elite as historical cause, the elite is never an entirely visible agency. It is, in fact, a secular substitute for the will of God, being realized in a sort of providential design, except that usually non-elite men are thought capable of opposing it and eventually overcoming it.

The opposite view—of the elite as impotent—is now quite popular among liberal-minded observers. Far from being omnipotent, the elites are thought to be so scattered as to lack any coherence as a historical force. Their invisibility is not the invisibility of secrecy but the invisibility of the multitude. Those who occupy the formal places of authority are so check-mated—by other elites exerting pressure, or by the public as an electorate, or by constitutional codes—that, although there may be upper classes, there is no ruling class; although there may be men of power, there is no power elite; although there may be a system of stratification, it has no effective top. In the extreme, this view of the elite, as weakened by compromise and disunited to the point of nullity, is a substitute for impersonal collective fate; for, in this view, the decisions of the visible men of the higher circles do not count in history.

Internationally, the image of the omnipotent elite tends to prevail. All good events and pleasing happenings are quickly imputed by the opinion-makers to the leaders of their own nation; all bad events and unpleasant experiences are imputed to the enemy abroad. In both cases, the omnipotence of evil rulers or of virtuous leaders is assumed. Within the nation, the use of such rhetoric is rather more complicated: when men speak of the power of their own party or circle, they and their leaders are, of course, impotent; only 'the people' are omnipotent. But, when they speak of the power of their opponent's party or circle, they impute to them omnipotence; 'the people' are now powerlessly taken in.

More generally, American men of power tend, by convention, to deny that they are powerful. No American runs for office in order to rule or even govern, but only to serve; he does not become a bureaucrat or even an official, but a public servant. And nowadays, as I have already pointed out, such postures have become standard features of the public-relations programs of all men of power. So firm a part of the style of power-wielding have they become that conservative writers readily misinterpret them as indicating a trend toward an 'amorphous power situation.'

But the 'power situation' of America today is less amorphous than is the perspective of those who see it as a romantic confusion. It is less a flat, momentary 'situation' than a graded, durable structure. And if those who occupy its top grades are not omnipotent, neither are they impotent. It is the form and the height of the gradation of power that we must examine if we would understand the degree of power held and exercised by the elite.

If the power to decide such national issues as are decided were shared in an absolutely equal way, there would be no power elite; in fact, there would be no *gradation* of power, but only a radical homogeneity. At the opposite extreme as well, if the power to decide issues were absolutely monopolized by one small group, there would be no gradation of power; there would simply be this small group in command, and below it, the undifferentiated, dominated masses. American society today represents neither the one nor the other of these extremes, but a conception of them is none the less useful: it makes us realize more clearly the question of the structure of power in the United States and the position of the power elite within it.

Within each of the most powerful institutional orders of modern society there is a gradation of power. The owner of a roadside fruit stand does not have as much power in any area of social or economic or political decision as the head of a multi-million-dollar fruit corporation; no lieutenant on the line is as powerful as the Chief of Staff in the Pentagon; no deputy sheriff carries as much authority as the President of the United States. Accordingly, the problem of defining the power elite concerns the level at which we wish to draw the line. By lowering the line, we could define the elite out of existence; by raising it, we could make the elite a very small circle indeed. In a preliminary and minimum way, we draw the line crudely, in charcoal as it were: By the power elite, we refer to those political, economic, and military circles which as an intricate set of overlapping cliques share decisions having at least national consequences. In so far as national events are decided, the power elite are those who decide them. . . .

6

It is not my thesis that for all epochs of human history and in all nations, a creative minority, a ruling class, an omnipotent elite, shape all historical events. Such statements, upon careful examination, usually turn out to be mere tautologies,[6] and even when they are not, they are so entirely general as to be useless in the attempt to understand the history of the present. The minimum definition of the power elite as those who decide whatever is decided of major consequence, does not imply

that the members of this elite are always and necessarily the history-makers; neither does it imply that they never are. We must not confuse the conception of the elite, which we wish to define, with one theory about their role: that they are the history-makers of our time. To define the elite, for example, as 'those who rule America' is less to define a conception than to state one hypothesis about the role and power of that elite. No matter how we might define the elite, the extent of its members' power is subject to historical variation. If, in a dogmatic way, we try to include that variation in our generic definition, we foolishly limit the use of a needed conception. If we insist that the elite be defined as a strictly coordinated class that continually and absolutely rules, we are closing off from our view much to which the term more modestly defined might open to our observation. In short, our definition of the power elite cannot properly contain dogma concerning the degree and kind of power that ruling groups everywhere have. Much less should it permit us to smuggle into our discussion a theory of history.

During most of human history, historical change has not been visible to the people who were involved in it, or even to those enacting it. Ancient Egypt and Mesopotamia, for example, endured for some four hundred generations with but slight changes in their basic structure. That is six and a half times as long as the entire Christian era, which has only prevailed some sixty generations; it is about eighty times as long as the five generations of the United States' existence. But now the tempo of change is so rapid, and the means of observation so accessible, that the interplay of event and decision seems often to be quite historically visible, if we will only look carefully and from an adequate vantage point.

When knowledgeable journalists tell us that 'events, not men, shape the big decisions,' they are echoing the theory of history as Fortune, Chance, Fate, or the work of The Unseen Hand. For 'events' is merely a modern word for these older ideas, all of which separate men from history-making, because all of them lead us to believe that history goes on behind men's backs. History is drift with no mastery; within it there is action but no deed; history is mere happening and the event intended by no one.[7]

The course of events in our time depends more on a series of human decisions than on any inevitable fate. The sociological meaning of 'fate' is simply this: that, when the decisions are innumerable and each one is of small consequence, all of them add up in a way no man intended—to history as fate. But not all epochs are equally fateful. As the circle of those who decide is narrowed, as the means of decision are centralized and the consequences of decisions become enormous, then the course of great events often rests upon the decisions of determinable circles. This does not necessarily mean that the same circle of men follow through from one event to another in such a way that all of history is merely their plot. The power of the elite does not necessarily mean that history is not also shaped by a series of small decisions, none of which are thought out. It does not mean that a hundred small arrangements and compromises and adaptations may not be built into the going policy and the living event. The idea of the power elite implies nothing about the process of decision-making as such: it is an attempt to delimit the social areas within which that process, whatever its character, goes on. It is a conception of who is involved in the process.

The degree of foresight and control of those who are involved in decisions that count may also vary. The idea of the power elite does not mean that the estimations and calculated risks upon which decisions are made are not often wrong and that the consequences are sometimes, indeed often, not those intended. Often those who make decisions are trapped by their own inadequacies and blinded by their own errors.

Yet in our time the pivotal moment does arise, and at that moment, small circles do decide or fail to decide. In either case, they are an elite of power. The dropping of the A-bombs over Japan was such a moment; the decision on Korea was such a moment; the

confusion about Quemoy and Matsu, as well as before Dienbienphu were such moments; the sequence of maneuvers which involved the United States in World War II was such a 'moment.' Is it not true that much of the history of our times is composed of such moments? And is not that what is meant when it is said that we live in a time of big decisions, of decisively centralized power?

Most of us do not try to make sense of our age by believing in a Greek-like, eternal recurrence, nor by a Christian belief in a salvation to come, nor by any steady march of human progress. Even though we do not reflect upon such matters, the chances are we believe with Burckhardt that we live in a mere succession of events; that sheer continuity is the only principle of history. History is merely one thing after another; history is meaningless in that it is not the realization of any determinate plot. It is true, of course, that our sense of continuity, our feeling for the history of our time, is affected by crisis. But we seldom look beyond the immediate crisis or the crisis felt to be just ahead. We believe neither in fate nor providence; and we assume, without talking about it, that 'we'—as a nation—can decisively shape the future but that 'we' as individuals somehow cannot do so.

Any meaning history has, 'we' shall have to give to it by our actions. Yet the fact is that although we are all of us within history we do not all possess equal powers to make history. To pretend that we do is sociological nonsense and political irresponsibility. It is nonsense because any group or any individual is limited, first of all, by the technical and institutional means of power at its command; we do not all have equal access to the means of power that now exist, nor equal influence over their use. To pretend that 'we' are all history-makers is politically irresponsible because it obfuscates any attempt to locate responsibility for the consequential decisions of men who do have access to the means of power.

From even the most superficial examination of the history of the western society we learn that the power of decision-makers is first of all limited by the level of technique, by the *means* of power and violence and organization that prevail in a given society. In this connection we also learn that there is a fairly straight line running upward through the history of the West; that the means of oppression and exploitation, of violence and destruction, as well as the means of production and reconstruction, have been progressively enlarged and increasingly centralized.

As the institutional means of power and the means of communications that tie them together have become steadily more efficient, those now in command of them have come into command of instruments of rule quite unsurpassed in the history of mankind. And we are not yet at the climax of their development. We can no longer lean upon or take soft comfort from the historical ups and downs of ruling groups of previous epochs. In that sense, Hegel is correct: we learn from history that we cannot learn from it.

Notes

1. Jacob Burckhardt, *Force and Freedom* (New York: Pantheon Books, 1943), pp. 303 ff.

2. Cf. Hans Gerth and C. Wright Mills, *Character and Social Structure* (New York: Harcourt, Brace, 1953), pp. 457 ff.

3. The statistical idea of choosing some value and calling those who have the most of it an elite derives, in modern times, from the Italian economist, Pareto, who puts the central point in this way: 'Let us assume that in every branch of human activity each individual is given an index which stands as a sign of his capacity, very much the way grades are given in the various subjects in examinations in school. The highest type of lawyer, for instance, will be given 10. The man who does not get a client will be given 1—reserving zero for the man who is an out-and-out idiot. To the man who has made his millions—honestly or dishonestly as the case may be—we will give 10. To the man who has earned his thousands we will give 6; to such as just manage to keep out of the poorhouse, 1, keeping zero for those who get in. . . . So let us make a class of people who have the highest indices in their branch of activity, and to that class give the name of *elite*.' Vilfredo Pareto, *The Mind and Society* (New York: Harcourt, Brace, 1935), par. 2027 and 2031. Those who follow this approach end up not with one elite, but with a number corresponding to the number of values they select. Like many rather abstract ways of reasoning, this one is useful because it forces us to think in a clear-cut way. For a skillful use of this approach, see the work of Harold D. Lasswell, in particular, *Politics: Who Gets What, When, How* (New York: McGraw-Hill, 1936); and for a more systematic use, H. D. Lasswell and Abraham Kaplan, *Power and Society* (New Haven: Yale University Press, 1950).

4. The conception of the elite as members of a top social stratum, is, of course, in line with the prevailing common-sense view of stratification. Technically, it is closer to 'status group' than to 'class,' and has been very well stated by Joseph A. Schumpeter, 'Social Classes in an Ethically Homogeneous Environment,' *Imperialism and Social Classes* (New York: Augustus M. Kelley, Inc., 1951), pp. 133 ff., especially pp. 137–47. Cf. also his *Capitalism, Socialism and Democracy*, 3rd ed. (New York: Harper, 1950), Part II. For the distinction between class and status groups, see *From Max Weber: Essays in Sociology* (trans. and ed. by Gerth and Mills; New York: Oxford University Press, 1946). For an analysis of Pareto's conception of the elite compared with Marx's conception of classes, as well as data on France, see Raymond Aron, 'Social Structure and Ruling Class,' *British Journal of Sociology*, vol. I, nos. 1 and 2 (1950).

5. The most popular essay in recent years which defines the elite and the mass in terms of a morally evaluated character-type is probably José Ortega y Gasset's, *The Revolt of the Masses*, 1932 (New York: New American Library, Mentor Edition, 1950), esp. pp. 91 ff.

6. As in the case, quite notably, of Gaetano Mosca, *The Ruling Class* (New York: McGraw-Hill, 1939). For a sharp analysis of Mosca, see Fritz Morstein Marx, 'The Bureaucratic State,' *Review of Politics*, vol. I, 1939, pp. 457 ff. Cf. also Mills, 'On Intellectual Craftsmanship,' April 1952, mimeographed, Columbia College, February 1955.

7. Cf. Karl Löwith, *Meaning in History* (Chicago: University of Chicago Press, 1949), pp. 125 ff. for concise and penetrating statements of several leading philosophies of history.

ANTHONY GIDDENS

Elites and Power

It is certainly one of the most characteristic emphases of the Marxian perspective that, in capitalism especially (but also, in a general sense, in the prior types of class system), the realm of the 'political' is subordinate to that of the 'economic'. What remains relatively obscure in Marx is the specific form of this dependence, and how it is expressed concretely in the domination of the ruling class.[1] The importance of this is not confined to the analysis of the social structure of capitalism, but bears directly upon the question of the classless character of socialism. It relates, in addition, to issues brought to the forefront by the critique of the Marxian standpoint advanced by the 'elite theorists' of the turn of the century. The substance of this critique, in the writings of such as Pareto and Mosca, may be expressed as an attempt to transmute the Marxian concept of class, as founded in the relations of production, into an essentially *political* differentiation between those 'who rule' and those who 'are ruled'—a transmutation which was, indeed, in part made possible by Marx's failure to specify in a systematic fashion the modes whereby the economic hegemony of the capitalist class becomes 'translated' into the political domination of the *ruling* class. For if it is simply the case that economic control directly yields political power, the way is open for the assertion that, in socialism, as in capitalism (indeed as in any

other conceivable type of complex society), whoever controls the means of production thereby achieves political domination as a ruling class. The movement of history from capitalism to socialism then becomes conceived of as a mere succession of 'ruling classes' ('elites'), as in classical 'elite theory', or more specifically as the emergence of the sort of 'managerial' or 'technocratic' ruling class described in Burnham's writings, and more recently in some of the variants of the theory of the 'technocratic society'.[2]

The points at issue between the Marxian standpoint and 'elite theory' have become further complicated in recent years by the use of concepts drawn from the latter, such as that of 'power elite', as if they were synonymous with that of 'ruling class'. It will be useful to clarify the usage of the terms 'ruling class', 'elite', 'power elite', 'governing class', etc., which involves, in part, looking more closely at the structuration of the upper class.

In the analysis which follows, I shall be interested primarily in developing a set of formulations which illuminate significant conceptual distinctions, rather than adhering to conventional terminological usage—if it can be said, in any case, that there is any conventional practice in a field in which there has been so much confusion.[3] I shall suggest that, given the distinctions set out below, there can exist a 'governing class' without it necessarily being a 'ruling class'; that there can exist a 'power elite' without there necessarily being either a 'ruling' or a 'governing class'; that there can be what I shall call a system of 'leadership groups' which constitutes neither a 'ruling class', 'governing class', nor 'power

Originally published in 1973. Please see complete source information beginning on page 891.

Recruitment

	Open	Closed
High	solidary elite	uniform elite
Low	abstract elite	established elite

Integration

elite'; and that *all* of these social formations are, in principle, compatible with the existence of a society which is 'capitalist' in its organisation. To begin with, a few elementary remarks are necessary about the notion of 'elite'. As it is sometimes employed, 'elite' may refer to those who 'lead' in any given category of activity: to actors and sportsmen as well as to political or economic 'leaders'. There is evidently a difference, however, between the first and the second, in that the former 'lead' in terms of some sort of scale of 'fame' or 'achievement', whereas the second usage may be taken to refer to persons who are at the head of a specific social organisation which has an internal authority structure (the state, an economic enterprise, etc.). I shall use the term 'elite group' in this latter sense, to designate those individuals who occupy positions of formal authority at the head of a social organisation or institution; and 'elite' very generally, to refer either to an elite group or cluster of elite groups.

In these terms, it can be said that a major aspect of the structuration of the upper class concerns, first, the process of mobility into or recruitment to, elite positions and, second, the degree of social 'solidarity' within and between elite groups. Mediate structuration thus concerns how 'closed' the process of recruitment to elite positions is, in favour of those drawn from propertied backgrounds. Proximate structuration depends primarily upon the frequency and nature of the social contacts between the members of elite groups. These may take various forms, including the formation of marriage connections or the existence of other kin ties, the prevalence of personal ties of acquaintance or friendship, etc. If the extent of social 'integration' of elite groups is high, there is also likely to be a high degree of moral solidarity characterising the elite as a whole and, probably, a low incidence of either latent or manifest conflicts between them. There has never been any elite, however solidary, which has been free of conflicts and struggles; but the degree and intensity of overt conflict has varied widely, and thus it is reasonable to speak broadly of differentials in the solidarity of elite groups.

Combining these two aspects of structuration, we can establish a typology of elite formations [see diagram this page].

A 'uniform' elite is one which shares the attributes of having a restricted pattern of recruitment and of forming a relatively tightly knit unity. It hardly needs emphasising that the classifications involved are not of an all-or-nothing character. The point has been made that even among traditional aristocracies there was never a completely 'closed' pattern of recruitment, something which has only been approached by the Indian caste system—all elites open their ranks, in some degree, to individuals from the lower orders, and may enhance their stability thereby. A relatively closed type of recruitment, however, is likely to supply the sort of coherent socialisation process producing a high level of solidarity between (and within) elite groups. But it is quite feasible to envisage the existence of instances which approximate more closely to the case of an 'established' elite, where there is a relatively closed pattern of recruitment, but only a low level of integration between elite groups. A 'solidary' elite, as defined in

Issue-strength

	Broad	Restricted
Consolidated power	autocratic	oligarchic
Diffused power	hegemonic	democratic

the classification, might also appear to involve an unlikely combination of elements, since it might seem difficult to attain a high degree of integration among elite groups whose members are drawn from diverse class backgrounds. But, while this type of social formation is probably rare in capitalist societies, at least some of the state socialist countries fit quite neatly into this category: the Communist Party is the main channel of access to elite positions, and while it provides an avenue of mobility for individuals drawn in substantial proportions from quite lowly backgrounds, at the same time it ensures a high degree of solidarity among elite groups. An 'abstract' elite, involving both relatively open recruitment and a low level of elite solidarity, whatever its empirical reality, approximates closely to the picture of certain contemporary capitalist societies as these are portrayed in the writings of the theorists of so-called 'pluralist democracy'.

The distinguishing of different types of elite formation does not, in itself, enable us to conceptualise the phenomenon of power. As in the case of class structuration itself, we may distinguish two forms of the mediation of power relationships in society. The first I shall call the *institutional* mediation of power; the other, the mediation of power in terms of *control*. By the institutional mediation of power, I mean the general form of state and economy within which elite groups are recruited and structured. This concerns, among other things, the role of property in the overall organisation of economic life, the nature of the legal framework defining economic and political rights and obligations, and the institutional structure of the state itself. The mediation of control refers to the actual (effective) power of policy-formation and decision-making held by the members of particular elite groups: how far, for example, economic leaders are able to influence decisions taken by politicians, etc. To express it another way, we can say that power has two aspects: a 'collective' aspect, in the sense that the 'parameters' of any concrete set of power relationships are contingent upon the overall system of organisation of a society; and a 'distributive' aspect, in the sense that certain groups are able to exert their will at the expense of others.[4] The mediation of control is thus expressed in terms of 'effective' power, manifest in terms of the capacity either to take or to influence the taking of decisions which affect the interests of two or more parties differentially.

We may conceptually separate two variable factors in analysing effective power (that is to say, power as differentiated from 'formal authority') in relation to types of elite formation. The first concerns how far such power is 'consolidated' in the hands of elite groups; the second refers to the 'issue-strength' of the power wielded by those in elite positions. While the former designates limitations upon effective power, deriving from constraints imposed from 'below', the latter concerns how far that power is limited *because it can only be exercised in relation to a range of restricted issues*. Thus it is often held to be characteristic of modern capitalist societies that there are quite narrowly defined limitations upon the issues over which elite groups are able to exercise control.[5] By combining these two aspects of effective power as exercised by elite groups, we can establish a classification of forms of power-structure [see diagram on this page]. Like the previous typology, this sets out

	Elite formation	Power-holding
Ruling class	uniform/established elite	autocratic/oligarchic
Governing class	uniform/established elite	hegemonic/democratic
Power elite	solidary elite	autocratic/oligarchic
Leadership groups	abstract elite	hegemonic/democratic

an abstract combination of possibilities; it goes almost without saying that this is no more than an elementary categorisation of a very complex set of phenomena, and the labels applied here in no way exhaust the variety of characteristics which are frequently subsumed under these terms.

According to these definitions, the consolidation of effective power is greatest where it is not restricted to clearly defined limits in terms of its 'lateral range' (broad 'issue-strength'), and where it is concentrated in the hands of the elite, or an elite group. Power-holding is 'oligarchic' rather than 'autocratic' where the degree of centralisation of power in the hands of elite groups is high, but where the issue-strength of that power is limited. In the case of 'hegemonic' control, those in elite positions wield power which, while it is not clearly defined in scope and limited to a restricted range of issues, is 'shallow'. A 'democratic' order, in these terms, is one in which the effective power of elite groups is limited in both respects.

Finally, bringing together both classifications formulated above, we can set up an overall typology of elite formations and power within the class structure [see diagram on this page]. This makes possible a clarification of the four concepts already mentioned—'ruling class', 'governing class', 'power elite' and 'leadership groups'. It must be emphasised that these partially cross-cut some of the existing usages in the literature on class and elite theory. The Paretian term 'governing class' is here not, as in Pareto's own writing, a replacement for the Marxian 'ruling class'; in this scheme, a governing class is 'one step down', both in terms of elite formation and power-holding, from a 'ruling class'.

In this scheme, the 'strongest' case of a ruling class is defined as that where a uniform elite wields 'autocratic' power; the weakest is where an established elite holds 'oligarchic' power. Where a relatively closed recruitment pattern is linked with the prevalence of defined restrictions upon the effective power of elite groups, a governing class exists, but not a ruling class. A governing class borders upon being a ruling class where a uniform elite possesses 'hegemonic' power; and comes closest to being a system of leadership groups where an established elite holds 'democratic' power. Where a governing class involves a combination of an established elite and 'hegemonic' power, it stands close to being a power elite. A power elite is distinguished from a ruling class in terms of pattern of recruitment, as is a governing class from a system of leadership groups. The latter exists where elite groups only hold limited power, and where, in addition, elite recruitment is relatively open in character.

In terms of the mediation of control, this classification leaves undefined the relative primacy of the power of any one elite group over others. This can be conceptually expressed as referring to the nature of the *hierarchy* which exists among elite groups. A hierarchy exists among elite groups in so far as one such group holds power of broader issue-strength than others, and is thereby able to exert a degree of control over decisions taken by those within them. Thus it may be that the economic elite, or certain sectors of the economic elite, are able to significantly condition political decisions through the use of 'influence', 'inducement', or the 'direct' control of political positions—i.e., through the fact that members of the economic elite are also incumbents of political positions. We may refer to all of these modes of obtaining, or striving for, control as the *media of interchange* between elite groups. It is precisely one of the major tasks of the analysis of elite formations to examine the media of interchange which operate between elite groups in any given society in order to determine what kinds of elite hierarchy exist.

Notes

1. Most subsequent Marxist authors have either been content with the most generalised assertions about this issue, or have wanted to have their cake and eat it by insisting that capitalism is dominated by a ruling class who do not actually 'rule'; cf. Nicos Poulantzas, *Pouvoir politique et classes sociales de l'état capitaliste* (Paris 1970), pp. 361ff.

2. James Burnham, *The Managerial Revolution* (New York 1941).

3. In this section of this chapter I have drawn upon part of my article 'Elites in the British class structure', *Sociological Review* 20, 1972.

4. cf. Talcott Parsons, 'On the concept of political power', *Proceedings of the American Philosophical Society* 107, 1963. The error in Parsons' analysis, however, is to take insufficient account of the fact that the 'collective' aspect of power is asymmetrical in its consequences for the different groupings in society.

5. As in Keller's 'strategic elites'. See Suzanne Keller, *Beyond the Ruling Class* (New York 1963).

E D W A R D   A .   S H I L S

The Political Class in the Age of Mass Society: Collectivistic Liberalism and Social Democracy

The very subject of the study of elites is anathema to the anti-elitists. Mosca and Pareto have always been suspect among progressivistic, collectivistic liberals and radicals, partly because they were suspected of having been Fascists, partly because some Fascists invoked them as witnesses to their oligarchical ideals and their admiration—and practice—of

Originally published in 1982. Please see complete source information beginning on page 891.

brutality. But, in fact, the study of elites is an evaluatively neutral subject. Insofar as it confines itself to the description of what happens between two or more generations, it is silent at the question as to whether inequality in the distribution of opportunities and rewards is inherent in the nature of societies. Indeed, the descriptive accounts contained in elite studies are quite compatible with the beliefs that inequalities are inevitable and with beliefs that they are necessary and useful or at least have advantages which more than compensate for their disadvantages. They are quite compatible with beliefs that the distributions which they disclose are good or evil.

Mosca certainly regarded the kinds of inequalities that he discovered in his studies as inevitable. He thought there could be no society without elites and that elites perform functions which are absolutely fundamental for the working of society. He thought moreover that they could not be dispensed with and that some of their vices were an inevitable concomitant of that existence. These did not seem to be controvertible issues to Mosca, nor indeed did they take a central position in his thought. He was more concerned with the conditions under which political elites were effective. This seems to me to set the proper problem in the study of elites. The demographic or "elite-recruitment" studies find their justification when the information that they bring is put to the task of explaining the success or failure of elites in maintaining their domination over their societies and avoiding violent disruptions in their tenure. Mosca did not conceive of the tenure of a particular set of individuals; he thought of tenure as running beyond the lifetime or the political careers of single individuals, conceived simply as individuals. He thought of the success of elites as political lineages or political classes. The ruling or political class was not the aggregate of all individuals participating in political life; it was not the aggregate of all those sections of the population whose members participated in politics. The ruling or political class was narrower than the latter; it was more a collective than the former. The political class was, according to Mosca, marked by a sense of political vocation, which was shared by its individual members who, at the same time, perceived that sense of vocation in the other members of the class. There was, on this basis, a sense of solidarity of individuals with each other, even though the political class as a whole was divided by rivalries.

The concept of a political class referred to a cluster of families or, to a lesser extent, professions and institutions from which the individuals who held important elective and appointive positions in the government came. Membership in these lineages or membership in these professions or the fact of having been a student at certain schools or colleges or universities offered to their members a sense of identity as parts of a loose collectivity whose "business" was ruling the society. The concept of a political class refers not only to the families, professions, and schools from which politicians and political organizers come; it refers to more than these and to the sense of identity focused on the shared right and obligation to rule. It is also a reference to an accumulating tradition of outlook and skill. The tradition provides each new generational group in the lineages, the professions, or the schools and the protégés of these groups, with the knowledge and skill that it needs to remain in power, to contend for power if it is not in power, and to do its job of exercising power with sufficient effectiveness to enable its collectivity to survive, to leave the peripheries of the ruled, in their significant parts, sufficiently satisfied and, if not satisfied, then sufficiently impotent so as to leave the political class at the center of society.

Mosca—and Schumpeter—seemed to think that these traditions of ruling provided the dispositions and attitudes needed to rule effectively, the self-confidence in confronting the decisions inherent in ruling, the ability to weigh and calculate the chances of success, and the knowledge of human beings with whom one must collaborate and against whom one must act. They thought that political experience is the best teacher of the art of politics and that the accumulated experiences of generations, concentrated into streams of traditions which flow into and through institutions, such as lineages, professions and schools, colleges and universities, are the sources of the knowledge which enables political classes to be successful. The idea of a political class is relevant to the understanding of politics because it implies that certain kinds of attitudes and knowledge are necessary for effective rule and that the sources of recruitment are connected with the qualities that make for effectiveness or ineffectiveness of rule.

Mosca wrote his great book a century ago, and he looked back over all of human history in the way in which an educated man in the

Italy of his time, well read in the classics and in history, could do. He wrote in a period that was on the verge of political and social developments which made the existence of the kind of political class which he had in mind more difficult. Political classes in Mosca's sense are greatly attenuated in the West, to the extent that they exist at all. And the tasks which they would have faced, and which their successors do face in the second half of the 20th century, render the efficacy of rulers more difficult. . . .

*   *   *

Whatever the complex of conditions that brought forth the present situation of "popular democracy," collectivistic liberalism, and social democracy and whatever the differences among these, the present situation is one that requires a tremendous concentration of power in the government to assemble and dispose of resources and to cope with a very high level of demands in various parts of the population.

Contemporary Western governments have taken the responsibility for full employment and economic growth, as well as for the provision of goods and services beyond those provided by the market, for the fostering of individual happiness and personal development, for the care of health and the conservation of nature, for the progress of scientific knowledge and the promotion of technological innovation, for the well-being of the arts and the quality of culture and for social justice—not just the rule of law—and for the remedying of past wrongs. This is a tremendous distance from the welfare state as it was conceived in Germany in the 19th century and by humanitarian reformers in the United States and Great Britain at the beginning of the 20th century. There is scarcely any sphere of life into which modern governments have not entered as a result of their own conception of their obligations and their sensitivity to the imperfections of man's life on earth and in response to the demands of various parts of the electorate and the prevailing intellectual opinion as to what governments should do and how they can do it.

No "political class," when political classes were still the reservoirs from which governing political elites came, ever had to cope with such a situation. The situation is a novel one; the tasks placed on and accepted by or actually sought by government are to some extent novel in substance and certainly unprecedented in scope. Moreover, the tasks change rapidly. Tasks are redefined. Failures must be remedied by renewed and more extensive measures. The undertakings of governments are so numerous and so comprehensive are the responsibilities that have been demanded of or proclaimed by governments as their "programs" that tasks of coordination of unexampled complexity arise. Governments have long ceased to regard governing as their first, perhaps even their only task; every government on its accession to office has a program of positive actions intended to carry further its past achievements, to broaden them and to improve on them. (Mistakes of one's own commission are seldom admitted.) On the rare occasions when an ostensibly less expansive government accedes to office, its program of undoing some of the arrangements instituted by its more expansive predecessors is as complicated as the positive program it would cancel. Furthermore, programs of cancellation of the arrangements of previous governments are never as comprehensive as the programs of preceding more positive administrations.

How different this is from the budget of tasks that political classes, when they still existed, accepted and were expected to accept! Even in the "absolute" monarchies of the *ancien régime,* government aspired to nothing comparable in scale and intensity to what contemporary Western governments accept as their objectives.

The great merit of the political class was its inheritance of a tradition of the arts of politics and ruling. The knowledge borne by that tradition was wisdom; it was not technical knowledge. Governments formed by political classes did not use much technical knowledge, and they used practically nothing of what would now be called scientific knowledge and scientific technology. Details of road building, the maintenance of waterways, the registration of titles to property, the construction of tax rolls, and the keeping of accounts of revenues and expenditures could be left to officials; decisions at the higher levels of government, insofar as they drew on this kind of knowledge, could be made by delegation of authority or by placing oneself in the hands of "expert advisors." Turgot and Colbert knew as much of the "science of economics" as anyone in France at that time. The fact is that there was little "science" which was thought to have bearing on the affairs of state; the challenge to know it and to incorporate it into decisions was not a burden which the "political class" had to bear. That burden is, however, one which contemporary politicians must bear.

The kinds of problems with which government dealt were not beyond the cognitive possessions of the political class. The failures of a political class could not be attributed to its failure to master and use an available stock of scientific knowledge. The problems political classes faced, to the extent that they faced them, did not lie outside the powers gained from the assimilation of the traditional political and governmental wisdom available to members of the political class and their own experience.

To do all the things which are demanded of them and to which they have committed themselves, legislators of the present century have called into being an immense bureaucracy. The bureaucracy, competent or incompetent though it might be in taking these tasks in hand, is certainly able to hold its own with the legislators who are constitutionally the rulers of Western societies, whether they be systems of parliamentary government dominated by a cabinet made up of the leaders of the dominant party or the presidential system which provides for an independent legislature and an independent executive. It was long ago pointed out by Max Weber that the bureaucracy would become the dominant power in government, unless it could be held in check by a system of competitive parties which, through elections and the competition in par-

liament, brought charismatic leaders to the fore. The American Congress, not knowing how to generate charismatic politicians, has sought a make-weight against the bureaucracy through the expansion of congressional staffs. They have now become dependent on a bureaucracy of their own making which is nearly as dominating over its superiors as the bureaucracy of the civil service. The President, to cope in his turn with the civil service on the one hand and with the legislature, which is increasingly wagged by the bureaucratic tail of its own creation, has created a large bureaucracy of his own in the Executive Office of the President. . . .

* * *

The Soviet Union is the only country that can be said to have a political class—a very limited circle of long duration from which the highest political elite is chosen by co-optation and calculation. It is not a political class in Mosca's sense because it lacks the element of recruitment from lineage, but this is a secondary matter. The present Soviet elite comes from a political class, the higher ranks of the Communist party of the Soviet Union; it comes primarily from Russia. Its members were not born into the Soviet political class, but they must enter it very early in their careers and make those careers within it and through the patronage of its then reigning leaders. It is a closed circle; intrusions from the outside are not compatible with its continued existence. Progress within the political class is dependent almost entirely on decisions within the political class which, having the formal organization of the Communist party of the Soviet Union as its frame, maintains—at least thus far—a strict control over succession.

Has the Communist political class been successful? In certain important respects, it has been successful. It has remained in power for about two thirds of a century; it has avoided subversion or replacement from outside itself. It has succeeded in achieving this success by ruthlessness, in brutal suppression of even mild-mannered internal criticism. In this sense, it goes beyond one of the features of political classes. Whereas political classes could assimilate some of their potential rivals or antagonists and could bring them into the system—this is how constitutional liberalism came to live together with monarchically centered conservatism in the 19th century in Western and Central Europe—the Soviet political elite suppresses potential rivals.

Since remaining in power is one of the tests of success of a political elite or of a political class (which is the variant of concern to us here), the Soviet elite has been successful. But one of the features of modern political elites is that they possess programs which they claim to be able to realize. The Soviet elite has certainly been quite successful in its external policies, in its intrusions into other countries. It has possessed the readiness to use force, corruption, manipulation, and conspiracy in the pursuit of its ends abroad, and it has done so with self-confidence. In this respect it has had all the qualities of relatively successful political classes of early modern times up to almost the end of the 19th century; these were the features of political classes which Mosca, and especially Pareto, admired.

Communism is, however, an ideal arrangement of the internal affairs of a society, and it is through the establishment everywhere of such a system that the Soviet elite justifies its extrusions beyond its own boundaries. There it has not been successful, neither within its own boundaries nor in the regimes which it has established and maintained in power outside those boundaries. There, all the qualities which are sustained by the culture of a political class have not helped it—with the exception of its readiness to suppress by the harshest methods those who appear to endanger it. In those fields of activity, like the economic sphere, in which force is not sufficient, the Soviet political class and those lesser political classes which it supports have not been at all successful. Being a political class is thus not anything like a guarantee of success, although it does have certain advantages.

*   *   *

When we turn away from Communist regimes and consider the political elites of modern Western countries, we contemplate a scene which is fairly devoid of the qualities of organization and culture characteristic of political classes. Modern liberalism, with its emphasis on individual achievement, modern taxation, and the changes in the technology and organization of agriculture have doomed one of the pillars of the system of political classes, namely the great landowning families which in many large societies supplied cultural centers of interaction and much of the personnel of the political classes.

The church, the religious orders, and lay, para-ecclesiastical organizations once constituted a set of adjuncts of the political class, particularly in Roman Catholic countries in the *anciens régimes* and to a smaller, but still some, extent in Protestant countries. This has changed greatly in Roman Catholic countries as a consequence of anticlericalism and more recently as a consequence of radicalism in the priesthood; priests in some Latin countries have become the enemies of what remains of the political class. In Protestant countries too there has been a clerical withdrawal from the political elite.

The political elites have become less self-enclosed, and their different and rival sectors have become less conciliatory toward each other than when they formed a political class. The fate of the system of *versuiling* which prevailed for more than a century in the Netherlands illustrates this process. As long as the political elites of the various "vertical" sectors of Dutch society maintained their ascendancy in consequence of the compliance of their following, they could collaborate more easily with their rivals or competitors of the other "vertical" sectors. When the rank and file of the various parties became more demanding, more consciously "self-esteeming," and more insistent on their being heeded by their leaders, the political class of the Netherlands lost some of its self-enclosedness, its control over recruitment, and its self-assurance. Similar developments, *mutatis mutandis,* have occurred in other Western countries. The churches have become uneasy about their links with the center of their respective societies. They have sought to disavow their participation in the earthly center in order to espouse the causes and to seek the approval of the peripheries of society, while claiming thereby to affirm their link with the transcendent center of all existence.

Lineages ceased to be as significant in the self-consciousness of individuals and in their influence on the conduct and loyalties of their members. Churches became somewhat dissociated from the centers of society—either by the constitutional separation of church and state or through voluntary withdrawal and disavowal by the churches.

Great Britain and France were the only countries in which educational institutions served to form and rally the political class. In the former, the great public schools—above all Eton, Harrow, Rugby, and a few others—and Oxford University (also Cambridge to a lesser degree) provided places for inculcation of the outlook of the political class, a sense of solidarity—the "old school tic"—and places of recruitment into the political class. In France, in different ways, a few of the great *lycées* in Paris, e.g., the Lycée Louis le Grand and the Ecole libre des sciences politiques and, around the time of the First World War, the Ecole normale supérieure, played a similar role.[1] More recently, the Ecole d'administration has been added to the set of formative institutions of the French political elite. (The Ecole polytechnique, important though it has been in the administration of the country, does not seem to have been quite as important in the formation and maintenance of the political elite in contemporary France, although it is conceivable that the technological, scientific training which it offers might lead to its displacement of the more humanistic Ecole normale supérieure. The same applies to the forward movement of the Ecole nationale d'administration.)

Neither the United States nor Germany have had any higher educational institutions which have performed approximately similar functions. No German university, despite the intellectual achievements and the nationalistic devotion (sometimes excessive) of German professors, ever played a role like that of Oxford in Great Britain. The role of the universities in the United States is somewhat similar. In some of the states, the state university played a part of some importance in the formation of a state-wide political elite. (I think particularly of the University of Wisconsin and, with less certainty, of the University of Minnesota.) Harvard University has never been in a position in national political life in the United States comparable to that of Oxford or the French *grandes écoles.* It has, from time to time, appeared to be on the verge of that situation, for example, during the administrations of Theodore Roosevelt, Franklin Roosevelt, and John Kennedy. Many of its members would have liked it to be such, and, recently, the Kennedy School of Public Affairs tries to perform a partial function of an institution which contributes to the formation of a political class through its courses for newly elected members of Congress. Nevertheless, despite aspirations and occasional flickerings, Harvard has not attained that position, and no other American educational institution has come even that near.

The United States is too large and, despite the recent aggrandizement of the national center, it is still too decentralized in its interests, functions, and loyalties for a political class to emerge. Populism would have resisted it. But even without populism and the diversity of American society, local and regional interests and the local and federal structure of the American governmental system would have prevented it. The local and state political machines did create some of the constitutive elements of a political class, but the weakness, between presidential elections, of the national institutions of the two major parties has also stood in the way of the fusion of these constituents into a national political class.

Insofar as the United States has a political class—and it has one only in a most rudimentary and partial form—it does so through its national legislative bodies. Of these, the Senate is by far the most important in many respects. The United States Senate and the British House of Commons have each claimed or, had claimed for them, the standing of "the best club in the world." A club has its atmosphere and its rules; it has its own distinctive culture which new members must acquire and through which they acquire "the art of politics." It is, however, another matter as to whether the "best club in the world" can generate and sustain the skill, knowledge, solidarity, and self-confidence necessary for keeping on top of the problems which the demands of the electorate and of the particular interests within it, and their own ideas about the rightful sphere of government, have presented to modern politicians for solution.

The strain on the political culture of the main centers of Western societies is aggravated by the unceasingly critical and demanding scrutiny which the contemporary apparatus of knowledge, on the one side, and demanding and increasingly aggrieved assertiveness of the mass of population on the other, directs toward the political elite.

When Mosca discussed a closed or a partially closed political class he had in mind primarily the reservoir of recruitment and the extent to which that reservoir was open to persons who came from outside the main political families, institutions, and circles. Modern political life under conditions of popular democracy is too open for the generation and maintenance of a political class. Mosca's emphasis on the partial closedness of recruitment as a condition of the existence and continuity of a political class might also have been extended, and it should now be extended to include closedness from external scrutiny.

Bentham conceived of the "eye of the public" as "the virtue of the statesman," but he never conceived of that eye as having such a depth of penetration, such brightness, and such constancy as the present eye of the public represented in the professional staffs of the mass media of communication. Like many of the critics of the closure of the political classes of the 18th and 19th centuries who wanted a pattern of government more open to the public gaze, he did not imagine how imaginative, how powerful, how detailed, and omnipresent that eye would become.

It would be very difficult for a political elite, nurtured by a combination of open and closed recruitment, to withstand that insistent eye, especially under conditions in which the minds and voices behind that eye demand so much and demand it so insistently and censoriously. The invention of sample surveys of the political attitudes of Western societies, the frequency of those surveys, and the specificity of the objects on which they seek to discover the distribution of attitudes mean that political elites have to think unceasingly about whether their measures are popular. Popularity of measures becomes a criterion of the success of a measure, long before it has had a chance to become effective. Effectiveness and popularity are not the same thing, and their divergence renders the formation of a political class in Mosca's sense impossible. A political class in Mosca's sense did not have to be continuously on the alert to its popularity, and since it did not try to do as much as contemporary political elites in societies dominated by collectivistic liberal and social democratic beliefs and demands, it was easier for it to be effective. Neither of these conditions is present today.

Note

1. Albert Thibaudet puts this thesis forward explicitly in *La Republique des professeurs* (Paris: Grasset, 1927).

MICHAEL USEEM

The Inner Circle

Recent studies of the politics of big business could hardly be more divided on the extent to which the corporate community is socially unified, cognizant of its classwide interests, and prepared for concerted action in the political arena. In a number of original investigations, for instance, G. William Domhoff finds "persuasive evidence for the existence of a socially cohesive national upper class."[1] These "higher circles," composed chiefly of corporate executives, primary owners, and their descendents, constitute, in his view, "the governing class in America," for these businesspeople and their families dominate the top positions of government agencies, the political parties, and the governing boards of nonprofit organizations. Drawing on studies of the U.S., Great Britain, and elsewhere, Ralph Miliband reaches a similar conclusion, finding that "'elite pluralism' does not . . . prevent the separate elites in capitalist society from constituting a dominant economic class, possessed of a high degree of cohesion and solidarity, with common interests and common purposes which far transcend their specific differences and disagreements."[2]

Yet other analysts have arrived at nearly opposite conclusions. In an extensive review of studies of business, Ivar Berg and Mayer Zald argue that "businessmen are decreasingly a coherent and self-sufficient autonomous elite; increasingly business leaders are differentiated by their heterogeneous interests and find it difficult to weld themselves into a solidified group."[3] Similarly, Daniel Bell contends that the disintegration of family capitalism in America has thwarted the emergence of a national "ruling class," and, as a result, "there are relatively few political issues on which the managerial elite is united."[4] Leonard Silk and David Vogel, drawing on their observations of private discussions among industrial managers, find that the "enormous size and diversity of corporate enterprise today makes it virtually impossible for an individual group to speak to the public or government with authority on behalf of the entire business community."[5]

Observers of the British corporate community express equally disparate opinion, though the center of gravity is closer to that of discerning cohesion than disorganization. Drawing on their own study of British business leaders during the past century, Philip Stanworth and Anthony Giddens conclude that "we may correctly speak of the emergence, towards the turn of the century, of a consolidated and unitary 'upper class' in industrial Britain."[6] More recently, according to John Westergaard and Henrietta Resler, "the core" of the privileged and powerful is "those who own and those who control capital on a large scale: whether top business executives or rentiers makes no difference in this context. Whatever divergences of interests there may be among them on this score and others, latent as well as manifest, they have a common stake in one overriding cause: to keep the working rule of the society capitalist."[7] The solidity is underpinned by a unique lattice-

Originally published in 1984. Please see complete source information beginning on page 891.

work of old school ties, exclusive urban haunts, and aristocratic traditions that are without real counterpart in American life. Thus, "a common background and pattern of socialization, reinforced through intermarriage, club memberships, etc. generated a community feeling among the members of the propertied class," writes another analyst, and "this feeling could be articulated into a class awareness by the most active members of the class."[8]

Yet even if the concept of "the establishment" originated in British attempts to characterize the seamless web at the top that seemed so obvious to many, some observers still discern little in British business on which to pin such a label. Scanning the corporate landscape in the early 1960s, for instance, J. P. Nettl finds that the "business community" is in "a state of remarkable weakness and diffuseness—compared, say, to organized labour or the professions," for British businessmen lack "a firm sense of their distinct identity, and belief in their distinct purpose."[9] The years since have brought little consolidation, according to Wyn Grant: business "is neither homogeneous in its economic composition nor united on the appropriate strategy and tactics to advance its interests." Thus, "businessmen in Britain are not bound by a strong sense of common political purpose."[10]

Scholarly disagreement on this question, not surprisingly, is reflected in the textbooks used in university social-science courses. Every year American undergraduate students enter courses whose main textbook declares that business leaders have "a strong sense of identity as a class and a rather sophisticated understanding of their collective interest on which they tend to act in a collective way."[11] But students on other campuses find themselves studying textbooks with entirely different conclusions. They will be taught that the capitalist class has ceased to exist altogether or, at the minimum, that the received wisdom is, at best, agnostic on its degree of cohesion. The required reading in some courses asserts that "the question of whether [the] upper class forms a unified, cohesive, dominant group is

still the subject of unresolved debate."[12] The correct view according to the assigned textbook in still other courses is that "until more data are gathered the question of whether national power is in the control of a power elite or veto group remains moot."[13] Still other students, especially those enrolled in management courses, are informed that fragmentation rather than cohesion now prevails. "A great deal of evidence," asserts a text for business school instruction, "suggests that our society is leaning toward the pluralistic model" rather than the "power-elite" model. "Few, if any, books are written about an 'establishment' anymore, suggesting that if one did exist it either has disappeared or is not influential enough to worry about."[14] The theory of the "power elite" is, according to another widely used textbook on business and society, "a gross distortion of reality and the conclusions derived from it are largely erroneous."[15]

Social theory itself divides along this very line. Both traditional pluralist thought and a neo-Marxist strand sometimes labeled "structuralism" have generally argued that the parochial concerns of individual firms receive far greater expression in the political process than do the general collective concerns of business. Competition among firms, sectoral cleavages, and executives' and directors' primary identification with their own enterprise all inhibit even the formation of classwide awareness, let alone an organizational vehicle for promoting their shared concerns. Business disorganization, it is argued, prevails. Arguments based on pluralism and those on structural Marxism radically diverge in the implications they draw from the presumed disunity. To the pluralists, the corporate elite is far too divided to be any more effective than any other interest group in imposing its views on the government, thus enabling the state to avoid having its prerogatives co-opted by business. But for structural Marxism, it is precisely because of this disorganization of big business that the state can and does (for other reasons) assume the role of protecting the common interests of its major corporations.

Counterposed to both of these theoretical perspectives is an equally familiar thesis, advanced by what are now known as "instrumental" neo-Marxists and by many non-Marxists as well: that the government is more responsive to the outlook of big business than to that of any other sector or class, certainly of labor. According to these theories, this responsiveness is the result, in part, of the social unity and political cohesion of the corporate elite. With such cohesion and coordination, business is able to identify and promote successfully those public policies that advance the general priorities shared by most large companies.[16]

Resolution of these opposing visions of the internal organization of the business community is essential if we are to understand how, and with what effect, business enters the political process, or, in Anthony Giddens's more abstract framing, how we are to comprehend "the modes in which . . . economic hegemony is translated into political domination."[17] But the resolution offered here is not one of establishing which of these competing views is more "correct," for either answer would be, as we shall see, incorrect; in their own limited and specific fashions, both descriptions are also partly true. . . .

The Inner Circle

I will argue that a politicized leading edge of the leadership of a number of major corporations has come to play a major role in defining and promoting the shared needs of large corporations in two of the industrial democracies, the United States and the United Kingdom. Rooted in intercorporate networks through shared ownership and directorship of large companies in both countries, this politically active group of directors and top managers gives coherence and direction to the politics of business. Most business leaders are not part of what I shall term here the *inner circle*. Their concerns extend little beyond the immediate welfare of their own firms. But those few whose positions make them sensi-

tive to the welfare of a wide range of firms have come to exercise a voice on behalf of the entire business community.

Central members of the inner circle are both top officers of large firms and directors of several other large corporations operating in diverse environments. Though defined by their corporate positions, the members of the inner circle constitute a distinct, semi-autonomous network, one that transcends company, regional, sectoral, and other politically divisive fault lines within the corporate community.

The inner circle is at the forefront of business outreach to government, nonprofit organizations, and the public. Whether it be support for political candidates, consultation with the highest levels of the national administration, public defense of the "free enterprise system," or the governance of foundations and universities, this politically dominant segment of the corporate community assumes a leading role, and corporations whose leadership involves itself in this pancorporate network assume their own distinct political role as well. Large companies closely allied to the highest circle are more active than other firms in promoting legislation favorable to all big business and in assuming a more visible presence in public affairs, ranging from philanthropy to local community service.

The inner circle has assumed a particularly critical role during the past decade. The 1970s and early 1980s were a period of unprecedented expansion of corporate political activities, whether through direct subvention of candidates, informal lobbying at the highest levels of government, or formal access to governmental decision-making processes through numerous business-dominated panels created to advise government agencies and ministries. This political mobilization of business can be traced to the decline of company profits in both the United States and the United Kingdom and to heightened government regulation in America and labor's challenge of management prerogatives in Britain. As large companies have increasingly sought to influence the political process, the inner circle has helped direct their activities toward political ends that will yield benefits for all large firms, not just those that are most active. This select group of directors and senior managers has thus added a coherence and effectiveness to the political voice of business, one never before so evident. The rise to power of governments attentive to the voice of business, if not always responsive to its specific proposals, is, in part, a consequence of the mobilization of corporate politics during the past decade and the inner circle's channeling of this new energy into a range of organizational vehicles.

Both the emergence of the inner circle and the degree to which it has come to define the political interests of the entire business community are unforeseen consequences of a far-reaching transformation of the ways in which large corporations and the business communities are organized. In the early years of the rise of the modern corporation, self-made entrepreneurs were at the organizational helm, ownership was shared with, but limited to, kin and descendents, and the owning families merged into a distinct, intermarrying upper class. It was the era of family capitalism, and upper-class concerns critically informed business political activity. In time, however, family capitalism was slowly but inexorably pushed aside by the emergence of a new pattern of corporate organization and control—managerial capitalism. Business political activity increasingly came to address corporate, rather upper-class, agendas, as the corporation itself became the central organizing force. If family capitalism was at its height at the end of the nineteenth century and managerial capitalism was ascendent during the first half of the twentieth, both are now yielding in this era to institutional capitalism, a development dating to the postwar period and rapidly gaining momentum in recent decades. In the era of institutional capitalism, it is not only family or individual corporate interests that serve to define how business political activity is organized and expressed but rather concerns much more classwide—the shared interests and needs of all large corporations taken together. Increasingly a consciousness of a generalized corporate outlook shapes the content of corporate political action.

The large business communities in Britain and America have thus evolved, for the most part without conscious design, the means for aggregating and promoting their common interests. While government agencies add further coherence to the policies sought, the inner circle now serves to fashion, albeit in still highly imperfect ways, the main elements of public policies suited to serve the broader requirements of the entire corporate community. This conclusion is not in accord with predominant thinking, nor with those theories about business-government relations more fully described below. Of these, most fall into one of two opposing schools. According to the first, corporate leadership is presumed to be either too-little organized to act politically at all, or, as the second goes, so fully organized that it acts as a single, politically unified bloc. This [essay] rejects both schools of thought and argues for a new perception, a new theory of the nature of the politics of big business in contemporary British and American society.

A new conception of the business firm is also needed. Most corporate business decisions are viewed, correctly, as a product of the internal logic of the firm. Yet when decisions are made on the allocation of company monies to political candidates, the direction of its philanthropic activities, and other forms of political outreach, an external logic is important as well. This is the logic of classwide benefits, involving considerations that lead to company decisions beneficial to all large companies, even when there is no discernible, direct gain for the individual firm. The inner circle is the carrier of this extracorporate logic; the strategic presence of its members in the executive suites of major companies allows it to shape corporate actions to serve the entire corporate community.

The power of the transcorporate network even extends into the selection of company senior managers. In considering an executive for promotion to the uppermost positions in a firm, the manager's reputation within the firm remains of paramount importance, but it is not the only reputation that has come to count. The executive's standing within the broader corporate community—as cultivated through successful service on the boards of several other large companies, leadership in major business associations, and the assumption of civic and public responsibilities—is increasingly a factor. Acceptance by the inner circle has thus become almost a prerequisite for accession to the stewardship of many of the nation's largest corporations. Our traditional conception of the firm must accordingly be modified. No longer is the large company an entirely independent actor, striving for its own profitable success without regard for how its actions are affecting the profitability of others. While it retains its independence in many areas of decision-making, its autonomy is compromised. And this is especially true for company actions targeted at improving the political environment. Through the agency of the inner circle, large corporations are now subject to a new form of collective political discipline by their corporate brethren. . . .

Principles of Social Organization

The organization is simultaneously structured by a number of distinct principles, of which three are of overriding importance.[18] Each contains a fundamentally different implication for the ways in which business enters the political arena.

The *upper-class principle* asserts that the first and foremost defining element is a social network of established wealthy families, sharing a distinct culture, occupying a common social status, and unified through intermarriage and common experience in exclusive settings, ranging from boarding schools to private clubs. This principle is the point of departure for virtually all analyses of the British "establishment," or the group that has sometimes been more termed "the great and

the good."[19] Yet the lesser visibility and heterogeneity of an American "establishment" has not discouraged scholars from treating the U.S. circles in terms analogous to those applied to the British upper class. This is evident, for instance, in E. Digby Baltzell's studies of the national and metropolitan "business aristocracies"; in G. William Domhoff's inquiries into America's "upper-social class"; in Randall Collins's treatment of the preeminence of upper-class cultural dominance in America; and in Leonard and Mark Silk's study of what they have simply called "the American establishment."[20]

Many, if not most members of the upper class also occupy positions in or around large companies. But from the standpoint of this principle, these corporate locations are useful but not defining elements. Individuals are primarily situated instead according to a mixture of such factors as family reputation, kinship connections, academic pedigree, social prominence, and patrician bearing. As the upper class enters politics, this principle supports the conclusions that its main objectives would be to preserve the social boundaries of the upper class, its intergenerational transmission of its position, and the privately held wealth on which its privileged station resides. Control of the large corporation is only one means to this end, though in the U.S. it has emerged as the single most important means. Thus, one "of the functions of upper class solidarity," writes Baltzell, "is the retention, within a primary group of families, of the final decision-making positions within the social structure. As of the first half of the twentieth century in America, the final decisions affecting the goals of the social structure have been made primarily by members of the financial and business community."[21]

A parallel movement into British industry is suggested by other analysts. "Without stigma," writes one observer, "peers, baronets, knights and country squires [accepted] directorships in the City, in banks, large companies and even in the nationalized industries." But the entry into commerce, necessitated by political and financial reality, was not at the price of assimilation, it is argued, for the upper class moved to rule business with the same self-confident sense of special mission with which it had long overseen land, politics, and the empire. Aristocratic identity ran far too deep to permit even capitalist subversion of traditional values: "Heredity, family connections, going to the same schools, belonging to the same clubs, the same social circle, going to the same parties, such were the conditions that enabled 'the charmed circle' to survive all change, unscathed, whether economic, political, religious or cultural."[22] Business enterprise is simply the newest means for preserving upper-class station, and, as such, is largely subordinated to that project.

The *corporate principle* of organization suggests by contrast that the primary defining element is the corporation itself. Location is determined not by patrician lineage, but by the individual's responsibilities in the firm and the firm's position in the economy. Coordinates for the latter include such standard dimensions as company size, market power, sector, organizational complexity, source of control, financial performance, and the like. Upper-class allegiances are largely incidental to this definition of location, for the manager is locked into corporate-determined priorities no matter what family loyalties may still be maintained. This is the point of departure, of course, for most journalists covering business, corporate self-imagery, and analysts working within the traditional organizational behavior paradigm.[23] Not only are upper-class commitments viewed as largely incidental, but loyalties to the corporate elite as a whole are taken to be faint by comparison with the manager's single-minded drive to advance the interests of his own firm ahead of those of his competitors. By implication, corporate leaders enter politics primarily to promote conditions favorable to the profitability of their own corporations. Policies designed to preserve upper-class station or the long-term collective interests of all large companies receive weak articulation at best. Capitalist competition and its political spillover might be described as

one of th few remaining illustrations of Hobbes's infamous state of a war of all against all.

The *classwide principle* resides on still different premises about the main elements defining the social organization of the corporate community. In this framework, location is primarily determined by position in a set of interrelated, quasiautonomous networks encompassing virtually all large corporations. Acquaintanceship circles, interlocking directorates, webs of interfirm ownership, and major business associations are among the central strands of these networks. Entry into the transcorporate networks is contingent on successfully reaching the executive suite of some large company, and it is further facilitated by old school ties and kindred signs of a proper breeding. But corporate credentials and upper-class origins are here subordinated to a distinct logic of classwide organization. . . .

Upper-class, corporate, and classwide principles of social organization distinctively shape the basic thrust of business political activity. Thus, their relative importance is of fundamental interest for comprehending contemporary corporate activity—from the orchestration of public opinion on behalf of "reindustrialization" to renewed assaults on organized labor and government regulation. The underlying theme of the present analysis is that the relative balance long ago shifted in the U.S. from upper-class to corporate principle, and that American business is currently undergoing still another transformation, this time from corporate to classwide principles of organization. By the middle of this century, family capitalism had largely given way to managerial capitalism, and in recent decades managerial capitalism itself has been giving way to institutional capitalism, bringing us into an era in which classwide principles are increasingly dominant. In the U.K., the corporate principle never quite so fully eclipsed the upper-class principle, but both logics are now yielding there as well to the rise of classwide organization within the business community. This transformation has profound implications for the power and ideology of big business in both countries. . . .

The Power Elite

Business, military, and the government—these were the three pillars of C. Wright Mills's famous American "power elite."[24] Since publication of this classic study in 1956, several generations of university students have been required to master its elements, even as, or perhaps because, they were soon themselves to become part of one of the three pillars. As contested as it was, Mills's thesis was assimilated into the shared perception of most educated circles, a touchstone for informed conversation about how our society governs itself, if not proven fact. In opening an article profiling the chief executives of the largest U.S. corporations some two decades after *The Power Elite* first appeared, *Fortune* magazine could still frame a question whose reference most readers were certain to comprehend: "Is [the chief executive], as often supposed outside the business world, an aristocrat of what C. Wright Mills called the Power Elite?"[25]

Less remembered than the general thesis, but more useful for understanding corporate politics, is Mills's prescient insight regarding why business had become a pillar of the establishment. American capitalism, he observed, has been marked by continuously increasing centralization and concentration. This process, in Mills's view, had led to the emergence of a new breed of corporate executives committed to industry-wide concerns reaching far beyond the interests of their own firms. Moreover, a fraction of these executives took an even broader view of business problems: "They move from the industrial point of interest and outlook to the interests and outlook of the class of all big corporate property as a whole."[26]

Mills identified two features of business organization as primarily responsible for the change in outlook. First, the personal and family investments of top managers and owners had become dispersed among a number of firms. As a result, he wrote, "the executives and owners who are in and of and for this propertied class cannot merely push the narrow interests of each property; their interests become engaged by the whole corporate class."[27]

Second, the emergence of an extensive network of interlocking directorships among the major corporations also meant that a number of managers had assumed responsibility for the prosperity of several corporations, and thus those holding multiple directorships constituted "a more sophisticated executive elite which now possesses a certain autonomy from any specific property interests. Its power is the power . . . of classwide property."[28] It is this power that had so well positioned the business elite to serve as a dominant pillar of the American power elite.

Surveying much the same landscape, other analysts have offered kindred hypotheses. Maurice Zeitlin has suggested that centralizing tendencies akin to those discussed by Mills are creating an overarching unity within the business community. Prominent among such tendencies is "the establishment of an effective organizational apparatus of interlocking directorates" cutting across both financial and industrial sectors. Such interlocking directorates may be very important in any effort to maintain the "cohesiveness of the capitalist class and its capacity for common action and unified policies."[29] The number of owners and managers holding diversified corporate investments and positions is viewed by both Zeitlin and Mills as a potentially dominant political segment of the business community, one that is increasingly in a position to impose its outlook as it recognizes itself as the national network that it is.

The growing concentration of economic power in this network has been recognized in official circles as well, with equanimity in some, alarm in others. A U.S. congressional study of shared directorships warns, for instance, that "the interlocking management device" could lead to a situation in which "inordinate control over the major part of the U.S. commerce would be concentrated in the hands of [a] few individuals," creating the possibility that "an 'inner group' would control the destiny of American commerce."[30]

Central to these analyses is the potentially critical political role played by top managers holding multi-firm connections. Executives with ties to several, often disparate, companies necessarily become concerned with the joint welfare of the several companies. Their indirect ties to other firms through the interlocking directorate further enlarges the scope of their concern. "Even more than other large corporation executives," writes one group of analysts, "those who sit at the center of the web of interlocking directorates must have an outlook and executive policies that, while yet serving particular and more narrow interests, conform to the general interests of the corporate community and of the principal owners of capital within it."[31] The inner circle, in short, constitutes a distinct, politicized business segment, if a segment is defined as a subset of class members sharing a specific social location with partially distinct interests.[32] Though members of the inner circle share with other corporate managers a common commitment to enhancing company profits, their heightened sensitivity to business interests more general than those that look solely to support individual company profits also sets them apart. . . .

The business pillar of the establishment is indeed a pillar, but as powerful as those who occupy the pillar's base may be within their own large corporation, they lack the means and incentives for shaping classwide policy. The top of the pillar does not. It has the power to act through its umbrella of intercorporate connections. It has the unity to act by virtue of its shared social cohesion. Its upperclass connections opens doors when it chooses to act. And at its disposal are the business associations when formal representation is needed.

The inner circle is not all powerful, however. Nor is it seamless. The upper-class credentials are partial, the ability to control the associations imperfect. Yet in all these respects it is more prepared to act than are

other individuals or groups of corporate managers and directors. The pluralist and structuralist claims of elite disorganization capture a relative truth when applied to the bulk of the corporate community. The claim of disunity is far less applicable, however, to the inner circle.

Even then the inner circle does not act as a committee of the whole. Political action is taken not by the inner circle, but by organized entities within it. Resources are actually mobilized through (1) the intercorporate and informal networks linking members of the inner circle, and (2) the formal associations over which the inner circle exercises substantial influence. The real unit of classwide corporate politics, then, is not the business elite as a whole, nor even this select stratum of the elite. As blocs, neither business nor the inner circle act on behalf of anything. But within the inner circle are a set of horizontally organized networks and vertically structured organizations that do act. These are the real motors of business political motion. The inner circle, then, refers not just to the company executive directors who constitute its membership, but also to the networks that constitute its internal structure. It is the power of these internal networks that propel members of the inner circle into leadership roles on behalf of the entire corporate community.

Notes

1. Domhoff 1974, p. 109; 1967; 1970; 1972; 1979.
2. Miliband 1969, p. 47.
3. Berg and Zald 1978, p. 137.
4. Bell 1962, pp. 62–63.
5. Silk and Vogel 1976, p. 181.
6. Stanworth and Giddens 1974, p. 100.
7. Westergaard and Resler 1975, p. 346.
8. Scott 1979, pp. 125–26.
9. Nettl 1965, p. 23.
10. Grant 1980, p. 146.
11. Szymanski 1978, p. 39.
12. Rothman 1978, p. 89.
13. Duberman 1976, p. 74.
14. Buchholz 1982, pp. 58–59.
15. Steiner and Steiner 1980, p. 9.

16. Many elements of the several perspectives are summarized in Alford (1975). The less well-known intra-Marxist debate is described within or exemplified by the works of Miliband (1969), Offe (1973), O'Connor (1973), Poulantzas (1973), Gold et al. (1975), Jessop (1977), Domhoff (1979), Whitt (1980, 1982), and Skocpol (1980).

17. Giddens 1974, p. xi.

18. Other principles are described in Useem (1980).

19. See, for instance, Cole (1955), pp. 101–23; Guttsman (1963); Perrott (1968); Sampson (1971); Johnson (1973); Giddens (1976).

20. Baltzell 1958, 1964, 1966, 1979; Domhoff 1967, 1970, 1974, 1979; Collins 1971, 1979; Silk and Silk 1980.

21. Baltzell 1966, p. 273.

22. Bedardia 1979, pp. 202–4.

23. Westhues (1976) provides a description of this approach.

24. Mills 1956.

25. Burck 1976, p. 173.

26. Mills 1956, p. 121.

27. Mills 1956, p. 121.

28. Mills 1956, p. 122.

29. Zeitlin 1974, p. 1, 112.

30. U.S. House Committee on the Judiciary, 1965, Antitrust Subcommittee, pp. 225–26.

31. Zeitlin et al. 1974, p. 4.

32. A helpful conceptualization of class segments within the business community can be found in Zeitlin et al. (1976).

References

Alford, Robert. 1975. "Paradigms of relations between state and society." In *Stress and Contradiction in Modern Capitalism,* Leon Lindberg et al., eds. Lexington, Ma.: Heath.

Baltzell, E. Digby. 1958. *Philadelphia Gentlemen: The Making of a National Upper Class.* New York: Free Press.

Baltzell, E. Digby. 1964. *The Protestant Establishment: Aristocracy and Caste in America.* New York: Random House.

Baltzell, E. Digby. 1966. "'Who's Who in America' and 'The Social Register': elite and upper class indexes in metropolitan America." Pp. 266–275 in *Class, Status, and Power,* Reinhard Bendix and Seymour Martin Lipset, eds. New York: Free Press, 2nd edition.

Baltzell, E. Digby. 1979. *Puritan Boston and Quaker Philadelphia.* New York: Free Press.

Bedardia, Francois. 1979. *A Social History of England, 1851–1975.* A. S. Foster, trans. London: Methuen.

Bell, Daniel. 1962. *The End of Ideology.* New York: Free Press.

Berg, Ivar, and Mayer N. Zald. 1978. "Business and society." *Annual Review of Sociology* 4: 115–143.

Buchholz, Rogene A. 1982. *Business Environment and Public Policy: Implications for Management.* Englewood Cliffs, N.J.: Prentice-Hall.

Burck, Charles G. 1976. "A group profile of the Fortune 500 chief executive." *Fortune,* May, pp. 173ff.

Cole, G. D. K. 1955. *Studies in Class Structure.* London: Routledge and Kegan Paul.

Collins, Randall. 1971. "Functional and conflict theories of educational stratification." *American Sociological Review* 36: 1002–1019.

Collins, Randall. 1979. *The Credential Society: An Historical Sociology of Education and Stratification.* New York: Academic Press.

Domhoff, G. William. 1967. *Who Rules America?* Englewood Cliffs, N.J.: Prentice-Hall.

Domhoff, G. William. 1970. *The Higher Circles: The Governing Class in America.* New York: Random House.

Domhoff, G. William. 1972. *Fat Cats and Democrats: The Role of the Big Rich in the Party of the Common Man.* Englewood Cliffs, N.J.: Prentice-Hall.

Domhoff, G. William. 1974. *The Bohemian Grove and Other Retreats: A Study of Ruling-Class Consciousness.* New York: Harper and Row.

Domhoff, G. William. 1979. *The Powers That Be: Processes of Ruling-Class Domination in America.* New York: Random House.

Duberman, Lucile. 1976. *Social Inequality: Class and Caste in America.* New York: Lippincott.

Giddens, Anthony. 1974. "Preface." In *Elites and Power in British Society,* Philip Stanworth and Anthony Giddens, eds. London: Cambridge University Press.

Giddens, Anthony. 1976. "The Rich." *New Society* 38 (October): 63–66.

Gold, David A., Clarence P. H. Lo, and Erik Olin Wright. 1975. "Recent developments in Marxist theories of the capitalist state." *Monthly Review* 27 (October): 29–43.

Grant, Wyn. 1980. "Business interests and the British Conservative Party." *Government and Opposition* 15: 143–161.

Guttsman, W. L. 1963. *The British Political Elite.* London: MacGibbon and Kee.

Jessop, Bob. 1977. "Recent theories about the capitalist state." *Cambridge Journal of Economics* 1: 353–373.

Johnson, R. W. 1973. "The British political elite, 1955–1972." *European Journal of Sociology* 14: 35–77.

Miliband, Ralph. 1969. *The State in Capitalist Society.* New York: Basic Books.

Mills, C. Wright. 1956. *The Power Elite.* New York: Oxford University Press.

O'Connor, James. 1973. *The Fiscal Crisis of the State.* New York: St. Martin's Press.

Offe, Claus. 1973. "The abolition of market control and the problem of legitimacy (I)." *Kapitalistate* 1: 109–116.

Nettl, J. P. 1965. "Consensus or elite domination: the case of business." *Political Studies* 8:22–44.

Perrott, Roy. 1968. *The Aristocrats.* London: Weidenfeld and Nicolson.

Poulantzas, Nicos. 1973. *Political Power and Social Classes.* Timothy O'Hagen, trans. London: New Left Books, and Sheed Ward.

Rothman, Robert A. 1978. *Inequality and Stratification in the United States.* Englewood Cliffs, N.J.: Prentice-Hall.

Sampson, Anthony. 1971. *The New Anatomy of Britain.* London: Hodder and Stoughton.

Scott, John. 1979. *Corporations, Classes and Capitalism.* London: Hutchinson.

Silk, Leonard, and David Vogel. 1976. *Ethics and Profits: The Crisis of Confidence in American Business.* New York: Simon and Schuster.

Silk, Leonard, and Mark Silk. 1980. *The American Establishment.* New York: Basic Books.

Skocpol, Theda. 1980. "Political response to capitalist crisis: Neo-Marxist theories of the state and the case of the New Deal." *Politics and Society* 10: 155–201.

Stanworth, Philip, and Anthony Giddens. 1974. "An economic elite: a demographic profile of company chairmen." In *Elites and Power in British Society,* Philip Stanworth and Anthony Giddens, eds. London: Cambridge University Press.

Steiner, George A., and John F. Steiner. 1980. *Business, Government, and Society: A Managerial Perspective.* New York: Random House.

Szymanski, Albert. 1978. *The Capitalist State and the Politics of Class.* Cambridge, Ma.: Winthrop Publishing Company.

U.S. House Committee on the Judiciary. 1965. Antitrust Subcommittee. *Interlocks in Corporate Management.* Washington, D.C.: U.S. Government Printing Office.

Useem, Michael. 1980. "Corporations and the corporate elite." In *Annual Review of Sociology,* Alex Inkeles, Neil J. Smelser, and Ralph Turner, eds. Palo Alto, Ca.: Annual Reviews.

Westergaard, John, and Henrietta Resler. 1975. *Class in Capitalist Society: A Study of Contemporary Britain.* London: Heinemann.

Westhues, Kenneth. 1976. "Class and organization as paradigms in social science." *The American Sociologist* 11: 38–49.

Whitt, J. Allen. 1980. "Can capitalists organize themselves?" In *Power Structure Research,* G. William Domhoff, ed. Beverly Hills, Ca.: Sage.

Zeitlin, Maurice, Richard Earl Ratcliff, and Lynda Ann Ewen. 1974. "The 'Inner Group': interlocking directorates and the internal differentiation of the capitalist class in Chile." Presented at the annual meeting of the American Sociological Association.

Zeitlin, Maurice, W. Lawrence Newman, and Richard Earl Ratcliff. 1976. "Class segments: agrarian property and political leadership in the capitalist class in Chile." *American Sociological Review* 41: 1006–1029.

GIL EYAL, IVÁN SZELÉNYI, AND ELEANOR TOWNSLEY

Post-Communist Managerialism

The unique feature of making capitalism from the ruins of state socialism in Central Europe is that it is happening without a propertied bourgeoisie. In all other historical sites where modern capitalism has developed, some form of private property and some class of private proprietors—no matter how embryonic, and no matter how different from modern capitalist entrepreneurs—already existed. In the classical case of transition, feudal landlords gradually converted their property into private ownership and began to be recruited into the new *grande bourgeoisie*. Urban artisans and merchants were busily accumulating capital, and were well positioned to transform themselves from the third estate of a feudal order into one of the fractions of the new dominant class in a capitalist mode of production. Postcommunism is the first situation where the transition to private property from a collective form of ownership is being attempted. Moreover, this project is being led by the second *Bildungsbürgertum*—by an uneasy alliance between former communist apparatchiks, technocrats, managers and their former left-wing critics, the dissident intellectuals. In short, capitalism is being made by a coalition of propertyless agents, who only yesterday outbid each other in their anticapitalism.

In 1988 two leading sociologists of the region, Jadwiga Staniszkis and Elemér Hankiss, formulated a provocative hypothesis, which [may be termed] the theory of political capitalism.[1] According to Staniszkis and Hankiss, the former communist *nomenklatura* knew by 1988 that the destruction of the old communist order was inevitable. They therefore designed a scheme to convert political office into private wealth, and attempted to transform themselves into a new *grande bourgeoisie*. Indeed, many commentators on the Central European transformation think that this is what happened after 1989: communist officials used political office to convert public goods into private individual wealth—*de facto,* they stole state property and became a 'kleptocracy'. . . .

The second theory we confront is Erzsébet Szalai's theory of 'technocratic revolution', which in some ways, can be viewed as a refinement of the general political capitalism thesis.[2] Szalai's argument is that the late state-socialist *nomenklatura* was highly fragmented, and that the dynamics of social change should be understood as an intense struggle between the bureaucratic and technocratic fractions of the old ruling estate. In this view, 1989 was a successful revolution of the late state-socialist technocracy against the bureaucratic fraction of the communist ruling estate. . . . Rather than the *nomenklatura* as a whole grasping power, one of its fractions—the technocratic-managerial elite—appeared to have established itself as the new propertied class. . . .

In 1990, we launched a survey in six East and Central European countries—Russia,

Originally published in 1998. Please see complete source information beginning on page 891.

Poland, the Czech Republic, Slovakia, Hungary and Bulgaria—to assess the empirical support for [these] forecasts. In 1993, in each country, we interviewed 1,000 people who were members of the 1988 *nomenklatura,* 1,000 people who belonged to the new economic, political, and cultural elites at the time; we also conducted personal life history interviews of 5,000 adults randomly selected from the population. In this chapter we present data from three Central European countries: the Czech Republic, Hungary, and Poland. We ask: what happened to the old *nomenklatura?* What are the social origins of members of the new elite? Is there any evidence for the existence of a propertied bourgeoisie by 1993? If so, how is this new class of domestic proprietors constituted? How much, and what, do they own?

Whatever Happened to the *Nomenklatura?*

Political capitalism theory expects to find that the old communist elite has turned itself into the new propertied bourgeoisie of post-communist society. Its most general proposition is that people who were in *nomenklatura* positions prior to 1989 were able to retain their power and privilege through the post-communist transition by converting their political capital into private economic wealth. Our data cast doubt on these predictions.

Table 1 describes the 1993 post-communist occupational destinations of those individuals who occupied *nomenklatura* positions in 1988 in Hungary, the Czech Republic, and Poland.[3] While there is some variation across the countries, the main finding in the table is one of massive downward mobility among *nomenklatura* members during the first five years of post-communism. Only half of those who occupied *nomenklatura* positions in 1988 were still in positions of authority in 1993, and this includes rather minor positions in low-level management. Indeed, the proportion of former *nomenklatura* members who occupied *any* authority position in 1993 was

rather low. And—rather surprisingly—in Hungary, which boasted the most advanced market reform policies of the late communist period, the loss of authority positions among former *nomenklatura* members has been even more marked than it has been in the other countries: only 43.1 percent of the Hungarian *nomenklatura* retained jobs in which they have subordinates. . . .

If we dig deeper into the data, the problems with the political capitalism thesis become even more serious. In its original formulation, this theory stated that political office had been used for the accumulation of private wealth in Central Europe. In order to test the accuracy of this statement, we need to disaggregate the '*nomenklatura*' category further. There were very different kinds of *nomenklatura* positions in the communist system, and good reason to think that they were divided among themselves. For this reason, a fair test of political capitalism theory should investigate whether or not any particular component of the *nomenklatura* has successfully negotiated the post-communist transition and become private proprietors. After all, some of our *nomenklatura* members in 1988 were top managers of large firms—thus they were 'technocrats', or what we term the 'economic elite' of the late communist period. In their case, it is not obvious that becoming a manager of a privately owned firm is a conversion of political capital into private wealth—managers and technocrats may simply have used their human capital and their managerial experience to maintain senior economic positions in the post-communist transition. Other former *nomenklatura* members belonged to the 'cultural elite'—they were rectors of universities, Members of the Academies of Sciences, or editors of daily newspapers—and these jobs in the cultural sector were not positions from which one could easily generate vast amounts of private wealth. Thus, political capitalism theory would not necessarily expect former members of the communist cultural elite to be those most able to convert political office into private wealth. Arguably, however, the political

TABLE 1

Occupational Destinations in 1993 of People Who Were in *Nomenklatura* Positions in 1988 by Country

Occupation in 1993	Czech Republic	Hungary	Poland
All in position of authority	51.7	43.1	51.2
High political office	3.0	6.4	9.0
High manager—public	16.2	11.2	13.4
High manager—private	12.8	2.4	9.1
High cultural office	1.1	4.4	7.1
Low-level managers	12.6	13.0	8.6
Entrepreneurs	6.0	5.7	4.0
Professionals	12.2	19.9	13.9
Workers	12.6	5.5	9.5
Retired early (younger than 65)	15.4	19.1	17.2
Other retired and unemployed	8.1	12.6	8.2
All respondents	100%	100%	100%
(n)	(468)	(803)	(849)

Note: Numbers may not add up to 100 percent due to rounding.

capitalism thesis should hold for members of the 'political elite'. These were people who held positions in the Communist Party apparatus or in the civil service, and of all the members of the *nomenklatura* they were the best placed to use their 'office' to enrich themselves through the mechanism of 'spontaneous privatization'.[4] With this disaggregation of the *nomenklatura* into its economic, cultural, and political components, we are now in a position to offer a crucial test of Staniszkis's and Hankiss's version of the political capitalism thesis by asking: to what extent has the 'bureaucratic' fraction of the ruling estate—the 'political elite'—benefited economically from the post-communist transition?

Table 2 documents the 1993 occupational destinations of former *nomenklatura* members for each component of the *nomenklatura*: the economic fraction, the cultural fraction, and the political fraction. It shows, first, that the political fraction of the *nomenklatura* was the least successful in weathering the post-communist transition. Only 39.3 percent of the political *nomenklatura* retained positions of authority between 1988 and 1993, compared to 44.2 percent of the cultural elite and 70.7 percent of the economic elite. Second, early retirement was also much

more common among the political fraction (20.9 percent) of the *nomenklatura* than among the economic and cultural fractions (14.7 and 11.1 percent respectively). This suggests that political capital was much less useful than cultural capital, and particularly cultural capital in the form of managerial expertise, for successfully navigating the pitfalls of post-communism. Third, Table 2 suggests that former Communist Party and state officials who comprised the political fraction of the *nomenklatura* in 1988 had less success in entering new private-sector positions than former communist managers. Among the former members of the economic *nomenklatura*, 24.6 percent (5.4 plus 19.2 percent) either owned or managed a private business in 1993, compared to only 9.8 percent (5.8 plus 4.0 percent) of members of the political fraction. These findings indicate that it was more advantageous to be a manager than a party or state official if one wanted to enter the new economic elite of post-communism. Moreover, these findings directly refute arguments by Staniszkis and Hankiss that it was the political fraction of the former communist elite who were best placed to take advantage of post-communist market reforms; rather, we find that members of the economic *nomen-*

TABLE 2

Occupational Destinations in 1993 of People Who Were in Economic, Political, and Cultural
Nomemklatura Positions in 1988 in All Three Countries (Czech Republic, Hungary, and Poland)

Occupation in 1993	Economic Elite, 1988	Political Elite, 1988	Cultural Elite, 1988
All in position of authority	70.7	39.3	44.2
High political office	1.5	10.8	1.3
High manager—public	33.4	5.9	7.8
High manager—private	19.2	4.0	1.4
High cultural office	0.4	1.8	19.3
Low-level managers	10.8	11.0	11.8
Entrepreneurs	5.4	5.8	2.5
Professionals	4.7	16.9	27.4
Workers	2.2	13.4	3.3
Retired early (younger than 65)	14.7	20.9	11.1
Other retired and unemployed	7.6	9.4	14.1
All respondents	100%	100%	100%
(n)	(536)	(1,186)	(398)

Note: Numbers may not add up to 100 percent due to rounding.

klatura were much bigger beneficiaries of the post-communist transition than members of the political *nomenklatura*. . . .

Diffuse Property Relations as the Context for Managerial Control

In one respect, however, our findings diverge from Szalai's predictions. Staniszkis and Hankiss anticipated that former communists would use their power to become the new corporate owners of post-communism, while Szalai argued more specifically that the technocratic-managerial elite was the most likely candidate to achieve this aim. Our data suggest that both these predictions miss the mark. Managerial ownership, or the management buy-out of state-owned firms, is not the major story in post-communism. Indeed, the majority of corporate and industrial managers have acquired no business property at all [for details, see Eyal, Szelényi and Townsley[5]]. Furthermore, fully half of those who own businesses possess stakes not in the firms

they manage, but in small subcontracting firms. Finally, we find that those who own shares in the businesses they manage are likely to be managers of smaller firms, and typically own only a small fraction of the assets of these firms. In other words, the former communist technocracy do not hold ultimate economic decision-making power as owners, as Szalai predicted; rather, they exercise power as experts and managers.

While data available to us on ownership relations in large firms are sketchy and may not be sufficiently representative, the evidence at our disposal supports hypotheses put forward on the basis of ethnographic observations by David Stark and Larry King.[6] Stark found that ownership in Central European corporations is 'recombinant', that is, it is neither private nor public. King found firms with 'recombinant' property, too, but he also identified a number of alternative strategies of privatization, most of which have not led to ownership by identifiable individuals. Our data on property also document diffuse patterns of ownership in post-communist

Central Europe, and with the exception of foreign-owned firms (which are really significant only in Hungary), it is not easy to tell who the real owners are. Direct or indirect public ownership, institutional cross-ownership, ownership by banks that are owned by the government or state privatization agencies, and self-ownership (firms owning firms, which own them) are all typical. Together, this creates the material base for the substantial autonomy and power exercised by non-propertied technocrats and managers.

Finally, while the big winners of the post-communist transition are former communist technocrats, we find that they cannot rule by themselves. They have been forced to create a hegemonic power bloc together with the new politocracy and the opinion-making intellectual elite, and these two groups are composed largely of former dissident intellectuals.[7] Immediately following the fall of communism, the new politocracy and opinion-making intellectual elite made an attempt to squeeze the former communist technocracy out of power. They soon learned, however, that neither fraction of the intellectual elite could rule alone. During the second post-communist elections, many former dissidents were dropped from the politocracy, and the late communist pragmatists joined the new political elite. These are strange bedfellows indeed, who form the 'unholy alliance' of post-communism. . . .

An Outline of a Theory of Managerial Capitalism

On the basis of the analyses presented above [and elsewhere],[8] we summarize our theory of managerial capitalism in the following six theses.

Thesis 1. Post-communist economies are characterized by *diffuse property relations*. At the present time it is impossible to identify individuals or groups of individuals with sufficient amounts of property who are able to exercise any-

thing even remotely similar to owners' control of economic decision-making.

Thesis 2. Ironically, it was precisely so-called 'privatization' which created these diffuse property relations. Privatization destroyed redistributive control over state firms, but it has not produced identifiable owners (yet).

Thesis 3. The dispersion of property rights is a *universal* phenomenon, but in market capitalist economies with an established propertied bourgeoisie it faces strict limits which do not exist in post-communism. Post-communist managers do not have to contend with a class of powerful capitalist proprietors; consequently, managerial power and decision-making are visible contributions to the prestige and 'distinction' of the new power bloc.

Thesis 4. Given the dispersion of property rights, the central representative of managerial power in Central Europe is not the manager of the industrial firm, but the finance manager. The most powerful people of the post-communist era are bank managers, managers of investment funds, experts at the Ministry of Finance, advisors at the IMF and the World Bank, and experts working for foreign and international financial agencies. In the absence of a class of big private proprietors, the power of finance managers is not a function of how many shares they own in the banks they manage, or in the firms their banks manage. Rather, their power is a form of 'cultural capital'; it is a function of their capacity to appropriate the sacred knowledge of the workings of the world capitalist system.

Thesis 5. Even though Central European managers are not limited by the power of a propertied bourgeoisie, we would emphasize that they do not exercise power in a vacuum. Rather, they occupy a historically distinctive post-communist class context, formed by ongoing struggles over privatization and the formation of new class actors. These struggles take place among members of the power bloc—managers, technocrats, and intellectuals, in the first instance—and between this power bloc and former bureaucrats, in the second. As we have argued [elsewhere],[9] no single class fraction has emerged as the decisive victor in these struggles, and as a consequence the power of managers and their capacity to control semi-public property comes to them by default.

Thesis 6. Managerial strategies reflect their knowledge that the current balance of class forces is precarious. They understand that they exercise power by default. In order to survive, therefore, managers have developed a diverse range of strategies to navigate the political and economic uncertainties of post-communism. Probably the most prevalent managerial strategy was not managerial 'buy-out' but, rather, an attempt to stand 'on as many legs as possible'. During the process of privatization most managers acquired *some* property, but this was typically a relatively small stake, and not even necessarily in the firms they managed. Indeed, as early as the late 1980s some members of management teams were busy setting up small subcontracting firms, owned by themselves or by members of their families. They subcontracted the most lucrative activities of the state firms they managed to these companies, they even sold some of the more valuable assets of the parent firms to these subcontracting units at undervalued prices. Still, it is probably the exception to the rule that these managers retired from their main firm altogether, that they 'jumped the boat' to run the subcontracting firms they own. The reason for their reluctance to do so is clear: why should they swap a *major* managerial job for the position of owner-

manager in a *minor* operation which employs only a handful of people? On the other hand, managers also have an interest in being more than *only* managers. In post-communist society, the managerial elite is closely intertwined with the politocracy; hence post-communist managers are even more dependent upon politicians than are capitalist managers in the West. State bureaucracies in East Central Europe often have the power, through direct or indirect state ownership of firms, to appoint and dismiss managers. As long as their position can be threatened by the political elite, it seems to be wise for managers to have their own small private firm in the background.

Notes

1. Jadwiga Staniszkis (1991a) *The Dynamics of Breakthrough*. Berkeley: University of California Press; Elemér Hankiss (1990) *East European Alternatives*. Oxford: Clarendon Press.

2. Erzsébet Szalai (1989) 'The New Elite'. *Across Frontiers* 5(Fall-Winter): 25–31. [In Hungarian: Beszélő 26, 1989].

3. The population of *nomenklatura* members was defined as those individuals occupying the top 3,000–5,000 positions in these countries in 1988, positions for which appointment usually required the approval of some organ or official of the Central Committee of the Communist Party.

4. In both Hungary and Poland during 1988, the regimes launched programs which were referred to as 'spontaneous privatization'. Communist elites acknowledged the necessity of changing property rights, and privatizing publicly held assets, but they initiated this process in a rather unregulated way. Under spontaneous privatization, firms could initiate their own privatization and negotiate their own terms with state organizations (in 1988, this still meant the Communist Party). Indeed, the initial hypotheses about political capitalism put forward by Staniszkis and Hankiss were formulated in reaction to these spontaneous privatization plans.

5. Gil Eyal, Iván Szelényi and Eleanor Townsley (1998) *Making Capitalism without Capitalists: The New Ruling Elites in Eastern Europe*. London: Verso.

6. David Stark (1996) 'Recombinant Property in East European Capitalism'. *American Journal of Sociology* 101(4): 993–1027; Larry King (1997). *Pathways from Socialism: The Transformation of Firms in Hungary, the Czech Republic and Slovakia*. Ph.D dissertation, Department of Sociology, UCLA.

7. Erzsébet Szalai (1994) 'The Power Structure in Hungary after the Political Transition'. pp. 120–43 in *The New Great Transformation*, ed.

Christopher G.A. Bryant and Edmund Mokrzycki. London and New York: Routledge; Erzsébet Szalai (1994) *Utelagazás. Hatalom és értelmiség az államszocializmus után* (At the crossroads: power and intellectuals after state socialism). Budapest: Pesti Szalon Kiadó.

8. Eyal, Szelényi and Townsley, *Making Capitalism Without Capitalists*.

9. Ibid.

Gradational Status Groupings

▶ R E P U T A T I O N ,   D E F E R E N C E ,   A N D   P R E S T I G E

W .   L L O Y D   W A R N E R ,   W I T H   M A R C H I A   M E E K E R
A N D   K E N N E T H   E E L L S

Social Class in America

Our great state papers, the orations of great men, and the principles and pronouncements of politicians and statesmen tell us of the equality of all men. Each school boy learns and relearns it; but most of us are dependent upon experience and indirect statement to learn about "the wrong side of the tracks," "the Gold Coast and the slums," and "the top and bottom of the social heap." We are proud of those facts of American life that fit the pattern we are taught, but somehow we are often ashamed of those equally important social facts which demonstrate the presence of social class. Consequently, we tend to deny them or, worse, denounce them and by so doing deny their existence and magically make them disappear from consciousness. We use such expressions as "the Century of the Common Man" to insist on our democratic faith; but we know that, ordinarily, for Common Men to exist as a class, un-Common superior and inferior men must also exist. We know that every town or city in the country has its "Country Club set" and that this group usually lives on its Gold Coast, its Main Line, North Shore, or Nob Hill, and is the top of the community's social heap. . . .

Originally published in 1960. Please see complete source information beginning on page 891.

Class Among the New England Yankees

Studies of communities in New England clearly demonstrate the presence of a well-defined social-class system.[1] At the top is an aristocracy of birth and wealth. This is the so-called "old family" class. The people of Yankee City say the families who belong to it have been in the community for a long time—for at least three generations and preferably many generations more than three. "Old family" means not only old to the community but old to the class. Present members of the class were born into it; the families into which they were born can trace their lineage through many generations participating in a way of life characteristic of the upper class back to a generation marking the lowly beginnings out of which their family came. Although the men of this level are occupied gainfully, usually as large merchants, financiers, or in the higher professions, the wealth of the family, inherited from the husband's or the wife's side, and often from both, has been in the family for a long time. Ideally, it should stem from the sea trade when Yankee City's merchants and sea captains made large fortunes, built great Georgian houses on elm-lined Hill Street, and filled their houses and gardens with the proper symbols of their high position. They became the 400, the Brahmins, the Hill Streeters to whom others looked up; and they, well-mannered or not, looked down on the rest. They counted themselves, and were so counted, equals of similar levels in Salem, Boston, Providence, and other New England cities. Their sons and daughters married into the old families from these towns and at times, when family fortune was low or love was great, they married wealthy sons and daughters from the newly rich who occupied the class level below them. This was a happy event for the fathers and mothers of such fortunate young people in the lower half of the upper class, an event well publicized and sometimes not too discreetly bragged about by the parents of the lower-upper-class children, an occasion to be explained by the mothers from the old families in terms of the spiritual demands of romantic love and by their friends as "a good deal and a fair exchange all the way around for everyone concerned."

The new families, the lower level of the upper class, came up through the new industries—shoes, textiles, silverware—and finance. Their fathers were some of the men who established New England's trading and financial dominance throughout America. When New York's Wall Street rose to power, many of them transferred their activities to this new center of dominance. Except that they aspire to old-family status, if not for themselves then for their children, these men and their families have a design for living similar to the old-family group. But they are consciously aware that their money is too new and too recently earned to have the sacrosanct quality of wealth inherited from a long line of ancestors. They know, as do those about them, that, while a certain amount of wealth is necessary, birth and old family are what really matter. Each of them can cite critical cases to prove that particular individuals have no money at all, yet belong to the top class because they have the right lineage and right name. While they recognize the worth and importance of birth, they feel that somehow their family's achievements should be

better rewarded than by a mere second place in relation to those who need do little more than be born and stay alive.

The presence of an old-family class in a community forces the newly rich to wait their turn if they aspire to "higher things." Meanwhile, they must learn how to act, fill their lives with good deeds, spend their money on approved philanthropy, and reduce their arrogance to manageable proportions.

The families of the upper and lower strata of the upper classes are organized into social cliques and exclusive clubs. The men gather fortnightly in dining clubs where they discuss matters that concern them. The women belong to small clubs or to the Garden Club and give their interest to subjects which symbolize their high status and evoke those sentiments necessary in each individual if the class is to maintain itself. Both sexes join philanthropic organizations whose good deeds are an asset to the community and an expression of the dominance and importance of the top class to those socially beneath them. They are the members of the Episcopalian and Unitarian and, occasionally, the Congregational and Presbyterian churches.

Below them are the members of the solid, highly respectable upper-middle class, the people who get things done and provide the active front in civic affairs for the classes above them. They aspire to the classes above and hope their good deeds, civic activities, and high moral principles will somehow be recognized far beyond the usual pat on the back and that they will be invited by those above them into the intimacies of upper-class cliques and exclusive clubs. Such recognition might increase their status and would be likely to make them members of the lower-upper group. The fact that this rarely happens seldom stops members of this level, once activated, from continuing to try. The men tend to be owners of stores and belong to the large proprietor and professional levels. Their incomes average less than those of the lower-upper class, this latter group having a larger income than any other group, including the old-family level.

These three strata, the two upper classes and the upper-middle, constitute the levels above the Common Man. There is a considerable distance socially between them and the mass of the people immediately below them. They comprise three of the six classes present in the community. Although in number of levels they constitute half the community, in population they have no more than a sixth, and sometimes less, of the Common Man's population. The three levels combined include approximately 13 per cent of the total population.

The lower-middle class, the top of the Common Man level, is composed of clerks and other white-collar workers, small tradesmen, and a fraction of skilled workers. Their small houses fill "the side streets" down from Hill Street, where the upper classes and some of the upper-middle live, and are noticeably absent from the better suburbs where the upper-middle concentrate. "Side Streeter" is a term often used by those above them to imply an inferior way of life and an inconsequential status. They have accumulated little property but are frequently home owners. Some of the more successful members of ethnic groups, such as the Italians, Irish, French-Canadians, have reached this level. Only a few members of these cultural minorities have gone beyond it; none of them has reached the old-family level.

The old-family class (upper-upper) is smaller in size than the new-family class (lower-upper) below them. It has 1.4 per cent, while the lower-upper class has 1.6 per cent, of the total population. Ten per cent of the population belongs to the upper-middle class, and 28 per cent to the lower-middle level. The upper-lower is the most populous class, with 34 per cent, and the lower-lower has 25 per cent of all the people in the town.

The prospects of the upper-middle-class children for higher education are not as good as those of the classes above. One hundred per cent of the children of the two upper classes take courses in the local high school that prepare them for college, and 88 per cent of the upper-middle do; but only 44 percent of the lower-middle take these courses, 28 per cent of the upper-lower, and 26 per cent of the lower-lower. These percentages provide a good index of the position of the lower-middle class, ranking it well below the three upper classes, but placing it well above the upper-lower and the lower-lower.[2]

The upper-lower class, least differentiated from the adjacent levels and hardest to distinguish in the hierarchy, but clearly present, is composed of the "poor but honest workers" who more often than not are only semi-skilled or unskilled. Their relative place in the hierarchy of class is well portrayed by comparing them with the classes superior to them and with the lower-lower class beneath them in the category of how they spend their money.

A glance at the ranking of the proportion of the incomes of each class spent on ten items (including such things as rent and shelter, food, clothing, and education, among others) shows, for example, that this class ranks second for the percentage of the money spent on food, the lower-lower class being first and the rank order of the other classes following lower-middle according to their place in the social hierarchy. The money spent on rent and shelter by upper-lower class is also second to the lower-lower's first, the other classes' rank order and position in the hierarchy being in exact correspondence. To give a bird's-eye view of the way this class spends its money, the rank of the upper-lower, for the percentage of its budget spent on a number of common and important items, has been placed in parentheses after every item in the list which follows: food (2), rent (2), clothing (4), automobiles (5), taxes (5), medical aid (5), education (4), and amusements (4–5). For the major items of expenditure the amount of money spent by this class out of its budget corresponds fairly closely with its place in the class hierarchy, second to the first of the lower-lower class for the major necessities of food and shelter, and ordinarily, but not always, fourth or fifth to the classes above for the items that give an opportunity for cutting down the amounts spent on them. Their feelings about doing the right thing, of being respectable and rearing their children to do better than they have, coupled with the limitations of their income, are well reflected in how they select and reject what can be purchased on the American market.[3]

The lower-lower class, referred to as "Riverbrookers" or the "low-down Yankees who live in the clam flats," have a "bad reputation" among those who are socially above them. This evaluation includes beliefs that they are lazy, shiftless, and won't work, all opposites of the good middle-class virtues belonging to the essence of the Protestant ethic. They are thought to be improvident and unwilling or unable to save their money for a rainy day and, therefore, often dependent on the philanthropy of the private or public agency and on poor relief. They are sometimes said to "live like animals" because it is believed that their sexual mores are not too exacting and that pre-marital intercourse, post-marital infidelity, and high rates of illegitimacy, sometimes too publicly mixed with incest, characterize their personal and family lives. It is certain that they deserve only part of this reputation. Research shows many of them guilty of no more than being poor and lacking in the desire to get ahead, this latter trait being common among those above them. For these reasons and others, this class is ranked in Yankee City below the level of the Common Man (lower-middle and upper-lower). For most of the indexes of status it ranks sixth and last.

Class in the Democratic Middle West and Far West

Cities large and small in the states west of the Alleghenies sometimes have class systems which do not possess an old-family (upper-upper) class. The period of settlement has not always been sufficient for an old-family level, based on the security of birth and inherited wealth, to entrench itself. Ordinarily, it takes several generations for an old-family class to gain and hold the prestige and power necessary to impress the rest of the community sufficiently with the marks of its "breeding" to be able to confer top status on those born into it. The family, its name, and its lineage must have had time to become identified in the public mind as being above ordinary mortals.

While such identification is necessary for the emergence of an old-family (upper-upper) class and for its establishment, it is also necessary for the community to be large enough for the principles of exclusion to operate. For example, those in the old-family group must be sufficiently numerous for all the varieties of social participation to be possible without the use of new-family members; the family names must be old enough to be easily identified; and above all there should always be present young people of marriageable age to become mates of others of their own class and a sufficient number of children to allow mothers to select playmates and companions of their own class for their children.

When a community in the more recently settled regions of the United States is sufficiently large, when it has grown slowly and at an average rate, the chances are higher that it has an old-family class. If it lacks any one of these factors, including size, social and economic complexity, and steady and normal growth, the old-family class is not likely to develop.

One of the best tests of the presence of an old-family level is to determine whether members of the new-family category admit, perhaps grudgingly and enviously and with hostile derogatory remarks, that the old-family level looks down on them and that it is considered a mark of advancement and prestige by those in the new-family group to move into it and be invited to the homes and social affairs of the old families. When a member of the new-family class says, "We've only been here two generations, but we still aren't old-family," and when he or she goes on to say that "they (old family) consider themselves better than people like us and the poor dopes around here let them get away with it," such evidence indicates that an old-family group is present and able to enforce recognition of its superior position upon its most aggressive and hostile competitors, the members of the lower-upper, or new-family, class.

When the old-family group is present and its position is not recognized as superordinate to the new families, the two tend to be co-ordinate and view each other as equals. The old-family people adroitly let it be known that their riches are not material possessions alone but are old-family lineage; the new families display their wealth, accent their power, and prepare their children for the development of a future lineage by giving them the proper training at home and later sending them to the "right" schools and marrying them into the "right" families.

Such communities usually have a five-class pyramid, including an upper class, two middle, and two lower classes.[4] . . .

The communities of the mountain states and Pacific Coast are new, and many of them have changed their economic form from mining to other enterprises; consequently, their class orders are similar to those found in the Middle West. The older and larger far western communities which have had a continuing, solid growth of population which has not destroyed the original group are likely to have the old-family level at the top with the other classes present; the newer and smaller communities and those disturbed by the destruction of their original status structure by large population gains are less likely to have an old-family class reigning above all others. San Francisco is a clear example of the old-family type; Los Angeles, of the more amorphous, less well-organized class structure.

Class in the Deep South

Studies in the Deep South demonstrate that, in the older regions where social changes until recently have been less rapid and less disturbing to the status order, most of the towns above a few thousand population have a six-class system in which an old-family elite is socially dominant.

For example, in a study of a Mississippi community, a market town for a cotton-growing region around it, Davis and the Gardners found a six-class system.[5] Perhaps the southern status order is best described by Chart I which gives the names used by the people of the community for each class and succinctly tells how the members of each class regard themselves and the rest of the class order.

The people of the two upper classes make a clear distinction between an old aristocracy and an aristocracy which is not old. There is no doubt that the first is above the other; the upper-middle class views the two upper ones much as the upper classes do themselves but groups them in one level with two divisions, the older level above the other; the lower-middle class separates them but considers them co-ordinate; the bottom two classes, at a greater social distance than the others, group all the levels above the Common Man as "society" and one class. An examination of the terms used by the several classes for the other classes shows that similar principles are operating.

The status system of most communities in the South is further complicated by a color-caste system which orders and systematically controls the relations of those categorized as Negroes and whites.

Although color-caste in America is a separate problem and the present [essay] does not deal with this American status system, it is necessary that we describe it briefly to be sure a clear distinction is made between it and social class. Color-caste is a system of values and behavior which places all people who are thought to be white in a superior position and those who are thought of as black in an inferior status. . . .

The members of the two groups are severely punished by the formal and informal rules of our society if they intermarry, and when they break this rule of "caste endogamy," their children suffer the penalties of our caste-like system by being placed in the lower color caste. Furthermore, unlike class, the rules of this system forbid the members of

CHART I
The social perspectives of the social classes*

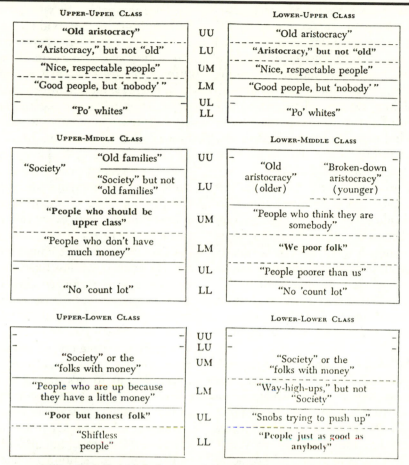

UPPER-UPPER CLASS		LOWER-UPPER CLASS
"Old aristocracy"	UU	"Old aristocracy"
"Aristocracy," but not "old"	LU	"Aristocracy," but not "old"
"Nice, respectable people"	UM	"Nice, respectable people"
"Good people, but 'nobody'"	LM	"Good people, but 'nobody'"
"Po' whites"	UL / LL	"Po' whites"

UPPER-MIDDLE CLASS		LOWER-MIDDLE CLASS
"Society" — "Old families"	UU	"Old aristocracy" (older) — "Broken-down aristocracy" (younger)
"Society" but not "old families"	LU	
"People who should be upper class"	UM	"People who think they are somebody"
"People who don't have much money"	LM	"We poor folk"
	UL	"People poorer than us"
"No 'count lot"	LL	"No 'count lot"

UPPER-LOWER CLASS		LOWER-LOWER CLASS
	UU / LU	
"Society" or the "folks with money"	UM	"Society" or the "folks with money"
"People who are up because they have a little money"	LM	"Way-high-ups," but not "Society"
"Poor but honest folk"	UL	"Snobs trying to push up"
"Shiftless people"	LL	"People just as good as anybody"

* Allison Davis, Burleigh B. Gardner, and Mary R. Gardner, *Deep South* (Chicago: University of Chicago Press, 1941), p. 65.

the lower caste from climbing out of it. Their status and that of their children are fixed forever. This is true no matter how much money they have, how great the prestige and power they may accumulate, or how well they have acquired correct manners and proper behavior. There can be no social mobility out of the lower caste into the higher one. (There may, of course, be class mobility within the Negro or white caste.) The rigor of caste rules varies from region to region in the United States.[6]

The Mexicans, Spanish Americans, and Orientals occupy a somewhat different status from that of the Negro, but many of the characteristics of their social place in America are similar.[7]

The social-class and color-caste hypotheses, inductively established as working principles for understanding American society, were developed in the researches which were reported in the "Yankee City" volumes, *Deep South*, and *Caste and Class in a Southern Town*. Gunnar Myrdal borrowed them, particularly color-caste, and made then known to a large, non-professional American audience.[8]

The Generalities of American Class

It is now time to ask what are the basic characteristics of social status common to the communities of all regions in the United States and, once we have answered this question, to inquire what the variations are among the several systems. Economic factors are significant and important in determining the class position of any family or person, influencing the kind of behavior we find in any class, and contributing their share to the present form of our status system. But, while significant and necessary, the economic factors are not sufficient to predict where a particular family or individual will be or to explain completely the phenomena of social class. Something more than a large income is necessary for high social position. Money must be translated into socially approved behavior and possessions, and they in turn must be translated into intimate participation with, and acceptance by, members of a superior class. . . .

The "right" kind of house, the "right" neighborhood, the "right" furniture, the proper behavior—all are symbols that can ultimately be translated into social acceptance by those who have sufficient money to aspire to higher levels than they presently enjoy.

To belong to a particular level in the social-class system of America means that a family or individual has gained acceptance as an equal by those who belong in the class. The behavior in this class and the participation of those in it must be rated by the rest of the community as being at a particular place in the social scale.

Although our democratic heritage makes us disapprove, our class order helps control a number of important functions. It unequally divides the highly and lowly valued things of our society among the several classes according to their rank. Our marriage rules conform to the rules of class, for the majority of marriages are between people of the same class. No class system, however, is so rigid that it completely prohibits marriages above and below one's own class. Furthermore, an open class system such as ours permits a person during his lifetime to move up or down from the level into which he was born. Vertical social mobility for individuals or families is characteristic of all class systems. The principal forms of mobility in this country are through the use of money, education, occupation, talent, skill, philanthropy, sex, and marriage. Although economic mobility is still important, it seems likely now that more people move to higher positions by education than by any other route. We have indicated before this that the mere possession of money is insufficient for gaining and keeping a higher social position. This is equally true of all other forms of mobility. In every case there must be social acceptance.

Class varies from community to community. The new city is less likely than an old one to have a well-organized class order; this is also true for cities whose growth has been rapid as compared with those which have not been disturbed by huge increases in population from other regions or countries or by the rapid displacement of old industries by new ones. The mill town's status hierarchy is more likely to follow the occupational hierarchy of the mill than the levels of evaluated participation found in market towns or those with diversified industries. Suburbs of large metropolises tend to respond to selective factors which reduce the number of classes to one or a very few. They do not represent or express all the cultural factors which make up the social pattern of an ordinary city.

Yet systematic studies from coast to coast, in cities large and small and of many economic types, indicate that, despite the variations and diversity, class levels do exist and that they conform to a particular pattern of organization.

Notes

1. See W. Lloyd Warner and Paul S. Lunt, *The Social Life of a Modern Community*, Vol. I, "Yankee City Series" (New Haven: Yale University Press, 1941); W. Lloyd Warner and Paul S. Lunt,

The Status System of a Modern Community, Vol. II, "Yankee City Series" (New Haven: Yale University Press, 1942).

2. See *The Social Life of a Modern Community,* pp. 58–72.

3. The evidence for the statements in this paragraph can be found in *The Social Life of a Modern Community,* pp. 287–300.

4. It is conceivable that in smaller communities there may be only three, or even two, classes present.

5. Allison Davis, Burleigh B. Gardner, and Mary R. Gardner, *Deep South* (Chicago: University of Chicago Press, 1941). Also read: John Dollard, *Caste and Class in a Southern Town* (New Haven: Yale University Press, 1937); Mozell Hill, "The All-Negro Society in Oklahoma" (Unpublished Ph.D. dissertation, University of Chicago, 1936); Harry J. Walker, "Changes in Race Accommodation in a Southern Community" (Unpublished Ph.D. dissertation, University of Chicago, 1945).

6. See St. Clair Drake and Horace R. Cayton, *Black Metropolis* (New York: Harcourt, Brace & Co., 1945), for studies of two contrasting caste orders; read the "Methodological Note" by Warner in *Black Metropolis* for an analysis of the difference between the two systems.

7. See W. Lloyd Warner and Leo Srole, *The Social Systems of American Ethnic Groups,* Vol. III, "Yankee City Series" (New Haven: Yale University Press, 1945). Chapter X discusses the similarities and differences and presents a table of predictability on their probable assimilation and gives the principles governing these phenomena.

8. Gunnar Myrdal, *An American Dilemma* (New York: Harper & Bros., 1944). For an early publication on color-caste, see W. Lloyd Warner, "American Caste and Class," *American Journal of Sociology,* XLII, No. 2 (September, 1936), 234–37, and "Formal Education and the Social Structure," *Journal of Educational Sociology,* IX (May, 1936), 524–31.

EDWARD SHILS

Deference

Into every action of one human being towards another there enters an element of appreciation or derogation of the 'partner' towards whom the action is directed. It enters in varying degrees; some actions contain very little of it, some consist almost entirely of appreciation or derogation, in most actions the appreciative or derogatory elements are mingled with others, such as commanding, coercing, cooperating, purchasing, loving, etc.

Appreciation and derogation are responses to properties of the 'partner', of the role which he is performing, of the categories into which he is classified or the relationships in which he stands to third persons or categories of persons—against the background of the actor's own image of himself with respect to these properties. This element of appreciation or derogation is different from those responses to the past or anticipated actions of the 'partner' which are commands, acts of obedience, the provision of goods or services, the imposition of injuries such as the withholding or withdrawal of goods and services, and acts of love or hatred.

These acts of appreciation or derogation I shall designate as *deference*. The term *deference* shall refer both to positive or high deference and to negative or low deference or derogation. Ordinarily, when I say that one person defers to another, I shall mean that he is acknowledging that person's worth or dig-

Originally published in 1968. Please see complete source information beginning on page 891.

nity but when I speak of a person's 'deference-position', that might refer either to a high or low deference-position. What I call deference here is sometimes called 'status' by other writers. There is nothing wrong with that designation, except that it has become associated with a conception of the phenomenon which I wish to modify. The term 'deference', with its clear intimation of a person who defers, brings out the aspect which has in my view not been made sufficiently explicit in work on this subject in recent years. . . .

The Bases of Deference

The disposition to defer and the performance of acts of deference are evoked by the perception, in the person or classes of persons perceived, of certain characteristics or properties of their roles or actions. These characteristics or properties I shall call deference-entitling properties or entitlements. While they do not by themselves and automatically arouse judgments of deference, they must be seen or believed to exist for deference to be granted. Deference-entitlements include: occupational role and accomplishment, wealth (including type of wealth), income and the mode of its acquisition, style of life, level of educational attainment, political or corporate power, proximity to persons or roles exercising political or corporate power, kinship connections, ethnicity, performance on behalf of the community or society in relation to external communities or societies, and the possession of 'objective acknowledgments' of deference such as titles or ranks.

It is on the basis of the perception of these entitlements that individuals and classes or more or less anonymous individuals who are believed to possess some constellation of these entitlements are granted deference; it is on the basis of the possession of these properties that they grant deference to themselves and claim it from others. It is on the basis of simultaneous assessments of their own and of others' deference-entitlements that they regulate their conduct towards others and anticipate the deferential (or derogatory) responses of others.

Why should these properties be singled out as pertinent to deference? What is it about them which renders them deference-relevant? Why are they and not kindness, amiability, humour, manliness, femininity, and other temperamental qualities which are so much appreciated in life, regarded as deference-relevant?

The cognitive maps which human beings form of their world include a map of their society. This map locates the primary or corporate groups of which they are active members and the larger society which includes these groups, but with which they have little active contact. The map which delineates this society entails a sense of membership in that society and a sense of the vital character of that membership. Even though the individual revolts against that society, he cannot completely free himself from his sense of membership in it. The society is not just an ecological fact or an environment; it is thought to possess a vitality which is inherent in it and membership in it confers a certain vitality on those who belong to it. It is a significant cosmos from which members derive some of their significance to themselves and to others. This significance is a charismatic significance; i.e. it signifies the presence and operation of what is thought to be of ultimate and determinative significance.

If we examine each of the deference-relevant properties with reference to this charismatic content, i.e. with reference to the extent to which it tends to have charisma attributed to it, we will see that each of these properties obtains its significance as an entitlement to deference primarily on these grounds.

Occupational role is ordinarily thought of as one of the most significant entitlements to deference. The most esteemed occupations in societies, for which there are survey or impressionistic data, are those which are in their internal structure and in their functions closest to the *centres*. The centres of society are those positions which exercise earthly power and which mediate man's relationship to the order of existence—spiritual forces, cosmic powers, values and norms—which legitimates or withholds legitimacy from the earthly powers or which dominates earthly existence. The highest 'authorities' in society—governors, judges, prime ministers and presidents and fundamental scientists—are those whose roles enable them to control society or to penetrate into the ultimate laws and forces which are thought to control the world and human life. Occupational roles are ranked in a sequence which appears approximately to correspond with the extent to which each role possesses these properties. The charismatic content of a given occupational role will vary with the centrality of the corporate body or sector in which it is carried on. The most authoritative role in a peripheral corporate body will carry less charisma than the same type of role in a more centrally located corporate body. The roles which exercise no authority and which are thought to have a minimum of contact with transcendent powers call forth least deference.

Of course, occupational roles and their incumbents are also deferred to on account of certain highly correlated deference-entitling properties such as the income which the practice of the occupation provides, the educational level of its practitioners, the ethnic qualities of its incumbents, etc. Conversely, occupational roles which are ill-remunerated and the incumbents of which have little education and are of derogatory ethnic stocks receive little deference on the grounds of these traits as well as on the grounds of the nature and functions of the occupational role itself. Nonetheless, occupational role is an independent entitlement to deference. . . .

Deference Behaviour

The term *status,* when it is used to refer to deference-position, ordinarily carries with it overtones of the stability, continuity and pervasiveness which are possessed by sex and age. A person who has a given status tends to be thought of as having that status at every moment of his existence as long as that particular status is not replaced by another status. One of the reasons why I have chosen to use the term 'deference-position' in place of 'status' is that it makes a little more prominent the fact that status is not a substantial property of the person arising automatically from the possession of certain entitlements but is in fact an element in a relationship between the person deferred to and the deferent person. Deference towards another person is an attitude which is manifested in behaviour.

Acts of deference judgments are evaluative classifications of self and other. As classifications they transcend in their reference the things classified. A person who is evaluatively classified by an act of deference on the basis of his occupation is in that classification even when he is not performing his occupational role. The classificatory deference judgment, because it is a generalization, attains some measure of independence from the intermittence of entitlements. It has an intermittence of its own which is not necessarily synchronized with that of the entitlements.

Overt concentrated acts of deference such as greetings and presentations are usually shortlived, i.e. they are performed for relatively short periods and then 'disappear' until the next appropriate occasion. The appropriate occasions for the performance of concentrated acts of deference might be regular in their recurrence, e.g. annually or weekly or even daily, but except for a few 'deference-occupations' they are not performed with the high frequency and density over extended periods in the way in which occupational roles are performed. But does deference consist exclusively of the performance of concentrated deferential actions? Is there a 'deference vacuum' when concentrated deferential actions are not being performed? Where does deference go when it is not being expressed in a grossly tangible action?

To answer this question, it is desirable to examine somewhat more closely the character of attenuated deference actions. There are concentrated, exclusively deferential actions which are nothing but deferential actions just as there are exclusively power or style of life or occupational actions but in a way different from these others. Occupational actions are substantial; all effort within a given space and time is devoted to their performance. They can be seen clearly by actor and observer as occupational actions; the exercise of authority has many of these features, especially when it is exercised in an authoritative occupational role. Expenditures of money are of shorter duration but they too are clearly definable. The acts of consumption and conviviality which are comprised in a style of life are of longer duration but they too are also clearly defined. On the other hand, level of educational attainment and kinship connection and ethnicity are not actual actions at all, they are classifications in which 'objectively' the classified person is continuously present although once present in the class he does nothing to manifest or affirm.

But deference actions—deferring to self and other, receiving deference from self and other—are actions. They result in and are performed with reference to classifications but they are actions nonetheless. They are not however always massive actions of much duration. They occur moreover mainly at the margin of other types of action. Deference actions performed alone are usually very short-lived; they open a sequence of interaction and they close it. Between beginning and end, deference actions are performed in fusion with non-deferential actions. Throughout the process of interaction they are attenuated in the substance of the relationship in which the performance of tasks appropriate to roles in corporate bodies, to civil roles, to personal relationships, etc., occurs. Deference actions have always been largely components of other actions; they are parts of the pattern of speaking to a colleague, a superior or an inferior about the business at hand in an authoritatively hierarchical corporate body, of speaking about or to a fellow citizen, of acting towards him over a distance (as in an election). In other words, deference actions seldom appear solely as deference actions and those which do are not regarded, especially in the United States,

as a particularly important part of interaction in most situations. Nonetheless, deference is demanded and it is accepted in an attenuated form.

This then is the answer to the question as to where deference goes when it ceases to be concentrated: it survives in attenuation, in a pervasive, intangible form which enters into all sorts of relationships through tone of speech, demeanour, precedence in speaking, frequency and mode of contradiction, etc. . . .

The Distribution of Deference

It has long been characteristic of the study of deference and of the deference-positions (status) which it helps to produce to ascribe to them a distribution similar in important respects to the distribution of entitlements such as occupational roles and power, income, wealth, styles of life, levels of educational attainment, etc. The entitlements are all relatively 'substantial' things which are not matters of opinion but rather 'objective', more or less quantifiable, conditions or attributes and as such capable of being ranged in a univalent and continuous distribution. Every individual has one occupation or another at any given period in time or for a specifiable duration; every individual has—if it could be measured—such and such an average amount of power over a specifiable time period. Every individual has some style of life, certain components of which at least are enduring and observable—and he either possesses them or does not possess them. There are of course cases of persons having two widely different kinds of occupational roles within the same limited time period ('moonlighting'), of persons having widely divergent incomes within a given period, but these and other anomalies can quite easily be resolved by specifiable procedures for the collection of data and for their statistical treatment and presentation.

Present-day sociological notions of deference (status, esteem, prestige, honour, etc.) grew up in association with the 'objective'[1] conception of social stratification. For reasons of convenience in research and also because common usage practised a system of classification into 'middle', 'upper', 'lower',[2] etc., classes, research workers and theorists attempted to construct a composite index which would amalgamate the positions of each individual in a number of distributions (in particular, the distributions of occupational role and education) into some variant of the three-class distribution. The resultant was called 'social-economic status' (sometimes, 'socio-economic status').

The 'subjective' conception of social stratification appreciated the 'opinion'-like character of deference but for reasons of convenience in research procedure and because of the traditional mode of discourse concerning social stratification, the 'subjective factor' itself tended to be 'substantialized' and it too was regarded as capable of being ranged in a univalent distribution.[3] Sometimes as in the Edwards classification in the United States or in the Registrar-General's classification in the United Kingdom, this 'subjective factor' impressionistically assessed by the research worker was amalgamated with the 'objective factors' in arriving at a single indicator of 'status'. Status was taken to mean a total status, which included both deference-position and entitlements, constructed by an external observer (not a participant in the system). But this conception has not found sufferance because it is patently unsatisfactory. Deference-position—or esteem, prestige or status—does belong to a different order of events in comparison with events like occupational distribution, income and wealth distribution, etc. It belongs to the realm of values; it is the outcome of evaluative judgments regarding positions in the distributions of 'objective' characteristics.

The improvement of techniques of field work in community studies and sample surveys has rendered it possible to collect data, relatively systematically, about these evaluations and to assign to each person in a small community or to each occupation on a list a single position in a distribution. Research technique has served to obscure a fundamen-

tal conceptual error. As a result, since each person possessed a status (or deference-position), they could be ranged in a single distribution. Such a distribution could occur, however, only under certain conditions. The conditions include (*a*) an evaluative consensus throughout the society regarding the criteria in accordance with which deference is allocated; (*b*) cognitive consensus throughout the society regarding the characteristics of each position in each distribution and regarding the shape of the distributions of entitlements; (*c*) consensus throughout the society regarding the weights to be assigned to the various categories of deference-entitling properties;[4] (*d*) equal attention to and equal differentiation by each member of the society of strata which are adjacent to his own and those which are remote from it;[5] (*e*) equal salience of deference judgments throughout the society; (*f*) univalence of all deference judgments.

Were these conditions to obtain, then the distribution of deference-positions in such a society might well have the form which the distributions of 'objective' entitlements possess. There are, however, numerous reasons why the distribution of deference-positions or status does not have this form. Some of these reasons are as follows: (*a*) Some consensus concerning the criteria for the assessment of entitlements might well exist but like any consensus it is bound to be incomplete. Furthermore criteria are so ambiguously apprehended that any existent consensus actually covers a wide variety of beliefs about the content of the criteria. (*b*) Cognitive consensus throughout the society regarding the properties of entitlements and the shape of their distributions is rather unlikely because of the widespread and unequal ignorance about such matters as the occupational roles, incomes, educational attainments of individuals and strata. (*c*) The weighting of the various criteria is not only ambiguous, it is likely to vary from stratum to stratum depending on the deference position of the various strata and their positions on the various distributions; it is likely that each stratum will give a heavier weight to that distribution on which it stands more highly or on which it has a greater chance of improving its position or protecting it from 'invaders'. (d) The perceptions of one's own stratum or of adjacent strata are usually much more differentiated and refined and involve more subsidiary criteria than is the case in their perceptions of remote strata. Thus even if they are compatible with each other there is no identity of the differentiations made by the various strata. (e) Some persons are more sensitive to deference than are others and this difference in the salience of deference occurs among strata as well. Some persons think frequently in terms of deference position, others think less frequently in those terms. Accordingly assessments of other human beings and the self may differ markedly within a given society, among individuals, strata, regions and generations with respect to their tendency to respond deferentially rather than affectionately or matter-of-factly or instrumentally. The arrangement of the members of a society into a stratified distribution as if each of them had a determinate quantity of a homogeneous thing called deference (or status or prestige) does violence to the nature of deference and deference-positions; it further obscures in any case sufficiently opaque reality. The possibility of dissensus in each of the component judgments—cognitive and evaluative—which go to make up a deference-judgment can, of course, be covered by the construction of measures which hide the dispersion of opinions. If all inter-individual disagreements are confined to differences in ranking within a given stratum, the procedure would perhaps be acceptable. But, if 80 per cent of a population place certain persons in stratum I and if 20 per cent place them in stratum II, is it meaningful to say that the persons so judged are in stratum I?

The dissensus which results in inter-individually discordant rankings seriously challenges the validity of procedures which construct univalent deference distributions and then disjoin them into strata. This difficulty would exist even if there were agreement about the location of the boundary lines which allegedly

separate one deference stratum from the other. But there is no certainty that there will be consensus on this matter, and the purpose of realistic understanding is not served by assuming that there is such consensus or by constructing measures which impose the appearance of such a consensus on the data. . . .

Deference Systems

Deference systems tend to become territorially dispersed into local systems which are more differentiated to those who participate in them than is the national system. I do not mean to say that the several systems ranging from local to national are in conflict with each other. Indeed they can be quite consensual and the local usually could not be constituted without reference to persons, roles and symbols of the centre. In the various zones and sectors of the periphery where the centre is more remote, the imagery of the centre still enters markedly into the deference system and local differentiations are often simply refined applications of perceptions and evaluations which have the centre as their point of reference. Thus, for example, local deference judgments will make more subtle internal distinctions about occupational role and authority, income and style of life than would judgments made from a distant point either peripheral or central. Still the distinctions will refer to distances from some standard which enjoys its highest fulfilment at the centre. It seems unlikely that centre-blindness can ever be complete in any society.

Nevertheless, the various systems do to some extent have lives of their own. The local deference system is probably more continuously or more frequently in operation than the national system—although as national societies become more integrated and increasingly incorporate with local and regional societies, the national deference system becomes more frequently and more intensely active.

In all societies, the deference system is at its most intense and most continuous at the centre. The high concentrations of power and wealth, the elaborateness of the style of life, all testify to this and call it forth. It is at the centre that deference institutions function and this gives an added focus and stimulus to deference behaviour. The centre adds the vividness of a local deference system to the massive deference-evoking powers of centrality. Within each local or regional deference system, there are some persons who are more sensitive than others to the centre and they infuse into the local system some awareness of and sensitivity to the centre.

At some times and at others, individuals whose preoccupations are mainly with the local deference systems—insofar as they are at all concerned with deference—place themselves on the macrosocial deference map. This self-location and the perception that others are also locating themselves is the precondition of a sense of affinity among those who place themselves macro-socially on approximately the same position in the distribution of deference. The placement of others is made of course on the basis of fragmentary evidence about occupational role, style of life, or elements of these and the sense of affinity is loose, the self-location very vague, very inarticulated and very approximate. In this way deference (or status) strata are constituted. They have no clear boundaries and membership cannot be certified or specified. It is largely a matter of sensing one's membership and being regarded by others as a member. Those one 'knows' are usually members, and beyond them the domain spreads out indefinitely and anonymously in accordance with vague cognitive stratification maps and an inchoate image of the 'average man'; within each stratum, an 'average man' possesses the proper combination of positions on the distribution of significant deference-entitlements.

Thus the formation of deference-strata is a process of the mutual assimilation of local deference systems into a national deference system. It is through class consciousness that deference-strata are formed.

In the course of its self-constitution a deference stratum also defines in a much vaguer way the other deference strata of its society. It draws boundary lines but, except for those it draws about itself, the boundaries are matters of minor significance. Boundary lines are of importance only or mainly to those who are affected by the location of the boundary, i.e. those who live close to it on one side or the other. The location of a line of division in the distribution of deference is regarded as important primarily by those who fear that they themselves are in danger of expulsion or who are refused admission to the company of members of a stratum to whom they regard themselves as equal or to whom they wish to be equal and whose company they regard as more desirable than the one to which they would otherwise be confined. The members of any deference stratum are likely to be ignorant about the location of deference stratum boundaries which are remote from them and if they are not ignorant, they are indifferent.

The various deference strata of local deference systems are in contact with each other through occasional face-to-face contacts. They are present in each others' imaginations and this deferential presence enters into all sorts of non-deferential actions of exchange, conflict and authority.

In national deference systems too the different strata are in contact with each other, not very much through face-to-face contact but through their presence in each other's imagination. This presence carries with it the awareness of one's distance from the centre and it entails some acceptance of the centrality of the centre and some acceptance of the greater dignity of the centre. It is an implicit belief that the centre embodies and enacts standards which are important in the assessment of oneself and one's own stratum.

In some sense, the centre 'is' the standard which is derived from the perception, correct or incorrect, of its conduct and bearing. These remote persons and strata which form the centre might be deferred to, or condemned in speech, and the pattern of their conduct, bearing, outlook, etc., might be emulated or avoided. An 'objective existence' is attributed to the rank ordering from centrality to peripherality of the other strata and within this rank ordering one's own stratum is located. The ontological, non-empirical reality which is attributed to position in the distribution of deference makes it different from 'mere' evaluation and sometimes even antithetical to it.

On a much more earthly level, contacts between deference strata occur and in many forms—particularly through the division of labour and its coordination through the market and within corporate bodies and in the struggle for political power. This does not mean that the strata encounter each other in corporately organized forms[6] or that, when there is interstratum contact in the encounter of corporate bodies, these bodies include all or most members of their respective strata. Much of this inter-stratum contact takes place through intermediaries who act as agents and who receive a deference which is a response both to their own deference-entitling properties and those of their principals. Those who act on behalf of these corporate bodies do so in a state of belief that they are 'representing' the deference-stratum to which they belong or feel akin.

A society can then have a deference system of relatively self-distinguishing and self-constituting deference strata, with the strata being in various kinds of relationship with each other. Such a situation is entirely compatible with the absence of the type of objective deference distribution which we rejected in the foregoing section. Each of the deference strata possesses in a vague form an image of a society-wide deference distribution but these images cannot be correct in the sense of corresponding to an objective deference distribution, which might or might not actually exist.

Notes

This paper is a further exploration of the theme of my earlier papers 'Charisma, order and status', *American Sociological Review,* vol. 30 (April 1965), pp. 199–213; 'Centre and periphery', in *The Logic of Personal Knowledge: Essays in Hon-*

our of Michael Polanyi (London: Routledge, Kegan Paul, 1961), pp. 117–30; 'The concentration and dispersion of charisma', *World Politics,* vol. XI, 1, pp. 1–19; and 'Metropolis and province in the intellectual community' in N. V. Sovani and V. M. Dandekar (eds.), *Changing India: Essays in Honour of Professor D. R. Cadgil* (Bombay: Asia Publishing House, 1961), pp. 275–94.

1. The 'objective' conception concerned itself with the relatively substantial entitlements, the 'subjective' with the 'opinion'-like elements.

2. The prevalence of the trichotomous classification and variations on it is probably of Aristotelian origin. There is no obvious reason why reflection on experience and observation alone should have resulted in three classes. This might well be a case where nature has copied art.

3. It is quite possible that this pattern of thought which emerged in the nineteenth century was deeply influenced by the conception of social class of the nineteenth-century critics of the *ancien régime* and of the bourgeois social order which succeeded it. In the *ancien régime* the most powerful ranks were designated by legally guaranteed titles which entered into the consciousness of their bearers and those who associated with or considered them. These designations were not 'material' or 'objective'. They did not belong to the 'substructure' of society. They were therefore 'subjective' but they were also unambiguous. They could be treated in the same way as 'objective' characteristics. By extension, the same procedure could be applied to the other strata.

4. Where these three conditions exist, there would also exist a consensus between the judgment which a person makes of his own deference-position and the judgments which others render about his position.

5. It also presupposes equal knowledge by all members of the society about all other members.

6. Corporate organizations, membership in which is determined by a sense of affinity of deference positions and of positions in other distributions, seldom enlist the active membership of all the members of the stratum or even of all the adult male members of the stratum. Those who are not members of the corporate body are not, however, to be regarded as completely devoid of the sense of affinity with other members of their stratum. 'Class consciousness' in this sense is very widespread but it is a long step from this type of 'class consciousness' to the aggressively alienated class consciousness which Marxist doctrine predicted would spread throughout the class of manual workers in industry and Marxist agitation has sought to cultivate.

PETER M. BLAU AND OTIS DUDLEY DUNCAN,
WITH THE COLLABORATION OF ANDREA TYREE

Measuring the Status of Occupations

Two approaches have dominated the investigations of occupational hierarchy carried out by students of social stratification. One is the effort to develop a socioeconomic classification scheme for occupations. Perhaps the most influential work here was that of the census statistician Alba M. Edwards.[1] His "social-economic grouping" of occupations has been widely used in studies of occupational stratification and mobility. With certain modifications it led to the "major occupation groups" used by the Bureau of the Census since 1940. . . . To suggest that his grouping supplied a "scale," Edwards contented himself with showing differences in average or typical levels of education and income of the workers included in the several categories: "Education is a very large factor in the social status of workers, and wage or salary income is a very large factor in their economic status."[2]

A more recent development is the derivation of scores for *detailed* census occupation titles representing a composite index of edu-

cation and income levels of workers in each such occupation. Priority for this specific technique probably belongs to social scientists in Canada,[3] with a similar approach being taken in this country by both a private researcher worker[4] and, lately, in official publications of the U. S. Bureau of the Census.[5]

The second approach to occupational stratification is to secure, from samples more or less representative of the general public, ratings of the "general standing" or "prestige" of selected occupations. Such ratings have been shown to be remarkably close to invariant with respect to (a) the composition and size of the sample of raters; (b) the specific instructions or form of the rating scale; (c) the interpretation given by respondents to the notion of "general standing"; and (d) the passage of time.[6] The high order of reliability and stability evidenced by prestige ratings would commend their use in problems requiring social distance scaling of the occupations pursued by a general sample of the working force, but for one fact: ratings have hitherto been available only for relatively small numbers of occupation titles. Many research workers have resorted to ingenious schemes for splicing *ad hoc* judgments into the series of rated occupations, but no general solution to the problem has been widely accepted.

Work currently in progress at the National Opinion Research Center promises to over-

Originally published in 1967. Please see complete source information beginning on page 891.

come this difficulty by supplying prestige ratings for a comprehensive list of occupations. In the absence of such ratings at the time of the Occupational Changes in a Generation (OCG) survey we fell back on the idea of a socioeconomic index of occupational status. The particular index we used, however, was one designed to give near-optimal reproduction of a set of prestige ratings. A full account of the construction of this index is given elsewhere,[7] and only a few general points need to be made before presenting some illustrations of the scale values assigned to occupations.

In the derivation of the socioeconomic index of occupational status, prestige ratings obtained from a sizable sample of the U.S. population in 1947 were taken as the criterion. These were available for 45 occupations whose titles closely matched those in the census detailed list. Data in the 1950 Census of Population were converted to two summary measures: per cent of male workers with four years of high school or a higher level of educational attainment, and per cent with incomes of $3,500 or more in 1949 (both variables being age-standardized). The multiple regression of per cent "excellent" or "good" prestige ratings on the education and income measures was calculated. The multiple correlation, with the 45 occupations as units of observation, came out as .91, implying that five-sixths of the variation in aggregate prestige ratings was taken into account by the combination of the two socioeconomic variables. Using the regression weights obtained in this calculation, all census occupations were assigned scores on the basis of their education and income distributions. Such scores may be interpreted either as estimates of (unknown) prestige ratings or simply as values on a scale of occupational socioeconomic status ("occupational status" for short). The scale is represented by two-digit numbers ranging from 0 to 96. It closely resembles the scales of Blishen, Bogue, and the U.S. Bureau of the Census mentioned earlier, although there are various differences in detail among the four sets of scores.

One of the most serious issues in using any index of occupational status in the study of mobility has to do with the problem of temporal stability. . . . Fortunately, we now have a detailed study of temporal stability in occupational prestige ratings. The results are astonishing to most sociologists who have given the matter only casual thought. A set of ratings obtained as long ago as 1925 is correlated to the extent of .93 with the latest set available, obtained in 1963. The analysts conclude, "There have been no substantial changes in occupational prestige in the United States since 1925."[8] Less complete evidence is available for the socioeconomic components of our index, but information available in the Censuses of 1940, 1950, and 1960 points to a comparably high order of temporal stability,[9] despite major changes in the value of the dollar and the generally rising levels of educational attainment. . . .

Two-digit status scores are available for 446 detailed occupation titles. Of these, 270 are specific occupation categories; the remainder are subgroupings, based on industry or class of worker, of 13 general occupation categories. The reader may consult the source publication for the scores of particular occupations of interest.[10] Here we shall only illustrate the variation of the scores by citing illustrative occupations, not always those of the greatest numerical importance (see Table 1). . . .

Table 1 makes it clear that occupations of very different character may have similar status scores. In particular, there is considerable overlap of scores of occupations in distinct major occupation groups. Indeed, only five points separate the lowest occupation in the "professional, technical, and kindred workers" group from the highest among "laborers, except farm and mine." Nevertheless, the major occupation group classification accounts for three-fourths of the variation in scores among detailed occupations. The status scores offer a useful refinement of the coarser classification but not a radically different pattern of grading.

TABLE 1
Occupations Illustrating Various Scores on the Index of Occupational Status*

Score Interval	Title of Occupation (Frequency per 10,000 Males in 1960 Experienced Civilian Labor Force in Parentheses)
90 to 96	Architects (7); dentists (18); chemical engineers (9); lawyers and judges (45); physicians and surgeons (47)
85 to 89	Aeronautical engineers (11); industrial engineers (21); salaried managers, banking and finance (30); self-employed proprietors, banking and finance (5)
80 to 84	College presidents, professors and instructors (31); editors and reporters (14); electrical engineers (40); pharmacists (19); officials, federal public administration and postal service (13); salaried managers, business services (11)
75 to 79	Accountants and auditors (87); chemists (17); veterinarians (3); salaried managers, manufacturing (133); self-employed proprietors, insurance and real estate (9)
70 to 74	Designers (12); teachers (105); store buyers and department heads (40); credit men (8); salaried managers, wholesale trade (41); self-employed proprietors, motor vehicles and accessories retailing (12); stock and bond salesmen (6)
65 to 69	Artists and art teachers (15); draftsmen (45); salaried managers, motor vehicles and accessories retailing (18); self-employed proprietors, apparel and accessories retail stores (8); agents, n.e.c. (29); advertising agents and salesmen (7); salesmen, manufacturing (93); foremen, transportation equipment manufacturing (18)
60 to 64	Librarians (3); sports instructors and officials (12); postmasters (5); salaried managers, construction (31); self-employed proprietors, manufacturing (35); stenographers, typists, and secretaries (18); ticket, station, and express agents (12); real estate agents and brokers (33); salesmen, wholesale trade (106); foremen, machinery manufacturing (28); photoengravers and lithographers (5)
55 to 59	Funeral directors and embalmers (8); railroad conductors (10); self-employed proprietors, wholesale trade (28); electrotypers and stereotypers (2); foremen, communications, utilities, and sanitary services (12); locomotive engineers (13)
50 to 54	Clergymen (43); musicians and music teachers (19); officials and administrators, local public administration (15); salaried managers, food and dairy products stores (21); self-employed proprietors, construction (50); bookkeepers (33); mail carriers (43); foremen, metal industries (28); toolmakers, and die-makers and setters (41)
45 to 49	Surveyors (10); salaried managers, automobile repair services and garages (4); office machine operators (18); linemen and servicemen, telephone, telegraph and power (60); locomotive firemen (9); airplane mechanics and repairmen (26); stationary engineers (60)
40 to 44	Self-employed proprietors, transportation (8); self-employed proprietors, personal services (19); cashiers (23); clerical and kindred workers, n.e.c. (269); electricians (77); construction foremen (22); motion picture projectionists (4); photographic process workers (5); railroad switchmen (13); policemen and detectives, government (51)

Table 1 probably does not illustrate adequately the variation by industry subclass of such occupation categories as "operatives, not elsewhere classified" and "laborers, not elsewhere classified." Such variation is fairly substantial. It must be understood, however, that particularly at these levels of the census classification scheme the occupation-industry categories represent groups of jobs with quite heterogeneous specifications, although the groups are thought to be somewhat homogeneous as to the degree of skill and experience required for their performance. No one has yet faced the question of what a study of occupational mobility would look like if all the 20,000 or more detailed titles in the *Dictionary of Occupational Titles* were coded without prior grouping.

TABLE 1

(continued)

Score Interval	Title of Occupation (Frequency per 10,000 Males in 1960 Experienced Civilian Labor Force in Parentheses)
35 to 39	Salaried and self-employed managers and proprietors, eating and drinking places (43); salesmen and sales clerks, retail trade (274); bookbinders (3); radio and television repairmen (23); firemen, fire protection (30); policemen and detectives, private (3)
30 to 34	Building managers and superintendents (7); self-employed proprietors, gasoline service stations (32); boilermakers (6); machinists (111); millwrights (15); plumbers and pipe fitters (72); structural metal workers (14); tinsmiths, coppersmiths, and sheet metal workers (31); deliverymen and routemen (93); operatives, printing, publishing and allied industries (13); sheriffs and bailiffs (5)
25 to 29	Messengers and office boys (11); newsboys (41); brickmasons, stonemasons, and tile setters (45); mechanics and repairmen, n.e.c. (266); plasterers (12); operatives, drugs and medicine manufacturing (2); ushers, recreation and amusement (2); laborers, petroleum refining (3)
20 to 24	Telegraph messengers (1); shipping and receiving clerks (59); bakers (21); cabinetmakers (15); excavating, grading, and road machine operators (49); railroad and car shop mechanics and repairmen (9); tailors (7); upholsterers (12); bus drivers (36); filers, grinders, and polishers, metal (33); welders and flame-cutters (81)
15 to 19	Blacksmiths (5); carpenters (202); automobile mechanics and repairmen (153); painters (118) attendants, auto service and parking (81); laundry and dry cleaning operatives (25); truck and tractor drivers (362); stationary firemen (20); operatives, metal industries (103); operatives, wholesale and retail trade (35); barbers (38); bartenders (36); cooks, except private household (47)
10 to 14	Farmers (owners and tenants)(521); shoemakers and repairers, except factory (8); dyers (4); taxicab drivers and chauffeurs (36); attendants, hospital and other institution (24); elevator operators (11); fishermen and oystermen (9); gardeners, except farm, and groundskeepers (46); longshoremen and stevedores (13); laborers, machinery manufacturing (10)
5 to 9	Hucksters and peddlers (5); sawyers (20); weavers, textile (8); operatives, footwear, except rubber, manufacturing (16); janitors and sextons (118); farm laborers, wage workers (241); laborers, blast furnaces, steel works, and rolling mills (26); construction laborers (163)
0 to 4	Coal mine operatives and laborers (31); operatives, yarn, thread and fabric mills (30); porters (33); laborers, saw mills, planing mills, and millwork (21)

*n.e.c. means "not elsewhere classified"

SOURCES: Reiss, op. cit., Table B-1; and U.S. Bureau of the Census, 1960 Census of Population, Final Report, PC(1)-1D, Table 201.

The use of occupational status scores carries a theoretical implication. We are assuming, in effect, that the occupation structure is more or less continuously graded in regard to status rather than being a set of discrete status classes. The justification of such an assumption is not difficult. One needs only to look at any tabulation of social and economic characteristics of persons engaged in each specific occupation (whatever the level of refinement in the system of occupational nomenclature). We discover that the occupations overlap—to a greater or lesser degree, to be sure—in their distributions of income, educational attainment, consumer expenditures, measured intelligence, political orientations, and residential locations (to mention but a few items). One may sometimes find evidence supporting the interpretation that there are "natural breaks" in such distributions. Interpretations of this kind were advanced [elsewhere][11] in respect to the dividing line between farm and nonfarm and between white-collar and manual occupations. The evidence did not permit the conclusion that such occupation categories are entirely disjunct. The analysis ... suggests that boundaries may be discerned between the three broad groups, [but] also shows that these are by no means sharp lines without any overlap.

If we choose to think of occupational status as exhibiting continuous variation, the appropriate analytical model is one that treats status as a quantitative variable. This point of view has far-reaching implications for the conceptualization of the process of mobility as well as for the analysis and manipulation of data purporting to describe the process.

Notes

1. Alba M. Edwards, *Comparative Occupation Statistics for the United States,* 1870 to 1940, Washington: Government Printing Office, 1943.

2. *Ibid.,* p. 180.

3. Enid Charles, *The Changing Size of the Family in Canada,* Census Monograph No. One, Eighth Census of Canada, 1941, Ottawa: The Kings Printer and Controller of Stationery, 1948; Bernard R. Blishen, "The Construction and Use of an Occupational Class Scale," *Canadian Journal of Economics and Political Science,* 24 (1958), 519–531.

4. Donald J. Bogue, *Skid Row in American Cities,* Chicago: Community and Family Study Center, University of Chicago, 1963, Chapter 14 and Appendix B.

5. U. S. Bureau of the Census, *Methodology and Scores of Socioeconomic Status,* Working Paper, No. 15 (1963); U. S. Bureau of the Census, "Socioeconomic Characteristics of the Population: 1960," *Current Population Reports,* Series P–23, No. 12 (July 31, 1964).

6. Albert J. Reiss, Jr., *et al., Occupations and Social Status,* New York: Free Press of Glencoe, 1961; Robert W. Hodge, Paul M. Siegel, and Peter H. Rossi, "Occupational Prestige in the United States, 1925–63," *American Journal of Sociology,* 70 (1964), 286–302.

7. Otis Dudley Duncan, "A Socioeconomic Index for All Occupations," in Reiss, *op. cit.,* pp. 109–138.

8. Hodge, Siegel, and Rossi, *op. cit.,* p. 296.

9. Reiss, *op. cit.,* p. 152. (Work in progress by Hodge and Treiman further supports this point.)

10. Duncan, *op. cit.,* Table B–1, pp. 263–275.

11. Peter M. Blau and Otis Dudley Duncan, *The American Occupational Structure,* New York: The Free Press, 1967, Chapter 2.

DONALD J. TREIMAN

Occupational Prestige in Comparative Perspective

In the three decades since World War II there have been some eighty-five studies of occupational prestige conducted in more than sixty countries throughout the world, ranging from highly industrialized places such as the U.S. to traditional societies such as India, Thailand, Nigeria, and New Guinea. Although these studies vary somewhat in their specific details, they all utilize the same basic procedure: a sample of the population is asked to rate or rank a set of occupational titles with respect to their prestige or social standing. These ratings are then aggregated into mean scores (or other measures of central tendency) and the scores are treated as indicators of the relative prestige of the evaluated occupations.

A remarkable feature of these studies is that they yield the same results regardless of the exact wording of the questionnaire. It does not matter whether respondents are asked about the "prestige" or "social standing" or "respect" accorded certain occupations, or whether they are asked to rate occupations on a scale or to rank them in any other way. The results are the same. A second striking feature is that the educated and uneducated, the rich and poor, the urban and rural, the old and

young, all on the average have the same perceptions of the prestige hierarchy. There is no systematic subgroup variation in the relative ratings of jobs. This is of considerable importance since it allows us to make use of data drawn from rather poor samples of the population—for example, students, members of voluntary organizations, representatives of special subcultures—without fear that if we had a different sample we would get different answers. The third noteworthy feature is that although the distribution of the labor force in various occupations varies substantially from place to place, the same sorts of occupations tend to exist everywhere. Even if there are not many airplane pilots or professors in a given country, there tend to be at least a few of them and the population at large knows what these jobs are. In general, the organization of work into specific jobs is amazingly uniform across societies. Pretty much everywhere there are distinctions between weavers and tailors, and between carpenters, painters, and plumbers. And the uniformity in occupations across societies is reflected in the uniformity of occupational titles appearing in prestige studies. As a result, matching occupational titles across countries is a less onerous task than might be expected.

These three features, uniform results regardless of measurement procedures, minimal subgroup variations, and similarity of occupational titles, make possible a systematic comparison of occupational prestige hierarchies among countries. The basic procedure is to match titles across countries, e.g., "physi-

Originally published in 1976. Please see complete source information beginning on page 891.

cian" in the U.S. with "doctor" in Australia, "medecin" in Mauritania, "medico" in Argentina, "laege" in Denmark, and then to compute a product moment correlation between the prestige scores for all matching titles for each pair of countries. The correlation coefficients thus generated can be taken as measures of the similarity of prestige evaluations between each pair of countries. The fundamental conclusion from such computations is that there is substantial uniformity in occupational evaluations throughout the world: the average intercorrelation between pairs of countries is .81.[1] As such numbers go, it is extremely high and fully justifies treatment of the prestige hierarchy in any given country as reflecting, in large part, a single worldwide occupational prestige hierarchy. On the basis of this result, and in view of the need for a standard occupational scaling procedure, it seemed desirable to attempt to construct a standard occupational prestige scale which could be applied to any country.

In order to match occupational titles across countries, it was necessary to devise a comprehensive occupational classification scheme. To do this, I took advantage of an already existing scheme: the *International Standard Classification of Occupations,* Revised Edition (ISCO).[2] This classification is a "nested" scheme which clusters occupations into nine major groups, eighty-three minor groups, 284 unit groups, and 1,506 specific occupations. It was developed by the International Labour Office as a guide for national census offices to encourage the comparability of occupational statistics. Many foreign census bureaus do, in fact, utilize the ISCO scheme and do publish occupational statistics according to its guidelines.

However, since the 1,506 ISCO occupational categories did not correspond very well to the occupational titles for which I had prestige ratings, I followed the ISCO scheme (with minor variations) down to the unit group level and then, within this level, made distinctions among specific occupations when they appeared warranted by my prestige data. The

resulting classification contains 509 distinct occupational titles.

To derive generic prestige scores for each of these occupations, I converted all the data to a standard metric and then simply averaged scores across all countries in which a given title appeared. Scores for higher levels of aggregation (unit groups, minor groups, and major groups) were derived by various averaging procedures.[3]

How good is the prestige scale created by this procedure? The answer is—very good. Evidence for contemporary societies is extremely convincing. The average correlation of the new Standard Scale with the reported prestige hierarchies of fifty-five countries is .91 and only seven of the correlations are less than .87. Thus the Standard Scale is, on the average, the best available predictor of the prestige of occupations in any contemporary society.[4] . . .

A Theory of the Determinants of Prestige

Analysis of the universally shared occupational prestige hierarchy suggests that high prestige is allocated to those occupations which require a high degree of skill or which entail authority over other individuals or control over capital. Moreover, the nature of occupational specialization is such that specific occupations are relatively invariant in these characteristics across time and space. As a result, the prestige of specific occupations is relatively invariant as well. In fact, it is so uniform that a single occupational prestige scale will capture the basic features of the occupational hierarchy of any society.

Specialization of functions into distinct occupational roles necessarily results in inequalities among occupations with respect to skill, authority, and control over capital. Some occupations, by their very definitions, require specific skills. For example, literacy is required of clerks because one cannot be a clerk if one is illiterate. Similarly, some occupations require control over capital or authority over other individuals as inherent definitions of their functions. For instance, a managerial job is one which involves "planning, direction, control, and co-ordination";[5] otherwise, it is not a managerial job but something else. Examples of these inherent inequalities can be located throughout the prestige hierarchy.

Skill, authority, and economic control are singled out as the basic resources which differentiate occupations because these are the fundamental aspects of power—they provide the crucial means to the achievement of desired goals. But the more powerful an occupation, the more important it is that it be performed well, since the consequences of competent or incompetent performances are more telling for such occupations. For example, if a garbage collector does his job poorly, little is lost; but if a surgeon is incompetent, a life can be lost. Or, similarly, if a chain store manager makes a poor business decision it may cost a firm a few hundred or at the most a few thousand dollars; but a poor decision on the part of a major executive can run into millions. Consequently, the more powerful an occupation, the greater the incentive to attract competent personnel to it. And since the basic mechanism for inducing people to perform tasks is to reward them, it follows that the most powerful positions will also be the most highly rewarded.

Other factors do enter into the determination of rewards, so that the relationship between power and privilege is not perfect. Some functions are in greater demand than others, depending upon the needs of society at any particular time. For example, in a hunting and gathering society, hunting is in greater demand than farming and thus hunting is more highly rewarded. And in a commercial economy, law is of great importance and therefore highly rewarded. But these differences are relatively minor compared to the differences in occupational requisites and perquisites which are inherent in the definitions of jobs and therefore stable across time and space.

Not only is the relative power and privilege of occupations essentially similar across soci-eties, but so is the prestige accorded them, for prestige is granted in recognition of power and privilege. Prestige is the metric of "moral worth," and the moral worth of positions reflects their control over socially valued resources and rewards, that is, their power and privilege.[6] Since occupations are differentiated with respect to power, they will in turn be differentiated with respect to privilege and prestige. Thus, if this theory of prestige determinants is correct, these attributes of occupations will be highly correlated across societies.[7] In particular, skill level, authority, economic power, wealth, income, and prestige will be highly intercorrelated with one another and will be highly correlated across countries.

In my work on occupational prestige in contemporary societies, I amassed data on the education levels of occupations for fifteen nations (as a surrogate measure for "skill") and on income levels of occupations for eleven countries; no comparable measures of authority or control of capital were available. These data indicate a striking uniformity in occupational hierarchies. Like occupational prestige evaluations, occupational variations in education and in income proved to be highly similar from society to society. When measures of the average level of schooling of incumbents of each occupation were computed for the U.S., Argentina, Canada, West Germany, Ghana, Great Britain, India, Israel, Japan, the Netherlands, Norway, Taiwan, the U.S.S.R., Yugoslavia, and Zambia and these measures were intercorrelated, the average intercorrelation was .76, which is almost as high as the average prestige intercorrelation reported above (.81). And when measures of the average income of incumbents of each occupation were computed for the U.S., Canada, Ceylon, Costa Rica, India, New Zealand, Pakistan, Surinam, Sweden, Taiwan, and Yugoslavia and these measures were intercorrelated, the average intercorrelation was .65, which is still a substantial correlation. Moreover, education, income, and prestige levels of occupations were highly correlated within each country: the average correlations were, respectively, .77 between education and income, .72 between education and prestige, and .69 between income and prestige. The average correlations with the Standard Scale were .79 for education and .70 for income.[8]

In short, the available data indicate that in the contemporary world occupational hierarchies are substantially invariant from place to place, even among countries varying widely in level of industrialization. This finding lends considerable empirical support to the theoretical argument outlined above.

Notes

This is a revised version of a paper presented at the Conference on International Comparisons of Social Mobility in Past Societies held in 1972. Preparation of the paper was supported by a grant from the National Science Foundation to Columbia University (NSF #28050). I am grateful to the following for making unpublished material available or for giving leads to the work of others: Peter Decker, Sigmund Diamond, Clyde Griffen, James Henretta, David Herlihy, Theodore Hershberg, Richard Hopkins, Michael Katz, William Sewell, Jr., James Smith, and Stephan Thernstrom. Thanks are also extended to Vincent Covello, Theodore Riccardi, Jr., Rose M. Cascio, Michael Freeman, John Hammond, Jr., Herbert Klein, and Jane Ferrar. The comments of the participants at the MSSB Conference, and especially those of Griffen, were extremely helpful in preparing the revision.

1. This average correlation was computed over all pairs of countries with at least 10 occupational titles rated in common.

2. International Labour Office (Geneva, 1969).

3. These are described more fully in Donald J. Treiman, *Occupational Prestige in Comparative Perspective* (New York, 1976), ch. 8.

4. I have shown that the Standard Scale does a uniformly better job of predicting occupational prestige hierarchies in individual countries than do occupational status scales developed specifically for use in occupational mobility studies in those countries. See Donald J. Treiman, "Problems of Concept and Measurement in the Comparative Study of Occupational Mobility," *Social Science Research,* IV (1975), 183–230.

5. I.L.O., *International Standard Classification,* 95.

6. Cf. Edward Shils, "Deference," in John A. Jackson (ed.), *Social Stratification* (Cambridge, 1968), 104–132.

7. Some readers will recognize the similarity between this theory and that of Kingsley Davis and Wilbert E. Moore, "Some Principles of Stratification," *American Sociological Review,* X (1945), 242–249. The principal difference between the two lies in the claim by Davis and Moore that prestige is granted by society as an inducement to competent people to fill important jobs. My claim is that occupational income may be seen as such an inducement but that prestige must be viewed as a measure of moral worth, that is, of the extent to which an occupation embodies that which is valued by members of society. Since power and privilege are universally valued and since hierarchies of power and privilege are relatively invariant, prestige will also be relatively invariant.

8. The education data typically derive from the population censuses of each of the countries in question. The income data also typically derive from population censuses, but in some cases they are from enterprise censuses. Ordinarily annual income was utilized but in some instances weekly or monthly wage rates were available rather than annual income. In practice, alternative measures of the relative income of occupational groups tend to be highly correlated, despite differences among occupations in part-time or seasonal employment rates. See Treiman, Occupational Prestige, ch. 5, Tables 5.1 and 5.2. Data on both income and education levels were available for only five countries: the U.S., Canada, India, Taiwan, and Yugoslavia.

JOHN H. GOLDTHORPE AND KEITH HOPE

Occupational Grading and Occupational Prestige

Introduction

Over the last forty years or so, there has accumulated in the literature of sociology and social psychology a relatively large number (probably several score) of studies in which respondents have been required to grade a selection of occupations in some hierarchical fashion. It has become customary to refer to such studies as being ones of 'occupational prestige'. Indeed, when the matter of occupational prestige is now considered, it is almost invariably in terms of studies of the kind in question. Furthermore, the data provided by these enquiries have come to play an important part both in theoretical discussion and in the conduct of empirical investigation in the general problem-area of social stratification and mobility. Yet, oddly enough, 'occupational prestige' studies have rarely been subjected to critical examination other than from a technical point of view. . . .

The Meaning of Prestige

An appropriate starting point for a more radical appraisal of 'occupational prestige' studies than seems hitherto to have been made is with the concept of 'prestige' itself. In a sociologi-

cal context, we would suggest, prestige can be most usefully understood as referring to a particular form of social advantage and power, associated with the incumbency of a role or membership of a collectivity: specifically, to advantage and power which are of a *symbolic,* rather than of an economic or political nature. That is to say, such advantage and power imply the ability of an actor to exploit—in the pursuit of his goals—*meanings* and *values,* rather than superior material resources or positions of authority or of *force majeure.*

From this conception it follows that a hierarchy of prestige is constituted by intersubjective communication among actors, and must therefore be characterized in attitudinal and relational terms. It cannot be characterized—other than misleadingly—as a distribution in which units have differing amounts of some particular substance or quality. As a provisional statement, a prestige hierarchy might be one in which actors

(i) *defer* to their superiors—that is, acknowledge by speech or other action their own social inferiority—and seek, or at least appreciate, association with superiors;

(ii) *accept* their equals as partners, associates etc. in intimate social interaction—entertainment, friendship, courtship, marriage, etc.;

(iii) *derogate*[1] their inferiors, if only by accepting their deference and avoiding association with them other than where their own superiority is confirmed.

Originally published in 1972. Please see complete source information beginning on page 891.

The attributes of roles or collectivities which differentiate actors in respect of their prestige are various. What they have in common is some symbolic significance—some generally recognised meaning—which, in conjunction with prevailing values, constitutes a claim to social superiority or, conversely, some stigma of inferiority. For example, having the role of doctor and working in a hospital or clinic implies having knowledge of, control over and close involvement with matters which are generally regarded as ones of ultimate concern—matters of life and death. Belonging to an aristocratic family and owning a landed estate signifies descent from illustrious forebears and participation in an historically-rooted, distinctive and exclusive way of life. Working as a clerk in a bank evokes such generally valued characteristics as honesty, trustworthiness, discretion and dependability, and again in relation to 'important'—in this case, financial—matters. In all of these cases, then, 'deference-entitlements' (Shils, 1968) exist, and are likely to be honoured at least by some actors in some contexts. In contrast, being, say, a gypsy scrap-metal dealer or a West Indian refuse-collector is likely to mean relatively frequent exposure to derogation, on account both of the symbolic significance of the ethnic memberships in question and of the implied occupational contact with what is spoiled, discarded and dirty.[2] In other words, prestige positions do not derive directly from the attributes of a role or collectivity 'objectively' considered, but rather from the way in which certain of these attributes are perceived and evaluated in some culturally determined fashion. . . .

Occupational Prestige

Assuming that a conception of prestige consistent with classical analyses is adopted, then the reference of 'occupational prestige' follows from it directly: it is to the chances of deference, acceptance and derogation associated with the incumbency of occupational roles and membership in occupational collec-

tivities. Such prestige will be related to the 'objective' attributes of occupations—their rewards, requisite qualifications, work-tasks, work environments etc.—but only indirectly: only, that is, in so far as these attributes carry symbolic significance of a kind that is likely to be interpreted as indicative of social superiority or inferiority, with corresponding interactional consequences.

We may, therefore, now go on to ask such questions as: (i) whether such a conception of occupational prestige has been that generally held by the authors of conventional occupational prestige studies; (ii) whether the results of such studies provide valid indicators of prestige in the sense in question; (iii) whether the uses to which results have been put have been appropriate ones. . . .

The Interpretation of Occupational Prestige Ratings

It has been regularly remarked that in occupational prestige ratings, as conventionally carried out, both cognitive and evaluative processes are involved. However, precisely what are supposed to be the objects of these processes has rarely been made clear. For example, if it really were occupational prestige in the sense we would favour which was being assessed, then what would have to be cognized (or, rather, *recognized*) and evaluated would be the symbolic significance of certain features of an occupation with regard to the chances of those engaged in the occupation meeting with deference, acceptance or derogation in their relations with others. If, for instance, the occupational 'stimulus' given were that of 'coal miner', a possible response might be on the lines of

'dirty, degrading work' →
'rough, uncultivated men' →
'likely to be looked down on by most groups'

or, alternatively perhaps

'difficult, dangerous work' →
'able, courageous men' →
'likely to be respected by many groups'

But is this in fact the kind of thing that usually happens? There is little reason to believe so, at least if we are guided by respondents' own accounts of what chiefly influenced their ratings.[3] Rather, we would suggest, the operation that most respondents have tended to perform (perhaps in accordance with the principle of least effort) is a far more obvious and simple one: namely, that of rating the occupations on the basis of what they know, or think they know, about a number of objective characteristics, evaluated in terms of what they contribute to the general 'goodness' of a job. In other words—and consistently with their own accounts—respondents in occupational prestige studies have not typically been acting within a distinctively 'prestige' frame of reference at all. The sensitivity to symbolic indications of social superiority and inferiority which this would imply has not usually been evoked by the task of grading set them. Rather, this task has led them to assess occupations only in some far less specific fashion, according to a composite judgment on an assortment of their attributes which might be thought of as more or less desirable.[4]

Such an interpretation of what 'occupational prestige' ratings are actually about would seem, moreover, to fit far better with what is known of the pattern of variation in such ratings than would the idea that they relate to prestige *stricto sensu*. The basic feature of this pattern is that while some considerable amount of disagreement in rating occurs as between *individuals*, differences between the mean ratings of age, sex, regional, occupational and other collectivities are never very great. If one assumes that in making their judgments, respondents more or less consciously (i) consider a number of different occupational attributes which they take as determining how 'good' a job is; (ii) attach some subjective 'weight' to each of these; (iii) for each occupation presented apply their rating 'formula' to what they know about the occu-

pation, and thus (iv) come to some overall assessment of it—then one might well anticipate some appreciable degree of variation in ratings at the individual level. Individuals are likely to differ in their familiarity with particular jobs and in their priorities as regards what makes a job 'good'. However, one would not expect—other than in somewhat special and limited cases[5]—that such differences would be socially structured in any very striking way. Knowledge about the more general characteristics of other than rather esoteric occupations is relatively 'open'; and, again in general terms, the kinds of thing thought of as 'good' in a job are unlikely to give rise to systematic differences in ratings, especially since there is, in any case, a clear tendency for such advantages to go together. To take a particular example—from the NORC data—it is not surprising, given an interpretation of the kind we have proposed, that individuals should quite often disagree about the ratings of 'building contractor' *vis-à-vis* 'welfare-worker'—*nor* that, at the same time, in the case of age, sex, regional, occupational or other categories, the former job should invariably have the higher *mean* rating. (See Reiss 1961, pp. 55–6, 225–8).[6]

On the other hand, if we were to suppose that 'occupational prestige' scores did give a valid indication of a structure of prestige relations, then the degree of consensus that is shown among different social groups would indeed be remarkable, at least in those societies where other research has indicated some notable diversity in value systems and in particular between members of different social strata. For in this case it would not be a matter of evaluative consensus simply on what attributes make a job 'good', but rather on certain symbolic criteria of generalized superiority and inferiority, with all their attitudinal and behavioural implications. As Shils has observed, the conditions necessary for an entirely, or even a largely, 'integrated' prestige order to exist are in fact demanding ones. It would seem, therefore, the safest assumption to make that, within modern industrial societies, such conditions will prevail only locally, transiently or imperfectly, and thus that social relations expressive of a prestige order will occur only in an intermittent or discontinuous fashion. On the basis of available empirical data, one might suggest that while derogation is still quite widely manifest—as, for example, in the form of differential association or status-group exclusivity—the claim to superiority thus made by one group is not necessarily, or even usually, acknowledged by those regarded as inferior; that is to say, the latter are often not inclined to display deference.[7] This refusal may be revealed passively—by disregard for the claim to superiority, in that no particular 'respect' is shown, and little concern to reduce social distance from the 'superior' group; or, perhaps, some direct challenge to the claim may be made where real interests are felt to be threatened by it—as, say, by 'exclusivity' in housing areas, use of amenities, etc. . . .

The Uses of 'Occupational Prestige' Ratings

One notable use of the data in question results from the fact that over the last two decades occupational prestige studies have been carried out in a steadily increasing number of countries at different levels of economic development. The opportunity has therefore arisen of making cross-national comparisons which, it has been supposed, can throw light on the relationship between value systems and social structural characteristics and are thus relevant to the thesis of the 'convergent' development of societies as industrialism advances. For example, Inkeles and Rossi (1956), comparing occupational prestige ratings in studies from six industrial societies, showed that a high degree of similarity prevailed. On this basis, they concluded that common structural features of these societies were of greater influence on the evaluation of occupations than were differences in cultural traditions. Subsequently, however, occupational prestige ratings from several countries as yet little industrialized have *also* been

shown to be broadly in line with the hierarchy found in economically advanced societies—in so far, that is, as comparisons can be made. This result has then led to the modified argument (Hodge, Treiman and Rossi, 1966) that what is chiefly reflected in prestige ratings is the set of structural features shared by national societies of *any* degree of complexity— 'specialized institutions to carry out political, religious, and economic functions, and to provide for the health, education and welfare of the population . . .'. Occupations at the top of these institutional structures, it is suggested, are highly regarded because of their functional importance and also because they are those which require the most training and ability and those to which the highest rewards accrue. Thus, 'any major prestige inversion would produce a great deal of inconsistency in the stratification system' (p. 310).

In this way, therefore, it is clearly indicated how occupational prestige data may further be employed in support of a general theory of social stratification of a structural-functional type. Such an application has in fact been made quite explicitly in the work of Barber (1957). Following a Parsonian approach, Barber takes the results of the Inkeles-Rossi study as the main empirical foundation for the view that the factual order of stratification in modern societies tends in the main to be consistent with the dominant normative order. Inequality in social rewards and relationships, it is held, is structured in accordance with functional 'needs', and this arrangement is then seen as receiving general moral support: 'functionally important roles are congruent with or partly determine a system of values' (p. 6).

Clearly, for occupational prestige data to be used in the ways in question, it is necessary to assume that such data reflect prevailing values and norms *of a particular kind*: ones pertaining to the 'goodness'—in the sense of the 'fairness' or 'justice'—of the existing distribution of social power and advantage. However, in view of our previous discussion, it is difficult to regard such an assumption as a valid one or indeed to understand why it ever should have been made. Even if it were to be supposed that data on publicly recognized occupational hierarchies do indicate a prestige order in something approximating the classical conception, it still then would not follow that they can provide evidence that the objective reality of stratification is morally legitimated. For while prestige relations do depend upon a certain range of shared understandings, consensus on principles of distributive justice is not necessarily involved.[8] Moreover, as we have argued, by far the most plausible interpretation is that occupational prestige ratings reflect prevailing ideas at a much lower level of abstraction: that is, ideas of what is 'good' in the sense simply of what is generally found desirable in an occupation. And if *this* is the case, then the consensus that exists is obviously of no very great moral or legitimatory significance at all. Apart from quite unsurprising agreement on such matters as, for example, that high pay is preferable to low pay, more security to less, qualifications to lack of qualifications, etc., the consensus that is implied is of a cognitive and perceptual kind, not an evaluative one. The fact that, on average, all groups and strata agree that certain occupations should be rated higher than others tells one nothing at all about whether the occupational hierarchy that is thus represented is regarded as that which *ought* to exist. And in so far as the publicly recognized hierarchy corresponds to that proposed by structural-functional theorists, this would seem to indicate no more than that broadly similar sets of rating criteria are being applied: i.e. occupational rewards and occupational requirements.[9]

Thus, as regards the utilization of occupational prestige data in the advancement of stratification theory, our view must be that this has been fundamentally misguided. What, now, of their application in research? Primarily, of course, occupational prestige ratings have been used in studies of social mobility, in which they have constituted the hierarchy—scalar or categorical—in the context of which mobility has been assessed. Assumptions about what prestige ratings rate are thus

necessarily involved in the interpretation of mobility patterns, and the crucial issues that arise are once more ones of 'validity'.

Concerning the question: What, in mobility studies, may occupational prestige ratings be taken to indicate?—three main positions can be distinguished. These can be usefully considered in turn, together with their implications and problems.

(i) Ratings may be taken—as, for example, by Svalastoga (1959)—as indicative of the position of an occupation within a prestige order; that is, as indicative of the chances of those holding that occupation encountering deference, acceptance or derogation in their social lives. In this case, therefore, mobility between different occupational levels, other than of a marginal kind, may be interpreted as involving the probability of subcultural and relational discontinuity. While such a perspective does not necessarily mean that society is seen as divided up into more or less discrete strata, it does imply that social mobility, as measured, is not just a matter of individuals gaining more qualifications, more income, more interesting work etc., but further of their experiencing changes in their life-styles and patterns of association. The difficulty is, however, as already remarked, that the validity of occupational prestige ratings construed in this way has never been established, and that there are indeed strong grounds for doubting their validity. In other words, we are simply not in a position to infer, with any acceptable degree of precision and certitude, what are the typical consequences of mobility, as measured via occupational prestige ratings, for the actual social experience of those deemed to be mobile.

(ii) Prestige ratings may be taken as indicative of the status of occupations in the generic sense—that is, as being in effect comparable with composite measures of 'socio-economic' status, derived from data on income, education, housing, possessions etc. Justification for this position is twofold: first, to [quote] the observation of Reiss (1961), respondents in prestige-rating studies appear 'to emphasize the relevance of indicators sociologists use to measure socio-economic status . . . '; secondly, as shown by Duncan (1961), it is possible, at least in the American case, to predict prestige ratings fairly accurately from census data on occupational income and education. If then, 'occupational prestige' is understood in the way in question, some reasonable basis may be claimed for interpreting occupationally-measured mobility in terms of movement between grades of occupation differentiated chiefly by their levels of rewards and requirements. At the same time, though, it must be emphasized that in this case no good grounds exist for any interpretation in terms of prestige *stricto sensu*, and, of course, no basis at all for any consideration of how far mobility may be incongruent from one form of stratification to another. Precisely because of the inevitably 'synthetic' nature (Ossowski, 1963) of socio-economic status, as indicated by prestige scores, the analysis of mobility must be strictly unidimensional. These limitations would lead one to suggest, therefore, that if it is accepted that occupational prestige ratings are not valid indicators of a prestige order but are being used simply to stand proxy for socio-economic status, then it would be preferable, where possible, to seek to measure the latter more directly—and without any concern to combine components so that a good 'fit' with prestige scores may be obtained. To discard the notion of prestige altogether would, in this case, mean losing nothing but the possibility of terminological confusion; and developing separate indices of occupational income, education etc., as well as some composite measure, would permit the analysis of mobility in a multi-dimensional manner. In short, there seems no good argument for basing mobility research on occupational prestige ratings, interpreted as socio-economic status scores, other than where a lack of data on the socio-economic attributes of occupations makes this procedure an unavoidable *pis aller*.

(iii) Prestige ratings may be taken as indicating popular evaluations of the relative 'goodness' of occupations in terms of the en-

tire range of prevailing criteria. In this case, related mobility data are open to interpretation as showing, basically, the chances of individuals entering more or less desirable grades of occupation, given certain grades of origin. While an interpretation of the data on these lines has rarely, if ever, been pursued consistently throughout a mobility study, it is that which, on grounds of validity, could best be defended. First, as we have already argued, grading occupations according to notions of their general 'goodness' is what respondents in occupational prestige studies appear, in the main, to be doing. Secondly, it is in regard to *this* understanding of prestige scores that it would seem most relevant to claim, following Duncan and Artis (1951) and Reiss (1961), that their validity lies in the degree of consensus which emerges, despite the use of quite various criteria of evaluation. The argument that this consensus points to 'the existence of an underlying and agreed upon structure of occupational prestige' is difficult to sustain once it is recognized just what consensus on a prestige order entails. But the idea of a broadly agreed upon ordering of occupations in terms of 'goodness' does, on the evidence in question, receive some clear—and not very surprising—support. Furthermore, if prestige ratings are taken as indicative of an occupational hierarchy of this kind, then the fact that they represent synthetic judgments and cannot be 'disaggregated' is no longer a problem in the analysis of mobility patterns. For if mobility is being interpreted as being simply between grades of occupation of differing desirability in some overall sense, a unidimensional approach would appear the appropriate one. However, it must be added that what would then be a dubious and potentially dangerous step would be to shift from such an interpretation of specifically occupational mobility to one in which conclusions were drawn regarding the stability of status groups, income classes, or social strata in any sense whatsoever; that is, conclusions regarding *social* mobility as generally understood. In effect, of course, a shift of this nature has been made in most large-scale mobility studies carried out in the recent past. But while it might reasonably be held that such a manoeuvre is unlikely to be very misleading so far as the 'gross' patterns of social mobility are concerned, the difficulty is (apart from the limitation of unidimensionality) that we have no way of knowing at just *what* point and in *what* ways it might turn out to be quite deceptive. Yet again, the problem of validity recurs.

The general—and rather pessimistic—conclusion to which one is led is, therefore, the following: that to the extent that the meaning of occupational prestige ratings is correctly construed, the less useful they appear to be as a basis for mobility studies which pursue the 'classical' sociological interests of mobility research.

Notes

1. We use 'derogate' in this context following Shils (1968). Were it not that its usual connotations go beyond its strict meaning, 'disparage'—literally 'to make unequal'—might be a preferable term.

2. On 'stigma symbols' as the obverse of 'prestige symbols', see Goffman (1963).

3. See Reiss (1961).

4. As regards the NORC [National Opinion Research Center] study, it is worth recalling what is usually forgotten: that this enquiry, at least in the view of those who devised it, was in fact specifically aimed at finding out what people thought were the best jobs, in the sense of the most desirable. Where 'prestige' and 'standing' are referred to in the initial report on the study, they are obviously equated with desirability. See NORC (1947).

5. E.g. where respondents are rating occupations within their own status or situs areas, c.f. Gerstl and Cohen (1964).

6. Our interpretation of the meaning of 'occupational prestige' ratings is also consistent with the fact that certain variations in the task set to respondents appear to make little difference to the results achieved: e.g. whether respondents are asked to rate occupations according to their 'social prestige', 'social standing', 'social status', 'general desirability' etc: or whether they are asked for their own opinions or what they believe are generally prevailing opinions. It seems reasonable to suppose that if respondents are required to grade occupations according to any one criterion which, while rather imprecise, implies a 'better-worse' dimension, they will produce results of the kind in question; and further, that the level of consensus in this respect is such that the distinction between personal and general opinion is of little consequence—provided that there is no suggestion of a normative judgment being required; that is, one in terms of which jobs *ought* to be the best.

7. Cf. for example, Goldthorpe, Lockwood, Bechhofer and Platt (1969), chapters 4 and 5.

8. In fact, one might suggest the hypothesis that societies of the kind in which an integrated and stable prestige order is to be found will tend to be ones in which the factual order of stratification is not commonly appraised in terms of distributive justice, or indeed envisaged as capable of being in any way substantially different from what it is.

The distinction between the recognition of prestige and the attribution of justice is foreshadowed—as are several other points in the above paragraph—by Gusfield and Schwartz (1963) in a paper that has been curiously neglected by subsequent American writers on occupational grading.

9. It is a well-known problem of the structural-functional theory of stratification that other usable criteria of the functional importance of occupational roles are hard to find: employing the two criteria in question does, of course, introduce a serious degree of circularity into the argument.

References

Barber, B. (1957). *Social stratification*. Harcourt, Brace & Co., New York.

Duncan, O.D. (1961). A socioeconomic index for all occupations. In A.J. Reiss, *Occupations and social status*. Free Press of Glencoe. New York.

Duncan, O.D. and Artis, J.W. (1951). *Social stratification in a Pennsylvania rural community*. Pennsylvania State College: Agricultural Experiment Station Bulletin 543.

Gerstl, J. and Cohen, L.K. (1964). Dissensus, situs and egocentrism in occupational ranking. *Brit. J. Sociol.*, 15, 254–61.

Goffman, E. (1963). *Stigma*. Prentice Hall, Englewood Cliffs.

Goldthorpe, J.H., Lockwood, D., Bechhofer, F. and Platt, J. (1969). *The affluent worker in the class structure*. Cambridge University Press.

Gusfield, J.R. and Schwartz, M. (1963). The meaning of occupational prestige: reconsideration of the NORC scale. *Amer. Sociol. Rev.*, 28, 265–71.

Hodge, R.W., Treiman, D.J. and Rossi, P. (1966). A comparative study of occupational prestige. In *Class, status and power* (2nd edn.). (ed. R.

Bendix and S.M. Lipset). Free Press of Glencoe, New York.

Inkeles, A. and Rossi, P. (1956). National comparisons of occupational prestige. *Amer. J. Sociol.,* 61, 329–39.

N.O.R.C. (1947). Jobs and occupations: a popular evaluation. *Opinion News,* 9th September. Reprinted in *Class, status and power* (1st edn.). (ed. R. Bendix and S.M. Lipset). Free Press of Glencoe, New York.

Ossowski, S. (1963). *Class structure in the social consciousness.* Routledge, London.

Reiss, A.J. (1961). *Occupations and social status.* Free Press of Glencoe, New York.

Shils, E.A. (1968). Deference. In *Social stratification* (ed. J.A. Jackson). Cambridge University Press.

Svalastoga, K. (1959). *Prestige, class and mobility.* Gyldendal, Copenhagen.

DAVID L. FEATHERMAN AND ROBERT M. HAUSER

Prestige or Socioeconomic Scales in the Study of Occupational Achievement?

At least in the United States and Australia, the processes of allocation to educational and occupational statuses from social origins (i.e., the process of stratification or of status attainment) seem largely socioeconomic in character (Featherman, Jones, and Hauser, 1975). Put another way, inter- and intragenerational movements of men among categories of their own and their parents' educations and occupations more closely follow the dimensions of social space defined by the "socioeconomic" distances among occupation groups than by the "prestige" distances among occupations. Evidence for this interpretation is drawn from parallel results for the United States and Australia in which estimates for the structural equations of "status attainment" models with occupations scaled in units of Duncan's (1961) socioeconomic index (SEI) yield higher coefficients of multiple determination (R^2)

than do estimates based on occupations scaled in units of NORC prestige (Siegel, 1971) or of Treiman's (1977) international prestige index. In addition, the canonical structure of generational and career occupational mobility in both societies more nearly approximates a socioeconomic "space," as the canonical weights for occupation categories correlated higher with mean SEI scores for these occupations than with mean Siegel or Treiman scores.

In interpreting these data we suggest that prestige scores for occupations are less valid indicators of the dimensions of occupations pertinent to occupational mobility in industrial societies and of the status attainment processes operating therein than are socioeconomic scores. We reason from evidence for the United States (Reiss, 1961; Siegel, 1971) and Great Britain (Goldthorpe and Hope, 1974) that occupational prestige scores represent a congeries of salient dimensions or occupational characteristics. For example, the British ratings of the "social standing" of occupations are a linear combination (to the extent of 97% of their variance) of four oblique dimensions: standard of living, power and in-

Originally published in 1976. Please see complete source information beginning on page 891.

fluence over other people, level of qualifications, and value to society (Goldthorpe and Hope, 1974: 14). Any two pairs of raters produce rankings which are modestly correlated at best (r = .4), consistent with the notion that unique variance in prestige gradings is quite high. Conversely, the mean ranks for the same occupations over socially and demographically defined groups correlate in the range of 0.8 and 0.9. This common variance appears to be socioeconomic; that is, over three-quarters of the linear variance in prestige scores is a reflection of the educational and economic properties of the ranked occupations. Thus, while raters in the United States and Britain used many and idiosyncratic features of occupations in assessing their relative social standing, apparently they all were aware of and utilized the socioeconomic "desirability" of titles, to some extent, in reaching their decisions.

The salience of the socioeconomic properties of occupations across persons, groups, and perhaps societies may follow from the rather similar social organization of occupations in functionally similar economic systems (e.g., industrial capitalism). But more to the point of the relative centrality of "prestige" or socioeconomic dimensions to the process of status attainment, we speculate that commonalities in prestige grades and in the responsiveness of these rankings to socioeconomic attributes of occupations may reflect popular awareness of (what further comparative research may show to be) similar processes of status allocation across societies. In at least the cases of Australia and the United States, the socioeconomic model, patterned after the work of Blau and Duncan (1967), yields estimates of effect parameters which are substantially the same. Moreover, log-linear adjustments of mobility matrices for the effects of differential occupation structures (to wit, as provided in the table margins) uncovers largely similar interactions within the tables (to wit, constant patterns of inflow and outflow both between and within generations for both societies).

Our provisional conclusion is that prestige scores are "error-prone" estimates of the socioeconomic attributes of occupations. Whatever it is that prestige scores scale—and this does not appear to be prestige in the classical sense of deference/derogation (see Goldthorpe and Hope, 1972)—it is substantively different from socioeconomic status. Yet one is best advised to use a scale for occupations which most accurately captures the features of occupations having force for the social process one is studying. In instances of occupational mobility and related processes of status allocation, socioeconomic dimensions and socioeconomic scores for occupations are the more central, and therefore are preferable over prestige scores.

Notes

This research was supported by NSF Grant #44336, NICHHD Grant #HD-05876 and institutional support from the College of Agricultural and Life Sciences, University of Wisconsin-Madison. Any opinions, findings, conclusions, or recommendations are those of the authors and do not necessarily reflect the views of the National Science Foundation.

References

Blau, P. M. and O. D. Duncan (1967) The American Occupational Structure. New York: Wiley.

Duncan, O.D. (1961) "A socioeconomic index for all occupations," pp. 139–161 in A. Reiss, Occupations and Social Status. New York: Free Press.

Featherman, D. L., F. L. Jones, and R. M. Hauser (1975) "Assumptions of social mobility research in the U.S.: the case of occupational status." Social Science Research 4 (December): 329–360.

Goldthorpe, J. and K. Hope (1974) The Social Grading of Occupations: A New Approach and Scale. Oxford: Oxford Univ. Press.

———. (1972) "Occupational grading and occupational prestige," pp. 19–79 in K. Hope (ed.) The Analysis of Social Mobility: Methods and Approaches. Oxford: Clarendon.

Reiss, A. J. (1961) Occupations and Social Status. New York: Free Press.

Siegel, P. M. (1971) "Prestige in the American occupational structure." Unpublished doctoral dissertation, University of Chicago.

Treiman, D. J. (1977) Occupational Prestige in Comparative Perspective. New York: Academic Press.

R O B E R T   W.   H O D G E

The Measurement of Occupational Status

Since the appearance of Blau and Duncan's monumental inquiry into "The American Occupational Structure" (1967), we have learned a great deal about processes of inter- and intrageneration occupational mobility. Indeed, there has been a virtual explosion of research on processes of status attainment. Much of this research rests upon the reduction of information about a person's detailed occupational pursuit to a single continuous variable, a transformation typically accomplished by utilizing Duncan's Socioeconomic Index for All Occupations (Duncan, 1961a) to assign status scores to the occupations held by fathers and sons at various points in their careers (see, for example, Blau and Duncan, 1967; Hauser and Featherman, 1977). Despite the reliance of most inquiries into processes of status attainment on Duncan's SEI scale, there has been little discussion of the properties and characteristics of this index by its users (see, however, Duncan, 1961b, and Featherman and Hauser, 1976). The purpose of this essay is to discuss the characteristics of Duncan's SEI scale, as

well as several difficulties encountered in its use in studies of occupational mobility. . . .

On the Interpretation of Duncan's Index

The conceptual meaning of Duncan's SEI scale is by no means clear; at least three alternative interpretations are available and none of these is entirely satisfactory. All of these interpretations rest upon features of the construction of Duncan's index and/or characteristics of the estimated weights of its components.

The most obvious interpretation of Duncan's SEI scale follows from the technique by which the weights of its components were derived. The reader will recall that they were established by regressing the percentage of excellent plus good ratings received by a few titles in the North-Hatt study which matched census lines on census-derived indicators of the age-standardized educational and income levels of these occupations. Scale values for all occupations were then obtained by substituting the education and income measures, available for all occupations from census data, into the resulting equation. Consequently, Duncan's SEI scale may be interpreted as *the expected percentage of excellent*

Originally published in 1981. Please see complete source information beginning on page 891.

plus good ratings an occupation would receive in a prestige inquiry of the North-Hatt type.

There are two defects with this interpretation of Duncan's SEI scale. First, the prediction equation for the prestige indicator is less than satisfactory. It accounts for a bit more than four-fifths of the variance in prestige ratings. One could, of course, regard the error variance as random, on the view that prestige ratings are just "error-prone" proxies for the education and income levels of occupations. However, such a view cannot be sustained in the light of the substantial consensus which exists between subgroups of raters. The education and income levels of occupations fail to account for the consensus observed between subgroups of raters differing in their own occupations, their sex, race, and so forth. Not only is there consensus between subgroups of raters about overall prestige ratings, there is also consensus about that part of the prestige of an occupation which is not accounted for by the income and educational levels of its incumbents. This fact enables one to discount the view that prestige scores are just "error-prone" indicators of the "socioeconomic" level of an occupation, a point which appears to have escaped Featherman and Hauser who state (1976, p. 405), "Our provisional conclusion is that prestige scores are 'error-prone' estimates of the socioeconomic attributes of occupations." This claim is quite possibly true *with respect to the intergenerational transmission of occupational status.* However, in view of the consensus over them from one subgroup of raters to the next, the "errors" themselves appear to be social facts in Durkheim's sense, rather than random disturbances which have no life of their own. For this reason, the interpretation of Duncan's SEI scale as a predicted prestige score flies in the face of what is known about occupational prestige.

Since the publication of Duncan's SEI scale, pure prestige scales have become available for all occupations (Siegel, 1971; Treiman, 1977). Comparisons of the performance of these scales with Duncan's index in studies of status

attainment leave no doubt that the association between the detailed occupations of fathers and their sons is captured more completely by their values on Duncan's index than on either Siegel's or Treiman's prestige scale (see, for example, Duncan *et al.*, 1972; Featherman and Hauser, 1976; Stevens and Featherman, 1981). This is yet another reason why the interpretation of Duncan's scale as expected prestige scores is dubious.

A second interpretation of Duncan's SEI scale pays no attention to the method of its construction and makes reference only to its components. Without specifying the precise meaning of either, sociologists commonly make a distinction between "social status" and "economic status." (These concepts, whatever they are, should not be confused with Weber's concepts of "status honor" and "class," which have quite specific meanings that are analytically, if not statistically, independent of the usual measures of "social status" and "economic status.") Education is frequently utilized as an indicator of "social status," while current income is a common measure of "economic status." Since aggregate measures of the educational and income levels of an occupation's incumbents enter into the computation of Duncan's index, it is natural to refer to the combination of them as a *socioeconomic index of occupational status.*

This interpretation of Duncan's SEI scale is, obviously, the one most frequently made in the literature. Duncan indicated his own preference for it by his decision to name his index as he did. The socioeconomic interpretation of Duncan's SEI scale is clearly embedded in its use in Blau and Duncan's study of occupational mobility (1967), Hauser and Featherman's replication of it (1977), and Featherman and Hauser's important discussion (1976) of the properties of socioeconomic and prestige indicators of occupational standing. Most users of the Duncan index have accepted this interpretation without serious consideration of alternatives. Despite the overwhelming consensus in the published literature about the proper interpretation of Duncan's scale, it is interesting to note that

Duncan himself, in his original presentation of the scale, is more than slightly ambiguous about its proper interpretation. At one point, he remarks (1961a, p. 115),

Our problem, then, is defined as that of obtaining a socioeconomic index for each of the occupations in the detailed classification of the 1950 Census of Population. This index is to have both face validity, in terms of its constituent variables, and *sufficient predictive efficiency with respect to the NORC occupational prestige ratings that it can serve as an acceptable substitute for them* [emphasis is added] in any research where it is necessary to grade or rank occupations in the way that the NORC score does but where some of the occupations are not on the NORC list.

This quotation seems to make clear that Duncan wanted to cut the cake both ways: the index was a socioeconomic one, but it was also a substitute for prestige ratings. Subsequently, Duncan made clear that he did not regard his index as the equivalent of a pure prestige scale, noting (1961a, p. 129) that, "It should be made perfectly clear that the socioeconomic index does *not* [Duncan's italics] purport to be a prediction of the prestige ratings that occupations excluded from the NORC list would receive in a similarly conducted study of prestige ratings." Subsequent research has clearly demonstrated that Duncan was absolutely correct in this judgment: his scale and prestige scales are very definitely not the same thing. But that still leaves open how his scale should be interpreted.

The interpretation of Duncan's SEI scale as a socioeconomic index is seemingly agreeable and consistent with what its constituent indicators are thought to measure at the individual level. Nonetheless, this interpretation of Duncan's and similar scales is not without its problems. In our view, there are two primary difficulties with socioeconomic indicators of an occupation's location in the social structure of work. First, the combination of indicators of social and economic status such as education and income into a composite index of socioeconomic level begs the question of whether or not the effects of these factors are proportional to their weights in the index—a crucial and necessary assumption whenever the index is subsequently employed in empirical research. There is ample evidence *at the individual level* that education and income can even have *effects of opposite sign* on some dependent variables such as fertility; combining them together with a person's occupational level into an overall index of an individual's socioeconomic level presumes unidimensionality where there is none and should be avoided. (For a further discussion of this point and additional examples, see Hodge, 1970.) But if it is sound practice to keep such variables as income and education separated at the individual level, one can at least question the wisdom of combining them *at the aggregate level* of occupations. It may well be that alternative, aggregate characteristics of occupations are not just alternative indicators of an occupation's location in a single hierarchy, but reflect somewhat different forces at work on an occupation's incumbents and their behavior.

What we regard, however, as an even greater difficulty with the socioeconomic interpretation of Duncan's SEI scale stems from the analytical status of the concept of "socioeconomic" level. As far as we can see, it has none: its relationship to such *well-defined*, though *poorly measured*, concepts of stratification theory as "class," "status," and "power" is at best vague and imprecise. The concept of socioeconomic status has no independent analytical status in stratification theory: at the individual level it is no more or no less than whatever is measured by a person's education, occupational pursuit, and income and, at the aggregate level of occupations, it is just some combination of whatever skills it takes to enter the occupation and whatever rewards are obtained from pursuing it at a given point in time within a given market structure. Socioeconomic status is what socioeconomic status scales measure; there is no underlying analytical concept to which we can refer a proposed indicator of socioeconomic status to decide whether it is well or ill conceived or to assess how it might be improved. For example, referring to "the choice of summary statistics to represent the education and income distributions of the occupations, and the adjustment of these statistics for age differences among occupations," Duncan observed (1961a, p. 119), "Reasonable procedures for accomplishing these two steps, different from the ones followed [in the construction of Duncan's index] are easily proposed." In a world like this, of course, there is no theoretical justification for the choice of one, as opposed to another plausible means of summarizing the constituent indicators and the choice of any one of the competing alternatives rests on the assumption that they all measure the same thing in approximately the same way. As Duncan put it (1961a, p. 119), ". . . it seems doubtful that the final result would be greatly altered by switching to one of the alternatives." Whether this is literally the case, we cannot say, for while students of status attainment have been especially diligent at exposing the weaknesses of pure prestige scales in the study of occupational mobility, they have devoted but limited energy to examining the properties of alternative socioeconomic scales, to exposing the behavior of the component variables in these scales, and to making these scales temporally relevant to their research, a fault remedied in considerable measure by the work of Stevens and Featherman (1981).

We offer now a third and final interpretation of Duncan's SEI scale. In Duncan's SEI index, the weights of the education and income variables are nearly equal and the intercept is close to zero. We can find the constant k which will center the coefficients of the income and education variables in Duncan's SEI scale around .5 by solving $.50 - .55k = .59k - .50$ for $K = (1)/(1.14) = .8772$.[1] Multiplying the values of Duncan's SEI scale (= D) by this value and adding $6(k) = 6(.8772) = 5.26$ to eliminate the constant term leaves us with

$$D' = k(D) + 6(k) = 8.772(D) + 5.26$$

$$= .4825(E) + 5.175(I),$$

a transformed index (= D') in which the education (= E) and income (= I) indicators are for all practical purposes simply averaged together. This transformation of Duncan's SEI scale is, of course, made possible only because the summary measures of the education and income distributions of the occupations receive nearly equal weights when prestige is regressed on them. Our ability to effect this transformation suggests another interpretation of the Duncan SEI scale scores, viz., *a linear transformation of the best guess we could make of the age-standardized percentage of an occupation's male incumbents either with at least a high school diploma or with 1949 incomes of $3500 or more if neither percentage was known.* In fact, one would not go far awry in interpreting the untransformed values of Duncan's SEI scale in this fashion, since the transformation required to effect this interpretation is roughly equal to the identity operator.

This interpretation of Duncan's SEI scale is, we believe, novel, though Cain (1974, p. 1501) comes close to making it. And while it sounds ridiculous, that is not necessarily a disadvantage. It keeps one's attention focused upon the essential feature of Duncan's SEI scale, to wit, the particular way it glues education and income together to construct "socioeconomic" status. Beyond that, it makes clear the inherent uncertainty which necessarily surrounds any results obtained by the use of Duncan's SEI scale: having used it, there is absolutely no way of knowing whether the observed effects are brought about by the economic rewards attached to occupations or by the skills required to pursue them. Instead, one must resort to casting the results in terms of an occupation's "socioeconomic" status—a concept which seems more nearly contrived for convenience than a social fact in Durkheim's sense. In keeping with the bulk of the literature on status attainment, we will continue throughout this paper to accept the *socioeconomic* interpretation of Duncan's SEI scale, but it should be obvious that the serious questions which can be raised about this or any other interpretation of Duncan's scale also make the interpretation of any findings based upon it problematical.

Occupation as a Contextual Variable

In recent years, a considerable amount of sociological inquiry has been directed toward detecting contextual effects on individual behavior. In this research tradition, individual behavior is seen in part as a function of the characteristics of the other individuals with whom the subject shares group memberships (see, e.g., Blau, 1957, 1960; Davis, Spaeth, and Huson, 1961; Tannenbaum and Bachman, 1964; Farkas, 1974). Research of this kind has not been without its critics, of which Hauser (1970a, 1970b, 1974) is by far the most outspoken.

There are several strategies of research for examining so-called group, contextual, and structural effects upon individual behavior. We need not detail these here, although we should note that the most general of all these models is the one embedded in the analysis of covariance. The particular strategy of interest in the present context is the one where the consequences for an individual's behavior of his membership in a social group or population aggregate are summarized by an indicator which reflects the average or some other measure of the central tendency on a particular trait of the individual members comprising the social groups or population aggregates to which he belongs. An example of this research strategy would be characterizing schoolchildren by the proportion of minority group members in the school they attend. Such a characterization of an individual has nothing to do with the structural features of the school he attends, such as library books per capita. Instead, it rests solely upon the individual characteristics of his fellow classmates.

The fundamental difficulty with this strategy for analyzing contextual or compositional effects is put quite simply: there is *no logically conceivable way in which one could run an experiment to test for any observed effects*. This is the fundamental defect with the analysis of all compositional effects; Hauser (1970a) comes close to stating this principle, but does not make it as explicit as he might have. To illustrate this principle, we may pursue the foregoing example. Suppose we wanted to run an experiment to examine the effects of minority composition on school achievement among white students. Now obviously, our first step would be to make random assignments of white students to schools; in this way the white students in each school would be expected to have equivalent means and variances on all characteristics save those we experimentally manipulate; this is the advantage we realize from experimentation. So far, so good. Now we must construct our experimental variable. To do this, we can again make random assignments, this time of minority students, of subjects to schools. However, while we can make random assignments of minority students to schools so that their expected means and variances on all variables are equal from school to school, *we must assign them in differential numbers*. If we failed to do this, the schools would not differ in their minority composition and there would be no between-school variance in our experimental variable. The situation is now this: by making random assignments we have secured an expected equality from school to school in the means and variances of both white and minority students on all variables. However, the ratio of white to minority students varies from school to school and that, necessary to conduct the experiment at all, proves fatal.

Minority and white students *do not differ on their minority status alone*. They differ in their socioeconomic backgrounds, in the numbers of their siblings, in the quality of their experiences, and almost surely in their attitudes and values as well. Because the schools vary in their minority composition, *they will necessarily vary in every individual level correlate of minority status as well*. Consequently, any observed effect of minority composition is confounded by every individual correlate of minority status and *there is no logically possible way of experimentally separating these confounding factors.* Having found an effect of minority composition, we can generate additional compositional effects by the carload lot. All we need to do is to refer to the individual level correlates of minority status. Furthermore, although it is not essential to the argument advanced herein, any attempt to separate these confounding factors via nonexperimental methods will certainly flounder on the barricade of multicollinearity, since the relevant associations are the typically high, ecological correlations across the units of the experiment—in this case schools.

The foregoing argument requires comment. First, there is nothing about it which denies the existence of contextual or compositional effects. Indeed, they may be large and substantial, but the argument clearly implies that *there is no logically possible way of isolating them.* Second, while *practically* speaking, most social-science findings are not subject to verification via experimentation, one can at least *logically* conceive of an experiment to test them. Contextual effects, however, are in a different ball park from most other social-science findings. There is no conceivable way of contriving an experiment to test them. That should give one pause, for it is far from clear that the limited resources for social-science research should be expended on discovering effects *whose causes can never be experimentally isolated.* Finally, while it is technically possible to detect a generalized contextual effect—indeed, the experiment outlined above could do that—the impossibility of specifying the precise causal force which generates the effect means that contextual analysis is profoundly and fundamentally irrelevant to policy decisions. Any effort to formulate policy on the basis of presumed, *specific* contextual effects is foolhardy, for there is no way of knowing whether the effects are generated by the specific causes one has identified or by one of their confounding correlates.

Occupation is not inherently a contextual variable. Although other considerations enter the picture, one can at least think of detailed occupational groupings as clusters of jobs whose incumbents are mutually substitutable. Thus, it is the similarity in the work required by the jobs forming an occupational group, rather than the similarity in the personal characteristics of their incumbents, which delineates one occupation from another. However, once occupational information is scored with a socioeconomic index like Duncan's, occupation *is turned into a contextual variable.* All of the reservations that one might have about contextual analysis similarly apply to the analysis of occupational information coded in this particular way. One can, of course, *logically* conceive of an experiment to test for the effects of occupation as such; though practically such an experiment might be unfeasible, at least logically one can imagine randomly assigning subjects to occupational groups. But there is no logical way to conduct an experiment about *occupational status.* Duncan's SEI scale includes the education and income levels of *incumbents* as its factors; if one tried to run an experiment on occupations by randomly assigning subjects to occupations, the expected means and variances in their educational and income levels would be identical from one occupation to the next and the occupations would no longer be differentiated according to their socioeconomic status as it is measured by Duncan's scale. In order to keep the Duncan scale scores of the occupations differentiated, one would have to assign relatively more high school graduates and high-income earners to some occupations than to others. Once one has done this, the entire advantage of experimentation is lost and one's experiment would be confounded by every individual level correlate of educational attainment and income. There is just no logically conceivable way to reproduce experimentally any results derived by scoring occupational data with Duncan's scale scores; this fact alone ought to give one pause before using such a scale, particularly in analyses which purport to be causal, rather than merely descriptive in character.

The educational component of Duncan's index strikes us as the most problematical in this regard. Although the income component refers to individuals and to total income, rather than earnings from one's main occupation, one can at least think of this component of Duncan's scale as a characteristic of *jobs* rather than of *people*. To the extent this is so, one could go ahead and make random assignments of persons to posts in an experimental situation without destroying the income differentiation of occupations. But education is another matter: it is attached to people not posts. There is no way around this fact and this component of Duncan's SEI scale indubitably means that its use, both conceptually and practically, serves to reduce "occupation" to a contextual variable. There is more than a little intellectual irony in the fact that perhaps the leading critic of contextual analysis (Hauser, 1970a, 1970b, 1974) is also one of the principal proponents of Duncan's SEI scale (Featherman, Jones, and Hauser, 1975; Featherman and Hauser, 1976). . . .

Prestige and Socioeconomic Status as Occupational Indicators

Prestige scores have two distinct advantages and one very definite disadvantage relative to socioeconomic indices in the study of status attainment and related phenomena. The most obvious advantage of prestige scores is that, unlike socioeconomic indices derived from the characteristics of an occupation's incumbents, they do not reduce occupation to a contextual variable. Because prestige scores are *operationally* independent of the characteristics of an occupation's incumbents, one can logically conceive of an experiment in which subjects are randomly allocated to occupations differing in the prestige they are accorded by the general public. Of course, it may well be that the individual characteristics of an occupation's incumbents are a source of its prestige, in which case one consequence of the experiment might be to reduce the between-occupational variance in prestige scores, since occupations would no longer differ in the characteristics of their incumbents.

If, however, the socioeconomic characteristics of an occupation's incumbents are merely *correlates* rather than *causes* of an occupation's prestige rating, then no change would be observed in their prestige ratings, a situation which would be obtained if prestige ratings are derived from, say, the desirability of the work performed in an occupation, the authority built into occupational positions regardless of their incumbents, and features of the typical work setting.

Another advantage of using prestige scores in the study of occupational stratification flows from its status as a well-defined analytical concept in stratification theory. Although Featherman and Hauser (1976, p. 404) conclude "that occupational prestige scores represent a congeries of salient dimensions or occupational characteristics," such a definition of occupational prestige has little to do with the concept as it is typically used in stratification theory. We would venture that the appropriate definition of occupational prestige is analytically parallel to Weber's definition of power. In this view, the relative prestige of two occupations may be defined as the expectation that a member of one will give (or receive) deference from a member of the other. The concept of expectation or probability is crucial to this definition, as it also is to Weber's definition of power, for it admits the possibility that some members of an occupation may receive deference from members of another occupation while others will give deference to members of the same occupation. In keeping with this view of the relative prestige of two occupations, we can think of the overall prestige of an occupation as the expectation that one of its members will receive (or give) deference to a randomly selected member of any other occupation.

The foregoing definition of occupational prestige implies that it has both a formal and informal component—a part that is built into an occupation by virtue of its formal authority relations with other occupations and a part that devolves upon an occupation by virtue of the performance of its members in situations which are not organized by authority relations. Prestige, in this view, is not identical with power, but it does represent a significant resource—viz., command over the respect of others—which can be mobilized in the effort to secure desired outcomes in the face of competing alternatives. Whether or not occupational prestige conceived in this way is, in fact, what prestige scales measure is, of course, another question. One advantage of using occupational prestige scales, however, rests precisely on one's ability to raise this question intelligibly. Because one analytically knows what prestige is, one can query whether one has measured it satisfactorily. A parallel question cannot be posed of socioeconomic scales, since as best we can tell the socioeconomic status of an occupation is whatever is measured by a socioeconomic scale of occupations.

But whatever analytical advantage prestige scales of occupational status may have is in large measure undercut by their performance, relative to socioeconomic scales, in empirical research. As we have already noted, whatever it is that socioeconomic scales of occupational status measure more nearly governs the process of intergenerational occupational mobility and the entire process of status attainment than do the occupational differences reflected in prestige scales. This is one very sound reason for preferring the former to the latter, even if one can be less than analytically clear about what it is that socioeconomic scales measure. It is, of course, possible that prestige scales perform poorly because they are inferior measures of the underlying analytical concept. We think a case to that effect could be sketched out, but space does not permit us to do so here.

Notes

1. This is because Duncan's SEI scale is constructed from the regression equation,

$$\hat{P} = 0.55(E) + 0.59(I) - 6.0,$$

where E is the age-standardized percentage of the male experienced civilian labor force with 4 years of high school or more, and I is the age-standardized percentage of males who had incomes in 1949 of $3500 or more.—Ed.

References

Blau, P. M. (1957), "Formal organization: Dimensions of analysis," American Journal of Sociology 63, 58–69.

Blau, P. M. (1960), "Structural effects," American Sociological Review 25, 178–193.

Blau, P. M., and Duncan, O. D. (1967), The American Occupational Structure, Wiley, New York.

Cain, G. G. (1974), "Review of Socioeconomic Background and Achievement by O. D. Duncan, D. L. Featherman, and B. Duncan," American Journal of Sociology 79, 1497–1509.

Davis, J. A., Spaeth, J. L., and Huson, C. (1961), "A technique for analyzing the effects of group composition," American Sociological Review 26, 215–226.

Duncan, O. D. (1961a), "A socioeconomic index for all occupations," in Occupations and Social Status (A. J. Reiss, Jr. et al., Eds.), pp. 109–138, The Free Press of Glencoe, New York.

Duncan, O. D. (1961b), "Properties and characteristics of the socioeconomic index," in Occupations and Social Status (A. J. Reiss, Jr. et al., Eds.), pp. 139–161, The Free Press of Glencoe, New York.

Duncan, O. D., Featherman, D. L., and Duncan, B. (1972), Socioeconomic Background and Achievement, Seminar, New York.

Farkas, G. (1974), "Specification, residuals, and contextual effects," Sociological Methods and Research 2, 333–363.

Featherman, D. L., and Hauser, R. M. (1976), "Prestige or socioeconomic scales in the study of occupational achievement?" Sociological Methods and Research 4, 403–422.

Featherman, D. L., Jones, F. L., and Hauser, R. M. (1975), "Assumptions of social mobility research in the U.S.: The case of occupational status," Social Science Research 4, 329–360.

Hauser, R. M. (1970a), "Context and consex: A cautionary tale," American Journal of Sociology 75, 645–664.

Hauser, R. M. (1970b), "Hauser replies," American Journal of Sociology 76, 517–520.

Hauser, R. M. (1974), "Contextual analysis revisited," Sociological Methods and Research 2, 365–375.

Hauser, R. M., and Featherman, D. L. (1977), The Process of Stratification: Trends and Analyses, Academic Press, New York.

Hodge, R. W. (1970), "Social integration, psychological well-being and their socioeconomic correlates," Sociological Inquiry 40, 182–206.

Siegel, P. M. (1971), Prestige in the American Occupational Structure, unpublished Ph.D. dissertation, University of Chicago Library, Chicago.

Stevens, G., and Featherman, D. L. (1981), "A revised socioeconomic index of occupational status," Social Science Research 10, 364–395.

Tannenbaum, A. S., and Bachman, J. G. (1964), "Structural versus individual effects," American Journal of Sociology 69, 585–595.

Treiman, D. J. (1977), Occupational Prestige in Comparative Perspective, Academic Press, New York.

ROBERT M. HAUSER AND JOHN ROBERT WARREN

Socioeconomic Indexes for Occupations: A Review, Update, and Critique

There are several reasons to focus more attention on the collection, scaling, and analysis of occupational data than has recently been the case. First, job-holding is the most important social role held by most adults outside their family or household. When we meet someone new, often our first question is, "What do you do?" and that is a very good question. Job-holding defines how we spend much of our time, and it provides strong clues about the activities and circumstances in which that time is spent. Second, job-holding tells us about the technical and social skills that we bring to the labor market, and for most people job-holding delimits current and future economic prospects. Thus, even for persons who are not attached to the labor market, past jobs or the jobs held by other members of the same family or household provide information about economic and social standing. Third, as market labor has become nearly universal among adult women as well as men, it is increasingly possible to characterize individuals in terms of their own current or past jobs. Fourth, once we have a good job description, it is possible to map jobs into many classifications, scales, and measures. Fifth, measurement of jobs and occupations does not entail the same problems of refusal, recall, reliability, and stability as occur in the measurement of income or wealth. Job descriptions—contemporary or retrospective, from job-holders or from their family members—are imperfect, but the reliability and validity of carefully collected occupational data are high enough to support sustained analysis (Hauser, Sewell, and Warren 1994). Thus, even if we are limited to retrospective questions, we can confidently trace occupational trajectories across the adult years. The same cannot be said of earnings trajectories, let alone other components of personal or household income or wealth.

Originally published in 1997. Please see complete source information beginning on page 891.

Conceptual Issues

It is important to distinguish between jobs and occupations. A job is a specific and sometimes unique bundle of activities carried out by a person in the expectation of economic remuneration. An occupation is an abstract category used to group and classify similar jobs. Such abstractions are often heterogeneous and idiosyncratic in construction, but they usually involve determinations of similarity in typical activities, in the sites where work is performed, in the form of job tenure, in the skill requirements of the job, or in the product or service that results from the job. There are multiple systems for the classification of jobs and complex interdependencies between occupational and industrial classifications. Most social scientific uses of occupational data are based either on (a) the classification systems of the U.S. Bureau of the Census, which are revised each decade at the time of the census, or (b) the *Dictionary of Occupational Titles,* which is produced by the Employment and Training Administration of the U.S. Department of Labor.

Some measures of social class reflect job or personal characteristics, whereas others depend on occupation. For example, consider two widely used conceptions of "social class." Wright's (1985, 88) class typology combines concepts of ownership, authority, and expertise. It requires information about a person's educational attainment as well as ownership, authority, supervision, and occupational classification. On the other hand, Erikson and Goldthorpe's (1992, 38–39) "class schema," is ultimately a grouping of occupational categories based upon Goldthorpe and Hope's (1974) study of occupational prestige in Great Britain (Goldthorpe 1980). Each author sees his scheme as a theoretically refined basis for identifying the membership of real and discrete social classes. In Wright's neo-Marxian classification, the aim is to identify modes of labor exploitation in the relations of production. In Erikson and Goldthorpe's neo-Weberian classification, the class categories are designed to identify distinct combinations of occupational function and employment status.

In our opinion, differences between the two class schemes and between them and our occupational status measures lie more in the proximity of constituent variables to jobs and persons than in other theoretical or conceptual distinctions that have been debated by their authors. Other things being equal, we should expect a classification based partly upon personal and job characteristics to be more direct and powerful in its influence than a classification based on occupational characteristics would be alone. Rather than relying on a predetermined combination of occupation and other social or economic characteristics, we suggest that investigators should use data on individual education and income, and on other job characteristics, as well as on occupational standing (see Jencks, Perman, and Rainwater 1988).

In working with measures of occupational social standing, we emphasize the social and economic grading of the occupational structure, rather than a priori constructions of distinct social classes. People are linked to jobs, not only through job-holding, but also through their relationships with others who hold or have held jobs. Jobs can be mapped into standard occupational classifications, and the categories of those classifications may be linked to occupational characteristics. By working back through this series of linkages, we can describe people in terms of occupational characteristics. Such characteristics will be valid as descriptions of jobs only to the degree that occupations are homogeneous and the intervening maps and linkages are sound. In our view, the remarkable thing about this way of measuring social and economic characteristics is not that it is error prone, which would seem obvious, but that it has such high reliability and validity. That it does so is a social fact, which rests both on skill and care in classification and coding but also on strong uniformities in social structure.

Occupational Prestige and Socioeconomic Indexes of Occupational Status

What are the relevant status characteristics of occupations? Many discussions of occupations in the stratification system begin with the concept of occupational prestige, the general level of social standing enjoyed by the incumbents of an occupation. In the United States there have been three major national surveys of occupational prestige, the most recent of which was carried out in conjunction with the 1989 General Social Survey (GSS) of the National Opinion Research Center (NORC; Nakao and Treas 1994). The main problem with all of these occupational prestige ratings is that they lack criterion validity. Prestige is not as highly correlated with other variables as are other measures of occupational social standing, specifically, measures of the socioeconomic status of occupations, as indicated by the average educational attainment and income of occupational incumbents.

Duncan (1961) created the first socioeconomic index (SEI) of occupational status. For forty-five census occupation lines, he ran the linear regression of the percentage of "good" or "excellent" ratings on measures of both occupational education and occupational income (see Duncan 1961 for details). This regression yielded roughly equal weights for the two regressors, a result that motivated some sociologists to characterize socioeconomic scales as a hybrid of "social status" (as indexed by occupational education) and economic status (see Hodge 1981).

The Duncan SEI has been updated or elaborated in several ways, and researchers should be cautious in using the updates because of their potential lack of comparability. Most recently, as part of their work with prestige scores obtained in the 1989 GSS, Nakao and Treas (1994) created socioeconomic scores for 1980-basis census occupational lines by regressing their prestige ratings on the charac-teristics of male and female occupational incumbents in the 1980 census. The obvious next step is to create another set of socioeconomic scores, using the 1989 prestige scores as a criterion, but based upon characteristics of the work force in the 1990 census.

In an earlier paper (see Hauser and Warren 1997), we made a special extract of occupational education and earnings from the 1990 census 5 percent public use sample. Throughout our analyses, we used the same definition of occupational education as Nakao and Treas (1994), namely, the percentage of people in an occupation who had completed one or more years of college. After experimenting with alternative treatments of earnings and income, we constructed the new socioeconomic indexes using occupational wage rates, whereas Duncan (1961) used the percentage of occupational incumbents who had reported incomes of $3500 or more. Our prestige criterion was the percentage of prestige ratings above a fixed threshold. However, for statistical reasons, we used a logistic transformation of the prestige criterion and of the educational level and wage rate of each occupation (see Hauser and Warren 1997, 203–17).

We then constructed socioeconomic indexes for the total work force and, separately, for men and for women. Our purpose in creating gender-specific indexes was to compare the behavior of occupational characteristics between men and women, especially in relation to occupational prestige. We do not recommend routine use of the gender-specific indexes in research. Although the indexes for all workers, men, and women have roughly the same range and are in the same metric, their statistical properties differ. Findings based on the total, male, and female indexes are not strictly comparable (Warren, Sheridan, and Hauser 1998), and, where researchers choose to use a composite socioeconomic index, we recommend the index based on the characteristics of all workers.

Chastened and instructed by the example of Fox's (1991) and Friendly's (1991) reanalyses of Duncan's data, we also paid a good deal of attention to issues of fit and functional form. In the final set of regression analyses, we used several types of residual plots to identify influential outliers. Based on these findings, we deleted several occupations from the regression analyses used to estimate weights for the socioeconomic scores. Several of the largest and most influential exceptions to typical relationships among occupational education, wage rates, and prestige occur in common and visible jobs: business owners, farmers, clergy, secretaries, teachers, waiters and waitresses, janitors, and truck drivers. This finding reminds us that occupational prestige is by no means the same as occupational socioeconomic status, and we should respect both the theoretical and empirical distinctions between them.

Using estimates from our preferred models, we computed total-based, male-based, and female-based SEI scores for all occupations. The combined three sets of scores were transformed to range between 0 and 100. Our 1990-basis and 1980-basis total (TSEI), male (MSEI), and female (FSEI) scores for all occupation lines, the socioeconomic components of those scores, and the 1989 Nakao-Treas prestige scores and ratings are available elsewhere (Hauser and Warren 1997; http://www.ssc.wisc.edu/cde/cdewp/1996papers.htm).

Structural Models of the Socioeconomic Index

Subsequent analyses—presented in detail in Hauser and Warren (1997)—reveal three potential weaknesses in composite socioeconomic indexes of occupational standing. First, gender differences appear both in the relationships between occupational socioeconomic standing and prestige and in the socioeconomic characteristics of occupational incumbents. Second, occupational wage rates appear to be far less highly correlated, both within and across generations, than occupa-

tional education. Third, the latter finding led us to wonder whether the use of prestige-validated socioeconomic indexes may overestimate the importance of the economic standing of occupations in the stratification process. Thus, we developed structural equation models in which the construction of socioeconomic indexes was embedded in the stratification process. These models were estimated using data for men and women in the 1994 GSS.

For example, one of our models considered relationships among father's occupational status, the status of a man or woman's first occupation, and the status of his or her current or last occupation. In this rudimentary model, we specified that the status of first occupation depends on that of father's occupation, whereas the status of current or last occupation depends upon father's occupation and first occupation. To be sure, this is scarcely a complete model of the stratification process, but it is sufficient to generate new estimates of the weights of the socioeconomic index components. At each of the three stages of the model—father's occupation, first occupation, and current or last occupation—we assume that an SEI composite is completely determined by measures of occupational education and occupational wages (Hauser and Warren 1997, 236). Figure 1 illustrates part of this model with measures of father's and child's occupational education and occupational wage. The effects of father on child identify the weights of occupational education, a, and occupational wage, b, in the SEI. To our surprise, we found that the weight of the wage rate is negligible, that is, b = 0. Thus, in the GSS data the process of occupational stratification is best described by relationships among occupation-based measures of educational attainment, not the combination of occupation-based measures of educational attainment and wage rates. Our findings from the socioeconomic model point to occupational differentiation by education as a central feature of the stratification process.

FIGURE 1
Illustrative Model of Intergenerational Stratification in Occupational Socioeconomic Status

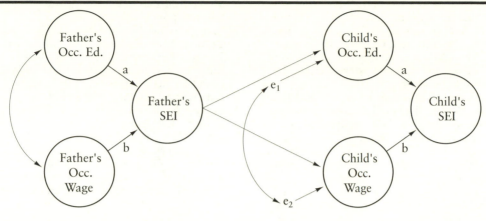

Discussion

We are thus led to question the value of traditional socioeconomic indexes of occupational standing, including those that we constructed. If the 1994 GSS data are a reliable guide, we would do better—in studies of the stratification process—to index occupations by their educational level alone than by any of the usual, weighted combinations of educational level and earnings. However, given the modest sensitivity of occupational status correlations to differences in model specification, we would not suggest any wholesale effort to reevaluate previous findings about levels, trends, and differentials in occupational stratification. It would be sufficient, we think, to suggest that previously estimated levels of correlation are slightly too low. Finally, we would caution that our findings about the relative importance of occupational education and occupational wage rates are specific to models of the stratification process. Just as the relative weights of occupational education and wage rates differ between prestige and socioeconomic outcomes, so they may also differ across other outcomes (e.g., health, well-being, social participation, or political choice). If there is any general conclusion to be drawn from our analysis, it is that we ought to move toward a more specific and disaggregated appraisal of the effects of occupational characteristics on social, psychological, economic, political, and health outcomes. Although composite measures of occupational status may have heuristic uses, the global concept of occupational status is scientifically obsolete.

References

Duncan, Otis Dudley. 1961. "A Socioeconomic Index for All Occupations." Pages 109–138 in *Occupations and Social Status*, edited by Albert J. Reiss, Jr.New York: Free Press.

Erikson, Robert, and John H. Goldthorpe. 1992. *The Constant Flux: A Study of Class Mobility in Industrial Societies*. Oxford: Clarendon Press.

Fox, John. 1991. *Regression Diagnostics*, edited by Michael S. Lewis-Beck. Quantitative Applications in the Social Sciences, Vol. 07–079. Newbury Park, CA: Sage.

Friendly, Michael. 1991. *SAS System for Statistical Graphics*. SAS Series in Statistical Applications. Cary, NC: SAS Institute.

Goldthorpe, John H. 1980. *Social Mobility and Class Structure in Modern Britain*. Oxford: Clarendon Press.

Goldthorpe, John, and Keith Hope. 1974. *The Social Grading of Occupations: A New Approach and Scale.* Oxford: Clarendon Press.

Hauser, Robert M., and John Robert Warren. 1997. "Socioeconomic Indexes of Occupational Status: A Review, Update, and Critique." Pages 177–298 in *Sociological Methodology, 1997,* edited by Adrian Raftery. Cambridge: Blackwell Publishers.

Hauser, Robert M., William H. Sewell, and John Robert Warren. 1994. "Education, Occupation, and Earnings in the Long Run: Men and Women from Adolescence to Midlife." Paper presented at the 1994 Meeting of the American Sociological Association. University of Wisconsin-Madison.

Hodge, Robert W. 1981. "The Measurement of Occupational Status." *Social Science Research* 10:396–415.

Jencks, Christopher, Lauri Perman, and Lee Rainwater. 1988. "What is a Good Job? A New Measure of Labor-Market Success." *American Journal of Sociology* 93:1322–57.

Nakao, Keiko, and Judith Treas. 1994. "Updating Occupational Prestige and Socioeconomic Scores: How the New Measures Measure Up." Pages 1–72 in *Sociological Methodology, 1994,* edited by Peter Marsden. Washington, D.C.: American Sociological Association.

Warren, John Robert, Jennifer T. Sheridan, and Robert M. Hauser. 1998. "Choosing a Measure of Occupational Standing: How Useful are Composite Measures in Analyses of Gender Inequality in Occupational Attainment?" *Sociological Methods and Research* 27:3–76.

Wright, Erik Olin. 1985. *Classes.* London: Verso.

AAGE B. SØRENSEN

The Basic Concepts of Stratification Research: Class, Status, and Power

Many good things come in three parts—God, Montesquieu's concept of the modern democratic state, and the major dimensions of social structure. All sociology students are told that class, status, and power are the main variables in stratification research. Weber's brief essay, in the English translation entitled "Class, Status, Party" (1946), is probably the closest thing to a universally required text for all sociologists. Most agree that these three variables are what sociologists use when they analyze processes and structures of stratification. Little else is agreed upon. There is wide disagreement about the relative importance of the three variables. There is equally wide disagreement over the concepts behind the variables. This essay attempts to sort out some of these disagreements and, it is hoped, provide some order.

In addition to the disagreements, there is unequal attention to the three variables. Power never has been a frequently used variable in empirical stratification research. It is a slippery concept and a difficult variable to measure. The study of elites is the main research tradition using power in stratification research; other empirical uses of the concept tend to be located in political science or political sociology. The elite studies make assumptions about the distribution of power and then examine only one part of the distribution, the elite. We have no agreed-upon mea-

sures that allow a test of these assumptions about the distribution, and there is surprisingly little attention given in stratification research to characterizing empirically the structure of power in society. Debates about the usefulness of elite studies tend to be debates about untestable assumptions concerning the distribution of power.

To Weber, studies of class and of status are studies of bases of power, in the sense that class or status positions may be seen as resources for affecting the action of others. However, matters are rarely conceived of that way in stratification research. Sociologists study class and status because they are interested in class and status. Marxists especially tend to think of the class structure as the most important thing about social structure from which everything else, including the power structure, derives. The discussions about the validity of this claim occur in debates about the relation between class and the state. These discussions usually take place in political sociology. The main application of the concept of power in stratification research is the frequent use of authority as an element in the concept of class.

I focus in this essay on class and status and survey some of the main distinctions and conceptual properties that dominate the literature and are well represented in the readings. Few concepts in sociology carry as much conceptual baggage as these two. For many sociologists, the choice between concepts of status and class is a fundamental choice between basic assumptions about the nature of society.

This is an original article prepared for this book.

Indeed, for some, it is a choice reflecting basic ideological positions. My main conclusion is that the choices are simpler to make and the conceptual baggage less burdensome than many claim. The essay devotes most attention to the concept of class, which is the most complicated and most ambitious concept in the field of stratification, if not in sociology (see, also, Sørensen 1996, 2000).

Basic Ideas

It is useful to think of distinct levels of status and class concepts. These levels are differentiated by how close the concepts are connected to theories of inequality. Most measures of status seem to capture overall welfare along several dimensions of inequality and have no theory of inequality implied. Not all status concepts are like this. Weber's original idea of status groups captures a one-dimensional concept of prestige or honor with more theoretical implications. In addition to the socioeconomic or welfare concept and the prestige concept of status, I distinguish among three concepts of class. The first one, a "stratum concept" of class, is not unlike socioeconomic status. It is meant to convey the idea of homogeneous groupings along several dimensions of inequality. Like socioeconomic status, the concept provides no theory of how inequality is obtained. The other two, which I call the market or Weberian concept of class and the Marxist concept of class, have theories of inequality attached to them. The Marxist concept also attaches antagonistic interests to class categories, while the Weberian concept is more ambiguous about this.

Theoretical power is related to the empirical requirements of the concept. The Marxist concept makes the most stringent requirements: A Marxist class category may or may not exist depending on whether or not positions in social structure have certain properties; in particular, positions should be associated with interests that are in conflict with the interests associated with other positions. The prestige concept of status also suggests empiri-

cal requirements in the form of strategies of exclusion. The socioeconomic status concept and the stratum concept of class make no such requirements; they are purely nominal classifications of people or positions and therefore especially simple to apply in empirical research. A main task for this essay is a critical review of some of the attempts to meet empirical requirements of such concepts, especially the classic Marxist class concept.

For purposes of this review, it is important to distinguish between positions in social structure and persons occupying these positions. This distinction is the main theoretical contribution of sociological theory about inequality—the distinction is, for example, completely absent from economic theory. A structural theory of inequality is one in which inequality is created by relationships between positions. The structural explanation may be complete, as in the Marxist theory of exploitation; or it may be partial with the theory positing an interaction between characteristics of position and characteristics of person. The most obvious examples of a partial explanation are functionalist theories of the Davis and Moore (1945) variety and organizational theories of inequality that emphasize motivational consequences of organizations, such as internal labor markets (e.g., Stinchcombe 1974; Sørensen 1983; Lazear and Rosen 1981).

In the discussion that follows, I detail the most important status and class concepts. I try to show that the basic choices are not between class and status but between concepts that are useful for different types of research tasks. There is more to say about class than about status. The claims about the theoretical power of the class concepts have been greater.

Social Status: Welfare or Honor?

Sociology students are often told that Weber's discussion of status groups is the original source for the concept of status. This is a bit bizarre. Weber did not use the word *status* or *status group*. He used the words *stand* and *ehre*, which most would translate as estate and honor, in describing what these groups were about. We are meant to be brought back to, or reminded of, the world of feudalism and knights. This world was not so far from Wilhelmian Germany as it is from the contemporary United States. In any event, Weber's ideas about this had little to do with the concept of socioeconomic status that produces the standard variable in all of status-attainment research and the standard independent variable in much other sociological research, especially of the survey variety.

Sorokin's discussion of the basic concepts of stratification is a much more accurate point of departure for the concept and variable that dominate modern stratification research under the name "social status." Sorokin (1927) explicitly adopts a spatial metaphor for society with vertical and horizontal dimensions. The vertical or status dimension has three components: economic status, political status, and occupational status. There are distances and movements (in the form of social mobility) along these dimensions. The vertical dimension is a measuring rod put through society to capture what inequality is about; it tells us what is up and what is down and how far up and down people and positions are.

Sorokin's status concept makes it possible to talk meaningfully about directions and distances. Weber's concept of honor does not. The differentiation of honor depends on who differentiates. Peasants are equally dishonorable to lords but unequally honorable to each other. This imbalance is not useful if one wants to measure distances and movements. Sorokin receives less honor than Weber from modern sociologists, so Weber remains the original source of wisdom about status despite the confusion it creates to compare his comments on the topic with the properties of the concept that is most often used in empirical research. This is the concept of socioeconomic status with the properties described by Sorokin.

It would have made more sense to translate *ehre* as prestige. The concepts of prestige employed by, for example, Goode (1978) and Shils (1970) are similar to the relational concept of *ehre*. Prestige as *ehre* is an extremely interesting variable and in certain institutions—academia, the arts, and the military—an extremely important variable. It is a concept with more theoretical implications than the concept of socioeconomic status. High prestige causes deference, and low prestige causes contempt. Prestige groups practice exclusion or closure, for example with respect to marriage. If prestige groups are to be equated with Weber's status groups, they must be seen as discrete groupings.

Prestige groups should be identified empirically by demonstrating practices of exclusion or closure. Not all occupational groups or categories of people with similar levels of socioeconomic status necessarily practice such explicit exclusion. Therefore, the identification of prestige groups poses the same type of empirical problems as the empirical identification of the higher-level class concepts, as discussed later. There is some theoretical work on the issue of closure and exclusion (Parkin 1979). Unfortunately, the measurement of prestige and the empirical identification of prestige groups are neglected because of the conceptual confusion created by a misleading translation of Weber and the neglect of Sorokin. The best work on the topic is qualitative (e.g., Goode 1978; Shils 1970).

Empirical research on prestige was derailed also because the concept was contaminated by loose usage in empirical practices. With the arrival of modern survey techniques, it became possible to have national samples rank occupations from one to five according to labels ranging from "excellent" to "poor." This was said to measure the prestige of occupations. However, the occupational ratings do not measure prestige in the sense of honor or deference. There is empirical evidence for this claim. Goldthorpe and Hope (1974) directly asked respondents about what they had in mind when rating occupations. They responded that they thought about things such as income, education, job security, and the like that enter into people's ideas of a good job. Thus, respondents seem to rate occupations according to the general level of welfare that they provide incumbents. The second piece of evidence is that it does not matter much who does the ratings. This is one of the most well established findings in all of sociology. Occupations are rated about the same by all, at all times, and wherever these occupations are found.[1] What is measured by occupational prestige is not a relational concept.

Duncan (1961) used the occupational prestige ratings to generate an index of socioeconomic status. The procedure is simple: For the subset of occupations for which ratings exist, regress the ratings of occupations on aggregate characteristics of those who occupy these occupations. (Duncan used income and education of incumbents.) Then use the regression equation to derive scores for all occupations. The result is called the Socioeconomic Index (SEI). Since SEI is based on occupational prestige scores, it can be seen as an approximation to such scores, with the degree of approximation reflecting the quality of the prediction. Although the approximation is generally quite good, for some occupations the SEI and occupational prestige scores differ, most notably for farmers. Farmers have low income and low formal education but are rated higher than other occupations with the same level of income and education. This may be the result of Americans' nostalgia for a rural past, or it may simply mean that Americans carry around images of farmers that overstate their true income and schooling. Featherman and Hauser (1976) find that SEI explains more variance in status-attainment models than occupational prestige measures, and they conclude from this that SEI is the better measure. This is really a conclusion about how best to measure the socioeconomic status of farmers; it has nothing to do with the difference between the concept of prestige as *ehre* and the concept of socioeconomic status.

Socioeconomic status and occupational prestige are characteristics of occupations. Older American sociology (Warner et al. 1949; Hollingshead and Redlick 1958) constructed measures of the socioeconomic status of persons using indexes based on education, occupation, type of residence, source of income, and other individual attributes. These synthetic measures of the socioeconomic status of persons should perform even better than the occupational-level socioeconomic status measure when the issue is to predict individual behavior, such as voting, deviance, school performance of children, and so forth.

Socioeconomic status measured at the level of occupation nevertheless remains the favorite independent variable in research on all kinds of individual behaviors and attitudes, probably because of the ease with which the measure is obtained. Much has been made of the difference between status, measured at the level of occupation, and class. It is claimed that the use of status assumes that the occupational structure is more fundamental than the class structure (Wright 1979). However, the relative merit of seeing occupations as the basic dimension of social structure has nothing to do with the usefulness of socioeconomic status in empirical research. It is research practice, not theory, that conflates socioeconomic status and occupation. One might equally well have a socioeconomic status measure based on the ranking of class categories.

Obversely, Grusky and Sørensen (1998) argue that detailed occupations ought not be reduced to a nominal socioeconomic scale, since the division of labor often breeds organic *gemeinschaftlich* groups with closely defended borders and well-developed cultures. This formulation involves treating detailed occupations as status groups in the true Weberian sense rather than as mere indicators of vertical "social status."

The Grusky-Sørensen proposal thus signals a turn away from conventional socioeconomic scaling. In recent years, socioeconomic scales have indeed declined in popularity, and Hauser and Warren (1997) have even suggested that "the global concept of occupational status is scientifically obsolete" (p. 251). The main rationale for this conclusion is that conventional scales based on a composite of educational attainment and wage rates are out-performed in models of stratification by occupational scales based wholly on education. If the socioeconomic tradition is now in some disarray, this is no doubt partly because the theoretical rationale for socioeconomic composites is poorly developed, even in the work of Sorokin (1927; also, see Hodge 1981).

Class

Most sociologists recognize that the concept of class is among our most important concepts. It is perhaps the most influential formulation of the central idea of sociology—that is, the idea of a social structure. Some claim the concept has a status as gravity does in physics. The analogy is imperfect: Physics without a concept of gravity is impossible, but some pursue sociology without ever employing the term *class* and claim the concept is not needed. Further, those who employ the term use it to denote quite different concepts. This is an expression of the well-known disagreements about what are the central ideas of sociology.

In much of modern sociology, class has come to mean nothing more than a homogeneous categorical grouping of social positions in contrast to the gradation provided by socioeconomic status. An explicit formulation of this emphasis on social homogeneity can be found in Geiger (1951) and Carlsson (1958). It appears to have been decisive for the formulation of the class scheme proposed by Goldthorpe (see Goldthorpe [1984] for an elaboration of the rationale). The difference, if any, between such a *stratum concept of class* and the welfare or socioeconomic concept of social status is the emphasis on the resources that are responsible for a person's welfare rather than the welfare dimensions themselves. This approach usually results in a class scheme that is not completely ordered as socioeconomic status is. A good example is Goldthorpe's class scheme (1987). Such stratum class schemes may be very useful in empirical research. They are nominal categories that do not imply theories of inequality. I concentrate on Marxist or market concepts of

class that do imply positional theories of inequality, in particular theories of exploitation.

Marxist Concept of Class

The core of the Marxist concept is a theory of exploitation that explains inequality between classes and the resulting antagonistic interests that generate conflict. Unfortunately, this theory has certain defects, and the concept cannot account for an important part of the inequality we observe—the inequality generated in the labor market. In this section, I first elaborate these points and then show that the defects perhaps can be overcome by identifying the circumstances when market mechanisms produce a form of inequality in which the advantages of some are obtained at the disadvantage of others.

In Marx's own analysis, the ability of one party to become better off at the expense of another is conferred by ownership of the means of production. The two components of ownership—authority and legal ownership—are the means to establish the exploitative relationship. It is the exploitative relationship that defines classes. If there are ways other than ownership of property to maintain a relationship of exploitation, classes presumably would be created.

Exploitation takes place in a social relationship without regard to who occupies this relationship. Capitalists exploit workers because the logic of capitalist production forces them to do so, not because they are evil or conservative or white males. Smart capitalists are no better at exploiting than dumb capitalists. Smart capitalists may get higher profits, but the relation between profits and the rate of exploitation is very complicated. Marx demonstrates this at great length in volume three of *Capital*. Class relations that are relations of exploitation create inequality independently of the personal characteristics of those who occupy class positions. Class positions are "empty places" (Simmel 1908). This is of fundamental importance for the relation between the class structure and the structure of inequality. Only by changing the class structure can the structure of inequality be changed. Therefore, class conflict will produce social change.

This does not mean that Marx did not recognize sources of inequality other than class. He describes but does not analyze inequality in the labor market by education, skills, and ability. These are all inequalities associated with personal characteristics and not with class positions. According to Marx, many inequalities will disappear with the advance of capitalism as the working class becomes more homogeneous. The inequalities caused by effort and ability will continue into socialism. These inequalities are less important for Marx. No tinkering with the structure of society will remove them.

Since exploitation is rooted in positions, class positions become associated with antagonistic interests. Those in positions to exploit wish to preserve their ability to obtain advantage; those being exploited want to destroy the relationship that creates their disadvantage. The model includes a scenario, called the formation of revolutionary class consciousness, describing how the "structural" interests are translated into collective action. The stages are class awareness, class conflict, class struggle, and eventually the destruction of the relationships that define classes.

To Marx, exploitation in capitalist society is created in the employment relationship, but he pays no systematic attention to variation in employment relationships that would form classes within the employed labor force. In fact, I argue later that Marx probably conceived of only one type of employment relationship, at least in advanced capitalism. This is the employment relationship conceived of in classical and neoclassical economics. Regardless of whether the original exploitation theory is valid, it is of little assistance in providing a structural theory of inequality among positions that are jobs. The Marxist concept is useless for analyzing inequality and conflict within the labor market as opposed to the inequality and conflict between capitalists and workers.

There is an even more important theoretical problem. It was Marx's great discovery that voluntary employment relationships create involuntary exploitation of one party by the other. The exploitation comes about by the appropriation by the capitalist of surplus value created by the worker. This assumes the validity of the labor theory of value. Unfortunately, this theory has been abandoned by everyone.[2] The labor theory of value generates a set of relationships among unobservables. It has great appeal as a claim of injustice but no appeal as an economic theory.

Abandoning the labor theory of value removes the basis for the whole theory of inequality and social change, unless some other concept of exploitation can be developed to explain inequality associated with class positions. This other concept should also make empirical requirements that can be met in analysis of labor market structures. The next section considers if the market power concept can provide such an alternative.

Class and Market Power

The Weberian concept of class as market power appears to provide a straightforward rationale for why classes create inequality. In light of the difficulties with the Marxist concept, it is understandable why the market power concept is appealing.

In the Weberian conception, classes are people with similar command over economic resources. The market creates inequality, and class is a proxy for variables that cause inequality in the market, such as occupation, skill, and property. Weberian classes group people according to their resources and their access to resources for obtaining welfare and well-being in the market, but class relations are usually not seen as the direct cause of inequality. Market mechanisms are responsible.

It is presumably to be expected that the market concept will identify positions in social structure associated with interests in preserving advantages and removing disadvantages caused by occupancy of these positions. However, since advantages and disadvantages are created in the market, the realizations of interests by different groups are not necessarily interdependent. In the market the advantage of some does not necessarily reduce the advantage of others. This will only happen when advantage is based on a mechanism of exploitation in the market. Identifying such a mechanism of exploitation is needed for the market concept to be useful in specifying class categories that are conflict groups rather than simply strata.

Roemer's (1982) reformulation of the Marxist exploitation idea is a useful starting point for such an effort. The basic idea is quite simple: Inequality in productive assets will produce exploitation in a market economy with private property and trade. Those with superior assets will need to work less to obtain the same level of welfare as those with inferior assets. If the superior assets were divided among the disadvantaged, they would be better off. Defining classes by absence and presence of property and by amount of property produces a class scheme correlating perfectly with the amount of exploitation.

Roemer's concept of exploitation creates a class concept in which inequalities among classes are created in the market. They are produced by returns to productive assets traded in the market. This market concept of class makes the theory consistent with modern economics. However, the development of the theory relies mainly on the consequences of returns to alienable productive assets—that is, physical property. Here the problem is to define a type of exploitation based on properties of positions in the labor market. This is not a matter dealt with extensively by Roemer (1982). Indeed, he does not emphasize the distinction between people and positions.

It is possible to derive some insights into the exploitation-creating properties of jobs by conceiving of exploitation as generated by economic rent. This seems consistent with Roemer's formulation. Returns on productive assets are payments for use of factors of production. It is important to note that there are two types of productive assets: assets in inherently fixed supply and "normal" assets in variable supply. In the case of normal assets, an increase in return or pay for their use will generate a corresponding increase in the supply of such assets. The increase in supply will then reduce returns to the level obtained for other factors of production. In the long run, therefore, such assets do not create the type of inequality in which the welfare of those possessing the asset is obtained at the expense of those not possessing the asset. All assets will tend to provide the same return, and these returns in turn compensate for the consumption forgone when making the investment. The advantage of some caused by the return on their investments will not reduce the advantage of others.

However, some assets, such as fertile land and superior ability, may be in fixed supply. These assets create a "rent"—a payment that is in addition to the one needed to employ the assets. They produce advantages that are not Pareto-optimal. Those individuals not obtaining the rent are worse off than they would have been without the rent payments to those owning the assets in fixed supply. Roemer's idea of exploitation is consistent with inequalities created by rent-generating assets. These assets will satisfy his test for exploitation. The test is that dividing the assets among owners and nonowners will make the nonowners better off.[3]

To create a positional theory of inequality in the labor market, it is therefore necessary to search for rent-generating assets attached to employment positions. These assets will provide an advantage to the incumbent of the position not available to those not in the position. I show later that many employment positions, including some treated by recent scholars as class categories in the labor market, do not form class positions. In fact, not even all forms of rents generated in employment relationships will create class positions.

Class Formation

While the market power concept of class does identify a source of antagonistic interests in certain labor market structures, exploitation does not unavoidably create the conditions in which latent antagonistic interests result in manifest collective action. Indeed, Roemer (1988) shows that exploitation in the abstract may produce a number of paradoxical consequences. The class formation analyses of Giddens (1973), Parkin (1979), and Goldthorpe (1987) are useful for the identification of the conditions that make exploitation produce class action.

Class formation analysis relies on a simple theory of the formation of collective action. The theory is that persons with the same location in the class structure might realize over time their common interests and form class movements. This is a Durkheimian theory of mechanical solidarity emphasizing similarity and time together. If the boundaries between classes are relatively rigid, class incumbents may come to identify with their class and act in its behalf. Therefore, the study of mobility patterns becomes a major vehicle for the identification of social classes that might become actors in changing social structure. This is an approach already suggested by Weber's remarks on the matter (Weber 1968). Although there are other sources of "class structuration" (Giddens 1973), such as residential segregation, the analysis of mobility processes represents the best-known empirical example of the class formation perspective.

The class formation approach assumes that some theory explains why classes are unequal and why they have antagonistic interests. While silent on the nature of this theory, it adds an important requirement to the definition of positions that create class categories. Incumbency in these positions must have some permanency over time. Thus, to identify class categories within the employed part of the labor force, we need to know the stability of the employment relationships that create the corresponding job categories. This dimen-sion of employment relationships is the major focus in the remainder of this essay.

In conclusion, exploitation among groups within the labor market has been argued to derive from rent-generating properties of jobs. The mere existence of exploitation is not sufficient for the formation of classes. The class formation perspective suggests identifying properties of jobs generating stable interests and stable membership.

Employment Relationships and Class Properties of Jobs

In this section, I briefly survey the properties of jobs that generate economic rents and stable membership and then ask if some of the proposals for defining class categories in the labor market satisfy these necessary conditions.

Jobs are defined by employment relationships. They form (often implicit) contracts between employer and employee about the execution of certain tasks in return for payment over a period of time. It is useful to characterize employment relations according to who typically has the initiative in terminating the contract. The result is a continuum ranging from employment relationships that are completely *open* (the employer will dismiss the worker whenever a better worker is available for the job) to those that are *closed* (the worker typically has the initiative and therefore high job security). For an elaboration of the distinction and the arguments for when open and closed jobs are likely to emerge, see Sørensen (1983) and Sørensen and Kalleberg (1981).

Open and Closed Relationships

Open employment relationships, of course, assume the employer knows that a different worker can do the job better and that there are no significant costs in dismissing the incumbent. They are assumed in the basic price theory applied to competitive labor markets that constitutes neoclassical economic theory of wage rates. In this scenario, wage rates are a function of individual productivity; equally productive persons should, except for short-term disequilibria, obtain the same wage.

Open employment relationships define jobs that do not satisfy the requirement of permanency needed to create class categories within the labor market. They are of considerable interest anyway. First, they establish a baseline for determining positional sources of inequality. This baseline is the market or competitive wage. Second, in the present context, it is of interest to note that Marx saw open employment relations as being typical of advanced capitalism.

Marx saw the essence of capitalist society in the treatment of labor as a commodity, purchased and sold on the market in the manner of other commodities. This is the very scenario assumed in neoclassical economic theory of the labor market. Such a theory was not available to Marx. Marginalism had not yet been invented. Further, the question of how different prices of labor are created in the labor market apparently was of little interest to him. Thus, we find nowhere in Marx an analysis of wage inequalities similar to the analysis presented by John Stuart Mill. There is, however, nothing to suggest that Marx would not have accepted the now-standard theory about this wage structure. In particular, Marx's analysis of the dynamics of capitalist society predicts the development of a labor market satisfying the assumptions made in neoclassical labor economics. As Roemer puts it: "The neoclassical model of the competitive economy is not a bad place for Marxists to start their study of idealized capitalism" (Roemer 1988, 196).

This view of Marx's "theory" of the labor market of course implies that Marxist theory will be the same as neoclassical theory in conceptualizing income differences among the employed. There will be no subclasses created in the labor market, consistent with the basic homogenization thesis of Karl Marx. The dynamics of capitalism will destroy those deviating employment relationships that survive from earlier modes of production, such as artisans. With this perspective, the emiseration thesis is not a prediction of wage equality. It is a prediction of a uniform labor market with no positional advantages but with inequality due to skill and ability that will remain also into socialism and only disappear with the ultimate compensating differentials introduced by communism.

It should be noted that open employment relationships may generate economic rents. Scarce and unusual abilities may command a rent so that the person with the rare ability has an advantage obtained at the expense of the welfare of others. Others might be better off if the scarce ability was equally distributed. This does not create classes. Abilities are attributes of people and not of positions, and no reorganization of labor market structures will change the distribution of innate and unique talents.

Skills acquired through training and experience create inequality, but they do not necessarily command rents. The main economic theory about the acquisition of skills—human capital theory—argues that training is undertaken at a cost and results in skills that increase the pay for the individual. Training will only be undertaken if the returns equal the costs. If returns exceed costs, more workers will seek training, thereby lowering the returns on skills. Therefore, in equilibrium, differentials caused by skills exactly compensate for training costs. The cumulated lifetime earnings of people with unequal skills will be equal, except for the variation due to compensating differentials, to effort, and to ability and other resources that affect training costs (such as family background). Skills of general usefulness in the labor market will produce cross-sectional inequality. However, when returns on training equal costs of training, skills do not generate rents and therefore cannot be a basis for exploitation.

Skills may generate rents if training opportunities are in fixed, limited supply because of restrictions of admissions to schools and apprenticeships. This will create an advantage that is a rent. It will be a higher return on the skill than would be necessary to bring about

training for the skill. There are numerous examples of situations in which this seems to occur: the training for medical doctors; for most
crafts and other skilled occupations; and for
artisans and other self-employed occupations
typical of the petit bourgeoisie. However, in
open employment relations, these rents do
not create class categories within the labor
market. Open jobs do not provide the needed
permanency. Furthermore—regardless of
whether skills are rent-generating—they are
not properties of positions.[4] The advantages
produced outside the labor market seem difficult to maintain unless the advantaged group
also can restrict access to the employment of
these skills or their substitutes.

Closed employment relationships satisfy
the requirement of permanency. Furthermore, closed employment creates the positions that have the potential of providing advantages that may be obtained independently
of the productivity of persons. However,
only when the resulting job rewards systematically differ from the competitive wage
over some period of time will these properties be class properties.

There is a considerable literature on the
causes of closed employment relationships.
Specific on-the-job training, financed by the
employer (Becker 1964), and transaction
costs (Williamson 1975) are among the most
important causes. These explanations suggest
that closed employment may be more efficient
than open employment in certain production
technologies. If this is so, closed employment
does not create rents and therefore does not
create the bases for separate classes within the
labor market.

If training opportunities are rationed and
employment relationships closed, economic
rents should emerge. It is indeed in such job
structures that collective action to preserve
positional advantage has been more successful. The resulting social organizations, such as
craft unions, are particularly important when
the use of credentials is underwritten by the
state in the form of licensing. This is also the
case for professions, such as medicine and
law, in which the restriction on employment

opportunities is not at the level of a job but at
the level of the occupation. It is important to
note that a measure of skill level, such as educational attainment, is not in itself informative as to whether skills are rent-generating or
not. We need information on the actual rationing of training opportunities.[5] This makes
many proposals to define "new" classes by
skills and education of quite dubious validity.

Classes in Internal Labor Markets

The use of authority and the use of incentives
are properties of closed employment relationships that are solutions to the main problem
for the employer involved: the problem of
how to match wage rates and productivity, especially effort, in the absence of open competition. Both solutions have been used to justify the emergence of class categories within
the labor market. What follows is a brief evaluation of a recent proposal to use authority
and incentive structures to define class categories within the labor market.

Authority relations are an inherent part of
the employment relationship. Marx emphasizes the importance of authority for employment contracts: That is, when workers sell
their labor power, they also sell control over
their own activities.[6] Indeed, authority is often identified as the basis for the formation of
class categories (Dahrendorf 1959; Wright
1979), and among many sociologists of the
labor market, authority has become the defining characteristic of "class" (Kalleberg and
Berg 1987).

The class schemes using authority relations
to define classes often do not provide a rationale in terms of exploitation mechanisms. It is
possible, for example, that Dahrendorf's
scheme (1959) may be justified by a justice
theory of exploitation, but the theory is not
presented. It is difficult to provide a rationale
in terms of an economic theory of exploitation. Wright (1985) suggests that there is an
advantage accruing to authority that derives
from having control over the organization of
production. The organization itself is seen as
a productive asset, and authority becomes a

measure of the asset. This approach is not convincing. The asset of organization is not in fixed supply and therefore does not necessarily generate rents. Further, those in authority in an organization do not "own" the organization of production; they execute it. Finally, authority is not a measure of the value of the asset—of the productive effectiveness of an organizational arrangement. It is difficult, without an incentive argument, to formulate a convincing theory for why those with authority should have higher wages than those who produce. Wright does not try.

Incentive systems provide a way of reducing the costs of exercising authority, in particular, the cost of wages to supervisors. Two such incentive systems have been suggested to create class categories. In "efficiency wage theory" (see, e.g., Akerlof and Yellen 1986), the argument is that paying above-market wages creates an incentive for high performance. Wright (1979) suggests the existence of such a "loyalty" wage for his class category of "semiautonomous employees." However, the efficiency wage increases the productivity of the worker. It therefore need not deviate from the competitive wage, that is, the wage obtained in the open labor market by the worker exercising the same level of effort. The efficiency wage is a solution to the possible inefficiency caused by closed employment relationships. If the solution works, there are no positional advantages caused by efficiency wages.

Promotion systems in internal labor markets are another important solution to the incentive problems created by closed employment relations. It is a common and old idea among sociologists (Weber 1968; Stinchcombe 1974) that promotion schemes can be important for generating effort. In promotion schemes, inequality in the cross section clearly is associated with occupancy of positions. The question is whether the advantages and disadvantages associated with positions constitute rents and therefore represent exploitation.

It is important to consider the career implications of the promotion scheme. The job ladders create an upward-sloping career trajec-tory. To the extent that the age slope in productivity is lower than the slope in wages, older workers will be paid more than their productivity would justify in a different job structure. If firms maximize profits, they should attempt to equalize total wages paid over the career to the overall productivity of the worker. Younger workers, therefore, will be paid less than their productivity would justify elsewhere.

The implications of this scenario for positional advantages and interests are straightforward but perhaps surprising. For the duration of the employment contract, the overall outcome may well be that there is no advantage in lifetime income of entering an internal labor market. In other words, access to an internal labor market does not necessarily provide a positional advantage that is a rent.[7] The situation is much the same as the one predicted by human capital theory for the returns to training, where the inequality observed in the cross section also misinforms about the overall advantage.

This leaves the use of rationed skills and credentials in matching persons to closed jobs as the main source of positional advantages that can form class categories within the labor market. There is nothing surprising in the proposition that closed skilled jobs for which training opportunities are rationed will form the main example of such categories. These are the positions that form the traditional basis of craft unions and professional organizations. Nevertheless, in recent work on the labor market, scholars employing class analysis strangely ignore these categories.

Conclusion

The general argument has been that the choice of basic concepts in stratification research is a question of balancing theoretical power and specificity with empirical requirements of concepts. The Marxist class concept is the most powerful, but it is also the most unsatisfactory concept for analyzing inequality and conflict within the large majority of the population of modern industrialized societies. The stratum concept of class and the concept of socioeconomic status pose the fewest empirical requirements. They are also least informative about the causes and consequences of inequality.

Some analysts see the choice between class and status concepts as a fundamental one. Certain class concepts indeed make stronger theoretical claims than the socioeconomic status concepts (which basically make none). Unless one believes that Marxist theory explains everything, this does not mean class concepts are more useful. It depends on what is being studied. The Marxist class concept and the market concept may be useful for studies of political processes and social movements, since they make claims about the sources of conflict and social change. However, in studies of attainment and in analyses that predict behavior or attitudes from the level of welfare obtained by individuals, the Marxist or market concepts of class are less useful than socioeconomic status. These class categories often are more heterogeneous than socioeconomic status categories. Further, since SEI and related measures form continuous variables, socioeconomic status is very convenient for use in the estimation of individual linear regression models. The stratum concept of class also emphasizes homogeneity, yet the discrete form may make it an awkward variable to use in attainment studies. Nevertheless, this discrete form may make it especially useful when the emphasis is on certain outcomes, as in mobility research, or when it is desired to study the consequences that changes in industrial structure have for the distribution of welfare.

I have tried to show that an economic theory of rent can be used to identify class categories that have the potential to form class actors. The Weberian idea of prestige or status groups also makes the claim that such groups practice exclusion. This suggests that status groups establish strategies to protect an advantage that is threatened because it is obtained at the expense of others. The market concept of class, therefore, may be seen as a

latent basis for status groups consistent with Weber's discussion. There is one difficulty. It has been argued that market-generated class categories form around rents and property, whereas status groups presumably are about honor or prestige. The transition from rents to honor needs analysis.

The controversies in sociology over the last twenty years have surrounded the choice of basic concepts with a minefield of ideological and epistemological connotations. This confusion has not been useful for research and theoretical development. The main message of this essay is to treat the basic concepts as tools useful for some purposes but not for every purpose.

Notes

I am indebted to Patricia Chang, Liah Greenfeld, Annemette Sørensen, and Jesper B. Sørensen for valuable comments and suggestions.

1. There are, of course, some variations, but they are relatively minor. A comprehensive treatment is provided by Treiman (1977).
2. The start of the demise of the Marxist labor theory of value is usually attributed to the German economist Eugene von Böhm-Bahwerk a hundred years ago. The history of the debate has been reviewed by many: See, for example, Gordon (1990) for a review that includes the attempt by so-called analytical Marxists (e.g., G. A. Cohen, Jon Elster, and John Roemer) to revise the basis for Marxist theory.
3. It is important to note that cross-sectional inequality, in my opinion, does not necessarily provide evidence for exploitation. When some individuals have higher income because of the returns they receive on earlier investments, they are being compensated for consumption forgone when making the investment. Those who do not receive the return, because they did not make the investment, would obviously gladly share in the returns. However, they should then also "pay back" the added gratification they received when choosing consumption over investment. This hypothetical exchange would only be advantageous to those owning assets when these assets are in fixed supply and rents are extracted. The need to consider lifetime incomes when identifying exploitation becomes important for my criticism later of recent formulations of class concepts within the labor market.

4. Roemer (1982) does not provide a discussion of this implication of human capital theory in his formulation of "skill assets" as a basis for exploitation. In fact, he does not present a precise definition of skills. In one place he seems to refer to any type of endowment that leads to unequal productivity (1982, 111); in another he explicitly states, "Let us treat skills as embodied and innate" (1982, 24). Only the latter should generate rents. Wright (1985) uses the former interpretation and therefore confuses returns with rents. Wright does attempt to make skills a property of positions by defining "skill requirements" of jobs.

5. Wright (1985) violates this principle by operationalizing skill assets as levels of educational attainment. He identifies what he calls skill requirements of positions in an attempt to implement Roemer's notion of exploitation based on skill assets. However, the concept of skill requirements does not distinguish between skills that generate true rents and those for which the income payoff is merely compensation for training costs.

6. The importance attached to authority in Marxist theory seems to contradict the argument presented previously that Marx would have accepted the neoclassical scenario for the labor market in which authority has no role. There is no doubt that Marx thought that the authority exercised by capitalists was important for the creation of classes. However, the importance of authority derives from Marx's belief in the labor theory of value. This theory implies that the wage paid to the worker is independent of his productivity—it represents the cost of reproducing the worker. Therefore, the amount of surplus generated will depend on how much work the employer extracts from the labor purchased. However, if the labor theory of value is abandoned, the need for authority disappears. In the open employment relationships assumed in modern marginal productivity theory, workers are paid according to their productivity, including their effort. As a result, effort is of no concern to the firm. Workers who do not work hard are simply paid less than workers who work hard.

7. Internal labor markets also create other problems for class analysis; see Sørensen (1991) for a discussion.

References

Akerlof, George A., and Janet L. Yellen. 1986. "Introduction." Pp. 1–21 in George A. Akerlof and Janet L. Yellen, eds., *Efficiency Wage Models of the Labor Market.* New York: Cambridge University Press.

Becker, Gary S. 1964. *Human Capital.* New York: National Bureau of Economic Research.

Carlsson, Gösta. 1958. *Social Mobility and Class Structure.* Lund: C.W.K. Gleerup.

Dahrendorf, Ralf. 1959. *Class and Class Conflict in Industrialized Society.* Stanford: Stanford University Press.

Davis, Kingsley, and Wilbert E. Moore. 1945. "Some Principles of Stratification." *American Sociological Review* 10:242–249.

Duncan, Otis D. 1961. "A Socioeconomic Index for All Occupations." Pp. 109–138 in A. J. Reiss, Jr., ed., *Occupations and Social Status.* New York: Free Press.

Featherman, David L., and Robert M. Hauser. 1976. "Prestige or Socioeconomic Scales in the Study of Occupational Achievement." *Sociological Methods and Research* 4:402–422.

Geiger, Theodor. 1951. *Soziale Umschichtungen in einer dänischer Mittelstadt.* Vol. 23 of *Acta Jutlandica.* Aarhus, Denmark: University of Aarhus.

Giddens, Anthony. 1973. *The Class Structure of Advanced Societies.* New York: Harper & Row.

Goldthorpe, John H. 1984. "Social Mobility and Class Formation: On the Renewal of a Tradition in Sociological Inquiry." CASMIN-Projekt. Institut für Sozialwissenschaften. Universität Mannheim.

———. 1987. *Social Class and Mobility in Modern Britain.* 2d ed. Oxford: Clarendon Press.

Goldthorpe, John H., and Keith Hope. 1974. *The Social Grading of Occupations: A New Approach and Scale.* Oxford: Clarendon Press.

Goode, William J. 1978. *The Celebration of Heroes: Prestige as a Control System.* Berkeley: University of California Press.

Gordon, David. 1990. *Resurrecting Marx: The Analytical Marxists on Freedom, Exploitation, and Justice.* New Brunswick, N.J.: Transaction Books.

Grusky, David B., and Jesper B. Sørensen. 1998. "Can Class Analysis Be Salvaged?" *American Journal of Sociology* 103: 1187–1234.

Hauser, Robert M., and John Robert Warren. 1997. "Socioeconomic Indexes for Occupations: A Review, Update, and Critique." Pp. 177–298 in Adrian E. Raftery, ed., *Sociological Methodology, Volume 27.* Washington, D.C.: American Sociological Association.

Hodge, Robert W. 1981. "The Measurement of Occupational Status." *Social Science Research* 10:396–415.

Hollingshead, August B., and Frederick C. Redlick. 1958. *Social Class and Mental Illness: A Community Study.* New York: Wiley.

Kalleberg, Arne L., and Ivar Berg. 1987. *Work and Industry: Structures, Markets, and Processes.* New York: Plenum.

Lazear, Edward P., and Sherwin Rosen. 1981. "Rank-Order Tournaments as Optimum Labor Contracts." *Journal of Political Economy* 89 (2):841–864.

Parkin, Frank. 1979. *Marxism and Class Theory: A Bourgeois Critique.* New York: Columbia University Press.

Roemer, John E. 1982. *A General Theory of Exploitation and Class.* Cambridge, Mass.: Harvard University Press.

———. 1988. "Should Marxists Be Interested in Exploitation?" Pp. 260–282 in John E. Roemer, ed., *Analytical Marxism.* New York: Cambridge University Press.

Shils, Edward A. 1970. "Deference." Pp. 420–448 in Edward O. Laumann, Paul M. Siegel, and Robert W. Hodge, eds., *The Logic of Social Hierarchies.* Chicago: Markham.

Simmel, Georg. 1908. *Soziologie.* Leipzig: Duncker and C. Humblot.

Sørensen, Aage B. 1983. "Processes of Allocation to Open and Closed Positions in Social Structure." *Zeitschrift für Soziologie* 12 (July): 203–224.

———. 1991. "On the Usefulness of Class Analysis in Research on Social Mobility and Socioeconomic Inequality." *Acta Sociologica* 34: 71–87.

———. 1996. "The Structural Basis of Social Inequality." *American Journal of Sociology* 101: 1333–65.

———. 2000. "Toward a Sounder Basis for Class Analysis." *American Journal of Sociology* 105:1523–1558.

Sørensen, Aage B., and Arne L. Kalleberg. 1981. "An Outline of a Theory of the Matching of Persons to Jobs." Pp. 49–74 in Ivar Berg, ed., *Sociological Perspectives on Labor Markets.* New York: Academic Press.

Sorokin, Pitirim. 1927. *Social Mobility.* New York: Harper & Bros.

Stinchcombe, Arthur L. 1974. *Creating Efficient Industrial Administrations.* New York: Academic Press.

Treiman, Donald J. 1977. *Occupational Prestige in Comparative Perspective.* New York: Academic Press.

Warner, W. Lloyd, Marchia Meeker, and Kenneth Eells. 1949. *Social Class in America.* New York: Science Research Associates.

Weber, Max. 1946. "Class, Status, and Party." Pp. 180–195 in Hans H. Gerth and C. Wright Mills, eds., *From Max Weber.* London: Routledge.

———. 1968. *Economy and Society.* New York: Bedminster Press.

Williamson, Oliver E. 1975. *Markets and Hierarchies: Analysis and Antitrust Implications.* New York: Free Press.

Wright, Erik O. 1979. *Class Structure and Income Determination.* New York: Academic Press.

———. 1985. *Classes.* London: Verso.

Part IV
Generating Inequality

Social Mobility
   Classical Viewpoints
   Modern Analyses of Class Mobility
   Modern Analyses of Income Mobility and Poverty Spells

Status and Income Attainment
   Basic Models
   Social Psychological Models
   The "New Structuralism"
   Social Capital, Networks, and Attainment
   Rational Action Approaches to Mobility and Attainment

PITIRIM A. SOROKIN

Social and Cultural Mobility

Conception of Social Mobility and Its Forms

By social mobility is understood any transition of an individual or social object or value—anything that has been created or modified by human activity—from one social position to another. There are two principal types of social mobility, *horizontal* and *vertical*. By horizontal social mobility or shifting, is meant the transition of an individual or social object from one social group to another situated on the same level. Transitions of individuals, as from the Baptist to the Methodist religious group, from one citizenship to another, from one family (as a husband or wife) to another by divorce and remarriage, from one factory to another in the same occupational status, are all instances of social mobility. So too are transitions of social objects, the radio, automobile, fashion, Communism, Darwin's theory, within the same social stratum, as from Iowa to California, or from any one place to another. In all these cases, "shifting" may take place without any noticeable change of the social position of an individual or social object in the vertical direction. By

Originally published in 1959. Please see complete source information beginning on page 891.

vertical social mobility is meant the relations involved in a transition of an individual (or a social object) from one social stratum to another. According to the direction of the transition there are two types of vertical social mobility: *ascending* and *descending,* or *social climbing* and *social sinking.* According to the nature of the stratification, there are ascending and descending currents of economic, political, and occupational mobility, not to mention other less important types. The ascending currents exist in two principal forms: as an *infiltration* of the individuals of a lower stratum into an existing higher one; and as a *creation of a new group by such individuals, and the insertion of such a group into a higher stratum instead of, or side by side with, the existing groups of this stratum.* Correspondingly, the descending current has also two principal forms: the first consists in a dropping of individuals from a higher social position into an existing lower one, without a degradation or disintegration of the higher group to which they belonged; the second is manifested in *a degradation of a social group as a whole, in an abasement of its rank among other groups, or in its disintegration as a social unit.* The first case of "sinking" reminds one of an individual falling from a ship; the second of the sinking of the ship itself with all on board, or of the ship as a wreck breaking itself to pieces. . . .

Immobile and Mobile Types of Stratified Societies

Theoretically, there may be a stratified society in which the vertical social mobility is nil. This means that within it there is no ascending or descending, no circulation of its members; that every individual is forever attached to the social stratum in which he was born; that the membranes or hymens which separate one stratum from another are absolutely impenetrable, and do not have any "holes" through which, nor any stairs and elevators with which, the dwellers of the different strata may pass from one floor to another. *Such a type of stratification may be styled as absolutely closed, rigid, impenetrable, or immobile.* The opposite theoretical type of the inner structure of the stratification of the same height and profile is that in which the vertical mobility is very intensive and general; here the membranes between the strata are very thin and have the largest holes to pass from one floor to another. Therefore, though the social building is as stratified as the immobile one, nevertheless, the dwellers of its different strata are continually changing; they do not stay a very long time in the same "social story," and with the help of the largest staircases and elevators are *en masse* moving "up and down." *Such a type of social stratification may be styled open, plastic, penetrable, or mobile.* Between these two extreme types there may be many middle or intermediary types of stratification. . . .

General Principles of Vertical Mobility

As far as the corresponding historical and other materials permit seeing, in the field of vertical mobility there seems to be no definite perpetual trend toward either an increase or a decrease of the intensiveness and generality of mobility. This is proposed as valid for the history of a country, for that of a large social body, and, finally, for the history of mankind.

In these dynamic times, with the triumph of the electoral system, with the industrial revolution, and especially a revolution in transportation, this proposition may appear strange and improbable. The dynamism of our epoch stimulates the belief that history has tended and will tend in the future toward a perpetual and "eternal" increase of vertical mobility. There is no need to say that many social thinkers have such an opinion.[1] And yet, if its bases and reasons are investigated it may be seen that they are far from convincing.

In the first place, the partisans of the acceleration and increase of mobility used to point out that in modern societies there are no juridical and religious obstacles to circulation, which existed in a caste—or in a feudal society. Granting for a moment that this statement is true, the answer is: first of all, it is impossible to infer an "eternal historical tendency" on the basis of an experience only of some 130 years; this is too short a period, beside the course of thousands of years of human history, to be a solid basis for the assertion of the existence of a perpetual trend. In the second place, even within this period of 130 years, the trend has not been manifested clearly throughout the greater part of mankind. Within the large social aggregates of Asia and Africa, the situation is still indefinite; the caste-system is still alive in India; in Tibet and Mongolia, in Manchuria and China, among the natives of many other countries, there has been either no alteration of the situation or only such as had happened many times before. In the light of these considerations reference to feudalism compared with the "free" modern times loses a great deal of its significance.

Grant that the removal of the juridical and religious obstacles tended to increase mobility. Even this may be questioned. It would have been valid if, in place of the removed obstacles, there were not introduced some other ones. In fact, such new obstacles were introduced. If in a caste-society it is rarely possible to be noble unless born from a noble family, it is possible nevertheless to be noble and privileged without being wealthy; in the present society it is possible to be noble without being born in a prominent family; but, as a general rule, it is necessary to be wealthy.[2] One obstacle gone, another has taken its place. In theory, in the United States of America, every citizen may become the President of the United States. In fact, 99.9 per cent of the citizens have as little chance of doing it as 99.9 per cent of the subjects of a monarchy have of becoming a monarch. One kind of obstacle removed, others have been established. By this is meant that the abolition of obstacles to an intensive vertical circulation, common in caste-society and feudal society, did not mean an absolute decrease of the obstacles, but only a substitution of one sort of impediment for another. And it is not yet known what kind of obstacles—the old or the new—is more efficient in restraining social circulation. . . .

Occupational Dispersion and Recruitment

In present Western societies different occupational groups are strongly interwoven, and the cleavages between them are considerably obliterated, or, more accurately, are somewhat indefinite and not clearly cut. Indeed, since one son of a family is an unskilled laborer, another a business man, and the third a physician, it is not easy to decide to what group such a family belongs. On the other hand, since the offspring of the same family or of many families of the same occupational status enter the most different occupations, the cleavages between occupations are thereby considerably obliterated, their "strangeness" toward each other is weakened; their social heterogeneity and repulsion diminished. As a result, the precipice between occupational groups becomes less than it is in a society where such dispersion of the children of fathers who belong to the same occupation does not take place, or is a very rare phenomenon. This means that there is a fallacy in the statement of many theorizers of class struggle who

continue to talk about the present social classes as though they were still a kind of caste. They forget completely about the fluid composition of present occupational groups. However, a part of the truth is in their statement. What is it? The answer is given in the next propositions.

In spite of the above-shown dispersion among different occupations, the "hereditary" transmission of occupation still exists, and, on the average, it is still high enough. It is likely also that the fathers' occupation is still entered by the children in a greater proportion than any other. This means that a part of the population, during one or two or more generations, still remains in a régime like a caste-system. Shall we wonder, therefore, that this part has habits, traditions, standards, mores, psychology, and behavior similar to that of a caste-society? Shall we wonder that the cleavages between such "rigid" parts of each occupation are quite clearly cut—economically, socially, mentally, morally, and even biologically? Under specific conditions, such a part of the population may give a real basis for the existence of a class psychology and class antagonisms. To this extent the partisans of the class struggle may have a reason for their theory and aspirations. As an illustration of this, the following fact may be mentioned. Among the German proletariat, the narrow-proletarian psychology and ideology—in the form of social-democratic and communist affiliations—have existed principally among those who have been "hereditary proletarians" or used to remain within this class throughout their life.[3] The same may be said of any "hereditary and non-shifting part" of any occupation.

The next basis for the aspirations of partisans of class theories is given by the fact which may be generalized as follows: *The closer the affinity between occupations, the more intensive among them is mutual interchange of their members; and,* vice versa, *the greater the difference between occupations the less is the number of individuals who shift from one group to another.* Since such is the case, it is natural that there are cleavages not so much between occupational groups in the narrow sense of the word, as between bigger social subdivisions going on along the lines of the "affine" and "non-affine" occupational subdivisions. In a class composed totally of the affine occupational groups, *e.g.*, of different groups of unskilled and semiskilled labor, there appears and exists a community of interests, habits, morals, traditions, and ideologies considerably different from those of another class composed totally of other affine occupational groups, *e.g.*, of different professional and business groups. These differences, being reinforced by differences in the economic status of such classes, create a basis for what is styled as the present class-differentiation, with its satellites in the form of the class antagonisms and class friction. Thus far the partisans of the class struggle may have a basis for their activity and propaganda. . . .

Mobility Facilitates Atomization and Diffusion of Solidarity and Antagonisms

In an immobile society the social solidarity of its members is concentrated within the social box to which they belong. It rarely surpasses its limits because the social contact of an individual with the members of other different "boxes" is very weak and rare. Under such conditions the members of different boxes are likely to be strangers or to be in quite neutral relations. But within each box the ties of solidarity of its members are most intensive; for the same reason that the solidarity of the members of an old-fashioned family is strong. They have a complete understanding and a complete community of interests, or a complete like-mindedness, elaborated in the closest face-to-face contacts throughout a life span. The same may be said of hatred and antagonisms. All these socio-psychical phenomena are "localized" within and "centered" around a definite social box. In a mobile social body a "delocalization," and "atomiza-

tion," and diffusion tend to take place. Since an individual belongs to different social groups and shifts from one box to another, his "area" of solidarity is not limited within one box. It becomes larger. It involves many individuals of different boxes. It ceases to "concentrate" within one box. It becomes "individualized" and selects not "boxes" but persons, or social atoms. The same may be said of the attitudes of hatred and antagonism. At the same time the phenomena of solidarity and antagonism are likely to lose their intensiveness. They become colder and more moderate. The reason for this is at hand: an individual now is not secluded for life in his box. He stays for a shorter time within each box; his face-to-face contacts with the members of each social group become shorter, the number of persons with whom he "lives together," more numerous: he becomes like a polygamist who is not obliged and does not invest all his love in one wife, but divides it among many women. Under such conditions, the attachment becomes less hot; the intensiveness of feeling, less concentrated.

In the social field this calls forth two important changes. In the first place, the map of solidarity and antagonisms within any mobile society becomes more complex and curved than in an immobile one. It is relatively clear in an immobile society. It goes along the lines separating one caste, order, or clear-cut stratum from another. The vertical and horizontal trenches are in general simple and conspicuous. In periods of social struggle, slaves fight with slaves against masters; serfs against their lords; plebeians, against patricians; peasants, against landlords. Much more complex is the map of solidarity and antagonism in a mobile society. Since the boxes are less clearly cut off from each other, and since each of them is filled by a fluid population from different strata, the lines of solidarity and antagonism become more whimsical, and assume the most fanciful character. During the World War the citizens of the United States showed a considerable difference in their attitudes toward the belligerent countries. Anglo-Saxon, French, and Slavic citizens sympathized with the Allies; the German-Americans, with the Central Powers. The unity of the citizenship did not prevent this splitting. If, further, is taken into consideration the difference in religion, political aspiration, economic and occupational status, the lines of solidarity and antagonism for and against the War appear to be most fanciful. People of the same nationality, or of the same religion, or occupational status, or economic status, or children of the same family, very often happen to be in opposite factions.

In the second place, the lines of solidarity and antagonism in a mobile society become more flexible and more changeable. A man, who yesterday was an antagonist of a definite measure, today becomes its partisan because his social position has been changed. Shifting from one social position to another calls forth a similar shifting of interests and solidarity. Fluidity of social groups facilitates the same result. Therefore, it is not strange when we see that yesterday's foes are today's friends. The group, which last year was an enemy to be exterminated, to-day turns out an ally. In the contemporary interrelations of groups and whole countries this flexibility of the map of solidarity and antagonism is conspicuous. . . .

Mobility Favors an Increase of Individualism Followed by a Vague Cosmopolitanism and Collectivism

Mobility facilitates an increase of individualism because it destroys this "seclusion for life in one social box" typical of an immobile society. When a man is for life attached to his "box," a knowledge of the box is enough to know the characteristics of the man. On the other hand, the man feels himself not so much as a particular personality, but only as a cell or a component of the group to which he belongs.[4] Under such conditions, the "boxes" but not the individuals are the social atoms or units. When the "boxes" are less definite and rigid, when their population is fluid, when an individual passes from position to position

and often belongs to several overlapping groups, his attachment to the box becomes less intensive; his characteristics cannot be decided through his temporary position; in order to know him one must take him as an individual and study his personality. This participation in many groups, shifting from one group to another, and impossibility of identification with any one group makes an individual something separate from a social box; awakens his personality, transforms him from the component of a group to an individual person. As he is shifting from group to group, he now must secure rights and privileges for himself, not for a specific group, because he himself does not know in what group he will be to-morrow. Hence the "Declaration of the Rights of Men" but not that of a group. Hence the demands of liberty of speech, religion, freedom, self-realization for a *man,* but not for a group. Hence the equality of all individuals before law; and individual responsibility instead of that of a group, as is the case in an immobile society. A mobile society inevitably must "invest" all rights and responsibilities in an individual but not in a group. . . .

Complete social isolation or loneliness is unbearable for the majority of people. It has been mentioned that mobility facilitates such an isolation. Detached from an intimate oneness with any group, losing even family shelter against loneliness, modern individuals try by every means to attach themselves to some social body to avoid their isolation. And the more the family is disintegrated, the stronger is this need. Some enter labor and occupational unions; some try to fight their isolation through an affiliation with political parties; some, through a participation in different societies, clubs, churches; some through a mad rush from one dancing hall to another. Some try to belong at once to many and often opposite groups. All these "collectivist tendencies" are nothing but the other side of individualism and isolation, created by mobility. They are attempts to substitute for the previous lost "boxes" something similar to them. To some extent all these unions, clubs, societies, and so forth, serve this purpose. But only to some extent. Shifting does not permit one to attach himself to such groups strongly. Hence arise the trends to go further in this direction. This trend is conspicuously manifested in the social schemes of Communists, revolutionary syndicalists, and guild socialists. They contemplate a complete engulfment of an individual within the commune, or syndicate, or a restored guild. They unintentionally try to reëstablish "the lost paradise" of an immobile society, and to make an individual again only a "finger of the hand" of a social body. The greater is the loneliness, the more urgent the need. I fear, however, that until social mobility is diminished, such attempts, even being realized, cannot give what is expected of them. In the best case they may create a kind of a compulsory "social box" which will be felt to be a prison by its members. In conditions of social mobility such a cell will be destroyed by its prisoners. In order to realize the program it is necessary to diminish the mobility. If we are entering such a period, then in some form these schemes may be realized. Are we entering one? I cannot confidently say. Some symptoms are in favor of such an hypothesis. But they are not quite clear as yet; the topic is too big to be discussed briefly, and the writer too much likes the mobile type of society to prophesy its funeral; therefore, he prefers to finish the discussion right here. Whatever may happen in the future, our mobile period is far from ended. And if our aristocracy would try to be a real aristocracy, strong in its rights and duties, creative in its achievements, less sensual in its proclivities and free from parasitism; if it would raise its fecundity; if the channels of climbing are open to every talent among the lower strata; if the machinery of social testing and selection is properly reorganized; if the lower strata are raised to levels as high as possible; and if we are not permeated by the ideologies of false sentimentality and "humanitarian impotency," then the chances for a long and *brilliant* existence of present mobile societies are great and high. Let history do what it has to do; and let us do what we ought to do without wavering and hesitation.

Notes

1. See, *e.g.*, Fahlbeck, "Les classes sociales"; "La noblesse de Suede"; "La décadence et la chute des peuples," in *Bull. de l'Inst. Int. de Stat.*, Vols. XII, XV, and XVIII; D'Aeth, F. G., "Present Tendencies of Class Differentiation," *The Sociological Review*, pp. 269–272 et seq., 1910.

2. Such is the condition necessary for a man to be included in the American "Social Register."

3. See Lurie, *Sostav Proletariata*, p. 9; see also the series "Auslese und Anpassung der Arbeiterschaft," *Schriften des Vereins für Sozialpolitik*.

4. Durkheim, E., *La division du travail social*, and Bouglé, Charles, "Revue générale des théories récentes sur la division du travail," *L'Année sociologique*, Vol. VI; Palant, *Les antinomies entre l'individu et société, passim.*

SEYMOUR MARTIN LIPSET, REINHARD BENDIX, AND HANS L. ZETTERBERG

Social Mobility in Industrial Society

Widespread social mobility has been a concomitant of industrialization and a basic characteristic of modern industrial society. In every industrial country, a large proportion of the population has had to find occupations considerably different from those of their parents. During the nineteenth century, the proportion of the labor force in urban occupations increased rapidly, while the proportion in agriculture decreased.

In the twentieth century the West has been characterized by a rapid growth of trade and of service industries, as well as of bureaucracy in industry and government; more people have become employed in white-collar work, and the comparative size of the rural population has declined even more rapidly than before.[1] These changes in the distribution of occupations from generation to generation mean that no industrial society can be viewed as closed or static.

This apparently simple statement runs counter to widely held impressions concerning the different social structures of American and Western European societies. According to these impressions, America has an "open society" with considerable social mobility, but the countries of Western Europe (specifically England, France, Italy, Germany, the Low Countries, and the Scandinavian nations) have soci-

eties that are "closed," in the sense that the children of workers are forced to remain in the social position of their parents. This judgment reflects earlier European beliefs. In the age of the French Revolution, America appeared to be a land free from traditional institutions and historical legacies: the country of the future, Hegel called it, where each man was master of his fate just as American democracy itself was the product of human reason. This notion has been reiterated in many analyses, all contrasting American and European societies.

For the most part these discussions deal with the differences between democratic and autocratic institutions; but they also express assumptions about contrasting patterns of social mobility. Sometimes the political and social aspects of the contrast between America and Europe have been linked as cause and effect: differences in political institutions and values have been cited as evidence for the assertion that the society of America is "open," those of Europe "closed"; and the supposedly greater rate of social mobility in American society has been viewed as a major reason for the success of American democracy. For example, some fifty years ago Werner Sombart referred to the opportunities abundant in America as the major reason why American workers rejected the Marxist view that there is little opportunity under capitalism, while European workers accepted it because their opportunities were more restricted.[2] Such judgments as Sombart's were, however, no more than inferences based on the general contrast between the American tradition

Originally published in 1959. Please see complete source information beginning on page 891.

which proclaimed the goal of opportunity for all and the European emphasis upon social stability and class differences.[3] For as a matter of fact, it is not really clear whether the different political orientation of the American and European worker reflects different opportunities for social mobility or only a difference in their ethos!

The questions implicit in these alternative interpretations can be answered today with somewhat more assurance than was possible even two decades ago because of recent research in social mobility. In this chapter we attempt to summarize the findings available for a number of countries. Since our object is to assemble a large amount of empirical evidence, it will be useful to state at the outset that *the overall pattern of social mobility appears to be much the same in the industrial societies of various Western countries.* This is startling—even if we discount the mistaken efforts to explain differences in political institutions by reference to different degrees of social mobility in the United States and in Western Europe. Further, although it is clear that social mobility is related in many ways to the economic expansion of industrial societies, it is at least doubtful that the rates of mobility and of expansion are correlated. Since a number of the countries for which we have data have had different rates of economic expansion but show comparable rates of social mobility, our tentative interpretation is that the social mobility of societies becomes relatively high once their industrialization, and hence their economic expansion, reaches a certain level.

Occupational Mobility

Before World War II, studies of social mobility were usually limited to investigations of the social origins of different occupational groups, employees of single factories, or inhabitants of single communities. Since World War II there have been at least fifteen different national surveys in eleven countries which have secured from representative samples of the population information that relates the occupations of the respondents to the occupations of their fathers. In addition, there have been a number of studies conducted in different cities of various countries. Taken together, these investigations permit the comparison of current variations in occupational mobility, as well as some estimate of differences during the past half century.

To make such comparisons and estimates is difficult. Few of the studies were made with the intention of facilitating the comparison of findings in different countries. Many of them employ systems of classifying occupations which cannot be compared with each other and the questions concerning the occupations of respondents and fathers are seldom similar. In order to use the results for a comparative analysis, we have reduced the occupational categories for most countries to the closest approximation of manual, nonmanual, and farm occupations. In presenting these materials, we make the assumption that a move from manual to nonmanual employment constitutes upward mobility among *males. . . .*

The lack of comparable classifications in nationwide surveys of social mobility makes it difficult to [reach] more than general impressions. Moreover, we must bear in mind that we deal here exclusively with a single index to complex and quite diverse societies, so that inferences can carry us only part of the way and should be made with caution. Yet, the value of a comparative approach to social mobility becomes apparent when we set side by side for each country the figures which are most clearly indicative of upward, downward, and total mobility across the line between the middle and the working class (table 1). Because of the varying systems of occupational classification the Italian figures cannot be compared with any of the others, and the British and Danish figures can be compared only with each other. The remainder, however, are reasonably comparable.

The figures in the first column give the proportion of all sons of manual workers who now occupy middle-class positions. In the second column the figures indicate the proportion of all sons of middle-class fathers who are now in manual occupations. In order to

TABLE 1

Comparative Indices of Upward and Downward Mobility (percentages)

NONFARM POPULATIONS

Country	Upward mobility (Nonmanual sons of manual fathers)	Downward mobility (Manual sons of nonmanual fathers)	Total vertical mobility (Nonfarm population mobile across the line between working and middle class)
United States[a]	33	26	30
Germany[b]	29	32	31
Sweden	31	24	29
Japan	36	22	27
France	39	20	27
Switzerland	45	13	23

POPULATIONS WITH RURAL AND URBAN OCCUPATIONS CLASSIFIED TOGETHER[a]

Country	High prestige occupation sons of fathers in low prestige occupations	Low prestige occupation sons of fathers in high prestige occupations	Proportion mobile across high and low occupation prestige lines
Denmark	22	44	31
Great Britain	20	49	29
Italy	8	34	16

SOURCES—UNITED STATES: Average of three studies [Natalie Rogoff, "Jobs and Occupations," *Opinion News*, September 1 (1947): 3–33; Survey Research Center, University of Michigan, 1952 Presidential Election Survey; R. Centers, "Occupational Mobility of Urban Occupational Strata," *American Sociological Review*, 13 (1948): 203]. GERMANY: Average of three studies [Erich Reigratski, *Soziale Verflechtungen in der Bundesrepublik* (Tubingen: Mohr-Siebeck, 1956); Institut für Demoskopie, Allensbach, Germany; DIVO, Frankfurt A.M.]. SWEDEN: Data collected by H.L. Zetterberg, partly reported in "Sveriges fem rangrullor," *Vecko-Journalen*, 48 (1957): 40. JAPAN: Research Committee on Stratification and Social Mobility of The Japanese Sociological Association, *Social Stratification and Mobility* (Tokyo: 1956, mimeographed), p. 13. FRANCE: M. Bresard, "Mobilité sociale et dimension de la famille," *Population*, 5 (1950): 553–566. SWITZERLAND: Recalculated from information supplied by Professor Roger Girod. DENMARK: Computed from data furnished by Professor K. Svalastoga, Copenhagen, Denmark. GREAT BRITAIN: Calculated from David V. Glass, *Social Mobility in Britain* (London: Routledge and Kegan Paul, 1954). ITALY: L. Livi, "Sur la mesure de la mobilité sociale," *Population*, 5 (1950): 65–76.

[a]Occupations of high prestige are high levels of nonmanual occupations and farm owners, except in the high-prestige data for Italy, which include all nonmanual occupations and well-to-do peasants. Occupations of low prestige include routine nonmanual occupations, manual occupations, and farm occupations, except the low-prestige data for Italy, which include only manual occupations (including farm workers) and poor peasants.

get some index of the total mobility in society, the figures in the third column were computed: out of all the sons of fathers in urban occupations who are themselves in urban occupations, those who were mobile in either direction were added together, and this figure was expressed as a percentage of the total.

For example, of those persons in the nonfarm population of the United States who were sons of fathers in nonfarm occupations, 30 per cent had either fallen into a manual position from their fathers' nonmanual position, or had risen from their fathers' working-class occupation into a middle-class one. Though this is, to be sure, a very crude index, it should give a rough indication of the fluidity of the urban occupational structure. It expresses the proportion of the native urban population which has, in one way or another, "changed class."

The first impression one gains from table 1 is that all the countries studied are characterized by a high degree of mobility. From one generation to another, a quarter to a third of the nonfarm population moves from working class to middle class or vice versa. Second, there is among the first six countries a high degree of similarity in this total mobility rate. The total range is between 23 and 31 per cent, and five of the six countries (United States, Germany, Sweden, Japan, France) range between 27 and 31 per cent. Such narrow differences lead quickly to one interpretation: total mobility rates in these countries are practically the same.

This similarity does not hold, of course, if the relationship between parental occupations and sons' occupations are compared in terms either of upward or of downward mobility, rather than the total amount of mobility. Then it appears that there is considerable variation among countries in the degree to which a father's occupation is an asset or a handicap. Thus, we see that the sons of middle-class fathers are more likely to fall in status in the United States and Germany than they are in Japan, France, or Switzerland. There is less variation in the degree to which a working-class family background handicaps a man in securing a nonmanual position; only Switzerland stands out as permitting higher rates of upward movement than the other countries. Given the variations in the methods of collecting data, it would be premature to place much reliance on these differences. . . .

Mobility Trends and Social Structure

Several different processes inherent in all modern social structures have a direct effect on the rate of social mobility, and help account for the similarities in rates in different countries:

(1) changes in the number of available vacancies; (2) different rates of fertility; (3) changes in the rank accorded to occupations; (4) changes in the number of inheritable status-positions; and (5) changes in the legal restrictions pertaining to potential opportunities.

By examining the relationship between these features of the social structure and the trends of mobility in different countries, we may be able to account for the similarities and differences among these trends.

1. The number of vacancies in a given stratum is not always, or even usually, constant. For example, in every industrialized or industrializing country, the increase in the proportion of professional, official, managerial, and white-collar positions and the decline in the proportion of unskilled-labor jobs creates a surge of mobility, which is upward—provided these positions retain their relative standing and income. More and more people are needed to manage industry, to distribute goods, to provide personal services, and to run the ever-growing state bureaucracy. A comparison of the ratio of administrative (white-collar) to production (manual) workers in manufacturing industries over the last half-century in the United States, the United Kingdom, and Sweden shows that the correspondence in trends is very great. Thus, in the United States in 1899 there were 8 administrative employees per 100 production workers, in 1947 there were 22 administrative employees per 100 production workers, and in 1957 there were 30 administrative employees per 100 production workers.[4] The corresponding rise in Britain between 1907 and 1948 is from 9 to 20 administrative employees per 100 production workers, and in Sweden the number rose from 7 to 21 between 1915 and 1950. In none of these countries did the proportion of those self-employed in urban occupations decline.

2. An important determinant of upward mobility is the difference in rates of fertility. In all industrialized countries for which we have data, fertility tends to vary inversely with income.[5] Although changes in the eco-

nomic structure are increasing the proportion of persons engaged in high-level occupations, the families of men who are now in such occupations are not contributing their proportionate share of the population. Consequently, even if every son of a high-status father were to retain that status, there would still be room for others to rise.

A similar consideration also applies to the process of urbanization. In all industrialized countries the urban centers continue to grow, requiring migrants to fill new positions or to replace urbanites, who characteristically fail to reproduce themselves. Although the urban birth rate is below reproduction level, the proportion of the population living in large cities (100,000 and over) grew in England from 26 per cent in 1871 to 38 per cent in 1951; in Germany from 5 per cent in 1870 to 27 per cent in 1950; in France, from 9 per cent in 1870 to 17 per cent in 1946; and in the United States from 11 per cent in 1870 to 30 per cent in 1950. And, as [shown elsewhere],[6] the process of migration into urban areas permits a large proportion of the sons of workers who grow up in metropolitan centers to fill the newly created or demographically vacated middle-class positions, while the manual jobs left open are filled by migrants from small towns or rural areas.

3. In our rapidly changing world some positions lose, some gain, prestige. Thus, a person can be mobile in the eyes of society without changing his job. Admittedly, most of these losses or gains are barely noticeable within one generation. For example, a rating of twenty-five occupations made in 1925 was compared with a rating made in 1947, and a correlation of .97 was obtained, indicating practically no change.[7] However, another study of the same period has indicated that government positions in the United States have enhanced their prestige since the 'twenties.[8] Moreover, the addition of new occupations may sometimes inadvertently alter the prestige of certain ranks; for example, the emergence of the occupation of airplane pilot during the last generation served to deglamorize such occupations as ship captain and loco-motive engineer. And significant changes in a given profession such as were effected in those of physicist, mathematician, and others by the atomic research programs during World War II, are also likely to better—or to lower—its prestige. However, we do not have studies with which to test such guesses.

4. In modern social structures there is a relative decline in the number of inheritable positions.[9] Many middle-class fathers in salaried positions have little to give their children except a good education and motivation to obtain a high-status position. If for any reason, such as the early death of the father or family instability, a middle-class child does not complete his higher education, he is obviously in a poorer position, in terms of prospective employment, than the son of a manual worker who completes college. Clearly, some of the children of the middle class are so handicapped, others simply do not have the ability to complete college or to get along in a bureaucratic hierarchy, and many of these fall into a status below that of their fathers. Whatever the reason, persons of middle-class origin who fall in status leave room for others of lower-class background to rise.

The importance of this factor is emphasized by the sharp increase in the educational level among the working classes. No nation approaches the United States in terms of the number of university students who come from the working class. Even sons of working-class Negroes in the United States are more likely to go to college than sons of European workers.[10] The effect of the difference in university attendance among workers on the two continents, of course, is reduced by the fact that higher education is a more certain way of achieving a privileged position in Europe than in the United States.

5. Many earlier legal restrictions upon the right of a person to create a new and higher occupational status for himself have been removed. The abolition of the guild system is the classic example of this. All the countries we have discussed in this chapter have legal guarantees of the freedom of occupational choice. A peculiar consequence of such guar-

antees is the phenomenon of "increased upward mobility" during depressions. In these periods many manual workers are fired and cannot find jobs in their normal occupations. To survive, many of them become small entrepreneurs and, thus, according to the conventional classification, move upward on the social ladder. . . .

The Consequences of Social Mobility

Although it appears, then, that the *amount* of social mobility is largely determined by the more or less uniform structural changes of industrialized societies and is therefore much the same in all such societies, it should be emphasized that the *consequences* of that mobility have been most diverse. To take an extreme example: if a Negro in South Africa obtains a nonmanual position, he is a ready candidate for leadership in a movement of radical protest. But if a white American from a working-class family makes the same move, he usually becomes politically and socially conservative. Perhaps the most important key to an explanation of such varying consequences of mobility across the line between manual and nonmanual occupations, is the concept of *status discrepancies*. Every society may be thought of as comprising a number of separate hierarchies—e.g., social, economic, educational, ethnic, etc.—each of which has its own status structure, its own conditions for the attainment of a position of prestige within that structure. There are likely to be a number of discrepancies among the positions in the different hierarchies that every person occupies simultaneously, for, as Georg Simmel pointed out, every person maintains a unique pattern of group affiliations. Mobility merely adds to these discrepancies by creating or accentuating combinations of a high position in one rank and a low one in another; for example, a high position in an occupation combined with a low ethnic status, or a high position in the social-class hierarchy (based on the status of people with whom one associates) combined with a low income.

The few analyses of the psychological dimension of this problem that have been made indicate that status discrepancies may cause difficulties in personal adjustment because high self-evaluations in one sphere of life conflict with low ones in another. Durkheim, for example, suggested that both upward and downward mobility result in increased suicide rates by increasing the number of persons who find themselves in an *anomic* situation, one in which they do not know how to react to the norms involved.[11] Studies of mental illness have suggested that people moving up in America are more likely to have mental breakdowns than the nonmobile.[12]

Since it is primary-group relations which give individuals the psychic support which "protects" them against suicide and mental illness, the hypotheses developed by Janowitz and Curtis on the social consequences of occupational mobility may help explain the above findings. They suggest that social mobility is likely to have disruptive consequences on primary group structures, such as family, clique, and friendships, but that the integration of secondary group structures is less likely to be influenced. They further suggest that primary group strains will be greatest for extreme upward-mobile and downward-mobile families and least for stable and moderately upward-mobile families; greater for intra-generational than for inter-generational mobility.[13]

Of greater interest in the present context are studies which focus attention upon structural sources of status discrepancies, rather than upon the psychological adjustment to the experiences which typically result from these discrepancies. For example, in a society in which there is a marked difference between the consumption patterns of the working class and the middle class, status discrepancies are more likely to arise from occupational mobility than in societies in which the consumption patterns of workers and middle-class persons are similar.[14] Unfortunately, only in the field of political values do we have comparative data on the differential consequences of social mobility. The data derived from a number of

TABLE 2
Party Choice of German, Finnish, Swedish, and American Middle-Class Men Related to Their Social Origin

Country and party choice	Father's occupation					
	Manual		Nonmanual		Farm	
	Per cent	Number in sample	Per cent	Number in sample	Per cent	Number in sample
Germany: 1953						
Social Democratic.........	32	200	20	142	22	58
Finland: 1949						
Social Democratic and						
Communist.............	23	357	6	356	10	183
Sweden: 1950						
Social Democratic.........	47	135	20	315	..	..
Norway: 1957						
Labor and Communist.....	49	61	29	73	24	46
United States: 1952						
Democratic..............	22	67	30	79	34	59

SOURCES: The German data are from a study made by UNESCO Institute at Cologne, Germany; the Finnish data were supplied by Dr. Erik Allerdt and were collected by the Finnish Gallup Poll; the Swedish data are from H. L. Zetterberg, "Overages Erlander?" *Vecko-Journalen*, 48 (1957): 18 and 36; the Norwegian figures are recomputed from data provided by the Oslo Institute for Social Research; the American data are from material supplied by the Survey Research Center of the University of Michigan.

European and American studies (table 2) indicate that in America the successfully mobile members of the middle class are more conservative (that is, more often Republican) than those class members who are in a social position comparable to that of their parents. In Germany, Finland, Norway, and Sweden, on the other hand, the former group is more radical (that is, more often Social Democratic or Communist).

The data from these five countries suggest that individuals moving up occupationally in Northern Europe where shifts from one class to another require major adjustments in living style are more likely than comparably successful Americans to retain links to their class of origin. In the United States there is also presumably less concern with personal background in much of the middle class, and more likelihood that the successful individual need only change his residential neighborhood to bring his economic and his social status into line. These findings seem related to variations in the working-class vote. In Germany and Sweden, the skilled workers are more radical than the semi- and unskilled; in America, Britain, and Australia, the skilled workers are

more conservative.[15] This leads us to the hypothesis that skilled workers experience more status rejection in these North European countries, so that their higher economic status results in frustrations, while the other countries mentioned may give the highly paid skilled worker more real opportunities to aspire to middle-class status. The differences between the working- and middle-class styles of life may also be an important factor, since in America it is presumably easier to take on middle-class consumption patterns. A suggestive indication that the retention of working-class political values by upward-mobile persons is related to other working-class elements in their style of life, is indicated by the following data (see table 3) from Sweden: white-collar workers who have risen from working-class backgrounds will generally continue to vote for the working-class party unless they change their style of consumption (symbolized here by the automobile); on assuming a middle-class consumption pattern, they also adopt the voting pattern of the middle class.

This attempt to interpret what little data we have on the consequences of upward mobility in different cultures rests on the unproven as-

TABLE 3

Relationship Between Social Origin, Consumption Patterns, and Voting Behavior Among Men in Sweden
(percentages)

Voting	Manual from manual homes		Nonmanual from manual homes		Nonmanual from nonmanual homes	
	Without car	With car	Without car	With car	Without car	With car
Non-Socialist.........	15	14	38	74	79	83
Socialist..............	85	86	63	26	21	17
Number in sample.....	221	72	78	55	170	145

SOURCE: From H. L. Zetterberg, "Overages Erlander?"

sumption that in Europe men who move up in the economic hierarchy find it difficult to adjust to the life style of higher levels, while in the United States men can more easily fulfill the requirements of the social position that corresponds to their economic success. . . .

Ideological Equalitarianism

The data presented in the preceding [section] raise questions about the validity of the widely-accepted belief that the United States is *the* land of opportunity. Yet how can we account for the persistence of the assumption that in this country the position of an individual's family is less likely to determine his social and economic destiny than in Europe? And how is this image related to patterns of social mobility? . . .

We can only speculate when we attempt to assess the effects of the absence of a feudal past in America. Clearly it has not meant the absence of status distinctions—which have frequently been every bit as invidious, though more surreptitiously introduced, on this side of the Atlantic as on the other. But it has led to, among other things, an ideological equalitarianism, which is not any the less important because it has been contradicted on every side by the existence of status differences. No act is perhaps as symbolic of this ideology as Thomas Jefferson's order to have a round table replace the rectangular one at the White

House because this would relieve him of the necessity of stipulating the order of precedence at official receptions. This act was not a denial of the existing differences in rank and authority; it was rather a testimony to the belief that these were the accidental, not the essential, attributes of man. Among men of equal worth it is not in good taste to insist on the accidental distinctions which divide them.

Such ideological equalitarianism has played, and continues to play, an important role in facilitating social mobility in the United States. It enables the person of humble birth to regard upward mobility as attainable for himself, or for his children. It facilitates his acceptance as a social equal if he succeeds in rising economically. It mitigates the emotional distance between persons of different social rank. And it fosters in any existing elite the persuasion (however mistaken this may be) that its eminence is the result of individual effort, and hence temporary. The point to emphasize is, not that these beliefs are often contradicted by the experience of those who hold them, but that this equalitarian ideology has persisted in the face of facts which contradict it. We would suggest that the absence of hereditary aristocracy has done much to foster this persistence. Americans have rarely been exposed to persons whose conduct displays a belief in an inherited and God-given superiority and also demands that others demonstrate (by deferential behavior) their recognition of this superiority.

The existence of ideological equalitarianism in the United States is generally acknowledged, but interpretations of its significance vary widely. One of these interpretations holds that this ideology is a delusion which must be dispelled by presenting the people with the hard facts of status differences. Accordingly, W. Lloyd Warner has called for systematic, explicit training to combat half-knowledge and confused emotions, in order that the adult student will learn "what he needs to know about our status order, how it operates, how he fits into the system, and what he should do to improve his position or make his present one more tolerable."[16] Whatever may be said of the usefulness of such studies, we find it difficult to believe that significant numbers of Americans are not aware of the existence of status differences. We doubt that instruction of the kind envisaged by Warner will have any notable effect upon the belief in equal opportunity. All the available evidence points, rather, to the fact that people continue to believe in the "equalitarianism" of American society despite their daily familiarity with economic inequality and status distinctions.

Another interpretation of ideological equalitarianism takes a much more optimistic view. In his great work on the American Negro, Gunnar Myrdal has pictured the dilemma which arises for every white American out of the profound contradiction between the theory of equal rights and the practice of racial segregation.[17] In the actions prompted by this deep moral conflict Myrdal sees the lever that can be used to bring about progressive social change. This too we find difficult to accept. It is our belief that *this* approach overemphasizes the urgency of a moral conflict. We would not deny that the conflict is present and that it has often led the way from equalitarian theory to equalitarian practice. Indeed, this conflict and its resultant social agitation is a mainspring of the American liberal tradition. Yet the available evidence indicates that the development of both the theory and the practice of "equalitarianism" among the white majority has been aided by the continued presence of large, ethnically segregated castes. That is, one of the reasons why the belief in this system has been sustained is because opportunities to rise socially and economically have been available to "majority-Americans," and a disproportionate share of poverty, unemployment, sickness and all forms of deprivation have fallen to the lot of minority groups, especially fifteen million Negro Americans.

Our own interpretation of "ideological equalitarianism" differs from these overpessimistic or overoptimistic views. We think that the equalitarianism of manners is not merely a matter of belief, but a reality: differences in status and power have no great effect upon the casual social contacts which set the tone of everyday human relations. This is linked to the fact that these differences have not been elaborated ideologically as they have in Europe. Surely this has not diminished these differences of status and power, but it has helped to prevent the ideological hardening of interest- and status-groups, so that the representation of collective interests is a thing apart from the intellectual life of the country. As a result, Americans frequently think of the differences of status and power, not as being what they really are, but rather as differences in the distribution of material goods. This well-known materialism of American society can also be thought of as an ideology—an ideology which purports to measure men by the single yardstick of material success. As such it is unlike the class and status ideologies of Europe; it involves instead quite an idealistic belief in equality, for all the differences in material status which it accentuates.

Such ideological equalitarianism implies an ideal which is best expressed by the familiar phrase, "equality of opportunity." It is conceivable that a people might adhere to such an ideal for some time even in the face of declining opportunities for occupational advancement. Some of the evidence concerning the response to the experience of the Great Depression suggests that the traditional belief in America as the land of opportunity imparted to people a spirit of resilience which helped to sustain them through great adversity.[18] However, it is our guess that *a sharp and lasting decline* in the opportunities for occupational advancement would jeopardize these beliefs and lead to a change in the system of values. Such a decline has not yet occurred.

Notes

1. See Colin Clark, *The Conditions of Economic Progress,* 3d ed. (London: Macmillan, 1957), pp. 490–520.

2. Werner Sombart, *Warum gibt es in den Vereinigten Staaten keinen Sozialismus?* (Tuebingen: J. C. B. Mohr, 1906), p. 135.

3. It may be noted, however, that Sombart also emphasized the subjective factor: "Consideration should also be given to the mere awareness of the worker that he could become an independent farmer at any time. This consciousness was bound to give the American worker a feeling of security and peace of mind which the European worker did not know. One can tolerate any coercive situation much more easily if one has at least the illusion that one could escape that situation if worse came to worst." *Ibid.,* p. 140. Such an awareness was, in Sombart's opinion, relatively independent of the actual number of workers who availed themselves of opportunities for upward mobility, though he did not develop this point further.

4. Reinhard Bendix, *Work and Authority in Industry* (New York: Wiley, 1956), pp. 211–226.

5. An exception is the big cities of Sweden in the earlier part of this century. However, data in the 1935 census indicate that differential fertility was at that time a characteristic of the nation as a whole.

6. Seymour M. Lipset and Reinhard Bendix, *Social Mobility in Industrial Society* (Berkeley and Los Angeles: University of California Press, 1964), chapter viii.

7. Martha E. Deeg and Donald G. Paterson, "Changes in the Social Status of Occupations," *Occupations,* 25 (1947): 205–208.

8. M. Janowitz and Deil Wright, "The Prestige of Public Employment: 1929 and 1954," *Public Administration Review,* 16 (1956): 15–21.

9. See S. M. Lipset and R. Bendix, *Social Mobility in Industrial Society,* chapters iii and iv.

10. C. Arnold Anderson, "The Social Status of University Students in Relation to Type of Economy: An International Comparison," in *Transactions of the Third World Congress of Sociology,* Vol. V (London: International Sociological Association, 1956), p. 57.

11. E. Durkheim, *Suicide* (Glencoe: The Free Press, 1951), pp. 246–254.

12. A. B. Hollingshead, R. Ellis, and E. Kirby, "Social Mobility and Mental Illness," *American Sociological Review,* 19 (1954): 577–584. A. B. Hollingshead and F. C. Redlich, "Schizophrenia and Social Structure," *American Journal of Psychiatry,* 110 (1954): 695–701. The possibility that the same factors cause social mobility that cause mental illness is suggested by Evelyn Ellis, "Social Psychological Correlates of Upward Social Mobility among Unmarried Career Women," *American Sociological Review,* 17 (1952): 558–563.

13. Morris Janowitz and Richard Curtis, "Sociological Consequences of Occupational Mobility in a U. S. Metropolitan Community," (Working Paper One submitted to the Fourth Working Conference on Social Stratification and Social Mobility, International Sociological Association, December, 1957).

14. See S. M. Lipset and R. Bendix, *Social Mobility in Industrial Society,* chapter iii.

15. See S. M. Lipset and J. Linz, *The Social Basis of Political Diversity* (Stanford: Center for Advanced Study in the Behavioral Sciences, 1956; mimeographed.) Data from the Swedish Gallup Poll for different Swedish elections, and from a 1953 study of German elections conducted by the UNESCO Institute at Cologne, and the 1957 study conducted by DIVO indicate that the better paid and higher skilled Swedish and German workers are much more likely to vote for the left parties than the lower paid and less skilled.

16. W. Lloyd Warner, *et al., Social Class in America* (Chicago: Science Research Associates, Inc., 1949), p. v. It is perhaps paradoxical that a theory of class which emphasizes reciprocal status evaluations, should, nevertheless, justify itself on these grounds. The very ambiguity of these evaluations is an important part of the evidence, and an approach that deliberately eliminates this ambiguity in the name of scientific accuracy may obscure this part of the evidence.

17. See G. Myrdal, *The American Dilemma* (New York: Harper, 1942).

18. See E. Wight Bakke, *The Unemployed Worker* (New Haven: Yale University Press, 1940), pp. 83–89, and by the same author, *Citizens Without Work* (New Haven: Yale University Press, 1940), pp. 66–68.

R A L P H   H .   T U R N E R

Sponsored and Contest Mobility and the School System

This paper suggests a framework for relating certain differences between American and English systems of education to the prevailing norms of upward mobility in each country. Others have noted the tendency of educational systems to support prevailing schemes of stratification, but this discussion concerns specifically the manner in which the *accepted mode of upward mobility* shapes the school system directly and indirectly through its effects on the values which implement social control.

Two ideal-typical normative patterns of upward mobility are described and their ramifications in the general patterns of stratification and social control are suggested. In addition to showing relationships among a number of differences between American and English schooling, the ideal-types have broader implications than those developed in this paper: they suggest a major dimension of stratification which might be profitably incorporated into a variety of studies in social class; and they readily can be applied in further comparisons between other countries.

The Nature of Organizing Norms

Many investigators have concerned themselves with rates of upward mobility in specific countries or internationally,[1] and with

the manner in which school systems facilitate or impede such mobility.[2] But preoccupation with the *extent* of mobility has precluded equal attention to the predominant *modes* of mobility. The central assumption underlying this paper is that within a formally open class system that provides for mass education the organizing folk norm which defines the accepted mode of upward mobility is a crucial factor in shaping the school system, and may be even more crucial than the extent of upward mobility. In England and the United States there appear to be different organizing folk norms, here termed *sponsored mobility* and *contest mobility,* respectively. *Contest* mobility is a system in which elite[3] status is the prize in an open contest and is taken by the aspirants' own efforts. While the "contest" is governed by some rules of fair play, the contestants have wide latitude in the strategies they may employ. Since the "prize" of successful upward mobility is not in the hands of an established elite to give out, the latter can not determine who shall attain it and who shall not. Under *sponsored* mobility elite recruits are chosen by the established elite or their agents, and elite status is *given* on the basis of some criterion of supposed merit and cannot be *taken* by any amount of effort or strategy. Upward mobility is like entry into a private club where each candidate must be "sponsored" by one or more of the members. Ultimately the members grant or deny upward mobility on the basis of whether they judge the candidate to have those qualities they wish to see in fellow members. . . .

Originally published in 1960. Please see complete source information beginning on page 891.

Social Control and the Two Norms

Every society must cope with the problem of maintaining loyalty to its social system and does so in part through norms and values, only some of which vary by class position. Norms and values especially prevalent within a given class must direct behavior into channels that support the total system, while those that transcend strata must support the general class differential. The way in which upward mobility takes place determines in part the kinds of norms and values that serve the indicated purposes of social control in each class and throughout the society.

The most conspicuous control problem is that of ensuring loyalty in the disadvantaged classes toward a system in which their members receive less than a proportional share of society's goods. In a system of contest mobility this is accomplished by a combination of futuristic orientation, the norm of ambition, and a general sense of fellowship with the elite. Each individual is encouraged to think of himself as competing for an elite position so that loyalty to the system and conventional attitudes are cultivated in the process of preparation for this possibility. It is essential that this futuristic orientation be kept alive by delaying a sense of final irreparable failure to reach elite status until attitudes are well established. By thinking of himself in the successful future the elite aspirant forms considerable identification with elitists, and evidence that they are merely ordinary human beings like himself helps to reinforce this identification as well as to keep alive the conviction that he himself may someday succeed in like manner. To forestall rebellion among the disadvantaged majority, then, a contest system must avoid absolute points of selection for mobility and immobility and must delay clear recognition of the realities of the situation until the individual is too committed to the system to change radically. A futuristic orientation cannot, of course, be inculcated successfully in all members of lower strata, but sufficient internalization of a norm of ambition tends to leave the unambitious as individual deviants

and to forestall the latters' formation of a genuine subcultural group able to offer collective threat to the established system. Where this kind of control system operates rather effectively it is notable that organized or gang deviancy is more likely to take the form of an attack upon the conventional or moral order rather than upon the class system itself. Thus the United States has its "beatniks"[4] who repudiate ambition and most worldly values and its delinquent and criminal gangs who try to evade the limitations imposed by conventional means,[5] but very few active revolutionaries.

These social controls are inappropriate in a system of sponsorship since the elite recruits are chosen from above. The principal threat to the system would lie in the existence of a strong group the members of whom sought to *take* elite positions themselves. Control under this system is maintained by training the "masses" to regard themselves as relatively incompetent to manage society, by restricting access to the skills and manners of the elite, and by cultivating belief in the superior competence of the elite. The earlier that selection of the elite recruits is made the sooner others can be taught to accept their inferiority and to make "realistic" rather than fantasy plans. Early selection prevents raising the hopes of large numbers of people who might otherwise become the discontented leaders of a class challenging the sovereignty of the established elite. If it is assumed that the difference in competence between masses and elite is seldom so great as to support the usual differences in the advantages accruing to each,[6] then the differences must be artificially augmented by discouraging acquisition of elite skills by the masses. Thus a sense of mystery about the elite is a common device for supporting in the masses the illusion of a much greater hiatus of competence than in fact exists.

While elitists are unlikely to reject a system that benefits them, they must still be restrained from taking such advantage of their favorable situation as to jeopardize the entire elite. Under the sponsorship system the elite recruits—who are selected early, freed from the strain of competitive struggle, and kept under close supervision—may be thoroughly indoctrinated in elite culture. A norm of paternalism toward inferiors may be inculcated, a heightened sensitivity to the good opinion of fellow elitists and elite recruits may be cultivated, and the appreciation of the more complex forms of aesthetic, literary, intellectual, and sporting activities may be taught. Norms of courtesy and altruism easily can be maintained under sponsorship since elite recruits are not required to compete for their standing and since the elite may deny high standing to those who strive for position by "unseemly" methods. The system of sponsorship provides an almost perfect setting for the development of an elite culture characterized by a sense of responsibility for "inferiors" and for preservation of the "finer things" of life.

Elite control in the contest system is more difficult since there is no controlled induction and apprenticeship. The principal regulation seems to lie in the insecurity of elite position. In a sense there is no "final arrival" because each person may be displaced by newcomers throughout his life. The limited control of high standing from above prevents the clear delimitation of levels in the class system, so that success itself becomes relative: each success, rather than an accomplishment, serves to qualify the participant for competition at the next higher level.[7] The restraints upon the behavior of a person of high standing, therefore, are principally those applicable to a contestant who must not risk the "ganging up" of other contestants, and who must pay some attention to the masses who are frequently in a position to impose penalties upon him. But any special norm of paternalism is hard to establish since there is no dependable procedure for examining the means by which one achieves elite credentials. While mass esteem is an effective brake upon over-exploitation of position, it rewards scrupulously ethical and altruistic behavior much less than evidence of fellow-feeling with the masses themselves.

Under both systems, unscrupulous or disreputable persons may become or remain members of the elite, but for different reasons. In contest mobility, popular tolerance of a little craftiness in the successful newcomer, together with the fact that he does not have to undergo the close scrutiny of the old elite, leaves considerable leeway for unscrupulous success. In sponsored mobility, the unpromising recruit reflects unfavorably on the judgments of his sponsors and threatens the myth of elite omniscience; consequently he may be tolerated and others may "cover up" for his deficiencies in order to protect the unified front of the elite to the outer world.

Certain of the general values and norms of any society reflect emulation of elite values by the masses. Under sponsored mobility, a good deal of the protective attitudes toward and interest in classical subjects percolates to the masses. Under contest mobility, however, there is not the same degree of homogeneity of moral, aesthetic, and intellectual values to be emulated, so that the conspicuous attribute of the elite is its high level of material consumption—emulation itself follows this course. There is neither effective incentive nor punishment for the elitist who fails to interest himself in promoting the arts or literary excellence, or who continues to maintain the vulgar manners and mode of speech of his class origin. The elite has relatively less power and the masses relatively more power to punish or reward a man for his adoption or disregard of any special elite culture. The great importance of accent and of grammatical excellence in the attainment of high status in England as contrasted with the twangs and drawls and grammatical ineptitude among American elites is the most striking example of this difference. In a contest system, the class order does not function to support the *quality* of aesthetic, literary, and intellectual activities; only those well versed in such matters are qualified to distinguish authentic products from cheap imitations. Unless those who claim superiority in these areas are forced to submit their credentials to the elite for evaluation, poor quality is often honored equally with high quality and class prestige does not serve to maintain an effective norm of high quality.

This is not to imply that there are no groups in a "contest" society devoted to the protection and fostering of high standards in art, music, literature, and intellectual pursuits, but that such standards lack the support of the class system which is frequently found when sponsored mobility prevails. In California, the selection by official welcoming committees of a torch singer to entertain a visiting king and queen and "can-can" dancers to entertain Mr. Khrushchev illustrates how American elites can assume that high prestige and popular taste go together.

Formal Education

Returning to the conception of an organizing ideal norm, we assume that to the extent to which one such norm of upward mobility is prevalent in a society there are constant strains to shape the educational system into conformity with that norm. These strains operate in two fashions: directly, by blinding people to alternatives and coloring their judgments of successful and unsuccessful solutions to recurring educational problems; indirectly, through the functional interrelationships between school systems and the class structure, systems of social control, and other features of the social structure which are neglected in this paper.

The most obvious application of the distinction between sponsored and contest mobility norms affords a partial explanation for the different policies of student selection in the English and American secondary schools. Although American high school students follow different courses of study and a few attend specialized schools, a major educational preoccupation has been to avoid any sharp social separation between the superior and inferior students and to keep the channels of movement between courses of study as open as possible. Recent criticisms of the way in which superior students may be thereby held back in their development usually are nevertheless qualified by the insistence that these students must not be withdrawn from the mainstream of student life.[8] Such segregation offends the sense of fairness implicit in the contest norm and also arouses the fear that the elite and future elite will lose their sense of fellowship with the masses. Perhaps the most important point, however, is that schooling is presented as an opportunity, and making use of it depends primarily on the student's own initiative and enterprise.

The English system has undergone a succession of liberalizing changes during this century, but all of them have retained the attempt to sort out early in the educational program the promising from the unpromising so that the former may be segregated and given a special form of training to fit them for higher standing in their adult years. Under the Education Act of 1944, a minority of students has been selected each year by means of a battery of examinations popularly known as "eleven plus," supplemented in varying degrees by grade school records and personal interviews, for admission to grammar schools.[9] The remaining students attend secondary modern or technical schools in which the opportunities to prepare for college or to train for the more prestigeful occupations are minimal. The grammar schools supply what by comparative standards is a high quality of college preparatory education. Of course, such a scheme embodies the logic of sponsorship, with early selection of those destined for middle-class and higher-status occupations, and specialized training to prepare each group for its destined class position. This plan facilitates considerable mobility, and recent research reveals surprisingly little bias against children from manual laboring-class families in the selection for grammar school, when related to measured intelligence.[10] It is altogether possible that adequate comparative study would show a closer correlation of school success with measured intelligence and a lesser correlation between school success and family background in England than in the United States. While selection of superior students for mobility opportunity is probably more efficient under such a system, the obstacles for persons not so selected of "making the grade" on the basis of their own initiative or enterprise are probably correspondingly greater. . . .

Effects of Mobility on Personality

Brief note may be made of the importance of the distinction between sponsored and contest mobility with relation to the supposed effects of upward mobility on personality development. Not a great deal is yet known about the "mobile personality" nor about the specific features of importance to the personality in the mobility experience.[11] However, today three aspects of this experience are most frequently stressed: first, the stress or tension involved in striving for status higher than that of others under more difficult conditions than they; second, the complication of interpersonal relations introduced by the necessity to abandon lower-level friends in favor of uncertain acceptance into higher-level circles; third, the problem of working out an adequate personal scheme of values in the face of movement between classes marked by somewhat variant or even contradictory value systems.[12] The impact of each of these three mobility problems, it is suggested, differ depending upon whether the pattern is that of the contest or of sponsorship.

Under the sponsorship system, recruits are selected early, segregated from their class peers, grouped with other recruits and with youth from the class to which they are moving, and trained specifically for membership in this class. Since the selection is made early, the mobility experience should be relatively free from the strain that comes with a series of elimination tests and long-extended uncertainty of success. The segregation and the integrated group life of the "public" school or grammar school should help to clarify the mobile person's social ties. (One investigator failed to discover clique formation along lines of social class in a sociometric study of a number of grammar schools.[13]) The problem of a system of values may be largely met when the elite recruit is taken from his parents and peers to be placed in a boarding school, though it may be less well clarified for the grammar school boy who returns each evening to his working-class family. Undoubtedly this latter limitation has something to do

with the observed failure of working-class boys to continue through the last years of grammar school and into the universities.[14] In general, then, the factors stressed as affecting personality formation among the upwardly mobile probably are rather specific to the contest system, or to incompletely functioning sponsorship system.

Notes

This is an expanded version of a paper presented at the Fourth World Congress of Sociology, 1959, and abstracted in the *Transactions* of the Congress. Special indebtedness should be expressed to Jean Floud and Hilde Himmelweit for helping to acquaint the author with the English school system.

1. A comprehensive summary of such studies appears in Seymour M. Lipset and Reinhard Bendix, *Social Mobility in Industrial Society*, Berkeley and Los Angeles: University of California Press, 1959.

2. *Cf.* C. A. Anderson, "The Social Status of University Students in Relation to Type of Economy: An International Comparison," *Transactions of the Third World Congress of Sociology*, London, 1956, Vol. V, pp. 51–63; J. E. Floud, *Social Class and Educational Opportunity*, London: Heinemann, 1956; W. L. Warner, R. J. Havighurst, and M. B. Loeb, *Who Shall Be Educated?* New York: Harper, 1944.

3. Reference is made throughout the paper to "elite" and "masses." The generalizations, however, are intended to apply throughout the stratification continuum to relations between members of a given class and the class or classes above it. Statements about mobility are intended in general to apply to mobility from manual to middle-class levels, lower-middle to upper-middle class, and so on, as well as into the strictly elite groups. The simplified expressions avoid the repeated use of cumbersome and involved statements which might otherwise be required.

4. See, e.g., Lawrence Lipton, *The Holy Barbarians*, New York: Messner, 1959.

5. *Cf.* Albert K. Cohen, *Delinquent Boys: The Culture of the Gang*, Glencoe, Ill.: Free Press, 1955.

6. D. V. Glass, editor, *Social Mobility in Britain*, Glencoe, Ill.: Free Press, 1954, pp. 144–145, reports studies showing only small variations in intelligence between occupational levels.

7. Geoffrey Gorer, *The American People*, New York: Norton, 1948, pp. 172–187.

8. See, e.g., *Los Angeles Times,* May 4, 1959, Part I, p. 24.

9. The nature and operation of the "eleven plus" system are fully reviewed in a report by a committee of the British Psychological Society and in a report of extensive research into the adequacy of selection methods. See P. E. Vernon, editor, *Secondary School Selection: A British Psychological Inquiry,* London: Methuen, 1957; and Alfred Yates and D. A. Pidgeon, *Admission to Grammar Schools,* London: Newnes Educational Publishing Co., 1957.

10. J. E. Floud, A. H. Halsey, and F. M. Martin, *Social Class and Educational Opportunity,* London: Heinemann, 1956.

11. *Cf.* Lipset and Bendix, *op. cit.,* pp. 250 ff.

12. See, e.g., August B. Hollingshead and Frederick C. Redlich, *Social Class and Mental Illness,* New York: Wiley, 1958; W. Lloyd Warner and James C. Abegglen, *Big Business Leaders in America,* New York: Harper, 1955; Warner *et al., Who Shall be Educated?, op. cit.;* Peter M. Blau, "Social Mobility and Interpersonal Relations," *American Sociological Review,* 21 (June, 1956), pp. 290–300.

13. A. N. Oppenheim, "Social Status and Clique Formation among Grammar School Boys," *British Journal of Sociology,* 6 (September, 1955), pp. 228–245. Oppenheim's findings may be compared with A. B. Hollingshead, *Elmtown's Youth,* New York: Wiley, 1949, pp. 204–242. See also Joseph A. Kahl, *The American Class Structure,* New York: Rinehart, 1957, pp. 129–138.

14. Floud *et al., op. cit.,* pp. 115 ff.

DAVID L. FEATHERMAN AND ROBERT M. HAUSER

A Refined Model of Occupational Mobility

In this [article] we describe and apply a log-linear model of the mobility table. . . . The model permits us to locate groups or clusters of cells in the classification that share similar chances of mobility or immobility, freed of the confounding influences of the relative numbers of men in each origin or destination category and of changes in those relative numbers between origin and destination distributions.

By modeling the mobility table in this way we obtain new insights into the process of mobility, changes in that process, and the interactions of the mobility process with changes in the occupational structure within one mobility classification or between two or more mobility classifications. For example, we take a fresh look at the differing tendencies toward immobility in the several occupational strata, at the existence of "class" boundaries limiting certain types of mobility, at differences in upward and downward exchanges between occupational strata, and at differences among strata in the dispersion of recruitment and supply. In these purposes our analysis parallels Blau and Duncan's treatment of manpower flows (1967:Chap. 2; also, see Blau, 1965).

Several sociologists have recently drawn attention to relationships between occupational mobility and class formation, for example, Giddens (1973), Parkin (1971), and Westergaard and Resler (1975). Goldthorpe and Llewellyn (1977) have critically reviewed these and related works in light of British mobility data collected in 1972. It would be easy to identify our present analytic interests with those of the class theorists, but we think such an inference unwarranted.

Although we are attempting a description of the mobility regime that is free of the distributions of occupational origins and destinations, we believe with Goldthorpe and Llewellyn that the class theorists are attempting to interpret what [might be] termed the gross flows of manpower. For the American case we have already described those flows [see Featherman and Hauser (1978:Chapter 3)], and our interest now centers on the net or underlying patterns of association in the mobility table.

We have approached the mobility table without strong theoretical presuppositions about affinities among occupational strata. Like Blau and Duncan, we have worked inductively, but our more refined analytic tools have led to substantively different conclusions than theirs about the major features of the mobility process in the United States.

Some readers may find the following discussion excessively technical, but we have tried to minimize the presentation of methodological detail. We have tried to avoid describing the methods by which empirical spec-

Originally published in 1978. Please see complete source information beginning on page 891.

ifications of the mobility table may be explored, although we believe these are interesting in their own right. We have focused on the rationale and interpretation of our model, including comparisons with other ways of looking at the mobility table that seem likely to elucidate the properties of the model.

Mobility Models

The record of sociological mobility studies is paralleled by a history of statistical analysis in which occupational mobility has often served as stimulus, object, or illustration of statistical ideas (for example, see Pearson, 1904; Chessa, 1911; Rogoff, 1953; Glass, 1954; Goodman, 1961, 1968, 1969a, 1972c; Tyree, 1973; White, 1963, 1970a; Singer and Spilerman, 1976). Indeed, it is consistent with the historical pattern that sociologists were introduced to the method of path analysis primarily by way of its successful application in studies of occupational mobility (Duncan and Hodge, 1963; Blau and Duncan, 1967). Devices for the statistical analysis of mobility data range from simple descriptive measures to complex analytic schemes. We make no systematic effort to review these measures and models, for there are several recent and comprehensive reviews (Boudon, 1973; Pullum, 1975; Bibby, 1975). We focus almost exclusively on multiplicative (loglinear) representations of the occupational mobility table. In so doing we do not intend to suggest that other methods and approaches are inferior, but to exploit features of the loglinear model that seem interesting and fruitful. . . .

In a series of papers, Goodman (1963, 1965, 1968, 1969a, 1969b, 1972c) developed and exposited methods for the analysis of contingency tables (including mobility tables) in which the significant interactions were localized in specified cells or sets of cells in the table (also, see Pullum, 1975). For example, in the case of highly aggregated (3 × 3 or 5 × 5) mobility tables Goodman showed that most of the interaction pertained to cells on or near the main diagonal (when the occupa-

tion categories of origin and destination were listed in order of increasing status). White (1963, 1970b) has made essentially the same suggestion, but some aspects of his models and methods are less appealing. Goodman (1965, 1969a) proposed that the analyst ignore or "blank out" those cells where interaction was greatest (where frequencies were thought to be especially dense or especially sparse) and attempt to fit a modified model of statistical independence, termed "quasi-independence," to the remaining frequencies in the table. In the case where only diagonal cells were blanked out in a mobility table, Goodman called the model one of "quasi-perfect mobility," after the term "perfect mobility," which had earlier been applied to the model of statistical independence in a mobility table. For an early application of this model to a large (17 × 17) table see Blau and Duncan (1967:64–67). Goodman (1965, 1968, 1969a) noted that quasi-independence might hold over all cells in a table whose entries were not ignored, or it might hold within, but not between certain subsets of cells whose entries were not ignored. . . .

Models of quasi-independence have provided important insights into the structure of mobility tables. Aside from Goodman's expository papers, they have been applied in cross-national, interurban, and cross-temporal analyses (Iutaka et al., 1975; Featherman et al., 1975; Pullum, 1975; Hauser et al., 1975; Ramsøy, 1977; Goldthorpe et al., 1978). Goodman (1969a) also has shown how related ideas may be supplied to test any specific hypothesis about the pattern of association in a mobility table.

At the same time the application of quasi-independence models in mobility analysis has been less than satisfying in some ways. Even where large numbers of cells are blocked, quasi-independence models do not fit large tables very well (Pullum, 1975; Hauser et al., 1975). That is, when mobility data are not highly aggregated, it appears that association is not limited to the small number of cells on or near the main diagonal. The larger the number of entries blocked (or fitted exactly) before a good fit is obtained, the less substantively appealing is the model of quasi-independence. Moreover, by treating departures from quasi-independence in the blocked or ignored cells as parameters or indices of mobility and departures in the unblocked cells as error, the quasi-independence model attaches too much theoretical importance to occupational inheritance (Hope, 1976). Of course, occupational inheritance is always defined by reference to a given classification of occupations, and the problem is exacerbated by the fact that the model of quasi-independence fits best when the mobility table is based on broad occupation groups. The model is of greatest validity in the measurement of immobility in classifications where the concept of occupational inheritance becomes vague.

The focus on fit on or near the main diagonal follows a traditional sociological interest in occupational inheritance, but it also draws our attention away from other aspects of association in the table. For example, one might hypothesize that certain types of mobility are as prevalent as other types of mobility or immobility. More generally, one might wish to construct a parametric model of mobility and immobility for the full table that would recognize the somewhat arbitrary character of occupational inheritance and the possible gradations of association throughout the table.

Goodman's (1972c) general multiplicative model of mobility tables and other cross-classifications substantially advanced the sophistication and precision of mobility analysis. For example, Goodman proposed and applied to the classic British and Danish mobility data a number of alternative specifications, all but two of which—the simple independence model and that of quasi-perfect mobility—assumed ordinality in the occupational categories. The models incorporated combinations of parameters for upward and downward mobility, for the number of boundaries crossed, and for barriers to crossing particular categoric boundaries. Many of these models—as well as problems in comparing their goodness of fit—are reviewed by Bishop *et*

al. (1975:Chaps. 5, 8, 9), and some of the same models are discussed by Haberman (1974:Chap. 6). Applying Goodman's (1972c) general model we take a slightly different approach in developing models of the mobility table. Elsewhere, Hauser (1978) has applied this approach in an analysis of the classic British mobility table, and Baron (1977) has used it in a reanalysis of Rogoff's (1953) Indianapolis data.

A Refined Multiplicative Model of the Mobility Table[1]

Let x_{ij} be the observed frequency in the ijth cell of the classification of men by their own occupations ($j = 1,\ldots,J$) and their own occupations or fathers' occupations at an earlier time ($i = 1,\ldots,I$). In the context of mobility analysis the same categories will appear in rows and columns, and the table will be square with $I = J$. For $k = 1,\ldots,K$, let H_k be a mutually exclusive and exhaustive partition of the pairs (i, j) in which

$$E[x_{ij}] = m_{ij} = \alpha\beta_i\gamma_j\delta_{ij} \qquad (1)$$

where $\delta_{ij} = \delta_k$ for $(i, j) \in H_k$, subject to the normalization $\prod_i\beta_i = \prod_i\gamma_j = \prod_i\prod_j\delta_{ij} = 1$. The normalization of parameters is a matter of convenience, and we choose the value of so that it will hold. Note that, unlike the usual set-up, the interaction effects are not constrained within rows or columns although the marginal frequencies are fixed. The model says the expected frequencies are a product of an overall effect (α), a row effect (β_i), a column effect (γ_j), and an interaction effect (δ_{ij}). The row and column parameters represent conditions of occupational supply and demand; they reflect demographic replacement processes and past and present technologies and economic conditions. The cells (i, j) are assigned to K mutually exclusive and exhaustive levels, and each of those levels shares a common interaction parameter δ_k. Thus, aside from total, row, and column effects, each expected frequency is determined by only one parameter, which reflects the level of mobility or immobility in that cell relative to that in other cells in the table.

The interaction parameters of the model correspond directly to our notions of variations in the density of observations (White, 1963:26). Unlike several models fitted by Goodman (1972c), this model does not assume ordinal measurement of occupations. Of course, the assumption of ordinality may help us interpret results, or our findings may be used to explore the metric properties of our occupational classification. For the model to be informative, the distribution of levels across the cells of the table must form a meaningful pattern, and one in which the parameters are identified (Mason *et al.*, 1973; Haberman, 1974: 217). Furthermore, the number of levels (K) should be substantially less than the number of cells in the table. These latter properties are partly matters of substantive and statistical interpretation and judgment, rather than characteristics of the model or of the data. We have found it difficult to interpret models where the number of levels is much greater than the number of categories recognized in the occupational classification. . . .

Mobility to First Jobs: An Illustration

Table 1 gives frequencies in a classification of son's first, full-time civilian occupation by father's (or other family head's) occupation at the son's sixteenth birthday among American men who were ages 20–64 in 1973 and were not currently enrolled in school.[2] Table 2 gives the design matrix of a model for the data of Table 1. Each numerical entry in the body of the table gives the level of H_k to which the corresponding entry in the frequency table was assigned. Formally, the entries are merely labels, but, for convenience in interpretation, the numerical values are inverse to the estimated density of mobility or immobility in the cells to which they refer.

On this understanding the design says that, aside from conditions of supply and demand, immobility is highest in farm occupations (Level 1) and next highest in the upper non-

manual category (Level 2). If we take the occupation groups as ranked from high to low in the order listed, we may say that there are zones of high and almost uniform density bordering the peaks at either end of the status distribution. There is one zone of high density that includes upward or downward movements between the two nonmanual groups and immobility in the lower nonmanual group. Mobility from lower to upper nonmanual occupations (Level 3) is more likely than the opposite movement, and the latter is as likely as stability in the lower nonmanual category (Level 4). Moreover, the densities of immobility in the lower nonmanual category and of downward mobility to it are identical to those in the second zone of relatively high density, which occurs at the lower end of the occupational hierarchy. The second zone includes movements from the farm to the lower manual group and back as well as immobility in the lower manual group. Last, there is a broad zone of relatively low density (Level 5) that includes immobility in the upper manual category, upward and downward mobility within the manual stratum, mobility between upper manual and farm groups, and all movements between nonmanual and either manual or farm groups. The design says that an upper manual worker's son is equally likely to be immobile or to move to the bottom or top of the occupational distribution; obversely, it says that an upper manual worker is equally likely to have been recruited from any location in the occupational hierarchy, including his own. Also, it is worth noting that four of the five density levels recognized in the model occur along the main diagonal, and two of these (Levels 4 and 5) are assigned both to diagonal and off-diagonal cells.

With a single exception the design is symmetric. That is, the upward and downward flows between occupations are assigned to the same density levels, except mobility from lower to upper nonmanual strata (Level 3) exceeds that from upper to lower nonmanual strata (Level 4). This asymmetry in the design is striking because it suggests the power of upper white-collar families to block at least one

TABLE 1

Frequencies in a Classification of Mobility from Father's (or Other Family Head's) Occupation to Son's First Full-Time Civilian Occupation: U.S. Men Aged 20–64 in March 1973

Father's occupation	Son's occupation					
	Upper nonmanual	Lower nonmanual	Upper manual	Lower manual	Farm	Total
Upper nonmanual	1414	521	302	643	40	2920
Lower nonmanual	724	524	254	703	48	2253
Upper manual	798	648	856	1676	108	4086
Lower manual	756	914	771	3325	237	6003
Farm	409	357	441	1611	1832	4650
Total	4101	2964	2624	7958	2265	19,912

NOTE: Frequencies are based on observations weighted to estimate population counts and compensate for departures of the sampling design from simple random sampling (see Featherman and Hauser [1978: Appendix B]). Broad occupation groups are upper nonmanual: professional and kindred workers, managers and officials, and non-retail sales workers; lower nonmanual: proprietors, clerical and kindred workers, and retail salesworkers; upper manual: craftsmen, foremen and kindred workers; lower manual: service workers, operatives and kindred workers, and laborers, except farm; farm: farmers and farm managers, farm laborers and foremen.

TABLE 2

Asymmetric 5-Level Model of Mobility from Father's Occupation to First Full-Time Civilian Occupation

Father's occupation	Son's occupation				
	(1)	(2)	(3)	(4)	(5)
1. Upper nonmanual	2	4	5	5	5
2. Lower nonmanual	3	4	5	5	5
3. Upper manual	5	5	5	5	5
4. Lower manual	5	5	5	4	4
5. Farm	5	5	5	4	1

NOTE: Broad occupation groups are upper nonmanual: professional and kindred workers, managers and officials, and non-retail sales workers; lower nonmanual: proprietors, clerical and kindred workers, and retail sales-workers; upper manual: craftsmen, foremen and kindred workers; lower manual: service workers, operatives and kindred workers, and laborers, except farm; farm: farmers and farm managers, farm laborers and foremen.

type of status loss and because it is the *only* asymmetry in the design. For example, Blau and Duncan (1967:58–67) suggest that there are semipermeable class boundaries separating white-collar, blue-collar, and farm occupations, which permit upward mobility but inhibit downward mobility. The only asymmetry in the present design occurs *within* one of the broad classes delineated by Blau and Duncan.

Overall, the design resembles a river valley in which two broad plains are joined by a narrow strip of land between two great peaks. The contours of the peaks differ in that the one forming one side of the valley is both taller and more nearly symmetric than that forming the other side. This representation appears in Figure 1.

In some respects, this design matrix parallels Levine's (1967:Chap. 4) description of the surface of the British mobility table as a saddle (also see Levine, 1972). However, our interpretation is more extreme, since the density reaches an absolute minimum in the center of the table, not merely a minimum among the diagonal cells. In this way our model for the American 5 × 5 table is closer to Goodman's (1969a:38, 1969b:846) conclusion that a British 5 × 5 table shows "status disinheritance" in the middle category. We show elsewhere (Featherman and Hauser, 1978) that Levine's interpretation of the British data is based on a confounding of marginal effects and interactions which parallels that entailed in the use of mobility ratios, even though Levine did not use mobility ratios.

The model of Table 2 provides less than a complete description of the mobility data in Table 1. Under the model of statistical independence we obtain a likelihood-ratio statistic, $G^2 = 6167.7$, which is asymptotically distributed as χ^2 with 16 *df*. With the model of Table 2 as null hypothesis we obtain $G^2 =$

FIGURE 1

Volume of mobility from father's occupation to first full-time civilian occupation: U.S. men aged 20–64 in March 1973. The base is a unit square, and the total volume under the surface is one. Length and breadth can be read as probabilities, and height is proportionate to probability. The vertical scale has been compressed by a factor of 10.

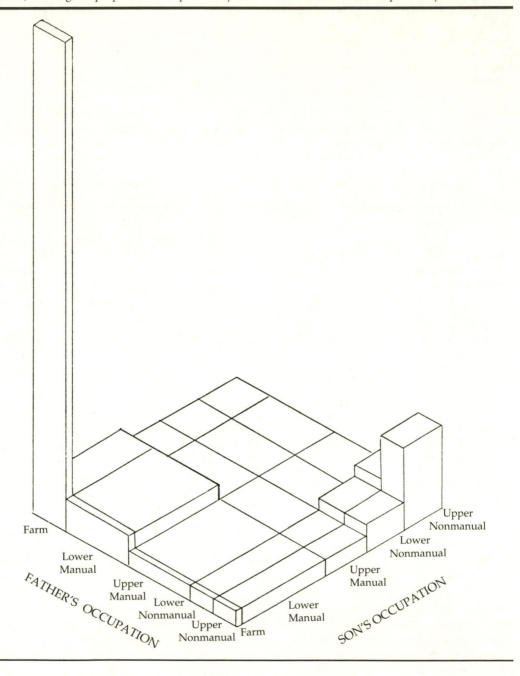

66.5 with 12 *df,* since we lose 4 *df* in creating the five categories of *H.* Clearly the model does not fit, if we take the probability associated with the test statistic as our only guide. On the other hand the model does account for 98.9% of the association in the data, that is, of the value of G^2 under independence. Given the extraordinarily large sample size we might expect small departures from frequencies predicted by the model to be statistically significant. . . .

The measures of fit we have examined have told us nothing about the several parameters of the model. That is, we have not shown that our suggested interpretation of the design matrix (Table 2) is substantively appealing, or even that the design correctly sorts the cells of the mobility table into zones of high and low density. Certainly, we want to look at the way in which the model fits and interprets the data as well as at deviations from fitted values.

The upper panel of Table 3 shows the row, column, and level parameters estimated under the model of Table 2 for mobility in the 1973 data from father's (or head's) occupation at son's sixteenth birthday to son's first full-time civilian occupation. The parameters are expressed in additive form, that is, they are effects on logs of frequencies under the model of Eq. (1). The row and column parameters clearly show an intergenerational shift out of farming and into white-collar or lower blue-collar occupations. Of course these parameters reflect a number of factors, including temporal shifts in the distribution of the labor force across occupations, differential fertility, and life cycle differences in occupational positions. The level parameters show very large differences in mobility and immobility across the several cells of the classification, and these differences closely follow our interpretation of the design matrix. Differences between level parameters may readily be interpreted as differences in logs of frequencies, net of row and column effects. For example, the estimates say that immobility in farm occupations is 3.40 = 3.044 − (−.356) greater (in the metric of logged frequencies) than the estimated mobility or immobility in cells assigned

to Level 5 in the design matrix. In multiplicative terms, immobility in farm occupations is $e^{3.40} = 29.96$ times greater than mobility or immobility at Level 5. It would be incorrect to attach too much importance to the signs of the level parameters as reported in Table 3, for they simply reflect our normalization rule that level parameters sum to zero (in the log-frequency metric) across the cells of the table. For example, while the parameters for Levels 4 and 5 each reflect relatively low densities, it is not clear that either parameter indicates "status disinheritance" in the diagonal cells to which it pertains (compare Goodman, 1969a, 1969b).

In any event the parameters do show a sharp density gradient across the levels of the design. The smallest difference, between Levels 3 and 4, indicates a relative density $e^{.549-.243} = e^{.306} = 1.36$ times as great at Level 3 than at Level 4. The heterogeneity of Level 5 is indicated by the fact that the difference in density between Levels 3 and 4 is about as large as the range of residuals within Level 5. Immobility in farm occupations and in upper nonmanual occupations is quite distinct from densities at other levels, but also immobility in the farm occupations is $e^{3.044-1.234} = e^{1.810} = 6.11$ times as great as in the upper nonmanual occupations.

We can write the sample counterpart of Eq. (1) as

$$\hat{m}_{ij} = \hat{\alpha}\hat{\beta}_i\hat{\gamma}_j\hat{\delta}_{ij}. \tag{2}$$

Recalling that

$$e_{ij} = x_{ij} / \hat{m}_{ij}, \tag{3}$$

we substitute Eq. (2) into (3) and rearrange terms to obtain

$$x_{ij} = \hat{\alpha}\hat{\beta}_i\hat{\gamma}_j\hat{\delta}_{ij}e_{ij}. \tag{4}$$

We divide both sides of Eq. (4) by the first three terms on the right-hand side to obtain

$$R^*_{ij} = \frac{x_{ij}}{\hat{\alpha}\hat{\beta}_i\hat{\gamma}_j} = \hat{\delta}_{ij}e_{ij}. \tag{5}$$

TABLE 3

Parameters and Residuals (in Additive Form) from Main, Row, and Column Effects in the Model of Table 2: Mobility from Father's (or Other Family Head's) Occupation to Son's First Full-Time Civilian Occupation, U.S. Men Aged 20–64 in March 1973

A. Additive parameters

	Category of row, column, or level				
Design factor	(1)	(2)	(3)	(4)	(5)
Rows (father's occupation)	−.466	−.451	.495	.570	−.148
Columns (son's occupation)	.209	.190	.240	1.020	−1.660
Levels (density)	3.044	1.234	.549	.243	−.356

Grand mean = 6.277

B. Level parameter plus residual (log R_{ij}^{*})

	Son's occupation				
Father's occupation	(1)	(2)	(3)	(4)	(5)
1. Upper nonmanual	1.23	.25	−.34	−.36	−.45
2. Lower nonmanual	.55	.25	−.53	−.29	−.29
3. Upper manual	−.30	−.49	−.26	−.37	−.43
4. Lower manual	−.43	−.22	−.44	.24	.28
5. Farm	−.32	−.44	−.28	.24	3.04

NOTE: See text for explanation.

We shall call R_{ij}^{*} the new mobility ratio, or, simply, the mobility ratio. In the case of diagonal cells R_{ij}^{*} is equivalent to the new immobility ratio proposed by Goodman (1969a,b, 1972c; also, see Pullum, 1975:7–8), but we suggest the ratio be computed for all cells of the table as an aid both to substantive interpretation and to the evaluation of model design.

The lower panel of Table 3 gives logs of the new mobility ratios for the model of Table 2 fitted to the classification of mobility to first jobs. While the entries in this panel depend on our specification of the model, neither need that specification rigidly govern our interpretation of the relative densities. Obviously, the pattern of relative densities does conform substantially to our earlier description of the design. The fit is good enough so there is no overlap in densities across levels recognized in the design, and all of the negative entries are neatly segregated in Level 5 of the design. If immobility among skilled workers—in cell (3, 3)—is high relative to mobility in other cells at Level 5, it is still clear that the immo-

bility in that category is substantially less than the immobility in any other occupation group. . . .

Mobility Chances: A New Perspective

As an alternative to the Blau-Duncan interpretation, we think our multiplicative models yield a cogent and parsimonious description of occupational mobility among American men. Unlike its precursor, our description does not reflect the shape of occupational distributions of origin or destination, but only the underlying patterns of immobility and exchange between occupational strata. It may be useful here to review the major features of this description that appear in mobility between generations and within the occupational career. In doing so, of course, we do some injustice to details reported in the preceding analysis.

First, there is great immobility at the top and at the bottom of the occupational hierarchy, here represented by upper nonmanual and by farm occupations, respectively. This immobility is far more extreme than has heretofore been supposed by most students of the mobility process; it may even be consistent with the beliefs of the more extreme critics of rigidity in the American class structure.

Second, surrounding the extremes of the occupational hierarchy at both top and bottom are transitional zones, within which there are relatively homogeneous chances of immobility and of exchange with adjacent extreme strata.

Third, taken as aggregates the extreme and transitional zones of the occupational hierarchy are relatively closed both to upward and to downward movements. That is, there are sharp breaks between the density of observations within the extreme and transitional zones and the density of mobility beyond those zones. In this sense (but not in others) we may say that the data suggest the existence of barriers to movement across class boundaries.

Fourth, once the boundaries of the transitional zones have been crossed, no social distance gradient seems to underly variations in long-distance mobility chances. These are surprisingly uniform, and observed variations in them show no consistent pattern.

Fifth, if immobility is very great at the extremes of the occupational hierarchy, it is almost nonexistent in the middle of the hierarchy. Contrary to widespread belief, men of upper blue-collar origin are about as likely to end up anywhere higher or lower in the occupational hierarchy as in their stratum of origin. Obversely, upper blue-collar workers are about as likely to have originated anywhere higher or lower in the occupational hierarchy as in their stratum of destination. Those who would find their beliefs about "class" rigidity confirmed by our estimates of immobility at the extremes of the occupational hierarchy must reconcile these with our finding that between generations immobility in upper manual occupations is no more prevalent than most types of extreme, long-distance mobility. There is no evidence of "class" boundaries limiting the chances of movement to or from the skilled manual occupations.

Sixth, there is a rough equality in the propensities to move in one direction or the other between occupational strata. There are several exceptions to this symmetric mobility pattern, some of which may be quite important, but none suggests a dominant tendency toward upward relative to downward mobility across or within class boundaries.

Last, from a methodological perspective, our description of the mobility regime is extremely simple. In broad outline it might be fitted to a 5×5 table with the expenditure of as few as 2 *df*. None of our analyses of American mobility tables required the expenditure of more than 6 of the 16 *df* left unused by the model of simple statistical independence.

We reemphasize that the present description of relative mobility chances does not conflict in any way with our earlier description (Featherman and Hauser 1978:Chapter 3) of occupational inflow and outflow patterns. Rather, relative mobility chances are components of inflows and outflows, but the latter are also affected by distributions of occupational origins and destinations. Major features of the inflow and outflow tables, like the pervasiveness of upward mobility between generations and within the occupational career, are absent from the present account because they are functions of changing distributions of occupational origins and destinations.

Notes

1. We assume the familiarity of the reader with loglinear models for frequency data. Fienberg (1970a, 1977) and Goodman (1972a,b) give useful introductions, as does the comprehensive treatise by Bishop *et al.* (1975). We rely heavily on methods for the analysis of incomplete tables, which have been developed by Goodman (1963, 1965, 1968, 1969a,b, 1971, 1972c), Bishop and Fienberg (1969), Fienberg (1970b, 1972), and Mantel (1970); again, Bishop *et al.* (1975, especially pp. 206–211, 225–228, 282–309, 320–324) is valuable. Our model is a special case of Goodman's (1972c) general model.

2. The reported frequencies are based on a complex sampling design and have been weighted to es-

timate population counts while compensating for certain types of survey nonresponse. The estimated population counts have been scaled down to reflect underlying sample frequencies, and an additional downward adjustment was made to compensate for departures of the sampling design from simple random sampling (see Featherman and Hauser [1978:Appendix B]). The frequency estimates in Table 1 have been rounded to the nearest integer, but our computations have been based on unrounded figures. We treat the adjusted frequencies as if they had been obtained under simple random sampling.

Bibliography

Baron, James N. 1977. "The structure of intergenerational occupational mobility: Another look at the Indianapolis mobility data." Unpublished masters thesis, University of Wisconsin—Madison.

Bibby, John. 1975. "Methods of measuring mobility." *Quality and Quantity* 9 (March): 107–136.

Bishop, Yvonne M. M., and Stephen E. Fienberg. 1969. "Incomplete two-dimensional contingency tables." *Biometrics* 25:119–128.

Bishop, Yvonne M. M., Stephen E. Fienberg, and Paul W. Holland. 1975. *Discrete Multivariate Analysis: Theory and Practice.* Cambridge: M.I.T. Press.

Blau, Peter M. 1965. "The flow of occupational supply and recruitment." *American Sociological Review* 30 (August):475–490.

Blau, Peter M., and Otis Dudley Duncan. 1967. *The American Occupational Structure.* New York: Wiley.

Boudon, Raymond. 1973. *Mathematical Structure of Social Mobility.* San Francisco: Jossey-Bass.

Chessa, Frederico. 1911. *La Trasmissione Erediteria delle Professioni.* Torino: Fratelli Bocca.

Duncan, Otis Dudley, and Robert W. Hodge. 1963. "Education and occupational mobility." *American Journal of Sociology* 68 (May): 629–644.

Featherman, David L., and Robert M. Hauser. 1978. *Opportunity and Change.* New York: Academic Press.

Featherman, David L., F. Lancaster Jones, and Robert M. Hauser. 1975. "Assumptions of social mobility research in the United States: the case of occupational status." *Social Science Research* 4:329–360.

Fienberg, Stephen E. 1970a. "The analysis of multidimensional contingency tables." *Ecology* 51:419–433.

———. 1970b. "Quasi-independence and maximum likelihood estimation in incomplete contingency tables." *Journal of the American Statistical Association* 65:1610–1616.

———. 1972. "The analysis of incomplete multiway contingency tables." *Biometrics* 23 (March):177–202.

———. 1977. *The Analysis of Cross-Classified Categorical Data.* Cambridge: M.I.T. Press.

Giddens, Anthony. 1973. *The Class Structure of the Advanced Societies.* New York: Harper and Row.

Glass, D. B. 1954. *Social Mobility in Britain.* London: Routledge and Kegan Paul.

Goldthorpe, John W., and Catriona Llewellyn. 1977. "Class mobility in modern Britain: three theses examined." *Sociology* 11 (May): 257–287.

Goldthorpe, John W., Clive Payne, and Catriona Llewellyn. 1978. "Trends in class mobility." *Sociology* 12 (September):441–468.

Goodman, Leo A. 1961. "Statistical methods for the mover-stayer model." *Journal of the American Statistical Association* 56 (December):841–868.

———. 1963. "Statistical methods for the preliminary analysis of transaction flows." *Econometrica* 31 (January):197–208.

———. 1965. "On the statistical analysis of mobility tables." *American Journal of Sociology* 70 (March):564–585.

———. 1968. "The analysis of cross-classified data: independence, quasi-independence, and interaction in contingency tables with or without missing entries." *Journal of the American Statistical Association* 63 (December): 1091–1131.

———. 1969a. "How to ransack social mobility tables and other kinds of cross-classification tables." *American Journal of Sociology* 75 (July): 1–39.

———. 1969b. "On the measurement of social mobility: an index of status persistence." *American Sociological Review* 34 (December): 831–850.

———. 1971. "A simple simultaneous test procedure for quasi-independence in contingency tables." *Applied Statistics* 20:165–177.

———. 1972a. "A general model for the analysis of surveys." *American Journal of Sociology* 77 (May):1035–1086.

———. 1972b. "A modified multiple regression approach to the analysis of dichotomous variables." *American Sociological Review* 37 (February):28–46.

———. 1972c. "Some multiplicative models for the analysis of cross-classified data." Pp. 649–696 in *Proceedings of the Sixth Berkeley Symposium on Mathematical Statistics and*

Probability. Berkeley: University of California Press.

Haberman, Shelby J. 1974. *The Analysis of Frequency Data.* Chicago: University of Chicago Press.

Hauser, Robert M. 1978. "A structural model of the mobility table." *Social Forces* 56 (March): 919–953.

Hauser, Robert M., Peter J. Dickinson, Harry P. Travis, and John M. Koffel. 1975. "Temporal change in occupational mobility: evidence for men in the United States." *American Sociological Review* 40 (June):279–297.

Hope, Keith. 1976. Review of Thomas W. Pullum's *Measuring Occupational Inheritance. American Journal of Sociology* 82 (November):726–730.

Iutaka, S., B. F. Bloomer, R. E. Burke, and O. Wolowyna. 1975. "Testing the quasi-perfect mobility model for intergenerational data: international comparison." *Economic and Social Review* 6:215–236.

Levine, Joel Harvey. 1967. Measurement in the study of intergenerational status mobility. Unpublished doctoral dissertation. Department of Social Relations. Harvard University.

———. 1972. "A two-parameter model of interaction in father-son status mobility." *Behavioral Science* 17 (September):455–465.

Mantel, Nathan. 1970. "Incomplete contingency tables." *Biometrics* 26:291–304.

Mason, Karen Oppenheim, William M. Mason, Halliman H. Winsborough, and Kenneth W. Poole. 1973. "Some methodological issues in cohort analysis of archival data." *American Sociological Review* 38 (April):242–258.

Parkin, Frank. 1971. *Class Inequality and Political Order: Social Stratification in Capitalist and Communist Societies.* New York: Praeger.

Pearson, Karl. 1904. "On the theory of contingency and its relation to association and normal correlation." Reprinted, 1948, in *Karl Pearson's Early Papers.* Cambridge: Cambridge University Press.

Pullum, Thomas. 1975. *Measuring Occupational Inheritance.* New York: Elsevier.

Ramsøy, Natalie. 1977. *Social Mobilitet i Norge (Social Mobility in Norway).* Oslo: Tiden Forlag.

Rogoff, Natalie. 1953. *Recent Trends in Occupational Mobility.* Glencoe, Illinois: Free Press.

Singer, Burton, and Seymour Spilerman. 1976. "The representation of social processes by Markov models." *American Journal of Sociology* 82 (July):1–54.

Tyree, Andrea. 1973. "Mobility ratios and association in mobility tables." *Population Studies* 27 (July):577–588.

Westergaard, John, and Henrietta Resler. 1975. *Class in a Capitalist Society: A Study of Contemporary Britain.* New York: Basic Books.

White, Harrison C. 1963. "Cause and effect in social mobility tables." *Behavioral Science* 8:14–27.

———. 1970a. *Chains of Opportunity: System Models of Occupational Mobility in Organizations.* Cambridge: Harvard University Press.

———. 1970b. "Stayers and movers." *American Journal of Sociology* 76 (September): 307–324.

DAVID B. GRUSKY AND ROBERT M. HAUSER

Comparative Social Mobility Revisited: Models of Convergence and Divergence in 16 Countries

The starting point for most mobility research is the thesis advanced by Lipset and Zetterberg (1959) that observed mobility rates are much the same in all Western industrialized societies. However, more recent and detailed data lend little support for this position (Hauser and Featherman, 1977; Erikson et al., 1979; Hope, 1982), and Featherman et al. (1975) thus suggested that variation in observed mobility rates might derive from historical and cultural differences in occupational structures, but not from differences in exchanges between occupations. This hypothesis, labelled the FJH revision by Erikson et al., leads to the prediction that mobility chances are invariant once variations in origin and destination distributions have been controlled. Although the FJH revision has been supported by pairwise or three-way comparisons (Erikson et al., 1982; McRoberts and Selbee, 1981; Hope, 1982; Portocarero, 1983; Hauser, 1983), research with a larger sample of countries has tended to emphasize cross-national variability (Tyree et al., 1979; Hazelrigg and Garnier, 1976; McClendon, 1980a).[1] There is also some disagreement about the degree to which "structural influences," reflected in the margins of the mobility table, can account for national differences in observed mobility rates. The FJH revision implies that variation in observed mobility must be attributed to marginal differences, yet McClendon (1980b) has recently reported a contrary finding for industrialized nations.

Among "second generation" mobility scholars (e.g., Treiman, 1970), the long-standing contention has been that mobility increases with industrialization, even after controls are introduced for changes in class or occupation distributions. This contention, typically labelled the "thesis of industrialism," is to be contrasted with the FJH revision; the latter allows an initial developmental effect on mobility, but it implies there is no further effect once a certain level of industrialization is reached. Unfortunately, evidence on the industrialism thesis is no more conclusive than that addressing the FJH revision. Some studies report a positive relationship between industrialization and mobility (Tyree et al., 1979; Hazelrigg, 1974; Cutright, 1968), but others report no significant association (Hazelrigg and Garnier, 1976; Hardy and Hazelrigg, 1978). In an effort to reconcile these findings, McClendon (1980a) claims that the positive relationship holds only when the sample is restricted to men of nonfarm origins. By virtue of his distinction among immobility parameters of different occupational strata, McClendon's research leads in a fruitful direction. . . .

Originally published in 1984. Please see complete source information beginning on page 891.

The data that we shall employ are 3×3 classifications of son's by father's occupation for sixteen countries; each table categorizes occupations as white-collar, blue-collar, or farm. The tables were originally assembled by Hazelrigg and Garnier (1976) from mobility surveys of the 1960s and early 1970s, but they have been reanalyzed extensively (Hardy and Hazelrigg, 1978; McClendon, 1980a, 1980b; Tyree et al., 1979; Heath, 1981; Urton, 1981; Raftery, 1983).[2] We will not discuss problems of validity and comparability associated with these data because they have been outlined by Hazelrigg and Garnier (1976:500). Suffice it to say that this three-stratum classification captures important barriers to occupational mobility and other significant differences in life chances (e.g., see Blau and Duncan, 1967:59). . . .

Using the quasi-perfect mobility model, we investigate differences between occupational strata in opportunities for mobility or inheritance. We believe that these differences in relative mobility chances arise primarily from variation in the resources and desirability accorded occupations. However, we emphasize variation in economic resources since their transmission is perhaps the most decisive and reliable mechanism of intergenerational inheritance (Goldthorpe, 1980:100). It follows that white-collar immobility should be strong since fathers within this stratum can transmit resources in the form of a business enterprise, professional practice, or privileged education. The desirability of white-collar positions strengthens inheritance further, as white-collar sons wish to retain their fathers' positions. In contrast, sons from the blue-collar stratum do not receive economic resources that bind them to their fathers' stratum, nor do they typically find inheritance as desirable as mobility to the white-collar stratum; the absence of these processes implies considerable mobility for sons of blue-collar origins. The structure of farm inheritance contrasts quite sharply with this blue-collar fluidity. Not only is land a tangible economic good, but there are strong cultural practices and traditions favoring its transfer from generation to genera-

tion.[3] Farm inheritance is further strengthened by spatial isolation from urban labor markets (Featherman and Hauser, 1978:188). Given the distinctive skills of farmers, traditions of land tenure, and spatial isolation, one might expect farm inheritance to be even stronger than that of the white-collar stratum.

Two implications follow from these observations about inheritance. First, the relative strengths of stratum-specific inheritance may be uniform across nations simply because there is substantial uniformity in the economic resources and desirability of occupations (Treiman, 1977).[4] It is commonly argued that the latter uniformities also account for the cross-national regularity in occupational prestige hierarchies (Treiman, 1977; Goldthorpe and Hope, 1974). Thus, invariance in mobility processes may be closely related to other constancies in stratification. Second, rather than deriving from the standardizing logic of industrialism, the common structure of mobility may apply to all societies regardless of their economic development. The FJH hypothesis may be broadened in this manner because occupational resources and desirability are similar in all complex societies, industrialized or not (Treiman, 1977). . . .

The Cross-National Structure of Mobility

There has been no direct test of the Lipset-Zetterberg hypothesis in earlier studies. To carry out this test, we set up a model of global equality between the mobility classifications in the full set of 16 nations and in the 9 most industrialized, nonsocialist nations. Within the more industrialized subsample, this model yields a highly significant likelihood-ratio chi-square test statistic, $L^2 = 3,201$ with 64 degrees of freedom (df), and the ratio of the test statistic to its degrees of freedom is $L^2/df = 50.0$. In the full sample, $L^2 = 18,390$ with 120 df and $L^2/df = 153.3$. There is no less evidence of heterogeneity among mobility classifications within the industrialized subsample than

TABLE 1

Selected Models of Mobility with and Without Cross-National Equality Constraints:
Sixteen-Country Sample and Industrialized Subsample[a]

Model	Full Sample			Industrialized Countries		
	L^2	df	L^2_H/L^2_T	L^2	df	L^2_H/L^2_T
A. Unconstrained Models						
1. Independence	42970	64	100.0	12020	36	100.0
2. Quasi-perfect mobility	150	16	0.3	77	9	0.6
3. Uniform inheritance	6222	48	14.5	2233	27	18.6
4. Perfect blue-collar mobility	841	32	2.0	206	18	1.7
5. Symmetry	24636	48	—	6748	27	—
B. Models with Cross-National Constraints						
6. Quasi-perfect mobility	1500	61	3.5	513	33	4.3
7. Uniform inheritance	7069	63	16.5	2429	35	20.2
8. Perfect blue-collar mobility	1640	62	3.8	538	34	4.5
9. All two-way interactions	1329	60	3.1	438	32	3.6
C. Contrasts Between Constrained and Unconstrained Models						
10. 2 vs. 6	1350	45	3.1	436	24	3.6
11. 3 vs. 7	847	15	2.0	196	8	1.6
12. 4 vs. 8	799	30	1.9	332	16	2.8

[a] The full sample includes Australia, Belgium, France, Hungary, Italy, Japan, Philippines, Spain, United States, West Germany, West Malaysia, Yugoslavia, Denmark, Finland, Norway and Sweden. The industrialized subsample includes Australia, Belgium, France, United States, West Germany, Denmark, Finland, Norway and Sweden.

within the full set of 16 countries, for there are 3 times as many observations in the full sample as in the industrialized subsample. Thus, we reject the Lipset-Zetterberg hypothesis. Not only is there highly significant variation in observed mobility rates among industrialized nations, but there is no less variation among these nations than among nations that vary widely in level of industrialization.

The remainder of our analysis focuses on the FJH revision of the Lipset-Zetterberg hypothesis, that is, on the measurement and explanation of intersocietal variation in social fluidity.[5] Table 1 shows the fit of selected models of mobility and immobility. The left-hand side of the table pertains to the full set of countries, while the right-hand side of the table pertains to nine highly industrialized nations. In Panel A, the models do not place any cross-country equality constraints on parameters, so the fit statistic for each model is simply the sum of the fit statistics for that model applied to each country separately. Panel B reports the fit of several of the models of Panel

A, each subject to the additional restriction that all of the interaction parameters of that model (but not the marginal effects) are the same in each country. Panel C displays contrasts between corresponding models in Panel A and in Panel B.

Models 1 through 4 in Table 1 are of the form

$$E[X_{ijk}] = \alpha_k \beta_{ik} \gamma_{jk} \delta_{ijk} \qquad (1)$$

where $\delta_{ijk} = \delta_{mk}$ for $(i,j) \in H_m$. In this context, X_{ijk} is the observed frequency in the ijk^{th} cell of the classification of father's stratum (i) by son's stratum (j) by country (k), and H_m is a partition of the pairs (i,j), which is mutually exclusive, exhaustive, and cross-nationally invariant. Subject to the usual normalizations, this model implies that expected frequencies in the kth country are the product of a grand mean (α_k), a row effect (β_{ik}), a column effect (γ_{jk}), and an interaction effect (δ_{ijk}). Models 1 through 4 differ only by partitioning the pairs (i,j) according to various theories of the structure of interaction. These partitions are displayed in Figure 1; cells sharing a numeric value within a matrix are assigned the same interaction parameter in the corresponding model. Note that we have specialized the model to impose the same partition of cells in each country, but not necessarily to specify the same interaction parameters in each country. Since this general model has been discussed in detail elsewhere (e.g., Hauser, 1978, 1979), we will not elaborate it further.

Model 1 specifies conditional independence of father's and son's stratum, so $\delta_{ijk} = 1$ for all pairs (i,j) in all countries (k); this says there is no intergenerational association in any of the 16 countries. Although the global chi-square statistic, $L^2 = 42,970$, reveals that independence is patently inconsistent with these data, this model provides a baseline statistic representing the association to be explained by subsequent models. Model 2, quasi-perfect mobility, fits a distinct inheritance parameter to each diagonal cell and posits independence among the remaining cells off the diagonal. This model fits extremely well, accounting for 99.7 percent of the association under the baseline model of independence. Indeed, the model cannot be rejected at the .05 level in ten of the sixteen countries, and in all countries it explains at least 97.3 percent of the association. Since this is one of our preferred models, we shall consider its implications in some detail.

First, quasi-perfect mobility implies quasi-symmetry in a 3×3 table. In a mobility classification, quasi-symmetry means that upward and downward moves are equally likely, net of differences in the prevalence of occupations. Thus, our results do not support the interpretation of semipermeable class boundaries advanced by Blau and Duncan (1967) for the United States. Featherman and Hauser (1978:184–87) and Hauser (1981) report a similar finding in disaggregated American mobility tables; we extend that finding to a larger set of countries.[6]

Symmetry in exchange mobility is entirely consistent with intergenerational occupational change and consequent differences between

FIGURE 1
Parameter displays describing the structure of association for selected models of mobility

Independence

Quasi-Perfect Mobility

Uniform Inheritance

Perfect Blue-Collar Mobility

observed inflow and outflow distributions. We can see this by contrasting the model of quasi-perfect mobility (quasi-symmetry) with that of complete symmetry (Model 5), which posits equal frequencies in corresponding cells above and below the main diagonal of each mobility classification, $E[X_{ijk}] = E[X_{jik}]$. The fit of Model 5, $L^2 = 24,636$, shows that observed frequencies are highly asymmetric. However, from the excellent fit of quasi-perfect mobility (quasi-symmetry), we know this observed asymmetry derives from heterogeneity between origin and destination distributions rather than an intrinsic asymmetry of exchange between occupational strata.

Second, the quasi-perfect mobility model says that mobility does not follow a social distance gradient. Those who move off the diagonal are equally likely to reach either of the two remaining strata regardless of distance or direction. The implication is that long-range mobility is no less frequent than short-range mobility after controlling for marginal effects. Featherman and Hauser (1978: Ch. 4) offer a similar interpretation of disaggregated American mobility tables.

Third, the parameters of the quasi-perfect mobility model reveal wide differences among strata in the strength of inheritance. For purposes of summary, it is instructive to consider Model 6, which constrains parameter estimates to be the same in all sixteen countries. Net of row and column effects, farm inheritance is 12.3 times more likely than mobility off the diagonal, white-collar inheritance is 5.2 times more likely than mobility, and blue-collar inheritance is only 1.2 times more likely than mobility. The picture that emerges is one of severe immobility at the two extremes of the occupational hierarchy and considerable fluidity in the middle (compare Featherman and Hauser, 1978: Ch. 4). Indeed, the United States and Hungary show significant blue-collar disinheritance.[7] A net propensity for mobility out of the blue-collar stratum was first noted by Goodman (1965:575, 1969a) in the classic British and Danish mobility tables of the early postwar period; the results presented here extend his finding to additional countries. Friendly critics have suggested to us that blue-collar disinheritance is implausible and, for that reason, should lead us to reject quasi-perfect mobility in favor of other equivalent models (Goodman, 1979; Hauser, 1979: 453–54, 1981; MacDonald, 1981). On the basis of our earlier discussion of mechanisms of stratum inheritance, we do not think it is possible to rule out blue-collar status disinheritance (see Featherman and Hauser 1978:179–89).

The remaining models in Panel A of Table 1 help us to test, elaborate, and qualify these interpretations. The uniform inheritance model (Line 3) posits a single inflation factor for the main diagonal; the model says that occupational strata share a uniform propensity for inheritance. This model fits poorly, confirming our observation of substantial variability among inheritance parameters. The model of perfect blue-collar mobility (Line 4) equates densities of mobility and immobility for men of blue-collar origin or destination (Goodman, 1965:569–71). Net of marginal effects, this model says that blue-collar workers are recruited equally from all three occupational

strata and that men of blue-collar origins are selected equally into all three strata. Further, the model says that blue-collar mobility and immobility are as likely as exchange between the white-collar and farm strata. This model does not fit satisfactorily ($L^2 = 841$ with 32 df), yet it does account for 98 percent of the test statistic under conditional independence (compare Lines 1 and 4). Moreover, Model 4 does fit well in 6 countries: Italy, West Malaysia, Yugoslavia, Denmark, Norway, and Sweden. The contrast between Models 2 and 4 tests whether there is significant blue-collar stratum inheritance or disinheritance. Although the global contrast between these models is clearly significant ($L^2 = 691$ with 16 df), the contrast is nonsignificant in Australia and in the other 6 countries where Model 4 fits the data. This provides further evidence for attenuated blue-collar inheritance; it is so weak that densities of mobility and blue-collar immobility can be equated in several of the countries in our data.

Convergence in Social Fluidity

The cross-national consistency in the fit of quasi-perfect mobility provides some evidence of similarity in processes of mobility, but we have not yet tested the cross-national variation in the parameters estimated under this model. If the same model fits, but its coefficients vary from country to country, then convergence obtains only in a limited sense. The remainder of Table 1 addresses this issue. Whereas each model in Panel A allows interactions between strata to vary across countries, each model in Panel B equates those interactions. The statistics in Panel B reflect lack of fit in the models of Panel A as well as cross-national differences in coefficients, whereas the contrasts between fit statistics in Panels A and B reflect the latter component alone. As shown in Panel C, each of these contrasts is highly significant statistically. At the same time, there is also a great deal of cross-national similarity in parameter estimates; no more than 3.6 percent of the chi-square statistic under conditional independence is attributable to variation in parameters. A similar conclusion may be drawn from the fit of the model of all two-way interactions, which allows 4 df for interaction between origin and outcome strata (Line 9 of Panel B).

These results make it quite clear that the "cross-nationally common element heavily predominates over the cross-nationally variable one" (Erikson et al., 1982:12). Not only does one simple model, quasi-perfect mobility, fit all of these data satisfactorily, but its coefficients do not vary greatly between countries. These findings of cross-national invariance support the FJH revision of the Lipset-Zetterberg hypothesis.

The results of Table 1 imply convergence among industrialized countries in our sample, but they also suggest that conclusions of invariance apply equally to the full sample. Under each of the models of Table 1, the share of association due to cross-national interaction effects (L^2_H/L^2_T) is virtually the same in the full sample as in the industrialized subsample. This suggests an extension of the scope of the FJH hypothesis to state that mobility regimes are much the same in all complex societies, regardless of economic development.[8]

Conclusions

We have gained new insights into the leading issues of comparative social mobility by reanalyzing a standard set of data. Although we know the limitations of these data, we think that our results set a provisional baseline for future comparative research with "second generation" studies. We expect and hope that many of our findings will be elaborated, challenged, and falsified in future work.

The preceding analysis provides considerable support for the FJH revision of the Lipset-Zetterberg hypothesis, which implies that historical and cultural variations affect the shape of the occupational structure but not the interactions between occupational strata; this invariance is perhaps stronger than

heretofore supposed. We have also proposed that the FJH revision might be elaborated in two respects. First, we suggested that uniformity in mobility regimes is not limited to highly industrialized societies but may extend across levels of economic development. Industrialized countries share a common pattern of mobility, but the pattern can not derive from the "logic of industrialism" if it applies equally to less-developed societies. This uniformity in mobility patterns may be the analogue to invariance in prestige hierarchies, in the sense that both may result from cross-national regularities in the resources and desirability accorded occupations.

Second, we provided greater substance to the FJH revision by specifying the structure of the shared mobility regime. Since the revision remains agnostic with regard to this structure, we proceeded inductively by fitting a series of mobility models. It is most striking that quasi-symmetry (and equivalent models) provided superior fit in nearly all the countries. This finding implies that Blau and Duncan's (1967) hypothesis of semipermeable class boundaries is not confirmed in the United States, nor in the other countries in our sample. Rather, there is a symmetry of exchanges between occupational strata, once intergenerational shifts in the marginal distributions are controlled.

Under the quasi-perfect mobility model, we find strong white-collar inheritance and even stronger farm inheritance, perhaps consonant with the beliefs of the more extreme critics of rigidity in the class structure. Although the strength of inheritance within these strata might lend the impression of distinct class boundaries, this must be reconciled with extreme fluidity in the blue-collar stratum. Indeed, in several countries there is actually a net propensity for blue-collar disinheritance; this finding extends Goodman's (1965, 1969a, 1969b) results on the classic British and Danish mobility tables. . . .

The need to extend and elaborate our analysis is accentuated by our finding that intersocietal differences in observed mobility are induced principally by variations in the marginal distributions of the mobility tables.

This suggests that future research should explore the effects of economic and political variables on the shape of the social hierarchy. Much the same conclusion was advanced by Hauser et al. (1975) in their longitudinal analysis of American mobility classifications. They argued that further research cannot treat marginal differences as a nuisance factor if they are the driving force behind temporal change in observed mobility rates. We might add that economic and political variables may well have a greater effect on the structure of occupational supply and demand than on social fluidity. Although issues of this nature may be addressed within the general analytic framework presented here, we leave this task for future research.

Notes

An earlier draft of this paper was presented at the 47th Annual Meeting of the Midwest Sociological Society, Kansas City, 1983. Computations were supported by a grant to the Center for Demography and Ecology of the University of Wisconsin-Madison from the National Institute for Child Health and Human Development (HD–5876). During the preparation of this paper Grusky was supported by a predoctoral fellowship from the National Science Foundation, and Hauser was supported by the Graduate School of the University of Wisconsin-Madison. We thank Lawrence Hazelrigg for furnishing the mobility data, and Peter Smith for providing sample counts for the Philippines table. We have benefited greatly from the comments of Michael Hout, O. D. Duncan, Clifford C. Clogg, Walter Mueller, Michael Sobel, Robert D. Mare, McKee J. McClendon, and from unpublished memoranda and correspondence with Leo A. Goodman that O. D. Duncan shared with us. The opinions expressed herein are those of the authors.

1. Of course, there is an element of subjectivity in any evaluation of the FJH revision; it is unclear how much similarity in mobility regimes is necessary to confirm the hypothesis.

2. Following McClendon (1980a, 1980b), Bulgaria was omitted from the data because the sample included both males and females. Some of the cited studies have supplemented these data with mobility classifications from other countries. We have revised the counts for the U.S., France, Hungary, and the Philippines to reflect the sizes and designs of those samples. These data are available from the authors by request.

3. Although there is intergenerational transfer of skills in the blue-collar stratum, we think it is far stronger in the farm sector, where the family is more often the unit of production.

4. This argument for uniformity may need qualification in the case of socialist societies to the degree that they accord greater desirability to blue-collar occupations and prohibit formal ownership of economic resources (Parkin, 1971; Giddens, 1973).

5. Goldthorpe (1980) uses the term social fluidity for mobility and immobility net of marginal effects. We use it to refer globally to interaction effects, rather than using "mobility" as an inclusive term.

6. For an explanation of quasi-symmetry, see Bishop et al. (1975: Ch. 8). Featherman and Hauser (1978:184–87) and Hauser (1981) discuss the relevance of quasi-symmetry to the interpretation of social mobility. Featherman and Hauser did find some asymmetries in their analysis of intergenerational mobility to current occupations, but the majority of these pertained to mobility within the broad strata of the present analysis.

7. On request the authors will provide estimates of stratum inheritance under quasi-perfect mobility in each of the sixteen countries. References to statistical significance in the text are based on the α = .05 level, two-tailed.

8. Since the data are primarily from Western industrialized nations, this finding is most tentative.

References

Bishop, Yvonne M., Stephen E. Fienberg and Paul W. Holland. 1975. Discrete Multivariate Analysis: Theory and Practice. Cambridge: MIT Press.

Blau, Peter M. and Otis D. Duncan. 1967. The American Occupational Structure. New York: Wiley.

Cutright, Phillips. 1968. "Occupational inheritance: a cross-national analysis." American Journal of Sociology 73:400–16.

Erikson, Robert, John H. Goldthorpe and Lucienne Portocarero. 1979. "Intergenerational class mobility in three Western European societies: England, France, and Sweden." British Journal of Sociology 30:415–41.

———. 1982. "Social fluidity in industrial nations: England, France, and Sweden." British Journal of Sociology 33:1–34.

Featherman, David L. and Robert M. Hauser. 1978. Opportunity and Change. New York: Academic Press.

Featherman, David L., F. Lancaster Jones and Robert M. Hauser. 1975. "Assumptions of mobility research in the United States: the case of occupational status." Social Science Research 4:329–60.

Giddens, Anthony. 1973. The Class Structure of the Advanced Societies. New York: Harper & Row.

Goldthorpe, John H. 1980. Social Mobility and Class Structure in Modern Britain. Oxford: Clarendon Press.

Goldthorpe, John H. and Keith Hope. 1974. The Social Grading of Occupations: A New Approach and Scale. Oxford: Clarendon Press.

Goodman, Leo A. 1965. "On the statistical analysis of mobility tables." American Journal of Sociology 70:564–85.

———. 1969a. "On the measurement of social mobility: an index of status persistence." American Sociological Review 34:831–50.

———. 1969b. "How to ransack social mobility tables and other kinds of cross-classification tables." American Journal of Sociology 75:1–39.

———. 1979. "Multiplicative models for the analysis of occupational mobility tables and other kinds of cross-classification tables." American Journal of Sociology 84:804–19.

Hardy, Melissa A. and Lawrence E. Hazelrigg. 1978. "Industrialization and the circulatory rate of mobility: further tests of some cross-sectional hypotheses." Sociological Focus 11:1–10.

Hauser, Robert M. 1978. "A structural model of the mobility table." Social Forces 56:919–53.

———. 1979. "Some exploratory methods for modeling mobility tables and other cross-classified data." Pp. 413–58 in Karl F. Schuessler (ed.), Sociological Methodology, 1980. San Francisco: Jossey-Bass.

———. 1981. "Hope for the mobility ratio." Social Forces 60:572–84.

———. 1983. "Vertical class mobility in Great Britain, France, and Sweden." Center for Demography and Ecology, University of Wisconsin—Madison: Working Paper 82–36.

Hauser, Robert M. and David L. Featherman. 1977. "Commonalities in social stratification and assumptions about status mobility in the United States." Pp. 3–50 in Robert M. Hauser and David L. Featherman (eds.), The Process of Stratification. New York: Academic Press.

Hauser, Robert M., John N. Koffel, Harry P. Travis and Peter J. Dickinson. 1975. "Temporal change in occupational mobility: evidence for men in the United States." American Sociological Review 40:279–97.

Hazelrigg, Lawrence E. 1974. "Cross-national comparisons of father-to-son occupational mobility." Pp. 469–93 in Joseph Lopreato and Lionel S. Lewis (eds.), Social Stratification. New York: Harper & Row.

Hazelrigg, Lawrence E. and Maurice A. Garnier. 1976. "Occupational mobility in industrial societies: a comparative analysis of differential access to occupational ranks in seventeen countries." American Sociological Review 41:498–511.

Heath, Anthony. 1981. Social Mobility. London: Fontana.

Hope, Keith. 1982. "Vertical and nonvertical class mobility in three countries." American Sociological Review 47:100–113.

Lipset, Seymour M. and Hans L. Zetterberg. 1959. "Social mobility in industrial societies." Pp. 11–75 in Seymour M. Lipset and Reinhard Bendix (eds.), Social Mobility in Industrial Society. Berkeley: University of California Press.

MacDonald, K. I. 1981. "On the formulation of a structural model of the mobility table." Social Forces 60:557–71.

McClendon, McKee J. 1980a. "Occupational mobility and economic development: a cross-national analysis." Sociological Focus 13:331–42.

———. 1980b. "Structural and exchange components of occupational mobility: a cross-national analysis." The Sociological Quarterly 21:493–509.

McRoberts, Hugh A. and Kevin Selbee. 1981. "Trends in occupational mobility in Canada and the United States: a comparison." American Sociological Review 46:406–21.

Parkin, Frank. 1971. Class Inequality and Political Order. New York: Praeger.

Portocarero, Lucienne. 1983. "Social fluidity in France and Sweden." Acta Sociologica 26:127–39.

Raftery, Adrian E. 1983. "Comment on 'Gaps and Glissandos . . .'" American Sociological Review 48:581–83.

Treiman, Donald J. 1970. "Industrialization and social stratification." Pp. 207–34 in Edward O. Laumann (ed.), Social Stratification: Research and Theory for the 1970s. New York: Bobbs-Merrill.

———. 1977. Occupational Prestige in Comparative Perspective. New York: Academic Press.

Tyree, Andrea, Moshe Semyonov and Robert Hodge. 1979. "Gaps and glissandos: inequality, economic development, and social mobility in 24 countries." American Sociological Review 44:410–24.

Urton, William L. 1981. "Mobility and economic development revisited." American Sociological Review 46:128–37.

ROBERT ERIKSON AND JOHN H. GOLDTHORPE

Trends in Class Mobility: The Post-War European Experience

Introduction

The issue of trends in class mobility in industrial societies is one characterised by a wide-ranging dissensus which, unfortunately, extends to matters of fact as well as of interpretation. We do not suppose that in this paper we will be able to resolve all the disagreements that are apparent. We do, however, believe that we can address the issue on the basis of comparative mobility data of a distinctively higher quality than those previously utilised, and that the results we report have significant consequences—positive or negative—for most of the rival positions that have been taken up.[1]

From the 1960s onwards, perhaps the dominant view on mobility trends has been that derived from what we will refer to as the 'liberal theory' of industrialism, as developed by various American authors (Kerr *et al.*, 1960, 1973; Kerr, 1969, 1983; Dunlop *et al.*, 1975; cf. also Parsons, 1960: chs. 3 and 4; 1967: chs. 4 and 15; 1971). This theory is a functionalist one which aims at establishing the distinctive properties of industrial societies in terms of the essential prerequisites for, or nec-

essary consequences of, the technical and economic rationality that is seen as their defining characteristic. What is implied so far as social mobility is concerned may be put in the form of the following three-part proposition.

In industrial societies, in comparison with preindustrial ones

(i) absolute rates of social mobility are generally high, and moreover upward mobility—i.e. from less to more advantaged positions—predominates over downward mobility;

(ii) relative rates of mobility—or, that is, mobility opportunities—are more equal, in the sense that individuals of differing social origins compete on more equal terms to attain (or to avoid) particular destinations; and

(iii) both the level of absolute rates of mobility and the degree of equality in relative rates tend to increase over time.

To explain *why* these contrasts between mobility in pre-industrial and industrial society should arise, a number of arguments are deployed which have, moreover, been elaborated and extended in the specialist literature by authors generally sympathetic to the liberal position (see esp. Blau and Duncan, 1967: ch. 12; Treiman, 1970). While all the arguments in question take on a functionalist form, one may usefully distinguish between those relating to three different kinds of effect—*structural, processual* and *compositional*.

Originally published in 1992. Please see complete source information beginning on page 891.

First, it is held that within industrial society the dynamism of a rationally developed technology calls for continuous, and often rapid, change in the structure of the social division of labour, which also tends to become increasingly differentiated. High rates of mobility thus follow as from generation to generation, and in the course of individual lifetimes, the redistribution of the active population is required: that is, among economic sectors—first, from agriculture to manufacturing and then from manufacturing to services—and, in turn, among industries and among a growing diversity of occupations. Furthermore, the overall tendency is for advancing technology to *upgrade* levels of employment. Although some skills are rendered obsolete, new ones are created and the *net* effect is a reduction in the number of merely labouring and routine occupations and a rising demand for technically and professionally qualified personnel. At the same time, both the increasing scale of production, dictated by economic rationality, and the expansion of the services sector of the economy promote the growth of large bureaucratic organisations in which managerial and administrative positions also multiply. Industrial societies become increasingly 'middle-class' or at least 'middle-mass' societies. Consequently, upward mobility is more likely than downward in both intergenerational and worklife perspective. Under industrialism, the chances of 'success' are steadily improved for all.

Secondly, it is further claimed that as well as thus reshaping the objective structure of opportunity, industrialism transforms the processes through which particular individuals are allocated to different positions within the division of labour. Most fundamentally, rational procedures of social selection require a shift away from *acription* and towards *achievement* as the leading criterion: what counts is increasingly what individuals can do, and not who they are. Moreover, the growing demand for highly qualified personnel promotes the expansion of education and training, and also the reform of educational institutions so as to increase their accessibility to indivduals of all social backgrounds. Human resources cannot be wasted; talent must be fully exploited wherever it is to be found. Thus, as within a society of widening educational provision 'meritocratic' selection comes to predominate, the association between individuals' social origins and their eventual destinations tends steadily to weaken and the society takes on a more 'open' character. And at the same time various other features of industrialism also serve to reduce the influence of social origins on individuals' future lives. For example, urbanisation and greater geographical mobility loosen ties of kinship and community; mass communications spread information, enlarge horizons and raise aspirations; and a greater equality of condition—that is, in incomes and living standards—means that the resources necessary for the realisation of ambition are more widely available.

Thirdly, it is argued that the foregoing effects interact with each other, in that the emphasis on achievement as the basis for social selection will be strongest within the expanding sectors of the economy—that is, the more technologically advanced manufacturing industries and services—and within the increasingly dominant form of large-scale bureaucratic organisation. Conversely, ascriptive tendencies will persist chiefly within declining sectors and organisational forms—for example, within agriculture or small-scale, family-based business enterprise. In other words, compositional effects on mobility occur in that, once a society begins to industrialise, the proportion of its population that is subject to the new 'mobility regime' characteristic of industrialism not only increases as that regime imposes itself, but further as those areas and modes of economic activity that are most resistant to it become in any event ever more marginal.

One reason that may then be suggested for the degree of dominance exerted by the liberal position is the coherent way in which the underlying theory has been developed. Another is the manifest failure of the main attempt made directly to controvert it. That is, the revision and extension of the Marxist theory of proletarianisation (cf. Braverman, 1974; Carchedi, 1977; Wright and Singelmann, 1982; Crompton and Jones, 1984) which sought to show the necessity for the systematic 'degrading', rather than upgrading, of labour under the exigencies of late capitalism—with the consequence of large-scale *downward* mobility of a collective kind. This undertaking lacked from start any secure empirical foundation, and the accumulation of results incompatible with the new theory resulted in its eventual abandonment even by those who had been among its most resourceful supporters (see e.g. Singelmann and Tienda, 1985; Wright and Martin, 1987). However, various other positions can still be identified that to a greater or lesser extent come into conflict with the liberal view and that continue to merit serious attention.

First of all, it should be noted that the theory of mobility in industrial society advanced by Lipset and Zetterberg (1956, 1959) and sometimes simply assimilated to the liberal theory (see e.g. Kerr, 1983: 53) does in fact differ from it in crucial respects. For example, Lipset and Zetterberg do not seek to argue that mobility steadily *increases* with industrial development: indeed, they remark that *among* industrial societies no association is apparent between mobility rates and rates of economic growth. What they propose (1959: 13) is, rather, some kind of 'threshold' effect: 'our tentative interpretation is that the social mobility of societies becomes relatively high once their industrialization, and hence their economic expansion, reaches a certain level'. And although Lipset and Zetterberg's claim that (absolute) mobility rates in industrial societies become *uniformly* high would now be generally regarded as empirically untenable, their suggestion that a historic upward shift in such rates tends to occur at some—perhaps quite early—stage in the industrialisation process has not been similarly disconfirmed. Again, it is not part of Lipset and Zetterberg's case that the high mobility that they see as characteristic of industrial societies is the result of a tendency towards greater openness. Rather, they

place the emphasis firmly on the effects of structural change, and in turn they are at pains to point out (1959: 27) that 'the fact that one country contains a greater percentage of mobile individuals than another does *not* mean that that country approximates a model of equal opportunity more closely'.

Secondly, a yet more radical challenge to the liberal view may be derived from the pioneering work of Sorokin (1927/1959). Taking a synoptic view, as much dependent on historical and ethnographic evidence as on contemporary social research, Sorokin was led to the conclusion that in modern western societies mobility was at a relatively high level, and he was further ready to acknowledge the possibility that, from the eighteenth century onwards, mobility rates had in general shown a tendency to rise. However, he was at the same time much concerned to reject the idea that what was here manifested was in effect 'the end of history' and the start of a 'perpetual and "eternal" increase of vertical mobility'. Rather, Sorokin argued, the present situation represented no more than a specific historical phase; in some societies in some periods mobility increased, while in other periods it declined. Overall, no 'definite perpetual trend' was to be seen towards either greater or less mobility, but only 'trendless fluctuation'. Those who were impressed by the distinctiveness of the modern era knew too little about historical societies and their diversity: 'What has been happening is only an alternation—the waves of greater mobility superseded by the cycles of greater immobility—and that is all' (1959: 152–4).

It might from the foregoing appear that Sorokin's position was merely negative. But, in fact, underlying his denial of developmental trends in mobility and his preference for a cyclical view, at least the elements of a theory can be discerned. In arguing against the supposition that rates of mobility in the modern period are quite unprecedented, one of the points Sorokin most stresses is that while certain barriers to mobility have been largely removed—for example, juridical and religious ones—it is important to recognise that other barriers have become more severe or have been newly introduced: for example, those represented by systems of educational selection and occupational qualification (1959: 153–4, 169–79). This, moreover, is what must always be expected: the forms of social stratification which provide the context for mobility are themselves structures expressing differential power and advantage, and thus possess important self-maintaining properties. Those who hold privileged positions will not readily cede them and, in the nature of the case, can draw on superior resources in their defence. Indeed, Sorokin remarks that if he *had* to believe in the existence of a permanent trend in mobility, it would be in a declining one, since social strata are often observed to become more 'closed' over time as the cumulative result of those in superior positions using their power and advantage to restrict entry from below (1959: 158–60). However, this propensity for closure—which we may understand as being *endogenous* to all forms of stratification—is not the only influence on mobility rates. A further point that Sorokin several times makes (see e.g. 1959: 141–152, 466–72) is that in periods of both political and economic upheaval—associated, say, with revolution or war or with rapid commercial, industrial and technological change—marked surges in mobility are typically produced as the social structure as a whole, including the previously existing distribution of power and advantage, is disrupted. In other words, increased mobility here results from the impact of factors that are *exogenous* to the stratification order.

Thirdly and finally, one may note a more recently developed position which, however, has evident affinities with that of Sorokin. Featherman, Jones and Hauser (1975) aim at presenting a reformulation of Lipset and Zetterberg's hypothesis that across industrial societies rates of social mobility display a basic similarity. This hypothesis cannot stand if expressed in terms of absolute rates but, they argue, becomes far more plausible if applied, rather, to relative rates. When mobility is considered at the 'phenotypical' level of absolute rates cross-national similarity can scarcely be expected. This is because these rates are greatly influenced by the structural context of mobility and, in turn, by effects deriving from a range of economic, technological and demographic circumstances which are known to vary widely and which, so far as particular individuals and families are concerned, must be regarded as 'exogenously determined'. When, however, mobility is considered *net of* all such effects, or that is, at the 'genotypical' level of relative rates, the likelihood of cross-national similarity being found is much greater. For at this level only those factors are involved that bear on the relative chances of individuals of differing social origin achieving or avoiding, in competition with each other, particular destination positions among those that are structurally given. And there is reason to suppose that in modern societies the conditions under which such 'endogenous mobility regimes' operate—for example, the degree of differentiation in occupational hierarchies and in job rewards and requirements—may not be subject to substantial variation.

For present purposes, then, the chief significance of the FJH hypothesis lies in the rather comprehensive challenge that it poses to the claims of liberal theorists. On the one hand, so far as absolute mobility rates are concerned, it implies a basic scepticism, essentially akin to that of Sorokin, about the possibility of *any* long-term, developmentally-driven trend; while, on the other hand, it stands directly opposed to the proposition that under industrialism a steady increase occurs in the equality of mobility chances. Although some initial developmental effect in this direction early in the industrialisation process might be compatible with the hypothesis, any continuing change in relative mobility rates is clearly precluded (cf. Grusky and Hauser, 1984: 20). Once societies can be deemed to have become industrial, their mobility regimes should stabilise in some approximation to the common pattern that the FJH hypothesis proposes, and should not thereafter reveal any specific or persistent tendencies, whether towards convergence on greater openness or otherwise. No forces are recognised inherent in the functional dynamics of industrialism that work systematically to expand mobility opportunities.

The divergent arguments concerning mobility trends that we have reviewed in this section will then provide the context within which we present our empirical analyses of data for European nations. First, though, we must say something about what we take to be the particular relevance to evaluating these arguments of the European experience over the post-war years.

The Relevance of the European Experience

It is not difficult to detect within the liberal theory of industrialism a degree of American or, more accurately perhaps, of Anglo-American, ethnocentricity. Historically, the origins of modern industrial society are traced back to late eighteenth- and early nineteenth-century England; and other western nations, including the USA, are then seen as having successively followed England's lead in breaking free of the constraints of a traditional social order and entering the industrial world.[2] Contemporaneously, it is the USA rather than England that is recognised as the vanguard nation; and with industrialisation now on the global agenda, the major differences between industrial and pre-industrial, or modern and traditional, society are seen as best revealed through explicit or implicit USA–Third World comparisons. Within these perspectives, therefore, the experience of industrialisation of the mainland European nations is viewed in only a rather restrictive way. It tends either to be taken for granted, as fitting unproblematically into the trajectories defined by the two paradigm cases, or alternatively as providing interesting instances of 'deviations', over which, however, the logic of industrialism has eventually to prevail.[3]

This schematic background to the liberal theory must be regarded as excessively simplified, and possibly misleading, in at least two respects. On the one hand, while England did indeed industrialise early, the supposition that other western nations then followed along the same path, being differentiated only by the degree of their 'retardation', is one that has no sound historiographic basis. What is chiefly significant about the process of industrialisation in England is that—in part *because* of England's priority, but for other reasons too—it took on a quite distinctive character which subsequent cases could scarcely reflect (cf. Kemp, 1978: ch. 1 esp.). Rather than having simply followed in England's wake, other European nations do in fact display in their recent economic histories a great diversity of developmental paths; and it is, furthermore, important to recognise that later industrialisation and economic retardation should not always be equated—as, for example, the French case can well illustrate (cf. O'Brien and Keyder, 1978).

On the other hand, it would also be mistaken to suppose that by the end of the nineteenth century the industrialisation of Europe was essentially completed. This would be to neglect the great economic and social importance that agriculture and also artisanal and other 'pre-industrial' forms of production continued to have throughout the nineteenth, and for well into the twentieth, century—and in many of the more advanced European nations as well as in those on the 'periphery'. It was in fact, as Bell has remarked (1980: 233), only in the period *after the second world war* that Europe as a whole became an industrial society. Indeed, various interpretations of the 'long boom' of this period have seen it as reflecting aspects of this culmination—for example, as being driven by the final phase of the supply of surplus rural labour (Kindleberger, 1967) or as marking the ultimate overcoming of the dualism of traditional and modern sectors within European economies (Lutz, 1984).[4]

The fact, then, that we here concentrate on the experience of European nations by no means implies that we will be treating questions of mobility trends within an unduly limited context. To the contrary, we have the advantage that while these nations can supply us with high quality data (far better, for example, than those usually available from Third World nations), they do also display a remarkably wide range of variation in their levels and patterns of industrial development—and even if we consider only that time-span to which our mobility data have some reference: that is, from the 1970s back to the first two decades of the century, in which the oldest respondents within our national samples were born. (For details of the surveys utilised, see Appendix Table 1). . . .

It will from the foregoing have become evident that, in seeking to exploit the historical richness of our European data, we are prepared to make a large assumption: namely, that valid inferences about the presence or absence of mobility trends can be drawn from the data of single inquiries. What we are in effect proposing is that age-groups distinguished within our samples from the 1970s can be treated as successive birth-cohorts, and that the mobility experience of their members can then be taken as indicative of whether or not change over time has occurred in mobility rates and patterns. In such an approach certain well-known difficulties arise, above all in treating intergenerational mobility, and in conclusion of this section we should therefore give these some attention.

To begin with, we must recognise that we are not in fact dealing with true birth cohorts within the nations we consider but only with what might better be called 'quasi-cohorts': that is, with the survivors of true cohorts, following on losses due to mortality and emigration, to whom immigrants will then be added. In such cases as those of the FRG, Ireland and Poland, the numbers here involved will obviously be substantial. This, however, is a situation that we can do little to remedy; we can only trust that no serious distortions will be introduced into our data of a kind that might affect our conclusions regarding trends.[5]

Further, there is the so-called 'identification problem'. If for the members of a national sample one compares their present class position (i.e. at time of inquiry) with their class of origin (i.e. father's class), the mobility experience of the individuals within successive 'quasi-cohorts' will be likely to reflect several different effects: not only those of the historical period through which they have lived but also those of their age and of their cohort membership *per se*. Thus, the problem is that of how we can assess 'period' effects—which are those relevant to questions of mobility trends—separately from effects of the other kinds. No clear-cut solution is, or can be, available (cf. Glenn, 1977), since birth-cohorts and age-groups are inescapably 'embedded' in historical time. However, several considerations would lead us to believe that in pursuing our present purposes we need not in fact be at so great a disadvantage in this respect as might initially appear.

First, it would seem empirically defensible to regard men of around 30–35 years of age as having reached a stage of 'occupational maturity', beyond which further major changes in their class positions become relatively unlikely (Goldthorpe, 1980, 1987: ch. 3; cf. also Blossfeld, 1986). Thus, we may take results for cohorts of this age or older as giving a reasonably reliable indication of the 'completed' pattern of the collective class mobility of their members.

Secondly, for all of our European nations except one, the Federal Republic of Germany, we have information on individuals' experience of mobility from their class of origin to their class of *first* employment. For this transition, therefore, age effects at least will obviously be much reduced, since attention is focused on a fairly well defined life-cycle stage. We would not wish to regard data on this transition as a very satisfactory basis for cross-national comparisons of intergenerational mobility, on grounds that we discuss elsewhere (Erikson and Goldthorpe, 1992: ch. 8). None the less, we are thus provided with the possibility of checking whether or not the conclusions that we reach on trends, or their absence, in mobility from class of origin to present class are consistent with ones that pertain to mobility rates of a more age-specific kind.[6]

Thirdly, it is important for us to emphasise that in the analyses that follow our concern will be not so much with the actual empirical description of mobility trends as with the evaluation of particular claims about such trends. What, therefore, we can always consider is whether, if we were to suppose some confounding of effects in our results, these would be of a kind that would tend unduly to favour or disfavour a given position. Thus, for example, in the case of the liberal claim that within industrial nations mobility and openness tend steadily to increase, it is difficult to see why any confounding of period effects by age effects should produce unfairly *negative* results: that is to say, it would appear unlikely that an actual increase in openness and mobility among the more recent cohorts within our national samples would be concealed by the fact that these cohorts are made up of young persons. If anything, one might expect the contrary, since younger persons will have benefited more widely from the expansion of educational provision which, according to the liberal theory, is one of the major sources of greater mobility and equality of opportunity. Likewise, there would seem no reason why age effects should obscure any trends within our data for the mobility rates of different nations to converge—as would be expected under the liberal theory as differences between nations' levels of industrial development are reduced. For if, as the theory maintains, the determinants and processes of mobility become increasingly standardised through the logic of industrialism, then convergence in mobility rates should, presumably, be *more* apparent among the younger than the older age groups in our samples (for an elaboration of this point, see Erikson, Goldthorpe and Portocarero, 1983: 307–10 and Figure 1).

As Glenn has observed (1977: 17), cohort analysis should never be a mechanical exercise, uninformed by theory and by additional 'external' evidence; and this point obviously applies *a fortiori* in the case of analyses, such as those we shall present, which rest only on 'quasi-cohorts'. But since we do have some knowledge about both the historical setting of the mobility that we consider and its life-course phasing, and since we are addressing a number of more or less specific and theoretically grounded hypotheses rather than proceeding quite empirically, our strategy is, we believe, one capable of producing results that can be interpreted in a reasonably reliable and consequential way. It is to these results that we now turn.

Absolute Rates

In seeking to assess the arguments that we have earlier reviewed, we start with evidence on intergenerational class mobility in the form of absolute rates: that is, rates based on differing versions of our class schema (see Appendix Table 2) and expressed in simple percentage terms. So as to avoid marked age effects in considering the transition from class of origin to present class, we restrict our attention to men in our national samples who were over age 30 at the time of inquiry (i.e. at some point in the early or mid–1970s; cf. Appendix Table 1). These men, we suppose, would be approaching, or would have attained, a stage of relative occupational maturity. The maximum age-limit that we apply here—and in all subsequent analyses—is 64.[7]

First of all, we consider *total* mobility rates. That is, the percentage of all men in our national samples found in cells off the main diagonal of the intergenerational mobility table based on the sevenfold version of the class schema; or, in other words, the percentage of all men whose 'present', or destination, class was different to their class of origin—the latter being indexed by the respondent's *father's* class at the time of the respondent's early adolescence.[8] In Figure 1 we seek to plot the course followed by the total mobility rate in each of our nine European nations on the basis of moving weighted averages of this rate for men *in successive birth years*, using a method of graduation that has been developed by Hoem and Linneman (1987).[9]

FIGURE 1
Total mobility rates for men in nine nations by birth year

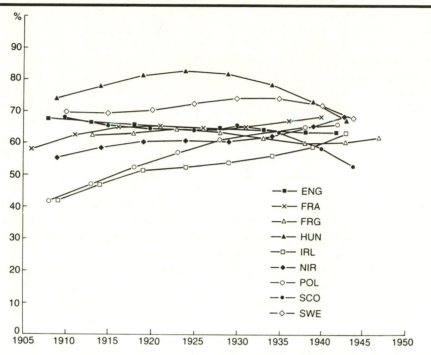

From inspection of Figure 1, the general impression gained must be one of support for the contention that absolute mobility rates display merely trendless change. It would, at all events, be difficult to ally the data here presented with the idea of mobility increasing steadily as industrialism advances. No regular tendency is apparent for the mobility of older respondents—of men born, say, in the first two decades of the century—to be exceeded by that of respondents who were born some twenty years later, and who would have reached occupational maturity during the long boom of the post-war years. And we may add that no essentially different picture emerges if, using the same technique, we plot total mobility rates from class of origin to class of *first* employment.[10] It would thus seem improbable that the failure of the graphs of Figure 1 to move upwards to the right, as would be expected from the liberal theory, can be explained simply in terms of the confounding of period by age effects.

The one possible pattern that might be discerned in Figure 1 is some tendency for total mobility rates to converge—even if not while steadily rising. That is to say, some narrowing down could be claimed in the cross-national range of mobility levels as between those displayed by the oldest and the youngest cohorts in our samples. For the former, as can be seen, the range of total mobility rates is from around 40 to over 70 percent, while for the latter it is from 50 to under 70 per cent—and, one might add, would be some ten percentage points narrower still if the one case of Scotland were to be discounted.

However, it is important to note how this convergence comes about. It is in fact to a large extent the result of an increase in total mobility in two nations, Ireland and Poland, in which the rate among older cohorts, at around the 40 per cent mark, was substantially lower than in other nations. Ireland and Poland are—together with Hungary—those nations in our sample in which, as we have earlier indicated, industrialisation was most delayed. An alternative interpretation of Figure 1 would therefore be that instead of revealing a general tendency towards convergence in mobility rates, it rather supports a hypothesis of the kind suggested by Lipset and Zetterberg: that is, of a specific upturn in mobility occurring at a stage relatively early in the industrialisation process when the first major impact of structural change is felt.

That Hungary would then appear as deviant, in showing a high total mobility rate even among the oldest men considered, need not be found surprising. This could be seen as the result of the quite exceptional amount of mobility imposed upon the Hungarian agricultural workforce through direct political intervention, and which is thus reflected across the experience of all age-groups alike. In the period immediately following the second world war, the land reforms of the provisional government created over half-a-million new peasant proprietors; but then, under the subsequent state socialist regime, agriculture was within a decade almost entirely collectivised through the establishment of co-operatives or state farms (Kulcsár, 1984: 78–84, 96–100; Brus, 1986a, 1986b). Thus, respondents to our 1973 survey who were the sons of agricultural proprietors—over a quarter of the total—held different class positions to their fathers more or less of necessity, and even in fact where they continued to work the same land.[11]

These findings on total mobility do, we believe, carry significant implications, to which we shall wish to return. It is, however, of further interest here to try to obtain a somewhat more detailed picture of tendencies in absolute rates by considering also intergenerational *outflow* rates. Unfortunately, the relative smallness of the sizes of certain of our national samples means that we cannot reliably base our examination of such rates on the seven-class version of our schema but must, for the most part, resort to the three-class version (cf. Appendix Table 2) which distinguishes simply between nonmanual, manual and farm classes.[12]

Figures 2 to 6, which are produced via the same procedures as Figure 1, show the course followed in each of our nations by five different outflow rates calculated from 3×3 intergenerational mobility tables (again for men aged 30–64). As is indicated, the rates in question are those for intergenerational immobility within the farm class, for mobility from farm origins to manual and to nonmanual destinations, and for mobility from manual origins to nonmanual destinations and *vice versa*. Of the other transitions possible within the 3×3 tables, those from manual and nonmanual origins to farm positions were generally followed by too few individuals to allow any reliable rates to be established; and the fact that the numbers involved here are more or less negligible means in turn that trends in the remaining rates—that is, rates of immobility within the manual and nonmanual classes—need scarcely be plotted separately, since they will be essentially the complements of those already examined of mobility between these two classes.

Figure 2 displays the changing proportions of men across birth-cohorts in our nine nations who were of farm origins and who were themselves found in farm work. A broad tendency is apparent for such intergenerational immobility to decline, which might be expected in consequence of the general contraction of agricultural employment. The decline in the cases of Ireland and Poland from farm immobility rates of upwards of 70 per cent in the oldest cohorts is of particular interest in view of the interpretation we have suggested of the increases in total mobility in these nations revealed in Figure 1. By resorting to the raw data, we can in fact show that changes within the farm sector here played a crucial part. Thus, the contribution of this sector to the total *im*mobility rate (i.e. the proportion of all cases in the mobility table found in cells on the main diagonal) fell in the Irish case from 69 per cent for men born before 1925 to only 27 per cent for those born after 1940, while in the Polish case the corresponding decline was from 77 to 35 per cent.

FIGURE 2
Outflow rates from farm origins to farm destinations for men in nine nations by birth year

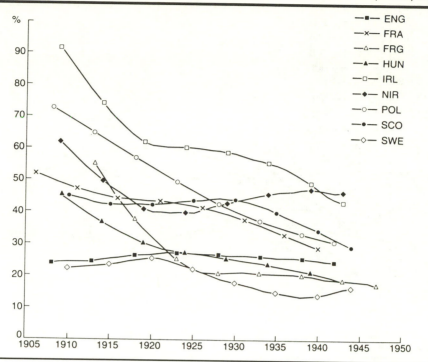

In two other nations, France and Hungary, the decline in farm immobility is also more or less continuous over the period to which our data refer. However, the cases of England, Scotland and Northern Ireland and likewise that of the FRG would suggest that, once the decline of agriculture has reached a certain point, rates of farm immobility tend to level out or to become rather variable. And Sweden appears quite distinctive in that farm immobility is shown at a low level—never more than 25 per cent—throughout the decades in which agricultural employment was falling. Here, though, we do have evidence to suggest some distortion in our results. Our corresponding plot for the transition to class of first employment indicates a strong decline in farm immobility; but, on account perhaps of the very rapidity of agricultural contraction in the post-war years, it would seem that many men also left the farm workforce at a quite late age, thus obscuring the downward trend when the transition to present class is considered.

Finally, it may be observed that in Figure 2, as in Figure 1, any impression of converging rates is created essentially by the rather dramatic Irish and Polish graphs. If these are disregarded, the cross-national range in rates of farm immobility merely fluctuates, being, for example, no narrower—at around 15 to 50 per cent—for men born from the mid–1930s onwards than it was for men born around 1920.

Figures 3 and 4 then display the course of outflow rates from farm origins to manual and nonmanual destinations respectively. Figure 3 would suggest that in those cases where declining trends in intergenerational immobility in farming were revealed in Figure 2, their counterpart has been increased outflows from farm origins into manual wage-earning positions in industry. France, Hungary, Ireland and Poland all show such increases of a continuous kind. In the remaining nations, however, trends are less readily discerned. In the cases of the FRG and Sweden, increasing pro-

FIGURE 3

Outflow rates from farm origins to manual destinations for men in nine nations by birth year

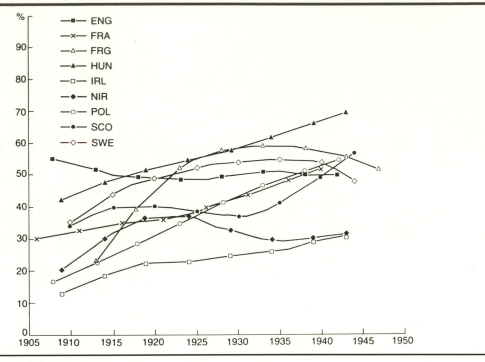

portions of men in the cohorts born up to about 1930 moved from farm origins into manual work—following what might perhaps be taken as a characteristic tendency of the drive to 'mature' industrialism. But in later cohorts this tendency is clearly not sustained, although for Sweden there is probably some underestimation of the rate in question as the converse of the distortion noted in regard to farm immobility. For England, Northern Ireland and Scotland, the graphs undulate in no readily interpretable way. Turning to the outflow rates from farm origins to nonmanual destinations presented in Figure 4, we find that trendless change is here still more manifest. The most remarkable feature of the graphs displayed is indeed their flatness, apart from the early rise from a near-zero level in the Irish case.[13]

The remaining point to be observed from Figures 3 and 4 together is that we find little indication at all of national mobility rates converging. Over the period covered, the

cross-national range for farm-to-manual outflows shifts upwards, but with little narrowing, from around 10 to 55 per cent to 30 to 70 per cent; while the rates for farm-to-nonmanual outflows are notable for being almost entirely confined within a range of 10 to 25 per cent.

The last two Figures in the series, 5 and 6, show changes in rates of intergenerational mobility between the broad manual and nonmanual classes that we distinguish. From inspection of the graphs, it would once again seem difficult to avoid the conclusion that no clear trends emerge. Although some impression may perhaps be given that, overall, mobility from manual origins to nonmanual destinations has decreased while that in the reverse direction has increased, it is in fact only in the Polish case that monotonic trends in these directions can be found. In general, fluctuating rates are displayed, and the graphs for different nations frequently cross. Moreover, as earlier remarked, the negligible vol-

FIGURE 4

Outflow rates from farm origins to non-manual destinations for men in nine nations by birth year

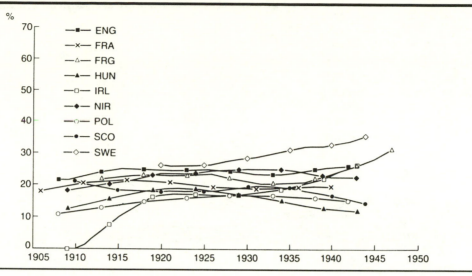

FIGURE 5

Outflow rates from manual origins to non-manual destinations for men in nine nations by birth year

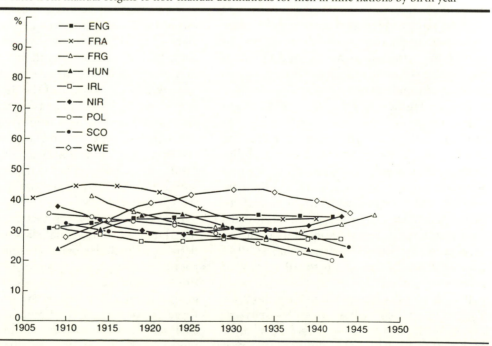

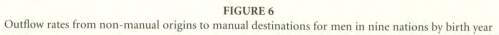

FIGURE 6

Outflow rates from non-manual origins to manual destinations for men in nine nations by birth year

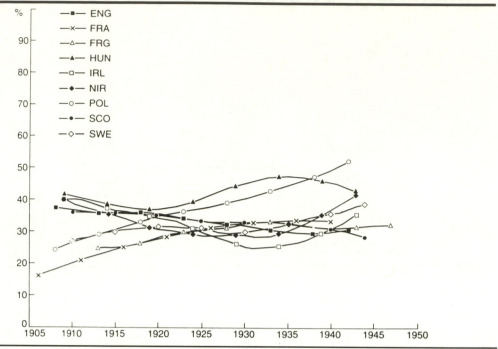

ume of outflows from both manual and non-manual origins to farm destinations means that the plots of Figures 5 and 6 can be taken as essentially the obverses of those relating to *im*mobility within our manual and nonmanual classes; so in the case of these rates too an absence of trends may be claimed.

Finally, Figures 5 and 6 again fail to provide evidence of cross-national convergence in mobility rates. Over the period covered, the cross-national range for rates of mobility from manual origins to nonmanual destinations narrows only slightly as it falls from around 30 to 55 per cent for the oldest cohorts down to 20 to 40 per cent for the youngest; and the range for mobility in the reverse direction shows no narrowing at all in moving from 20 to 45 up to 30 to 55 per cent.[14]

It is the results contained in these last two Figures—and also in Figure 4—that may occasion most surprise among those presented so far. It would be generally accepted that nonmanual work tends to grow and manual work to contract as industrial societies reach the more advanced stages of their development—regardless of whether this is seen as contributing to a net degrading or upgrading of the employment structure overall. And thus, within the context of the three-class version of our schema, increasing mobility into nonmanual destinations from farm and manual origins alike should be 'structurally' favoured. Yet, in our data, no consistent indication of such tendencies is to be found, even within the more advanced nations or among the younger cohorts.

However, it must in this connection be noted that our nonmanual class is very widely defined. It includes some groupings, such as routine nonmanual employees in administration, commerce and services, which have grown primarily through the greater workforce participation of women; and others, such as small proprietors and other self-employed workers, which, over the period that

FIGURE 7
Outflow rates from farm origins to service class destinations for men in nine nations by birth year

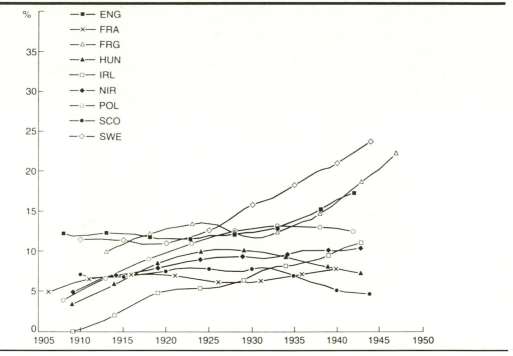

our data cover, were typically in decline. If, then, we wish to consider mobility flows into the nonmanual groupings that have most clearly expanded among the male workforce, which are in fact mostly at the higher levels of the white-collar range, we need to draw on data from mobility tables of a more elaborated kind. Although, as we have explained, we cannot go over entirely to the seven-class version of our schema, we can, for present purposes, make a useful compromise: we can construct mobility tables that apply the seven-class version to destinations while retaining the three-class version for origins.

In Figures 7 and 8 we show the course followed by two outflow rates derived from such 3 × 7 tables: that is, outflow rates from farm and from manual origins respectively into Class I+II of the seven-class version—the service class of primarily professional, higher technical, administrative and managerial employees. In other words, we here focus on subsets of the rates presented in Figures 4 and

5 where the mobility in question is into types of employment that *have* been in general expansion. Furthermore, we can also in this way examine changes in mobility flows which, in the light of the hierarchical divisions that we make within our class schema (cf. Appendix Table 3), could be regarded as representing mobility *upwards* from less to more advantaged class positions.[15]

A preliminary point to be noted about Figures 7 and 8 is that, because the rates we are here concerned with are generally lower and less differentiated than those presented in previous figures, we have doubled the vertical scale, thus of course 'enlarging' the changes that are depicted. Even so, they do not appear as highly dramatic.

In Figure 7, some increase in mobility from farm origins into the service class is shown up among younger cohorts in several nations—that is, in England, the FRG and Sweden and, more weakly, in Ireland. But in the remainder any increase that can be detected occurs

FIGURE 8

Outflow rates from manual origins to service class destinations for men in nine nations by birth year

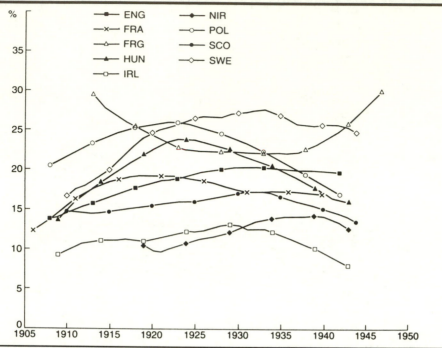

among older cohorts, and the trend then fades out—so that cross-national differences in rates in fact *widen*. In Figure 8, rates of mobility from manual origins into the service class likewise display an increase in England and Sweden which is at least held, and in the FRG they turn sharply upwards among the youngest cohorts. But again, too, the other nations differ, with the most common tendency being for rates first to rise but then at some later point to decline. It is of interest to note that this tendency is most marked in Figure 8, and also appears in Figure 7, in the graphs for our two eastern European nations. Upward mobility into the service class among Hungarian and Polish men born in the early 1920s—who would reach occupational maturity in the period of post-war 'socialist reconstruction'—rose to a level that later cohorts quite fail to match.

Where, among younger cohorts, the graphs of Figures 7 and 8 level out or turn down, we cannot preclude the possibility that this is in some part the result of age effects—so that in

fact, as the men in these cohorts become older, a larger proportion will enter into service-class positions. However, what we would doubt is that such effects are likely to an extent that would make the graphs seriously misleading. There are good empirical grounds for supposing—and the liberal theory would certainly predict—that the younger the men in our samples, the more probable it is that they will achieve upward mobility through education, so that this mobility will be apparent at a relatively early stage in their working lives. And in this connection, it is then further relevant to emphasise that the graphs corresponding to those of Figures 7 and 8 which depict mobility to class of first employment similarly fail to reveal consistently rising trends. It emerges rather that even if one considers only men born from the 1920s onwards, a steady increase in mobility into the service class from farm and manual origins alike is found in just one nation—namely, Sweden.

What, we believe, should be emphasised here is that although the service class does show a general tendency to expand within modern societies, it does not do so at a steady pace simply in response to the exigencies of industrial development. Periods of relatively rapid growth and of stasis will alternate under the influence of other factors, not least political ones, thus producing rises and falls in rates of upward mobility into this class of a kind which the Hungarian and Polish cases do no more perhaps than exemplify at their most striking.[16]

How, then, can we best sum up the foregoing findings in regard to trends in absolute rates? To begin with, we can say that our investigation of outflow rates points to certain trends which seem likely to have occurred in most, if not all, of the nations we consider at *some* stage of their industrial development:

(i) a decline in intergenerational immobility within the farm sector;

(ii) an increase in mobility from farm origins into manual employment in industry; and

(iii) some upturn in mobility from farm and manual origins into service-class positions.

To this extent, therefore, we might stop short of an extreme antinomianism of the kind that Sorokin could be taken to represent, and recognise that industrialism does carry typical implications for the direction of several broad mobility flows—as indeed Carlsson (1963) argued some time ago in a critique of Sorokin's position.

However, we must then also say that the trends that we are able to identify have rarely appeared as continuous over the period to which our data refer; that from nation to nation their phasing within the developmental process evidently differs; and moreover that changes in all other rates that we have examined would appear to be essentially directionless. In turn, therefore, we can produce little evidence that within our European nations mobility rates overall are moving steadily towards some relatively well defined 'industrial' pattern in the way that the liberal theory would suggest—and certainly not towards one that is characterised by steadily rising

mobility. The outflow rates that we have considered show no clear tendency to converge; and, whatever course they may follow, they are not associated with any consistent upward trend in total mobility rates. In the light of the evidence presented, and in particular of that of Figure 1, it could not be claimed that men in our national samples whose working lives began, say, after the second world war have generally lived in more mobile societies than those who first entered employment in the 1920s.

The one possible qualification that might here be made is suggested by our findings for Ireland and Poland. These could be taken as meeting the expectation that an upward shift in the level of total mobility will occur in the course of industrialisation where a rapid decline in agricultural employment or, more specifically perhaps, the break-up of a predominantly peasant economy, goes together with a rising demand for industrial labour. But even if, as Lipset and Zetterberg would hold, a shift of this kind can be regarded as a general characteristic of the emergence of industrial societies, at least two further points would still, on our evidence, need to be made. First, the upturn in mobility has to be seen as being of a delimited, once-and-for-all kind; and secondly, it still leaves ample room for subsequent variation in absolute mobility rates and patterns as nations proceed to the further stages of their development.[17]

Relative Rates

We move on now to consider trends in intergenerational class mobility from the standpoint of relative rates, which we shall treat in terms of odds ratios. That is, ratios which show the relative odds of individuals in two different classes of origin being found in one rather than another of two different classes of destination; or, alternatively, one could say, which show the degree of *net* association that exists between the classes of origin and of destination involved. Two further points concerning such ratios may here be noted.

First, the total set of odds ratios that can be calculated within a mobility table may be taken as representing the 'endogenous mobility regime' or 'pattern of social fluidity' that the table embodies. And since odds ratios are 'margin insensitive' measures, it is then possible for this underlying regime or pattern to remain unaltered as between two or more mobility tables even though their marginal distributions differ and, thus, all absolute rates that can be derived from them. Further, we might add, it would be possible for relative rates as expressed by odds ratios to differ from table to table in some systematic way without this being readily apparent from an inspection of absolute rates.

Secondly, odds ratios are the elements of loglinear models; and, thus, where these ratios are taken as the measure of relative mobility rates, hypotheses about the latter can be presented and formally tested through the application of such models. This is the approach that we shall here follow.

In examining relative rates, we shall attempt, in the same way as we did with absolute rates, to make inferences about the extent of changes over time from the mobility experience of successive birth-cohorts within our national samples. However, instead of here working with yearly cohorts, we distinguish four ten-year birth-cohorts, which can then be regarded, given the closeness of the dates of the inquiries from which the samples derive, as having more or less comparable locations within the broad sweep of recent European economic history.

The first—that is, the earliest—of these cohorts comprises men aged 55 to 64, who were thus mostly born in the first two decades of the century, and who entered employment before or during the inter-war depression years. The second is of men aged 45 to 54, the majority of whom were born in the 1920s and entered employment in the later 1930s or the war years. The third is that of men aged 35 to 44, who were born between the late 1920s and the early 1940s, and whose working lives have fallen very largely within the post-war period. And finally the fourth cohort is that of men aged 25 to 34, who were born from the end of the 1930s onwards and who mostly entered employment while the long boom was in train. This last cohort is clearly made up of respondents who could not be generally assumed to have reached a stage of occupational maturity, and this we must recall where it might be relevant to the interpretation of our results.

When we thus divide our national samples into cohorts, we again have a potential problem of unduly low cell counts in the mobility tables for each cohort. To obviate this, we base our analyses throughout on the five-class version of our schema (cf. Appendix Table 2).

As regards relative rates, there is, as we have noted, an obvious opposition between the expectations that follow from the liberal theory and those that may be derived from the FJH hypothesis. According to the former, a tendency should be found in the course of the development of industrial societies for relative rates to become more equal—or, one could say, for all odds ratios to move closer to the value of 1, which signifies the complete independence of class origins and destinations or 'perfect mobility'. According to the latter, relative rates will be basically the same across all societies that have market economies and (at least) nuclear family systems, whatever stage their level of industrial development may have reached; and thus, when examined over time within particular industrial societies, relative rates should reveal little change at all.

We may then start off from an attempt at evaluating these rival positions, and, to this end, we introduce a rather simple loglinear model which is, however, able to provide a direct representation of expectations under the FJH hypothesis, at least if this is taken *stricto sensu*. This model, which we have earlier labelled the 'constant social fluidity' (CnSF) model (Goldthorpe, 1980, 1987: ch.3; Erikson, Goldthorpe and Portocarero, 1983) may, for present purposes, be written as

$$\log F_{ijk} = \mu + \lambda_i^o + \lambda_j^D + \lambda_k^C \qquad (1)$$

$$+ \lambda_{ik}^{OC} + \lambda_{jk}^{DC} + \lambda_{ij}^{OD}$$

where F_{ijk} is the expected frequency in cell ijk of a three-way table comprising class of origin (O), class of destination (D) and cohort (C) and, on the right-hand side of the equation, μ is a scale factor, λ_i^o, λ_j^D and λ_k^C represent the 'main' effects of the distribution of individuals over origins, destinations and cohorts respectively, and the remaining terms represent the effects for the three possible two-way associations in the table.

Thus, the model entails a number of substantive propositions, most of which are unproblematic: for example, that an association exists between class of origin and class of destination; and that further associations exist between class of origin and cohort and between class of destination and cohort—in other words, men in different cohorts have different origin and destination distributions. It is, however, a further proposition that is critical. Since no *three-way* association is provided for in the model (the λ_{ijk}^{ODC} term does not appear), it is also entailed that the level of association between class of origin and of destination is *constant across cohorts* or, one could alternatively say, that over the mobility tables for successive cohorts all corresponding relative rates, as measured by odds ratios, are identical.

We can then consider our nine nations separately, and in each case fit the above CnSF model to a three-way table which comprises the five classes of origin, five classes of destination and four cohorts that we propose to distinguish. The results of so doing are presented in Table 1.

In this table we also report the results of applying a model that represents the hypothesis of the (conditional) independence of class origins and destinations; that is, the CnSF model minus the λ_{ij}^{OD} term. We do not expect this independence model to fit the data—and, as can be seen, in no case does it; but it serves as a useful baseline, by reference to which we can assess, through the rG^2 statistic in the fourth column of the table, how much of the total association between class of origin and class of destination the CnSF model is able to account for.[18]

Also in addition to the more usual 'goodness of fit' statistics, we give in the last column of Table 1 values for the statistic $G^2(S)$. This we introduce here to attempt to deal with a difficulty arising from the large variation in the sizes of our national samples. In consequence of this variation, our national mobility tables differ quite widely in their capacity to show up as statistically significant relatively small deviations from models that we fit to them. It is as if we were looking at slides through microscopes of greatly differing power: we have the possibility of seeing far more detail in some cases than in others. Thus, there is the evident danger that we do not evaluate a model in an evenhanded way from nation to nation. We could, for example, be led to reject a model in the Polish case on account of deviations which, were they present also in the case of, say, Ireland, we would simply not observe. Thus, we evidently need some measure of goodness of fit that is standardised by sample size. One possibility would be to take G^2/N. However, we prefer, as a more refined measure, Schwartz's suggestion of $G2(S)$ which is given by $((G^2 - df)/N) \times K + df$, where K is the sample size which is to be taken as standard.[19] We will follow the conservative practice of setting K equal to the size of the *smallest* of the national samples with which we are concerned—and thus, in Table 1, at 1746. To help remind the reader of the hypothetical nature of $G^2(S)$—that it is the G^2 value that we would expect from a sample of size K, all other things being equal—we report it only to the nearest integer.

What, then, can we learn from the content of Table 1? It would in fact appear that the CnSF model performs fairly well. It is true that the p values reported indicate that in only four of the nine nations—England, Ireland, Northern Ireland and Sweden—would one retain this model, taken as the null hypothesis, according to the conventional 0.05 criterion. However, it is also evident that much of the variation in the G^2 and p values returned is attributable to differences in sample size. When one examines the $G^2(S)$ values in the final column of the table, one finds that these are in

TABLE 1
Results of Fitting the CnSF Model to Intergenerational Class Mobility for Four Birth-Cohorts

Model*	G^2	df	p	$rG^{2†}$	$\Delta^‡$	$G^2(S)$ (1,746)
ENG						
(N = 8,343)						
OC DC (con. ind.)	1,695.0	64	0.00	—	16.1	405
OC DC OD (CnSF)	53.1	48	0.28	96.9	2.6	49
FRA						
(N = 16,431)						
OC DC	6,370.6	64	0.00	—	24.7	734
OC DC OD	96.7	48	0.00	98.5	·2.0	53
FRG						
(N = 3,570)						
OC DC	1,092.0	64	0.00	—	21.2	567
OC DC OD	81.9	48	0.00	92.5	4.4	65
HUN						
(N = 10,319)						
OC DC	2,386.0	64	0.00	—	19.2	457
OC DC OD	69.9	48	0.02	97.1	2.4	52
IRL						
(N = 1,746)						
OC DC	902.3	64	0.00	—	29.2	902
OC DC OD	60.2	48	0.11	93.3	5.2	60
NIR						
(N = 1,808)						
OC DC	780.6	64	0.00	—	25.5	756
OC DC OD	44.5	48	>0.50	94.3	5.0	45
POL						
(N = 27,993)						
OC DC	7,357.7	64	0.00	—	19.6	519
OC DC OD	66.7	48	0.04	99.1	1.4	49
SCO						
(N = 3,985)						
OC DC	1,146.6	64	0.00	—	18.1	538
OC DC OD	66.3	48	0.04	94.2	4.4	56
SWE						
(N = 1,882)						
OC DC	403.9	64	0.00	—	17.3	379
OC DC OD	45.2	48	>0.50	88.8	5.1	45

Notes:
   * O = origin class; D = destination class; C = cohort.
   † rG^2 shows the percentage reduction in the G^2 for a model taken as baseline (here the conditional independence model) that is achieved by a more complex model (here the CnSF model). For further discussion of this statistic, see n. 18.
   ‡ Δ is the dissimilarity index, showing the percentage of all cases in the table analysed that are misclassified—that is, allocated to the wrong cell—by a particular model.

fact contained within a rather narrow range, and moreover that in no case do they exceed the 65 mark, thus implying, with df = 48, p values of above 0.05. In other words, if we were restricted throughout to sample sizes of 1746, such as that we have for Ireland, we would find it difficult to reject the CnSF model for any nation—although the FRG would have to be regarded as a borderline case.

What could therefore be claimed on the basis of the foregoing is that while significant deviations from the CnSF model do have to be recognised in some at least of our nations, such deviations would not appear to be at all substantial. In this connection, it is of further relevance to note that in all cases but one the CnSF model accounts for more than 90 per cent of the total association existing between class of origin and of destination—the exception being Sweden, where the independence model fits least badly; and again, that within the different national mobility tables the CnSF model leads to the misclassification of, at most, only a little over 5 per cent of all cases.[20]. . .

Conclusions

We have sought in this paper to use data from European nations in order to evaluate various arguments concerning mobility trends within industrial societies. The major outcome, it might be said, has been a negative one: that is, considerable doubt has been thrown on claims associated with what we have called the liberal theory of industrialism. We have found no evidence of general and abiding trends towards either higher levels of total mobility or of social fluidity within the nations we have considered; nor evidence that mobility rates, whether absolute or relative, are changing in any other consistent direction; nor again evidence that such rates show a tendency over time to become cross-nationally

more similar. The most that could be said on the side of arguments proposing some linkage between industrial development and increased and more standardised mobility rates would be that structural changes—most importantly, the decline in agriculture—appear likely to generate upturns in total, and also perhaps in certain outflow rates over periods of limited duration and of very variable phasing.

Such results are all the more damaging to the liberal theory since, as we earlier emphasised, Europe over the middle decades of the twentieth century, and above all in the postwar era, provides a context in which the theory should have every chance of showing its force. Furthermore, we may reiterate the point that any distortions in our findings that derive from our reliance on (quasi-) cohort analysis, and in particular from the confounding of age and period effects, are unlikely to be ones that tell unfairly against liberal claims: if anything, the contrary should be supposed.

We would therefore believe that the attempt to represent changes in mobility rates in modern societies as displaying regular developmental patterns, driven by a functional logic of industrialism, is one that faces serious empirical difficulties; and, in turn, we would argue that the need must be recognised to search for ways in which these changes might be more satisfactorily understood. In this connection, there is then one further outcome of the analyses of the present chapter which should, in our judgment, be seen as having major significance: namely, that while it appears that liberal expectations of directional tendencies in absolute and relative mobility rates are in both respects largely unfounded, *the nature of the contrary evidence is quite different from one case to the other: with absolute rates it is evidence of trendless, though often quite wide, fluctuation, but with relative rates it is evidence of considerable stability.* What is thus suggested is that in attempts to go beyond the liberal theory, the treatment of absolute and of relative rates is likely to set quite different kinds of problem and of analytical task.

As regards absolute rates, liberal expectations most obviously fail, we would suggest, because changes in structural influences on mobility do not themselves have the regularity that liberal theorists have been wont to suppose. Analyses of economic growth advanced in the 1950s and 1960s by authors such as Clark (1957), Rostow (1960) and Kuznets (1966) were taken as demonstrating clear sequences of change in the sectoral and occupational, and hence in the class, composition of labour forces. However, it would by now be widely accepted that, whatever theoretical insights the work of these authors may provide, it does *not* allow one to think, at a historical level, in terms of a well-defined series of developmental stages through which the structure of the labour forces of different nations will pass in turn as industrialisation proceeds. While certain very general tendencies of change may in this respect be identified, considerable variation still prevails from case to case in relation to the speed with which change occurs and the extent to which different aspects of change are separated in time or overlap (Singelmann, 1978; Gagliani, 1985).

The European experience of industrialisation, which has provided the setting for our analyses in this paper, itself well illustrates the variety of paths that the development of labour forces may follow; and it does, moreover, bring out the diversity of the causal factors at work here—by no means all of which can be plausibly seen as part of some englobing developmental process. Thus, the historical formation of national class structures has to be seen as reflecting not only early or late industrialisation but, in addition, important influences stemming, on the one hand, from the international political economy and, on the other, from the various strategies pursued by national governments in response to both external and internal pressures. To take but one example here, the contraction of agricul-

ture—which we have found to play a major part in the pattern of change in absolute class mobility rates—cannot be understood, as it has occurred in particular cases, simply in terms of the shifting marginal productivity of sectors and differences in the elasticities of demand for their products that the theory of economic growth would emphasise. As the agrarian histories of our nations can amply show (see, e.g., Priebe, 1976), the pace and timing of agricultural contraction also—and often far more decisively—reflects whether nations were at the centre or on the periphery of international trading relations, in a position of economic dominance or dependence; and, further, the policies that their governments adopted towards agriculture both in regard to its social organisation and its protection against or exposure to market forces.[21]

Once, therefore, the variability and complexity of the determination of the structural contexts of mobility is appreciated, the extent to which the movement of absolute rates over time appears as merely trendless can no longer be found especially surprising. If changes in such rates do largely express the shifting conjunctures of a diversity of exogenous effects, then 'trendlessness' as suggested by Sorokin, is indeed what must be expected. It is noteworthy that it is essentially an argument on these lines that has been pursued by the several European economic and social historians who have sought to join in the sociological debate. In rejecting 'the idea of a sustained growth in social mobility during industrialization', these authors have emphasised the 'multitude of factors' which affect mobility levels; and, in place of developmental stages, they have sought rather to establish empirically a number of different 'eras' or 'phases' of both rising *and falling* mobility within the period in which European industrialisation has occurred (see esp. Kaelble, 1984: 490; also Kaelble, 1981; Mendels, 1976; Kocka, 1980).

Thus, we would maintain, the crucial issue that arises so far as absolute rates of mobility are concerned is that of whether, or how far the course of change they follow is in fact a phenomenon open to explanation in macrosociological terms. Investigators who have been impressed by the degree of temporal variation in absolute, as compared with relative, rates have gone on to conclude that the dynamism of the former must lie primarily in structural effects, and in turn they have urged that these should not be treated as merely a 'nuisance factor' but should become themselves the focus of inquiry (e.g. Hauser *et al.*, 1975; Grusky and Hauser, 1984; Goldthorpe, 1985). However, while this argument has an evident logic, it does leave quite undecided the question of just what *kind* of understanding of structural effects—and thence of change in absolute rates—it might be possible to achieve. In so far as generalisations about such effects can be made, will they prove to be of any great explanatory value when applied to particular instances? Or may one be in this respect forced back willy-nilly to a reliance largely on specific historical descriptions—as a position such as that of Sorokin would in effect imply? Or again are there perhaps intermediate possibilities?

Turning now to relative rates, we meet with a very different situation. In this case, the liberal theory is undermined because, instead of the anticipated trend of change, in the direction of greater equality, we find evidence of an essential stability. Although shifts in relative rates can in some cases be detected [see Erikson and Goldthorpe 1992: 90–101], these are not only ones which go in various directions but, more importantly, ones which, as against those observed in absolute rates, are of very limited magnitude—so that one might wish to speak more of 'oscillation' than of fluctuation. In other words, the liberal theory would here appear to fail because the logic of industrialism has not in fact automatically generated the changes within processes of social selection which were expected of it, and through which a steady increase in fluidity and openness would be promoted.

It is in this connection of interest to note that of late exponents of the liberal theory appear to have modified their position in regard to relative rates quite significantly. Thus, for example, Treiman initially sought to provide the hypothesis of a trend towards greater openness with a rationale largely in terms of the functional exigencies of industrialism (1970: 218). However, in a recent paper (with Yip), he puts much stronger emphasis on the part that is played in creating greater openness and equality of opportunity by the more proximate factor of greater *equality of condition*—that is, by a greater equality in the economic, cultural and social resources that families possess. And while it is still maintained that this increase in equality of condition itself ultimately derives from the development of industrialism, it is at the same time accepted that 'industrialization and inequality do not move in perfect concert' and, further, that *other* factors, especially political ones—for example, whether a nation has a socialist regime—may also affect the degree of inequality that exists (Treiman and Yip, 1989: 376–7). That is to say, it would here seem to be recognised that even in cases where a trend towards greater fluidity may be empirically established, this cannot be regarded as simply a matter of developmental necessity but must rather be explained as the contingent outcome of quite complex patterns of social action (cf. also Ganzeboom, Luijkx and Treiman, 1989; Simkus *et al.*, 1990). And conversely, this revised, and evidently much weaker, position is then of course able to accommodate the alternative possibility that, in particular instances, no trend of this kind is observed—because countervailing forces have in fact proved too strong.

The stability in relative rates that we have shown gains in significance, we may add, not only because the period that our data cover comprised decades of unprecedented economic growth but also because it was, of course, one of major political upheavals, in which, in the train of war and revolution, national frontiers were redrawn and massive shifts of population occurred.[22] The fact that the relative rates underlying the mobility experience of cohorts within our national samples should then reveal so little change—whether directional or otherwise—becomes all the more remarkable. While we have not been able to support the claim of a sustained developmental trend, we have, it appears, found indications of something of no less sociological interest: that is, of a constancy in social process prevailing within our several nations over decades that would in general have to be characterised in terms of the transformation and turbulence that they witnessed.

Furthermore, this finding is, as we have indicated, one which may be related to a larger sociological argument, namely, that represented by the FJH hypothesis. We have presented analyses which indicate that *some* variation in fluidity patterns does in fact occur among nations—indeed, more than within nations over time—and also that this variation shows no tendency to diminish [see Erikson and Goldthorpe 1992: 90–101]. Thus, expectations of convergence are not met. However, neither would cross-national varia-

tion appear to be increasing; and, more importantly, as we have elsewhere sought to show (Erikson and Goldthorpe 1987, 1992: ch. 5), it could not be reckoned as sufficiently wide to rule out the possibility that the 'basic' similarity in relative rates that the FJH hypothesis claims is the major source of the temporal stability that we have observed; or, that is, the possibility that *constancy* above all reflects *commonality*.

In other words, in so far as the degree of similarity proposed by the FJH hypothesis is established, we may think of temporal shifts in fluidity within nations as being no more than oscillations occurring around the standard pattern that the hypothesis implies or, at all events, as being restricted in their frequency and extent by whatever set of effects it is that generates this pattern. And in this regard, then, the ultimate task becomes that of understanding these effects; or, that is, of seeking to explain not variance, to which, as Lieberson (1987) has observed, analytical strategies within macrosociology have thus far been chiefly oriented, but rather a *lack* of variance—for which, unfortunately, appropriate strategies remain largely to be devised.

APPENDIX TABLE 1

National Inquiries Used as Data Sources

	Inquiry	Date	References for survey details
England & Wales (ENG)	Oxford National Occupational Mobility Inquiry	1972	Goldthorpe (1980)
France (FRA)	INSEE Enquête Formation-Qualification Professionelle	1970	Pohl, Thélot and Jousset (1974)
Federal Republic of Germany (FRG)	ZUMA Superfile	1976–1978	Erikson *et al.* (1988)
Hungary (HUN)	Social Mobility and Occupational Change in Hungary	1973	Andorka and Zagórski (1980)
Irish Republic (IRL)	Determinants of Occupational Mobility	1973–1974	O'Muircheartaigh and Wiggins (1977)
Northern Ireland (NIR)	Determinants of Occupational Mobility	1973–1974	O'Muircheartaigh and Wiggins (1977)
Poland (POL)	Change in the Socio-Occupational Structure	1972	Zagórski (1977–8)
Scotland (SCO)	Scottish Mobility Study	1974–1975	Payne (1987)
Sweden (SWE)	Level of Living Survey	1974	Andersson (1987)

APPENDIX TABLE 2
The Class Schema

Full version		Collapsed versions					
		Seven-class*		Five-class		Three-class	
I	Higher-grade professionals, administrators, and officials; managers in large industrial establishments; large proprietors	I+II	Service class: professionals, administrators and managers; higher-grade technicians; supervisors of non-manual workers				
II	Lower-grade professionals, administrators, and officials; higher-grade technicians; managers in small industrial establishments; supervisors of non-manual employees			I–III	White-collar workers		
IIIa	Routine non-manual employees, higher grade (administration and commerce)	III	Routine non-manual workers: routine non-manual employees in administration and commerce; sales personnel; other rank-and-file service workers			Non-manual workers	
IIIb	Routine non-manual employees, lower grade (sales and services)						
IVa	Small proprietors, artisans, etc., with employees	IVa+b	Petty bourgeoisie: small proprietors and artisans, etc., with and without employees	IVa+b	Petty bourgeoisie		
IVb	Small proprietors, artisans, etc., without employees						
IVc	Farmers and smallholders; other self-employed workers in primary production	IVc	Farmers: farmers and smallholders and other self-employed workers in primary production	IVc+VIIb	Farm workers	Farm workers	
V	Lower-grade technicians; supervisors of manual workers	V+VI	Skilled workers: lower-grade technicians; supervisors of manual workers; skilled manual workers	V+VI	Skilled workers		
VI	Skilled manual workers					Manual workers	
VIIa	Semi- and unskilled manual workers (not in agriculture, etc.)	VIIa	Non-skilled workers: semi- and unskilled manual workers (not in agriculture, etc.)	VIIa	Non-skilled workers		
VIIb	Agricultural and other workers in primary production	VIIb	Agricultural labourers: agricultural and other workers in primary production				

APPENDIX TABLE 3

Scores for Classes of the Schema on Different Occupational Scales as a Basis for a Threefold Hierarchical Division

Scale*	Class						
	I+II	III	IVa+b	IVc	V+VI	VIIa	VIIb
Treiman	56	35	42	44	35	29	24
Hope–Goldthorpe (England)	63	36	39	47	40	29	31
Wegener (FRG)	92	50	49	50	49	39	30
Irish Occupational Index (all Ireland)	58	30	42	42	37	24	26
de Lillo–Schizzerotto (Italy)	71	41	51	48	34	20	11
Naoi (Japan)	62	41	37	37	41	33	30
Duncan (USA)	66	27	46	25	33	17	14
Division	1			2			3

Note:

    * The international Treiman scale and those for the FRG, Ireland, and Japan are intended as scales of occupational prestige, although constructed in different ways; the English scale and also, it would seem, the Italian, are intended as ones of the general desirability of occupations in popular estimation; and the US scale, while originally constructed as a proxy for a prestige scale, is now generally interpreted as one of the socio-economic status of occupations. For further details, see Treiman (1977), Goldthorpe and Hope (1974), Wegener (1988), Boyle (1976), de Lillo and Schizzerotto (1985), Naoi (1979), and Duncan (1961).

Notes

1. This paper is based on chapter 3 of Robert Erikson and John H. Goldthorpe, *The Constant Flux: A Study of Class Mobility in Industrial Societies*, The Clarendon Press, Oxford, 1992. The research on which this book reports was carried out under the auspices of the CASMIN-Projekt, based at the Institüt für Sozialwissenschaften of the University of Mannheim and funded by grants from the Stiftung Volkswagenwerk, Hanover. Readers are referred to the above work (chapter 2 esp.) for full details of the comparative methodology followed in research.

2. The influence here of the 'stages-of-growth' model of Rostow (1960: see esp. Chart 1) would seem to be of particular importance and also, perhaps—though the evidence is indirect—the interpretation of European industrial development provided by Landes (1957, 1965, 1972), which places major emphasis upon the rate and pattern of diffusion of techniques of production from Britain to the more 'backward' economies of the European mainland.

3. Thus, for example, in Kerr *et al.* (1960) discussion of France and Italy is largely concerned with the impediments to industrial development that result from the persisting importance of 'family-dominated enterprises' with 'patrimonial management' (see e.g. pp. 80, 141–2; and cf. Landes, 1957); and discussion of Germany, with difficulties of social rigidity and authoritarianism, following from the promotion of industrialisation by a dynastic elite (e.g. pp. 54–5, 150–1).

4. It is of interest that Bell should refer to the situation on which he comments as one 'that has gone relatively unexamined'. This statement may well be true for American theorists of industrialism, but it can scarcely hold in the case of European economic and social historians. See, for example, the discussion of issues central to the 'reperiodisation' of the development of industrial society in Europe that are found in Wrigley (1972) and Mayer (1981).

5. So far as emigration is concerned, a detailed review of the possible and likely effects on mobility rates and propensities is provided in Hout (1989), with special reference to the Irish case.

6. For our present purposes, it is the confounding of period by age effects that is most likely to create problems. To the extent that cohort effects are present in the data, this may be regarded as valid evidence against the occurrence of secular trends.

7. This is in fact the highest maximum age that we could apply across all nine of our national samples.

8. The wording of the questions from which this information was derived varied somewhat from one national inquiry to another but not, we believe, in ways likely to have any significant effects on the comparability of data. In this and all similar instances full details of question wording, construction of variables, etc. are to be found in the documentation to the CASMIN International Social Mobility Superfile (Erikson *et al.*, 1988).

9. We are greatly endebted to Jan Hoem for his most generous help in this aspect of our work.

10. These plots are not shown but in what follows it may be assumed that where no reference is made to rates of mobility from class origins to class of first employment, our findings in this respect would not lead us seriously to qualify those we have obtained for rates from class origins to present class.

11. The results that we report here for Hungary do of course depend on our treating workers on agricultural co-operatives or state farms as having a different class position (VIIb) from that of peasant proprietors (IVc). Some analysts of mobility in Hungary have not made this distinction; but we would argue the desirability of so doing, wherever it is practically feasible. It was, after all, precisely the aim both of the immediate post-war land reform and of the subsequent collectivisation programme to *change* agrarian class relations. In the Polish case, it should be noted, the attempt to collectivise agriculture that the regime launched at the end of the 1940s met with fierce peasant opposition and was finally abandoned in 1956 (cf. Lewis, 1973).

12. Although, then, we are here forced back to the obviously rather crude three-class basis of much earlier comparative research, we must stress that we still do achieve a much higher standard of data comparability. As a result of our systematic recoding of the original unit-record data (see Erikson and Goldthorpe, 1992: ch. 2), we have a reasonable assurance that the categories of 'nonmanual', 'manual' and 'farm' are being applied in a consistent manner from nation to nation, rather than providing comparability of a merely nominal kind.

13. It may be noted that in Figure 4 the left tail of the curve for Sweden has been deleted. This is on account of its unreliability, as determined by a test developed by Hoem (see Erikson and Goldthorpe, 1992: ch. 3, Annex). For the same reason, we have also deleted the left tail of the curve for Northern Ireland in Figure 8.

14. These results are of direct relevance to the Lipset-Zetterberg hypothesis of cross-national similarity in absolute rates, since this was in fact formulated in terms of outflow rates from nonmanual to manual positions and *vice versa*. We do not take up this issue here (but see further Erikson and Goldthorpe, 1992: ch. 6).

15. Following the hierarchical levels that we propose, a further upward flow—that our 3×7 tables do not enable us to distinguish—would be represented by men entering Class I + II positions from Class III origins.

16. Thus, for example, in the English case the more or less continuous rise in upward mobility into the service class across the cohorts we distinguish can be related to a corresponding steady expansion of this class from a time somewhere between 1931 and 1951 (there was no 1941 Census)—following, however, on several decades in which it grew scarcely at all (see Goldthorpe, 1980, 1987: ch. 2 esp.). As regards socialist societies, it may further be noted that evidence of a 'parabolic' curve for upward mobility, similar to that we record in Hungary and Poland, is also found for post-war Czechoslovakia in data from a survey conducted in 1984 (personal communication from Marek Boguszak and cf. Boguszak, 1990).

17. It would, moreover, be mistaken simply to equate a peasant economy—or society—with a 'traditional' one. Thus, while one may with justification speak of a peasant economy existing in substantial areas of Ireland at least up to the 1940s, many of its key institutional features—most importantly, perhaps, non-partible inheritance—were relatively new (cf. Hannan, 1979). The Irish peasant community, as classically depicted by Arensberg and Kimball (1940, 1968), has in fact to be seen as the historical product of economic and social conditions in Ireland following the Great Famine of 1846–9 and then of the land reform legislation introduced between 1870 and the First World War.

18. It is important that rG^2, referred to by Goodman (1972) as the 'coefficient of multiple determination', should be interpreted within the particular context of loglinear modelling, rather than being taken as the equivalent of the perhaps more familiar R^2 of regression analysis. As Schwartz has pointed out (1985), the fact that R^2s are typically much lower than rG^2s reflects the fact that in regression the units of analysis are usually individuals while in loglinear modelling they are the cells of cross-tabulations and the scores are the numbers of individuals in a cell. Such aggregate data must then be expected to reveal stronger regularities than individual-level data. Schwartz's summary (1985: 2–3) is apt: rG^2 'measures how adequately a model accounts for the observed *associations* among a pre-specified set of variables while R^2 and Eta^2 measure the amount of *variation* in one variable that can be accounted for by its (linear) association with specified independent variables'. The point

may be added that the substantive meaning of rG[2] will of course depend on the model that is chosen as baseline.

19. This suggestion was made to us by Joseph E. Schwartz in a personal communication, for which we are duly grateful.

20. We may add that results from equivalent analyses of data referring to mobility from class of origin to class of first employment are essentially similar. In only one case, that of Ireland, would the CnSF model be rejected on the basis of the G[2](S) statistic; and again only in the Swedish case does the model not account for at least 90 per cent of the total origin-destination association, while at most only a little over 5 per cent of all cases are misclassified. It should, however, be recalled that we cannot undertake an analysis of the kind in question for the FRG, owing to lack of information on first employment.

21. Moreover, while we would believe that 'demand side' factors are generally of major importance in promoting structural change, 'supply side' ones may also have to be taken into account—for example, the effects of demographic change, including in- and out-migration, and of changes in the workforce participation rates of women and of different age-groups. And in these respects too political intervention may obviously play a crucial role.

22. Most importantly, in the aftermath of World War II the FRG was created out of the division of the Third Reich, and Poland's frontiers were moved some 150–200 miles to the west—both changes being accompanied by large population movements. In addition, one may note the truncation of Hungary in 1920 (with the loss of almost 70 per cent of its area and 60 per cent of its population); and the partition of Ireland in 1920–2, following the War of Independence and the Civil War, so as to create the Irish Free State (which became the Irish Republic in 1949) and the six counties of Northern Ireland, a constituent element of the United Kingdom with, up to 1973, its own parliament and executive.

Bibliography

Andersson, L. (1987): 'Appendix A: Sampling and Data Collection' in R. Erikson and R. Åberg eds., *Welfare in Transition: A Survey of Living Conditions in Sweden 1968–1981*. Oxford: Clarendon Press.

Andorka, R. and K. Zagórski (1980): *Socio-Occupational Mobility in Hungary and Poland*. Warsaw: Polish Academy of Sciences.

Arensberg, C.M. and S.T. Kimball (1940, 2nd ed. 1968): *Family and Community in Ireland*. Cambridge, Mass.: Harvard University Press.

Bell, D. (1980): 'Liberalism in the Post-Industrial Society' in *Sociological Journeys*. London: Heinemann.

Blau, P.M. and O.D. Duncan (1967): *The American Occupational Structure*. New York: Wiley.

Blossfeld, H.-P. (1986): 'Career Opportunities in the Federal Republic of Germany'. *European Sociological Review* 2.

Boguszak, M. (1990): 'Transition to Socialism and Intergenerational Class Mobility: The Model of Core Social Fluidity Applied to Czechoslovakia' in M. Haller ed., *Class Structure in Europe*. Armonk, N.Y.: Sharpe.

Boyle, J.F. (1976): 'Analysis of the Irish Occupational Index'. Department of Social Studies, The Queen's University, Belfast.

Braverman, H. (1974): *Labor and Monopoly Capitalism*. New York: Monthly Review Press.

Brus, W. (1986a): 'Postwar Reconstruction and Socio-Economic Transformation' in M.C. Kaser and E.A. Radice eds., *The Economic History of Eastern Europe, 1919–1975*, vol. 2. Oxford: Clarendon Press.

Brus, W. (1986b): '1950 to 1953: The Peak of Stalinism' in M.C. Kaser ed., *The Economic History of Eastern Europe, 1919–1975*, vol. 3. Oxford: Clarendon Press.

Carchedi, G. (1977): *On the Economic Identification of Classes*. London: Routledge.

Carlsson, G. (1963): 'Sorokin's Theory of Social Mobility' in P.J. Allen ed., *Pitirim A. Sorokin in Review*. Durham, N.C.: Duke University Press.

Clark, C. (3rd ed., 1957): *The Conditions of Economic Progress*. London: Macmillan.

Crompton, R. and G. Jones (1984): *White-Collar Proletariat: Deskilling and Gender in Clerical Work*. London: Macmillan.

Duncan, O.D. (1961): 'A Socioeconomic Index for All Occupations' in A.J. Reiss ed., *Occupations and Social Status*. New York: Free Press.

Dunlop, J.T., F.H. Harbison, C. Kerr and C.A. Myers (1975): *Industrialism and Industrial Man Reconsidered*. Princeton: Inter-University Study of Human Resources in National Development.

Erikson, R. and J.H. Goldthorpe (1987): 'Commonality and Variation in Social Fluidity in Industrial Nations. Part I: A Model for Evaluating the 'FJH Hypothesis'; Part II: The Model of Core Social Fluidity Applied'. *European Sociological Review* 3.

Erikson, R. and J.H. Goldthorpe (1992): *The Constant Flux: A Study of Class Mobility in Industrial Societies*. Oxford: Clarendon Press.

Erikson, R., J.H. Goldthorpe and L. Portocarero (1983): 'Intergenerational Class Mobility and the Convergence Thesis'. *British Journal of Sociology* 34.

Erikson, R., J.H. Goldthorpe, W. König, P. Lüttinger and W. Müller (1988): 'CASMIN International Mobility Superfile: Documentation'. Mannheim: Institut für Sozialwissenschaften, University of Mannheim.

Featherman, D.L., F.L. Jones and R.M. Hauser (1975): 'Assumptions of Social Mobility Research in the US: The Case of Occupational Status'. *Social Science Research* 4.

Gagliani, G. (1985): 'Long-Term Changes in the Occupational Structure'. *European Sociological Review* 1.

Ganzeboom, H., R. Luijkx and D.J. Treiman (1989): 'Intergenerational Class Mobility in Comparative Perspective'. *Research in Social Stratification and Mobility* 8.

Glenn, N.D. (1977): *Cohort Analysis*. Beverly Hills: Sage.

Goldthorpe, J.H. (with Catriona Llewellyn and Clive Payne) (1980, 2nd ed. 1987): *Social Mobility and Class Structure in Modern Britain*. Oxford: Clarendon Press.

Goldthorpe, J.H. (1985): 'On Economic Development and Social Mobility'. *British Journal of Sociology* 36.

Goldthorpe, J.H. and K. Hope (1974): *The Social Grading of Occupations: A New Approach and Scale*. Oxford: Clarendon Press.

Goodman, L.A. (1972): 'A General Model for the Analysis of Surveys'. *American Journal of Sociology* 77.

Grusky, D.B. and R.M. Hauser (1984): 'Comparative Social Mobility Revisited: Models of Convergence and Divergence in 16 Countries'. *American Sociological Review* 49.

Hannan, D.F. (1979): *Displacement and Development: Class, Kinship and Social Change in Irish Rural Communities*. Dublin: The Economic and Social Research Institute.

Hauser, R.M., P.J. Dickinson, H.P. Travis and J.M. Koffel (1975): 'Temporal Change in Occupational Mobility: Evidence for Men in the United States'. *American Sociological Review* 40.

Hoem, J.M. and P. Linneman (1987): 'The Tails in Moving Average Graduation'. Stockholm: Research Reports in Demography 37, University of Stockholm.

Hout, M. (1989): *Following in Father's Footsteps: Social Mobility in Ireland*. Cambridge, Mass.: Harvard University Press.

Kaelble, H. (1981): *Historical Research on Social Mobility*. London: Croom Helm.

Kaelble, H. (1984): 'Eras of Social Mobility in 19th and 20th Century Europe'. *Journal of Social History* 17.

Kemp, T. (1978): *Historical Patterns of Industrialization*. London: Longman.

Kerr, C. (1969): *Marshall, Marx and Modern Times*. Cambridge: Cambridge University Press.

Kerr, C. (1983): *The Future of Industrial Societies*. Cambridge, Mass.: Harvard University Press.

Kerr, C., J.T. Dunlop, F.H. Harbison and C.A. Myers (1960, 2nd ed. 1973): *Industrialism and Industrial Man*. Cambridge, Mass.: Harvard University Press.

Kindleberger, C.P. (1967): *Europe's Postwar Growth: The Role of Labor Supply*. Cambridge, Mass.: Harvard University Press.

Kocka, J. (1980): 'The Study of Social Mobility and the Formation of the Working Class in the 19th Century'. *Le mouvement social* 111.

Kulcsár, K. (1984): *Contemporary Hungarian Society*. Budapest: Corvina.

Kuznets, S. (1966): *Modern Economic Growth*. New Haven: Yale University Press.

Landes, D.S. (1957): 'Observations on France: Economy, Society and Politics'. *World Politics*, April.

Landes, D.S. (1965, 2nd ed. 1972): *The Unbound Prometheus: Technological Change and Industrial Development in Western Europe from 1750 to the Present*. Cambridge: Cambridge University Press.

Lewis, P. (1973): 'The Peasantry' in D. Lane and G. Kolankiewicz eds., *Social Groups in Polish Society*. London: Macmillan.

Lieberson, S. (1985, 2nd ed. 1987): *Making It Count*. Berkeley, University of California Press.

de Lillo, A. and A. Schizzerotto (1985): *La valutazione sociale delle occupazioni*. Bologna: II Mulino.

Lipset, S.M. and H.L. Zetterberg (1956): 'A Theory of Social Mobility'. *Transactions of the Third World Congress of Sociology*, vol. 3. London: International Sociological Association.

Lipset, S.M. and H.L. Zetterberg (1959): 'Social Mobility in Industrial Societies' in S.M. Lipset and R. Bendix, *Social Mobility in Industrial Society*. Berkeley: University of California Press.

Lutz, B. (1984): *Der kurze Traum immerwährender Prosperität*. Frankfurt: Campus.

Mayer, A.J. (1981): *The Persistence of the Old Regime: Europe to the Great War*. New York: Pantheon.

Mendels, F.F. (1976): 'Social Mobility and Phases of Industrialisation'. *Journal of Interdisciplinary History* 7.

Naoi, A. (1979): 'Shokugyoteki Chiishakudo no Kosei' (The Construction of the Occupational Status Scale) in K. Tominaga ed., *Nihon no Kaiso Kozo* (The Stratification Structure in Japan). Tokyo: Todai Shuppan Kai.

O'Brien, P. and C. Keyder (1978): *Economic Growth in Britain and France, 1780–1914*. London: Allen and Unwin.

O'Muircheartaigh, C.A. and R.D. Wiggins (1977): 'Sample Design and Evaluation for an

Occupational Mobility Study'. *Economic and Social Review* 8.

Parsons, T. (1960): *Structure and Process in Modern Societies*. Glencoe: Free Press.

Parsons, T. (1967): *Sociological Theory and Modern Society*. New York: Free Press.

Parsons, T. (1971): *The System of Modern Societies*. Englewood Cliffs: Prentice-Hall.

Payne, G. (1987): *Employment and Opportunity*. London: Macmillan.

Pohl, R., C. Thélot and M-F. Jousset (1974): *L'Enquête Formation-Qualification Professionelle de 1970*. Paris: INSEE.

Priebe, H. (1976): 'The Changing Role of Agriculture, 1920–1970' in C.M. Cipolla ed., *Fontana Economic History of Europe*, vol. 5 (ii). London: Fontana.

Rostow, W.W. (1960): *The Stages of Economic Growth: A Non-Communist Manifesto*. Cambridge: Cambridge University Press.

Schwartz, J.E. (1985): 'Goodman's Coefficient of Multiple Determination: Why it is *Not* Analogous to R^2'. Stockholm: Swedish Institute for Social Research.

Simkus, A.A., R. Andorka, J. Jackson, K-B. Yip and D.J. Treiman (1990): 'Changes in Social Mobility in Two Societies in the Crux of Transition: A Hungarian-Irish Comparison, 1943–1973'. *Research in Social Stratification and Mobility* 9.

Singelmann, J. (1978): *From Agriculture to Services: The Transformation of Industrial Employment*. Beverly Hills: Sage.

Singelmann, J. and M. Tienda (1985): 'The Process of Occupational Change in a Service Society: The Case of the United States, 1960–1980' in B. Roberts, R. Finnegan and D. Gallie, eds., *New Approaches to Economic Life*. Manchester: Manchester University Press.

Sorokin, P.A. (1927, 2nd ed. 1959): *Social and Cultural Mobility*. Glencoe: Free Press.

Treiman, D.J. (1970): 'Industrialisation and Social Stratification' in E.O. Laumann ed., *Social Stratification: Research and Theory for the 1970s*. Indianapolis: Bobbs Merrill.

Treiman, D.J. (1977): *Occupational Prestige in Comparative Perspective*. New York: Academic Press.

Treiman, D.J. and K-B. Yip (1989): 'Educational and Occupational Attainment in 21 Countries' in M.L. Kohn ed., *Cross-National Research in Sociology*. Newbury Park: Sage.

Wegener, B. (1988): *Kritik des Prestiges*. Opladen: Westdeutscher Verlag.

Wright, E.O. and J. Singelmann (1982): 'Proletarianization in the Changing American Class Structure'. *American Journal of Sociology* 88.

Wright, E.O. and B. Martin (1987): 'The Transformation of the American Class Structure, 1960–1980'. *American Journal of Sociology* 93.

Wrigley, E.A. (1972): 'The Process of Modernization and the Industrial Revolution in England'. *Journal of Interdisciplinary History* 3.

Zagórski, K. (1977–8): 'Transformations of Social Structure and Social Mobility in Poland'. *International Journal of Sociology* 7.

PETER GOTTSCHALK

Inequality, Income Growth, and Mobility: The Basic Facts

During the 1950s and 1960s, mean wages in the United States grew rapidly, and the dispersion around this growing mean changed very little. Starting in the 1970s and continuing into the 1980s and 1990s, these patterns were reversed: mean wages grew slowly, and inequality increased rapidly.

These changes in labor markets were reflected in changes in the distribution of family income.[1] The mean of the distribution of family income did increase after 1973, in spite of the near constancy of mean real wages, as family members increased the number of hours they worked. However, the increase in inequality of wages was mirrored by an increase in the dispersion of family income. A large descriptive literature has documented the rise in inequality, while a smaller behavioral literature has sought to delineate the causes of this rise.[2]

These changes in the distribution of family income affected rates of poverty directly. During the 1950s and 1960s, temporary increases in poverty during recessions were more than offset by declines in poverty during economic expansions. As long as the poor gained along with everyone else from the secular growth in the mean, one could be confident that poverty rates would ratchet down. This is exactly what happened as poverty rates fell from 22.4 percent in 1959 to 11.1 percent in 1973.

But these patterns in mean family income, poverty and inequality came to an end in the 1970s. Figure 1 plots real mean per capita income, the official poverty rate and the ratio of the income of the household at the 80th percentile to the income at the 20th percentile, which is a commonly used measure of inequality. Percentile ratios are often used as the overall measure of inequality, partly because they are not influenced by the problem that at the very top of the income distribution, most surveys report income higher than a certain amount as being "top-coded." Changes in percentile ratios avoid this problem of top-coding by only requiring knowledge of the income at the 80th or 90th percentile, which is below the top-coded values. But other measures and other ratios display largely similar patterns.

Over the last two decades, poverty rates have continued to increase during recessions and decline during expansions, just as they had in the 1960s. However, the declines in poverty during expansions have failed to offset the increases during recessions, and poverty rates ratcheted up 31 percent from 1973 to 1994 (that is, from 11.1 percent of the population to 14.5 percent) in spite of a

Originally published in 1997. Please see complete source information beginning on page 891.

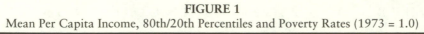

FIGURE 1
Mean Per Capita Income, 80th/20th Percentiles and Poverty Rates (1973 = 1.0)

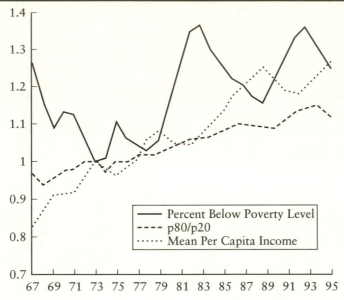

Source: Tables B-3 and B-5 Current Population Reports—Consumer Income Series P60-193 and Table C-1 of P60-194. Mean per capita income is a weighted average of male and female persons, including persons with zero income.

27 percent increase in mean per capita income. The coexistence of rising poverty and increases in mean incomes indicates that the poverty-reducing effects of growing mean income were being offset by the growth in inequality, as well as demographic changes. Changes in the demographic composition of the population, such as the increase in female-headed households, are also partially responsible for the rise in poverty rates. But these changes are no more important to the rise in poverty than the increase in wage inequality (Danzinger and Gottschalk, 1995). . . .

Conceptual Issues: Inequality, Economic Growth, Mobility

For many people, growth in inequality is considered a distributional "problem" only if it results in a decline in the economic position of persons at the bottom of the distribution. If incomes grow throughout the distribution,

but the growth is higher at the top than at the bottom, then inequality increases, but the absolute incomes of those at the bottom improve.

Changes in the absolute incomes of those at the bottom are affected by the amount of economic growth, changes in inequality and changes in mobility. While this essay makes sharp distinctions among these three concepts, the ideas are often confused, especially in the popular press. Increases in the mean, increases in inequality and increases in mobility each describe a particular aspect of the joint distribution of income, Y_t, over T periods: $f(Y_1, Y_2 \ldots Y_T)$. Economic growth between period t and $t + k$ reflects differences in the means of the marginal distributions of Y in the two years. Increases in inequality reflect changes in the variance (and in higher level moments) of the marginal distributions. Changes in mobility reflect changes in the covariance of income across years.

TABLE 1
Earnings Mobility in the United States

One Year Mobility (1974–1975)

		1975 Quintiles					
		1	*2*	*3*	*4*	*5*	*Total*
	1	0.687	0.221	0.079	0.013	0.000	1.000
	2	0.215	0.491	0.222	0.069	0.003	1.000
1974	3	0.065	0.236	0.497	0.176	0.026	1.000
Quintiles	4	0.033	0.049	0.159	0.584	0.175	1.000
	5	0.000	0.005	0.040	0.158	0.798	1.000

Seventeen Year Mobility (1974–1991)

		1991 Quintiles					
		1	*2*	*3*	*4*	*5*	*Total*
	1	0.421	0.228	0.143	0.130	0.078	1.000
	2	0.287	0.360	0.193	0.092	0.067	1.000
1974	3	0.147	0.206	0.321	0.205	0.120	1.000
Quintiles	4	0.097	0.120	0.242	0.324	0.217	1.000
	5	0.031	0.073	0.102	0.254	0.539	1.000

Source: Author's tabulation of the PSID.

Increases in mean income will reduce the proportion of people falling below a fixed poverty threshold as long as there are no other changes in the distribution. This insight lies at the heart of the proposition that economic growth can benefit everyone. However, if the mean and the variance of the distribution both increase, then there is no assurance that all will be better off. The U.S. experience of recent decades shows that increases in inequality of labor market income can fully offset the effects of increase in the mean, leading to a decline in absolute (as well as relative) earnings at the bottom of the distribution.

Measures of mobility capture how incomes are correlated across periods. Without information on mobility it is impossible to tell what proportion of low earners in one cross-section also had low earnings in a subsequent cross-section. If many low earners in one year have high earnings in other years, then the cross-sectional earnings distribution is not very informative. Only longitudinal data can

yield that information. Likewise, cross-section data cannot reveal whether people with low earnings in one year are getting poorer, nor for that matter whether the rich are getting richer. Cross-sectional data can only be used to compare the characteristics and number of persons with low earnings in one year with those in another year. . . .

Changes in Mobility

Table 1 uses the University of Michigan's Panel Survey of Income Dynamics (PSID) to document the extent of mobility. These data show that while earnings mobility is clearly evident, there is also substantial persistence. The table shows the probability that a person in a certain quintile in 1974 (the first year for which we have valid earnings data) was in a particular quintile in 1975 (top panel) and in 1991 (bottom panel).[3] Of those in the lowest quintile in 1974, 68.7 percent were still in the lowest quintile one year later and fully 90.8 percent were in the two lowest quintiles.[4] Thus, while there is mobility out of the lowest quintile in one year, it is small and movement was not very far.

Mobility rates are naturally higher when persons have 17 years to climb out of the bottom of the distribution. But a substantial proportion still remain in the lowest quintile. Of those who started in the lowest quintile in 1974, 42.1 percent found themselves in the lowest quintile 17 years later. This degree of persistence is consistent with the well-documented finding that the transitory component of earnings dies off after roughly three years. Therefore, of those who experience a transitory increase in earnings in one year, many will tend to fall back a few years later. To put it another way, the probability of being out of the bottom quintile after 17 years is much lower than would be implied by a calculation that took the one-year transition rates and assumed that movement would occur independently for each of the next 17 years.[5] Of those who did exit the bottom quintile, most did not make large progress, with the largest group moving to the next quintile. Similarly, the probability of staying in the highest quintile was .539, with .793 staying in the two highest quintiles.

Whether this mobility should be viewed as large or small depends on the question being asked. It is certainly high enough to make the point that people are not stuck at the bottom or the top of the earnings distribution; after all, most people's earnings increase as they gain labor market experience. Thus, one should be careful not to assume that those in a certain quintile in one year remained in that quintile the next year. However, mobility is too low to wash out the effects of yearly inequality. Even when earnings are averaged over a 17-year period, inequality is only reduced by roughly a third, as measured by the 90/10 ratio.[6] Thus, even based on average earnings over 17 years, substantial inequality of "permanent" earnings would remain.[7]

Another basis on which to judge whether the United States has a lot or a little mobility is by comparisons with other industrialized countries for which we have longitudinal data. While the United States has substantially more inequality than other OECD countries, it is not an outlier when it comes to mobility (Burkhauser, Holtz-Eakin and Rhody, forthcoming; OECD, 1996).[8] U.S. mobility rates resemble those of countries as different as France, Italy and Sweden. The fact that the United States has a more decentralized labor market than does the United Kingdom does not carry over into greater economic mobility. Likewise, the more centralized wage setting institutions in Germany and the Nordic countries do not translate into significantly less mobility in those countries than in the United States.

Thus far, the focus has been on the amount of mobility, not the trend in mobility. Even if the United States had a high *level* of mobility, this would reveal nothing about the *trend* in inequality of income measured over multiple periods. The existence of mobility reduces the level of inequality of income measured over multiple years. However, mobility reduces the *trend* toward greater inequality only if mobility *increases*. If mobility were constant, then we would simply have two different measures of inequality: a one-year measure based on the evolving cross-section evidence and a permanent income measure based on multiple years. The amount of inequality will be lower, but both measures will display the same rising trend.

Has mobility increased? Measuring changes in mobility makes substantial demands on the data. Mobility itself can only be estimated with two or more years of data. Therefore, at a very minimum it takes three years of data to measure changes in mobility. Furthermore, one needs many years of data to estimate mobility patterns even in a world where mobility is not changing. The data requirements are further compounded when trying to measure changes in mobility. Only a few studies have looked at changes in earnings mobility. Some have found declines, most have found no change, and none has found any increase (Gottschalk and Moffitt, 1994; Buchinsky and Hunt, 1995). Therefore, taking mobility into account does nothing to reverse the *trend* toward greater inequality.

which we have data. However, since the United States has greater inequality, change between quintiles in the United States does require larger percentage changes in earnings.

Notes

1. Changes in the distribution of family income reflected other changes as well, including demographic shifts and changes in the distribution of other sources of incomes such as transfer income and earnings of spouses.

2. For a review of this literature, see Levy and Murnane (1992) and Gottschalk and Smeeding (1997). For a discussion of patterns of inequality before the 1950s, the interested reader might begin with Goldin and Margo (1992).

3. The sample for the top panel consists of males 20 to 58 in 1974. The sample for the bottom panel is restricted to males 20 to 42, which insures that sample members are 59 or younger in 1991.

4. Reported annual earnings includes measurement error, which tends to overstate the amount of inequality and the amount of mobility. Averaging income over three years to reduce the measurement error reduces mobility out of the lowest quintile by about 10 percent.

5. If the probability of exiting in each period were $(1-.687)$ and no one who exited from the lowest quintile returned, then the probability of remaining in the lowest quintile for 16 years would be $.687^{17}$ instead of the observed .421.

6. Based on author's tabulation of the 90/10 ratio based on 17-year average earnings, PSID.

7. Since people with low permanent earnings are very likely to face borrowing constraints over this long a period, it is in no way obvious that this long an accounting period is more appropriate than a one-year accounting period. In fact, an accounting period shorter than a year might be most appropriate for people with very low earnings.

8. The probability of changing quintiles is similar in the United States and in OECD countries for

References

Buchinsky, Moshe, and Jennifer Hunt, "Wage Mobility in the United States." NBER Working Paper No. 5455, 1996.

Burkhauser, Richard V., Douglas Holtz-Eakin, and Stephen E. Rhody, "Mobility and Inequality in the 1980s: A Cross-National Comparison of the United States and Germany." In Jenkins, Stephen, Arie Kapteyn, and Bernard van Praag, eds., *The Distribution of Welfare and Household Production: International Perspectives.* Cambridge, Mass.: Cambridge University Press, forthcoming.

Danziger, Sheldon, and Peter Gottschalk, *America Unequal.* Cambridge, Mass.: Harvard University Press, 1995.

Goldin, Claudia, and Robert A. Margo, "The Great Compression: The Wage Structure in the United States at Mid-Century," *Quarterly Journal of Economics,* February 1992, *107*, 1–34.

Gottschalk, Peter, and Robert Moffitt, "The Growth of Earnings Instability in the U.S. Labor Market," *Brookings Papers on Economic Activity,* 1994, 2, 217–72.

Gottschalk, Peter, and Timothy M. Smeeding, "Cross-National Comparisons of Earnings and Income Inequality," *Journal of Economic Literature,* forthcoming, June 1997, *35*.

Levy, Frank, and Richard J. Murnane, "U.S. Earnings Levels and Earnings Inequality: A Review of Recent Trends and Proposed Explanations," *Journal of Economic Literature,* September 1992, *30*, 1333–81.

OECD, "Earnings Inequality, Low-Paid Employment and Earnings Mobility," *Employment Outlook,* July 1996, 59–108.

PETER GOTTSCHALK, SARA MCLANAHAN,
AND GARY D. SANDEFUR

The Dynamics and Intergenerational Transmission of Poverty and Welfare Participation

The traditional approach to the measurement of poverty has been to examine the size and composition of the poverty population by analyzing cross-sectional data on yearly income. Yet a good part of the poverty policy debate focuses on issues that cannot be addressed with data on yearly income. There is substantial interest, for example, in long-term poverty or the welfare dependence of a single generation and the links between the outcomes of parents and their children. Statistics on who is poor (or who receives welfare) during a single year provide no information on the total number of years that individuals and families are poor (or receiving welfare). Nor do they tell us if today's poor (or welfare recipients) grew up in households that were poor or received public assistance. Here we examine the recent empirical research on poverty and welfare dynamics and the emerging research on the links between generations.

The vision of a permanently dependent underclass, mired in poverty and dependency, gained considerable attention during the 1980s. Conservative analysts such as Charles Murray (1984) argued that a "welfare trap" robbed recipients of the will to better their

lot. Welfare offered the opportunity to drop out of the labor market and to abandon the traditional family model by making it possible to raise children while unemployed and unmarried. Furthermore, the resulting debilitating effects of welfare were asserted to be passed on to successive generations. According to this view, welfare programs were a cause of the problem, rather than part of the solution to poverty. The way to save people from long-term poverty and dependence was to scale back the welfare system.

Ironically, the notion that people were trapped in long-term poverty was one of the motivations for the War on Poverty. Drawing on the work of Oscar Lewis (1961) and Michael Harrington (1962), liberals used the idea of an intergenerational poverty to galvanize public support for the creation of work and training programs for youth. These programs promised to reunite the poor with the rest of society. In effect, the War on Poverty was waged on behalf of the children of the poor, who were assumed to be trapped by poverty rather than by welfare. According to this view, welfare provided the transitional financial support necessary to allow the poor to gain the skills to become self-sufficient.

That the specter of a permanently poor class has been used to justify both the creation and the dismantling of social programs is indicative of the controversy surrounding these issues. Moreover, just as both liberals and conservatives have used the existence of the

Originally published in 1994. Please see complete source information beginning on page 891.

permanently poor to promote their policy agendas, both groups have also denied or downplayed the existence of permanent poverty at one point or another.

Two factors have contributed to the conservatives' emphasis at times on the transitory nature of poverty. The first is their belief in the openness of society. Sensitive to criticisms that markets lead to a rigid class division among social and economic classes, they have argued that there is considerable mobility across the income distribution and, hence, that for many families poverty is not a permanent status. Second is their belief that official measures of yearly poverty seriously exaggerate the amount of poverty. One of the primary defects of annual income as a measure of the distribution of well-being is that it ignores offsetting changes in incomes in other years.[1] Milton Friedman makes the case most forcefully by asking us to consider two societies that have the same distribution of annual income: "In one there is great mobility and change so that the position of particular families in the income hierarchy varies widely from year to year. In the other, there is great rigidity, each family stays in the same position year after year. Clearly, in any meaningful sense, the second one would be the more unequal society" (1962, p. 171). According to this view, we should be most concerned with the distribution of lifetime well-being. If many of the poor in one year are not poor in the following year, then the truly needy, or truly poor, are a small subset of the poor in a single year.[2]

Liberals have also at times downplayed the existence of permanent poverty, though for two somewhat different reasons. First, their belief that income is largely determined by factors outside the control of the individual, such as the health of the economy, leads them to stress the transitory nature of poverty and welfare recipiency. Families fall upon hard times. During these bleak periods the less fortunate fall into poverty and may need to participate in government programs. Outside conditions may change, however, leading to exits from both poverty and welfare.

Second, liberals are also reluctant to embrace the notion of an underclass because of their experience with the debate over the "culture of poverty" in the late 1960s. Although the concept of a dysfunctional culture was originally proposed as a critique of capitalism, the culture of poverty argument soon came to be viewed as "blaming the victims" for conditions beyond their control. According to this view, it was not "the system" but rather the poor's lack of will to avoid the "welfare trap" that caused long-term poverty.[3] As black clients became an increasing proportion of the welfare caseload, this argument became open to charges of racial bias. As a result, liberals backed off from any discussion of long-term or intergenerational poverty during the 1970s for fear of being labeled racist or unsympathetic to the poor.

That liberals and conservatives have such different views on intragenerational and intergenerational dynamics is due, in part, to their very different models of the causes of long-term poverty and the role of welfare in reducing or exacerbating poverty. The causal explanation, put forward by conservatives, is that welfare programs create dependency and, therefore, perpetuate poverty (Murray, 1984; Mead, 1986). The availability of welfare encourages women to bear children out of wedlock, encourages families to break up, and eliminates the need for absentee fathers to contribute to the economic and social requirements of their children, thereby encouraging long-term dependency. Furthermore, long-term dependency is assumed to be passed from one generation to the next.

For liberals, long-term poverty and welfare participation have generally been explained in terms of the lack of employment opportunities or the existence of jobs that do not provide earnings sufficient for a family to have a minimally adequate standard of living (Harrington, 1962; Wilson and Neckerman, 1986). If employment opportunities continue to be inadequate, then parents will not be able to earn enough to support their children. Poverty will continue, and in some cases, dependency on welfare will also result from the inadequate economic environment.

William Julius Wilson and Kathryn Neckerman (1986) have further broadened the focus to the connections between inadequate employment opportunities, family structure, and poverty. They argue that the lack of employment opportunities, especially for black men, has led to a lower rate of marriage and a higher rate of out-of-wedlock childbearing among black women. Inadequate employment opportunities thus produce poverty and welfare dependence indirectly through effects on family structure as well as directly through reduced income.

From this brief review, we can see that conservatives are likely to view long-term poverty as evidence of the dangers of welfare. At the same time they stress that American society is fairly open, so that many of the poor are only temporarily poor. Liberals are likely to point to the problems faced by the long-term poor as a way of marshaling sympathy for the poor and garnering support for government interventions to combat poverty, including policies to improve market opportunities and to expand programs. At the same time, liberals downplay any negative behavioral effects of long-term welfare participation.

Who is correct in this debate is still a highly contested issue. Part of the debate rests on logical arguments. Liberals argue that because welfare is freely chosen by recipients, it can hardly be called a "trap." Recipients obviously believe that welfare is the best of the bad options they face. There is no logical basis for arguing that the mother herself would freely choose welfare if it formed a "trap" that she wished to avoid. Welfare provides a steady, if meager, source of income, which must be preferred to the option of working and raising a family as a single parent or the option of marrying the father, who may not be able to support his children financially. Although it is possible to argue that the children or taxpayers are worse off when the mother accepts assistance, it is not consistent to argue that recipients make choices and that these choices make them worse off.

Similarly, conservatives argue that liberals deny the inevitable work and marriage disincentives inherent in the welfare system. By paying a mother more if she doesn't work and doesn't marry, the welfare system discourages mothers from following either of these socially desirable activities. Because both marriage and work lead to higher income, the welfare system creates long-term poverty and dependency. Therefore, according to conservatives, the logical outcome of a more generous welfare system is to form a trap that locks recipients into long-term poverty.

The relevant question, however, is not whether a trap exists or whether there are disincentives, for it is certainly true that some families receive welfare for protracted periods and that there are disincentives. The question is the quantitative magnitude of these factors. We approach this highly ideological debate by examining two central issues: the prevalence of long-term poverty and welfare participation and the disincentives caused by public assistance; and the relationship between poverty, income, and welfare use in one generation and the next.

Evidence on Intragenerational Mobility

Dynamic issues have received less attention than the static measures of poverty, in part because longitudinal data sets such as the Panel Study of Income Dynamics (PSID) and the National Longitudinal Survey of Youth (NLSY) have been widely available only since the late 1960s. These data sets only now have enough years of data to study both long-term poverty and welfare recipiency and to observe the outcomes over multiple generations.

Income and Poverty Dynamics

We begin by documenting the extent to which poverty is a permanent or transitory condition. Figure 1 presents data on the length of poverty spells. This figure, based on data from the Panel Study of Income Dynamics,

FIGURE 1
Annual poverty spell distribution.
(Author's tabulation of Panel Study of Income Dynamics, 1968–1987, distribution of first observed spell.)

a. All races

Proportion

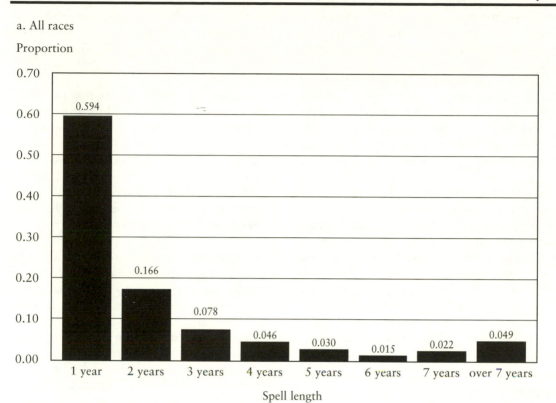

Spell length

b. By race

Proportion

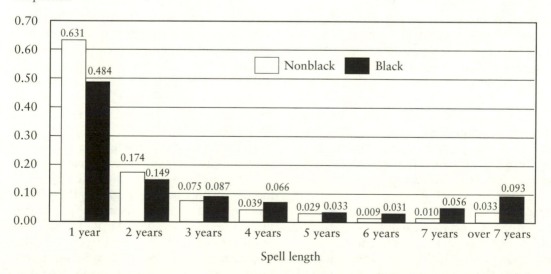

Spell length

counts the number of consecutive years that a person lived in a family with an annual income below the family's annual poverty line. It asks the question, "If you follow a group of people who have just started new poverty spells, how long will these poverty spells last?"

Figure 1a shows data for persons of all races. It shows that 59.4 percent of poverty spells last only one year.[4] An additional 16.6 percent last only two years. Thus nearly three-quarters of all poverty spells are shorter than two years. At the other extreme only 7.1 percent of the spells last seven or more years. Figure 1b shows the corresponding data for persons disaggregated by race. From this figure it is clear that blacks stay in poverty longer than nonblacks. Of the poverty spells of nonblacks, 63.1 percent last less than one year; the corresponding figure for blacks is only 48.4. Blacks also have considerably more long spells. Almost 15 percent of their poverty spells last seven or more years, while only 4.3 percent of the spells for nonblacks are this long. . . .

Welfare Dynamics

The public debate during the 1980s over welfare reform was largely driven by the perception that a large number of welfare recipients were incapable of becoming self-sufficient without either a large carrot to persuade them off the program or a large stick to force them off. Conservatives charged that welfare recipients stayed on welfare for long periods, soaking up tax dollars and living in perpetual dependency. Liberals downplayed long-term dependency, acknowledging that a small proportion of the welfare population had long welfare spells but emphasizing that most recipients used welfare on a temporary basis.

Duration of single AFDC spells. We begin by answering the following question: If all the Aid to Families with Dependent Children cases that opened in a given year were followed for their duration, how long would each spell last?[5] Figure 2 shows that most

AFDC spells are short. For blacks, 33.7 percent of spells last only a year, and an additional 16.2 percent end in the second year.[6] For nonblacks, the corresponding figures are 44.0 and 22.8 percent.[7] By the end of two years, half of the welfare spells for blacks and two-thirds of the spells for nonblacks have ended.

These data provide evidence that most welfare entrants are not trapped in perpetual dependency.[8] But Figure 2 also shows that although most cases are not long, a substantial minority of cases remain open for protracted periods. At the end of seven years, 5.8 percent of the AFDC spells of nonblacks were still in progress and 25.4 percent of the AFDC spells of blacks were still in progress.

Recidivism and duration of multiple spells. Roughly half of the families leaving AFDC or Food Stamps will return to these programs at some future date. The duration of a single spell thus gives only a partial picture. To know whether recipients use AFDC for extensive parts of their child-rearing years, one must take account of recidivism and the combined length of multiple spells. Data on multiple spells, however, are limited.

An alternative measure of participation across multiple spells is to estimate the number of years a family receives AFDC, without regard to breaks in spells. Figure 3 (see page 384) shows our estimates of the number of years a woman who received welfare would receive AFDC in the first nine years after the birth of her first child.[9] These distributions are shown separately by race for all women who received AFDC (Figure 3a for blacks and 3b for nonblacks).[10]

As expected, the number of total years on welfare is substantially higher than the number of years on welfare in the first spell. Although roughly half the initial spells of blacks last two years or less, just 27.7 percent of black recipients received AFDC for only two of the ten years when multiple spells are taken into account.[11] For nonblacks the proportion of spells of two years or less drops from 66.8 to 41.3 when multiple spells are included. The

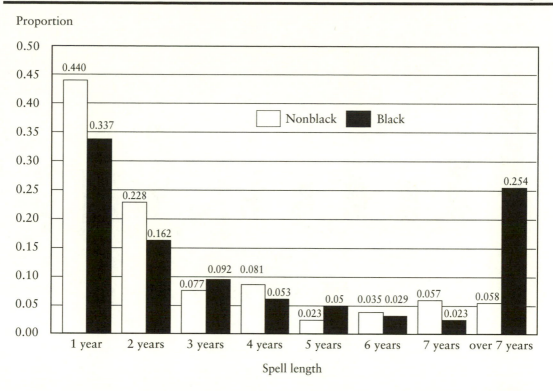

FIGURE 2
Distribution of AFDC spell length by race, 1974–1987.
(Author's tabulation of Panel Study of Income Dynamics, 1974–1987, distribution of first observed spell.)

short spells are partially replaced by spells of three to four years as people with short spells exit and return for short periods. Including multiple spells, however, also increases the proportion of long spells. The proportion of initial spells that lasted seven to ten years is 21.1 percent for blacks and 11.7 percent for nonblacks. When multiple spells are included, these figures increase to 34.4 and 18.0 percent. . . .

Evidence on Intergenerational Dynamics

We now extend our analysis to poverty and welfare dynamics across generations. Again this issue has a political context. Liberals tend to focus on the intergenerational transmission of family background, income, and poverty. If low-income families have few resources to pass on to their children or to use to finance their children's education, then their children will be more likely to become poor adults themselves. Inasmuch as poverty leads to welfare participation, this will also lead to intergenerational welfare participation. According to this view, the intergenerational transmission of poverty causes the intergenerational correlation in welfare participation. Conservatives tend to argue the opposite. Welfare perpetuates poverty and dependence across generations by promoting out-of-wedlock childbearing, by breaking up families, and by eroding the work ethic. These early childhood experiences lower children's achievement and lead to poverty and welfare participation in the next generation.

FIGURE 3

Estimated distribution of years a mother receives AFDC in the first ten years after conception of her first child. (Authors' calculations based on the Panel Study of Income Dynamics, 1974–1987.)

a. All black recipients

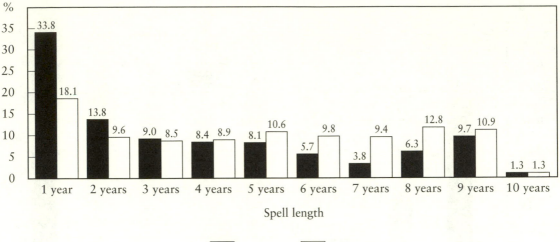

b. All nonblack recipients

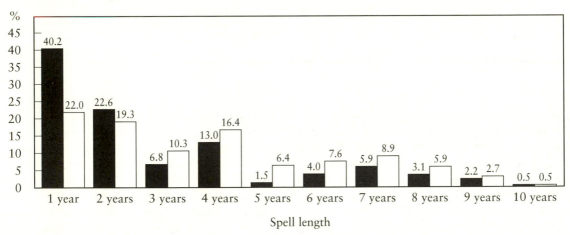

Intergenerational Correlations in Poverty and Income

If successive generations have similar incomes, then parents and their children are likely to have similar probabilities of falling into poverty.[12] Although early studies of intergenerational income mobility tended to find relatively low correlations, recent evidence suggests the correlation is substantial.[13] For example, Donald Treiman and Robert Hauser (1977) estimated that the intergenerational correlation of income was between .24 and .36 for men aged 25 to 34; Jere Behrman and Paul Taubman (1990) and Gary Solon (1992) found correlations of father's and son's income of .58 and .40 respectively. Such a high intergenerational correlation in income implies relatively little mobility in incomes across generations.

What do these correlations imply for someone who is born in a low-income family? Solon (1992) estimates (assuming an intergenerational correlation in income of .40) that the probability that a son whose father was in the bottom quintile (20 percent) of the income distribution will remain in the bottom quintile of the income distribution as an adult is .42. Growing up at the bottom of the income distribution poses a significant disadvantage in American society.[14] Similarly, Mary Corcoran and her colleagues (1987) find that children growing up in families that experience long-term poverty have significantly lower education, wages, and incomes. . . .

The Role of Family Background and Family Structure

The research on the intergenerational relationships in the experience of poverty can be viewed as part of a larger body of sociological research on the effects of family background on social and economic achievement in adulthood. The research shows that, in addition to income and father's occupation, family background characteristics, such as parents' education, whether or not parents remained married, and number of siblings, significantly affect children's achievement (Jencks et al., 1972; Featherman and Hauser, 1978).

The effects of family background factors as well as of family income are mediated by other variables, among the most important of which is an individual's education. In other words, background has a strong effect on education, which in turn has a strong effect on income.

Although family structure—whether or not a child grew up in a "broken family"—has long been included in status attainment models, interest in family instability as a possible mechanism for explaining the intergenerational transmission of poverty increased in the 1980s.[15] Today most of the background characteristics known to affect children's well-being have changed in ways that would be expected to benefit children. Parents are more educated than they were several decades ago; fathers' occupational status has risen; and the number of siblings in the family has declined. In contrast, family instability, which is believed to reduce children's well-being, has become increasingly common since 1950. Hence researchers have focused on the role of family structure in reproducing poverty across generations.

Does family instability harm children? If we ask whether growing up in a nonintact family is associated with being poor in adulthood, the answer is yes. Figure 4 shows the likelihood of experiencing several "high-risk" events—dropping out of school, having a child out of wedlock before age twenty, and being idle in late adolescence—for children who grow up in intact and nonintact families. Each of these events increases the risk of poverty and welfare dependence in adulthood, and each is a fairly good proxy for children's lifetime income.

Children from nonintact families are more than twice as likely to drop out of high school as children from intact families. Young women from nonintact families are between two and four times as likely to give birth out of wedlock as young women from intact families, and young men from nonintact families are about 1.5 times as likely to become idle as their peers from intact families. About half of the association between family instability and child well-being is due to difference in family income. Most of the rest is due to differences in parenting behavior (such as helping with school work and supervising social activities) and residential mobility.

Although family structure has a sizable impact, family disruption does not automatically relegate children to long-term poverty or welfare dependence. Most children finish high school, delay childbearing, and become attached to the labor force regardless of whether they live with one or both parents while growing up. . . .

FIGURE 4

Family stability and children's attainment. (Estimates are based on four nationally representative surveys:
the National Longitudinal Survey–Youth Cohort (NLSY), the Panel Study of Income Dynamics (PSID),
the High School and Beyond Study (HSB), and the National Survey of Families and Households (NSFH).
The bars represent "predicted values" based on models that control for race, parents' education, number
of siblings, and region of residence at age sixteen.)

a. High school dropout (males and females)

Proportion

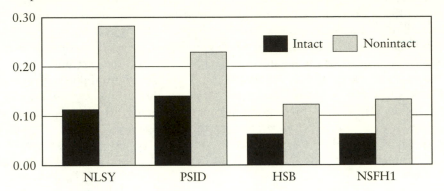

b. Teen premarital birth (females)

Proportion

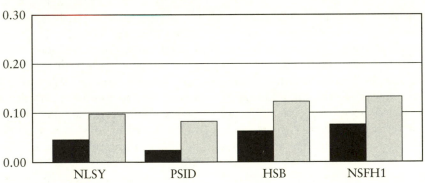

c. Idleness (males)

Proportion

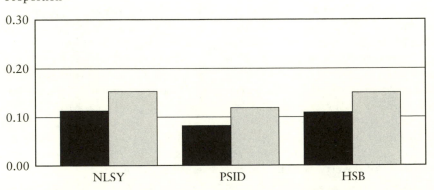

Intergenerational Correlations in Welfare Participation

The research on intergenerational welfare participation suggests common patterns across generations. Peter Gottschalk (1992) finds that although a substantial proportion of the daughters of welfare recipients do not receive welfare themselves as adults, their risk is substantially greater than the risk of daughters whose mothers did not receive welfare. The probability that a nonblack daughter has a child and receives welfare is .261 if the mother received welfare, whereas it is only .066 if the mother never received AFDC. The comparable figures for blacks are .486 and .136.[16] McLanahan (1988) finds that coming from a family that received 50 percent or more of its annual income from welfare while the daughter was between the ages of twelve and sixteen has the strongest effect among welfare indicators on AFDC participation for whites, while a simple measure of welfare receipt during the ages twelve to sixteen has the strongest effect for blacks.

Because of the lack of data on full welfare histories of both generations, few studies attempt to construct measures of long-term welfare use in both generations. Greg Duncan, Martha Hill, and Saul Hoffman (1988) measure welfare dependence as heavy use, defined as receiving welfare continuously for a three-year period. They find that 64 percent of the women whose families were highly dependent during their adolescence (defined as ages thirteen to fifteen) did not use welfare themselves between the ages of twenty-one and twenty-three. Only 20 percent were heavy welfare users themselves. When the analyses are adjusted for differences in the background of the individuals (income and family structure), the relationship between family of origin's welfare use and children's welfare use declines but remains positive.

Moffitt (1992) reviews these and other studies and concludes that there is consistent evidence of strong correlations between parental welfare receipt and daughter's welfare receipt, even though this preliminary research has not yet explained the causes of the strong intergenerational correlation. Because families receiving welfare are poor—indeed, poverty is a condition of welfare receipt—we would expect children from welfare families to have higher rates of poverty and welfare use as adults than children from nonpoor, nonwelfare families. Intergenerational correlation, therefore, does not necessarily indicate a causal relationship. Daughters and their mothers may simply share characteristics that increase the probability of their both receiving assistance.[17] For example, if both the mother and the daughter grow up in neighborhoods with poor-quality schools, both will be more likely to have lower earnings and, hence, a greater need for income assistance. In this case, taking the mother off of welfare will not lower the probability that the daughter will receive assistance. Changing the quality of the school the daughter attends, however, will raise her income and, in turn, lower the probability that she receives public assistance.

*   *   *

We have focused on two broad issues: (1) the extent to which individuals and families are poor for long periods of time or use welfare for extended periods; and (2) the extent to which the experiences of individuals as children are associated with their economic situation as adults or, more specifically, the extent to which poverty and welfare use are passed on across generations.

The results regarding the first issue suggest that a majority of the poor remain poor for short periods of time, and that a majority of welfare recipients receive welfare for only a few years. There is, however, a minority who experience long-term poverty or welfare dependence. By most accounts, nevertheless, temporary dips into poverty and short-term participation in welfare are much more common than long-term spells of poverty and dependence.

The results regarding the second issue—whether poverty and welfare dependence are passed along from generation to generation—also suggest that the media and some scholars have overstated the extent to which poverty and welfare are traps in which individuals and families are caught. The large majority of families and individuals who are poor or who use welfare are not trapped, and neither are their children. It is true that individuals who lived in poor families as children are more likely to experience poverty as adults, and it is true that individuals whose families participated in welfare programs when they were children are more likely to receive welfare as adults. But it is also true that as many as two-thirds of the children from these families manage to escape poverty and dependence when they grow up.

Notes

1. Annual income would be the proper measure if people could only save or borrow to smooth income within each year.

2. Note that this argument implicitly assumes that people can smooth their consumption by either saving or borrowing against future income. The argument for extending the accounting period beyond a year becomes much weaker if many poverty spells occur early in life when income smoothing through saving may not be possible.

3. This view is still often reflected in public statements. For example, in his famous "Murphy Brown" speech, Vice President Dan Quayle stated that "the intergenerational poverty that troubles us so much today is predominately a poverty of values." *Boston Globe*, May 21, 1992.

4. We find more one-year spells than reported in Bane and Ellwood (1986). This reflects our use of the official poverty line rather than 125 percent of the official thresholds, our inclusion of post–1982 data, our inclusion of persons over sixty-five, and their exclusion of some one-year spells. Using their procedure reduces the frequency of one-year spells by .084.

5. This question differs from the question that asks how long spells currently in progress will last.

6. Our results differ from those of Ellwood (1986) who used fewer years of data and who looked only at spells of both receiving AFDC and being a female head of household.

7. Blank (1989) finds somewhat shorter durations because she uses monthly data.

8. Although AFDC receives by far the most attention, the Food Stamp program provides assistance to a much larger caseload. Burstein and Visher (1989) show that there is even more turnover in the Food Stamp caseload than in the AFDC caseload. At the end of one year, roughly two-thirds of all Food Stamp cases have been closed. If long-term recipiency is defined as a Food Stamp spell that lasts for three years or more, then only 15 percent of all Food Stamp cases could be classified as long term.

9. Because AFDC is available to pregnant women, we include the year prior to birth and the following nine years in the ten-year window.

10. These data are generated by estimating discrete time duration models for spells on and off of welfare and simulating the predicted spell durations over the ten-year period. The data on the first spell differ from the data in Figure 2, which samples all spells.

11. Duncan, Laren, and Yeung (1991) examined families in the PSID that received AFDC at least once during the first eighteen years of their child's life. Although their conclusions are based on smaller samples that do not allow for disaggregation, they find similar overall patterns.

12. Furthermore, a focus on the association in income across generations may be more informative, as individuals who experience childhood poverty may experience near-poverty as adults. They would not be counted as poor, but analyzing income, rather than poverty status, overcomes the problem of living standards above the poverty line.

13. Becker and Tomes (1986) concluded that the intergenerational correlation in income was somewhere around .17, based on their review of some early studies. This finding suggests a fairly small effect of parental income on the income of children later as adults.

14. If the intergenerational correlation in income were zero, the probability that the child of a poor family would fall into poverty would be the same as the probability for the child of a rich family, namely .20.

15. For a review of this literature, see McLanahan and Booth (1989).

16. These patterns are attenuated but not eliminated after controlling for a large number of factors that may also affect the daughter's participation.

17. Gottschalk (1992) finds some evidence that the relationship is not just spurious.

References

Bane, Mary Jo, and David T. Ellwood. 1986. "Slipping into and out of Poverty: The Dynamics of Spells." *Journal of Human Resources* 21 (Winter): 1–23.

Becker, Gary S., and Nigel Tomes. 1986. "Human Capital and the Rise and Fall of Families."

Journal of Labor Economics 4 (2, pt. 2): S1–S39.

Behrman, Jere R., and Paul Taubman. 1990. "The Intergenerational Correlation between Children's Adult Earnings and Their Parents' Income: Results from the Michigan Panel Study of Income Dynamics." *Review of Income and Wealth* 36: 115–127.

Blank, Rebecca M. 1989. "Analyzing the Length of Welfare Spells." *Journal of Public Economics* 39: 245–273.

Burstein, Nancy R., and Mary G. Visher. 1989. "The Dynamics of Food Stamp Program Participation." U.S. Department of Agriculture, Food, and Nutrition Service, Washington, D.C. March. Mimeo.

Corcoran, Mary, Roger H. Gordon, Deborah Laren, and Gary Solon. 1987. "Intergenerational Transmission of Education, Income, and Earnings." University of Michigan, Institute of Public Policy Studies, Mimeo.

Duncan, Greg J., Martha S. Hill, and Saul D. Hoffman. 1988. "Welfare Dependence within and across Generations." *Science* 239: 467–471.

Duncan, Greg J., Deborah Laren, and W.J.J. Yeung. 1991. "How Dependent Are America's Children on Welfare? Recent Findings from the PSID." Institute for Social Research, University of Michigan, Ann Arbor. Mimeo.

Ellwood, David T. 1986. *Targeting "Would-Be" Long-Term Recipients of AFDC*. Princeton, NJ.: Mathematica Policy Research.

Featherman, David L., and Robert M. Hauser. 1978. *Opportunity and Change*. New York: Academic Press.

Freidman, Milton. 1962. *Capitalism and Freedom*. Chicago: University of Chicago Press.

Gottschalk, Peter. 1992. "Is the Correlation in Welfare Participation across Generations Spurious? Department of Economics, Boston College. Mimeo.

Harrington, Michael. 1962. *The Other America: Poverty in the United States*. New York: Macmillan.

Jencks, Christopher, Marshall Smith, Henry Acland, Mary Jo Bane, David Cohen, Herbert Gintis, Barbara Heyns, and Stephan Michelson. 1972. *Inequality*. New York: Basic Books.

Lewis, Oscar. 1961. *The Children of Sanchez*. New York: Random House.

McLanahan, Sara S. 1988. "Family Structure and Dependency: Early Transitions to Female Household Headship." *Demography* 25: 1–16.

McLanahan, Sara S., and Karen Booth. 1989. "Mother-Only Families: Problems, Prospects, and Politics." *Journal of Marriage and the Family* 51: 557–580.

Mead, Lawrence M. 1986. *Beyond Entitlement: The Social Obligations of Citizenship*. New York: Free Press.

Moffitt, Robert. 1992. "The Effect of the Medicaid Program on Welfare Participation and Labor Supply." *Review of Economics and Statistics* 74 (4): 615–626.

Murray, Charles. 1984. *Losing Ground: American Social Policy, 1950–1980*. New York: Basic Books.

Solon, Gary. 1992. "Intergenerational Income Mobility in the United States." *American Economic Review* 82 (3): 393–408.

Treiman, Donald J., and Robert M. Hauser. 1977. "Intergenerational Transmission of Income: An Exercise in Theory Construction." In *The Process of Stratification: Trends and Analyses*, ed. Robert M. Hauser and David L. Featherman. New York: Academic Press.

Wilson, William Julius, and Kathryn M. Neckerman. 1986. "Poverty and Family Structure: The Widening Gap Between Evidence and Public Policy Issues." In *Fighting Poverty: What Works and What Doesn't*, ed. Sheldon H. Danziger and Daniel H. Weinberg. Cambridge, Mass.: Harvard University Press.

Status and Income Attainment

BASIC MODELS

PETER M. BLAU AND OTIS DUDLEY DUNCAN,
WITH THE COLLABORATION OF ANDREA TYREE

The Process of Stratification

Stratification systems may be characterized in various ways. Surely one of the most important has to do with the processes by which individuals become located, or locate themselves, in positions in the hierarchy comprising the system. At one extreme we can imagine that the circumstances of a person's birth—including the person's sex and the perfectly predictable sequence of age levels through which he is destined to pass—suffice to assign him unequivocally to a ranked status in a hierarchical system. At the opposite extreme his prospective adult status would be wholly problematic and contingent at the time of birth. Such status would become entirely determinate only as adulthood was reached, and solely as a consequence of his own actions taken freely—that is, in the absence of any constraint deriving from the circumstances of his birth or rearing. Such a pure achievement system is, of course, hypothetical, in much the same way that motion without friction is a purely hypothetical possibility in the physical world. Whenever the stratification system of any moderately large and com-

plex society is described, it is seen to involve both ascriptive and achievement principles.

In a liberal democratic society we think of the more basic principle as being that of achievement. Some ascriptive features of the system may be regarded as vestiges of an earlier epoch, to be extirpated as rapidly as possible. Public policy may emphasize measures designed to enhance or to equalize opportunity—hopefully, to overcome ascriptive obstacles to the full exercise of the achievement principle.

The question of how far a society may realistically aspire to go in this direction is hotly debated, not only in the ideological arena but in the academic forum as well. Our contribution, if any, to the debate will consist largely in submitting measurements and estimates of the strength of ascriptive forces and of the scope of opportunities in a large contemporary society. The problem of the relative importance of the two principles in a given system is ultimately a quantitative one. We have pushed our ingenuity to its limit in seeking to contrive relevant quantifications.

The governing conceptual scheme in the analysis is quite a commonplace one. We think of the individual's life cycle as a sequence in time that can be described, however partially and crudely, by a set of classificatory or quantitative measurements taken at succes-

Originally published in 1967. Please see complete source information beginning on page 891.

sive stages. Ideally we should like to have under observation a cohort of births, following the individuals who make up the cohort as they pass through life. As a practical matter we resorted to retrospective questions put to a representative sample of several adjacent cohorts so as to ascertain those facts about their life histories that we assumed were both relevant to our problem and accessible by this means of observation.

Given this scheme, the questions we are continually raising in one form or another are: how and to what degree do the circumstances of birth condition subsequent status? and, how does status attained (whether by ascription or achievement) at one stage of the life cycle affect the prospects for a subsequent stage? The questions are neither idle nor idiosyncratic ones. Current policy discussion and action come to a focus in a vaguely explicated notion of the "inheritance of poverty." Thus a spokesman for the Social Security Administration writes:

It would be one thing if poverty hit at random and no one group were singled out. It is another thing to realize that some seem destined to poverty almost from birth—by their color or by the economic status or occupation of their parents.[1]

Another officially sanctioned concept is that of the "dropout," the person who fails to graduate from high school. Here the emphasis is not so much on circumstances operative at birth but on the presumed effect of early achievement on subsequent opportunities. Thus the "dropout" is seen as facing "a lifetime of uncertain employment,"[2] probable assignment to jobs of inferior status, reduced earning power, and vulnerability to various forms of social pathology.

In this study we do not have measurements on all the factors implicit in a full-blown conception of the "cycle of poverty" nor all those variables conceivably responding unfavorably to the achievement of "dropout" status. . . . This limitation, however, is not merely an analytical convenience. We think of the selected quantitative variables as being sufficient to describe the major outlines of status changes in the life cycle of a cohort. Thus a study of the relationships among these variables leads to a formulation of a basic model of the process of stratification.

A Basic Model

To begin with, we examine only five variables. For expository convenience, when it is necessary to resort to symbols, we shall designate them by arbitrary letters but try to remind the reader from time to time of what the letters stand for. These variables are:

V: Father's educational attainment
X: Father's occupational status
U: Respondent's educational attainment
W: Status of respondent's first job
Y: Status of respondent's occupation in 1962

Each of the three occupational statuses is scaled by the [socioeconomic] index described [elsewhere],[3] ranging from 0 to 96. The two education variables are scored on the following arbitrary scale of values ("rungs" on the "educational ladder") corresponding to specified numbers of years of formal schooling completed:

0: No school
1: Elementary, one to four years
2: Elementary, five to seven years
3: Elementary, eight years
4: High school, one to three years
5: High school, four years
6: College, one to three years
7: College, four years
8: College, five years or more (i.e., one or more years of postgraduate study)

Actually, this scoring system hardly differs from a simple linear transformation, or "coding," of the exact number of years of school completed. In retrospect, for reasons given [elsewhere],[4] we feel that the score implies too great a distance between intervals at the lower end of the scale; but the resultant distortion is minor in view of the very small proportions scored 0 or 1.

A basic assumption in our interpretation of regression statistics—though not in their calculation as such—has to do with the causal or temporal ordering of these variables. In terms of the father's career we should naturally assume precedence of V (education) with respect to X (occupation when his son was 16 years old). We are not concerned with the father's career, however, but only with his statuses that comprised a configuration of background circumstances or origin conditions for the cohorts of sons who were respondents in the Occupational Changes in a Generation (OCG) study. Hence we generally make no assumption as to the priority of V with respect to X; in effect, we assume the measurements on these variables to be contemporaneous from the son's viewpoint. The respondent's education, U, is supposed to follow in time—and thus to be susceptible to causal influence from—the two measures of father's status. Because we ascertained X as of respondent's age 16, it is true that some respondents may have completed school before the age to which X pertains. Such cases were doubtlessly a small minority and in only a minor proportion of them could the father (or other family head) have changed status radically in the two or three years before the respondent reached 16.

The next step in the sequence is more problematic. We assume that W (first job status) follows U (education). The assumption conforms to the wording of the questionnaire, which stipulated "the first full-time job you had after you left school." In the years since the OCG study was designed we have been made aware of a fact that should have been considered more carefully in the design. Many students leave school more or less definitively, only to return, perhaps to a different school, some years later, whereupon they often finish a degree program.[5] The OCG questionnaire contained information relevant to this problem, namely the item on age at first job. Through an oversight no tabulations of this item were made for the present study. Tables

prepared for another study[6] using the OCG data, however, suggest that approximately one-eighth of the respondents report a combination of age at first job and education that would be very improbable unless (a) they violated instructions by reporting a part-time or school-vacation job as the first job, or (b) they did, in fact, interrupt their schooling to enter regular employment. (These "inconsistent" responses include men giving 19 as their age at first job and college graduation or more as their education; 17 or 18 with some college or more; 14, 15, or 16 with high-school graduation or more; and under 14 with some high school or more.) When the two variables are studied in combination with occupation of first job, a very clear effect is evident. Men with a given amount of education beginning their first jobs early held lower occupational statuses than those beginning at a normal or advanced age for the specified amount of education.

Despite the strong probability that the U-W sequence is reversed for an appreciable minority of respondents, we have hardly any alternative to the assumption made here. If the bulk of the men who interrupted schooling to take their first jobs were among those ultimately securing relatively advanced education, then our variable W is downwardly biased, no doubt, as a measure of their occupational status immediately after they finally left school for good. In this sense, the correlations between U and W and between W and Y are probably attenuated. Thus, if we had really measured "job after completing education" instead of "first job," the former would in all likelihood have loomed somewhat larger as a variable intervening between education and 1962 occupational status. We do not wish to argue that our respondents erred in their reports on first job. We are inclined to conclude that their reports were realistic enough, and that it was our assumption about the meaning of the responses that proved to be fallible.

The fundamental difficulty here is conceptual. If we insist on *any* uniform sequence of the events involved in accomplishing the transition to independent adult status, we do violence to reality. Completion of schooling, departure from the parental home, entry into the labor market, and contracting of a first marriage are crucial steps in this transition, which all normally occur within a few short years. Yet they occur at no fixed ages nor in any fixed order. As soon as we aggregate individual data for analytical purposes we are forced into the use of simplifying assumptions. Our assumption here is, in effect, that "first job" has a uniform significance for all men in terms of its temporal relationship to educational preparation and subsequent work experience. If this assumption is not strictly correct, we doubt that it could be improved by substituting any other *single* measure of initial occupational status. (In designing the OCG questionnaire, the alternative of "job at the time of first marriage" was entertained briefly but dropped for the reason, among others, that unmarried men would be excluded thereby.)

One other problem with the *U-W* transition should be mentioned. Among the younger men in the study, 20 to 24 years old, are many who have yet to finish their schooling or to take up their first jobs or both—not to mention the men in this age group missed by the survey on account of their military service.[7] Unfortunately, an early decision on tabulation plans resulted in the inclusion of the 20 to 24 group with the older men in aggregate tables for men 20 to 64 years old. We have ascertained that this results in only minor distortions by comparing a variety of data for men 20 to 64 and for those 25 to 64 years of age. Once over the *U-W* hurdle, we see no serious objection to our assumption that both *U* and *W* precede *Y*, except in regard to some fraction of the very young men just mentioned.

In summary, then, we take the somewhat idealized assumption of temporal order to represent an order of priority in a causal or processual sequence, which may be stated diagrammatically as follows:

$$(V, X) - (U) - (W) - (Y).$$

In proposing this sequence we do not overlook the possibility of what Carlsson calls "delayed effects,"[8] meaning that an early variable may affect a later one not only via intervening variables but also directly (or perhaps through variables not measured in the study).

In translating this conceptual framework into quantitative estimates the first task is to establish the pattern of associations between the variables in the sequence. This is accomplished with the correlation coefficient. Table 1 supplies the correlation matrix on which much of the subsequent analysis is based. In discussing causal interpretations of these correlations, we shall have to be clear about the distinction between two points of view. On the one hand, the simple correlation—given our assumption as to direction of causation—measures the gross magnitude of the effect of the antecedent upon the consequent variable. Thus, if $r_{YW} = .541$, we can say that an increment of one standard deviation in first job status produces (whether directly or indirectly) an increment of just over half of one standard deviation in 1962 occupational status. From another point of view we are more concerned with net effects. If both first job and 1962 status have a common antecedent cause—say, father's occupation—we may want to state what part of the effect of *W* on *Y* consists in a transmission of the prior influence of *X*. Or, thinking of *X* as the initial cause, we may focus on the extent to which its influence on *Y* is transmitted by way of its prior influence on *W*.

We may, then, devote a few remarks to the pattern of gross effects before presenting the apparatus that yields estimates of net direct

TABLE 1

Simple Correlations for Five Status Variables

	Variable				
Variable	Y	W	U	X	V
Y: 1962 occ. status		.541	.596	.405	.322
W: First-job status		...	.538	.417	.332
U: Education			...	.438	.453
X: Father's occ. status				...	.516
V: Father's education					...

and indirect effects. Since we do not require a causal ordering of father's education with respect to his occupation, we may be content simply to note that $r_{XV} = .516$ is somewhat lower than the corresponding correlation, $r_{YU} = .596$, observed for the respondents themselves. The difference suggests a heightening of the effect of education on occupational status between the fathers' and the sons' generations. Before stressing this interpretation, however, we must remember that the measurements of V and X do not pertain to some actual cohort of men, here designated "fathers." Each "father" is represented in the data in proportion to the number of his sons who were 20 to 64 years old in March 1962.

The first recorded status of the son himself is education (U). We note that r_{UV} is just slightly greater than r_{UX}. Apparently both measures on the father represent factors that may influence the son's education.

In terms of gross effects there is a clear ordering of influences on first job. Thus $r_{WU} > r_{WX} > r_{WV}$. Education is most strongly correlated with first job, followed by father's occupation, and then by father's education.

Occupational status in 1962 (Y) apparently is influenced more strongly by education than by first job; but our earlier discussion of the first-job measure suggests we should not overemphasize the difference between r_{YW} and r_{YU}. Each, however, is substantially greater than r_{YX}, which in turn is rather more impressive than r_{YV}.

Figure 1 is a graphic representation of the system of relationships among the five variables that we propose as our basic model. The numbers entered on the diagram, with the exception of r_{XV}, are path coefficients, the estimation of which will be explained shortly. First we must become familiar with the conventions followed in constructing this kind of diagram. The link between V and X is shown as a curved line with an arrowhead at both ends. This is to distinguish it from the other lines, which are taken to be paths of influence. In the case of V and X we may suspect an influence running from the former to the latter.

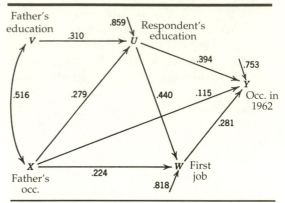

FIGURE 1
Path coefficients in basic model of the process of stratification

But if the diagram is logical for the respondent's generation, we should have to assume that for the fathers, likewise, education and occupation are correlated not only because one affects the other but also because common causes lie behind both, which we have not measured. The bidirectional arrow merely serves to sum up all sources of correlation between V and X and to indicate that the explanation thereof is not part of the problem at hand.

The straight lines running from one measured variable to another represent *direct* (or net) influences. The symbol for the path coefficient, such as p_{YW}, carries a double subscript. The first subscript is the variable at the head of the path, or the effect; the second is the causal variable. (This resembles the convention for regression coefficients, where the first subscript refers to the "dependent" variable, the second to the "independent" variable.)

Finally, we see lines with no source indicated carrying arrows to each of the effect variables. These represent the residual paths, standing for all other influences on the variable in question, including causes not recognized or measured, errors of measurement, and departures of the true relationships from additivity and linearity, properties that are assumed throughout the analysis.

An important feature of this kind of causal scheme is that variables recognized as effects of certain antecedent factors may, in turn, serve as causes for subsequent variables. For example, U is caused by V and X, but it in turn influences W and Y. The algebraic representation of the scheme is a system of equations, rather than the single equation more often employed in multiple regression analysis. This feature permits a flexible conceptualization of the *modus operandi* of the causal network. Note that Y is shown here as being influenced directly by W, U, and X, but not by V (an assumption that will be justified shortly). But this does not imply that V has no influence on Y. V affects U, which does affect Y both directly and indirectly (via W). Moreover, V is correlated with X, and thus shares in the gross effect of X on Y, which is partly direct and partly indirect. Hence the gross effect of V on Y, previously described in terms of the correlation r_{YV}, is here interpreted as being entirely indirect, in consequence of V's effect on intervening variables and its correlation with another cause of Y.

Path Coefficients

Whether a path diagram, or the causal scheme it represents, is adequate depends on both theoretical and empirical considerations. At a minimum, before constructing the diagram we must know, or be willing to assume, a causal ordering of the observed variables (hence the lengthy discussion of this matter earlier in this chapter). This information is external or *a priori* with respect to the data, which merely describe associations or correlations. Moreover, the causal scheme must be complete, in the sense that all causes are accounted for. Here, as in most problems involving analysis of observational data, we achieve a formal completeness of the scheme by representing unmeasured causes as a residual factor, presumed to be uncorrelated with the remaining factors lying behind the variable in question. If any factor is known or

presumed to operate in some other way it must be represented in the diagram in accordance with its causal role, even though it is not measured. Sometimes it is possible to deduce interesting implications from the inclusion of such a variable and to secure useful estimates of certain paths in the absence of measurements on it, but this is not always so. A partial exception to the rule that all causes must be explicitly represented in the diagram is the unmeasured variable that can be assumed to operate strictly as an intervening variable. Its inclusion would enrich our understanding of a causal system without invalidating the causal scheme that omits it. Sociologists have only recently begun to appreciate how stringent are the logical requirements that must be met if discussion of causal processes is to go beyond mere impressionism and vague verbal formulations.[9] We are a long way from being able to make causal inferences with confidence, and schemes of the kind presented here had best be regarded as crude first approximations to adequate causal models.

On the empirical side, a minimum test of the adequacy of a causal diagram is whether it satisfactorily accounts for the observed correlations among the measured variables. In making such a test we employ the fundamental theorem in path analysis, which shows how to obtain the correlation between any two variables in the system, given the path coefficients and correlations entered on the diagram.[10] Without stating this theorem in general form we may illustrate its application here. For example,

$$r_{YX} = p_{YX} + p_{YU}r_{UX} + p_{YW}r_{WX};$$

and

$$r_{WX} = p_{WX} + p_{WU}r_{UX}.$$

We make use of each path leading to a given variable (such as Y in the first example) and the correlations of each of its causes with all other variables in the system. The latter correlations, in turn, may be analyzed; for example, r_{WX}, which appeared as such in the first equation, is broken down into two parts in the second. A complete expansion along these lines is required to trace out all the indirect connections between variables; thus,

$$r_{YX} = p_{YX} + p_{YU}p_{UX} + p_{YU}p_{UV}r_{VX} + p_{YW}p_{WX} + p_{YW}p_{WU}p_{UX} + p_{YW}p_{WU}p_{UV}r_{VX}.$$

Now, if the path coefficients are properly estimated, and if there is no inconsistency in the diagram, the correlations calculated by a formula like the foregoing must equal the observed correlations. Let us compare the values computed from such a formula with the corresponding observed correlations:

$$r_{WV} = p_{WX}r_{XV} + p_{WU}r_{UV}$$

$$= (.224)(.516) + (.440)(.453)$$

$$= .116 + .199 = .315$$

which compares with the observed value of .332; and

$$r_{YV} = p_{YU}r_{UV} + p_{YX}r_{XV} + p_{YW}r_{WV}$$

$$= (.394)(.453) + (.115)(.516) + (.281)(.315)$$

$$= .326$$

(using here the calculated rather than the observed value of r_{WV}), which resembles the actual value, .322. Other such comparisons— for r_{YX}, for example—reveal, at most, trivial discrepancies (no larger than .001).

We arrive, by this roundabout journey, at the problem of getting numerical values for the path coefficients in the first place. This involves using equations of the foregoing type inversely. We have illustrated how to obtain correlations if the path coefficients are known, but in the typical empirical problem we know the correlations (or at least some of them) and have to estimate the paths. For a diagram of the type of Figure 1 the solution involves equations of the same form as those of linear multiple regression, except that we work with a recursive system of regression equations[11] rather than a single regression equation.

TABLE 2

Partial Regression Coefficients in Standard Form (Beta Coefficients) and Coefficients of Determination, for Specified Combinations of Variables

Dependent Variable[a]	Independent Variables[a]				Coefficient of Determination (R^2)
	W	U	X	V	
U[b]	...	...	.279	.310	.26
W	...	.433	.214	.026	.33
W[b]	...	.440	.224	...	.33
Y	.282	.397	.120	-.014	.43
Y[b]	.281	.394	.115	...	.43
Y	.311	.428	...	...	.42

[a] V: Father's education.
   X: Father's occ. status.
   U: Respondent's education.
   W: First-job status.
   Y: 1962 occ. status.
[b] Beta coefficients in these sets taken as estimates of path coefficients for Figure 1.

Table 2 records the results of the regression calculations. It can be seen that some alternative combinations of independent variables were studied. It turned out that the net regressions of both W and Y on V were so small as to be negligible. Hence V could be disregarded as a direct influence on these variables without loss of information. The net regression of Y on X was likewise small but, as it appears, not entirely negligible. Curiously, this net regression is of the same order of magnitude as the proportion of occupational inheritance in this population—about 10 per cent, as discussed [elsewhere].[12] We might speculate that the direct effect of father's occupation on the occupational status of a mature man consists of this modest amount of strict occupational inheritance. The remainder of the effect of X on Y is indirect, inasmuch as X has previously influenced U and W, the son's education and the occupational level at which he got his start. For reasons noted [elsewhere][13] we do not assume that the full impact of the tendency to take up the father's occupation is registered in the choice of first job.

With the formal properties of the model in mind we may turn to some general problems confronting this kind of interpretation of our results. One of the first impressions gained from Figure 1 is that the largest path coefficients in the diagram are those for residual factors, that is, variables not measured. The residual path is merely a convenient representation of the extent to which measured causes in the system fail to account for the variation in the effect variables. (The residual is obtained from the coefficient of determination; if $R^2_{Y(WUX)}$ is the squared multiple correlation of Y on the three independent variables, then the residual for Y is $\sqrt{1 - R^2_{Y(WUX)}}$.) Sociologists are often disappointed in the size of the residual, assuming that this is a measure of their success in "explaining" the phenomenon under study. They seldom reflect on what it would mean to live in a society where nearly perfect explanation of the dependent variable could be secured by studying causal variables like father's occupation or respondent's education. In such a society it would indeed be true that some are "destined to poverty almost from birth . . . by the economic status or occupation of their parents" (in the words of the reference cited in endnote 1). Others, of course, would be "destined" to affluence or to modest circumstances. By no effort of their own could they materially alter the course of destiny, nor could any stroke of fortune, good or ill, lead to an outcome not already in the cards.

Thinking of the residual as an index of the adequacy of an explanation gives rise to a serious misconception. It is thought that a high multiple correlation is presumptive evidence that an explanation is correct or nearly so, whereas a low percentage of determination means that a causal interpretation is almost certainly wrong. The fact is that the size of the residual (or, if one prefers, the proportion of variation "explained") is *no* guide whatever to the validity of a causal interpretation. The best-known cases of "spurious correlation"—a correlation leading to an egregiously wrong interpretation—are those in which the coefficient of determination is quite high.

The relevant question about the residual is not really its size at all, but whether the unobserved factors it stands for are properly represented as being uncorrelated with the measured antecedent variables. We shall entertain [elsewhere][14] some conjectures about unmeasured variables that clearly are not uncorrelated with the causes depicted in Figure 1. It turns out that these require us to acknowledge certain possible modifications of the diagram, whereas other features of it remain more or less intact. A delicate question in this regard is that of the burden of proof. It is all too easy to make a formidable list of unmeasured variables that someone has alleged to be crucial to the process under study. But the mere existence of such variables is already acknowledged by the very presence of the residual. It would seem to be part of the task of the critic to *show*, if only hypothetically, but *specifically*, how the modification of the causal scheme to include a new variable would disrupt or alter the relationships in the original diagram. His argument to this effect could then be examined for plausibility and his evidence, if any, studied in terms of the empirical possibilities it suggests.

Our supposition is that the scheme in Figure 1 is most easily subject to modification by introducing additional measures of the same kind as those used here. If indexes relating to socioeconomic background other than V and X are inserted we will almost certainly estimate differently the direct effects of these particular variables. If occupational statuses of the respondent intervening between W and Y were known we should have to modify more or less radically the right-hand portion of the diagram. Yet we should argue that such modifications may amount to an enrichment or extension of the basic model rather than an invalidation of it. The same may be said of other variables that function as intervening causes. In theory, it should be possible to specify these in some detail, and a major part of the research worker's task is properly defined as an attempt at such specification. In the course of such work, to be sure, there is always the possibility of a discovery that would require a fundamental reformulation, making the present model obsolete. Discarding the model would be a cost gladly paid for the prize of such a discovery.

Postponing the confrontation with an altered model, the one at hand is not lacking in interest. An instructive exercise is to compare the magnitudes of gross and net relationships. Here we make use of the fact that the correlation coefficient and the path coefficient have the same dimensionality. The correlation r_{YX} = .405 (Table 1) means that a unit change (one standard deviation) in X produces a change of 0.4 unit in Y, in gross terms. The path coefficient, p_{YX} = .115 (Figure 1), tells us that about one-fourth of this gross effect is a result of the direct influence of X on Y. (We speculated above on the role of occupational inheritance in this connection.) The remainder (.405 − .115 = .29) is indirect, via U and W. The sum of all indirect effects, therefore, is given by the difference between the simple correlation and the path coefficient connecting two variables. We note that the indirect effects on Y are generally substantial, relative to the direct. Even the variable temporally closest (we assume) to Y has "indirect effects"—actually, common antecedent causes—nearly as large as the direct. Thus r_{YW} = .541 and p_{YW} = .281, so that the aggregate of "indirect effects" is .26, which in this case are common determinants of Y and W that spuriously inflate the correlation between them.

To ascertain the indirect effects along a given chain of causation we must multiply the path coefficients along the chain. The procedure is to locate on the diagram the dependent variable of interest, and then trace back along the paths linking it to its immediate and remote causes. In such a tracing we may reverse direction once but only once, following the rule "first back, then forward." Any bidirectional correlation may be traced in either direction. If the diagram contains more than one such correlation, however, only one may be used in a given compound path. In tracing the indirect connections no variable may be

intersected more than once in one compound path. Having traced all such possible compound paths, we obtain the entirety of indirect effects as their sum.

Let us consider the example of effects of education on first job, U on W. The gross or total effect is r_{WU} = .538. The direct path is p_{WU} = .440. There are two indirect connections or compound paths: from W back to X then forward to U; and from W back to X, then back to V, and then forward to U. Hence we have:

$$r_{WU} = p_{WU} + \underbrace{p_{WX}p_{UX} + p_{WX}r_{XV}p_{UV}}$$
$$\text{(gross)} \quad \text{(direct)} \qquad \text{(indirect)}$$

or, numerically,

$$.538 = .440 + (.224)(.279) + (.224)(.516)(.310)$$

$$= .440 + .062 + .036$$

$$= .440 + .098.$$

In this case all the indirect effect of U on W derives from the fact that both U and W have X (plus V) as a common cause. In other instances, when more than one common cause is involved and these causes are themselves interrelated, the complexity is too great to permit a succinct verbal summary.

A final stipulation about the scheme had best be stated, though it is implicit in all the previous discussion. The form of the model itself, but most particularly the numerical estimates accompanying it, are submitted as valid only for the population under study. No claim is made that an equally cogent account of the process of stratification in another society could be rendered in terms of this scheme. For other populations, or even for subpopulations within the United States, the magnitudes would almost certainly be different, although we have some basis for supposing them to have been fairly constant over the last few decades in this country. The technique of path analysis is not a method for discovering causal laws but a procedure for giving a quantitative interpretation to the manifestations of a known or assumed causal system as it operates in a particular population. When the

The Process of Stratification

same interpretive structure is appropriate for two or more populations there is something to be learned by comparing their respective path coefficients and correlation patterns. We have not yet reached the stage at which such comparative study of stratification systems is feasible. . . .

The Concept of a Vicious Circle

Although the concept of a "cycle of poverty" has a quasi-official sanction in U. S. public policy discussion, it is difficult to locate a systematic explication of the concept. As clear a formulation as any that may be found in academic writing is perhaps the following:[15]

Occupational and social status are to an important extent self-perpetuating. They are associated with many factors which make it difficult for individuals to modify their status. Position in the social structure is usually associated with a certain level of income, education, family structure, community reputation, and so forth. These become part of a vicious circle in which each factor acts on the other in such a way as to preserve the social structure in its present form, as well as the individual family's position in that structure. . . . The cumulation of disadvantages (or of advantages) affects the individual's entry into the labor market as well as his later opportunities for social mobility.

The suspicion arises that the authors in preparing this summary statement were partly captured by their own rhetoric. Only a few pages earlier they had observed that the "widespread variation of educational attainment within classes suggests that one's family background plays an enabling and motivating rather than a determining role."[16] But is an "enabling and motivating role" logically adequate to the function of maintaining a "vicious circle"? In focusing closely on the precise wording of the earlier quotation we are not interested in splitting hairs or in generating a polemic. It merely serves as a convenient point of departure for raising the questions of

what is specifically meant by "vicious circle," what are the operational criteria for this concept, and what are the limits of its usefulness.

To begin with, there is the question of fact—or, rather, of how the quantitative facts are to be evaluated. How "difficult" is it, in actuality, "for individuals to modify their status" (presumably reference is to the status of the family of orientation)? We have found that the father-son correlation for occupational status is of the order of .4. (Assuming attenuation by errors of measurement, this should perhaps be revised slightly upward.) Approaching the measurement problem in an entirely different way, we find that the amount of intergenerational mobility between census major occupation groups is no less than seven-eighths as much as would occur if there were no statistical association between the two statuses whatsoever, or five-sixths as much as the difference between the "minimum" mobility involved in the intergenerational shift in occupation distributions and the amount required for "perfect" mobility.[17] Evidently a very considerable amount of "status modification" or occupational mobility does occur. (There is nothing in the data exhibited by Lipset and Bendix to indicate the contrary.) If the existing amount of modification of status is insufficient in terms of some functional or normative criterion implicitly employed, the precise criterion should be made explicit: *How much mobility must occur to contradict the diagnosis of a "vicious circle"?*

Next, take the postulate that occupational status (of origin) is "associated with many factors" and that "each factor acts on the other" so as "to preserve . . . the individual family's position." Here the exposition virtually cries out for an explicit *quantitative* causal model; if not one of the type set forth in the first section of this chapter, then some other model that also takes into account the way in which several variables combine their effects. Taking our own earlier model, for want of a better alternative, as representative of the situation, what do we learn about the "associated factors"? Family "position" is, indeed, "associated with . . . education," and education in turn makes a sizable difference in early and subsequent occupational achievement. Yet of the total or gross effect of education (U) on Y, occupational status in 1962 ($r_{YU} = .596$), only a minor part consists in a transmission of the prior influence of "family position," at least as this is indicated by measured variables V (father's education) and X (father's occupation). . . . A relevant calculation concerns the compound paths through V and X linking Y to U. Using data for men 20 to 64 years old with nonfarm background, we find:

$$p_{YX}p_{UX} = .025$$

$$p_{YX}r_{XV}p_{UV} = .014$$

$$p_{YX}p_{WX}p_{UX} = .014$$

$$p_{YW}p_{WX}r_{XV}p_{UV} = .008$$

$$\text{Sum} = .061$$

This is the *entire* part of the effect of education that has to do with "perpetuating" the "family's position." By contrast, the direct effect is $p_{YU} = .407$ and the effect via W (exclusive of prior influence of father's education and occupation on respondent's first job) is $p_{YW}p_{WU} = .128$, for a total of .535. Far from serving in the main as a factor perpetuating initial status, education operates *primarily* to induce variation in occupational status that is independent of initial status. The simple reason is that the large residual factor for U is an indirect cause of Y. But by definition it is quite uncorrelated with X and V. This is not to gainsay the equally cogent point that the degree of "perpetuation" (as measured by r_{YX}) that does occur is mediated in large part by education.

This conclusion is so important that we should not allow it to rest on a single calculation. The reader accustomed to a calculus of "explained variation" may prefer the following. For men 35 to 44 years of age with nonfarm background (a convenient and not unrepresentative illustration), we have these

pertinent results: $r_{YX} = .400$; $R_{Y(XV)} = .425$; $R_{Y(UXV)} = .651$. Note that adding the "associated factor" of father's education to father's occupation increases very slightly our estimate of the influence of "family position" on occupational achievement. Including respondent's education, however, makes quite a striking difference. Squaring these coefficients to yield an accounting of the total variation in respondent's 1962 occupational status (Y), we obtain these percentages:

(*i*) Gross (or total) effect of father's education and occupation	18.06
(*ii*) Education of respondent, independent of (*i*)	24.32
(*iii*) All other factors, independent of (*i*) and (*ii*)	57.62
TOTAL	100.00

An analogous calculation, derived from multiple-classification rather than linear-regression statistics, was offered [elsewhere].[18] The results are rather similar. Here we have imputed to the measures of "family position," X and V, their *total* influence, including such part of this as works through education; the 24 per cent contribution of respondent's education refers only to the part of the effect of education that is net of the background factors. Still, education has a greater influence, *independent of these factors*, than they have themselves, operating both directly and indirectly. Overshadowing both these components, of course, is the unexplained variation of nearly 58 per cent, which can have nothing to do with "perpetuating status."

Whatever the merit of these observations, they should at least make clear that statistical results do not speak for themselves. Rather, the findings of a statistical analysis must be controlled by an interpretation—one that specifies the form the analysis will take—and be supplemented by further interpretations that (ideally) make explicit the assumptions on which the analyst is proceeding. The form in which our results are presented is dictated by a conception of status achievement as a temporal process in which later statuses depend, in part, on earlier statuses, intervening achievements, and other contingent factors. In such a framework it may not be a meaningful task to evaluate the relative importance of different causal factors. Instead, attention is focused on how the causes combine to produce the end result. From this point of view we can indicate, first, the gross effect of the measured background factors or origin statuses of a cohort of men on their adult achievement. We can then show how and to what extent this effect is transmitted via measured intervening variables and, finally, to what extent such intervening variables contribute to the outcome, independently of their role in transmission of prior statuses. In a balanced interpretation all these questions should be dealt with explicitly.

Our treatment seems to indicate the advisability of keeping in perspective the magnitude of the gross relationship of background factors and status of origin to subsequent achievement. The relationship is not trivial, nor is it, on the other hand, great enough in itself to justify the conception of a system that insures the "inheritance of poverty" or otherwise renders wholly ineffectual the operation of institutions supposedly based on universalistic principles.

Our model also indicates where the "vicious circle" interpretation is vulnerable. In the passage on the vicious circle quoted there seems to be an assumption that because of the substantial inter-correlations between a number of background factors, each of which has a significant relationship to subsequent achievement, the total effect of origin on achievement is materially enhanced. Here, in other words, the concept of "cumulation" appears to refer to the intercorrelations of a collection of independent variables. But the effect of such intercorrelations is quite opposite to what the writers appear to suppose. They are not alone in arguing from a fallacious assumption that was caustically analyzed by Karl Pearson half a century ago.[19] The crucial point is that if the several determinants are indeed substantially intercorrelated with each

other, then their combined effect will consist largely in redundancy, not in "cumulation." This circumstance does not relieve us from the necessity of trying to understand better *how* the effects come about (a point also illustrated in a less fortunate way in Pearson's work). It does imply that a refined estimate of how much effect results from a combination of "associated factors" will not differ greatly from a fairly crude estimate based on the two or three most important ones. Sociologists have too long followed the mirage of "increasing the explained variance.". . .

We do not wish to imply that the idea of cumulation of influences, or even the particular form of cumulation describable as a "vicious circle," is without merit. Our aim is to call attention to the necessity of specifying the actual mechanism that is only vaguely suggested by such terms. One legitimate meaning of cumulation is illustrated by the model of a synthetic cohort presented [elsewhere].[20] In this case what is cumulative is the experience of an individual or a cohort of individuals over the life cycle, so that in the latter part of the life cycle achieved status depends heavily on prior achievements, whatever the factors determining those achievements may have been. The cumulation here consists in large measure of the effects of contingent factors not related to social origins or measured background factors.

The situation of the Negro American, which is analyzed [elsewhere],[21] exemplifies mechanisms inviting the label of a vicious circle. What is crucial in this case is not merely that Negroes begin life at a disadvantage and that this initial disadvantage, transmitted by intervening conditions, has adverse effects on later careers. Rather, what happens is that, in addition to the initial handicap, the Negro experiences further handicaps at each stage of the life cycle. When Negroes and whites are equated with respect to socioeconomic circumstances of origin and rearing, Negroes secure inferior education. But if we allow for this educational disadvantage as well as the disadvantage of low social origins, Negroes find their way into first jobs of lower status than whites. Again, allowing for the handicap of inferior career beginnings, the handicap of lower education, and the residual effect of low socioeconomic origins—even with all these allowances—Negroes do not enjoy comparable occupational success in adulthood. Indeed, even though we have not carried our own analysis this far, there is good evidence that Negroes and whites do not have equal incomes even after making allowance for the occupational status difference and the educational handicap of Negroes.[22] Thus there surely are disadvantaged minorities in the United States who suffer from a "vicious circle" that is produced by discrimination. But not all background factors that create occupational handicaps are necessarily indicative of such a vicious circle of *cumulative* disadvantages; the handicaps of the Southern whites, for example, are not cumulative in the same sense.[23] A vicious circle of cumulative impediments is a distinctive phenomenon that should not be confused with any and all forms of differential occupational achievement.

As noted earlier, the issue of equalitarianism is one that has generally been more productive of debate than of cogent reasoning from systematized experience. Without becoming fully involved in such a debate here, we must at least attempt to avoid having our position misunderstood. We have *not* vouchsafed a "functional interpretation" that asserts that somehow American society has just the right amount of stratification and just the appropriate degree of intergenerational status transmission. We *have* indicated that it is easy to exaggerate the latter and, in particular, that it is possible seriously to misconstrue the nature of the causal relationships in the process that characterizes status transmission between generations.

In conclusion, one question of policy may be briefly mentioned, which pertains to the distinction between the plight of the minorities who do suffer disadvantages due to their ascribed status and the influence of ascribed factors on occupational life in general. To help such minorities to break out of the vi-

cious circle resulting from discrimination and poverty is a challenge a democratic society must face, in our opinion. To advocate this policy, however, is not the same as claiming that *all* ascriptive constraints on opportunities and achievements could or should be eliminated. To eliminate all *dis*advantages that flow from membership in a family of orientation—with its particular structure of interpersonal relationships, socioeconomic level, community and regional location, and so on—would by the same token entail eliminating any *advantages* the family can confer or provide. If parents, having achieved a desirable status, can *ipso facto* do nothing to make comparable achievement easier for their offspring, we may have "equal opportunity." But we will no longer have a family system—at least not in the present understanding of the term. (This point has not been misunderstood in radical, particularly Marxist, ideologies.)

We do not contemplate an effortless equilibrium at some optimum condition where the claims of egalitarian values and the forces of family attachment are neatly balanced to the satisfaction of all. A continuing tension between these ultimately incompatible tendencies may, indeed, be a requisite for social progress. We do contend that both equity and effectiveness in the policy realm call for a deeper understanding of the process of stratification than social science and politics yet can claim.

Notes

1. Mollie Orshansky, "Children of the Poor," *Social Security Bulletin*, 26(July 1963).

2. Forrest A. Bogan, "Employment of High School Graduates and Dropouts in 1964," *Special Labor Force Report*, No. 54 (U. S. Bureau of Labor Statistics, June 1965), p. 643.

3. Peter M. Blau and Otis Dudley Duncan, *The American Occupational Structure*, New York: The Free Press, 1967, ch. 4.

4. *Ibid.*

5. Bruce K. Eckland, "College Dropouts Who Came Back," *Harvard Educational Review,* 34 (1964), 402–420.

6. Beverly Duncan, *Family Factors and School Dropout: 1920–1960,* U. S. Office of Education, Cooperative Research Project No. 2258, Ann Arbor: Univ. of Michigan, 1965.

7. Blau and Duncan, *op. cit.,* Appendix C.

8. Gösta Carlsson, *Social Mobility and Class Structure,* Lund: CWK Gleerup, 1958, p. 124.

9. H. M. Blalock, Jr., *Causal Inferences in Nonexperimental Research,* Chapel Hill: Univ. of North Carolina Press, 1964.

10. Sewall Wright, "Path Coefficients and Path Regressions," *Biometrics,* 16(1960), 189–202; Otis Dudley Duncan, "Path Analysis," *American Journal of Sociology,* 72(1966), 1–16.

11. Blalock, *op. cit.,* pp. 54ff.

12. Blau and Duncan, *op. cit.,* ch. 4.

13. *Ibid.,* ch. 3.

14. *Ibid.,* ch. 5.

15. Seymour M. Lipset and Reinhard Bendix, *Social Mobility in Industrial Society,* Berkeley: Univ. of California Press, 1959, pp. 198–199.

16. *Ibid.,* p. 190.

17. U. S. Bureau of the Census, "Lifetime Occupational Mobility of Adult Males: March 1962," *Current Population Reports,* Series P–23, No. 11 (May 12, 1964), Table B.

18. Blau and Duncan, *op. cit.,* ch. 4.

19. Karl Pearson, "On Certain Errors with Regard to Multiple Correlation Occasionally Made by Those Who Have Not Adequately Studied This Subject," *Biometrika,* 10(1914), 181–187.

20. Blau and Duncan, *op. cit.,* ch. 5.

21. *Ibid.,* ch. 6.

22. See Herman P. Miller, *Rich Man, Poor Man,* New York: Crowell, 1964, pp. 90–96.

23. Blau and Duncan, *op. cit.,* ch. 6.

CHRISTOPHER JENCKS, MARSHALL SMITH, HENRY ACLAND, MARY JO BANE, DAVID COHEN, HERBERT GINTIS, BARBARA HEYNS, AND STEPHAN MICHELSON

Inequality: A Reassessment of the Effect of Family and Schooling in America

Most Americans say they believe in equality. But when pressed to explain what they mean by this, their definitions are usually full of contradictions. Many will say, like the Founding Fathers, that "all men are created equal." Many will also say that all men are equal "before God," and that they are, or at least ought to be, equal in the eyes of the law. But most Americans also believe that some people are more competent than others, and that this will always be so, no matter how much we reform society. Many also believe that competence should be rewarded by success, while incompetence should be punished by failure. They have no commitment to ensuring that everyone's job is equally desirable, that everyone exercises the same amount of political power, or that everyone receives the same income.

But while most Americans accept inequality in virtually every sphere of day-to-day life, they still believe in what they often call "equal opportunity." By this they mean that the rules determining who succeeds and who fails should be fair. People are, of course, likely to disagree about precisely what is "fair" and what is "unfair." Still, the general principle of fair competition is almost universally endorsed.

Originally published in 1972. Please see complete source information beginning on page 891.

During the 1960s, many reformers devoted enormous effort to equalizing opportunity. More specifically, they tried to eliminate inequalities based on skin color, and to a lesser extent on economic background. They also wanted to eliminate absolute deprivation: "poverty," "ignorance," "powerlessness," and so forth. But only a handful of radicals talked about eliminating inequality per se. Almost none of the national legislation passed during the 1960s tried to reduce disparities in adult status, power, or income in any direct way. There was no significant effort, for example, to make taxation more progressive, and very little effort to reduce wage disparities between highly paid and poorly paid workers. Instead, attention focused on helping workers in poorly paid jobs to move into better paid jobs. Nor was there much effort to reduce the social or psychological distance between high- and low-status occupations. Instead, the idea was to help people in low-status occupations leave these occupations for more prestigious ones. Even in the political arena, "maximum feasible participation" implied mainly that more "leaders" should be black and poor, not that power should be equally distributed between leaders and followers.

Because the reforms of the 1960s did not tackle the problem of adult inequality directly, they accomplished only a few of their goals. Equalizing opportunity is almost impossible without greatly reducing the absolute level of inequality, and the same is true of eliminating deprivation.

Consider the case of equal opportunity. One can equalize the opportunities available to blacks and whites without equalizing anything else, and considerable progress was made in this direction during the late 1960s. But equalizing the opportunities available to different children of the same race is far more difficult. If a society is competitive and rewards adults unequally, some parents are bound to succeed while others fail. Successful parents will then try to pass along their advantages to their children. Unsuccessful parents will inevitably pass along some of their disadvantages. Unless a society completely eliminates ties between parents and children, inequality among parents guarantees some degree of inequality in the opportunities available to children. The only real question is how serious these inequalities must be.

Or consider the problem of deprivation. When the war on poverty began in late 1963, it was conceived as an effort to raise the living standards of the poor. The rhetoric of the time described the persistence of poverty in the midst of affluence as a "paradox," largely attributable to "neglect." Official publications all assumed that poverty was an absolute rather than a relative condition. Having assumed this, they all showed steady progress toward the elimination of poverty, since fewer and fewer people had incomes below the official "poverty line."

Yet despite all the official announcements of progress, the feeling that lots of Americans were poor persisted. The reason was that most Americans define poverty in relative rather than absolute terms. Public opinion surveys show, for example, that when people are asked how much money an American family needs to "get by," they typically name a figure about half what the average American family actually receives.[1] This has been true for the last three decades, despite the fact that real incomes (i.e. incomes adjusted for inflation) have doubled in the interval.

Political definitions of poverty have reflected these popular attitudes. During the Depression, the average American family was living on about $30 a week. A third of all families were living on less than half this amount, i.e. less than $15 a week. This made it natural for Franklin Roosevelt to speak of "one third of a nation" as ill-housed, ill-clothed, and ill-fed. One third of the nation was below what most people then regarded as the poverty line.

By 1964, when Lyndon Johnson declared war on poverty, incomes had risen more than fivefold. Even allowing for inflation, living standards had doubled. Only about 10 percent of all families had real incomes as low as the bottom third had had during the Depression. But popular conceptions of what it took to "get by" had also risen since the Depression. Mean family income was about $160 a week, and popular opinion now held that it took $80 a week for a family of four to make ends meet. About a quarter of all families were still poor by this definition. As a matter of political convenience, the Administration set the official poverty line at $60 a week for a family of four rather than $80, ensuring that even conservatives would admit that those below the line were poor. But by 1970 inflation had raised mean family income to about $200 a week, and the National Welfare Rights Organization was rallying liberal support for a guaranteed income of $100 a week for a family of four.

These political changes in the definition of poverty were not just a matter of "rising expectations" or of people's needing to "keep up with the Joneses." The goods and services that made it possible to live on $15 a week during the Depression were no longer available to a family with the same "real" income (i.e. $40 a week) in 1964. Eating habits had changed, and many cheap foods had disappeared from the stores. Most people had enough money to buy an automobile, so public transportation had atrophied, and families without automobiles were much worse off than during the Depression. The labor market had also changed, and a person without a telephone could not get or keep many jobs. A home without a telephone was more cut off socially than when few people had telephones and more people "dropped by." Housing arrangements had changed, too. During the Depression, many people could not afford indoor plumbing and "got by" with a privy. By the 1960s, privies were illegal in most places. Those who could not afford an indoor toilet ended up in buildings which had broken toilets. For this they paid more than their parents had paid for privies.

Examples of this kind suggest that the "cost of living" is not the cost of buying some fixed set of goods and services. It is the cost of participating in a social system. The cost of participation depends in large part on how much other people habitually spend to participate.

Those who fall far below the norm, whatever it may be, are excluded. It follows that raising the incomes of the poor will not eliminate poverty if the incomes of other Americans rise even faster. If people with incomes less than half the national average cannot afford what "everyone" regards as "necessities," the only way to eliminate poverty is to make sure everyone has an income at least half the average.

This line of reasoning applies to wealth as well as poverty. The rich are not rich because they eat filet mignon or own yachts. Millions of people can now afford these luxuries, but they are still not "rich" in the colloquial sense. The rich are rich because they can afford to buy other people's time. They can hire other people to make their beds, tend their gardens, and drive their cars. These are not privileges that become more widely available as people become more affluent. If all workers' wages rise at the same rate, the highly paid professional will have to spend a constant percentage of his income to get a maid, a gardener, or a taxi. The number of people who are "rich," in the sense of controlling more than their share of other people's time and effort, will therefore remain the same, even though consumption of yachts and filet mignon is rising.

If the distribution of income becomes more equal, as it did in the 1930s and 1940s, the number of people who are "rich" in this sense of the term will decline, even though absolute incomes are rising. If, for example, the wages of domestic servants rise faster than the incomes of their prospective employers, fewer families will feel they can afford full-time servants. This will lower the living standards of the elite to some extent, regardless of what happens to consumption of yachts and filet mignon.

This same logic applies not only to income but to the cognitive skills taught in school. Young people's performance on standardized tests rose dramatically between World War I and World War II, for example. But the level of competence required for many adult roles rose too. When America was a polyglot nation of immigrants, all sorts of jobs were open to those who could not read English. Such people could, for example, join the army, drive a truck, or get a job in the construction industry. Today, when almost everyone can read English, the range of choices open to nonreaders has narrowed. The military no longer takes an appreciable number of illiterates, a driver's license requires a written examination, and apprenticeships in the construction trades are restricted to those who can pass tests. Those who cannot read English are at a disadvantage, simply because they are atypical. America is not organized with their problems in mind. The same thing applies to politics. If the average citizen's vocabulary expands, the vocabulary used by politicians and newspapers will expand too. Those with very limited vocabularies relative to their neighbors will still have trouble following events, even though their vocabulary is larger than, say, their parents' vocabulary was.

Arguments of this kind suggest that it makes more sense to think of poverty and ignorance as relative than as absolute conditions. They also suggest that eliminating poverty and ignorance, at least as these are usually defined in America, depends on eliminating, or at least greatly reducing, inequality. This is no simple matter. Since a competitive system means that some people "succeed" while others "fail," it also means that people will end up unequal. If we want to reduce inequality, we therefore have two options. The first possibility is to make the system less competitive by reducing the benefits that derive from success and the costs paid for failure. The second possibility is to make sure that everyone enters the competition with equal advantages and disadvantages.

The basic strategy of the war on poverty during the 1960s was to try to give everyone entering the job market or any other competitive arena comparable skills. This meant placing great emphasis on education. Many people imagined that if schools could equalize people's cognitive skills this would equalize their bargaining power as adults. In such a system nobody would end up very poor—or, presumably, very rich.

This strategy rested on a series of assumptions which went roughly as follows:

1. Eliminating poverty is largely a matter of helping children born into poverty to rise out of it. Once families escape from poverty, they do not fall back into it. Middle-class children rarely end up poor.

2. The primary reason poor children do not escape from poverty is that they do not acquire basic cognitive skills. They cannot read, write, calculate, or articulate. Lacking these skills, they cannot get or keep a well-paid job.

3. The best mechanism for breaking this vicious circle is educational reform. Since children born into poor homes do not acquire the skills they need from their parents, they must be taught these skills in school. This can be done by making sure that they attend the same schools as middle-class children, by giving them extra compensatory programs in school, by giving their parents a voice in running their schools, or by some combination of all three approaches.

So far as we can discover, each of these assumptions is erroneous.

1. Poverty is not primarily hereditary. While children born into poverty have a higher-than-average chance of ending up poor, there is still an enormous amount of economic mobility from one generation to the next. Indeed, there is nearly as much economic inequality among brothers raised in the same homes as in the general population. This means that inequality is recreated anew in each generation, even among people who start life in essentially identical circumstances.

2. The primary reason some people end up richer than others is not that they have

more adequate cognitive skills. While children who read well, get the right answers to arithmetic problems, and articulate their thoughts clearly are somewhat more likely than others to get ahead, there are many other equally important factors involved. Thus there is almost as much economic inequality among those who score high on standardized tests as in the general population. Equalizing everyone's reading scores would not appreciably reduce the number of economic "failures."

3. There is no evidence that school reform can substantially reduce the extent of cognitive inequality, as measured by tests of verbal fluency, reading comprehension, or mathematical skill. Neither school resources nor segregation has an appreciable effect on either test scores or educational attainment.

Our work suggests, then, that many popular explanations of economic inequality are largely wrong. We cannot blame economic inequality primarily on genetic differences in men's capacity for abstract reasoning, since there is nearly as much economic inequality among men with equal test scores as among men in general. We cannot blame economic inequality primarily on the fact that parents pass along their disadvantages to their children, since there is nearly as much inequality among men whose parents had the same economic status as among men in general. We cannot blame economic inequality on differences between schools, since differences between schools seem to have very little effect on any measurable attribute of those who attend them.

Economic success seems to depend on varieties of luck and on-the-job competence that are only moderately related to family background, schooling, or scores on standardized tests. The definition of competence varies greatly from one job to another, but it seems in most cases to depend more on personality than on technical skills. This makes it hard to imagine a strategy for equalizing competence.

A strategy for equalizing luck is even harder to conceive.

The fact that we cannot equalize luck or competence does *not* mean that economic inequality is inevitable. Still less does it imply that we cannot eliminate what has traditionally been defined as poverty. It only implies that we must tackle these problems in a different way. Instead of trying to reduce people's capacity to gain a competitive advantage on one another, we would have to change the rules of the game so as to reduce the rewards of competitive success and the costs of failure. Instead of trying to make everyone equally lucky or equally good at his job, we would have to devise "insurance" systems which neutralize the effects of luck, and income-sharing systems which break the link between vocational success and living standards.

This could be done in a variety of ways. Employers could be constrained to reduce wage disparities between their best- and worst-paid workers.[2] The state could make taxes more progressive, and could provide income supplements to those who cannot earn an adequate living from wages alone. The state could also provide free public services for those who cannot afford to buy adequate services in the private sector. Pursued with vigor, such a strategy would make "poverty" (i.e. having a living standard less than half the national average) virtually impossible. It would also make economic "success," in the sense of having, say, a living standard more than twice the national average, far less common than it now is. The net effect would be to make those with the most competence and luck subsidize those with the least competence and luck to a far greater extent than they do today.

This strategy was rejected during the 1960s for the simple reason that it commanded relatively little popular support. The required legislation could not have passed Congress. Nor could it pass today. But that does not mean it was the wrong strategy. It simply means that until we change the political and moral premises on which most Americans now operate, poverty and inequality of opportunity will persist at pretty much their present level.

At this point the reader may wonder whether trying to change these premises is worthwhile. Why, after all, should we be so concerned about economic equality? Is it not enough to ensure equal opportunity? And does not the evidence we have described suggest that opportunities are already quite equal in America? If economic opportunities are relatively equal, and if the lucky and the competent then do better for themselves than the unlucky and incompetent, why should we feel guilty about this? Such questions cannot be answered in any definitive way, but a brief explanation of our position may help avoid misunderstanding.

We begin with the premise that every individual's happiness is of equal value. From this it is a short step to Bentham's dictum that society should be organized so as to provide the greatest good for the greatest number. In addition, we assume that the law of diminishing returns applies to most of the good things in life. In economic terms this means that people with low incomes value extra income more than people with high incomes.[3] It follows that if we want to maximize the satisfaction of the population, the best way to divide any given amount of money is to make everyone's income the same. Income disparities (except those based on variations in "need") will always reduce overall satisfaction, because individuals with low incomes will lose more than individuals with high incomes gain.

The principal argument against equalizing incomes is that some people contribute more to the general welfare than others, and that they are therefore entitled to greater rewards. The most common version of this argument is that unless those who contribute more than their share are rewarded (and those who contribute less than their share punished) productivity will fall and everyone will be worse off. A more sophisticated version is that people will only share their incomes on an equal basis if all decisions that affect these incomes are made collectively. If people are left free to make decisions on an individual basis, their

neighbors cannot be expected to pay the entire cost of their mistakes.

We accept the validity of both these arguments. We believe that men need incentives to contribute to the common good, and we prefer monetary incentives to social or moral incentives, which tend to be inflexible and very coercive. We believe, in other words, that virtue should be rewarded, and we assume that there will be considerable variation in virtue from one individual to another. This does not, however, mean that incomes must remain as unequal as they are now. Even if we assume, for example, that the most productive fifth of all workers accounts for half the Gross National Product, it does not follow that they need receive half the income. A third or a quarter might well suffice to keep both them and others productive.

Most people accept this logic to some extent. They believe that the rich should pay more taxes than the poor, although they often disagree about how much more. Conversely, they believe that the poor should not starve, even if they contribute nothing to the general welfare. They believe, in other words, that people should not be rewarded solely for their contribution to the general welfare, but that other considerations, such as need, should also be taken into account. Our egalitarianism is simply another way of saying that we think need should play a larger role than it now does in determining what people get back from society. We do not think it can or should be the sole consideration.

When we turn from the distribution of income to the distribution of other things, our commitment to equality is even more equivocal. We assume, for example, that occupational prestige resembles income in that those who have low-prestige occupations usually value additional prestige more than those who have high-prestige occupations. Insofar as prestige is an end in itself, then, the optimal distribution is again egalitarian. But occupational prestige derives from a variety of factors, most of which are more difficult to redistribute than income. We cannot imagine a social system in which all occupations have equal prestige, except in a society where all workers are equally competent. Since we do not see any likelihood of equalizing competence, we regard the equalization of occupational prestige as a desirable but probably elusive goal.

When we turn from occupational prestige to educational attainment and cognitive skills, the arguments for and against equality are reversed. If schooling and knowledge are thought of strictly as ends in themselves, it is impossible to make a case for distributing them equally. We can see no reason to suppose, for example, that people with relatively little schooling value additional schooling more than people who have already had a lot of schooling. Experience suggests that the reverse is the case. Insofar as schooling is an end in itself, then, Benthamite principles imply that those who want a lot should get a lot, and those who want very little should get very little. The same is true of knowledge and cognitive skills. People who know a lot generally value additional knowledge and skills more than those who know very little. This means that insofar as knowledge or skill is valued for its own sake, an unequal distribution is likely to give more satisfaction to more people than an equal distribution.

The case for equalizing the distribution of schooling and cognitive skill derives not from the idea that we should maximize consumer satisfaction, but from the assumption that equalizing schooling and cognitive skill is necessary to equalize status and income. This puts egalitarians in the awkward position of trying to impose equality on people, even though the natural demand for both cognitive skill and schooling is very unequal. Since we have found rather modest relationships between cognitive skill and schooling on the one hand and status and income on the other, we are much less concerned than most egalitarians with making sure that people end up alike in these areas.

Our commitment to equality is, then, neither all-embracing nor absolute. We do not believe that everyone can or should be made equal to everyone else in every respect. We assume that some differences in cognitive skill and vocational competence are inevitable, and that efforts to eliminate such differences can never be 100 percent successful. But we also believe that the distribution of income can be made far more equal than it is, even if the distribution of cognitive skill and vocational competence remains as unequal as it is now. We also think society should get on with the task of equalizing income rather than waiting for the day when everyone's earning power is equal.

Notes

1. This material has been collected and analyzed by Lee Rainwater at Harvard University, as part of a forthcoming study of the social meaning of low income.

2. Lester C. Thurow and Robert E.B. Lucas, in "The American Distribution of Income" [Washington, D.C.: U.S. Government Printing Office, March 17, 1972], discuss the possibility of such constraints in some detail. The principal virtue of this approach is that it reduces the incomes of the rich *before* they are defined as "income" rather than afterwards. This means that the recipient is less conscious of what he is giving up and less likely to feel he is being cheated of his due.

3. If everyone had equal earning power we could assume that people "chose" their incomes voluntarily and that those with low incomes were those who were maximizing something else (e.g. leisure, autonomy, etc.). But as we note [elsewhere], people's concern with income as against other objectives has no apparent effect on their actual income, at least while they are young [see Christopher Jencks, Marshall Smith, Henry Acland, Mary Jo Bane, David Cohen, Herbert Gintis, Barbara Heyns, and Stephan Michelson, *Inequality: A Reassessment of the Effect of Family and Schooling in America,* New York: Harper and Row, 1972, ch. 7, note 64]. Thus we infer that income differences derive largely from differences in earning power and luck.

WILLIAM H. SEWELL, ARCHIBALD O. HALLER, AND ALEJANDRO PORTES

The Educational and Early Occupational Attainment Process

Blau and Duncan (1967:165–172) have recently presented a path model of the occupational attainment process of the American adult male population. This basic model begins with two variables describing the early stratification position of each person; these are his father's educational and occupational attainment statuses. It then moves to two behavioral variables; these are the educational level the individual has completed and the prestige level of his first job. The dependent variable is the person's occupational prestige position in 1962. That the model is not without power is attested by the fact that it accounts for about 26 percent of the variance in educational attainment, 33 percent of the variance in first job, and 42 percent of the variance in 1962 level of occupational attainment. Various additions to the basic model are presented in the volume, but none is clearly shown to make much of an improvement in it. These include nativity, migration, farm origin, subgroup position, marriage, and assortative mating. Without detracting from the excellence of the Blau and Duncan analysis, we may make several observations.

1. Because the dependent behaviors are occupational prestige attainments—attainment levels in a stratification system, it is appropriate to single out variables indicating father's stratification position as the most relevant social structural inputs. It is unfortunate that practical considerations prevented the inclusion of psychological inputs in their model, especially considering the repeated references to one such—mental ability—in the literature on differential occupational attainment (Lipset and Bendix, 1959:203–226; Sewell and Armer, 1966). More recently, this gap has been partially filled (Duncan, 1968a).

2. Also omitted are social psychological factors which mediate the influence of the input variables on attainment. This, too, is unfortunate in view not only of the speculative theory but also the concrete research in social psychology, which suggests the importance of such intervening variables as reference groups (Merton, 1957:281–386), significant others (Gerth and Mills, 1953:84–91), self-concept (Super, 1957:80–100), behavior expectations (Gross et al., 1958), levels of educational and occupational aspiration (Haller and Miller, 1963; Kuvlesky and Ohlendorf, 1967; Ohlendorf et al., 1967), and experiences of success or failure in school (Parsons, 1959; Brookover et al., 1965).

It remains to be seen whether the addition of such psychological and social psychological variables is worthwhile, although there are

Originally published in 1969. Please see complete source information beginning on page 891.

reasons for believing that at least some of them may be. First, an explanation of a behavior system requires a plausible causal argument, not just a set of path coefficients among temporally ordered variables. As indicated in Duncan's (1969) recent work, the introduction of social psychological mediating variables offers this possibility, but it does not guarantee it. As it stands, the Blau-Duncan model fails to indicate why any connection at all would be expected between the input variables, father's education and occupation, and the three subsequent factors: respondent's education, respondent's first job, and respondent's 1962 occupation. Granting differences among social psychological positions, they all agree that one's cognitions and motivations (including, among others, knowledge, self-concept and aspirations) are developed in structured situations (including the expectations of others), and that one's actions (attainments in this case) are a result of the cognitive and motivational orientations one brings to the action situation, as well as the factors in the new situation itself. Second, if valid, a social psychological model will suggest new points at which the causal system may be entered in order to change the attainment behaviors of persons, an issue not addressed by the Blau and Duncan volume. Variables such as the expectations of significant others offer other possibilities for manipulating the outcomes, including educational attainments. Third, in addition to the above advantages, a social psychological model of educational and occupational attainment might add to the explanation of variance in the dependent variables.

The Problem

The present report extends the attempts of the writers (Sewell and Armer, 1966; Sewell and Orenstein, 1965; Sewell and Shah, 1967; Sewell, 1964; Haller and Sewell, 1967; Portes *et al.*, 1968; Haller, 1966; Haller and Miller, 1963; Miller and Haller, 1964; Sewell *et al.*, 1957) to apply social psychological concepts

to the explanation of variation in levels of educational and occupational attainment. We assume (1) that certain social structural and psychological factors—initial stratification position and mental ability, specifically—affect both the sets of significant others' influences bearing on the youth, and the youth's own observations of his ability; (2) that the influence of significant others, and possibly his estimates of his ability, affect the youth's levels of educational and occupational aspiration; (3) that the levels of aspiration affect subsequent levels of educational attainment; (4) that education in turn affects levels of occupational attainment. In the present analysis we assume that all effects are linear; also, that the social psychological variables perform only mediating functions.

More specifically, we present theory and data regarding what we believe to be a logically consistent social psychological model. This provides a plausible causal argument to link stratification and mental ability inputs through a set of social psychological and behavioral mechanisms to educational and occupational attainments. One compelling feature of the model is that some of the inputs may be manipulated through experimental or other purposive interventions. This means that parts of it can be experimentally tested in future research and that practical policy agents can reasonably hope to use it in order to change educational and occupational attainments.

A Social Psychological Model

The model treats causal relationships among eight variables. X_1 is the occupational prestige level attained by the adult person, or *occupational attainment* (OccAtt); X_2 is the educational level he had previously attained, or *educational attainment* (EdAtt); X_3 is the occupational prestige level to which he aspired as a youth, or *level of occupational aspiration* (LOA); X_4 is his *level of educational aspiration* as a youth (LEA); X_5 is the influence for educational achievement exerted upon him by significant others while still in

DIAGRAM 1
Path coefficients of antecedents of educational and occupational attainment levels

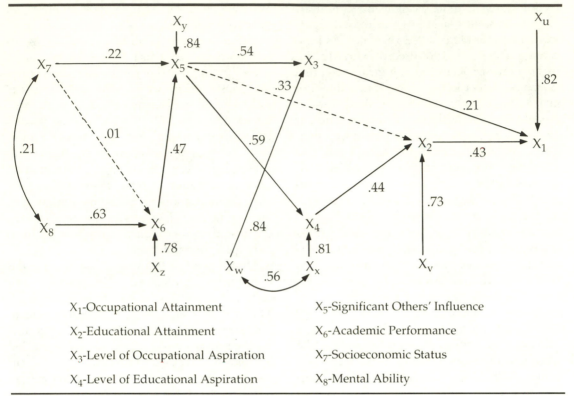

X_1-Occupational Attainment

X_2-Educational Attainment

X_3-Level of Occupational Aspiration

X_4-Level of Educational Aspiration

X_5-Significant Others' Influence

X_6-Academic Performance

X_7-Socioeconomic Status

X_8-Mental Ability

high school, or *significant others' influence* (SOI); X_6 is the quality of his *academic performance* in high school (AP); X_7 is the level of his family in the stratification system, or *socioeconomic status* (SES); and X_8 is his *mental ability* as measured while he was in high school (MA). Path models (Blau and Duncan, 1967:165–172; Wright, 1934; Wright, 1960; Heise, 1969) require a knowledge of the causal order among the variables. Beyond the causal arguments presented below, additional credibility is suggested by the existence of a plausible temporal order among variables. X_7 (SES) and X_8 (MA) precede everything else. X_5 (SOI) and X_6 (AP) precede both aspirations and attainments, and it can be assumed that for the most part X_6 precedes X_5. Youthful aspirations obviously precede later educational and occupational attainments. Pre-adult educational attainments precede adult occupational attainments.

By no means do all of the possible causal linkages seem defensible. The most likely ones are indicated in Diagram 1. In it straight solid lines stand for causal lines that are to be theoretically expected, dotted lines stand for possible but theoretically debatable causal lines, and curved lines represent unanalyzed correlations among variables which cannot be assigned causal priority in present data.

Commencing from the left of the diagram, we assume, as has often been found before (Sewell and Shah, 1967; Sewell *et al.*, 1957), that a low positive correlation, r_{78}, exists between the youth's measured mental ability (MA) and his parents' socioeconomic status (SES). This is the case: $r_{78} = .21$. We anticipate the existence of substantial effect of MA on academic performance (AP). We theorize that significant others' influence (SOI) is controlled by AP, and by socioeconomic status, as well as by exogenous factors, that they exert profound effects on aspiration, and that the latter in turn influences later attainments. A more detailed examination of the theory follows.

Working with partial conceptions of SOI (and using different terminology), Bordua (1960) and Sewell and Shah (1968) have shown that parents' expectations for the youths' attainments are important influences on later aspirations and attainment. Similarly, Cramer (1967), Alexander and Campbell (1964), Campbell and Alexander (1965), Haller and Butterworth (1960), and Duncan *et al.* (1968) have investigated peer influences on aspirations and attainments. Each of these sets of actors, plus some others, may be seen as a special case of reference group influence. Building on such thinking, we have concluded that the key variable here is significant others' influence. Significant others are the specific persons from whom the individual obtains his level of aspiration, either because they serve as models or because they communicate to him their expectations for his behavior (Woelfel, 1967). The term "significant others" is more appropriate than that of "reference group" because it eliminates the implication that collectivities such as one's friends, or work groups, or parents are necessarily the influential agents for all individuals. Experimental research, beginning with Sherif's work (1935), has shown the importance of other persons in defining one's own situation. One obtains his social behavior tendencies largely through the influence of others. Herriott (1963) has carried this line of thinking into the present area of research. He has shown that one's conception of the educational behavior others think appropriate to him is highly correlated with his level of educational aspiration. Thus, significant others' influence is a central variable in a social psychological explanation of educational and occupational attainment. It is obviously important to discover the causal paths determining SOI, as well as those by which it exerts its effects on attainment. We hypothesize a substantial direct path (p_{57}) from socioeconomic status (SES) to SOI. We also hypothesize a substantial effect of mental ability on SOI. This is be-

cause we expect that the significant others with whom the youth interacts base their expectations for his educational and occupational attainments in part on his demonstrated abilities. In turn, this implies that the path from mental ability (MA) to SOI is indirect by way of academic performance (AP). Thus, we hypothesize the existence of a pronounced path from MA to AP (p_{68}) and another from AP to SOI (p_{56}). So far we assume that one's grades in school are based on the quality of his performance. A strong undercurrent in the literature seems to have held, however, that the youth's family's SES has a direct influence on his grades (Havighurst and Neugarten, 1957:236–237). To our knowledge, this has not been adequately demonstrated, and in large high schools, often far removed from the youth's home and neighborhood, this may well be debatable. Nevertheless, since it is at least possible that school grades (the evidences of performance) are partly determined by teachers' desires to please prestigious parents or to reward "middle-class" behavior, we have drawn a dotted path (p_{67}) from SES to AP, allowing for the possibility of such an influence.

We hypothesize that the major effects of significant others' influence (SOI) on attainment are mediated by its effects on levels of aspiration. Thus, we have indicated a path (p_{35}) from SOI to level of occupational aspiration (LOA) and another (p_{45}) from SOI to level of educational aspiration (LEA). It is not inconsistent with this to suspect the possibility that SOI might have a direct influence on later educational attainment (EdAtt); we have thus included a dotted or debatable path (p_{25}) from SOI to EdAtt. Because we are here referring to SOI during late high school, it must necessarily refer largely to college education. There is, therefore, no reason to include such a path from SOI to occupational attainment.

Levels of educational aspiration (LEA) and occupational aspirations (LOA) are known to be highly correlated, since education is widely, and to some extent validly, considered to be a necessary condition for high occupational attainment (Haller and Miller, 1963:30, 39–42,

96). But LOA and LEA are not identical. (In these data, $r_{34.5} = r_{WX} = .56$.) We expect that LEA will have a pronounced effect on EdAtt (p_{24}), and that its entire effect on level of occupational attainment will be expressed through EdAtt. On the other hand, we do not hypothesize any effect of LOA on EdAtt which is not already contained in its correlation with LEA. Hence, there is no hypothetical path for LOA to EdAtt. A direct effect of LOA on OccAtt (p_{13}) is hypothesized, however.

There are 26 possible paths, given the sequence laid out above. As one can see by counting the paths (straight lines) in Diagram 1, we hypothesize noteworthy effects for only eight of these—ten if the dotted lines are counted. If this were a rigorous theoretical model, path coefficients would be calculated only for these eight (or ten) supposed causal connections. We believe that because of the fact that it is not rigorous, and at this stage of our knowledge probably cannot be, it would be well to calculate all of the possible 26 path coefficients, using the calculated values as rough indicators of the influences operating in the system. If the theoretic reasoning is a fair description of the reality to which it is addressed, the path coefficients for the eight (or ten) predicted causal lines should be considerably greater than those for the remainder where no causal prediction was made. Also, it is entirely possible that some unhypothesized causal lines might turn out to be of importance. This, too, argues for calculating the whole set of 26. These data are presented in tabular form (Table 3) below.

Method

In 1957 all high school seniors in Wisconsin responded to an extensive questionnaire concerning their educational and occupational aspirations and a number of potentially related topics. In 1964 one of the authors (Sewell) directed a follow-up in which data on later educational and occupational attainments were collected from an approximately one-third random sample of the respondents in the original survey.

This study is concerned with those 929 subjects for whom data are available at both times, in 1957 and 1964, and who (a) are males and (b) whose fathers were farmers in 1957. Zero-order correlations are computed on all 929 cases, using a computer program which accepts missing data. All higher order coefficients are based on 739 cases for whom data on each variable were complete. (The matrices of zero-order correlations between all eight variables for those two sets of cases are practically identical.)

Variables

Level of occupational attainment (X_1—OccAtt) was measured by Duncan's (1961) socioeconomic index of occupational status.

Level of educational attainment (X_2—EdAtt) was operationalized with data obtained in 1964 by dividing the sample into those who have had at least some college education and those who have not had any at all.[1]

Level of occupational aspiration (X_3—LOA) was determined by assigning Duncan's (1961) socioeconomic index scores to the occupation indicated by the respondent as the one he desired to fill in the future.

Level of educational aspiration (X_4—LEA) is a dichotomous variable corresponding to the respondent's statement in 1957 of whether or not he planned to attend college after graduating from high school.

Index of significant others' influence (X_5—SOI) is a simple summated score (range: zero to three) of three variables: (a) The youth's report of his parents' encouragement for college, dichotomized according to whether or not the respondent perceived direct parental encouragement for going to college. (b) The youth's report of his teachers' encouragement for college, dichotomized in a similar manner, according to whether or not direct teacher encouragement for college was perceived by the respondent. (c) Friends' college plans, dichotomized according to the respondent's statement that most of his close friends planned or did not plan to go to college. These variables, all emphasizing education, were combined because they reflect the same conceptual dimension, and that dimension is theoretically more relevant than any of its component parts. That the three components do in fact measure the same dimension is attested by the positive correlations among them and a subsequent factor analysis. These correlations and the correlation of each with the summated variable, significant others' influence, are shown in Table 1. It may be relevant to point out the composition of this significant others' index in the light of Kelley's distinction (1952). Clearly, the perceptions of direct parental and teacher pressures toward college conform to the classic case of normative reference groups. The educational plans of close friends, on the other hand, may be thought of as having mixed functions. First, close peer groups may exercise pressure toward conformity, and second, friends' plans also serve for the individual's cognitive comparison of himself with "people like himself." Therefore, though the main character of the dimension indicated by this index is clearly normative, it can be thought of as containing some elements of an evaluative function as well.

Quality of academic performance (X_6—AP) is measured by a reflected arc sine transformation of each student's rank in his high school class.

Socioeconomic status (X_7—SES) is measured by a factor-weighted combination of the education of the respondent's father and mother, his perception of the economic status of the family, his perception of possible parental support should he choose to go to college and the approximate amount of such support, and the occupation of his father.[2]

Measured mental ability (X_8—MA) is indexed by Henmon-Nelson test scores (1942). The data were taken when the youths were in the junior year of high school. The scores, originally recorded as percentile-ranks, were treated with an arc sine transformation to approximate a normal distribution.[3]

TABLE 1

Zero-Order Correlations Between Indicators of Significant Others' Influence Regarding College

	Teachers' Influence	Friends' Influence	Index of Significant Others' Influence
Parental Influence	.37	.26	.74
Teachers' Influence	...	.32	.72
Friends' Influence	...	...	.68
Significant Others' Influence	...	...	...

Results

The zero-order correlation coefficients among eight variables are presented in Table 2. A complete path diagram would involve too many lines to be intelligible, because path coefficients presented in Diagram 1 were calculated for all 26 possible lines implied in the causal order specified above. With the exception of the theoretically dubious direct path from SES to AP, which turned out to be $p_{67} = .01$, each of the path coefficients for causal lines hypothesized in Diagram 1 is larger than those not hypothesized. Both sets of standardized beta (or path) coefficients are presented in Table 3.

This table shows that the reasoning presented in the above section, offering a social psychological explanation for educational and occupational attainment, cannot be too far off the mark. We had hypothesized that SOI (significant others' influence) was of central importance. In fact, it has notable direct effects on three subsequent variables, each of which bears ultimately on prestige level of occupational attainment. Both theory and data agree that SOI has direct effects on levels of educational and occupational aspiration, as well as educational (*i.e.,* college) attainment. In turn, each aspiration variable appears to have the predicted substantial effects on its respective attainment variable. Looking at its antecedents, we note theory and data again agree that SOI is affected directly by SES and indirectly by measured mental ability through

TABLE 2
Zero-Order Correlations

	X_1 Occupational Attainment (Prestige Scores—Duncan)	X_2 Educational Attainment (Years College)	X_3 Level of Occupational Aspiration	X_4 Level of Educational Aspiration	X_5 Significant Others' Influence	X_6 Academic Performance (Grade Point)	X_7 Socioeconomic Status	X_8 Measured Mental Ability
X_1-Occ. Att.	...	.52	.43	.38	.41	.37	.14	.33
X_2-Ed. Att.	...	...	.53	.61	.57	.48	.23	.40
X_3-LOA	...	...	...	.70	.53	.43	.15	.41
X_4-LEA	...	...	...	...	.59	.46	.26	.40
X_5-SOI	...	...	...	...	...	.49	.29	.41
X_6-AP	...	...	...	...	...	...	.16	.62
X_7-SES	...	...	...	...	...	...	...	.21
X_8-MA	...	...	...	...	...	...	...	...

TABLE 3
Standardized Beta Coefficients for Hypothesized and Non-Hypothesized Causal Paths*

Dependent Variables	Independent Variables						
	X_2 EdAtt	X_3 LOA	X_4 LEA	X_5 SOI	X_6 AP	X_7 SES	X_9 MA
X_6 AP	...	...	...	...	...	(.01)	.62
X_5 SOI	...	...	...	...	.39	.21	.13
X_4 LEA	...	...	...	.45	.18	.07	.08
X_3 LOA	...	...	...	.42	.12	—.02	.16
X_2 EdAtt	...	.07	.34	(.23)	.17	.05	.03
X_1 OccAtt	.38	.19	—.10	.11	.06	.00	.04

* Figures in italics are coefficients for paths hypothesized in Diagram 1.
Figures in parentheses refer to theoretically debatable causal lines.

the latter's effect on the youth's academic performance. The latter variable is crucial because it provides (or is correlated with) palpable evidence that significant others can observe and, thus to a degree, align their expectations for the youth with his demonstrated ability.

None of the unpredicted paths is very strong, but we must recognize that there may be more operating in such a system than we were able to anticipate from previous thinking. There is a pair of perhaps consequential direct paths from academic performance to educational aspiration ($p_{46} = .18$) and to educational attainment ($p_{26} = .17$). There are several possibilities. The data might imply the existence of a mediating factor, such as one's self

conception of his ability, a factor which could influence both educational aspirations and attainment. They also suggest that not all of the effect of ability on educational aspiration and attainments is mediated by SOI. Finally, one's ability may exert a continuing effect on his educational attainments quite apart from the mediation of either significant others or aspirations—and therefore apart from one's conception of his ability. Arguments such as these, however, should not be pressed too far because the figures are small. Another unexpected but noteworthy path links mental ability directly to level of occupational aspiration. We offer no speculation regarding it.

So far we have seen that a consistent and plausible social psychological position is at least moderately well borne out by the analysis of lines of apparent influence of its variables when they are arranged in causal order. How well does the total set of independent variables work in accounting for variance in the attainment variables? In brief, $R^2_{1.2345678} = .34$ and $R^2_{2.345678} = .50$. Thus, the variables account for 34 percent of the variance in level of occupational attainment and 50 percent of the variance in level of educational attainment. Obviously, variables X_3 through X_8 are much more effective in accounting for educational attainment than in accounting for occupational attainment. Indeed, educational attainment alone accounts for 27 percent of the variance in occupational attainment (from Table 3, $r^2_{12} = .52^2 = .27$). What we have here, then, is a plausible causal system functioning primarily to explain variation in educational attainment. This, in turn, has considerable effect on occupational attainment. The same set of variables adds a small but useful amount to the explanation of occupational attainment variance beyond that contributed by its explanation of educational attainment.[4]

Discussion and Conclusions

Using father's occupational prestige, the person's educational attainment, and his first job level, Blau and Duncan (1967:165–172) were able to account for 33 percent of the variance in occupational attainment of a nationwide sample of American men. Neither our sample nor our variables are identical with theirs; so it is impossible to assess the total contribution of this study to the state of knowledge as reflected in their work. Educational attainment is strategic in both studies and in this regard the studies are fairly comparable. The present model adds a great deal to the explanation of the social psychological factors affecting that variable. The prospects seem good, too, that if the present model were to be applied to a sample coming from a wider range of the American stratification system with greater age variation, it might prove to be more powerful than it appears with our sample of young farm-reared men. In general, the present take-off on the Blau-Duncan approach to occupational attainment levels seems worthy of further testing and elaboration.

Several comments are appropriate regarding the social psychological position and data presented here. (1) Clearly, the variable we have called significant others' influence is an important factor. The present evidence appears to show that once formed its effects are far-reaching. Also, besides being a powerful explanatory factor, significant others' influence should be amenable to manipulation. It thus suggests itself as a point at which external agents might intervene to change educational and occupational attainment levels. This means that at least part of the system is theoretically amenable to experimental testing. The parts of the present model which are hypothetically dependent upon this variable might be more securely tested if such experiments can be worked out. Also, practical change agents might be able to change levels of attainment, either by inserting themselves or others as new significant others or by changing the expectations existing significant others have for the individual. There may well be a substantial payoff from more refined work with this variable.

(2) The results seem to indicate, too, that aspirations (a special class of attitudes) are in fact performing mediational functions in transmitting anterior factors into subsequent behaviors. This has been a subject of recent debate, much of which has in effect held that attitudinal variables are useless epiphenomena. This was recently discussed by Fendrich (1967).

Such encouraging results do not, however, mitigate the need for (a) general experimental determination of the supposed effects of attitudes on behaviors, and (b) specific experimental determination of the effects of aspirations on attainments.

(3) The question may be raised as to the extent to which this system is inherently culture-bound. One might wonder whether attainment behavior within an institutionalized pattern of "sponsored" rather than "contest"

achievement (Turner, 1960) would change the path model. Besides this (and perhaps other institutionalized types of achievement patterns), there is also the question of the relevance of the model for ascribed occupational attainment systems. Obviously we do not have data bearing on these questions but we may at least discuss them. Let us suppose that the same eight variables are measured on youth in a "sponsored" achievement context. We speculate that if measured mental ability is the basis of selection of those who are to be advanced, then the direct path from mental ability to significant others' influence would increase because sponsors are significant others. (This would require a more general measure of significant others' influence than was used here.) If a variable other than mental ability or socioeconomic status is important to the sponsors, then the residual effect of unmeasured variables on significant others' influence would increase. Since one's sponsors presumably influence one's aspirations and aspirations in turn mediate attainment, the rest of the model probably would not change much.

Consider the case of ascribed attainment. Here one's parents' position determines what one's significant others will expect of one; mental ability is either irrelevant or controlled by family position; and one's aspirations are controlled by the family. The importance of higher education may vary among basically ascribed systems: in one it may be unimportant, in another it may merely validate one's status, or in still another it may train ascribed elites to fulfill the key social roles in the society. If educational attainment is important within the social system, aspirations will mediate the influence of significant others upon it, and it in turn will mediate occupational attainment. If not, occupational aspirations will mediate occupational attainment and educational attainment will drop out of the path model. In short, by allowing for variations in the path coefficients, the same basic social psychological model might work well to describe attainment in stratification and mobility systems quite different from that of the present sample.

(4) The linear model used here seems to be an appropriate way to operationalize social psychological positions holding that the function of "intervening" attitudinal variables is to mediate the influence of more fundamental social structural and psychological variables on behavior. By assuming linear relations among variables and applying a path system to the analysis, we have cast the attainment problem in such a framework. It seems to have worked quite well. We are sufficiently encouraged by this attempt to recommend that a parallel tack might be made on problems in which the overt behavior variables are quite different from educational and occupational attainment.

(5) Nonetheless, satisfactory as such a linear model and its accompanying theory seems to be, there is still the possibility that other techniques flowing from somewhat different social psychological assumptions might be better. It is possible that, in the action situation, enduring attitudes (such as educational and occupational aspirations) may function as independent forces which express themselves in relevant overt behaviors to the degree that other personality and situational variables permit. Linear models would thus be effective to the degree that the persons modify their aspirations to bring them in line with potentials for action offered by the latter variables. More importantly, the combined effects of aspirational and facilitational variables would produce non-linear accelerating curves of influence on behavior variables. For the present types of data, this would imply that parental stratification position, mental ability, and significant others' influence not only produce aspirations, but also, to the extent to which these influences continue more or less unchanged on into early adulthood, they function as differential facilitators for the expression of aspirations in attainments. If this is true, a nonlinear system of statistical analysis handling interaction effects would be even more powerful than the one used in this paper.

(6) It should be remembered that the most highly educated of these young men had just

begun their careers when the final data were collected. If the distance between them and the less educated widens, the occupational attainment variance accounted for by the model may well increase. The direct relations of some of the antecedents to occupational attainment may also change. In particular, mental ability may show a higher path to occupational attainment.

(7) Finally, although the results reported in this paper indicate that the proposed model has considerable promise for explaining educational and early occupational attainment of farm boys, its adequacy should now be tested on populations with a more differentiated socioeconomic background. It is quite possible that in such populations the effects of socioeconomic status on subsequent variables may be significantly increased. The effects of other variables in the system may also be altered when the model is applied to less homogeneous populations.

The present research appears to have extended knowledge of the causal mechanism influencing occupational attainment. Most of this was accomplished by providing a consistent social psychological model which adds to our ability to explain what is surely one of its key proximal antecedents, educational attainment.

Notes

Revision of paper originally prepared for delivery at the joint sessions of the Rural Sociological Society and the American Sociological Association, San Francisco, August, 1967. The research reported here was supported by the University of Wisconsin Graduate School, by the Cooperative State Research Service and the University's College of Agriculture for North Central Regional Research Committee NC–86, by funds to the Institute for Research on Poverty at the University of Wisconsin provided by the Office of Economic Opportunity pursuant to the provisions of the Economic Opportunity Act of 1964, and by a grant from the National Institute of Health, U. S. Public Health Service (M–6275). The writers wish to thank Otis Dudley Duncan for his careful reading and incisive criticisms and Vimal P. Shah for help in the statistical analysis. The conclusions are the full responsibility of the authors.

1. It is important to note that the timing of the follow-up was such as to allow most individuals to complete their education up to the bachelor's degree and beyond. It is unlikely that the educational attainment of the sample as a whole will change much in the years to come. On the other hand, while the span of seven years allowed those individuals who did not continue their education to find a stable position in the occupational structure and even improve upon it, there was not enough time for those who continued their education to do the same. A few of the latter were still in school; most had just begun their occupational careers. It is therefore possible that a follow-up taken five or ten years from now would show greater differentiation in attainments as the educated group gathers momentum and moves up in the occupational world.

2. Naturally, father's occupation is a constant in this subsample of farm-reared males. It is important to note that the SES mean and standard deviations for this subsample are considerably lower than for the total sample. The low and homogeneous SES levels of this subsample may yield atypical relations among the variables.

3. Our previous research (Sewell and Armer, 1966; Haller and Sewell, 1967) has led us to be skeptical of claims that local ecological and school class compositional factors influence aspirations and attainments. Nevertheless the zero-order intercorrelations of five such variables and their correlations with X_1-X_8 are available (although they are not presented here). Two of these pertain to the county in which the youth attended high school: county level of living and degree of urbanization. Three pertain to his high school senior class: average SES of the class, percentage of the class members whose fathers attended college, and percentage of the class members whose fathers had professional-level occupations. Though substantially correlated with each other, the variables are uncorrelated with the variables in the above model.

4. Some readers will be interested in the path coefficients as calculated only for the lines hypothesized in the diagram. For this reason and because of the diagram's parsimony, we have calculated the values for each of its eight paths (or ten, including dubious ones). The restricted model explains 47 and 33 percent of the variance in X_2 and X_1, respectively. Data not presented here show that the model reproduces the zero-order correlation matrix quite well. For this reason and because the model is an effective predictor of X_2 and X_1, it may be considered to be fairly valid. Nonetheless, it seems more prudent to rest our case on the less presumptuous data already presented in Table 3. This is why the coefficients presented in the diagram are not discussed here.

References

Alexander, C. Norman, Jr., and Ernest Q. Campbell. 1964. "Peer influences on adolescent educational aspirations and attainments." American Sociological Review 29 (August):568–575.

Blau, Peter M., and Otis Dudley Duncan. 1967. The American Occupational Structure. New York: Wiley.

Bordua, David J. 1960. "Educational aspirations and parental stress on college." Social Forces 38 (March):262–269.

Brookover, Wilbur B., Jean M. LePere, Don E. Hamachek, Shailer Thomas, and Edsel L. Erickson. 1965. Self-concept of Ability and School Achievement. East Lansing: Michigan State University, Bureau of Educational Research Services.

Campbell, Ernest Q., and C. Norman Alexander. 1965. "Structural effects and interpersonal relationships." American Journal of Sociology 71 (November):284–289.

Cramer, M. R. 1967. "The relationship between educational and occupational plans of high school students." Paper presented at the meeting of the Southern Sociological Society, Atlanta (unpublished).

Duncan, Otis Dudley. 1961. "A socioeconomic index for all occupations." Pp. 109–138 in Albert J. Reiss, Jr. (ed.), Occupations and Social Status. New York: Free Press.

———. 1968a. "Ability and achievement." Eugenics Quarterly 15 (March):1–11.

———. 1969. "Contingencies in the construction of causal models," Edgar F. Borgatta, (ed.), Sociological Methodology.

Duncan, Otis Dudley, Archibald O. Haller, and Alejandro Portes. 1968. "Peer influences on aspirations: a reinterpretation." American Journal of Sociology 74 (September):119–137.

Fendrich, James M. 1967. "Perceived reference group support: racial attitudes and overt behavior." American Sociological Review 32 (December):960–970.

Gerth, Hans, and C. Wright Mills. 1953. Character and Social Structure. New York: Harcourt, Brace and World.

Gross, Neal, Ward S. Mason, and Alexander W. McEachern. 1958. Explorations in Role Analysis. New York: Wiley.

Haller, Archibald O. 1966. "Occupational choices of rural youth." Journal of Cooperative Extension 4 (Summer):93–102.

Haller, Archibald O., and Charles E. Butterworth. 1960. "Peer influences on levels of occupational and educational aspiration." Social Forces 38 (May):289–295.

Haller, Archibald O., and Irwin W. Miller. 1963. The Occupational Aspiration Scale: Theory, Structure and Correlates. East Lansing: Michigan Agricultural Experiment Station Bulletin 288.

Haller, Archibald O., and William H. Sewell. 1967. "Occupational choices of Wisconsin farm boys." Rural Sociology 32 (March): 37–55.

Havighurst, Robert J., and Bernice L. Neugarten. 1957. Society and Education. Boston: Allyn and Bacon.

Heise, David R. 1969. "Problems in path analysis and causal inference," Edgar F. Borgatta, (ed.), Sociological Methodology.

Henmon, V. A. C., and M. J. Nelson. 1942. The Henmon-Nelson Test of Mental Ability. Boston: Houghton Mifflin Company.

Herriott, Robert E. 1963. "Some social determinants of educational aspiration." Harvard Educational Review 33 (Spring):157–177.

Kelley, Harold H. 1952. "Two functions of reference groups." Pp. 410–414 in Guy E. Swanson, et al. (eds.), Readings in Social Psychology. New York: Henry Holt and Company.

Kuvlesky, William P., and George W. Ohlendorf. 1967. A Bibliography of Literature on Status Projections of Youth: I. Occupational Aspirations and Expectations. College Station: Texas A&M University, Department of Agricultural Economics and Sociology.

Lipset, Seymour M., and Reinhard Bendix. 1959. Social Mobility in Industrial Society. Berkeley: University of California Press.

Merton, Robert K. 1957. Social Theory and Social Structure. New York: Free Press.

Miller, I. W., and Archibald O. Haller. 1964. "The measurement of level of occupational aspiration." Personnel and Guidance Journal 42 (January):448–455.

Ohlendorf, George W., Sherry Wages, and William P. Kuvlesky. 1967. A Bibliography of Literature on Status Projections of Youth: II. Educational Aspirations and Expectations. College Station: Texas A and M University, Department of Agricultural Economics and Sociology.

Parsons, Talcott. 1959. "The school class as a social system." Harvard Educational Review 29 (Summer):297–318.

Portes, Alejandro, Archibald O. Haller, and William H. Sewell. 1968. "Professional-executive vs. farming as unique occupational choices." Rural Sociology 33 (June):153–159.

Sewell, William H. 1964. "Community of residence and college plans." American Sociological Review 29 (February):24–38.

Sewell, William H., and J. Michael Armer. 1966. "Neighborhood context and college plans." American Sociological Review 31 (April): 159–168.

Sewell, William H., Archibald O. Haller, and Murray A. Straus. 1957. "Social status and educational and occupational aspiration." American Sociological Review 22 (February):67–73.

Sewell, William H., and Alan M. Orenstein. 1965. "Community of residence and occupational choice." American Journal of Sociology 70 (March):551–563.

Sewell, William H., and Vimal P. Shah. 1967. "Socioeconomic status, intelligence, and the attainment of higher education." Sociology of Education 40 (Winter):1–23.

————. 1968. "Social class, parental encouragement, and educational aspirations." American Journal of Sociology 73 (March):559–572.

Sherif, Muzafer. 1935. "A study of some social factors in perception." Archives of Psychology Number 187.

Super, Donald E. 1957. The Psychology of Careers. New York: Harper.

Turner, Ralph H. 1960. "Sponsored and contest mobility and the school system." American Sociological Review 25 (December):855–867.

Woelfel, Joseph. 1967. "A paradigm for research on significant others." Paper presented at the Joint Session of the Society for the Study of Social Problems and the American Sociological Association, San Francisco (unpublished).

Wright, Sewall. 1934. "The method of path coefficients." Annals of Mathematical Statistics 5 (September):161–215.

————. 1960. "Path coefficients and regression coefficients: alternative or complementary concept?" Biometrics 16 (June):189–202.

JAY MACLEOD

Ain't No Makin' It: Leveled Aspirations in a Low-income Neighborhood

"Any child can grow up to be president." So maintains the dominant ideology in the United States. This perspective characterizes American society as an open one in which barriers to success are mainly personal rather than social. In this meritocratic view, education ensures equality of opportunity for all individuals, and economic inequalities result from differences in natural qualities and in one's motivation and will to work. Success is based on achievement rather than ascription. Individuals do not inherit their social status—they attain it on their own. Because schooling mitigates gender, class, and racial barriers to success, the ladder of social mobility is there for all to climb. A favorite Hollywood theme, the rags-to-riches story resonates in the psyche of the American people. We never tire of hearing about Andrew Carnegie, for his experience validates much that we hold dear about America, the land of opportunity. Horatio Alger's accounts of the spectacular mobility achieved by men of humble origins through their own unremitting efforts occupy a treasured place in our national folklore. The American Dream is held out as a genuine prospect for anyone with the drive to achieve it.

"I ain't goin' to college. Who wants to go to college? I'd just end up gettin' a shitty job anyway." So says Freddie Piniella,[1] an intelligent eleven-year-old boy from Clarendon Heights, a low-income housing development in a northeastern city. This statement, pro-

Originally published in 1987. Please see complete source information beginning on page 891.

nounced with certitude and feeling, completely contradicts our achievement ideology. Freddie is pessimistic about his prospects for social mobility and disputes schooling's capacity to "deliver the goods." Such a view offends our sensibilities and seems a rationalization. But Freddie has a point. What of Carnegie's grammar school classmates, the great bulk of whom no doubt were left behind to occupy positions in the class structure not much different from those held by their parents? What about the static, nearly permanent element in the working class, whose members consider the chances for mobility remote and thus despair of all hope? These people are shunned, hidden, forgotten—and for good reason—because just as the self-made man is a testament to certain American ideals, so the very existence of an "underclass" in American society is a living contradiction to those ideals.

Utter hopelessness is the most striking aspect of Freddie's outlook. Erik H. Erikson writes that hope is the basic ingredient of all vitality;[2] stripped of hope, there is little left to lose. How is it that in contemporary America a boy of eleven can feel bereft of a future worth embracing? This is not what the United States is supposed to be. The United States is the nation of hopes and dreams and opportunity. As Ronald Reagan remarked in his 1985 State of the Union Address, citing the accomplishments of a young Vietnamese immigrant, "Anything is possible in America if we have the faith, the will, and the heart."[3] But to Freddie Piniella and many other Clarendon Heights young people who grow up in households where their parents and older siblings are unemployed, undereducated, or imprisoned, Reagan's words ring hollow. For them the American Dream, far from being a genuine prospect, is not even a dream. It is a hallucination.

I first met Freddie Piniella in the summer of 1981 when as a student at a nearby university I worked as a counselor in a youth enrichment program in Clarendon Heights. For ten weeks I lived a few blocks from the housing project and worked intensively with nine boys, aged eleven to thirteen. While engaging them in recreational and educational activities, I was surprised by the modesty of their aspirations. The world of middle-class work was entirely alien to them; they spoke about employment in construction, factories, the armed forces, or, predictably, professional athletics. In an ostensibly open society, they were a group of boys whose occupational aspirations did not even cut across class lines. . . .

The male teenage world of Clarendon Heights is populated by two divergent peer groups. The first group, dubbed the Hallway Hangers because of the group's propensity for "hanging" in a particular hallway in the project [i.e., outside doorway #13], consists predominantly of white boys. Their characteristics and attitudes stand in marked contrast to the second group, which is composed almost exclusively of black youths who call themselves the Brothers. Surprisingly, the Brothers speak with relative optimism about their futures, while the Hallway Hangers are despondent about their prospects for social mobility. . . .

Before describing the boys' orientation toward work [in more detail], I would like to make an analytical distinction between aspirations and expectations. Both involve assessments of one's desires, abilities, and the character of the opportunity structure. In articulating one's aspirations, an individual weighs his or her preferences more heavily; expectations are tempered by perceived capabilities and available opportunities. Aspirations are one's preferences relatively unsullied by anticipated constraints; expectations take these constraints squarely into account.[4]

The Hallway Hangers: Keeping a Lid on Hope

Conventional, middle-class orientations toward employment are inadequate to describe the Hallway Hangers' approach to work. The notion of a career, a set of jobs that are connected to one another in a logical progression, has little relevance to these boys. They are hesitant when asked about their aspirations and expectations. This hesitancy is not the result of indecision; rather it stems from the fact that these boys see little choice involved in getting a job. No matter how hard I pressed him, for instance, Jinks refused to articulate his aspirations: "I think you're kiddin' yourself to have any. We're just gonna take whatever we can get." Jinks is a perceptive boy, and his answer seems to be an accurate depiction of the situation. Beggars cannot be choosers, and these boys have nothing other than unskilled labor to offer on a credential-based job market.

It is difficult to gauge the aspirations of most of the Hallway Hangers. Perhaps at a younger age they had dreams for their futures. At ages sixteen, seventeen, and eighteen, however, their own job experiences as well as those of family members have contributed to a deeply entrenched cynicism about their futures. What is perceived as the cold, hard reality of the job market weighs very heavily on the Hallway Hangers; they believe their preferences will have almost no bearing on the work they actually will do. Their expectations are not merely tempered by perceptions of the opportunity structure; even their aspirations are crushed by their estimation of the job market. These generalizations may seem bold and rather extreme, but they do not lack ethnographic support.

The pessimism and uncertainty with which the Hallway Hangers view their futures emerge clearly when the boys are asked to speculate on what their lives will be like in twenty years.

(all in separate interviews)
STONEY: Hard to say. I could be dead tomorrow. Around here, you gotta take life day by day.
BOO-BOO: I dunno. I don't want to think about it. I'll think about it when it comes.
FRANKIE: I don't fucking know. Twenty years. I may be fucking dead. I live a day at a time. I'll probably be in the fucking pen.
SHORTY: Twenty years? I'm gonna be in jail.

These responses are striking not only for the insecurity and despondency they reveal, but also because they do not include any mention of work. It is not that work is unimportant—for people as strapped for money as the Hallway Hangers are, work is crucial. Rather, these boys are indifferent to the issue of future employment. Work is a given; they all hope to hold jobs of one kind or another in order to support themselves and their families. But the Hallway Hangers believe the character of work, at least all work in which they are likely to be involved, is essentially the same: boring, undifferentiated, and unrewarding. Thinking about their future jobs is a useless activity for the Hallway Hangers. What is there to think about?

For Steve and Jinks, although they do see themselves employed in twenty years, work is still of tangential importance.

JM: If you had to guess, what do you think you'll be doing twenty years from now?

(in separate interviews)
STEVE: I don't fucking know. Working probably. Have my own pad, my own house. Bitches, kids. Fucking fridge full of brewskies. Fine wife, likes to get laid.
JINKS: Twenty years from now? Probably kicked back in my own apartment doing the same shit I'm doing now—getting high. I'll have a job, if I'm not in the service, if war don't break out, if I'm not dead. I just take one day at a time.

Although the Hallway Hangers expect to spend a good portion of their waking hours on the job, work is important to them not as an end in itself, but solely as a means to an end—money.

In probing the occupational aspirations and expectations of the Hallway Hangers, I finally was able to elicit from them some specific hopes. Although Shorty never mentions his expectations, the rest of the Hallway Hangers have responded to my prodding with some definite answers. The range of answers as well as how they change over time are as significant as the particular hopes each boy expresses.

Boo-Boo's orientation toward work is typical of the Hallway Hangers. He has held a number of jobs in the past, most of them in the summer. During his freshman year in high school Boo-Boo worked as a security guard at school for $2.50 an hour in order to make restitution for a stolen car he damaged. Boo-Boo also has worked on small-scale construction projects through a summer youth employment program called Just-A-Start, at a pipe manufacturing site, and as a clerk in a gift shop. Boo-Boo wants to be an automobile mechanic. Upon graduating from high school, he studied auto mechanics at a technical school on a scholarship. The only black student in his class, Boo-Boo was expelled early in his first term after racial antagonism erupted into a fight. Boo-Boo was not altogether disappointed, for he already was unhappy with what he considered the program's overly theoretical orientation. (Howard London found this kind of impatience typical of working-class students in the community college he studied.[5]) Boo-Boo wanted hands-on training, but "all's they were doing was telling me about how it's made, stuff like that." Boo-Boo currently is unemployed, but he recently had a chance for a job as a cook's helper. Although he was not hired, the event is significant nevertheless because prior to the job interview, Boo-Boo claimed that his ambition now was to work in a restaurant. Here we have an example of the primacy of the opportunity structure in determining the aspirations of the Hallway Hangers. One job opening in another field was so significant that the opening prompted Boo-Boo to redefine totally his aspirations.

In contrast to the rest of the Hallway Hangers who are already on the job market, Steve wants to stay in school for the two years required to get his diploma. Yet he has a similar attitude toward his future work as do the other youths. He quit his summer job with the Just-A-Start program and has no concrete occupational aspirations. As for expectations, he believes he might enlist in the Air Force af-

ter graduation but adds, "I dunno. I might just go up and see my uncle, do some fuckin' construction or something."

Many of these boys expect to enter military service. Jinks and Frankie mention it as an option; Stoney has tried to enlist, but without success. Although Jinks refuses to think in terms of aspirations, he will say what he expects to do after he finishes school.

JM: What are you gonna do when you get out?
JINKS: Go into the service, like everybody else. The navy.
JM: What about after that?
JINKS: After that, just get a job, live around here.
JM: Do you have any idea what job you wanna get?
JINKS: No. No particular job. Whatever I can get.

Jinks subsequently quit school. He had been working twenty hours a week making clothes-racks in a factory with his brother. He left school with the understanding that he would be employed full-time, and he was mildly content with his situation: "I got a job. It ain't a good job, but other things will come along." Two weeks later, he was laid off. For the past three months he has been unemployed, hanging full-time in doorway #13.

Shorty has worked construction in the past and has held odd jobs such as shoveling snow. Shorty, an alcoholic, has trouble holding down a steady job, as he freely admits. He was enrolled in school until recently. Ordered by the court to a detoxification center, Shorty apparently managed to convince the judge that he had attended enough Alcoholics Anonymous meetings in the meantime to satisfy the court. He has not returned to school since, nor has he landed a job. Given that Shorty is often on the run from the police, he is too preoccupied with pressing everyday problems to give serious thought to his long-term future. It is not surprising that my ill-timed query about his occupational aspirations met with only an impatient glare. . . .

The definitions of aspirations and expectations given [earlier] suggest that an assessment of the opportunity structure and of one's capabilities impinge on one's preferences for the future. However, the portrait of the Hallway Hangers painted in these pages makes clear that "impinge" is not a strong enough word. But are the leveled aspirations and pessimistic expectations of the Hallway Hangers a result of strong negative assessments of their capabilities or of the opportunity structure?

This is not an easy question to answer. Doubtless, both factors come into play, but in the case of the Hallway Hangers, evaluation of the opportunity structure has the dominant role. Although in a discussion of why they do not succeed in school, the Hallway Hangers point to personal inadequacy ("We're all just fucking burnouts"; "We never did good anyways"), they look to outside forces as well. In general, they are confident of their own abilities.

(In a group interview)

JM: If you've got five kids up the high school with all A's, now are you gonna be able to say that any of them are smarter than any of you?

SLICK: *(immediately)* No.

JM: So how'd that happen?

SLICK: Because they're smarter in some areas just like we're smarter in some areas. You put them out here, right? And you put us up where they're living—they won't be able to survive out here.

SHORTY: But we'd be able to survive up there.

FRANKIE: See, what it is—they're smarter more academically because they're taught by teachers that teach academics.

JM: Not even streetwise, just academically, do you think you could be up where they are?

FRANKIE: Yeah.

CHRIS: Yeah.

SHORTY: Yeah.

JM: When it comes down to it, you're just as smart?

FRANKIE: Yeah.

SLICK: *(matter-of-factly)* We could be smarter.

FRANKIE: Definitely.

CHRIS: On the street, like.

FRANKIE: We're smart, we're smart, but we're just smart [inaudible]. It's fucking, y'know, we're just out to make money, man. I know if I ever went to fucking high school and college in a business course . . .

SLICK: And concentrated on studying . . .

FRANKIE: I know I could make it. I am a businessman.

JM: So all of you are sure that if you put out in school . . .

FRANKIE: Yeah! If I went into business, I would, yeah. If I had the fucking money to start out with like some of these fucking rich kids, I'd be a millionaire. Fucking right I would be.

Although these comments were influenced by the dynamics of the group interview, they jibe with the general sense of self-confidence the Hallway Hangers radiate and indicate that they do not have low perceptions of their own abilities.

If their assessments of their own abilities do not account for the low aspirations of the Hallway Hangers, we are left, by way of explanation, with their perceptions of the job opportunity structure. The dominant view in the United States is that American society is an open one that values and differentially rewards individuals on the basis of their merits. The Hallway Hangers question this view, for it runs against the grain of their neighbors' experiences, their families' experiences, and their own encounters with the labor market.

The Clarendon Heights community, as a public housing development, is by definition made up of individuals who do not hold even modestly remunerative jobs. A large majority are on additional forms of public assistance; many are unemployed. Like most old housing projects, Clarendon Heights tends to be a cloistered, insular neighborhood, isolated from the surrounding community. Although younger residents certainly have external points of reference, their horizons are nevertheless very narrow. Their immediate world is composed almost entirely of people who have not "made it." To look around at a great variety of people—some lazy, some alcoholics, some energetic, some dedicated, some clever, some resourceful—and to realize all of them have been unsuccessful on the job market is powerful testimony against what is billed as an open society.

The second and much more intimate contact these boys have with the job market is through their families, whose occupational histories only can be viewed as sad and disillusioning by the Hallway Hangers. These are not people who are slothful or slow-witted; rather, they are generally industrious, intelligent, and very willing to work. With members of their families holding low-paying, unstable jobs or unable to find work at all, the Hallway Hangers are unlikely to view the job opportunity structure as an open one.

The third level of experience on which the Hallway Hangers draw is their own. These boys are not newcomers to the job market. As we have seen, all have held a variety of jobs. All except Steve are now on the job market year round, but only Stoney has a steady job. With the exceptions of Chris, who presently is satisfied with his success peddling drugs, and Steve, who is still in school, the Hallway Hangers are actively in search of decent work. Although they always seem to be following up on some promising lead, they are all unemployed. Furthermore, some who were counting on prospective employment have had their hopes dashed when it fell through. The work they have been able to secure typically has been in menial, dead-end jobs paying minimum wage.

Thus, their personal experience on the job market and the experiences of their family members and their neighbors have taught the Hallway Hangers that the job market does not necessarily reward talent or effort. Neither they nor their parents, older siblings, and friends have shared in the "spoils" of economic success. In short, the Hallway Hangers are under no illusions about the openness of the job opportunity structure. They are conscious, albeit vaguely, of a number of class-based obstacles to economic and social advancement. Slick, the most perceptive and articulate of the Hallway Hangers, points out particular barriers they must face.

SLICK: Out here, there's not the opportunity to make money. That's how you get into stealin' and all that shit.

(*in a separate interview*)
SLICK: That's why I went into the army—cuz there's no jobs out here right now for people that, y'know, live out here. You have to know somebody, right?

In discussing the problems of getting a job, both Slick and Shorty are vocal.

SLICK: All right, to get a job, first of all, this is a handicap, out here. If you say you're from the projects or anywhere in this area, that can hurt you. Right off the bat: reputation.
SHORTY: Is this dude gonna rip me off, is he . . .
SLICK: Is he gonna stab me?
SHORTY: Will he rip me off? Is he gonna set up the place to do a score or somethin'? I tried to get a couple of my buddies jobs at a place where I was working construction, but the guy says, "I don't want 'em if they're from there. I know you; you ain't a thief or nothing."

Frankie also points out the reservations prospective employers have about hiring people who live in Clarendon Heights. "A rich kid would have a better chance of getting a job than me, yeah. Me, from where I live, y'know, a high crime area, I was prob'ly crime-breaking myself, which they think your nice honest rich kid from a very respected family would never do."

Frankie also feels that he is discriminated against because of the reputation that attaches to him because of his brothers' illegal exploits. "Especially me, like I've had a few opportunities for a job, y'know. I didn't get it cuz of my name, because of my brothers, y'know. So I was deprived right there, bang.

Y'know they said, 'No, no, no, we ain't havin' no Dougherty work for us.'" In a separate discussion, Frankie again makes this point. Arguing that he would have almost no chance to be hired as a fireman, despite ostensibly meritocratic hiring procedures, even if he scored very highly on the test, Frankie concludes, "Just cuz fuckin' where I'm from and what my name is."

The Hallway Hangers' belief that the opportunity structure is not open also emerges when we consider their responses to the question of whether they have the same chance as a middle- or upper-class boy to get a good job. The Hallway Hangers generally respond in the negative. When pushed to explain why, Jinks and Steve made these responses, which are typical.

(in separate interviews)
JINKS: Their parents got pull and shit.
STEVE: Their fucking parents know people.

Considering the boys' employment experiences and those of their families, it is not surprising that the Hallway Hangers' view of the job market does not conform to the dominant belief in the openness of the opportunity structure. They see a job market where rewards are based not on meritocratic criteria, but on "who you know." If "connections" are the keys to success, the Hallway Hangers know that they are in trouble.

Aside from their assessment of the job opportunity structure, the Hallway Hangers are aware of other forces weighing on their futures. A general feeling of despondency pervades the group. As Slick puts it, "The younger kids have nothing to hope for." The Hallway Hangers often draw attention to specific incidents that support their general and vague feelings of hopelessness and of the futility of nurturing aspirations or high expectations. Tales of police brutality, of uncaring probation officers and callous judges, and of the "pull and hook-ups of the rich kids" all have a common theme, which Chris summarizes, "We don't get a fair shake and shit." Although they sometimes internalize the blame

for their plight (Boo-Boo: "I just screwed up"; Chris: "I guess I just don't have what it takes"; Frankie: "We've just fucked up"), the Hallway Hangers also see, albeit in a vague and imprecise manner, a number of hurdles in their path to success with which others from higher social strata do not have to contend.

Insofar as contemporary conditions under capitalism can be conceptualized as a race by the many for relatively few positions of wealth and prestige, the low aspirations of the Hallway Hangers, more than anything else, seem to be a decision, conscious or unconscious, to withdraw from the running. The competition, they reason, is not a fair one when some people have an unobstructed lane. As Frankie maintains, the Hallway Hangers face numerous barriers: "It's a steeplechase, man. It's a motherfucking steeplechase." The Hallway Hangers respond in a way that suggests only a "sucker" would compete seriously under such conditions.

Chris's perspective seems a poignant, accurate description of the situation in which the Hallway Hangers find themselves.

CHRIS: I gotta get a job, any fucking job. Just a job. Make some decent money. If I could make a hundred bucks a week, I'd work. I just wanna get my mother out of the projects, that's all. But I'm fucking up in school. It ain't easy, Jay. I hang out there [in doorway #13] 'til about one o'clock every night. I never want to go to school. I'd much rather hang out and get high again. It's not that I'm dumb. You gimme thirty bucks today, and I'll give you one hundred tomorrow. I dunno. It's like I'm in a hole I can't get out of. I guess I could get out, but it's hard as hell. It's fucked up.

The Brothers: Ready at the Starting Line

Just as the pessimism and uncertainty with which the Hallway Hangers view their futures emerges when we consider what they perceive their lives will be like in twenty years, so do the Brothers' long-term visions serve as a valuable backdrop to our discussion of their aspirations. The ethos of the Brothers' peer group is a positive one; they are not resigned to a bleak future but are hoping for a bright one. Nowhere does this optimism surface more clearly than in the Brothers' responses to the question of what they will be doing in twenty years. Note the centrality of work in their views of the future.

(*all in separate interviews*)

SUPER: I'll have a house, a nice car, no one bothering me. Won't have to take no hard time from no one. Yeah, I'll have a good job, too.

JUAN: I'll have a regular house, y'know, with a yard and everything. I'll have a steady job, a good job. I'll be living the good life, the easy life.

MIKE: I might have a wife, some kids. I might be holding down a regular business job like an old guy. I hope I'll be able to do a lot of skiing and stuff like that when I'm old.

CRAIG: I'll probably be having a good job on my hands, I think. Working in an office as an architect, y'know, with my own drawing board, doing my own stuff, or at least close to there.

James takes a comic look into his future without being prompted to do so. "The ones who work hard in school, eventually it's gonna pay off for them and everything, and they're gonna have a good job and a family and all that. Not me though! I'm gonna have *myself*. I'm gonna have some money. And a different girl every day. And a different car. And be like this (*poses with one arm around an imaginary girl and the other on a steering wheel*)."

The Brothers do not hesitate to name their occupational goals. Although some of the Brothers are unsure of their occupational aspirations, none seems to feel that nurturing an aspiration is a futile exercise. The Brothers have not resigned themselves to taking whatever they can get. Rather, they articulate specific occupational aspirations (although these often are subject to change and revision).

Like all the Brothers, Super has not had extensive experience on the job market; he only has worked at summer jobs. For the past three summers, he has worked for the city doing maintenance work in parks and school buildings through a CETA-sponsored summer youth employment program. During the last year, Super's occupational aspirations have fluctuated widely. His initial desire to become a doctor was met with laughter from his friends. Deterred by their mocking and by a realization of the schooling required to be a doctor, Super immediately decided that he would rather go into business: "Maybe I can own my own shop and shit." This aspiration, however, also was ridiculed. "Yeah, right," commented Mokey, "Super'll be pimping the girls, that kinda business." In private, however, Super still clings to the hope of becoming a doctor, although he cites work in the computer field as a more realistic hope. "Really, I don't know what I should do now. I'm kinda confused. First I said I wanna go into computers, right? Take up that or a doctor." The vagueness of Super's aspirations is important; once again, we get a glimpse of how little is known about the world of middle-class work, even for somebody who clearly aspires to it. Of one thing Super is certain: "I just know I wanna get a good job."

Although Super does not distinguish between what constitutes a good job and what does not, he does allude to criteria by which the quality of a job can be judged. First, a good job must not demand that one "work on your feet," a distinction, apparently, between white and blue-collar work. Second, a good job implies at least some authority in one's workplace, a point Super makes clearly, if in a disjointed manner. "Bosses—if you don't come on time, they yell at you and stuff like that. They want you to do work and not sit down and relax and stuff like that, y'know. I want to try and be a boss, y'know, tell people what to do. See, I don't always want people telling me what to do, y'know—the low rank. I wanna try to be with people in the high rank." Although Super does not know what occupation he would like to enter, he is certain that he wants a job that is relatively high up in a vaguely defined occupational hierarchy. . . .

The Brothers display none of the cockiness about their own capabilities that the Hallway Hangers exhibit. Instead, they attribute lack of success on the job market exclusively to personal inadequacy. This is particularly true when the Brothers speculate about the future jobs the Hallway Hangers and their own friends will have. According to the Brothers, the Hallway Hangers (in Super's words) "ain't gonna get nowhere," not because of the harshness of the job market but because they are personally lacking. The rest of the Brothers share this view.

JM: Some of those guys who hang with Frankie, they're actually pretty smart. They just don't channel that intelligence into school, it seems to me.
CRAIG: I call that stupid, man. That's what they are.
JM: I dunno.
CRAIG: Lazy.

(*in a separate interview*)
SUPER: They think they're so tough they don't have to do work. That don't make sense, really. You ain't gonna get nowhere; all's you gonna do is be back in the projects like your mother. Depend on your mother to give you money every week. You ain't gonna get a good job. As you get older, you'll think about that, y'know. It'll come to your mind. "Wow, I can't believe, I should've just went to school and got my education."

(*in a separate interview*)
MOKEY: They all got attitude problems. They just don't got their shit together. Like Steve. They have to improve themselves.

In the eyes of the Brothers, the Hallway Hangers have attitude problems, are incapable of considering their long-term future, and are lazy or stupid.

Because this evidence is tainted (no love is lost between the two peer groups), it is significant that the Brothers apply the same criteria in judging each other's chances to gain meaningful employment. James thinks Mokey is headed for a dead-end job because he is immature and undisciplined. He also blames Juan for currently being out of work. "Juan's outta school, and Juan does *not* have a job (*said with contempt*). Now that's some kind of a senior. When I'm a senior, I'm gonna have a job already. I can see if you're gonna go to college right when you get out of school; but Juan's not doin' nothin'. He's just stayin' home." Juan, in turn, thinks that Mokey and Super will have difficulty finding valuable work because of their attitudes. He predicts that Derek and Craig will be successful for the same reason.

These viewpoints are consistent with the dominant ideology in America; barriers to success are seen as personal rather than social. By attributing failure to personal inadequacy, the Brothers exonerate the opportunity structure. Indeed, it is amazing how often they affirm the openness of American society.

(*all in separate interviews*)
DEREK: If you put your mind to it, if you want to make a future for yourself, there's no reason why you can't. It's a question of attitude.
SUPER: It's easy to do anything, as long as you set your mind to it, if you wanna do it. If you really want to do it, if you really want to be something. If you don't want to do it . . . you ain't gonna make it. I gotta get that through my mind: I wanna do it. I wanna be somethin'. I don't wanna be livin' in the projects the rest of my life.
MOKEY: It's not like if they're rich they get picked [for a job]; it's just mattered by the knowledge of their mind.
CRAIG: If you work hard, it'll pay off in the end.
MIKE: If you work hard, really put your mind to it, you can do it. You can make it.

This view of the opportunity structure as an essentially open one that rewards intelligence, effort, and ingenuity is shared by all the Brothers. Asked whether their chances of securing a remunerative job are as good as those of an upper-class boy from a wealthy district of the city, they all responded affirmatively. Not a single member of the Hallway Hangers, in contrast, affirms the openness of American society. . . .

Reproduction Theory Reconsidered

This basic finding—that two substantially different paths are followed within the general framework of social reproduction—is a major challenge to economically determinist theories. Two groups of boys from the same social stratum who live in the same housing project and attend the same school nevertheless experience the process of social reproduction in fundamentally different ways. This simple fact alone calls into question many of the theoretical formulations of Bowles and Gintis.[6] If, as they argue, social class is the overriding determinant in social reproduction, what accounts for the variance in the process between the Brothers and Hallway Hangers? Bowles and Gintis, in considering a single school, maintain that social reproduction takes place primarily through educational tracking. Differential socialization through educational tracking prepares working-class students for working-class jobs and middle-class students for middle-class jobs. But the Hallway Hangers and the Brothers, who are from the same social class background and exposed to the curricular structure of the school in the same manner, undergo the process of social reproduction in substantially different manners. The theory of Bowles and Gintis cannot explain this difference.

Bourdieu's notion of habitus, however, can be used to differentiate the Hallway Hangers and the Brothers.[7] The habitus, as defined by Giroux, is "the subjective dispositions which reflect a class-based social grammar of taste,

knowledge, and behavior inscribed in . . . each developing person."[8] According to Bourdieu, the habitus is primarily a function of social class. Bourdieu does not give an adequate sense of the internal structure of the habitus, but there is some precedent in his work for incorporating other factors into constructions of the habitus; for example, he differentiates people not only by gender and class, but also by whether they come from Paris or not. Although Bourdieu sometimes gives the impression of a homogeneity of habitus within the boundaries of social class, I understand habitus to be constituted at the level of the family and thus can include, as constitutive of the habitus, factors such as ethnicity, educational histories, peer associations, and demographic characteristics (e.g., geographical mobility, duration of tenancy in public housing, sibling order, and family size) as these shape individual action. Although Bourdieu never really develops the notion along these lines, he does allude to the complexity and interplay of mediations within the habitus. "The habitus acquired in the family underlies the structuring of school experiences, and the habitus transformed by schooling, itself diversified, in turn underlies the structuring of all subsequent experiences (e.g. the reception and assimilation of the messages of the culture industry or work experiences), and so on, from restructuring to restructuring."[9] When understood along the lines I have indicated, the concept of habitus becomes flexible enough to accommodate the interactions among ethnicity, family, schooling, work experiences, and peer associations that have been documented [here].

Although we may accept the notion of habitus as a useful explanatory tool, we must reject the inevitability of its *function* in Bourdieu's theoretical scheme. According to Bourdieu, the habitus functions discreetly to integrate individuals into a social world geared to the interests of the ruling classes; habitus engenders attitudes and conduct that are compatible with the reproduction of class inequality. The outstanding example of this process is the development by working-class individuals of depressed aspirations that mirror their actual chances for social advancement.

The circular relationship Bourdieu posits between objective opportunities and subjective hopes is incompatible with the findings [presented here]. The Brothers, whose objective life chances probably were lower originally than those available to the Hallway Hangers because of racial barriers to success, nevertheless nurture higher aspirations than do the Hallway Hangers. By emphasizing structural determinants at the expense of mediating factors that influence subjective renderings of objective probabilities, Bourdieu presumes too mechanistic and simplistic a relationship between aspiration and opportunity. This component of his theory fails to fathom how a number of factors lie between and mediate the influence of social class on individuals; Bourdieu cannot explain, for instance, how ethnicity intervenes in the process of aspiration formation and social reproduction.

Thus, the theoretical formulations of Bowles and Gintis and the deterministic elements of Bourdieu's theory, although elegant and intuitively plausible, are incapable of accounting for the processes of social reproduction as they have been observed and documented in Clarendon Heights. These theories give an excellent account of the hidden structural and ideological determinants that constrain members of the working class and limit the options of Clarendon Heights teenagers. What the Hallway Hangers and the Brothers demonstrate quite clearly, however, is that the way in which individuals and groups respond to structures of domination is open-ended. Although there is no way to avoid class-based constraints, the outcomes are not predefined. Bowles and Gintis and Bourdieu pay too little attention to the active, creative role of individual and group praxis. As Giroux maintains, what is missing from such theories "is not only the issue of resistance, but also any attempt to delineate the complex ways in which working-class subjectivities are constituted."[10]

From Ethnography to Theory

Once we descend into the world of actual human lives, we must take our theoretical bearings to make some sense of the social landscape, but in doing so we invariably find that the theories are incapable of accounting for much of what we see. The lives of the Hallway Hangers and the Brothers cannot be reduced to structural influences or causes; although structural forces weigh upon the individuals involved, it is necessary, in the words of Willis, "to give the social agents involved some meaningful scope for viewing, inhabiting, and constructing their own world in a way which is recognizably human and not theoretically reductive."[11] We must appreciate both the importance and the relative autonomy of the cultural level at which individuals, alone or in concert with others, wrest meaning out of the flux of their lives.

The possibilities open to these boys as lower-class teenagers are limited structurally from the outset. That they internalize the objective probabilities for social advancement to some degree is beyond question. The process by which this takes place, however, is influenced by a whole series of intermediate factors. Because gender is constant in the study discussed in these pages, race is the principal variable affecting the way in which these youths view their situation. Ethnicity introduces new structurally determined constraints on social mobility, but it also serves as a mediation through which the limitations of class are refracted and thus apprehended and understood differently by different racial groups. The Brothers comprehend and react to their situation in a manner entirely different from the response the Hallway Hangers make to a similar situation; ethnicity introduces a new dynamic that makes the Brothers more receptive to the achievement ideology. Their acceptance of this ideology affects their aspirations but also influences, in tandem with parental encouragement, their approach to school and the character of their peer group, factors that in turn bear upon their aspirations.

If we modify the habitus by changing the ethnicity variable and altering a few details of family occupational and educational histories and duration of tenancy in public housing, we would have the Hallway Hangers. As white lower-class youths, the Hallway Hangers view and interpret their situation in a different light, one that induces them to reject the achievement ideology and to develop aspirations and expectations quite apart from those the ideology attempts to generate. The resultant perspective, which is eventually reinforced by the Hallway Hangers' contact with the job market, informs the boys' approach to school and helps us understand the distinctive attributes of this peer group. Thus, although social class is of primary importance, there are intermediate factors at work that, as constitutive of the habitus, shape the subjective responses of the two groups of boys and produce quite different expectations and actions.

Having grown up in an environment where success is not common, the Hallway Hangers see that the connection between effort and reward is not as clearcut as the achievement ideology would have them believe. Because it runs counter to the evidence in their lives and because it represents a forceful assault on their self-esteem, the Hallway Hangers repudiate the achievement ideology. Given that their parents are inclined to see the ideology in the same light, they do not counter their sons' rejection of the American Dream.

A number of important ramifications follow from the Hallway Hangers' denial of the dominant ideology: the establishment of a peer group that provides alternative means of generating self-esteem, the rejection of school and antagonism toward teachers, and, of course, the leveling of aspirations. In schematizing the role of the peer group, it is difficult not to appear tautological, for the group does wield a reciprocal influence on the boys: It attracts those who are apt to reject school and the achievement ideology and those with low aspirations and then deepens these individuals' initial proclivities and further shapes them to fit the group. But at the same time, the peer

subculture itself, handed down from older to younger boys, is the product of the particular factors that structure the lives of white teenagers in Clarendon Heights.

In addition to the peer group, the curricular structure of the school solidifies the low aspirations of the Hallway Hangers by channeling them into programs that prepare students for manual labor jobs. Low aspirations, in turn, make the Hallway Hangers more likely to dismiss school as irrelevant. Once on the job market, the Hallway Hangers' inability to secure even mediocre jobs further dampens their occupational hopes. Thus although each individual ultimately retains autonomy in the subjective interpretation of his situation, the leveled aspirations of the Hallway Hangers are to a large degree a response to the limitations of social class as they are manifest in the Hallway Hangers' social world.

The Brothers' social class origins are only marginally different from those of the Hallway Hangers. Being black, the Brothers also must cope with racially rooted barriers to success that, affirmative action measures notwithstanding, structurally inhibit the probabilities for social advancement, although to a lesser degree than do shared class limitations. What appears to be a comparable objective situation to that of the Hallway Hangers, however, is apprehended in a very different manner by the Brothers.

As black teenagers, the Brothers interpret their families' occupational and educational records in a much different light than do the Hallway Hangers. Judging by the Brothers' constant affirmation of equality of opportunity, the boys believe that racial injustice has been curbed in the United States in the last twenty years. Whereas in their parents' time the link between effort and reward was very tenuous for blacks, the Brothers, in keeping with the achievement ideology, see the connection today as very strong: "If you work hard, it'll pay off in the end" (Craig). Hence, the achievement ideology is more compatible with the Brothers' attitudes than with those of the Hallway Hangers, for whom it cannot succeed against overwhelming contrary evidence. The ideology is not as emotionally painful for the Brothers to accept because past racial discrimination can help account for their families' poverty, whereas the Hallway Hangers, if the ideology stands, are afforded no explanation outside of laziness and stupidity for their parents' failures. The optimism that acceptance of the achievement ideology brings for the Brothers is encouraged and reinforced by their parents. Thus, we see how in the modified habitus ethnicity affects the Brothers' interpretation of their social circumstances and leads to acceptance of the achievement ideology, with all the concomitant results.

Postscript: The Hallway Hangers and Brothers Eight Years Later

"Hey, Jay, what the fuck brings you back to the Ponderosa?" Greeted by Steve in July 1991, I surveyed a Clarendon Heights that had changed considerably since 1983. Steve jerked his thumb over his shoulder at a group of African American teenagers lounging in the area outside doorway #13, previously the preserve of the Hallway Hangers. "How do you like all the new niggers we got here? Motherfuckers've taken over, man." I asked Steve about Frankie, Slick, and the other Hallway Hangers. "I'm the only one holding down the fort," he answered. "Me and Jinks—he lives in the back. The rest of 'em pretty much cut loose, man."

In their mid-twenties, the seven Hallway Hangers should be in the labor force full time. Most of them aren't: They are unemployed or imprisoned, or are working sporadically either for firms "under the table" or for themselves in the drug economy. . . . The Hallway Hangers have been trapped in what economists call the secondary labor market— the subordinate segment of the job structure where the market is severely skewed against workers. Jobs in the primary labor markets provide wages that can support families and an internal career structure, but the rules of

the game are different in the secondary labor market. Wages are lower, raises are infrequent, training is minimal, advancement is rare, and turnover is high.

When the legitimate job market fails them, the Hallway Hangers can turn to the underground economy. Since 1984 almost all of the Hallway Hangers have at least supplemented their income from earnings in the burgeoning, multibillion-dollar drug market. The street economy promises better money than does conventional employment. It also provides a work site that does not demean the Hallway Hangers or drain their dignity. As workers in the underground economy, they won't have to take orders from a boss's arrogant son, nor will they have to gossip with office colleagues and strain to camouflage their street identities. . . .

Although they have certainly fared better than the Hallway Hangers, the Brothers have themselves stumbled economically in the transition to adulthood. Even more so than the Hallway Hangers, the Brothers have been employed in the service sector of the economy. They have bagged groceries, stocked shelves, flipped hamburgers, delivered pizzas, repaired cars, serviced airplanes, cleaned buildings, moved furniture, driven tow trucks, pumped gas, delivered auto parts, and washed dishes. They have also worked as mail carriers, cooks, clerks, computer operators, bank tellers, busboys, models, office photocopiers, laborers, soldiers, baggage handlers, security guards, and customer service agents. Only Mike, as a postal service employee, holds a unionized position. Although their experiences on the labor market have been varied, many of the Brothers have failed to move out of the secondary labor market. Instead, like the Hallway Hangers, they have been stuck in low-wage, high-turnover jobs. . . .

These results are depressing. The experiences of the Hallway Hangers since 1984 show that opting out of the contest—neither playing the game nor accepting its rules—is not a viable option. Incarceration and other less explicit social penalties are applied by society when the contest is taken on one's own terms. There is no escape: The Hallway Hangers must still generate income, build relationships, and establish households. Trapped inside the game, the Hallway Hangers now question their youthful resistance to schooling and social norms. Granted the opportunity to do it over again, the Hallway Hangers say they would have tried harder to succeed.

But the Brothers *have* always tried, which is why their experiences between 1984 and 1991 are as disheartening as the Hallway Hangers'. If the Hangers show that opting out of the contest is not a viable option, the Brothers show that dutifully playing by the rules hardly guarantees success either. Conservative and liberal commentators alike often contend that if the poor would only apply themselves, behave responsibly, and adopt bourgeois values, then they will propel themselves into the middle class. The Brothers followed the recipe quite closely, but the outcomes are disappointing. They illustrate how rigid and durable the class structure is. Aspiration, application, and intelligence often fail to cut through the firm figurations of structural inequality. Though not impenetrable, structural constraints on opportunity, embedded in both schools and job markets, turn out to be much more debilitating than the Brothers anticipated. Their dreams of comfortable suburban bliss currently are dreams deferred, and are likely to end up as dreams denied.

Notes

1. All names of neighborhoods and individuals have been changed to protect the anonymity of the study's subjects.

2. Erik H. Erikson, *Gandhi's Truth* (New York: Norton, 1969), p. 154.

3. Ronald Reagan, "State of the Union Address to Congress," *New York Times,* 6 February 1985, p. 17.

4. Kenneth I. Spenner and David L. Featherman, "Achievement Ambitions," *Annual Review of Sociology* 4 (1978):376–378.

5. Howard B. London, *The Culture of a Community College* (New York: Praeger, 1978).

6. Samuel Bowles and Herbert Gintis, *Schooling in Capitalist America* (New York: Basic Books, 1976).

7. See Pierre Bourdieu, *Outline of a Theory of Practice* (Cambridge: Cambridge University Press, 1977).

8. Henry A. Giroux, *Theory & Resistance in Education* (London: Heinemann Educational Books, 1983), p. 89.

9. Bourdieu, *Outline of a Theory of Practice*, p. 87.

10. Giroux, *Theory & Resistance*, p. 85.

11. Paul E. Willis, *Learning to Labor* (Aldershot: Gower, 1977), p. 172.

MICHAEL J. PIORE

The Dual Labor Market: Theory and Implications

The central tenet of [my] analysis is that the role of employment and of the disposition of manpower in perpetuating poverty can be best understood in terms of a dual labor market. One sector of that market, which I have termed elsewhere the primary market,[1] offers jobs which possess several of the following traits: high wages, good working conditions, employment stability and job security, equity and due process in the administration of work rules, and chances for advancement. The secondary sector has jobs that are decidedly less attractive, compared with those in the primary sector. They tend to involve low wages, poor working conditions, considerable variability in employment, harsh and often arbitrary discipline, and little opportunity to advance. The poor are confined to the secondary labor market. Eliminating poverty requires that they gain access to primary employment.

The factors that generate the dual market structure and confine the poor to the secondary sector are complex. With some injustice to that complexity, they may be summarized: First, the most important characteristic distinguishing primary from secondary jobs appears to be the behavioral requirements they impose upon the work force, particularly that of employment stability. Insofar as secondary workers are barred from primary jobs by a real qualification, it is generally their inability to show up for work regularly and on time. Secondary employers are far more tolerant of lateness and absenteeism, and many secondary jobs are of such short duration that these do not matter. Work skills, which receive considerable emphasis in most discussions of poverty and employment, do not appear a major barrier to primary employment (although, because regularity and punctuality are important to successful learning in school and on the job, such behavioral traits tend to be highly correlated with skills).

Second, certain workers who possess the behavioral traits required to operate efficiently in primary jobs are trapped in the secondary market because their superficial characteristics resemble those of secondary workers. This identification occurs because employment decisions are generally made on the basis of a few readily (and hence inexpensively) assessed traits like race, demeanor, accent, educational attainment, test scores, and the like. Such traits tend to be statistically correlated with job performance but not necessarily (and probably not usually) causally related to it. Hence, a number of candidates who are rejected because they possess the

Originally published in 1970. Please see complete source information beginning on page 891.

"wrong" traits are actually qualified for the job. Exclusion on this basis may be termed *statistical discrimination*. In addition to statistical discrimination, workers are also excluded from primary employment by *discrimination pure and simple*.

Discrimination of any kind enlarges the labor force that is captive in the secondary sector, and thus lowers the wages that secondary employers must pay to fill their jobs. Such employers thus have an economic stake in perpetuating discrimination. Since it limits the supply of labor in the primary sector and raises the wages of workers who have access to jobs there, primary workers also have a stake in discrimination. Discrimination pure and simple is not generally of economic value to primary employers, since it forces them to pay higher wages without obtaining corresponding economic gains. In statistical discrimination, however, the higher wages are compensated by the reduced cost of screening job candidates, and here primary employers share the interest of secondary employers and primary workers in perpetuating such discrimination.

Third, the distinction between primary and secondary jobs is not, apparently, technologically determinate. A portion—perhaps a substantial proportion—of the work in the economy can be organized for either stable or unstable workers. Work normally performed in the primary sector is sometimes shifted to the secondary sector through subcontracting, temporary help services, recycling of new employees through probationary periods, and the like. Nor is the primary-secondary distinction necessarily associated with a given enterprise. Some enterprises, most of whose jobs constitute primary employment and are filled with stable, committed workers, have subsections or departments with inferior job opportunities accommodated to an unstable work force. Secondary employers generally have a few primary jobs, and some have a large number of them. Nonetheless, despite a certain degree of elasticity in the distribution of work between the primary and secondary sections,

shifts in the distribution generally involve changes in the techniques of production and management and in the institutional structure and procedures of the enterprises in which the work is performed. The investment necessary to effect these changes acts to strengthen resistance to antipoverty efforts.

Fourth, the behavioral traits associated with the secondary sector are reinforced by the process of working in secondary jobs and living among others whose life-style is accommodated to that type of employment. Hence, even people initially forced into the secondary sector by discrimination tend, over a period of time, to develop the traits predominant among secondary workers. Thus, a man who works in a world where employment is intermittent and erratic tends to lose habits of regularity and punctuality. Similarly, when reward and punishment in the work place are continually based upon personal relationships between worker and supervisor, workers forget how to operate within the impersonal, institutional grievance procedures of the primary sector. When such workers do gain access to primary jobs, they are frustrated by the system's failure to respond on a personal basis and by their own inability to make it respond on an institutional basis.

Finally, among the poor, income sources other than employment, especially public assistance and illicit activity, tend to be more compatible with secondary than with primary employment. The public assistance system discourages full-time work and forces those on welfare either into jobs that are part-time or into jobs that pay cash income which will not be reported to the social worker or can be quickly dropped or delayed when the social worker discovers them or seems in danger of doing so. The relationship between social worker and client builds upon the personal relationship that operates in the secondary sector, not on the institutional mechanisms that tend to operate in the primary sector. Illegitimate activity also tends to follow the intermittent work pattern prevalent in secondary employment, and the attractions of such activity, as well as life patterns and role models it presents to those not themselves involved but associating with people who are, foster behavioral traits antagonistic to primary employment.

The dual market interpretation of poverty has some central implications: the poor do participate in the economy; the manner of their participation, not the question of participation as such, constitutes the manpower problem of the poor; and their current mode of participation is ultimately a response to a series of pressures—economic, social, and technical—playing upon individuals and labor market institutions. This suggests that a distinction can be drawn between policies that are designed to alleviate the pressures which generate the dual market structure and those that attempt to attack the problem directly by moving individuals from secondary to primary employment. The latter policies combat prevailing pressures but leave intact the forces that generate them. The thrust of [my] argument is that in concentrating upon training, counseling, and placement services for the poor, manpower policy has overemphasized direct approaches, and that more weight should be placed upon policies which affect the environment in which employment decisions are made and the pressures which the environment generates. Among such policies are antidiscrimination policy, occupational licensing reform, and the structure of public assistance.

Analysis of the dual labor market suggests a further implication: because the "poor" do participate in the economy, certain groups are interested in that participation and how it occurs. Policies aimed at moving the poor out of the secondary market work against the interests of these groups and therefore are in danger of being subverted by them. This danger is a major reason for concentrating on indirect approaches that are not susceptible to the same kind of subversion; in fact, because such approaches alleviate the pressures generating the dual market structure, they reduce the resistance to policies that move directly

against that structure. The dangers to which existing institutions subject programs designed to move the poor directly out of the secondary market are twofold. The new institutions created by these programs can be rejected by the prevailing economic system and isolated off to one side; a program, for example, would then recruit workers for training in skills that are little utilized in either the secondary or the primary market. Alternatively, the new institutions may be captured by the prevailing economic system and used to facilitate its operation; for example, neighborhood employment offices may recruit secondary workers for secondary jobs, and training may be provided in primary employment to workers who would have gotten it anyway in establishments that would have financed it themselves. The central problem in the design of direct approaches to manpower programs is to organize them in such a way that they can resist this two-fold threat of rejection on the one hand and capture on the other.

These conclusions follow directly from the dual market interpretation of the poverty problem but they are not uniquely dependent upon it. The dual labor market is one of a class of theoretical constructs which views poverty in the United States in terms of a dichotomy in the economic and social structures. Such a dichotomy is implicit in the concept of a "culture of poverty" and in the expression of public policy goals associated with poverty in terms of an income cutoff. Most such views of poverty entertain the idea that the dichotomy is a product of forces endogenous to the economy (or, more broadly, the society as a whole). It follows that attempts to eliminate poverty will tend to run counter to the natural operation of the economy, and that they will be resisted by existing institutions and are in danger of rejection. To say all this is perhaps to say simply that if poverty were easy to eliminate, it wouldn't be around in the first place. But it does at least identify as a certain problem in the program design the task of equipping the institution which works with the poor to withstand the rejection pressures.

What the dual labor market interpretation implies that is not implicit in other dichotomous interpretations is that the poor are separated from the nonpoor not only in the negative sense of exclusion from activities and institutions to which the nonpoor have access, but also in the positive sense that they have economic value where they are; that, in other words, *there are groups actively interested in the perpetuation of poverty.* It is this interest that makes new institutions created to work with the poor in the labor market subject to threats of capture as well as of rejection.

Notes

1. See Michael J. Piore, "On-The-Job Training in the Dual Labor Market," in Arnold Weber, *et al., Public-Private Manpower Policies* (Madison, Wisc.: Industrial Relations Research Association, 1969), pp. 101–132.

A A G E   B .   S Ø R E N S E N   A N D   A R N E   L .   K A L L E B E R G

An Outline of a Theory of the Matching of Persons to Jobs

Much recent research in sociology has focused on labor market processes. These concerns include analysis of the processes that produce variation in individual earnings by characteristics of people and their jobs; the analysis of career patterns and job mobility processes; and the analysis of employment and unemployment patterns of various population groups. Sociologists share many of these concerns with economists, and there is much overlap in research topics among sociologists and economists.

Despite similarities in methodology and research design, the research traditions in sociology and economics have quite different intellectual backgrounds. Most empirical research on labor market processes in economics is guided by the dominant school of labor economics—the neoclassical theory of wage determination and labor supply, with marginal productivity theory accounting for the demand side and human capital theory taking care of the supply side. In contrast, sociological research on labor market phenomena has its origin in research describing socioeconomic attainment and social mobility processes for various population groups. Sociological research on attainment and mobility has not employed an explicitly stated conceptual apparatus that informs the choice of variables and the interpretation of parameters. Although there is a growing body of findings about the magnitude of the influences of various variables on the outcomes of labor market processes, particularly income attainment, there are few efforts by sociologists to identify the mechanisms that create the influences of personal and job characteristics on income and earnings or on the other labor market outcomes.

Originally published in 1981. Please see complete source information beginning on page 891.

There is no need for sociologists to develop a unique theory of labor market processes if the neoclassical economic theory adequately accounts for the findings of empirical research. With respect to a favorite variable of both economists and sociologists—that is, education—human capital theory does provide an interpretation of results. However, the economic theory does not provide a rationale for the sociological concern for occupational attainment. Job characteristics, including those presumably captured by the Socioeconomic Index (SEI) or prestige scores of occupations, play little or no role in the orthodox economic theory. Still, occupational status accounts for a substantial fraction of the explained variance in sociological income attainment models.

The amount of variance added to income attainment models by occupation is not necessarily a strong argument for replacing or supplementing the economic theory. Sociologists have not been able to account for very much variance in income attainment. Research informed by human capital theory (e.g., Mincer, 1974) has in fact been able to do as well or better without including occupation. A measure of occupational status must necessarily show some relation to income, reflecting the between-occupation variance in income that it captures. An observed effect of job characteristics on income or earnings may be attributed to a misspecification of sociological models, both with respect to functional form and omitted variables, and need not be considered a challenge to the economic theory.

There are, however, other reasons for critically evaluating the neoclassical or orthodox economic theory. The economic theory is powerful, and numerous predictions can be derived from it regarding the earnings attainment process and other labor market processes, particularly labor supply. (A list of such predictions is presented by Becker, 1964.) Some of these predictions are borne out by empirical observations; some are not. Thurow (1975, pp. 56–70) presents a list of deviations from the theory, pertaining to such issues as the relationship between wages and

unemployment, changes in the distribution of earnings, and the relationship between the distribution of education and the distribution of income. Numerous others have identified features of the earnings attainment process and of labor markets that deviate from the assumptions and predictions of the neoclassical theory. A review of these challenges to orthodox theory has been presented by Cain (1976). Particularly important are those critiques that argue that labor markets are segmented and that stress the differences between either so-called primary and secondary jobs (cf. Doeringer & Piore, 1971); or monopoly, competitive, and state economic sectors (cf. Averitt, 1968; Bluestone, 1970; O'Connor, 1973); or wage competition and job competition sectors (Thurow, 1975); or internal and external markets (Doeringer & Piore, 1971; Kerr, 1954). These critiques all observe that jobs and job structures differ, contrary to the assumption about the homogeneous nature of labor markets made by the economic theory. They stress qualitative differences among jobs relevant for employment and earnings processes and claim to be able to account for the observations that deviate from the orthodox economic theory, as well as to provide different explanations for labor market processes that also can be explained by the orthodox theory. An example of such an alternative explanation is Thurow's (1975) interpretation of the relationship between education and earnings.

Most of the criticism comes from within economics, though there are examples of research and conceptual elaboration by sociologists pertaining to the issues raised by the segmented labor market theory (Sørensen, 1977; Spilerman, 1977; Stolzenberg, 1975). The issues are clearly relevant for sociological research, and more so since the alternatives to the neoclassical theory provide a rationale for introducing job characteristics sociologists are likely to continue to emphasize.

The classical sociological theorists did not leave labor market analysis to economists. Marx and Weber spent lifetimes analyzing the relation between economy and society, and their concerns in many ways parallel the issues raised in recent controversies. Marx's analysis of capitalist society is an analysis of the implications of the fundamental condition of capitalist production: Labor is treated as a commodity bought and sold freely in a market. This conception of the labor market, we shall argue in the following pages, parallels the conception of the orthodox economic theory.

Marx treated labor in capitalist society as a homogeneous abstract category, and though there are occasional remarks concerning deviations from this model of labor as a commodity and their relevance for class conflict (e.g., Marx, 1961, Vol. 1, chap. 14), no systematic analysis of alternative labor market structures is presented. Weber's long analysis of the sociological categories of economic action (Weber, 1947, Pt. I, chap. 2) provides, in contrast, numerous concepts relevant for the analysis of labor market structures (including nonmarket relationships), particularly in the sections on the social division of labor. The concepts are highly relevant for the issues raised by the challenges to orthodox economic theory, and some of Weber's basic concepts will be used extensively in this chapter.

The following pages provide a conceptual framework for the analysis of labor markets. Labor markets are arenas for the matching of persons to jobs. The conditions that determine the earnings outcome of this matching process are of primary interest here, particularly the identification of what determines the influence of job and personal characteristics on earnings. The purpose of this chapter is not to show the neoclassical theory to be wrong, but rather to identify the conditions for the emergence of the matching process associated with the labor market structure assumed in the orthodox economic theory. It will be argued that the conditions for the emergence of this matching process are not present in some segments of the labor market. The absence of these conditions leads to alternative matching processes, and a model of one important alternative matching process will be presented. The two contrasting matching processes will be shown to have very different implications for the earnings determination process and for other labor market processes.

Basic Concepts

The theory proposed in this chapter will rely on Weber's notion of open and closed social relationships (Weber, 1947, p. 139) to identify different job structures characterized by different matching processes.[1] The degree of closure, in turn, is seen as determined by the bargaining power of employers and employees. We shall, therefore, refer to the employment relationship as the crucial determinant of the notion of the matching process and its earnings outcome.

Employment relationships are social relationships created in the production of goods and services between an employer (or his agent) and an employee. We concentrate on employment relationships typical of capitalist production in which the employer appropriates the output from the production process and has complete possession over the nonhuman means of production. Our analysis will focus on the consequences for the earnings determination process and other labor market processes of variation in control over the job by the employer versus the employee. Two aspects of control over the job may be distinguished. One is control over the activities of the job, resulting in more or less autonomy for the employee; the other is control over access to the job, resulting in a more or less closed employment relationship. These two dimensions may vary independently. Particularly, control over access to the job will be considered crucial, because it influences the nature of competition among employees.

The degree of control over access is a continuum. At one extreme, the employee "owns" the job and no one else can get access unless the current incumbent voluntarily leaves it and a vacancy is established. The length of the employment is then completely controlled by the employee, and the employment relationship is closed to outsiders. At the other extreme, the employer may replace the incumbent at any time. The employment contract is reestablished in every short interval of time, and the employment relationship is completely open to outsiders.

The employment relationship is established in a process assumed to involve purposive actors as employers and employees where both parties are attempting to maximize earnings. The earnings of the employer are determined by the value of the product of the job-person combination in relation to costs of production. The value of production is a question of prices of products and quantity produced. Quantity produced in turn reflects the performance of the employee and the technology used, including the technical division of labor adopted. For purposes of this analysis, the main variable of interest is the performance of the employee and the main costs of production of interest are the wages paid to the employee and the costs of supervision.

The performance of employees or the quantity of labor supplied will be taken as determined by such attributes of the employees as their skills, abilities, and effort. The employer's return from production evidently depends on his or her ability to obtain the highest output at the lowest costs. While numerous factors may influence the overall level of wages, the employer's ability to minimize costs of production depends not only on the overall level of wages but also on the ability to tie variations in wages paid to variations in the employee's productivity. The main argument of this chapter is that the mechanisms the employer can use to relate wages to performance depend on the employment relationship, particularly the employee's control over access to the job, and that these different mechanisms identify important differences in labor market structures relevant also for labor market processes other than earnings.

The orthodox economic theory identifies a particular set of mechanisms for relating the productivity of employees to their earnings. We shall first consider these mechanisms and the employment relationships needed for these mechanisms to be effective.

The Neoclassical Theory of Earnings Determination

In the economic theory, a wage rate is generated by a labor market as a result of the demand and supply schedules of labor. Demand for labor varies with the derived demand for products, as reflected in their value. The link between wages and the value of products is established through the concept of marginal productivity, since profit-maximizing firms will be in equilibrium when the value of the marginal product equals the marginal cost or price of labor as a factor of production. This should produce different wage rates for identical labor supply because of differences in demand. However, the neoclassical theory emphasizes supply differences as a source of differences in wage rates and earnings, in particular those supply differences resulting from different skills and other individual characteristics related to an employee's productive capacity.

Differences in skills, according to human capital theory, determine different levels of productive capacity resulting in different wage rates. If skills were acquired at no cost, those wage differentials would soon lead to equalizing skill acquisition. But skills are acquired at costs. These costs are partly direct in the form of tuition and living expenses and partly opportunity costs in the form of earnings foregone. No one should undertake training if the returns from this training, in the form of increased earnings accumulated over the working life, are not at least equal to the costs of training.

If only skills acquired through training are relevant, earnings differentials would be exactly off-setting the differences in training costs. However, it is usually recognized that earnings differentials also capture variations in ability, where ability is used to refer to such characteristics as IQ, motivation, and creativity. Ability may be incorporated in the theory by recognizing that persons with different abilities have different investment costs and hence need different earnings to induce the undertaking of training. In addition, some aptitudes may be innate and scarce; these will command a rent because of their fixed supply. Finally, some variation in earnings can be attributed to different opportunities for financing training, particularly as a result of the unequal distribution of parental wealth in combination with the unwillingness of lenders to take collateral in human capital.

The basic proposition derived from the neoclassical theory is then that differences in earnings reflect differences in the productive capacity of persons as a result of their training, abilities, and training opportunities. There may be transient variations in earnings as a result of differences in derived demand in combination with market imperfections, but the basic source of inequality in earnings is unequal endowments in productive capacities among persons. In other words, identical persons are assumed to obtain almost identical earnings, regardless of the characteristics of the jobs they are in.

This theory can be used to account for a number of features of observed earnings attainment processes. Most importantly, it provides an explanation for the relation between education and earnings that interprets education as a source of marketable skills. Also, the theory predicts growth patterns for earnings, where earnings increase rapidly in the younger years and then gradually reach a stable level, with growth after entry into the labor market explained by investment in on-the-job training. Empirically, the theory fares well in accounting for variations in earnings among persons, using schooling and time in the labor force (as a proxy for on-the-job training and experience) as the main independent variables (Mincer, 1974).

The economic theory also emphasizes supply in accounting for other market processes. Most importantly, unemployment is seen as mostly voluntary, except in certain population groups (youngsters, blacks) where minimum wage laws make it impossible for employers to pay the market wage.

The focus in human capital theory on the supply side—that is, on characteristics of persons—reflects the job structure assumed in the theory—that is, one of a competitive and perfectly functioning labor market. To distinguish the neoclassical theory of the earnings determination process from the alternative model of the matching process that will be formulated later in the chapter, we will refer to the neoclassical theory as the *wage competition* model (following Thurow, 1975) to emphasize the focus on competition among employees for wages. . . .

A competitive labor market that determines wage rates is one where employers make wage offers and workers bid for employment on the basis of their productivity. The match is made when the value of the marginal product demanded equals the wage rate of the employee. This presupposes that employees paid more than their value can be replaced by others who are willing to work at the wage rate that equals marginal productivity, whereas employees who are paid less than their value can get access to jobs where the wage rate reflects their productivity. Only when the employment relationship is completely open will such a clearing of the market through wage rates be possible. Closed employment relationships, where new recruits can only get access if the incumbent leaves, insulate incumbents from competition. Employers cannot resolve discrepancies between productivity and wage rates by threatening to replace or actually replacing the current employee by someone who is more productive at the same wage rate or who is willing to work at a lower wage rate.

It could be argued that the existence of closed employment relationships does not prevent the employer from relating wages to performance, even in the absence of the ability to replace an employee. Most importantly, the employer can use promotion schemes to reward performance and in this way obtain efficient production. This is correct. Our argument is not that closed employment relationships necessarily prevent efficient production, but that promotion systems represent very different mechanisms for relating wages to performance than the use of competition among employees in open employment relationships where employers make wage offers and employees bid for employment on the basis of their productivity. Promotions can take place only when there is a vacancy in a higher level job and are meaningless as rewards for performance unless jobs at different levels provide different wages, so that wages become attributes of jobs rather than of people. Although a firm with closed employment relationships may operate efficiently because of the overall match between job assignments and performance of employees, the wages for individual employees will reflect the jobs they hold and therefore, not only their performance, but also the rate at which vacancies appear, the organization of jobs, and the seniority of employees. A very different labor market structure exists from the one assumed in the neoclassical theory when wages are tied to jobs and not to individual variations in performance. . . .

Vacancy Competition

When employees have control over access to the job, others can only get access to the job when incumbents leave. Hence, a vacancy must exist for a person to get access to a job. We will refer to the resulting matching process as *vacancy competition*. We do not wish to argue that this is the only alternative matching process to the wage competition model described by neoclassical economics. At least one other alternative employment relationship can be identified: This is the often met arrangement when employees are directly involved in the disposition of goods to the market, and the "salesperson" is paid some fraction of total earnings. But such relationships presuppose that jobs are not highly interdependent and that the salesperson is pri-

marily involved in the disposition, rather than in the production, of goods.[2] Vacancy competition in contrast is likely to emerge in closed employment relationships where jobs are interdependent in a technical and social division of labor around production.

In vacancy competition, as in wage competition, employers are assumed to be concerned about hiring the most productive employee at the least cost. But because of the indeterminate length of the employment relationship and the lack of competition among employees over wages, it will not be possible for the employer to link marginal productivity to the wage rate. This has important consequences for (a) the determination of who should be hired; (b) the determination of earnings; and (c) the organization of jobs in job ladders. These consequences all follow from the employer's attempt to secure the highest possible return from production when faced with employee control over the job.

In wage competition, the employer can rely on the wage rate as a measure of a person's productive capacity. The employer need only be concerned that the value of marginal productivity equals the wage rate and can be indifferent to the relationship between personal characteristics of employees and their performances. In contrast, in vacancy competition, the employer should be very much concerned about the relationship between personal characteristics and productive capacity, because once hired the employee cannot be easily dismissed. Furthermore, it is a person's potential performance that will be of concern, including the person's ability to fulfill the training requirements of jobs. Previous experience, education, and such ascriptive characteristics as race and sex will be used as indicators of potential performance; the main requirements are that the indicators chosen are visible and in the employer's experience show some relationship to performance. Based on the information provided by these indicators, the employer will hire the most promising candidate among those available for a job. In other words, access to a vacancy will be determined by a ranking of job candidates. As proposed by Thurow (1975), the situation may be conceived of as one where a queue of job candidates is established for vacant jobs. A person's position in the labor queue will be determined, not by his or her absolute level of productive capacity, but by the rank order in relation to other job candidates according to characteristics deemed relevant by employers.

As there is a queue of persons for jobs, there will be a rank order or a queue of vacant jobs, where the rank order is established by the earnings provided by vacant jobs, the career trajectories they imply, and such other characteristics as status, pleasantness, and convenience. The matching process, then, is a matching of the queue of persons to the queue of vacant jobs. The highest placed person in the labor queue will get the best job in the job queue. Changes in the supply of persons with certain characteristics (say a change in the distribution of education) and changes in the availability of jobs at different levels of rewards will change the rank orderings. As a result, whenever there is a change in the labor and job queues, persons with similar characteristics will tend to be hired into different jobs and persons in similar jobs may have different personal characteristics. The organization of jobs into career trajectories (discussed later) will further reinforce these tendencies.

Wage rates in vacancy competition are characteristics of jobs, not of persons. Because employers have no effective way of enforcing a translation of productivity variations into wage rates other than by promotions, wages will tend to become heavily influenced by such institutional forces as collective bargaining and employee desire to preserve traditional relative wage differentials. Internally, wage differentials will reflect the organization of jobs into job ladders.

The creation of job ladders in internal labor markets is, as already mentioned, a way for the employer to create an incentive structure in the absence of open employment relationships. The organization of jobs into promotion schedules further acts as a screening device, inducing low-performance employees to

leave on their own decision by denying or delaying promotion in relation to other employees. To be effective, jobs at the same level in a promotion schedule should provide identical earnings, whereas jobs at different levels should provide a differential large enough to induce employees to compete for promotion opportunities. This further reinforces the tendency in vacancy competition for earnings to become a characteristic of jobs so that similar jobs provide similar earnings regardless of characteristics of the incumbents.

Actual promotion opportunities are created when persons leave the firm or a new job is added, setting in motion chains of vacancies (White, 1970). The number of job levels, the distribution of jobs at various levels, the seniority distribution of employees, and the demand for products influencing the creation of new jobs (or the elimination of jobs), all interact to produce promotion schedules governing the careers of employees. These promotion schedules will under certain conditions result in career lives that are similar to those predicted by human capital theory, even though the mechanisms are quite different (Sørensen, 1977).

In wage competition, employees can change their earnings only by changing their performance. In vacancy competition, changes in earnings are generated by moves in mobility regimes that are chains of vacancies in internal labor markets. There is, in vacancy competition, no automatic correspondence between the creation of promotion opportunities and whatever changes take place in a person's productive capacity. Employees may be promoted without a preceding change in productivity, and a change in productive capacity need not result in a promotion. This means that the cross-sectional association between personal characteristics and earnings will be attenuated, even though personal characteristics are crucial for access to jobs. (A formal derivation of this conclusion and an empirical illustration is presented by Wise, 1975.)

In vacancy competition, variations in earnings reflect variations in job characteristics and the organization of jobs in internal labor markets. This is in contrast to the situation in the neoclassical model of wage competition, where the primary source of variation is the variation in personal characteristics that determine a person's productive capacity.

Vacancy competition structures are likely to be similar to the job structures identified as primary jobs (e.g., Doeringer & Piore, 1971). However, the dualist literature has a very descriptive character, and there is also some confusion as to whether the labor market segmentation is a segmentation of jobs or of persons (blacks, poor, and women in the secondary sector, white skilled workers in the primary sector). The main conclusion derived from this literature is that there are good jobs and bad jobs.

Constraints on Growth in Earnings

The two polar models of the matching process suggest different constraints on a person's ability to increase his or her earnings. In wage competition, earnings directly reflect performance and hence the skills and abilities of a person. Increases in earnings then are obtained by increasing the skill level of a person, and the major constraint on growth in earnings will be limitations on acquiring additional human capital. In wage competition markets, the amount of training that can be provided in jobs will be low, since on-the-job training is a major cause of the emergence of vacancy competition (Thurow, 1975). Hence, the major source of income inequality among persons lies outside the labor market—that is, in the educational and other training institutions that produce skill differentiation.

In vacancy competition sectors, the major constraint on the attainment of income is access to jobs. If no job is available, a person will not be able to obtain earnings. Growth in earnings is produced by the utilization of opportunities for mobility to better jobs, and this opportunity structure, not changes in skills, governs the earnings variations over time. The major source of variation in earnings is then the restriction of access to jobs

and the level of derived demand that determines the availability of jobs.

The different constraints on growth in earnings in wage competition and vacancy competition jobs imply that quite different policies will have to be used in an attempt to increase pretransfer earnings of poverty groups. In wage competition sectors, policies aimed at increasing skill levels either through schooling or—for those already having entered the labor market—through various off-the-job training programs would presumably be effective. In vacancy competition sectors such policies would be quite ineffective since such training would not make jobs available.

The rather limited success of worker training programs suggests that job vacancy competition indeed is predominant in the U.S. economy. More correctly, the fate of such programs suggests that it is indeed difficult to prepare low-skilled workers for jobs that demand high skill levels, since such jobs tend to be vacancy competition jobs.

Notes

This research was supported in part by funds granted to the Institute for Research on Poverty at the University of Wisconsin by the Office of Economic Opportunity pursuant to the provisions of the Economic Opportunity Act of 1964. The conclusions expressed herein are those of the authors.

1. The definitions are given in paragraph 10 in the section on "Basic Concepts" in *Economy and Society*, Volume 1. "A social relationship . . . will be known as 'open' to those on the outside, if . . . participation . . . is . . . not denied to anyone who is inclined to participate and is actually in a position to do so. The relationship will be known as 'closed' [if] participation of certain persons is excluded, limited or subject to conditions [Weber, 1947, p. 139]." Weber argues that market relationships are open and gives as an example of a closed relationship the "establishment of rights to and possession of particular jobs on the part of the worker [Weber, 1947, p. 141]." This identification of open relationships with market relationships (for the exchange of labor for wages) and of closed relationships with control over the job by the worker (and the absence of market relationships) will be relied on heavily in this chapter.

2. A similar arrangement accounts for the apparent contradiction of the argument presented here exemplified by the existence of wage competition among faculty at elite universities despite tenure. Here the individual scholar, and not the employer (i.e., the university), disposes himself of the products (articles and other contributions) to a competitive market and obtains himself the returns from this activity (i.e., prestige in the profession).

References

Averitt, R. T. 1968. *The Dual Economy*. New York: Norton.

Becker, G. S. 1964. *Human Capital*. New York: National Bureau of Economic Research.

Bluestone, B. 1970. "The tripartite economy: Labor markets and the working poor." *Poverty and Human Resources Abstracts* (5 March–April):15–35.

Cain, G. G. 1976. "The challenge of segmented labor market theories to orthodox theory: A survey." *Journal of Economic Literature* 14:1215–1257.

Doeringer, P. B., and M. J. Piore. 1971. *Internal Labor Markets and Manpower Analysis*. Lexington, Massachusetts: Heath.

Kerr, C. 1954. "The Balkanization of labor markets." In E. W. Bakke, P. M. Hauser, G. L. Palmer, C. A. Myers, D. Yoder, and C. Kerr (eds.), *Labor Mobility and Economic Opportunity*. Cambridge, Massachusetts: Technology Press of MIT.

Marx, K. 1961. *Capital* (Vol. 1–3). Moscow: Foreign Language Press. (Originally published in English, 1887)

Mincer, J. 1974. *Schooling, Experience and Earnings*. New York: National Bureau of Economic Research.

O'Connor, J. 1973. *The Fiscal Crisis of the State*. New York: St. Martin's.

Sørensen, A. B. 1977. "The structure of inequality and the process of attainment." *American Sociological Review* 42:965–978.

Spilerman, S. 1977. "Careers, labor market structure, and socioeconomic achievement." *American Journal of Sociology* 83:551–593.

Stolzenberg, R. M. 1975. "Occupations, labor markets and the process of wage attainment." *American Sociological Review* 40:645–665.

Thurow, L. C. 1975. *Generating Inequality*. New York: Basic.

Weber, M. 1947. [*The Theory of Social and Economic Organization*] (A. M. Henderson and T. Parsons, Trans.). New York: Oxford Univ. Press.

White, H. C. 1970. *Chains of Opportunity: System Models of Mobility in Organizations*. Cambridge, Massachusetts: Harvard Univ. Press.

Wise, D. A. 1975. "Personal attributes, job performance and probability of promotion." *Econometrica* 43:913–931.

MARK S. GRANOVETTER

The Strength of Weak Ties

Most intuitive notions of the "strength" of an interpersonal tie should be satisfied by the following definition: the strength of a tie is a (probably linear) combination of the amount of time, the emotional intensity, the intimacy (mutual confiding), and the reciprocal services which characterize the tie. Each of these is somewhat independent of the other, though the set is obviously highly intracorrelated. Discussion of operational measures of and weights attaching to each of the four elements is postponed to future empirical studies. It is sufficient for the present purpose if most of us can agree, on a rough intuitive basis, whether a given tie is strong, weak, or absent.

Consider, now, any two arbitrarily selected individuals—call them A and B—and the set, $S = C, D, E, \ldots$, of all persons with ties to either *or* both of them. The hypothesis which enables us to relate dyadic ties to larger structures is: the stronger the tie between A and B, the larger the proportion of individuals in S to whom they will *both* be tied, that is, connected by a weak or strong tie. This overlap in their friendship circles is predicted to be least when their tie is absent, most when it is strong, and intermediate when it is weak.

The proposed relationship results, first, from the tendency (by definition) of stronger ties to involve larger time commitments. If A-B and A-C ties exist, then the amount of time C spends with B depends (in part) on the amount A spends with B and C, respectively. (If the events "A is with B" and "A is with C" were independent, then the event "C is with A and B" would have probability equal to the product of their probabilities. For example, if A and B are together 60% of the time, and A and C 40%, then C, A, and B would be together 24% of the time. Such independence would be less likely after than before B and C became acquainted.) If C and B have no relationship, common strong ties to A will probably bring them into interaction and generate one. Implicit here is Homans's idea that "the more frequently persons interact with one another, the stronger their sentiments of friendship for one another are apt to be" (1950, p. 133).

The hypothesis is made plausible also by empirical evidence that the stronger the tie connecting two individuals, the more similar they are, in various ways (Berscheid and Walster 1969, pp. 69–91; Bramel 1969, pp. 9–16; Brown 1965, pp. 71–90; Laumann 1968; Newcomb 1961, chap. 5; Precker 1952). Thus, if strong ties connect A to B and A to C, both C and B, being similar to A, are probably similar to one another, increasing the likelihood of a friendship once they have met. Applied in reverse, these two factors—time and similarity—indicate why weaker A-B and A-C ties make a C-B tie less likely than strong

Originally published in 1973. Please see complete source information beginning on page 891.

ones: C and B are less likely to interact and less likely to be compatible if they do. . . .

To derive implications for large networks of relations, it is necessary to frame the basic hypothesis more precisely. This can be done by investigating the possible triads consisting of strong, weak, or absent ties among A, B, and any arbitrarily chosen friend of either or both (i.e., some member of the set S, described above). A thorough mathematical model would do this in some detail, suggesting probabilities for various types. This analysis becomes rather involved, however, and it is sufficient for my purpose in this paper to say that the triad which is most unlikely to occur, under the hypothesis stated above, is that in which A and B are strongly linked, A has a strong tie to some friend C, but the tie between C and B is absent. This triad is shown in figure 1. To see the consequences of this assertion, I will exaggerate it in what follows by supposing that the triad shown never occurs—that is, that the B-C tie is always present (whether weak or strong), given the other two strong ties. Whatever results are inferred from this supposition should tend to occur in the degree that the triad in question tends to be absent.

Some evidence exists for this absence. Analyzing 651 sociograms, Davis (1970, p. 845) found that in 90% of them triads consisting of two mutual choices and one nonchoice occurred less than the expected random number of times. If we assume that mutual choice indicates a strong tie, this is strong evidence in the direction of my argument. Newcomb (1961, pp. 160–65) reports that in triads consisting of dyads expressing mutual "high attraction," the configuration of three strong ties became increasingly frequent as people knew one another longer and better; the frequency of the triad pictured in figure 1 is not analyzed, but it is implied that processes of cognitive balance tended to eliminate it.

The significance of this triad's absence can be shown by using the concept of a "bridge"; this is a line in a network which provides the *only* path between two points (Harary, Norman, and Cartwright 1965, p. 198). Since, in

FIGURE 1
Forbidden triad

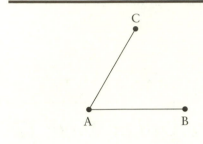

general, each person has a great many contacts, a bridge between A and B provides the only route along which information or influence can flow from any contact of A to any contact of B, and, consequently, from anyone connected *indirectly* to A to anyone connected indirectly to B. Thus, in the study of diffusion, we can expect bridges to assume an important role.

Now, if the stipulated triad is absent, it follows that, except under unlikely conditions, *no strong tie is a bridge.* Consider the strong tie A-B: if A has another strong tie to C, then forbidding the triad of figure 1 implies that a tie exists between C and B, so that the path A-C-B exists between A and B; hence, A-B is not a bridge. A strong tie can be a bridge, therefore, *only if* neither party to it has any *other* strong ties, unlikely in a social network of any size (though possible in a small group). Weak ties suffer no such restriction, though they are certainly not automatically bridges. What is important, rather, is that all bridges are weak ties.

In large networks it probably happens only rarely, in practice, that a specific tie provides the *only* path between two points. The bridging function may nevertheless be served *locally.* In figure 2a, for example, the tie A-B is not strictly a bridge, since one can construct the path A-E-I-B (and others). Yet, A-B *is* the shortest route to B for F, D, and C. This function is clearer in figure 2b. Here, A-B is, for C, D, and others, not only a local bridge to B, but, in most real instances of diffusion, a

FIGURE 2
Local bridges. (a) Degree 3; (b) Degree 13. Straight line = strong tie; dotted line = weak tie.

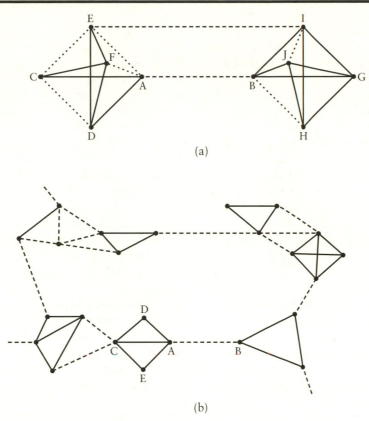

(a)

(b)

much more likely and efficient path. Harary et al. point out that "there may be a distance [length of path] beyond which it is not feasible for *u* to communicate with *v* because of costs or distortions entailed in each act of transmission. If *v* does not lie within this critical distance, then he will not receive messages originating with *u*" (1965, p. 159). I will refer to a tie as a "local bridge of degree *n*" if *n* represents the shortest path between its two points (other than itself), and *n* > 2. In figure 2*a*, A-B is a local bridge of degree 3, in 2*b*, of degree 13. As with bridges in a highway system, a local bridge in a social network will be more significant as a connection between two sectors to the extent that it is the only alternative for many people—that is, as its degree in-

creases. A bridge in the absolute sense is a local one of infinite degree. By the same logic used above, only weak ties may be local bridges.

Suppose, now, that we adopt Davis's suggestion that "in interpersonal flows of most any sort the probability that 'whatever it is' will flow from person *i* to person *j* is (*a*) directly proportional to the number of all-positive (friendship) paths connecting *i* and *j*; and (*b*) inversely proportional to the length of such paths" (1969, p. 549). The significance of weak ties, then, would be that those which are local bridges create more, and shorter, paths. Any given tie may, hypothetically, be removed from a network; the number of paths broken and the changes in average path length resulting between arbitrary pairs of points (with some limitation on length of path considered) can then be computed. The contention here is that removal of the average weak tie would do more "damage" to transmission probabilities than would that of the average strong one.

Intuitively speaking, this means that whatever is to be diffused can reach a larger number of people, and traverse greater social distance (i.e., path length), when passed through weak ties rather than strong. If one tells a rumor to all his close friends, and they do likewise, many will hear the rumor a second and third time, since those linked by strong ties tend to share friends. If the motivation to spread the rumor is dampened a bit on each wave of retelling, then the rumor moving through strong ties is much more likely to be limited to a few cliques than that going via weak ones; bridges will not be crossed. . . .

I will develop this point empirically by citing some results from a labor-market study I have recently completed. Labor economists have long been aware that American blue-collar workers find out about new jobs more through personal contacts than by any other method. (Many studies are reviewed by Parnes 1954, chap. 5.) Recent studies suggest that this is also true for those in professional, technical, and managerial positions (Shapero, Howell, and Tombaugh 1965; Brown 1967; Granovetter 1970). My study of this question laid special emphasis on the nature of the *tie* between the job changer and the contact person who provided the necessary information.

In a random sample of recent professional, technical, and managerial job changers living in a Boston suburb, I asked those who found a new job through contacts how often they *saw* the contact around the time that he passed on job information to them. I will use this as a measure of tie strength. A natural a priori idea is that those with whom one has strong ties are more motivated to help with job information. Opposed to this greater motivation are the structural arguments I have been making: those to whom we are weakly tied are more likely to move in circles different from our own and will thus have access to information different from that which we receive.

I have used the following categories for frequency of contact: often = at least twice a week; occasionally = more than once a year but less than twice a week; rarely = once a year or less. Of those finding a job through contacts, 16.7% reported that they saw their contact often at the time, 55.6% said occasionally, and 27.8% rarely ($N = 54$). The skew is clearly to the weak end of the continuum, suggesting the primacy of structure over motivation.

In many cases, the contact was someone only marginally included in the current network of contacts, such as an old college friend or a former workmate or employer, with whom sporadic contact had been maintained (Granovetter 1970, pp. 76–80). Usually such ties had not even been very strong when first forged. For work-related ties, respondents almost invariably said that they never saw the person in a nonwork context. Chance meetings or mutual friends operated to reactivate such ties. It is remarkable that people receive crucial information from individuals whose very existence they have forgotten. . . .

From the individual's point of view, then, weak ties are an important resource in making possible mobility opportunity. Seen from a more macroscopic vantage, weak ties play a role in effecting social cohesion. When a man changes jobs, he is not only moving from one network of ties to another, but also establishing a link between these. Such a link is often of the same kind which facilitated his own movement. Especially within professional and technical specialties which are well defined and limited in size, this mobility sets up elaborate structures of bridging weak ties between the more coherent clusters that constitute operative networks in particular locations.

References

Berscheid, E., and E. Walster. 1969. *Interpersonal Attraction*. Reading, Mass.: Addison-Wesley.

Bramel, D. 1969. "Interpersonal Attraction, Hostility and Perception." In *Experimental Social Psychology,* edited by Judson Mills. New York: Macmillan.

Brown, David. 1967. *The Mobile Professors.* Washington, D.C.: American Council on Education.

Brown, Roger. 1965. *Social Psychology.* New York: Free Press.

Davis, James A. 1969. "Social Structures and Cognitive Structures." In R. P. Abelson et al., *Theories of Cognitive Consistency.* Chicago: Rand McNally.

———. 1970. "Clustering and Hierarchy in Interpersonal Relations." *American Sociological Review* 35 (October): 843–52.

Granovetter, M. S. 1970. "Changing Jobs: Channels of Mobility Information in a Suburban Community." Doctoral dissertation, Harvard University.

Harary, F., R. Norman, and D. Cartwright. 1965. *Structural Models.* New York: Wiley.

Homans, George. 1950. *The Human Group.* New York: Harcourt, Brace & World.

Laumann, Edward. 1968. "Interlocking and Radial Friendship Networks: A Cross-sectional Analysis." Mimeographed. Ann Arbor: University of Michigan.

Newcomb, T. M. 1961. *The Acquaintance Process.* New York: Holt, Rinehart & Winston.

Parnes, Herbert. 1954. *Research on Labor Mobility.* New York: Social Science Research Council.

Precker, Joseph. 1952. "Similarity of Valuings as a Factor in Selection of Peers and Near-Authority Figures." *Journal of Abnormal and Social Psychology* 47, suppl. (April): 406–14.

Shapero, Albert, Richard Howell, and James Tombaugh. 1965. *The Structure and Dynamics of the Defense R & D Industry.* Menlo Park, Calif.: Stanford Research Institute.

NAN LIN

Social Networks and Status Attainment

Status attainment can be understood as a process by which individuals mobilize and invest resources for returns in socioeconomic standings. These resources can be classified into two types: personal resources and social resources. *Personal resources* are possessed by the individual who can use and dispose of them with freedom and without much concern for compensation. *Social resources* are resources accessible through one's direct and indirect ties. The access to and use of these resources are temporary and borrowed. For example, a friend's occupational or authority position, or such positions of this friend's friends, may be ego's social resource. The friend may use his or her position or network to help ego to find a job. These resources are "borrowed" and useful to achieve ego's certain goal, but they remain the property of the friend or his or her friends.

The theoretical and empirical work for understanding and assessing the status attainment process can be traced to the seminal study reported by Blau and Duncan (1967). Their major conclusion was that, even accounting for both the direct and indirect effects of ascribed status (parental status), achieved status (education and prior occupational status) remained the most important factor accounting for the ultimate attained status. The study thus set the theoretical baseline for further modifications and expansions. All subsequent theoretical revisions and expansions must be evaluated for their contribution to the explanation of status attainment beyond those accounted for by the Blau-Duncan

Originally published in 1999. Please see complete source information beginning on page 891.

paradigm (Kelley 1990; Smith 1990). Several lines of contributions since then, including the addition of sociopsychological variables (Sewell and Hauser 1975), the recasting of statuses into classes (Wright 1979; Goldthorpe 1980), the incorporation of "structural" entities and positions as both contributing and attained statuses (Baron and Bielby 1980; Kalleberg 1988), and the casting of comparative development or institutions as contingent conditions (Treiman 1970), have significantly amplified rather than altered the original Blau-Duncan conclusion concerning the relative merits of achieved versus ascribed personal resources in status attainment.

In the last three decades, a research tradition has focused on the effects on attained statuses of social resources. The principal proposition is that social resources exert an important and significant effect on attained statuses, beyond that accounted for by personal resources. Systematic investigations of this proposition have included efforts in (1) developing theoretical explanations and hypotheses, (2) developing measurements for social resources, (3) conducting empirical studies verifying the hypotheses, and (4) assessing the relative importance of social resources as compared to personal resources in the process of status attainment. . . .

Contributions of social network analysis to status attainment can be traced to the seminal study conducted by Mark Granovetter (1974), who interviewed 282 professional and managerial men in Newton, Massachusetts. The data suggested that those who used interpersonal channels seemed to land more satisfactory and better (e.g., higher income) jobs. Inferring from this empirical research, substantiated with a review of job search studies, Granovetter proposed (1973) a network theory for information flow. The hypothesis of "the strength of weak ties" was that weaker ties tend to form bridges that link individuals to other social circles for information not likely to be available in their own circles, and such information should be useful to the individuals.

However, Granovetter never suggested that access to or help from weaker rather than stronger ties would result in better statuses of jobs thus obtained (1995:148). Clues about the linkage between strength of ties and attained statuses came indirectly from a small world study conducted in a tri-city metropolitan area in upstate New York (Lin, Dayton, and Greenwald 1978). The task of the participants in the study was to forward packets containing information about certain target persons to others they knew on a first-name basis so that the packets might eventually reach the target persons. The study found that successful chains (those packets successfully forwarded to the targets) involved higher-status intermediaries until the last nodes (dipping down in the hierarchy toward the locations of the targets). Successful chains also implicated nodes that had more extensive social contacts (who claimed more social ties), and yet these tended to forward the packets to someone they had not seen recently (weaker ties). The small world study thus made two contributions. First, it suggested that access to hierarchical positions might be the critical factor in the process of status attainment. Thus, the possible linkage between strength of ties and status attainment might be indirect: The strength of weak ties might lie in their accessing social positions vertically higher in the social hierarchy, which had the advantage in facilitating the instrumental action. Second, the study implicated behavior rather than a paper-and-pencil exercise, as each step in the packet-forwarding process required actual actions from each participant. Thus, the study results lend behavioral validity to those found in previous status attainment paper-pencil studies.

Based on these studies, a theory of social resources has emerged (Lin 1982, 1990). The theory begins with an image of the macro-social structure consisting of positions ranked according to certain normatively valued resources such as wealth, status, and power. This structure has a pyramidal shape in terms of accessibility and control of such resources: The higher the position, the fewer the occupants; and the higher the position, the better the view it has of the structure (especially down below). The pyramidal structure suggests advantages for positions nearer to the top, both in terms of number of occupants (fewer) and accessibility to positions (more). Individuals within these structural constraints and opportunities take actions for expressive and instrumental purposes. For instrumental actions (attaining status in the social structure being one prime example), the better strategy would be for ego to reach toward contacts higher up in the hierarchy. These contacts would be better able to exert influence on positions (e.g., recruiter for a firm) whose actions may benefit ego's interest. This reaching-up process may be facilitated if ego uses weaker ties, because weaker ties are more likely to reach out vertically (presumably upward) rather than horizontally relative to ego's position in the hierarchy.

References

Baron, J. N., and W. T. Bielby. 1980. "Bringing the Firm Back in: Stratification, Segmentation, and the Organization of Work." *American Sociological Review* 45:737–65.

Blau, P. M., and O. D. Duncan. 1967. *The American Occupational Structure.* New York: Wiley.

Goldthorpe, J. H. 1980. *Social Mobility and Class Structure in Modern Britain.* New York: Oxford University Press.

Granovetter, M. 1973. "The Strength of Weak Ties." *American Journal of Sociology* 78: 1360–80.

Granovetter, M. 1974. *Getting a Job.* Cambridge, MA: Harvard University Press.

Granovetter, M. 1995. *Getting a Job.* Rev. ed. Chicago: University of Chicago Press.

Kalleberg, A. 1988. "Comparative Perspectives on Work Structures and Inequality." *Annual Review of Sociology* 14:203–25.

Kelley, J. 1990. "The Failure of a Paradigm: Log-Linear Models of Social Mobility." Pages 319–46, 349–57 in *John H. Goldthorpe: Consensus and Controversy,* edited by J. Clark, C. Modgil, and S. Modgil. London: Falmer.

Lin, N. 1982. "Social Resources and Instrumental Action." Pages 131–45 in *Social Structure and Network Analysis,* edited by P. V. Marsden and N. Lin. Beverly Hills, CA: Sage Publications.

Lin, N. 1990. "Social Resources and Social Mobility: A Structural Theory of Status Attainment." Pages 247–71 in *Social Mobility and Social Structure,* edited by R. L. Breiger. New York: Cambridge University Press.

Lin, N., P. Dayton, and P. Greenwald. 1978. "Analyzing the Instrumental Use of Relations in the Context of Social Structure." *Sociological Methods and Research* 7:149–66.

Sewell, W. H., and R. M. Hauser. 1975. *Education, Occupation & Earnings: Achievement in the Early Career.* New York: Academic Press.

Smith, M. R. 1990. "What Is New in New Structuralist Analyses of Earnings?" *American Sociological Review* 55:827–41.

Treiman, D. J. 1970. "Industrialization and Social Stratification." Pages 207–34 in *Social Stratification: Research and Theory for the 1970s,* edited by E. O. Laumann. Indianapolis: Bobbs-Merrill.

Wright, E. O. 1979. *Class Structure and Income Determination.* New York: Academic Press.

RONALD S. BURT

Structural Holes

Some people enjoy higher incomes than others. Some are promoted faster. Some are leaders on more important projects. The human capital explanation is that inequality results from differences in individual ability. The usual evidence is on general populations, as is Becker's (1975) pioneering analysis of income returns to education, but the argument is widely applied by senior managers to explain who gets to the top of corporate America—managers who make it to the top are smarter or better educated or more experienced. But, while human capital is surely necessary to success, it is useless without the social capital of opportunities in which to apply it.

Social capital can be distinguished in its etiology and consequences from human capital (e.g., Coleman, 1990; Bourdieu and Wacquant, 1992; Burt, 1992; Putnam, 1993; Lin, 1998). With respect to etiology, social capital is a quality created between people, whereas human capital is a quality of individuals. Investments that create social capital are therefore different in fundamental ways from the investments that create human capital (Coleman, 1988, 1990). I focus in this paper on consequences, a focus in network analysis for many years (Breiger, 1995). With respect to consequences, social capital is the contextual complement to human capital. Social capital predicts that returns to intelligence, education, and seniority depend in some part on a person's location in the social structure of a market or hierarchy. While human capital refers to individual ability, social capital refers to opportunity. Some portion of the value a manager adds to a firm is his or her ability to coordinate other people: identifying opportunities to add value within an organization and getting the right people together to develop the opportunities. Knowing who, when, and how to coordinate is a function of the manager's network of contacts within and beyond the firm. Certain network forms deemed social capital can enhance the manager's ability to identify and develop opportunities. Managers with more social capital get higher returns to their human capital because they are positioned to identify and develop more rewarding opportunities.

The Network Structure of Social Capital

Structural hole theory gives concrete meaning to the concept of social capital. The theory describes how social capital is a function of brokerage opportunities in a network (see Burt, 1992, for detailed discussion). The structural hole argument draws on several lines of network theorizing that emerged in sociology during the 1970s, most notably, Granovetter (1973) on the strength of weak ties, Freeman (1977) on betweenness centrality, Cook and Emerson (1978) on the power of having exclusive exchange partners, and Burt (1980) on the structural autonomy created by network complexity. More generally, sociological ideas elaborated by Simmel

Originally published in 1997. Please see complete source information beginning on page 891.

(1955) and Merton (1968), on the autonomy generated by conflicting affiliations, are mixed in the structural hole argument with traditional economic ideas of monopoly power and oligopoly to produce network models of competitive advantage. In a perfect market, one price clears the market. In an imperfect market, there can be multiple prices because disconnections between individuals, holes in the structure of the market, leave some people unaware of the benefits they could offer one another. Certain people are connected to certain others, trusting certain others, obligated to support certain others, dependent on exchange with certain others. Assets get locked into suboptimal exchanges. An individual's position in the structure of these exchanges can be an asset in its own right. That asset is social capital, in essence, a story about location effects in differentiated markets. The structural hole argument defines social capital in terms of the information and control advantages of being the broker in relations between people otherwise disconnected in social structure. The disconnected people stand on opposite sides of a hole in social structure. The structural hole is an opportunity to broker the flow of information between people and control the form of projects that bring together people from opposite sides of the hole.

Information Benefits

The information benefits are access, timing, and referrals. A manager's network provides access to information well beyond what he or she could process alone. It provides that information early, which is an advantage to the manager acting on the information. The network that filters information coming to a manager also directs, concentrates, and legitimates information received by others about the manager. Through referrals, the manager's interests are represented in a positive light, at the right time, and in the right places.

The structure of a network indicates the redundancy of its information benefits. There are two network indicators of redundancy.

The first is cohesion. Cohesive contacts—contacts strongly connected to each other—are likely to have similar information and therefore provide redundant information benefits. Structural equivalence is the second indicator. Equivalent contacts—contacts who link a manager to the same third parties—have the same sources of information and therefore provide redundant information benefits.

Nonredundant contacts offer information benefits that are additive rather than redundant. Structural holes are the gaps between nonredundant contacts (see Burt, 1992: 25–30, on how Granovetter's weak ties generalize to structural holes). The hole is a buffer, like an insulator in an electric circuit. A structural hole between two clusters in a network need not mean that people in the two clusters are unaware of one another. It simply means that they are so focused on their own activities that they have little time to attend to the activities of people in the other cluster. A structural hole indicates that the people on either side of the hole circulate in different flows of information. A manager who spans the structural hole, by having strong relations with contacts on both sides of the hole, has access to both information flows. The more holes spanned, the richer the information benefits of the network.

Figure 1 provides an example. James had a network that spanned one structural hole. The hole is the relatively weak connection between the cluster reached through contacts 1, 2, and 3 and the cluster reached through contacts 4 and 5. Robert took over James's job and expanded the social capital associated with the job. He preserved connection with both clusters in James's network but expanded the network to a more diverse set of contacts. Robert's network, with the addition of three new clusters of people, spans ten structural holes.

Information benefits in this example are enhanced in several ways. The volume is higher in Robert's network simply because he reaches more people indirectly. Also, the diversity of his contacts means that the quality of his information benefits is higher. Each

FIGURE 1
Illustrative manager's networks*

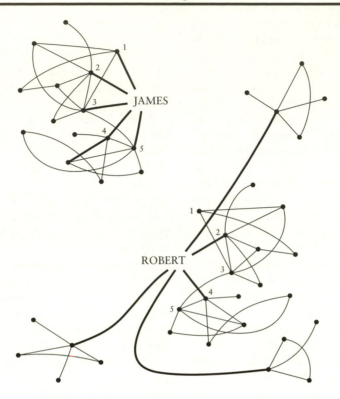

*Thick lines represent a manager's direct contacts.

cluster of contacts is a single source of information because people connected to one another tend to know the same things at about the same time. Nonredundant clusters provide Robert with a broader information screen and, therefore, greater assurance that he will be informed of opportunities and impending disasters (access benefits). Further, since Robert's contacts are only linked through him at the center of the network, he is the first to see new opportunities created by needs in one group that could be served by skills in other groups (timing benefits). He stands at the crossroads of social organization. He has the option of bringing together otherwise disconnected individuals in the network when it would be rewarding. And because Robert's contacts are more diverse, he is more likely to be a candidate for inclusion in new opportunities (referral benefits). These benefits are compounded by the fact that having a network that yields such benefits makes Robert more attractive to other people as a contact in their own networks.

Control Benefits

The manager who creates a bridge between otherwise disconnected contacts has a say in whose interests are served by the bridge. The disconnected contacts communicate through the manager, giving the manager an opportunity to adjust his or her image with each contact, which is the structural foundation for managerial robust action (Padgett and Ansell, 1993). Simmel and Merton introduced the sociology of people who derive control benefits from structural holes: The ideal type is the *tertius gaudens* (literally, "the third who benefits"), a person who benefits from brokering the connection between others (see Burt, 1992: 30–32, for review). As the broker between otherwise disconnected contacts, a manager is an entrepreneur in the literal sense of the word—a person who adds value by brokering the connection between others (Burt, 1992: 34–36; see also Martinelli, 1994). There is a tension here, but not the hostility of combatants. It is merely uncertainty. In the swirling mix of preferences characteristic of social networks, where no demands have absolute authority, the *tertius* negotiates for favorable terms. Structural holes are the setting for *tertius strategies*, and information is the substance. Accurate, ambiguous, or distorted information is strategically moved between contacts by the *tertius*. The information and control benefits reinforce one another at any moment in time and cumulate together over time.

Networks rich in structural holes present opportunities for entrepreneurial behavior. The behaviors by which managers develop these opportunities are many and varied, but the opportunity itself is at all times defined by a hole in the social structure around the manager. In terms of the structural hole argument, networks rich in the entrepreneurial opportunities of structural holes are entrepreneurial networks, and entrepreneurs are people skilled in building the interpersonal bridges that span structural holes.

Predicted Social Capital Effect

Managers with contact networks rich in structural holes know about, have a hand in, and exercise control over the more rewarding opportunities. They monitor information more effectively than it can be monitored bureaucratically. They move information faster, and to more people, than memos. These entrepreneurial managers know the parameters of organization problems early. They are highly mobile relative to people working through a bureaucracy, easily shifting network time and energy from one solution to another. More in control of their immediate surroundings, entrepreneurial managers tailor solutions to the specific individuals being coordinated, replacing the boiler-plate solutions of formal bureaucracy. There is also the issue of costs: entrepreneurial managers offer inexpensive coordination relative to the bureaucratic alternative. Managers with networks rich in structural holes operate somewhere between the force of corporate authority and the dexterity of markets, building bridges between disconnected parts of the firm where it is valuable to do so. They have more opportunity to add value, are expected to do so, and are accordingly expected to enjoy higher returns to their human capital. The prediction is that in comparisons between otherwise similar people like James and Robert in Figure 1, it is people like Robert who should be more successful.

References

Becker, Gary. 1975 Human Capital, 2d ed. Chicago: University of Chicago Press.

Bourdieu, Pierre, and Loïc J. D. Wacquant. 1992 An Invitation to Reflexive Sociology. Chicago: University of Chicago Press.

Breiger, Ronald L. 1995 "Socioeconomic achievement and social structure." In Annual Review of Sociology, 21: 115–136. Palo Alto, CA: Annual Reviews.

Burt, Ronald S. 1980 "Autonomy in a social topology." American Journal of Sociology, 85: 892–925.

———. 1992 Structural Holes. Cambridge, MA: Harvard University Press.

Coleman, James S. 1988 "Social capital in the creation of human capital." American Journal of Sociology, 94: S95–S120.

———. 1990 Foundations of Social Theory. Cambridge, MA: Harvard University Press.

Cook, Karen S., and Richard M. Emerson. 1978 "Power, equity and commitment in exchange networks." American Sociological Review, 43: 712–739.

Freeman, Linton C. 1977 "A set of measures of centrality based on betweenness." Sociometry, 40: 35–40.

Granovetter, Mark S. 1973 "The strength of weak ties." American Journal of Sociology, 78: 1360–1380.

Lin, Nan. 1998 Social Resources and Social Action. New York: Cambridge University Press (forthcoming).

Martinelli, Alberto. 1994 "Entrepreneurship and management." In Neil J. Smelser and Richard Swedberg (eds.), The Handbook of Economic Sociology: 476–503. Princeton, NJ: Princeton University Press.

Merton, Robert K. 1968 "Continuities in the theory of reference group behavior." In Robert K. Merton, Social Theory and Social Structure: 335–440. New York: Free Press.

Padgett, John F., and Christopher K. Ansell. 1993 "Robust action and the rise of the Medici, 1400–1434." American Journal of Sociology, 98: 1259–1319.

Putnam, Robert D. 1993 Making Democracy Work: Civic Traditions in Modern Italy. Princeton, NJ: Princeton University Press.

Simmel, Georg. 1955 Conflict and the Web of Group Affiliations. Trans. by Kurt H. Wolff and Reinhard Bendix. New York: Free Press.

RICHARD BREEN AND JOHN H. GOLDTHORPE

Explaining Educational Differentials: Towards a Formal Rational Action Theory

Introduction

In the light of recent research in the sociology of education, which has involved extensive over-time and cross-national analyses (see esp. Shavit and Blossfeld 1993; Erikson and Jonsson 1996b), it would seem that the following empirical generalizations can reliably be made and constitute *explananda* that pose an evident theoretical challenge.

Over the last half-century at least, all economically advanced societies have experienced a process of educational expansion. Increasing numbers of young people have stayed on in full-time education beyond the minimum school leaving age, have taken up more academic secondary courses, and have entered into some form of tertiary education.

Over this same period, *class* differentials in educational attainment, considered net of all effects of expansion per se, have tended to display a high degree of stability, i.e. while children of all class backgrounds have alike participated in the process of expansion, the pattern of association between class origins and the relative chances of children staying on in education, taking more academic courses

or entering higher education has, in most societies, been rather little altered. Children of less advantaged class origins have not brought their take-up rates of more ambitious educational options closer to those of their more advantaged counterparts.

It has, though, to be recognized that this latter generalization is not entirely without exception. In one national case at least, that of Sweden, there can be little doubt that class differentials in educational attainment have indeed declined over several decades (Erikson and Jonsson 1993); and, while some conflict of evidence remains, a similar decline has been claimed for The Netherlands (De Graaf and Ganzeboom 1993) and for Germany (Müller and Haun 1994; Jonsson, Mills and Müller 1996). Thus, any theory that is put forward in order to explain the more typical persistence of class differentials should be one that can at the same time be applied *mutatis mutandis* to such 'deviant' cases.

It would in addition be desirable that such a theory should be capable of yet further extension in order to account for a third regularity that has emerged from the research referred to.

Over a relatively short period—in effect, from the 1970s onwards—*gender* differentials in levels of educational attainment, favouring males over females, have in nearly all advanced societies declined sharply and, in some instances, have been virtually eliminated or

Originally published in 1997. Please see complete source information beginning on page 891.

even reversed. In other words, while the process of educational expansion has not in the main led to children from less advantaged family backgrounds catching up with those from more advantaged backgrounds in their average levels of attainment, in families across the class structures of contemporary societies daughters have tended rather rapidly to catch up with sons.

In an earlier paper (Goldthorpe 1996), a theory of persisting class differentials in educational attainment, sensitive to the further requirements previously indicated, was developed from a 'rational action' standpoint. In the present paper, our aim is to refine this theory and to express it in a formal model. In this way we would hope to clarify its central arguments and in turn the wider implications that it carries. Since such attempts at the formalization of theory are still not very common in sociology, the paper may also serve to stimulate discussion of the merits or demerits of this kind of endeavour. Readers interested in the more general *problematik* in the context of which the theory was initially conceived are referred to the earlier paper. In the remainder of this introductory section we set out certain 'background' assumptions of our subsequent exposition that will not be further discussed. The more specific assumptions on which our model rests will be introduced, and their significance considered, as the paper proceeds.

We assume, to begin with, that class differentials in educational attainment come about through the operation of two different kinds of effect which, following Boudon (1974), we label as 'primary' and 'secondary'. Primary effects are all those that are expressed in the association that exists between children's class origins and their average levels of demonstrated academic ability. Children of more advantaged backgrounds are in fact known to perform better, on average, than children of less advantaged backgrounds on standard tests, in examinations, etc. Primary effects, as will be seen, enter into our model but, fortunately, in such a way that we need not take up

the vexed and complex question of the extent to which they are genetic, psychological or cultural in character. It is, rather, secondary effects that for us play the crucial role. These are effects that are expressed in the actual choices that children, together perhaps with their parents, make in the course of their careers within the educational system—including the choice of exit. Some educational choices may of course be precluded to some children through the operation of primary effects: i.e. because these children lack the required level of demonstrated ability. But, typically, a set of other choices remains, and it is further known that the overall patterns of choice that are made, are in themselves—over and above primary effects—an important source of class differentials in attainment.

We then further assume that, *in their central tendencies*, these patterns of educational choice reflect action on the part of children and their parents that can be understood as rational, i.e. they reflect evaluations made of the costs and benefits of possible alternatives—e.g. to leave school or to stay on, to take a more academic or a more vocational course—and of the probabilities of different outcomes, such as educational success or failure. These evaluations, we further suppose, will be in turn conditioned by differences in the typical constraints and opportunities that actors in different class positions face and in the level of resources that they command. However, what we seek to dispense with is any assumption that these actors will also be subject to systematic influences of a (sub)cultural kind, whether operating through class differences in values, norms or beliefs regarding education or through more obscure 'subintentional' processes. Not only do we thus gain in theoretical parsimony, but we would in any event regard the 'culturalist' accounts of class differentials in educational attainment that have so far been advanced, as in various ways unsatisfactory (see further Goldthorpe 1996).

Finally, two other assumptions, regarding the structural context of action, should also be spelled out. On the one hand, we do of course suppose the existence of a class structure, i.e. a structure of positions defined by relations in labour markets and production units. And, in addition, we need to assume that within this structure classes are in some degree hierarchically ordered in terms of the resources associated with, and the general desirability of the positions they comprise. On the other hand, we suppose an educational system—i.e. a set of educational institutions that serve to define the various options that are open to individuals at successive stages in their educational careers. And here, too, we have a more specific requirement. That is, that this system should possess a diversified structure that provides options not just for more or less education but also for education of differing kinds, and that in turn entails individuals making choices at certain 'branching points' that they may not be able later to modify, or at least not in a costless way. It might be thought that this latter requirement will tend to limit the applicability of our model to educational systems of the more traditional European, rather than, say, the American variety, i.e. to ones where the type of school attended is likely to be more consequential than the total number of years spent in education. However, we would argue that, on examination, educational systems such as that of the USA, turn out to be more diversified than is often supposed, so that children do in fact face educational choices that involve considerations that go beyond simply 'more' or 'less': for example, in the American case, with the choice at secondary level between academic and vocational tracks. It is further of interest to note how two American authors have specified in this regard the divergence between assumptions that we and they would share and those of most economists working within the 'human capital' paradigm. While for the latter education appears as a 'fungible linear accumulation, like a financial investment', a more realistic view would be that educational systems, the American included, 'offer an array of choices

and constraints that defy . . . simple linear formulations' (Arum and Hout 1995, 1).

A Model of Educational Decisions

The model that we present is intended to be generic: that is, as one applicable in principle to the entire range of decisions that young people may be required to make over the course of their educational careers as regards leaving or staying on or as regards which educational option to pursue. However, in the interests of simplicity, we will here set out the model as it would apply just to the choice of leaving or continuing in education. The salient elements of the exposition are shown in Figure 1 by means of a decision tree. Here we assume that pupils must choose whether to continue in education—i.e. follow the 'stay' branch of the tree—to the completion of a further level (as, say, in the decision of whether or not to continue to A-level after GCSE) or to leave and enter the labour market, i.e. follow the 'leave' branch. Continuing in education has two possible outcomes, which we take to be success or failure. Because remaining at school often leads to an examination, we equate success with passing such an examination. This is indicated by the node labelled P in Figure 1, while failing the examination is indicated by the node labelled F. Leaving is then the third educational outcome in our model, that is, in addition to those of staying in education and passing and staying and failing, and is indicated by node L.

In deciding whether to continue in education or leave, parents and their children, we suppose, take into account three factors. The first of these is the cost of remaining at school. Continuing in full-time education will impose costs on a family which they would not have to meet were their child to leave school: these include the direct costs of education and earnings forgone. We can therefore express these costs relative to the costs of leaving by setting the latter to be zero and the former as $c > 0$. The second factor is the likeli-

FIGURE 1
Single decision tree

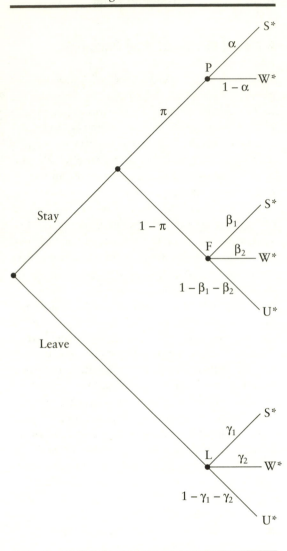

FIGURE 1
Single decision tree

hood of success if a pupil continues in education. Since we distinguish only between success and failure, subjective beliefs about the chances of success at the next stage of education can be captured in our model by a single parameter, which we label π. This parameter measures the subjective conditional probability of passing the relevant examination given continuation. The third factor is then the value or utility that children and their families attach to the three educational outcomes rep-

resented by P, F and L in Figure 1. In our model this factor is expressed in terms of beliefs about the chances of access that each outcome affords to three possible destination classes.

For the purposes of our exposition, we take these classes as being the service class or salariat of professionals, administrators and managers (S^* in Figure 1), the working class (W^*) and the underclass, (U^*)—the class, say, of those with only a precarious place in the labour market and in only the lowest grades of employment if not unemployed. However, it should be emphasized that nothing of significance attaches to this choice of classes, except that, as earlier noted, we need to have a hierarchical ordering. Thus, the service class is regarded as comprising the most advantaged and most desirable positions and the underclass the least advantaged and least desirable, with the working class falling in-between. This ranking of classes is, moreover, assumed to be universally recognized or, at all events, not to vary across the population in any socially structured way.

As we have said, each of the three possible educational outcomes in our model has attached to it subjective probabilities of access to each of the three possible destination classes. So, as Figure 1 shows, for pupils who remain at school and pass their examination, node P, the probability of access to the service class is given by α. There is no path linking this educational outcome to the underclass. This means that anyone who reaches this particular outcome is believed to be certain to avoid this class. It follows, therefore, that the probability of entering the working class, conditional on having been educationally successful, is given by $1 - \alpha$. At the other two outcome nodes, F and L, there is a positive probability of entering all three destination classes. So, for the outcome F (remaining at school and failing) the probability of access to the service class is given by β_1, the probability of access to the working class by β_2 and the probability of access to the underclass by $1 - \beta_1 - \beta_2$. For the L outcome the corresponding probabilities are then given by the γ parameters.

We repeat that these are all subjective probabilities. Just as with π, the values for our various α, β and γ parameters reflect people's beliefs, in this case, about the returns to various educational outcomes conceptualized in terms of access to more or less desirable locations in the class structure. In principle, therefore, these parameters could vary widely across individuals and families. Again, though, we assume a societal consensus in regard to a set of beliefs that then serve as conditions on the parameters in question and that may be stated as follows:

i. $\alpha > \beta_1$ and $\alpha > \gamma_1$. It is generally believed that remaining at school and succeeding affords a better chance of access to the service class than does remaining at school and failing or leaving school. Our model does not require that we make any assumptions about the relative magnitude of β_1 and γ_1. It could, for example, be the case that a young person's chances of access to the service class are improved simply by acquiring more years of education, even if this does not lead to examination success. Alternatively, such time spent in education may be wasted in the sense that leaving school and embarking earlier on a career will yield a better chance of access to the service class.

ii. $\gamma_1 + \gamma_2 > \beta_1 + \beta_2$. Remaining at school and failing increases the chances of entering the underclass. This means that there is a risk involved in choosing to continue to the next level of education.

iii. $\gamma_2/\gamma_1 > 1$; $(\gamma_2/\gamma_1) \geq (\beta_2/\beta_1)$. Those who leave school immediately have a better chance of entry to the working class than to the service class. This may or may not be the case among those who remain at school and fail though, if it is, their odds of entering the working class rather than the service class are no greater than for those who leave school immediately.

iv. $\alpha > 0.5$. Staying on at school and passing the examination makes entry to the service class more likely than entry to the working class.[1]

In the interests of realism, especially as regards (ii) and (iii) above, it ought to be noted that 'leaving' and entering the labour market need not in most educational systems be equated with a definitive ending of the individual's educational career. Taking this option could in fact lead to further vocational courses pursued in conjunction with employment.

The Generation of Class Differentials

Given the model previously outlined, we can now turn to the question of explaining why differences exist across classes in the proportions of young people who make one kind of educational decision rather than another. For ease of exposition here we consider only two classes of origin, the service class, S, and the working class, W. In all of what follows we assume that these classes differ in only two ways. First (and it is here that we give recognition to 'primary' effects) children of the two classes differ in their average ability. Ability is taken to be normally distributed within each class with means $a_s > a_w$ and variance given by σ_a^2. Secondly, the two classes have different levels of resources, r, which they can use to meet c, the costs of education. Resources are taken to have a logistic distribution with mean values $r_s > r_w$ for the two classes and a common dispersion parameter, σ_r^2. Throughout, we make no other assumptions about differences between the classes. In particular, and as earlier noted, we do not suppose any class-specific cultural values or social norms nor any class differences in the subjective α, β and γ parameters of our model.

We then propose three mechanisms through which class differentials in educational attainment may arise at the level of 'secondary' effects. Of these three, we would wish to stress the particular importance of the first, since this provides an account of how these differentials may be created and sustained through the apparently 'free' choices made by those in less advantaged classes. Our second and third mechanisms can be understood as accentuating the differing patterns of choice that derive from this initial source.

Relative Risk Aversion

We begin with an assumption regarding aspirations: that is, that families in both classes alike seek to ensure, so far as they can, that their children acquire a class position at least as advantageous as that from which they originate or, in other words, they seek to avoid downward social mobility. This means that the educational strategy pursued by parents in the service class is to maximize the chances of their children acquiring a position in this class. In terms of our model their strategy is to maximize the probability of access to S^*. For working-class parents the implication is that they should seek for their children a place in either the working or the service class, since either meets the criterion of being at least as good as the class from which they originate. In terms of our model their strategy is then to maximize the probability of access to S^* or W^*, which is the same as minimizing the probability of access to U^*. This establishes families in both classes as having identical *relative* risk aversion: they want to avoid, for their children, any position in life that is worse than the one from which they start.

To see the consequence of these two strategies, maximize $pr(S^*)$ for those of service-class origins and minimize $pr(U^*)$ for those of working-class origins—assume, for the moment, that continuing in education is costless ($c = 0$). Then we find that whether or not a pupil believes it to be in his or her best interests to continue in education rather than leave depends on the value p_i (where i indicates the ith pupil) given by

$$p_{iS} = \frac{\pi_i \alpha + (1 - \pi_i)\beta_1}{\pi_i \alpha + (1 - \pi_i)\beta_1 + \gamma_1} \quad (1)$$

for the ith service class pupil and

$$p_{iW} = \frac{\pi_i + (1 - \pi_i)(\beta_1 + \beta_2)}{\pi_i + (1 - \pi_i)(\beta_1 + \beta_2) + (\gamma_1 + \gamma_2)}$$

$$(2)$$

for the ith working class pupil. Here we have allowed π to vary between pupils but we have assumed the values of α, β and γ to be common to all. If p takes a value greater than one-half this indicates that the expected returns to remaining at school exceed those of leaving. Thus, without taking account, as yet, of the costs of pursuing the former strategy, pupils for whom $p_i > 0.5$, can be said to prefer to remain in education. Even if subjective expectations of future success, as captured by π, do not differ between the two classes it will nevertheless be the case that, given conditions (1) to (4), $p_{iS} > p_{iW}$ for any value of π less than one.[2]

Proof: $p_{iS} > p_{iW} \; \forall \; \pi \leq 1$ if and only if

$$\frac{\pi\alpha + (1 - \pi)\beta_1}{\gamma_1} > \frac{\pi + (1 - \pi)(\beta_1 + \beta_2)}{(\gamma_1 + \gamma_2)} \quad (3)$$

Taking the first term on the left hand side of (3) we have

$$\frac{\pi\alpha}{\gamma_1} = \frac{\pi}{\frac{1}{\alpha}\gamma_1} > \frac{\pi}{\gamma_1 + \gamma_2} \quad (3a)$$

by conditions (3) and (4). Taking the second term on the left hand side of (3) we have

$$\frac{(1 - \pi)\beta_1}{\gamma_1} \geq \frac{(1 - \pi)(\beta_1 + \beta_2)}{(\gamma_1 + \gamma_2)} \quad (3b)$$

by conditions (ii) and (iii). Together (3a) and (3b) imply (3) which in turn implies $p_s > p_w$ as required.

This result establishes that if continuing in education is costless and there are no class differences in the subjective probability parameters α, β, γ and π, children from middle-class backgrounds will more strongly 'prefer' (in the sense of perceiving it to be in their best interests) to remain in school to a further level of education rather than leave.

The proportions in each class who prefer to stay are derived as follows. Assume that p has an unspecified distribution with means in each class p_s and p_w and dispersion parameters σ_{pS} and σ_{pW}. Because $p_{iS} > p_{iW}$ for any common value of π_i, and assuming, for the moment, no class difference in the distribution of π, it follows that $p_s > p_w$. Then, given that only those pupils for whom p exceeds one-half prefer to stay at school, the proportions in each class preferring this outcome are given by the area under the unspecified distribution function above the point

$$z_s = \frac{\frac{1}{2} - p_s}{\sigma_{pS}}$$

for the service class and analogously for the working class.

Differences in Ability and Expectations of Success

Thus far we have been assuming that the option of continuing in education is open to all pupils. But, of course, this is often not the case and successive levels of education may only be open to those who meet some criterion, such as a given level of performance in a previous examination. Let us assume, for the sake of simplicity, that this criterion can be expressed directly in terms of ability, so that, for example, a pupil may only continue in education if his or her ability level exceeds some threshold, k: i.e. we impose the condition that a_i must be greater than k. Recalling our assumption regarding primary effects that the mean level of ability is higher in the service class than in the working class but that both have the same variance in ability, it follows that the proportion of service-class children who meet this condition exceeds the proportion of working-class children.

However, we might also suppose that pupils' own knowledge of their ability helps shape the subjective probability they attach to being successful in the next stage of education, which we labelled π_i. So we can write $\pi_i = g(a_i)$, where g indicates that π is a function of a. If we then denote by π_s^* and π_w^* the re-

quired minimum subjective probabilities compatible with continuing in education (these are the smallest values of π_i for which $p_i > 0.5$) we can write the probability of continuing in education as

$$pr(a_i > k)pr(\pi_i > \pi^* \mid a_i > k)$$

$$= pr(a_i > k, \pi_i > \pi^*)$$

$$= pr(a_i > k, g(a_i) > \pi^*) \tag{4}$$

If

$$pr(g(a_i) > \pi^*) \leq pr(a_i > k)$$

then (4) reduces to

$$pr(\pi_i > \pi^*).$$

If pupils' expectations about how well they will perform at the next level of education are upwardly bounded by how well they have performed in their most recent examination—for example, if there are no pupils who, although they have failed to exceed the threshold k are nevertheless sufficiently optimistic about their future examination performance to wish to continue in education—then ability differences will be wholly captured in differences in the subjective parameter π. This will cause the average value of π to be lower among working- than service-class pupils because of the class difference in average ability levels.

Differences in Resources

Thus far we have assumed education to be costless. If we relax this assumption we need to take account of class differences in the resources that families in different locations in the class structure can devote to their children's education. Assume, therefore, that pupils can continue in education if and only if $r_i > c$ where r_i is the level of resources available for children's education in the ith family. Given that service-class families have, on average, greater resources than working-class families ($r_s > r_w$) and that resources have the same dispersion within each class, it follows that the proportion of service-class pupils for whom this resource requirement is met will exceed the proportion of working-class pupils.

We have now suggested three mechanisms which, taken together, give rise to class differentials in the proportions of children who choose to stay on in education. Our first mechanism shows how, solely because of the relative risk aversion that is seen as being common across classes, there will be a stronger preference among service- than working-class pupils for remaining in education given that no costs attach to doing so. Our second mechanism then allows for class differences in average ability levels and in turn in expectations of success. The effect of this is to introduce class differences in the values of π (the subjective probability of future educational success), which further widen class differences in the value of p and thus in the strength of the preference for staying on in education. Finally, our third mechanism takes account of the costs of continuing in education and allows for a further source of class differentials, the average resource levels available to meet these costs. The effect of this is to promote class differences via the proportion of families in each class whose resources exceed the costs of their children continuing in education or, more simply, who can afford to allow their children to continue. . . .

Explaining Empirical Generalizations

We may now seek to apply our model to the explanation of the empirical generalizations that were set out in the Introduction, beginning with that of the widely observed persistence of class differentials in educational attainment in the context of an overall increase in educational participation rates. To account for the latter trend is fairly easy: the relative costs of education have declined over time in all economically advanced countries. As the period of compulsory schooling has been extended, the costs of successively higher levels of education have been reduced through the abolition of fees, the introduction of maintenance grants, soft loans, etc. In our model this change is treated via mechanism (iii)—class differences in resources—and is captured in a decline in the size of the parameter c. This will lead to an increase in the proportions of children from both service- and working-class origins continuing in education, providing, of course, that the preference for continuing (given by our p parameter) does not decline. However, far from p_i declining over time it is more plausible to believe that there is a widespread increase in the desire to remain in full-time education as educational credentials come to take on increasing importance in the labour market and in securing a relatively advantaged class position. Indeed, in so far as education is regarded as a 'positional' good, p_i could be expected to rise steadily simply as a consequence of educational expansion itself.

At the same time our model can provide an explanation of how, within a context of educational expansion, class differentials may none the less persist. To see this, recall that class differences in educational attainment are usually measured by odds ratios which compare the odds of continuing in education versus leaving for pairs of origin classes. Under our model, the odds ratio between the service and the working class is equal to

$$\frac{\phi_S / (1 - \phi_S)}{\phi_W / (1 - \phi_W)}$$

where we use ϕ_S to mean the proportion of service class pupils who remain in education and similarly for ϕ_W. It is then possible to show (see Breen and Goldthorpe 1997, 300–2) that, given a decline over time in c, together with an increase in the proportion of both service- and working-class pupils who consider it in their best interests to remain in education, the odds of continuing in education increase by a roughly constant amount for each class, and so preserve a similar constancy in the odds ratio. This tells us that, under these circumstances, a uniform decline in the costs of education, i.e. uniform across classes, will result in the odds for children of all classes choosing to continue being multiplied by something like a common factor. So if, for example, some level of education is made free of charge (in the sense that fees are no longer levied) class differences in participation (as measured by odds ratios) at this level will remain more or less unchanged even though the overall participation rate will increase.

Our model also sheds some new light on the concept of 'maximally maintained inequality' in education (Raftery and Hout 1990; Hout, Raftery and Bell 1993). These authors argue that class differences in educational attainment will only begin to decline when participation in a given level of education of children of more advantaged backgrounds reaches saturation. In our model, such a reduction will occur once c declines to the value at which all members of the service class have resources that exceed it. At this point, all service-class families will possess resources that exceed the costs of remaining in education and thus the proportion in this class who choose to continue in education will be equal to the proportion who perceive it to be in their interests (i.e. for whom $p_i > 0.5$). *Further* reductions in c will then have no influence on the numbers of service-class children who choose to continue but will still increase the proportion of working-class children who do so. Under these conditions, the relevant odds ratio could be expected to move towards unity.[3] However, it should be recognized that, as understood in terms of our model, maximally maintained inequality does not imply that a decline in class differentials can only commence at the point at which all children of more advantaged class origins continue in education. Rather, this effect occurs once all such children whose p_i is greater than one-half continue, in other words, once all those who perceive it to be in their best interests to continue are able to act accordingly. It is true that in some instances the achievement of this latter condition will, in fact, give rise to 100 percent continuation among children of more advantaged classes.[4] But further declines in c, even if they lead to $r_{iW} > c$ for all members of the working class, will not lead to equality in the proportions continuing in edu-

cation in each class so long as there still remains a class difference in the proportion who prefer to continue.

It further follows from our model that class differentials in educational attainment will also respond to changes in the costs of education which, rather than being uniform, have a variable impact across classes. Such changes could be brought about directly through the selective subsidization of young people according to their class of origin, as occurred, for example, in some post-war Communist societies. However, essentially the same effect could follow from a general reduction in inequality of condition between classes. Specifically, if class differences in resources, r, become smaller, our model would predict that differentials in educational attainment, as measured by odds-ratios, would in turn decline.

It is then in this way that the model may be seen as applying to the national case that most obviously deviates from the typical pattern of persisting class inequalities in education, i.e. that of Sweden, in which, as earlier noted, a narrowing of such inequalities over the post-war decades is well attested. There is indeed further extensive evidence (for reviews, see Erikson and Jonsson 1996a; Goldthorpe 1996) that in this same period the average income levels of different classes in Sweden became more equal, while the degree of economic insecurity experienced by members of the working class was steadily reduced. And through time-series analysis, correlations can in fact be established between these latter tendencies and the growing equality in educational outcomes that are at all events consistent with the hypothesis of a causal influence (Erikson 1996).

As against the constancy in class differentials in educational attainment, to which exceptions are few, the decline in gender differentials that has occurred in virtually all advanced societies since the 1970s must appear as rather dramatic. Because gender differentials arise within, rather than between, families, neither changes in the costs of education nor in inequalities in resources among families are appropriate to explaining their reduction. In the light of our model, this may rather be seen as resulting from shifts in the perception of educational returns that have been prompted by changes in women's labour market participation. It would be fair comment to say that the pattern of returns to different educational decisions that we have thus far envisaged would, for most of the 20th century, be more applicable to young men than to young women. Until quite recently, it is likely that educational decisions in the case of girls were shaped in the main by the expectation that their primary social roles would be those of wife and mother, and that their class positions would therefore be determined more by whom they married than by how they themselves fared in the labour market. In so far as this were the case, then the relative returns to education for women would be somewhat different to those we have supposed in the exposition of our model: at all events, the returns associated with any particular educational decision would be less highly differentiated than for men. So, for example, young women of service-class origins could be thought best able to retain their position in this class through marriage; but to meet young service-class men did not necessitate that they themselves should acquire the educational qualifications that led to a service-class occupation. Rather, their qualifications had to be such as to provide them with employment that would bring them into contact with potential service-class husbands, and this requirement might be met through only relatively modest levels of educational attainment, leading to a job as, say, a secretary or nurse. And within both the home and the educational system alike, as much emphasis was indeed placed on the acquisition of social and domestic skills as on skills that would have value in the labour market.

Such a flatter 'gradient' in the returns to different educational pathways would, if incorporated into our model, have two consequences. First, the proportion of women choosing to remain in education at each decision point would be smaller than the proportion of men; and, second, class differentials would tend to be less among women than among men. The former result follows from the lesser incentive to continue in successively higher levels of education that would be held out to women of all class origins alike; the latter comes about because the magnitude of the class differences among those choosing to remain in education (for given values of ability and resources) is directly proportional to the differences in returns associated with the various possible educational outcomes. If we consider equations (1) and (2) shown earlier, then as the difference between, say, α_1, β_1 and γ_1 diminishes, so the difference between p_{iS} and p_{iW} will also diminish.

Over the past 20 years, we would suggest, the pattern of returns to education for women has drawn closer to that for men, as rates of women's labour market participation and, especially rates for married women, have increased and as a woman's own employment has taken on greater significance in determining the standard of living enjoyed by her family and further, perhaps, her own class position. In other words, our model as expressed in Figure 1 has come increasingly to apply to women: the 'gradient' in their returns to education has steepened. According to our model, then, such a change should have two effects: gender differentials in educational attainment should decline, as indeed they have, and at the same time the magnitude of class differences among women should increase.

Conclusions: Theoretical Implications of the Model

As regards the theoretical implications of our model, we would see these as being of main significance in their bearing on explanatory strategy. The model represents children and their families as acting in a (subjectively) rational way, i.e. as choosing among the different educational options available to them on the basis of evaluations of their costs and benefits and of the perceived probabilities of more or less successful outcomes. It then accounts for stability, or change, in the educational differentials that ensue by reference to a quite limited range of situational features. For example, in the case of persisting class differentials, the explanatory emphasis falls on similarly persisting inequalities in the resources that members of different classes can command in the face of the constraints and opportunities that their class positions typically entail. Class differences in demonstrated academic ability are also recognized, but not—as we have emphasized—class differences of a (sub)cultural character.

To the extent, then, that our model holds good, i.e. that it can provide an adequate account of the regularities we have considered and that its further empirical implications are not rejected—the relatively parsimonious strategy of the rational action approach is supported; and, we might add, in an area in which 'culturalist' theories of one kind or another have hitherto enjoyed great popularity—even if not great explanatory success (see Goldthorpe 1996). In turn, the case for attempting to pursue this strategy in other areas of sociological enquiry is strengthened.

Finally, though, we would wish to allude to certain theoretical implications that might be regarded as following from our model but that do not in fact do so. To begin with, we are not required to suppose that, in making educational choices, children and their parents in fact go through the processes of ratiocination that the model might appear to attribute to them. We do take it to be the case that the actors in question have some knowledge of how their society works, have some concern for their own, or for family interests, and seek to use the former to promote the latter. But we can at the same time accept that the decisions they make may only rarely result from any entirely explicit procedures, rather than, say, 'emerging' over a period of time and, in all probability, reflecting also various non-rational influences. What underlies our approach is the idea that it is rational considerations that are, not the only, but the main common factor at work across individual instances, and that will therefore shape patterns

of educational choices in aggregate and, in turn, the regularities that constitute our *explananda*. Our model then aims to represent these considerations in an 'idealized' way, so as to capture the key generative processes involved, rather than to represent decision-making as it actually occurs at the level of particular families.

Further, while we do not in explaining class differentials in education invoke systematic variation in values or derived norms, this does not mean that we have to deny their very existence. Thus, in so far as class-specific norms may be identified—which is an empirical issue—we could recognize them as serving as *guides* to rational action that have evolved over time out of distinctive class experience and that may substitute for detailed calculation when educational choices arise. Understood in this way, such norms could conceivably be of some explanatory significance as inertial forces in cases where the structure of constraints and opportunities or the distribution of resources is changing. But what we would in fact expect, and the decline in gender differentials would, at least by analogy, lend support, is that norms, in being essentially epiphenomenal, would rather quickly come into line with patterns of action that display a rational adaptation to the new circumstances that have come into being.

In sum, our model implies an explanatory strategy that is undoubtedly 'reductionist' so far as the relation of norms to rational action is concerned (see Elster 1991). However, we do not in this regard seek what Popper (1972: Ch. 8) has criticized as reduction by fiat, but only reduction in so far as it is warranted by the empirical support that our theoretical arguments can obtain in the particular area in which they have been applied.[5]

Notes

1. Strictly speaking the mathematics of our model require a slightly weaker condition, namely that $\alpha \geq \gamma_1 / (\gamma_1 + \gamma_2)$. This imposes a condition on the magnitude of the difference in the chances of

access to the service class as between remaining at school and passing the examination and leaving immediately. The conditional probability of access to the service class for those who leave immediately should not be greater than $\gamma_1 + \gamma_2$ times the conditional probability of access to the service class for those who remain at school and pass the examination. However, because of condition (iii), condition (iv) will always be met if $\alpha > 0.5$.

2. Note that, whereas p_{iW} can take any value between zero and one depending on the value of π, if $\beta_1 \geq \gamma_1$ then p_{iS} will exceed one-half for all values of π.

3. Though empirically this will be observed only if the proportion of service-class children who consider it in their best interests to remain in education does not change for other reasons. For example, given an increase over time in the importance of educational qualifications in obtaining jobs we might see changes in the relative values of the α, β and γ parameters causing the proportion for whom $p_i > 0.5$ to increase in both classes. Under these conditions a narrowing of the odds-ratio will not necessarily follow.

4. In our model this will be the case for the service class if (in addition to conditions (i) to (iv)) $\beta_1 \geq \gamma_1$ but it need not be so if this inequality does not hold.

5. Elster (1991) criticizes several different versions of the argument that action taken in conformity with social norms is reducible to rational action. However, his efforts to show that no version entails that such a reduction is always possible are of greater philosophical than sociological interest. One could entirely agree with Elster, yet still wish to maintain that, in a particular instance of sociological explanation, a reductionist view could in fact be upheld; or, more generally, that it is good strategy to start from a reductionist position and to modify it only in so far as the evidence requires.

References

Arum, R. and M. Hout. 1995. 'The Early Returns: The Transition from School to Work in the United States.' European University Institute, School-to-Work Conference, Florence.

Boudon, R. 1974. *Education, Opportunity and Social Inequality.* New York: Wiley.

Breen, R. and J.H. Goldthorpe. 1997. 'Explaining Educational Differentials. Towards a Formal Rational Action Theory.' Rationality and Society 9: 275–305.

De Graaf, P.M. and H.G.B. Ganzeboom. 1993. 'Family Background and Educational Attainment in the Netherlands for the 1891–1960 Birth Cohorts.' In *Persistent Inequality: Chang-*

ing Educational Attainment in Thirteen Countries, eds Y. Shavit and H.-P. Blossfeld. Boulder: Westview Press.

Elster, J. 1991. 'Rationality and Social Norms.' *Archives Européennes de Sociologie* 32: 109–29.

Erikson, R. 1996. 'Can We Account for the Change in Inequality of Educational Opportunity?' In *Can Education be Equalised? The Swedish Case in Comparative Perspective,* eds R. Erikson and J.O. Jonsson. Boulder: Westview Press.

Erikson, R. and J.O. Jonsson. 1993. *Ursprung och Utbildning.* Stockholm: Statens Offentliga Utredningar.

Erikson, R. and J.O. Jonsson. 1996a. 'Explaining Class Inequality in Education: the Swedish Test Case.' In *Can Education be Equalised? The Swedish Case in Comparative Perspective,* eds R. Erikson and J.O. Jonsson. Boulder: Westview Press.

Erikson, R. and J.O. Jonsson. (eds). 1996b. *Can Education be Equalised? The Swedish Case in Comparative Perspective.* Boulder: Westview Press.

Goldthorpe, J.H. 1996. 'Class Analysis and the Reorientation of Class Theory: The Case of Persisting Differentials in Educational Attainment.' *British Journal of Sociology* 45(3): 481–506.

Hout, M., A.E. Raftery and E.O. Bell. 1993. 'Making the Grade: Educational Stratification in the United States, 1925–1989.' In *Persistent Inequality: Changing Educational Attainment in Thirteen Countries,* eds Y. Shavit and H.-P. Blossfeld. Boulder: Westview Press.

Jonsson, J.O., C. Mills and W. Müller. 1996. 'A Half Century of Increasing Educational Openness? Social Class, Gender and Educational Attainment in Sweden, Germany and Britain.' In *Can Education be Equalised? The Swedish Case in Comparative Perspective,* eds R. Erikson and J.O. Jonsson. Boulder: Westview Press.

Müller, W. and D. Haun. 1994. 'Bildungsungleichheit im Sozialen Wandel.' *Kölner Zeitschrift für Soziologie und Sozialpsychologie* 46: 1–42.

Popper, K.R. 1972. *Objective Knowledge.* Oxford: Clarendon Press.

Raftery, A.E. and M. Hout. 1990. 'Maximally Maintained Inequality: Expansion, Reform and Opportunity in Irish Education, 1921–1975.' ISA Research Committee on Social Stratification and Mobility, Madrid.

Shavit, Y. and H.-P. Blossfeld. (eds). 1993. *Persistent Inequality: Changing Educational Attainment in Thirteen Countries.* Boulder, Westview Press.

JOHN ALLEN LOGAN

Rational Choice and the TSL Model of Occupational Opportunity

Introduction

Logan (1996b) introduces a new statistical method, the two-sided logit (TSL) model, for studying the empirical determinants of occupational opportunity and choice in a general labor market. Applying this model gives estimates of the importance of individual workers' attributes in determining opportunities for employment in broad occupational categories, and of the importance of job characteristics in determining workers' choices of occupations. In this paper I consider the TSL model from a rational-choice perspective which was not developed in the original introduction (1996b).

I consider the model as a relatively complete, but still empirically estimable, representation of rational choice in the occupational context. As Hechter (1994) notes, rational choice models in principle make choice a function of both objective and subjective elements, which for the worker are respectively external constraints on job availabilities and the worker's own preferences for types of job. Hechter emphasizes that preferences among alternatives depend on both instrumental and immanent properties of the alternatives, and that stable, internalized preferences for these properties can usefully be called instrumental and immanent values. But most empirical

work, he says, simplifies the choice situation in such a way that immanent and instrumental values become irrelevant, leaving differences in constraints as the sole explanation of differences in behavior. TSL, by contrast, retains much more of the full context of choice, by making the constraints facing actors a matter for estimation, and by allowing both instrumental and immanent properties of alternatives to be considered. In retaining these aspects of choice, the TSL model seems particularly suited for extra-economic, sociological explanations of opportunity and choice. . . .

The Two-sided Logit Model

The TSL model proposed in Logan (1996b) is now described. The model has two sides, one for workers and one for employers. Each employer may employ more than one worker, while each worker takes at most one job. In an idealization of the actual process by which matches occur, employers initially evaluate workers before deciding whether to make job offers, using this utility function:

$$U_j(i) = \beta_j^* x_i^* + m_j + \varepsilon_{1ij} \tag{1}$$

Here β is a row vector of employer j's preferences for relevant characteristics of workers, and x_i^* is a column vector of worker i's observed values on those characteristics. In addition to the direct evaluation of i's characteristics, the equation also includes a scalar quantity m_j to represent the net effect of any systematic contributions to j's utility for mak-

Originally published in 1996. Please see complete source information beginning on page 891.

ing a hire which are unrelated to i's characteristics. Generally speaking, these are market influences, which are considered exogenous factors with respect to the matching situation of the modeled employers and workers. It is assumed that the value of m_j cannot be observed directly by the researcher. The term e_{1ij} is a random disturbance representing utility-relevant factors which are not known to the observer (i.e. the researcher), but which are known to employer j and influence its evaluation of i.

The model specifies that employer j makes a decision regarding i by comparing (1) with the utility of *not* hiring i:

$$U_j(\neg i) = b_j + s_j + \varepsilon_{0ij} \qquad (2)$$

Here b_j is the baseline utility the employer would obtain without an additional hire, and $s_j \geq 0$ is a strategic increment over this baseline utility which the employer may require before making an offer.[1] The strategic increment keeps the employer from offering a job to the first applicant who would make any addition whatsoever to its utility; how the employer might set its value is discussed later. The quantities on the right side of (2) do not depend on the characteristics of worker i, but may depend on the characteristics of employer j itself; therefore they are j-subscripted rather than i-subscripted. Neither b_j nor s_j is directly observable. The term ε_{0ij} is a random disturbance indicating influences on the utility of not hiring i which are unknown to the observer.

When expression (1) is greater in value than expression (2), employer j makes a job offer:

$$o_{ij} = \begin{cases} = 1 \text{ if } U_j(i) > U_j(\neg i) \\ = 0 \text{ otherwise} \end{cases} \qquad (3)$$

The dummy variable o_{ij} is 1 when employer j makes an offer to i, and 0 otherwise. This model of employer j's decision is called a random utilities model because it represents the decision as a function of utilities which have

random components, the disturbance terms in (1) and (2).

The individual's choice of his/her most preferred offer from the available set is in turn specified as a second random utilities model. The utility which i would obtain from the job offered by j is defined as:

$$V_i(j) = \alpha_i z_j + v_{ij} \qquad (4)$$

for $j = 0, 1, \ldots, J$. Vector z_j contains the observed characteristics of an offered job when $j > 0$, while it contains the characteristics of unemployment when $j = 0$. Vector α_i contains the preferences of the individual, and v_{ij} is a random disturbance representing unknown influences on the utility. The decision rule for the individual is to select the single alternative j which offers the highest utility.

In practice it is not possible to estimate a separate utility function for each individual. If $V_i(j) = \alpha z_{ij} + v_{ij}$ is substituted for (4), then dummy variables representing the individual's membership in different groups can be introduced in interaction with the original z_j variables to estimate preferences which vary among groups.

Equations (1) through (4), together with the decision rules given for employers and workers, and with particular distributional assumptions for the disturbances, lead to a model of the probability each worker has of accepting a job with each employer.[2] Because of the decision rules, this probability has the following two interpretations:

$P(A_{ij})$ = probability that worker i will accept job j
= probability that worker i prefers job j to all other jobs available to him or her, and that employer j prefers i to all other workers available to it.   (5)

The second interpretation of $P(A_{ij})$ is valid because the joint pattern of preferences it describes requires i to accept j's job under the rules, and i will not accept j's job unless the joint pattern holds.

The model requires observations of x_i, z_j and the observed outcome matching (i, j), but does not require observations of m_j, b_j, s_j, or the pattern of offers made to each worker by employers. For computational reasons, this model cannot be applied directly to data on individual jobs, but instead must be estimated using the average characteristics of jobs in occupational categories. Logan (1996a) describes an EM algorithm used to obtain maximum likelihood estimates of parameters with such data, and Logan (1996b) discusses the estimates and their interpretation in more detail. Note that the estimates of the workers' (but not the employers') preferences may be downwardly biased when the model is estimated on average occupational characteristics, though this should not affect the qualitative results from the model.

Table 1 reproduces TSL estimates for women and men from the 1972–80 General Social Survey data, as analyzed in Logan (1996b). Five occupational categories are used in the models: professional; managerial; clerical and service; manufacturing blue collar; and other blue collar. Unemployment, defined here as the state of being without a formal job, is a sixth outcome category. In the models shown, workers rate employers by the prestige and autonomy of offered jobs, and employers rate workers by years of education, age and race (non-white = 1). The estimates use the mean prestige and autonomy in occupational categories as data on the employers, and individual-level measures on the workers. In addition to the preference coefficients appearing in the preceding equations, the TSL method estimates employer-specific intercept terms, β_{j0}, centered here to represent the tendencies of employers to hire white workers with average values of education and age. The asterisks indicate the strengths of evidence for particular coefficients according to the BIC criterion described in Raftery (1995).

Panel A of Table 1 shows estimates of the preferences of men and women for job prestige and autonomy (as measured by occupational category means). The implication of the estimates is that, in the 1970s, women preferred autonomy more than prestige, by comparison with the pattern seen for men. The preference coefficients of autonomy for women and men were .143 and .034 respec-

tively, while the coefficients of prestige were .037 and .099.[3]

Panel B of Table 1 presents estimates of the preferences of employers hiring in each of the five occupational categories. As might be expected, employers in different categories appear to differ in their preferences, with professional and managerial employers strongly valuing education, for example, while manufacturing blue-collar employers show a distaste either for formal education itself or for some quality of workers which covaries with education. Only employers of male managers show strong preferences regarding age or race. Age is valued as a characteristic of managers, perhaps because experience and/or accumulated financial capital is a prerequisite for many jobs. However, non-white race is a property of workers which employers of managers seem strongly to avoid. Logan (1996b) discusses these results in more detail, giving several specific meanings which can be attached to the magnitudes of the estimates.

Depiction of Rational Choice

This section considers how the model just described corresponds to a standard rational-choice framework. As Hechter (1994) observed, rational-choice theory involves both objective and subjective components from the point of view of the actor. The objective component is a set of external constraints on the actor's choices, while the subjective component is the actor's utility, which determines his/her preferences among alternatives. Actors may value either instrumental or immanent goods in choosing among alternatives, instrumental goods being means for obtaining other things which are valued for themselves, the immanent goods. When the rational-choice model is considered in this basic form, the provision that actors may value immanent goods allows for the possibility that such non-economic influences as norms, habits, traditions and value-rational motives may be important influences on the choices of alternatives, regardless of market values.

TABLE 1
Two-sided Logit Estimates of Employers' and Workers' Preferences (1972–80 General Social Survey)

A. Workers' preferences for job characteristics (α coefficients):

	Women (N = 2632)	Men (N = 2149)
Prestige	.037**	.099**
	(5.22)	(9.95)
Autonomy	.143**	.034
	(11.64)	(3.21)

B. Employers' preferences for worker characteristics (β coefficients):

	Women (N = 2632)					Men (N = 2149)				
	Prof.	Mgmt.	Clerical/ Service	Mfg. Blue	Other Blue	Prof.	Mgmt.	Clerical/ Service	Mfg. Blue	Other Blue
Intercept	-2.605**	-2.570**	.304	-.174	-3.078**	-1.831**	-6.22**	-5.24*	1.123	1.011
	(15.87)	(20.19)	(1.86)	(0.47)	(18.41)	(15.82)	(5.10)	(4.02)	(2.23)	(3.56)
Education	.988**	.228**	.242*	-1.068**	-.140	.674**	.349**	.138	-.735**	-.449**
	(12.23)	(5.46)	(4.19)	(4.25)	(2.59)	(14.87)	(9.91)	(3.21)	(4.58)	(4.64)
Age	.011	.036	.011	.007	.005	.027	.091**	-.005	.032	.007
	(0.65)	(2.05)	(0.81)	(0.16)	(0.21)	(1.87)	(6.64)	(0.28)	(0.69)	(0.20)
Non-white	.214	-1.155	.723	1.382	.174	-.529	-1.570**	.096	-.228	-.819
	(0.72)	(-2.46)	(2.82)	(1.19)	(0.45)	(1.90)	(5.02)	(0.36)	(0.39)	(2.15)

Notes: Absolute values of t = (est./s.e.) in parentheses. * = strong evidence of effect: $|t| > \sqrt{(\ln N + 6)}$; ** = very strong evidence: $|t| > \sqrt{(\ln N + 10)}$.
Source: Logan (1996b).

However, in most empirical applications, Hechter says, this threefold determination of choice by constraints, immanent values and instrumental values is radically simplified through 'the typical value assumption' of rational-choice theory. The assumption is that actors value alternatives on the basis of instrumental goods, such as money, which may then be exchanged for immanent goods of intrinsic value. The power of this assumption lies in the fact that all actors may plausibly be held to value all instrumental (but not all immanent) goods positively and equally, since by definition they can be exchanged for immanent goods. This granted, it becomes unnecessary to measure the common value placed on instrumental goods, and rational-choice models may be expressed as functions of constraints only, a great simplification over the fundamental threefold model. Hechter lists several fruitful branches of applied rational-choice theory which he says rely on this reduction, and also considers circumstances which may undercut or support it use. He does not consider the possibility of applied rational-choice models which preserve the threefold structure.

Imposing assumptions such as the typical value assumption is a primary means by which strong rational-choice *theories* are derived from the basic rational-choice framework. Such strong assumptions are undoubtedly sometimes necessary to simplify deductions and generate predictions. However, the typical value assumption is nothing less than the assertion that *everything is for sale,* since only if all immanent goods can be obtained through exchanges for instrumental goods will the assumption be persuasive. This may seem close enough to reality for the economist, but gives pause to the sociologist.

The TSL model is less a theory of occupational attainment, something obtained by making restrictive assumptions on the basic framework, than an attempt to translate the framework into an estimable model directly. This is not to say that no assumptions are ultimately required for estimation, but that the model mathematically represents the independent contributions of constraints, immanent values and instrumental values. The assumptions needed for estimation arise from data and computational requirements but do not reduce the threefold framework of rational choice to a single principle.

Constraints on choice in the TSL model can be considered from either the worker's or the employer's side of the model. For the worker, constraints are imposed by the choices of employers not to make certain jobs available. The model of these constraints is given in the combination of equations (1) and (2) implied by decision rule (3). Both exogenous market forces, m_j, and the characteristics of the worker him/herself, x_i^*, help determine the constraints the worker faces. On the other hand, from the employer's side of the model it is the decisions of workers which create constraints on hiring. These constraints are affected by the characteristics of the employer's offered job, z_j, as well as by workers' preferences, α_i, as equation (4) shows. The constraints each side faces are therefore functions in part of the other side's preferences.

Unlike models making the typical value assumption, TSL allows the preferences of workers and employers to be functions of any mix of characteristics of the alternatives, whether instrumental or immanent, or both. The example in Table 1 shows just such a mix. Prestige, as Hechter specifically mentions, may be considered an instrumental good, at least in part, since it can be used to obtain other goods. Autonomy, by contrast, is an immanent good, something to be enjoyed on the job, but not to be exchanged in another context for a different good.

Employers derive instrumental goods from their employees indirectly, in the form of increased production. To the extent that certain properties of workers increase production, they have instrumental value. Education may be such a property. But other properties of workers, such as congeniality in the work situation or racial or ethnic similarity to present workers, may have little instrumental or production value, and be valued instead primarily as immanent goods. Education and race, arguably instrumental and immanent properties, appear together in the model of Table 1.

Asking what the TSL model would look like if the typical value assumption were imposed may help clarify the issue. Say, then, that it is decided that to a useful approximation all workers prefer jobs according to their instrumental characteristics; this would drop autonomy from the model as irrelevant a priori. Then, if it is further held that the value placed on instrumental characteristics is common to all workers, there is no need to estimate a coefficient for prestige (or other instrumental characteristics). Instead, the occupational categories could be ranked in unambiguous ascending order by their average instrumental utilities. Equation (4) would disappear, replaced conceptually by the proviso that all workers prefer higher utility occupations according to the universally shared ranking. Under this condition, the TSL model can be shown to reduce mathematically to a sequential logit model (Logan 1996b). Only the firms' preferences in equations (1) and (2) would affect the attainment of workers, and their effects would be as constraints on workers' choices, which to the workers would appear objective.

No statistical model, TSL included, seems capable of distinguishing the mode of valuation by data analysis alone, that is, whether a particular characteristic has instrumental or immanent value to the actor. The best TSL can do is to detect the relative influences of measured characteristics on matching behavior, leaving it for the analyst to interpret which values are instrumental and which immanent, as earlier.

In summary, TSL is a relatively complete representation of rational choice in the occupational attainment situation, containing the three fundamental elements described by Hechter. TSL's two-sided approach contains a duality between constraints and preferences, so that one side's preferences become the other side's constraints. It is only while looking at the choice situation from the point of view of a particular side that constraints seem purely objective.

Notes

1. Strictly speaking, (2) is only a utility when $s_j = 0$, since a non-zero s_j represents no actual increment to the baseline utility. However, I will refer to (2) as a utility whether or not $s_j = 0$, for convenience.

2. The key assumptions are that the disturbances are independent across firms and workers, and that they have type I extreme value (Gumbel) distributions. See Logan (1996b) for details.

3. The coefficients are interpreted more concretely as the log-odds that a unit difference in the value of a job characteristic will produce a concordant difference in a worker's rankings of two otherwise similar opportunities.

References

Hechter, Michael. 1994. 'The Role of Values in Rational Choice Theory.' *Rationality and Society* 6: 318–33.

Logan, John Allen. 1996a. 'Estimation of Two-sided Logit Models. Working Paper 96–07, Center for Demography and Ecology, University of Wisconsin, Madison.

———. 1996b. 'Opportunity and Choice in a Socially Structured Labor Market.' *American Journal of Sociology.*

Raftery, Adrian E. 1995. 'Bayesian Model Selection in Social Research.' In *Sociological Methodology 1995*, ed. Peter V. Marsden, 111–63. Cambridge, MA: Basil Blackwell.

ROBERT D. MARE

Observations on the Study of Social Mobility and Inequality[1]

Although classical discussions of social mobility focused on the macro-level connections among mobility, social inequality, and the potential for society-wide class conflict (e.g., Sorokin [this volume]), modern mobility research tends to dwell on an important but more limited set of individual-level relationships. How rigid is the connection between social origins and destinations, and how does this vary across time and place? Who gets ahead in the world of work? What mechanisms link social statuses and positions early in life to those that come later? The readings in this section illustrate some of the key approaches to questions of this sort. They cover well-established lines of investigation of occupational mobility and the process of socioeconomic attainment, as well as new work on social networks, the dynamics of poverty, and models of rational action. A main line of development during the past 20 years has been the growth of "structural" approaches to stratification, which attempt to break away from abstract occupational categories and single-dimensional approaches to work hierarchies. These contributions are based on empirically grounded categories of social class that stress the authority position of work roles (Wright 1997; Erikson and Goldthorpe [this volume]); classifications of work roles by labor market sector (e.g., Piore [this volume];

Doeringer and Piore 1971); taxonomies of work governed by the types of organizations where it is done (e.g., Baron and Bielby 1980, 1984); more detailed examinations of occupations (Sørensen and Grusky, 1996); models of how social mobility depends on job vacancies in organizations (Sørensen and Kalleberg [this volume]; White 1970) or in the economy as a whole (Keyfitz 1973; Sørensen 1977); and models of how workers and employers are matched (Mortensen 1988; Logan [this volume]). (See Baron 1994 for a more thorough review of these developments.)

Given our abiding curiosity about who gets ahead and the fairness of the process, the centrality of work to most adult lives, and the fundamental role of the economy in society, politics, and culture, it is understandable that stratification research emphasizes the labor market, including its rewards, institutions, and formal and informal organization. Yet this emphasis, by itself, leads to an incomplete view of how social stratification and inequality are generated. This essay focuses on aspects of social mobility and inequality not emphasized in other articles in this section. I first discuss other key institutions of stratification on which substantial research relevant to mobility and inequality has been done and then sketch an agenda for future work that I believe will enrich our understanding of how inequality is generated. In so doing I argue for (1) a richer form of institutional analysis of

---

This is an original article prepared for this book.

stratification that focuses on families and households, schooling, and spatially structured hierarchies at the local, national, and global levels; (2) the development of more sophisticated models of human behavior related to stratification as it unfolds in these institutional settings; and (3) the development of dynamic models that link these two levels of analysis.

Other Institutions of Stratification

At the most elementary level, to focus exclusively on work institutions and economic mobility overlooks the stratification of the large nonworking part of the population, including (1) children and teenagers; (2) "working-age" persons who do not hold jobs because they are homekeepers, caregivers, students, disabled, incarcerated, independently affluent, or simply unable to find work; and (3) retired persons who are past the conventional working age. Although some of these persons are linked to the labor market because they worked recently or because of family ties to a worker, many have no connection to work organizations and live entirely outside of the processes of occupational mobility. Additionally, to focus on labor markets is to overlook how other institutions, such as families and schools, generate stratification in ways that are more complex than simply affecting the resources that individuals bring to the labor market (see below). A further consequence of focusing on the labor market is that we tend to regard stratification as fundamentally about the movement and distributions of individuals, even when we acknowledge the causal importance of the structure of labor markets, jobs, and social networks (Baron 1994). This reflects our preoccupation with our own epoch, in which jobs belong to individuals, rather than families, neighborhoods, or other communal units. Although these supra-individual units cannot be employed, they can nonetheless be stratified, and their structural features may have substantial effects on stratification. Indeed, because they

"survive" beyond the lifetimes of biological individuals, these units, in concert with work institutions, maintain and transform systems of inequality. I elaborate on these observations below by considering in turn two institutions, families and schools, that play an especially important role in stratification systems.

Families, Households, and Social Stratification

In most empirical studies of social mobility and attainment, "family background" is viewed as a multidimensional index of individuals' resources or statuses at an early stage of life and is derived from measurements of their parents' characteristics. Family relationships are typically measured at the individual level and viewed as a personal trait rather than an aspect of social structure. Yet this emphasis minimizes the ways in which family demography and organization are interdependent with social stratification. Consider the following connections between family and stratification:

1. The size and structure of the family of orientation affect educational and occupational attainment, even among families with similar socioeconomic characteristics. Children's school performance and ultimate educational attainment vary inversely with sibship size in most societies, presumably because per capita resources are scarcer in large families (Blau and Duncan 1967; Blake 1989; but see Shavit and Pierce 1991). Parents also affect their offspring through the *timing* of fertility: offspring born to older parents go farther in school than those born to younger parents (Mare and Tzeng 1989). Family structure, as defined by the number of parents present in a household, also affects offsprings' educational attainments and other outcomes in early adult life (e.g., McLanahan and Sandefur 1994). Children raised by single mothers fare worse than children raised in two-parent families. The effect of fathers' so-

cioeconomic characteristics on the success of their sons may also be weakened in single-mother households inasmuch as absent fathers make less of a difference to the socioeconomic standing of the household than those who are present. Finally, depending on the strength of kin relationships, adult relatives such as grandparents or fathers-in-law may affect the socioeconomic success of young persons. The evidence for grandparent effects on achievement is largely negative for the contemporary United States (e.g., Warren and Hauser 1997), but one can envision rules of inheritance in which such effects may be important. In Brazil, fathers-in-law exert a substantial influence on the economic success of their sons-in-law, even when the characteristics of fathers are controlled (Lam and Schoeni 1993).

2. The association between the socioeconomic characteristics of parents and offspring is just one out of a large number of possible socioeconomic associations between pairs of kin, which include siblings, spouses, individuals and their parents-in-law, parents and parents-in-law, cousins, and grandparents and grandchildren. Although the association between the socioeconomic characteristics of each of these kin pairs contains information about the possible "transmission" of status from one family member to another or the socioeconomic "barriers" within the population, each association also depends on the strength and meaning of the kin relationship. The association between father's and son's occupation, for example, is a measure of the rigidity of the social stratification system, but it also reflects the general strength of the bond between father and son. In populations in which many boys live apart from their fathers for some of their childhood, the association between father's and son's occupation may be weaker than in populations in which two-parent households are universal (Biblarz and Raftery 1993). Likewise, variation in educational homogamy between husbands and wives reflects, to some degree, variation in the social barriers to marriage across educational lines, but it also may result from variation in the meaning, organization, and timing of

marriages (Oppenheimer 1988; Mare 1991). When comparing socioeconomic associations between kin across societies or over time, it is important to realize that the rigidity of systems of stratification is affected in part by the strength of kin ties, which may in turn be affected by demographic and cultural factors normally viewed as outside of social stratification per se. By the same token, the rigidity of social stratification, as indicated by the association between the socioeconomic characteristics of kin, may have a large effect on bonds of kinship more generally.

3. Social mobility research emphasizes the roles of individuals as economic producers. Yet we should consider the distribution of resources among consumer units as well. (See Szelényi [this volume] for a fuller discussion of units of analysis in stratification.) Inasmuch as consumption is carried out in households, trends in income and consumption distribution must be assessed, at least in part, at the household level, the unequal distribution of resources within families and households notwithstanding (e.g., Karoly 1994; Lazear and Michael 1988; Mayer and Jencks 1993). This suggests that we should broaden mobility research to include movement among poverty, income, or consumption strata at the family or household level (e.g., Musick and Mare 1999). Yet the formation of families and households is not exogenous to the social mobility process. Decisions about when to leave the parental home; whether, when, and whom to marry; how many children to have; and, in older ages, with whom to live are interdependent with socioeconomic success and mobility (as well as the network of available kin and friends). Socioeconomic success or failure often cause individuals to form or dissolve couples, families, or households. In short, our units of analysis in the study of stratification may be created by the very processes that we seek to understand. Despite the good efforts of social scientists to unravel this puzzle, few clear solutions to these problems have been found.

4. It is families rather than individuals that provide demographic continuity of social

stratification from one generation to the next. In the occupational mobility table, the distribution of sons' or daughters' occupations measures the occupational structure for a well-defined population at a particular time. Because parents are known only by the offspring who report on them, however, the distribution of parents' occupations has no clear time or population reference. The distribution of fathers' occupations depends on both a sequence of occupation distributions that existed at a variety of times in the past and on differentials in level and timing of fertility across occupation groups (Duncan 1966). Thus the family backgrounds of individuals are created by both the socioeconomic levels of parents and a set of decisions about whom to marry (which establish the distribution of father's and mother's socioeconomic characteristics), how many children to have (which establish sibship size), and whether to remain married (which establish family and household structure). The stratification scholar should therefore bear in mind that socioeconomic reproduction combines intergenerational social mobility with demographic reproduction, including differential fertility, fertility timing, mortality, assortative mating, and family stability (for example, Mare 1997a; 1997b; Musick and Mare 1998).

Educational Stratification

As Blau and Duncan (1967) illustrate in their "Basic Model" of stratification, educational attainment is a pivotal mechanism governing social mobility and socioeconomic attainment. It is the first socioeconomic "outcome" for a cohort of persons entering adulthood and a key determinant of later success in the labor market. The importance of educational stratification and the socioeconomic "returns" to schooling is twofold. First, in most societies, variation in educational attainment accounts for a large part of the association between the socioeconomic characteristics of parents and their offspring. That is, schooling "transmits" most of the effect of family background on later socioeconomic achievement.

Second, however, the moderate-sized correlations between social background and education on the one hand and between education and occupational or earnings attainment on the other imply that education introduces substantial variation in socioeconomic attainment that cannot merely be reduced to variation in family backgrounds. This interpretation of the role of schooling applies irrespective of how it actually affects economic standing, whether through the accumulation of human capital (Becker 1962), through socialization for the workplace (Bowles and Gintis 1976), through a "signal" of otherwise hidden potential productivity (Spence 1974), or through the establishment of a queue that, for whatever reason, employers use to match workers to positions (e.g., Thurow 1975; Sørensen 1977).

In Blau and Duncan's model, educational attainment is viewed as a status, the cumulation of an individual's educational experience. The schooling process, however, in fact comprises a series of transitions between successive levels of schooling that are structured by the family, peer group, school, labor market, and cultural influences that may change while an individual remains in school (Mare 1980; 1981). This view is implicit in the distinction between sponsored and contest mobility systems, which differ essentially in whether students are selected (by social class or ability) early or late in the schooling process (Turner [this volume]). It is also the empirical counterpart to behavioral models of decisions about whether to continue in school (Breen and Goldthorpe [this volume]; Breen 2000). By viewing schooling as a series of transitions (e.g., attendance in high school given completion of elementary school, high school graduation given high school attendance), one can see which stages of schooling depend most on socioeconomic background and at which stages intercohort changes in socioeconomic effects occur (Mare 1980; 1981).

Analyses of school transitions also show how the effects of family background on total educational attainment may decline over time because of (1) secular growth in educational attainment, combined with (2) a tendency for the effects of parents' socioeconomic characteristics to be weaker at later stages of schooling. These two empirical tendencies, taken together, imply that growing fractions of birth cohorts face transitions that are only weakly dependent on social origins (Mare 1981). This approach is especially suited to the cross-national comparison of systems that may vary in the meaning of total years completed but nonetheless make broadly comparable institutional distinctions, such as those among primary, secondary, and post-secondary schooling (Shavit and Blossfeld 1993; Rijken 1999). Breen and Jonsson (in press) extend the analysis of school transitions to nations that have multidimensional educational hierarchies (e.g., Sweden) in which students make transitions within and between parallel academic and vocational streams.

The analysis of school transitions also leads to a reappraisal of how parents' educational attainments affect those of their offspring. In contrast to the linear relationships between parents' and offsprings' schooling in Blau and Duncan's model, families may try to ensure that children go *at least* as far as their parents, implying that parental educational attainment constitutes a threshold for the attainment of offspring. The avoidance of downward educational mobility is central to Breen and Goldthorpe's [this volume] model of educational decision making. Whether parents have completed a particular school transition does in fact strongly affect whether their offspring make that transition, over and above the effect of parents' level of completed schooling (Mare and Chang 1998).[2]

The Future of Stratification Research

Many breakthroughs in stratification research have resulted from innovative adaptation of technical methods that refine and expand the purview of the field and lead to superior formulation of research questions. Examples of these innovations include log-linear models,

which make it possible to operationalize the distinction between absolute and relative rates of occupational mobility; structural equation models, which elucidate the causal pathways by which family, school, and labor market experiences are connected; event history methods, which reveal the time dependence of socioeconomic events and statuses; and multilevel analyses, which clarify the interdependent causal processes that occur among individuals, families, neighborhoods, schools, or nations. Innovation in stratification research also comes from major social changes, such as women's increased participation in the paid labor force, the rapid growth in single-parent households, the fall of communism in Eastern Europe, and the emergence of private markets in China. These developments spawn the revision of empirical models of mobility, attainment, and inequality (e.g., Bernhardt, Morris, and Handcock 1995; McLanahan and Sandefur 1994; Róna-Tas 1994; Walder, Li, and Treiman 2000). Future innovations in stratification research, including the ones called for in the remaining sections of this essay, are also likely to come from both technical innovation and ongoing social change. As shall be evident, the suggestions that follow also reflect the view that progress in the field requires attending not only to the institutional forces at work, but additionally to the role of human agency (i.e., purposive behavior) as it plays out in the context of these institutional constraints.

Agency and Endogeneity in Behavioral and Statistical Models

The emphasis in sociological research on mobility and inequality has been to describe stratification phenomena in demographic and social structural terms and to eschew models of human agency. In our standard models, individuals are not viewed as purposive agents, but rather as passive beings, heavily constrained by socializing agents, social networks, and large-scale forces. By virtue of this passive conception of human behavior, the causal ordering of variables is assumed to follow their temporal order (e.g., family and schooling factors are causes of occupational status or earnings), and structural positions are assumed to cause individual attitudes, behaviors, and resources (e.g., labor market sector is a cause of earnings). These simplifying causal assumptions work hand in hand with the assumed lack of purposive behavior. Purposive behavior, in contrast, creates the possibility that events or statuses that are realized in a temporal sequence may in fact be jointly determined by prior decisions. Likewise, it creates the possibility that individuals choose (or self-select into) structural positions because of the anticipated benefits connected to those positions.

These issues are pervasive in the analysis of socioeconomic achievement. Consider two examples:

1. A large estimated negative effect of sibship size on educational attainment is almost universal. That sibship size is usually fixed well before a young person leaves school makes it appear that size of sibship is a cause of educational attainment, if by "cause" one means that an intervention to lower average family size would, *ceteris paribus*, raise average levels of education. But an alternative interpretation is that, when women or couples plan their fertility, they take account of their expectations about the kinds of costs they will bear and investments they will make in their children. In the parlance of family economics, they make a "quality-quantity tradeoff" in balancing their level of fertility with the advantages that they will provide their children (Becker 1991; Caldwell, Reddy, and Caldwell 1988). By this interpretation, basic stratification models must be revised to allow for the joint determination of sibship size and offspring's education.

2. Perhaps the most extensively studied relationship in social science is the effect of educational attainment on earnings or wages. Whether schooling embodies human capital or is merely a signal to employers of otherwise hidden attributes of workers, it is typi-

cally assumed that, at the margin, positive increments to schooling raise the wages of workers. Yet linear models of the effect of education on earnings may give misleading estimates of the economic return to schooling. If individuals decide whether to continue in school with expectations about the wages that alternative amounts of schooling will bring, then educational attainment and wage are *jointly* determined and their relationship can only be correctly assessed by models that take school decision making, expected wages, and ultimate wages into account (Willis and Rosen 1979). Similar issues arise in the relationship between academic tracking and student achievement (Gamoran and Mare 1989) and between labor market sector or occupation and earnings (Cain 1976; Sakamoto and Chen 1991). Each of these relationships raises hard questions of behavioral theory and model specification for which standard statistical approaches do not suffice. For the purpose of describing the joint distributions of socioeconomic variables, these problems can often be ignored. To understand the causal mechanisms that underpin stratification at the individual level, however, more sophisticated structural models must be developed.

The largest obstacle to model development in sociology is the absence of well-developed theories of human behavior. Absent strong theoretical assumptions, it is usually impossible to make much headway on estimating complex relationships among stratification variables. Within economics, the assumption of utility maximization guides the development and estimation of models for intergenerational processes, family decision making, and income determination (Becker 1991). For good reasons, however, few sociologists are willing to accept these models uncritically. Instead, insofar as sociologists acknowledge the role of purposive action and its consequences for empirical research on stratification, they tend to adopt more informal approaches (e.g., Gamoran and Mare 1989). Although this is preferable to ignoring purposive behavior altogether, it is questionable how far one can go in the absence of stronger theory. One promising line of work, which eschews theories based on utility maximization but provides a formal structure for the interpretation of market phenomena, is empirical models for two-sided matching processes (Roth and Sotomayer 1990). Logan (this volume; 1996a; 1996b) proposes statistical models for matching workers to jobs. These models represent the mutually restrictive effects of employer preferences on the behavior of workers and worker preferences on the behavior of employers, show how worker characteristics are rewarded in the market and how the characteristics of jobs attract workers, and lead to a substantially revised assessment of how labor market structure affects achievement. The power of these models derives from the assumption that job-worker matches are approximately in equilibrium, which implies that workers and employers strive to make the best match that they can, but not necessarily one that maximizes an assumed utility function. These models have broad potential applicability to stratification phenomena, including intergenerational and intragenerational occupational mobility, assortative mating, ethnic competition in the labor market, and educational stratification.

Spatial Issues in Mobility and Inequality

The field would also profit from exploring how spatially structured hierarchies at the local, national, and global levels provide the context within which such purposive behavior plays out. At the dawn of the current era of stratification research analysts turned away from local community studies and focused instead on national systems of mobility and inequality. Assuming that individuals were not confined by local hierarchies and mobility opportunities, researchers obtained national-level data with measurements that followed, as far as possible, national statistical agency guidelines (Pfautz and Duncan 1950; Blau and Duncan 1967). The contextual properties and even the identity of regions and local communities became marginal to the main line of mobility investigation and, when these factors were recognized, they were inevitably treated as exogenous "background" characteristics of individuals. These nation-level studies have been conducted in many countries, thereby permitting relatively systematic cross-national comparisons and multilevel investigations of processes at both the nation and individual levels (Treiman and Ganzeboom 1999). These developments have crystallized into paradigmatic spatial assumptions of contemporary stratification research, namely, that subnational geographic variation is of minor importance to stratification, geography may affect individuals and societies but only as an exogenous factor, nation states define the boundaries of stratification systems, and nation states are independent cases in comparative analysis.

As useful as these simplifying assumptions may have been for the development of national and comparative research, they should be reassessed. Economic globalization implies that national labor markets are increasingly interdependent. International migration of labor, often tied to the prospects for socioeconomic mobility in both origin and destination countries, creates demographic links between national systems of stratification. These developments undermine the assumptions that nations are independent entities and that nation of residence is exogenous to the process of social stratification. Although nations are becoming increasingly interdependent, some are, de facto or de jure, also splitting up. The breakups of the Soviet Union and Czechoslovakia are obvious examples, but geographically concentrated minorities in other nations, such as Canada or Spain, often advocate some form of (spatial) separatism. We need, therefore, a more flexible approach to the definition of geographic units. Whether research conclusions are robust to alternative assumptions about geographic boundaries and national interdependencies should be topics for empirical research rather than fixed assumptions.

We can also benefit from the reincorporation of space into the analysis of single societies. A substantial literature explores the possibility of "neighborhood effects" on individual socioeconomic outcomes (e.g., Jencks and Mayer 1990). Although the effects of neighborhoods reported in this literature are often weak or poorly specified, geographic location is nonetheless highly relevant to social stratification. In recent decades in the United States, residential segregation among socioeconomic groups has increased (Jargowsky 1997), suggesting a stronger interdependence of residential mobility and social mobility at the individual level and neighborhood segregation and inequality at the population level (Quillian 1999). The links among these phenomena, however, are not well understood. Studies of social mobility and attainment, of neighborhood effects, of residential mobility, and of residential segregation occupy largely distinct literatures. Empirical and theoretical research that attempts to elucidate the links among these processes has the potential of revealing important mechanisms through which inequality is generated.

From Micro-Level to Macro-Level Processes of Stratification and Inequality

The final and most ambitious agenda for the field involves developing models that specify how micro-level processes and behavior are parlayed into macro-level stratificational change. Much contemporary mobility research involves little more than micro-level accounting for the success and failure of individuals in the labor market, even when researchers give primacy to macro-level organizational, network, and market mechanisms. By its very nature, this type of research, taken alone, cannot tell us much about how and why systems of stratification are maintained and evolve. Nor can it reveal much about the determinants of inequality, an inherently aggregate concept. A partial exception to these generalizations is studies that analyze system-

atic variations across countries and over time in social mobility and the process of socioeconomic attainment (Treiman and Ganzeboom 1999). Yet despite the concern of comparative scholars with change in stratification systems, they are typically guided by general propositions, such as those linking industrialization and stratification, that discriminate poorly between cross-section and temporal variation (Treiman 1970). The resulting studies typically do not examine how the stratification process itself may affect other societal-level conditions, and they treat macro-level influences as empirically separate from and irreducible to the behavior and characteristics of individuals. As a result, these studies pay scant attention to the *dynamics* of change in stratification or inequality; that is, they are exercises in comparative statics, rather than efforts to elucidate the ways in which an existing regime of stratification may hold the seeds of transformation into a subsequent regime. This limitation of comparative studies arises, in part, because the process of socioeconomic attainment, as typically conceived, is not a closed system; technological, political, and demographic factors impinge on stratification in ways that we typically regard as exogenous rather than as consequences of past regimes of mobility and inequality alone. This limitation also arises because we have a very weak understanding of the dynamics of stratification systems.

One limited attempt to embed social mobility within a dynamic context is the study of demographic and socioeconomic reproduction. This is an effort to account for changes in the distributions of socioeconomic characteristics through the use of models of renewal in heterogeneous populations, combined with information on intergenerational mobility across social strata (e.g, Kremer 1997; Mare 1997a; 1997b; Preston and Campbell 1993). These models elucidate the mechanisms through which social mobility and demographic processes—including differential fertility, mortality, marriage, and immigration—may effect changes in socioeconomic hierarchies. They also provide an explicit link between the behaviors of individuals and aggregate features of populations. The limitation of these models, however, is that they are narrow in scope and, in their current state of development, ill-suited to the analysis of the effects of market constraints, technology, and work organization. Nonetheless, they illustrate the sort of analysis that will be needed if we are to understand the dynamics of stratification and inequality.

From Social Mobility to Social Inequality

The classical motivation for mobility studies (e.g., Sorokin [this volume]) involved tracing out connections between social mobility and social inequality. I am thus suggesting a return to this concern and correspondingly increased appreciation that social mobility and social inequality are linked by a welter of conceptual and empirical relationships. Consider, for example, the following:

1. When inequality is high, there is much more at stake in the study of mobility than when inequality is low.
2. The pattern of social inequality may influence rates of mobility: For example, when many persons are self-employed and hence have substantial capital investments in their job, intergenerational mobility may be lower than when most persons work for wages (Simkus 1984).
3. The impact of inequality on people's lives and their likely response to inequality depends on whether they regard their positions in the stratification system as more or less permanent (Sombart [1903]1976; Sorokin [this volume]; Sibley 1942).
4. Mobility itself may change inequality through supply and demand in the labor market. When a change in mobility patterns affects the relative numbers of workers trained for various positions, the relative wages of these skill groups may change and, in turn, change employers' demands for workers of varying types and the resulting job and wage distributions (Freeman 1971; 1976).
5. Intragenerational job and wage mobility may affect earnings inequality through the creation of "transitory" variance in earnings (versus the variance in workers' "permanent" earnings). Inequality in earnings at any time is greater in markets where workers make frequent moves than in markets with limited labor mobility (Gottschalk and Moffit 1994).

The articles in this section do not attend adequately to relationships of the foregoing sort. In view of the interdependence of mobility and inequality, not to mention the dramatic and poorly understood growth in inequality in Western industrial societies during the past quarter century (Levy and Murnane 1992; Morris and Western 1999), one hopes that future stratification studies will redress this imbalance.

The scientific understanding of stratification will grow if we take a broad view of the institutional and demographic mechanisms that govern mobility and inequality, welcome new efforts to blend formal behavioral theories with empirical analysis, think flexibly about the ways that spatial relations create and reflect inequalities, and look for ways to study the dynamic relationships between individual behavior and the characteristics of populations and institutions. This is a tall order, but we must face these challenges if we are to move beyond the question of who gets ahead to the broader issue of how systems of social mobility and inequality are generated.

Notes

1. David Grusky, Judith Seltzer, and Donald Treiman made very helpful comments on an earlier draft of this essay. This work was supported by the John D. and Catherine T. MacArthur Foundation and by the Council on Research of the UCLA Academic Senate.

2. Space limitations preclude discussion of the various ways in which social stratification also occurs within schools. Academic tracking, for example, can broaden or narrow pre-existing inequalities in academic achievement among students and thus affect variation in ultimate educational attainment (e.g., Gamoran and Mare 1989; Kerckhoff 1993).

References

Baron, James N. 1994. "Reflections on Recent Generations of Mobility Research." Pages 384–93 in *Social Stratification: Class, Race, and Gender in Sociological Perspective,* edited by D. B. Grusky. Boulder, CO: Westview Press.

Baron, James N., and William T. Bielby. 1980. "Bringing the Firms Back In: Stratification, Segmentation, and the Organization of Work." *American Sociological Review* 45:737–65.

Baron, James N., and William T. Bielby. 1984. "The Organization of Work in a Segmented Economy." *American Sociological Review* 49:454–73.

Becker, Gary S. 1962. "Investment in Human Capital: A Theoretical Analysis." *Journal of Political Economy* 70 (Supplement):9–49.

Becker, Gary S. 1991. *A Treatise on the Family.* Cambridge: Harvard University Press.

Bernhardt, Annette, Martina Morris, and Mark S. Handcock. 1995. "Women's Gains or Men's Losses? A Closer Look at the Shrinking Gender Gap in Earnings." *American Journal of Sociology* 101:302–28.

Biblarz, Timothy J., and Adrian E. Raftery. 1993. "The Effects of Family Disruption on Social Mobility." *American Sociological Review* 58:97–109.

Blake, Judith. 1989. *Family Size and Achievement.* Berkeley: University of California Press.

Blau, Peter M., and Otis Dudley Duncan. 1967. *The American Occupational Structure.* New York: Wiley.

Bowles, Samuel, and Herbert Gintis. 1976. *Schooling in Capitalist America.* New York: Basic Books.

Breen, Richard. 2000. "A Rational Choice/Bayesian Learning Model of Educational Inequality." Paper presented to the meetings of the Research Committee on Social Stratification of the International Sociological Association (RC 28), Libourne, France.

Breen, Richard, and John H. Goldthorpe. 1997. "Explaining Educational Differentials: Toward a Formal Theory of Rational Action." *Rationality and Society* 9:275–306.

Breen, Richard, and Jan O. Jonsson. In press. "A Multinomial Transition Model for Analyzing Educational Careers." *American Sociological Review.*

Cain, Glen G. 1976. "The Challenge of Segmented Labor Market Theories to Orthodox Theory." *Journal of Economic Literature* 12:1215–57.

Caldwell, John C., P. H. Reddy, and Pat Caldwell. 1988. *The Causes of Demographic Change: Experimental Research in South India.* Madison: University of Wisconsin Press.

Doeringer, P. B, and M. J. Piore. 1971. *Internal Labor Markets and Manpower Analysis.* Lexington, MA: D. C. Heath.

Duncan, Otis Dudley. 1966. "Methodological Issues in the Analysis of Social Mobility." Pages 51–97 in *Social Structure and Mobility in Economic Development,* edited by N. J. Smelser and S. M. Lipset. Chicago: Aldine.

Erikson, Robert, and John H. Goldthorpe. 1992. *The Constant Flux.* New York: Clarendon Press Oxford.

Freeman, Richard B. 1971. *The Labor Market for College-Trained Manpower.* Cambridge: Harvard University Press.

Freeman, Richard B. 1976. *The Overeducated American.* New York: Academic Press.

Gamoran, A., and Robert D. Mare. 1989. "Secondary School Tracking and Stratification: Compensation, Reinforcement, or Neutrality?" *American Journal of Sociology* 94:1146–83.

Gottschalk, Peter, and Robert Moffitt. 1994. "The Growth of Earnings Instability in the U.S. Labor Market." *Brookings Papers on Economic Activity* 2:217–72.

Jargowsky, Paul A. 1997. *Poverty and Place: Ghettos, Barrios, and the American City.* New York: Russell Sage Foundation.

Jencks, Christopher, and Susan E. Mayer. 1990. "The Social Consequences of Growing up in a Poor Neighborhood." In *Inner City Poverty in the United States,* edited by Laurence E. Lynn, Jr. and Michael G. H. McGeary. Washington, DC: National Academy Press.

Karoly, Lynn A. 1994. "The Trend in Inequality Among Families, Individuals, and Workers in the United States: A Twenty-Five Year Perspective." Pages 19–97 in *Uneven Tides: Rising Inequality in America,* edited by S. Danziger and P. Gottschalk. New York: Russell Sage Foundation.

Kerckhoff, Alan C. 1993. *Diverging Pathways: Social Structure and Career Deflections.* Cambridge: Cambridge University Press.

Keyfitz, Nathan. 1973. "Individual Mobility in a Stationary Population." *Population Studies* 27:335–52.

Kremer, Michael. 1997. "How Much Does Sorting Increase Inequality?" *Quarterly Journal of Economics* 112:115–39.

Lam, David, and Robert F. Schoeni. 1993. "Effects of Family Background on Earnings and Returns to Schooling: Evidence from Brazil." *The Journal of Political Economy* 101:710–40.

Lazear, Edward P., and Robert T. Michael. 1988. *Allocation of Income Within the Household.* Chicago: University of Chicago Press.

Levy, Frank, and Richard Murnane. 1992. "U.S. Earnings Levels and Earnings Inequality: A Review of Recent Trends and Proposed Explanations." *Journal of Economic Literature* 30: 1333–81.

Logan, John Allen. 1996a. "Opportunity and Choice in Socially Structured Labor Markets." *American Journal of Sociology* 102: 114–60.

Logan, John Allen. 1996b. "Rules of Access and Shifts in Demand: A Comparison of Log-Linear and Two-Sided Logit Models." *Social Science Research* 25:174–99.

Logan, John Allen. 1996c. "Rational Choice and the TSL Model of Occupational Opportunity." *Rationality and Society* 8:207–30.

Mare, Robert D. 1980. "Social Background and School Continuation Decisions." *Journal of the American Statistical Association* 75:295–305.

Mare, Robert D. 1981. "Change and Stability in Educational Stratification." *American Sociological Review* 46:72–87.

Mare, Robert D. 1991. "Five Decades of Educational Assortative Mating." *American Sociological Review* 56:15–32.

Mare, Robert D. 1997a. "Differential Fertility, Intergenerational Educational Mobility, and Racial Inequality." *Social Science Research* 26:263–91.

Mare, Robert D. 1997b. "Assortative Mating, Intergenerational Mobility, and Educational Inequality." Paper presented to Population Association of America, Washington, DC.

Mare, Robert D., and Huey-Chi Chang. 1998. "Family Strategies and Educational Attainment Norms in Taiwan and the United States: Some New Models for Educational Stratification." Paper presented to Research Committee on Social Stratification and Mobility of the International Sociological Association, Montreal.

Mare, Robert D., and Meei-Shenn Tzeng. 1989. "Fathers' Ages and the Social Stratification of Sons." *American Journal of Sociology* 95: 108–31.

Mayer, Susan E., and Christopher Jencks. 1993. "Recent Trends in Economic Inequality in the United States: Income vs. Expenditures vs. Material Well-Being." In *Poverty and Prosperity in America at the Close of the Twentieth Century*, edited by Dimitri Papadimitriou and Edward Wolfe. London: Macmillan.

McLanahan, Sara S., and Gary D. Sandefur. 1994. *Growing up with a Single Parent.* Cambridge: Harvard University Press.

Morris, Martina, and Bruce Western. 1999. "Inequality in Earnings at the Close of the Twentieth Century." *Annual Review of Sociology* 28:623–57.

Mortensen, Dale T. 1988. "Matching: Finding a Partner for Life or Otherwise." *American Journal of Sociology* 94 (Supplement):S215–S240.

Musick, Kelly, and Robert D. Mare. 1998. "Family Structure, Intergenerational Mobility, and the Reproduction of Poverty: Evidence for Increasing Polarization?" Paper presented to Population Association of America, Chicago.

Musick, Kelly, and Robert D. Mare. 1999. "Recent Trends in the Inheritance of Poverty and Family Structure." Paper presented to Population Association of America, New York.

Oppenheimer, Valerie K. 1988. "A Theory of Marriage Timing: Assortative Mating under Varying Degrees of Uncertainty." *American Journal of Sociology* 96:563–91.

Pfautz, Harold W., and Otis Dudley Duncan. 1950. "A Critical Evaluation of Warner's Work in Community Stratification." *American Sociological Review* 15:205–15.

Piore, Michael J. 1970. "The Dual Labor Market: Theory and Implications." In *The State and the Poor*, edited by Samuel H. Beer and Richard E. Barringer. Cambridge: Winthrop Publishers.

Preston, Samuel H., and Cameron Campbell. 1993. "Differential Fertility and the Distribution of Traits: The Case of IQ." *American Journal of Sociology* 98:997–1019.

Quillian, Lincoln. 1999. "Migration Patterns and the Growth of High Poverty Neighborhoods, 1970–1990." *American Journal of Sociology* 105:1–37.

Rijken, Susanne. 1999. *Educational Expansion and Status Attainment.* Utrecht: Interuniversity Center for Social Science Theory and Methodology.

Róna-Tas, Ákos. 1994. "The First Shall Be Last? Entrepreneurship and Communist Cadres in the Transition from Socialism." *American Journal of Sociology* 100:40–69.

Roth, Alvin E., and Marilda A. Oliveira Sotomayor. 1990. *Two-Sided Matching: A Study in Game-Theoretic Modeling and Analysis.* Cambridge: Cambridge University Press.

Sakamoto, Arthur, and Meichu D. Chen. 1991. "Sample Selection and the Dual Labor Market." *Research in Social Stratification and Mobility* 10:171–98.

Shavit, Yossi and Hans-Peter Blossfeld, eds. 1993. *Persistent Inequality: Changing Educational Attainment in Thirteen Countries*. Boulder, CO: Westview Press.

Shavit, Yossi, and Jennifer L. Pierce. 1991. "Sibship Size and Educational Attainment in Nuclear and Extended Families: Arabs and Jews in Israel." *American Sociological Review* 56: 321–30.

Sibley, Elbridge. 1942. "Some Demographic Clues to Stratification." *American Sociological Review* 3:322–30.

Simkus, Albert. 1984. "Structural Transformation and Social Mobility in Hungary: 1938–1973." *American Sociological Review* 49:291–307.

Sombart, Werner. [1903]1976. *Why Is There No Socialism in the United States?* White Plains, NY: M. E. Sharpe.

Sørensen, Aage B. 1977. "The Structure of Inequality and the Process of Attainment." *American Sociological Review* 42:965–78.

Sørensen, Aage B., and Arne L. Kalleberg. 1981. "An Outline of a Theory of the Matching of Persons to Jobs." In *Sociological Perspectives on Labor Markets*, edited by Ivar Berg. New York: Academic Press.

Sørensen, Jesper B., and David B. Grusky. 1996. "The Structure of Career Mobility in Microscopic Perspective." Pages 83–114 in *Social Differentiation and Social Inequality: Essays in Honor of John C. Pock*, edited by J. N. Baron, D. B. Grusky, and D. J. Treiman. Boulder, CO: Westview Press.

Sorokin, Pitrim A. 1959. *Social and Cultural Mobility*. New York: The Free Press.

Spence, A. Michael. 1974. *Market Signaling: Informational Transfer in Hiring and Related Screening Processes*. Cambridge: Harvard University Press.

Thurow, Lester C. 1975. *Generating Inequality*. New York: Basic Books.

Treiman, Donald J. 1970. "Industrialization and Social Stratification." Pages 207–34 in *Social Stratification: Research and Theory for the 1970s*, edited by Edward O. Lauman. Indianapolis: Bobbs-Merrill.

Treiman, Donald J., and Harry B. G. Ganzeboom. 1999. "The Fourth Generation of Comparative Stratification Research." In *Sociological Research at the End of the Century*, edited by Stella Quah and Arnaud Sales. London: Sage.

Turner, Ralph H. 1960. "Sponsored and Contest Mobility and the School System." *American Sociological Review* 25:855–66.

Walder, Andrew G., Bobai Li, and Donald J. Treiman. 2000. "Politics and Life Chances in State Socialist Regimes: Dual Career Paths into the Urban Chinese Elite, 1949–1996." *American Sociological Review* 65:191–209.

Warren, John Robert, and Robert M. Hauser. 1997. "Social Stratification across Three Generations: New Evidence from the Wisconsin Longitudinal Study." *American Sociological Review* 62:561–72.

White, Harrison. 1970. *Chains of Opportunity: System Models of Mobility in Organizations*. Cambridge: Harvard University Press.

Willis, Robert J., and Sherwin Rosen. 1979. "Education and Self-Selection." *Journal of Political Economy* 87 (Supplement):S7–S36.

Wright, Erik Olin. 1997. *Class Counts*. Cambridge: Cambridge University Press.

Part V
The Consequences of Stratification

Lifestyles and Consumption Patterns

Interests, Attitudes, and Personalities

Lifestyles and Consumption Patterns

THORSTEIN VEBLEN

The Theory of the Leisure Class

Pecuniary Emulation

The end of acquisition and accumulation is conventionally held to be the consumption of the goods accumulated—whether it is consumption directly by the owner of the goods or by the household attached to him and for this purpose identified with him in theory. This is at least felt to be the economically legitimate end of acquisition, which alone it is incumbent on the theory to take account of. Such consumption may of course be conceived to serve the consumer's physical wants—his physical comfort—or his so-called higher wants—spiritual, æsthetic, intellectual, or what not; the latter class of wants being served indirectly by an expenditure of goods, after the fashion familiar to all economic readers.

But it is only when taken in a sense far removed from its naïve meaning that consumption of goods can be said to afford the incentive from which accumulation invariably proceeds. The motive that lies at the root of ownership is emulation; and the same motive of emulation continues active in the further development of the institution to which it has given rise and in the development of all those features of the social structure which this in-

stitution of ownership touches. The possession of wealth confers honor; it is an invidious distinction. Nothing equally cogent can be said for the consumption of goods, nor for any other conceivable incentive to acquisition, and especially not for any incentive to the accumulation of wealth.

It is of course not to be overlooked that in a community where nearly all goods are private property the necessity of earning a livelihood is a powerful and ever-present incentive for the poorer members of the community. The need of subsistence and of an increase of physical comfort may for a time be the dominant motive of acquisition for those classes who are habitually employed at manual labor, whose subsistence is on a precarious footing, who possess little and ordinarily accumulate little; but it will appear in the course of the discussion that even in the case of these impecunious classes the predominance of the motive of physical want is not so decided as has sometimes been assumed. On the other hand, so far as regards those members and classes of the community who are chiefly concerned in the accumulation of wealth, the incentive of subsistence or of physical comfort never plays a considerable part. Ownership began and grew into a human institution on grounds unrelated to the subsistence minimum. The dominant incentive was from the outset the invidious distinction attaching to wealth, and, save temporarily and by exception, no other motive has usurped the primacy at any later stage of the development. . . .

Originally published in 1973. Please see complete source information beginning on page 891.

In any community where goods are held in severalty it is necessary, in order to ensure his own peace of mind, that an individual should possess as large a portion of goods as others with whom he is accustomed to class himself; and it is extremely gratifying to possess something more than others. But as fast as a person makes new acquisitions, and becomes accustomed to the resulting new standard of wealth, the new standard forthwith ceases to afford appreciably greater satisfaction than the earlier standard did. The tendency in any case is constantly to make the present pecuniary standard the point of departure for a fresh increase of wealth; and this in turn gives rise to a new standard of sufficiency and a new pecuniary classification of one's self as compared with one's neighbors. So far as concerns the present question, the end sought by accumulation is to rank high in comparison with the rest of the community in point of pecuniary strength. So long as the comparison is distinctly unfavorable to himself, the normal, average individual will live in chronic dissatisfaction with his present lot; and when he has reached what may be called the normal pecuniary standard of the community, or of his class in the community, this chronic dissatisfaction will give place to a restless straining to place a wider and ever-widening pecuniary interval between himself and this average standard. The invidious comparison can never become so favorable to the individual making it that he would not gladly rate himself still higher relatively to his competitors in the struggle for pecuniary reputability.

In the nature of the case, the desire for wealth can scarcely be satiated in any individual instance, and evidently a satiation of the average or general desire for wealth is out of the question. However widely, or equally, or "fairly," it may be distributed, no general increase of the community's wealth can make any approach to satiating this need, the ground of which is the desire of everyone to excel everyone else in the accumulation of goods. If, as is sometimes assumed, the incentive to accumulation were the want of subsistence or of physical comfort, then the aggre-

gate economic wants of a community might conceivably be satisfied at some point in the advance of industrial efficiency; but since the struggle is substantially a race for reputability on the basis of an invidious comparison, no approach to a definitive attainment is possible.

What has just been said must not be taken to mean that there are no other incentives to acquisition and accumulation than this desire to excel in pecuniary standing and so gain the esteem and envy of one's fellowmen. The desire for added comfort and security from want is present as a motive at every stage of the process of accumulation in a modern industrial community; although the standard of sufficiency in these respects is in turn greatly affected by the habit of pecuniary emulation. To a great extent this emulation shapes the methods and selects the objects of expenditure for personal comfort and decent livelihood.

Besides this, the power conferred by wealth also affords a motive to accumulation. That propensity for purposeful activity and that repugnance to all futility of effort which belong to man by virtue of his character as an agent do not desert him when he emerges from the naïve communal culture where the dominant note of life is the unanalyzed and undifferentiated solidarity of the individual with the group with which his life is bound up. When he enters upon the predatory stage, where self-seeking in the narrower sense becomes the dominant note, this propensity goes with him still, as the pervasive trait that shapes his scheme of life. The propensity for achievement and the repugnance to futility remain the underlying economic motive. The propensity changes only in the form of its expression and in the proximate objects to which it directs the man's activity. Under the regime of individual ownership the most available means of visibly achieving a purpose is that afforded by the acquisition and accumulation of goods; and as the self-regarding antithesis between man and man reaches fuller consciousness, the propensity for achievement—the instinct of workmanship—tends more and more to shape itself into a straining to excel others in pecuniary achievement. Relative success, tested by an invidious pecuniary comparison with other men, becomes the conventional end of action. The currently accepted legitimate end of effort becomes the achievement of a favorable comparison with other men; and therefore the repugnance to futility to a good extent coalesces with the incentive of emulation. It acts to accentuate the struggle for pecuniary reputability by visiting with a sharper disapproval all shortcoming and all evidence of shortcoming in point of pecuniary success. Purposeful effort comes to mean, primarily, effort directed to or resulting in a more creditable showing of accumulated wealth. Among the motives which lead men to accumulate wealth, the primacy, both in scope and intensity, therefore, continues to belong to this motive of pecuniary emulation.

In making use of the term "invidious," it may perhaps be unnecessary to remark, there is no intention to extol or depreciate, or to commend or deplore any of the phenomena which the word is used to characterize. The term is used in a technical sense as describing a comparison of persons with a view to rating and grading them in respect of relative worth or value—in an æsthetic or moral sense—and so awarding and defining the relative degrees of complacency with which they may legitimately be contemplated by themselves and by others. An invidious comparison is a process of valuation of persons in respect of worth.

Conspicuous Leisure

If its working were not disturbed by other economic forces or other features of the emulative process, the immediate effect of such a pecuniary struggle as has just been described in outline would be to make men industrious and frugal. This result actually follows, in some measure, so far as regards the lower classes, whose ordinary means of acquiring goods is productive labor. This is more especially true of the laboring classes in a sedentary community which is at an agricultural stage of industry, in which there is a considerable subdivision of property, and whose laws and customs secure to these classes a more or less definite share of the product of their industry. These lower classes can in any case not avoid labor, and the imputation of labor is therefore not greatly derogatory to them, at least not within their class. Rather, since labor is their recognized and accepted mode of life, they take some emulative pride in a reputation for efficiency in their work, this being often the only line of emulation that is open to them. For those for whom acquisition and emulation is possible only within the field of productive efficiency and thrift, the struggle for pecuniary reputability will in some measure work out in an increase of diligence and parsimony. But certain secondary features of the emulative process, yet to be spoken of, come in to very materially circumscribe and modify emulation in these directions among the pecuniarily inferior classes as well as among the superior class.

But it is otherwise with the superior pecuniary class, with which we are here immediately concerned. For this class also the incentive to diligence and thrift is not absent; but its action is so greatly qualified by the secondary demands of pecuniary emulation, that any inclination in this direction is practically overborne and any incentive to diligence tends to be of no effect. The most imperative of these secondary demands of emulation, as well as the one of widest scope, is the requirement of abstention from productive work. . . . During the predatory culture labor comes to be associated in men's habits of thought with weakness and subjection to a master. It is therefore a mark of inferiority, and therefore comes to be accounted unworthy of man in his best estate. By virtue of this tradition labor is felt to be debasing, and this tradition has never died out. On the contrary, with the advance of social differentiation it has acquired the axiomatic force due to ancient and unquestioned prescription.

In order to gain and to hold the esteem of men it is not sufficient merely to possess wealth or power. The wealth or power must be put in evidence, for esteem is awarded only on evidence. And not only does the evidence of wealth serve to impress one's importance on others and to keep their sense of importance alive and alert, but it is of scarcely less use in building up and preserving one's self-complacency. In all but the lowest stages of culture the normally constituted man is comforted and upheld in his self-respect by "decent surroundings" and by exemption from "menial offices." Enforced departure from his habitual standard of decency, either in the paraphernalia of life or in the kind and amount of his everyday activity, is felt to be a slight upon his human dignity, even apart from all conscious consideration of the approval or disapproval of his fellows.

The archaic theoretical distinction between the base and the honorable in the manner of a man's life retains very much of its ancient force even today. So much so that there are few of the better class who are not possessed of an instinctive repugnance for the vulgar forms of labor. We have a realizing sense of ceremonial uncleanness attaching in an especial degree to the occupations which are associated in our habits of thought with menial service. It is felt by all persons of refined taste that a spiritual contamination is inseparable from certain offices that are conventionally required of servants. Vulgar surroundings, mean (that is to say, inexpensive) habitations, and vulgarly productive occupations are unhesitatingly condemned and avoided. They are incompatible with life on a satisfactory spiritual plane—with "high thinking." From the days of the Greek philosophers to the present, a degree of leisure and of exemption from contact with such industrial processes as serve the immediate everyday purposes of human life has ever been recognized by thoughtful men as a prerequisite to a worthy or beautiful, or even a blameless, human life. In itself and in its consequences the life of leisure is beautiful and ennobling in all civilized men's eyes.

This direct, subjective value of leisure and of other evidences of wealth is no doubt in great part secondary and derivative. It is in part a reflex of the utility of leisure as a means of gaining the respect of others, and in part it is the result of a mental substitution. The performance of labor has been accepted as a conventional evidence of inferior force; therefore it comes itself, by a mental shortcut, to be regarded as intrinsically base. . . .

Conspicuous Consumption

In the earlier phases of the predatory culture the only economic differentiation is a broad distinction between an honorable superior class made up of the able-bodied men on the one side, and a base inferior class of laboring women on the other. According to the ideal scheme of life in force at that time it is the office of the men to consume what the women produce. Such consumption as falls to the women is merely incidental to their work; it is a means to their continued labor, and not a consumption directed to their own comfort and fullness of life. Unproductive consumption of goods is honorable, primarily as a mark of prowess and a perquisite of human dignity; secondarily it becomes substantially honorable in itself, especially the consumption of the more desirable things. The consumption of choice articles of food, and frequently also of rare articles of adornment, becomes tabu to the women and children; and if there is a base (servile) class of men, the tabu holds also for them. With a further advance in culture this tabu may change into simple custom of a more or less rigorous character; but whatever be the theoretical basis of the distinction which is maintained, whether it be a tabu or a larger conventionality, the features of the conventional scheme of consumption do not change easily. When the quasi-peaceable stage of industry is reached, with its fundamental institution of chattel slavery, the general principle, more or less rigorously applied, is that the base, industrious class should consume only what may be necessary to their subsistence. In the nature of things, luxuries and the comforts of life belong to the leisure class. Under the tabu, certain victuals, and more particularly certain beverages, are strictly reserved for the use of the superior class. . . .

As wealth accumulates, the leisure class develops further in function and structure, and there arises a differentiation within the class. There is a more or less elaborate system of rank and grades. This differentiation is furthered by the inheritance of wealth and the consequent inheritance of gentility. With the inheritance of gentility goes the inheritance of obligatory leisure; and gentility of a sufficient potency to entail a life of leisure may be inherited without the complement of wealth required to maintain a dignified leisure. Gentle blood may be transmitted without goods enough to afford a reputably free consumption at one's ease. Hence results a class of impecunious gentlemen of leisure. These half-caste gentlemen of leisure fall into a system of hierarchical gradations. Those who stand near the higher and the highest grades of the wealthy leisure class, in point of birth, or in point of wealth, or both, outrank the remoter-born and the pecuniarily weaker. These lower grades, especially the impecunious, or marginal, gentlemen of leisure, affiliate themselves by a system of dependence or fealty to the great ones; by so doing they gain an increment of repute, or of the means with which to lead a life of leisure, from their patron. They become his courtiers or retainers, servants; and being fed and countenanced by their patron they are indices of his rank and vicarious consumers of his superfluous wealth. Many of these affiliated gentlemen of leisure are at the same time lesser men of substance in their own right; so that some of them are scarcely at all, others only partially, to be rated as vicarious consumers. So many of them, however, as make up the retainers and hangers-on of the patron may be classed as vicarious consumers without qualification. Many of these again, and also many of the other aristocracy of less degree, have in turn attached to their persons a more or less comprehensive group of vicarious consumers in the persons of their wives and children, their servants, retainers, etc.

Throughout this graduated scheme of vicarious leisure and vicarious consumption the rule holds that these offices must be performed in some such manner, or under some such circumstance or insignia, as shall point plainly to the master to whom this leisure or consumption pertains, and to whom therefore the resulting increment of good repute of right inures. The consumption and leisure executed by these persons for their master or patron represents an investment on his part with a view to an increase of good fame. . . .

With the disappearance of servitude, the number of vicarious consumers attached to any one gentleman tends, on the whole, to decrease. The like is of course true, and perhaps in a still higher degree, of the number of dependents who perform vicarious leisure for him. In a general way, though not wholly nor consistently, these two groups coincide. The dependent who was first delegated for these duties was the wife, or the chief wife; and, as would be expected, in the later development of the institution, when the number of persons by whom these duties are customarily performed gradually narrows, the wife remains the last. In the higher grades of society a large volume of both these kinds of service is required; and here the wife is of course still assisted in the work by a more or less numerous corps of menials. But as we descend the social scale, the point is presently reached where the duties of vicarious leisure and consumption devolve upon the wife alone. In the communities of the Western culture, this point is at present found among the lower middle class.

And here occurs a curious inversion. It is a fact of common observance that in this lower middle class there is no pretense of leisure on the part of the head of the household. Through force of circumstances it has fallen into disuse. But the middle-class wife still carries on the business of vicarious leisure, for the good name of the household and its master. In descending the social scale in any modern industrial community, the primary fact—the conspicuous leisure of the master of the household—disappears at a relatively high point. The head of the middle-class household has been reduced by economic circumstances to turn his hand to gaining a livelihood by occupations which often partake largely of the character of industry, as in the case of the ordinary business man of today. But the derivative fact—the vicarious leisure and consumption rendered by the wife, and the auxiliary vicarious performance of leisure by menials—remains in vogue as a conventionality which the demands of reputability will not suffer to be slighted. It is by no means an uncommon spectacle to find a man applying himself to work with the utmost assiduity, in order that his wife may in due form render for him that degree of vicarious leisure which the common sense of the time demands.

The leisure rendered by the wife in such cases is, of course, not a simple manifestation of idleness or indolence. It almost invariably occurs disguised under some form of work or household duties or social amenities, which prove on analysis to serve little or no ulterior end beyond showing that she does not occupy herself with anything that is gainful or that is of substantial use. The greater part of the customary round of domestic cares to which the middle-class housewife gives her time and effort is of this character. Not that the results of her attention to household matters, of a decorative and mundificatory character, are not pleasing to the sense of men trained in middle-class proprieties; but the taste to which these effects of household adornment and tidiness appeal is a taste which has been formed under the selective guidance of a canon of propriety that demands just these evidences of wasted effort. The effects are pleasing to us chiefly because we have been taught to find them pleasing. There goes into these domestic duties much solicitude for a proper combination of form and color, and for other ends that are to be classed as æsthetic in the proper sense of the term; and it is not denied that effects having some substantial æsthetic value are sometimes attained. Pretty much all that is here insisted on is that, as regards these amenities of life, the housewife's efforts are under the guidance of traditions that have been shaped by the law of conspicuously wasteful expenditure of time and substance. If beauty or comfort is achieved—and it is a more or less for-

tuitous circumstance if they are—they must be achieved by means and methods that commend themselves to the great economic law of wasted effort. The more reputable, "presentable" portion of middle-class household paraphernalia are, on the one hand, items of conspicuous consumption, and on the other hand, apparatus for putting in evidence the vicarious leisure rendered by the housewife.

The requirement of vicarious consumption at the hands of the wife continues in force even at a lower point in the pecuniary scale than the requirement of vicarious leisure. At a point below which little if any pretense of wasted effort, in ceremonial cleanness and the like, is observable, and where there is assuredly no conscious attempt at ostensible leisure, decency still requires the wife to consume some goods conspicuously for the reputability of the household and its head. So that, as the latter-day outcome of this evolution of an archaic institution, the wife, who was at the outset the drudge and chattel of the man, both in fact and in theory—the producer of goods for him to consume—has become the ceremonial consumer of goods which he produces. But she still quite unmistakably remains his chattel in theory; for the habitual rendering of vicarious leisure and consumption is the abiding mark of the unfree servant.

This vicarious consumption practiced by the household of the middle and lower classes can not be counted as a direct expression of the leisure-class scheme of life, since the household of this pecuniary grade does not belong within the leisure class. It is rather that the leisure-class scheme of life here comes to an expression at the second remove. The leisure class stands at the head of the social structure in point of reputability; and its manner of life and its standards of worth therefore afford the norm of reputability for the community. The observance of these standards, in some degree of approximation, becomes incumbent upon all classes lower in the scale. In modern civilized communities the lines of demarcation between social classes have grown vague and transient, and wherever this happens the norm of reputability imposed by the upper class extends its coercive influence with but slight hindrance down through the social structure to the lowest strata. The result is that the members of each stratum accept as their ideal of decency the scheme of life in vogue in the next higher stratum, and bend their energies to live up to that ideal. On pain of forfeiting their good name and their self-respect in case of failure, they must conform to the accepted code, at least in appearance.

The basis on which good repute in any highly organized industrial community ultimately rests is pecuniary strength; and the means of showing pecuniary strength, and so of gaining or retaining a good name, are leisure and a conspicuous consumption of goods. Accordingly, both of these methods are in vogue as far down the scale as it remains possible; and in the lower strata in which the two methods are employed, both offices are in great part delegated to the wife and children of the household. Lower still, where any degree of leisure, even ostensible, has become impracticable for the wife, the conspicuous consumption of goods remains and is carried on by the wife and children. The man of the household also can do something in this direction, and indeed, he commonly does; but with a still lower descent into the levels of indigence—along the margin of the slums—the man, and presently also the children, virtually cease to consume valuable goods for appearances, and the woman remains virtually the sole exponent of the household's pecuniary decency. No class of society, not even the most abjectly poor, forgoes all customary conspicuous consumption. The last items of this category of consumption are not given up except under stress of the direst necessity. Very much of squalor and discomfort will be endured before the last trinket or the last pretense of pecuniary decency is put away. There is no class and no country that has yielded so abjectly before the pressure of physical want as to deny themselves all gratification of this higher or spiritual need.

From the foregoing survey of the growth of conspicuous leisure and consumption, it ap-

pears that the utility of both alike for the purposes of reputability lies in the element of waste that is common to both. In the one case it is a waste of time and effort, in the other it is a waste of goods. Both are methods of demonstrating the possession of wealth, and the two are conventionally accepted as equivalents. The choice between them is a question of advertising expediency simply, except so far as it may be affected by other standards of propriety, springing from a different source. On grounds of expediency the preference may be given to the one or the other at different stages of the economic development. The question is, which of the two methods will most effectively reach the persons whose convictions it is desired to affect. Usage has answered this question in different ways under different circumstances.

So long as the community or social group is small enough and compact enough to be effectually reached by common notoriety alone—that is to say, so long as the human environment to which the individual is required to adapt himself in respect of reputability is comprised within his sphere of personal acquaintance and neighborhood gossip—so long the one method is about as effective as the other. Each will therefore serve about equally well during the earlier stages of social growth. But when the differentiation has gone farther and it becomes necessary to reach a wider human environment, consumption begins to hold over leisure as an ordinary means of decency. This is especially true during the later, peaceable economic stage. The means of communication and the mobility of the population now expose the individual to the observation of many persons who have no other means of judging of his reputability than the display of goods (and perhaps of breeding) which he is able to make while he is under their direct observation.

The modern organization of industry works in the same direction also by another line. The exigencies of the modern industrial system frequently place individuals and households in juxtaposition between whom there is little contact in any other sense than that of juxtaposition. One's neighbors, mechanically speaking, often are socially not one's neighbors, or even acquaintances; and still their transient good opinion has a high degree of utility. The only practicable means of impressing one's pecuniary ability on these unsympathetic observers of one's everyday life is an unremitting demonstration of ability to pay. In the modern community there is also a more frequent attendance at large gatherings of people to whom one's everyday life is unknown; in such places as churches, theaters, ballrooms, hotels, parks, shops, and the like. In order to impress these transient observers, and to retain one's self-complacency under their observation, the signature of one's pecuniary strength should be written in characters which he who runs may read. It is evident, therefore, that the present trend of the development is in the direction of heightening the utility of conspicuous consumption as compared with leisure. . . .

Pecuniary Canons of Taste

The requirements of pecuniary decency have, to a very appreciable extent, influenced the sense of beauty and of utility in articles of use or beauty. Articles are to an extent preferred for use on account of their being conspicuously wasteful; they are felt to be serviceable somewhat in proportion as they are wasteful and ill adapted to their ostensible use. . . .

By habituation to an appreciative perception of the marks of expensiveness in goods, and by habitually identifying beauty with reputability, it comes about that a beautiful article which is not expensive is accounted not beautiful. In this way it has happened, for instance, that some beautiful flowers pass conventionally for offensive weeds; others that can be cultivated with relative ease are accepted and admired by the lower middle class, who can afford no more expensive luxuries of this kind; but these varieties are rejected as vulgar by those people who are better able to pay for expensive flowers and who are educated to a higher schedule of pecuniary beauty in the florist's products; while still other flowers, of no greater intrinsic beauty than these, are cultivated at great cost and call out much admiration from flower-lovers whose tastes have been matured under the critical guidance of a polite environment.

The same variation in matters of taste, from one class of society to another, is visible also as regards many other kinds of consumable goods, as, for example, is the case with furniture, houses, parks, and gardens. This diversity of views as to what is beautiful in these various classes of goods is not a diversity of the norm according to which the unsophisticated sense of the beautiful works. It is not a constitutional difference of endowments in the æsthetic respect, but rather a difference in the code of reputability which specifies what objects properly lie within the scope of honorific consumption for the class to which the critic belongs. It is a difference in the traditions of propriety with respect to the kinds of things which may, without derogation to the consumer, be consumed under the head of objects of taste and art. With a certain allowance for variations to be accounted for on other grounds, these traditions are determined, more or less rigidly, by the pecuniary plane of life of the class.

PIERRE BOURDIEU

Distinction: A Social Critique of the Judgement of Taste

The Social Space

The distribution of the different classes (and class fractions) runs from those who are best provided with both economic and cultural capital to those who are most deprived in both respects (see figures 1 and 2). The members of the professions, who have high incomes and high qualifications, who very often (52.9 percent) originate from the dominant class (professions or senior executives), who receive and consume a large quantity of both material and cultural goods, are opposed in almost all respects to the office workers, who have low qualifications, often originate from the working or middle classes, who receive little and consume little, devoting a high proportion of their time to care maintenance and home improvement; and they are even more opposed to the skilled or semi-skilled workers, and still more to unskilled workers or farm labourers, who have the lowest incomes, no qualifications, and originate almost exclusively (90.5 percent of farm labourers, 84.5 percent of unskilled workers) from the working classes.[1]

The differences stemming from the total volume of capital almost always conceal, both

from common awareness and also from 'scientific' knowledge, the secondary differences which, within each of the classes defined by overall volume of capital, separate class fractions, defined by different asset structures, i.e., different distributions of their total capital among the different kinds of capital [economic and cultural].

Once one takes account of the structure of total assets—and not only, as has always been done implicitly, of the dominant kind in a given structure, 'birth', 'fortune' or 'talents', as the nineteenth century put it—one has the means of making more precise divisions and also of observing the specific effects of the structure of distribution between the different kinds of capital. This may, for example, be symmetrical (as in the case of the professions, which combine very high income with very high cultural capital) or asymmetrical (in the case of higher-education and secondary teachers or employers, with cultural capital dominant in one case, economic capital in the other). One thus discovers two sets of homologous positions. The fractions whose reproduction depends on economic capital, usually inherited—industrial and commercial employers at the higher level, craftsmen and shopkeepers at the intermediate level—are opposed to the fractions which are least endowed (relatively, of course) with economic capital, and whose reproduction mainly depends on cultural capital—higher-education and secondary teachers at the higher level, primary teachers at the intermediate level. . . .

Originally published in 1984. Please see complete source information beginning on page 891.

FIGURE 1 The space of social positions (shown in black)
FIGURE 2 The space of life-styles (shown in grey)

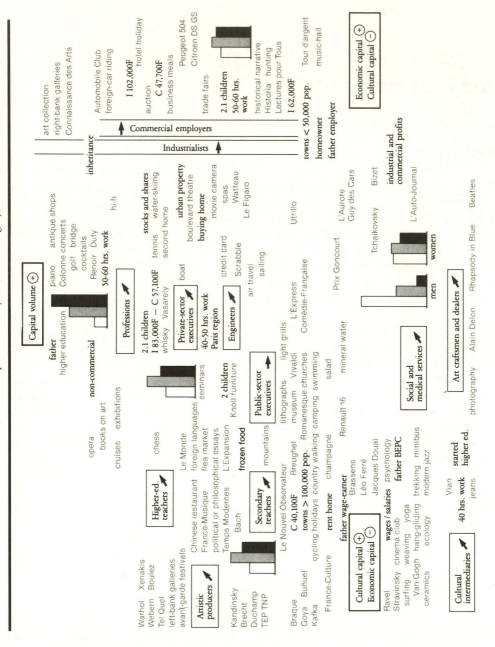

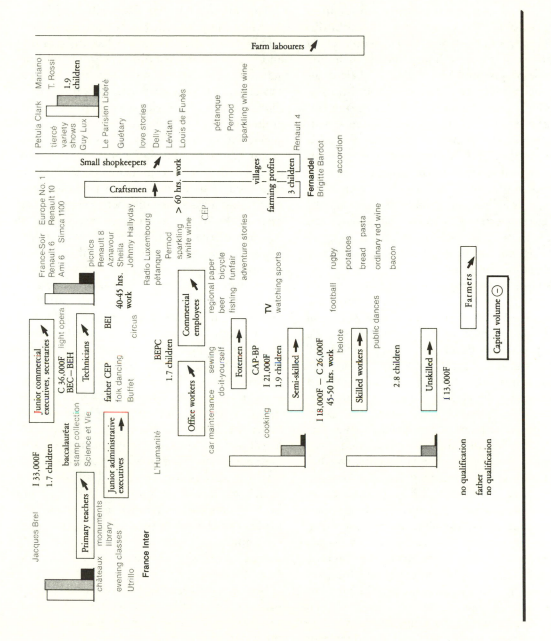

The Habitus

The mere fact that the social space described here can be presented as a diagram indicates that it is an abstract representation, deliberately constructed, like a map, to give a bird's-eye view, a point of view on the whole set of points from which ordinary agents (including the sociologist and his reader, in their ordinary behaviour) see the social world. Bringing together in simultaneity, in the scope of a single glance—this is its heuristic value—positions which the agents can never apprehend in their totality and in their multiple relationships, social space is to the practical space of everyday life, with its distances which are kept or signalled, and neighbours who may be more remote than strangers, what geometrical space is to the 'travelling space' (*espace hodologique*) of ordinary experience, with its gaps and discontinuities.

But the most crucial thing to note is that the question of this space is raised within the space itself—that the agents have points of view on this objective space which depend on their position within it and in which their will to transform or conserve it is often expressed. Thus many of the words which sociology uses to designate the classes it constructs are borrowed from ordinary usage, where they serve to express the (generally polemical) view that one group has of another. As if carried away by their quest for greater objectivity, sociologists almost always forget that the 'objects' they classify produce not only objectively classifiable practices but also classifying operations that are no less objective and are themselves classifiable. The division into classes performed by sociology leads to the common root of the classifiable practices which agents produce and of the classificatory judgements they make of other agents' practices and their own. The habitus is both the generative principle of objectively classifiable judgements and the system of classification (*principium divisionis*) of these practices. It is in the relationship between the two capacities which define the habitus, the capacity to produce classifiable practices and works, and the capacity to differentiate and appreciate these practices and products (taste), that the represented social world, i.e., the space of life-styles, is constituted.

The relationship that is actually established between the pertinent characteristics of economic and social condition (capital volume and composition, in both synchronic and diachronic aspects) and the distinctive features associated with the corresponding position in the universe of life-styles only becomes intelligible when the habitus is constructed as the generative formula which makes it possible to account both for the classifiable practices and products and for the judgements, themselves classified, which make these practices and works into a system of distinctive signs. When one speaks of the aristocratic asceticism of teachers or the pretension of the petite bourgeoisie, one is not only describing these groups by one, or even the most important, of their properties, but also endeavouring to name the principle which generates all their properties and all their judgements of their, or other people's, properties. The habitus is necessity internalized and converted into a disposition that generates meaningful practices and meaning-giving perceptions; it is a general, transposable disposition which carries out a systematic, universal application—beyond the limits of what has been directly learnt—of the necessity inherent in the learning conditions. That is why an agent's whole set of practices (or those of a whole set of agents produced by similar conditions) are both systematic, inasmuch as they are the product of the application of identical (or interchangeable) schemes, and systematically distinct from the practices constituting another life-style.

Because different conditions of existence produce different habitus—systems of generative schemes applicable, by simple transfer, to the most varied areas of practice—the practices engendered by the different habitus appear as systematic configurations of properties expressing the differences objectively inscribed in conditions of existence in the form of systems of differential deviations

FIGURE 3
Conditions of existence, habitus, and life-style

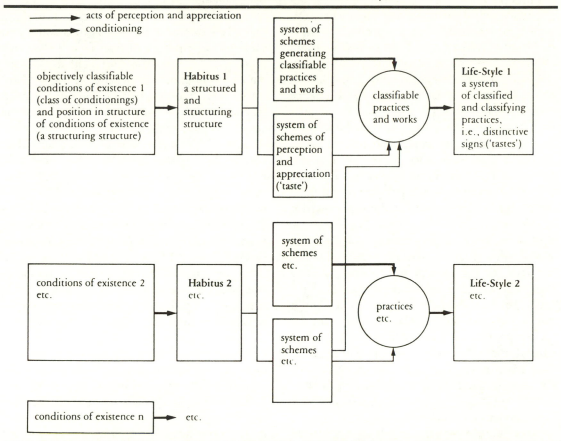

which, when perceived by agents endowed with the schemes of perception and appreciation necessary in order to identify, interpret and evaluate their pertinent features, function as life-styles (see figure 3).[2]

The habitus is not only a structuring structure, which organizes practices and the perception of practices, but also a structured structure: the principle of division into logical classes which organizes the perception of the social world is itself the product of internalization of the division into social classes. Each class condition is defined, simultaneously, by its intrinsic properties and by the relational properties which it derives from its position in the system of class conditions, which is also a system of differences, differential positions, i.e., by everything which distinguishes it from what it is not and especially from everything it is opposed to; social identity is defined and asserted through difference. This means that inevitably inscribed within the dispositions of the habitus is the whole structure of the system of conditions, as it presents itself in the experience of a life-condition occupying a particular position within that structure. The most fundamental oppositions in the structure (high/low, rich/poor etc.) tend to establish themselves as the fundamental structuring principles of practices and the perception of practices. As a system of practice-generating schemes which expresses systematically the necessity and freedom inherent in its class condition and the difference constituting that position, the habitus apprehends differences between conditions, which it grasps in the form of differences between classified, classifying practices (products of other habitus), in accordance with principles of differentiation which, being themselves the product of these differences, are objectively attuned to them and therefore tend to perceive them as natural.

While it must be reasserted, against all forms of mechanism, that ordinary experience of the social world is a cognition, it is equally important to realize—contrary to the illusion of the spontaneous generation of consciousness which so many theories of the 'awakening of class consciousness' (*prise de conscience*) amount to—that primary cognition is misrecognition, recognition of an order which is also established in the mind. Life-styles are thus the systematic products of habitus, which, perceived in their mutual relations through the schemes of the habitus, become sign systems that are socially qualified (as 'distinguished', 'vulgar' etc.). The dialectic of conditions and habitus is the basis of an alchemy which transforms the distribution of capital, the balance-sheet of a power relation, into a system of perceived differences, distinctive properties, that is, a distribution of symbolic capital, legitimate capital, whose objective truth is misrecognized.

As structured products (*opus operatum*) which a structuring structure (*modus operandi*) produces through retranslations according to the specific logic of the different *fields,* all the practices and products of a given agent are objectively harmonized among themselves, without any deliberate pursuit of coherence, and objectively orchestrated, without any conscious concertation, with those of all members of the same class. The habitus continuously generates practical metaphors, that is to say, transfers (of which the transfer of motor habits is only one example) or, more precisely, systematic transpositions required by the particular conditions in which the habitus is 'put into practice' (so that, for example, the ascetic ethos which might be expected always to express itself in saving may, in a given context, express itself in a particular way of using credit). The practices of the same agent, and, more generally, the practices of all agents of the same class, owe the stylistic affinity which makes each of them a metaphor of any of the others to the fact that they are the product of transfers of the same schemes of action from one field to another. An obvious paradigm would be the disposition called 'handwriting', a singular way of tracing letters which always produces the same writing, i.e., graphic forms which, in spite of all the differences of size, material or colour due to the surface (paper or blackboard) or the instrument (pen or chalk)—in spite, therefore, of the different use of muscles—present an immediately perceptible family resemblance, like all the features of style or manner whereby a painter or writer can be recognized as infallibly as a man by his walk.

Systematicity is found in the opus operatum because it is in the modus operandi.[3] It is found in all the properties—and property—with which individuals and groups surround themselves, houses, furniture, paintings, books, cars, spirits, cigarettes, perfume, clothes, and in the practices in which they manifest their distinction, sports, games, entertainments, only because it is in the synthetic unity of the habitus, the unifying, generative principle of all practices. Taste, the propensity and capacity to appropriate (materially or symbolically) a given class of classified, classifying objects or practices, is the generative formula of life-style, a unitary set of distinctive preferences which express the same expressive intention in the specific logic of each of the symbolic subspaces, furniture, clothing, language or body hexis. Each dimension of life-style 'symbolizes with' the others, in Leibniz's phrase, and symbolizes them. An old cabinetmaker's world view, the way he manages his budget, his time or his body, his use of language and choice of clothing are fully present in his ethic of scrupulous, impeccable craftsmanship and in the aesthetic of work for work's sake which leads him to measure the beauty of his products by the care and patience that have gone into them.

The system of matching properties, which includes people—one speaks of a 'well-matched couple', and friends like to say they have the same tastes—is organized by taste, a system of classificatory schemes which may only very partially become conscious although, as one rises in the social hierarchy, life-style is increasingly a matter of what Weber calls the 'stylization of life'. Taste is the basis of the mutual adjustment of all the features associated with a person, which the old aesthetic recommended for the sake of the mutual reinforcement they give one another; the countless pieces of information a person consciously or unconsciously imparts endlessly underline and confirm one another, offering the alert observer the same pleasure an art-lover derives from the symmetries and correspondences produced by a harmonious distribution of redundancies. The over-determination that results from these redundancies is felt the more strongly because the different features which have to be isolated for observation or measurement strongly interpenetrate in ordinary perception; each item of information imparted in practice (e.g., a judgement of a painting) is contaminated—and, if it deviates from the probable feature, corrected—by the effect of the whole set of features previously or simultaneously perceived. That is why a survey which tends to isolate features—for example, by dissociating the things said from the way they are said—and detach them from the system of correlative features tends to minimize the deviation, on each point, between the classes, especially that between the petit bourgeois and the bourgeois. In the ordinary situations of bourgeois life, banalities about art, literature or cinema are inseparable from the steady tone, the slow, casual diction, the distant or self-assured smile, the measured gesture, the well-tailored suit and the bourgeois salon of the person who pronounces them.

Taste is the practical operator of the transmutation of things into distinct and distinctive signs, of continuous distributions into discontinuous oppositions; it raises the differences inscribed in the physical order of bodies to the symbolic order of significant distinctions. It transforms objectively classified practices, in which a class condition signifies itself (through taste), into classifying practices, that is, into a symbolic expression of class position, by perceiving them in their mutual relations and in terms of social classificatory schemes. Taste is thus the source of the system of distinctive features which cannot fail to be perceived as a systematic expression of a particular class of conditions of existence, i.e., as a distinctive life-style, by anyone who possesses practical knowledge of the relationships between distinctive signs and positions in the distributions—between the universe of objective properties, which is brought to light by scientific construction, and the no less objective universe of life-styles, which exists as such for and through ordinary experience.

This classificatory system, which is the product of the internalization of the structure of social space, in the form in which it impinges through the experience of a particular position in that space, is, within the limits of economic possibilities and impossibilities (which it tends to reproduce in its own logic), the generator of practices adjusted to the regularities inherent in a condition. It continuously transforms necessities into strategies, constraints into preferences, and, without any mechanical determination, it generates the set of 'choices' constituting life-styles, which derive their meaning, i.e., their value, from their position in a system of oppositions and correlations.[4] It is a virtue made of necessity which continuously transforms necessity into virtue by inducing 'choices' which correspond to the condition of which it is the product. As can be seen whenever a change in social position puts the habitus into new conditions, so that its specific efficacy can be isolated, it is taste—the taste of necessity or the taste of luxury—and not high or low income which commands the practices objectively adjusted to these resources. Through taste, an agent has what he likes because he likes what he has, that is, the properties actually given to him in the distributions and legitimately assigned to him in the classifications.[5]

The Homology Between the Spaces

Bearing in mind all that precedes, in particular the fact that the generative schemes of the habitus are applied, by simple transfer, to the most dissimilar areas of practice, one can immediately understand that the practices or goods associated with the different classes in the different areas of practice are organized in accordance with structures of opposition which are homologous to one another because they are all homologous to the structure of objective oppositions between class conditions. Without presuming to demonstrate here in a few pages what the whole of the rest of this work will endeavour to establish—but lest the reader fail to see the wood for the trees of detailed analysis—I shall merely indicate, very schematically, how the two major organizing principles of the social space govern the structure and modification of the space of cultural consumption, and, more generally, the whole universe of life-styles.

In cultural consumption, the main opposition, by overall capital value, is between the practices designated by their rarity as distinguished, those of the fractions richest in both economic and cultural capital, and the practices socially identified as vulgar because they are both easy and common, those of the fractions poorest in both these respects. In the intermediate position are the practices which are perceived as pretentious, because of the manifest discrepancy between ambition and possibilities. In opposition to the dominated condition, characterized, from the point of view of the dominant, by the combination of forced poverty and unjustified laxity, the dominant aesthetic—of which the work of art and the aesthetic disposition are the most complete embodiments—proposes the combination of ease and asceticism, i.e., self-imposed austerity, restraint, reserve, which are affirmed in that absolute manifestation of excellence, relaxation in tension.

This fundamental opposition is specified according to capital composition. Through the mediation of the means of appropriation available to them, exclusively or principally cultural on the one hand, mainly economic on the other, and the different forms of relation to works of art which result from them, the different fractions of the dominant class are oriented towards cultural practices so different in their style and object and sometimes so antagonistic (those of 'artists' and 'bourgeois')[6] that it is easy to forget that they are variants of the same fundamental relationship to necessity and to those who remain subject to it, and that each pursues the exclusive appropriation of legitimate cultural goods and the associated symbolic profits. Whereas the dominant fractions of the dominant class (the 'bourgeoisie') demand of art a high degree of denial of the social world and incline towards a hedonistic aesthetic of ease and facility, symbolized by boulevard theatre or Impressionist painting, the dominated fractions (the 'intellectuals' and 'artists') have affinities with the ascetic aspect of aesthetics and are inclined to support all artistic revolutions conducted in the name of purity and purification, refusal of ostentation and the bourgeois taste for ornament; and the dispositions towards the social world which they owe to their status as poor relations incline them to welcome a pessimistic representation of the social world.

While it is clear that art offers it the greatest scope, there is no area of practice in which the intention of purifying, refining and sublimating facile impulses and primary needs cannot assert itself, or in which the stylization of life, i.e., the primacy of form over function, which leads to the denial of function, does not produce the same effects. In language, it gives the opposition between popular outspokenness and the highly censored language of the bourgeois, between the expressionist pursuit of the picturesque or the rhetorical effect and the choice of restraint and false simplicity (litotes). The same economy of means is found in body language: here too, agitation and haste, grimaces and gesticulation are opposed to slowness—'the slow gestures, the slow glance' of nobility, according to Nietzsche[7]—to the restraint and impassivity which signify elevation. Even the field of primary tastes is organized according to the fundamental opposition, with the antithesis between quantity and quality, belly and palate, matter and manners, substance and form.

Form and Substance

The fact that in the realm of food the main opposition broadly corresponds to differences in income has masked the secondary opposition which exists, both within the middle classes and within the dominant class, between the fractions richer in cultural capital and less rich in economic capital and those whose assets are structured in the opposite way. Observers tend to see a simple effect of income in the fact that, as one rises in the social hierarchy, the proportion of income spent on food diminishes, or that, within the food budget, the proportion spent on heavy, fatty, fattening foods, which are also cheap—pasta, potatoes, beans, bacon, pork—declines (C.S. III), as does that spent on wine, whereas an increasing proportion is spent on leaner, lighter (more digestible), non-fattening foods (beef, veal, mutton, lamb, and especially fresh fruit and vegetables).[8] Because the real principle of preferences is taste, a virtue made of necessity, the theory which makes consumption a simple function of income has all the appearances to support it, since income plays an important part in determining distance from necessity. However, it cannot account for cases in which the same income is associated with totally different consumption patterns. Thus, foremen remain attached to 'popular' taste although they earn more than clerical and commercial employees, whose taste differs radically from that of manual workers and is closer to that of teachers.

For a real explanation of the variations which J. F. Engel's law merely records, one has to take account of all the characteristics of social condition which are (statistically) associated from earliest childhood with posses-

sion of high or low income and which tend to shape tastes adjusted to these conditions.[9] The true basis of the differences found in the area of consumption, and far beyond it, is the opposition between the tastes of luxury (or freedom) and the tastes of necessity. The former are the tastes of individuals who are the product of material conditions of existence defined by distance from necessity, by the freedoms or facilities stemming from possession of capital; the latter express, precisely in their adjustment, the necessities of which they are the product. Thus it is possible to deduce popular tastes for the foods that are simultaneously most 'filling' and most economical[10] from the necessity of reproducing labour power at the lowest cost which is forced on the proletariat as its very definition. The idea of taste, typically bourgeois, since it presupposes absolute freedom of choice, is so closely associated with the idea of freedom that many people find it hard to grasp the paradoxes of the taste of necessity. Some simply sweep it aside, making practice a direct product of economic necessity (workers eat beans because they cannot afford anything else), failing to realize that necessity can only be fulfilled, most of the time, because the agents are inclined to fulfil it, because they have a taste for what they are anyway condemned to. Others turn it into a taste of freedom, forgetting the conditionings of which it is the product, and so reduce it to pathological or morbid preference for (basic) essentials, a sort of congenital coarseness, the pretext for a class racism which associates the populace with everything heavy, thick and fat.[11] Taste is *amor fati*, the choice of destiny, but a forced choice, produced by conditions of existence which rule out all alternatives as mere daydreams and leave no choice but the taste for the necessary.

The taste of necessity can only be the basis of a life-style 'in-itself', which is defined as such only negatively, by an absence, by the relationship of privation between itself and the other life-styles. For some, there are elective emblems, for others stigmata which they bear in their very bodies. 'As the chosen people bore in their features the sign that they were the property of Jehovah, so the division of labour brands the manufacturing worker as the property of capital'.[12] The brand which Marx speaks of is nothing other than lifestyle, through which the most deprived immediately betray themselves, even in their use of spare time; in so doing they inevitably serve as a foil to every distinction and contribute, purely negatively, to the dialectic of pretension and distinction which fuels the incessant changing of taste. Not content with lacking virtually all the knowledge or manners which are valued in the markets of academic examination or polite conversation nor with only possessing skills which have no value there, they are the people 'who don't know how to live', who sacrifice most to material foods, and to the heaviest, grossest and most fattening of them, bread, potatoes, fats, and the most vulgar, such as wine; who spend least on clothing and cosmetics, appearance and beauty; those who 'don't know how to relax', 'who always have to be doing something', who set off in their Renault 5 or Simca 1000 to join the great traffic jams of the holiday exodus, who picnic beside major roads, cram their tents into overcrowded campsites, fling themselves into the prefabricated leisure activities designed for them by the engineers of cultural mass production; those who by all these uninspired 'choices' confirm class racism, if it needed to be confirmed, in its conviction that they only get what they deserve.

The art of eating and drinking remains one of the few areas in which the working classes explicitly challenge the legitimate art of living. In the face of the new ethic of sobriety for the sake of slimness, which is most recognized at the highest levels of the social hierarchy, peasants and especially industrial workers maintain an ethic of convivial indulgence. A bon vivant is not just someone who enjoys eating and drinking; he is someone capable of entering into the generous and familiar—that is, both simple and free—relationship that is encouraged and symbolized by eating and drinking together, in a conviviality which sweeps away restraints and reticence.

The boundary marking the break with the popular relation to food runs, without any doubt, between the manual workers and the clerical and commercial employees (C.S. II). Clerical workers spend less on food than skilled manual workers, both in absolute terms (9,376 francs as against 10,347 francs) and in relative terms (34.2 percent as against 38.3 percent); they consume less bread, pork, pork products (*charcuterie*), milk, cheese, rabbit, poultry, dried vegetables and fats, and, within a smaller food budget, spend as much on meat—beef, veal, mutton and lamb—and slightly more on fish, fresh fruit and aperitifs. These changes in the structure of spending on food are accompanied by increased spending on health and beauty care and clothing, and a slight increase in spending on cultural and leisure activities. When it is noted that the reduced spending on food, especially on the most earthly, earthy, down-to-earth foods, is accompanied by a lower birth-rate, it is reasonable to suppose that it constitutes one aspect of an overall transformation of the relationship to the world. The 'modest' taste which can defer its gratifications is opposed to the spontaneous materialism of the working classes, who refuse to participate in the Benthamite calculation of pleasures and pains, benefits and costs (e.g., for health and beauty). In other words, these two relations to the 'fruits of the earth' are grounded in two dispositions towards the future which are themselves related in circular causality to two objective futures. Against the imaginary anthropology of economics, which has never shrunk from formulating universal laws of 'temporal preference', it has to be pointed out that the propensity to subordinate present desires to future desires depends on the extent to which this sacrifice is 'reasonable', that is, on the likelihood, in any case, of obtaining future satisfactions superior to those sacrificed.[13]

Among the economic conditions of the propensity to sacrifice immediate satisfactions to expected satisfactions one must include the probability of these future satisfactions which is inscribed in the present condition. There is still a sort of economic calculation in the unwillingness to subject existence to economic calculation. The hedonism which seizes day by day the rare satisfactions ('good times') of the immediate present is the only philosophy conceivable to those who 'have no future' and, in any case, little to expect from the future.[14] It becomes clearer why the practical materialism which is particularly manifested in the relation to food is one of the most fundamental components of the popular ethos and even the popular ethic. The being-in-the-present which is affirmed in the readiness to take advantage of the good times and take time as it comes is, in itself, an affirmation of solidarity with others (who are often the only present guarantee against the threats of the future), inasmuch as this temporal immanentism is a recognition of the limits which define the condition. This is why the sobriety of the petit bourgeois is felt as a break: in abstaining from having a good time and from having it with others, the would-be petit bourgeois betrays his ambition of escaping from the common present, when, that is, he does not construct his whole self-image around the opposition between his home and the café, abstinence and intemperance, in other words, between individual salvation and collective solidarities.

The café is not a place a man goes to for a drink but a place he goes to in order to drink in company, where he can establish relationships of familiarity based on the suspension of the censorships, conventions and proprieties that prevail among strangers. In contrast to the bourgeois or petit-bourgeois café or restaurant, where each table is a separate, appropriated territory (one asks permission to borrow a chair or the salt), the working-class café is a site of companionship (each new arrival gives a collective greeting, 'Salut la compagnie!' etc.). Its focus is the counter, to be leaned on after shaking hands with the landlord—who is thus defined as the host (he often leads the conversation)—and sometimes shaking hands with the whole company; the ta-

bles, if there are any, are left to 'strangers', or women who have come in to get a drink for their child or make a phone call. In the café free rein is given to the typically popular art of the joke—the art of seeing everything as a joke (hence the reiterated 'Joking apart' or 'No joke', which mark a return to serious matters or prelude a second-degree joke), but also the art of making or playing jokes, often at the expense of the 'fat man'. He is always good for a laugh, because, in the popular code, his fatness is more a picturesque peculiarity than a defect, and because the good nature he is presumed to have predisposes him to take it in good heart and see the funny side. The joke, in other words, is the art of making fun without raising anger, by means of ritual mockery or insults which are neutralized by their very excess and which, presupposing a great familiarity, both in the knowledge they use and the freedom with which they use it, are in fact tokens of attention or affection, ways of building up while seeming to run down, of accepting while seeming to condemn—although they may also be used to test out those who show signs of stand-offishness.[15]

Three Styles of Distinction

The basic opposition between the tastes of luxury and the tastes of necessity is specified in as many oppositions as there are different ways of asserting one's distinction vis-à-vis the working class and its primary needs, or—which amounts to the same thing—different powers whereby necessity can be kept at a distance. Thus, within the dominant class, one can, for the sake of simplicity, distinguish three structures of the consumption distributed under three items: food, culture and presentation (clothing, beauty care, toiletries, domestic servants). These structures take strictly opposite forms—like the structures of their capital—among the teachers as against the industrial and commercial employers (see table 1). Whereas the latter have exceptionally high expenditure on food (37 percent of

TABLE 1

Yearly Spending by Teachers, Professionals, and Industrial and Commercial Employers, 1972

Type of spending	Teachers (higher and secondary)		Professionals		Industrial and commercial employers	
	Francs	% of total	Francs	% of total	Francs	% of total
Food[a]	9,969	24.4	13,956	24.4	16,578	37.4
Presentation[b]	4,912	12.0	12,680	22.2	5,616	12.7
Culture[c]	1,753	4.3	1,298	2.3	574	1.3

Source: C.S. II (1972).

a. Includes restaurant or canteen meals.

b. Clothes, shoes, repairs and cleaning, toiletries, hairdressing, domestic servants.

c. Books, newspapers and magazines, stationery, records, sport, toys, music, entertainments.

the budget), low cultural costs and medium spending on presentation and representation, the former, whose total spending is lower on average, have low expenditure on food (relatively less than manual workers), limited expenditure on presentation (though their expenditure on health is one of the highest) and relatively high expenditure on culture (books, papers, entertainments, sport, toys, music, radio and record-player). Opposed to both these groups are the members of the professions, who devote the same proportion of their budget to food as the teachers (24.4 percent), but out of much greater total expenditure (57,122 francs as against 40,884 francs), and who spend much more on presentation and representation than all other fractions, especially if the costs of domestic service are included, whereas their cultural expenditure is lower than that of the teachers (or even the engineers and senior executives, who are situated between the teachers and the professionals, though nearer the latter, for almost all items).

The system of differences becomes clearer when one looks more closely at the patterns of spending on food. In this respect the industrial and commercial employers differ markedly from the professionals, and a fortiori from the teachers, by virtue of the importance they give to cereal-based products (especially cakes and pastries), wine, meat preserves (foie gras, etc.) and game, and their relatively low spending on meat, fresh fruit and vegetables. The teachers, whose food purchases are almost identically structured to those of office workers, spend more than all other fractions on bread, milk products, sugar, fruit preserves and non-alcoholic drinks, less on wine and spirits and distinctly less than the professions on expensive products such as meat—especially the most expensive meats, such as mutton and lamb—and fresh fruit and vegetables. The members of the professions are mainly distinguished by the high proportion of their spending which goes on expensive products, particularly meat (18.3 percent of their food budget), and especially the most expensive meat (veal, lamb, mutton), fresh fruit and vegetables, fish and shellfish, cheese and aperitifs.[16]

Thus, when one moves from the manual workers to the industrial and commercial employers, through foremen, craftsmen and small shopkeepers, economic constraints tend to relax without any fundamental change in the pattern of spending (see figure 4). The opposition between the two extremes is here established between the poor and the rich (nouveau riche), between *la bouffe* and *la grande bouffe*;[17] the food consumed is increasingly rich (both in cost and in calories) and increasingly heavy (game, foie gras). By contrast, the taste of the professionals or senior executives defines the popular taste, by negation, as the taste for the heavy, the fat and the coarse, by tending towards the light, the refined and the delicate (see table 2). The disappearance of

FIGURE 4
The food space

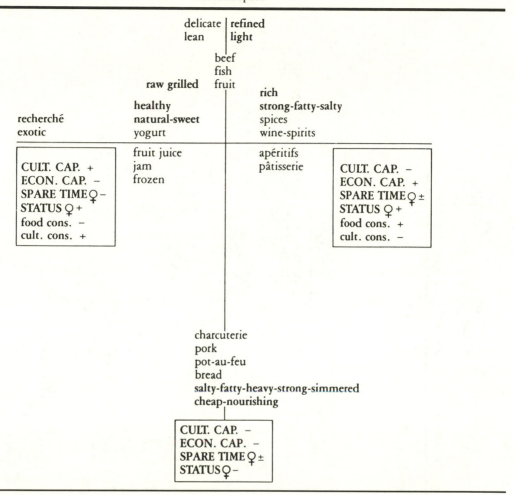

economic constraints is accompanied by a strengthening of the social censorships which forbid coarseness and fatness, in favour of slimness and distinction. The taste for rare, aristocratic foods points to a traditional cuisine, rich in expensive or rare products (fresh vegetables, meat). Finally, the teachers, richer in cultural capital than in economic capital, and therefore inclined to ascetic consumption in all areas, pursue originality at the lowest economic cost and go in for exoticism (Italian, Chinese cooking etc.)[18] and culinary populism (peasant dishes). They are thus almost consciously opposed to the (new) rich with their rich food, the buyers and sellers of *grosse bouffe,* the 'fat cats',[19] gross in body

and mind, who have the economic means to flaunt, with an arrogance perceived as 'vulgar', a life-style which remains very close to that of the working classes as regards economic and cultural consumption.

Eating habits, especially when represented solely by the produce consumed, cannot of course be considered independently of the whole life-style. The most obvious reason for this is that the taste for particular dishes (of which the statistical shopping-basket gives only the vaguest idea) is associated, through preparation and cooking, with a whole conception of the domestic economy and of the division of labour between the sexes. A taste for elaborate casserole dishes (pot-au-feu,

TABLE 2

Annual Household Expenditures on Food: Fractions of the Dominant Class, 1972

	Teachers (higher and secondary)		Senior executives		Professions		Engineers		Industrial and commercial employers	
Average number persons per household	3.11		3.6		3.5		3.6		3.6	
Average total household expenditure (francs)	40,844		52,156		57,122		49,822		44,339	
Average total household expenditure on food (francs)	9,969		13,158		13,956		12,666		16,578	
Expenditure on food as % of total expenditure	24.4		25.2		24.4		25.4		37.4	
	Average exp.		Average exp.		Average exp.		Average exp.		Average exp.	
Type of Food	Francs	As % of all food exp.	Francs	As % of all food exp.	Francs	As % of all food exp.	Francs	As % of all food exp.	Francs	As % of all food exp.
Cereals	865	8.7	993	7.5	1,011	7.2	951	7.5	1,535	9.2
bread	322	3.2	347	2.6	326	2.3	312	2.5	454	2.5
cakes, pastries	452	4.5	552	4.1	548	4.0	539	4.2	989	5.6
rusks	16	0.2	27	0.2	33	0.2	28	0.2	29	0.1
rice	35	0.3	32	0.2	62	0.4	41	0.3	33	0.1
flour	40	0.4	35	0.2	41	0.3	31	0.2	28	0.1
Vegetables	766	7.7	1,015	7.7	1,100	7.9	899	7.1	1,222	7.4
potatoes	81	0.8	94	0.7	95	0.7	98	0.7	152	0.8
fresh vegetables	555	5.6	729	5.5	811	5.8	647	5.1	915	5.1
dried or canned	131	1.3	191	1.4	216	1.5	154	1.2	153	0.8
Fruit	632	6.3	871	6.6	990	7.2	864	6.8	877	5.2
fresh fruit	295	2.9	405	3.1	586	4.2	424	3.3	547	3.1
citrus fruit, bananas	236	2.4	343	2.6	303	2.2	324	2.5	256	1.4
dried	102	1.0	122	0.9	98	0.7	116	0.9	72	0.4
Butcher's meat	1,556	15.6	2,358	18.0	2,552	18.3	2,073	16.4	2,323	14.0
beef	814	8.1	1,291	9.8	1,212	8.7	1,144	9.0	1,273	7.2
veal	335	3.4	452	3.4	630	4.5	402	3.1	377	2.3
mutton, lamb	156	1.6	315	2.3	438	3.2	242	1.9	390	2.2
horse	31	0.3	49	0.3	31	0.2	37	0.3	94	0.5
pork (fresh)	221	2.2	251	1.7	239	1.7	247	1.9	187	1.3

Pork products	634	6.3	741	5.6	774	5.5	705	5.6	812	4.9
Meat preserves	336	3.4	350	2.6	233	1.7	310	2.4	1,362	8.0
Fish, shellfish	336	3.4	503	3.8	719	5.1	396	3.1	588	3.5
Poultry	235	2.3	311	2.4	399	2.8	310	2.4	333	2.0
Rabbit, game	36	0.3	97	0.7	148	1.1	89	0.7	289	1.7
Eggs	149	1.4	172	1.3	190	1.4	178	1.4	185	1.1
Milk	299	3.0	271	2.0	249	1.8	287	2.3	309	1.9
Cheese, yogurt	692	6.9	776	5.9	843	6.0	785	6.1	1,090	6.5
Fats	399	4.0	564	4.3	525	3.8	504	4.0	551	3.3
butter	320	3.2	408	3.1	379	2.7	371	2.9	405	2.4
oil	66	0.6	136	1.0	132	1.0	103	0.8	112	0.6
margarine	12	0.1	17	0.1	12	0.1	29	0.2	19	0.1
lard	1	0	2	0	1	0	1	0	13	0.1
Sugar, confectionery, cocoa	304	3.0	395	3.0	265	1.9	327	2.6	407	2.4
Alcohol	711	7.1	1,365	10.3	1,329	9.5	937	7.4	2,218	13.4
wine	457	4.6	869	6.6	899	6.4	392	3.1	1,881	11.8
beer	82	0.8	91	0.7	40	0.3	184	1.4	93	0.5
cider	13	0.1	12	0	0	0	8	0	5	0
apéritifs, liqueurs etc.	157	1.6	391	3.0	389	2.8	352	2.8	237	1.4
Non-alcoholic drinks	344	3.4	342	2.6	267	1.9	295	2.3	327	2.0
Coffee, tea	152	1.5	215	1.5	291	2.1	178	1.4	298	1.8
Restaurant meals	829	8.3	1,863	13.0	1,562	11.2	1,372	10.8	1,179	7.1
Canteen meals	745	7.5	562	4.0	221	1.6	773	6.1	299	1.8
Miscellaneous	264	2.6	379	2.7	258	1.8	432	3.4	324	1.9

Source: C.S. II (1972).

blanquette, daube), which demand a big investment of time and interest, is linked to a traditional conception of woman's role. Thus there is a particularly strong opposition in this respect between the working classes and the dominated fractions of the dominant class, in which the women, whose labour has a high market value (and who, perhaps as a result, have a higher sense of their own value) tend to devote their spare time rather to child care and the transmission of cultural capital, and to contest the traditional division of domestic labour. The aim of saving time and labour in preparation combines with the search for light, low-calorie products, and points towards grilled meat and fish, raw vegetables ('*salades composées*'), frozen foods, yogurt and other milk products, all of which are diametrically opposed to popular dishes, the most typical of which is pot-au-feu, made with cheap meat that is boiled (as opposed to grilled or roasted), a method of cooking that chiefly demands time. It is no accident that this form of cooking symbolizes one state of female existence and of the sexual division of labour (a woman entirely devoted to housework is called 'pot-au-feu'), just as the slippers put on before dinner symbolize the complementary male rôle.

Small industrial and commercial employers, the incarnation of the 'grocer' traditionally execrated by artists, are the category who most often (60 percent) say they change into their carpet slippers every day before dinner, whereas the professions and the senior executives are most inclined to reject this petit-bourgeois symbol (35 percent say they never do it). The particularly high consumption of carpet slippers by working-class women (both urban and rural) no doubt reflects the relation to the body and to self-presentation entailed by confinement to the home and to domestic life. (The wives of craftsmen, shopkeepers and manual workers are those who most often say that their choice of clothes is mainly guided by a concern to please their husbands.)

It is among manual workers that most time and interest is devoted to cooking: 69 percent of those questioned say they like doing elaborate cooking (*la grande cuisine*), as against 59 percent of the junior executives, 52 percent of the small shopkeepers and 51 percent of the senior executives, professionals and industrialists (C.S. V). (Another indirect index of these differences as regards the sexual division of labour is that whereas the teachers and senior executives seem to give priority to a washing machine and a dishwasher, for the professionals and industrial or commercial employers priority seems to go rather to a TV set and a car—C.S. II.) Finally, when invited to choose their two favourite dishes from a list of seven, the farm workers and manual workers, who, like all other categories, give the highest rank to roast leg of lamb, are the most inclined (45 percent and 34 percent, as against 28 percent of the clerical workers, 20 percent of the senior executives and 19 percent of the small employers) to choose pot-au-feu (the farm workers are almost the only ones who choose *andouillette*—pork tripe sausage—14 percent of them, as against 4 percent of the manual workers, clerical workers and junior executives, 3 percent of the senior executives and 0 percent of the small employers). Manual workers and small employers also favour coq au vin (50 percent and 48 percent), a dish typical of small restaurants aiming to be 'posh', and perhaps for this reason associated with the idea of 'eating out' (compared with 42 percent of the clerical workers, 39 percent of the senior executives and 37 percent of the farm workers). The executives, professionals and big employers clearly distinguish themselves solely by choosing—from a list which for them is particularly narrow—the dish which is both relatively 'light' and symbolically marked (in contrast to the ordinary routine of petit-bourgeois cooking), bouillabaisse (31 percent, as against 22 percent of the clerical workers, 17 percent of the small employers, 10 percent of the manual workers, 7 percent of the farm workers), in which the opposition between fish and meat (especially the pork in sauerkraut or *cassoulet*) is clearly strengthened by regionalist and touristic connotations (C.S. IV). It is obvious that the imprecise classifications used in this survey prevent one from seeing the effects of the secondary opposition between the fractions, and that the tendencies observed would have been more marked if, for example, it had been possible to isolate the teachers or if the list of dishes had been more diversified in the sociologically pertinent respects.

Tastes in food also depend on the idea each class has of the body and of the effects of food on the body, that is, on its strength, health and beauty; and on the categories it uses to evaluate these effects, some of which may be important for one class and ignored by another, and which the different classes may rank in very different ways. Thus, whereas the working classes are more attentive to the strength of the (male) body than its shape, and tend to go for products that are both cheap and nutritious, the professions prefer products that are tasty, health-giving, light and not fattening. Taste, a class culture turned into nature, that is, *embodied,* helps to shape the class body. It is an incorporated principle of classification which governs all forms of incorporation, choosing and modifying everything that the body ingests and digests and assimilates, physiologically and psychologically. It follows that the body is the most indisputable materialization of class taste, which it manifests in several ways. It does this first in the seemingly most natural features of the body, the dimensions (volume, height, weight) and shapes (round or square, stiff or supple, straight or curved) of its visible forms, which express in countless ways a whole relation to the body, i.e., a way of treating it, caring for it, feeding it, maintaining it, which reveals the deepest dispositions of the habitus. It is in fact through preferences with regard to food which may be perpetuated beyond their social conditions of production (as, in other areas, an accent, a walk etc.),[20] and also, of course, through the uses of the body in work and leisure which are bound up with them, that the class distribution of bodily properties is determined.

The quasi-conscious representation of the approved form of the perceived body, and in particular its thinness or fatness, is not the only mediation through which the social definition of appropriate foods is established. At a deeper level, the whole body schema, in particular the physical approach to the act of eating, governs the selection of certain foods. For example, in the working classes, fish tends to be regarded as an unsuitable food for men, not only because it is a light food, insufficiently 'filling', which would only be cooked for health reasons, i.e., for invalids and children, but also because, like fruit (except bananas) it is one of the 'fiddly' things which a man's hands cannot cope with and which make him childlike (the woman, adopting a maternal role, as in all similar cases, will prepare the fish on the plate or peel the pear); but above all, it is because fish has to be eaten in a way which totally contradicts the masculine way of eating, that is, with restraint, in small mouthfuls, chewed gently, with the front of the mouth, on the tips of the teeth (because of the bones). The whole masculine identity— what is called virility—is involved in these two ways of eating, nibbling and picking, as befits a woman, or with whole-hearted male gulps and mouthfuls, just as it is involved in the two (perfectly homologous) ways of talking, with the front of the mouth or the whole mouth, especially the back of the mouth, the throat (in accordance with the opposition, noted in an earlier study, between the manners symbolized by *la bouche* and *la gueule*).[21]

This opposition can be found in each of the uses of the body, especially in the most insignificant-looking ones, which, as such, are predisposed to serve as 'memory joggers' charged with the group's deepest values, its most fundamental 'beliefs'. It would be easy to show, for example, that Kleenex tissues, which have to be used delicately, with a little sniff from the tip of the nose, are to the big cotton handkerchief, which is blown into sharply and loudly, with the eyes closed and the nose held tightly, as repressed laughter is to a belly laugh, with wrinkled nose, wide-open mouth and deep breathing ('doubled up with laughter'), as if to amplify to the utmost an experience which will not suffer containment, not least because it has to be shared, and therefore clearly manifested for the benefit of others.

And the practical philosophy of the male body as a sort of power, big and strong, with enormous, imperative, brutal needs, which is asserted in every male posture, especially when eating, is also the principle of the division of foods between the sexes, a division which both sexes recognize in their practices and their language. It behooves a man to drink and eat more, and to eat and drink stronger things. Thus, men will have two rounds of aperitifs (more on special occasions), big ones in big glasses (the success of Ricard or Pernod is no doubt partly due to its being a drink both strong and copious—not a dainty 'thimbleful'), and they leave the tit-bits (savoury biscuits, peanuts) to the children and the women, who have a small measure (not enough to 'get tipsy') of homemade aperitif (for which they swap recipes). Similarly, among the hors d'oeuvres, the *charcuterie* is more for the men, and later the cheese, especially if it is strong, whereas the *crudités* (raw vegetables) are more for the women, like the salad; and these affinities are marked by taking a second helping or sharing what is left over. Meat, the nourishing food par excellence, strong and strong-making, giving vigour, blood, and health, is the dish for the men, who take a second helping, whereas the women are satisfied with a small portion. It is not that they are stinting themselves; they really don't want what others might need, especially the men, the natural meat-eaters, and they derive a sort of authority from what they do not see as a privation. Besides, they don't have a taste for men's food, which is reputed to be harmful when eaten to excess (for example, a surfeit of meat can 'turn the blood', over-excite, bring you out in spots etc.) and may even arouse a sort of disgust.

Strictly biological differences are underlined and symbolically accentuated by differences in bearing, differences in gesture, posture and behaviour which express a whole relationship to the social world. To these are added all the deliberate modifications of appearance, especially by use of the set of marks—cosmetic (hairstyle, make-up, beard, moustache, whiskers etc.) or vestimentary— which, because they depend on the economic and cultural means that can be invested in them, function as social markers deriving their meaning and value from their position in the system of distinctive signs which they constitute and which is itself homologous with the system of social positions. The sign-bearing, sign-wearing body is also a producer of signs which are physically marked by the relationship to the body: thus the valorization of virility, expressed in a use of the mouth or a pitch of the voice, can determine the whole of working-class pronunciation. The body, a social product which is the only tangible manifestation of the 'person', is commonly perceived as the most natural expression of innermost nature. There are no merely 'physical' facial signs; the colour and thickness of lipstick, or expressions, as well as the shape of the face or the mouth, are immediately read as indices of a 'moral' physiognomy, socially characterized, i.e., of a 'vulgar' or 'distinguished' mind, naturally 'natural' or naturally 'cultivated'. The signs constituting the perceived body, cultural products which differentiate groups by their degree of culture, that is, their distance from nature, seem grounded in nature. The legitimate use of the body is spontaneously perceived as an index of moral uprightness, so that its opposite, a 'natural' body, is seen as an index of *laisser-aller* ('letting oneself go'), a culpable surrender to facility.

Thus one can begin to map out a universe of class bodies, which (biological accidents apart) tends to reproduce in its specific logic the universe of the social structure. It is no accident that bodily properties are perceived through social systems of classification which are not independent of the distribution of these properties among the social classes. The prevailing taxonomies tend to rank and contrast the properties most frequent among the dominant (i.e., the rarest ones) and those most frequent among the dominated.[22] The social representation of his own body which each agent has to reckon with,[23] from the very beginning, in order to build up his subjective image of his body and his bodily hexis, is thus obtained by applying a social system of classification based on the same principle as the social products to which it is applied. Thus, bodies would have every likelihood of receiving a value strictly corresponding to the positions of their owners in the distribution of the other fundamental properties—but for the fact that the logic of social heredity sometimes endows those least endowed in all other respects with the rarest bodily properties, such as beauty (sometimes 'fatally' attractive, because it threatens the other hierarchies), and, conversely, sometimes denies the 'high and mighty' the bodily attributes of their position, such as height or beauty.

Unpretentious or Uncouth?

It is clear that tastes in food cannot be considered in complete independence of the other dimensions of the relationship to the world, to others and to one's own body, through which the practical philosophy of each class is enacted. To demonstrate this, one would have to make a systematic comparison of the working-class and bourgeois ways of treating food, of serving, presenting and offering it, which are infinitely more revelatory than even the nature of the products involved (especially since most surveys of consumption ignore differences in quality). The analysis is a difficult one, because each life-style can only really be constructed in relation to the other, which is its objective and subjective negation, so that the meaning of behaviour is totally reversed depending on which point of view is adopted and on whether the common words which have to be used to name the conduct (e.g., 'manners') are invested with popular or bourgeois connotations.

Plain speaking, plain eating: the working-class meal is characterized by plenty (which does not exclude restrictions and limits) and above all by freedom. 'Elastic' and 'abundant' dishes are brought to the table—soups or sauces, pasta or potatoes (almost always included among the vegetables)—and served

with a ladle or spoon, to avoid too much measuring and counting, in contrast to everything that has to be cut and divided, such as roasts.[24] This impression of abundance, which is the norm on special occasions, and always applies, so far as is possible, for the men, whose plates are filled twice (a privilege which marks a boy's accession to manhood), is often balanced, on ordinary occasions, by restrictions which generally apply to the women, who will share one portion between two, or eat the leftovers of the previous day; a girl's accession to womanhood is marked by doing without. It is part of men's status to eat and to eat well (and also to drink well); it is particularly insisted that they should eat, on the grounds that 'it won't keep', and there is something suspect about a refusal. On Sundays, while the women are on their feet, busily serving, clearing the table, washing up, the men remain seated, still eating and drinking. These strongly marked differences of social status (associated with sex and age) are accompanied by no practical differentiation (such as the bourgeois division between the dining room and the kitchen, where the servants eat and sometimes the children), and strict sequencing of the meal tends to be ignored. Everything may be put on the table at much the same time (which also saves walking), so that the women may have reached the dessert, and also the children, who will take their plates and watch television, while the men are still eating the main dish and the 'lad', who has arrived late, is swallowing his soup.

This freedom, which may be perceived as disorder or slovenliness, is adapted to its function. Firstly, it is labour-saving, which is seen as an advantage. Because men take no part in housework, not least because the women would not allow it—it would be a dishonour to see men step outside their rôle—every economy of effort is welcome. Thus, when the coffee is served, a single spoon may be passed around to stir it. But these short cuts are only permissible because one is and feels at home, among the family, where ceremony would be an affectation. For example, to save washing up, the dessert may be handed out on improvised plates torn from the cake-box (with a joke about 'taking the liberty', to mark the transgression), and the neighbour invited in for a meal will also receive his piece of cardboard (offering a plate would exclude him) as a sign of familiarity. Similarly, the plates are not changed between dishes. The soup plate, wiped with bread, can be used right through the meal. The hostess will certainly offer to 'change the plates', pushing back her chair with one hand and reaching with the other for the plate next to her, but everyone will protest ('It all gets mixed up inside you') and if she were to insist it would look as if she wanted to show off her crockery (which she is allowed to if it is a new present) or to treat her guests as strangers, as is sometimes deliberately done to intruders or 'scroungers' who never return the invitation. These unwanted guests may be frozen out by changing their plates despite their protests, not laughing at their jokes, or scolding the children for their behaviour ('No, no, *we* don't mind', say the guests; 'They ought to know better by now', the parents respond). The common root of all these 'liberties' is no doubt the sense that at least there will not be self-imposed controls, constraints and restrictions—especially not in eating, a primary need and a compensation—and especially not in the heart of domestic life, the one realm of freedom, when everywhere else, and at all other times, necessity prevails.

In opposition to the free-and-easy working-class meal, the bourgeoisie is concerned to eat with all due form. Form is first of all a matter of rhythm, which implies expectations, pauses, restraints; waiting until the last person served has started to eat, taking modest helpings, not appearing over-eager. A strict sequence is observed and all coexistence of dishes which the sequence separates, fish and meat, cheese and dessert, is excluded: for example, before the dessert is served, everything left on the table, even the salt-cellar, is removed, and the crumbs are swept up. This extension of rigorous rules into everyday life (the bourgeois male shaves and dresses first

thing every morning, and not just to 'go out'), refusing the division between home and the exterior, the quotidian and the extra-quotidian, is not explained solely by the presence of strangers—servants and guests—in the familiar family world. It is the expression of a habitus of order, restraint and propriety which may not be abdicated. The relation to food—*the* primary need and pleasure—is only one dimension of the bourgeois relation to the social world. The opposition between the immediate and the deferred, the easy and the difficult, substance (or function) and form, which is exposed in a particularly striking fashion in bourgeois ways of eating, is the basis of all aestheticization of practice and every aesthetic. Through all the forms and formalisms imposed on the immediate appetite, what is demanded—and inculcated—is not only a disposition to discipline food consumption by a conventional structuring which is also a gentle, indirect, invisible censorship (quite different from enforced privations) and which is an element in an art of living (correct eating, for example, is a way of paying homage to one's hosts and to the mistress of the house, a tribute to her care and effort). It is also a whole relationship to animal nature, to primary needs and the populace who indulge them without restraint; it is a way of denying the meaning and primary function of consumption, which are essentially common, by making the meal a social ceremony, an affirmation of ethical tone and aesthetic refinement. The manner of presenting and consuming the food, the organization of the meal and setting of the places, strictly differentiated according to the sequence of dishes and arranged to please the eye, the presentation of the dishes, considered as much in terms of shape and colour (like works of art) as of their consumable substance, the etiquette governing posture and gesture, ways of serving oneself and others, of using the different utensils, the seating plan, strictly but discreetly hierarchical, the censorship of all bodily manifestations of the act or pleasure of eating (such as noise or haste), the very refinement of the things consumed, with quality more important than quantity—this whole commitment to stylization tends to shift the emphasis from substance and function to form and manner, and so to deny the crudely material reality of the act of eating and of the things consumed, or, which amounts to the same thing, the basely material vulgarity of those who indulge in the immediate satisfactions of food and drink.[25]

Given the basic opposition between form and substance, one could re-generate each of the oppositions between the two antagonistic approaches to the treatment of food and the act of eating. In one case, food is claimed as a material reality, a nourishing substance which sustains the body and gives strength (hence the emphasis on heavy, fatty, strong foods, of which the paradigm is pork—fatty and salty—the antithesis of fish—light, lean and bland); in the other, the priority given to form (the shape of the body, for example) and social form, formality, puts the pursuit of strength and substance in the background and identifies true freedom with the elective asceticism of a self-imposed rule. And it could be shown that two antagonistic world views, two worlds, two representations of human excellence are contained in this matrix. Substance—or matter—is what is substantial, not only 'filling' but also real, as opposed to all appearances, all the fine words and empty gestures that 'butter no parsnips' and are, as the phrase goes, purely symbolic; reality, as against sham, imitation, window-dressing; the little eating-house with its marble-topped tables and paper napkins where you get an honest square meal and aren't 'paying for the wallpaper' as in fancy restaurants; being, as against seeming, nature and the natural, simplicity (pot-luck, 'take it as it comes', 'no standing on ceremony'), as against embarrassment, mincing and posturing, airs and graces, which are always suspected of being a substitute for substance, i.e., for sincerity, for feeling, for what is felt and proved in actions; it is the free-speech and language of the heart which make the true 'nice guy', blunt, straightforward, unbending, honest, genuine, 'straight down the line' and 'straight as a die',

as opposed to everything that is pure form, done only for form's sake; it is freedom and the refusal of complications, as opposed to respect for all the forms and formalities spontaneously perceived as instruments of distinction and power. On these moralities, these world views, there is no neutral viewpoint; what for some is shameless and slovenly, for others is straightforward, unpretentious; familiarity is for some the most absolute form of recognition, the abdication of all distance, a trusting openness, a relation of equal to equal; for others, who shun familiarity, it is an unseemly liberty.

The popular realism which inclines working people to reduce practices to the reality of their function, to do what they do, and be what they are ('That's the way I am'), without 'kidding themselves' ('That's the way it is'), and the practical materialism which inclines them to censor the expression of feelings or to divert emotion into violence or oaths, are the near-perfect antithesis of the aesthetic disavowal which, by a sort of essential hypocrisy (seen, for example, in the opposition between pornography and eroticism) masks the interest in function by the primacy given to form, so that what people do, they do as if they were not doing it.

The Visible and the Invisible

But food—which the working classes place on the side of being and substance, whereas the bourgeoisie, refusing the distinction between inside and outside or 'at home' and 'for others', the quotidian and the extra-quotidian, introduces into it the categories of form and appearance—is itself related to clothing as inside to outside, the domestic to the public, being to seeming. And the inversion of the places of food and clothing in the contrast between the spending patterns of the working classes, who give priority to being, and the middle classes, where the concern for 'seeming' arises, is the sign of a reversal of the whole world view. The working classes make a realistic or, one might say, functionalist use of clothing. Looking for substance and function rather than form, they seek 'value for money' and choose what will 'last'. Ignoring the bourgeois concern to introduce formality and formal dress into the domestic world, the place for freedom—an apron and slippers (for women), bare chest or a vest (for men)—they scarcely mark the distinction between top clothes, visible, intended to be seen, and underclothes, invisible or hidden—unlike the middle classes, who have a degree of anxiety about external appearances, both sartorial and cosmetic, at least outside and at work (to which middle-class women more often have access).

Thus, despite the limits of the data available, one finds in men's clothing (which is much more socially marked, at the level of what can be grasped by statistics on purchases, than women's clothing) the equivalent of the major oppositions found in food consumption. In the first dimension of the space, the division again runs between the office workers and the manual workers and is marked particularly by the opposition between grey or white overalls and blue dungarees or boiler-suits, between town shoes and the more relaxed moccasins, kickers or sneakers (not to mention dressing-gowns, which clerical workers buy 3.5 times more often than manual workers). The increased quantity and quality of all purchases of men's clothing is summed up in the opposition between the suit, the prerogative of the senior executive, and the blue overall, the distinctive mark of the farmer and industrial worker (it is virtually unknown in other groups, except craftsmen); or between the overcoat, always much rarer among men than women, but much more frequent among senior executives than the other classes, and the fur-lined jacket or lumber jacket, mainly worn by agricultural and industrial workers. In between are the junior executives, who now scarcely ever wear working clothes but fairly often buy suits.

Among women, who, in all categories (except farmers and farm labourers), spend more than men (especially in the junior and senior executive, professional and other high-income categories), the number of purchases increases

as one moves up the social hierarchy; the difference is greatest for suits and costumes—expensive garments—and smaller for dresses and especially skirts and jackets. The topcoat, which is increasingly frequent among women at higher social levels, is opposed to the 'all-purpose' raincoat, in the same way as overcoat and lumber jacket are opposed for men. The use of the smock and the apron, which in the working classes is virtually the housewife's uniform, increases as one moves down the hierarchy (in contrast to the dressing-gown, which is virtually unknown among peasants and industrial workers).

The interest the different classes have in self-presentation, the attention they devote to it, their awareness of the profits it gives and the investment of time, effort, sacrifice and care which they actually put into it are proportionate to the chances of material or symbolic profit they can reasonably expect from it. More precisely, they depend on the existence of a labour market in which physical appearance may be valorized in the performance of the job itself or in professional relations; and on the differential chances of access to this market and the sectors of this market in which beauty and deportment most strongly contribute to occupational value. A first indication of this correspondence between the propensity to cosmetic investments and the chances of profit may be seen in the gap, for all forms of beauty care, between those who work and those who do not (which must also vary according to the nature of the job and the work environment). It can be understood in terms of this logic why working-class women, who are less likely to have a job and much less likely to enter one of the occupations which most strictly demand conformity to the dominant norms of beauty, are less aware than all others of the 'market' value of beauty and much less inclined to invest time and effort, sacrifices and money in cultivating their bodies.

It is quite different with the women of the petite bourgeoisie, especially the new petite bourgeoisie, in the occupations involving presentation and representation, which often impose a uniform (*tenue*) intended, among other things, to abolish all traces of heterodox taste, and which always demand what is called *tenue*, in the sense of 'dignity of conduct and correctness of manners', implying, according to the dictionary, 'a refusal to give way to vulgarity or facility'. (In the specialized 'charm schools' which train hostesses, the working-class girls who select themselves on the basis of 'natural' beauty undergo a radical transformation in their way of walking, sitting, laughing, smiling, talking, dressing, making-up etc.) Women of the petite bourgeoisie who have sufficient interests in the market in which physical properties can function as capital to recognize the dominant image of the body unconditionally without possessing, at least in their own eyes (and no doubt objectively) enough body capital to obtain the highest profits, are, here too, at the site of greatest tension.

The self-assurance given by the certain knowledge of one's own value, especially that of one's body or speech, is in fact very closely linked to the position occupied in social space (and also, of course, to trajectory). Thus, the proportion of women who consider themselves below average in beauty, or who think they look older than they are, falls very rapidly as one moves up the social hierarchy. Similarly, the ratings women give themselves for the different parts of their bodies tend to rise with social position, and this despite the fact that the implicit demands rise too. It is not surprising that petit-bourgeois women—who are almost as dissatisfied with their bodies as working-class women (they are the ones who most often wish they looked different and who are most discontented with various parts of their bodies), while being more aware of the usefulness of beauty and more often recognizing the dominant ideal of physical excellence—devote such great investments, of self-denial and especially of time, to improving their appearance and are such unconditional believers in all forms of cosmetic voluntarism (e.g., plastic surgery).

As for the women of the dominant class, they derive a double assurance from their bod-

ies. Believing, like petit-bourgeois women, in the value of beauty and the value of the effort to be beautiful, and so associating aesthetic value and moral value, they feel superior both in the intrinsic, natural beauty of their bodies and in the art of self-embellishment and everything they call *tenue*, a moral and aesthetic virtue which defines 'nature' negatively as sloppiness. Beauty can thus be simultaneously a gift of nature and a conquest of merit, as much opposed to the abdications of vulgarity as to ugliness.

Thus, the experience par excellence of the 'alienated body', embarrassment, and the opposite experience, ease, are clearly unequally probable for members of the petite bourgeoisie and the bourgeoisie, who grant the same recognition to the same representation of the legitimate body and legitimate deportment, but are unequally able to achieve it. The chances of experiencing one's own body as a vessel of grace, a continuous miracle, are that much greater when bodily capacity is commensurate with recognition; and, conversely, the probability of experiencing the body with unease, embarrassment, timidity grows with the disparity between the ideal body and the real body, the dream body and the 'looking-glass self' reflected in the reactions of others (the same laws are also true of speech).

Although it is not a petit-bourgeois monopoly, the petit-bourgeois experience of the world starts out from timidity, the embarrassment of someone who is uneasy in his body and his language and who, instead of being 'as one body with them', observes them from outside, through other people's eyes, watching, checking, correcting himself, and who, by his desperate attempts to reappropriate an alienated being-for-others, exposes himself to appropriation, giving himself away as much by hyper-correction as by clumsiness. The timidity which, despite itself, realizes the objectified body, which lets itself be trapped in the destiny proposed by collective perception and statement (nicknames etc.), is betrayed by a body that is subject to the representation of others even in its passive, unconscious reactions (one feels oneself blushing). By contrast, ease, a sort of indifference to the objectifying gaze of others which neutralizes its powers, presupposes the self-assurance which comes from the certainty of being able to objectify that objectification, appropriate that appropriation, of being capable of imposing the norms of apperception of one's own body, in short, of commanding all the powers which, even when they reside in the body and apparently borrow its most specific weapons, such as 'presence' or charm, are essentially irreducible to it. This is the real meaning of the findings of the experiment by W. D. Dannenmaier and F. J. Thumin, in which the subjects, when asked to assess the height of familiar persons from memory, tended to overestimate most of the height of those who had most authority or prestige in their eyes.[26] It would seem that the logic whereby the 'great' are perceived as physically greater than they are applies very generally, and that authority of whatever sort contains a power of seduction which it would be naive to reduce to the effect of self-interested servility. That is why political contestation has always made use of caricature, a distortion of the bodily image intended to break the charm and hold up to ridicule one of the principles of the effect of authority imposition.

Charm and charisma in fact designate the power, which certain people have, to impose their own self-image as the objective and collective image of their body and being; to persuade others, as in love or faith, to abdicate their generic power of objectification and delegate it to the person who should be its object, who thereby becomes an absolute subject, without an exterior (being his own Other), fully justified in existing, legitimated. The charismatic leader manages to be for the group what he is for himself, instead of being for himself, like those dominated in the symbolic struggle, what he is for others. He 'makes' the opinion which makes him; he constitutes himself as an absolute by a manipulation of symbolic power which is constitutive of his power since it enables him to produce and impose his own objectification.

The Universes of Stylistic Possibles

Thus, the spaces defined by preferences in food, clothing or cosmetics are organized according to the same fundamental structure, that of the social space determined by volume and composition of capital. Fully to construct the space of life-styles within which cultural practices are defined, one would first have to establish, for each class and class fraction, that is, for each of the configurations of capital, the generative formula of the habitus which retranslates the necessities and facilities characteristic of that class of (relatively) homogeneous conditions of existence into a particular life-style. One would then have to determine how the dispositions of the habitus are specified, for each of the major areas of practice, by implementing one of the stylistic possibles offered by each field (the field of sport, or music, or food, decoration, politics, language etc.). By superimposing these homologous spaces one would obtain a rigorous representation of the space of life-styles, making it possible to characterize each of the distinctive features (e.g., wearing a cap or playing the piano) in the two respects in which it is objectively defined, that is, on the one hand by reference to the set of features constituting the area in question (e.g., the system of hairstyles), and on the other hand by reference to the set of features constituting a particular life-style (e.g., the working-class lifestyle), within which its social significance is determined.

Sources

The survey on which the work was based was carried out in 1963, after a preliminary survey by extended interview and ethnographic observation, on a sample of 692 subjects (both sexes) in Paris, Lille and a small provincial town. To obtain a sample large enough to make it possible to analyse variations in practices and opinions in relation to sufficiently homogeneous social units, a complementary survey was carried out in 1967–68, bringing the total number of subjects to 1,217. Because the survey measured relatively stable dispositions, this time-lag does not seem to have affected the responses (except perhaps for the question on singers, an area of culture where fashions change more rapidly).

The following complementary sources (C.S.) were also used:

I. The 1966 survey on 'businessmen and senior executives' was carried out by SOFRES (Société française d'enquêtes par sondages) on behalf of the Centre d'études des supports de publicité (CESP). The sample consisted of 2,257 persons aged 15 and over, each living in a household the head of which was a large industrial or commercial employer, a member of the professions, a senior executive, an engineer or a secondary or higher-education teacher. The questionnaire included a set of questions on reading habits and the previous few days' reading of daily, weekly and monthly newspapers and magazines, use of radio and TV, standard of living, household equipment, life-style (holidays, sport, consumption), professional life (conferences, travel, business meals), cultural practices and the principal basic data (educational level, income, population of place of residence etc.). I had access to the whole set of distributions by the socio-occupational category of the head of household or individual.

II. The regular survey by INSEE (Institut national de la statistique et des études economiques) on household living conditions and expenditure was based in 1972 on a representative sample of 13,000 households. It consists of a survey by questionnaire dealing with the characteristics of the household (composition, ages, occupation of the head), accommodation and facilities, major expenditure (clothing, fuel etc.), periodic expenditure (rent, service charges etc.), combined with analysis of account books for current expenditure, left with each household for a week, collected and checked by the interviewer. This survey makes it possible to assess the whole range of expenditure (except certain major and infrequent items such as air travel, removal expenses etc.), as well as items of consumption not preceded by purchase (food in the case of farmers, items drawn from their stocks by craftsmen and shopkeepers), which are evaluated at their retail price to allow comparison with the other categories of households. This explains why consumption is considerably higher than income in the case of farmers and small businessmen (categories which are always particularly prone to under-declare their income). For the overall findings, see G. Bigata and B. Bouvier, 'Les conditions de vie des ménages en 1972', *Collections de l'IN-SEE*, ser. M, no. 32 (February 1972). The data presented here come from secondary analysis of tables by narrow categories produced at my request.

The other surveys consulted are simply listed below. These studies, almost always devoted to a particular area of cultural activity, are generally based on relatively limited samples. They mostly use a classification which groups the occupations into five categories: (1) *agriculteurs* (farmers and farm labourers); (2) *ouvriers* (industrial manual workers); (3) industrial and commercial employers; (4) clerical workers and junior executives; (5) senior executives and the 'liberal professions'.

III. INSEE, 'La consommation alimentaire des Français', *Collections de l'INSEE*. (The regular INSEE surveys on eating habits.)

IV. SOFRES, *Les habitudes de table des Français* (Paris, 1972).

V. SOFRES, *Les Français et la gastronomie*, July 1977. (Sample of 1,000.)

Notes

1. The gaps are more clear-cut and certainly more visible as regards education than income, because information on incomes (based on tax declarations) is much less reliable than information on qualifications. This is especially true of industrial and commercial employers (who, in the CESP survey—C.S. I—provided, along with doctors, the highest rate of non-response to the questions about income), craftsmen, shopkeepers and farmers.

2. It follows from this that the relationship between conditions of existence and practices or the meaning of practices is not to be understood in terms either of the logic of mechanism or of the logic of consciousness.

3. In contrast to the atomistic approach of social psychology, which breaks the unity of practice to establish partial 'laws' claiming to account for the products of practice, the opus operatum, the aim is to establish general laws reproducing the laws of production, the modus operandi.

4. Economic theory, which treats economic agents as interchangeable actors, paradoxically fails to take account of the economic dispositions, and is thereby prevented from really explaining the systems of preferences which define incommensurable and independent subjective use-values.

5. An ethic, which seeks to impose the principles of an ethos (i.e., the forced choices of a social condition) as a universal norm, is another, more subtle way of succumbing to *amor fati*, of being content with what one is and has. Such is the basis of the felt contradiction between ethics and revolutionary intent.

6. 'Bourgeois' is used here as shorthand for 'dominant fractions of the dominant class', and 'intellectual' or 'artist' functions in the same way for 'dominated fractions of the dominant class'.

7. F. Nietzsche, *Der Wille zur Macht* (Stuttgart, Alfred Kröner, 1964), no. 943, p. 630.

8. Bananas are the only fruit for which manual workers and farm workers have higher annual per capita spending (FF 23.26 and FF 25.20) than all other classes, especially the senior executives, who spend most on apples (FF 31.60 as against FF 21.00 for manual workers), whereas the rich, expensive fruits—grapes, peaches and nuts—are mainly eaten by professionals and industrial and commercial employers (FF 29.04 for grapes, 19.09 for peaches and 17.33 for nuts, as against FF 6.74, 11.78 and 4.90 respectively, for manual workers).

9. This whole paragraph is based on secondary analysis of the tables from the 1972 INSEE survey on household expenditure on 39 items by socio-occupational category (C.S. II).

10. A fuller translation of the original text would include: "'les *nourritures* à la fois les plus *nourrissantes* et les plus *économiques*'" (the double tautology showing the reduction to pure economic function).' (Translator's note.)

11. In the French: 'le gros et le gras, gros rouge, gros sabots, gros travaux, gros rire, grosses blagues, gros bon sens, plaisanteries grasses'— cheap red wine, clogs (i.e., obviously), heavy work, belly laughs, crude common sense, crude jokes (translator).

12. K. Marx, *Capital*, I (Harmondsworth, Penguin, 1976), 482 (translator).

13. One fine example, taken from Böhm-Bawerk, will demonstrate this essentialism: 'We must now consider a *second* phenomenon of human experience—one that is heavily fraught with consequence. That is the fact that we feel less concerned about future sensations of joy and sorrow simply because they do lie in the future, and the lessening of our concern is in proportion to the remoteness of that future. Consequently we accord to goods which are intended to serve future ends a value which falls short of the true intensity of their future marginal utility. *We systematically undervalue our future wants and also the means which serve to satisfy them.*' E. Böhm-Bawerk, *Capital and Interest*, II (South Holland, Ill., 1959), 268, quoted by G. L. Stigler and G. S. Becker, 'De gustibus non est disputandum', *American Economic Review*, 67 (March 1977), 76–90.

14. We may assume that the deep-seated relation to the future (and also to one's own person—which is valued more at higher levels of the social hierarchy) is reflected in the small proportion of manual workers who say that 'there is a new life after death' (15 percent, compared with 18 percent of craftsmen and shopkeepers, office workers and middle managers, and 32 percent of senior executives).

15. It is not superfluous to point out that this art, which has its recognized virtuoso, the 'life and soul of the party', can sink into the caricature of jokes or remarks that are defined as stereotyped, stupid or coarse in terms of the criteria of popular taste.

16. The oppositions are much less clear-cut in the middle classes, although homologous differences are found between primary teachers and office workers on the one hand and shopkeepers on the other.

17. *La bouffe:* 'grub', 'nosh'; *grande bouffe:* 'blow-out' (translator).

18. The preference for foreign restaurants—Italian, Chinese, Japanese and, to a lesser extent, Russian—rises with level in the social hierarchy. The only exceptions are Spanish restaurants, which are associated with a more popular form of tourism, and North African restaurants, which are most favoured by junior executives (C.S. IV).

19. *Les gros:* the rich; *grosse bouffe:* bulk food (cf. *grossiste:* wholesaler, and English 'grocer'). See also note 17 above (translator).

20. That is why the body designates not only present position but also trajectory.

21. In 'The Economics of Linguistic Exchanges', *Social Science Information,* 26 (December 1977), 645–668, Bourdieu develops the opposition between two ways of speaking, rooted in two relations to the body and the world, which have a lexical reflection in the many idioms based on two words for 'mouth': *la bouche* and *la gueule*. *La bouche* is the 'standard' word for the mouth; but in opposition to *la gueule*—a slang or 'vulgar' word except when applied to animals—it tends to be restricted to the lips, whereas *la gueule* can include the whole face or the throat. Most of the idioms using *la bouche* imply fastidiousness, effeminacy or disdain; those with *la gueule* connote vigour, strength or violence (translator's note).

22. This means that the taxonomies applied to the perceived body (fat/thin, strong/weak, big/small etc.) are, as always, at once arbitrary (e.g., the ideal female body may be fat or thin, in different economic and social contexts) and necessary, i.e., grounded in the specific reason of a given social order.

23. More than ever, the French possessive pronouns—which do not mark the owner's gender— ought to be translated 'his or her'. The 'sexism' of the text results from the male translator's reluctance to defy the dominant use of a sexist symbolic system (translator).

24. One could similarly contrast the bowl, which is generously filled and held two-handed for unpretentious drinking, and the cup, into which a little is poured, and more later ('Would you care for a little more coffee?'), and which is held between two fingers and sipped from.

25. Formality is a way of denying the truth of the social world and of social relations. Just as

popular 'functionalism' is refused as regards food, so too there is a refusal of the realistic vision which leads the working classes to accept social exchanges for what they are (and, for example, to say, without cynicism, of someone who has done a favour or rendered a service, 'She knows I'll pay her back'). Suppressing avowal of the calculation which pervades social relations, there is a striving to see presents, received or given, as 'pure' testimonies of friendship, respect, affection, and equally 'pure' manifestations of generosity and moral worth.

26. W. D. Dannenmaier and F. J. Thumin, 'Authority Status as a Factor in Perceptual Distortion of Size', *Journal of Social Psychology*, 63 (1964), 361–365.

Interests, Attitudes, and Personalities

MICHAEL HOUT, JEFF MANZA, AND CLEM BROOKS

The Realignment of U.S. Presidential Voting, 1952–1992

American presidential elections since the 1960s have offered ample material for political scientists and political sociologists who have contended that the stable class politics of industrial capitalism is giving way to a new, 'postmaterial' politics (e.g. Inglehart 1977, 1990; Lipset 1981; Clark and Lipset 1991; Abramson and Inglehart 1995). They point to newer cleavages based on gender, identity, and 'postmaterialist' values which—they argue— have taken on more electoral importance. In a world of new political movements and politicians standing for office who are completely outside traditional party systems, claims of class dealignment ring true. Others have countered that conclusions of 'dealignment' do not square with the empirical evidence and/or exaggerate the significance of these developments. The rise of one set of cleavages does not imply the fall of others. Instead of class dealignment, defenders of class analysis argue that the association between class and vote is merely subject to patterns of 'trendless fluctuation' (Heath *et al.* 1985, 1991) or class realignment (Hout *et al.* 1995). . . .

Originally published in 1999. Please see complete source information beginning on page 891.

Class Voting and Class Politics

Interest in class voting goes back to the dawn of contemporary understandings of class in the nineteenth century. The roots of contemporary debates are planted in data, however, not in class theory. The national election surveys that accumulated in many countries since the 1960s yielded a harvest of class-voting studies over lengthy time-series, and most findings through the early 1970s suggested that class had a strong—if variable—influence on voting behaviour (Lipset 1981 (1st edn. 1960); Alford 1963; Lipset and Rokkan 1967; Rose 1974). Lipset and Rokkan's influential theoretical synthesis argued that two revolutions, the National Revolution and the Industrial Revolution, initiated everywhere processes of social differentiation and conflict. The two revolutions produced four basic sets of cleavages: (1) church(es) versus the state, (2) dominant versus subject cultures, (3) agriculture versus manufacturing, and (4) employers versus workers (1967: 14). The precise political articulation of these cleavages varied from country to country, depending on geopolitical structures and the timing of political and economic development, but all countries were subject to the same basic pattern. Further industrialization led to the decline of most types of social cleavage other than class, magnifying the importance of the democratic class struggle.

In many Western European countries and Australia the cleavage structure was 'frozen' in an institutional structure dominated by class-based parties (Lipset and Rokkan 1967; also Rose and Urwin 1970; Bartolini and Mair 1990). Where this occurred, it is appropriate to talk of a 'class politics' (Mair 1993, 1999). But even in places like the United States where class-based parties have not emerged, the long-run pattern of class voting calls for our attention. In particular, as our analysis of the US case has shown, the absence of a 'class politics' actually raises a new possibility of class realignment. In the United States, classes have shifted their allegiance from one party to another, while parties have sought to revise their traditional appeals in order to attract voters from classes that may be 'available'. In many ways it is a two-sided dance in which both partners try to lead.

This process has been explicit in the elections of 1992 and 1996. Mr Clinton dropped the Democrats' familiar appeals to 'working people' in favour of direct calls to 'the middle class'. It is well known that many blue-collar workers identify with the middle class (Halle 1984). Mr Clinton appealed to them and to insecure white-collar workers in 1992 with proposals to reform health care and welfare, and in 1996 with promises to defend middle-class entitlements like old-age pensions and health care (Social Security and Medicaid), and pledges to subsidize higher education by giving tax credits to students' parents.

Unions used to be the agents that bound the working class to the Democrats in the United States. The Democratic Party gave the unions an important voice in the selection of candidates from 1936 to 1968. In exchange, the unions delivered their share of the working-class vote to the Democrats. That tie was effectively broken by electoral reforms in the 1970s. The demise of unions' political brokerage was hastened by a crisis in public trust of unions and the trend away from union membership. Scandals rocked organized labour in the 1960s and 1970s, eroding public trust

(Lipset and Schneider 1983) and making identification with unions more of a liability than an asset for a politician. All the while firms were leaving states with long union traditions and moving to 'right-to-work' states that promised to block union organizing. At the same time, the National Labor Relations Board made it harder for workers to organize new union locals (Fischer *et al.* 1996: ch. 6).

Some of these shifts in presidential politics may have encouraged rising class voting on the right. Republican candidates promised to cut government spending and regulation in ways designed to appeal to managers and entrepreneurs. The emphasis on 'taming the unions' presumably has a constituency among those who oppose unions in the workplace.

Our analysis of class voting in the United States distinguishes between what we term 'traditional' and 'total' class voting and develops statistical models appropriate to each (Hout *et al.* 1995). Traditional models of class voting hinge on the theoretical assumption that there should be a close correspondence between the working class and parties of the left and between the middle class and parties of the centre or right. This assumption can be embedded in models of class voting that identify the 'natural' party of a given class (Rose and McAllister 1986; Weakliem 1995), or models that array classes and parties as ordered points on latent continua and examine the degree to which the latent variables are associated (Weakliem and Heath 1999). Whatever its particular form, the traditional assumption is, however, only appropriate to understanding the historically significant but specific pattern of the relationship between classes and parties that has tended to characterize capitalist democracies in the twentieth century.

Class voting need not be limited to the combinations embedded in the traditional conception. First, class affects turnout as well as partisan choice (Verba *et al.* 1978). This class skew in participation is likely to have important consequences for the party system and public policy (Burnham 1982; Piven and Cloward 1986). Yet analyses of class voting in the United States almost never simultaneously consider voting and nonvoting (Weakliem and Heath (1999) and Hout *et al.* (1995) provide exceptions). Secondly, even within the ambit of partisan choice, traditional alliances need not be the only class differences we consider. In other words, total class voting—the sum of all class differences in voting behaviour—is more inclusive than 'traditional' class voting. Traditional class voting, while clearly important to the study of class voting, is a specific configuration in the comparative and historical alignment of classes and parties, but not the *only* way in which classes can differ at the polls. Traditional class voting contributes to total class voting, but the patterns of voting and partisanship can and do shift. Shifts in traditional class voting patterns are typically interpreted as *dealignment* (i.e. as confirmation of the declining importance of class for voting behaviour). Our 'total' class-voting approach allowed us to see that while the traditional linkages between classes and parties have undergone *realignment*, the effect of class location on voting behaviour remains significant.

Our distinction between traditional and total class voting is related to Mair's (1999) distinction between 'class politics' and 'class voting'. According to Mair, class voting signifies a tendency for classes to ally themselves with different parties in a given election; class politics requires that the coalitions persist over several elections and become institutionalized. Total class voting as we have defined it here requires only class voting. Discussions of the decline of traditional class voting implicitly assume—but do not demonstrate—an erosion of class politics.

The concept of traditional class voting is deeply rooted in the literature. It is unavoidable when class is conceived or operationalized as a dichotomy. A multi-class approach implied by contemporary theories of class and stratification invites the distinction between total and traditional class voting as does the

simultaneous consideration of several voting outcomes (including nonvoting). In our analysis of class voting in the United States since the Second World War (Hout *et al.* 1995) we specify statistical models predicated on both conceptions, show how models predicated on the total class-voting conception fit the data better, and conclude that the data contradict the thesis of declining political significance of class. We shall review those results in this essay. . . .

Data and Methods

The data come from the American National Election Study (ANES)—a time-series that stretches back to the presidential election of 1952. The 1952 ANES also included a question about voting in the 1948 election. The ANES is a stratified random sample of voting-age Americans, with the sample size varying from approximately 1,200 to 2,500 respondents in a given year.

The dependent variable in our analyses is self-reported vote for president. Self-reports exaggerate turnout but reproduce the partisan split well in each election (e.g. Abramson *et al.* 1994).

We measure the effect of elections using dummy variables. We use two strategies to assess changes in the effects of other variables. The first is to test for the statistical interaction between the election dummy variables and each of the socio-demographic variables in our model. The other is to test for the interaction between a linear time variate and each of the socio-demographic variables. We prefer the simpler linear change specification whenever it fits the data acceptably well, but we are not inclined to extrapolate the trends beyond the observed time-series.

We use one class scheme in all elections. It is the six-class scheme we devised for our previous analyses of voting in US presidential elections (Hout *et al.* 1995). To the familiar five-class version of the Erikson-Goldthorpe (1992) scheme, we add a distinction between managers and professionals among the so-called 'salariat.' Thus, our class categories are: (1) professional (including self-employed), (2) manager, (3) nonmanagerial white-collar employee,[1] (4) self-employed (except professional), (5) skilled blue collar, and (6) less skilled blue collar. The key variables are self-employment (yes or no) and occupation.

We use a combination of graphical displays and logistic regression methods to analyse the ANES data. In our logistic regressions, we combine data on all elections into a single dataset and estimate the main effects of election, class, gender, age, region, education, and race. The general form of the logistic regression equation is:

$$y_i = \ln(p_i/(1 - p_i))$$
$$= \beta_0 + \Sigma_{j=1}^{11}(\beta_j T_{ij}) + \Sigma_{j=12}^{16}(\beta_j X_{i(j-11)})$$
$$+ \Sigma_{j=17}^{P}(\beta_j Z_{i(j-16)}) \tag{1}$$

where y_i is the log odds on person i voting for the Democratic candidate in an election, T_{ij} ($t = 1, \ldots, 11$) is a dummy variable for election, $X_{i(j-11)}$ ($J = 12, \ldots, 16$) is a dummy variable for class, and $Z_{i(j-16)}$ ($J = 17, \ldots, P$) represents the other variables in the model. We then selectively introduce interaction effects—especially those involving time—and keep only the significant ones.

The Realignment of Class Voting

The traditional pattern of class voting held in the US presidential elections of 1948 up until 1960.[2] With the exception of the self-employed, middle-class voters supported the Republican candidates and working-class voters supported the Democrats. The self-employed split evenly between the two parties. After 1964 professionals shifted rapidly towards the Democrats; routine white-collar workers followed at a slower pace. At about the same time, the self-employed and skilled blue-collar workers shifted in the Republican

direction. The self-employed had split between Democrats and Republicans; they became strong Republicans. The skilled blue-collar workers had been strong Democrats; they began to split their votes and were actually strong Republicans in 1988. Managers and less-skilled blue-collar workers showed no significant trend, although the lower working-class vote became more volatile after 1960.

We summarize these results in two forms in Figure 1 (from Hout *et al.* 1995: fig. 2). The data in the figure are coefficients from two logistic regression models. The simpler model fits a linear trend that varies by class to the voting time-series; the coefficients are connected by the straight lines in each panel of the figure. The more complicated model allows each class parameter to take its best-fitting value in each election; the coefficients are shown as dots in the figure. The simpler linear interaction model is preferred for these data, even though the dots spread around the lines.[3]

The most important feature of these trends is the bifurcation of the 'salariat'. Managers and professionals have followed different political paths since the 1960s. Managers' interests cling closely to the low-tax, deregulation agenda of the Republican Party. Professionals have less of a stake in those policies for several reasons. Although their incomes have been as high as managers' in recent years and were actually slightly higher in the 1970s (Levy 1995), professionals are not as worried about government spending or regulation as managers are (Brooks and Manza 1997). Strikes and wage demands of trade unions seldom affect professionals' work. Thus, these mild material interests have been overtaken by professionals' concerns with civil rights, civil liberties, and the environment. In one sense, the impact of social issues on professionals' voting is a point in favour of postmaterialist accounts of electoral change. But a postmaterialist argument implies that class no longer correlates with vote. Here we see that one class responded to these concerns by

FIGURE 1
Total effect of class on partisan choice by year, class, and model: United States, 1948–1992

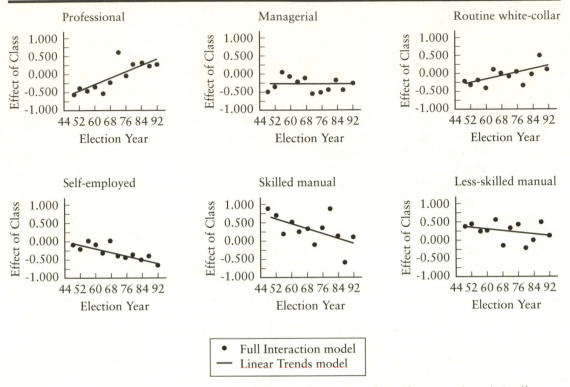

Note: Total effect controls for gender, race, region, age, education, and significant trends in their effects.

switching allegiance from one party to the other—as a class.

The other politically significant feature of the post–1960s class-voting profile is the volatility of the working class, especially the skilled craft workers. The main trend is away from the Democrats and towards the Republicans, but they swing widely around that trend line. Exactly why is unclear. Some accounts cited the special appeal of Ronald Reagan. But it is 1956 (Eisenhower's second campaign), 1972 (Nixon's second campaign), and 1988 (Bush's first campaign) that are the strong Republican showings among skilled blue-collar workers. Two of these are reelection bids. Skilled workers also strongly backed the incumbent—Carter—in 1980. But it is more than an attraction to the incumbent as neither Johnson in 1964 nor Reagan in 1984 did better than the trend would suggest. . . .

Conclusions

To understand the changing class coalitions of postwar American politics, analysts will need to [investigate] party strategies and class-specific changes in public opinion. The Democratic and Republican parties themselves have changed their appeals. Since the late 1960s, the Republicans have frequently played on skilled workers' economic self-interest to lure their votes. They have met with varying degrees of success. These appeals have lost them some support among routine white-collar workers and professionals. Explicit appeals by Democrats and 'new Democrats' have shored up that latent support. In recent presidential campaigns, the Democrats have explicitly invoked the 'middle class' as their primary electoral target. Further research, perhaps combining qualitative and quantitative research on the bases of party appeals, is called for to explore these possibilities (for the few existing efforts to explore the party coalitions, see Stanley *et al.* 1986 and Carmines and Stanley 1992).

Research on the class effects of changes in public opinion are also appropriate. In our own earlier work (Brooks and Manza 1997), we have found that the increased salience of liberal attitudes on social issues explains much of the shift of professionals towards the Democratic Party. Other studies focusing on attitudes may continue to reveal class-specific differences which can help account for class realignment.

Notes

1. This class is mostly composed of clerical and sales workers. In the United States, this class is sometimes called 'pink collar' because the majority of clerical, sales, and white-collar service workers are women. Workers in this category are also distinct from other white-collar employees because they tend to be paid hourly wages instead of a salary. They are also more unionized than other white-collar classes.

2. The 1948 data are from the retrospective reports of respondents to the 1952 ANES.

3. The likelihood ratio test (the difference between −2 log-likelihood for the full interaction and linear change models) is 45 with 61 degrees of freedom (with a *bic* value of −501).

References

Abramson, P.R., and Inglehart, R. 1995. *Value Change in Global Perspective*. Ann Arbor: University of Michigan Press.

Abramson, P.R., Aldrich, J.H., and Rhode, D.W. 1994. *Change and Continuity in the 1992 Elections*. Washington, D.C.: Congressional Quarterly Press.

Alford, R. 1963. *Party and Society: The Anglo-American Democracies*. Westport, Conn.: Greenwood Press.

Bartolini, S., and Mair, P. 1990. *Identity, Competition and Electoral Availability: The Stabilisation of European Electorates, 1885–1985*. Cambridge: Cambridge University Press.

Brooks, C., and Manza, J. 1997. "The social and ideological bases of middle class political realignment in the United States, 1972–1992." *American Sociological Review* 62: 91–108.

Burnham, W.D. 1982. *The Current Crisis in American Politics*. New York: Oxford University Press.

Carmines, E.G., and Stanley, H.W. 1992. "The transformation of the New Deal party system: social groups, political ideology, and changing partisanship among northern whites, 1972–1988." *Political Behavior* 14: 213–37.

Clark, T.N., and Lipset, S.M. 1991. "Are social classes dying?" *International Sociology* 6: 397–410.

Erikson, R., and Goldthorpe, J.H. 1992. *The Constant Flux: A Study of Class Mobility in Industrial Societies*. Oxford: Clarendon Press.

Fischer, C.S., Hout, M., Sánchez Jankowski, M., Lucas, S.R., Swidler, A., and Voss, K. 1996. *Inequality by Design: Cracking the Bell Curve Myth*. Princeton: Princeton University Press.

Halle, D. 1984. *America's Working Man: Work, Home, and Politics Among Blue-collar Property Owners*. Chicago: University of Chicago Press.

Heath, A.F., Jowell, R., and Curtice, J. 1985. *How Britain Votes*. Oxford: Pergamon Press.

Heath, A.F., Evans, G., Field, J., and Witherspoon, S. 1991. *Understanding Political Change: The British Voter, 1964–1987*. Oxford: Pergamon Press.

Hout, M., Brooks, C., and Manza, J. 1995. "The democratic class struggle in the United States." *American Sociological Review* 60: 805–28.

Inglehart, R. 1977. *The Silent Revolution: Changing Values and Political Styles among Western Publics*. Princeton: Princeton University Press.

Inglehart, R. 1990. *Culture Shift in Advanced Industrial Society*. Princeton: Princeton University Press.

Levy, F. 1995. "Incomes and income inequality." In *State of the Union: America in the 1990's, Volume One: Economic Trends*, ed. R. Farley. New York: Russell Sage Foundation. 1–57.

Lipset, S.M. 1981. *Political Man: The Social Bases of Politics* (expanded and updated edn.). London: Heinemann.

Lipset, S.M., and Rokkan, S. 1967. "Cleavage structures, party systems and voter alignments: an introduction." In *Party Systems and Voter Alignments: Cross National Perspectives*, eds. S.M. Lipset and S. Rokkan. New York: The Free Press. 1–64.

Lipset, S.M., and Schneider, W.S. 1983. *The Confidence Gap: Business, Labor, and Government in the Public Mind*. New York: Free Press.

Mair, P. 1999. "Critical Commentary." In *The End of Class Politics? Class Voting in Compar-*

ative Context, ed. Geoffrey Evans. Oxford: Oxford University Press. 308–12.

Piven, F.F., and Cloward, R.A. 1986. *Why Americans Don't Vote.* New York: Pantheon.

Rose, R. (ed.) 1974. *Electoral Behavior: A Comparative Handbook.* New York: Free Press.

Rose, R., and McAllister, I. 1986. *Voters Begin to Choose: From Closed-Class to Open Elections in Britain.* London: Sage.

Rose, R., and Urwin, D. 1970. "Persistence and change in western party systems since 1945." *Political Studies* 18: 287–319.

Stanley, H.W., Bianco, W.T., and Niemi, R.G. 1986. "Partisanship and group support over time: a multivariate analysis." *American Political Science Review* 80: 969–76.

Verba, S., and Kim, J. 1978. *Participation and Political Equity.* Cambridge: Cambridge University Press.

Weakliem, D.L. 1995. "Two models of class voting." *British Journal of Political Science* 25: 254–70.

Weakliem, D.L., and Heath, A.F. 1999. "The secret life of class voting: Britain, France, and the United States since the 1930s." In *The End of Class Politics? Class Voting in Comparative Context,* ed. Geoffrey Evans. Oxford: Oxford University Press. 97–136.

MELVIN L. KOHN

Job Complexity and Adult Personality

There have been several distinct approaches to the study of work, each of them emphasizing some aspect that bears on a particular theoretical concern of the investigator. Rarely, though, has that concern been the effect of work on personality. Sociologists have learned much about social stratification and mobility, for example, by focusing on the dimension of work most pertinent to the stratificational system, the status of the job (Blau and Duncan, 1967; Duncan, Featherman, and Duncan, 1972; Sewell, Hauser, and Featherman, 1976). But however important status may be for studies of mobility, it would be unwise to assume—as is often done—that the status of a job is equally pertinent for personality. In terms of impact on personality, job status serves mainly as a gross indicator of the job's location in the hierarchical organiza-

tion of the economic and social system. The status of the job is closely linked to such structural conditions of work as how complex it is, how closely it is supervised, and what sorts of pressures it entails. It is these structural realities, not status as such, that affect personality (Kohn and Schooler, 1973).

It is also indisputable that economists have learned much about the functioning of the economic system by focusing on the extrinsic rewards the job confers—in particular, income. Just as with occupational status, though, it would be incorrect to assume that because income is important for an understanding of the economic system qua system, income is also the most significant aspect of the job in terms of the meaning of work to the worker or the impact of work on his sense of self and orientation to the rest of the world (Whyte, 1955; Kohn and Schooler, 1973).

Organizational theorists, both the Weberian sociologists and those more applied scholars who call themselves administrative scientists, have, by studying formal organizational structure, undoubtedly contributed much to our understanding of how organizations function (Blau and Schoenherr, 1971). But the

Originally published in 1980. Please see complete source information beginning on page 891.

very strength of their approach—its systematic attention to how formal organizations function as systems, regardless of the personalities of those who play the various organizational roles—means that they largely ignore the effect of organizational structure on the individual worker and his work. When they do pay attention to the individual worker, their interest rarely goes beyond his role as worker.

The human-relations-in-industry approach, in deliberate juxtaposition to the formal organizational approach, focuses on informal, interpersonal relationships and the symbolic systems that emerge out of such relationships (Whyre, 1961; 1969). Scholars using this approach supply a needed corrective to the formal organizational perspective. But they sometimes seem unaware that people not only relate to one another on the job; they also work. Moreover, this perspective has been concerned almost exclusively with the implications of work for on-the-job behavior, paying little attention to the effects of the job on other realms of life.

Occupational psychologists come close to understanding the relationship between work and personality, but there are two major limitations to their studies. First, many of them misinterpret Kurt Lewin (and, I would add, W. I. Thomas) by dealing exclusively with how people perceive their work while neglecting the actual conditions under which that work is performed. (This criticism applies as well to most sociological studies of alienation in work.) Thus, they measure boredom rather than routinization, interest in the work rather than its substantive complexity, and "alienation in work" rather than actual working conditions. Such an approach ignores the possibilities that there can be a gap between the conditions to which a person is subjected and his awareness of those conditions; that the existence or nonexistence of such a gap is itself problematic and may be structurally determined; and that conditions felt by the worker to be benign can have deleterious consequences, while conditions felt to be onerous can have beneficial consequences. The second

limitation is the preoccupation of most occupational psychologists with job satisfaction, as if this were the only psychological consequence of work. I am less disturbed by the technical difficulties in measuring job satisfaction—a notoriously slippery concept—than I am by the assumption that work has no psychological ramifications beyond the time and place during and within which it occurs. Work affects people's values, self-conceptions, orientation to social reality, even their intellectual functioning. Job satisfaction is only one, and far from the most important, psychological consequence of work.

The research that comes closest of all to dealing straightforwardly with work and its consequences for personality employs an old tradition of sociological study—case studies of occupations. Practitioners of this art have sometimes done a magnificent job of depicting the reality of work as it impinges on the worker. Unfortunately, though, their studies cannot determine which aspects of work are most pertinent for which aspects of psychological functioning. W. Fred Cottrell's (1940) classic study of railroaders, for example, pointed out a multitude of ways that the job conditions of men who operate trains differ from those of men in many other occupations—including the unpredictability of working hours, geographical mobility, precision of timing, outsider status in the home community, and unusual recruitment and promotion practices. Since all these conditions are tied together in one occupational package, it is not possible to disentangle the psychological concomitants of each. More recent comparative studies face similar interpretative problems. For example, Robert Blauner's (1964) study of alienation among blue-collar workers in four industries, chosen to represent four technological levels, showed that differences in working conditions are systematically associated with the stage of technological development of the industry. But these differences, too, come in packages: Printing differs from automobile manufacture not only in technology and in the skill levels of workers but also in pace of the work, closeness of supervision, freedom of physical movement, and a multitude of other conditions. One cannot tell which, if any, of these interlocked occupational conditions are conducive to alienation.

Disentangling Occupational Conditions

Disentangling occupational conditions to assess their psychological impact requires a mode of research different from that employed in studies of particular occupations and particular industries. Carmi Schooler and I have dealt with the problem by shifting the focus from named occupations—carpenter, surgeon, or flight engineer—to dimensions of occupation (Kohn, 1969; Kohn and Schooler, 1969; 1973). Our strategy has been to secure a large and representative sample of employed men, who necessarily work in many occupations and many industries.[1] We have inventoried the men's job conditions and then differentiated the psychological concomitants of each facet of occupation by statistical analysis. In our most recent research, my colleagues and I have done comparable analyses for employed women (Miller et al., 1979).

Even though occupational conditions are intercorrelated, they are not perfectly intercorrelated. Thus, substantively complex jobs are likely also to be time-pressured; but there are enough jobs that are substantively complex yet not time-pressured, and enough that are substantively simple yet time-pressured, for us to examine the relationship between substantive complexity and, say, receptiveness or resistance to change, while statistically controlling time pressure. We can also look for statistical interaction between the two, asking whether the impact of substantive complexity on, let us say, stance toward change is different for men who are more time-pressured and for men who are less time-pressured. And, at the same time, we can statistically control many other occupational conditions, as well as important nonoccupational variables, for example, education,

which usually precedes and is often a prerequisite for the job.

In all, we have indexed more than fifty separable dimensions of occupation, including such diverse aspects of work experience as the substantive complexity of work, the routinization or diversity of the flow of work, relationships with co-workers and with supervisors, pace of work and control thereof, physical and environmental conditions, job pressures and uncertainties, union membership and participation, bureaucratization, job protections, and fringe benefits. (For complete information, see Kohn, 1969, pp. 236, 244–253.) These indices provide the basis for a broad descriptive picture of the principal facets of occupations, as experienced by men in all types of industries and at all levels of the civilian economy.

I must admit that this approach—based as it is on a sample survey of all men employed in civilian occupations—is not optimum for securing some kinds of job information. Men may have only limited information about certain aspects of their jobs, such as the overall structure of the organization in which they work. Moreover, a sample of men scattered across many occupations and many work places does not contain enough people in any occupation or any workplace to trace out interpersonal networks and belief systems. Similarly, the method is not well adapted for studying the industrial and technological context in which the job is embedded. The method is most useful for studying the immediate conditions of a man's own job—what he does, who determines how he does it, in what physical and social circumstances he works, to what risks and rewards he is subject.

We found that nearly all of the more than fifty occupational conditions that we had inventoried are correlated with at least some of the several aspects of values, self-conception, social orientation, and intellectual functioning that we had measured (Kohn and Schooler, 1973).[2] But most of these statistical relationships reflect the interrelatedness of occupational conditions with one another and with education. Only twelve of the occupational conditions we studied appear to have any substantial relationship to men's psychological functioning when education and all other pertinent occupational conditions are statistically controlled. Few though they are, these twelve occupational conditions are sufficient to define the "structural imperatives of the job," in that they identify a man's position in the organizational structure, his opportunities for occupational self-direction, the principal job pressures to which he is subject, and the principal uncertainties built into his job.[3] These job conditions are "structural" in two senses: they are built into the structure of the job and they are largely determined by the job's location in the structures of the economy and the society.

Substantive Complexity

Because of its theoretical and empirical importance, I devote the remainder of this essay to one of the twelve structural imperatives of the job, the substantive complexity of work.[4] By the substantive complexity of work, I mean the degree to which the work, in its very substance, requires thought and independent judgment. Substantively complex work by its very nature requires making many decisions that must take into account ill-defined or apparently conflicting contingencies. Although, in general, work with data or with people is likely to be more complex than work with things, this is not always the case, and an index of the overall complexity of work should reflect its degree of complexity in each of these three types of activity. Work with things can vary in complexity from ditch digging to sculpting; similarly, work with people can vary in complexity from receiving simple directions or orders to giving legal advice; and work with data can vary from reading instructions to synthesizing abstract conceptual systems. Thus, the index of substantive complexity that we have generally employed is based on the degree of complexity of the person's work with things, with data, and with people; our appraisal of the overall complexity of his work, regardless of whether he works primarily with things, with data, or with people; and estimates of the amount of time he spends working at each type of activity (Kohn and Schooler, 1973; Kohn, 1976). The several components receive weightings based on a factor analysis.[5]

I focus on substantive complexity for two reasons. The first is that I conceive substantive complexity to be central to the experience of work. The other structural imperatives of the job—even closeness of supervision and routinization—set the conditions under which work is done but they do not characterize the work itself. The substantive complexity of work, by contrast, is at the heart of the experience of work. More than any other occupational condition, it gives meaning to this experience.

The second reason for my preoccupation with substantive complexity is empirical. Our analyses show that substantive complexity of work is strongly related to a wide range of psychological variables. The substantive complexity of work is of course correlated with job satisfaction and with occupational commitment. It also bears on many facets of off-the-job psychological functioning, ranging from valuation of self-direction to self-esteem to authoritarian conservatism to intellectual flexibility. It is even related to the intellectual demands of men's leisure-time pursuits. Moreover, these correlations remain statistically significant and large enough to be meaningful even when education and all other pertinent dimensions of occupation are statistically controlled. Thus, the substantive complexity of work has a strong, independent relationship to many facets of psychological functioning, a relationship stronger than that of any other dimension of occupation we have studied. This is true for men, and our most recent analyses show it to be equally true for employed women (Miller et al., 1979).

The Direction of Causal Effects

There is evidence that the substantive complexity of work is not only correlated with, but has a causal impact on, psychological functioning. The evidence of causal directionality is of two types. The more extensive but less definitive evidence comes from our analyses of cross-sectional data, derived from a large sample of men employed in civilian occupations. Social scientists have long recognized that one cannot make inferences about the direction of causal effects from cross-sectional data unless some of the described phenomena clearly preceded others in their time of occurrence. But where one can realistically assume reciprocity—that *a* affects *b* and *b* also affects *a*—it is possible to assess the magnitude of these reciprocal effects, using econometric techniques for solving simultaneous equations. The simplest of these, which we used, is called two-stage least squares.[6] With this technique, we have assessed the relationships between the substantive complexity of work and many facets of psychological functioning: occupational commitment, job satisfaction, valuation of self-direction or of conformity to external authority, anxiety, self-esteem, receptiveness or resistance to change, standards of morality, authoritarian conservatism, intellectual flexibility, the intellectuality of leisure-time activities, and three types of alienation—powerlessness, self-estrangement, and normlessness.

Our findings indicate that the substantive complexity of men's work affects all these facets of psychological functioning, independent of the selection processes that draw men into particular fields of work and independent of their efforts to mold their jobs to fit their needs, values, and capacities. Moreover, the substantive complexity of work in every instance affects psychological functioning more—often, much more—than the particular facet of psychological functioning affects the substantive complexity of work. This evidence is not definitive—only longitudinal studies can provide definitive evidence—but it does establish a strong prima facie case that the substantive complexity of work has a real and meaningful effect on a wide range of psychological phenomena.

More definitive, albeit less extensive, evidence comes from a follow-up study we conducted with a representative subsample of men in the original study ten years after the initial survey (Kohn and Schooler, 1978). Analyses of longitudinal data require the development of "measurement models" that separate unreliability of measurement from change in the phenomena studied. The essence of the method employed in constructing these models is the use of multiple indicators for each principal concept, inferring from the covariation of the indicators the degree to which each reflects the underlying concept that they are all hypothesized to reflect and the degree to which each reflects anything else, which for measurement purposes is considered to be error (see Jöreskog, 1969, and other papers cited in Kohn and Schooler, 1978). These models permit us to take into account that errors in the measurement of any indicator at the time of the initial survey may well be correlated with errors in the measurement of that same indicator at the time of the follow-up survey. Disregarding such correlated errors in the indicators might make the underlying concept seem more stable or less stable than it really is—thereby distorting any causal analysis in which that index is employed. . . .

We chose intellectual flexibility as the first aspect of psychological functioning to be assessed because it offers us the greatest challenge—intellectual flexibility obviously affects recruitment into substantively complex jobs, and there is every reason to expect it to be resistant to change. Still, intellectual flexibility—though not much studied by sociologists—is so important a part of psychological functioning that we must not unthinkingly assume it to be entirely the product of genetics and early life experience. Rather, we should empirically test the possibility that intellectual flexibility may be responsive to adult occupational experience.

Our index of intellectual flexibility is meant to reflect men's actual intellectual performance in the interview situation. We used a variety of indicators—including the men's answers to seemingly simple but highly revealing cognitive problems, their handling of perceptual and projective tests, their propensity to agree when asked "agree-disagree" questions, and the impression they made on the interviewer during a long session that required a great deal of thought and reflection. None of these indicators is believed to be completely valid; but we do believe that all the indicators reflect, to some substantial degree, men's flexibility in coping with an intellectually demanding situation.

The stability of intellectual flexibility, thus measured, is remarkably high over time: The correlation between men's intellectual flexibility at the time of the original study and their intellectual flexibility ten years later, shorn of measurement error, is 0.93. It would be erroneous to assume, though, that the high over-time stability of intellectual flexibility means that it is unaffected by adult experience; it might even be that this stability reflects unchanging life circumstances. In fact, we find that the effect of the substantive complexity of work on intellectual flexibility is striking—on the order of one-fourth as great as that of the men's ten-year-earlier levels of intellectual flexibility. This effect is essentially contemporaneous: The path from the substantive complexity of the job held at the time of the initial survey to intellectual flexibility at the time of the follow-up survey ten years later is small and statistically nonsignificant, while the path from the substantive complexity of the current job to current intellectual flexibility is much more substantial and is statistically significant.[7]

The reciprocal effect of intellectual flexibility on substantive complexity is still more impressive than the effect of substantive complexity on intellectual flexibility. This effect is entirely lagged, that is, it is the men's intellectual flexibility at the time of the initial survey that significantly affects the substantive complexity of their current jobs, and not their current intellectual flexibility. The longitudinal analysis thus demonstrates something that no cross-sectional analysis could show—that, over time, the relationship between substantive complexity and intellectual flexibility is truly reciprocal. The effect of substantive complexity on intellectual flexibility is more immediate: current job demands affect current thinking processes. Intellectual flexibility, by contrast, has a time-lagged effect on substantive complexity: current intellectual flexibility has scant effect on current job demands, but considerable effect on the future course of one's career. Cross-sectional analyses portray only part of this process, making it seem that the relationship between the substantive complexity of work and intellectual functioning were mainly unidirectional, with work affecting intellectual functioning but not the reverse. Longitudinal analysis portrays a more intricate and more interesting, truly reciprocal process.

The data thus demonstrate, beyond reasonable doubt, what heretofore could be stated only as a plausible thesis buttressed by presumptive evidence—that the substantive complexity of work both considerably affects, and is considerably affected by, intellectual flexibility.

My colleagues and I have recently completed two further analyses that extend these conclusions. A much more extensive longitudinal analysis of job conditions and intellectual flexibility (Kohn and Schooler, 1981) confirms that the substantive complexity of work affects intellectual flexibility not only when prior levels of intellectual flexibility and pertinent aspects of social background are taken into account but also when all other structural imperatives of the job are taken into account as well. We further find that substantive complexity is not the only job condition that affects intellectual flexibility; several other job conditions that stimulate and challenge the individual are conducive to intellectual flexibility. But, clearly, substantive complexity plays a key role, not only because it has such a great effect on intellectual flexibility, but also because it provides the principal mechanism through which other job conditions affect intellectual functioning.

In another analysis (Miller et al., 1979), we found that the substantive complexity of work is as important for women's psychological functioning as it is for men's. In particular, a causal analysis using measurement models similar to those described above, but limited to cross-sectional data, shows the contemporaneous effect of substantive complexity on intellectual flexibility to be at least as great for employed women as for employed men.

These findings come down solidly in support of those who hold that occupational conditions affect personality and in opposition to those who believe that the relationship between occupational conditions and personality results solely from selective recruitment and job molding. Admittedly, personality has great importance in determining who go into what types of jobs and how they perform those jobs; in fact, our analyses underline the importance of these processes. But that has never been seriously at issue. What has been disputed is whether the reverse phenomenon—of job conditions molding personality—also occurs. The evidence of our longitudinal analysis supports the position that it does occur.

In particular, this analysis adds to and helps specify the growing evidence that the structure of the environment has an important effect on cognitive development (Rosenbaum, 1976) and that cognitive processes do not become impervious to environmental influence after adolescence or early adulthood but continue to show "plasticity" throughout the life span (Baltes, 1968; Horn and Donaldson, 1976; Baltes and Schaie, 1976). Our findings reinforce this conclusion by showing that intellectual flexibility continues to be responsive to experience well into midcareer. In fact, it appears that the remarkable stability of intellectual flexibility reflects, at least in part, stability in people's life circumstances. Intellectual flexibility is ever responsive to changes in the substantive complexity of people's work; for most people, though, the substantive complexity of work does not fluctuate markedly.

This analysis demonstrates as well the importance of intellectual flexibility for substantive complexity. I think it noteworthy that this effect appears to be lagged rather than contemporaneous. The implication is that the structure of most jobs does not permit any considerable variation in the substantive complexity of the work: job conditions are not readily modified to suit the needs or capacities of the individual worker. But over a long enough time—certainly over a period as long as ten years—many men either modify their jobs or move on to other jobs more consonant with their intellectual functioning. Thus, the long-term effects of intellectual flexibility on substantive complexity are considerable, even though the contemporaneous effects appear to be negligible.

Our models, of course, deal mainly with the events of midcareer or later. I think it reasonable to assume that men's intellectual flexibility in childhood, adolescence, and early adulthood have had a considerable effect on their educational attainments, and our data show that educational attainment is very important for the substantive complexity of the early jobs in men's careers. Since the substantive complexity of early jobs is a primary determinant of the substantive complexity of later jobs, it seems safe to infer that intellectual flexibility's long-term, indirect effects on the substantive complexity of later jobs has been even greater than our analysis depicts.

The reciprocal relationship between substantive complexity and intellectual flexibility implies an internal dynamic by which relatively small differences in substantive complexity at early stages of a career may become magnified into larger differences in both substantive complexity and intellectual flexibility later in the career. If two men of equivalent intellectual flexibility were to start their careers in jobs differing in substantive complexity, the man in the more complex job would be likely to outstrip the other in further intellectual growth. This, in time, might lead to his attaining jobs of greater complexity, further affecting his intellectual growth. Meantime, the man in the less complex job would develop intellectually at a slower pace, perhaps not at all, and in the extreme case might even decline in his intellectual functioning. As a result, small differences in the substantive complexity of early jobs might lead to increasing differences in intellectual development. . . .

Processes of Learning and Generalization

Why does substantive complexity have such wide-spread ramifications for personality? This question is still largely unanswered. Our findings suggest that the simplest type of learning-generalization process is operating here: that there is a direct translation of the lessons of the job to outside-the-job realities, rather than some indirect process, such as reaction formation or compensation (Breer and Locke, 1965). Thus, men who do complex work come to exercise their intellectual prowess not only on the job but also in their nonoccupational lives. They become more open to new experience. They come to value self-direction more highly. They even come to engage in more intellectually demanding leisure-time activities. In short, the lessons of work are directly carried over to nonoccupational realms.

Several alternative interpretations have been advanced, but none has been adequately tested. One such interpretation is that doing more (or less) substantively complex work leads to a stronger (or weaker) sense of control over the forces that affect one's life, and that this sense of controlling or not controlling those forces influences one's self-concept, in particular, one's self-esteem. But why is it necessary to accord so strategic a role in the causal chain to "locus of control"? Why not say, more directly, that people who do substantively complex work come to think of themselves as capable of doing difficult and challenging tasks—and thus deserve respect in everyone's eyes, including their own? Similarly, people who do substantively simple work come to think of themselves as capable of nothing more than this simple-minded stuff.

I think the most reasonable hypothesis is the most straightforward: that in an industrial society, where work is central to people's lives, what people do in their work directly affects their values, their conceptions of self, and their orientation to the world around them—"I do, therefore I am." Hence, doing substantively complex work tends to increase one's respect for one's own capacities, one's valuation of self-direction, one's intellectuality (even in leisure-time pursuits), and one's sense that the problems one encounters in the world are manageable. There is no need to posit that locus of control or any other aspect of values and orientation plays a necessary intermediary role in this process; the substantive complexity of work can directly affect all aspects of people's conceptions of reality. . . .

Still another possible interpretation is that occupational conditions do not affect all people similarly, but differently, depending on the individual's own needs, values, and abilities—the so-called "fit" hypothesis. Our analyses do not support this interpretation. We repeatedly find, for example, that the substantive complexity of work has much the same effects regardless of whether men value intrinsic or extrinsic aspects of their work more highly (Kohn and Schooler, 1973; Kohn, 1976). But these analyses have been broad-gauge, and more detailed analyses of pertinent subpopulations might require us to modify our views. Moreover, our analyses of this issue have thus far not been longitudinal. But since our data demonstrate that people's values and even their abilities are affected by their job conditions, it is clear that only longitudinal assessments can be conclusive.

Our studies have led me to conclude that the intrinsic meaning and psychological impact of a job result not just from the status or income or interpersonal relationships that the job provides but also—and especially—from the meaningful challenges the work itself poses (or fails to pose). The most important challenge is that of mastering complex tasks, that is, the substantive complexity of the work. Our data indicate that substantive complexity affects people's psychological functioning regardless of their needs, values, and personal capacities and regardless of their social class (but, of course, the type of work one does is intimately related to one's social class; so, too, are one's values). What matters most about work, in short, is not any of its attendant rewards or social experiences, but the work itself.

Moreover, the relationship between work and psychological functioning is quintessentially reciprocal. There is an ongoing process, throughout all of adult life, whereby the occupational conditions encountered by the individual both mold his psychological processes and in turn are molded by his personality and behavior. No theory of adult personality development that fails to take account of the ongoing effects of occupational (and, presumably, other social) conditions can be regarded as realistic. By the same token, no social psychology of occupations that fails to take account of the ongoing effects of individual psychological functioning can be regarded as realistic.

Notes

1. Our primary source of data is a sample survey of 3,101 men, representative of all men employed in civilian occupations in the United States. These men were interviewed for us by the National Opinion Research Center (NORC) in the spring and summer of 1964. For more detailed information on sample and research design, see Kohn, 1969, pp. 235–264. In 1974 NORC reinterviewed a representative subsample of these men for us; this time, the wives (and, where applicable, one of the children) were interviewed, too. For detailed information on the follow-up study, see Kohn and Schooler (1978) and Kohn (1977).

2. Our principal indices of psychological functioning measure subjective reactions to the job itself (that is, job satisfaction and occupational commitment), valuation of self-direction or of conformity to external authority (both for oneself and for one's children), self-conception (self-confidence, self-deprecation, fatalism, anxiety, and idea conformity), social orientation (authoritarian conservatism, criteria of morality, trustfulness, and receptiveness or resistance to change), alienation (powerlessness, self-estrangement, and normlessness), and intellectual functioning (intellectual flexibility, intellectuality of leisure-time activities). For

detailed information about our definitions of these concepts and our methods of indexing them, see Kohn, 1969, pp. 47–58, 73–84, 265–269; Kohn and Schooler, 1973, pp. 99–101; Kohn, 1976, pp. 114–118.

3. Specifically, these twelve crucial occupational conditions are: (1) ownership/nonownership; (2) bureaucratization; (3) position in the supervisory hierarchy; (4) closeness of supervision; (5) routinization of the work; (6) substantive complexity of the work; (7) frequency of time-pressure; (8) heaviness of work; (9) dirtiness of work; (10) the likelihood, in this field, of there occurring a sudden and dramatic change in a person's income, reputation, or position; (11) the probability, in this line of work, of being held responsible for things outside one's control; and (12) the risk of loss of one's job or business.

4. The concept "substantive complexity" has been the subject of much research that goes considerably beyond the issues addressed in this essay. Many writers have adopted the concept and used it for such diverse purposes as reinterpreting the status-attainment model (Spaeth, 1976), proposing a new method of classifying the occupational structure of the U.S. economy (Temme, 1975), reassessing the psychological effects of complex role sets (Coser, 1975), interpreting the effects of fathers' occupational experiences on their sons' occupational choices (Mortimer, 1974; 1976), and searching out the sources of powerlessness (Tudor, 1972).

5. To validate this index, which is specifically tailored to each respondent's description of his own job, we have compared it to assessments of the average level of complexity of work with things, with data, and with people for the entire occupation, made by trained occupational analysts for the *Dictionary of Occupational Titles* (United States Department of Labor, 1965). The multiple correlation between our index of substantive complexity and the independently coded *Dictionary* ratings is 0.78—sufficiently high to assure us that our appraisals of substantive complexity accurately reflect the reality of people's work.

6. The two-stage least squares technique is described in detail by Kohn and Schooler (1973) and the references cited therein. This method attempts to "purge" each variable of the effects of all others with which it is reciprocally related by estimating from other pertinent data what each individual's score on that variable would have been if the other variables had not had an opportunity to affect it. These estimated scores are then used as independent variables in the (second stage) multiple-regression equations.

7. Concretely, the time-lagged path (that is, from substantive complexity in 1964 to intellectual flexibility in 1974) is 0.05 and the contemporaneous path is 0.18. A path of 0.18 might not under ordinary circumstances be considered striking; but a

continuing effect of this magnitude on so stable a phenomenon as intellectual flexibility is impressive, because the cumulative impact will be much greater than the immediate effect at any one time. Continuing effects, even small-to-moderate continuing effects, on highly stable phenomena become magnified in importance. The effect of the substantive complexity of work on intellectual flexibility is especially noteworthy when we take into account that we are dealing with men who are at least ten years into their occupational careers.

References

Baltes, Paul B. 1968. Longitudinal and cross-sectional sequences in the study of age and generation effects. *Human Development*, 11:145–171.

Baltes, Paul B., and K. Warner Schaie. 1976. On the plasticity of intelligence in adulthood and old age. *American Psychologist*, 31:720–725.

Blau, Peter M., and Otis Duncan. 1967. *The American occupational structure*. New York: Wiley.

Blau, Peter M., and Richard A. Schoenherr. 1971. *The structure of organizations*. New York: Basic Books.

Blauner, Robert. 1964. *Alienation and freedom: the factory worker and his industry*. Chicago: University of Chicago Press.

Breer, Paul E., and Edwin A. Locke. 1965. *Task experience as a source of attitudes*. Homewood, Ill.: Dorsey.

Coser, Rose Laub. 1975. The complexity of roles as a seedbed of individual autonomy. In *The idea of social structure: papers in honor of Robert K. Merton*, ed. L. A. Coser. New York: Harcourt Brace Jovanovich.

Cottrell, W. Fred. 1940. *The railroader*. Stanford: Stanford University Press.

Duncan, Otis D., David L. Featherman, and Beverly Duncan. 1972. *Socioeconomic background and achievement*. New York: Seminar Press.

Horn, John L., and Gary Donaldson. 1976. On the myth of intellectual decline in adulthood. *American Psychologist*, 31:701–719.

Jöreskog, Karl G. 1969. A general approach to confirmatory maximum likelihood factor analysis. *Psychometrika*, 34:183–202.

Kohn, Melvin L. 1977. Reassessment, 1977. In *Class and conformity: a study in values*. 2nd ed. Chicago: University of Chicago Press.

———. 1976. Occupational structure and alienation. *American Journal of Sociology* 82:111–130.

———. 1969. *Class and conformity: a study in values*. Homewood, Ill.: Dorsey. (2nd ed., Chicago: University of Chicago Press, 1977.)

Kohn, Melvin L., and Carmi Schooler. 1981. Job conditions and intellectual flexibility: a longitudinal assessment of their reciprocal effects. In *Factor analysis and measurement in sociological research: a multidimensional perspective*, ed. E. F. Borgatta and D. J. Jackson. Beverly Hills: Sage Publications.

———. 1978. The reciprocal effects of the substantive complexity of work and intellectual flexibility: a longitudinal assessment. *American Journal of Sociology*, 84:24–52.

———. 1973. Occupational experience and psychological functioning: an assessment of reciprocal effects. *American Sociological Review*, 38:97–118.

———. 1969. Class, occupation, and orientation. *American Sociological Review*, 34:659–678.

Miller, Joanne, Carmi Schooler, Melvin L. Kohn, and Karen A. Miller. 1979. Women and work: the psychological effects of occupational conditions. *American Journal of Sociology*, 85:66–94.

Mortimer, Jeylan T. 1976. Social class, work, and the family: some implications of the father's occupation for familial relationships and sons' career decisions. *Journal of Marriage and the Family*, 38:241–256.

———. 1974. Patterns of intergenerational occupational movements: a smallest-space analysis. *American Journal of Sociology*, 79:1278–1299.

Rosenbaum, James E. 1976. *Making inequality: the hidden curriculum of high school tracking*. New York: Wiley.

Sewell, William H., Robert M. Hauser, and David L. Featherman, eds. 1976. *Schooling and achievement in American society*. New York: Academic Press.

Spaeth, Joe L. 1976. Cognitive complexity: a dimension underlying the socioeconomic achievement process. In *Schooling and achievement in American society*, ed. William H. Sewell, Robert M. Hauser, and David L. Featherman. New York: Academic Press.

Temme, Lloyd V. 1975. *Occupation: meanings and measures*. Washington, D.C.: Bureau of Social Science Research.

Tudor, Bill. 1972. A specification of relationships between job complexity and powerlessness. *American Sociological Review*, 37:596–604.

United States Department of Labor. 1965. *Dictionary of occupational titles*. Washington, DC: United States Government Printing Office. 3rd ed.

Whyte, William F. 1969. *Organizational behavior: theory and application*. Homewood, Ill.: Richard D. Irwin.

———. 1961. *Men at work*. Homewood, Ill.: Dorsey.

———. 1955. *Money and motivation: an analysis of incentives in industry*. New York: Harper.

PAUL DIMAGGIO

Social Stratification, Life-Style, Social Cognition, and Social Participation

Measures of class and related variables, as well as such other axes of stratification as gender and race, have long been the crack troops in sociologists' war on unexplained variance. Hardly an aspect of human experience—the clothes one wears, the number of siblings one has, the diseases one is likely to contract, the music to which one listens, the chances that one will serve in the armed forces or fall prey to violent crime—is uncorrelated with some dimension of social rank.

This section focuses on three well-developed literatures: on the relationship among stratification, lifestyle, and consumption patterns; on the interactions among class, personality, and attitudes; and on the connection between class position and political attitudes and participation. Such work considers the consequences of stratification for the cultural styles, personalities, and political preferences of individuals and groups, but it goes beyond this to assess the *effects* of cultural style, personality, and political behavior on people's life chances. Moreover, scholars in each tradition have explored the role of history and social structure in constituting the relationships observed in studies in which individuals are the units of analysis. In each case, we see not only that social inequality shapes important

This is an original article prepared for this book.

aspects of lifestyle, cognition, social membership, and participation, but that these differences in turn reinforce patterns of material advantage and disadvantage. We also see that the stratification system works through a combination of individual choice and institutional structures (e.g., legal-regulatory regimes, political parties) that affect how those choices are perceived, understood, and resolved.

Culture, Lifestyle, and Consumption

The starting point for any discussion of lifestyles and consumption patterns must be the work of Thorstein Veblen and Pierre Bourdieu. Although both of these authors believe that social stratification has profound effects on lifestyle, beyond this their approaches vary. First, they call attention to different aspects of stratification. Veblen (1973) uses the term *class* rhetorically, but his emphasis is on a continuous prestige hierarchy, "rated and graded" by similarity to a "leisure-class" cultural ideal. Bourdieu (1984), by contrast, posits discrete "class fractions" sharing similar positions with respect to education, income, and occupation, each united by a *habitus* or world view derived from similar life experiences and common images of the way of life appropriate for people "like us." Moreover, the social functions of taste are less complicated for Veblen than for Bourdieu. Veblen portrays pecuniary emulation and conspicuous consumption as strategies that individuals employ to compete for status against their peers. By contrast, like Max Weber (on status groups, 1968; Collins 1979) and Mary Douglas (Douglas and Isherwood 1979), Bourdieu views tastes as signs of group affiliation, of horizontal connections as well as vertical distinctions (Bourdieu 1983).

Bourdieu's work has inspired a body of empirical research on the origins and effects of "cultural capital," usually operationalized by measures of survey respondents' knowledge of, interest in, or experience with the arts. Studies in Australia, Brazil, Bulgaria, the Czech Republic, Greece, Hungary, the Netherlands, Poland, Slovakia, Sweden, and the United States have all documented robust intergenerational transmission of cultural capital (Amaral 1991; DiMaggio and Mohr 1985; DeGraaf 1986; Ganzeboom, DeGraaf, and Robert 1990; Katsillas and Rubinson 1990; Kraaycamp and Nieuwbeerta 1999; Lamb 1989; Mohr and DiMaggio 1995; Roe 1983; Van Eijck 1997). Similarly, researchers agree that adults' tastes (and related behaviors) are associated with educational attainment and, to a lesser extent, occupation (DiMaggio and Ostrower 1989; Hughes and Peterson 1983; Robinson and Godbey 1997). Significant effects of students' cultural capital on such outcomes as school grades (Amaral 1991; Aschaffenburg and Maas 1997; Attewell and Battle 1999; DiMaggio 1982a; Roe 1983), educational aspirations (Lamb 1989) and attainment (DiMaggio and Mohr 1985), and marital selection (DiMaggio and Mohr 1985; Kalmijn 1994) have been demonstrated by most, but not all (e.g., DeGraaf 1986; Katsillas and Rubinson 1990) studies of these topics. Research in five former socialist countries reported a significant effect of parents' cultural participation (net of parents' education) on their adult children's material well-being (Kraaykamp and Nieuwbeerta 2000). The results are more consistent with Bourdieu's than with Veblen's formulation of the

problem. Research on the predictors of cultural capital finds that schooling, which Bourdieu views as the key institution controlling access and rewards to cultural capital, is a far better predictor of taste than income, which Veblen regarded as central. Similarly, using direct measures of home cultural climate, Mohr and DiMaggio (1995) demonstrate that these affect strongly the cultural capital of adolescents, mediating most of the effects of parental education and occupation. At the same time, other results are consistent with *both* Veblen and Bourdieu's orientations. For example, research supports status-competitive over cognitive explanations of class differences: Tastes cluster more by the prestige of goods (e.g., liking fine art and classical music) than by their formal similarities (e.g., liking all kinds of music); attitudes toward high culture and arts attendance predict achievement better than what students actually know about the arts; and early socialization in the arts has been found to be more strongly related to educational attainment than to subsequent arts attendance (DiMaggio 1982a).

Not all the evidence is consistent with Bourdieu's argument, however, and some of the evidence that is consistent is also relatively weak. Much evidence, for example, suggests that although inherited cultural capital sustains the reproduction of privilege for many children of the well educated and well to do, inherited or achieved cultural capital also serves as a means of upward mobility for some working-class youth (DiMaggio 1982a; DeGraaf, DeGraaf, and Kraaykamp 1998). Moreover, although taste is *differentiated* by social status, there is no sign of discrete taste classes with sharply *segmented* preferences. In a study of a local industry, Erickson (1996) demonstrates that the more complex are people's social networks, the more diverse and highly differentiated are their interests and tastes. She suggests that whereas classical forms of cultural capital may be used to dominate and exclude, a broader range of tastes and interests serves to bridge difference and enable persons to inhabit multiple social worlds. Consistent with this intuition, educational attainment is strongly related not just to participation in prestigious art forms but also to consumption of most kinds of popular culture as well (Gans 1986; Bryson 1996; Peterson and Kern 1996; Robinson and Godbey 1997).

The definition of cultural capital has also suffered from some ambiguity (Lamont and Lareau 1988). On theoretical grounds, the use of the "capital" metaphor is potentially misleading insofar as it suggests an analogy with human capital. Whereas human capital comprises individual skills that are task-related, the components of cultural capital are socially constructed or, as Bourdieu has put it, "arbitrary." At the societal level, stocks of human capital contribute directly to the economic productivity of labor; indeed, human-capital theory emerged as a way of explaining surprising positive residuals in gross national products during periods of educational expansion (Schultz 1961). By contrast, there is no intrinsic reason that "stocks" of cultural capital should boost aggregate productivity; any positive economic effect is likely to be incidental and to operate on economic institutions (primarily by increasing levels of trust) rather than in the realm of production. At the individual level, human capital is a product of investment, whereas cultural capital is more likely to be acquired effortlessly as a by-product of socialization. To put it another way, the acquisition of human capital expresses an individual logic of strategic competition, whereas the acquisition and maintenance of cultural capital express a collective logic of monopolistic closure at the level of the status group.

Unresolved questions also attend the operationalization of "cultural capital." Most studies have followed Bourdieu in using measures of participation in the high-culture arts, although the concept is potentially much broader. Why aesthetic measures have performed so well is not entirely clear. The arts are arguably the most thoroughly institutionalized form of prestigious culture in modern industrial societies (DiMaggio 1982a). However, it remains unclear whether aesthetic orientations affect status attainment directly or are proxies for generalized skill in navigating status hierarchies (Swidler 1986); orientation to such hierarchies (Hagan 1991); moral stances (Lamont 1992); broader intellectual interests (DeGraaf, DeGraaf, and Kraaykamp 1998); or other unmeasured forms of cultural capital, such as self-presentation or linguistic skills (Bernstein 1977; Erickson and Schultz 1982).

Insofar as the "capital" metaphor can be justified, it is in calling attention to the institutional apparatus that guarantees the wide legitimacy of certain cultural signals. For example, local or ephemeral cultural resources (e.g., those related to cuisine or styles of dress) tend to lack such institutional backing, whereas other, more fully institutionalized, cultural resources (e.g., the high culture arts or, earlier, forms of religious expression) constitute a currency ("cultural capital" proper) of wide social, geographic, and temporal scope. Ultimately, combining fine-grained studies of social interaction and national surveys with a broader than customary range of cultural measures will be necessary to resolve these operational issues.

Finally, we need to understand why certain tastes or styles become valued more highly than others. The contemporary hierarchy of aesthetic taste, for example, was the product of early-industrial class formation and political change, varying in detail but similar in result in Europe and the United States (DiMaggio 1982b). It is clear that cultural hierarchies are maintained by economic investments (e.g., expenditures on humanities courses) and state power (e.g., government grants to high-cultural arts organizations or laws mandating the use of a single language in linguistically diverse communities). It is equally plain that other processes (e.g., increases in the proportion of cultural goods financed through market exchange as opposed to elite philanthropy) erode hierarchy. But we still lack a comprehensive theory of the manner in which such hierarchies change.

Personality as a Product of Social Class

In the long history of research on the relationship between class and personality, there is no more creative and influential work than the research program of Melvin Kohn and his colleagues (Schooler 1987). Whereas the readings from Veblen and Bourdieu emphasize class differences in consumption, Kohn explores the relationship between one's place in the stratification order and the inner self of values and attitudes.

Actually, Kohn's work has more in common with Bourdieu's than this implies, for *Distinction* (Bourdieu 1984) not only treats class fractions as differing in tastes, but also in both *ethos* (underlying evaluative dispositions) and *habitus* (experience-based schema that generate consistent behaviors across an infinite range of situations). These authors agree that both normative and cognitive orientations are linked to class and occupational positions because shared experiences associated with these positions are generalized by social learning and shaped into enduring dispositions.

Beyond this, though, the two differ markedly. Whereas Bourdieu emphasizes struggle among class fractions and strategic interaction in complex social "fields," Kohn and his colleagues rely on learning theory to the exclusion of strategic mechanisms and focus on the individual level of analysis. In addition, although each views human personalities or *habitus* as both stable and plastic, Bourdieu places relatively more weight on the role of the family and the broader social environment, whereas Kohn and his colleagues focus almost exclusively on the influence of work.

Both approaches have generated impressive long-term research programs. The work of Melvin Kohn, Carmi Schooler, and their colleagues spans five decades from the publication of Kohn's first paper on social class and parental values in 1959 to the present. The early studies (e.g., Kohn and Schooler 1969) documented moderate but robust associations between men's SES (a weighted combination of education and occupational position) and numerous values and orientations: the extent to which they valued self-directedness or conformity in their children; the characteristics they valued in themselves; the extent to which they judged their work according to intrinsic standards or extrinsic rewards; their attitudes toward morality and change; and their authoritarianism, self-confidence, and confidence in others. Social class was related to more self-directed, optimistic, and flexible responses in all these areas, with educational attainment and occupation (but not income) playing independent roles in predicting orientations and values. Most effects of occupation were captured by measures of opportunities for self-directedness inherent in the job.

Kohn and Schooler reinterviewed many of the same men 10 years later and used the results to test the causal inferences in their earlier work (Kohn and Schooler 1978; 1982). Analyzing data from both time periods, they reported that, although values and orientations were stable over time, men whose jobs were complex and who exercised considerable self-direction actually became *more* flexible, whereas men who did simple work and were highly supervised became less so. These findings have been sustained, extended, and elaborated in subsequent comparative work carried out on Polish men, Japanese and Ukrainian men and women, American women working in the paid labor force and at home, and students in U.S. schools (Miller et al. 1979; Schooler et al. 1984; Miller, Kohn, and Schooler 1986; Kohn et al. 1990; Naoi and Schooler 1990; Kohn et al. 1997). Based on re-interviews of the original 1964 sample 30 years later, Schooler, Mulatu, and Oates (1999) have demonstrated even greater effects of complexity on cognitive function among aging workers.

Whereas scholars of cultural capital have long emphasized the larger institutional framework within which such capital is defined and transmitted, those of work and personality have focused more narrowly on teasing out individual-level effects of class, albeit in various national contexts. However, scholars within the latter research tradition have occasionally stepped back to explore social-structural, as well as individual-level, effects on values. For example, Schooler (1976) has argued that the strength and endurance of feudalism is associated with lower levels of individualism in both Europe and the Far East; Kohn et al. (1997) have examined whether radical forms of social change (e.g., the post-socialist transition) modify the relationship between social structure and personality.

This work has yielded a substantial body of knowledge. Perhaps most notable, given the mass of research documenting statistical associations between measures of social rank and almost everything else, is the success with which Kohn, Schooler, and colleagues have identified *what it is about class* (and occupation) that makes the difference. Rarely has stratification been defined and operationalized with such theoretical precision. Equally important, as with research on "cultural capital," the work demonstrates that the *effects* of desirable positions in the stratification order are themselves *resources* that help men and women get ahead.

A few questions remain open. The effects of self-direction and complexity on values are more notable for their ubiquity and robustness than for their strength. We know little about the factors that may account for the variance that work content does not explain. Moreover, the research has focused on men's and women's occupational lives; it has yet to explicate the role of schooling and early childhood socialization in setting men and women on trajectories that later occupational experience may either moderate or, more likely, reinforce.

Social Inequality, Political Attitudes, and Political Participation

Our political culture portrays voting as an individual choice, as well as the ultimate ritual of citizenship. Yet social scientists have long noted that people's votes, as well as their political attitudes, are shaped by one's place in the class system. As Michael Hout, Jeff Manza, and Clem Brooks note in their chapter, the traditional view portrayed a polity in which industrial workers supported candidates of the left, whereas employers, tradespersons, and professionals voted for candidates of the right and center. Indeed, because the literature was so deeply oriented toward European systems in which social democratic parties represented the interests of labor against the forces of conservatism, many observers felt it necessary to explain the *absence* of a working-class socialist political movement in the United States. Even in the United States, President Franklin Roosevelt's social reformist policies and embrace of organized labor built a strong alliance between working people and the Democratic Party, so that for a while, at least, the United States had a loose but recognizable form of class politics.

As union members and blue-collar Americans defected from the Democratic Party with greater frequency (and as highly educated members of the professional labor force began to vote routinely for Democrats), pundits and political scientists announced the end of class voting. Hout and colleagues, however, note that class (or, more precisely, occupational sector) can matter even if people have stopped voting in ways associated with the "class politics" of the industrial era. Instead they show us that class has come to matter in a different way: that we have witnessed not a dealignment but a realignment. For the blue-collar workers at the heart of the New Deal coalition, class voting does appear to have declined between 1944 and 1992. For the self-employed, it increased. By contrast, the votes of professionals and less-skilled white-collar workers are about as strongly influenced by their jobs now as at mid-century, but the object of their political allegiance has changed.

What accounts for these shifts? One pivotal question concerns the extent to which patterns of class voting reflect rational assessment of self-interest, status concerns, or the politics of identity (Page and Shapiro 1992). Although Hout and colleagues do not address this issue directly, they suggest (in their discussion of the attraction of professionals to "postmaterialist" positions) that no single process of preference formation can account for all of the changes they identify.

The traditional approach viewed class politics as rooted in class antagonisms intrinsic to the capitalist social order. Once one acknowledges that the effects of class are potentially more complicated, one recognizes that political strategies and institutions shape the association between class position and political allegiance, perhaps more so than the narrowly construed "interests" that conventional models emphasize. Politicians struggle not only over policies but also over agendas and framing. Franklin Roosevelt's pro-labor policies and legislation were central to attracting workers to the New Deal coalition. Republicans won back some working-class voters through a combination of racial politics and populist appeals. All this transpired under an institutional regime marked by the absence of working-class parties, parliamentary democracy, or proportional representation, and by the presence of a strong federal system in which party discipline is weak and local issues often dominate national concerns.

The literature on class and politics is of course far broader than the single selection reproduced in this section can convey. Although Hout and colleagues focus on the effects of occupation, other scholars have shown effects on political views and behavior of other dimensions of stratification, especially educational attainment and race. "New class" theorists (Gouldner 1979) have argued that highly educated workers, especially those employed by public and nonprofit organizations, share a "culture of critical discourse" that engenders oppositional and anti-authoritarian political beliefs. In his assessment of the theory, Brint (1984) reported that tolerance was associated not with upper-middle-class status per se, but with particular locations within that class: Cultural and social-service professionals, for example, were more tolerant than technical professionals or business managers.

Social inequality does not merely shape people's votes and their attitudes, it shapes every aspect of political participation. More educated, higher-income citizens vote more than other Americans, give more money to political candidates, contact their representatives more frequently, and participate more in social-movement activity. The most comprehensive recent study summarizes its findings this way: "The voices of the well-educated and the well-heeled . . . sound more loudly" in political affairs (Verba, Schlozman, and Brady 1995, 512; see also Manza, Hout and Brooks 1995, 155–57). The burgeoning literature on "social capital" also demonstrates that dimensions of stratification influence rates of participation in many kinds of community activities (Putnam 2000). Although evidence of declining social capital in society as a whole has received more attention (at least in the United States), *inequality* in social capital also rose during the late twentieth century: Wuthnow (forthcoming) reports that "virtually all the decline in association memberships between 1974 and 1991 took place in the more marginalized segments of the population rather than among people who had the most privileges already" (Wuthnow forthcoming).

This line of research, like those reviewed above, provides many examples of how institutional forces condition the relationship between class and individual-level behavior. As noted previously, scholars have long sought to provide institutional accounts of differences between Europe and the United States in class-based voting, with the classical contributions being those of Sombart ([1906] 1976) and Lipset (1981; for a more recent contribution, see Evans 1999). There is also much research exploring the effects of institutional variability within as well as between nation-states. For example, Hill and Leighley (1996) report that working-class voters are more likely to participate in elections in states where the Democratic Party is relatively liberal and elections are competitive.

Conclusions

Each literature reviewed here demonstrates the effects of aspects of stratification on culture, lifestyle, attitudes, or social participation. Each reports reciprocal effects on life chances of tastes, cognitive capacities, or behavior patterns with which hierarchically advantaged people are especially well endowed. And each has explored the role of institutional and social-structural change in accounting for relationships observed at the individual level.

The same is true of many other literatures that demonstrate effects of stratification on noneconomic outcomes. Research on physical and mental health, for example, reveals that illness, mortality, and emotional distress are unequally allocated throughout the stratification system, with those at the bottom receiving far more than their share (Williams and Collins 1995; Robert and House 1999). Studies of access to social networks similarly find that Euro-Americans, men, and people with more education have wider social networks, and more resourceful connections, than African Americans, women, and the less educated (Marsden 1987; Lin 2001). Still other research suggests that these findings are related: When poor people face misfortune, they have weaker social support on which to rely and therefore experience even more distress (Williams 1990). Like values and lifestyles, health and networks are predictors as well as consequences of success. Emotional distress and illness keep people from getting ahead; robust social networks help them push forward (Granovetter 1995; Lin 1999).

A similar feedback loop is suggested by research on social inequality and access to the new digital technologies, the so-called digital divide. As the Internet spread from its academic origins to become a mass medium in the late 1990s, researchers found that the people who use it (like those who use computers of any kind) are richer, better educated, more urban, and more likely to be of European or Asian descent than those who do not (Roper/Starch 1998; National Telecommuni-cations and Information Administration 1999; Nie and Erbring 2000). (The one hierarchy the Internet *did* subvert—and this may be typical of new technologies—was age: young people gained access before older ones, and studies reported that users were more frequently getting assistance from their children than from their parents.)

Such differences don't simply reflect patterns of inequality; they may also reinforce them (Schiller 1996). Research on computer use, which diffused to homes and workplaces a few years ahead of the Internet, suggests that computers boost workers' earnings (Krueger 1993) and high school students' SAT scores (Attewell and Battle 1999). Just as Bourdieu posits higher returns to cultural capital for higher-status students, Attewell and Battle (1999) find that home computers pay off more handsomely for students from high socioeconomic status backgrounds.

Will differences in access persist, or do they simply reflect class differences in rates of adoption of new technologies? There is some evidence that gaps associated with race, gender, and age have declined with time, but those associated with educational attainment remain high. Still, there is reason to believe that rising availability of community-based access, declining connection price, and more user-friendly technologies may all soften inequalities in the short run. However, as always, institutional factors will do much to determine the outcome. Government investment in public programs that place numerous, high-quality computers with fast download capacity in libraries, community organizations, or senior centers in low-income communities would reduce inequality. Intellectual property legislation that limits the scope of what Web sites can distribute or exchange without payment, Internet service providers' business strategies that herd unsophisticated users into portals that provide easy access to corporate infotainment sites and impede access to everything else, and technological developments that place some of the Internet's riches beyond the reach of users without the most expensive equipment will all exacerbate social inequality in the capacity to extract value from the Internet, even as differences in formal access decline (DiMaggio et al. forthcoming).

Taken together, the findings of research on noneconomic consequences of stratification (and the reciprocal effects of these consequences) demonstrate processes of cumulative advantage and disadvantage that are sometimes referred to as *social reproduction* (Bourdieu and Passeron 1977). We must distinguish between *micro-* and *macro-reproduction* to pursue this point.

A social process is "reproductive" in the micro sense insofar as attitudes, values, tastes, and behaviors linked to social origins are themselves causally related to hierarchical position at some later point, in a manner that reinforces initial advantage or disadvantage. Micro-reproduction occurs both intra- and intergenerationally. It entails both direct reciprocal relationships between pairs of variables (e.g., job complexity and intellectual flexibility) and more complex causal chains (e.g., having middle-class parents gives one a wide-ranging social network that makes it easier to get an attractive and complex job, thus increasing one's intellectual flexibility).

The strength of micro-reproduction is an open question. Although studies of the relationship between class and particular kinds of lifestyles or attitudes often find significant but relatively small effects, we have been remiss in investigating the ways in which such myriad small effects cumulate and interact. Rarely, if ever, do researchers explore the relationship between position in the stratification order and a wide range of "lifestyle" variables (attitudes, values, cultural capital, linguistic capital, social networks, and health) in a single set of models featuring reciprocal effects and appropriate interaction terms. The extent to which such analyses would reveal stronger micro-reproductive processes than appear in more limited studies is an empirical question. Addressing it, and thus taking micro-reproduction seriously, requires that we relax otherwise productive barriers of specialization between different research subfields, each

with its own set of dependent variables, in the interest of theoretical and empirical synthesis.

Whatever the results of such studies in particular national contexts, the effects of class on attitudes and lifestyle is likely to vary over time and cross-nationally as a result of macrostructural factors. By macro-reproduction, I refer to large-scale structural change (e.g., the rise and fall of industries or communities), political decisions (e.g., those that alter the redistributive effects of the tax system), legal factors (e.g., definitions of property rights), or institutional developments (e.g., the emergence of formal organizations devoted to "high culture") that strengthen individual-level relationships between social origin and individual life chances.

There are many macrostructural processes that merit further study. How might the effect (or character) of pecuniary emulation vary between Western societies, where highly differentiated consumer goods are allocated on the basis of price, and socialist (or post-socialist) societies, where narrower selections of goods are allocated on the basis of queuing and rationing? What are the effects of macrostructural conditions (e.g., level of economic development or degree of religious and racial heterogeneity) on the extent to which individual political attitudes are stratified by occupational and educational attainment? How do economic policies or government regulations shape access to information technologies that may in turn facilitate the acquisition of human and social capital? If we are to answer such questions, historical and international comparative work must assume even more central places in the study of stratification.

References

Amaral, Ana Lúcia 1991. *Cultural Capital and School Success: A Study of Brazilian Normal Schools.* Ph.D. diss., Graduate School of Education, Stanford University.

Aschaffenburg, Karen, and Ineke Maas. 1997. "Cultural and Educational Careers: The Dynamics of Social Reproduction." *American Sociological Review* 62:573–87.

Attewell, Paul, and Juan Battle. 1999. "Home Computers and School Performance." *The Information Society* 15:1–10.

Bernstein, Basil. 1977. *Class, Codes and Control.* Vol. 3. London: Routledge & Kegan Paul.

Bourdieu, Pierre. 1983. "The Forms of Capital." Pages 241–58 in *Handbook of Theory and Research for the Sociology of Education,* edited by J. G. Richardson. Westport, CT: Greenwood.

Bourdieu, Pierre. 1984. *Distinction: A Social Critique of the Judgment of Taste.* Cambridge: Harvard University Press.

Bourdieu, Pierre, and Jean-Claude Passeron. 1977. *Reproduction in Education, Society and Culture.* Beverly Hills: Sage Publications.

Brint, Steven. 1984. "'New Class' and Cumulative Trend Explanations of Liberal Political Attitudes of Professionals." *American Journal of Sociology* 90:30–71.

Bryson, Bethany. 1996. "Anything But Heavy Metal: Symbolic Exclusion and Musical Dislikes." *American Sociological Review* 61:884–99.

Collins, Randall. 1979. *The Credential Society: An Historical Sociology of Education.* New York: Academic Press.

DeGraaf, Nan Dirk, Paul M. DeGraaf, and Gerbert Kraaykamp. 1998. "How Does Parental Cultural Capital Affect Educational Outcomes in the Netherlands?" Paper presented at the 1998 meetings of the American Sociological Association.

DeGraaf, Paul M. 1986. "The Impact of Financial and Cultural Resources on Educational Attainment in the Netherlands." *Sociology of Education* 59:237–46.

DiMaggio, Paul. 1982a. "Cultural Capital and School Success: The Impact of Status Culture Participation on the Grades of U.S. High School Students." *American Sociological Review* 47:189–201.

DiMaggio, Paul. 1982b. "Cultural Entrepreneurship in Nineteenth-Century Boston, I: The Creation of an Organizational Base for High Culture in America." *Media, Culture and Society* 4:33–50.

DiMaggio, Paul, Eszter Hargittai, W. Russell Neuman, and John Robinson. Forthcoming. "Social Implications of the Internet." *Annual Review of Sociology.*

DiMaggio, Paul, and John Mohr. 1985. "Cultural Capital, Educational Attainment and Marital Selection." *American Journal of Sociology* 90:1231–61.

DiMaggio, Paul, and Francie Ostrower. 1990. "Participation in the Arts by Black and White Americans." *Social Forces* 68:753–78.

Douglas, Mary, and Baron Isherwood. 1979. *The World of Goods: Toward an Anthropology of Consumption.* New York: W. W. Norton.

Erickson, Bonnie H. 1996. "Culture, Class and Connections." *American Journal of Sociology* 102:217–51.

Erickson, Fred, and Jeffrey Schultz. 1982. *The Counselor as Gatekeeper: Social Interaction in Interviews.* New York: Academic Press.

Evans, Geoffrey, ed. 1999. *The End of Class Politics? Class Voting in Comparative Context.* Oxford: Oxford University Press.

Gans, Herbert J. 1986. "American Popular Culture and High Culture in a Changing Class Structure." Pages 17–38 in *Prospects: An Annual of American Cultural Studies.* Vol. 10. New York: Cambridge University Press.

Ganzeboom, Harry B. G., Paul M. DeGraaf, and Peter Robert. 1990. "Cultural Reproduction Theory on Socialist Ground." *Research in Social Stratification and Mobility* 9:79–104.

Gouldner, Alvin. 1979. *The Future of Intellectuals and the Rise of the New Class.* New York: Seabury Press.

Granovetter, Mark S. 1995. *Getting a Job: A Study of Contacts and Careers.* 2d ed. Chicago: University of Chicago Press.

Hagan, John. 1991. "Density and Drift: The Risks and Rewards of Youth." *American Sociological Review* 56: 567–82.

Hill, Kim Quaile, and Jay Leighley. 1996. "Political Parties and Class Mobilization in Contemporary U.S. Elections." *American Journal of Political Science* 40:787–804.

Hughes, Michael, and Richard A. Peterson. 1983. "Isolating Cultural Choice Patterns in a U.S. Population." *American Behavioral Scientist* 26:459–78.

Kalmijn, M. 1994. "Assortative Mating by Cultural and Economic Occupational Status." *American Journal of Sociology* 100:422–52.

Katsillas, John, and Richard Rubinson. 1990. "Cultural Capital, Student Achievement, and Educational Reproduction in Greece." *American Sociological Review* 55:270–79.

Kohn, Melvin. 1959. "Social Class and Parental Values." *American Journal of Sociology* 64: 337–51.

Kohn, Melvin L., and Carmi Schooler. 1969. "Class, Occupation, and Orientation." *American Sociological Review* 34:659–78.

Kohn, Melvin L., and Carmi Schooler. 1978. "The Reciprocal Effects of the Substantive Complexity of Work and Intellectual Flexibility: A Longitudinal Assessment." *American Journal of Sociology* 84:24–52.

Kohn, Melvin L., and Carmi Schooler. 1982. "Job Conditions and Personality: A Longitudinal Assessment of Their Reciprocal Effects." *American Journal of Sociology* 87:1257–86.

Kohn, Melvin L., Atsushi Naoi, Carrie Schoenbach, Carmi Schooler, and Kazimierz M. Slomczynski. 1990. "Position in the Class Structure and Psychological Functioning in the United States, Japan, and Poland." *American Journal of Sociology* 94:964–1008.

Kohn, Melvin L., K. M. Slomczynski, K. Janica, V. Khmelko, B.WE. Mach, V. Paniotto, W. Zaborowski, Ramon Gutierrez, and Charles Heyman. 1997. "Social Structure and Personality under Conditions of Radical Social Change: A Comparative Analysis of Poland and Ukraine." *American Sociological Review* 62: 614–38.

Kraaykamp, Gerbert, and Paul Nieuwbeerta. 2000. "Parental Background and Life-Style Differentiation in Eastern Europe: Social, Political and Cultural Intergenerational Reproduction in Five Former Socialist Societies." *Social Science Research* 29:92–122.

Krueger, Alan B. 1993. "How Computers Have Changed the Wage Structure: Evidence from Micro Data." *Quarterly Journal of Economics* 108: 33–60.

Lamb, Stephen. 1989. "Cultural Consumption and the Educational Plans of Australian Secondary School Students." *Sociology of Education* 62:95–108.

Lamont, Michele. 1992. *Money, Mortals, and Manners: Symbolic Boundaries in French and American Upper-Middle Class Culture.* Chicago: University of Chicago Press.

Lamont, Michele, and Annette Lareau. 1988. "Cultural Capital: Allusions, Gaps, and Glissandos in Recent Theoretical Developments." *Sociological Theory* 6:153–68.

Lin, Nan. 1999. "Social Networks and Status Attainment." *Annual Review of Sociology* 225: 467–87.

Lin, Nan. 2001. *Social Capital: A Theory of Social Structure and Action.* New York: Cambridge University Press.

Lipset, Seymour Martin. 1981. *Political Man: The Social Bases of Politics.* Baltimore: Johns Hopkins University Press.

Manza, Jeff, Michael Hout, and Clem Brooks. 1995. "Class Voting in Capitalist Democracies Since World War II: Dealignment, Realignment or Trendless Fluctuation." *Annual Review of Sociology* 21:137–62.

Marsden, Peter V. 1987. "Core Discussion Networks of Americans." *American Sociological Review* 52:122–31.

Miller, Joanne, Carmi Schooler, Melvin Kohn, and K. A. Miller. 1979. "Women and Work: The Psychological Effects of Occupational Conditions." *American Journal of Sociology* 85:66–94.

Miller, Karen, Melvin L. Kohn, and Carmi Schooler. 1986. "Educational Self-Direction and Personality." *American Sociological Review* 51:372–90.

Mohr, John, and Paul DiMaggio. 1995. "The Intergenerational Transmission of Cultural Capital." *Research in Social Stratification and Mobility* 14:167–99.

Naoi, Michiko, and Carmi Schooler. 1990. "Psychological Consequences of Occupational Conditions among Japanese Wives." *Social Psychology Quarterly* 58:100–16.

National Telecommunications and Information Administration. 1999. *Falling Through the Net: Defining the Digital Divide.* Washington, DC: U.S. Department of Commerce.

Nie, Norman H., and Lutz Erbring. 2000. *Internet and Society: A Preliminary Report.* Palo Alto, CA: Stanford Institute for the Quantitative Study of Society.

Page, Benjamin I., and Robert Y. Shapiro. 1992. *The Rational Public: Fifty Years of Trends in Americans' Policy Preferences.* Chicago: University of Chicago Press.

Peterson, Richard A., and Roger M. Kern. 1996. "Changing Highbrow Taste: From Snob to Omnivore." *American Sociological Review* 61: 900–7.

Putnam, Robert D. 2000. *Bowling Alone: The Collapse and Revival of American Community.* New York: Simon & Shuster.

Robert, Stephanie, and James House. 1999. "Socioeconomic Inequalities in Health: An Enduring Sociological Problem." In *Handbook of Medical Sociology,* edited by C. E. Bird, Peter Conrad, and A. M. Fremont. Englewood Cliffs, NJ: Prentice Hall.

Robinson, John, and Jane Godbey. 1997. *Time for Life.* State College: Pennsylvania State Univeristy Press.

Roe, Keith. 1983. *Mass Media and Adolescent Schooling: Conflict or Co-Existence?* Stockholm: Almqvist & Wiksell.

Roper/Starch Inc. 1998. *American Online/Roper Starch Cyberstudy.* New York: Roper/Starch Worldwide.

Schiller, Herbert I. 1996. *Information Inequality: The Deepening Social Crisis in America.* New York: Routledge.

Schooler, Carmi. 1976. "Serfdom's Legacy: An Ethnic Continuum." *American Journal of Sociology* 81:1265–86.

Schooler, Carmi. 1987. "Psychological Effects of Complex Environments During the Life Span: A Review and Theory." Pages 24–49 in *Cognitive Functioning and Social Structure Over the Life*

Course, edited by Carmi Schooler and K. Warner Schaie. Norwood, NJ: Ablex.

Schooler, Carmi, Mesfin Mulatu, and Gary Oates. 1999. "The Continuing Effects of Substantively Complex Work on the Intellectual Functioning of Older Workers." *Psychology and Aging* 14: 280–94.

Schooler, Carmi, Joanne Miller, K. A. Miller, and C. N. Richard. 1984. "Work for the Household: Its Nature and Consequences for Husbands and Wives." *American Journal of Sociology* 90:97–124.

Schultz, T. W. 1961. "Investment in Human Capital." *American Economic Review* 51:1–7.

Sombart, Werner. [1906] 1976. *Why Is There No Socialism in the United States?* White Plains, NY: M. E. Sharpe.

Swidler, Ann. 1986. "Culture in Action: Symbols and Strategies." *American Sociological Review* 51:273–86.

Van Eijck, Koen. 1997. "The Impact of Family Background and Educational Attainment on Cultural Consumption." *Poetics* 25: 195–224.

Veblen, Thorstein. [1899] 1973. *The Theory of the Leisure Class.* Boston: Houghton Mifflin.

Verba, Sidney, Kay Lehman Schlozman, and Henry E. Brady. 1995. *Voice and Equality: Civic Voluntarism in American Politics.* Cambridge: Harvard University Press.

Weber, Max. 1968. *Economy and Society.* Berkeley: University of California Press.

Williams, David R. 1990. "Socioeconomic Differentials in Health: A Review and Reflection." *Social Psychology Quarterly* 53:81–99.

Williams, David R., and Chiquita Collins. 1995. "U.S. Socioeconomic and Racial Differences in Health: Patterns and Explanations." *Annual Review of Sociology* 21:349–86.

Wuthnow, Robert. Forthcoming. "The Changing Character of Social Capital in the United States." *The Dynamics of Social Capital in Comparative Perspective,* edited by Robert Putnam. Princeton: University of Princeton Press.

Part VI
Ascriptive Processes

Racial and Ethnic Inequality

Gender Stratification

Racial and Ethnic Inequality

▶ MODES OF INCORPORATION

EDNA BONACICH

A Theory of Ethnic Antagonism: The Split Labor Market

Societies vary considerably in their degree of ethnic and racial antagonism. Such territories as Brazil, Mexico, and Hawaii are generally acknowledged to be relatively low on this dimension; while South Africa, Australia, and the United States are considered especially high. Literally hundreds of variables have been adduced to account for these differences, ranging from religions of dominant groups, to whether the groups who migrate are dominant or subordinate, to degrees of difference in skin color, to an irreducible "tradition" of ethnocentrism. While some writers have attempted to synthesize or systematize some subset of these (e.g., Lieberson, 1961; Mason, 1970; Noel, 1968; Schermerhorn, 1970; van den Berghe, 1966), one is generally struck by the absence of a developed theory accounting for variations in ethnic antagonism.

One approach to this problem is to consider an apparent anomaly, namely that ethnic antagonism has taken two major, seemingly antithetical forms: exclusion movements, and so-called caste systems.[1] An example of the former is the "white Australia" policy; while South Africa's color bar illustrates the latter. The United States has shown both forms, with a racial caste system in the South and exclusion of Asian and "new" immigrants[2] from the Pacific and eastern seaboards respectively. Apart from manifesting antagonism between ethnic elements, exclusion and caste seem to have little in common. In the one, an effort is made to prevent an ethnically different group from being part of the society. In the other, an ethnically different group is essential to the society: it is an exploited class supporting the entire edifice. The deep south felt it could not survive without its black people; the Pacific coast could not survive with its Japanese. This puzzle may be used as a touchstone for solving the general problem of ethnic antagonism, for to be adequate a theory must be able to explain it.

The theory presented here is, in part, a synthesis of some of the ideas used by Oliver Cox to explain the Japanese-white conflict on the U.S. Pacific coast (Cox, 1948:408–22), and by Marvin Harris to analyze the difference between Brazil and the deep south in rigidity of

Originally published in 1972. Please see complete source information beginning on page 891.

the "color line" (Harris, 1964:79–94). It stresses the role of a certain kind of economic competition in the development of ethnic antagonism. Economic factors have, of course, not gone unnoticed, though until recently sociological literature has tended to point them out briefly, then move on to more "irrational" factors (even such works as The Economics of Discrimination, Becker, 1957). A resurgence of Marxian analysis (e.g. Blauner, 1969; Reich, 1971) has thrust economic considerations to the fore, but I shall argue that even this approach cannot adequately deal with the problem posed by exclusion movements and caste systems. In addition, both Marxist and non-Marxist writers assume that racial and cultural differences in themselves prompt the development of ethnic antagonism. This theory challenges that assumption, suggesting that economic processes are more fundamental.

No effort is made to prove the accuracy of the following model. Such proof depends on a lengthier exposition. Historical illustrations are presented to support it.

Ethnic Antagonism

"Ethnic" rather than "racial" antagonism was selected as the dependent variable because the former is seen to subsume the latter. Both terms refer to groups defined socially as sharing a common ancestry in which membership is therefore inherited or ascribed, whether or not members are currently physically or culturally distinctive.[3] The difference between race and ethnicity lies in the size of the locale from which a group stems, races generally coming from continents, and ethnicities from national sub-sections of continents. In the past the term "race" has been used to refer to both levels, but general usage today has reversed this practice (e.g. Schermerhorn, 1970; Shibutani and Kwan, 1965). Ethnicity has become the generic term.

Another reason for choosing this term is that exclusion attempts and caste-like arrangements are found among national groupings within a racial category. For example, in

1924 whites (Europeans) attempted to exclude whites of different national backgrounds from the United States by setting up stringent immigration quotas.

The term "antagonism" is intended to encompass all levels of intergroup conflict, including ideologies and beliefs (such as racism and prejudice), behaviors (such as discrimination, lynchings, riots), and institutions (such as laws perpetuating segregation). Exclusion movements and caste systems may be seen as the culmination of many pronouncements, actions, and enactments, and are continuously supported by more of the same. "Antagonism" was chosen over terms like prejudice and discrimination because it carries fewer moralistic and theoretical assumptions (see Schermerhorn, 1970:6–9). For example, both of these terms see conflict as emanating primarily from one side: the dominant group. Antagonism allows for the possibility that conflict is mutual; i.e. a product of interaction.

The Split Labor Market

The central hypothesis is that ethnic antagonism first germinates in a labor market split along ethnic lines. To be split, a labor market must contain at least two groups of workers whose price of labor differs for the same work, or would differ if they did the same work. The concept "price of labor" refers to labor's total cost to the employer, including not only wages, but the cost of recruitment, transportation, room and board, education, health care (if the employer must bear these), and the costs of labor unrest. The degree of worker "freedom" does not interfere with this calculus; the cost of a slave can be estimated in the same monetary units as that of a wage earner, from his purchase price, living expenses, policing requirements, and so on.

The price of a group of workers can be roughly calculated in advance and comparisons made even though two groups are not engaged in the same activity at the same time. Thus in 1841 in the colony of New South Wales, the Legislative Council's Committee

TABLE 1

Estimated Cost of Three Types of Labor to Be
Shepherds in New South Wales, 1841*

	Free Man (White)			Prisoner (White)			Coolie (Indian)		
	£	s.	d.	£	s.	d.	£	s.	d.
Rations	16	18	0	13	14	4	9	6	4
Clothing	—	—	—	3	3	0	1	1	8
Wages	25	0	0	—	—	—	6	0	0
Passage from India	—	—	—	—	—	—	2	0	0
Total per Annum	41	18	0	16	17	4	18	8	0

*From Yarwood (1968:13).

on Immigration estimated the relative costs of recruiting three groups of laborers to become shepherds. Table 1 shows their findings. The estimate of free white labor, for example, was based on what it would take to attract these men from competing activities.

Factors Affecting the Initial Price of Labor

Labor markets that are split by the entrance of a new group develop a dynamic which may in turn affect the price of labor. One must therefore distinguish initial from later price determinants. The initial factors can be divided into two broad categories: resources and motives.

1. Resources

Three types of resources are important price determinants. These are:

a. Level of Living, or Economic Resources. The ethnic groups forming the labor market in a contact situation derive from different economic systems, either abroad or within a conquered territory. For members of an ethnic group to be drawn into moving, they must at least raise their wage level. In general, the poorer the economy of the recruits, the less the inducement needed for them to enter the new labor market. Crushing poverty may

drive them to sell their labor relatively cheaply. For example, Lind (1968:199) describes the effect of the living level on the wage scale received by immigrant workers to Hawaii:

In every case [of labor importations] the superior opportunities for gaining a livelihood have been broadcast in regions of surplus manpower, transportation facilities have been provided, and finally a monetary return larger than that already received has been offered to the prospective laborer. The monetary inducement has varied considerably, chiefly according to the plane of living of the population being recruited, and the cheapest available labor markets have, of course, been most extensively drawn upon.

Workers need not accept the original wage agreement for long after they have immigrated, since other opportunities may exist; for instance, there may be ample, cheap land available for individual farming. One capitalist device for keeping wages low at least for a time is to bind immigrants to contracts before they leave the old economy. The Indian indenture system, for example, rested on such an arrangement (Gillion, 1962:19–38).

b. Information. Immigrants may be pushed into signing contracts out of ignorance. They may agree to a specific wage in their homeland not knowing the prevailing wage in the new country, or having been beguiled by a false account of life and opportunity there. Williams (1944:11), for example, describes some of the false promises made to draw British and Germans as workers to West Indian sugar plantations before the advent of African slavery. Chinese labor to Australia was similarly "obtained under 'false and specious pretenses'" (Willard, 1967:9).

The possibilities for defrauding a population lacking access to the truth are obvious. In general, the more people know about conditions obtaining in the labor market to which they are moving, the better can they protect themselves against disadvantageous wage agreements.

c. Political Resources. By political resources I mean the benefits to a group of organizing. Organization can exist at the level of labor, or it can occur at higher levels, for example, in a government that protects them. These levels are generally related in that a strong government can help organize its emigrants. There are exceptions, however: strong emigrant governments tend not to extend protection to their deported convicts or political exiles; and some highly organized groups, like the Jews in the United States, have not received protection from the old country.

Governments vary in the degree to which they protect their emigrants. Japan kept close watch over the fate of her nationals who migrated to Hawaii and the Pacific coast; and the British colonial government in India tried to guard against abuses of the indenture system (for example, by refusing to permit Natal to import Indian workers for their sugar plantations until satisfactory terms had been agreed to; cf. Ferguson-Davie, 1952:4–10). In contrast Mexican migrant workers to the United States have received little protection from their government, and African states were unable to intervene on behalf of slaves brought to America. Often the indigenous populations of colonized territories have been politically weak following conquest. Thus African nations in South Africa have been unable to protect their migrant workers in the cities.

In general, the weaker a group politically, the more vulnerable it is to the use of force, hence to an unfavorable wage bargain (or to no wage bargain at all, as with slavery). The price of a labor group varies inversely with the amount of force that can be used against it, which in turn depends on its political resources.

2. Motives

Two motives affect the price of labor, both related to the worker's intention of not remaining permanently in the labor force. Temporary workers tend to cost less than permanent workers for two reasons. First, they are more willing to put up with undesirable work conditions since these need not be endured forever. If they are migrants, this tolerance may extend to the general standard of living. Often migrant temporary workers are males who have left the comforts of home behind and whose employers need not bear the cost of housing and educating their families. Even when families accompany them, such workers tend to be willing to accept a lower standard of living since it is only short term.

Second, temporary workers avoid involvement in lengthy labor disputes. Since they will be in the labor market a short while, their main concern is immediate employment. They may be willing to undercut wage standards if need be to get a job and are therefore ripe candidates for strike-breaking. Permanent workers also stand to lose from lengthy conflict, but they hope for benefits to their progeny. If temporary workers are from elsewhere, they have no such interest in future business-labor relations. Altogether, temporary workers have little reason to join the organizations and unions of a permanent work force, and tend not to do so.

a. Fixed or Supplementary Income Goal. Some temporary workers enter the market either to supplement family income, or to work toward a specific purchase. The worker's standard of living does not, therefore, depend on his earnings on the job in question, since his central source of employment or income lies elsewhere. Examples of this phenomenon are to be found throughout Africa:

. . . the characteristic feature of the labor market in most of Africa has always been the massive circulation of Africans between their villages and paid employment outside. In some places villagers engage in wage-earning seasonally. More commonly today they work for continuous though short-term periods of roughly one to three years, after which they return to the villages. . . . the African villager, the potential migrant into paid employment, has a relatively low, clearly-defined and rigid income goal; he wants money to pay head and hut taxes, to make marriage payments required of prospective bridegrooms, or to purchase some specific consumer durable (a bicycle, a rifle, a sewing machine, a given quantity of clothing or textiles, etc.) (Berg, 1966:116–8).

Such a motive produces the "backward-sloping labor supply function" characteristic of many native peoples in colonized territories. In addition to the general depressing effects on wages of being temporary, this motive leads to a fairly rapid turnover in personnel, making organization more difficult and hindering the development of valuable skills which could be used for bargaining. If wages were to rise, workers would reach their desired income and withdraw more quickly from the market, thereby lessening their chances of developing the political resources necessary to raise their wages further.

b. Fortune Seeking. Many groups, commonly called sojourners (see Siu, 1952), migrate long distances to seek their fortune, with the ultimate intention of improving their position in their homeland. Such was the case with Japanese immigrants on the west coast and Italian immigrants in the east. Such workers stay longer in the labor market, and can develop political resources. However, since they are temporary they have little incentive to join the organizations of the settled population. Instead they tend to create competing organizations composed of people who will play a part in their future in the homeland, i.e. members of the same ethnic group.

Sojourner laborers have at least three features which affect the price of labor: lower wages, longer hours, and convenience to the employer. The Japanese show all three. Millis (1915:45) cites the U.S. Immigration Commission on the question of relative wages:

The Japanese have usually worked for a lower wage than the members of any other race save the Chinese and the Mexican. In the salmon canneries the Chinese have been paid higher wages than the Japanese engaged in the same occupations. In the lumber industry, all races, including the East Indian, have been paid higher wages than the Japanese doing the same kind of work. As section hands and laborers in railway shops they have been paid as much or more than the Mexicans, but as a rule less than the white men of many races.

And so on. The lower wage level of Japanese workers reflects both a lower standard of living, and a desire to get a foothold in the labor market. As Iwata (1962:27) puts it: "Their willingness to accept even lower wages than laborers of other races enabled the Japanese to secure employment readily."

Millis (1915:155) describes a basket factory in Florin, California, where Japanese workers had displaced white female workers because the latter were unwilling to work more than ten hours a day or on weekends. The Japanese, anxious to return to Japan as quickly as possible, were willing to work twelve to fourteen hours per day and on weekends, thereby saving their employers the costs of a special overtime work force.

The Japanese immigrants developed political resources through a high degree of community organization. This could be used for the convenience of the employer, by solving his recruitment problems, seeing that work got done, and providing workers with board and lodging. In the case of seasonal labor, the Japanese community could provide for members during the off-season by various boarding arrangements and clubs, and by transporting labor to areas of demand (Ichihashi, 1932:172–6; Millis, 1915:44–5). These conveniences saved the employer money.[4]

As the reader may have noted, I have omitted a factor usually considered vital in determining the price of labor, i.e. differences in skills. I would contend, however, that this does not in itself lead to that difference in price for the same work which distinguishes a split labor market. While a skilled worker may be able to get a higher paying job, an unskilled laborer of another ethnicity may be trained to fill that job for the same wage. Skills are only indirectly important in that they can be used to develop political resources, which in turn may lead to a difference in wage level for the same work.

Price of Labor and Ethnicity

Ethnic differences need not always produce a price differential. Thus, if several ethnic groups who are approximately equal in resources and/or goals enter the same economic system, a split labor market will not develop. Alternatively, in a two-group contact situation, if one ethnic group occupies the position of a business elite and has no members in the labor force (or in a class that could easily be pushed into the labor force, e.g. low-capital farmers) then regardless of the other group's price, the labor market will not be split. This statement is a generalization of the point made by Harris (1964) that the critical difference in race relations between the deep south and Brazil was that the former had a white yeomanry in direct competition with ex-slaves, while the Portuguese only occupied the role of a business elite (plantation owners).

Conversely, a split labor force does not only stem from ethnic differences. For example, prison and female labor have often been cheaper than free male labor in western societies. Prison labor has been cheap because prisoners lack political resources, while women often labor for supplementary incomes (cf. Hutchinson, 1968:59–61; Heneman and Yoder, 1965:543–4).

That initial price discrepancies in labor should ever fall along ethnic lines is a function of two forces. First, the original wage agreement arrived at between business and new labor often takes place in the labor group's point of origin. This is more obviously a feature of immigrant labor, but also occurs within a territory when conquered peoples enter their conquerors' economy. In other words, the wage agreement is often concluded within a national context, these nationalities coming to comprise the ethnic elements of the new labor market. One would thus expect the initial wages of co-nationals to be similar.

Second, nations or peoples that have lived relatively separately from one another are likely to have developed different employment motives and levels of resources (wealth, organization, communication channels.) In other words, the factors that affect the price of labor are likely to differ grossly between nations, even though there may be considerable variation within each nation, and overlap between nations. Color differences in the initial price of labor only seem to be a factor because resources have historically been roughly correlated with color around the world.[5] When color and resources are not correlated in the "expected" way, then I would predict that price follows resources and motives rather than color.

In sum, the prejudices of business do not determine the price of labor, darker skinned or culturally different persons being paid less because of them. Rather, business tries to pay as little as possible for labor, regardless of ethnicity, and is held in check by the resources and motives of labor groups. Since these often vary by ethnicity, it is common to find ethnically split labor markets.

The Dynamics of Split Labor Markets

In split labor markets, conflict develops between three key classes: business, higher paid labor, and cheaper labor. The chief interests of these classes are as follows:

1. Business or Employers

This class aims at having as cheap and docile a labor force as possible to compete effectively with other businesses. If labor costs are too high (owing to such price determinants as unions), employers may turn to cheaper sources, importing overseas groups or using indigenous conquered populations. In the colony of Queensland in Australia, for example, it was believed that cotton farming would be the most suitable economic enterprise:

However, such plantations (being too large) could not be worked, much less cleared, by their owners; neither could the work be done by European laborers because sufficient numbers of these were not available—while even had there been an adequate supply, the high rates of wages would have been prohibitive. This was a consideration which assumed vast importance when it was realized that cotton would have to be cultivated in Queensland at a considerably lower cost than in the United States in order to compensate for the heavier freights from Queensland—the more distant country from England. It seemed then that there was no possibility of successful competition with America unless the importation of some form of cheap labor was permitted (Moles, 1968:41).

Cheaper labor may be used to create a new industry having substantially lower labor costs than the rest of the labor market, as in Queensland. Or they may be used as strikebreakers or replacements to undercut a labor force trying to improve its bargaining position with business. If cheap labor is unavailable, business may turn to mechanization, or try to relocate firms in areas of the world where the price of labor is lower.

2. Higher Paid Labor

This class is very threatened by the introduction of cheaper labor into the market, fearing that it will either force them to leave the territory or reduce them to its level. If the labor market is split ethnically, the class antagonism takes the form of ethnic antagonism. It is my contention (following Cox, 1948:411n) that, while much rhetoric of ethnic antagonism concentrates on ethnicity and race, it really in large measure (though probably not entirely) expresses this class conflict.

The group comprising higher paid labor may have two components. First, it may include current employees demanding a greater share of the profits or trying to maintain their position in the face of possible cuts. A second element is the small, independent, entrepreneur, like the subsistence farmer or individual miner. The introduction of cheaper labor into these peoples' line can undermine their position, since the employer of cheaper labor can produce at lower cost. The independent operator is then driven into the labor market. The following sequence occurs in many colonies: settlement by farmers who work their own land, the introduction of intensive farming using cheaper labor, a rise in land value and a consequent displacement of independent farmers. The displaced class may move on (as occurred in many of the West Indies when African slave labor was introduced to raise sugar), but if it remains, it comes to play the role of higher paid labor.

The presence of cheaper labor in areas of the economy where higher paid labor is not currently employed is also threatening to the latter, since the former attract older industries. The importance of potential competition cannot be over-stressed. Oftentimes writers assert the irrationality of ethnic antagonism when direct economic competition is not yet in evidence owing to few competitors having entered the labor market, or to competitors having concentrated in a few industries. Thus Daniels (1966:29) belittles the role of trade unions in the Asiatic Exclusion League by describing one of the major contributors as "an organization whose members, like most trade unionists in California, were never faced with job competition from Japanese." It does not take direct competition for members of a higher priced labor group to see the possible threat to their well-being, and to try to prevent its materializing. If they have reason to believe many more low-priced workers are likely to follow an initial "insignificant trickle" (as Daniels, 1966:1, describes the Japanese immigration, failing to mention that it was insignificant precisely because a larger anticipated flow had been thwarted, and diverted to Brazil), or if they see a large concentration of cheaper labor in a few industries which could easily be used to undercut them in their own, they will attempt to forestall undercutting.

Lest you think this fear misguided, take note that, when business could override the interests of more expensive labor, the latter have indeed been displaced or undercut. In British Guiana the local labor force, composed mainly of African ex-slaves, called a series of strikes in 1842 and 1847 against planters' attempts to reduce their wages. Plantation owners responded by using public funds to import over 50,000 cheaper East Indian indentured workers (Despres, 1969). A similar situation obtained in Mississippi, where Chinese were brought in to undercut freed blacks. Loewen (1971:23) describes the thinking of white land-owners: "the 'Chinaman' would not only himself supply a cheaper and less troublesome work force but in addition his presence as a threatening alternative would intimidate the Negro into resuming his former docile behavior." Such displacement has occurred not only to nonwhite more expensive labor, but, as the effects of slavery in the West Indies show, to whites by white capitalists.

3. Cheaper Labor

The employer uses this class partly to undermine the position of more expensive labor, through strikebreaking and undercutting. The forces that make the cheaper group cost less permit this to occur. In other words, either they lack the resources to resist an offer or use of force by business, or they seek a quick return to another economic and social base.

With the possible exception of sojourners, cheaper labor does not intentionally undermine more expensive labor; it is paradoxically its weakness that makes it so threatening, for business can more thoroughly control it. Cox makes this point (1948:417–8) in analyzing why Pacific coast white and Asian workers could not unite in a coalition against business:

. . . the first generation of Asiatic workers is ordinarily very much under the control of labor contractors and employers, hence it is easier for the employer to frustrate any plans for their organization. Clearly this cultural bar helped antagonize white workers against the Asiatics. The latter were conceived of as being in alliance with the employer. It would probably have taken two or three generations before, say, the East Indian low-caste worker on the Coast became sufficiently Americanized to adjust easily to the policies and aims of organized labor.

Ethnic antagonism is specifically produced by the competition that arises from a price differential. An oversupply of equal-priced labor does not produce such antagonism, though it too threatens people with the loss of their job. However, hiring practices will not necessarily fall along ethnic lines, there being no advantage to the employer in hiring workers of one or another ethnicity. All workingmen are on the same footing, competing for scarce jobs (cf. Blalock, 1967:84–92, who uses this model of labor competition). When one ethnic group is decidedly cheaper than another (i.e. when the labor market is split) the higher paid worker faces more than the loss of his job; he faces the possibility that the wage standard in all jobs will be undermined by cheaper labor.

Victory for More Expensive Labor

If an expensive labor group is strong enough (strength generally depending on the same factors that influence price), they may be able to resist being displaced. Both exclusion and caste systems represent such victories for higher paid labor.

1. Exclusion

Exclusion movements generally occur when the majority of a cheaper labor group resides outside a given territory but desires to enter it (often at the request of business groups). The exclusion movement tries to prevent the physical presence of cheaper labor in the employment area, thereby preserving a non-split, higher priced labor market.

There are many examples of exclusion attempts around the world. In Australia, for instance, a group of white workers was able to prevent capitalists from importing cheaper labor from India, China, Japan and the Pacific Islands. Attempts at importation were met with strikes, boycotts, petitions and deputations (Willard, 1967:51–7). Ultimately, organized white labor pressed for strong exclusion measures, and vigilantly ensured their enforcement. As Yarwood (1964:151–2) puts it: "A comparison of the records of various governments during our period [1896–1923] leaves no doubt as to the special role of the Labour Party as the guardian of the ports." In other words, a white Australia policy (i.e. the exclusion of Asian and Polynesian immigrants) appears to have sprung from a conflict of interests between employers who wanted to import cheap labor, and a labor force sufficiently organized to ward off such a move.

California's treatment of Chinese and Japanese labor is another example of exclusion. A socialist, Cameron H. King, Jr., articulates the threatened labor group's position:

Unskilled labor has felt this competition [from the Japanese] for some time being compelled to relinquish job after job to the low standard of living it could not endure. The unskilled laborers are largely unorganized and voiceless. But as the tide rises it is reaching the skilled laborers and the small merchants. These are neither unorganized nor voiceless, and viewing the menace to their livelihood they loudly demand protection of their material interests. We of the Pacific Coast certainly know that exclusion is an effective solution. In the seventh decade of the nineteenth century the problem arose of the immigration of Chinese laborers. The Republican and Democratic parties failed to give heed to the necessities of the situation and the Workingman's party arose and swept the state with the campaign cry of "The Chinese must go." Then the two old parties woke up and have since realized that to hold the labor vote they must stand for Asiatic exclusion (King, 1908:665–6).

King wrote this around the time of the Gentlemen's Agreement, an arrangement of the U.S. and Japanese governments to prevent further immigration of Japanese labor to the Pacific Coast (Bailey, 1934). The Agreement was aimed specifically at labor and not other Japanese immigrants, suggesting that economic and not racial factors were at issue.

Exclusion movements clearly serve the interests of higher paid labor. Its standards are protected, while the capitalist class is deprived of cheaper labor.

2. Caste

If cheaper labor is present in the market, and cannot be excluded, then higher paid labor will resort to a caste arrangement, which depends on exclusiveness rather than exclusion. Caste is essentially an aristocracy of labor (a term borrowed from Lenin, e.g. 1964), in which higher paid labor deals with the undercutting potential of cheaper labor by excluding them from certain types of work. The higher paid group controls certain jobs exclusively and gets paid at one scale of wages, while the cheaper group is restricted to another set of jobs and is paid at a lower scale. The labor market split is submerged because the differentially priced workers ideally never occupy the same position.

Ethnically distinct cheaper groups (as opposed to women, for example, who face a caste arrangement in many Western societies) may reside in a territory for two reasons: either they were indigenous or they were imported early in capitalist-labor relations, when the higher paid group could not prevent the move. Two outstanding examples of labor aristocracies based on ethnicity are South Africa, where cheaper labor was primarily indigenous, and the U.S. south, where they were imported as slaves.

Unlike exclusion movements, caste systems retain the underlying reality of a price differential, for if a member of the subordinate group were to occupy the same position as a member of the stronger labor group he would be paid less. Hence, caste systems tend to become rigid and vigilant, developing an elaborate battery of laws, customs and beliefs aimed to prevent undercutting. The victory has three facets. First, the higher paid group tries to ensure its power in relation to business by monopolizing the acquisition of certain essential skills, thereby ensuring the effectiveness of strike action, or by controlling such important resources as purchasing power. Second, it tries to prevent the immediate use of cheaper labor as undercutters and strikebreakers by denying them access to general education thereby making their training as quick replacements more difficult, or by ensuring through such devices as "influx control" that the cheaper group will retain a base in their traditional economies. The latter move ensures a backward-sloping labor supply function (cf. Berg, 1966) undesirable to business. Third, it tries to weaken the cheaper group politically, to prevent their pushing for those resources that would make them useful as undercutters. In other words, the solution to the devastating potential of weak, cheap labor is, paradoxically, to weaken them further, until it is no longer in business' immediate interest to use them as replacements.

South Africa is perhaps the most extreme modern example of an ethnic caste system. A split labor market first appeared there in the mining industry. With the discovery of diamonds in 1869, a white working class emerged.[6] At first individual whites did the searching, but, as with the displacement of small farms by plantations, they were displaced by consolidated, high-capital operations, and became employees of the latter (Doxey, 1961:18). It was this class together with imported skilled miners from Cornwall (lured to Africa by high wages) which fought the capitalists over the use of African labor. Africans were cheaper because they came to the mines with a fixed income goal (e.g. the price of a rifle) and did not view the mines as their main source of livelihood. By contrast, European workers remained in the mines and developed organizations to further their interests.

Clearly, it would have been to the advantage of businessmen, once they knew the skills involved, to train Africans to replace the white miners at a fraction of the cost; but this did not happen. The mining companies accepted a labor aristocracy, not out of ethnic solidarity with the white workers but:

(as was to be the case throughout the later history of mining) they had little or no choice because of the collective strength of the white miners. . . . The pattern which was to emerge was that of the Europeans showing every sign of preparedness to use their collective strength to ensure their exclusive supremacy in the labour market. Gradually the concept of trade unionism, and, for that matter, of socialism, became accepted in the minds of the European artisans as the means of maintaining their own position against non-white inroads (Doxey, 1961:23–4).

The final showdown between mine owners and white workers occurred in the 1920's when the owners tried to substitute cheaper non-white labor for white labor in certain semi-skilled occupations. This move precipitated the "Rand Revolt," a general strike of white workers on the Witwatersrand, countered by the calling in of troops and the declaration of martial law. The result was a coalition between Afrikaner nationalists (predominantly workers and small-scale farmers being pushed off the land by larger, British owned farms) and the English-speaking Labor Party (Van der Horst, 1965:117–8). The Revolt "showed the lengths to which white labour was prepared to go to defend its privileged position. From that time on, mine managements have never directly challenged the colour-bar in the mining industry" (Van der Horst, 1965:118).

The legislative history of much of South Africa (and of the post-bellum deep south) consists in attempts by higher priced white labor to ward off undercutting by cheaper groups, and to entrench its exclusive control of certain jobs.[7]

This interpretation of caste contrasts with the Marxist argument that the capitalist class purposefully plays off one segment of the working class against the other (e.g. Reich, 1971). Business, I would contend, rather than desiring to protect a segment of the working class supports a liberal or laissez faire ideology that would permit all workers to compete freely in an open market. Such open competition would displace higher paid labor. Only under duress does business yield to labor aristocracy, a point made in Deep South, a book written when the depression had caused the displacement of white tenant farmers and industrial workers by blacks:

The economic interests of these groups [employers] would also demand that cheaper colored labor should be employed in the "white collar" jobs in business offices, governmental offices, stores, and banks. In this field, however, the interests of the employer group conflict not only with those of the lower economic group of whites but also with those of the more literate and aggressive middle group of whites. A white store which employed colored clerks, for example, would be boycotted by both these groups. The taboo upon the employment of colored workers in such fields is the result of the political and purchasing power of the white middle and lower groups (Davis, *et. al.,* 1941:480).

In sum, exclusion and caste are similar reactions to a split labor market. They represent victories for higher paid labor. The victory of exclusion is more complete in that cheaper labor is less available to business. For this reason I would hypothesize that a higher paid group prefers exclusion to caste, even though exclusion means they have to do the dirty work. Evidence for this comes from Australia where, in early attempts to import Asian labor, business tried to buy off white labor's opposition by offering to form them into a class of "mechanics" and foremen over the "coolies" (Yarwood, 1968:16, 42). The offer was heartily rejected in favor of exclusion. Apartheid in South Africa can be seen as an attempt to move from caste to the exclusion of the African work force.

Most of our examples have contained a white capitalist class, a higher paid white labor group, and a cheaper, non-white labor group. Conditions in Europe and around the world, and not skin color, yield such models. White capitalists would gladly dispense with and undercut their white working-class brethren if they could, and have done so whenever they had the opportunity. In the words of one agitator for excluding Chinese from the U.S. Pacific coast: "I have seen men . . . American born, who certainly would, if I may use a strong expression, employ devils from Hell if the devils would work for 25 cents less than a white man" (cited in Daniels and Kitano, 1970:43).

In addition, cases have occurred of white workers playing the role of cheap labor, and facing the same kind of ethnic antagonism as non-white workers. Consider the riots against Italian strike-breakers in the coal fields of Pennsylvania in 1874 (Higham, 1965:47–8). In the words of one writer: "Unions resented the apparently inexhaustible cheap and relatively docile labor supply which was streaming from Europe obviously for the benefit of their employers" (Wittke, 1953:10).

Even when no ethnic differences exist, split labor markets may produce ethnic-like antagonism. Carey McWilliams (1945:82–3) describes an instance:

During the depression years, "Old Stock"—that is, white, Protestant, Anglo-Saxon Americans, from Oklahoma, Arkansas, and Texas—were roundly denounced in California as "interlopers." The same charges were made against them that were made against the Japanese: they were "dirty"; they had "enormous families"; they engaged in unfair competition; they threatened to "invade" the state and to "undermine" its institutions. During these turgid years (1930–1938) California attempted *to exclude,* by various extra-legal devices, those yeoman farmers just as it had excluded the Chinese and Japanese. "Okies" were "inferior" and "immoral." There was much family discord when Okie girl met California boy, and vice versa. . . . The prejudice against the Okies was obviously not "race" prejudice; yet it functioned in much the same manner.

Conclusion

Obviously, this type of three-way conflict is not the only important factor in ethnic relations. But it does help explain some puzzles, including, of course, the exclusion-caste anomaly. For example, Philip Mason (1970:64) develops a typology of race relations and finds that it relates to numerical proportions without being able to explain the dynamic behind this correlation. Table 2 presents a modified version of his chart. My theory can explain these relationships. Paternalism arises in situations where the cleavage between business and labor corresponds to an ethnic difference. A small business elite rules a large group of workers who entered the labor market at approximately the same price or strength. No split labor market existed, hence no ethnic caste system arises. The higher proportion of the dominant ethnicity under "Domination" means that part of the dominant group must be working class. A labor element that shares ethnicity with people who have sufficient resources to become the business elite is generally likely to come from a fairly wealthy country and have resources of its own. Such systems are likely to develop split labor markets. Finally, competition has under it societies whose cheaper labor groups have not been a major threat because the indigenous population available as cheap labor has been small and/or exclusion has effectively kept business groups from importing cheap labor in large numbers.

This theory helps elucidate other observations. One is the underlying similarity in the situation of blacks and women. Another is the history of political sympathy between California and the South. And, a third is the conservatism of the American white working class, or what Daniels and Kitano (1970:45) consider to be an "essential paradox of American life: [that] movements for economic democracy have usually been violently opposed to a thorough-going ethnic democracy." Without having to resort to psychological constructs like "authoritarianism," this theory is able to explain the apparent paradox.

In sum, in comparing those countries with the most ethnic antagonism with those having the least, it is evident that the difference does not lie in the fact that the former are Protestant and the latter Catholic: Protestants are found in all three of Mason's types, and Hawaii is a Protestant dominated territory. It

TABLE 2

Numerical Proportion of Dominant to Subordinate Ethnic Groups*

	Category	
Domination	Paternalism	Competition
	Situations	
South Africa (1960) 1–4	Nigeria (1952) 1–2000	Britain (1968) 50–1
U.S. South (1960) 4–1	Nyasaland (1966) 1–570	U.S. North (1960) 15–1
Rhodesia (1960) 1–16	Tanganyika 1–450	New Zealand 13–1
	Uganda 1–650	

*Adapted from Mason (1970:64).

does not lie in whether the dominant or subordinate group moves: South Africa and the deep south show opposite patterns of movement. It is evident that some of the most antagonistic territories have been British colonies, but not all British colonies have had this attribute. The characteristic that those British colonies and other societies high on ethnic antagonism share is that they all have a powerful white, or more generally higher paid, working class.

Notes

1. I do not wish to enter the debate over the applicability of the term "caste" to race relations (cf. Cox, 1948; Davis, et al., 1941). It is used here only for convenience and implies no particular theoretical bent.

2. The term "exclusion" has not usually been applied to immigrant quotas imposed on eastern and southern European immigrants; but such restrictions were, in effect, indistinguishable from the restrictions placed on Japanese immigration.

3. This usage contrasts with that of van den Berghe (1967a:9–10) who reserves the term "ethnic" for groups socially defined by cultural differences. In his definition, ethnicity is not necessarily inherited. I would contend that, while persons of

mixed ancestry may be problematic and are often assigned arbitrarily by the societies in which they reside, inheritance is implied in the common application of the word.

4. Sojourners often use their political resources and low price of labor to enter business for themselves (a process which will be fully analyzed in another paper). This does not remove the split in the labor market, though it makes the conflict more complex.

5. It is, of course, no accident that color and resources have been historically related. Poverty among non-white nations has in part resulted from European imperialism. Nevertheless, I would argue that the critical factor in the development of ethnic segmentation in a country is the meeting that occurs in the labor market of that country. The larger economic forces help determine the resources of entering parties, but it is not such forces to which workers respond. Rather they react to the immediate conflicts and threats in their daily lives.

6. Such a split was not found in the early Cape Colony, where business was one ethnicity—white, and labor another—non-white. Actually in neither case was the ethnic composition simple or homogeneous; but the important fact is that, among the laborers, who included so-called Hottentots, and slaves from Madagascar, Moçambique and the East Indies (cf. van den Berghe, 1967b:14), no element was significantly more expensive. The early Cape is thus structurally similar, in terms of the variables I consider important, to countries like Brazil and Mexico. And it is also noted for its "softened" tone of race relations as reflected in such practices as intermarriage.

7. Ethnically based labor aristocracies are much less sensitive about cheap labor in any form than are systems that do not arrive at this resolution because they are protected from it. Thus, Sutherland and Cressey (1970:561–2) report that both the deep south and South Africa continue to use various forms of prison contract labor, in contrast to the northern U.S. where the contract system was attacked by rising labor organizations as early as 1880.

References

Bailey, Thomas A. 1934. Theodore Roosevelt and the Japanese-American Crises. Stanford: Stanford University Press.

Becker, Gary. 1957. The Economics of Discrimination. Chicago: University of Chicago Press.

Berg, E. J. 1966. "Backward-sloping labor supply functions in dual economies—the Africa case." Pp. 114–36 in Immanuel Wallerstein (ed.), So-cial Change: The Colonial Situation. New York: Wiley.

Blalock, H. M., Jr. 1967. Toward a Theory of Minority-Group Relations. New York: Wiley.

Blauner, Robert. 1969. "Internal colonialism and ghetto revolt." Social Problems 16 (Spring): 393–408.

Cox, Oliver C. 1948. Caste, Class and Race. New York: Modern Reader.

Daniels, Roger. 1966. The Politics of Prejudice. Gloucester, Massachusetts: Peter Smith.

Daniels, Roger, and Harry H. L. Kitano. 1970. American Racism. Englewood Cliffs: Prentice-Hall.

Davis, Allison W., B. B. Gardner and M. R. Gardner. 1941. Deep South. Chicago: University of Chicago Press.

Despres, Leo A. 1969. "Differential adaptations and micro-cultural evolution in Guyana." Southwestern Journal of Anthropology 25 (Spring):14–44.

Doxey, G. V. 1961. The Industrial Colour Bar in South Africa. Cape Town: Oxford University Press.

Ferguson-Davie, C. J. 1952. The Early History of Indians in Natal. Johannesburg: South African Institute of Race Relations.

Gillion, K. L. 1962. Fiji's Indian Migrants. Melbourne: Oxford University Press.

Harris, Marvin. 1964. Patterns of Race in the Americas. New York: Walker.

Heneman, H. G., and Dale Yoder. 1965. Labor Economics. Cincinnati: Southwestern.

Higham, John. 1965. Strangers in the Land. New York: Athenium.

Hutchison, Emilie J. 1968. Women's Wages. New York: Ams Press.

Ichihashi, Yamato. 1932. Japanese in the United States. Stanford: Stanford University Press.

Iwata, Masakazu. 1962. "The Japanese immigrants in California agriculture." Agricultural History 36 (January):25–37.

King, Cameron H., Jr. 1908. "Asiatic exclusion." International Socialist Review 8 (May): 661–669.

Lenin, V. I. 1964. "Imperialism and the split in socialism." Pp. 105–120 in Collected Works, Volume 23, August 1916-March 1917. Moscow: Progress.

Lieberson, Stanley. 1961. "A societal theory of race and ethnic relations." American Sociological Review 26 (December):902–910.

Lind, Andrew W. 1968. An Island Community. New York: Greenwood.

Loewen, James W. 1971. The Mississippi Chinese. Cambridge: Harvard University Press.

Mason, Philip. 1970. Patterns of Dominance. London: Oxford University Press.

McWilliams, Carey. 1945. Prejudice: Japanese-Americans. Boston: Little, Brown.

Millis, H. A. 1915. The Japanese Problem in the United States. New York: Macmillan.

Moles, I. N. 1968. "The Indian coolie labour issue." Pp. 40–48 in A. T. Yarwood (ed.), Attitudes to Non-European Immigration. Melbourne: Cassell Australia.

Noel, Donald L. 1968. "A theory of the origin of ethnic stratification." Social Problems 16 (Fall):157–172.

Reich, Michael. 1971. "The economics of racism." Pp. 107–113 in David M. Gordon (ed.), Problems in Political Economy. Lexington, Massachusetts: Heath.

Schermerhorn, R. A. 1970. Comparative Ethnic Relations. New York: Random House.

Shibutani, Tamotsu, and Kian M. Kwan. 1965. Ethnic Stratification. New York: Macmillan.

Siu, Paul C. P. 1952. "The sojourner." American Journal of Sociology 58 (July):34–44.

Sutherland, Edwin H., and Donald R. Cressey. 1970. Criminology. Philadelphia: Lippincott.

van den Berghe, Pierre L. 1966. "Paternalistic versus competitive race relations: an ideal-type approach." Pp. 53–69 in Bernard E. Segal (ed.), Racial and Ethnic Relations. New York: Crowell.

———. 1967a. Race and Racism. New York: Wiley.

———. 1967b. South Africa: A Study in Conflict. Berkeley: University of California Press.

Van der Horst, Sheila T. 1965. "The effects of industrialization on race relations in South Africa." Pp. 97–140 in Guy Hunter (ed.), Industrialization and Race Relations. London: Oxford University Press.

Willard, Myra. 1967. History of the White Australia Policy to 1920. London: Melbourne University Press.

Williams, Eric. 1944. Capitalism and Slavery. Chapel Hill: University of North Carolina Press.

Wittke, Carl. 1953. "Immigration policy prior to World War I." Pp. 1–10 in Benjamin M. Ziegler (ed.), Immigration: An American Dilemma. Boston: Heath.

Yarwood, A. T. 1964. Asian Immigration to Australia. London: Cambridge University Press.

Yarwood, A. T. (ed.). 1968. Attitudes to Non-European Immigration. Melbourne: Cassell Australia.

ALEJANDRO PORTES AND ROBERT D. MANNING

The Immigrant Enclave: Theory and Empirical Examples

I. Introduction

The purpose of this chapter is to review existing theories about the process of immigrant adaptation to a new society and to recapitulate the empirical findings that have led to an emerging perspective on the topic. This emerging view revolves around the concepts of different modes of structural incorporation and of the immigrant enclave as one of them. These concepts are set in explicit opposition to two previous viewpoints on the adaptation process, generally identified as assimilation theory and the segmented labor markets approach.

The study of immigrant groups in the United States has produced a copious historical and sociological literature, written mostly from the assimilation perspective. Although the experiences of particular groups varied, the common theme of these writings is the unrelenting efforts of immigrant minorities to surmount obstacles impeding their entry into

Originally published in 1986. Please see complete source information beginning on page 891.

the "mainstream" of American society (Handlin, 1941, 1951; Wittke, 1952; Child, 1943; Vecoli, 1977). From this perspective, the adaptation process of particular immigrant groups followed a sequential path from initial economic hardship and discrimination to eventual socioeconomic mobility arising from increasing knowledge of American culture and acceptance by the host society (Warner and Srole, 1945; Gordon, 1964; Sowell, 1981). The focus on a "core" culture, the emphasis on consensus-building, and the assumption of a basic patterned sequence of adaptation represent central elements of assimilation theory.

From this perspective. the failure of individual immigrants or entire ethnic groups to move up through the social hierarchies is linked either to their reluctance to shed traditional values or to the resistance of the native majority to accept them because of racial, religious, or other shortcomings. Hence, successful adaptation depends, first of all, on the willingness of immigrants to relinquish a "backward" way of life and, second, on their acquisition of characteristics making them acceptable to the host society (Eisenstadt; 1970). Throughout, the emphasis is placed on the social psychological processes of motivation, learning, and interaction and on the cultural values and perceptions of the immigrants themselves and those who surround them.

The second general perspective takes issue with this psychosocial and culturalist orientation as well as with the assumption of a single basic assimilation path. This alternative view begins by noting that immigrants and their descendants do not necessarily "melt" into the mainstream and that many groups seem not to want to do so, preferring instead to preserve their distinct ethnic identities (Greeley, 1971; Glazer and Moynihan, 1970). A number of writers have focused on the resilience of these communities and described their functions as sources of mutual support and collective political power (Suttles, 1968; Alba and Chamlin, 1983; Parenti, 1967). Others have gone beyond descriptive

accounts and attempted to establish the causes of the persistence of ethnicity. Without exception, these writers have identified the roots of the phenomenon in the economic sphere and, more specifically, in the labor-market roles that immigrants have been called on to play.

Within this general perspective, several specific theoretical approaches exist. The first focuses on the situation of the so-called unmeltable ethnics—blacks, Chicanos, and American Indians—and finds the source of their plight in a history of internal colonialism during which these groups have been confined to specific areas and made to work under uniquely unfavorable conditions. In a sense, the role of colonized minorities has been to bypass the free labor market, yielding in the process distinct benefits both to direct employers of their labor and, indirectly, to other members of the dominant racial group (Blauner, 1972; Geschwender, 1978). The continuation of colonialist practices to our day explains, according to this view, the spatial isolation and occupational disadvantages of these minorities (Barrera, 1980).

A second approach attempts to explain the persistence of ethnic politics and ethnic mobilization on the basis of the organization of subordinate groups to combat a "cultural division of labor." The latter confined members of specific minorities to a quasi-permanent situation of exploitation and social inferiority. Unlike the first view, this second approach does not envision the persistence of ethnicity as a consequence of continuing exploitation, but rather as a "reactive formation" on the part of the minority to reaffirm its identity and its interests (Hechter, 1977; Despres, 1975). For this reason, ethnic mobilizations are often most common among groups who have already abandoned the bottom of the social ladder and started to compete for positions of advantage with members of the majority (Nagel and Olzak, 1982).

A final variant focuses on the situation of contemporary immigrants to the United States. Drawing on the dual labor market literature, this approach views recent immigrants as the latest entrants into the lower tier of a segmented labor market where women and other minorities already predominate. Relative to the latter, immigrants possess the advantages of their lack of experience in the new country, their legal vulnerability, and their greater initial motivation. All of these traits translate into higher productivity and lower labor costs for the firms that employ them (Sassen-Koob, 1980). Jobs in the secondary labor market are poorly paid, require few skills, and offer limited mobility opportunities. Hence, confinement of immigrants to this sector insures that those who do not return home are relegated to a quasi-permanent status as disadvantaged and discriminated minorities (Piore, 1975, 1979).

What these various structural theories have in common is the view of resilient ethnic communities formed as the result of a consistently disadvantageous economic position and the consequent absence of a smooth path of assimilation. These situations, ranging from slave labor to permanent confinement to the secondary labor market, are not altered easily. They have given rise, in time, either to hopeless communities of "unmeltable" ethnics or to militant minorities, conscious of a common identity and willing to support a collective strategy of self-defense rather than rely on individual assimilation.

These structural theories have provided an effective critique of the excessively benign image of the adaptation process presented by earlier writings. However, while undermining the former, the new structural perspective may have erred in the opposite direction. The basic hypothesis advanced in this chapter is that several identifiable modes of labor-market incorporation exist and that not all of them relegate newcomers to a permanent situation of exploitation and inferiority. Thus, while agreeing with the basic thrust of structural theories, we propose several modifications that are necessary for an adequate understanding of the different types of immigrant flows and their distinct processes of adaptation.

II. Modes of Incorporation

In the four decades since the end of World War II, immigration to the United States has experienced a vigorous surge reaching levels comparable only to those at the beginning of the century (National Research Council, 1985, chapter 2). Even if one restricts attention to this movement, disregarding multiple other migrations elsewhere in the world, it is not the case that the inflow has been of a homogeneous character. Low-wage labor immigration itself has taken different forms, including temporary contract flows, undocumented entries, and legal immigration. More importantly, it is not the case that all immigrants have been directed to the secondary labor market. For example, since the promulgation of the Immigration Act of 1965, thousands of professionals, technicians, and craftsmen have come to the United States, availing themselves of the occupational preference categories of the law. This type of inflow, dubbed "brain drain" in the sending nations, encompasses today sizable contingents of immigrants from such countries as India, South Korea, the Philippines, and Taiwan, each an important contributor to U.S. annual immigration.

The characteristics of this type of migration have been described in detail elsewhere (Portes, 1976, 1981). Two such traits deserve mention, however. First, occupationally skilled immigrants—including doctors, nurses, engineers, technicians, and craftsmen—generally enter the "primary" labor market; they contribute to alleviate domestic shortages in specific occupations and gain access, after a period of time, to the mobility ladders available to native workers. Second, immigration of this type does not generally give rise to spatially concentrated communities; instead, immigrants are dispersed throughout many cities and regions, following different career paths.

Another sizable contingent of entrants whose occupational future is not easily characterized *a priori* are political refugees.

Large groups of refugees, primarily from Communist-controlled countries, have come to the United States, first after the occupation of Eastern Europe by the Soviet Army, then after the advent of Fidel Castro to power in Cuba, and finally in the aftermath of the Vietnam War. Unlike purely "economic" immigrants, refugees have often received resettlement assistance from various governmental agencies (Zolberg, 1983; Keely, 1981). All the available evidence runs contrary to the notion of a uniform entry of political refugees into low-wage secondary occupations; on the contrary, there are indications of their employment in many different lines of work.

A third mode of incorporation has gained the attention of a number of scholars in recent years. It consists of small groups of immigrants who are inserted or insert themselves as commercial intermediaries in a particular country or region. These "middleman minorities" are distinct in nationality, culture, and sometimes race from both the superordinate and subordinate groups to which they relate (Bonacich, 1973; Light, 1972). They can be used by dominant elites as a buffer to deflect mass frustration and also as an instrument to conduct commercial activities in impoverished areas. Middlemen accept these risks in exchange for the opportunity to share in the commercial and financial benefits gained through such instruments as taxation, higher retail prices, and usury. Jews in feudal and early modern Europe represent the classic instance of a middleman minority. Other examples include Indian merchants in East Africa, and Chinese entrepreneurs in Southeast Asia and throughout the Pacific Basin (Bonacich and Modell, 1980, chapter 1). Contemporary examples in the United States include Jewish, Korean, and other Oriental merchants in inner-city ghetto areas and Cubans in Puerto Rico (Kim, 1981; Cobas, 1984).

Primary labor immigration and middleman entrepreneurship represent two modes of incorporation that differ from the image of an homogeneous flow into low-wage employment. Political refugees, in turn, have followed a variety of paths, including both of the above as well as insertion into an ethnic enclave economy. The latter represents a fourth distinct mode. Although frequently confused with middleman minorities, the emergence and structure of an immigrant enclave possess distinct characteristics. The latter have significant theoretical and practical implications, for they set apart groups adopting this entry mode from those following alternative paths. We turn now to several examples of immigrant enclaves to clarify their internal dynamics and causes of their emergence.

III. Immigrant Enclaves

Immigration to the United States before World War I was, overwhelmingly, an unskilled labor movement. Impoverished peasants from southern Italy, Poland, and the eastern reaches of the Austro-Hungarian Empire settled in dilapidated and crowded areas, often immediately adjacent to their points of debarcation, and took any menial jobs available. From these harsh beginnings, immigrants commenced a slow and often painful process of acculturation and economic mobility. Theirs was the saga captured by innumerable subsequent volumes written from both the assimilation and the structural perspectives.

Two sizable immigrant groups did not follow this pattern, however. Their most apparent characteristic was the economic success of the first generation, even in the absence of extensive acculturation. On the contrary, both groups struggled fiercely to preserve their cultural identity and internal solidarity. Their approach to adaptation thus directly contradicted subsequent assimilation predictions concerning the causal priority of acculturation to economic mobility. Economic success and "clannishness" also earned for each minority the hostility of the surrounding population. These two immigrant groups did not have a language, religion, or even race in common and they never overlapped in significant numbers in any part of the United States. Yet, arriving at opposite ends of the continent, Jews and Japanese pursued patterns of economic adaptation that were quite similar both in content and in their eventual consequences.

A. Jews in Manhattan

The first major wave of Jewish immigration to the United States consisted of approximately 50,000 newcomers of German origin, arriving between 1840 and 1870. These immigrants went primarily into commerce and achieved, in the course of a few decades, remarkable success. By 1900, the average income of German-Jewish immigrants surpassed that of the American population (Rischin, 1962). Many individuals who started as street peddlers and small merchants had become, by that time, heads of major industrial, retail, and financial enterprises.

The second wave of Jewish immigration exhibited quite different characteristics. Between 1870 and 1914, over two million Jews left the Pale of Settlement and other Russian-dominated regions, escaping Czarist persecution. Major pogroms occurred before and during this exodus (Dinnerstein, 1977). Thus, unlike most immigrants of the period, the migration of Russian and Eastern Europe Jews was politically motivated and their move was much more permanent. In contrast to German Jews, who were relatively well educated, the Yiddish-speaking newcomers came, for the most part, from modest origins and had only a rudimentary education. Although they viewed the new Russian wave with great apprehension, German Jews promptly realized that their future as an ethnic minority depended on the successful integration of the newcomers (Rischin, 1962). Charitable societies were established to provide food, shelter, and other necessities, and private schools were set up to teach immigrants English, civics, and the customs of the new country (Howe and Libo, 1979).

Aside from its size and rapidity of arrival, turn-of-the-century Jewish immigration had two other distinct characteristics. First was its strong propensity toward commerce and self-employment in general in preference to wage labor: as German Jews before them, many Russian immigrants moved directly into street peddling and other commercial activities of the most modest sort. Second was its concentration into a single, densely populated urban area—the lower East Side of Manhattan. Within this area, those who did not become storekeepers and peddlers from the start found employment in factories owned by German Jews, learning the necessary rudiments for future self-employment (Sowell, 1981, chapter 4).

The economic activities of this population created, in the course of two decades, a dense network of industrial, commercial, and financial enterprises. Close physical proximity facilitated exchanges of information and access to credit and raw materials. Characteristic of this emerging Jewish enclave is that production and marketing of goods was not restricted to the ethnic community, but went well beyond it into the general economy. Jews entered the printing, metal, and building trades; they became increasingly prominent in jewelry and cigar-making; above all, the garment industry became the primary domain of Jewish entrepreneurship, with hundreds of firms of all sizes engaged in the trade (Rischin, 1962; Howe and Libo, 1979).

The economic success of many of these ventures did not require and did not entail rapid acculturation. Immigrants learned English and those instrumental aspects of the new culture required for economic advancement. For the rest, they preferred to remain with their own and maintained, for the most part, close adherence to their original religion, language, and values (Wirth, 1956; Howe, 1976). Jewish enclave capitalism depended, for its emergence and advancement, precisely on those resources made available by a solidaristic ethnic community: protected access to labor and markets, informal sources of credit, and business information. It was through these resources that upstart immigrant enterprises could survive and eventually compete effectively with better-established firms in the general economy.

The emergence of a Jewish enclave in East Manhattan helped this group bypass the conventional assimilation path and achieve significant economic mobility in the course of the first generation, well ahead of complete acculturation. Subsequent generations also pursued this path, but the resources accumulated through early immigrant entrepreneurship were dedicated primarily to further the education of children and their entry into the professions. It was at this point that outside hostility became most patent, as one university after another established quotas to prevent the onrush of Jewish students. The last of these quotas did not come to an end until after World War II (Dinnerstein, 1977).

Despite these and other obstacles, the movement of Jews into higher education continued. Building on the economic success of the first generation, subsequent ones achieved levels of education, occupation, and income that significantly exceed the national average (Featherman, 1971; Sowell, 1981, chapter 4). The original enclave is now only a memory, but it provided in its time the necessary platform for furthering the rapid social and economic mobility of the minority. Jews did enter the mainstream of American society, but they did not do so starting uniformly at the bottom, as most immigrant groups had done; instead, they translated resources made available by early ethnic entrepreneurship into rapid access to positions of social prestige and economic advantage.

B. Japanese on the West Coast

The specific features of Japanese immigration differ significantly from the movement of European Jews, but their subsequent adaptation and mobility patterns are similar. Beginning in 1890 and ending with the enactment of the Gentlemen's Agreement of 1908, approximately 150,000 Japanese men immigrated to the West Coast. They were followed primarily by their spouses until the Immigration Act of 1924 banned any further Asiatic immigration.

Although nearly 300,000 Japanese immigrants are documented in this period (Daniels, 1977), less than half of this total remained in the United States (Petersen, 1971). This is due, in contrast to the case of the Jews, to the sojourner character of Japanese immigrants: the intention of many was to accumulate sufficient capital for purchasing farm land or settling debts in Japan. Hence this population movement included commercial and other members of the Japanese middle class who, not incidentally, were explicitly sponsored by their national government.

The residential patterns of Japanese immigrants were not as concentrated as those of Jews in Manhattan, but they were geographically clustered. Almost two-thirds of the 111,010 Japanese reported in the U.S. Census of 1920 lived in California. Further, one-third of California's Japanese residents lived in Los Angeles County in 1940, while another one-third lived in six nearby counties (Daniels, 1977). However, it was not the residential segregation of Japanese immigrants but rather their occupational patterns that eventually mobilized the hostility of the local population.

Japanese immigrants were initially welcomed and recruited as a form of cheap agricultural labor. Their reputation as thrifty and diligent workers made them preferable to other labor sources. Nativist hostilities crystallized, however, when Japanese immigrants shifted from wage labor to independent ownership and small-scale farming. This action not only reduced the supply of laborers but it also increased competition for domestic growers in the fresh-produce market. In 1900, only about 40 Japanese farmers in the entire United States leased or owned a total of 5000 acres of farmland. By 1909, the number of Japanese farmers had risen to 6000 and their collective holdings exceeded 210,000 acres (Petersen, 1971). Faced with such "unfair" competition, California growers turned to the political means at their disposal. In 1913, the state legislature passed the first Alien Land Law, which restricted land ownership by foreigners. This legislation did not prove sufficient, however, and, in subsequent years, the ever-accommodating legislature passed a series of acts closing other legal loopholes to Japanese farming (Petersen, 1971).

These proscriptions, which barred most of the Japanese from the lands, accelerated their entry into urban enterprise. In 1909, Japanese entrepreneurs owned almost 3000 small shops in several Western cities. Forty percent of Japanese men in Los Angeles were self-employed. They operated businesses such as dry-cleaning establishments, fisheries, lunch counters, and produce stands that marketed the production of Japanese farms (Light, 1972).

The ability of the first-generation *Issei* to escape the status of stoop labor in agriculture was based on the social cohesion of their community. Rotating credit associations offered scarce venture capital, while mutual-aid organizations provided assistance in operating farms and urban businesses. Light (1972) reports that capitalizations as high as $100,000 were financed through ethnic credit networks. Economic success was again accompanied by limited instrumental acculturation and by careful preservation of national identity and values. It was the availability of investment capital, cooperative business associations, and marketing practices (forward and backward economic linkages) within the ethnic enclave that enabled Japanese entrepreneurs to expand beyond its boundaries and compete effectively in the general economy. This is illustrated by the production and marketing of fresh produce. In 1920, the value of Japanese crops was about 10% of the total for California, when the Japanese comprised less than 1% of the state's population; many retail outlets traded exclusively with a non-Japanese clientele (Light, 1972; Petersen, 1971).

During the early 1940s, the Japanese ethnic economy was seriously disrupted but not eliminated by the property confiscations and camp internments accompanying World War II. After the war, economic prosperity and other factors combined to reduce local hostility toward the Japanese. Older *Issei* and many of their children returned to small business,

while other second-generation *Nisei*, like their Jewish predecessors, pursued higher education and entered the white-collar occupations *en masse*. This mobility path was completed by the third or *Sansei* generation, with 88% of their members attending college. Other third-generation Japanese have continued, however, the entrepreneurial tradition of their parents (Bonacich and Modell, 1980). Like Jews before them, Japanese-Americans have made use of the resources made available by early immigrant entrepreneurship to enter the mainstream of society in positions of relative advantage. The mean educational and occupational attainment of the group's 600,000 members surpasses at present all other ethnic and native groups, while its average family income is exceeded among American ethnic groups only by the Jews (Sowell, 1981).[1] . . .

IV. Conclusion: A Typology of the Process of Incorporation

We can now attempt a summary description of the characteristics of immigrant enclaves and how they differ from other paths. The emergence of an ethnic enclave economy has three prerequisites: first, the presence of a substantial number of immigrants, with business experience acquired in the sending country; second, the availability of sources of capital; and third, the availability of sources of labor. The latter two conditions are not too difficult to meet. The requisite labor can usually be drawn from family members and, more commonly, from recent arrivals. Surprisingly perhaps, capital is not a major impediment either since the sums initially required are usually small. When immigrants did not bring them from abroad, they could be accumulated through individual savings or pooled resources in the community. It is the first condition that appears critical. The presence of a number of immigrants skilled in what Franklin Frazier (1949) called the art of "buying and selling" is common [not only to the Jewish and Japanese cases reviewed above but also to contemporary enclave economies among Koreans and Cubans]. Such an entrepreneurial-commercial class among early immigrant cohorts can usually overcome other obstacles; conversely, its absence within an immigrant community will confine the community to wage employment even if sufficient resources of capital and labor are available.

Enclave businesses typically start small and cater exclusively to an ethnic clientele. Their expansion and entry into the broader market requires, as seen above, an effective mobilization of community resources. The social mechanism at work here seems to be a strong sense of reciprocity supported by collective solidarity that transcends the purely contractual character of business transactions. For example, receipt of a loan from a rotating credit association entails the duty of continuing to make contributions so that others can have access to the same source of capital. Although, in principle, it would make sense for the individual to withdraw once his loan is received, such action would cut him off from the very sources of community support on which his future business success depends (Light, 1972).

Similarly, relations between enclave employers and employees generally transcend a contractual wage bond. It is understood by both parties that the wage paid is inferior to the value of labor contributed. This is willingly accepted by many immigrant workers because the wage is only *one* form of compensation. Use of their labor represents often the key advantage making poorly capitalized enclave firms competitive. In reciprocity, employers are expected to respond to emergency needs of their workers and to promote their advancement through such means as on-the-job training, advancement to supervisory positions, and aid when they move into self-employment. These opportunities represent the other part of the "wage" received by enclave workers. The informal mobility ladders thus created are, of course, absent in the secondary labor market where there is no primary bond between owners and workers or no common ethnic community to enforce the norm of reciprocity.

Paternalistic labor relations and strong community solidarity are also characteristic of middleman minorities. Although both modes of incorporation are similar and are thus frequently confused, there are three major structural differences between them. First, immigrant enclaves are not exclusively commercial. Unlike middleman minorities, whose economic role is to mediate commercial and financial transactions between elites and masses, enclave firms include in addition a sizable productive sector. The latter may comprise agriculture, light manufacturing, and construction enterprises; their production, marketed often by coethnic intermediaries, is directed toward the general economy and not exclusively to the immigrant community.

Second, relationships between enclave businesses and established native ones are problematic. Middleman groups tend to occupy positions complementary and subordinate to the local owning class; they fill economic niches either disdained or feared by the latter. Unlike them, enclave enterprises often enter in direct competition with existing domestic firms. There is no evidence, for example, that domestic elites deliberately established or supported the emergence of the Jewish, Japanese, Korean, or Cuban business communities as means to further their own economic interests. There is every indication, on the other hand, that this mode of incorporation was largely self-created by the immigrants, often in opposition to powerful domestic interests. Although it is true that enclave entrepreneurs have been frequently employed as subcontractors by outside firms in such activities as garment and construction (Bonacich, 1978), it is incorrect to characterize this role as the exclusive or dominant one among these enterprises.

Third, the enclave is concentrated and spatially identifiable. By the very nature of their activities, middleman minorities must often be dispersed among the mass of the population. Although the immigrants may live in certain limited areas, their businesses require proximity to their mass clientele and a measure of physical dispersion within it. It is true that middleman activities such as money-lending have been associated in several historical instances with certain streets and neighborhoods, but this is not a necessary or typical pattern. Street peddling and other forms of petty commerce require merchants to go into the areas where demand exists and avoid excessive concentration of the goods and services they offer. This is the typical pattern found today among middleman minorities in American cities (Cobas, 1984; Kim, 1981).

Enclave businesses, on the other hand, are spatially concentrated, especially in their early stages. This is so for three reasons: first, the need for proximity to the ethnic market which they initially serve; second, proximity to each other which facilitates exchange of information, access to credit, and other supportive activities; third, proximity to ethnic labor supplies on which they crucially depend. Unlike the Jewish, Korean, or Cuban cases, the Japanese enclave economy does partially depart from the pattern of high physical concentration. This can be attributed to the political persecution to which this group was subjected. Originally, Japanese concentration was a rural phenomenon based on small farms linked together by informal bonds and cooperative associations. Forced removal of this minority from the land compelled their entry into urban businesses and their partial dispersal into multiple activities.

Physical concentration of enclaves underlies their final characteristic. Once an enclave economy has fully developed, it is possible for a newcomer to live his life entirely within the confines of the community. Work, education, and access to health care, recreation, and a variety of other services can be found without leaving the bounds of the ethnic economy. This institutional completeness is what enables new immigrants to move ahead economically, despite very limited knowledge of the host culture and language. Supporting empirical evidence comes from studies showing low levels of English knowledge among enclave minorities and the absence of a net effect of knowledge of English on their average income levels (Light, 1980; Portes and Bach, 1985).

Table 1 summarizes this discussion by presenting the different modes of incorporation and their principal characteristics. Two caveats are necessary. First, this typology is not exhaustive, since other forms of adaptation have existed and will undoubtedly emerge in the future. Second, political refugees are not included, since this entry label does not necessarily entail a unique adaptation path. Instead, refugees can select or be channelled in many different directions, including self-employment, access to primary labor markets, or confinement to secondary sector occupations.

Having discussed the characteristics of enclaves and middleman minorities, a final word must be said about the third alternative to employment in the lower tier of a dual labor market. As a mode of incorporation, primary sector immigration also has distinct advantages, although they are of a different order from those pursued by "entrepreneurial" minorities. Dispersal throughout the receiving country and career mobility based on standard promotion criteria makes it imperative for immigrants in this mode to become fluent in the new language and culture (Stevens, Goodman, and Mick, 1978). Without a supporting ethnic community, the second generation also becomes thoroughly steeped in the ways of the host society. Primary sector immigration thus tends to lead to very rapid social and cultural integration. It represents the path that approximates most closely the predictions of assimilation theory with regard to (1) the necessity of acculturation for social and economic progress and (2) the subsequent rewards received by immigrants and their descendants for shedding their ethnic identities.

Clearly, however, this mode of incorporation is open only to a minority of immigrant groups. In addition, acculturation of professionals and other primary sector immigrants is qualitatively different from that undergone by others. Regardless of their differences, immigrants in other modes tend to learn the new language and culture with a heavy "local" content. Although acculturation may be slow, especially in the case of enclave groups, it car-

TABLE 1
Typology of Modes of Incorporation

Variable	Primary sector immigration	Secondary sector immigration	Immigrant enclaves	Middleman minorities
Size of immigrant population	Small	Large	Large	Small
Spatial concentration, national	Dispersed	Dispersed	Concentrated	Concentrated
Spatial concentration, local	Dispersed	Concentrated	Concentrated	Dispersed
Original class composition	Homogeneous: skilled workers and professionals	Homogeneous: manual laborers	Heterogeneous: entrepreneurs, professionals, and workers	Homogeneous: merchants and some professionals
Present occupational status distribution	High mean status/low variance	Low mean status/low variance	Mean status/high variance	Mean status/low variance
Mobility opportunities	High: formal promotion ladders	Low	High: informal ethnic ladders	Average: informal ethnic ladders
Institutional diversification of ethnic community	None	Low: weak social institutions	High: institutional completeness	Medium: strong social and economic institutions
Participation in ethnic organizations	Little or none	Low	High	High
Resilience of ethnic culture	Low	Average	High	High
Knowledge of host country language	High	Low	Low	High
Knowledge of host country institutions	High	Low	Average	High
Modal reaction of host community	Acceptance	Discrimination	Hostility	Mixed: elite acceptance/mass hostility

ries with it elements unique to the surrounding community—its language inflections, particular traditions, and loyalties (Greeley, 1971; Suttles, 1968). On the contrary, acculturation of primary sector immigrants is of a more cosmopolitan sort. Because career requirements often entail physical mobility, the new language and culture are learned more rapidly and more generally, without strong attachments to a particular community. Thus, while minorities entering menial labor, enclave, or middleman enterprise in the United States have eventually become identified with a certain city or region, the same is not true for immigrant professionals, who tend to "disappear," in a cultural sense, soon after their arrival (Stevens *et al.*, 1978; Cardona and Cruz, 1980).

Awareness of patterned differences among immigrant groups in their forms of entry and labor market incorporation represents a significant advance, in our view, from earlier undifferentiated descriptions of the adaptation process. This typology is, however, a provisional effort. Just as detailed research on the condition of particular minorities modified or replaced earlier broad generalizations, the propositions advanced here will require revision. New groups arriving in the United States at present and a revived interest in immigration should provide the required incentive for empirical studies and theoretical advances in the future.

Note

1. The original article from which this excerpt was drawn includes a further discussion of contemporary Korean and Cuban enclaves.—ED.

References

Alba, Richard D., and Chamlin, Mitchell B. (1983). Ethnic identification among whites. *American Sociological Review* 48:240–47.

Barrera, Mario (1980). *Race and class in the Southwest: A theory of racial inequality.* Notre Dame, Indiana: Notre Dame University Press.

Blauner, Robert (1972). *Racial oppression in America.* New York: Harper and Row.

Bonacich, Edna (1973). A theory of middleman minorities. *American Sociological Review* 38(October):583–594.

Bonacich, Edna (1978). U.S. capitalism and Korean immigrant small business. Riverside, California: Department of Sociology, University of California—Riverside, mimeographed.

Bonacich, Edna, and Modell, John (1980). *The economic basis of ethnic solidarity: Small business in the Japanese-American community.* Berkeley, California: University of California Press.

Cardona, Ramiro C., and Cruz, Carmen I. (1980). *El exodo de Colombianos.* Bogota: Ediciones Tercer Mundo.

Child, Irving L. (1943). *Italian or American? The second generation in conflict.* New Haven, Connecticut: Yale University Press.

Cobas, Jose (1984). Participation in the ethnic economy, ethnic solidarity and ambivalence toward the host society: The case of Cuban emigres in Puerto Rico. Presented at the American Sociological Association Meeting, San Antonio, Texas: August.

Daniels, Roger (1977). The Japanese-American experience: 1890–1940. In *Uncertain Americans* (L. Dinnerstein and F. C. Jaher, eds.), pp. 250–267. New York: Oxford University Press.

Despres, Leo (1975). Toward a theory of ethnic phenomena. In *Ethnicity and resource competition* (Leo Despres, ed.), pp. 209–212. The Hague: Mouton.

Dinnerstein, Leonard (1977). The East European Jewish migration. In *Uncertain Americans* (L. Dinnerstein and F. C. Jaher, eds.), pp. 216–231. New York: Oxford University Press.

Eisenstadt, S. N. (1970). The process of absorbing new immigrants in Israel. In *Integration and development in Israel* (S. N. Eisenstadt, RivKah Bar Yosef, and Chaim Adler, eds.), pp. 341–367. Jerusalem: Israel University Press.

Featherman, David L. (1971). The socio-economic achievement of white religio-ethnic sub-groups: Social and psychological explanations. *American Sociological Review* 36 (April): 207–222.

Frazier, E. Franklin (1949). *The Negro in the United States.* New York: Macmillan.

Geschwender, James A. (1978). *Racial stratification in America.* Dubuque, Iowa: William C. Brown.

Glazer, Nathan, and Moynihan, Daniel P. (1970). *Beyond the melting pot: The Negroes, Puerto Ricans, Jews, Italians and Irish of New York City.* Cambridge, Massachusetts: M.I.T. Press.

Gordon, Milton M. (1964). *Assimilation in American life: The role of race, religion, and national origins.* New York: Oxford University Press.

Greeley, Andrew (1971). *Why can't they be like us? America's white ethnic groups.* New York: Dutton.

Handlin, Oscar (1941). *Boston's immigrants: A study of acculturation.* Cambridge: Harvard University Press.

Handlin, Oscar (1951). *The uprooted: The epic story of the great migrations that made the American people.* Boston: Little Brown.

Hechter, Michael (1977). *Internal colonialism, the Celtic fringe in British national development, 1536–1966.* Berkeley, California: University of California Press.

Howe, Irving (1976). *World of our fathers.* New York: Harcourt, Brace, Jovanovich.

Howe, Irving, and Libo, Kenneth (1979). *How we lived, a documentary history of immigrant Jews in America.* New York: Richard March.

Keely, Charles B. (1981). *Global refugee policy: The case for a development-oriented strategy.* New York: The Population Council.

Kim, Illsoo (1981). *New urban immigrants, the Korean community in New York.* Princeton, New Jersey: Princeton University Press.

Light, H. Ivan (1972). *Ethnic enterprise in America: Business and welfare among Chinese, Japanese, and Blacks.* Berkeley, California: University of California Press.

Light, H. Ivan (1980). Asian enterprise in America: Chinese, Japanese, and Koreans in small business. In *Self-help in urban America* (Scott Cummings, ed.) pp. 33–57. New York: Kennikat Press.

Nagel, Joane, and Olzak, Susan (1982). Ethnic mobilization in new and old states: An extension of the competition model. *Social Problems* 30:127–143.

National Research Council (1985). Immigration statistics: A story of neglect. Report of the Panel on Immigration Statistics. Washington, D.C.: National Academy of Sciences.

Parenti, Michael (1967). Ethnic politics and the persistence of ethnic identification. *American Political Science Review* 61:717–726.

Petersen, William (1971). *Japanese Americans, oppression and success.* New York: Random House.

Piore, Michael J. (1975). Notes for a theory of labor market stratification. In *Labor market segmentation* (Richard C. Edwards, Michael Reich, and David M. Gordon, eds.), pp. 125–171. Lexington, Massachusetts: Heath.

Piore, Michael J. (1979). *Birds of passage, migrant labor and industrial societies.* New York: Cambridge University Press.

Portes, Alejandro (1976). Determinants of the brain drain. *International Migration Review* 10(Winter):489–508.

Portes, Alejandro (1981). Modes of structural incorporation and theories of labor immigration. In *Global Trends in Migration, Theory and Research on International Population Movements* (Mary M. Kritz, Charles B. Keely, and Silvano M. Tomasi, eds.), pp. 279–297. New York: Center for Migration Studies.

Portes, Alejandro, and Bach, Robert L. (1985). *Latin journey, Cuban and Mexican immigrants in the United States.* Berkeley, California: University of California Press.

Rischin, Moses (1962). *The promised city, New York Jews 1870–1914.* Cambridge, Mass.: Harvard University Press.

Sassen-Koob, Saskia (1980). Immigrant and minority workers in the organization of the labor process. *Journal of Ethnic Studies* (1/Spring): 1–34.

Sowell, Thomas (1981). *Ethnic America: A history.* New York: Basic Books.

Stevens, Rosemary, Goodman, Louis W., and Mick, Stephen (1978). *The alien doctors, foreign medical graduates in American hospitals.* New York: Wiley.

Suttles, Gerald D. (1968). *The social order of the slum, ethnicity and territory in the inner city.* Chicago: University of Chicago Press.

Vecoli, Rudolph (1977). The Italian Americans. In *Uncertain Americans* (L. Dinnerstein and F. C. Jaher, eds.), pp. 201–215. New York: Oxford University Press.

Warner, W. Lloyd, and Srole, Leo (1945). *The social systems of American ethnic groups.* New Haven: Yale University Press.

Wirth, Louis (1956). *The ghetto.* Chicago: University of Chicago Press.

Wittke, Carl (1952). *Refugees of revolution: The German Forty-eighters in America.* Philadelphia: University of Pennsylvania Press.

Zolberg, Aristide (1983). Contemporary transnational migrations in historical perspective: Patterns and dilemmas. In *U.S. immigration and refugee policy* (Mary M. Kritz, ed.), pp. 15–51. Lexington, Massachusetts: Heath.

STANLEY LIEBERSON

A Piece of the Pie: Blacks and White Immigrants Since 1880

The source of European migrants to the United States shifted radically toward the end of the last century; Northwestern Europe declined in relative importance, thanks to the unheralded numbers arriving from the Southern, Central, and Eastern parts of Europe. These "new" sources, which had contributed less than one-tenth of all immigrants as late as 1880, were soon sending the vast majority of newcomers, until large-scale immigration was permanently cut off in the 1920s. For example, less than 1 percent of all immigrants in the 1860s had come from Italy, but in the first two decades of the twentieth century more migrants arrived from this one nation than from all of the Northwestern European countries combined (Lieberson, 1963, p. 550). These new European groups piled up in the slums of the great urban centers of the East and Midwest, as well as in the factory towns of those regions, and in the coal-mining districts of Pennsylvania and elsewhere. They were largely unskilled, minimally educated, poor, relegated to undesirable jobs and residences, and life was harsh.

The descendants of these South-Central-Eastern (SCE) European groups have done relatively well in the United States. By all accounts, their education, occupations, and incomes are presently close to—or even in excess of—white Americans from the earlier Northwestern European sources.[1] To be sure, there are still areas where they have not quite "made it." Americans of Italian and Slavic origin are underrepresented in *Who's Who in America,* although their numbers are growing (Lieberson and Carter, 1979, table 1). Every president of the United States has thus far been of old European origin. Likewise, a study of the 106 largest Chicago-area corporations found Poles and Italians grossly underrepresented on the boards or as officers when compared with their proportion in the population in the metropolitan area (Institute of Urban Life, 1973).[2] There is also evidence of discrimination in the upper echelons of banking directed at Roman Catholics and Jews, to say nothing of nonwhites and women generally (United States Senate Committee on Banking, Housing and Urban Affairs, 1976, pp. 218–219, 223). For example, as of a few years ago there were only a handful of Jews employed as senior officers in all of New York City's eight giant banks and there were *no* Jews employed as senior officers in any of the nation's 50 largest non-New York banks (Mayer, 1974, p. 11).

Nevertheless, it is clear that the new Europeans have "made it" to a degree far in excess of that which would have been expected or predicted at the time of their arrival here. It is also equally apparent that blacks have not. Whether it be income, education, occupation, self-employment, power, position in major corporations, residential location, health, or living conditions, the average black status is distinctly below that held by the average

Originally published in 1980. Please see complete source information beginning on page 891.

white of SCE European origin. Numerous exceptions exist, of course, and progress has occurred: There are many blacks who have made it. But if these exceptions should not be overlooked, it is also the case that blacks and new Europeans occupy radically different average positions in society.

Since the end of slavery occurred about 20 years before the new Europeans started their massive move to the United States and because the latter groups seem to have done so well in this nation, there are numerous speculations as to why the groups have experienced such radically different outcomes. Most of these end up in one of two camps: either blacks were placed under greater disadvantages by the society and other forces outside of their control; or, by contrast, the new Europeans had more going for them in terms of their basic characteristics. Examples of the former explanation include: the race and skin color markers faced by blacks but not by SCE Europeans; greater discrimination against blacks in institutions ranging from courts to unions to schools; the preference that dominant whites had for other whites over blacks; and the decline in opportunities by the time blacks moved to the North in sizable numbers. Interpretations based on the assumption that the differences in success reflect superior new European attributes include speculations regarding family cohesion, work ethic, intelligence, acceptance of demeaning work, and a different outlook toward education as a means of mobility. Not only is it possible for both types of forces to be operating but their relative role could easily change over time, since a period of about 100 years is long enough to permit all sorts of feedback processes as well as broad societal changes which have consequences for the groups involved. Hence the problem is extremely complex. As one might expect, those sympathetic to the difficulties faced by blacks tend to emphasize the first factor; those emphasizing the second set of forces tend to be less sympathetic.

The answer to this issue is relevant to current social policies because an understanding of the causes would affect the ways proposed for dealing with the present black—white gap. In addition, there is the related issue of whether the SCE groups provide an analogy or a model for blacks. Finally, the historical causes of present-day circumstances are of grave concern to all those who are enmeshed in these events. Is the relatively favorable position enjoyed by the descendants of new European immigrants to be seen as purely a function of more blood, sweat, and tears such that easy access to the same goodies will in some sense desecrate all of these earlier struggles—let alone mean sharing future opportunities with blacks? If, on the other hand, the position held by blacks vis-à-vis the new Europeans is due to their skin color and the fact that blacks experience more severe forms of discrimination, then the present-day position of blacks is proof of the injustices that exist and the need to redress them. . . .

A Theory of Intrinsic Differences

Ignoring blacks and new Europeans for a moment, consider the forces generating contact between racial and ethnic groups. These can be crudely divided into voluntary and involuntary forms of contact. Blacks were brought to the New World involuntarily as slaves; American Indians were already here but their contact with the white settlers was also involuntary insofar as they were overrun. By way of contrast, the movement of the new Europeans to the United States and the later migration of blacks from the South to the North are both examples of voluntary migration, international and internal, respectively. What do we know about voluntary migration? As a general rule, we can say that it is driven by economic forces, that is, people move from areas of low opportunity to areas of better opportunity. This is all relative, to be sure, but it means that the opportunity structure for a set of voluntary migrants is more favorable in the receiving area than in the sending area.[3] Because there is a lot of ignorance in these matters, as well as other satisfactions involved, a secondary counterflow to the sending area is sometimes rather substantial. Nevertheless, a net movement on the part of a group from one nation to another, or from one subarea within a nation to another subarea, is generally due to superior opportunities in the receiving area.

We also know that a set of potential sending areas differ from one another in their levels of living and opportunity structure. This means that the residents of countries (or subareas) A, B, C, . . . , N will vary in their evaluation of the options available to them in the United States (or urban North for blacks in the South) because they will be affected by the different opportunity structures available in their respective homelands (or the South for potential black migrants to the North). Migrants arriving in the United States from various sources will therefore differ in what is an acceptable job, depending on the options that exist for them in their homeland for the skills that they possess. A low-level menial job that might prove an attractive income alternative to someone with minimal skills from an extremely poor country would not be a migration "pull" for someone with more attractive alternatives in another homeland either because the level of living is higher or because the person possesses skills that can command a better job. Further, insofar as nations differ in their levels of development, it means that their labor forces will vary in the levels of skill for which they are capable as well as in their average educational levels.

Two important conclusions follow from these assumptions. First, there is an inherent reason for expecting differences between groups at the initial point of contact simply because the migrant groups differ in the alternatives available to them in the areas from which they are migrating. Ignoring special situations such as famine, social unrest, and oppression, emigrants from a nation with a relatively high level of living will tend to be both qualified for better jobs and have more attractive alternatives in their homeland than will those migrating from a nation with a lower level of living. Work acceptable to one group, in the sense of being a superior alternative to the opportunities available in the homeland, will not be attractive to members of another group (or to only a much smaller segment). Hence migrants from different sources will vary in their jobs and incomes not necessarily because of discrimination or work orientation but because of the alternatives available to them at home. Such groups at the initial point of contact in the United States differ not in their aspirations, but rather in the minimum they will settle for. And they differ in how little they will accept because of the alternatives at home that they must weight them against. The second point is one well recognized in the work of Bonacich (1972, 1976), namely, workers in the receiving country will view migrants from nations with lower levels of living as potential competitors willing to work for less because of the alternatives at home.

However, of special interest here is the first issue, namely, whether earlier in this century and late in the last one the level of living in South-Central-Eastern Europe differed from the level of living for blacks in the South. If so, then the theory leads one to expect the group living in the poorer situation to have a lower minimum standard and so to accept working conditions and jobs that the other would reject. Deriving this conclusion is easier than testing it because to my knowledge there are no solid data on wages for the groups in comparable work which also take into account the cost of living encountered in each nation and the South at that time. Moreover, I cannot find data sets for per capita GNP during those periods for each of the countries. Consequently, I am obliged to rely on a reasonably good surrogate measure of the nature of life in these places, namely, life expectancy.

Table 1 compares life expectancy at birth for blacks circa 1900, 1910, and 1920 with various nations in South, Central, and Eastern Europe. In addition, the average life table values in four southern cities in 1880 are compared with those for these same European nations. In 1880, when the sources of European migration first started to shift, life expectancy at birth in SCE Europe was generally superior

TABLE 1
Life Expectancy at Birth in South, Central, and Eastern Europe and Among Blacks in the United States,
1880–1920

Nation	Sex	Year			
		1880	1900–1902	1909–1911	1919–1920
Austria	Male	32.64	39.06	41.16	47.43
	Female	35.26	41.19	43.36	50.54
Bulgaria	Male	—	41.27	44.18	45.18
	Female	—	41.85	43.70	45.39
Finland	Male	—	44.13	46.53	49.08
	Female	—	46.52	49.68	53.03
Greece	Male	36.23	41.86	44.27	46.81
	Female	37.73	43.49	45.96	48.56
Italy	Male	34.33	43.60	45.66	48.64
	Female	34.84	44.11	46.50	50.01
Russia	Male	26.69	32.05	35.86	39.36
	Female	29.36	33.74	39.10	43.53
Black	Male	22.04	32.54	34.05	40.45
	Female	26.22	35.04	37.67	42.35

SOURCES: European nations from Dublin, Lotka, and Spiegelman, 1949, tables 87 and 88
(data interpolated to correspond to years above). Black data for original registration states
in twentieth century are from Dublin, Lotka, and Spiegelman, 1949, tables 81 and 83. Data
for blacks in 1880 are based on median figures for colored in four southern cities,
Washington, D.C., Baltimore, Charleston, and New Orleans. Derived from data reported
in Billings, 1886, pp. cxliv-cxlv.

to that experienced by blacks in the South. The expectation of life at birth for both black men and women in 1880, respectively, 22 and 26 years, is below that for any of the new European sources listed, the closest being Russia (males, 27; females, 29). Insofar as these life table values indicate general living conditions, one can infer that there would be jobs attractive to blacks that would not be attractive to the new Europeans.

Life expectancy was higher for Austrians, Bulgarians, Finns, Greeks, and Italians when compared with blacks in each of the four periods (Table 1). The only exception were the Russians who had lower levels in 1900–1902 and who had mixed results in the 1919–1920 comparison.[4] Incidentally, comparisons between Northwestern European nations and the South-Central-Eastern nations are consistent with this perspective; the former have

generally more favorable mortality than do the new European sources.

In short, if the European and black life table values represent differences in levels of living, then there is some reason to expect that the new Europeans might start off in a more favorable position than would blacks in the North even if there was no discrimination. Namely, if the average level of living for southern blacks was lower than that for whites residing in SCE Europe, then the relative attractiveness of certain job options in the North would differ for the groups. This does not mean that the upper end of their aspirations would differ, but it does mean that there is an intrinsic reason why blacks might start off lower. Of course, this situation is exacerbated by an additional force, the existence of even more discrimination against blacks than against SCE Europeans both in their initial jobs and later mobility. The "theory of intrinsic differences" developed here is sufficient to explain why groups will start off occupying different socioeconomic niches, but it does not account for their continuation over time. Indeed, without discrimination or other factors one would expect such initial gaps to narrow progressively if there is intergenerational mobility (Lieberson and Fuguitt, 1967).[5] Accordingly, one must look elsewhere to understand why more discrimination was directed at blacks as well as why other forces have maintained these gaps.

Composition, the Latent Structure of Race Relations, and North-South Differences

Many have observed that the position of blacks started to deteriorate in this century as their numbers increased in the North. Basically two explanations for this have been offered: a shift in the "quality" of black migration and the response of whites to the radical increase in the numbers of blacks. In evaluating these explanations and offering an alternative, we should come closer to understanding the general forces that for so many decades have kept blacks from closing the initial gaps.

The quality interpretation is simply that migration northward became less selective over time, particularly after the decline in southern agriculture forced blacks to move in more or less helter-skelter fashion. There are two bodies of data that sharply challenge this thesis. Starting with the work of Bowles, Bacon, and Ritchey (1973) there is evidence to indicate that southern black migrants to the North in recent years have done relatively well when compared with northern-born blacks in terms of welfare, employment rates, earnings after background factors are taken into account, and so on. There is reason for this pattern to occur (Lieberson, 1978a), but the point here is that the results do not support the notion that the black position in the North was undermined by these migrants because of their

qualities. A second data set, covering earlier decades as well, involves a comparison in each decade between the educational level of blacks living in the North in each decade with what would have occurred if there had been no migration into or out of the North during the preceding ten years. At most, the educational level of blacks in the North was only slightly different in each period from what it would have been without migration. This is due to the highly selective nature of black outmigration from the South (see Lieberson, 1978b).

As for the second explanation, namely, that changes in racial composition caused the black position to deteriorate, we know there was a massive increase in both the absolute number of blacks and their relative proportion of the population living in northern cities. The analysis of residential segregation in Lieberson (1980, chapter 9) fits in rather nicely with this perspective, with changes in the indexes accounted for by changes in population composition. But the segregation analysis involves a subtle difference from the assumption that the structure of race relations changed; it assumes that such dispositions were always present in a latent form and simply unfurl in accordance with shifts in population composition. To draw an analogy, if an automobile changes speed as we vary the pressure on the gas pedal, we do not assume that the engine changes in character with more or less gas. Rather we assume that the potential range of speeds was always there and is simply altered by the amount of gas received. In similar fashion, it is fruitful to assume that the reason for race relations changing with shifts in composition is not due to a radical alteration in the dispositions of whites, but rather that changes in composition affect the dispositions that existed all along. In other words, there is a latent structure to the race relations pattern in a given setting, with only certain parts of this structure observed at a given time. This fits in well with a long-standing ecological perspective on the influence of compositional changes on race and ethnic relations and competition (see, for example, Hawley, 1944). It also provides a rather novel perspective on North-South differences.

This way of thinking about the linkage between composition and race and ethnic relations has important consequences when approaching the deterioration in the position of blacks in the North and, indeed, the assumptions implicit to notions about the black position in various regions of the United States. How different was the situation for blacks in the South and non-South earlier in the century? Obviously there were very important historical differences between the regions. Even if there was far more to the Civil War than freeing the slaves, still the regions differed sharply in their history regarding slavery and their disposition toward the institution. Likewise, the customs were quite different in these regions with respect to such matters as poll taxes, Jim Crow laws, lynching, racial "etiquette," and the like. Some of these regional differences can probably be explained by the establishment of antiblack traditions that remain firm even after the causes have disappeared. Social events have a life of their own: once established, the customs persist long after causes vanish (see Lieberson, 1982).

But these important differences should not keep one from realizing that the North and South were still part of the same nation and shared certain qualities that were hidden only because the black composition in the regions was so radically different and because of historical forces. To be sure, if the small number of blacks living in a northern city had the vote, then they were unlikely to lose it when their proportion of the population increased to the point where it was of potential consequence to elections. But the latent structure of race relations in the North was not much different from the South on a variety of features. This has not been widely appreciated (a noteworthy exception being the analysis of the black position in the North before the end of slavery in the South by Litwack, 1961). It was not appreciated by those wanting to understand the changes in race relations as either

due to the changing quality of blacks living in the North or some fundamental shifts in the United States. To be sure, there are a lot of complications affecting this comparison, witness the fact that the level of living was generally higher in the North and there were a number of institutional heritages in the South which blacks could avoid elsewhere. Hence there were strong incentives for migration from the South. But it is extremely helpful to recognize that the differences between regions with respect to bread-and-butter matters were not as radical as one would think by focusing exclusively on lynchings, poll taxes, race-baiting politicians, and legally sanctioned forms of segregation.

As noted [earlier], normally one does not ask why blacks in the South did not do as well as South-Central-Eastern Europeans. Until recently, circumstances were incredibly difficult for blacks in the South—witness, for example, the educational situation [described in Lieberson (1980, chapter 6)]. However, I believe there is reason to suspect that a substantial part of the North-South gap was really due to the much smaller proportion blacks were of the urban population in the North and their virtual absence from the rural North. As a consequence, certain similarities in disposition toward blacks and the conflict between lower and higher wage rates were concealed by these compositional factors. In other words, underlying the two regions were a large number of common dispositions. This, I might add, also helps us understand some of the shifts that have occurred in the North when the black proportion of the population began to increase.

The Flow of Migrants

For more than a half century immigration from Europe has not been a significant factor in the SCE groups' growth, whereas the flow of blacks from South to North has been of importance in nearly all of this period. The significance of this widely cited difference is great. There are many more blacks who are recent migrants to the North whereas the immigrant component of the new Europeans drops off over time. Hence, at the very least it is important to make sure that generational factors are taken into account when comparing the ethnic groups. This is clearly an important consideration. For example, the median education of Japanese-American men increased massively between 1940 and 1960 in the United States—from 8.8 to 12.4 years of schooling. Almost all of this was due to changes in the generational composition of the group. With no immigration of any consequence for a number of decades, the foreign-born component dropped from 80 to 27 percent of the group. The actual shift in median education within the birthplace-specific components was rather small; from 8.3 to 8.8 years for the foreign-born and from 12.2 to 12.4 years for the American-born. In other words, almost all of the changes were simply due to shifts in generational composition (see Lieberson, 1973, pp. 562–563).

It is also argued that migration patterns are of significance because minimally skilled people no longer encounter the opportunities that once existed when the new Europeans were coming. This is not too convincing because there is every indication that occupational mobility is every bit as great now as it used to be. Second, black-white gaps in education are now narrowing rapidly. Finally, there is some reason to believe that intergenerational mobility in the North was never as good for blacks even in decades past (Thernstrom, 1973, pp. 183–194). I might add that the high unemployment rates among blacks in the North are not as novel as some have suggested. This is because smaller black-white gaps in earlier periods were a reflection of the substantial concentration of blacks in the rural South and the hidden underemployment that represented (see Lieberson, 1980, chapter 8).

Notwithstanding the importance of drawing generational distinctions, there is another way of thinking about the end of European immigration and the continuous flow of blacks. Theoretically, such shifts have consequences of their own in a regular and orderly way. In terms of the occupational queuing notion [see Thurow, 1969, chapter 4], the increase in the black component means a rise in the median black occupational position in the community, but it will at the same time widen the gap between blacks and new Europeans. Assuming that there is an occupational queue in which blacks are at the bottom and the new Europeans are just above them, consider the hypothetical data shown in table 2. In the first period, 5 percent of the work force is black and 10 percent is new European. The median black job is at the 2.5 percentile because they hold the bottom 5 percent of the jobs; the median new European job is at the tenth percentile, because they hold the jobs that range from the fifth to the fifteenth percentiles. Suppose in each period the new European component of the work force remains at 10 percent whereas blacks go to 10, then 20, and finally 30 percent of the work force. In each period, the average black percentile goes up but in each period the magnitude of the absolute gain in the average new European percentile goes up even faster. For example, from time 1 to time 2, the average black percentile goes up from 2.5 to 5, but the new European percentile goes up 5 points from 10 to 15. In similar fashion the new Europeans rise more rapidly when blacks go from 10 to 20 to 30 percent of the work force. This model ignores the fact that there will be some positive feedback as their component goes up because blacks will create a market for blacks pursuing such highly prestigious jobs as, for example, physicians, lawyers, dentists, merchants geared to blacks, and the like. Also, it assumes that the queuing is perfect such that the lowest SCE European enjoys a better job than the most highly placed black. Clearly this is false. But I believe the model does give one a clear understanding of how increases in the black component would upgrade the new Europeans at a more rapid rate as long as the queuing process remains intact. In effect, this queuing notion is compatible with the long-standing ladder model that holds that increases in a lower-ranked population would tend to upgrade the populations above them.

TABLE 2
Consequences of Black Population Increase for SCE European Jobs (queuing model)

Time	Percentage of population		Median percentile of jobs held		Increase in median percentile over previous time	
	Black	SCE European	Black	SCE European	Black	SCE European
1	5	10	2.5	10	—	—
2	10	10	5	15	2.5	5
3	20	10	10	25	5	10
4	30	10	15	35	5	10

NOTE: Median job percentile held is based on assumption that blacks received the lowest jobs in the community and that SCE European groups received the next lowest.

In this sense, the growing presence of blacks did indeed benefit the new Europeans—not because they were more likely to discriminate against blacks than were other segments of the white population, but because blacks were lower on the hierarchy. This all operates insofar as there are strong enough barriers through unions, employers, and other discriminatory forces to stave off the potential undercutting of whites through the acceptance of lower wages by blacks.

The spectacular events since World War II should be seen in the context of these changes in the flow of migrants. The continuation of black migration to the North and the cessation of new European immigration helped upgrade the SCE groups in two additional ways besides the queuing process discussed above. These are the impact that newer segments of a group have on older segments and the overloading of special niches that each group tends to develop in the labor market. (None of this is to overlook the employment opportunities generated in the 1940s due to the massive demands of the war and in the post–World War II period. Bear in mind that there was a depression prior to the war and hence these demands not only meant new opportunities for blacks but also for the SCE European groups who were still higher on the queue.)

As for special niches, it is clear that most racial and ethnic groups tend to develop concentrations in certain jobs which either reflect

some distinctive cultural characteristics, special skills initially held by some members, or the opportunity structure at the time of their arrival. In 1950 among the foreign-born men of different origins there were many such examples: 3.9 percent of Italians in the civilian labor force were barbers, eight times the level for all white men; 2.5 percent of the Irish were policemen or firemen, three times the rate for all white men; more than 2 percent of Scottish immigrants were accountants, about two and one-half times the level for whites; 9.4 percent of Swedish immigrants were carpenters, nearly four times the national level; 14.8 percent of Greek immigrant men ran eating and drinking establishments, 29 times the national level; and 3.3 percent of Russian immigrant men were tailors or furriers, 17 times the rate for all white men.[6] These concentrations are partially based on networks of ethnic contacts and experiences that in turn direct other compatriots in these directions. Each group does this and, because the job hierarchy is not a perfect system, such activities help give each group certain special niches that it might not otherwise have in a pure system of queues altered only by ethnic compatriot demands. In these cases, the group develops an "export" market in the sense of being able to supply needs and wants for other groups.

When the migration of a group accelerates, the ability to develop and exploit these special niches is badly handicapped. Such specialties can only absorb a small part of a group's total work force when its population grows rapidly or is a substantial proportion of the total population. After all, not everyone of Chinese origin could open a restaurant in a city where they are a sizable segment of the population, just as not all Jews could have opened stores in New York City. By contrast, when the numbers stabilize or increase at only a moderate clip, then the possibilities due to these ingroup concentrations are more sanguine. Thus, in communities where the group is a sizable segment of the population, it is more difficult for such niches to absorb much of the group.

The cessation of immigration, whether it involved the Japanese and Chinese or the South-Central-Eastern European groups, had long-run advantages to those members of the group already in the nation. (To be sure, there were certain negative costs such as the group's own natural market for compatriots' services or the expansion of demographically based power.) But these events help explain why blacks were unable to participate with the new Europeans in the massive socioeconomic shifts experienced in recent decades. In other words, it is more difficult to overcome the negative consequences of discrimination through special niches when the group is growing rapidly and/or is a large segment of the total population.

There is another way through which newcomers have a harmful effect on earlier arrivals and longer-standing residents from the same group. Sizable numbers of newcomers raise the level of ethnic and/or racial consciousness on the part of others in the city; moreover, if these newcomers are less able to compete for more desirable positions than are the longer-standing residents, they will tend to undercut the position of other members of the group. This is because the older residents and those of higher socioeconomic status cannot totally avoid the newcomers, although they work at it through subgroup residential isolation. Hence, there is some de-

terioration in the quality of residential areas, schools, and the like for those earlier residents who might otherwise enjoy more fully the rewards of their mobility. Beyond this, from the point of view of the dominant outsiders, the newcomers may reinforce stereotypes and negative dispositions that affect all members of the group.

Finally, I suspect that group boundaries shift and float in multiethnic or multiracial settings more than some recognize. Antagonisms and dispositions change in accordance with the group context. In this case, the movement of blacks to the North in sizable numbers reduced the negative disposition other whites had toward the new European groups. If the new Europeans rank higher in a queue, then the negative dispositions toward them would be muffled and modified in a setting where they would be viewed as relatively more desirable as neighbors, co-workers, political candidates, and so on than blacks. Ethnic ties and allegiances float and shift in accordance with the threats and alternatives that exist. The presence of blacks made it harder to discriminate against the new Europeans because the alternative was viewed even less favorably.

Under these circumstances, the rapid growth of the black population in the urban North during the last half century or so, accompanied by the opposite trend for the new Europeans, has significantly contributed to the differences in outcome experienced by these groups. These differences would be expected even if one ignores the latent structure of race relations tapped by these demographic changes in the North.

Further Analysis of Race

I believe there is further reason for speculating that race was not as crucial an issue as is commonly supposed for understanding the black outcome relative to the new Europeans. In order to avoid being misunderstood by the casual reader, let me reiterate that such a conclusion does not mean that other nonwhite groups or the new Europeans possessed certain favorable characteristics to a greater degree than did blacks. There is an alternative way of interpreting these events, namely, a substantial source of the disadvantage faced by blacks is due to their position with respect to certain structural conditions that affect race relations generally. Having been reviewed in this chapter, one should now make sense of black–new European gaps, but what about comparisons of blacks with other nonwhites? There are eight important factors to consider.

1. Although hard quantitative data are not available, there is every reason to believe that the response to Chinese and Japanese in the United States was every bit as severe and as violent initially as that toward blacks when the latter moved outside of their traditional niches.

2. There was a cessation of sizable immigration from Japan and China for a number of decades before these groups were able to advance in the society.

3. The cessation was due to the intense pressures within the United States against Asian migration, particularly by those whites who were threatened by these potential competitors.

4. This meant that the number of these groups in the nation is quite small relative to blacks. In the 1970 census there were 22,580,000 blacks recorded compared with 591,000 Japanese and 435,000 Chinese.

5. Because of factors 2 and 4 above, the opportunity for these Asian groups to occupy special niches was far greater than for blacks. Imagine more than 22 million Japanese Americans trying to carve out initial niches through truck farming!

6. Because of factor 2 there has been less negative effect on the general position of these groups due to recent immi-

grants (a situation that is now beginning to change somewhat for the Chinese).

7. Ignoring situations generated by direct competition between Asians and whites such as existed in the West earlier, there is some evidence that the white disposition toward blacks was otherwise even more unfavorable than that toward Asians. This is due to the ideologies that developed in connection with slavery as well as perhaps the images of Africa and its people stemming from exploration of the continent. Whatever the reason, one has the impression that whites have strikingly different attitudes toward the cultures of China and Japan than toward those of blacks or of Africa.

8. The massive economic threat blacks posed for whites earlier in the century in both the South and North was not duplicated by the Asians except in certain parts of the West.

I am suggesting a general process that occurs when racial and ethnic groups have an inherent conflict—and certainly competition for jobs, power, position, maintenance of different subcultural systems, and the like are such conflicts. Under the circumstances, there is a tendency for the competitors to focus on differences between themselves. The observers (in this case the sociologists) may then assume that these differences are the sources of conflict. In point of fact, the rhetoric involving such differences may indeed inflame them, but we can be reasonably certain that the conflict would have occurred in their absence. To use a contemporary example, if Protestants in Northern Ireland had orange skin color and if the skin color of Roman Catholics in that country was green, then very likely these physical differences would be emphasized by observers seeking to explain the sharp conflict between these groups. Indeed, very likely such racial differences would be emphasized by the combatants themselves. No doubt such physical differences would enter into the situation as a secondary cause because the rhetoric would inflame that difference, but we can be reasonably certain that the conflict would occur in their absence. In the same fashion, differences between blacks and whites—real ones, imaginary ones, and those that are the product of earlier race relations—enter into the rhetoric of race and ethnic relations, but they are ultimately secondary to the conflict for society's goodies.

This certainly is the conclusion that can be generated from the classic experiment by Sherif and Sherif (1953) in which a homogeneous group of children at camp were randomly sorted into two groups and then competition and conflict between the groups was stimulated. The experiment resulted in each of the groups developing all sorts of images about themselves and the other group. Yet, unknown to them, the groups were identical in their initial distribution of characteristics.

In order to avoid a misunderstanding of a position that is radically different from that held by most observers, whether they be black or white, oriented toward one group or the other, let me restate this part of my thesis. There is powerful evidence that blacks were victims of more severe forms of discrimination than were the new Europeans—although the latter also suffered from intense discrimination. Much of the antagonism toward blacks was based on racial features, but one should not interpret this as the ultimate cause. Rather the racial emphasis resulted from the use of the most obvious feature(s) of the group to support the intergroup conflict generated by a fear of blacks based on their threat as economic competitors. If this analysis is correct, it also means that were the present-day conflict between blacks and dominant white groups to be resolved, then the race issue could rapidly disintegrate as a crucial barrier between the groups just as a very profound and deep distaste for Roman Catholics on the part of the dominant Protestants has diminished rather substantially (albeit not disappeared).

The Great Non Sequitur

The data comparing blacks and the new Europeans earlier in this century lead one to a rather clear conclusion about the initial question. The early living conditions of the new Europeans after their migration to the United States were extremely harsh and their point of entry into the socioeconomic system was quite low. However, it is a non sequitur to assume that new Europeans had it as bad as did blacks or that the failure of blacks to move upward as rapidly reflected some ethnic deficiencies. The situation for new Europeans in the United States, bad as it may have been, was not as bad as that experienced by blacks at the same time. Witness, for example, the differences in the disposition to ban openly blacks from unions at the turn of the century (Lieberson, 1980, chapter 11), the greater concentration of blacks in 1900 in service occupations and their smaller numbers in manufacturing and mechanical jobs (Lieberson, 1980, chapter 10), the higher black death rates in the North (Lieberson, 1980, chapter 2), and even the greater segregation of blacks with respect to the avenues of eminence open to them (Lieberson and Carter, 1979). It is a serious mistake to underestimate how far the new Europeans have come in the nation and how hard it all was, but it is equally erroneous to assume that the obstacles were as great as those faced by blacks or that the starting point was the same.

Notes

1. Compare the data on Italian, Polish, and Russian education in younger ages, occupation, and income with that for Americans of British origin in *Population Characteristics* (United States Bureau of the Census, 1973, tables 6–9). The traditional basis for allocating European sources into the old and new categories is somewhat arbitrary and, in some cases, does not correspond with the period of greatest immigration. For example, several Scandinavian sources were more important between 1880 and 1920 than they were in earlier decades. In

keeping with traditional analysis, Germany is an old source and included with the Northwestern European nations even though it is a central European nation (Lieberson, 1963, p. 551).

2. This is a bit of an unfair comparison because these are national corporations and hence may tend to draw to some degree on the national market for executive recruitment and board members.

3. The distinction between "voluntary" and "involuntary" is sometimes not entirely clear, as in the case of starvation or political pressures in the sending country. Nevertheless, in those cases one can still argue that the motivation to move stems from more attractive conditions in the receiving country or subarea.

4. The original ten registration states used to provide data on black mortality in 1900, 1910, and 1920 were the six New England states and four elsewhere in the North. The reader may wonder if this is an appropriate measure for blacks because it is the living conditions of blacks in the South that are relevant here as an index for determining the jobs that they would accept in the North. Regional life tables, first available for 1930–1939, indicate that the three southern regions all have higher expectation of life at birth for nonwhite males than do either the North Atlantic or North-Central regions; this is also the case for two of the southern regions when compared to the Mountain and Pacific category. The gaps are not as great for nonwhite females (see Dublin, Lotka, and Spiegelman, 1949, tables 81, 83). The same sources also indicate that nonwhites in the rural South in 1939 had higher expectations of life than did nonwhites in either different regions or in different types of communities. A special adjustment that takes into account this difficulty still supports the conclusion that life expectancy at birth for South-Central-Eastern European countries was generally more favorable. Because the West-South-Central states had the highest and the North-Central region the lowest life expectancy at birth, the black data shown in table 1 were multiplied by the ratio of West-South-Central to North-Central regional black life table values in 1930–1939. This gave the most favorable increase to black values. In all periods the majority of SCE European nations still had higher life expectancy at birth even after this adjustment.

5. Another force probably operating in the same direction stems from the fact that the South was, of course, much closer to the North than was South-Central-Eastern Europe. If it is reasonable to assume that the minimum improvement necessary to stimulate migration will vary directly with distance, expressed in time-cost factors, then this

force will also work toward generating an initial difference favoring the white groups.

6. Based on data reported in Hutchinson, 1956, table A–2a. See the table for detailed titles of the occupations described in the text.

References

Billings, John S. *Report on the Mortality and Vital Statistics of the United States, Part 2.* Washington, D.C.: Government Printing Office, 1886.

Bonacich, Edna. "A Theory of Ethnic Antagonism: The Split Labor Market." *American Sociological Review* 37 (1972): 547–559.

———. "Advanced Capitalism and Black/White Race Relations in the United States: A Split Labor Market Interpretation." *American Sociological Review* 41 (1976): 34–51.

Bowles, Gladys K., A. L. Bacon, and P. N. Ritchey. *Poverty Dimensions of Rural-to-Urban Migration: A Statistical Report.* Washington, D.C.: Economic Research Service, U.S. Department of Agriculture, 1973.

Dublin, Louis I., Alfred J. Lotka, and Mortimer Spiegelman. *Length of Life: A Study of the Life Table.* 2nd ed., rev. New York: Ronald Press, 1949.

Hawley, Amos H. "Dispersion Versus Segregation: Apropos of a Solution of Race Problems." Papers of the Michigan Academy of Science, Arts, and Letters 30 (1944): 667–674. Adopted in *Race: Individual and Collective Behavior,* edited by Edgar T. Thompson and Everett C. Hughes, pp. 199–204. Glencoe, Ill.: Free Press, 1958.

Hutchinson, E. P. *Immigrants and Their Children, 1850–1950.* New York: Wiley, 1956.

Institute of Urban Life. "Report on the Representation of Poles, Italians, Latins and Blacks in the Executive Suites of Chicago's Largest Corporations." Chicago: Institute of Urban Life, 1973.

Lieberson, Stanley. "The Old-New Distinction and Immigrants in Australia." *American Sociological Review* 28 (1963): 550–565.

———. "Generational Differences Among Blacks in the North." *American Journal of Sociology* 79 (1973): 550–565.

———. "A Reconsideration of the Income Differences Found Between Migrants and Northern-Born Blacks." *American Journal of Sociology* 83 (1978a): 940–966.

———. "Selective Black Migration from the South: A Historical View." In *Demography of Racial and Ethnic Groups,* edited by Frank D.

Bean and W. Parker Frisbie, pp. 119–141. New York: Academic Press, 1978b.

———. *A Piece of the Pie: Blacks and White Immigrants Since 1880.* Berkeley: University of California Press, 1980.

———. "Forces Affecting Language Spread: Some Basic Propositions." In *Language Spread: Studies in Diffusion and Social Change,* edited by Robert L. Cooper, pp. 37–62. Bloomington: Indiana University Press, 1982.

Lieberson, Stanley, and Donna K. Carter. "Making It in America: Differences Between Eminent Blacks and White Ethnic Groups." *American Sociological Review* 44 (1979): 347–366.

Lieberson, Stanley, and Glenn V. Fuguitt. "Negro-White Occupational Differences in the Absence of Discrimination." *American Journal of Sociology* 73 (1967): 188–200.

Litwack, Leon F. *North of Slavery: The Negro in the Free States, 1790–1860.* Chicago: University of Chicago Press, 1961.

Mayer, Martin. *The Bankers.* New York: Weybright & Talley, 1974.

Sherif, Muzafer, and Carolyn W. Sherif. *Groups in Harmony and Tension: An Integration of Studies on Intergroup Relations.* New York: Harper & Brothers, 1953.

Thernstrom, Stephan. *The Other Bostonians: Poverty and Progress in the American Metropolis, 1880–1970.* Cambridge, Mass.: Harvard University Press, 1973.

Thurow, Lester C. *Poverty and Discrimination.* Washington, D.C.: Brookings Institution, 1969.

United States Bureau of the Census. *Population Characteristics.* "Characteristics of the Population by Ethnic Origin: March 1972 and 1971." Series P–20, No. 249. Washington, D.C.: Government Printing Office, 1973.

United States Senate Committee on Banking, Housing and Urban Affairs. *Treasury Department's Administration of the Contract Compliance Program for Financial Institutions.* Washington, D.C.: Government Printing Office, 1976.

ROGER WALDINGER

Still the Promised City? African-Americans and New Immigrants in Postindustrial New York

New York's brush with fiscal insolvency in the mid–1970s signaled the end for the old industrial cities of the United States. Its revival in the 1980s heralded the emergence of the nation's largest cities as world service centers. The smokestack cities of the industrial heartland unfortunately have no replacement for their run-of-the-mill production activities, steadily eroding under the twin impact of computerization and foreign competition. But in the largest urban agglomerations—Chicago, Los Angeles, Philadelphia, and, especially, New York—the advent of a postindustrial economy has triggered a new phase of growth. The key activities of the new economy—information processing, the coordination of large organizations, and the management of volatile financial markets—are overwhelmingly urban-based. And their dynamism has yanked these largest cities out of the economic torpor into which they had sunk.

The new urban vitality notwithstanding, cities remain deeply troubled—perhaps more so than before. The paradox of urban plenty

Originally published in 1996. Please see complete source information beginning on page 891.

is that comparatively few of the city's residents have been able to enjoy the fruits of growth. The number of poor people living in central cities has not fallen but risen, and dramatically so. Instead of arresting social dislocation, the economic turnaround has exacerbated the urban social problems identified thirty years ago. Though right and left differ on social policy responses, both camps agree that a sizable segment of the poor has been lopped off into an "urban underclass"—persistently poor and with no connection to legitimate ways of making a living.[1]

Demography is the subtext to the contemporary tale of urban woe. "Back to the city" has been the catchword of the new urban professionals—today's huddled masses, piled up in neighborhoods in and around the downtown business centers. But the influx of this much maligned gentry never matched the attention it received in the press. The tide of people flowing cityward remains what it has been for the past forty years: America's big cities attract mainly nonwhites. First came blacks, displaced from the technological backwaters of the agrarian South. Then came a wave of immigrants from the labor-surplus areas of the developing world: today's urban newcomers are arriving in numbers that rival the great migrations of a century ago.[2]

Thus the city of services is also a "majority minority" city. But how does this population base fit into the urban economy of today?

The received academic wisdom maintains that there is no fit at all. The industrial city grew because it possessed labor, and what it demanded of its labor was willing hands and strong muscles—not diplomas or technical expertise. But in the city of information processing and the transaction of high-level business deals, these qualities count no more. The equation between the city's economic function and its population base has no place for the unlettered, no matter how willing. The decline of the industrial city has left minorities high and dry.[3]

But a dissenting interpretation, now sufficiently repeated to have become a conventional wisdom, tells a different tale. Modern

urban development simultaneously generates high-level professional and managerial jobs and a proliferation of low-skilled, low-income "service" jobs. The polarized metropolis leaves minorities far from useless; instead, they serve as the new drawers of water and hewers of wood. In this version, it is not the poor who depend on the rich for their beneficence or for jobs and income to trickle down. Rather, the rich need the poor—to provide low-cost services, to maintain the city's underbelly, and to prop up what remains of the depressed manufacturing sector.[4]

In this chapter I argue that both stories—however intuitively appealing they may be separately or together—have it wrong. Neither metaphor, of polarization or of dislocation, captures the impact of the postindustrial urban transformation.[5] At root, both depict faceless, impersonal structures inexorably performing their actions on an inert urban mass. Not subjected to analysis, the structures are instead taken for granted, abstracted from any historical context, and divorced from the specific interests and forces that might have given them shape. Conflict and politics do not enter into these accounts of the making of the postindustrial economic world. Passing over dominant groups and their interests, these rival stories treat the new polyglot working and middle classes as an undifferentiated mass, helplessly playing out the scripts written for them by history.

But no *deus ex machina* determines which people get jobs, how they do so, and whether they then move ahead. The mechanisms of matching and mobility are social arrangements, shaped by the historical contexts in which they have grown up and subject to change—not simply as a result of pressures from the impersonal forces of the world economy, but in response to the actions of contending parties in specific societies and places. . . .

In briefest compass, my argument reads like this: The story of ethnics in America's cities is a collective search for mobility, in which the succession of one migrant wave after another alternatively stabilizes and disrupts the labor queue. In a market economy, employers allocate jobs to the most desirable workers they can recruit; but each market economy bears the imprint of the social structure in which it is embedded. In a race-conscious society like the United States, employers rank entire groups of people in terms of their ethnic and racial characteristics. All things being equal, members of the core cultural group stand at the top, followed by others.

The instability of America's capitalist economy subjects the labor queue's ordering to change. Growth pulls the topmost group up the totem pole; lower-ranking groups then seize the chance to move up the pecking order; in their wake, they leave behind vacancies at the bottom, which employers fill by recruiting workers from outside the economy—namely, migrants. The structure of the labor queue goes unchallenged as long as these newest arrivals are content to work in the bottom-level jobs for which they were initially recruited. But the economic orientations of the newcomers inevitably change, and when they do, complementarity is likely to be replaced by competition—which fans continuing ethnic strife over access to good jobs.

Competition between newcomers and insiders takes the form of conflict over the ethnic niche. Although migrants start at the bottom, they enter the economy under the auspices of friends or kin, which means that they begin with connections. Networks funnel the newcomers into specialized economic activities: as newcomers flow into the workplaces where earlier settlers have already gotten established, ethnic concentrations, or niches, gradually develop. The path up from the bottom involves finding a good niche and dominating it—which means that good jobs are reserved for insiders, leaving the next wave of outsiders excluded. Thus, the search by an earlier migrant group for labor market shelters eventuates in barriers that the next round of arrivals must confront.

Of course, economic life in America's cities is not all conflict. In some cases, the queue process simply pulls insider groups up the totem pole, leading them to abandon niches

that a new group of outsiders can take over. In other instances, conditions in the niche undergo relative deterioration, in which case the barriers to outsiders get relaxed. These conditions ensure that ethnics in the labor market are sometimes noncompeting, segmented groups. But the scarcity of good jobs relative to the surplus of job seekers guarantees that competition never disappears.

Thus, the structures that African-Americans and new immigrants confront result from America's serial incorporation of outsider groups and from those groups' attempts to create protective economic shelters. The continuous recourse to migration as a source of low-level labor, so characteristic of the United States, has made ethnicity the crucial and enduring mechanism that sorts groups of categorically different workers into an identifiably distinct set of jobs. For this reason, the ethnic division of labor stands as the central division of labor in the cities of twentieth-century America; the fates of new immigrants and African-Americans are bound up in its making and remaking. . . .

The conventional wisdom attributes urban disaster to the loss of white city residents. In fact, the outflow of white New Yorkers is what has given newcomers their chance. During economic downturns, whites fled the city faster than the rate of decline. And when the economy reheated, the outward seepage of whites slowed down but never stopped.

Over the years, the disproportionately declining white presence produced a ladder effect, creating empty spaces for newcomers up and down—though mainly down—the economic totem pole. Reflecting the influence of *prior* migration histories, the impact of white population decline rippled through New York's diversified economic complex in an uneven way. With the exception of those in construction and a few other skilled trades, New York's white ethnic proletariat disappeared after 1970, though a myriad of blue-collar jobs remained. Consequently, ethnic succession generated opportunities both in declining industries, where the rate of white outflows often outpaced the rate of job erosion, and in growth industries, where whites poured out of bottom-level positions even as demand for low-skilled workers increased. New York's small-business sector experienced the same round of musical chairs: newcomers moved in as white ethnics abandoned petty retailing, garment contracting, and other less remunerative business lines. A similar sequence of events occurred in many parts of the public sector, especially after 1975, when whites left municipal service for better opportunities elsewhere.

Since succession provides the backdrop for the economic stories of new immigrant and African-American New Yorkers, the central question concerns who got which jobs and why. In the 1970s and 1980s, black New Yorkers built up and consolidated the niche they had earlier established in government work. Public sector employment offered numerous advantages, including easier access to jobs and an employer that provided better, more equitable treatment. But convergence on government employment had the corollary effect of heightening the skill thresholds of the chief black economic base. To be sure, connections helped in gaining access to municipal jobs; and my case studies show that black civil servants networked as much as anyone else. However, civil service positions held promise only to those members of the community with the skills, experience, and credentials that government required—qualities not shared by the many African-American New Yorkers who have found themselves at economic risk.

Of course, work in the bowels of New York's economy could have been a possibility. Yet the data and the case studies demonstrate a steady erosion of African-Americans' *share* of the large number of remaining, low-skilled jobs—even as the *number* of low-level jobs held by minorities, native and immigrant, steadily grew. The African-American concentrations of old, from the most menial occupations in domestic service to later clusters like garment or hotel work, largely faded away. And African-Americans simultaneously failed to make headway in those low-skilled sectors

where competition with whites had previously kept them locked out.

The immigrants, by contrast, responded to ethnic succession in ways that expanded their economic base. Initially, the match between their aspirations and broader labor market dynamics created openings that the newcomers could fill. On the one hand, the immigrants' social origins predisposed them to embrace jobs that native New Yorkers would no longer accept; meager as they appeared to New Yorkers, the paychecks in the city's garment, restaurant, or retail sectors looked good in comparison to the going rate in Santo Domingo, Hong Kong, or Kingston. On the other hand, the city's factory sector was suffering a hemorrhage of older, native workers that outpaced the leakage of jobs, leading employers to take on new hands.

The initial portals into New York's economy channeled the newcomers into bottom-level jobs. The links between the workplace and the immigrant community helped convert these positions into platforms for upward movement. Immigrants were simply tied to others who would help them, right from the start. The connections among newcomers and settlers provided an informal structure to immigrant economic life; that structure, in turn, furnished explicit and implicit signposts of economic information and mechanisms of support that helped ethnics acquire skills and move ahead through business and other means.

In the end, new immigrant and African-American New Yorkers shaped their own fates by creating distinctive ethnic economic niches. But history had much to do with where each group could find a place. Looking over their shoulders toward conditions in the societies from which they have just departed, migrants move into industrial economies at the very bottom, taking up the jobs that natives will no longer do. While today's immigrants follow this traditional pattern, African-Americans, by contrast, are the migrants of a generation ago. The earlier pattern of rejections and successes shapes their searches of today, foreclosing options that immigrants, with their very different experiences and orientations, will pursue. Unlike the immigrants, African-Americans aspire to the rewards and positions enjoyed by whites. But the niches that African-Americans have carved out require skills that the least-educated members of that community simply don't have; African-American networks no longer provide connections to these more accessible jobs; and relative to the newcomers, employers find unskilled African-Americans to be much less satisfactory recruits. As for better-skilled African-Americans, they often compete with whites on unequal terrain, since past and present discrimination in housing and schools makes African-American workers less well prepared than whites. In this way, the mismatch between the aspirations of the *partly* disadvantaged and the requirements of the jobs to which they aspire provides the spark for persistent economic racial conflict between blacks and whites.

By contrast, immigrants have moved into noncompeting positions, taking over jobs that whites have deserted in their move up the occupational pecking order. Once the immigrants gain a lock on low-level jobs, ethnic connections funnel a steady stream of newcomers, excluding black New Yorkers who are not members of the same ethnic club.

Thus, the advent of a majority minority economy marks the emergence of a new division of labor, in which the various groups of new New Yorkers play distinct economic roles. Niche creation by African-Americans and immigrants has evolved into a mutually exclusive carving up of the pie: in carving out a place in the ethnic division of labor, the two groups effectively open or foreclose opportunities for each other. As in the past, control over good jobs and desired resources is subject to contest. Thus, the various components of New York's polyglot working and middle classes follow the example of their predecessors, continuing in, and reinvigorating, the pattern of interethnic economic competition that long characterized the city's white ethnic groups.

Notes

1. William J. Wilson, *The Truly Disadvantaged: The Inner City, the Underclass, and Public Policy* (Chicago: University of Chicago Press, 1987); Christopher Jencks and Paul Peterson, eds., *The Urban Underclass* (Washington, D.C.: Brookings Institution, 1991).

2. Sharon Zukin, "Gentrification," *Annual Review of Sociology,* 13 (1987): 129–147; William Frey and Alden Speare, *Regional and Metropolitan Growth and Decline in the United States* (New York: Russell Sage Foundation, 1988).

3. George Sternlieb and James Hughes, "The Uncertain Future of the Central City," *Urban Affairs Quarterly,* 18, no. 4 (1983): 455–472; John Kasarda, "Jobs, Mismatches, and Emerging Urban Mismatches," in M. G. H. Geary and L. Lynn, eds., *Urban Change and Poverty* (Washington, D.C.: National Academy Press, 1988), pp. 148–198.

4. Saskia Sassen, *The Mobility of Capital and Labor* (New York: Cambridge University Press, 1988) and *The Global City: New York, London, Tokyo* (Princeton: Princeton University Press, 1992); Bennett Harrison and Barry Bluestone, *The Great U-Turn* (New York: Basic Books, 1988).

5. The two perspectives also contradict each other on the issue of the direction of job change: is the problem the disappearance or the proliferation of low-level jobs? The answer is that neither polarization nor mismatch proponents are sure. Thus William Wilson and his collaborators emphasize the decline of manufacturing but then point out the "explosion of low-pay, part-time work" (L. J. Wacquant and W. J. Wilson, "The Cost of Racial and Class Exclusion in the Inner City," *Annals,* 501 [January 1989]: 11), the growth of sweatshops, and the "peripheralization and recomposition of the core," code words for economic polarization (L. J. Wacquant, "The Ghetto, the State, and the New Capitalist Economy," *Dissent,* 36, no. 4 [1989]: 512).

ALEJANDRO PORTES AND MIN ZHOU

The New Second Generation: Segmented Assimilation and Its Variants

My name is Herb
and I'm not poor;
I'm the Herbie that you're looking for,
like Pepsi,
a new generation
of Haitian determination—
I'm the Herbie that you're looking for.

A beat tapped with bare hands, a few dance steps, and the Haitian kid was rapping. His song, titled "Straight Out of Haiti," was being performed at Edison High, a school that sits astride Little Haiti and Liberty City, the largest black area of Miami. The lyrics captured well the distinct outlook of his immigrant community. The panorama of Little Haiti contrasts sharply with the bleak inner city. In Miami's Little Haiti, the storefronts leap out at the passersby. Bright blues, reds, and oranges vibrate to Haitian merengue blaring from sidewalk speakers.[1] Yet, behind the gay Caribbean exteriors, a struggle goes on that will define the future of this community. As we will see later on, it involves the second generation— children like Herbie—subject to conflicting pressure from parents and peers and to pervasive outside discrimination.

Growing up in an immigrant family has always been difficult, as individuals are torn by conflicting social and cultural demands while they face the challenge of entry into an unfamiliar and frequently hostile world. And yet the difficulties are not always the same. The process of growing up American oscillates between smooth acceptance and traumatic confrontation depending on the characteristics that immigrants and their children bring along and the social context that receives them. In this article, we explore some of these factors and their bearing on the process of social adaptation of the immigrant second generation. We propose a conceptual framework for understanding this process and illustrate it with selected ethnographic material and survey data from a recent survey of children of immigrants.

Research on the new immigration—that which arose after the passage of the 1965 Immigration Act—has been focused almost exclusively on the first generation, that is, on adult men and women coming to the United States in search of work or to escape political persecution. Little noticed until recently is the fact that the foreign-born inflow has been

Originally published in 1993. Please see complete source information beginning on page 891.

rapidly evolving from single adult individuals to entire family groups, including infant children and those born to immigrants in the United States. By 1980, 10 percent of dependent children in households counted by the census were second-generation immigrants.[2] In the late 1980s, another study put the number of students in kindergarten through twelfth grade in American schools who spoke a language other than English at home at 3 to 5 million.[3]

The great deal of research and theorizing on post–1965 immigration offers only tentative guidance on the prospects and paths of adaptation of the second generation because the outlook of this group can be very different from that of their immigrant parents. For example, it is generally accepted among immigration theorists that entry-level menial jobs are performed without hesitation by newly arrived immigrants but are commonly shunned by their U.S.-reared offspring. This disjuncture gives rise to a race between the social and economic progress of first-generation immigrants and the material conditions and career prospects that their American children grow to expect.[4]

Nor does the existing literature on second-generation adaptation, based as it is on the experience of descendants of pre-World War I immigrants, offer much guidance for the understanding of contemporary events. The last sociological study of children of immigrants was Irving Child's *Italian or American? The Second Generation in Conflict,* published fifty years ago.[5] Conditions at the time were quite different from those confronting settled immigrant groups today. Two such differences deserve special mention. First, descendants of European immigrants who confronted the dilemmas of conflicting cultures were uniformly white. Even if of a somewhat darker hue than the natives, their skin color reduced a major barrier to entry into the American mainstream. For this reason, the process of assimilation depended largely on individual decisions to leave the immigrant culture behind and embrace American ways. Such an advantage obviously does not exist for the black, Asian, and mestizo children of today's immigrants.

Second, the structure of economic opportunities has also changed. Fifty years ago, the United States was the premier industrial power in the world, and its diversified industrial labor requirements offered to the second generation the opportunity to move up gradually through better-paid occupations while remaining part of the working class. Such opportunities have increasingly disappeared in recent years following a rapid process of national deindustrialization and global industrial restructuring. This process has left entrants to the American labor force confronting a widening gap between the minimally paid menial jobs that immigrants commonly accept and the high-tech and professional occupations requiring college degrees that native elites occupy.[6] The gradual disappearance of intermediate opportunities also bears directly on the race between first-generation economic progress and second-generation expectations, noted previously. . . .

Assimilation As a Problem

The Haitian immigrant community of Miami is composed of some 75,000 legal and clandestine immigrants, many of whom sold everything they owned in order to buy passage to America. First-generation Haitians are strongly oriented toward preserving a strong national identity, which they associate both with community solidarity and with social networks promoting individual success.[7] In trying to instill national pride and an achievement orientation in their children, they clash, however, with the youngsters' everyday experiences in school. Little Haiti is adjacent to Liberty City, the main black inner-city area of Miami, and Haitian adolescents attend predominantly inner-city schools. Native-born youths stereotype Haitians as too docile and too subservient to whites and they make fun of French and Creole and of the Haitians' accent. As a result, second-generation Haitian children find themselves torn between conflicting ideas and values: to remain Haitian they would have to face social ostracism and continuing attacks in school; to become American—black American in this case—they would have to forgo their parents' dreams of making it in America on the basis of ethnic solidarity and preservation of traditional values.[8]

An adversarial stance toward the white mainstream is common among inner-city minority youths who, while attacking the newcomers' ways, instill in them a consciousness of American-style discrimination. A common message is the devaluation of education as a vehicle for advancement of all black youths, a message that directly contradicts the immigrant parents' expectations. Academically outstanding Haitian American students, "Herbie" among them, have consciously attempted to retain their ethnic identity by cloaking it in black American cultural forms, such as rap music. Many others, however, have followed the path of least effort and become thoroughly assimilated. Assimilation in this instance is not into mainstream culture but into the values and norms of the inner city. In the process, the resources of solidarity and mutual support within the immigrant community are dissipated.

An emerging paradox in the study of today's second generation is the peculiar forms that assimilation has adopted for its members. As the Haitian example illustrates, adopting the outlooks and cultural ways of the native-born does not represent, as in the past, the first step toward social and economic mobility but may lead to the exact opposite. At the other end, immigrant youths who remain firmly ensconced in their respective ethnic communities may, by virtue of this fact, have a better chance for educational and economic mobility through use of the material and social capital that their communities make available.[9]

This situation stands the cultural blueprint for advancement of immigrant groups in American society on its head. As presented in innumerable academic and journalistic writings, the expectation is that the foreign-born and their offspring will first acculturate and then seek entry and acceptance among the native-born as a prerequisite for their social and economic advancement. Otherwise, they remain confined to the ranks of the ethnic lower and lower-middle classes.[10] This portrayal of the requirements for mobility, so deeply embedded in the national consciousness, stands contradicted today by a growing number of empirical experiences.

A closer look at these experiences indicates, however, that the expected consequences of assimilation have not entirely reversed signs, but that the process has become segmented. In other words, the question is into what sector of American society a particular immigrant group assimilates. Instead of a relatively uniform mainstream whose mores and prejudices dictate a common path of integration, we observe today several distinct forms of adaptation. One of them replicates the time-honored portrayal of growing acculturation and parallel integration into the white middle-class; a second leads straight in the opposite direction to permanent poverty and assimilation into the underclass; still a third associates rapid economic advancement with deliberate preservation of the immigrant community's values and tight solidarity. This pattern of segmented assimilation immediately raises the question of what makes some immigrant groups become susceptible to the downward route and what resources allow others to avoid this course. In the ultimate analysis, the same general process helps explain both outcomes. We advance next our hypotheses as to how this process takes place and how the contrasting outcomes of assimilation can be explained. This explanation is then illustrated with recent empirical material in the final section.

Vulnerability and Resources

Along with individual and family variables, the context that immigrants find upon arrival in their new country plays a decisive role in the course that their offspring's lives will follow. This context includes such broad variables as political relations between sending and receiving countries and the state of the economy in the latter and such specific ones as the size and structure of preexisting coethnic communities. The concept of modes of incorporation provides a useful theoretical tool to understand this diversity. As developed in prior publications, modes of incorporation consist of the complex formed by the policies of the host government; the values and prejudices of the receiving society; and the characteristics of the coethnic community. These factors can be arranged in a tree of contextual situations, illustrated by Figure 1. This figure provides a first approximation to our problem.[11]

To explain second-generation outcomes and their segmented character, however, we need to go into greater detail into the meaning of these various modes of incorporation from the standpoint of immigrant youths. There are three features of the social contexts encountered by today's newcomers that create vulnerability to downward assimilation. The first is color, the second is location, and the third is the absence of mobility ladders. As noted previously, the majority of contemporary immigrants are nonwhite. Although this feature may appear at first glance as an individual characteristic, in reality it is a trait belonging to the host society. Prejudice is not intrinsic to a particular skin color or racial type, and, indeed, many immigrants never experienced it in their native lands. It is by virtue of moving into a new social environment, marked by different values and prejudices, that physical features become redefined as a handicap.

The concentration of immigrant households in cities and particularly in central cities, as documented previously, gives rise to a second source of vulnerability because it puts new arrivals in close contact with concentrations of native-born minorities. This leads to the identification of the condition of both groups—immigrants and the native poor—as the same in the eyes of the majority. More important, it exposes second-generation children to the adversarial subculture devel-

oped by marginalized native youths to cope with their own difficult situation.[12] This process of socialization may take place even when first-generation parents are moving ahead economically and, hence, their children have no objective reasons for embracing a counter-cultural message. If successful, the process can effectively block parental plans for intergenerational mobility.

The third contextual source of vulnerability has to do with changes in the host economy that have led to the evaporation of occupational ladders for intergenerational mobility. As noted previously, new immigrants may form the backbone of what remains of labor-intensive manufacturing in the cities as well as in their growing personal services sector, but these are niches that seldom offer channels for upward mobility. The new hourglass economy, created by economic restructuring, means that children of immigrants must cross a narrow bottleneck to occupations requiring advanced training if their careers are to keep pace with their U.S.-acquired aspirations. This race against a narrowing middle demands that immigrant parents accumulate sufficient resources to allow their children to effect the passage and to simultaneously prove to them the viability of aspirations for upward mobility. Otherwise, assimilation may not be into mainstream values and expectations but into the adversarial stance of impoverished groups confined to the bottom of the new economic hourglass.

The picture is painted in such stark terms here for the sake of clarity, although in reality things have not yet become so polarized. Middle-level occupations requiring relatively modest educational achievements have not completely vanished. By 1980, skilled blue-collar jobs—classified by the U.S. census as "precision production, craft, and repair occupations"—had declined by 1.1 percent relative to a decade earlier but still represented 13 percent of the experienced civilian labor force, or 13.6 million workers. Mostly clerical administrative support occupations added another 16.9 percent, or 17.5 million jobs. In 1980, occupations requiring a college degree

FIGURE 1

Modes of Incorporation: A Typology

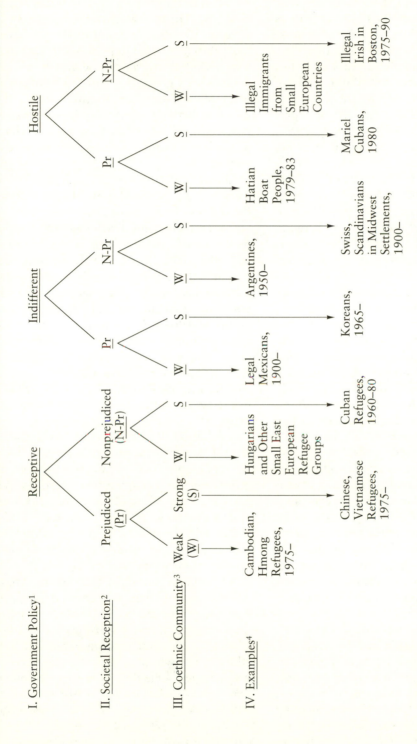

Source: Adapted from Alejandro Portes and Rubén G. Rumbaut, *Immigrant America: A Portrait* (Berkeley: University of California Press, 1990), p. 91. Copyright © 1990 by The Regents of the University of California.

1. Receptive policy is defined as legal entry with resettlement assistance, indifferent as legal entry without resettlement assistance, hostile as active opposition to a group's entry or permanence in the country; 2. Prejudiced reception is defined as that accorded to nonphenotypically white groups; nonprejudiced is that accorded to European and European-origin whites; 3. Weak coethnic communities are either small in numbers or composed primarily of manual workers; strong communities feature sizable numerical concentrations and a diversified occupational structure including entrepreneurs and professionals; 4. Examples include immigrant groups arriving from the start of the century to the present. Dates of migration are approximate. Groups reflect broadly but not perfectly the characteristics of each ideal type.

had increased by 6 percent in comparison with 1970, but they still employed less than a fifth—18.2 percent—of the American labor force.[13] Even in the largest cities, occupations requiring only a high school diploma were common by the late 1980s. In New York City, for example, persons with 12 years or less of schooling held just over one half of the jobs in 1987. Clerical, service, and skilled blue-collar jobs not requiring a college degree represented 46 percent.[14] Despite these figures, there is little doubt that the trend toward occupational segmentation has increasingly reduced opportunities for incremental upward mobility through well-paid blue-collar positions. The trend forces immigrants today to bridge in only one generation the gap between entry-level jobs and professional positions that earlier groups took two or three generations to travel.

Different modes of incorporation also make available, however, three types of resources to confront the challenges of contemporary assimilation. First, certain groups, notably political refugees, are eligible for a variety of government programs including educational loans for their children. The Cuban Loan Program, implemented by the Kennedy administration in connection with its plan to resettle Cuban refugees away from South Florida, gave many impoverished first- and second-generation Cuban youths a chance to attend college. The high proportion of professionals and executives among Cuban American workers today, a figure on a par with that for native white workers, can be traced, at least in part, to the success of that program.[15] Passage of the 1980 Refugee Act gave to subsequent groups of refugees, in particular Southeast Asians and Eastern Europeans, access to a similarly generous benefits package.[16]

Second, certain foreign groups have been exempted from the traditional prejudice endured by most immigrants, thereby facilitating a smoother process of adaptation. Some political refugees, such as the early waves of exiles from Castro's Cuba, Hungarians and Czechs escaping the invasions of their respective countries, and Soviet Jews escaping religious persecution, provide examples. In other cases, it is the cultural and phenotypical affinity of newcomers to ample segments of the host population that ensures a welcome reception. The Irish coming to Boston during the 1980s are a case in point. Although many were illegal aliens, they came into an environment where generations of Irish Americans had established a secure foothold. Public sympathy effectively neutralized governmental hostility in this case, culminating in a change of the immigration law directly benefiting the newcomers.[17]

Third, and most important, are the resources made available through networks in the coethnic community. Immigrants who join well-established and diversified ethnic groups have access from the start to a range of moral and material resources well beyond those available through official assistance programs. Educational help for second-generation youths may include not only access to college grants and loans but also the existence of a private school system geared to the immigrant community's values. Attendance at these private ethnic schools insulates children from contact with native minority youths, while reinforcing the authority of parental views and plans.

In addition, the economic diversification of several immigrant communities creates niches of opportunity that members of the second generation can occupy, often without a need for an advanced education. Small-business apprenticeships, access to skilled building trades, and well-paid jobs in local government bureaucracies are some of the ethnic niches documented in the recent literature.[18] In 1987, average sales per firm of the smaller Chinese, East Indian, Korean, and Cuban enterprises exceeded $100,000 per year and they jointly employed over 200,000 workers. These figures omit medium-sized and large ethnic firms, whose sales and work forces are much larger.[19] Fieldwork in these communities indicates that up to half of recently arrived immigrants are employed by coethnic firms and that self-employment offers a prime avenue for mobility to second-generation youths.[20] Such community-mediated opportunities provide a solution to the race between material resources and second-generation aspirations not available through competition in the open labor market. Through creation of a capitalism of their own, some immigrant groups have thus been able to circumvent outside discrimination and the threat of vanishing mobility ladders.

In contrast to these favorable conditions are those foreign minorities who either lack a community already in place or whose coethnics are too poor to render assistance. The condition of Haitians in South Florida, cited earlier, provides an illustration of one of the most handicapped modes of incorporation encountered by contemporary immigrants, combining official hostility and widespread social prejudice with the absence of a strong receiving community.[21] From the standpoint of second-generation outcomes, the existence of a large but downtrodden coethnic community may be even less desirable than no community at all. This is because newly arrived youths enter into ready contact with the reactive subculture developed by earlier generations. Its influence is all the more powerful because it comes from individuals of the same national origin, "people like us" who can more effectively define the proper stance and attitudes of the newcomers. To the extent that they do so, the first-generation model of upward mobility through school achievement and attainment of professional occupations will be blocked.

Three Examples

Mexicans and Mexican Americans

Field High School (the name is fictitious) is located in a small coastal community of central California whose economy has long been tied to agricultural production and immigrant farm labor. About 57 percent of the student population is of Mexican descent. An intensive ethnographic study of the class of 1985 at Field High began with school records

that showed that the majority of U.S.-born Spanish-surname students who had entered the school in 1981 had dropped out by their senior year. However, only 35 percent of the Spanish-surname students who had been originally classified by the school as limited English proficient (LEP) had dropped out. The figure was even lower than the corresponding one for native white students, 40 percent. LEP status is commonly assigned to recently arrived Mexican immigrants.[22]

Intensive ethnographic fieldwork at the school identified several distinct categories in which the Mexican-origin population could be classified. Recent Mexican immigrants were at one extreme. They dressed differently and unstylishly. They claimed an identity as Mexican and considered Mexico their permanent home. The most academically successful of this group were those most proficient in Spanish, reflecting their prior levels of education in Mexico. Almost all were described by teachers and staff as courteous, serious about their schoolwork, respectful, and eager to please as well as naive and unsophisticated. They were commonly classified as LEP.

The next category comprised Mexican-oriented students. They spoke Spanish at home and were generally classified as fluent English proficient (FEP). They had strong bicultural ties with both Mexico and the United States, reflecting the fact that most were born in Mexico but had lived in the United States for more than five years. They were proud of their Mexican heritage but saw themselves as different from the first group, the *recién llegados* (recently arrived), as well as from the native-born Chicanos and Cholos, who were derided as people who had lost their Mexican roots. Students from this group were active in soccer and the Sociedad Bilingue and in celebrations of May 5th, the anniversary of the Mexican defeat of French occupying forces. Virtually all of the Mexican-descent students who graduated in the top 10 percent of their class in 1981 were identified as members of this group.

Chicanos were by far the largest Mexican-descent group at Field High. They were mostly

U.S.-born second- and third-generation students whose primary loyalty was to their in-group, seen as locked in conflict with white society. Chicanos referred derisively to successful Mexican students as "schoolboys" and "schoolgirls" or as "wannabes." According to M. G. Matute-Bianchi,

> To be a Chicano meant in practice to hang out by the science wing . . . *not* eating lunch in the quad where all the "gringos" and "schoolboys" hang out . . . cutting classes by faking a call slip so you can be with your friends at the 7–11 . . . sitting in the back of classes and not participating . . . *not* carrying your books to class . . . *not* taking the difficult classes . . . doing the minimum to get by.[23]

Chicanos merge imperceptibly into the last category, the Cholos, who were commonly seen as "low riders" and gang members. They were also native-born Mexican Americans, easily identifiable by their deliberate manner of dress, walk, speech, and other cultural symbols. Chicanos and Cholos were generally regarded by teachers as "irresponsible," "disrespectful," "mistrusting," "sullen," "apathetic," and "less motivated," and their poor school performance was attributed to these traits.[24] According to Matute-Bianchi, Chicanos and Cholos were faced with what they saw as a forced-choice dilemma between doing well in school or being a Chicano. To act white was regarded as disloyalty to one's group.

The situation of these last two groups exemplifies losing the race between first-generation achievements and later generations' expectations. Seeing their parents and grandparents confined to humble menial jobs and increasingly aware of discrimination against them by the white mainstream, U.S.-born children of earlier Mexican immigrants readily join a reactive subculture as a means of protecting their sense of self-worth. Participation in this subculture then leads to serious barriers to their chances of upward mobility because school achievement is defined as antithetical to ethnic solidarity. Like Haitian students at Edison High, newly arrived Mexican students are at risk of being socialized into the same reactive stance, with the aggravating factor that it is other Mexicans, not native-born strangers, who convey the message. The principal protection of *mexicanos* against this type of assimilation lies in their strong identification with home-country language and values, which brings them closer to their parents' cultural stance.

Punjabi Sikhs in California

Valleyside (a fictitious name) is a northern California community where the primary economic activity is orchard farming. Farm laborers in this area come often from India; they are mainly rural Sikhs from the Punjab. By the early 1980s, second-generation Punjabi students already accounted for 11 percent of the student body at Valleyside High. Their parents were no longer only farm laborers, since about a third had become orchard owners themselves and another third worked in factories in the nearby San Francisco area. An ethnographic study of Valleyside High School in 1980–82 revealed a very difficult process of assimilation for Punjabi Sikh students. According to its author, M. A. Gibson, Valleyside is "redneck country," and white residents are extremely hostile to immigrants who look different and speak a different language: "Punjabi teenagers are told they stink . . . told to go back to India . . . physically abused by majority students who spit at them, refuse to sit by them in class or in buses, throw food at them or worse."[25]

Despite these attacks and some evidence of discrimination by school staff, Punjabi students performed better academically than majority Anglo students. About 90 percent of the immigrant youths completed high school, compared to 70–75 percent of native whites. Punjabi boys surpassed the average grade point average, were more likely to take advanced science and math classes, and expressed aspirations for careers in science and engineering. Girls, on the other hand, tended to enroll in business classes, but they paid less attention to immediate career plans, reflecting parental wishes that they should marry first. This gender difference is indicative of the continuing strong influence exercised by the immigrant community over its second generation. According to Gibson, Punjabi parents pressured their children against too much contact with white peers who may "dishonor" the immigrants' families, and defined "becoming Americanized" as forgetting one's roots and adopting the most disparaged traits of the majority, such as leaving home at age 18, making decisions without parental consent, dating, and dancing. At the same time, parents urged children to abide by school rules, ignore racist remarks and avoid fights, and learn useful skills, including full proficiency in English.[26]

The overall success of this strategy of selective assimilation to American society is remarkable because Punjabi immigrants were generally poor on their arrival in the United States and confronted widespread discrimination from whites without the benefit of either governmental assistance or a well-established coethnic community. In terms of our typology of vulnerability and resources, the Punjabi Sikh second generation was very much at risk except for two crucial factors. First, immigrant parents did not settle in the inner city or in close proximity to any native-born minority whose offspring could provide an alternative model of adaptation to white-majority discrimination. In particular, the absence of a downtrodden Indian American community composed of children of previous immigrants allowed first-generation parents to influence decisively the outlook of their offspring, including their ways of fighting white prejudice. There was no equivalent of a Cholo-like reactive subculture to offer an alternative blueprint of the stance that "people like us" should take.

Second, Punjabi immigrants managed to make considerable economic progress, as attested by the number who had become farm owners, while maintaining a tightly knit ethnic community. The material and social capital created by this first-generation community compensated for the absence of an older co-

ethnic group and had decisive effects on second-generation outlooks. Punjabi teenagers were shown that their parents' ways paid off economically, and this fact, plus their community's cohesiveness, endowed them with a source of pride to counteract outside discrimination. Through this strategy of selective assimilation, Punjabi Sikhs appeared to be winning the race against the inevitable acculturation of their children to American-style aspirations.

Caribbean Youths in South Florida

Miami is arguably the American city that has been most thoroughly transformed by post–1960 immigration. The Cuban Revolution had much to do with this transformation, as it sent the entire Cuban upper class out of the country, followed by thousands of refugees of more modest backgrounds. Over time, Cubans created a highly diversified and prosperous ethnic community that provided resources for the adaptation process of its second generation. Reflecting this situation are average Cuban family incomes that, by 1989, approximated those of the native-born population; the existence in 1987 of more than 30,000 Cuban-owned small businesses that formed the core of the Miami ethnic enclave; and the parallel rise of a private school system oriented toward the values and political outlook of this community.[27] In terms of the typology of vulnerability and resources, well-sheltered Cuban American teenagers lack any extensive exposure to outside discrimination, they have little contact with youths from disadvantaged minorities, and the development of an enclave creates economic opportunities beyond the narrowing industrial and tourist sectors on which most other immigrant groups in the area depend. Across town, Haitian American teenagers face exactly the opposite set of conditions, as has been shown.

Among the other immigrant groups that form Miami's ethnic mosaic, two deserve mention because they represent intermediate situations between those of the Cubans and Haitians. One comprises Nicaraguans escaping the Sandinista regime during the 1980s. They were not as welcomed in the United States as were the Cuban exiles, nor were they able to develop a large and diversified community. Yet they shared with Cubans their language and culture, as well as a militant anti-Communist discourse. This common political outlook led the Cuban American community to extend its resources in support of their Nicaraguan brethren, smoothing their process of adaptation.[28] For second-generation Nicaraguans, this means that the preexisting ethnic community that provides a model for their own assimilation is not a downtrodden group but rather one that has managed to establish a firm and positive presence in the city's economy and politics.

The second group comprises West Indians coming from Jamaica, Trinidad, and other English-speaking Caribbean republics. They generally arrive in Miami as legal immigrants, and many bring along professional and business credentials as well as the advantage of fluency in English. These individual advantages are discounted, however, by a context of reception in which these mostly black immigrants are put in the same category as native-born blacks and discriminated against accordingly. The recency of West Indian migration and its small size have prevented the development of a diversified ethnic community in South Florida. Hence new arrivals experience the full force of white discrimination without the protection of a large coethnic group and with constant exposure to the situation and attitudes of the inner-city population. Despite considerable individual resources, these disadvantages put the West Indian second generation at risk of bypassing white or even native black middle-class models to assimilate into the culture of the underclass. . . .

Conclusion

Fifty years ago, the dilemma of Italian American youngsters studied by Irving Child consisted of assimilating into the American main-

stream, sacrificing in the process their parents' cultural heritage in contrast to taking refuge in the ethnic community from the challenges of the outside world. In the contemporary context of segmented assimilation, the options have become less clear. Children of non-white immigrants may not even have the opportunity of gaining access to middle-class white society, no matter how acculturated they become. Joining those native circles to which they do have access may prove a ticket to permanent subordination and disadvantage. Remaining securely ensconced in their coethnic community, under these circumstances, may be not a symptom of escapism but the best strategy for capitalizing on otherwise unavailable material and moral resources. As the experiences of Punjabi Sikh and Cuban American students suggest, a strategy of paced, selective assimilation may prove the best course for immigrant minorities. But the extent to which this strategy is possible also depends on the history of each group and its specific profile of vulnerabilities and resources. The present analysis represents a preliminary step toward understanding these realities.

Notes

1. Alejandro Portes and Alex Stepick, *City on the Edge: The Transformation of Miami* (Berkeley: University of California Press, 1993), chap. 8.

2. Defined as native-born children with at least one foreign-born parent or children born abroad who came to the United States before age 12.

3. Joan N. First and John W. Carrera, *New Voices: Immigrant Students in U.S. Public Schools* (Boston: National Coalition of Advocates for Students, 1988).

4. Michael Piore, *Birds of Passage* (New York: Cambridge University Press, 1979); Herbert Gans, "Second-Generation Decline: Scenarios for the Economic and Ethnic Futures of the Post–1965 American Immigrants," *Ethnic and Racial Studies* 15:173–92 (Apr. 1992).

5. Irving L. Child, *Italian or American? The Second Generation in Conflict* (New Haven, CT: Yale University Press, 1943).

6. See, for example, Saskia Sassen, "Changing Composition and Labor Market Location of Hispanic Immigrants in New York City, 1960–1980," in *Hispanics in the U.S. Economy,* ed. George J. Borjas and Marta Tienda (New York: Academic Press, 1985), pp. 299–322.

7. See Alex Stepick, "Haitian Refugees in the U.S." (Report no. 52, Minority Rights Group, London, 1982); Alex Stepick and Alejandro Portes, "Flight into Despair: A Profile of Recent Haitian Refugees in South Florida," *International Migration Review,* 20:329–50 (Summer 1986).

8. This account is based on fieldwork in Miami conducted in preparation for a survey of immigrant youths in public schools.

9. On the issue of social capital, see James S. Coleman, "Social Capital in the Creation of Human Capital," *American Journal of Sociology,* supplement, 94:S95–121 (1988); Alejandro Portes and Min Zhou, "Gaining the Upper Hand: Economic Mobility among Immigrant and Domestic Minorities," *Ethnic and Racial Studies,* 15:491–522 (Oct. 1992). On ethnic entrepreneurship, see Ivan H. Light, *Ethnic Enterprise in America: Business and Welfare among Chinese, Japanese, and Blacks* (Berkeley: University of California Press, 1972); Kenneth Wilson and W. Allen Martin, "Ethnic Enclaves: A Comparison of the Cuban and Black Economies in Miami," *American Journal of Sociology,* 88:135–60 (1982).

10. See W. Lloyd Warner and Leo Srole, *The Social Systems of American Ethnic Groups* (New Haven, CT: Yale University Press, 1945); Thomas Sowell, *Ethnic America: A History* (New York: Basic Books, 1981).

11. See Alejandro Portes and Rubén G. Rumbaut, *Immigrant America: A Portrait* (Berkeley: University of California Press, 1990), chap. 3.

12. See Mercer L. Sullivan, *"Getting Paid": Youth, Crime, and Work in the Inner City* (Ithaca, NY: Cornell University Press, 1989), chaps. 1, 5.

13. U.S., Department of Commerce, Bureau of the Census, *Census of Population and Housing, 1980: Public Use Microdata Samples A (MRDF)* (Washington, DC: Department of Commerce, 1983).

14. Thomas Bailey and Roger Waldinger, "Primary, Secondary, and Enclave Labor Markets: A Training System Approach," *American Sociological Review,* 56:432–45 (1991).

15. Professionals and executives represented 25.9 percent of Cuban-origin males aged 16 years and over in 1989; the figure for the total adult male population was 26 percent. See Jesus M. García and Patricia A. Montgomery, *The Hispanic Population of the United States: March 1990,* Current Population Reports, ser. P–20, no. 449 (Washington, DC: Department of Commerce, 1991).

16. Portes and Rumbaut, *Immigrant America,* pp. 23–25; Robert L. Bach et al., "The Economic Adjustment of Southeast Asian Refugees in the United States," in *World Refugee Survey, 1983* (Geneva: United Nations High Commission for Refugees, 1984), pp. 51–55.

17. The 1990 Immigration Act contains tailor-made provisions to facilitate the legalization of Irish immigrants. Those taking advantage of the provisions are popularly dubbed "Kennedy Irish" in honor of the Massachusetts Senator who coauthored the act. On the 1990 act, see Michael Fix and Jeffrey S. Passel, "The Door Remains Open: Recent Immigration to the United States and a Preliminary Analysis of the Immigration Act of 1990" (Working paper, Urban Institute and RAND Corporation, 1991). On the Irish in Boston, see Karen Tumulty, "When Irish Eyes Are Hiding . . . ," *Los Angeles Times,* 29 Jan. 1989.

18. Bailey and Waldinger, "Primary, Secondary, and Enclave Labor Markets"; Min Zhou, *New York's Chinatown: The Socioeconomic Potential of an Urban Enclave* (Philadelphia: Temple University Press, 1992); Wilson and Martin, "Ethnic Enclaves"; Suzanne Model, "The Ethnic Economy: Cubans and Chinese Reconsidered" (Manuscript, University of Massachusetts at Amherst, 1990).

19. U.S. Department of Commerce, Bureau of the Census, *Survey of Minority-Owned Business Enterprises, 1987,* MB–2 and MB–3 (Washington, DC: Department of Commerce, 1991).

20. Alejandro Portes and Alex Stepick, "Unwelcome Immigrants: The Labor Market Experiences of 1980 (Mariel) Cuban and Haitian Refugees in South Florida," *American Sociological Review,* 50:493–514 (Aug. 1985); Zhou, *New York's Chinatown;* Luis E. Guarnizo, "One Country in Two: Dominican-Owned Firms in New York and the Dominican Republic" (Ph.D. diss. Johns Hopkins University, 1992); Bailey and Waldinger, "Primary, Secondary, and Enclave Labor Markets."

21. Stepick, "Haitian Refugees in the U.S."; Jake C. Miller, *The Plight of Haitian Refugees* (New York: Praeger, 1984).

22. M. G. Matute-Bianchi, "Ethnic Identities and Patterns of School Success and Failure among Mexican-Descent and Japanese-American Students in a California High School," *American Journal of Education,* 95:233–55 (Nov. 1986). This study is summarized in Rubén G. Rumbaut, "Immigrant Students in California Public Schools: A Summary of Current Knowledge" (Report no. 11, Center for Research on Effective Schooling for Disadvantaged Children, Johns Hopkins University, Aug. 1990).

23. Matute-Bianchi, "Ethnic Identities and Patterns," p. 253.

24. Rumbaut, "Immigrant Students," p. 25.

25. M. A. Gibson, *Accommodation without Assimilation: Sikh Immigrants in an American High School* (Ithaca, NY: Cornell University Press, 1989), p. 268.

26. Gibson, *Accommodation without Assimilation*. The study is summarized in Rumbaut, "Immigrant Students," pp. 22–23.

27. García and Montgomery, Hispanic Population; U.S. Department of Commerce, Bureau of the Census, *Survey of Minority-Owned Business Enterprises*, MB–2.

28. Portes and Stepick, *City on the Edge*, chap. 7.

M A R Y   C .   W A T E R S

Black Identities: West Indian Immigrant Dreams and American Realities

A key proposition of the new models of immigrant incorporation studies how the social capital immigrants bring with them, and the racial and ethnic definitions of nonwhite immigrants as minorities, combine to create a situation where becoming American in terms of culture and identity and achieving economic success are decoupled. Some immigrants and their children do better economically by maintaining a strong ethnic identity and culture and by resisting American cultural and identity influences. In fact, many authors now suggest that remaining immigrant- or ethnic-identified eases economic and social incorporation into the United States. These new assumptions turn models of identity change on their head—now those who resist becoming American do well and those who lose their immigrant ethnic distinctiveness become downwardly mobile. West Indians, it turns out, fit this model very well because when West Indians lose their distinctiveness as immigrants or ethnics they become not just Americans, but black Americans. Given the ongoing prejudice and discrimination in American society, this represents downward mobility for the immigrants and their children. . . .

The main argument of this chapter is that black immigrants from the Caribbean come to the United States with a particular identity/culture/worldview that reflects their unique history and experiences. This culture and identity are different from the immigrant identity and culture of previous waves of European immigrants because of the unique history of the origin countries and because of the changed contexts of reception the immigrants face in the United States. This culture and identity are also different from the culture and identity of African Americans.

At first, two main aspects of the culture of West Indians help them to be successful in America. First, because they are immigrants they have a different attitude toward employment, work, and American society than native-born Americans. Employers value this highly. Their background characteristics, including human capital and social network ties, ease their entry into the U.S. labor force. Middle-class immigrants come with qualifications and training that are needed in the U.S. economy (nurses, for example). Because English is their native language, they are able

Originally published in 1999. Please see complete source information beginning on page 891.

to transfer their foreign qualifications (teaching credentials, nursing degrees) into American credentials. In addition, working-class immigrants have extensive networks of contacts that facilitate their entry into low-level jobs.

Second, the immigrants' unique understanding and expectations of race relations allow them to interact with American racial structures in a successful way. Specifically, their low anticipation of sour race relations allows them to have better interpersonal interactions with white Americans than many native African Americans. Because they come from a society with a majority of blacks and with many blacks in high positions, the immigrants have high ambitions and expectations. Yet their experience with blocked economic mobility due to race and their strong racial identities lead them to challenge blocked mobility in a very militant fashion when they encounter it. This combination of high ambitions, friendly relations with whites on an interpersonal level, and strong militance in encountering any perceived discrimination leads to some better outcomes in the labor market for West Indians than for black Americans.

Ultimately, however, the structural realities of American race relations begin to swamp the culture of the West Indians. Persistent and obvious racial discrimination undermines the openness toward whites the immigrants have when they first arrive. Low wages and poor working conditions are no longer attractive to the children of the immigrants, who use American, not Caribbean, yardsticks to measure how good a job is. Racial discrimination in housing channels the immigrants into neighborhoods with inadequate city services and high crime rates. Inadequate public schools undermine their hopes for their children's future. Over time the distinct elements of West Indian culture the immigrants are most proud of—a willingness to work hard, a lack of attention to racialism, a high value on education, and strong interests in saving for the future—are undermined by the realities of life in the United States.

These changes are particularly concentrated among the working-class and poor immigrants. Middle-class immigrants are able to pass along aspects of their culture and worldview to their children, but the majority of the working-class immigrants are not. Race as a master status in the United States soon overwhelms the identities of the immigrants and their children, and they are seen as black Americans. Many of the children of the immigrants develop "oppositional identities" to deal with that status. These identities stress that doing well in school is "acting white." The cultural behaviors associated with these oppositional identities further erode the life chances of the children of the West Indian immigrants.

While many white conservatives blame the culture of African Americans for their failures in the economy, the experiences of the West Indians show that even "good culture" is no match for racial discrimination. Over the course of one generation the structural realities of American race relations and the American economy undermine the cultures of the West Indian immigrants and create responses among the immigrants, and especially their children, that resemble the cultural responses of African Americans to long histories of exclusion and discrimination. . . .

The key factor brought to fresh light by the West Indian immigrants' experiences is the role of continuing racial inequality—the institutional failures in our inner cities to provide jobs, education, and public safety—in sustaining a cultural response of disinvestment in the face of discrimination rather than increased striving. A lifetime of interpersonal attacks based on race can lead to bitterness and anger on the part of an individual. A community of people coping with economic marginality and a lack of any avenues of institutional support for individual mobility leads to a culture of opposition. That culture might serve individuals well for those times when it protects them from the sting of racism and discrimination, but ultimately as a long-term political response to discrimination and exclusion it serves to prevent people from taking advantage of the new opportunities that do arise. Those opportunities are reserved by whites in power for immigrants who make them feel less uncomfortable about relations between the races and especially about taking orders from white supervisors or customers.

One of the African-American teachers [interviewed in this study] eloquently describes how even one act of cruelty or disdain by a white person can have long-standing effects on a young black person and on the whole cycle of black-white race relations:

I have had this happen to me so let me relate this incident. I have been going or coming from a building and held the door for some old white person and had them walk right past me, as if I am supposed to hold the door for them. Not one word, a thank-you, or an acknowledgment of your presence was made. A seventeen-year-old, when he has something like that happen to him, the next time he is going to slam that door in the old lady's face, because I had that tendency myself. I had the hostility build up in me. The next time it happens I won't do that because I am older, but when I was seventeen it might not have made any difference to me that this was a different old lady. I would have flashed back to that previous incident and said I am not holding that door for you. Now that old lady who may have been a perfectly fine individual, who got this door slammed in her face by this young black person, her attitude is "boy, all those people are really vicious people." Her not understanding how it all came to pass. That on a large scale is what is happening in our country today. That's why our young people are very aggressive and very, very hostile when they are put in a situation of black-white confrontation. They say to themselves, "I am not going to let you treat me the way you treated my grandparents, or the way I have read or seen in books or movies that they were treated." I would rather for you to hate me than to disrespect me, is the attitude I think is coming out from our black youth today. (Black American male teacher, age 41)

The policy implications of this study lie in the ways in which the economic and cultural dis-

investment in American cities erodes the social capital of immigrant families. The families need recognition of their inherent strengths and the supports necessary to maintain their ambitions. The erosion of the optimism and ambition of the first generation that I saw in their children could be stopped if job opportunities were more plentiful, inner-city schools were nurturing and safe environments that provided good educations, and neighborhoods were safer. Decent jobs, effective schools, and safe streets are not immigrant- or race-based policies. They are universal policies that would benefit all urban residents. Indeed, the strengths these immigrant families have may be in part due to their immigrant status, but the problems they face are much more likely to be due to their class status and their urban residence. Policies that benefit immigrants would equally benefit Americans.

But, in addition, the experience of these immigrants tells us that we must recognize the continuing significance of interpersonal racism in creating psychological tensions and cultural adaptations in the black community. The cycle of attack and disrespect from whites, anger and withdrawal from blacks, and disengagement and blaming behaviors by whites must be broken by changing whites' behaviors. This involves policies that specifically address racial discrimination. The immigrants' tales of blatant housing and job discrimination directly point to needed vigilance in protecting all blacks in the United States from unequal treatment in the private sector. The more difficult problem is dealing with the everyday subtle forms of prejudice and discrimination that also plague foreign-born and American-born blacks. We cannot pass laws forbidding white women from clutching their handbags when black teenagers walk past them. We cannot require old white women to thank young black men who show them courteous behavior. Those kinds of behaviors can only change when whites no longer automatically fear blacks and when whites begin to perceive the humanity and diversity of the black people they encounter.

WILLIAM JULIUS WILSON

The Declining Significance of Race:
Blacks and Changing American Institutions

Race relations in America have undergone fundamental changes in recent years, so much so that now the life chances of individual blacks have more to do with their economic class position than with their day-to-day encounters with whites. In earlier years the systematic efforts of whites to suppress blacks were obvious to even the most insensitive observer. Blacks were denied access to valued and scarce resources through various ingenious schemes of racial exploitation, discrimination, and segregation, schemes that were reinforced by elaborate ideologies of racism. But the situation has changed. However determinative such practices were for the previous efforts of the black population to achieve racial equality, and however significant they were in the creation of poverty-stricken ghettoes and a vast underclass of black proletarians—that massive population at the very bottom of the social class ladder plagued by poor education and low-paying, unstable jobs—they do not provide a meaningful explanation of the life chances of black Americans today. The traditional patterns of interaction between blacks and whites, particularly in the labor market, have been fundamentally altered.

In the antebellum period, and in the latter half of the nineteenth century through the first half of the twentieth century, the continuous and explicit efforts of whites to construct racial barriers profoundly affected the lives of black Americans. Racial oppression was deliberate, overt, and is easily documented, ranging from slavery to segregation, from the endeavors of the white economic elite to exploit black labor to the actions of the white masses to eliminate or neutralize black competition, particularly economic competition.[1] As the nation has entered the latter half of the twentieth century, however, many of the traditional barriers have crumbled under the weight of the political, social, and economic changes of the civil rights era. A new set of obstacles has emerged from basic structural shifts in the economy. These obstacles are therefore impersonal but may prove to be even more formidable for certain segments of the black population. Specifically, whereas the previous barriers were usually designed to control and restrict the entire black population, the new barriers create hardships essentially for the black underclass; whereas the old barriers were based explicitly on racial motivations derived from intergroup contact, the new barriers have racial significance only in their consequences, not in their origins. In short, whereas the old barriers bore the per-

Originally published in 1978. Please see complete source information beginning on page 891.

vasive features of racial oppression, the new barriers indicate an important and emerging form of class subordination.

It would be shortsighted to view the traditional forms of racial segregation and discrimination as having essentially disappeared in contemporary America; the presence of blacks is still firmly resisted in various institutions and social arrangements, for example, residential areas and private social clubs. However, in the economic sphere, class has become more important than race in determining black access to privilege and power. It is clearly evident in this connection that many talented and educated blacks are now entering positions of prestige and influence at a rate comparable to or, in some situations, exceeding that of whites with equivalent qualifications. It is equally clear that the black underclass is in a hopeless state of economic stagnation, falling further and further behind the rest of society. . . .

Three Stages of American Race Relations

My basic thesis is that American society has experienced three major stages of black-white contact and that each stage embodies a different form of racial stratification structured by the particular arrangement of both the economy and the polity. Stage one coincides with antebellum slavery and the early post-bellum era and may be designated the period of *plantation economy and racial-caste oppression*. Stage two begins in the last quarter of the nineteenth century and ends at roughly the New Deal era and may be identified as the period of *industrial expansion, class conflict, and racial oppression*. Finally, stage three is associated with the modern, industrial, post–World War II era, which really began to crystallize during the 1960s and 1970s, and may be characterized as the period of *progressive transition from racial inequalities to class inequalities*. For the sake of brevity I shall identify the different periods respectively as

the preindustrial, industrial, and modern industrial stages of American race relations.

Although this abbreviated designation of the periods of American race relations seems to relate racial change to fundamental economic changes rather directly, it bears repeating that the different stages of race relations are structured by the unique arrangements and interactions of the economy and the polity. Although I stress the economic basis of structured racial inequality in the preindustrial and industrial periods of race relations, I also attempt to show how the polity more or less interacted with the economy either to reinforce patterns of racial stratification or to mediate various forms of racial conflict. Moreover, for the modern industrial period, I try to show how race relations have been shaped as much by important economic changes as by important political changes. Indeed, it would not be possible to understand fully the subtle and manifest changes in race relations in the modern industrial period without recognizing the dual and often reciprocal influence of structural changes in the economy and political changes in the state. Thus, my central argument is that different systems of production and/or different arrangements of the polity have imposed different constraints on the way in which racial groups have interacted in the United States, constraints that have structured the relations between racial groups and that have produced dissimilar contexts not only for the manifestation of racial antagonisms but also for racial group access to rewards and privileges.

In contrast to the modern industrial period in which fundamental economic and political changes have made economic class affiliation more important than race in determining Negro prospects for occupational advancement, the preindustrial and industrial periods of black-white relations have one central feature in common, namely, overt efforts of whites to solidify economic racial domination (ranging from the manipulation of black labor to the neutralization or elimination of black economic competition) through various forms of juridical, political, and social discrimination. Since racial problems during these two periods were principally related to group struggles over economic resources, they readily lend themselves to the economic class theories of racial antagonisms that associate racial antipathy with class conflict. A brief consideration of these theories, followed by a discussion of their basic weaknesses, will help to raise a number of theoretical issues that will be useful for analyzing the dynamics of racial conflict in the preindustrial and industrial stages of American race relations. However, in a later section of this chapter I shall attempt to explain why these theories are not very relevant to the modern industrial stage of American race relations.

Economic Class Theories

Students of race relations have paid considerable attention to the economic basis of racial antagonism in recent years, particularly to the theme that racial problems in historical situations are related to the more general problems of economic class conflict. A common assumption of this theme is that racial conflict is merely a special manifestation of class conflict. Accordingly, ideologies of racism, racial prejudices, institutionalized discrimination, segregation, and other factors that reinforce or embody racial stratification are seen as simply part of a superstructure determined and shaped by the particular arrangement of the class structure.[2] However, given this basic assumption, which continues to be the most representative and widely used economic class argument,[3] proponents have advanced two major and somewhat divergent explanations of how class conflicts actually shape and determine racial relations—the orthodox Marxist theory of capitalist exploitation,[4] and the *split labor-market theory* of working class antagonisms.[5]

The orthodox Marxist theory, which is the most popular variant of the Marxists' explanations of race,[6] postulates that because the

ultimate goal of the capitalist class is to maximize profits, efforts will be made to suppress workers' demands for increased wages and to weaken their bargaining power by promoting divisions within their ranks. The divisions occur along racial lines to the extent that the capitalist class is able to isolate the lower-priced black labor force by not only supporting job, housing, and educational discrimination against blacks, but also by developing or encouraging racial prejudices and ideologies of racial subjugation such as racism. The net effect of such a policy is to insure a marginal working class of blacks and to establish a relatively more privileged position for the established white labor force. Since discrimination guarantees a situation where the average wage rate of the black labor force is less than the average wage rate of the established white labor force, the probability of labor solidarity against the capitalist class is diminished.

At the same time, orthodox Marxists argue, the members of the capitalist class benefit not only because they have created a reserved army of labor that is not united against them and the appropriation of surplus from the black labor force is greater than the exploitation rate of the white labor force,[7] but also because they can counteract ambitious claims of the white labor force for higher wages either by threatening to increase the average wage rate of black workers or by replacing segments of the white labor force with segments of the black labor force in special situations such as strikes. The weaker the national labor force, the more likely it is that it will be replaced by lower-paid black labor especially during organized strikes demanding wage increases and improved working conditions. In short, orthodox Marxists argue that racial antagonism is designed to be a "mask for privilege" that effectively conceals the efforts of the ruling class to exploit subordinate minority groups and divide the working class.

In interesting contrast to the orthodox Marxist approach, the split labor-market theory posits the view that rather than attempting to protect a segment of the laboring class, business "supports a liberal or *laissez faire* ideology that would permit all workers to compete freely in an open market. Such open competition would displace higher paid labor. Only under duress does business yield to a labor aristocracy [i.e., a privileged position for white workers]."[8]

The central hypothesis of the split labor-market theory is that racial antagonism first develops in a labor market split along racial lines. The term "antagonism" includes all aspects of intergroup conflict, from beliefs and ideologies (e.g., racism), to overt behavior (e.g., discrimination), to institutions (e.g., segregationist laws). A split labor market occurs when the price of labor for the same work differs for at least two groups, or would differ if they performed the same work. The price of labor "refers to labor's total cost to the employer, including not only wages, but the cost of recruitment, transportation, room and board, education, health care (if the employer must bear these), and the cost of labor unrest."[9]

There are three distinct classes in a split labor market: (1) business or employers; (2) higher-paid labor; and (3) cheaper labor. Conflict develops between these three classes because of different interests. The main goal of business or employers is to maintain as cheap a labor force as possible in order to compete effectively with other businesses and to maximize economic returns. Employers will often import laborers from other areas if local labor costs are too high or if there is a labor shortage. Whenever a labor shortage exists, higher-paid labor is in a good bargaining position. Accordingly, if business is able to attract cheaper labor to the market place, the interests of higher-paid labor are threatened. They may lose some of the privileges they enjoy, they may lose their bargaining power, and they may even lose their jobs. Moreover, the presence of cheaper labor in a particular job market may not only represent actual competition but potential competition as well. An "insignificant trickle" could be seen as the beginning of a major immigration. If the labor market is split along ethnic lines, for example,

if higher-paid labor is white and lower-paid labor is black, class antagonisms are transformed into racial antagonisms. Thus, "while much rhetoric of ethnic antagonism concentrates on ethnicity and race, it really in large measure (though probably not entirely) expresses this class conflict."[10]

In some cases members of the lower-paid laboring class, either from within the territorial boundaries of a given country or from another country, are drawn into or motivated to enter a labor market because they feel they can improve their standard of living. As Edna Bonacich points out, "the poorer the economy of the recruits, the less the inducement needed for them to enter the new labor market."[11] In other cases, individuals are forced into a new labor-market situation, such as the involuntary migration of blacks into a condition of slavery in the United States. In this connection, the greater the employer's control over lower-priced labor, the more threatening is lower-paid labor to higher-paid labor.

However, if more expensive labor is strong enough, that is, if it possesses the power resources to preserve its economic interests, it can prevent being replaced or undercut by cheaper labor. On the one hand it can exclude lower-paid labor from a given territory. "Exclusion movements clearly serve the interests of higher paid labor. Its standards are protected, while the capitalist class is deprived of cheaper labor."[12] On the other hand, if it is not possible for higher-paid labor to rely on exclusion (cheaper labor may be indigenous to the territory or may have been imported early in business-labor relations when higher-paid labor could not prevent the move) then it will institutionalize a system of ethnic stratification which could (1) monopolize skilled positions, thereby ensuring the effectiveness of strike action; (2) prevent cheaper labor from developing the skills necessary to compete with higher-paid labor (for example, by imposing barriers to equal access to education); and (3) deny cheaper labor the political resources that would enable them to undercut higher-paid labor through, say, governmental regulations. "In other words, the solution to the devastating potential of weak, cheap labor is, paradoxically, to weaken them further, until it is no longer in business' immediate interest to use them as replacement."[13] Thus, whereas orthodox Marxist arguments associate the development and institutionalization of racial stratification with the motivations and activities of the capitalist class, the split labor-market theory traces racial stratification directly to the powerful, higher-paid working class.

Implicit in both of these economic class theories is a power-conflict thesis associating the regulation of labor or wages with properties (ownership of land or capital, monopolization of skilled positions) that determine the scope and degree of a group's ability to influence behavior in the labor market. Furthermore, both theories clearly demonstrate the need to focus on the different ways and situations in which various segments of the dominant racial group perceive and respond to the subordinate racial group. However, as I examine the historical stages of race relations in the United States, I find that the patterns of black/white interaction do not consistently and sometimes do not conveniently conform to the propositions outlined in these explanations of racial antagonism. In some cases, the orthodox Marxian explanation seems more appropriate; in other instances, the split labor-market theory seems more appropriate; and in still others, neither theory can, in isolation, adequately explain black-white conflict.

If we restrict our attention for the moment to the struggle over economic resources, then the general pattern that seems to have characterized race relations in the United States during the preindustrial and industrial stages was that the economic elite segments of the white population have been principally responsible for those forms of racial inequality that entail the exploitation of labor (as in slavery), whereas whites in the lower strata have been largely responsible for those forms of imposed racial stratification that are designed to eliminate economic competition (as in job segregation). Moreover, in some situations, the capitalist class and white workers form an alliance to keep blacks suppressed. Accordingly, restrictive arguments to the effect that racial stratification was the work of the capitalist class or was due to the "victory" of higher-paid white labor obscure the dynamics of complex and variable patterns of black-white interaction.

However, if we ignore the more categorical assertions that attribute responsibility for racial stratification to a particular class and focus seriously on the analyses of interracial contact in the labor market, then I will be able to demonstrate that, depending on the historical situation, each of the economic class theories provides arguments that help to illuminate race relations during the preindustrial and industrial periods of black-white contact. By the same token, I hope to explain why these theories have little application to the third, and present, stage of modern industrial race relations. My basic argument is that the meaningful application of the arguments in each theory for any given historical period depends considerably on knowledge of the constraints imposed by the particular systems of production and by the particular laws and policies of the state during that period, constraints that shape the structural relations between racial and class groups and which thereby produce different patterns of intergroup interaction. . . .

The Influence of the System of Production

The term "system of production" not only refers to the technological basis of economic processes or, in Karl Marx's terms, the "forces of production," but it also implies the "social relations of production," that is, "the interaction (for example, through employment and property arrangement) into which men enter at a given level of the development of the forces of production."[14] As I previously indicated, different systems of production impose constraints on racial group interaction. In the remainder of this section I should like to provide a firmer analytical basis for this distinction as it applies specifically to the three stages of American race relations, incorporating in my discussion relevant theoretical points raised in the foregoing sections of this chapter.

It has repeatedly been the case that a non-manufacturing or plantation economy with a simple division of labor and a small aristocracy that dominates the economic and political life of a society has characteristically generated a paternalistic rather than a competitive form of race relations, and the antebellum South was no exception.[15] Paternalistic racial patterns reveal close symbiotic relationships marked by dominance and subservience, great social distance and little physical distance, and clearly symbolized rituals of racial etiquette. The southern white aristocracy created a split labor market along racial lines by enslaving blacks to perform tasks at a cheaper cost than free laborers of the dominant group. This preindustrial form of race relations was not based on the actions of dominant-group laborers, who, as we shall see, were relatively powerless to effect significant change in race relations during this period, but on the structure of the relations established by the aristocracy. Let me briefly amplify this point.

In the southern plantation economy, public power was overwhelmingly concentrated in the hands of the white aristocracy. This power was not only reflected in the control of economic resources and in the development of a juridical system that expressed the class interests of the aristocracy, but also in the way the aristocracy was able to impose its viewpoint on the larger society.[16] This is not to suggest that these aspects of public power have not been disproportionately controlled by the economic elite in modern industrialized Western societies; rather it indicates that the hegemony of the southern ruling elite was much greater in degree, not in kind, than in these societies. The southern elite's hegemony was embodied in an economy that required little horizontal or vertical mobility. Further, because of the absence of those gradations of labor power associated with complex divisions of labor, white workers in the antebellum and early postbellum South had little opportunity to challenge the control of the aristocracy. Because white laborers lacked power resources in the southern plantation economy, their influence on the form and quality of racial stratification was minimal throughout the antebellum and early postbellum periods. Racial stratification therefore primarily reflected the relationships established between blacks and the white aristocracy, relationships which were not characterized by competition for scarce resources but by the exploitation of black labor.[17] Social distance tended to be clearly symbolized by rituals of racial etiquette: gestures and behavior reflecting dominance and subservience. Consequently, any effort to impose a system of public segregation was superfluous. Furthermore, since the social gap between the aristocracy and black slaves was wide and stable, ideologies of racism played less of a role in the subordination of blacks than they subsequently did in the more competitive systems of race relations following the Civil War. In short, the relationship represented intergroup paternalism because it allowed for "close symbiosis and even intimacy, without any threat to status inequalities."[18] This was in sharp contrast to the more competitive forms of race relations that accompanied the development of industrial capitalism in the late nineteenth century and first few decades of the twentieth century (the industrial period of American race relations), wherein the complex division of labor and opportunities for greater mobility not only produced interaction, competition, and labor-market conflict between blacks and the white working class, but also provided the latter with superior resources (relative to those they possessed under the plantation economy) to exert greater influence on the form and content of racial stratification.

The importance of the system of production in understanding race relations is seen in a comparison of Brazil and the southern United States during the postslavery periods. In the United States, the southern economy experienced a fairly rapid rate of expansion during the late nineteenth century, thereby creating various middle level skilled and un-skilled positions that working-class whites attempted to monopolize for themselves. The efforts of white workers to eliminate black competition in the south generated an elaborate system of Jim Crow segregation that was reinforced by an ideology of biological racism. The white working class was aided not only by its numerical size, but also by its increasing accumulation of political resources that accompanied changes in its relation to the means of production.

As white workers gradually translated their increasing labor power into political power, blacks experienced greater restrictions in their efforts to achieve a satisfactory economic, political, and social life. In Brazil, on the other hand, the large Negro and mulatto population was not thrust into competition with the much smaller white population over access to higher-status positions because, as Marvin Harris notes, "there was little opportunity for any member of the lower class to move upward in the social hierarchy."[19] No economic-class group or racial group had much to gain by instituting a rigid system of racial segregation or cultivating an ideology of racial inferiority. Racial distinctions were insignificant to the landed aristocracy, who constituted a numerically small upper class in what was basically a sharply differentiated two-class society originally shaped during slavery. The mulattoes, Negroes, and poor whites were all in the same impoverished lower-ranking position. "The general economic stagnation which has been characteristic of lowland Latin America since the abolition of slavery," observes Marvin Harris, "tends to reinforce the pattern of pacific relationships among the various racial groups in the lower ranking levels of the social hierarchy. Not only were the poor whites out-numbered by the mulattoes and Negroes, but there was little of a significant material nature to struggle over in view of the generally static condition of the economy."[20] Accordingly, in Brazil, segregation, discrimination, and racist ideologies failed to crystallize in the first several decades following the end of slavery. More recently, however, industrial-ization has pushed Brazil toward a competitive type of race relations, particularly the southern region (for example, São Paulo) which has experienced rapid industrialization and has blacks in economic competition with many lower-status white immigrants.[21]

Whereas the racial antagonism in the United States during the period of industrial race relations (such as the Jim Crow segregation movement in the South and the race riots in northern cities) tended to be either directly or indirectly related to labor-market conflicts, racial antagonism in the period of modern industrial relations tends to originate outside the economic order and to have little connection with labor-market strife. Basic changes in the system of production have produced a segmented labor structure in which blacks are either isolated in the relatively non-unionized, low-paying, basically undesirable jobs of the noncorporate sector, or occupy the higher-paying corporate and government industry positions in which job competition is either controlled by powerful unions or is restricted to the highly trained and educated, regardless of race. If there is a basis for labor-market conflict in the modern industrial period, it is most probably related to the affirmative action programs originating from the civil rights legislation of the 1960s. However, since affirmative action programs are designed to improve job opportunities for the talented and educated, their major impact has been in the higher-paying jobs of the expanding government sector and the corporate sector. The sharp increase of the more privileged blacks in these industries has been facilitated by the combination of affirmative action and rapid industry growth. Indeed despite the effectiveness of affirmative action programs the very expansion of these sectors of the economy has kept racial friction over higher-paying corporate and government jobs to a minimum.

Unlike the occupational success achieved by the more talented and educated blacks, those in the black underclass find themselves locked in the low-paying and dead-end jobs of the noncorporate industries, jobs which are not in high demand and which therefore do not generate racial competition or strife among the national black and white labor force. Many of these jobs go unfilled, and employers often have to turn to cheap labor from Mexico and Puerto Rico. As Nathan Glazer has pointed out, "Expectations have changed, and fewer blacks and whites today will accept a life at menial labor with no hope for advancement, as their fathers and older brothers did and as European immigrants did."[22]

Thus in the modern industrial era neither the corporate or government sectors nor the noncorporate low-wage sector provide the basis for the kind of interracial competition and conflict that has traditionally plagued the labor market in the United States. This, then, is the basis for my earlier contention that the economic class theories which associate labor-market conflicts with racial antagonism have little application to the present period of modern industrial race relations.

The Polity and American Race Relations

If the patterned ways in which racial groups have interacted historically have been shaped in major measure by different systems of production, they have also been undeniably influenced by the changing policies and laws of the state. For analytical purposes, it would be a mistake to treat the influences of the polity and the economy as if they were separate and unrelated. The legal and political systems in the antebellum South were effectively used as instruments of the slaveholding elite to strengthen and legitimate the institution of slavery. But as industrialization altered the economic class structure in the postbellum South, the organizing power and political consciousness of the white lower class increased and its members were able to gain enough control of the political and juridical systems to legalize a new system of racial domination (Jim Crow segregation) that clearly reflected their class interests.

In effect, throughout the preindustrial period of race relations and the greater portion of the industrial period the role of the polity was to legitimate, reinforce, and regulate patterns of racial inequality. However, it would be unwarranted to assume that the relationship between the economic and political aspects of race necessarily implies that the latter is simply a derivative phenomenon based on the more fundamental processes of the former. The increasing intervention, since the mid-twentieth century, of state and federal government agencies in resolving or mediating racial conflicts has convincingly demonstrated the political system's autonomy in handling contemporary racial problems. Instead of merely formalizing existing racial alignments as in previous periods, the political system has, since the initial state and municipal legislation of the 1940s, increasingly created changes leading to the erosion of traditional racial alignments; in other words, instead of reinforcing racial barriers created during the preindustrial and industrial periods, the political system in recent years has tended to promote racial equality.

Thus, in the previous periods the polity was quite clearly an instrument of the white population in suppressing blacks. The government's racial practices varied, as I indicated above, depending on which segment of the white population was able to assert its class interests. However, in the past two decades the interests of the black population have been significantly reflected in the racial policies of the government, and this change is one of the clearest indications that the racial balance of power has been significantly altered. Since the early 1940s the black population has steadily gained political resources and, with the help of sympathetic white allies, has shown an increasing tendency to utilize these resources in promoting or protecting its group interests.

By the mid-twentieth century the black vote had proved to be a major vehicle for political pressure. The black vote not only influenced the outcome of national elections but many congressional, state, and municipal elections as well. Fear of the Negro vote produced enactment of public accommodation and fair employment practices laws in northern and western municipalities and states prior to the passage of federal civil rights legislation in 1964. This political resurgence for black Americans increased their sense of power, raised their expectations, and provided the foundation for the proliferation of demands which shaped the black revolt during the 1960s. But there were other factors that helped to buttress Negro demands and contributed to the developing sense of power and rising expectations, namely, a growing, politically active black middle class following World War II and the emergence of the newly independent African states.

The growth of the black middle class was concurrent with the growth of the black urban population. It was in the urban areas, with their expanding occupational opportunities, that a small but significant number of blacks were able to upgrade their occupations, increase their income, and improve their standard of living. The middle-class segment of an oppressed minority is most likely to participate in a drive for social justice that is disciplined and sustained. In the early phases of the civil rights movement, the black middle class channeled its energies through organizations such as the National Association for the Advancement of Colored People, which emphasized developing political resources and successful litigation through the courts. These developments were paralleled by the attack against traditional racial alignments in other parts of the world. The emerging newly independent African states led the assault. In America, the so-called "leader of the free world," the manifestation of racial tension and violence has been a constant source of embarrassment to national government officials. This sensitivity to world opinion made the national government more vulnerable to pressures of black protest at the very time when blacks had the greatest propensity to protest.

The development of black political resources that made the government more sensitive to Negro demands, the motivation and morale of the growing black middle class that resulted in the political drive for racial equality, and the emergence of the newly independent African states that increased the federal government's vulnerability to civil rights pressures all combined to create a new sense of power among black Americans and to raise their expectations as they prepared to enter the explosive decade of the 1960s. The national government was also aware of this developing sense of power and responded to the pressures of black protest in the 1960s with an unprecedented series of legislative enactments to protect black civil rights.

The problem for blacks today, in terms of government practices, is no longer one of legalized racial inequality. Rather the problem for blacks, especially the black underclass, is that the government is not organized to deal with the new barriers imposed by structural changes in the economy. With the passage of equal employment legislation and the authorization of affirmative action programs the government has helped clear the path for more privileged blacks, who have the requisite education and training, to enter the mainstream of American occupations. However, such government programs do not confront the impersonal economic barriers confronting members of the black underclass, who have been effectively screened out of the corporate and government industries. And the very attempts of the government to eliminate traditional racial barriers through such programs as affirmative action have had the unintentional effect of contributing to the growing economic class divisions within the black community.

Class Stratification and Changing Black Experiences

The problems of black Americans have always been compounded because of their low position in both the economic order (the average economic class position of blacks as a group) and the social order (the social prestige or honor accorded individual blacks because of their ascribed racial status). It is of course true that the low economic position of blacks has helped to shape the categorical social definitions attached to blacks as a racial group, but it is also true that the more blacks become segmented in terms of economic class position, the more their concerns about the social significance of race will vary.

In the preindustrial period of American race relations there was of course very little variation in the economic class position of blacks. The system of racial caste oppression relegated virtually all blacks to the bottom of the economic class hierarchy. Moreover, the social definitions of racial differences were heavily influenced by the ideology of racism and the doctrine of paternalism, both of which clearly assigned a subordinate status for blacks vis-à-vis whites. Occasionally, a few individual free blacks would emerge and accumulate some wealth or property, but they were the overwhelming exception. Thus the uniformly low economic class position of blacks reinforced and, in the eyes of most whites, substantiated the social definitions that asserted Negroes were culturally and biogenetically inferior to whites. The uniformly low economic class position of blacks also removed the basis for any meaningful distinction between race issues and class issues within the black community.

The development of a black middle class accompanied the change from a preindustrial to an industrial system of production. Still, despite the fact that some blacks were able to upgrade their occupation and increase their education and income, there were severe limits on the areas in which blacks could in fact advance. Throughout most of the industrial period of race relations, the growth of the black middle class occurred because of the expansion of institutions created to serve the needs of a growing urbanized black population. The black doctor, lawyer, teacher, minister, businessman, mortician, excluded from the white community, was able to create a

niche in the segregated black community. Although the income levels and life-styles of the black professionals were noticeably and sometimes conspicuously different from those of the black masses, the two groups had one basic thing in common, a racial status contemptuously regarded by most whites in society. If E. Franklin Frazier's analysis of the black bourgeosie is correct, the black professionals throughout the industrial period of American race relations tended to react to their low position in the social order by an ostentatious display of material possessions and a conspicuous effort to disassociate themselves from the black masses.[23]

Still, as long as the members of the black middle class were stigmatized by their racial status; as long as they were denied the social recognition accorded their white counterparts; more concretely, as long as they remained restricted in where they could live, work, socialize, and be educated, race would continue to be a far more salient and important issue in shaping their sense of group position than their economic class position. Indeed, it was the black middle class that provided the leadership and generated the momentum for the civil rights movement during the mid-twentieth century. The influence and interests of this class were clearly reflected in the way the race issues were defined and articulated. Thus, the concept of "freedom" quite clearly implied, in the early stages of the movement, the right to swim in certain swimming pools, to eat in certain restaurants, to attend certain movie theaters, and to have the same voting privileges as whites. These basic concerns were reflected in the 1964 Civil Rights Bill which helped to create the illusion that, when the needs of the black middle class were met, so were the needs of the entire black community.

However, although the civil rights movement initially failed to address the basic needs of the members of the black lower class, it did increase their awareness of racial oppression, heighten their expectations about improving race relations, and increase their impatience with existing racial arrangements. These feelings were dramatically manifested in a series of violent ghetto outbursts that rocked the nation throughout the late 1960s. These outbreaks constituted the most massive and sustained expression of lower-class black dissatisfaction in the nation's history. They also forced the political system to recognize the problems of human survival and de facto segregation in the nation's ghettoes—problems pertaining to unemployment and underemployment, inferior ghetto schools, and deteriorated housing.

However, in the period of modern industrial race relations, it would be difficult indeed to comprehend the plight of inner-city blacks by exclusively focusing on racial discrimination. For in a very real sense, the current problems of lower-class blacks are substantially related to fundamental structural changes in the economy. A history of discrimination and oppression created a huge black underclass, and the technological and economic revolutions have combined to insure it a permanent status.

As the black middle class rides on the wave of political and social changes, benefiting from the growth of employment opportunities in the growing corporate and government sectors of the economy, the black underclass falls behind the larger society in every conceivable respect. The economic and political systems in the United States have demonstrated remarkable flexibility in allowing talented blacks to fill positions of prestige and influence at the same time that these systems have shown persistent rigidity in handling the problems of lower-class blacks. As a result, for the first time in American history class issues can meaningfully compete with race issues in the way blacks develop or maintain a sense of group position.[24]

Conclusion

The foregoing sections of this chapter present an outline and a general analytical basis for the arguments that will be systematically explored [elsewhere].[25] I have tried to show that race relations in American society have been historically characterized by three major stages and that each stage is represented by a unique form of racial interaction which is shaped by the particular arrangement of the economy and the polity. My central argument is that different systems of production and/or different policies of the state have imposed different constraints on the way in which racial groups interact—constraints that have structured the relations between racial groups and produced dissimilar contexts not only for the manifestation of racial antagonisms but also for racial-group access to rewards and privileges. I emphasized in this connection that in the preindustrial and industrial periods of American race relations the systems of production primarily shaped the patterns of racial stratification and the role of the polity was to legitimate, reinforce, or regulate these patterns. In the modern industrial period, however, both the system of production and the polity assume major importance in creating new patterns of race relations and in altering the context of racial strife. Whereas the preindustrial and industrial stages were principally related to group struggles over economic resources as different segments of the white population overtly sought to create and solidify economic racial domination (ranging from the exploitation of black labor in the preindustrial period to the elimination of black competition for jobs in the industrial period) through various forms of political, juridical, and social discrimination; in the modern industrial period fundamental economic and political changes have made economic class position more important than race in determining black chances for occupational mobility. Finally, I have outlined the importance of racial norms or belief systems, especially as they relate to the general problem of race and class conflict in the preindustrial and industrial periods.

My argument that race relations in America have moved from economic racial oppression to a form of class subordination for the less privileged blacks is not meant to suggest that racial conflicts have disappeared or have even been substantially reduced. On the contrary, the basis of such conflicts have shifted from the economic sector to the sociopolitical order and therefore do not play as great a role in determining the life chances of individual black Americans as in the previous periods of overt economic racial oppression.

Notes

1. See, William J. Wilson, *Power, Racism and Privilege: Race Relations in Theoretical and Sociohistorical Perspectives* (New York: The Free Press, 1973).

2. In Marxist terminology, the "superstructure" refers to the arrangements of beliefs, norms, ideologies, and noneconomic institutions.

3. However, not all theorists who emphasize the importance of economic class in explanations of race relations simply relegate problems of race to the superstructure. The Marxist scholars Michael Burawoy and Eugene Genovese recognize the reciprocal influence between the economic class structure and aspects of the superstructure (belief systems, political systems, etc.), a position which I also share and which is developed more fully in subsequent sections of this chapter. See Eugene D. Genovese, *Roll, Jordan, Roll: The World the Slaves Made* (New York: Pantheon, 1974); idem, *In Red and Black: Marxian Explorations in Southern and Afro-American History* (New York: Vintage Press, 1971); and Michael Burawoy, "Race, Class, and Colonialism," *Social and Economic Studies* 23 (1974): 521–50.

4. Oliver C. Cox, *Caste, Class and Race: A Study in Social Dynamics* (Garden City, New York: Doubleday, 1948); Paul A. Baran and Paul M. Sweezy, *Monopoly Capital: An Essay on the American Economic and Social Order* (Harmondsworth: Penguin, 1966); Michael Reich, "The Economics of Racism," in *Problems in Political Economy*, ed. David M. Gordon (Lexington, Mass.: Heath, 1971); and M. Nikolinakos, "Notes on an Economic Theory of Racism," *Race: A Journal of Race and Group Relations* 14 (1973): 365–81.

5. Edna Bonacich, "A Theory of Ethnic Antagonism: The Split Labor Market," *American Sociological Review* 37 (October 1972): 547–59; idem, "Abolition, The Extension of Slavery and the Position of Free Blacks: A Study of Split Labor Markets in the United States," *American Journal of Sociology* 81 (1975): 601–28.

6. For examples of alternative and less orthodox Marxist explanations of race, see Eugene D. Gen-

ovese, *The Political Economy of Slavery: Studies in the Economy and Society of the Slave South* (New York: Pantheon, 1966); idem, *The World the Slaveholders Made: Two Essays in Interpretation* (New York: Pantheon, 1969); idem, *In Red and Black;* idem, *Roll, Jordan, Roll;* and Burawoy, "Race, Class, and Colonialism."

7. "Exploitation," in Marxian terminology, refers to the difference between the wages workers receive and the value of the goods they produce. The size of this difference, therefore, determines the degree of exploitation.

8. Bonacich, "A Theory of Ethnic Antagonism," p. 557.

9. Ibid., p. 549.

10. Ibid., p. 553.

11. Ibid., p. 549.

12. Ibid., p. 555.

13. Ibid., p. 556.

14. Neil J. Smelser, *Karl Marx on Society and Social Change* (Chicago: University of Chicago Press, 1974), p. xiv. According to Smelser, Marx used the notions "forces of production" and "social relations of production" as constituting the "mode of production." However, in Marx's writings the mode of production is often discussed as equivalent only to the "forces of production." To avoid confusion, I have chosen the term "system of production" which denotes the interrelation of the forces of production and the mode of production.

15. Pierre L. van den Berghe, *Race and Racism: A Comparative Perspective* (New York: John Wiley and Sons, 1967), p. 26.

16. See, for example, Genovese, *Roll, Jordan, Roll.*

17. An exception to this pattern occurred in the cities of the antebellum South, where nonslaveholding whites played a major role in the development of urban segregation. However, since an overwhelming majority of the population resided in rural areas, race relations in the antebellum southern cities were hardly representative of the region.

18. van den Berghe, *Race and Racism*, p. 27.

19. Marvin Harris, *Patterns of Race in the Americas* (New York: Walker, 1964), p. 96.

20. Ibid., p. 96.

21. van den Berghe, *Race and Racism*, p. 28.

22. Nathan Glazer, "Blacks and Ethnic Groups: The Difference, and the Political Difference It Makes," in *Key Issues in the Afro-American Experience*, ed. Nathan I. Huggins, Martin Kilson, and Daniel M. Fox (New York: Harcourt Brace Jovanovich, 1971), 2: 209.

23. E. Franklin Frazier, *Black Bourgeoisie* (New York: The Free Press, 1957). See also Nathan Hare, *Black Anglo-Saxons* (New York: Collier, 1965).

24. The theoretical implications of this development for ethnic groups in general are discussed by Milton Gordon under the concept "ethclass." See Milton M. Gordon, *Assimilation in American Life* (New York: Oxford University Press, 1964).

[25]. See William Julius Wilson, *The Declining Significance of Race: Blacks and Changing American Institutions* (Chicago and London: University of Chicago Press, 1978).

CHARLES HIRSCHMAN AND C. MATTHEW SNIPP

The State of the American Dream: Race and Ethnic Socioeconomic Inequality in the United States, 1970–1990

America is a nation of immigrants, but not all immigrant groups have experienced the same reception and opportunities or have been accorded the same influence. American ideals and cultural values were largely shaped by the Anglo heritage of the founding settlers. For most of the nation's history, those ideals have continued to define the American experience for subsequent waves of arrivals. The millions of new immigrants were expected—as were native American Indians and African slaves—to assimilate into American society and to conform to Anglo-American ideals and values. They were also expected to discard their ethnic heritage as quickly as possible. Economic incentives, including hope for their own and their children's upward mobility, motivated the immigrants' acceptance of cultural change and adaptation.

Despite the massive immigration during the late nineteenth and early twentieth centuries, the image of American society as an extension of English society persisted throughout the first six decades of the twentieth century. As we near the end of the twentieth century and envision the future of American society, the patterns in the first half of the century—the exchange of cultural conformity for a chance at upward mobility, the American Dream—seem obsolete. There appears to be less societal pressure on new immigrants to surrender their culture, language, and traditions. In fact, group identities, including race, ethnicity, and gender, now frame claims to political power and political participation. Sensing this shift in political roles, other groups, such as American Indians, have made a concerted effort to assert the importance of their ethnic ancestry. Many traditionalists see these trends as divisive forces, while others view the emphasis on cultural diversity as the defining character of contemporary American society.

It is important to assess the state of the American Dream as the twentieth century ends—to chart where we have been and to anticipate where we are going. In this chapter, we analyze patterns and trends in social and economic inequality among the major racial and ethnic groups in American society. We track occupational and earnings attainment among men from seven major racial and ethnic groups between 1970 and 1990. The years from 1970 to 1990 represent an especially im-

Originally published in 1999. Please see complete source information beginning on page 891.

portant period in American history, given the government activism of the preceding decade. In the 1960s, federal and local governments enacted civil rights laws, created affirmative action procedures, and developed equal employment opportunity programs. For the first time in American history, public policy prohibited discrimination against Americans who did not fit Anglo standards of appearance, beliefs, and behavior. From the vantage point of the present, we look back over history to see if there has been progress in the uplifting of groups that historically have been outside the economic mainstream.

We find that there has indeed been progress in the reduction of socioeconomic inequality across race and ethnic groups over the twenty years from 1970 to 1990. With the exception of Japanese Americans, however, there remain wide socioeconomic gaps between minority populations and the majority. In 1989, African Americans, Latinos, and American Indians had an income gap from the majority population that was still around $10,000 for working men—only slightly less than the gap in 1969. . . .

Inequality in American Society

The persistence of inequality is linked to the ideal of *assimilation*. The stratification literature in sociology (and especially studies of status attainment) has traditionally viewed a reduction in economic differentials as an important gauge of socioeconomic assimilation (Hirschman 1983). For example, recent data from the General Social Survey show that black-white differences persist although their magnitude has declined (Grusky and DiPrete 1990). The presence of black-white differences in education, income, occupational status, or other measures of economic well-being are prima facie evidence that socioeconomic assimilation has not occurred.

Over the years, the ideal of assimilation has endured a hail of criticism. Some of these criticisms were anticipated, even prior to the development of assimilation theory. Horace

Kallen (1924) argued that immigrants should not be expected to surrender their culture and identity as a condition for participation in American society. Critics, in the 1960s, argued that ethnicity plays a central role in the lives of even the most acculturated groups (Glazer and Moynihan 1970). For many groups in American society, ethnicity is largely a symbolic construction and has a relatively minor role in their lives (Gans 1979; Waters 1990). Alba (1985), for example, wrote about the "twilight of ethnicity" among Americans of Italian descent. More recently, the phenomenon of ethnic resurgence has challenged the idea that assimilation is inevitable. There has been a remarkable revival of ethnic awareness, even among groups whose cultural identities were once considered destined for extinction, such as American Indians (Cornell 1988; Nagel 1996).

Why does ethnicity seem to matter for some groups and not for others? Gordon's theory suggests that prejudice and discrimination are critical. Acculturation is not sufficient for full participation in American society as long as "gatekeepers" continue to restrict access to neighborhoods, primary group associations, and opportunities for economic mobility. One prominent hypothesis is that "race"—physiological differences in skin color and other outward features—defines the essential difference between minority groups that are allowed to assimilate and those that are not (Cox 1948; Jordan 1974). Other perspectives suggest that racism (the differential treatment of persons of different "races") is contingent on historical conditions and that American society holds the potential to assimilate persons of different races as well as of different ethnic groups (Myrdal 1944; Wilson 1978).

There is a large body of empirical research on various dimensions of assimilation, including studies of socioeconomic assimilation, segregation in schools and housing, intermarriage, and prejudice (Hirschman 1983). Socioeconomic assimilation (as measured by occupational and earnings attainment) is widely considered an indicator of secondary-group structural assimilation (Gordon 1964;

Lieberson 1980). Although it is not possible to present a comprehensive review of the empirical studies of ethnic assimilation in American society, there are some important themes in the literature on socioeconomic assimilation that inform and guide our study.

Our analysis compares Anglo and other "white" Americans with African Americans; American Indians; Chinese, Filipino, and Japanese Americans; and Americans of Hispanic origin. European immigrants and their descendants have generally enjoyed considerable upward mobility throughout the twentieth century (Greeley 1978; Lieberson 1980). This is not to say that none were affected by bigotry and discrimination. On the contrary, there is a long history of ethnic antagonism in this country (e.g., anti-Semitic and anti-Catholic sentiment; see Baltzell 1964; Higham 1970). Nevertheless, the large socioeconomic differences that existed among these European ethnics in 1900 had virtually disappeared by the 1960s (Duncan and Duncan 1968; Neidert and Farley 1985; Lieberson and Waters 1988).

Compared with immigrants from Europe, American Indians, African Americans, and nonwhite immigrants from Asia and Latin America have not fared as well. The American Indian population is small and has experienced discrimination, forced isolation, and intense pressure from the federal government to assimilate into American society. Despite these efforts, many (perhaps most) American Indians remain outside the mainstream (i.e., the modern, largely urban) U.S. economy (Hoxie 1984; Fixico 1986; Gundlach and Roberts 1978; Snipp 1989; Snipp and Sandefur 1989). Racial discrimination and segregation have been major barriers to the advancement of blacks in American society (Duncan 1969; Featherman and Hauser 1976; Farley and Allen 1987; Massey and Denton 1993).

Hispanic and Asian groups warrant separate consideration, as they have experienced explosive population growth since the immigration reforms of 1965 and 1986 (Chiswick and Sullivan 1995). The Latino population (particularly Mexican Americans) is an old and established American ethnic group. During the 1960s and 1970s they also comprised the largest and fastest-growing immigrant group. It is difficult to make generalizations about the assimilation of Latinos because of their ethnic heterogeneity and the disparate circumstances of their immigration, internal migration, and settlement patterns (Bean and Tienda 1987). Even within a small group like Cuban Americans, there are substantial differences with respect to the circumstances of their immigration and the extent to which they have become assimilated (Portes and Bach 1985).

Although there is considerable diversity in the Latino population, there are also commonalties such as language. However, compared with Latinos, the so-called Asian and Pacific Islander population has spectacular diversity. Except for the continent of origin, there are few visible similarities. Many of these groups are exceedingly small in number, making it difficult to obtain reliable data on their socioeconomic characteristics. However, in the 1980s, Asian and Pacific Islanders were the fastest growing segment of the American population (Barringer, Gardner, and Levin 1993).

Asians, especially those of Japanese and Chinese descent, pose an anomaly for assimilationist thinking about racial and ethnic inequality. Despite long histories of discrimination and persecution, Americans of Japanese and Chinese descent have, in fact, attained even *higher* levels of social and economic well-being than the white population. Only part of this success can be linked to their high levels of schooling and concentration in urban areas (Hirschman and Wong 1984; Nee and Sanders 1985). Some observers who attribute their success to hard work and ingenuity describe Asians as "model minorities." But the evidence of the successful assimilation of all groups of Asians is mixed. Some recent Asian immigrants, especially those who were forced to flee in the aftermath of the Vietnam War, have had a much more difficult experience. Whether these disadvantages will persist into the future is an open question.

Finally, there is compelling evidence to suggest that there is growing socioeconomic diversity *within* each of these groups—African Americans, Latinos, American Indians, and Asians. For example, studies have shown that in recent years, some segments of the African American population have enjoyed greater opportunities and attained a middle-class lifestyle, while many more are left behind in inner city ghettos (Landry 1987; Wilson 1987; Farley and Allen 1987). The increasing socioeconomic inequality within minority group populations is a crucial issue (but is not addressed directly in our subsequent analysis).

In this research, we measure the socioeconomic differences between groups and estimate how much of the interethnic gap can be "explained" by antecedent characteristics. Interethnic inequality is measured as the differences between the mean occupational and earnings attainment of each minority group (African Americans, American Indians, Chinese, Japanese, Filipinos, and Latinos) and those of non-Hispanic whites (Hirschman 1980).

Data and Methods

Data

We use data from the Public Use Microdata Sample (PUMS) files of the decennial censuses of 1970, 1980, and 1990. These data permit us to examine recent trends in the socioeconomic achievements of seven racial and ethnic minorities. Census data have virtues and liabilities. Large samples are a primary virtue. They allow us to study relatively small populations that are usually not represented in national surveys. Our analyses include comparisons of the socioeconomic characteristics of whites, African Americans, Latinos, Japanese, Chinese, Filipinos, and American Indians. The primary liability of census data is the paucity of background variables that might explain relative levels and trends in race and ethnic inequality.

We restrict the sample to men between the ages of twenty-five to sixty-four who were working at the time of the census and received positive earnings the previous year. This sample does not completely represent these ethnic populations or even all adult men in these ethnic groups. But important theoretical and practical considerations led us to restrict the analysis to this subset of the population.

First, women's roles, and particularly their participation in the economy, have changed dramatically since 1970. The question of gender stratification is intertwined with changes in racial and ethnic stratification in such complex ways that a full study of the topic would exceed the scope of this chapter. Second, the age range was dictated by the fact that we are most interested in persons who are *economically active*. Many persons younger than twenty-five years old are either still in school or just entering the workforce. Persons age sixty-five and older are likely to be retired or very close to retirement. Third, we selected men who were employed in order to facilitate comparisons with earlier studies of race and ethnic assimilation (Duncan 1969; Hirschman and Wong 1984). These restrictions limit our results to a select segment of the population, but other work leads us to believe that our estimates of ethnic differences will be conservative. In our prior study, we found that the restricted sample (only those in the labor force and with earnings last year) excluded 15 percent of white men in the working years, but excluded 25 percent of black men (Hirschman and Wong 1984, 589). Ethnic differences reported below would in all likelihood be larger if we included persons who were not active members of the workforce.

Variables

Our study focuses on ethnic differences in two indicators of economic well-being: occupational status and earnings, and changes in these indicators from 1970 to 1990. We estimate a series of regression models that include age, education, residence, immigration status, and other variables as covariates. A complete list and description of these variables is presented in Table 1. Our measure of occupational status is the Duncan Socioeconomic In-

TABLE 1
Definition and Measurement of Demographic and Socioeconomic Characteristics

Ethnicity	Self-reported racial identification. Hispanic is self-identified in a separate item in the 1980 and 1990 censuses and based on a composite measure in the 1970 census. Whites are non-Hispanic whites; black Hispanics are coded black.
Age	Age at last birthday: 25–34; 35–44; 45–64.
Birthplace/length of U.S. residence	A composite measure based on country of birth and place of residence five years ago. Coded as native born; foreign born, in U.S. five years ago; foreign born, not in U.S. five years ago.
Place of residence	State or region of residence April 1, 1970, 1980, 1990. Coded for California; New York; Hawaii; South, metropolitan area; South, nonmetropolitan area; rest of U.S., metropolitan; rest of U.S., nonmetropolitan.
Years of schooling	Number of years of formal schooling completed. Coded as 0–8; 9–11; 12; 13–15; 16 or more.
Occupational SEI	Duncan's Socioeconomic Index, updated for 1980 and 1990.
Sector	Composite variable based on class of worker and industry classification. Coded as self-employed; government employed; retail trade, not self-employed; other periphery, not self-employed, not government employed, not in retail trade; other core, not self-employed, not government employed.
Weeks worked last year	Number of weeks worked in 1969, 1979, and 1989. Coded as less than fifty weeks, fifty or more weeks.
Hours worked last week	Hours worked during the week before the census (April 1). Coded as less than forty, forty, more than forty.
Earnings	Total income received from wages and salaries, self-employment income from farm and nonfarm sources. Earners with zero or negative incomes were excluded from each sample.

dex (SEI), which has been updated to reflect changes in the occupational structures reflected in the 1980 and 1990 censuses (Duncan 1961; Hauser and Warren 1997). Earnings are defined as wage and salary income as well as income received from farm or nonfarm self-employment. We use the consumer price index to adjust for inflation and express income in constant 1989 dollars.

Many of our independent variables are conventionally scaled, such as education, which is measured in years of completed schooling. However, there are several others which merit clarification. We use self-reported responses to the "race" question on the census form to create ethnic categories. We added an additional category for Hispanic. In 1970, this item was a composite based on Spanish surname, Puerto Rican birthplace or parentage, and Spanish language. For 1980 and 1990, the Hispanic category was based on a self-identification question on Spanish or His-

panic origin. The white category is the residual and properly refers to non-Hispanic whites.

We combined the variables for place of birth and "place of residence 5 years ago" to construct a measure of immigrant status. Foreign-born persons who were not living in the United States five years before the decennial census (1965, 1975, and 1985) are presumed to be recent immigrants. Place of residence is measured with a classification that uses information on region, state, and metropolitan location. This coding was used previously by Hirschman and Wong (1984) in an attempt to identify geographical locations of ethnic concentrations and of greater and lesser economic opportunity.

The economic sector variable identifies those who are self-employed—a common means of economic adaptation for immigrants—and those in retail trade (a low-wage sector). The balance are classified according to a widely used classification for core and periphery industries (Tolbert, Horan, and Beck 1980). The measures for residence and sector are admittedly crude approximations, but we contend that they reflect differential access to opportunities in the American stratification system.

Any empirical analysis requires compromises based on the quality of data and measurement. We acknowledge that the Hispanic category covers a broad array of ethnic heritages, but inconsistent measurement across the three censuses and small numbers in particular groups do not permit disaggregation. An equally thorny problem concerns the difficulty of separating out the impact of immigration and ethnicity. Major fractions of the Hispanic and Asian populations are foreign born whereas almost all blacks, American Indians, and a majority of whites are native born. One solution would be to limit our analysis to native-born ethnic populations, but this would exclude significant shares (sometime a majority) of some ethnic groups.

Analytical Strategy

We present descriptive data in Table 2. Equations in Tables 3 and 4 model the economic well-being of ethnic minorities, estimating three sets of ethnic effects: (1) gross, (2) total, and (3) direct and indirect effects. The *gross effect* is the level of ethnic inequality between whites and ethnic minorities on either Duncan SEI points or 1990 dollars. The *total effect* is the level of ethnic inequality net of age and birthplace. The remaining effects are based on a detailed decomposition of the total effect of ethnicity on attainment. *Direct effects* measure the level of ethnic inequality on occupational attainment and earnings after the effects of the remaining covariates (e.g., residence, education, and industrial sector) are removed. *Indirect effects* are the effects of ethnicity on occupational attainment and earnings that are mediated through the covariates in our models. We calculate indirect effects by estimating successive regression equations and subtracting the ethnic coeffi-

cients with the intervening variable from the ethnic coefficients in the preceding equation without the intervening variable (Alwin and Hauser 1975).

Results: Ethnic Differences in Socioeconomic Attainments

Table 2[1] shows the means and standard deviations for SEI and earnings for each ethnic group for the years 1970, 1980, and 1990. The SEI and earnings of Japanese workers and the SEI of the Chinese exceed those of the white sample. On the other hand, the earnings and occupational status of Hispanics, blacks, American Indians, and, to a lesser degree, Filipinos are well below the earnings and occupational status of whites.

The results are remarkably stable. The rankings of groups on SEI and earnings are virtually *unchanged* between 1970 and 1990. The average SEI of all groups increased between 1970 and 1990. Most of the gains were in the four- to six-point range except for Japanese workers who gained nine points. There was little net change in the earnings hierarchy. However, the pattern is more mixed than that for occupational status. In constant dollars, white earnings were stagnant from 1970 to 1990. Blacks, on the other hand, enjoyed modest gains in each decade since 1970. The same is true for Japanese workers. Other groups experienced modest gains in one decade and declines in another. This instability might be the result of compositional differences due to immigration, changing racial self-identification (in the case of American Indians), or reporting errors in the earnings data.

Models of Ethnic Stratification, 1970–90

The patterns in Table 2 reveal the relative status (and change in status) of ethnic minorities in American society. They do not take into account ethnic differences in education, place of

TABLE 2

Indicators of Socioeconomic Attainment among Men Aged Twenty-Five to Sixty-Four by Ethnicity: 1970, 1980, and 1990

	Mean SEI			Mean Annual Earnings*			N		
	1970	1980	1990	1970	1980	1990	1970	1980	1990
White	36.5	39.4	40.1	$35,125	$35,278	$35,523	3,139	3,063	3,013
Black	24.0	28.3	30.2	$20,436	$23,061	$23,172	2,726	2,540	2,482
Am. Ind.	27.4	31.9	31.2	$22,149	$25,925	$21,511	939	2,272	2,585
Japanese	38.4	44.7	47.4	$35,429	$37,205	$42,750	1,130	1,647	3,037
Chinese	42.9	46.7	46.1	$32,243	$31,424	$32,017	911	1,859	2,977
Filipino	33.7	39.1	38.2	$25,044	$30,463	$28,945	611	1,379	3,029
Hispanic	28.6	29.7	32.7	$27,304	$23,797	$25,760	1,394	2,231	2,841

	Standard Deviation (SEI)			Coefficient of Variation (SEI)			Standard Deviation (earnings)			Coefficient of Variation (earnings)		
	1970	1980	1990	1970	1980	1990	1970	1980	1990	1970	1980	1990
White	20.0	20.5	20.9	0.55	0.52	0.52	23,726	23,042	31,477	0.68	0.65	0.89
Black	13.9	16.4	17.7	0.58	0.58	0.59	12,500	14,898	18,127	0.61	0.65	0.78
Am. Ind.	16.4	18.3	17.6	0.60	0.57	0.56	16,054	19,334	17,293	0.72	0.75	0.80
Japanese	21.9	21.3	20.9	0.57	0.48	0.44	22,189	23,245	33,909	0.63	0.62	0.79
Chinese	24.1	23.5	23.2	0.56	0.50	0.50	22,959	24,307	30,035	0.71	0.77	0.94
Filipino	23.2	22.7	21.2	0.69	0.58	0.55	17,473	23,807	26,332	0.70	0.78	0.91
Hispanic	17.5	17.5	18.8	0.61	0.59	0.57	19,561	17,163	23,803	0.72	0.72	0.92

	Ratio of SEI to White Mean			White Minority Gap (SEI)			Ratio of Mean Earnings to White Mean			White Minority Gap (earnings in thousands of dollars)		
	1970	1980	1990	1970	1980	1990	1970	1980	1990	1970	1980	1990
White	100	100	100	—	—	—	100	100	100	—	—	—
Black	66	72	75	−12.5	−11.1	−9.9	58	65	65	−$14.7	−$12.2	−$12.4
Am. Ind.	75	81	78	−9.1	−7.5	−8.9	63	73	61	−$13.0	−$9.4	−$14.0
Japanese	105	113	118	1.9	5.3	7.3	101	105	120	$0.3	$1.9	$7.2
Chinese	118	119	115	6.4	7.3	6.0	92	89	90	−$2.9	−$3.9	−$3.5
Filipino	92	99	95	−2.8	−0.3	−1.9	71	86	81	−$10.1	−$4.8	−$6.6
Hispanic	78	75	82	−7.9	−9.7	−7.4	78	67	73	−$7.8	−$11.5	−$9.8

Am. Ind. = American Indian; SEI = socioeconomic index.

*Adjusted to constant 1989 dollars.

Sources: Public Use Microdata Sample (PUMS) files of the 1970, 1980, and 1990 *Census of Population*, U.S. Bureau of the Census.

residence, or other attributes that may affect socioeconomic attainment entirely apart from any consideration of ethnic relations. For example, some ethnic groups may have higher earnings because they are more heavily concentrated in higher paying urban labor markets, not because they receive different rewards for their work. We use regression analysis to decompose the ethnic effects on occupational and earnings achievements.

TABLE 3

Effects of Ethnicity on Occupational Attainment of Men Aged Twenty-Five to Sixty-Four
in the Labor Force 1970, 1980, and 1990 (average SEI points)

		Black	American Indian	Japanese	Chinese	Filipino	Hispanic
Gross	1970	−13	−9	2	6	−3	−8
	1980	−11	−8	5	7	0	−10
	1990	−10	−9	7	6	−2	−7
Total	1970	−13	−10	2	5	−4	−9
	1980	−11	−8	6	8	0	−10
	1990	−10	−9	8	7	−1	−7
Indirect via:							
Residence	1970	0	−1	−2	−1	−3	−1
	1980	1	−1	−3	−1	−2	−1
	1990	0	−1	−6	−4	−5	−1
Schooling	1970	−7	−6	6	5	2	−6
	1980	−6	−4	7	6	5	−7
	1990	−5	−5	10	7	7	−5
Sector	1970	1	0	0	0	0	0
	1980	0	0	0	0	0	0
	1990	0	0	0	0	0	0
Direct	1970	−7	−3	−2	1	−3	−2
	1980	−6	−3	2	3	−3	−2
	1990	−5	−3	4	4	−3	−1

SEI = socioeconomic index.

Occupational Attainment

The coefficients in Table 3 show the gross, total, direct, and indirect effects of ethnicity on
occupational SEI for the years of 1970, 1980,
and 1990. The first panel shows the *gross* differences in SEI for each ethnic group compared to white men. In spite of the overall
upgrading of average occupational status (reported in Table 2), there has been remarkably
little change in ethnic inequality over the
twenty years observed here. The average employed black man was thirteen SEI points behind the average employed white man in
1970 and ten points behind in 1990. The situation of American Indian and Hispanic men
was similar to that of black men, although
both groups were generally two to three SEI
points closer to the status of white men. All
three of these established minority groups

held substantially lower-status occupations
than white men. In contrast, Asian American
men were in occupations that were, on average, as good as or better than those of white
men. Whereas Filipino men held slightly lower
status jobs in 1990, Chinese and Japanese
American men worked at higher-status positions than did white men.

The second panel shows ethnic differences
net of the effects of age and immigrant status.
The total effects are almost identical to the
gross effects. Because there are important ethnic differences in immigrant status (Asians
and Hispanics are more likely to be foreign
born), one could conclude that there is little
occupational handicap for immigrants.

The third panel presents indirect effects
(through which ethnic differences are mediated) in residence, schooling, and industrial

sector. The parameter estimates are dependent on the order in which the variables are entered in successive equations. Although the temporal sequence of these variables cannot be specified with any assurance, we have estimated three equations by adding each variable in a sequential and cumulative order. First, place of current residence is added to the model with ethnicity, age, and immigrant status as independent variables. In turn, the same exercise is repeated for years of schooling and sector—adding the variable to the prior equation and measuring the change in the ethnic coefficients. The final equation shows the "direct effects" of ethnicity that remain after all these other considerations are held constant.

Current place of residence has an unexpected role as a mediator of ethnic advantage/disadvantage in occupational attainment. There is a slight disadvantage for American Indians and Hispanics because they live in geographical areas with a lower average SEI. The effect on the black-white differential is negligible. Residence appears to be a more serious handicap for Asian Americans, especially in 1990. Japanese, Filipino, and Chinese Americans have an average occupation that is four to six SEI points lower in 1990 than they would have if their geographical distribution was the same as for the population as a whole.

Educational composition plays two quite different roles for the six ethnic minorities in our samples. For the three disadvantaged minorities (blacks, American Indians, and Hispanics), having less education is the single most important reason for their lower occupational attainment. The absolute levels of occupational disadvantage associated with education are four to seven SEI points, and this accounts for about half or more of their total SEI ethnic-disadvantaged status in 1990.

In contrast, Asian Americans have much higher average levels of education than the general population, and all other things being equal, this boosts their occupational attainments. Indeed the occupational advantage associated with above-average levels of school-

ing for Asians has risen a bit over the two decades, and there was about a seven-point SEI advantage for Chinese and Filipinos and a ten-point SEI advantage for Japanese Americans in 1990.

In spite of the great attention given to "sector" or industry in the sociological literature, this variable plays no role in mediating ethnic differences in occupational attainment for any of the ethnic groups across the three time periods represented here.

The last panel in Table 3 shows the direct effects of ethnicity on occupational attainment after all the relevant variables from the census files are included in the equations. The coefficients are modest, at least relative to gross (or total) differences in occupational attainment. In 1990, holding all measured variables constant, the average employed black man held an occupation five SEI points lower than the average white man; American Indian and Filipino men were three points lower; and Hispanics were one point lower. The comparable direct effect of being Japanese or Chinese was four SEI points above the white level.

Some interpret the net or direct effect as a measure of ethnic discrimination, but all we can really say is that the relationship is unexplained. Discrimination (e.g., negative and positive preferences within certain labor markets) may play a role, but other unmeasured factors, including family background and social networks, may also account for some of the differences. Moreover, discrimination may also be operating indirectly through the intervening variables (e.g., in funding for inner city or reservation schools, funding that affects the quantity and quality of schooling).

Earnings Attainment

Table 4 presents comparable results for earnings attainment. The twenty years from 1970 to 1990 was a period of stagnant wages and rising inequality in the American economy (Karoly 1993; Levy 1995). How did the state of the economy play out in terms of wage differences among various subgroups of work-

TABLE 4
Effects of Ethnicity on the Earnings Attainment of Men Aged Twenty-Five to Sixty-Four in the Labor Force 1969, 1979, and 1989

		Black	American Indian	Japanese	Chinese	Filipino	Hispanic
Gross	1969	−$14,691	−$12,965	$301	−$2,885	−$10,083	−$7,820
	1979	−$12,216	−$9,351	$1,930	−$3,852	−$4,815	−$11,481
	1989	−$12,351	−$14,012	$7,227	−$3,507	−$6,578	−$9,763
Total	1969	−$14,664	−$12,772	$547	−$1,858	−$8,232	−$7,398
	1979	−$11,934	−$9,017	$2,524	−$2,582	−$3,339	−$10,665
	1989	−$12,062	−$13,326	$7,634	−$3,502	−$7,138	−$9,329
Indirect via:							
Residence	1969	−$115	−$1,307	$2,466	$1,682	$2,017	−$1,307
	1979	$67	−$488	−$266	$12	$5	$174
	1989	−$465	−$843	−$3,911	−$2,451	−$3,398	−$561
Schooling	1969	−$4,084	−$3,476	$3,138	$2,689	$166	−$4,165
	1979	−$3,360	−$2,571	$3,758	$3,020	$2,726	−$4,516
	1989	−$3,276	−$3,777	$6,822	$5,092	$4,742	−$3,518
Sector	1969	−$1,000	−$1,118	$456	$220	−$1,118	−$730
	1979	−$1,081	−$849	−$145	−$921	−$541	−$629
	1989	−$1,355	−$912	−$327	−$1,023	−$1,178	−$539
Occupation	1969	−$2,023	−$1,030	−$571	$348	−$959	−$763
	1979	−$1,638	−$835	$601	$953	−$798	−$673
	1989	−$1,635	−$992	$1,405	$1,361	−$877	−$421
Weeks and Hours Worked	1969	−$980	−$1,118	$20	−$318	−$652	−$763
	1979	−$1,353	−$1,344	−$46	−$514	−$1,071	−$721
	1989	−$1,618	−$2,011	$162	−$594	−$1,114	−$747
Direct	1969	−$9,036	−$5,793	−$2,723	−$10,151	−$7,329	−$8,506
	1979	−$6,342	−$8,183	$5,951	−$10,055	−$8,183	−$6,051
	1989	−$3,713	−$4,791	$3,484	−$5,887	−$5,313	−$3,543

ers? The first panel of Table 4 shows that ethnic differentials in male earnings were largely unchanged over the same period. The black-white differential actually dropped a bit (from $14,700 in 1969 to $12,200 in 1979) and remained at $12,400 by 1989. American Indian earnings fluctuated over the period, but their disadvantage relative to whites of almost $13,000 in 1969 grew to $14,000 by 1989. Unlike all other ethnic groups, Japanese men reached parity with the earnings of whites in 1969 and had pulled ahead (by $7,000) in 1989. Chinese, Filipino, and Hispanic men earned less than whites in 1969 and contin-

ued to do so in 1989, although the size of the differences peaked in 1979.

Holding constant age composition and immigrant status reveals the total effects of ethnicity on earnings in the second panel of Table 4. By and large, the pattern of ethnic advantage and disadvantage is similar to the gross effects. Black and American Indian men are the most disadvantaged—about $12,000 to $13,000 below the average for white men. Hispanic men are only slightly better off with a $9,300 earnings gap in 1989. Next are Filipinos and Chinese with deficits of $7,100 and $3,500 below white men. Japanese Americans earned $7,600 more than white men in 1989.

We decompose the total effects of each ethnic group on earnings (actually the ethnic-white earnings gap) in the third panel. Place of residence plays an unexpected role for Asian Americans. In 1969, the geographical concentration of Japanese, Chinese, and Filipinos in Hawaii and California was a distinct economic advantage—about $1,700 to $2,500—in comparison to whites. By 1989, these locations were a liability, with Asians suffering a $2,500 to $3,900 deficit because of their concentrations in these same areas. The geographic distribution of black, American Indian, and Hispanic men was a modest liability of several hundred dollars.

As with occupational attainment, education is the single most important variable mediating ethnic differentials in earnings. In 1989, about 25 to 33 percent of the economic gap between black, American Indian, and Hispanic men and white men can be explained by the lower educational attainment of these minority groups; the difference is about $3,500 dollars. In contrast, the higher education (compared to white men) of Japanese, Chinese, and Filipino men is the major reason for their higher earnings ($4,700 for Filipino men, $5,100 for Chinese men, and $6,800 for Japanese men).

Holding constant all of the measured background variables, including education, minorities were usually found in occupations and sectors that paid substantially less than those occupied by white men. The sum of the indirect effects of ethnicity on earnings via both occupation and sector was about $3,000 for black men, $2,000 for American Indians, and $1,000 for Hispanic men. The job sorting process for Filipino men reveals an economic disadvantage comparable to American Indian men. On the other hand, Chinese and Japanese do relatively well in finding well-paying occupations. However, all groups, with the exception of Japanese men, have a problem finding jobs that employ them for enough hours per week and weeks per year to

close the gap with white men. For black and American Indian men, the problems of unemployment and underemployment cost them about $2,000 relative to white men. The economic penalty for the other groups is less, ranging from $600 to $1,100.

The final panel of Table 4 shows the direct effects of ethnicity after controlling for all of the covariates included in prior models. The magnitude of the deficits due to direct effects is substantial: in the range of $5,000 to $10,000 for all ethnic groups (except Japanese) in 1969. There have been changes, mainly in reducing the size of the deficit, for the twenty-year period measured here. However, by 1989, all minority groups (with the exception of Japanese) still experienced very substantial direct deficits relative to whites—in the range of $3,500 to $5,900.

Rather than speculate on the reasons for the residual net effects, it may be more instructive to consider the overall magnitude and patterns of ethnic inequality. There are three ethnic "patterns" of earnings inequality. The first is represented by blacks, American Indians, and Hispanics. These groups suffer substantial inequality relative to whites (about $10,000 per year) and there has been little moderation over time. About 25 to 33 percent of the gap is due to lower educational levels, but the remainder is due to differences on labor market factors: occupation, industry, weeks and hours worked, and other unmeasured factors. The second type or pattern is illustrated by Chinese and Filipinos. The size of the deficit for these groups is about half the size of that for blacks, Hispanics, and American Indians. The sources of the Chinese and Filipino disadvantage are current residence, labor market positions, and unmeasured factors. Their potential disadvantage is reduced by their higher levels of schooling. In fact, their educational advantage over whites generates (all else being equal) about a $5,000 gain. Without this educational "boost," their economic situations would be similar to the level of blacks, American Indians, and Hispanics. Finally, the third pattern is represented by the Japanese. Japanese have higher incomes than whites in 1979 and 1989. In large part, this is due to their higher educational attainment, but they also experience an "advantage" that is not measured by the variables in the model.

Conclusions

There was much talk in the 1990s about *reverse* discrimination, the problems of white men who are unable to find jobs or obtain promotions because of preferences given to minorities. These perceptions seem quite at odds with the findings of this chapter, findings which show only modest changes in race and ethnic stratification among male workers over the two decades from 1970 to 1990.

However, we show that the patterns of race and ethnic inequality are complex. Looking first at occupational attainment, black, American Indian, and Hispanic men suffer about a ten-point SEI occupational deficit relative to whites, while Asian American men are equal to or above white men in their occupational positions.

For the groups that are behind whites, the "problem" is primarily educational deficits. If black, American Indian, and Hispanic men had educational attainments equal to whites, the results here suggest that they would only experience modest occupational disadvantages. There would still be a five-point SEI deficit for black men, but this would be half of their current handicap. The reason for the higher occupational attainment of Asian American men is simply their educational level. If the Asian American men had the same education as white men, there would be only modest ethnic occupational differences.

Turning to differences in income, earnings inequality is a much deeper problem for racial and ethnic minorities in America. All minorities, with the exception of Japanese, earn less than whites. For blacks, American Indians, and Hispanics, the financial shortfall relative to whites is huge—about $10,000 per male worker for the period under study—and there has been little sign of progress. Chinese and

Filipino men are also behind, but the gap is somewhat less.

These results—the persistence of race and ethnic differentials in late twentieth-century America—challenge conventional theories about the declining role of ascribed factors in the American stratification system. . . . However, the economy of the latter half of the 1990s has been characterized by rising opportunity, with a record low unemployment rate. Will this reduce the kinds of persistent racial and ethnic inequalities we have documented for the 1970s and 1980s? Perhaps. Tight labor markets make it more costly for employers to make invidious distinctions among workers. But the slow pace of change during the 1970s and 1980s suggests that racial inequality is woven deeply into the fabric of American society.

Notes

The authors wish to acknowledge the support provided to the second author by the Vilas Trust of the University of Wisconsin, support that was used for the processing and analysis of the data presented herein. Some of the data presented in this paper also appear in an unpublished manuscript, "Assimilation in American Society: Occupational Achievement and Earnings for Ethnic Minorities in the United States, 1970 to 1990," by the same authors.

1. To present descriptive statistics, we selected a representative sample of whites and blacks in the public use files and included all PUMS observations of the smaller populations such as American Indians and Asian Americans.

Bibliography

Alba, Richard. 1985. *Italian Americans: Into the Twilight of Ethnicity.* Englewood Cliffs, NJ: Prentice Hall.

Alwin, Duane F., and Robert M. Hauser. 1975. "The Decomposition of Effects in Path Analysis." *American Sociological Review* 40 (February):37–47.

Baltzell, E. Digby. 1964. *The Protestant Establishment: Aristocracy and Caste in America.* New York: Vintage.

Barringer, Herbert, Robert W. Gardner, and Michael Levin. 1993. *Asians and Pacific Is-*

landers in the United States. New York: Russell Sage.

Bean, Frank, and Marta Tienda. 1987. *The Hispanic Population of the United States.* New York: Russell Sage.

Chiswick, Barry, and Teresa Sullivan. 1995. "The New Immigrants." In *State of the Union: America in the 1990s,* edited by R. Farley, 2: 211–70. New York: Russell Sage.

Cornell, Stephen. 1988. *The Return of the Native.* New York: Oxford.

Cox, Oliver C. 1948. *Caste, Class, and Race: A Study in Social Dynamics.* Garden City, NJ: Doubleday.

Duncan, Beverly, and Otis Dudley Duncan. 1968. "Minorities and the Process of Stratification." *American Sociological Review* 33(3):356–64.

Duncan, Otis Dudley. 1961. "A Socioeconomic Index for All Occupations." In *Occupations and Social Status,* edited by Albert J. Reiss, Jr., 109–38. Glencoe: Free Press.

———. 1969. "Inheritance of Poverty or Inheritance of Race." In *On Understanding Poverty,* edited by D. P. Moynihan, 85–110. New York: Basic.

Farley, Reynolds, and Walter R. Allen. 1987. *The Color Line and the Quality of Life in America.* New York: Russell Sage.

Featherman, David, and Robert Hauser. 1976. "Changes in the Socioeconomic Stratification of the Races, 1962–1973." *American Journal of Sociology* 82(3):621–51.

Fixico, Donald L. 1986. *Termination and Relocation: Federal Indian Policy, 1945–1960.* Albuquerque: University of New Mexico Press.

Gans, Herbert J. 1979. "Symbolic Ethnicity: The Future of Ethnic Groups and Cultures in America." *Ethnic and Racial Studies* 2(January): 1–20.

Glazer, Nathan, and Daniel Patrick Moynihan. 1970. *Beyond the Melting Pot.* Cambridge, MA: MIT Press.

Gordon, Milton M. 1964. *Assimilation in American Life.* New York: Oxford University Press.

Greeley, Andrew. 1978. *Ethnicity, Denomination, and Inequality.* Beverly Hills: Sage.

Grusky, David, and Thomas DiPrete. 1990. "Recent Trends in the Process of Stratification." *Demography* 27:617–37.

Gundlach, James, and Alden Roberts. 1978. "Native American Indian Migration and Relocation: Success or Failure." *Pacific Sociological Review* 12:117–28.

Hauser, Robert M., and John Robert Warren. 1997. "Socioeconomic Indexes of Occupational Status: A Review, Update, and Critique." In *Sociological Methodology 1997,* edited by A. Raftery, 177–298. Cambridge, U.K.: Blackwell.

Higham, John. 1970. *Strangers in the Land: Patterns of American Nativism, 1860–1925.* New York: Atheneum.

Hirschman, Charles. 1980. "Theories and Models in Ethnic Inequality." In *Research in Race and Ethnic Relations,* edited by C. B. Marrett and C. Leggon, 2:1–20. Greenwich, CT: JAI Press.

———. 1983. "The Melting Pot Reconsidered." *Annual Review of Sociology* 9:397–423.

Hirschman, Charles, and Morrison G. Wong. 1984. "Socioeconomic Gains of Asian Americans, Blacks, and Hispanics: 1960–1976." *American Journal of Sociology* 90(3): 584–607.

Hoxie, Frederick E. 1984. *A Final Promise—The Campaign to Assimilate the Indians, 1880–1920.* Lincoln: University of Nebraska Press.

Jordan, Winthrop. 1974. *The White Man's Burden: Historical Origins of Racism in the United States.* New York: Oxford University Press.

Kallen, Horace M. 1924. *Culture and Democracy in the United States.* New York: Boni and Liveright.

Karoly, Lynn. 1993. "The Trend in Inequality among Families, Individuals, and Workers in the United States: A Twenty-Five Year Perspective." In *Uneven Tides: Rising Inequality in America,* edited by S. Danziger and P. Gottschalk, 19–97. New York: Russell Sage.

Landry, Bart. 1987. *The New Black Middle Class.* Berkeley: University of California Press.

Levy, Frank. 1995. "Incomes and Income Inequality." In *State of the Union: America in the 1990s,* edited by R. Farley, 1:1–58. New York: Russell Sage.

Lieberson, Stanley. 1980. *A Piece of the Pie: Black and White Immigrants since 1880.* Berkeley: University of California Press.

Lieberson, Stanley, and Mary Waters. 1988. *From Many Strands: Ethnic and Racial Groups in Contemporary America.* New York: Russell Sage.

Massey, Douglas S., and Nancy Denton. 1993. *American Apartheid: Segregation and the Making of the Underclass.* Cambridge, MA: Harvard University Press.

Myrdal, Gunnar. 1944. *An American Dilemma.* New York: Harper & Row.

Nagel, Joanne. 1996. *American Indian Ethnic Renewal.* New York: Oxford.

Nee, Victor, and Jimy Sanders. 1985. "The Road to Parity: Determinants of the Socioeconomic Achievements of Asian Americans." *Ethnic and Racial Studies* 8(1):75–93.

Neidert, Lisa S., and Reynolds Farley. 1985. "Assimilation in the United States: An Analysis of Ethnic and Generational Differences in Status and Achievement." *American Sociological Review* 50(6):840–50.

Portes, Alejandro, and Robert L. Bach. 1985. *Latin Journey: Cuban and Mexican Immigrants in the United States.* Berkeley: University of California Press.

Snipp, C. Matthew. 1989. *American Indians: The First of the This Land.* New York: Russell Sage.

Snipp, C. Matthew, and Gary Sandefur. 1989. "Earnings of American Indians and Alaska Natives: The Effects of Residence and Migration." *Social Forces* 66:994–1008.

Tolbert, Charles, Patrick M. Horan, and E. M. Beck. 1980. "The Structure of Economic Segmentation: A Dual Economy Approach." *American Journal of Sociology* 85:1095–116.

Waters, Mary C. 1990. *Ethnic Options: Choosing Identities in America.* Berkeley: University of California Press.

Wilson, William Julius. 1978. *The Declining Significance of Race: Blacks and Changing American Institutions.* Chicago: University of Chicago Press.

———. 1987. *The Truly Disadvantaged: The Inner City, The Underclass, and Public Policy.* Chicago: University of Chicago Press.

MELVIN L. OLIVER AND THOMAS M. SHAPIRO

Black Wealth / White Wealth: A New Perspective on Racial Inequality

Each year two highly publicized news reports capture the attention and imagination of Americans. One lists the year's highest income earners. Predictably, they include glamorous and highly publicized entertainment, sport, and business personalities. For the past decade that list has included many African Americans: musical artists such as Michael Jackson, entertainers such as Bill Cosby and Oprah Winfrey, and sports figures such as Michael Jordan and Magic Johnson. During the recent past as many as half of the "top ten" in this highly exclusive rank have been African Americans.

Another highly publicized list, by contrast, documents the nation's wealthiest Americans. The famous *Forbes* magazine profile of the nation's wealthiest 400 focuses not on income, but on wealth.[1] This list includes those people whose assets—or command over monetary resources—place them at the top of the American economic hierarchy. Even though this group is often ten times larger than the top earners list, it contains few if any African Americans. An examination of these two lists creates two very different perceptions of the well-being of America's black community on the eve of the twenty-first century. The large number of blacks on the top income list generates an optimistic view of how black Americans have progressed economically in American society. The near absence of blacks in the *Forbes* listing, by contrast, presents a much more pessimistic outlook on blacks' economic progress.

This chapter develops a perspective on racial inequality that is based on the analysis of private wealth. Just as a change in focus from income to wealth in the discussion above provides a different perspective on racial inequality, our analysis reveals deep patterns of racial imbalance not visible when

Originally published in 1997. Please see complete source information beginning on page 891.

viewed only through the lens of income. This analysis provides a new perspective on racial inequality by exploring how material assets are created, expanded, and preserved.

The basis of our analysis is the analytical distinction between wealth and other traditional measures of economic status, of how people are "making it" in America (for example, income, occupation, and education). Wealth is a particularly important indicator of individual and family access to life chances. Income refers to a flow of money over time, like a rate per hour, week, or year; wealth is a stock of assets owned at a particular time. Wealth is what people own, while income is what people receive for work, retirement, or social welfare. Wealth signifies the command over financial resources that a family has accumulated over its lifetime along with those resources that have been inherited across generations. Such resources, when combined with income, can create the opportunity to secure the "good life" in whatever form is needed—education, business, training, justice, health, comfort, and so on. Wealth is a special form of money not used to purchase milk and shoes and other life necessities. More often it is used to create opportunities, secure a desired stature and standard of living, or pass class status along to one's children. In this sense the command over resources that wealth entails is more encompassing than is income or education, and closer in meaning and theoretical significance to our traditional notions of economic well-being and access to life chances.

More important, wealth taps not only contemporary resources but material assets that have historic origins. Private wealth thus captures inequality that is the product of the past, often passed down from generation to generation. Given this attribute, in attempting to understand the economic status of blacks, a focus on wealth helps us avoid the either-or view of a march toward progress or a trail of despair. Conceptualizing racial inequality through wealth revolutionizes our conception of its nature and magnitude, and of whether it is declining or increasing. While most recent

analyses have concluded that contemporary class-based factors are most important in understanding the sources of continuing racial inequality, our focus on wealth sheds light on both the historical and the contemporary impacts not only of class but of race. . . .

The argument for class, most eloquently and influentially stated by William Julius Wilson in his 1978 book *The Declining Significance of Race,* suggests that the racial barriers of the past are less important than present-day social class attributes in determining the economic life chances of black Americans. Education, in particular, is the key attribute in whether blacks will achieve economic success relative to white Americans. Discrimination and racism, while still actively practiced in many spheres, have marginally less effect on black Americans' economic attainment than whether or not blacks have the skills and education necessary to fit in a changing economy. In this view, race assumes importance only as the lingering product of an oppressive past. As Wilson observes, this time in his *Truly Disadvantaged,* racism and its most harmful injuries occurred in the past, and they are today experienced mainly by those on the bottom of the economic ladder, as "the accumulation of disadvantages . . . passed from generation to generation."[2]

We believe that a focus on wealth reveals a crucial dimension of the seeming paradox of continued racial inequality in American society. Looking at wealth helps solve the riddle of seeming black progress alongside economic deterioration. Black wealth has grown, for example, at the same time that it has fallen further behind that of whites. Wealth reveals an array of insights into black and white inequality that challenge our conception of racial and social justice in America.

The empirical heart of our analysis resides in an examination of differentials in black and white wealth holdings. This focus paints a vastly different empirical picture of social inequality than commonly emerges from analyses based on traditional inequality indicators. The burden of our claim is to demonstrate not simply the taken-for-granted assumption that wealth reveals "more" inequality—income multiplied x times is not the correct equation. More importantly we show that wealth uncovers a qualitatively different pattern of inequality on crucial fronts. Thus the goal of this work is to provide an analysis of racial differences in wealth holding that reveals dynamics of racial inequality otherwise concealed by income, occupational attainment, or education. It is our argument that wealth reveals a particular network of social relations and a set of social circumstances that convey a unique constellation of meanings pertinent to race in America. This perspective significantly adds to our understanding of public policy issues related to racial inequality; at the same time it aids us in developing better policies for the future. In stating our case, we do not discount the important information that the traditional indicators provide, but we argue that by adding to the latter an analysis of wealth a more thorough, comprehensive and powerful explanation of social inequality can be elaborated. . . .

Economists argue that racial differences in wealth are a consequence of disparate class and human capital credentials (age, education, experience, skills), propensities to save, and consumption patterns. A sociology of wealth seeks to properly situate the social context in which wealth generation occurs. Thus the sociology of wealth accounts for racial differences in wealth holding by demonstrating the unique and diverse social circumstances that blacks and whites face. One result is that blacks and whites also face different structures of investment opportunity, which have been affected historically and contemporaneously by both race and class. We develop three concepts to provide a sociologically grounded approach to understanding racial differentials in wealth accumulation. These concepts highlight the ways in which this opportunity structure has disadvantaged blacks and helped contribute to massive wealth inequalities between the races.

Our first concept, "racialization of state policy," refers to how state policy has impaired the ability of many black Americans to accumulate wealth—and discouraged them from doing so—from the beginning of slavery throughout American history. From the first codified decision to enslave African Americans to the local ordinances that barred blacks from certain occupations to the welfare state policies of today that discourage wealth accumulation, the state has erected major barriers to black economic self-sufficiency. In particular, state policy has structured the context within which it has been possible to acquire land, build community, and generate wealth. Historically, policies and actions of the United States government have promoted homesteading, land acquisition, home ownership, retirement, pensions, education, and asset accumulation for some sectors of the population and not for others. Poor people—blacks in particular—generally have been excluded from participation in these state-sponsored opportunities. In this way, the distinctive relationship between whites and blacks has been woven into the fabric of state actions. The modern welfare state has racialized citizenship, social organization, and economic status while consigning blacks to a relentlessly impoverished and subordinate position within it.

Our second focus, on the "economic detour," helps us understand the relatively low level of entrepreneurship among and the small scale of the businesses owned by black Americans. While blacks have historically sought out opportunities for self-employment, they have traditionally faced an environment, especially from the postbellum period to the middle of the twentieth century, in which they were restricted by law from participation in business in the open market. Explicit state and local policies restricted the rights of blacks as free economic agents. These policies had a devastating impact on the ability of blacks to build and maintain successful enterprises. While blacks were limited to a restricted African American market to which others (for example, whites and other ethnics) also had easy access, they were unable to tap the more lucrative and expansive mainstream white markets. Blacks thus had fewer opportunities to develop successful businesses. When businesses were developed that competed in size and scope with white businesses, intimidation and ultimately, in some cases, violence were used to curtail their expansion or get rid of them altogether. The lack of important assets and indigenous community development has thus played a crucial role in limiting the wealth-accumulating ability of African Americans.

The third concept we develop is synthetic in nature. The notion embodied in the "sedimentation of racial inequality" is that in central ways the cumulative effects of the past have seemingly cemented blacks to the bottom of society's economic hierarchy. A history of low wages, poor schooling, and segregation affected not one or two generations of blacks but practically all African Americans well into the middle of the twentieth century. Our argument is that the best indicator of the sedimentation of racial inequality is wealth. Wealth is one indicator of material disparity that captures the historical legacy of low wages, personal and organizational discrimination, and institutionalized racism. The low levels of wealth accumulation evidenced by current generations of black Americans best represent the economic status of blacks in the American social structure.

To argue that blacks form the sediment of the American stratificational order is to recognize the extent to which they began at the bottom of the hierarchy during slavery, and the cumulative and reinforcing effects of Jim Crow and de facto segregation through the mid-twentieth century. Generation after generation of blacks remained anchored to the lowest economic status in American society. The effect of this inherited poverty and economic scarcity for the accumulation of wealth has been to "sediment" inequality into the social structure. The sedimentation of inequality occurred because the investment opportunity that blacks faced worked against their quest for material self-sufficiency. In contrast, whites in general, but well-off whites in particular, were able to amass assets and use their secure financial status to pass their wealth

from generation to generation. What is often not acknowledged is that the same social system that fosters the accumulation of private wealth for many whites denies it to blacks, thus forging an intimate connection between white wealth accumulation and black poverty. Just as blacks have had "cumulative disadvantages," many whites have had "cumulative advantages." Since wealth builds over a lifetime and is then passed along to kin, it is, from our perspective, an essential indicator of black economic well-being. By focusing on wealth we discover how black's socioeconomic status results from a socially layered accumulation of disadvantages passed on from generation to generation. In this sense we uncover a racial wealth tax.

Our empirical analysis enables us to raise and answer several key questions about wealth: How has wealth been distributed in American society over the twentieth century? What changes in the distribution of wealth occurred during the 1980s? And finally, what are the implications of these changes for black-white inequality?

During the eighties the rich got much richer, and the poor and middle classes fell further behind. Why? The Reagan tax cuts provided greater discretionary income for middle- and upper-class taxpayers. One asset whose value grew dramatically during the eighties was real estate, an asset that is central to the wealth portfolio of the average American. Home ownership makes up the largest part of wealth held by the middle class, whereas the upper class more commonly hold a greater degree of their wealth in financial assets. Owning a house is the hallmark of the American Dream, but it is becoming harder and harder for average Americans to afford their own home and fewer are able to do so.

In part because of the dramatic rise in home values, the wealthiest generation of elderly people in America's history is in the process of passing along its wealth. Between 1987 and 2011 the baby boom generation stands to inherit approximately $7 trillion. Of course, all will not benefit equally, if at all. One-third of the worth of all estates will be divided by the richest 1 percent, each legatee receiving an average inheritance of $6 million. Much of this wealth will be in the form of property, which, as the philosopher Robert Nozick is quoted as saying in a 1990 *New York Times* piece, "sticks out as a special kind of unearned benefit that produces unequal opportunities."[3] Kevin, a seventy-five-year-old retired homeowner interviewed for this study, captures the dilemma of unearned inheritance:

You heard that saying about the guy with a rich father? The kid goes through life thinking that he hit a triple. But really he was born on third base. He didn't hit no triple at all, but he'll go around telling everyone he banged the fucking ball and it was a triple. He was born there!

Inherited wealth is a very special kind of money imbued with the shadows of race. Racial difference in inheritance is a key feature of our story. For the most part, blacks will not partake in divvying up the baby boom bounty. America's racist legacy is shutting them out. The grandparents and parents of blacks under the age of forty toiled under segregation, where education and access to decent jobs and wages were severely restricted. Racialized state policy and the economic detour constrained their ability to enter the post–World War II housing market. Segregation created an extreme situation in which earlier generations were unable to build up much, if any, wealth. The average black family headed by a person over the age of sixty-five has no net financial assets to pass down to its children. Until the late 1960s there were few older African Americans with the ability to save much at all, much less invest. And no savings and no inheritance meant no wealth.

The most consistent and strongest common theme to emerge in interviews conducted with white and black families was that family assets expand choices, horizons, and opportunities for children while lack of assets limit opportunities. Because parents want to give their children whatever advantages they can, we wondered about the ability of the average American household to expend assets on their

children. We found that the lack of private assets intrudes on the dreams that many Americans have for their children. Extreme resource deficiency characterizes several groups. It may surprise some to learn that 62 percent of households headed by single parents are without savings or other financial assets, or that two of every five households without a high school degree lack a financial nest egg. Nearly one-third of all households—and 61 percent of all black households—are without financial resources. These statistics lead to our focus on the most resource-deficient households in our study—African Americans.

We argue that, materially, whites and blacks constitute two nations. One of the analytic centerpieces of this work tells a tale of two middle classes, one white and one black. Most significant, the claim made by blacks to middle-class status depends on income and not assets. In contrast, a wealth pillar supports the white middle class in its drive for middle-class opportunities and a middle-class standard of living. Middle-class blacks, for example, earn seventy cents for every dollar earned by middle-class whites but they possess only fifteen cents for every dollar of wealth held by middle-class whites. For the most part, the economic foundation of the black middle class lacks one of the pillars that provide stability and security to middle-class whites—assets. The black middle class position is precarious and fragile with insubstantial wealth resources. This analysis means it is entirely premature to celebrate the rise of the black middle class. The glass is both half empty and half full, because the wealth data reveal the paradoxical situation in which blacks' wealth has grown while at the same time falling further behind that of whites.

The social distribution of wealth discloses a fresh and formidable dimension of racial inequality. Blacks' achievement at any given level not only requires that greater effort be expended on fewer opportunities but also bestows substantially diminished rewards. Examining blacks and whites who share similar socioeconomic characteristics brings to light persistent and vast wealth discrepancies. Take education as one prime example: the most equality we found was among the college educated, but even here at the pinnacle of achievement whites control four times as much wealth as blacks with the same degrees. This predicament manifests a disturbing break in the link between achievement and results that is essential for democracy and social equality.

The central question of this study is, Why do the wealth portfolios of blacks and whites vary so drastically? The answer is not simply that blacks have inferior remunerable human capital endowments—substandard education, jobs, and skills, for example—or do not display the characteristics most associated with higher income and wealth. We are able to demonstrate that even when blacks and whites display similar characteristics—for example, are on a par educationally and occupationally—a potent difference of $43,143 in home equity and financial assets still remains. Likewise, giving the average black household the same attributes as the average white household leaves a $25,794 racial gap in financial assets alone.

The extent of discrimination in institutions and social policy provides a persuasive index of bias that undergirds the drastic differences between blacks and whites. We show that skewed access to mortgage and housing markets and the racial valuing of neighborhoods on the basis of segregated markets result in enormous racial wealth disparity. Banks turn down qualified blacks much more often for home loans than they do similarly qualified whites. Blacks who do qualify, moreover, pay higher interest rates on home mortgages than whites. Residential segregation persists into the 1990s, and we found that the great rise in housing values is color-coded.[4] Why should the mean value of the average white home appreciate at a dramatically higher rate than the average black home? Home ownership is without question the single most important means of accumulating assets. The lower values of black homes adversely affect the ability of blacks to utilize their residences as collateral for obtaining personal, business, or educational loans. We estimate that institutional biases in the residential arena have cost the current generation of blacks about $82 billion. Passing inequality along from one generation to the next casts another racially stratified shadow on the making of American inequality. Institutional discrimination in housing and lending markets extends into the future the effects of historical discrimination within other institutions.

Placing these findings in the larger context of public policy discussions about racial and social justice adds new dimensions to these discussions. A focus on wealth changes our thinking about racial inequality. The more one learns about wealth differences, the more mistaken current policies appear. To take these findings seriously, as we do, means not shirking the responsibility of seeking alternative policy ideas with which to address issues of inequality. We might even need to think about social justice in new ways. In some key respects our analysis of disparities in wealth between blacks and whites forms an agenda for the future, the key principle of which is to link opportunity structures to policies promoting asset formation that begin to close the racial wealth gap.

Closing the racial gap means that we have to target policies at two levels. First, we need policies that directly address the situation of African Americans. Such policies are necessary to speak to the historically generated disadvantages and the current racially based policies that have limited the ability of blacks, as a group, to accumulate wealth resources.

Second, we need policies that directly promote asset opportunities for those on the bottom of the social structure, both black and white, who are locked out of the wealth accumulation process. More generally, our analysis clearly suggests the need for massive redistributional policies in order to reforge the links between achievement, reward, social equality, and democracy. These policies must take aim at the gross inequality generated by those at the very top of the wealth distribution. Policies of this type are the most difficult ones on which to gain consensus but the most important in creating a more just society.

This chapter's underlying goal is to establish a way to view racial inequality that will serve as a guide in securing racial equality in the twenty-first century. Racial equality is not an absolute or idealized state of affairs, because it cannot be perfectly attained. Yet the fact that it can never be perfectly attained in the real world is a wholly insufficient excuse for dismissing it as utopian or impossible. What is important are the bearings by which a nation chooses to orient its character. We can choose to let racial inequality fester and risk heightened conflict and violence. Americans can also make a different choice, a commitment to equality and to closing the gap as much as possible.

Notes

1. Harold Senecker, 1993, "The *Forbes* 400: The Richest People in America," *Forbes,* 18 October, pp. 110–113.

2. William J. Wilson, 1987, *The Truly Disadvantaged,* Chicago: University of Chicago Press.

3. Nick Ravo, 1990, "A Windfall Nears in Inheritances from the Richest Generation," *New York Times,* 22 July E4.

4. Reynolds Farley and William H. Frey, 1994, "Changes in the Segregation of Whites from Blacks During the 1980s: Small Steps Toward a More Integrated Society," *American Sociological Review* 59: 23–45. Douglas S. Massey and Nancy A. Denton, 1993, *American Apartheid: Segregation and the Making of the Underclass,* Cambridge: Harvard University Press.

HERBERT J. GANS

The Possibility of a New Racial Hierarchy in the Twenty-first-century United States

Over the last decade, a number of social scientists writing on race and ethnicity have suggested that the country may be moving toward a new racial structure (Alba 1990; Sanjek 1994; Gitlin 1995). If current trends persist, today's multiracial hierarchy could be replaced by what I think of as a dual or bimodal one consisting of "nonblack" and "black" population categories, with a third, "residual," category for the groups that do not, or do not yet, fit into the basic dualism.[1]

Originally published in 1999. Please see complete source information beginning on page 891.

More important, this hierarchy may be based not just on color or other visible bodily features, but also on a distinction between undeserving and deserving, or stigmatized and respectable, races.[2] The hierarchy is new only insofar as the old white-nonwhite dichotomy may be replaced by a nonblack-black one, but it is hardly new for blacks, who are likely to remain at the bottom once again. I fear this hierarchy could develop even if more blacks achieve educational mobility, obtain professional and managerial jobs, and gain access to middle-class incomes, wealth, and other "perks." Still, the hierarchy could also end, particularly if the black distribution of income and wealth resembles that of the then-dominant races, and if interracial marriage eliminates many of the visible bodily features by which Americans now define race. . . .

The Dual Racial Hierarchy

Before what is now described, somewhat incorrectly, as the post–1965 immigration, the United States was structured as a predominantly Caucasian, or white, society, with a limited number of numerically and otherwise inferior races, who were typically called Negroes, Orientals, and American Indians— or blacks, yellows, and reds to go with the pinkish-skinned people called whites. There was also a smattering of groups involving a huge number of people who were still described by their national or geographic origins rather than language, including Filipinos, Mexicans and Puerto Ricans, Cubans, etc.[3]

After 1965, when many other Central and Latin American countries began to send migrants, the Spanish-speaking groups were all recategorized by language and called Hispanics. Newcomers from Southeast Asia were classified by continental origin and called Asians, which meant that the later Indian, Pakistani, and Sri Lankan newcomers had to be distinguished regionally, and called South Asians.

At the end of the twentieth century, the country continues to be dominated by whites. Nevertheless, both the immigrants who started to arrive after the end of World War II and the political, cultural, and racial changes that took place in the wake of their arrival have further invalidated many old racial divisions and labels. They have also set into motion what may turn out to be significant transformations in at least part of the basic racial hierarchy.

These transformations are still in an early phase but one of the first has been the elevation of a significant, and mostly affluent, part of the Asian and Asian-American population into a "model minority" that also bids to eradicate many of the boundaries between it and whites. Upward socioeconomic mobility

and increasing intermarriage with whites may even end up in eliminating the boundary that now constructs them as a separate race. Thus, one possible future trend may lead to all but poor Asians and Asian-Americans being perceived and even treated so much like whites that currently visible bodily differences will no longer be judged negatively or even noticed, except when and where Asians or Asian-Americans threaten white interests (e.g., Newman 1993). The same treatment as quasi whites may spread to other successfully mobile and intermarrying immigrants and their descendants, for example Filipinos and white Hispanics.[4]

What these minorities have in common now with Asians, and might have in common even more in the future, is that they are all nonblack, although not as many are currently as affluent as Asians. Nonetheless, by the middle of the twenty-first century, as whites could perhaps become, or will worry about becoming, a numerical minority in the country, they might cast about for political and cultural allies.[5] Their search for allies, which may not even be conscious or deliberate, could hasten the emergence of a new, nonblack racial category, whatever it is named, in which skin color, or in the case of "Hispanics," racially constructed ethnic differences, will be ignored, even if whites would probably remain the dominant subcategory.

The lower part of the emerging dual hierarchy will likely consist of people classified as blacks, including African-Americans, as well as Caribbean and other blacks, dark-skinned or black Hispanics, Native Americans, and anyone else who is dark skinned enough and/or possessed of visible bodily features and behavior patterns, actual or imagined, that remind nonblacks of blacks. Many of these people will also be poor, and if whites and other nonblacks continue to blame America's troubles on a low-status scapegoat, the new black category will be characterized as an undeserving race.

In effect, class will presumably play nearly as much of a role in the boundary changes as race, but with some important exceptions. For example, if a significant number of very poor whites remain as the twenty-first-century equivalent of today's "white trash," they will probably be viewed as less undeserving than equally poor blacks simply because they are whites.[6]

Furthermore, the limits of class are indicated, at least for today, by the continued stigmatization of affluent and otherwise high-status blacks, who suffer some of the same indignities as poor blacks (Feagin and Sykes 1994).[7] So, of course, do moderate- and middle-income members of the working class, who constitute the majority of blacks in America even if whites do not know it. The high visibility of "black" or Negroid physical features renders class position invisible to whites, so that even affluent blacks are suspected of criminal or pathological behavior that is actually found only among a minority of very poor blacks.

Despite continuing white hatreds and fears of blacks that continue almost 150 years after the Civil War, racial classification systems involving others have been more flexible. When the first Irish immigrants came to New York, they were so poor that they were perceived by Anglo-Saxon whites as the black Irish and often treated like blacks. Even so, it did not take the Irish long to separate themselves from blacks, and more important, to be so separated by the city's Anglo-Saxons. A generation later, the Irish were whites (Roediger 1991; Ignatiev 1995).

Perhaps their new whiteness was reinforced by the arrival of the next set of newcomers: people from Eastern and Southern Europe who were often described as members of "swarthy races." Even though the word *race* was used the way we today use *ethnicity*, the newcomers were clearly not white in the Anglo-Saxon sense, and Southern Italians were sometimes called "guineas" because of their dark skin. Nonetheless, over time, they too became white, thanks in part to their acculturation, their integration into the mainstream economy, and after World War II, their entry into the middle class. Perhaps the disappearance of their swarthiness was also reinforced by the arrival in the cities of a new wave of Southern blacks during and after World War II.

A less typical racial transformation occurred about that time in Mississippi, where whites began to treat the Chinese merchants who provided stores for poor blacks as near whites. As Loewen (1988) tells the story, increased affluence and acculturation were again relevant factors. Although whites neither socialized nor intermarried with the Chinese, they accorded them greater social deference and political respect than when they had first arrived. They turned the Chinese into what I previously called a residual category, and in the process created an early version of the nonblack-black duality that may appear in the United States in the next century.

As the Mississippi example suggests, changes in racial classification schemes need not require racial or class equality, for as long as scarce resources or positions remain, justifications for discrimination also remain and physical features that are invisible in some social settings can still become visible in others. Glass ceilings supply the best example, because they seem to change more slowly than some other hierarchical boundaries. Even ceilings for Jews, non-Irish Catholics, and others long classified as whites are still lower than those for WASPs in the upper reaches of the class and prestige structures.

I should note that the racial hierarchy I have sketched here, together with the qualifications that follow, are described both from the perspective of the (overtly) detached social scientist, and also from the perspective of the populations that end up as dominant in the structure. A longer paper would analyze how very differently the people who are fitted into the lower or residual parts of the hierarchy see it.[8]

Qualifications to the Dual Hierarchy

Even if the country would someday replace its current set of racial classifications, the result would not be a simple dual structure, and this model needs to be qualified in at least three ways.

Residuals

The first qualification is the near certainty of a residual or middle category that includes groups placed in a waiting position by the dominant population until it becomes clear whether they will be allowed to become non-black, face the seemingly permanent inferiority that goes with being black, or become long-term residuals.

If such a structure were to develop in the near future, those likely to be placed in a residual category would include the less affluent members of today's Asian, Hispanic and Filipino, Central and South American Indian, and mixed Indian-Latino populations. The future of the dark-skinned members of the South Asian newcomers is harder to predict. Indeed, their treatment will become an important test of how whites deal with the race-class nexus when the people involved are very dark skinned but are not Negroid—and when their class position is so high that in 1990 it outranked that of all other immigrants (Rumbaut 1997, table 1.4).[9]

Who is classified as residual will, like all other categorizations, be shaped by both class and race. To borrow Milton Gordon's (1964) useful but too rarely used notion of "ethclass," what may be developing are "race-classes," with lower-class members of otherwise racially acceptable groups and higher-class members of racially inferior ones being placed in the residual category.

It is also possible for two or more residual categories to emerge, one for nonwhite and Hispanic populations of lower- and working-class position, and another for nonwhites and Hispanics of higher-class position, with the latter more likely to be eligible eventually to join whites in the nonblack portion of a dual hierarchy. Yet other variations are conceivable, however, for white America has not yet given any clues about how it will treat middle-class Latinos of various skin colors and other bodily features. Perhaps today's ad hoc solution, to treat nonblack Hispanics as a quasi-racial ethnic group that is neither white nor black, may survive for another generation or more, particularly if enough Hispanics remain poor or are falsely accused of rejecting linguistic Americanization.

Being placed in a residual classification means more than location in a middle analytic category; it is also a socially enforced, even if covert, category, and it will be accompanied by all the social, political, and emotional uncertainties that go with being placed in a holding pattern and all the pains these create (Marris 1996). True, residuals may not know they are waiting, but then the second-generation white ethnic "marginal men" identified by Stonequist (1937) did not know they were waiting for eventual acculturation and assimilation.

Multiracials

A second qualification to the dual model is created by the emergence of biracials or multiracials that result from the rising intermarriage rates among Asian, Hispanic, and black and white immigrants as well as black and white native-born Americans.[10] Interracial marriages increased from 1 percent of all marriages in 1960 to 3 percent in 1990 (Harrison and Bennett 1995, 165).[11] They are expected to increase much faster in the future, particularly Asian-white ones, since even now, about a third of all Asian marriages, and more than half of all Japanese ones, are intermarriages.[12] If Hispanic-white marriages were also counted, they would exceed all the rest in current number and expected growth, but these are usually treated as ethnic rather than racial intermarriages.

Another set of recruits for a residual position includes the light-skinned blacks, once called mulattos, who today dominate the African-American upper class, some of whom may be sufficiently elite and light-skinned to be viewed as nonblack. Even now, the most prominent among the light-skinned black-white biracials, including business and civic leaders, celebrities and entertainers, are already treated as honorary whites, although many refuse this option and take special pride in their blackness and become "race leaders."[13]

Meanwhile, "multiracial" is in the process of slowly becoming a public racial category, and someday it could become an official one codified by the U.S. Census.[14] At this writing, however, many people of mixed race are not ready to define themselves publicly as such, and those who can choose which racial origin to use are sometimes flexible on instrumental grounds, or may choose different racial origins on different occasions.[15] How people of various racial mixtures construct themselves in the longer run is impossible to tell, since issues of their identification and treatment by others, their own identity, and the social, occupational, financial, and political benefits and costs involved cannot be predicted either.

As far as the country's long-term future racial structure is concerned, however, what matters most is how whites will eventually view and treat multiracial people. This will be affected by the variations in class and visible physical features among multiracial people— for example, how closely they resemble whites or other deserving races. Another question is the future of the traditional identification of race with "blood," which counts all nonwhites in halves, quarters, or even eighths, depending on how many and which ancestors intermarried with whom.[16] If the late twentieth-century belief in the power of genes continues, blood might simply be replaced by genes someday.

Mixed race is a particularly complex category, for several reasons. In any racial intermarriage with more than one offspring, each sibling is likely to look somewhat different racially from the others, ranging from darker to lighter or more and less nonwhite. Thus, one black-white sibling could be viewed as black and another as nonblack—even before they decide how they view themselves. What happens in subsequent generations is virtually unimaginable, since even if mixed-race individuals marry others of the same mixture, their children will not resemble their grand-parents and some may barely resemble their parents. Eventually, a rising number will be treated as, and will think of themselves as, white or nonblack, but this is possible only when people of multiracial origin can no longer bear children who resemble a black ancestor.

Empirical evidence about the effects of racial intermarriage from countries where it has taken place for a long time is unfortunately not very relevant. The closest case, the Caribbean islands, are for the most part, tiny. They are also former plantation societies, with a small number of white and light-skinned elites, and a large number of non-whites—and a differential conception of white and nonwhite from island to island.[17] Caribbean nonwhites appear to intermarry fairly freely but skin color does count and the darkest-skinned peoples are invariably lowest in socioeconomic class and status (Mintz 1989; Rodriguez 1989).

The only large country, Brazil, also began as a plantation society, and it differs from the United States particularly in that the Brazilian state eschewed racial legislation. As a result, Brazil never passed Jim Crow laws, but as of this writing (January 1998) it has not passed civil rights legislation either. Racial stratification, as well as discrimination and segregation, has persisted nonetheless, but it has been maintained through the class system. Drastic class inequalities, including a high rate of illiteracy among the poor, have enabled whites to virtually monopolize the higher class and status positions.

The absence of state involvement has given Brazil an undeserved reputation as a society that encourages intermarriage but ignores racial differences, a reputation the state has publicized as "racial democracy." The reality is not very different from that of the United States, however, for while there has been more intermarriage, it appears to have taken place mainly among blacks and black-white biracials, who together make up about half the country's population. Moreover, biracials gain little socioeconomic advantage from their lighter skins, even as the darkest-skinned blacks are kept at the bottom, forced into slums and prisons as in the United States.[18]

In effect, the Brazilian experience would suggest an empirical precedent for my hypothesis that blacks will remain a separate, and discriminated-against, population in the United States of the future. Indeed, in just about every society in which blacks first arrived as slaves, they are still at the bottom, and the political, socioeconomic, and cultural mechanisms to keep them there remain in place. Although blacks obtain higher incomes and prestige than Asians or white Hispanics in a number of American communities, the descendants of nonblack immigrants are, with some notable exceptions, still able to overtake most blacks in the long run.

Since parts of the United States were also a plantation society in which the slaves were black, the leftovers of the racial stratification pattern will likely continue here as well. Thus, children of black-white intermarriages who turn out to be dark skinned are classified as blacks, even if the United States is on the whole kinder to light-skinned biracials than Brazil.

The future of Asian-white biracials remains more unpredictable, in part because no empirical data exist that can be used to shore up guesses about them. The same observation applies to the endless number of other multiracial combinations that will be created when the children of multiracial parents intermarry with yet other multiracials. There will be few limits to new variations in bodily features, though which will be visible or noticed, and which of the latter will be stigmatized or celebrated as exotic cannot be guessed now.[19] Most likely, however, the larger the number of multiracials and of multiracial variations, the more difficult it will be for nonblacks to define and enforce racial boundaries, or to figure out which of the many darker-skinned varieties of multiracials had black ancestors. In that case, an eventual end to racial discrimination is possible.

If future racial self-identification patterns will also resemble today's ethnic ones, the racial equivalent of today's voluntary white ethnicity and its associated lack of ethnic loyalty may mean that many future triracial, quadriracial, and other multiracial people may eventually know little, and care even less, about the various racial mixtures they have inherited. It is even conceivable that this change will extend to black multiracials, and should race become voluntary for them as well, the possibility of an end to racial discrimination will be increased. Unfortunately, at the moment such extrapolations are far closer to utopian thinking than to sociological speculation.

Regional Variations

A third qualification to the dual model is that the portrait I have drawn is national, but given the regional variations in old racial groups and new immigrant populations, it fits no single U.S. region. Moreover, some parts of the country are now still so devoid of new immigrants, with the exception of the handful who come to establish "ethnic" restaurants, that the present racial hierarchies, categories, and attitudes, many of them based on stereotypes imported from elsewhere, could survive unchanged for quite a while in such areas. Furthermore, some areas that have experienced heavy immigration from Asia and Latin America are currently seeing an outmigration of whites, especially lower-income ones (Frey 1996). Thus, even current patterns in the racial makeup of U.S. regions could change fairly quickly.

In addition, regional differences remain in the demography of the lowest strata. The racial hierarchy of the Deep South will probably continue to bear many direct marks of slavery, although the de facto black experience elsewhere in the country has so far not been totally different. Moreover, in some regions, Latin American and other poor nonblack immigrants have already been able to jump over the poor black population economically and socially, partly because whites, including institutions such as banks, are less hostile—or less necessary—to them than they are to blacks.

In the Southwest, Mexicans and other Hispanics remain at the socioeconomic bottom,
although in California, they may be joined by
the Hmong, Laotians, and other very poor
Asians. And Native Americans still occupy
the lowest socioeconomic stratum in the
handful of mostly rural parts of the country
where they now live, although tribes with
gambling casinos may be able to effect some
changes in that pattern.

Even though some of the new immigrants
can by now be found just about everywhere in
America, the Los Angeles and New York City
areas not only remain the major immigrant
arrival centers but also contain the most diverse populations. As a result, a number of
the issues discussed in this paper will be
played out there, even as they are barely noticeable in the many smaller American cities
that may have attracted only a handful of the
newcomers. Since these two cities are also
the country's prime creators of popular culture, however, their distinctive racial and
ethnic characteristics will probably be diffused in subtle ways through the country as a
whole. . . .

Conclusion

Since no one can even guess much less model
the many causal factors that will influence the
future, the observations above are not intended to be read as a prediction but as an exercise in speculative analysis. The weakness of
such an analysis is its empirical reliance on
the extrapolation of too many current trends
and the assumed persistence of too many current phenomena. The analysis becomes a justifiable exercise, however, because it aims only
to speculate about what future "scenarios"
are possible, and what variables might shape
these.

Obviously, the observations about such a
hierarchy are not meant to suggest that it is
desirable. Indeed, I wrote the paper with the
hope that if such a future threatens to become
real, it can be prevented.

Notes

I am grateful for comments on earlier drafts of this
paper from Margaret Chin, Jennifer Lee, an anonymous reviewer—and from my fellow authors in the
volume *The Cultural Territories of Race: Black
and White Boundaries,* edited by Michèle Lamont
(Chicago and New York: University of Chicago
Press and Russell Sage Foundation, 1999).

1. These categories are constructions, but they
also contain populations experiencing all the pleasures and pains of being located in a hierarchy. And
although I am often discussing constructions, I will
forgo the practice of putting all racial, national,
and related names and labels between quotes, except for unusual racial stereotypes.

2. The two races may not be called that openly,
but ambiguous pejoratives have long been part of
the American vocabulary, for example *underclass*
now, and *pauper* a century earlier (Gans 1995).
Since races are social constructions, their names
will depend in large part on who does the nam-
ing—and whose names become dominant in the
public vocabulary.

3. Puerto Ricans are still often described as immigrants, even though they have been American
citizens for a long time and their move from the island to the mainland is a form of interstate mobility. Racial, class, and linguistic considerations have
undoubtedly influenced this labeling.

The same dominant-race thinking led Irving
Kristol and other neoconservatives to argue in the
1960s that blacks were similar enough to the white
European immigrants to be able to adopt and act
on immigrant values. They also assumed that
blacks would then assimilate like immigrants, ignoring such facts as that blacks had originally
come as slaves, not immigrants; had been here several centuries; and had not yet been allowed by
whites to assimilate. Thirty years later, many
whites ignore the same facts to propose the newest
immigrants as role models for blacks.

4. Much less is said about black Hispanics, including Puerto Ricans, who suffer virtually all of
the discriminatory and other injustices imposed on
African-Americans.

5. Some highly placed whites are already worrying, for example in a *Time* cover story by William
Henry III (1990), but then similar whites worried a
century earlier what the then arriving Catholic and
Jewish newcomers would do to *their* country. The
current worries are as meaningless as the old ones,
since they are based on extrapolations of current
patterns of immigration, not to mention current
constructions of (nonwhite) race and (Hispanic)
ethnicity.

6. Hacker (1996) notes, for example, that the
term "white trash" is no longer in common use. In-

deed, for reasons worth studying, the more popular term of the moment is "trailer trash," which nonetheless seems to be applied solely to poor whites.

7. In this respect, the United States differs from many other countries in the Western hemisphere, where blacks who have managed to become affluent are treated, within limits, as whites.

8. Not only might they perceive it more angrily than I am here doing, but they might be angrier about it than about the present hierarchy, simply because it is new but no great improvement. One result could be their constructions of new racial identities for themselves that depart drastically from the ones future nonblacks consider reasonable.

9. Being far fewer than Asians in number, South Asians are nationally not very visible now. Moreover, for religious and other reasons, South Asian immigrants have so far often been able to discourage their children from intermarrying.

10. My observations on multiracial constructions and people have benefited from many conversations with Valli Rajah.

11. Between 1970 and 1994, the number of people in interracial marriages grew from 676,000 to more than three million (Fletcher 1997). In 1990, biracial children made up 4 percent of all children, increasing from half a million in 1970 to about two million that year. The largest number were Asian-white children, followed by Native American-white and African American-white ones (Harrison and Bennett 1995).

12. Some observers currently estimate that 70 percent of all Japanese and Japanese-Americans are intermarried, mostly with whites. Since they came to the United States as families long before 1965, this estimate may supply a clue about what will happen to second-, third-, and later-generation descendants of other Asian-American populations.

13. Presumably class position will affect how other descendants of old Southern mulatto and creole populations (Dominguez 1986) will be classified.

14. In the political debates over the racial categories to be used in the Year 2000 Census, vocal multiracials preferred to be counted as and with various people of color. African-Americans and other officially recognized racial groups also indicated their opposition to a multiracial category, being reluctant to reduce the power of their numbers or the federal benefits that now go to racial minorities (e.g., Holmes 1996).

15. Kohne (1996) reports that light-skinned biracial Columbia University students who identify as whites also apply for scholarships as blacks. But then, four decades earlier, I met Italian-Americans in Boston's West End who took Irish names in order to obtain jobs in Irish-dominated city hall.

16. The practice of quantifying racial bloods has a long history in Europe and the United States, thanks to both eugenics and slavery. Perhaps it will disappear when enough people have to start counting three or more races. However, people also still use blood fractions when they marry across religions, so that the notion of racial, ethnic, or religious "blood" is by no means obsolete.

17. They are also different, for "one and the same person may be considered white in the Dominican Republic or Puerto Rico . . . 'colored' in Jamaica, Martinique, or Curacao . . . [and] a 'Negro' in Georgia" (Hoetink 1967, xii).

18. This account is based mainly on the data summarized in Fiola 1990 and Skidmore 1992, the classic analysis of the Brazilian racial system in Skidmore 1993, Adamo's 1983 case study of race and class in Rio de Janeiro, and the sociopolitical analyses by Marx (1995, 1996). I am indebted to Anthony Marx for guiding me into the literature on Brazil, although there is still precious little social research, especially with current data, in English.

19. No one has so far paid much attention to who is constructed as exotic and why, except the multiracial people, mostly women, to whom it is applied. Some of them benefit because they are sought by industries that hire workers with exotic facial features; but women without these occupational interests resent such labeling because it turns them into sexual objects.

Industries that employ workers with exotic features, facial and otherwise, such as the fashion and entertainment industries, play an interesting, and probably unduly influential, role in the country's public racial construction.

References

Adamo, Samuel C. 1983. "The Broken Promise: Race, Health and Justice in Rio de Janeiro, 1890–1940." Ph.D. diss., University of New Mexico.

Alba, Richard D. 1990. *Ethnic Identity*. New Haven: Yale University Press.

Dominguez, Virginia R. 1986. *White by Definition*. New Brunswick: Rutgers University Press.

Feagin, Joe R., and Michael P. Sykes. 1994. *Living with Racism*. Boston: Beacon.

Fiola, Jan. 1990. "Race Relations in Brazil: A Reassessment of the 'Racial Democracy' Thesis." Occasional Papers Series no. 34. University of Massachusetts Latin American Studies Program, Amherst.

Fletcher, Michael A. 1997. "More Than a Black-White Issue." *Washington Post National Weekly Edition,* May 26, 34.

Frey, William H. 1996. "Immigration, Domestic Migration and Demographic Balkanization in America." *Population and Development Review* 22:741–63.

Gans, Herbert J. 1995. *The War against the Poor.* New York: Basic.

Gitlin, Todd. 1995. *The Twilight of Common Dreams.* New York: Metropolitan.

Gordon, Milton M. 1964. *Assimilation in American Life.* New York: Oxford University Press.

Hacker, Andrew. 1996. Foreword to *The Coming Race War?* by Richard Delgado. New York: New York University Press.

Harrison, Roderick J., and Claudette Bennett. 1995. "Racial and Ethnic Diversity." In *State of the Union: America in the 1990s,* vol. 2, *Social Trends,* edited by Reynolds Farley. New York: Russell Sage Foundation.

Henry, William, III. 1990. "Beyond the Melting Pot." *Time,* April 9, 29–32.

Hoetink, Harry. 1967. *The Two Variants in Caribbean Race Relations.* London: Oxford University Press.

Holmes, Steven. 1996. "Census Tests New Category to Identify Racial Groups." *New York Times,* December 4, A25.

Ignatiev, Noel. 1995. *How the Irish Became White.* New York: Routledge.

Kohne, Natasha G. 1996. "The Experience of Mixed-Race Women: Challenging Racial Boundaries." Unpublished senior thesis, Department of Sociology, Columbia University, New York.

Loewen, James W. 1988. *The Mississippi Chinese.* 2d ed. Prospect Heights, Ill.: Waveland.

Marris, Peter. 1996. *The Politics of Uncertainty.* New York: Routledge.

Marx, Anthony W. 1995. "Contested Citizenship: The Dynamics of Racial Identity and Social Movements." *International Review of History* 40, supplement 3: 159–83.

———. 1996. "Race-Making and the Nation-State." *World Politics,* January, 180–208.

Mintz, Sidney W. 1989. *Caribbean Transformations.* New York: Columbia University Press.

Newman, Katherine. 1993. *Declining Fortunes.* New York: Basic.

Rodriguez, Clara E. 1989. *Puerto Ricans: Born in the U.S.A.* Boston: Unwin Hyman.

Roediger, David R. 1991. *Wages of Whiteness.* London: Verso.

Rumbaut, Ruben G. 1997. "Ties that Bind: Immigration and Immigrant Families in the United States." In *Immigration and the Family,* edited by Alan Booth, Ann C. Crouter, and Nancy Landale. Mahwah, N.J.: Erlbaum.

Sanjek, Roger. 1994. "Intermarriage and the Future of the Races in the United States." In *Race,* edited by Steven Gregory and Roger Sanjek. New Brunswick: Rutgers University Press.

Skidmore, Thomas L. 1992. "Fact and Myth: Discovering a Racial Problem in Brazil." Working paper 173. Helen Kellogg Institute for International Studies, University of Notre Dame.

———. 1993. *Black into White.* Durham: Duke University Press.

Stonequist, Everett V. 1937. *The Marginal Man.* New York: Scribner's.

WILLIAM JULIUS WILSON

Jobless Poverty: A New Form of Social Dislocation in the Inner-City Ghetto

In September 1996 my book, *When Work Disappears: The World of the New Urban Poor,* was published. It describes a new type of poverty in our nation's metropolises: poor, segregated neighborhoods in which a majority of adults are either unemployed or have dropped out of the labor force altogether. What is the effect of these "jobless ghettos" on individuals, families, and neighborhoods? What accounts for their existence? I suggest several factors and conclude with policy recommendations: a mix of public and private sector projects is more effective than relying on a strategy of employer subsidies.

The Research Studies

When Work Disappears was based mainly on three research studies conducted in Chicago between 1986 and 1993. The first of these three studies included a variety of data: a random survey of nearly 2,500 poor and non-poor African American, Latino, and white residents in Chicago's poor neighborhoods; a more focused survey of 175 participants who were reinterviewed and answered open-ended

questions; a survey of 179 employers selected to reflect distribution of employment across industry and firm size in the Chicago metro-politan areas; and comprehensive ethnographic research, including participant-observation research and life-history interviews by ten research assistants in a representative sample of inner-city neighborhoods.

The first of the two remaining projects also included extensive data: a survey of a representative sample of 546 black mothers and up to two of their adolescent children (aged eleven to sixteen—or 887 adolescents) in working-class, middle-class, and high-poverty neighborhoods; a survey of a representative sample of 500 respondents from two high-joblessness neighborhoods on the South Side of Chicago; and six focus-group discussions involving the residents and former residents of these neighborhoods.

Jobless Ghettos

The jobless poverty of today stands in sharp contrast to previous periods. In 1950, a substantial portion of the urban black population was poor but they were working. Urban poverty was quite extensive but people held jobs. However, as we entered the 1990s most adults in many inner-city ghetto neighborhoods were not working. For example, in 1950 a significant majority of adults held jobs in a typical week in the three neighborhoods

---

Originally published in 1999. Please see complete source information beginning on page 891.

that represent the historic core of the Black Belt in Chicago—Douglas, Grand Boulevard, and Washington Park. But by 1990, only four in ten in Douglas worked in a typical week, one in three in Washington Park, and one in four in Grand Boulevard.[1] In 1950, 69 percent of all males aged fourteen and older who lived in these three neighborhoods worked in a typical week, and in 1960, 64 percent of this group were so employed. However, by 1990 only 37 percent of all males aged sixteen and over held jobs in a typical week in these three neighborhoods.

The disappearance of work has had negative effects not only on individuals and families, but on the social life of neighborhoods as well. Inner-city joblessness is a severe problem that is often overlooked or obscured when the focus is mainly on poverty and its consequences. Despite increases in the concentration of poverty since 1970, inner cities have always featured high levels of poverty. But the levels of inner-city joblessness reached during the first half of the 1990s were unprecedented.

Joblessness versus Informal Work Activity

I should note that when I speak of "joblessness" I am not solely referring to official unemployment. The unemployment rate represents only the percentage of workers in the *official* labor force—that is, those who are *actively* looking for work. It does not include those who are outside of or have dropped out of the labor market, including the nearly six million males aged twenty-five to sixty who appeared in the census statistics but were not recorded in the labor market statistics in 1990 (Thurow 1990).

These uncounted males in the labor market are disproportionately represented in the inner-city ghettos. Accordingly, in *When Work Disappears,* I use a more appropriate measure of joblessness, a measure that takes into account both official unemployment and

non–labor-force participation. That measure is the employment-to-population ratio, which corresponds to the percentage of adults aged sixteen and older who are working. Using the employment-to-population ratio we find, for example, that in 1990 only one in three adults aged sixteen and older held a job in the ghetto poverty areas of Chicago, areas representing roughly 425,000 men, women, and children. And in the ghetto tracts of the nation's one hundred largest cities, for every ten adults who did not hold a job in a typical week in 1990 there were only six employed persons (Kasarda 1993).

The consequences of high neighborhood joblessness are more devastating than those of high neighborhood poverty. A neighborhood in which people are poor but employed is much different than a neighborhood in which people are poor and jobless. *When Work Disappears* shows that many of today's problems in the inner-city ghetto neighborhoods—crime, family dissolution, welfare, low levels of social organization, and so on—are fundamentally a consequence of the disappearance of work.

It should be clear that when I speak of the disappearance of work, I am referring to the declining involvement in or lack of attachment to the formal labor market. It could be argued that, in the general sense of the term, "joblessness" does not necessarily mean "nonwork." In other words, to be officially unemployed or officially outside the labor market does not mean that one is totally removed from all forms of work activity. Many people who are officially jobless are nonetheless involved in informal kinds of work activity, ranging from unpaid housework to work that draws income from the informal or illegal economies.

Housework is work, baby-sitting is work, even drug dealing is work. However, what contrasts work in the formal economy with work activity in the informal and illegal economies is that work in the formal economy is characterized by, indeed calls for, greater regularity and consistency in schedules and hours. Work schedules and hours are formalized. The demands for discipline are greater. It is true that some work activities outside the formal economy also call for discipline and regular schedules. Several studies reveal that the social organization of the drug industry is driven by discipline and a work ethic, however perverse.[2] However, as a general rule, work in the informal and illegal economies is far less governed by norms or expectations that place a premium on discipline and regularity. For all these reasons, when I speak of the disappearance of work, I mean work in the formal economy, work that provides a framework for daily behavior because of the discipline, regularity, and stability that it imposes.

Effect of Joblessness on Routine and Discipline

In the absence of regular employment, a person lacks not only a place in which to work and the receipt of regular income but also a coherent organization of the present—that is, a system of concrete expectations and goals. Regular employment provides the anchor for the spatial and temporal aspects of daily life. It determines where you are going to be and when you are going to be there. In the absence of regular employment, life, including family life, becomes less coherent. Persistent unemployment and irregular employment hinder rational planning in daily life, a necessary condition of adaptation to an industrial economy (Bourdieu 1965).

Thus, a youngster who grows up in a family with a steady breadwinner and in a neighborhood in which most of the adults are employed will tend to develop some of the disciplined habits associated with stable or steady employment—habits that are reflected in the behavior of his or her parents and of other neighborhood adults. These might include attachment to a routine, a recognition of the hierarchy found in most work situations, a sense of personal efficacy attained through the routine management of financial affairs, endorsement of a system of personal and material rewards associated with dependability and responsibility, and so on. Accordingly, when this youngster enters the labor market, he or she has a distinct advantage over the youngsters who grow up in households without a steady breadwinner and in neighborhoods that are not organized around work—in other words, a milieu in which one is more exposed to the less disciplined habits associated with casual or infrequent work.

With the sharp recent rise of solo-parent families, black children who live in inner-city households are less likely to be socialized in a work environment for two main reasons. Their mothers, saddled with child-care responsibilities, can prevent a slide deeper into poverty by accepting welfare. Their fathers, removed from family responsibilities and obligations, are more likely to become idle as a response to restricted employment opportunities, which further weakens their influence in the household and attenuates their contact with the family. In short, the social and cultural responses to joblessness are reflected in the organization of family life and patterns of family formation; there they have implications for labor-force attachment as well.

Given the current policy debates that assign blame to the personal shortcomings of the jobless, we need to understand their behavior as responses and adaptations to chronic subordination, including behaviors that have evolved into cultural patterns. The social actions of the jobless—including their behavior, habits, skills, styles, orientations, attitudes—ought not to be analyzed as if they are unrelated to the broader structure of their opportunities and constraints that have evolved over time. This is not to argue that individuals and groups lack the freedom to make their own choices, engage in certain conduct, and develop certain styles and orientations; but I maintain that their decisions and actions occur within a context of constraints and opportunities that are drastically different from those in middle-class society.

Explanations of the Growth of Jobless Ghettos

What accounts for the growing proportion of jobless adults in inner-city communities? An easy explanation would be racial segregation. However, a race-specific argument is not sufficient to explain recent changes in such neighborhoods. After all, these historical Black Belt neighborhoods were *just as segregated by skin color in 1950* as they are today, yet the level of employment was much higher then. One has to account for the ways in which racial segregation interacts with other changes in society to produce the recent escalating rates of joblessness. Several factors stand out: the decreasing demand for low-skilled labor, the suburbanization of jobs, the social deterioration of ghetto neighborhoods, and negative employer attitudes. I discuss each of these factors next.

Decreasing Demand for Low-Skilled Labor

The disappearance of work in many inner-city neighborhoods is in part related to the nationwide decline in the fortunes of low-skilled workers. The sharp decline in the relative demand for unskilled labor has had a more adverse effect on blacks than on whites because a substantially larger proportion of African Americans are unskilled. Although the number of skilled blacks (including managers, professionals, and technicians) has increased sharply in the last several years, the proportion of those who are unskilled remains large, because the black population, burdened by cumulative experiences of racial restrictions, was overwhelmingly unskilled just several decades ago (Schwartzman 1997).[3]

The factors involved in the decreased relative demand for unskilled labor include changes in skill-based technology, the rapid growth in college enrollment that increased the supply and reduced the relative cost of skilled labor, and the growing internationalization of economic activity, including trade liberalization policies, which reduced the price of imports and raised the output of export industries (Schwartzman 1997). The increased output of export industries aids skilled workers, simply because they are heavily represented in export industries. But increasing imports, especially those from developing countries that compete with labor-intensive industries (for example, apparel, textile, toy, footwear, and some manufacturing industries), hurts unskilled labor (Schwartzman 1997).

Accordingly, inner-city blacks are experiencing a more extreme form of the economic marginality that has affected most unskilled workers in America since 1980. Unfortunately, there is a tendency among policy makers, black leaders, and scholars alike to separate the economic problems of the ghetto from the national and international trends affecting American families and neighborhoods. If the economic problems of the ghetto are defined solely in racial terms they can be isolated and viewed as only requiring race-based solutions as proposed by those on the left, or as only requiring narrow political solutions with subtle racial connotations (such as welfare reform), as strongly proposed by those on the right.

Overemphasis on Racial Factors

Race continues to be a factor that aggravates inner-city black employment problems as we shall soon see. But the tendency to overemphasize the racial factors obscures other more fundamental forces that have sharply increased inner-city black joblessness. As the late black economist Vivian Henderson put it several years ago, "[I]t is as if racism having put blacks in their economic place steps aside to watch changes in the economy destroy that place" (Henderson 1975, 54). To repeat, the concentrated joblessness of the inner-city poor represents the most dramatic form of the growing economic dislocations among the unskilled stemming in large measure from changes in the organization of the economy, including the global economy.

Suburbanization of Jobs

But inner-city workers face an additional problem: the growing suburbanization of jobs. Most ghetto residents cannot afford an automobile and therefore have to rely on public transit systems that make the connection between inner-city neighborhoods and suburban job locations difficult and time consuming.

Although studies based on data collected before 1970 showed no consistent or convincing effects on black employment as a consequence of this spatial mismatch, the employment of inner-city blacks relative to suburban blacks has clearly deteriorated since then. Recent research (conducted mainly by urban labor economists) strongly shows that the decentralization of employment is continuing and that employment in manufacturing, most of which is already suburbanized, has decreased in central cities, particularly in the Northeast and Midwest (Holzer 1996).

Blacks living in central cities have less access to employment (as measured by the ratio of jobs to people and the average travel time to and from work) than do central-city whites. Moreover, unlike most other groups of workers across the urban-suburban divide, less-educated central-city blacks receive lower wages than suburban blacks who have similar levels of education. And the decline in earnings of central-city blacks is related to the decentralization of employment—that is, the movement of jobs from the cities to the suburbs—in metropolitan areas (Holzer 1996).

Social Deterioration of Ghetto Neighborhoods

Changes in the class, racial, and demographic composition of inner-city neighborhoods have also contributed to the high percentage of jobless adults in these neighborhoods. Because of the steady out-migration of more advantaged families, the proportion of nonpoor families and prime-age working adults has decreased sharply in the typical inner-city ghetto since 1970 (Wilson 1987). In the face of in-

creasing and prolonged joblessness, the declining proportion of nonpoor families and the overall depopulation has made it increasingly difficult to sustain basic neighborhood institutions or to achieve adequate levels of social organization. The declining presence of working- and middle-class blacks has also deprived ghetto neighborhoods of key structural and cultural resources. Structural resources include residents with income high enough to sustain neighborhood services, and cultural resources include conventional role models for neighborhood children.

On the basis of our research in Chicago, it appears that what many high jobless neighborhoods have in common is a relatively high degree of social integration (high levels of local neighboring while being relatively isolated from contacts in the broader mainstream society) and low levels of informal social control (feelings that they have little control over their immediate environment, including the environment's negative influences on their children). In such areas, not only are children at risk because of the lack of informal social controls, they are also disadvantaged because the social interaction among neighbors tends to be confined to those whose skills, styles, orientations, and habits are not as conducive to promoting positive social outcomes (academic success, pro-social behavior, employment in the formal labor market, etc.) as those in more stable neighborhoods. Although the close interaction among neighbors in such areas may be useful in devising strategies, disseminating information, and developing styles of behavior that are helpful in a ghetto milieu (teaching children to avoid eye-to-eye contact with strangers and to develop a tough demeanor in the public sphere for self-protection), they may be less effective in promoting the welfare of children in society at large.

Despite being socially integrated, the residents in Chicago's ghetto neighborhoods shared a feeling that they had little informal social control over the children in their environment. A primary reason is the absence of a strong organizational capacity or an institutional resource base that would provide an extra layer of social organization in their neighborhoods. It is easier for parents to control the behavior of the children in their neighborhoods when a strong institutional resource base exists and when the links between community institutions such as churches, schools, political organizations, businesses, and civic clubs are strong or secure. The higher the density and stability of formal organizations, the less illicit activities such as drug trafficking, crime, prostitution, and the formation of gangs can take root in the neighborhood.

Few Community Institutions

A weak institutional resource base is what distinguishes high jobless inner-city neighborhoods from stable middle-class and working-class areas. As one resident of a high jobless neighborhood on the South Side of Chicago put it, "Our children, you know, seems to be more at risk than any other children there is, because there's no library for them to go to. There's not a center they can go to, there's no field house that they can go into. There's nothing. There's nothing at all." Parents in high jobless neighborhoods have a much more difficult task controlling the behavior of their adolescents and preventing them from getting involved in activities detrimental to pro-social development. Given the lack of organizational capacity and a weak institutional base, some parents choose to protect their children by isolating them from activities in the neighborhood, including avoiding contact and interaction with neighborhood families. Wherever possible, and often with great difficulty when one considers the problems of transportation and limited financial resources, they attempt to establish contacts and cultivate relations with individuals, families, and institutions, such as church groups, schools, and community recreation programs, outside their neighborhood. A note of caution is necessary, though. It is just as indefensible to treat inner-city residents as super heroes who overcome racist oppression as it is to view them as helpless victims. We should, however, appreciate the range of choices, including choices representing cultural influences, that are available to inner-city residents who live under constraints that most people in the larger society do not experience.

Effect of Joblessness on Marriage and Family

It is within the context of labor-force attachment that the public policy discussion on welfare reform and family values should be couched. The research that we have conducted in Chicago suggests that as employment prospects recede, the foundation for stable relationships becomes weaker over time. More permanent relationships such as marriage give way to temporary liaisons that result in broken unions, out-of-wedlock pregnancies, and, to a lesser extent, separation and divorce. The changing norms concerning marriage in the larger society reinforce the movement toward temporary liaisons in the inner city, and therefore economic considerations in marital decisions take on even greater weight. Many inner-city residents have negative outlooks toward marriage, outlooks that are developed in and influenced by an environment featuring persistent joblessness.

The disrupting effect of joblessness on marriage and family causes poor inner-city blacks to be even more disconnected from the job market and discouraged about their role in the labor force. The economic marginality of the ghetto poor is cruelly reinforced, therefore, by conditions in the neighborhoods in which they live.

Negative Employer Attitudes

In the eyes of employers in metropolitan Chicago, the social conditions in the ghetto render inner-city blacks less desirable as workers, and therefore many are reluctant to hire them. One of the three studies that provided the empirical foundation for *When Work Disappears* included a representative sample of employers in the greater Chicago area who provided entry-level jobs. An overwhelming majority of these employers, both white and black, expressed negative views about inner-city ghetto workers, and many stated that they were reluctant to hire them. For example, a president of an inner-city manufacturing firm expressed a concern about employing residents from certain inner-city neighborhoods:

If somebody gave me their address, uh, Cabrini Green I might unavoidably have some concerns. *Interviewer:* What would your concerns be? *Respondent:* That the poor guy probably would be frequently unable to get to work and ... I probably would watch him more carefully even if it wasn't fair, than I would with somebody else. I know what I should do though is recognize that here's a guy that is trying to get out of his situation and probably will work harder than somebody else who's already out of there and he might be the best one around here. But I, I think I would have to struggle accepting that premise at the beginning. (Wilson 1996, field notes)

In addition to qualms about the neighborhood milieu of inner-city residents, the employers frequently mentioned concerns about applicants' language skills and educational training. An employer from a computer software firm in Chicago expressed the view "that in many businesses the ability to meet the public is paramount and you do not talk street talk to the buying public. Almost all your black welfare people talk street talk. And who's going to sit them down and change their speech patterns?" (Wilson 1996, field notes) A Chicago real estate broker made a similar point:

A lot of times I will interview applicants who are black, who are sort of lower class. ... They'll come to me and I cannot hire them because their language skills are so poor. Their speaking voice for one thing is poor ... they have no verbal facility with the language ... and these ... you know, they just don't know how to speak and they'll say "salesmens" instead of "salesmen" and that's a

problem. ... They don't know punctuation, they don't know how to use correct grammar, and they cannot spell. And I can't hire them. And I feel bad about that and I think they're being very disadvantaged by the Chicago Public School system. (Wilson 1996, field notes)

Another respondent defended his method of screening out most job applicants on the telephone on the basis of their use of "grammar and English":

I have every right to say that that's a requirement for this job. I don't care if you're pink, black, green, yellow or orange, I demand someone who speaks well. You want to tell me that I'm a bigot, fine, call me a bigot. I know blacks, you don't even know they're black. (Wilson 1996, field notes)

Finally, an inner-city banker claimed that many blacks in the ghetto "simply cannot read. When you're talking our type of business, that disqualifies them immediately, we don't have a job here that doesn't require that somebody have minimum reading and writing skills" (Wilson 1996, field notes).

How should we interpret the negative attitudes and actions of employers? To what extent do they represent an aversion to blacks *per se* and to what degree do they reflect judgments based on the job-related skills and training of inner-city blacks in a changing labor market? I should point out that the statements made by the African American employers concerning the qualifications of inner-city black workers did not differ significantly from those of the white employers. Whereas 74 percent of all the white employers who responded to the open-ended questions expressed negative views of the job-related traits of inner-city blacks, 80 percent of the black employers did so as well.

This raises a question about the meaning and significance of race in certain situations—in other words, how race intersects with other factors. A key hypothesis in this connection is that given the recent shifts in the economy, employers are looking for workers with a broad range of abilities: "hard" skills (literacy, numerical ability, basic mechanical ability, and other testable attributes) and "soft" skills (personalities suitable to the work environment, good grooming, group-oriented work behaviors, etc.). While hard skills are the product of education and training—benefits that are apparently in short supply in inner-city schools—soft skills are strongly tied to culture, and are therefore shaped by the harsh environment of the inner-city ghetto. For example, our research revealed that many parents in the inner-city ghetto neighborhoods of Chicago wanted their children not to make eye-to-eye contact with strangers and to develop a tough demeanor when interacting with people on the streets. While such behaviors are helpful for survival in the ghetto, they hinder successful interaction in mainstream society.

Statistical Discrimination

If employers are indeed reacting to the difference in skills between white and black applicants, it becomes increasingly difficult to discuss the motives of employers: are they rejecting inner-city black applicants out of overt racial discrimination or on the basis of qualifications?

Nonetheless, many of the selective recruitment practices do represent what economists call "statistical discrimination": employers make assumptions about the inner-city black workers *in general* and reach decisions based on those assumptions before they have had a chance to review systematically the qualifications of an individual applicant. The net effect is that many black inner-city applicants are never given the chance to prove their qualifications on an individual level because they are systematically screened out by the selective recruitment process.

Statistical discrimination, although representing elements of class bias against poor workers in the inner city, is clearly a matter of race both directly and indirectly. Directly, the selective recruitment patterns effectively screen out far more black workers from the inner city than Hispanic or white workers

from the same types of backgrounds. But indirectly, race is also a factor, even in those decisions to deny employment to inner-city black workers on the basis of objective and thorough evaluations of their qualifications. The hard and soft skills among inner-city blacks that do not match the current needs of the labor market are products of racially segregated communities, communities that have historically featured widespread social constraints and restricted opportunities.

Thus the job prospects of inner-city workers have diminished not only because of the decreasing relative demand for low-skilled labor in the United States economy, the suburbanization of jobs, and the social deterioration of ghetto neighborhoods, but also because of negative employer attitudes. This combination of factors presents a real challenge to policy makers. Indeed, considering the narrow range of social policy options in the "balance-the-budget" political climate, how can we immediately alleviate the inner-city jobs problem—a problem which will undoubtedly grow when the new welfare reform bill takes full effect and creates a situation that will be even more harmful to inner-city children and adolescents?

Public Policy Dilemmas

What are the implications of these studies on public policy? A key issue is public-sector employment. If firms in the private sector cannot hire or refuse to hire low-skilled adults who are willing to take minimum-wage jobs, then policy makers should consider a policy of public-sector employment-of-last-resort. Indeed, until current changes in the labor market are reversed or until the skills of the next generation of workers can be upgraded before they enter the labor market, many workers, especially those who are not in the official labor force, will not be able to find jobs unless the government becomes an employer-of-last-resort (Danziger and Gottschalk 1995). This argument applies especially to low-skilled inner-city black workers. It is bad enough that they face the problem of shifts in labor-market demand shared by all low-skilled workers; it is even worse that they confront negative employer perceptions about their work-related skills and attitudes.

For all these reasons, the passage of the 1996 welfare reform bill, which did not include a program of job creation, could have very negative social consequences in the inner city. Unless something is done to enhance the employment opportunities of inner-city welfare recipients who reach the time limit for the receipt of welfare, they will flood a pool already filled with low-skilled, jobless workers. . . .

West Virginia, a state that has been plagued with a severe shortage of work opportunities, has provided community service jobs to recipients of welfare for several years. In Wisconsin, Governor Thompson's welfare reform plan envisions community service jobs for many parents in the more depressed areas of the state, and the New Hope program in Milwaukee provides community service jobs for those unable to find employment in the private sector (Center on Budget and Policy Priorities 1996). It is especially important that this mixed strategy include a plan to make *adequate* monies available to localities or communities with high jobless and welfare dependency rates.

Obviously, as more people become employed and gain work experience, they will have a better chance of finding jobs in the private sector when jobs become available. The attitudes of employers toward inner-city workers could change, in part because they would be dealing with job applicants who have steady work experience and who could furnish references from their previous supervisors. Children are more likely to be socialized in a work-oriented environment and to develop the job readiness skills that are seen as important even for entry-level jobs.

Thus, given the recent welfare reform legislation, *adequate* strategies to enhance the employment opportunities of inner-city residents should be contemplated, strategies that would be adequately financed and designed to ad-dress the employment problems of low-skilled workers not only in periods of tight labor markets, but, even more important, in periods when the labor market is slack.

Notes

1. The figures on adult employment are based on calculations from data provided by the 1990 U.S. Bureau of the Census (1993) and the *Local Community Fact Book for Chicago—1950* (1953) and the *Local Community Fact Book for Chicago—1960* (1963). The adult employment rates represent the number of employed individuals (aged fourteen and older in 1950 and sixteen and older in 1990) among the total number of adults in a given area. Those who are not employed include both the individuals who are members of the labor force but are not working and those who have dropped out or are not part of the labor force.

2. See, for example, Bourgois (1995) and Venkatesh (1996).

3. The economist David Schwartzman defines "unskilled workers to include operators, fabricators, and laborers, and those in service occupations, including private household workers, those working in protective service occupations, food service, and cleaning and building service." On the basis of this definition he estimates that 80 percent of all black workers and 38 percent of all white workers were unskilled in 1950. By 1990, 46 percent of black workers and 27 percent of white workers were employed in unskilled occupations (Schwartzman 1997).

Bibliography

Bourdieu, Pierre. 1965. *Travail et Travailleurs en Algerie*. Paris: Editions Mouton.

Bourgois, Philippe. 1995. *In Search of Respect: Selling Crack in El Barrio*. New York: Cambridge University Press.

Center on Budget and Policy Priorities. 1996. *The Administration's $3 Billion Jobs Proposal*. Washington, DC: Center on Budget and Policy Priorities.

Danziger, Sheldon H., and Peter Gottschalk. 1995. *America Unequal*. Cambridge, MA: Harvard University Press.

Henderson, Vivian. 1975. "Race, Economics, and Public Policy." *Crisis* 83 (Fall):50–55.

Holzer, Harry J. 1996. *What Employers Want: Job Prospects for Less-Educated Workers*. New York: Russell Sage.

Kasarda, John D. 1993. "Inner-City Concentrated Poverty and Neighborhood Distress: 1970–1990." *Housing Policy Debate* 4(3): 253–302.

Local Community Fact Book for Chicago—1950. 1953. Chicago: Community Inventory, University of Chicago.

Local Community Fact Book for Chicago—1960. 1963. Chicago: Community Inventory, University of Chicago.

Schwartzman, David. 1997. *Black Unemployment: Part of Unskilled Unemployment.* Westport, CT: Greenwood.

Thurow, Lester. 1990. "The Crusade That's Killing Prosperity." *American Prospect* March/April:54–59.

U.S. Bureau of the Census. 1993. *Census of Population: Detailed Characteristics of the Population.* Washington, DC: U.S. Government Printing Office.

Venkatesh, Sudhir. 1996. "Private Lives, Public Housing: An Ethnography of the Robert Taylor Homes." Ph.D. dissertation., University of Chicago.

Wilson, William Julius. 1987. *The Truly Disadvantaged: The Inner City, The Underclass, and Public Policy.* Chicago: University of Chicago Press.

———. 1996. *When Work Disappears: The World of the New Urban Poor.* New York: Alfred A. Knopf.

D O U G L A S   S.   M A S S E Y   A N D   N A N C Y   A.   D E N T O N

American Apartheid: Segregation and the Making of the Underclass

It is quite simple. As soon as there is a group area then all your uncertainties are removed and that is, after all, the primary purpose of this Bill [requiring racial segregation in housing].

—Minister of the Interior, Union of South Africa legislative debate on the Group Areas Act of 1950

During the 1970s and 1980s a word disappeared from the American vocabulary.[1] It was not in the speeches of politicians decrying the multiple ills besetting American cities. It was not spoken by government officials responsible for administering the nation's social programs. It was not mentioned by journalists reporting on the rising tide of homelessness, drugs, and violence in urban America. It was not discussed by foundation executives and think-tank experts proposing new programs for unemployed parents and unwed mothers. It was not articulated by civil rights leaders speaking out against the persistence of racial inequality; and it was nowhere to be found in the thousands of pages written by social scientists on the urban underclass. The word was segregation.

Most Americans vaguely realize that urban America is still a residentially segregated society, but few appreciate the depth of black segregation or the degree to which it is maintained by ongoing institutional arrangements and contemporary individual

Originally published in 1993. Please see complete source information beginning on page 891.

actions. They view segregation as an unfortunate holdover from a racist past, one that is fading progressively over time. If racial residential segregation persists, they reason, it is only because civil rights laws passed during the 1960s have not had enough time to work or because many blacks still prefer to live in black neighborhoods. The residential segregation of blacks is viewed charitably as a "natural" outcome of impersonal social and economic forces, the same forces that produced Italian and Polish neighborhoods in the past and that yield Mexican and Korean areas today.

But black segregation is not comparable to the limited and transient segregation experienced by other racial and ethnic groups, now or in the past. No group in the history of the United States has ever experienced the sustained high level of residential segregation that has been imposed on blacks in large American cities for the past fifty years. This extreme racial isolation did not just happen; it was manufactured by whites through a series of self-conscious actions and purposeful institutional arrangements that continue today. Not only is the depth of black segregation unprecedented and utterly unique compared with that of other groups, but it shows little sign of change with the passage of time or improvements in socioeconomic status.

If policymakers, scholars, and the public have been reluctant to acknowledge segregation's persistence, they have likewise been blind to its consequences for American blacks. Residential segregation is not a neutral fact; it systematically undermines the social and economic well-being of blacks in the United States. Because of racial segregation, a significant share of black America is condemned to experience a social environment where poverty and joblessness are the norm, where a majority of children are born out of wedlock, where most families are on welfare, where educational failure prevails, and where social and physical deterioration abound. Through prolonged exposure to such an environment, black chances for social and economic success are drastically reduced.

Deleterious neighborhood conditions are built into the structure of the black community. They occur because segregation concentrates poverty to build a set of mutually reinforcing and self-feeding spirals of decline into black neighborhoods. When economic dislocations deprive a segregated group of employment and increase its rate of poverty, socioeconomic deprivation inevitably becomes more concentrated in neighborhoods where that group lives. The damaging social consequences that follow from increased poverty are spatially concentrated as well, creating uniquely disadvantaged environments that become progressively isolated—geographically, socially, and economically—from the rest of society.

The effect of segregation on black well-being is structural, not individual. Residential segregation lies beyond the ability of any individual to change; it constrains black life chances irrespective of personal traits, individual motivations, or private achievements. For the past twenty years this fundamental fact has been swept under the rug by policymakers, scholars, and theorists of the urban underclass. Segregation is the missing link in prior attempts to understand the plight of the urban poor. As long as blacks continue to be segregated in American cities, the United States cannot be called a race-blind society.

The Forgotten Factor

The present myopia regarding segregation is all the more startling because it once figured prominently in theories of racial inequality. Indeed, the ghetto was once seen as central to black subjugation in the United States. In 1944 Gunnar Myrdal wrote in *An American Dilemma* that residential segregation "is basic in a mechanical sense. It exerts its influence in an indirect and impersonal way: because Negro people do not live near white people, they cannot . . . associate with each other in the many activities founded on common neighborhood. Residential segregation . . . becomes reflected in uni-racial schools, hospitals, and other institutions" and creates "an artificial city . . . that permits any prejudice on the part of public officials to be freely vented on Negroes without hurting whites."[2]

Kenneth B. Clark, who worked with Gunnar Myrdal as a student and later applied his research skills in the landmark *Brown v. Topeka* school integration case, placed residential segregation at the heart of the U.S. system of racial oppression. In *Dark Ghetto,* written in 1965, he argued that "the dark ghetto's invisible walls have been erected by the white society, by those who have power, both to confine those who have *no* power and to perpetuate their powerlessness. The dark ghettos are social, political, educational, and—above all—economic colonies. Their inhabitants are subject peoples, victims of the greed, cruelty, insensitivity, guilt, and fear of their masters."[3]

Public recognition of segregation's role in perpetuating racial inequality was galvanized in the late 1960s by the riots that erupted in the nation's ghettos. In their aftermath, President Lyndon B. Johnson appointed a commission chaired by Governor Otto Kerner of Illinois to identify the causes of the violence and to propose policies to prevent its recurrence. The Kerner Commission released its report in March 1968 with the shocking admonition that the United States was "moving toward two societies, one black, one white—separate and unequal."[4] Prominent among the causes that the commission identified for this growing racial inequality was residential segregation.

In stark, blunt language, the Kerner Commission informed white Americans that "discrimination and segregation have long permeated much of American life; they now threaten the future of every American."[5] "Segregation and poverty have created in the racial ghetto a destructive environment totally unknown to most white Americans. What white Americans have never fully understood—but what the Negro can never forget—is that white society is deeply implicated in the ghetto. White institutions created it, white institutions maintain it, and white society condones it."[6]

The report argued that to continue present policies was "to make permanent the division of our country into two societies; one, largely Negro and poor, located in the central cities; the other, predominantly white and affluent, located in the suburbs."[7] Commission members rejected a strategy of ghetto enrichment coupled with abandonment of efforts to integrate, an approach they saw "as another way of choosing a permanently divided country."[8] Rather, they insisted that the only reasonable choice for America was "a policy which combines ghetto enrichment with programs designed to encourage integration of substantial numbers of Negroes into the society outside the ghetto."[9]

America chose differently. Following the passage of the Fair Housing Act in 1968, the problem of housing discrimination was declared solved, and residential segregation dropped off the national agenda. Civil rights leaders stopped pressing for the enforcement of open housing, political leaders increasingly debated employment and educational policies rather than housing integration, and academicians focused their theoretical scrutiny on everything from culture to family structure, to institutional racism, to federal welfare systems. Few people spoke of racial segregation as a problem or acknowledged its persisting consequences. By the end of the 1970s residential segregation became the forgotten factor in American race relations.[10]

While public discourse on race and poverty became more acrimonious and more focused on divisive issues such as school busing, racial quotas, welfare, and affirmative action, conditions in the nation's ghettos steadily deteriorated.[11] By the end of the 1970s, the image of poor minority families mired in an endless cycle of unemployment, unwed childbearing, illiteracy, and dependency had coalesced into a compelling and powerful concept: the urban underclass.[12] In the view of many middle-class whites, inner cities had come to house a large population of poorly educated single mothers and jobless men—mostly black and Puerto Rican—who were unlikely to exit poverty and become self-sufficient. In the ensuing national debate on the causes for this persistent poverty, four theoretical explanations gradually emerged: culture, racism, economics, and welfare.

Cultural explanations for the underclass can be traced to the work of Oscar Lewis, who identified a "culture of poverty" that he felt promoted patterns of behavior inconsistent with socioeconomic advancement.[13] According to Lewis, this culture originated in endemic unemployment and chronic social immobility, and provided an ideology that allowed poor people to cope with feelings of hopelessness and despair that arose because their chances for socioeconomic success were remote. In individuals, this culture was typified by a lack of impulse control, a strong present-time orientation, and little ability to defer gratification. Among families, it yielded an absence of childhood, an early initiation into sex, a prevalence of free marital unions, and a high incidence of abandonment of mothers and children.

Although Lewis explicitly connected the emergence of these cultural patterns to structural conditions in society, he argued that once the culture of poverty was established, it became an independent cause of persistent poverty. This idea was further elaborated in 1965 by the Harvard sociologist and then Assistant Secretary of Labor Daniel Patrick Moynihan, who in a confidential report to the President focused on the relationship between male unemployment, family instability, and the intergenerational transmission of poverty, a process he labeled a "tangle of pathology."[14] He warned that because of the structural absence of employment in the ghetto, the black family was disintegrating in a way that threatened the fabric of community life.

When these ideas were transmitted through the press, both popular and scholarly, the connection between culture and economic structure was somehow lost, and the argument was popularly perceived to be that "people were poor because they had a defective culture." This position was later explicitly adopted by the conservative theorist Edward Banfield, who argued that lower-class culture—with its limited time horizon, impulsive need for gratification, and psychological self-doubt—was primarily responsible for persistent urban poverty.[15] He believed that these cultural traits were largely imported, arising primarily because cities attracted lower-class migrants.

The culture-of-poverty argument was strongly criticized by liberal theorists as a self-serving ideology that "blamed the victim."[16] In the ensuing wave of reaction, black families were viewed not as weak but, on the contrary, as resilient and well adapted survivors in an oppressive and racially prejudiced society.[17] Black disadvantages were attributed not to a defective culture but to the persistence of institutional racism in the United States. According to theorists of the underclass such as Douglas Glasgow and Alphonso Pinkney, the black urban underclass came about because deeply imbedded racist practices within American institutions—particularly schools and the economy—effectively kept blacks poor and dependent.[18]

As the debate on culture versus racism ground to a halt during the late 1970s, conservative theorists increasingly captured public attention by focusing on a third possible cause of poverty: government welfare policy. According to Charles Murray, the creation of the underclass was rooted in the liberal welfare state.[19] Federal antipoverty programs altered the incentives governing the behavior of poor men and women, reducing the desirability of marriage, increasing the benefits of unwed childbearing, lowering the attractiveness of menial labor, and ultimately resulted in greater poverty.

A slightly different attack on the welfare state was launched by Lawrence Mead, who argued that it was not the generosity but the permissiveness of the U.S. welfare system that was at fault.[20] Jobless men and unwed mothers should be required to display "good citizenship" before being supported by the state. By not requiring anything of the poor, Mead argued, the welfare state undermined their independence and competence, thereby perpetuating their poverty.

This conservative reasoning was subsequently attacked by liberal social scientists, led principally by the sociologist William Julius Wilson, who had long been arguing for the increasing importance of class over race in understanding the social and economic problems facing blacks.[21] In his 1987 book *The Truly Disadvantaged,* Wilson argued that persistent urban poverty stemmed primarily from the structural transformation of the inner-city economy.[22] The decline of manufacturing, the suburbanization of employment, and the rise of a low-wage service sector dramatically reduced the number of city jobs that paid wages sufficient to support a family, which led to high rates of joblessness among minorities and a shrinking pool of "marriageable" men (those financially able to support a family). Marriage thus became less attractive to poor women, unwed childbearing increased, and female-headed families proliferated. Blacks suffered disproportionately from these trends because, owing to past discrimination, they were concentrated in locations and occupations particularly affected by economic restructuring.

Wilson argued that these economic changes were accompanied by an increase in the spatial concentration of poverty within black neighborhoods. This new geography of poverty, he felt, was enabled by the civil rights revolution of the 1960s, which provided middle-class blacks with new opportunities outside the ghetto.[23] The out-migration of middle-class families from ghetto areas left behind a destitute community lacking the institutions, resources, and values necessary for success in post-industrial society. The urban underclass thus arose from a complex interplay of civil rights policy, economic restructuring, and a historical legacy of discrimination.

Theoretical concepts such as the culture of poverty, institutional racism, welfare disincentives, and structural economic change have all been widely debated. None of these explanations, however, considers residential segregation to be an important contributing cause of urban poverty and the underclass. In their

principal works, Murray and Mead do not mention segregation at all;[24] and Wilson refers to racial segregation only as a historical legacy from the past, not as an outcome that is institutionally supported and actively created today.[25] Although Lewis mentions segregation sporadically in his writings, it is not assigned a central role in the set of structural factors responsible for the culture of poverty, and Banfield ignores it entirely. Glasgow, Pinkney, and other theorists of institutional racism mention the ghetto frequently, but generally call not for residential desegregation but for race-specific policies to combat the effects of discrimination in the schools and labor markets. In general, then, contemporary theorists of urban poverty do not see high levels of black-white segregation as particularly relevant to understanding the underclass or alleviating urban poverty.[26]

The purpose of this book is to redirect the focus of public debate back to issues of race and racial segregation, and to suggest that they should be fundamental to thinking about the status of black Americans and the origins of the urban underclass. Our quarrel is less with any of the prevailing theories of urban poverty than with their systematic failure to consider the important role that segregation has played in mediating, exacerbating, and ultimately amplifying the harmful social and economic processes they treat.

We join earlier scholars in rejecting the view that poor urban blacks have an autonomous "culture of poverty" that explains their failure to achieve socioeconomic success in American society. We argue instead that residential segregation has been instrumental in creating a structural niche within which a deleterious set of attitudes and behaviors—a culture of segregation—has arisen and flourished. Segregation created the structural conditions for the emergence of an oppositional culture that devalues work, schooling, and marriage and that stresses attitudes and behaviors that are antithetical and often hostile to success in the larger economy. Although poor black neighborhoods still contain many people who lead conventional, productive lives, their example has been overshadowed in recent years by a growing concentration of poor, welfare-dependent families that is an inevitable result of residential segregation.

We readily agree with Douglas, Pinkney, and others that racial discrimination is widespread and may even be institutionalized within large sectors of American society, including the labor market, the educational system, and the welfare bureaucracy. We argue, however, that this view of black subjugation is incomplete without understanding the special role that residential segregation plays in enabling all other forms of racial oppression. Residential segregation is the institutional apparatus that supports other racially discriminatory processes and binds them together into a coherent and uniquely effective system of racial subordination. Until the black ghetto is dismantled as a basic institution of American urban life, progress ameliorating racial inequality in other arenas will be slow, fitful, and incomplete.

We also agree with William Wilson's basic argument that the structural transformation of the urban economy undermined economic supports for the black community during the 1970s and 1980s.[27] We argue, however, that in the absence of segregation, these structural changes would not have produced the disastrous social and economic outcomes observed in inner cities during these decades. Although rates of black poverty were driven up by the economic dislocations Wilson identifies, it was segregation that confined the increased deprivation to a small number of densely settled, tightly packed, and geographically isolated areas.

Wilson also argues that concentrated poverty arose because the civil rights revolution allowed middle-class blacks to move out of the ghetto. Although we remain open to the possibility that class-selective migration did occur,[28] we argue that concentrated poverty would have happened during the 1970s with or without black middle-class migration. Our principal objection to Wilson's

focus on middle-class out-migration is not that it did not occur, but that it is misdirected: focusing on the flight of the black middle class deflects attention from the real issue, which is the limitation of black residential options through segregation.

Middle-class households—whether they are black, Mexican, Italian, Jewish, or Polish—always try to escape the poor. But only blacks must attempt their escape within a highly segregated, racially segmented housing market. Because of segregation, middle-class blacks are less able to escape than other groups, and as a result are exposed to more poverty. At the same time, because of segregation no one will move into a poor black neighborhood except other poor blacks. Thus both middle-class blacks and poor blacks lose compared with the poor and middle class of other groups: poor blacks live under unrivaled concentrations of poverty and affluent blacks live in neighborhoods that are far less advantageous than those experienced by the middle class of other groups.

Finally, we concede Murray's general point that federal welfare policies are linked to the rise of the urban underclass, but we disagree with his specific hypothesis that generous welfare payments, by themselves, discouraged employment, encouraged unwed childbearing, undermined the strength of the family, and thereby caused persistent poverty.[29] We argue instead that welfare payments were only harmful to the socioeconomic well-being of groups that were residentially segregated. As poverty rates rose among blacks in response to the economic dislocations of the 1970s and 1980s, so did the use of welfare programs. Because of racial segregation, however, the higher levels of welfare receipt were confined to a small number of isolated, all-black neighborhoods. By promoting the spatial concentration of welfare use, therefore, segregation created a residential environment within which welfare dependency was the norm, leading to the intergenerational transmission and broader perpetuation of urban poverty.

Coming to Terms
with American Apartheid

Our fundamental argument is that racial segregation—and its characteristic institutional
form, the black ghetto—are the key structural
factors responsible for the perpetuation of
black poverty in the United States. Residential
segregation is the principal organizational
feature of American society that is responsible
for the creation of the urban underclass. . . . It
can be shown that any increase in the poverty
rate of a residentially segregated group leads
to an immediate and automatic increase in the
geographic concentration of poverty. When
the rate of minority poverty is increased under conditions of high segregation, all of the
increase is absorbed by a small number of
neighborhoods. When the same increase in
poverty occurs in an integrated group, the
added poverty is spread evenly throughout
the urban area, and the neighborhood environment that group members face does not
change much.

During the 1970s and 1980s, therefore,
when urban economic restructuring and inflation drove up rates of black and Hispanic
poverty in many urban areas, underclass
communities were created only where increased minority poverty coincided with a
high degree of segregation—principally in
older metropolitan areas of the northeast and
the midwest. Among Hispanics, only Puerto
Ricans developed underclass communities,
because only they were highly segregated; and
this high degree of segregation is directly attributable to the fact that a large proportion
of Puerto Ricans are of African origin.

The interaction of intense segregation and
high poverty leaves black neighborhoods extremely vulnerable to fluctuations in the urban economy, because any dislocation that
causes an upward shift in black poverty rates
will also produce a rapid change in the concentration of poverty and, hence, a dramatic
shift in the social and economic composition
of black neighborhoods. The concentration of
poverty, for example, is associated with the
wholesale withdrawal of commercial institutions and the deterioration or elimination of
goods and services distributed through the
market.

Neighborhoods, of course, are dynamic
and constantly changing, and given the high
rates of residential turnover characteristic of
contemporary American cities, their well-
being depends to a great extent on the characteristics and actions of their residents. Decisions taken by one actor affect the subsequent
decisions of others in the neighborhood. In
this way isolated actions affect the well-being
of the community and alter the stability of the
neighborhood.

Because of this feedback between individual and collective behavior, neighborhood stability is characterized by a series of thresholds, beyond which various self-perpetuating
processes of decay take hold. Above these
thresholds, each actor who makes a decision
that undermines neighborhood well-being
makes it increasingly likely that other actors
will do the same. Each property owner who
decides not to invest in upkeep and maintenance, for example, lowers the incentive for
others to maintain their properties. Likewise,
each new crime promotes psychological and
physical withdrawal from public life, which
reduces vigilance within the neighborhood
and undermines the capacity for collective organization, making additional criminal activity more likely.

Segregation increases the susceptibility of
neighborhoods to these spirals of decline.
During periods of economic dislocation, a
rising concentration of black poverty is associated with the simultaneous concentration of
other negative social and economic conditions. Given the high levels of racial segregation characteristic of American urban areas,
increases in black poverty such as those observed during the 1970s can only lead to a
concentration of housing abandonment,
crime, and social disorder, pushing poor
black neighborhoods beyond the threshold of
stability.

By building physical decay, crime, and social disorder into the residential structure of
black communities, segregation creates a

harsh and extremely disadvantaged environment to which ghetto blacks must adapt. In concentrating poverty, moreover, segregation also concentrates conditions such as drug use, joblessness, welfare dependency, teenage childbearing, and unwed parenthood, producing a social context where these conditions are not only common but the norm. By adapting to this social environment, ghetto dwellers evolve a set of behaviors, attitudes, and expectations that are sharply at variance with those common in the rest of American society.

As a direct result of the high degree of racial and class isolation created by segregation, for example, Black English has become progressively more distant from Standard American English, and its speakers are at a clear disadvantage in U.S. schools and labor markets. Moreover, the isolation and intense poverty of the ghetto provides a supportive structural niche for the emergence of an "oppositional culture" that inverts the values of middle-class society. Anthropologists have found that young people in the ghetto experience strong peer pressure not to succeed in school, which severely limits their prospects for social mobility in the larger society. Quantitative research shows that growing up in a ghetto neighborhood increases the likelihood of dropping out of high school, reduces the probability of attending college, lowers the likelihood of employment, reduces income earned as an adult, and increases the risk of teenage childbearing and unwed pregnancy.

Segregation also has profound political consequences for blacks, because it so isolates them geographically that they are the only ones who benefit from public expenditures in their neighborhoods. The relative integration of most ethnic groups means that jobs or services allocated to them will generally benefit several other groups at the same time. Integration thus creates a basis for political coalitions and pluralist politics, and most ethnic groups that seek public resources are able to find coalition partners because other groups can anticipate sharing the benefits. That blacks are the only ones to benefit from resources allocated to the ghetto—and are the only ones harmed when resources are removed—makes it difficult for them to find partners for political coalitions. Although segregation paradoxically makes it easier for blacks to elect representatives, it limits their political influence and marginalizes them within the American polity. Segregation prevents blacks from participating in pluralist politics based on mutual self-interest.

Because of the close connection between social and spatial mobility, segregation also perpetuates poverty. One of the primary means by which individuals improve their life chances—and those of their children—is by moving to neighborhoods with higher home values, safer streets, higher-quality schools, and better services. As groups move up the socioeconomic ladder, they typically move up the residential hierarchy as well, and in doing so they not only improve their standard of living but also enhance their chances for future success. Barriers to spatial mobility are barriers to social mobility, and by confining blacks to a small set of relatively disadvantaged neighborhoods, segregation constitutes a very powerful impediment to black socioeconomic progress.

Despite the obvious deleterious consequences of black spatial isolation, policymakers have not paid much attention to segregation as a contributing cause of urban poverty and have not taken effective steps to dismantle the ghetto. Indeed, for most of the past two decades public policies tolerated and even supported the perpetuation of segregation in American urban areas. Although many political initiatives were launched to combat discrimination and prejudice in the housing and banking industries, each legislative or judicial act was fought tenaciously by a powerful array of people who believed in or benefited from the status quo.

Although a comprehensive open housing bill finally passed Congress under unusual circumstances in 1968, it was stripped of its enforcement provisions as its price of enactment, yielding a Fair Housing Act that was structurally flawed and all but doomed to fail. As documentation of the law's defects accumulated in multiple Congressional hearings, government reports, and scholarly studies, little was done to repair the situation until 1988, when a series of scandals and political errors by the Reagan Administration finally enabled a significant strengthening of federal antidiscrimination law.

Yet even more must be done to prevent the permanent bifurcation of the United States into black and white societies that are separate and unequal. As of 1990, levels of racial segregation were still extraordinarily high in the nation's large urban areas, particularly those of the north. Segregation has remained high because fair housing enforcement relies too heavily on the private efforts of individual victims of discrimination. Whereas the processes that perpetuate segregation are entrenched and institutionalized, fair housing enforcement is individual, sporadic, and confined to a small number of isolated cases.

As long as the Fair Housing Act is enforced individually rather than systemically, it is unlikely to be effective in overcoming the structural arrangements that support segregation and sustain the ghetto. Until the government throws its considerable institutional weight behind efforts to dismantle the ghetto, racial segregation will persist. . . .

Ultimately, however, dismantling the ghetto and ending the long reign of racial segregation will require more than specific bureaucratic reforms; it requires a moral commitment that white America has historically lacked. The segregation of American blacks was no historical accident; it was brought about by actions and practices that had the passive acceptance, if not the active support, of most whites in the United States. Although America's apartheid may not be rooted in the legal strictures of its South African relative, it is no less effective in perpetuating racial inequality, and whites are no less culpable for the socioeconomic deprivation that results.

As in South Africa, residential segregation in the United States provides a firm basis for a broader system of racial injustice. The geographic isolation of Africans within a narrowly circumscribed portion of the urban environment—whether African townships or American ghettos—forces blacks to live under extraordinarily harsh conditions and to endure a social world where poverty is endemic, infrastructure is inadequate, education is lacking, families are fragmented, and crime and violence are rampant.[30] Moreover, segregation confines these unpleasant by-products of racial oppression to an isolated portion of the urban geography far removed from the experience of most whites. Resting on a foundation of segregation, apartheid not only denies blacks their rights as citizens but forces them to bear the social costs of their own victimization.

Although Americans have been quick to criticize the apartheid system of South Africa, they have been reluctant to acknowledge the consequences of their own institutionalized system of racial separation. The topic of segregation has virtually disappeared from public policy debates; it has vanished from the list of issues on the civil rights agenda; and it has been ignored by social scientists spinning endless theories of the underclass. Residential segregation has become the forgotten factor of American race relations, a minor footnote in the ongoing debate on the urban underclass. Until policymakers, social scientists, and private citizens recognize the crucial role of America's own apartheid in perpetuating urban poverty and racial injustice, the United States will remain a deeply divided and very troubled society.[31]

Notes

1. Epigraph from Edgar H. Brookes, *Apartheid: A Documentary Study of Modern South Africa* (London: Routledge and Kegan Paul, 1968), p. 142.

2. Gunnar Myrdal, *An American Dilemma*, vol. 1 (New York: Harper and Brothers, 1944), p. 618; see also Walter A. Jackson, *Gunnar Myrdal and America's Conscience* (Chapel Hill: University of North Carolina Press, 1990), pp. 88–271.

3. Kenneth B. Clark, *Dark Ghetto: Dilemmas of Social Power* (New York: Harper and Row, 1965), p. 11.

4. U.S. National Advisory Commission on Civil Disorders, *The Kerner Report* (New York: Pantheon Books, 1988), p. 1.

5. Ibid.

6. Ibid., p. 2.

7. Ibid., p. 22.

8. Ibid.

9. Ibid.

10. A few scholars attempted to keep the Kerner Commission's call for desegregation alive, but their voices have largely been unheeded in the ongoing debate. Thomas Pettigrew has continued to assert the central importance of residential segregation, calling it the "linchpin" of American race relations; see "Racial Change and Social Policy," *Annals of the American Academy of Political and Social Science* 441 (1979):114–31. Gary Orfield has repeatedly pointed out segregation's deleterious effects on black prospects for education, employment, and socioeconomic mobility; see "Separate Societies: Have the Kerner Warnings Come True?" in Fred R. Harris and Roger W. Wilkins, eds., *Quiet Riots: Race and Poverty in the United States* (New York: Pantheon Books, 1988), pp. 100–122; and "Ghettoization and Its Alternatives," in Paul E. Peterson, ed., *The New Urban Reality* (Washington, D.C.: Brookings Institution, 1985), pp. 161–96.

11. See Thomas B. Edsall and Mary D. Edsall, *Chain Reaction: The Impact of Race, Rights, and Taxes on American Politics* (New York: Norton, 1991).

12. For an informative history of the evolution of the concept of the underclass, see Michael B. Katz, *The Undeserving Poor: From the War on Poverty to the War on Welfare* (New York: Pantheon, 1989), pp. 185–235.

13. Oscar Lewis, *La Vida: A Puerto Rican Family in the Culture of Poverty—San Juan and New York* (New York: Random House, 1965); "The Culture of Poverty," *Scientific American* 215 (1966): 19–25; "The Culture of Poverty," in Daniel P. Moynihan, ed., *On Understanding Poverty: Perspectives from the Social Sciences* (New York: Basic Books, 1968), pp. 187–220.

14. The complete text of this report is reprinted in Lee Rainwater and William L. Yancey, *The Moynihan Report and the Politics of Controversy* (Cambridge: MIT Press, 1967), pp. 39–125.

15. Edward C. Banfield, *The Unheavenly City* (Boston: Little, Brown, 1970).

16. William Ryan, *Blaming the Victim* (New York: Random House, 1971).

17. Carol Stack, *All Our Kin: Strategies of Survival in a Black Community* (New York: Harper and Row, 1974).

18. Douglas C. Glasgow, *The Black Underclass: Poverty, Unemployment, and Entrapment of Ghetto Youth* (New York: Vintage, 1981), p. 11; Alphonso Pinkney, *The Myth of Black Progress* (Cambridge: Cambridge University Press, 1984), pp. 78–80.

19. Charles Murray, *Losing Ground: American Social Policy, 1950–1980* (New York: Basic Books, 1984).

20. Lawrence M. Mead, *Beyond Entitlement: The Social Obligations of Citizenship* (New York: Free Press, 1986).

21. William Julius Wilson, *The Declining Significance of Race: Blacks and Changing American Institutions* (Chicago: University of Chicago Press, 1978).

22. William Julius Wilson, *The Truly Disadvantaged: The Inner City, the Underclass, and Public Policy* (Chicago: University of Chicago Press, 1987), pp. 1–108.

23. Ibid., pp. 49–62.

24. The subject indices of *Losing Ground* and *Beyond Entitlement* contain no references at all to residential segregation.

25. The subject index of *The Truly Disadvantaged* contains two references to pre–1960s Jim Crow segregation.

26. Again with the exception of Thomas Pettigrew and Gary Orfield.

27. We have published several studies documenting how the decline of manufacturing, the suburbanization of jobs, and the rise of low-wage service employment eliminated high-paying jobs for manual workers, drove up rates of black male unemployment, and reduced the attractiveness of marriage to black women, thereby contributing to a proliferation of female-headed families and persistent poverty. See Mitchell L. Eggers and Douglas S. Massey, "The Structural Determinants of Urban Poverty," *Social Science Research* 20 (1991): 217–55; Mitchell L. Eggers and Douglas S. Massey, "A Longitudinal Analysis of Urban Poverty: Blacks in U.S. Metropolitan Areas between 1970 and 1980," *Social Science Research* 21 (1992): 175–203.

28. The evidence on the extent of middle-class out-migration from ghetto areas is inconclusive. Because racial segregation does not decline with rising socioeconomic status, out-movement from poor black neighborhoods certainly has not been to white areas. When Kathryn P. Nelson measured rates of black out-migration from local "zones" within forty metropolitan areas, however, she found higher rates of out-movement for middle- and upper-class blacks compared with poor blacks; but her "zones" contained more than 100,000 inhabitants, making them considerably larger than neighborhoods (see "Racial Segregation, Mobility, and Poverty Concentration," paper presented at the annual meetings of the Population Association of America, Washington, D.C., March 19–23, 1991). In contrast, Edward Gramlich and Deborah Laren found that poor and middle-class blacks dis-

played about the same likelihood of out-migration from poor census tracts (see "Geographic Mobility and Persistent Poverty," Department of Economics, University of Michigan, Ann Arbor, 1990).

29. See Eggers and Massey, "A Longitudinal Analysis of Urban Poverty."

30. See International Defense and Aid Fund for Southern Africa, *Apartheid: The Facts* (London: United Nations Centre against Apartheid, 1983), pp. 15–26.

31. We are not the first to notice the striking parallel between the institutionalized system of racial segregation in U.S. cities and the organized, state-sponsored system of racial repression in South Africa. See John H. Denton, *Apartheid American Style* (Berkeley, Calif.: Diablo Press, 1967); James A. Kushner, "Apartheid in America: An Historical and Legal Analysis of Contemporary Racial Residential Segregation in the United States," *Howard Law Journal* 22 (1979):547–60.

Gender Stratification

▶ GENDER AND CLASS

SHULAMITH FIRESTONE

The Dialectic of Sex

The immediate assumption of the layman that the unequal division of the sexes is "natural" may be well-founded. We need not immediately look beyond this. Unlike economic class, sex class sprang directly from a biological reality: men and women were created different, and not equally privileged. Although, as Simone de Beauvoir points out [in *The Second Sex*], this difference of itself did not necessitate the development of a class system—the domination of one group by another—the reproductive *functions* of these differences did. The biological family is an inherently unequal power distribution. The need for power leading to the development of classes arises from the psychosexual formation of each individual according to this basic imbalance, rather than, as Freud, Norman O. Brown, and others have, once again overshooting their mark, postulated, some irreducible conflict of Life against Death, Eros vs. Thanatos.

The *biological family*—the basic reproductive unit of male/female/infant, in whatever form of social organization—is characterized by these fundamental—if not immutable—facts:

1. That women throughout history before the advent of birth control were at the continual mercy of their biology—menstruation, menopause, and "female ills," constant painful childbirth, wet-nursing and care of infants, all of which made them dependent on males (whether brother, father, husband, lover, or clan, government, community-at-large) for physical survival.
2. That human infants take an even longer time to grow up than animals, and thus are helpless and, for some short period at least, dependent on adults for physical survival.
3. That a basic mother/child interdependency has existed in some form in every society, past or present, and thus has shaped the psychology of every mature female and every infant.
4. That the natural reproductive difference between the sexes led directly to the first division of labor at the origins of class, as well as furnishing the paradigm of caste (discrimination based on biological characteristics).

These biological contingencies of the human family cannot be covered over with anthropological sophistries. Anyone observing animals mating, reproducing, and caring for

Originally published in 1970. Please see complete source information beginning on page 891.

their young will have a hard time accepting the "cultural relativity" line. For no matter how many tribes in Oceania you can find where the connection of the father to fertility is not known, no matter how many matrilineages, no matter how many cases of sex-role reversal, male housewifery, or even empathic labor pains, these facts prove only one thing: the amazing *flexibility* of human nature. But human nature is adaptable *to* something, it is, yes, determined by its environmental conditions. And the biological family that we have described has existed everywhere throughout time. Even in matriarchies where woman's fertility is worshipped, and the father's role is unknown or unimportant, if perhaps not on the genetic father, there is still some dependence of the female and the infant on the male. And though it is true that the nuclear family is only a recent development, one which only intensifies the psychological penalties of the biological family, though it is true that throughout history there have been many variations on this biological family, the contingencies I have described existed in all of them, causing specific psychosexual distortions in the human personality.

But to grant that the sexual imbalance of power is biologically based is not to lose our case. We are no longer just animals. And the Kingdom of Nature does not reign absolute. As Simone de Beauvoir herself admits:

The theory of historical materialism has brought to light some important truths. Humanity is not an animal species, it is a historical reality. Human society is an antiphysis—in a sense it is against nature; it does not passively submit to the presence of nature but rather takes over the control of nature on its own behalf. This arrogation is not an inward, subjective operation; it is accomplished objectively in practical action.

Thus, the "natural" is not necessarily a "human" value. Humanity has begun to outgrow nature: we can no longer justify the maintenance of a discriminatory sex class system on grounds of its origins in Nature. Indeed, for pragmatic reasons alone it is beginning to look as if we *must* get rid of it.

The problem becomes political, demanding more than a comprehensive historical analysis, when one realizes that, though man is increasingly capable of freeing himself from the biological conditions that created his tyranny over women and children, he has little reason to want to give this tyranny up. As Engels said, in the context of economic revolution:

It is the law of division of labor that lies at the basis of the division into classes [Note that this division itself grew out of a fundamental biological division]. But this does not prevent the ruling class, once having the upper hand, from consolidating its power at the expense of the working class, from turning its social leadership into an intensified exploitation of the masses.

Though the sex class system may have originated in fundamental biological conditions, this does not guarantee once the biological basis of their oppression has been swept away that women and children will be freed. On the contrary, the new technology, especially fertility control, may be used against them to reinforce the entrenched system of exploitation.

So that just as to assure elimination of economic classes requires the revolt of the underclass (the proletariat) and, in a temporary dictatorship, their seizure of the means of *production*, so to assure the elimination of sexual classes requires the revolt of the underclass (women) and the seizure of control of *reproduction*: not only the full restoration to women of ownership of their own bodies, but also their (temporary) seizure of control of human fertility—the new population biology as well as all the social institutions of childbearing and childrearing. And just as the end goal of socialist revolution was not only the elimination of the economic class *privilege* but of the economic class *distinction* itself, so the end goal of feminist revolution must be, unlike that of the first feminist movement, not just the elimination of male *privilege* but of the sex *distinction* itself: genital differences between human beings would no longer matter culturally. (A reversion to an unobstructed *pansexuality*—Freud's "polymorphous perversity"—would probably supersede hetero/

homo/bi-sexuality.) The reproduction of the species by one sex for the benefit of both would be replaced by (at least the option of) artificial reproduction: children would be born to both sexes equally, or independently of either, however one chooses to look at it; the dependence of the child on the mother (and vice versa) would give way to a greatly shortened dependence on a small group of others in general, and any remaining inferiority to adults in physical strength would be compensated for culturally. The division of labor would be ended by the elimination of labor altogether (cybernation). The tyranny of the biological family would be broken.

And with it the psychology of power. As Engels claimed for strictly socialist revolution:

The existence of not simply this or that ruling class but of any ruling class at all [will have] become an obsolete anachronism.

That socialism has never come near achieving this predicated goal is not only the result of unfulfilled or misfired economic preconditions, but also because the Marxian analysis itself was insufficient: it did not dig deep enough to the psychosexual roots of class. Marx was onto something more profound than he knew when he observed that the family contained within itself in embryo all the antagonisms that later develop on a wide scale within the society and the state. For unless revolution uproots the basic social organization, the biological family—the vinculum through which the psychology of power can always be smuggled—the tapeworm of exploitation will never be annihilated. We shall need a sexual revolution much larger than—inclusive of—a socialist one to truly eradicate all class systems.

HEIDI HARTMANN

The Unhappy Marriage of Marxism and Feminism: Towards a More Progressive Union

We can usefully define patriarchy as a set of social relations between men, which have a material base, and which, though hierarchical, establish or create interdependence and solidarity among men that enable them to dominate women. Though patriarchy is hierarchical and men of different classes, races, or ethnic groups have different places in the patriarchy, they also are united in their shared

Please see complete source information beginning on page 891.

relationship of dominance over their women; they are dependent on each other to maintain that domination. Hierarchies "work" at least in part because they create vested interests in the status quo. Those at the higher levels can "buy off" those at the lower levels by offering them power over those still lower. In the hierarchy of patriarchy, all men, whatever their rank in the patriarchy, are bought off by being able to control at least some women. There is some evidence to suggest that when patriarchy was first institutionalized in state societies, the ascending rulers literally made men the heads of their families (enforcing their control over their wives and children) in exchange for the men's ceding some of their tribal resources to the new rulers.[1] Men are dependent on one another (despite their hierarchical ordering) to maintain their control over women.

The material base upon which patriarchy rests lies most fundamentally in men's control over women's labor power. Men maintain this control by excluding women from access to some essential productive resources (in capitalist societies, for example, jobs that pay living wages) and by restricting women's sexuality. Monogamous heterosexual marriage is one relatively recent and efficient form that seems to allow men to control both these areas. Controlling women's access to resources and their sexuality, in turn, allows men to control women's labor power, both for the purpose of serving men in many personal and sexual ways and for the purpose of rearing children. The services women render men, and which exonerate men from having to perform many unpleasant tasks (like cleaning toilets) occur outside as well as inside the family setting. Examples outside the family include the harassment of women workers and students by male bosses and professors as well as the common use of secretaries to run personal errands, make coffee, and provide "sexy" surroundings. Rearing children, whether or not the children's labor power is of immediate benefit to their fathers, is nevertheless a crucial task in perpetuating patriarchy as a system. Just as class society must be reproduced by schools, work places, consumption norms, etc., so must patriarchal social relations. In our society children are generally reared by women at home, women socially defined and recognized as inferior to men, while men appear in the domestic picture only rarely. Children raised in this way generally learn their places in the gender hierarchy well. Central to this process, however, are the areas outside the home where patriarchal behaviors are taught and the inferior position of women enforced and reinforced: churches, schools, sports, clubs, unions, armies, factories, offices, health centers, the media, etc.

The material base of patriarchy, then, does not rest solely on childrearing in the family,

but on all the social structures that enable men to control women's labor. The aspects of social structures that perpetuate patriarchy are theoretically identifiable, hence separable from their other aspects. Gayle Rubin has increased our ability to identify the patriarchal element of these social structures enormously by identifying "sex/gender systems":

a "sex/gender system" is the set of arrangements by which a society transforms biological sexuality into products of human activity, and in which these transformed sexual needs are satisfied.[2]

We are born female and male, biological sexes, but we are created woman and man, socially recognized genders. *How* we are so created is that second aspect of the *mode* of production of which Engels spoke, "the production of human beings themselves, the propagation of the species."[3]

How people propagate the species is socially determined. If, biologically, people are sexually polymorphous, and society were organized in such a way that all forms of sexual expression were equally permissible, reproduction would result only from some sexual encounters, the heterosexual ones. The strict division of labor by sex, a social invention common to all known societies, creates two very separate genders and a need for men and women to get together for economic reasons. It thus helps to direct their sexual needs toward heterosexual fulfillment, and helps to ensure biological reproduction. In more imaginative societies, biological reproduction might be ensured by other techniques, but the division of labor by sex appears to be the universal solution to date. Although it is theoretically possible that a sexual division of labor not imply inequality between the sexes, in most known societies, the socially acceptable division of labor by sex is one which accords lower status to women's work. The sexual division of labor is also the underpinning of sexual subcultures in which men and women experience life differently; it is the material base of male power which is exercised (in our society) not just in not doing housework and in securing superior employment, but psychologically as well.

How people meet their sexual needs, how they reproduce, how they inculcate social norms in new generations, how they learn gender, how it feels to be a man or a woman—all occur in the realm Rubin labels the sex/gender system. Rubin emphasizes the influence of kinship (which tells you with whom you can satisfy sexual needs) and the development of gender specific personalities via childrearing and the "oedipal machine." In addition, however, we can use the concept of the sex/gender system to examine all other social institutions for the roles they play in defining and reinforcing gender hierarchies. Rubin notes that theoretically a sex/gender system could be female dominant, male dominant, or egalitarian, but declines to label various known sex/gender systems or to periodize history accordingly. We choose to label our present sex/gender system patriarchy, because it appropriately captures the notion of hierarchy and male dominance which we see as central to the present system.

Economic production (what marxists are used to referring to as *the* mode of production) and the production of people in the sex/gender sphere both determine "the social organization under which the people of a particular historical epoch and a particular country live," according to Engels. The whole of society, then, can be understood by looking at both these types of production and reproduction, people and things. There is no such thing as "pure capitalism," nor does "pure patriarchy" exist, for they must of necessity coexist. What exists is patriarchal capitalism, or patriarchal feudalism, or egalitarian hunting/gathering societies, or matriarchal horticultural societies, or patriarchal horticultural societies, and so on. There appears to be no necessary connection between *changes* in the one aspect of production and changes in the other. A society could undergo transition from capitalism to socialism, for example, and remain patriarchal. Common sense, history, and our experience tell us, however, that these two aspects of production are so closely

intertwined, that change in one ordinarily creates movement, tension, or contradiction in the other.

Racial hierarchies can also be understood in this context. Further elaboration may be possible along the lines of defining color/race systems, arenas of social life that take biological color and turn it into a social category, race. Racial hierarchies, like gender hierarchies, are aspects of our social organization, of how people are produced and reproduced. They are not fundamentally ideological; they constitute that second aspect of our mode of production, the production and reproduction of people. It might be most accurate then to refer to our societies not as, for example, simply capitalist, but as patriarchal capitalist white supremacist.

Capitalist development creates the places for a hierarchy of workers, but traditional marxist categories cannot tell us who will fill which places. Gender and racial hierarchies determine who fills the empty places. *Patriarchy is not simply hierarchical organization,* but hierarchy in which *particular* people fill *particular* places. It is in studying patriarchy that we learn why it is women who are dominated and how. While we believe that most known societies have been patriarchal, we do not view patriarchy as a universal, unchanging phenomenon. Rather patriarchy, the set of interrelations among men that allow men to dominate women, has changed in form and intensity over time. It is crucial that the hierarchy among men, and their differential access to patriarchal benefits, be examined. Surely, class, race, nationality, and even marital status and sexual orientation, as well as the obvious age, come into play here. And women of different class, race, national, marital status, or sexual orientation groups are subjected to different degrees of patriarchal power. Women may themselves exercise class, race, or national power, or even patriarchal power (through their family connections) over men lower in the patriarchal hierarchy than their own male kin.

To recapitulate, we define patriarchy as a set of social relations which has a material base and in which there are hierarchical relations between men and solidarity among them which enable them in turn to dominate women. The material base of patriarchy is men's control over women's labor power. That control is maintained by excluding women from access to necessary economically productive resources and by restricting women's sexuality. Men exercise their control in receiving personal service work from women, in not having to do housework or rear children, in having access to women's bodies for sex, and in feeling powerful and being powerful. The crucial elements of patriarchy as we *currently* experience them are: heterosexual marriage (and consequent homophobia), female childrearing and housework, women's economic dependence on men (enforced by arrangements in the labor market), the state, and numerous institutions based on social relations among men—clubs, sports, unions, professions, universities, churches, corporations, and armies. All of these elements need to be examined if we are to understand patriarchal capitalism. . . .

Industrialization and the Development of Family Wages

Marxists made quite logical inferences from a selection of the social phenomena they witnessed in the nineteenth century. But marxists ultimately underestimated the strength of the preexisting patriarchal social forces with which fledgling capital had to contend and the need for capital to adjust to these forces. The industrial revolution was drawing all people into the labor force, including women and children; in fact the first factories used child and female labor almost exclusively. That women and children could earn wages separately from men both undermined authority relations and kept wages low for everyone. Kautsky, writing in 1892, described the process this way:

[Then with] the wife and young children of the working-man . . . able to take care of themselves,

the wages of the male worker can safely be reduced to the level of his own personal needs without the risk of stopping the fresh supply of labor power.

The labor of women and children, moreover, affords the additional advantage that these are less capable of resistance than men [sic]; and their introduction into the ranks of the workers increases tremendously the quantity of labor that is offered for sale in the market.

Accordingly, the labor of women and children . . . also diminishes [the] capacity [of the male worker] for resistance in that it overstocks the market; owning to both these circumstances it lowers the wages of the working-man.[4]

The terrible effects on working class family life of low wages and of forced participation of all family members in the labor force were recognized by marxists. Kautsky wrote:

The capitalist system of production does not in most cases destroy the single household of the workingman, but robs it of all but its unpleasant features. The activity of woman today in industrial pursuits . . . means an increase of her former burden by a new one. *But one cannot serve two masters.* The household of the working-man suffers whenever his wife must help to earn the daily bread.[5]

Working men as well as Kautsky recognized the disadvantages of female wage labor. Not only were women "cheap competition" but working women were their very wives, who could not "serve two masters" well.

Male workers resisted the wholesale entrance of women and children into the labor force, and sought to exclude them from union membership and the labor force as well. In 1846 the *Ten-Hours' Advocate* stated:

It is needless for us to say, that all attempts to improve the morals and physical condition of female factory workers will be abortive, unless their hours are materially reduced. Indeed we may go so far as to say, that married females would be much better occupied in performing the domestic duties of the household, than following the never-tiring motion of machinery. We therefore hope the day is not distant, when the husband will be able to provide for his wife and family, without sending the former to endure the drudgery of a cotton mill.[6]

In the United States in 1854 the National Typographical Union resolved not to "encourage by its act the employment of female compositors." Male unionists did not want to afford union protection to women workers; they tried to exclude them instead. In 1879 Adolph Strasser, president of the Cigarmakers International Union, said: "We cannot drive the females out of the trade, but we can restrict their daily quota of labor through factory laws."[7]

While the problem of cheap competition could have been solved by organizing the wage earning women and youths, the problem of disrupted family life could not be. Men reserved union protection for men and argued for protective labor laws for women and children. Protective labor laws, while they may have ameliorated some of the worst abuses of female and child labor, also limited the participation of adult women in many "male" jobs. Men sought to keep high wage jobs for themselves and to raise male wages generally. They argued for wages sufficient for their wage labor alone to support their families. This "family wage" system gradually came to be the norm for stable working class families at the end of the nineteenth century and the beginning of the twentieth. Several observers have declared the non–wage-working wife to be part of the standard of living of male workers. Instead of fighting for equal wages for men and women, male workers sought the family wage, wanting to retain their wives' services at home. In the absence of patriarchy a unified working class might have confronted capitalism, but patriarchal social relations divided the working class, allowing one part (men) to be bought off at the expense of the other (women). Both the hierarchy between men and the solidarity among them were crucial in this process of resolution. Family wages may be understood as a resolution of the conflict over women's labor power which was occurring between patriarchal and capitalist interests at that time.

Family wages for most adult men imply men's acceptance, and collusion in, lower wages for others, young people, women and socially defined inferior men as well (Irish, blacks, etc., the lowest groups in the patriarchal hierarchy who are denied many of the patriarchal benefits). Lower wages for women and children and inferior men are enforced by job segregation in the labor market, in turn maintained by unions and management as well as by auxiliary institutions like schools, training programs, and even families. Job segregation by sex, by insuring that women have the lower paid jobs, both assures women's economic dependence on men and reinforces notions of appropriate spheres for women and men. For most men, then, the development of family wages secured the material base of male domination in two ways. First, men have the better jobs in the labor market and earn higher wages than women. The lower pay women receive in the labor market both perpetuates men's material advantage over women and encourages women to choose wifery as a career. Second, then, women do housework, childcare, and perform other services at home which benefit men directly. Women's home responsibilities in turn reinforce their inferior labor market position.

The resolution that developed in the early twentieth century can be seen to benefit capitalist interests as well as patriarchal interests. Capitalists, it is often argued, recognized that in the extreme conditions which prevailed in the early nineteenth century industrialization, working class families could not adequately reproduce themselves. They realized that housewives produced and maintained healthier workers than wage-working wives and that educated children became better workers than noneducated ones. The bargain, paying family wages to men and keeping women home, suited the capitalists at the time as well as the male workers. Although the terms of the bargain have altered over time, it is still true that the family and women's work in the family serve capital by providing a labor force and serve men as the space in which they exercise their privilege. Women, working to serve men and their families, also serve capital as consumers.[8] The family is also the place where dominance and submission are learned, as Firestone, the Frankfurt School, and many others have explained.[9] Obedient children become obedient workers; girls and boys each learn their proper roles.

While the family wage shows that capitalism adjusts to patriarchy, the changing status of children shows that patriarchy adjusts to capital. Children, like women, came to be excluded from wage labor. As children's ability to earn money declined, their legal relationship to their parents changed. At the beginning of the industrial era in the United States, fulfilling children's need for their fathers was thought to be crucial, even primary, to their happy development; fathers had legal priority in cases of contested custody. As children's ability to contribute to the economic well-being of the family declined, mothers came increasingly to be viewed as crucial to the happy development of their children, and gained legal priority in cases of contested custody.[10] Here patriarchy adapted to the changing economic role of children: when children were productive, men claimed them; as children became unproductive, they were given to women. . . .

The Family and the
Family Wage Today

We argued above that, with respect to capitalism and patriarchy, the adaptation, or mutual accommodation, took the form of the development of the family wage in the early twentieth century. The family wage cemented the partnership between patriarchy and capital. Despite women's increased labor force participation, particularly rapid since World War II, the family wage is still, we argue, the cornerstone of the present sexual division of labor—in which women are primarily responsible for housework and men primarily for wage work. Women's lower wages in the labor market (combined with the need for children to be

reared by someone) assure the continued existence of the family as a necessary income pooling unit. The family, supported by the family wage, thus allows the control of women's labor by men both within and without the family.

Though women's increased wage work may cause stress for the family (similar to the stress Kautsky and Engels noted in the nineteenth century), it would be wrong to think that as a consequence, the concepts and the realities of the family and of the sexual division of labor will soon disappear. The sexual division of labor reappears in the labor market, where women work at women's jobs, often the very jobs they used to do only at home—food preparation and service, cleaning of all kinds, caring for people, and so on. As these jobs are low-status and low-paying patriarchal relations remain intact, though their material base shifts somewhat from the family to the wage differential, from family-based to industrially-based patriarchy.[11]

Industrially based patriarchal relations are enforced in a variety of ways. Union contracts which specify lower wages, lesser benefits, and fewer advancement opportunities for women are not just atavistic hangovers—a case of sexist attitudes or male supremacist ideology—they maintain the material base of the patriarchal system. While some would go so far as to argue that patriarchy is already absent from the family (see, for example, Stewart Ewen, *Captains of Consciousness*),[12] we would not. Although the terms of the compromise between capital and patriarchy are changing as additional tasks formerly located in the family are capitalized, and the location of the deployment of women's labor power shifts, it is nevertheless true, as we have argued above, that the wage differential caused by extreme job segregation in the labor market reinforces the family, and, with it, the domestic division of labor, by encouraging women to marry. The "ideal" of the family wage—that a man can earn enough to support an entire family—may be giving way to a new ideal that both men and women contribute through wage earning to the cash income of the family. The wage differential, then, will become increasingly necessary in perpetuating patriarchy, the male control of women's labor power. The wage differential will aid in *defining* women's work as secondary to men's at the same time it necessitates women's actual continued economic dependence on men. The sexual division of labor in the labor market and elsewhere should be understood as a manifestation of patriarchy which serves to perpetuate it.

Many people have argued that though the partnership between capital and patriarchy exists now, it may *in the long run* prove intolerable to capitalism; capital may eventually destroy both familial relations and patriarchy. The argument proceeds logically that capitalist social relations (of which the family is not an example) tend to become universalized, that women will become increasingly able to earn money and will increasingly refuse to submit to subordination in the family, and that since the family is oppressive particularly to women and children, it will collapse as soon as people can support themselves outside it.

We do not think that the patriarchal relations embodied in the family can be destroyed so easily by capital, and we see little evidence that the family system is presently disintegrating. Although the increasing labor force participation of women has made divorce more feasible, the incentives to divorce are not overwhelming for women. Women's wages allow very few women to support themselves and their children independently and adequately. The evidence for the decay of the traditional family is weak at best. The divorce rate has not so much increased, as it has evened out among classes; moreover, the remarriage rate is also very high. Up until the 1970 census, the first-marriage age was continuing its historic decline. Since 1970 people seem to have been delaying marriage and childbearing, but most recently, the birth rate has begun to increase again. It is true that larger proportions of the population are now living outside traditional families. Young people, especially, are leaving their parents'

homes and establishing their own households before they marry and start traditional families. Older people, especially women, are finding themselves alone in their own households, after their children are grown and they experience separation or death of a spouse. Nevertheless, trends indicate that the new generations of young people will form nuclear families at some time in their adult lives in higher proportions than ever before. The cohorts, or groups of people, born since 1930 have much higher rates of eventual marriage and childrearing than previous cohorts. The duration of marriage and childrearing may be shortening, but its incidence is still spreading.[13]

The argument that capital destroys the family also overlooks the social forces which make family life appealing. Despite critiques of nuclear families as psychologically destructive, in a competitive society the family still meets real needs for many people. This is true not only of long-term monogamy, but even more so for raising children. Single parents bear both financial and psychic burdens. For working class women, in particular, these burdens make the "independence" of labor force participation illusory. Single parent families have recently been seen by policy analysts as transitional family formations which become two-parent families upon remarriage.[14]

It could be that the effects of women's increasing labor force participation are found in a declining sexual division of labor within the family, rather than in more frequent divorce, but evidence for this is also lacking. Statistics on who does housework, even in families with wage-earning wives, show little change in recent years; women still do most of it.[15] The double day is a reality for wage-working women. This is hardly surprising since the sexual division of labor outside the family, in the labor market, keeps women financially dependent on men—even when they earn a wage themselves. The future of patriarchy does not, however, rest solely on the future of familial relations. For patriarchy, like capital, can be surprisingly flexible and adaptable.

Notes

1. See Viana Muller, "The Formation of the State and the Oppression of Women: Some Theoretical Considerations and a Case Study in England and Wales," *Review of Radical Political Economics,* Vol. 9, no. 3 (Fall 1977), pp. 7–21.

2. Gayle Rubin, "The Traffic in Women," in *Toward an Anthropology of Women,* ed. Rayna Rapp Reiter (New York: Monthly Review Press, 1975), p. 159.

[3]. Frederick Engels, "Preface to the First Edition," *The Origin of the Family, Private Property and the State,* edited, with an introduction by Eleanor Burke Leacock (New York: International Publishers, 1972). The first aspect of the mode of production is, according to Engels, "the production of the means of existence, of food, clothing, and shelter and the tools necessary for that production."—ED.

4. Karl Kautsky, *The Class Struggle* (New York: Norton, 1971), pp. 25–26.

5. We might add, "outside the household." Kautsky, *Class Struggle,* p. 26, our emphasis.

6. Cited in Neil Smelser, *Social Change and the Industrial Revolution* (Chicago: University of Chicago Press, 1959), p. 301.

7. These examples are from Heidi I. Hartmann, "Capitalism, Patriarchy, and Job Segregation by Sex," *Signs: Journal of Women in Culture and Society,* Vol. 1, no. 3, pt. 2 (Spring 1976), pp. 162–163.

8. See Batya Weinbaum and Amy Bridges, "The Other Side of the Paycheck: Monopoly Capital and the Structure of Consumption," *Monthly Review,* Vol. 28, no. 3 (July-August 1976), pp. 88–103, for a discussion of women's consumption work.

9. Shulamith Firestone, *The Dialectic of Sex* (New York: Bantam Books, 1971). For the view of the Frankfurt School, see Max Horkheimer, "Authority and the Family," in *Critical Theory* (New York: Herder & Herder, 1972) and Frankfurt Institute of Social Research, "The Family," in *Aspects of Sociology* (Boston: Beacon, 1972).

10. Carol Brown, "Patriarchal Capitalism and the Female-Headed Family," *Social Scientist* (India); no. 40–41 (November-December 1975), pp. 28–39.

11. Carol Brown, in "Patriarchal Capitalism," argues, for example, that we are moving from "family based" to "industrially-based" patriarchy within capitalism.

12. Stewart Ewen, *Captains of Consciousness* (New York: Random House, 1976).

13. For the proportion of people in nuclear families, see Peter Uhlenberg, "Cohort Variations in Family Life Cycle Experiences of U.S. Females," *Journal of Marriage and the Family,* Vol. 36, no. 5 (May 1974), pp. 284–92. For remarriage rates see Paul C. Glick and Arthur J. Norton, "Perspectives on the Recent Upturn in Divorce and Remarriage," *Demography,* Vol. 10 (1974), pp. 301–14. For divorce and income levels see Arthur J. Norton and Paul C. Glick, "Marital Instability: Past, Present, and Future," *Journal of Social Issues,* Vol. 32, no. 1 (1976), pp. 5–20. Also see Mary Jo Bane, *Here to Stay: American Families in the Twentieth Century* (New York: Basic Books, 1976).

14. Heather L. Ross and Isabel B. Sawhill, *Time of Transition: The Growth of Families Headed by Women* (Washington, D.C.: The Urban Institute, 1975).

15. See Kathryn E. Walker and Margaret E. Woods, *Time Use: A Measure of Household Production of Family Goods and Services* (Washington, D.C.: American Home Economics Association, 1976); and Heidi I. Hartmann, "The Family as the Locus of Gender, Class, and Political Struggle: The Example of Housework," *Signs: Journal of Women in Culture and Society,* Vol. 6, no. 3 (Spring 1981)., pp. 366–394.

SZONJA SZELÉNYI

The "Woman Problem" in Stratification Theory and Research

There is a long history of debates addressing whether the primitive unit underlying stratification systems is the family or the individual. Although the modern history of the debate now extends over two decades, it continues to be unresolved and to attract some of the very best scholars in the field (e.g., Baxter 1994; Baxter and Western forthcoming; Crompton 1999; Sørensen 1994; Wright 1997).[1]

The purpose of this chapter is to review, juxtapose, and critique the various class models that have emerged out of this debate, as well as to propose a new approach. In the course of doing so, several themes will emerge. The first is that most of the theoretical contributions to the debate over the class position of women have taken place within very narrowly defined research traditions; and, consequently, the various participants in this debate rarely feel obliged to pit their own approach against the entire range of positions on record. Second, scholars coming from quite different political and theoretical positions often adopt rather similar views on the gender-class debate, thus making for ideological bedfellows that seem unlikely. Finally, the most disturbing feature of these debates is that protagonists typically fail to identify the theoretical underpinnings of their classification exercises, and the sociological consumer is therefore left without a yardstick against which the contributions might be assessed.

_____

This is an original article prepared for this book.

Most participants in the class-gender debate have so far left the following question unanswered: Does the entry of women into the labor force in increasing numbers render standard models of class less tenable? I first explore whether the so-called conventional model of class can be salvaged and then ask whether various revised formulations might be preferred. As my review unfolds, readers may find it useful to refer to Figure 1.

Conventional View

The position that has dominated stratification theory and research from the 1950s to the early 1970s rests on the assumptions that (1) the family rather than the individual forms the basic unit of sociological analysis, and (2) the social position of the family is properly indexed by the status of its (usually) male head. According to Parsons (1954), the occupational structure constitutes the main axis of social inequality and, as a result, the status of families is defined by their ranking within the occupational hierarchy. Moreover, because most wives do not have the opportunity to participate in the formal economy, the class position of their family is determined by their husband's occupation. The distinctive feature of Parsons is his resolutely functionalist interpretation of the sources of this gender-based division of labor. That is, he argues that segregating women in this fashion contributes to

FIGURE 1

A typology of approaches to locating women in the class structure

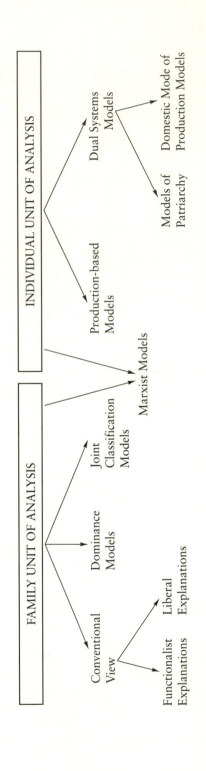

the stability of the family by eliminating competition for status between spouses and by allowing husbands to freely pursue labor market opportunities wherever they may arise without concern for their wives' careers.

Although the conventional viewpoint is routinely identified with a functionalist stance of this kind, it should be kept in mind that other theoretical orientations are also consistent with its propositions (Goldthorpe 1983). For example, Goldthorpe (1983) would agree with Parsons that the position of women in the class structure is merely derivative, but for Goldthorpe this arises from gender inequalities in power and advantage rather than any functional need to reduce competition between husbands and wives. Whereas some feminists have argued that the conventional view is a prime example of "intellectual sexism" (Acker 1973), Goldthorpe maintains that precisely the opposite is the case because his liberal rendition of the conventional view recognizes the derivative position of women and, therefore, underscores the importance of patriarchy.

The conventional view can nonetheless be criticized on other grounds. The most obvious difficulty is that it fails to appreciate the simple fact that women are entering the labor force in ever-increasing numbers. Although Goldthorpe would argue that the male head nonetheless continues to maintain "the greatest commitment to, and continuity in, labor market participation" (1983, 470), this fallback position is unlikely to attract a large following given the (seemingly) revolutionary changes in the market position of women. The following facts are especially relevant here: (1) the proportion of all women who are unmarried has been on the increase since the 1970s, (2) women are marrying at older ages and are delaying the birth of their first child, (3) increasing numbers of women participate in the labor force on a continuous basis and with greater commitment to a career, and (4) full-time participation in the labor force is on the rise even among married women. Taken together, these trends indicate that women's life chances are increasingly defined by their own careers, not by their husbands' careers.

Furthermore, if one follows Lockwood (1989) and Goldthorpe (1987) in defining classes as aggregates of occupations with similar market and work situations, the conventional viewpoint cannot be readily justified. To be sure, insofar as families pool income and function as unitary consumption classes, one might regard housewives as having the same market situation as their husbands.[2] However, when the wife is employed, the pooled income for the family no longer reflects the income of the husband alone. The conceptual standing of the conventional model scarcely improves when the work conditions of spouses are compared. Although employed women may possibly have work conditions that are similar to those of their (employed) husbands, it is implausible in the extreme to assume that this equivalence will also hold for women working at home. It follows that the conventional view is tenable only if classes are defined solely in terms of market situation, and even here one must impose the further condition that wives are not employed and thus contribute no income to the family.

Dominance Model

Although many critics assume that the conventional view is the only family-based approach to defining the class position of women (e.g., Wright 1989), there are in fact several such approaches on offer, and not all of these treat the position of women as wholly derivative. In the so-called dominance model, Erikson (1984) identifies the class position of the family with that of the individual who is most highly ranked within a "dominance hierarchy," where this hierarchy is established by ordering family members in terms of their labor force participation and work situation. Under this formulation, the worker with the strongest attachment to the labor force always dominates; in dual-career families the worker with the highest socioeconomic status dominates.

In evaluating this approach, one again has to ask whether it captures the market and work situation of families adequately. Although the total income of the family (and thus its situation in commodity markets) will probably be better approximated by the income of the dominant family member than by that of the male head, it should be obvious that no single individual can possibly capture the total income of the family when both spouses are working. It is likewise the case that no single individual can adequately represent the work situations of all family members. In raising issues of this sort, we do not wish to prejudge which underlying model of class Erikson prefers, but regardless of what his preferences might be the dominance model appears to be inadequate to the task. If, for example, the purpose of his model is to capture patterns of deference and derogation between families, then one must ask whether the (seemingly) arbitrary rules that Erikson uses to establish dominance truly capture the social processes by which families are evaluated. Unfortunately, we know of no empirical work that addresses this issue directly, but classical theory (e.g., Shils 1970) does suggest that processes of status evaluation are somewhat more complex than the dominance model would imply.

Joint Classification Model

The second family-based approach that is often overlooked by critics of the conventional view is the joint classification model proposed by Britten and Heath (1983). As the label suggests, Britten and Heath classify families in terms of the employment situation of both spouses, with the result thus being a "joint classification" that represents all possible combinations of their individual work statuses. If the intent of Britten and Heath is to capture the market and work situation of families, this approach is obviously superior to other family-based models because, by definition, the class position of the family is no longer reduced to that of any single family member.[3]

For our present purposes, the more important point is that Britten and Heath introduce, if only implicitly, a new definition of what constitutes a family-based approach. Whereas the conventional view seemingly implies that husbands and wives will have identical attitudes, behaviors, and consumption practices, the joint classification approach no longer imposes this kind of cross-spouse equality constraint. If the Britten-Heath approach were used to predict class outcomes (e.g., attitudes, behaviors, consumption practices), it would evidently allow for (1) an individual-level effect for the respondent's occupation, (2) a contextual effect for the spouse's occupation, and (3) a possible interaction effect between the two. The viability of the Britten-Heath model therefore turns on the presence of contextual effects for both husbands and wives. By contrast, if the conventional view is recast in the same language of contextual effects, it implies a "mixed model" in which only individual effects are fitted for men, and only contextual effects are fitted for women.

Marxist Models

Just as the family-based approach takes on many competing forms, so too there is no single individualistic model of class. The individualistic tradition nonetheless encompasses a somewhat less heterogeneous array of positions; at a minimum, all commentators within this tradition incorporate at least some women into their models of the class structure, even if they differ somewhat in their approaches to doing so. The common theme in all Marxist analyses, for example, is that both male and female wage workers are classified by the relationship of their individual jobs to the means of production. The variability within the Marxist camp arises only in their approaches to locating the class position of housewives. For classical Marxists (Engels 1968), housewives are seen as having no class position at all, because they have no direct relationship to the means of production. To be sure, these theorists did not ignore altogether the subordination of women, but they viewed this as a mere remnant of past social relations and argued that it would disappear with the incorporation of women into the formal economy.

Among Marxists of the postwar era, housewives are no longer treated as peripheral to the class system, but rather as explicitly involved in sustaining capitalist relations of production. This position takes on several forms. Whereas critical Marxists argue that housewives socialize children into a submissive role within capitalist relations of authority (Horkheimer 1982), other Marxists suggest that they provide male workers with an "emotional refuge in a cold and competitive society" (Lasch 1977, 6), and yet others claim that they constitute a reserve army of labor and thereby drive male wages down and undermine their strike potential (Beechey 1977). Under all of these viewpoints, women thus facilitate the exploitation of men, but are not themselves exploited in a classical Marxian sense. By contrast, the domestic labor theorists argue that housewives are indirectly exploited by capital because their husbands are paid a "family wage" that reimburses them not only for their direct contribution to profit on the shopfloor, but also for the daily reproduction of their labor power at home (Secombe 1974). This approach therefore converges with the conventional view because the position of housewives, albeit *not* employed women, again becomes derivative—or, as contemporary Marxists would put it, their position becomes "mediated" (Baxter and Western forthcoming; Wright 1989; 1997). It is in this sense, then, that the debate over the class position of women produces rather strange bedfellows.

Production-Based Models

The same sort of irony appears when attention is turned to "mainstream" stratification research and the production-based models that such research typically deploys. Although feminist critics (Acker 1973) often assume that practitioners within this tradition mechanically embrace the conventional view, in fact their treatment of women bears a more striking similarity to the position taken by classical Marxists. In models of attainment, attitudes, and the like, such mainstream researchers typically assign employed women to a class position that reflects their own job but treat housewives as outside the labor force and therefore ignore them. This is not to suggest that exclusively male analyses are no longer carried out; however, the men in these studies are not usually regarded as straightforward proxies for their families, but instead are seen as representing only themselves and therefore constituting only "half the story" (Grusky 1987, 7). It should finally be noted that many stratification researchers have taken further steps to distance themselves from the conventional view by devising occupational scales that reflect the socioeconomic standing of employed women as well as that of employed men (e.g., Hauser and Warren 1997). Although the "production-based" view elaborated here has not been explicitly theorized, it should be clear that contemporary research practices among most quantitative researchers are no longer consistent with the conventional view.

Dual Systems Models

The dual systems approach considers economic and sex-based inequalities simultaneously and posits that "a healthy and strong partnership exists between patriarchy and capital" (Hartmann 1981a, 19). Whereas Marxists see patriarchy as the handmaiden of capitalism (Horkheimer 1982), and radical feminists see capitalism as the handmaiden of patriarchy (Firestone 1971), dual systems theorists emphasize the reciprocal relationship between these two structures of inequality. For example, Hartmann (1981a) argues that women's domestic responsibilities make it difficult for them to compete for lucrative jobs, and this in turn generates a sex-segregated occupational structure. However, with the institutionalization of such segregation and the consequent emergence of a wage gap between genders, women have no choice but to be economically dependent on men (England forthcoming). By emphasizing this reciprocal link between production and reproduction, the dual systems approach provides a fruitful conceptual framework.

The difficulty with this approach, at least for present purposes, is that it is pitched at a highly abstract level and its classificatory implications are correspondingly unclear. It is possible, however, to identify two approaches to locating men and women in the stratification system that might be seen, albeit only indirectly, as having a dual systems heritage. The first such approach identifies the main line of patriarchal cleavage as being between men and women; the main lines of class cleavage are presumably captured by the conventional model of class (Firestone 1971). In most versions of this approach (e.g., models of patriarchy), the principal focus is on the structure of patriarchal relations, whereas little attention is paid to the nature of women's participation in the formal labor force (Millet 1970; Chodorow 1978; O'Brien 1981). The second such approach also adopts a dual systems framework, with the main line of patriarchal cleavage again occurring between men and women. However, in describing the economic sphere, proponents of this view no longer see the conventional model of class as satisfactory, and they explicitly incorporate housewives within a *domestic mode of production* (Delphy 1984; Szelényi 1992). With this reformulation of the concept of class, these analysts theorize household labor as constituting a distinctive economic sphere and thereby recover a large segment of the working population that has been routinely ignored by previous class schemes.

Is This a "Woman Problem?"

I close by underlining just three points. First, family-based models of class are especially difficult to evaluate, because their proponents sometimes fail to specify the dimensions of inequality that they ultimately seek to capture.

The conceptual underpinnings of Marxist and other individualistic models are well-specified by comparison. For example, when a Marxist asks whether housewives are properly conceived as members of the working class, this is clearly tantamount to asking whether they are exploited by capital. Although one might quarrel with the claim that exploitation should be the criterion by which classes are defined, the conceptual "yardstick" against which the Marxist model can be evaluated is at least clear.

Second, the joint classification model appears to take us in a fruitful direction, if only because it begins to recast the class-gender debate in the language of contextual effects. If this language is adopted and extended, one might reasonably ask whether the conjugal family is the only context of interest. As Parsons points out, it is perhaps high time to "divorce the concept of social class from its historic relation to both kinship and property" (1970, 24), given that individuals in modern society are embedded in a complex web of social communities (e.g., family of origin, family of procreation, work organization, neighborhood, friendship networks), all of which may give rise to contextual effects.[4] This reconceptualization suggests that the total effects of class on various stratification outcomes (e.g., lifestyles, consumption practices, political attitudes) are generated in two ways: *directly* by the class position of the actor, and *indirectly* through his or her affiliative ties to various significant others, including not merely the spouse but also parents, friends, coworkers, and children. The complex nature of these class effects is illustrated in Figure 2. In the language of path analysis, the direct effect of class (for the actor) equals d, and the indirect effects equal ac and be. The total effect of class is, therefore, $d+ac+be$. I doubt that much headway can be made in the gender-class debate without operationalizing the model in Figure 2. Although this contextualist framework has often been adopted in modeling patterns of class identification (e.g., Baxter 1994), there is much to be said for applying it to a wider range of outcomes.

FIGURE 2
Direct and affiliative class effects on lifestyles, behavior, and values

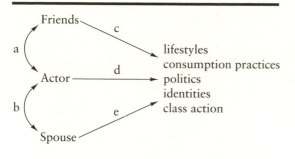

sticks," including not merely the achievements of their fathers but also of coworkers and friends.

The third and final point is that the presence and strength of such contextual effects, including those pertaining to the family, are ultimately an empirical matter. It follows that the gender-class debate has neither been resolved (Wright forthcoming) nor superseded (Baxter and Western, forthcoming). If we are to make further progress, we need to rethink the debate as pertaining not so much to the "woman problem" as to the strength of contextual effects, especially those embedded in the family. The model that is presented in Figure 2 is perhaps a useful step in this direction.

Notes

1. For older reviews that are still useful, see Acker (1973), Crompton and Mann (1986), and Abbot and Sapsford (1987).

2. Needless to say, the idea that such families function as unitary consumption classes is highly suspect, given the well-established presence of gender inequality *within* families (e.g., see Hartmann 1981b; Curtis 1986).

3. The irony here is that Goldthorpe (1983) in fact denies that the Britten-Heath approach is a viable *class* model. This conclusion could only be reached because Goldthorpe appears to abandon his earlier premise that classes should be defined in terms of market and work situations.

4. The complex nature of these contextual effects is perhaps best illustrated by Goldthorpe's (1987) study of the subjective experiences of social mobility in Great Britain. In an illuminating analysis, he shows that individuals evaluate their occupational success or failure via quite various "yard-

References

Abbott, Pamela, and Roger Sapsford. 1987. *Women and Social Class*. London: Tavistock.

Acker, Joan. 1973. "Women and Social Stratification: A Case of Intellectual Sexism." *American Journal of Sociology* 78:936–45.

Baxter, Janeen. 1994. "Is Husband's Class Enough? The Effect of Husband's Class on Women's Working Class Identity in the United States, Sweden, Norway, and Australia." *American Sociological Review* 59:220–35.

Baxter, Janeen, and Mark Western. Forthcoming. *Reconfigurations of Class and Gender*. Stanford: Stanford University Press.

Beechey, Veronica. 1977. "Some Notes on Female Wage Labour in Capitalist Production." *Capital and Class* 3:45–66.

Britten, Nicky, and Anthony Heath. 1983. "Women, Men, and Social Class." Pages 46–60 in *Gender, Class, and Work*, edited by Eva Gamarnikow, David Morgan, June Purvis, and Daphne Taylorson. London: Heinemann.

Chodorow, Christine. 1978. *The Reproduction of Mothering*. Berkeley: University of California Press.

Crompton, Rosemary. 1999. *Class and Stratification*. London: Polity.

Crompton, Rosemary, and Michael Mann. 1986. *Gender and Stratification*. London: Polity.

Curtis, Richard F. 1986. "Household and Family in Theory on Inequality." *American Sociological Review* 51:168–83.

Delphy, Christine. 1984. "The Main Enemy." Pages 57–77 in *Close to Home*, by Christine Delphy. Amherst: University of Massachusetts Press.

Engels, Frederick. 1968. "The Origin of the Family, Private Property, and the State." Pages 449–583 in *Selected Works*, by Karl Marx and Frederick Engels. Moscow: Progress.

England, Paula. Forthcoming. "Gender and Access to Money: What Do Trends in Earnings and Household Poverty Tell Us?" Chap. 8 in *Reconfigurations of Class and Gender*, edited by Janeen Baxter and Mark Western. Stanford: Stanford University Press.

Erikson, Robert. 1984. "Social Class of Men, Women, and Families." *Sociology* 18:500–14.

Firestone, Shulamith. 1971. *The Dialectic of Sex*. New York: Bantam.

Goldthorpe, John H. 1983. "Women and Class Analysis: In Defense of the Conventional View." *Sociology* 17:465–88.

Goldthorpe, John H. 1987. *Social Mobility and Class Structure in Modern Britain.* 2nd ed. Oxford: Clarendon Press.

Grusky, David B. 1987. "American Social Mobility in the 19th and 20th Centuries." Working Paper 86–28, University of Wisconsin–Madison, Center for Demography and Ecology.

Hartmann, Heidi. 1981a. "The Unhappy Marriage of Marxism and Feminism: Towards a More Progressive Union." Pages 2–41 in *Women and Revolution,* edited by Lydia Sargent. Boston: South End.

Hartmann, Heidi. 1981b. "The Family as the Locus of Gender, Class, and Political Struggle: The Example of Housework." *Signs* 1:137–69.

Hauser, Robert M., and John Robert Warren. 1997. "Socioeconomic Indexes of Occupational Status: A Review, Update, and Critique." Pages 177–298 in *Sociological Methodology, 1997,* edited by Adrian Raftery. Cambridge: Blackwell Publishers.

Horkheimer, Max. 1982. *Critical Theory.* New York: Continuum.

Lasch, Christopher. 1977. *Haven in a Heartless World.* New York: Basic Books.

Lockwood, David. 1989. *The Blackcoated Worker.* 2nd ed. Oxford: Clarendon Press.

Millett, Kate. 1970. *Sexual Politics.* New York: Ballantine Books.

O'Brien, Mary. 1981. *The Politics of Reproduction.* Boston: Routledge & Kegan Paul.

Parsons, Talcott. 1954. *Essays in Sociological Theory.* New York: Free Press.

Parsons, Talcott. 1970. "Equality and Inequality in Modern Society, or Social Stratification Revisited." Pages 13–72 in *Social Stratification,* edited by Edward O. Laumann. Indianapolis: Bobbs-Merrill.

Secombe, Wally. 1974. "The Housewife and Her Labour Under Capitalism" *New Left Review* 83:3–24.

Shils, Edward A. 1970. "Deference." Pages 420–48 in *The Logic of Social Hierarchies,* edited by Edward O. Laumann, Paul M. Siegel, and Robert W. Hodge. Chicago: Markham.

Sørensen, Annemette. 1994. "Women, Family, and Class." *Annual Review of Sociology* 20:27–47.

Szelényi, Szonja. 1992. "Economic Subsystems and the Occupational Structure: A Comparison of Hungary and the United States." *Sociological Forum* 7:563–85.

Szelényi, Szonja, and Jacqueline Olvera. 1996. "The Declining Significance of Class: Does Gender Complicate the Story?" *Theory and Society* 25:725–30.

Wright, Erik Olin. 1989. "Women in the Class Structure." *Politics and Society* 17:35–66.

Wright, Erik Olin. 1997. *Class Counts: Comparative Studies in Class Analysis.* Cambridge: Cambridge University Press.

Wright, Erik Olin. Forthcoming. "A Conceptual Menu for Studying the Interconnections of Class and Gender." Chap. 3 in *Reconfigurations of Class and Gender,* edited by Janeen Baxter and Mark Western. Stanford: Stanford University Press.

DAVID B. GRUSKY AND MARIA CHARLES

Is There a Worldwide Sex Segregation Regime?

As the field of gender stratification matures, it remains as fashionable as ever to debate the sources and causes of occupational segregation, while the logically prior task of mapping the descriptive contours of segregation continues to attract rather less attention. By virtue of this emphasis, the field has yet to provide a truly comprehensive portrait of sex segregation within industrial market economies, nor has it resolved whether a broad similarity in segregation regimes might be produced through diffusion, socio-biological imperatives, or the functional requisites of modernity. Although there is of course a standing literature on these matters, much of the existing work suffers from problems of data, methods, or conceptualization, and there is evidently no great rush among sex segregation scholars to move the field beyond these formidable problems. In the present chapter, we take matters of description more seriously than has heretofore been the case, with our main objective being to provide a detailed portrait of the underlying structure of sex segregation within industrial and advanced industrial market economies. This descriptive portrait will allow us to adjudicate, albeit only partially, between competing accounts of the sources of cross-national variability and commonality in segregation regimes.

There are three lines of research directly relevant to these objectives. The dominant

This is an original article prepared for this book.

approach, at least among American scholars, has been to apply conventional segregation indices (e.g., the index of dissimilarity) to aggregate classifications available from international statistical abstracts, most notably the *Yearbook of Labour Statistics* published by the International Labour Office (e.g., Anker 1998; Jacobs and Lim 1995; 1992; Blau and Ferber 1998; Blackman, Jarman, and Siltanen 1993). This research tradition has the great virtue of representing a relatively broad cross-section of countries, but it is necessarily flawed given that conventional indices conflate the underlying pattern of sex segregation with the structure of labor supply and demand (see Charles and Grusky 1995). At the other end of the continuum, one might cite the great many qualitative case studies of sex segregation, some of which suggest that occupational gender-typing can be highly idiosyncratic and path dependent (e.g., Reskin and Roos 1990; Bradley 1989; Lapidus 1985; Sanday 1981; Boserup 1970). This line of research, although quite revealing, perforce suffers from the limitations of all case studies; namely, one cannot know whether the discrepant patterns are indeed isolated idiosyncrasies or instead indicate more pervasive cross-national variation, nor is it possible to systematically control for cross-national variability in labor supply and demand. In recent years, a third tradition of log-multiplicative modeling has emerged, with the conventional data source for such research again being the aggregate compilations of the

International Labour Office (e.g., Charles and Grusky 1995; Charles 1992; Semyonov and Jones 1999; Cartmill 2000; Chang 2000). For all its methodological rigor, this line of research is vulnerable to the possibility that aggregate categories comprise widely different types of detailed occupations, thereby creating the appearance of real cross-national variability in segregation when in fact the occupational structure alone is variable. This possibility, if borne out, directly undermines our long-standing interest in mapping patterns of sex segregation after purging the confounding effects of variability in labor supply and demand.

We shall thus proceed by applying our log-multiplicative approach (Charles and Grusky 1995) to a new archive of carefully harmonized and highly detailed cross-classifications of sex by occupation. Although our principal contribution involves, then, the application of new methods to new disaggregate data, we also make conceptual headway by distinguishing between various types of cross-national variability and specifying the social forces and processes that underlie these types.

The Forms and Sources of Cross-National Similarity

In our prior critiques of segregation analysis (e.g., Charles and Grusky 1995), we have noted that conventional segregation indices

are problematic not merely for various methodological reasons but also because they focus exclusively on the *degree* of segregation, thereby concealing qualitative differences between segregation regimes. As indicated in Table 1, one might usefully distinguish between five types of cross-national similarity and variability, each of which may be associated with a specific "theory" about the forces accounting for sex segregation. The purpose of the present section is to contrast these various types of similarity and to elaborate the competing theories of sex segregation that might be regarded as underlying these types.

The first model of Table 1 allows the forces of supply and demand (i.e., the gender and occupation margins) to vary by country, whereas the residual densities of sex-by-occupation association are constrained to be invariant. This model implies that a genotypical pattern of sex segregation emerges after controlling for cross-national variability in (1) the relative sizes of occupations (i.e., the "demand for labor") and (2) rates of female labor force participation (i.e., the "supply of labor"). In motivating this model, one cannot rely directly on conventional explanatory theories of sex segregation (e.g., queuing, sex-role theories), because these speak to the generic and universal causes of segregation without addressing whether such causes will be modified or transformed as they play out in particular countries. Although most ex-

TABLE 1
The Structure of Cross-National Similarity and Variability in Sex Segregation Regimes

Forms of Invariance	Sources of Residual Variability	Examples of Relevant Scholars
1. Complete invariance	None	Chodorow; Reskin & Roos
2. Profile invariance	Variability in the diffusion of egalitarian values and institutions	Parsons; Goode
3. Micro-level invariance	Macro-level structural forces	Chang; Charles; Brinton
4. Macro-level invariance	Occupation-specific institutional and historical forces	Charles & Grusky
5. Complete variability	All of the above	Tilly; Scott; Bradley

planatory theorists have not, therefore, directly taken up issues of cross-national variability, their long-standing emphasis on the generic forces making for segregation suggests that the cross-nationally common element is expected to dominate and overwhelm the idiosyncratic component. That is, insofar as the forces making for segregation indeed operate similarly in all countries, one would necessarily anticipate a worldwide family resemblance in the basic features of segregation.[1]

In the above sense, conventional explanatory theories may be seen as consistent with type 1 invariance, but of course only with the additional caveat that the contours of the (putatively) shared regime are themselves a matter of disagreement. The main lines of contention are easily summarized; namely, one might distinguish between (1) theories of sex-typing that emphasize the deep-rooted and near universal identification of women with tasks involving service, reproduction, and nurturing (e.g., Chodorow 1978; Beck-Gernsheim and Ostner 1978), and (2) theories of male privilege (or "patriarchy") that emphasize the power of men to dominate the most desirable occupations (e.g., Reskin and Roos 1990; Walby 1986; Strober 1984; Hartmann 1976) as well as the incentives for women, in the context of such patriarchy, to opt for "undesirable" occupations that require a less substantial commitment to the labor force (e.g., Becker 1985; Mincer and Polachek 1974). The former theories speak principally to the "sectoral segregation" of women into non-manual occupations that emulate and reproduce their service-providing role in the domestic sphere; and the latter theories speak principally to the "gradational segregation" of women into undesirable manual and non-manual positions that can be reconciled with their domestic responsibilities. The advocates for these various theories naturally wish to represent them as complete and self-standing accounts; however, we suspect that the shared segregation profile will reveal the interleaving of sectoral and gradational forces that, for the most part, may be regarded as complementary rather than mutually exclusive.

If type 1 invariance proves inconsistent with the data, it is still possible that a more limited form of profile invariance will obtain. As indicated in Table 1, the underlying segregation profile may take on the same basic shape in all countries, whereas the degree of segregation may vary from country to country (see line 2). This formulation is consistent with the long-standing presumption of stratification scholars that any residual cross-national variability in segregation will necessarily take the form of differences in degree rather than kind. The logic underlying this assumption has not, however, been laid out in any careful or sustained way, no doubt because the available measures have all been scalar and hence scholars have naturally defaulted to them without any consideration of (unavailable) alternatives. As new measures and methods emerge, it is perhaps useful to ask whether a type 2 formulation can be reconciled with contemporary understandings of segregation regimes and their internal operation. We have suggested in Table 1 that such a reconciliation is indeed feasible; as shown here, one need merely assume that segregation systems are tightly coupled and well-integrated, with local patterns of segregation thus reflecting a wider system logic rather than purely occupation-specific dynamics. The resulting imagery suggests, then, a neo-Parsonian approach in which segregation practices throughout the occupational structure are the institutional realization of systemwide values regarding the legitimacy or illegitimacy of inequality (Parsons 1970; Goode 1963). The foregoing account might be contrasted with one that treats segregation regimes as more loosely coupled; that is, egalitarian practices in one sector of the occupational structure may sometimes be conjoined with highly discriminatory practices in another, thereby leading to more complex patterns of cross-national difference than a type 2 formulation allows.

If a type 2 model fails to fit the data, we are unwilling to resort directly to simple historicist formulations emphasizing that past arrangements live on and persist in unique country-specific form. We have instead suggested the fallback position (see line 3) that cross-national variability may be principally expressed at the level of major occupational categories (e.g., professional, clerical, craft; see Table 4 in the Appendix for a full listing). Under this formulation, the residue of segregation at the micro-level of highly detailed occupations (e.g., professor, office clerk, cabinetmaker) is regarded as less mutable, because it reflects the universal facts of patriarchy that allow males everywhere to dominate the most desirable occupations. This line of argumentation, although not explicitly laid out in the literature, is nonetheless consistent with conventional institutionalist approaches focusing on cross-national variability in aggregate patterns of segregation (see especially Chang 2000). For example, Brinton (1988) has suggested that Japanese women are disproportionately found in the semiskilled manual sector, where the returns to firm-specific capital are so limited that workers returning from extended family-related leaves are only trivially penalized. We might cite similarly prominent stories about female "overcrowding" in the Scandinavian service sector (Ruggie 1984; Charles 1992), the American managerial sector (Chang 2000), and the Turkish professional sector (Charles and Grusky 1995). Although countries may differ, then, in patterns of labor supply to major occupational groupings, such institutional variability is presumably overlaid on the more fundamental conditions of patriarchy that guarantee micro-level male advantage in the competition for desirable occupations *within* major categories.

It is a striking indication of how poorly the field is developed that the obverse position is no less credible (see line 4). That is, one might plausibly argue that macro-level patterns of segregation take on much the same shape everywhere, whereas labor practices at the micro-occupational level are subject to idiosyncrasies of all sorts, most notably those reflecting (1) the particular constellation of tasks assigned to an occupation (and the associated desirability of that occupation); (2) the types of labor that were available when the occupation expanded and carried out its formative recruiting; and (3) the types of firms, industries, or occupations that served as "models" for employment practices when the occupation was established or expanded (see Stinchcombe 1965 for a related argument). The foregoing considerations imply a form of path dependency whereby early decisions regarding the gender-typing of an occupation are definitively shaped by quite local and nation-specific considerations. By contrast, segregation at the macro-level may be determined by more fundamental and less variable forces, such as the worldwide diffusion of traditional gender roles. This line of reasoning suggests that the deep structure in segregation data will only be uncovered by first filtering out nation-specific noise at the detailed occupational level.

We are left, finally, with the extreme position that no deep structure exists and that cross-national variability is accordingly too complex to be captured even by the weakened formulations that we have just rehearsed (see line 5). The historical record indicates, of course, that segregation of some kind is universal, yet many scholars have emphasized that it takes on historically contingent forms that can only be understood through careful qualitative study (Blekher 1979; Dodge 1971; see also Bradley 1989; Scott 1986; Tilly and Scott 1978). This position has been compellingly argued; however, given that its adherents draw principally on case studies, one cannot know whether the cited idiosyncrasies are isolated examples or indicative of more pervasive variation, nor can one formally test for the more complex and subtle forms of cross-national similarity that we have outlined in Table 1. The results presented below provide, then, the first comprehensive evidence of the extent to which the distinctive cultures, histories, and institutions of countries live on in ways that shape their segregation profiles.

Sex Segregation Models

We proceed by fitting models that correspond to the various formulations listed in Table 1. For example, model 1 allows for cross-national variability in the occupational structure and in female labor supply, but constrains all sex-by-occupation interaction to be cross-nationally invariant. This model of all two-way interactions can be represented as follows:

$$m_{ijk} = \alpha_k \beta_{ik} \gamma_{jk} \delta_{ij}, \qquad (1)$$

where i indexes sex, j indexes occupation, k indexes country, α_k is the grand mean in the kth country, β_{ik} is the country-specific marginal effect for the ith gender, γ_{jk} is the country-specific marginal effect for the jth occupation, and δ_{ij} is the sex-by-occupation interaction for the ij^{th} cell in each country.[2]

If this model fails to fit, we might ask whether cross-national variability arises principally from simple differences in the *degree* of sex segregation (see line 2, Table 1). The centerpiece of our modeling approach is a multiplicative shift model that is consistent with the conventional practice of summarizing cross-national variability in a single parameter (i.e., an index). This model takes the form:

$$m_{ijk} = \alpha_k \beta_{ik} \gamma_{jk} e^{\Phi_k Z_i v_j} \qquad (2)$$

where Φ_k is the multiplicative shift effect for the kth country, Z_i is an indicator variable for gender (i.e., $Z_1 = 0$ and $Z_2 = 1$), and v_j is the scale value for the jth occupation. If this specification fits the data, it follows that Φ_k can be used to represent variability in the underlying strength of sex segregation.[3] We thus reject the common practice of simply assuming that a scalar index is empirically viable. Indeed, the frequently issued platitude that segregation indices should be selected on the basis of "research interests" is insufficiently stringent, because it makes no allowance for the possibility that the preferred measure fails to adequately characterize the data at hand. It is high time that ad-

vocates of particular indices be held accountable for the data reduction that their indices imply.

If the model of equation (2) also fails to fit, we can conclude that the occupation-specific contours of sex segregation (i.e., the "segregation profile") are variable across countries. The main problem with conventional index-based approaches is that qualitative differences in the segregation profile are ignored altogether and emphasis is instead placed on simple differences in the degree of segregation. The models presented in Charles and Grusky (1995) serve to properly refocus attention on the underlying profile itself. Although the task of modeling such profiles is not always an easy one, we can simplify matters for our present illustrative purposes by relying, without loss of generality, on the following saturated model:

$$m_{ijk} = \alpha_k \beta_{ik} \gamma_{jk} e^{Z_i v_{jk}}. \qquad (3)$$

Under this specification, the scale values (v_{jk}) are now subscripted by k, thus implying that the segregation profile freely varies by country. These scale values can be used to calculate a summary index, A, that allows for qualitative variability in the underlying structure of segregation.[4]

We consider, finally, a closely related model that estimates the net residue of segregation at the aggregate level after the data are purged of all lower-order compositional effects (see Charles and Grusky 1995, 952–53). This simple multilevel model, which is also saturated, can be represented as:

$$m_{ijk} = \alpha_k \beta_{ik} \gamma_{jk} e^{Z_i v_{jk} + Z_i \varphi_{ck}} \qquad (4)$$

where φ_{ck} refers to the scale values for major occupational categories (indexed by c), and v_{jk} refers to the scale values for detailed occupations nested in these major categories.[5] In estimating this model, we opt to parameterize the structure of segregation at multiple levels, thus allowing us to determine whether a deep commonality emerges for either major or minor occupational categories (see Grusky and Charles 1998).

A New Cross-National Data Archive

Although the foregoing models have been applied previously (e.g., Charles and Grusky 1995), our occupational classification is altogether new. We apply a 64-category classification that relies heavily on recent efforts of the National Statistical Institutes of the European Union to establish a single harmonized variant of the 1988 International Standard Classification of Occupations (see the Appendix for a listing of our classification). The resulting classification, dubbed ISCO–COM, has garnered widespread support within the European Union, but most member countries have not yet published sex segregation arrays based on the new protocol. We have nonetheless moved forward by (1) commissioning national statistical agencies to process individual-level census data as mandated by ISCO–COM, (2) securing highly detailed segregation arrays and recoding them in accord with such translation keys as are presently available, or (3) developing translation keys of our own and applying them to detailed segregation data. By virtue of ISCO–COM, it thus becomes feasible to standardize more rigorously than was heretofore possible, but of course some misclassification inevitably remains because of inadequate detail in the in-

digenous schemes or because of real cross-national variability in the division of labor itself (Elias and Birch 1993; 1994).[6] For the present study, we carry out analyses for 10 countries (see Table 2) that can be coded into our ISCO–COM classification with relatively little error, as this insistence on high-quality data constitutes our main comparative advantage relative to previous, more inclusive studies.

Tests of Cross-National Invariance

We begin our analysis by testing the simple claim that patterns of sex segregation are cross-nationally invariant once the confounding effects of labor supply and demand are parsed out (see equation 1). The L^2 statistic for this model registers as high as 1,763,819 (with 567 df), while the index of dissimilarity (Δ) indicates that 5.5 percent of the respondents must be reclassified to bring about a perfect correspondence between the observed values and those implied by the model. Although some scholars might characterize this fit as adequate (especially because $\Delta = 5.5$), it bears emphasizing that our more complicated models (see below) reveal rather substantial cross-national differences in both the underlying strength and pattern of segregation. We can conclude that the model of complete invariance suppresses much variability in the basic parameters of segregation.

In our next model, we allow the overall level of segregation to be cross-nationally variable, but continue to constrain the underlying segregation curve to take on the same shape in each country (see equation 2). Under this specification, we find that only 14 percent of the total cross-national variability in sex segregation is explained, with the remaining variability attributable to cross-national differences in the segregation profile itself.[7] The latter result implies that gender stratification systems are only poorly integrated and that pockets of extreme segregation and integration can therefore coexist in the same country. The standard presumption that the nation-

TABLE 2
Sources and Sample Characteristics
for Ten-Nation Data Set

Country	Census Year	Sample Size	Percent Female
Italy	1991	21,071,282	35.7
United States	1990	1,152,885	45.7
West Germany	1993	128,912	41.2
Portugal	1991	4,037,130	40.5
Sweden	1990	4,059,813	48.6
Switzerland	1990	3,076,445	38.0
Japan	1990	12,220,974	39.8
France	1990	900,255	43.0
Belgium	1991	3,418,512	39.8
United Kingdom	1991	2,405,091	44.3

state is a natural (or at least adequate) unit of analysis must accordingly be questioned; that is, attempts to understand cross-national variability in sex segregation as an outgrowth of either "woman-friendly" or "male-centered" national policies, institutions, and cultures are overly simplistic. The poor fit of this model implies either that (1) national values, policies, and institutions have occupation-specific effects (e.g., occupationally targeted affirmative action policies), or (2) segregation is driven not by national variables but by local occupation-specific forces (e.g., occupation-specific cultures, union practices). These interpretations are consistent with our premise that conventional index-based approaches should be supplemented with more careful study of segregation profiles.

The preceding results suggest, then, that cross-national variability at the detailed level cannot be characterized in any simple fashion, but it is still possible that a deeper commonality obtains at the aggregate level of major occupational groups. This hypothesis can be tested by fitting a model that estimates the net residue of segregation at the aggregate level after purging the data of lower-order compositional effects (see equation 4). The macro-level estimates from this model, as graphed in Figures 1A and 1B, do indeed reveal a rather striking similarity in the segregation curves.[8] Although the underlying profile is not cross-nationally identical, such variability as exists may be interpreted as a simple strengthening or weakening of a fundamentally shared pattern (compare Figures 1A and 1B). In this sense, modern segregation has a deep structure underlying it, albeit one that only emerges when all micro-level variability is stripped away.[9]

In characterizing these figures, we would suggest that sectoral and gradational principles are simultaneously at work, with the former principle accounting for the crowding of women into the nonmanual sector, and the latter principle accounting for the tendency of men to dominate the most desirable occupations in both sectors (i.e., managerial and craft occupations). The combination of these two forces yields the characteristic "leaning–N" profile of Figures 1A and 1B. This pattern emerges because, within both the manual and nonmanual sectors, the major occupational categories have been listed in order of declining desirability, or at least approximately so. The upward-sloping lines within each sector thus reveal that men are advantaged in securing the most desirable occupations (i.e., the gradational principle). However, a simple gradational story cannot fully explain the observed profile, because we also find a marked disjuncture in scale values at the manual–nonmanual barrier. This disjuncture reflects the operation of the sectoral principle; that is, there is a characteristic crowding of women into the nonmanual sector, even though the occupations within that sector are *more* desirable, on average, than those in the manual sector.

The observed commonalities can be attributed, then, to primitive segregating principles that are operative in all societies but expressed to varying degrees. As noted above, the same "leaning–N" pattern appears in both figures, yet is clearly attenuated in the case of Figure 1B. This attenuation appears both in the form of a diminished between-sector disjuncture (i.e., a weakened sectoral effect) as well as diminished within-sector slopes (i.e., a weakened gradational effect). It is striking in this regard that our two less-developed countries (i.e., Portugal and Italy) both appear in the moderate segregation profile. This result is consistent with arguments suggesting that, as industrialism advances, many traditionally female tasks differentiate out of the household economy and are incorporated into the paid economy (e.g., childcare), thereby drawing increasing numbers of women into highly segregated sectors of the labor market (see Charles 1992 for details).

The micro-level estimates from our model are next graphed in Figure 2. As might be anticipated, the scale values for virtually all occupations are quite widely scattered, thus suggesting that the forces of micro-level segregation manifest themselves in highly variable ways. The segregation of detailed occupations

FIGURE 1A

Aggregate profile for extreme segregation pattern

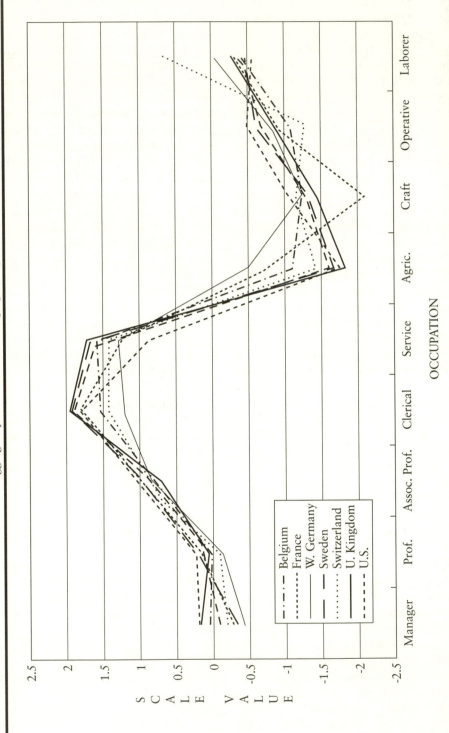

FIGURE 1B

Aggregate profile for moderate segregation pattern

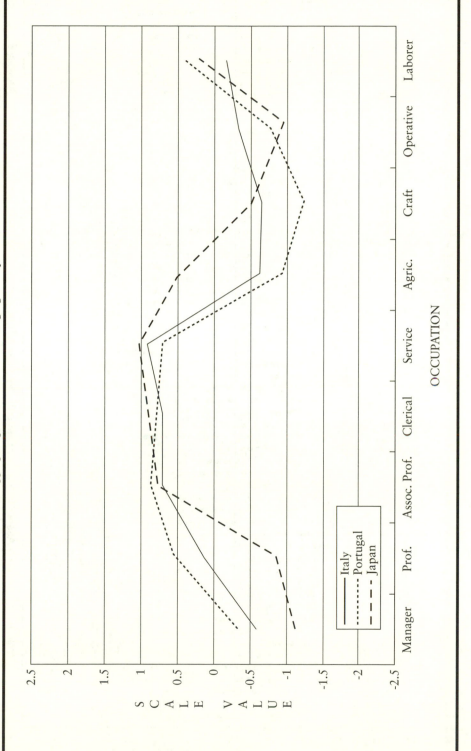

698

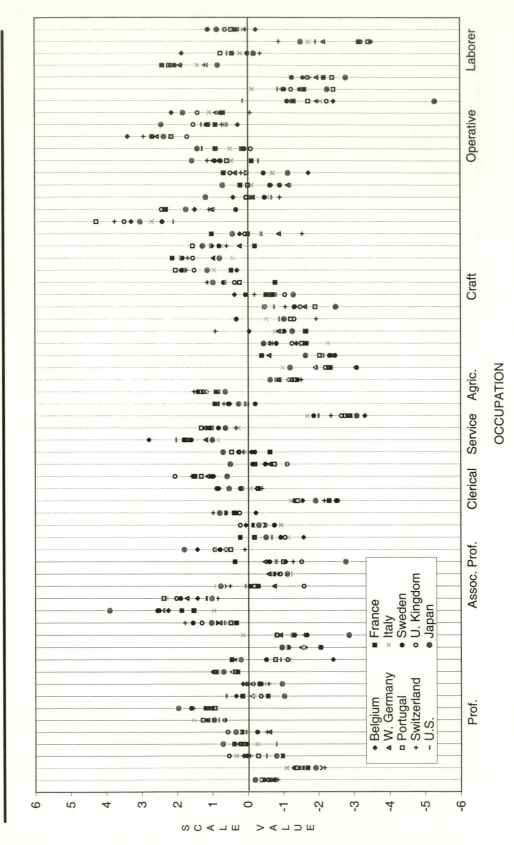

FIGURE 2
Cross-national dispersion in purged scale values

may reflect such idiosyncratic processes as (1) the types of firms, industries, or occupations that served as models for hiring practices when the occupation was established or expanded; (2) the closure strategies (e.g., unionization, credentialing) that occupational incumbents seized upon in attempting to monopolize skilled tasks; (3) the "women-friendliness" of the owners, unions, and managers involved in occupational staffing and recruitment; and (4) the gender composition of the labor force when the occupation expanded and carried out its formative recruiting. These processes all suggest a form of path dependency whereby local and particularistic forces influence the initial gender-typing of occupations and shape the subsequent trajectory of development (Stinchcombe 1965; Weeden and Sørensen forthcoming). The resulting cross-national variability is accordingly more complicated than that prevailing at the macro-level.

The foregoing results make it clear that all sex segregation indices, conventional or otherwise, are inappropriate for the present data. If summary measures are still insisted upon, we would do well to rely on a margin-free measure that does not condition on a common segregation profile (i.e., A). For each of our 10 countries, we have thus presented A as well as the more conventional index of dissimilarity (D), the latter serving as a useful point of comparison. As shown in Table 3, our association index reveals considerable cross-national variability not merely in the patterning of segregation, but also in its underlying strength. The United Kingdom, for example, is nearly twice as segregated as Italy; that is, males or females are overrepresented in the typical occupation by a factor of 6.28 in the United Kingdom, but only by a factor of 3.31 in Italy. The values of A for Belgium and France are nearly as high (i.e., A = 6.10), whereas Japan, Switzerland, Sweden, and Portugal assume a middling position in the hierarchy. Although Japanese segregation has been characterized in the past as surprisingly weak (e.g., Brinton and Ngo 1993), the present results indicate that, when A is applied to

TABLE 3
Scalar Measures of Sex Segregation

Country	Segregation Index	
	A	D
Italy	3.31	43.0
United States	4.39	45.1
West Germany	4.50	50.9
Portugal	5.26	47.7
Sweden	5.47	60.2
Switzerland	5.52	55.5
Japan	5.87	44.8
France	6.10	54.5
Belgium	6.10	51.2
United Kingdom	6.28	56.5

Note: A = Association Index; D = Index of Dissimilarity.

disaggregate data, Japan is restored to its rightful place as a moderately segregated country. By contrast, the United States joins Italy at the low end of the continuum, with A implying in this case that males or females are overrepresented in the typical occupation by a factor of only 4.39. This is nonetheless a strikingly high level of segregation insofar as the universalistic and egalitarian values of modern societies are taken seriously.

Conclusions

We led off this chapter by suggesting that segregation analysts have turned prematurely to explanatory modeling without first establishing the most basic descriptive contours of sex segregation. In accounting for this state of affairs, it is surely relevant that the requisite data have until now been unavailable, but it is equally problematic that adequate models and methods have likewise been lacking. We have sought to make progress on all fronts by distinguishing between different types of similarity and difference, by developing log-multiplicative models that correspond to these types, and by applying our models to a new archive of rigorously harmonized segregation data. This approach allows us to produce the first detailed mapping of sex segregation within industrial and advanced industrial market economies.

The results from our mapping exercise reveal so much variability in patterns of micro-level segregation that we are naturally led to historicist and institutionalist accounts of the more radical variety (e.g., Scott 1986). Although a long tradition of case study scholarship has identified discrepant sex-typing among particular occupations (e.g., Lapidus 1985), it was unclear whether the cited idiosyncrasies were isolated examples or indicative of more pervasive variation. We can now suggest that the distinctive histories and institutions of countries live on in ways that fundamentally shape their segregation profiles. The imagery that emerges, then, is that of loosely coupled segregation systems cobbled together from many occupation-specific "solutions" to the exigencies of modern industrial production and competing segregative and egalitarian cultural mandates.

This is not to suggest that the model of complete variability (line 5, Table 1) is to be preferred. Although observed patterns of segregation are indeed cross-nationally variable and idiosyncratic, a deeper commonality is detectable once the more chaotic features of micro-level segregation are statistically removed. The resulting macro-level segregation curves are fundamentally hybrid in character; that is, the "sectoral principle" accounts for the disproportionate allocation of women into the service-based nonmanual sector, and the "gradational principle" accounts for the simultaneous channeling of women into the least desirable occupations within both the manual and nonmanual sectors (see Charles and Grusky forthcoming). The first principle is consistent with models suggesting a reproduction of domestic gender roles in the formal economy, and the second principle is consistent with queuing models of male advantage. These two principles operate to varying degrees in all societies and hence produce fundamental commonality in the underlying structure of segregation.

Notes

This chapter was presented in draft form to the annual meeting of the American Sociological Association (Los Angeles, 1994). We are grateful for research support from the Faculty Career Development Office at the University of California—San Diego, the Hellman Faculty Fellowship Program (1995–1996 award), the National Science Foundation (NSF SBE-9808038), the Stanford Center for the Study of Families, Children, and Youth (1993–1994 grant), and the Stanford University Dean's Research Fund. The data analyzed here were assembled with the assistance of Sylvie Lagarde (France), Ulrich Greiner (Germany), Leif Haldorson (Sweden), Jan Boruvka (Switzerland), Margaret Wort (United Kingdom), and Mariko Lin Chang and Joon Han (Japan). The data were entered and cleaned by Max Draitser, Mark Jones, Karen Lee, Lida Nedilsky, and Jeanne Powers. This chapter further profited from the comments and advice of Karen Aschaffenburg, Lisa Catanzarite, Mariko Lin Chang, Peter Elias, Joon Han, Winifred Poster, Jesper Sørensen, Szonja Szelényi, and Kimberly Weeden. The opinions expressed herein are nonetheless the sole responsibility of the authors.

1. This is not to suggest that segregation regimes evolve in strict isolation from one another. To the contrary, the gender labels that are characteristically attached to occupations may well diffuse across national borders, thus generating cross-national similarities in the discriminatory tastes of employers and the sex-typed aspirations of workers. The foregoing process is likely fueled by the proliferation of transnational business networks as well as the growing normative authority of international political and social organizations (e.g., United Nations, World Bank).

2. The marginal effects for this model are identified by constraining the parameters for the first row and column to equal 1 (in each country), and the sex-by-occupation interaction effects are identified by constraining the parameters in the first row and column to equal 1 (in each country).

3. The scale values for this model are identified by constraining them to sum to 0, and the marginal and shift effects are identified by constraining the parameters for the first row, column, or level to equal 1 (see Charles and Grusky 1995, 938–39).

4. We follow Charles and Grusky (1995, 945) in defining A as $\exp(1/J \times \Sigma_{jk}^2)^{1/2}$. The closed-form solution for A is $\exp(1/J \times \Sigma\{\ln(F_{jk}/M_{jk}) - [1/J \times \Sigma\ln(F_{jk}/M_{jk})]\}^2)^{1/2}$, where M_{jk} and F_{jk} refer to the number of males and females in the jth occupation and k^{th} country.

APPENDIX
Recording Rules for Translating ISCO–88 into 64-Category Classification

Occupation	ISCO-88 Codes	Occupation	ISCO-88 Codes
A. Manager (MA)	111, 112, 114,	*F. Agric. & Fishery (AG)*	
Manager	121–123, 131	Farmer	611–613, 921
		Forestry & Fishery	614, 615
B. Professional (PR)			
Physical Science	211–213	*G. Craft (CR)*	
Architect & Engineer	214	Miner & Cutter	711, 712
Life Science	221	Building Finisher	713
Health	222	Painter & Related	714
Professor	231	Metal Moulder & Related	721
Secondary Teacher	232	Blacksmith & Related	722
Other Teacher	234, 235	Machinery Mechanic	723
Business Professional	241	Electrical Mechanic	724
Lawyer & Related	242	Metal Precision	731
Social Science & Related	243–245, 247	Handicraft	732, 733
Religious Professional	246, 348	Printing & Related	734
		Food Processing	741
C. Associate Prof. (AP)		Cabinet-Maker	742
Physical Science	311, 312	Textile & Garment	743
Inspector & Related	313–315	Pelt, Leather, & Shoe	744
Life Science & Health	321, 322		
Nursing & Midwife	223, 323	*H. Operative (OP)*	
Primary Teacher	233, 331, 332	Wood Processing	814
Other Teacher	333, 334	Other Stationary-Plant	811–813, 815–817
Finance & Sales	341	Metal & Mineral	821
Agent & Broker	342	Chemical & Related	822, 823
Admin. & Social Work	343, 346	Wood Product Operative	824, 825
Customs, Tax, & Related	344, 345	Textile & Related	826
Art, Entertaining, & Sport	347	Food & Related	827
		Assembler	828, 829
D. Clerical (CL)		Locomotive	831
Office Clerk	411, 412, 414, 419	Motor Vehicle	832
Material-recording	413	Mobile Plant Operator	833, 834
Cashier & Teller	421		
Client Information	422	*I. Laborer (LA)*	
		Vendor & Domestic	911–914, 916
E. Service & Sales (SS)		Messenger & Related	915
Travel Attendant	511	Mining & Construction	931
Housekeeping & Related	512	Manufacturing & Related	932, 933
Personal Care & Related	513		
Other Personal Service	514		
Protective Service	516		
Salesperson & Related	521, 522		

5. The micro-level scale values (v_{jk}) can be identified by constraining them to sum to 0 within each major occupational category, and the macro-level scale values (φ_{ck}) can be identified by constraining them to sum to 0 within each country.

6. These errors in coding, classification, and aggregation are addressed elsewhere in more detail (Charles and Grusky forthcoming).

7. The L^2 value for this model is 1,517,231 (with 558 df) and the index of dissimilarity (Δ) is 5.1.

8. In all of our figures, positive scale values indicate female overrepresentation, and negative scale values indicate male overrepresentation.

9. These graphs do of course reveal *some* macro-level variability that is consistent with the arguments of Chang (2000), Charles (1998; 1992), Brinton (1988), and others.

References

Anker, Richard. 1998. *Gender and Jobs: Sex Segregation of Occupations in the World*. Geneva: ILO.

Beck-Gernsheim, Elisabeth, and I. Ostner. 1978. "Frauen verändern—Berufe nicht?" *Soziale Welt* 29:257–87.

Becker, Gary S. 1985. "Human Capital, Effort, and the Sexual Division of Labor." *Journal of Labor Economics* 3:33–58.

Blackburn, Robert M., Jennifer Jarman, and Janet Siltanen. 1993. "The Analysis of Occupational Gender Segregation Over Time and Place: Considerations of Measurement and Some New Evidence." *Work, Employment, and Society* 7:335–62.

Blau, Francine D., and Marianne A. Ferber. 1998. *The Economics of Women, Men, and Work*. Upper Saddle River, NJ: Prentice Hall.

Blekher, Feiga. 1979. *The Soviet Woman in the Family and in Society*. New York: Wiley.

Boserup, Ester. 1970. *Woman's Role in Economic Development*. London: Allen & Unwin.

Bradley, Harriet. 1989. *Men's Work, Women's Work: A Sociological History of the Sexual Division of Labour in Employment*. Minneapolis: University of Minnesota Press.

Brinton, Mary C. 1988. "The Social-Institutional Bases of Gender Stratification: Japan as an Illustrative Case." *American Journal of Sociology* 94:300–34.

Brinton, Mary C., and Hang-Yue Ngo. 1993. "Age and Sex in the Occupational Structure: A United States–Japan Comparison." *Sociological Forum* 8:93–111.

Cartmill, Randi. 2000. "Occupational Sex Segregation in Global Perspective: Comparative Analyses of Industrialized and Less Developed Nations." Unpublished manuscript, Department of Sociology, University of Wisconsin– Madison.

Chang, Mariko Lin. 2000. "The Evolution of Sex Segregation Regimes." *American Journal of Sociology* 105:1658–1701.

Charles, Maria. 1992. "Cross-National Variation in Occupational Sex Segregation." *American Sociological Review* 57:483–502.

Charles, Maria. 1998. "Structure, Culture, and Sex Segregation in Europe." *Research in Social Stratification and Mobility* 16:89–116.

Charles, Maria, and David B. Grusky. 1995. "Models for Describing the Underlying Structure of Sex Segregation." *American Journal of Sociology* 100:931–71.

Charles, Maria, and David B. Grusky. Forthcoming. *Sex Segregation in Comparative Perspective*. Stanford: Stanford University Press.

Chodorow, Nancy. 1978. *The Reproduction of Mothering: Psychoanalysis and the Sociology of Gender*. Berkeley: University of California Press.

Dodge, Norton. 1971. "Women in the Soviet Economy." Pages 207–23 in *The Professional Woman*, edited by Athena Theodore. Cambridge: Schenkman.

Elias, Peter, and Margaret Birch. 1993. "Establishment of Community-Wide Occupational Statistics." Working paper, Institute for Employment Research, University of Warwick.

———. 1994. "Harmonising Occupational Information Across the European Union: Progress on the Labour Force Survey. Working paper, Institute for Employment Research, University of Warwick.

Goode, William J. 1963. *World Revolution and Family Patterns*. New York: Free Press.

Grusky, David B., and Maria Charles. 1998. "The Past, Present, and Future of Sex Segregation Methodology." *Demography* 35:497–504.

Hartmann, Heidi I. 1976. "Capitalism, Patriarchy, and Job Segregation by Sex." *Signs* 1:137-69.

Jacobs, Jerry A., and Suet T. Lim. 1992. "Trends in Occupational and Industrial Sex Segregation in 56 Countries, 1960-1980." *Work and Occupations* 19:450-86.

———. 1995. "Trends in Occupational and Industrial Sex Segregation in 56 Countries, 1960–1980." Pages 259–93 in *Gender Inequality at Work*, edited by Jerry A. Jacobs. Thousand Oaks: Sage Publications.

Lapidus, Gail W. 1985. "The Soviet Union." Pages 13–32 in *Women Workers in Fifteen Countries*, edited by Jennie Farley. New York: ILR Press.

Mincer, Jacob, and Solomon W. Polachek. 1974. "Family Investments in Human Capital: Earnings of Women." *Journal of Political Economy* 82:S76–S108.

Parsons, Talcott A. 1970. "Equality and Inequality in Modern Society, or Social Stratification Revisited." Pages 13–72 in *Social Stratification: Research and Theory for the 1970s*, edited by Edward O. Lauman. Indianapolis: Bobbs-Merrill.

Reskin, Barbara F., and Patricia A. Roos. 1990. *Job Queues, Gender Queues: Explaining Women's Inroads into Male Occupations*. Philadelphia: Temple University Press.

Ruggie, Mary. 1984. *The State and Working Women: A Comparative Study of Britain and Sweden*. Princeton: Princeton University Press.

Sanday, Peggy Reeves. 1981. *Female Power and Male Dominance: On the Origins of Sexual Inequality*. London: Cambridge University Press.

Scott, Alison MacEwen. 1986. "Industrialization, Gender Segregation and Stratification Theory." Pages 154–89 in *Gender and Stratification*, edited by Rosemary Crompton and Michael Mann. Cambridge: Polity Press.

Semyonov, Moshe, and Frank Jones. 1999. "Dimensions of Gender Occupational Differentiation in Segregation and Inequality: A Cross-National Analysis." *Social Indicators Research* 46:225–47.

Stinchcombe, Arthur L. 1965. "Social Structure and Organizations." Pages 142–93 in *Handbook of Organizations*, edited by James G. March. Chicago: Rand McNally.

Strober, Myra H. 1984. "Toward a General Theory of Occupational Sex Segregation: The Case of Public School Teaching." Pages 144–56 in *Sex Segregation in the Workplace*, edited by Barbara F. Reskin. Washington, D.C.: National Academy.

Tilly, Louise A., and Joan W. Scott. 1978. *Women, Work, and Family*. New York: Holt, Rinehart, & Winston.

Walby, Sylvia. 1986. *Patriarchy at Work*. Cambridge: Polity Press.

Weeden, Kimberly, and Jesper Sørensen. Forthcoming. "Two-Dimensional Models of Sex Segregation: Industries and Occupations." In *Sex Segregation in Comparative Perspective*, edited by Maria Charles and David B. Grusky. Stanford: Stanford University Press.

W I L L I A M   T.   B I E L B Y

The Structure and Process of Sex Segregation

My work seeks to understand the persistence of occupational segregation by sex and the sex gap in earnings. Neoclassical economists, of course, have an elegant, coherent theory of the sources of both occupational segregation by sex and earnings differentials: they come from the rational, utility-maximizing behavior of men and women within households and labor markets.

Sociologists view the situation differently. Indeed, depending on whom you ask, a sociologist might offer any of a number of explanations for sex differences in labor-market outcomes. Social psychologists would stress sex-role socialization. Feminist scholars would emphasize the "patriarchal" interests of male employers and workers. Marxists would tell a story about capitalists creating divisions in the work force in order to control labor and boost profits. Organizational theorists might talk about the unintended consequences of bureaucratic rules and procedures. Not surprisingly, sociologists from different camps often talk past one another.

However, sociologists are increasingly taking the work of neoclassical economists seri-

Originally published in 1991. Please see complete source information beginning on page 891.

ously. The language of "human capital," "statistical discrimination," and the like is increasingly part of the sociological discourse on gender and work. However, sociologists do not accept the neoclassical account uncritically. In this chapter, I first summarize how my research with James Baron and Denise Bielby challenges neoclassical explanations and then raise some issues concerning the promise and limitations of recent interdisciplinary approaches to the study of job segregation by sex and other forms of discrimination.

I. Neoclassical Views

In a sense, it all starts with the household division of labor. Women prefer, get stuck with, or have a comparative advantage caring for children and the home. Because of that, they invest less in market human capital. For example, intermittent labor-force participation leads to less work experience and thus to lower productivity and flatter age-earnings profiles. Women rationally *choose* occupations that are easy to leave and reenter, where skills do not atrophy, and so on. These choices lead to occupational segregation and wage differentials (see Polachek and Kao [1991]; Polachek [1979]).

Becker [1985] has offered a clever twist on this explanation. People do not simply allocate time between household and market activities. They also allocate *effort*. Since women allocate more effort to household activities, they have less effort to allocate to work outside the home. So, even when men and women have the same *amount* of work experience, training, etc., women are less productive. An additional hour of women's work is less effort-intensive than one of men's work. As a result, women are worth less to employers and accumulate less market human capital with each additional hour of work. This leads to an explanation for both occupational segregation by sex and earnings differentials within occupations. Women choose less effort-intensive jobs, and they are less productive than men working on the same jobs.

There is, of course, another view of occupational segregation that admits to a certain kind of "discrimination," but only a *rational* kind of "statistical discrimination." In a world filled with uncertainty, employers cannot always know the relevant traits of job applicants. Suppose that there are important traits that are difficult to measure, but we know that, on average, women exhibit more (or less) of them than men. One example often cited is the likelihood of job turnover. Suppose also that there are two kinds of jobs—those for which it is costly to replace a worker who quits and those for which it is not. Not knowing actual quit propensities, rational, profit-maximizing employers will reserve the former jobs for men and fill the latter with women, even if there is considerable overlap in the underlying distributions of quit propensities of men and women (Phelps [1972]; Aigner and Cain [1977]).

My research in collaboration with Denise Bielby (Bielby and Bielby [1988]) and James Baron (Bielby and Baron [1986]) suggests that despite the elegance of the neoclassical accounts, the world just does not work that way. Men and women employees do not act in a way that is consistent with neoclassical accounts, nor do employers.

II. Empirical Challenges to Neoclassical Views: The Allocation of Effort

Denise Bielby and I, using the 1973 and 1977 Quality of Employment Surveys, attempted to operationalize a human-capital model of the allocation of work effort (Bielby and Bielby [1988]). Here I summarize the findings relevant to the issue of job segregation and earnings disparities.

Contrary to the clear implication from Becker's model, women do not exert less effort than men in the workplace in order to conserve effort for household activities. Compared to men with similar household responsibilities, market human capital, earnings, promotion opportunities, and job responsibilities, women allocate substantially more effort to work activities; the net sex difference is nearly one-half a standard deviation on the scale we use. To the extent that women do allocate effort away from the workplace in order to meet family demands, these trade-offs bring their work effort back to the level of the typical male with no such family responsibilities.

How could this be? We believe that the neoclassical model of the allocation of work effort is seriously flawed in several ways. First, it may be inappropriate to assume that the "stock" of effort to be allocated by an individual is fixed, analogous to a fixed stock of physical capital. For women to work just as hard as men, if not harder, despite their greater household responsibilities, women must be able to draw on a reserve of energy that is either not available to the typical male, or more realistically, that men choose not to draw upon. Stephen Marks, a sociologist who has written on this topic [1977: 927], cites physiological evidence in support of his claim that "individuals have abundant and perpetually renewing [energy] resources." He suggests that individuals generate the energy needed to participate in activities to which they are committed and that they often feel more "energetic" after engaging in them. Our findings imply that as women add work roles to their family roles, they generate the energy necessary to fulfill their commitments to the two sets of activities.

A second factor ignored by human capital models is what social psychologists call "entitlement norms." The allocation to effort at work is influenced by internalized norms of a "fair day's work," which may differ by sex. Determinations of fairness are based on perceptions of contributions relative to rewards. Experiments show that men and women differ in how they invoke equity considerations in allocating effort and rewards. On average, women pay themselves less than men performing the same task, and women tend to undervalue their efforts relative to men (Lenney [1977]; Callahan-Levy and Messe [1979]; Major, McFarlin, and Gagnon

[1984]). It appears that, on average, women have lower internal standards of "personal entitlement," and, in the absence of salient external comparison standards, they make fairness judgments based on application of same-sex norms about appropriate rewards (Berger et al. [1972], Crosby [1982]).

In a laboratory experiment designed specifically to examine sex differences in effort and standards of personal entitlement, Major, McFarlin, and Gagnon [1984] asked men and women to do as much work as they thought was fair for a fixed amount of money. They collected objective measures of the accuracy and efficiency of performance on the task as well as information on each subject's perceptions of his or her level of performance. They discovered that, on average, "women worked longer, did more work, completed more correct work, and were more efficient than men" (1409). At the same time, men and women did *not* differ in their self-evaluations of their performance, despite women's superior objective performance. Nor did men and women differ in their reports of satisfaction from the task. In short, laboratory research on sex differences in internal standards of personal entitlement suggests that, all else constant, women can be expected to allocate more effort than men to work activities.

Third, structural features of workplaces might reinforce sex differences in entitlement norms. For example, research on sex segregation in the workplace suggests why same-sex norms about rewards for performance persist. Most men and women work in sex-segregated jobs (Bielby and Baron [1984], [1986]; Reskin and Hartmann [1986]). Consequently, many women lack information on both the numerator and the denominator of the "equity ratio" of reward to effort for men's work. According to social psychologists, it is precisely when external bases of social comparison are unavailable that individuals rely on internal, same-sex norms (Berger, Zelditch, Anderson, and Cohen [1972]; Berger, Rosenholtz, and Zelditch [1980]; Austin [1977]). Major, McFarlin, and Gagnon found that when external comparison information was available, neither sex relied on same-sex norms to make judgments of fair pay for a given task. Thus equity research suggests why employers might have a stake in a sex-segregated workforce: as long as women lack information about the reward structure for men, they will be willing to work for less pay. (Moreover, husbands of working women benefit by avoiding responsibility for household activities, despite the fact that their wives expend as much or more energy as they do at work.)

Fourth, another aspect of our analysis calls into question the extent to which decisions about work and family are made in a deliberately self-conscious, rational manner. Bielby and Bielby [1988] found that men's work effort is greatly influenced by family demands, while the effects of "human-capital" investments such as schooling and labor-market experience are relatively weak. In contrast, compared to men, women's work effort is less strongly influenced by family demands, but is more strongly affected by investments in market human capital. For example, a man with child-care responsibilities reduces his work effort, but a woman in the same situation does not. At the same time, a man with meager investments in "market human capital"—education and labor-market experience—does not decrease his work effort, but a woman with comparable investments does decrease her work effort. This suggests that individuals take sex-specific culturally prescribed roles for granted. Women do not adjust their effort allocations in response to household responsibilities, and men do not adjust their effort allocations in response to workplace investments.

It appears that individuals *do* rationally reflect upon their efforts when they cannot fall back upon culturally prescribed roles. Men confronted with household responsibilities reduce their work efforts, as do women with meager investments in market human capital. For men, some level of work effort may be culturally prescribed and "taken for granted" regardless of investments in education and training. For women, a certain level of work effort may be culturally prescribed and

"taken for granted" regardless of the level of household responsibilities. Moreover, the level of effort allocated to work by a woman with heavy household responsibilities is at least as large as that allocated by men with no such responsibilities at home.

In sum, Becker's human-capital model of the allocation of work effort provides a plausible explanation for both sex segregation and wage differentials by sex. However, our research and other social psychological studies call into question some basic premises of this model. The assumption of a fixed stock of effort may be unrealistic, the social psychological processes may be more complex than what is typically assumed about "economic man," and segregation of men's and women's jobs may reinforce sex differences in social psychological processes.

III. Empirical Challenges to Neoclassical Views: Noneconomic Bases of Statistical Discrimination

James Baron and I set out to analyze how men and women in the same general line of work are sorted into different firms and into different jobs within firms (Bielby and Baron [1984], [1986], [1987]; Baron and Bielby [1985]). Figure 1 shows the issue schematically. Consider an occupation like "electronics assembler" that is 40 percent female. Suppose that three firms in an industry employ electronics assemblers and that each of these firms uses assemblers in three of its job titles. In the hypothetical example, firm 1 relies disproportionately on male workers, firm 2 relies disproportionately on female workers, and firm 3 relies on a balanced mix of male and female workers. In firm 1, each of the jobs is staffed disproportionately by men, and in firm 2, the opposite is true. In firm 3, however, the first job is staffed exclusively by men, and the second and third jobs exclusively by women. We can imagine other patterns besides the one depicted in figure 1 for an occupation that is 40 percent female. For example, in a world without statistical discrimination, we might

FIGURE 1
Hypothetical distribution of workers in a mixed occupation across firms and jobs

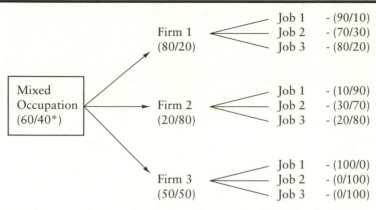

*Ratio of Male Workers to Female Workers

find the sex composition of specific jobs normally distributed around 40 percent female. In any case, according to neoclassical models of the labor market, knowledge of differences between firms and jobs in work requirements and differences between the sexes in job traits should explain how men and women in mixed occupations get distributed across firms and jobs.

Baron and I assembled data like this for several hundred California firms studied by the U.S. Employment Service in the late 1960s and 1970s. That is, we looked at how firms hiring from a sex-mixed labor pool staffed their jobs as a function of firm and job characteristics. Neoclassical models suggested the following hypotheses: scale, bureaucratization, and job-specific training are related to turnover costs, so if women are more likely to quit, they should be underrepresented in firms and jobs where these costs are high. If employers statistically discriminate based on turnover costs, women should be excluded altogether from jobs where these costs are high. The remaining job traits we looked at are job-relevant skills. Women have been shown to perform better, on average, on traits such as verbal skills, motor coordination, finger dexterity, interpersonal skills, and stamina under repetitive, monotonous working conditions. Men have been shown to perform better, on average, on numerical skills, spatial skills, and upper body strength. Thus the distribution of men and women across jobs should reflect differences in jobs in the extent to which they require these sex-linked traits.

Our most startling finding was that California firms in the late 1960s and 1970s rarely employed men and women in the same job titles. Even when drawing from a sex-mixed labor pool for a work role like "electronics assembler," firms reserved some job titles exclusively for men and others exclusively for women. That is, firms either employed male workers exclusively or female workers exclusively, or, if they employed both, men and women were completely segregated by job title, as in firm 3 in figure 1.

In addition, we found that the relationships between firm and job traits and the sex composition of work were exactly as hypothesized. "Male" traits were positively related to the likelihood of excluding women from a job and the effects of "female" traits were in the opposite direction. Our research indicates that employers exclude women from some jobs and men from others (in the same general line of work) based on their perceptions of group differences between men and women in job-related traits. That is, employers statistically discriminate.

However, our findings did not support the neoclassical version of statistical discrimination. Statistical discrimination is efficient only when it is costly to measure the actual job-relevant traits of individual workers. The factors that made the greatest difference in whether men or women were employed were not the subtle and difficult-to-measure factors like turnover costs. They were physical demands and finger dexterity. Men are assigned the jobs perceived to involve heavy work and women—*in the same occupation*—are assigned the "light" work. Women are assigned jobs defined as "detail" work, and men are not.

According to neoclassical economists, employers are sacrificing profits in order to sustain the type of sex segregation we observed. Our measure of physical demands was whether a job required lifting more than twenty five pounds. In most of the firms we studied, no woman would be assigned to these jobs, regardless of that woman's own physical strength. Yet it is simple and inexpensive to devise a test to learn whether a female (or male) job applicant is capable of lifting twenty five pounds. Similarly, it should be easy to devise a simple test that would allow an employer to observe whether a male (or female) job applicant could successfully complete a task requiring finger dexterity. Given that they were drawing from sex-mixed labor pools, why did employers persist in sustaining almost complete job segregation by sex? We had access to narrative material about the employment practices in these California firms, and analyses of these qualitative materials suggested several important factors.

Policies. In many of the firms studied by the Employment Service, it was a matter of company policy not to employ women in certain jobs and to favor employing women in others. Jobs closed to women were typically perceived to be physically demanding and those

favoring women usually involved "detail" work. Curiously, while we often came across policies specifying that women were preferred for certain jobs, we rarely encountered official *prohibitions* against men being employed in these jobs. Yet in practice, men rarely were employed in predominantly female jobs unless they were supervisors and in that case, they would almost always have distinct job titles.

There are at least two reasons for the lack of any explicit prohibition against using men in specific jobs, despite the nearly perfect segregation in practice. First, if female labor is less expensive, employers have no incentive to employ men in the same job categories as women, even if the company has no policy against doing so. Second, prohibitions against women working in certain jobs often originated in protective legislation (even if these regulations no longer applied), and thus complying with government regulations was often the original rationale for having a policy on women's work. No similar regulations mandated policies on men's work.

Organizational Inertia. Once a sex-based division of labor is established, it becomes "taken for granted," sustained over the years unless some deliberate effort is taken to undo it. This was especially evident in the exclusion of women from jobs perceived to be physically demanding. California laws prohibited the employment of women in jobs requiring heavy lifting until these laws were struck down in 1971. Yet our data showed that the exclusion of women from so-called physically demanding jobs was just as widespread through the late 1970s—when the practice was illegal—as it was during the period before 1971. We also saw this inertia in data from firms analyzed by the Employment Service at two points in time, typically six or seven years apart. The sex-based division of labor rarely changed over that six- or seven-year period, even when total employment fluctuated substantially, *unless* there was some deliberate effort taken to undo sex segregation.

Cultural Stereotypes. Cognitive psychologists have demonstrated that we all use stereotypes, or cognitive schema, as a cognitive shorthand we invoke to achieve economy in perception (Ashmore and Del Boca [1981]). Of course, the particular stereotypes we hold about sex roles are widely shared and continually reinforced in our culture. Despite what is assumed by neoclassical models of discrimination, the profit motive is not necessarily strong enough to overcome the cognitive processes that lead to the use of stereotypes. Thus it may be that employers make hiring decisions based on widely shared *misperceptions* of differences in the average traits of men and women. To complicate matters further, statistical discrimination can lead to "self-fulfilling prophecies," or what social psychologists call "expectancy confirmation sequences" (Darley and Fazio [1980]). That is, employers expect certain behaviors from women and assign them to routine tasks and dead-end jobs. Women respond by exhibiting the very behaviors employers expect, reinforcing the stereotype. Moreover, social psychological research suggests that employers are more likely to attend to and retain information that confirms stereotypes, ignoring behavior by women that does not fit their expectations.

Given the kind of data available to Baron and me, we had no direct evidence of cultural stereotypes held by specific employers or managers about men's work and women's work. However, such stereotypes were invoked quite often in policies regarding the employment of women in "heavy" work and in "detail" work. Indeed, it was not uncommon to encounter a policy prohibiting employment of women in certain jobs because of heavy lifting requirements and to then find in detailed job analyses by the Employment Service that these jobs required no heavy physical labor. In other words, the work is often labelled as "heavy work" because it is done by men.

Interests. Finally, the extreme sex segregation we discovered within mixed occupations could not have been sustained without someone's interests being served. It is not difficult to see how employers might have an interest in sex segregation. For example, our research on the allocation of effort suggests that segregation sustains sex-specific norms of entitlement. Male employees who view integration as a threat to their wages may resist the assignment of women to the job titles they hold. However, not at all clear from existing research are the circumstances under which male workers have the capacity to act on these interests, given employers' economic incentive to substitute cheap female labor for expensive male labor. Although my research with Baron on statistical discrimination did not get at the interests issue directly, other work we have done suggests a slight tendency for greater segregation in settings where male workers have substantial market power (Bielby and Baron [1984]).

IV. Conclusion: Reconciling Alternative Perspectives on the Structure and Process of Sex Segregation

We can identify six more or less distinct kinds of explanations for a single phenomenon: sex segregation in the workplace. These explanations are (1) neoclassical, based on models of statistical discrimination and investments in human capital; (2) social psychological, emphasizing socialization and internalized norms; (3) institutional, emphasizing the intended and unintended consequences and inertia of organizational arrangements; (4) cultural, emphasizing taken-for-granted notions of men's work and women's work, often shared by both men and women; (5) political, stressing the different interests of male employers and employees with respect to maintaining the status quo; and (6) patriarchal, emphasizing the common interests of male workers and employers in maintaining a sex-based division of labor.

The research my colleagues and I have pursued has sought to test neoclassical explanations of gender differences in the workplace, not to offer fully developed alternatives. In posing tentative accounting for our findings, we have drawn on both institutional approaches to the structure of work and social psychological theories of entitlement norms. Of course, these areas are no longer beyond the purview of neoclassical economics. For example, Williamson ([1975], [1985]) explains variation in organizational structures with the concept of economizing on transaction costs, and "efficiency wage" theorists invoke entitlement norms to explain interindustry wage differentials (Krueger and Summers [1987]; Akerlof and Yellen [1988]).

It is customary to applaud cross-disciplinary efforts, and the blurring of the boundaries between sociology and neoclassical economics may eventually lead to a comprehensive explanation of job segregation by sex that is consistent with the empirical evidence on the subject. By incorporating "sociological factors" (e.g., institutional barriers, entitlement norms), neoclassical models may be able to more faithfully represent the factors that slow the rate at which market forces erode discrimination in pay and job assignment. Moving in that direction requires continued commitment to the neoclassical assumption that were it not for various "drags" on the system, market forces would inevitably discount ascriptive factors like race and gender in valuing otherwise comparable labor inputs.

Adapting the neoclassical model in this way has appeal due to the power of the model's formal analytical properties. However, the pervasiveness and persistence of job segregation by sex seems too far at odds with the imagery of even the most extreme adaptations of the model (for a similar view, see Darity [1991]). For example, it is difficult to imagine what kinds of "transaction costs" could explain the nearly universal job segregation of men and women *within the same occupation* that Baron and I found across a wide variety of organizational settings. That such segregation would persist is especially problematic

from a neoclassical perspective, since the rationale was typically based on stereotypical perceptions of men's and women's job aptitudes, often with little basis in the actual duties men and women performed on the job. Indeed, on more than one occasion a labor economist has suggested to me that the kind of uniform sex segregation within occupations that Baron and I detected simply cannot exist in the real world!

Radical and Marxist economists who study discrimination have always been more open than their more orthodox colleagues to incorporating concepts and findings of sociologists. Furthermore, the kind of persistent job segregation by sex detected in my research with Baron is fully consistent with their models. Radical and Marxist models are built upon an imagery of conflict and struggle over control of the workplace among contending groups defined by race, class, and gender. In attempting to account for the persistence of the racial gap in unemployment, Shulman [1991] moves this line of theorizing forward by addressing the economic and social costs of dismantling discrimination. According to this perspective, job segregation and other forms of discrimination are likely to persist in the absence of any exogenous shock or direct intervention that changes the social relations among contending groups.

However, while radical and Marxist approaches appear more consistent with the findings of our research, I am not yet prepared to accept their models. My reservation is based on the absence of gender as a cultural or ideological phenomenon in their explanations of segregation and other forms of discrimination. Instead, their models are driven by the logic of systemic properties like concentration and monopolization and the self-interested, rational action of social groups (e.g., employers, white male workers) intent on preserving their privileged positions in the division of labor (Darity and Williams [1985]). Based on my research and my reading of the work of other sociologists, I have come to believe that gender is more than a dimension along which the labor force is segmented and that gender ideologies are a strong, semiautonomous force shaping segregation and other manifestations of socioeconomic inequality. I have yet to see this notion of gender and ideology incorporated into formal models of discrimination, but I can illustrate the empirical reality of the issue with two examples.

The first concerns the circumstances under which women were demobilized from factory jobs in the automobile industry after World War II. In the most definitive study to date on the topic, Milkman [1987] documented that the women who held these jobs performed at least as capably as the men they replaced. She also showed that many of the women mobilized by the automobile industry during the war wanted to keep their jobs. Moreover, at the war's end, the automobile manufacturers could no longer rely on "cost-plus" government contracts and therefore should have been more sensitive to labor costs after the war than during the war. Furthermore, Milkman showed that the unions that represented the interests of white male workers had virtually no power to influence management policy regarding hiring preferences and job assignments. In short, management appeared to have both the incentive and the ability to rely disproportionately on women during the tremendous expansion in employment during the years following the war.

Such behavior by employers would be consistent with both neoclassical and neo-Marxist approaches to the labor market. Instead, Milkman showed that management acted on a strong preference for young, male veterans and went to great lengths to purge women from all but the traditionally female job classifications. Perhaps management feared that female substitution in the automobile factories would destabilize labor relations and were taking into account one of the costs of dismantling discrimination emphasized in Shulman [1991]. However, there is little evidence that the very decisive actions taken by management to demobilize women were based on an informed view of the costs of possible resistance by male workers. Instead, for reasons that are difficult to explain from any perspective emphasizing economic self-

interest (or class interest), employers concluded that women ought not to hold these jobs once men returned from war.

My second example comes from research I have done in collaboration with Denise Bielby (Bielby and Bielby [1991]) empirically testing Jacob Mincer's [1978] neoclassical model of family migration decisions among dual-earner couples. According to the model, couples maximize family well-being. When a husband or wife is confronted with a job advancement requiring geographic relocation, the couple migrates when that person's gain is greater than the cost of disrupting his or her spouse's career. Otherwise, there is no net gain to the family, and family well-being is maximized by forgoing the job opportunity at the new location.

Presumably, the risk to joint family earnings due to a relocation increases with the level of earnings of the spouse whose career will be disrupted. If so, then the neoclassical model predicts that reluctance to relocate for a new job should increase directly with the level of the spouse's earnings. Accordingly, it was not surprising when data from the 1977 Quality of Employment Survey showed spouse's earnings to be the strongest predictor of a reluctance to relocate for a much better job in a new location. What was surprising (from the neoclassical perspective) was that the net effect of spouse's earnings was highly contingent upon both gender and gender-role beliefs. As figure 2 illustrates, traditional males—those who believed in the primacy of the husband's role as provider and who disapproved of working mothers—were not influenced at all by their wives' earnings. In contrast, traditional females were extremely sensitive to their husbands' earnings. In effect, such women expressed reluctance to relocate for job advancement unless their husbands earned very little. Holding nontraditional gender-role beliefs had opposite effects on men and women. Compared to traditional women, nontraditional women were more inclined to pursue job advancement at a new location, while the opposite was true for nontraditional men compared to traditional men. In other words, our results showed that

FIGURE 2

Reluctance to relocate due to family considerations, by sex, spouse's earnings, and gender-role beliefs

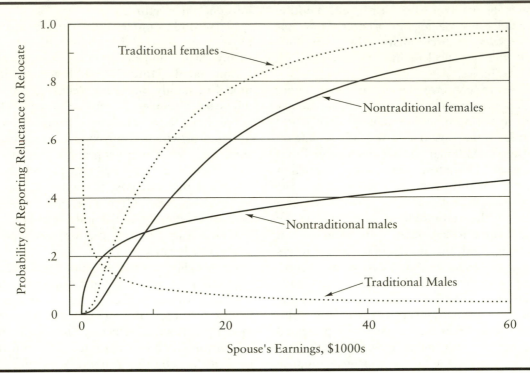

among those holding traditional beliefs, men were likely to put their private career interests ahead of the interest of overall family economic well-being (contrary to the assumption of the neoclassical model), while women behaved altruistically toward the family, maximizing family well-being instead of personal well-being (consistent with Mincer's assumption). However, the relationship was sharply mediated by gender-role beliefs, and the sex differences in orientation toward self and family were substantially attenuated among those holding nontraditional beliefs.

Thus our research suggests that traditional gender-role ideologies sustain women's disadvantages in both workplace and family dynamics. Traditional notions of women's role provide a rationale for job segregation and statistical discrimination in the workplace, and those same beliefs make it more difficult for women than men to pursue job opportunities (which in turn can reinforce stereotypes

and provide a rationale for statistical discrimination). In short, gender-role ideologies appear to directly shape the extent to which husbands and wives define and act upon their interests.

In sum, in an important sense, the economic theories of segregation and discrimination—neoclassical supply-side, demand-side, radical, and neo-Marxist—are neutral with respect to gender (and race). In these theories, whichever group happens to have fewer resources or less predictable traits or arrived last when either capital or "good jobs" were being allocated happens to end up disadvantaged. The ideological content of cultural idioms of gender and race have no causal impact in any of these theories. Curiously, this is true even when these theories are borrowed by sociologists, who, in recent years, have been captivated by theories that purport to explain social behavior as the outcome of "rational action" (Hechter [1983]; Coleman [1990]).

Yet the examples I have cited suggest that culture and ideology might have considerable explanatory power in more fully accounting for both persistence and change in job segregation and other forms of discrimination. At least at a descriptive level, sociocultural factors are impossible to ignore in any close empirical investigation of these phenomena. However, it is quite clear that we have a long way to go before such factors are fully incorporated into our theoretical and analytical models of discrimination.

References

Aigner, Dennis J. and Glen C. Cain. 1977. "Statistical Theories of Discrimination in Labor Markets." *Industrial and Labor Relations Review* 30, 2 (January): 175–187.

Akerlof, George A. and Janet L. Yellen. 1988. "Fairness and Unemployment." *American Economic Review* 78, 2 (May): 44–49.

Ashmore, Richard D. and Frances K. Del Boca. 1981. "Conceptual Approaches to Stereotypes and Stereotyping." pp. 1–35 in D. L. Hamilton (ed.), *Cognitive Procession Stereotyping and Intergroup Behavior.* Hillsdale, N.J.: Erlbaum.

Austin, William. 1977. "Equity Theory and Social Comparison Processes." pp. 279–305 in J. Suls and R. Miller (eds.) *Social Comparison Theory: Theoretical and Empirical Perspectives.* Washington, D.C.: Hemisphere Publishing.

Baron, James N. and William T. Bielby. 1985. "Organizational Barriers to Gender Equality: Sex Segregation of Jobs and Opportunities." pp. 233–251 in A. S. Rossi (ed.) *Gender and the Life Course.* New York: Aldine.

Berger, Joseph, Susan J. Rosenholtz, and Morris Zelditch. 1980. "Status Organizing Processes." *Annual Review of Sociology* 6: 479–508.

Berger, Joseph, Morris Zelditch, Jr., Bo Anderson, and Bernard P. Cohen. 1972. "Structural Aspects of Distributive Justice: A Status Value Formulation." pp. 119–146 in J. Berger, M. Zelditch, and B. Anderson (eds.) *Sociological Theories in Progress,* vol. 2. Boston: Houghton Mifflin.

Bielby, William T. and James N. Baron. 1984. "A Woman's Place Is with Other Women: Sex Segregation within Organizations." pp. 27–55 in B. F. Reskin (ed.), *Sex Segregation in the Workplace: Trends, Explanations, Remedies.* Washington, D.C.: National Academy Press.

———. 1986. "Men and Women at Work: Sex Segregation and Statistical Discrimination." *American Journal of Sociology* 91, 4 (January): 759–799.

———. 1987. "Undoing Discrimination: Comparable Worth and Job Integration." in Christine Bose and Glenna Spitze (eds.) *Ingredients for Women's Employment Policy.* Albany: State University of New York Press.

Bielby, William T. and Denise D. Bielby. 1988. "She Works Hard for the Money: Household Responsibilities and the Allocation of Work Effort." *American Journal of Sociology* 93, 5 (March): 1031–1059.

———. 1991. "I will Follow Him: Family Ties, Gender-Role Beliefs, and Reluctance to Relocate for a Better Job." Forthcoming, *American Journal of Sociology* 94.

Becker, Gary S. 1985. "Human Capital, Effort, and the Sexual Division of Labor." *Journal of Labor Economics* 3, 1, pt. 2 (January): 33–58.

Callahan-Levy, Charlene M. and Lawrence A. Messe. 1979. "Sex Differences in the Allocation of Pay." *Journal of Personality and Social Psychology* 37, 3 (March): 433–446.

Coleman, James S. 1990. *Foundations of Social Theory.* Cambridge, Mass.: Harvard University Press.

Crosby, F. 1982. *Relative Deprivation and Working Women.* New York: Oxford University Press.

Darity, William A., Jr. 1991. "Efficiency Wage Theory: Critical Reflections on the Neokeynesian Theory of Unemployment and Discrimination." pp. 39–53 in R.R. Cornwall and Phanindra V. Wunnava (eds.) *New Approaches to Economic and Social Analyses of Discrimination.* New York: Praeger Publishers.

Darity, William A., and Rhonda A. Williams. 1985. "Peddlars Forever? Culture, Competition, and Discrimination." *American Economic Review: Papers and Proceedings* 75, 2 (May): 256–261.

Darley, J. M. and R. H. Fazio. 1980. "Expectancy Confirmation Sequences." *American Psychologist* 35, 10 (October): 867–881.

Hechter, Michael. 1983. *The Microfoundations of Macrosociology.* Philadelphia: Temple University Press.

Krueger, Alan B. and Lawrence H. Summers. 1987. "Reflections on the Inter-Industry Wage Structure." ch. 2, pp. 17–47, in K. Lang and J. S. Leonard (eds.), *Unemployment and the Structure of Labor Markets.* New York: Basil Blackwell.

Lenney, Ellen. 1977. "Women's Self-Confidence in Achievement Settings." *Psychological Bulletin* 84, 1 (January): 1–13.

Major, Brenda, Dean B. McFarlin, and Diana Gagnon. 1984. "Overworked and Underpaid: On the Nature of Gender Differences in Personal Entitlement." *Journal of Personality and Social Psychology* 47, 6 (December): 1399–1412.

Marks, Stephen R. 1977. "Multiple Roles and Role Strain: Some Notes on Human Energy, Time, and Commitment." *American Sociological Review* 42, 6.

Milkman, Ruth. 1987. *Gender at Work: The Dynamics of Job Segregation by Sex During World War II.* Urbana: University of Illinois Press.

Mincer, Jacob. 1978. "Family Migration Decisions." *Journal of Political Economy* 86, no. 5 (October): 749–773.

Phelps, E. S. 1972. "The Statistical Theory of Racism and Sexism." *American Economic Review* 62, 4 (September): 659–661.

Polachek, Solomon W. 1979. "Occupational Segregation Among Women: Theory, Evidence, and a Prognosis." pp. 137–157 in C. B. Lloyd, E. S. Andrews, and C. L. Gilroy (eds.) *Women in the Labor Market.* New York: Columbia University Press.

Polachek, Solomon W. and Charng Kao. 1991. "Lifetime Work Expectations and Estimates of Gender Discrimination." pp. 199–238 in R.R. Cornwall and P.V. Wunnava (eds.) *New Approaches to Economic and Social Analyses of Discrimination.* New York: Praeger Publishers.

Reskin, Barbara F. and Heidi I. Hartmann (eds.) 1986. *Women's Work, Men's Work: Sex Segregation on the Job.* Washington, D.C.: National Academy Press.

Shulman, Steven. 1991. "Why is The Black Unemployment Rate Always Twice as High as The White Unemployment Rate?" pp. 5–37 in R.R. Cornwall and P.V. Wunnava (eds.) *New Approaches to Economic and Social Analyses of Discrimination.* New York: Praeger Publishers.

Williamson, Oliver E. 1975. *Markets and Hierarchies.* New York: Free Press.

———. 1985. *The Economic Institutions of Capitalism.* New York: Free Press.

J E R R Y   A .   J A C O B S

Revolving Doors: Sex Segregation and Women's Careers

This chapter is an effort to understand why women do "women's work." In 1985, over two-thirds of the women in the U.S. civilian labor force worked in occupations that were 70 percent or more female.[1] The study of women's work has attracted scholars from many disciplines, from psychology (Gutek, 1985) to history (Kessler-Harris, 1982) to anthropology (Sanday, 1981) to economics (Bergmann, 1986) to sociology (Reskin, 1984). A flurry of recent papers has addressed

such topics as trends in occupational segregation (Bianchi and Rytina, 1986; Jacobs, 1986), sex segregation among teenagers in the workplace (Greenberger and Steinberg, 1983), and sex segregation within voluntary organizations (McPherson and Smith-Lovin, 1986), between industries (Tienda, Smith, and Ortiz, 1987), across cities (Abrahamson and Sigelman, 1987), and within firms (Bielby and Baron, 1986). (See Reskin and Hartmann, 1985, for discussion of sex segregation in the workplace.)

This interest has undoubtedly been spurred by the growth in women's labor force participation (Goldin, 1983; Smith and Ward, 1984). Over 70 percent of women between the ages of 20 and 44 worked for pay in 1985, including nearly half of those with chil-

Originally published in 1989. Please see complete source information beginning on page 891.

dren under one year old. The overall rate of women's labor force participation has grown from 33.9 percent in 1950 to 54.5 percent in 1985 (U.S. Bureau of the Census, 1986). The women's movement has also heightened interest in working women. Legislative policies such as affirmative action, as well as the entry of feminist scholars into academia, have generated research on the disadvantaged position of working women. Most recently, calls for equal pay for work of comparable value have brought public and research attention to the concentration of women in low-paid, female-dominated occupations (Remick, 1984).

This chapter investigates the way women's careers intersect with the sexual division of labor in the workplace. We follow women's (and men's) life histories in order to understand the gender tracking system. We ask whether there is a decisive moment during women's lives when they are channeled into female-dominated occupations, or whether the process is more gradual. Is sex segregation principally due to a single life-course event, such as meeting with a guidance counselor in high school or becoming a parent, or is it the result of a cumulative process extending throughout much of the women's (and men's) lives?

As the title of this chapter suggests, we find surprising rates of mobility for women among male-dominated, sex-neutral, and female-dominated occupations (see Jacobs, 1989). This pattern of change is also evident when the dynamics of sex segregation of career aspirations and college majors are analyzed. Individual mobility is common, yet change in the structure of sex segregation is quite slow. This paradox is the central puzzle of this chapter.

The mobility described here and elsewhere (Jacobs, 1989) does not imply the existence of equal opportunity for women. Quite the contrary. The rates of mobility we document are roughly proportionate to the distribution of *women* across occupations; they do not imply that women have the same chances as men. For example, the probability of a woman starting her career in a male-dominated occupation is approximately one in three for re-

cent cohorts of women entering the labor force. Our data indicate that, for a woman who changes her occupation, the probability of moving into a male-dominated occupation is close to one in three, no matter whether her previous occupation was in a female-dominated, sex-neutral, or male-dominated field (Jacobs, 1989, chapter 7). This pattern suggests that women in female-dominated occupations who are able to change occupations stand a good chance of moving into a male-dominated occupation. Yet by the same token, women in male-dominated fields who change occupations also stand a good chance of moving to a sex-neutral or female-dominated occupation. Indeed, one of the more disturbing findings documented here (also, see Jacobs, 1989, chapter 7) is a startling rate of attrition of women in male-dominated occupations, even as these occupations appear to be opening their doors to them.

The revolving-door metaphor does not imply that women are getting nowhere. Rather, it suggests that gross mobility far exceeds the overall net change in opportunities for women. In recent years, for every 100 women in male-dominated occupations who were employed in two consecutive years, 90 remained in a male-dominated occupation, while 10 left for either a sex-neutral or female-dominated occupation. At the same time, 11 entered a male-dominated occupation from one of these other occupation groups. Thus, the revolving door sends 10 out for every 11 it lets in.[2] There has been a slow net accumulation of women in male-dominated occupations, but the net change is small compared to the size of the flows in both directions. If there were less attrition of women from male-dominated occupations, there would be more progress toward integrating men and women in the workplace. . . .

Sex Segregation and Social Control

To maintain any sexual division of labor, a society has to develop mechanisms for slotting men into male-dominated positions and women into female-dominated positions. Once positions or tasks are defined as masculine or feminine, societies must enforce these definitions. Sociologists refer to mechanisms by which societies bring about these results as mechanisms of social control.

The earliest stage of social control is socialization, during which society imbues the young with its prevailing values and beliefs. Central to our interest is vocational socialization, the development of gender identity that bears on the pursuit of careers. While the reproduction of social values may seem a simple matter in preindustrial societies, socialization is problematic in our own society. We argue that social control continues well beyond early socialization, involving the educational system, the decisions and behavior of employees and employers in the labor market, and the influences of family and friends throughout life. We raise questions about the efficacy of various gender-tracking mechanisms that are often assumed to be responsible for the maintenance of sex segregation.

The central thesis of this chapter is that the maintenance of sex segregation depends on a lifelong system of social control. While sex-role socialization is important, since it instills values and goals, it is inadequate by itself to maintain the system of sex segregation. Vocational aspirations have short life-expectancies, and young women frequently aspire to female-dominated occupations at one point in time and male-dominated jobs at another (see Jacobs, 1989, chapter 5). Further, the relationship between the sex type of young women's vocational goals and the sex type of the jobs they obtain is weak (see Jacobs, 1989, chapter 5). These patterns suggest that the influence of sex-role socialization is limited. Thus, sex-role socialization can be viewed as a system of social control for the early years, necessary but not sufficient to account for the persistence of occupational sex segregation.

For those men and women who attend college, social control continues during higher education. Many consider the educational system to be the realm of universalism, the

paramount social institution in our society for promoting opportunities for all. Indeed, the declines in sex segregation in higher education have surpassed those in the labor force. Yet, as shown in Jacobs (1989, chapter 6), important gender differences persist in America's colleges. Men and women pursue different majors, and informal social control plays a prominent role on campus.

The field of study in college is an important but not decisive component of gender tracking. Segregation remains fluid during the college years as many students move among male-dominated, sex-neutral, and female-dominated majors. Further, the link between a person's major in college and subsequent occupational pursuits is far from direct for many fields. Thus, the sex segregation of college majors resembles in both structure and process the segregation of aspirations and the segregation of occupations. Like sex-role socialization, sex segregation in the educational system is a necessary but not sufficient cause of gender inequality in the labor force.

Sex segregation in the labor force is the most durable of any context we consider, yet sex-role assignments are not fixed when women and men enter the labor force. Many women move among male-dominated, sex-neutral, and female-dominated occupations. The entry of women into male-dominated fields often does not immediately follow schooling, but instead may follow a period of employment in a female-dominated field or a spell as a homemaker. The patterns of stability and change in sex segregation are strikingly similar in aspirations, college majors, and careers, at both the aggregate and the individual level.

The problem, then, is accounting for the persistence of sex segregation at the societal or macro level despite its instability or permeability at the individual or micro level. Our resolution of this paradox is that sex roles are subject to continual, systematic, but imperfect control throughout life. Individuals move, but the system remains segregated, owing to the cumulative force of social pressures. . . .

Cumulative Disadvantage Versus Revolving Doors

Two competing versions of the lifelong social control perspective must be distinguished. The more familiar is what we label the "cumulative disadvantage" view, which we contrast with the "revolving door" perspective. The cumulative disadvantage model holds that occupational segregation by sex is the result of the accumulation of obstacles women face in their pursuit of careers. Thus, socialization is compounded by educational inequality and labor market discrimination, the cumulative force of which leaves women in a segregated set of occupations.

This view is clearly implicit in Berryman's discussion of women in science and engineering (1983). Women face obstacles beginning with ambivalent socialization about the importance of careers and the stereotype that science is an unfeminine pursuit. Women are underrepresented in science and engineering professions because of inadequate preparation in high school, attrition from science and engineering fields in college, and minority status and hostility on the job for those women who pursue such careers.

If the obstacles women confront in pursuing science and engineering careers are characteristic of male-dominated occupations, this model implies a number of specific predictions concerning sex segregation. The first is that segregation would increase over women's lifetimes as women continually leave male-dominated pursuits. One would expect to find more segregation as a cohort ages, as the disadvantages women face accumulate. Second, mobility observed between male-dominated and female-dominated occupations would take the form of attrition of women from male-dominated pursuits. Delayed entry into male-dominated occupations would be difficult; at the very least, delayed entries of women into male-dominated occupations should be less frequent than exits. Finally, if declines in sex segregation were to occur, this change would primarily take the form of changes between cohorts. The best one could

expect for those already in the pipeline is to reduce the rate of attrition; real change must await a new cohort that is exposed to different socialization, broader opportunities in school, and less hostility on the job. One would not expect increased integration among those already in the labor force, since the cumulative effects of these social control processes are essentially irreversible.

While the cumulative disadvantage model is attractive because of its recognition of the pervasive nature of social control, three striking findings suggest that while social control is continuous, its effects do not increase over the life course. First, occupational segregation by sex does not increase as men and women grow older (see Jacobs 1989, chapter 2). Second, sex-type mobility involves substantial rates of midcareer entry into, as well as exit from, male-dominated occupations (see Jacobs 1989, chapter 7). Third, overall change in segregation is observed across different age groups, and is not simply the result of cohort replacement (see Jacobs 1989, chapter 2). In other words, where the cumulative disadvantage view holds that change must come about principally because a new cohort has different experiences, the evidence suggests that a general weakening of the system of controls broadens opportunities for those already in the labor force. There is as much change in young women's aspirations over time as there is across new cohorts of women in the process of forming their aspirations. There is as much change for people already in college as there is among those entering college. In recent years, there has been a notable decline in segregation among those already in the labor market (see Jacobs 1989, chapter 2). The insight of the cumulative disadvantage view is that it recognizes the range of constraints imposed on women throughout their lives. Its limitation is that it assumes that the effects of barriers to women's opportunities are permanent and irreversible.

Thus we arrive at a lifelong social control perspective that is not characterized by cumulative disadvantage. In recognition of the dramatic levels of mobility we find, we refer to this view as the "revolving door" model of sex segregation. The revolving door perspective can account for extensive sex-type mobility because it recognizes a variety of stages in the career development process, and it recognizes a host of pressures women face. Most women will face one or more barriers to the pursuit of a career at some point; they are likely to overcome some of these and not others. Thus there are reasons to expect substantial flows of women into and out of male-dominated occupations, while overall the system changes only gradually.

This perspective also accounts for the patterns of change in sex segregation we are beginning to see. If social control is exercised throughout life, social change is likely to be experienced by women of different ages. Change should affect those already in the labor force as well as those entering it and those in the educational system. Theories that emphasize labor market entry as the decisive time for segregation cannot account for decreasing segregation among those already in the labor force. As shown elsewhere (Jacobs 1989, chapter 2), the declines in labor market segregation by sex in the 1970's occurred throughout the age structure and were not simply restricted to labor market entrants.

There is a striking similarity in the dynamics of sex segregation in the development of aspirations, in the segregation of college majors, and in the sex segregation of the occupational structure. All three are characterized by change occurring among different age groups, and all three have striking levels of mobility between male-dominated, sex-neutral, and female-dominated fields. The similarities of these patterns in these diverse contexts and across different stages of life convince us of the utility of the social control/revolving door perspective.

Notes

1. Calculated from data in *Employment and Earnings* (U.S. Bureau of Labor Statistics, 1986).

2. These figures reflect the analysis of Current Population Survey data discussed in Jacobs (1989, chapter 7).

Bibliography

Abrahamson, Mark, and Lee Sigelman. 1987. "Occupational Sex Segregation in Metropolitan Areas," *American Sociological Review*, 52(5): 588–97.

Bergmann, Barbara. 1986. *The Economic Emergence of Women*. New York: Basic Books.

Berryman, Sue R. 1983. *Who Will Do Science?* New York: Rockefeller Foundation.

Bianchi, Suzanne M., and Nancy Rytina. 1986. "The Decline in Occupational Sex Segregation During the 1970's: Census and CPS Comparisons," *Demography*, 23(1): 79–86.

Bielby, William T., and James N. Baron. 1986. "Men and Women at Work: Sex Segregation and Statistical Discrimination," *American Journal of Sociology*, 91(4): 759–99.

Goldin, Claudia. 1983. "The Changing Economic Role of Women: A Quantitative Approach," *Journal of Interdisciplinary History*, 13(4): 707–33.

Greenberger, Ellen, and Laurence D. Steinberg. 1983. "Sex Differences in Early Labor Force Experience: Harbinger of Things to Come," *Social Forces*, 62(2): 467–86.

Gutek, Barbara. 1985. *Sex and the Workplace*. San Francisco: Jossey-Bass.

Jacobs, Jerry A. 1986. "Trends in Contact Between Men and Women at Work, 1971–1981," *Sociology and Social Research*, 70(3): 202–6.

——. 1989. *Revolving Doors: Sex Segregation and Women's Careers*. Stanford, CA: Stanford University Press.

Kessler-Harris, Alice. 1982. *Out to Work: A History of Wage-Earning Women in the United States*. New York: Oxford University Press.

McPherson, J. Miller, and Lynn Smith-Lovin. 1986. "Sex Segregation in Voluntary Associations," *American Sociological Review*, 51(1): 61–79.

Remick, Helen, ed. 1984. *Comparable Worth and Wage Discrimination: Technical Possibilities and Political Realities*. Philadelphia: Temple University Press.

Reskin, Barbara, ed. 1984. *Sex Segregation in the Workplace: Trends, Explanations, Remedies*. Washington, D.C.: National Academy of Sciences.

Reskin, Barbara F., and Heidi I. Hartmann. 1985. *Women's Work, Men's Work: Sex Segregation on the Job*. Washington, D.C.: National Academy of Sciences.

Sanday, Peggy R. 1981. *Female Power and Male Dominance: On the Origins of Sexual Inequality.* Cambridge: Cambridge University Press.

Smith, James P., and Michael P. Ward. 1984. *Women's Wages and Work in the Twentieth Century.* Santa Monica, Calif.: Rand Corporation.

Tienda, Marta, Shelley A. Smith, and Vilma Ortiz. 1987. "Industrial Restructuring, Gender Segregation, and Sex Differences in Earnings," *American Sociological Review,* 52(2): 195–210.

U.S. Bureau of the Census. 1986. "Women in the American Economy," *Current Population Reports,* P–23, no. 146. Washington, D.C.: U.S. Government Printing Office.

U.S. Bureau of Labor Statistics. 1986. *Employment and Earnings.* Washington, D.C.: U.S. Government Printing Office.

BARBARA F. RESKIN

Labor Markets as Queues: A Structural Approach to Changing Occupational Sex Composition

The historic persistence of sex segregation (Gross 1968; Beller 1984) made women's dramatic gains during the 1970s in such diverse male occupations as pharmacy, bank management, bartending, and typesetting noteworthy. Why did women disproportionately enter these and a few other male occupations when they made only modest progress in most and lost ground in a few? To answer this question, Patricia Roos and I conducted a two-part study: multivariate analyses of the changing sex composition in all detailed census occupations and in-depth case studies of 14 occupations in which women's representation increased at least twice as much as it had in the labor force as a whole (see Table 1). This chapter draws on those case studies: bank managers (Bird 1990), bartenders (Detman 1990), systems analysts (Donato 1990a), public relations specialists (Donato 1990b), phar-macists (Phipps 1990a), insurance adjusters/examiners (Phipps 1990b), typesetters/compositors (Roos 1990), insurance salespersons (Thomas 1990), real estate salespersons (Thomas and Reskin 1990), bakers (Steiger and Reskin 1990), book editors (Reskin and Roos 1990), print and broadcast reporters, and accountants.[1] Although the case studies revealed that widely different factors precipitated these occupations' feminization, the process of change can be encompassed in a single perspective—queuing. This chapter begins by outlining the queuing approach. It then shows how the determinants of occupational feminization conformed to queuing processes. Finally, it argues that the queue model as I have developed it offers a structural approach to understanding change in job composition.

Queuing: an Overview

Simply stated, a queuing perspective views labor markets as composed of labor queues and job queues that reflect, respectively, employers' ranking of possible workers and workers'

Originally published in 1991. Please see complete source information beginning on page 891.

TABLE 1
Percent Females in Feminizing Occupations, 1970, 1980, 1988

Occupation	1970 %	1980 %	1988 %	1970–88 Increase %
Financial managers	19.4	31.4	42.4	23.0
Accountants/auditors	24.6	38.1	49.6	25.0
Operations/systems analysts	11.1	27.7	39.6	28.5
Pharmacists	12.1	24.0	31.9	19.8
Public relations specialists	26.6	48.8	59.1	32.5
Editors and reporters	41.6	49.3	n.a.	n.a.
Insurance sales	12.9	25.4	29.7	16.8
Real estate sales	31.2	45.2	48.5	17.3
Insurance adjusters/examiners	29.6	60.2	72.2	42.6
Bartenders	21.2	44.3	49.6	28.4
Bakers	25.4	40.7	47.8	22.4
Bus drivers	28.3	45.8	48.5	20.2
Typesetters/compositors	16.8	55.7	73.9	57.1
Labor Force	38.0	42.6	45.0	7.0

ranking of jobs.[2] The idea of the *labor* queue originated in Lester Thurow's (1969) work on race differences in unemployment and was elaborated by Hodge (1973) and Lieberson (1980). Rotella's (1977) analysis of the feminization of clerical work, Lieberson's (1980) study of racial and ethnic inequality, and Strober's (1984) theory of sex segregation implicitly invoked *job* as well as *labor* queues. The queuing perspective presented here views occupational composition as resulting from the simultaneous operation of job and labor queues (also see Reskin and Roos 1990). Employers hire workers from as high in the labor queue as possible, and workers accept the best jobs available to them, so the most desirable jobs go to the most preferred workers, less attractive jobs go to workers lower in the labor queue, and the most lowly workers end up jobless or in jobs others have rejected.

Three structural properties characterize both job and labor queues: (a) the ordering of their elements, (b) whether or not their elements overlap, and (c) their shape. By *elements,* I mean the constituent units—groups of potential workers or jobs. Thus the *ordering of elements* simply indicates in what order workers rank possible jobs and employers

rank prospective workers. I pass over how workers order jobs in the labor queue as something both sociologists and workers understand. In ordering the labor queue, employers consider potential productivity and cost.[3] However, the indirect effect of workers' sex on employers' estimations of the former and its direct influence on how employers rank workers result in labor queues that encompass and often act as *gender queues*.

The absolute and relative numbers of elements in a queue determine its *shape*. Thus the number of prospective workers in each subgroup in a labor market sets the shape of the labor queue, and the number of jobs at each level in the job queue fixes its shape. Panels A and B of Figure 1 show how the shape of labor and job queues can vary while their order remains constant. This variation influences each group's probable access to occupations of varying desirability. (Put differently, it shows how a queue's shape influences each occupation's chance of recruiting workers from particular groups.) For example, in a society with relatively few workers in the preferred group (A2) and few desirable jobs (B2), preferred groups will monopolize good jobs. A mismatch in the relative numbers of jobs

FIGURE 1
Illustration of variation in the shape of labor and job queues

Panel A. Hypothetical labor queues ordered by race for predominantly white and predominantly black labor markets, respectively

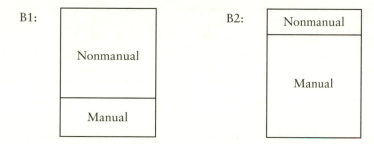

Panel B. Hypothetical job queues ordered by nonmanual-manual work for predominantly nonmanual and predominantly manual occupational structures, respectively

and workers at corresponding levels of the respective queues means that some workers will get better or worse jobs than persons from their group normally command. In consequence, when good jobs sharply outnumber highly ranked workers as in panels A2 and B1, employers must fill the better jobs with workers from lower in the labor queue than they usually hire. In contrast, when the *job queue* is bottom heavy, only the highest-ranked workers get desirable jobs, and workers moderately high in the labor queue are forced to settle for less. As Lieberson (1980, p. 297) has shown, both the *absolute* and the *relative* sizes of each group in the labor queue affect lower-ranked workers' chances of getting desirable jobs. The larger a subordinate group relative to the size of the preferred group, the more costly it is for employers to deny its members good jobs (Hodge 1973).

Whether or not *elements overlap* denotes the strength of rankers' preferences for one element over another. Among some employers, group membership is the overriding consideration in ordering the labor queue, and rankers favor persons from the group they prefer, regardless of qualifications. For other labor queues, employers are indifferent to group membership except to break ties between otherwise equally qualified prospects. Figure 2 illustrates variation in the intensity of raters' preferences with respect to workers' race in three hypothetical labor queues. The space between the races in panel A depicts the ranking for employers who invariably hire the lowest-ranked white worker over the best black worker; the overlapping groups in panel B depict the situation in which raters' aversion to blacks is slight. Panel C illustrates an intermediate situation in which employers

FIGURE 2
Illustration of variation in the intensity of raters' preferences with respect to race

Panel A. Racial group membership is an overriding consideration to rankers. Employers hire applicants as qualified as possible, but hire unqualified whites before hiring highly qualified blacks.

Blacks Low	Blacks Moderate	Blacks High	Whites Low	Whites Moderate	Whites High

Level of Qualification

Panel B. Racial group membership is a minor consideration to rankers. Employers hire the most qualified applicants, but within levels of qualification, give white applicants an edge over equally qualified blacks.

Blacks Low	Whites Low	Blacks Moderate	Whites Moderate	Blacks High	Whites High

Level of Qualification

Panel C. Racial group membership is an intermediate consideration to rankers. Employers will prefer a more qualified white over a less qualified black, but will hire very qualified blacks over unqualified whites.

Blacks Low	Blacks Moderate	Whites Low	Blacks High	Whites Moderate	Whites High

Level of Qualification

prefer white workers over equally qualified blacks but will set aside racial biases to hire very talented blacks over mediocre whites. Where preferences are weak, substantial job-level integration exists. In contrast, when preferences are overriding, all members of the favored group precede all members of the disfavored group in the labor queue, and the labor market is totally segmented.

Workers' job preferences also vary in intensity. Some workers may categorically prefer any job in a high-ranked occupation to working in a lower occupation (expressed, for example, in rejecting manual jobs in favor of nonmanual work). Alternatively, they may be more attuned to specific job characteristics than their overall rank, occasionally eschewing jobs in occupations usually reserved for the preferred group and appropriating more desirable jobs within lower-ranked occupations that usually go to less preferred groups. Strong preferences mean that workers invariably prefer one type of job (e.g., professional or nonmanual work) over another.

Changes in any of these structural features of queues—employers' rankings of workers or workers' ranking of jobs, the intensity of either groups' preferences, and the relative distributions of workers or jobs—can transform occupations' composition. Below, I show how they did so in the 1970s and 1980s.

Factors Promoting Occupational Feminization

I turn now to the factors that led the occupations we studied to feminize. Although this chapter emphasizes the role of these factors in explaining women's inroads into customarily male occupations, they also accounted for women's ghettoization *within* feminizing occupations into a few specialties, work settings, and industries. In order of importance for women's entry were job deterioration (reflecting changes in the ordering of the job queue), job growth (reflecting changes in the shape of the job queue), emergence of a sex-specific demand for women (reflecting changes in the ordering of the labor queue), and declining preference for men or aversion to women (reflecting changes in strength of employers' preferences). Women's increasing share of the labor queues for specific occupations or jobs (denoting a change in the shape of the labor queue), although it contributed to their inroads into male occupations, was itself in part a response to the increasing demand for women.

Occupational Growth. Although scholars recognize the potential of occupational growth to open male occupations to women (Oppenheimer 1970; Doeringer and Piore 1971; Bielby and Baron 1984; Fields and Wolff 1989), it does so only when it depletes the supply of acceptable candidates from the preferred group. In growing male occupations in which qualified male prospects were plentiful—that is, desirable occupations for which

workers could easily qualify such as driving trucks—employers had no need to resort to women. Only when occupations grow faster than the traditional labor supply must employers resort to nontraditional sources of labor. This is especially likely for jobs whose high entry requirements limit the number of qualified male prospects. Among the occupations we studied, this played a role in the feminization of accounting and systems analysis. As the computer industry served an increasingly broad range of users, the demand for systems analysts skyrocketed, creating almost 100,000 new jobs during the 1970s. Accounting registered even greater growth as expanding American corporations rationalized business functions, small firms became more dependent on accounting services, and complex tax laws made accountants indispensable to many taxpayers. Both occupations required credentials that took time to acquire, and in each the supply of qualified men proved inadequate, forcing employers to look lower in the labor queue for qualified workers. Thus occupational growth meant that employers reached women who had acquired the necessary credentials in the labor queue before filling all job openings. Rapidly growing occupations provide men with mobility opportunities (e.g., Strom 1987, p. 74), so an invasion by women is less threatening, especially if they are confined to female ghettos.

Job Deterioration. Most of the occupations we studied feminized after their work process or rewards changed to render them less attractive than competing possibilities open to men. In every occupation we studied, men's real earnings declined during the 1970s. For example, bartenders' earnings dropped after a 1966 amendment to the Fair Labor Standards Act allowed employers to pay tipped employees subminimum wages. Several changes reduced the earnings in residential real estate sales: New tax laws prompted brokers to transfer sales agents from employees to independent contractors to whom they paid no salaries or benefits. The erratic housing market left agents with low-income spells, and real earnings declined appreciably in residential sales. As a result, many male agents left residential real estate, and few entered to replace them.

Technological Change, Occupational Transformation, and Deskilling. Technological change often means the transformation and sometimes the deskilling of jobs. The resulting job deterioration has historically been the agent of feminization. A middle-aged male machinist summarized the pattern: "I've seen it happen more than once. Work gets simple enough, and they turn it over to the girls" (Astrachan 1986). The feminization of insurance adjusting/examining, typesetting/composing, and baking all justify his concern. Indeed, insurance adjusting epitomizes how transforming an occupation's work process feminized it. Throughout the 1960s, adjusters—virtually all of whom were male—worked in the field where they enjoyed the right to schedule their work, the use of a company car, and reasonable prospects for upward mobility. To increase profits in response to a decade of high inflation, firms shifted adjusting into the office, where "inside" adjusters handled claims by telephone and VDTs, had limited autonomy and promotion prospects, and earned low wages. With the transformation and clericalization of adjusting, the number of male adjusters dropped by 6,447 between 1970 and 1980, while an additional 73,744 women became adjusters.

Automation and computerization also figured into the feminization of typesetting/composing by adversely affecting work content and rewards. Electronic advances computerized the work of typesetters and compositors, transforming it to clerical work. However, given the propensity to devalue women's work (Phillips and Taylor 1980; Reskin 1988), we must be cautious in assuming that transformed jobs in typesetting/composing and adjusting/examining were necessarily less skilled than those involving the methods male workers formerly used to produce the same product.

Technical advances that allowed manufacturing bakeries to ship unbaked goods to retail outlets created less skilled, often part-time, minimum-wage jobs "baking off" these products in retail settings. These jobs attracted few men, but, as Hartmann (1989) has noted and Beechey and Perkins (1987) have shown for Britain, employers structure jobs with the object of filling them with one sex or the other. For example, employers deliberately structured bake-off baking to use an inexperienced female labor pool rather than creating full-time jobs that would have attracted more men.

Thus technological change can create jobs for women in customarily male occupations when it reduces rather than raises skill requirements (Hacker 1979). However, technically based deskilling does not inevitably lead to feminization (Roos 1986; Cockburn 1988; Rose 1988; Walsh 1989). Whether it does so depends on male workers' ability and desire to retain the jobs.

Industrial Change. Some occupations changed because of events in the industries that housed them. For example, following deregulation of the banking industry, banks tried to compete with savings and loan institutions by providing more services and easily accessible branches. This created thousands of new service-oriented management jobs in personal banking. However, they lacked prestige and the opportunity to acquire skills for promotion so they did not attract many men. Industrial change in book publishing resulted from conglomerization that commercialized the industry and robbed the job of editor of its primary attractions: a cultural image and the chance to shape American literature. As the number of qualified male applicants dropped, employers gave women the editorial jobs they had long sought. Industrial change in retail pharmacy made it less attractive to men as drugstore chains (as well as pharmacy outlets in discount stores, supermarkets, and health maintenance organizations) replaced independent pharmacies, thus eliminating the most lucrative aspect of pharmacy, the chance to be an entrepreneur.

In sum, men eschewed these declining occupations, and the ensuing labor shortages—sometimes exacerbated by occupational growth—drove employers to look lower in the labor queue, where they found women. As Joan Smith (1989) paraphrased Carter and Carter (1981), "Women [got] a ticket to ride *because* the gravy train has left the station."

Sex-specific Demand for Women. Antidiscrimination regulations of the 1960s and early 1970s restricted employers' freedom to downrank women because of their sex. In particular, a 1971 revised presidential executive order barred federal contractors from discriminating against women and required affirmative action to eliminate the effects of past discrimination. Despite limited enforcement, in a few industries, the Office for Federal Contract Compliance helped women enter male occupations. For example, women's headway in bank management resulted partly because Office for Federal Contract Compliance programs targeted the banking industry.

Regulatory agencies fostered women's gains in public relations by requiring employers to provide equal employment data on employees' sex across broad occupational groups. Employers improved their EEO statistics by placing women in public relations jobs, line positions most men shunned because they seldom offered a path to top-management posts.

Action by individual women or women's organizations also raised the costs employers risked for preferring men. Litigation or pressure by employee groups enhanced women's access to jobs as newspaper and magazine reporters, book editors, insurance agents, bank managers, and bartenders. For example, in 1971 women successfully challenged state "protective" laws that prohibited women from tending bar under Title VII of the Civil Rights Act. This was by far the most important reason for the feminization of bartending. Credit for women's progress in broadcast reporting goes to women's groups who challenged renewal-license applications to the Federal Communications Commission from stations that did not employ women in professional capacities and to pressure from women employees at the networks (Lewis 1986; Sanders and Rock 1988). Thus a few of the occupations we studied feminized because employers reordered or weakened the gender queue within the labor queue, placing women ahead of men for jobs in which they risked costly sanctions for preferring men. Integration prompted by regulatory agency pressure is unstable as long as the beneficiaries remain downranked in the labor queue (Collins 1983).

Changing Social Attitudes and Declining Discrimination. Until a generation ago, the public tolerated sex discrimination, but the civil rights movement and the feminist movement challenged white men's birthright to first place in the labor queue. Together, these movements reshaped attitudes about the propriety of excluding people from jobs because of their color and sex. Changed public sentiments prompted employers to espouse equal employment practices, regardless of whether their own attitudes had changed, and gave women permission to aspire to occupations formerly off limits to them. Large numbers of women, anticipating equal treatment, began to prepare for traditionally male jobs.

The only occupation in which new attitudes directly contributed to feminization was bartending. Women's exclusion had depended partly on male unionists' claims that mixing drinks would corrupt women (Cobble forthcoming). The women's liberation movement and the "sexual revolution" as well as changing courtship practices and delayed marriage of the late 1960s and 1970s appear to have transformed public attitudes about women's corruptibility and hence their need for protection. In the other feminizing occupations, changing attitudes did not spur employers to hire large numbers of women. In general, public sentiments about the kinds of work appropriate for women change after rather than before occupational feminization (Rotella 1977). For example, broadcasters long barred women from reporting the news because their voices allegedly lacked authority. What opened news reporting to women was not more enlightened attitudes by radio and television stations but the risk of losing their broadcast licenses.

Given the sources of feminization in the occupations we studied, it should come as no surprise that occupational-level desegregation did not bring job-level integration. In almost every occupation we studied, informants indicated that discrimination restricted women's access to the best jobs. For example, the personnel manager explained to a young female bank manager that her rapid career rise had leveled out because "the chairman and president want . . . people that they are comfortable with, and they are not . . . comfortable with women" (Bird 1990).

Women's Labor Supply and Preferences. With women's continued influx into the labor force during the 1970s, their share of the labor queue grew. However, what enlarged the female labor pools on which feminizing occupations drew was shortages of qualified male applicants that resulted from men's disdain for available jobs and from occupational growth. In short, women's growing proportion in the recruitment pools for sex-atypical occupations was largely a *response* to having a shot at jobs higher in the queue.

Women's beliefs that affirmative action and equal employment regulations ensured their access to jobs encouraged thousands to study to be pharmacists, systems analysts, accountants, and financial managers. Moreover, women's presence in sex-typical jobs in many industries that were home to feminizing occupations made them available for recruitment into male jobs. "Generating" a supply of female candidates often simply involved transferring women from sex-typical to sex-atypical jobs. For example, banks promoted women from clerk or teller to manager, publishers promoted women from secretary or editorial assistant to editor. In intensively female industries, such as banking, insurance, publishing, and real estate, as in the labor force as a whole, women were queued up—positioned to take advantage of a demand for their labor.

Explaining women's willingness to take customarily male occupations is easy: The available jobs paid better and offered better chances for advancement than female-dominated occupations that demanded comparable credentials. Although women's increasing need to support themselves and their dependents no doubt exacerbated their need for sex-atypical jobs, women were equally responsive to the attraction of higher wages during World War II when fewer women headed households. However, the contraction of female occupations in the 1970s pushed women toward male occupations (Blau 1989). Moreover, the greater attractiveness of these male occupations compared with those customarily open to women probably would have sufficed to draw women from female jobs even if the female labor force had not grown during the 1970s. Thus, while women's growing share of the labor queue played a role in their entry into formerly male jobs, without increased demand, the increased supply of female labor would not have feminized these male occupations.[4]

Queuing Models as Structural Approaches to Occupational Composition

Queuing emphasizes how employers rank groups of potential workers as well as how workers rank jobs. Because rankings simply boil down to preferences, is *queuing* not simply a fancy way to say that workers' and employers' preferences affect their labor market decisions? What does the queuing perspective add to the neoclassical economic approach to occupational segregation?

The neoclassical economic approach assumes (a) that workers' labor market decisions represent attempts to maximize their lifetime earnings, (b) that differences in the sexes' distributions across jobs stem primarily from women's family responsibilities, (c) that employers act to maximize revenues, and (d) that, in the short run, discriminatory "tastes" sometimes divert employers from their economic best interests, but, in the long run, competitive disadvantages that accrue from indulging economically irrational tastes lead discrimination to decline over time (Becker 1957). Thus traditional economic analysis treats sex segregation as the *aggregate* outcome of the mostly rational choices of *individual* workers and employers.

A queuing approach to changing occupational sex composition differs in several ways. First, queuing emphasizes the *collective* nature of sex segregation that results from *socially structured rankings* by *groups in conflict.* In contrast to the neoclassical perspective, queuing highlights the roles played by power and conflict between groups with contradictory interests in shaping occupations' composition. As I show below, the queuing perspective elucidates the role of group power in determining occupational access.

Second, it takes seriously the effects of noneconomic factors on workers' rankings of occupations and employers' rankings of prospective workers. It reminds us that working conditions, autonomy, social standing, career opportunities, and sex composition influence how workers appraise jobs and that employers' prejudices, stereotypes, and desire to preserve their own and other men's advantages influence how they rank workers.

Third, the queuing perspective assumes that the sexes rank most occupations similarly, so it predicts women's influx into accessible male occupations in view of their superior rewards. In explaining occupational feminization, it directs our attention to changes in employers' need for women and to declining barriers to women's access to traditionally male jobs. In other words, the queuing perspective redirects us from characteristics of female workers to structural properties of labor markets that in turn are shaped by the preferences of employers and male workers.

Power and Coalitions in Ordering the Labor Queue

In examining how conflict affects occupations' composition, we must bear in mind three points: First, three groups with competing interests have a stake in which sex predominates in an occupation—employers (who are overwhelmingly male), male workers, and female workers. Second, the greater social and economic power of employers and of men give them a substantial advantage in the struggle over what sex heads the queue for desirable occupations. Third, the outcome of the struggle over what sex dominates an occupation—occupations' sex compositions—represents a de facto coalition between competing groups.

Employers. Given their orientation toward minimizing costs and maximizing labor docility, employers should prefer female workers for all jobs. That so few have done so reminds us that other considerations affect male employers' labor decisions. Foremost among these is the personal stake of both male employers and male workers in excluding women from male-labeled jobs to preserve sex differentiation and hence male privilege in all spheres. Because sex differentiation both legitimates and facilitates unequal treatment, physically segregating the sexes at work and assigning them different tasks preserves male dominance by legitimating unequal wages, insulating men from female competition, supporting men's dominance in other public realms and the home, and shoring up myths of essential sex differences and male superiority (Reskin 1988). As Cockburn (1988, p. 41) put it, "Behind occupational segregation is gender differentiation, and behind that is male power."

Other considerations inclining employers to preserve good jobs for men include (a) the ability of male workers—and sometimes customers—to penalize employers for hiring women for "men's" jobs (Bergmann and Darity 1981; Strober 1988); (b) organizational inertia that makes following standard practices the course of least resistance; (c) custom—in other words, jobs' sex labels—combined with the uncertainties attendant on radically altering employment practices (Cohn 1985; Strom 1987; Figart and Bergmann 1989, p. 36); (d) gender solidarity with male workers;[5] and (e) forestalling later threats to their own jobs. As long as employers can operate profitably, preserving male jobs can be a fairly cheap amenity, especially if their competitors also practice male preference (Stolzenberg 1982; Strober 1988). Thus, in reserving male-dominated jobs for men, employers at once appease male workers, who could make hiring women costly; simplify organizational decisions; and shore up the gender hierarchy from which they benefit.

Male Workers. Male workers' disadvantaged economic position vis-à-vis employers and their advantaged sex status divide their interests. They stand to gain in the long run from acting collectively with *all* workers, but, in the short run, men are vulnerable to job and wage competition from women who must settle for lower wages. Equal job opportunities for women can also cost men domestic benefits they derive from sex inequality in the workplace and can threaten the gender hierarchy from which working men benefit (Hartmann 1976; Reskin 1988). Thus, for the most part, male workers do better in the short run by monopolizing male jobs than by welcoming female coworkers with whom they could collectively fight for better pay. Only when large numbers of women already have their foot in the door, or when labor shortages or outside agencies have imposed integration, are male workers freed to pursue their class interests collectively with female workers (Hirsch 1986; Milkman 1987; Cobble forthcoming). Under such conditions, male unions have tried to organize women and advocated equal pay.

Coalitions Between Employers and Male Workers. Male workers' monopoly of most occupations stems from the de facto coalition between male employers and male workers. Although I use the term *coalition* figuratively, employers' power to hire workers and assign them jobs means that ordinarily male workers can resist women's entry only with their male bosses' active contrivance (Baker 1964; Hartmann 1976; Cockburn 1988). The result of this coalition between male workers and employers is also seen in feminizing occupations in women's confinement to the least desirable jobs, thereby providing male workers a refuge from integration in still-male jobs (Cockburn 1988). For example, when outside pressure forced a large publishing firm to promote women to jobs as editorial assistants, it created a new, higher rank into which it promoted male former editorial assistants (Osterman 1979).

Despite the forces that preserve sex segregation, it broke down in the occupations we studied when male employers or male workers withdrew from their coalition. Employers never violated a coalition by directly substituting women for men, but they set aside customary practices, their own sex biases, and concern with the reactions of male workers when their firms' survival depended on cutting labor costs or averting unionization. In the occupations we studied, increased competition and the concomitant need to cut costs as well as vulnerability to work disruptions by unions precipitated this action. For example, industrywide demand for increased profits during the high-inflation 1970s prompted insurance companies to cut costs by standardizing the work of insurance adjusters and examiners. As I noted above, heightened competition for customers following deregulation forced banks to provide more customer services while trying to increase productivity and keep the lid on wages. In typesetting and composing, the International Typographical Union's frequent recourse to strikes spurred newspaper publishers to develop a printing technology that the union could not control, and then they hired women for the newly clericalized typesetting and composing jobs. It is important, however, that, in occupations that became less attractive to men for reasons not tied to employers' actions (book editing, real estate sales, retail pharmacy, and bartending), employers did not counter by improving male jobs. Employers' economic interests prevailed, and they replaced men with cheaper women.

In sum, the case studies suggested that employers put women ahead of men in labor queues *only* when labor costs became a pressing concern or when action by women or government regulators raised the cost of male preference.[6] Faced with economic exigencies, employers' willingness to donate profits to support white male privilege went by the wayside, and they struck a bargain with women workers.

Coalitions Between Male Employers and Female Workers. Why women should enter into de facto coalitions with male employers is no mystery. Disadvantaged relative to both male workers and male employers, women stand to gain from cooperating with either group. Employers are more likely to accept a coalition with women when their numbers are large. Cobble's (forthcoming) comparison of women's efforts early in this century to preserve the right to serve drinks with their efforts to tend bar illustrates the importance of numbers. Women waitresses' moderate representation within union locals gave them the clout to block proposed restrictions against their serving alcoholic drinks. In contrast, women's small numbers doomed their efforts to tend bar until they could invoke the Civil Rights Act. In the 1970s, women capitalized on their numbers in the book publishing, newspaper, broadcasting, and banking industries to challenge their exclusion from male jobs or their confinement in low-status posts. Large numbers mean that women can better spot their concentration in the least desirable jobs and more effectively protest it. Thus women's increased share in labor queues for male occupations contributed to their gains both by increasing the odds that employers would get down to women in the hiring queue

and by making them more powerful adversaries.

Resistance by Male Workers. Male workers' stake in monopolizing the best jobs encourages them to oppose employers' efforts to integrate women. To this end, they may try to reduce women's productivity by denying them training and information or withhold their own labor (Doeringer and Piore 1971; Bergmann and Darity 1981).[7] Whether men win the battle depends on their power base. For example, early in the Industrial Revolution, before strong unions existed, employers could easily feminize jobs (Kessler-Harris 1982, p. 266; Cohn 1985; Milkman 1987; Cockburn 1988). However, once unions were well established, they could preserve their domains. They did so in bartending, baking, and typesetting and composing as well as many other occupations throughout most of the century.

Obviously, men did not ultimately prevent women's entry in the occupations we studied. In most of those occupations, by abandoning jobs, male workers gave employers the go-ahead to hire women. Sometimes men do not see women as a threat. For instance, although men fought women's integration into clerical jobs in the British railroads (Cohn 1985), they did not resist women's movement in similar jobs in the United States because integration occurred slowly, and Pullman reserved the best jobs for men (Hirsch 1986, p. 33). In rapidly growing occupations, men did not resist women's entry because growth ensured that good jobs were plentiful, and within-occupation segregation assured men's access to the best jobs.

Thus the case studies of accounting and systems analysis revealed no systematic efforts to exclude women. Male incumbents in high-turnover occupations like book editing, bartending, and residential real estate sales had no stake in what happened in the long run. High turnover also means workers were too poorly organized to resist integration. Finally, in reorganizing work, employers had an effective tool in phasing out men. By changing the work process to incorporate female-labeled tasks, employers could disguise the fact that they were filling what had been men's jobs with women (Davies 1975, p. 282; Rotella 1977, pp. 162, 165) and recast them as women's work. For instance, after transforming the work of adjusters, industry trade journals construed the ideal insurance adjuster as a woman.[8]

However, men did effectively resist women's employment in the most desirable specialties within desegregating occupations, such as production baking, commercial real estate, and industrial pharmacy—partly by informal pressures that discouraged women's entry. I suspect, however, that women's continued exclusion depended more on employer discrimination in job assignment and promotion practices than on male workers' actions.

Conclusions

In summary, the queuing model proposed here holds that (a) employers rank prospective workers in terms of their potential productivity as well as their personal characteristics, but that they are also influenced by current employees and others who can impose costs for hiring or failing to hire women; (b) shortages—whether from job growth or from a job's inability to attract enough customary workers—prompt employers to hire workers from lower in the labor queue; (c) male workers affect women's access to jobs through their ability to preempt jobs, their power to enforce their monopoly over desirable jobs, and their ability, in abandoning jobs, to bestow them on workers lower in the labor queue; and (d) women's search for better jobs leads them to individually and collectively challenge their exclusion from men's jobs and to move into male lines of work that become open. The case study data support these predictions. I caution readers that our selection of case studies of occupations in which women's gains were exceptionally large limits the generalizability of these findings. However, most occupations included specialties or work settings that had feminized at varying rates, so the case studies provide variation on the dependent variable. Nonetheless, the bases for women's movement into occupations not marked by rapid feminization may have differed. Patricia Roos and I addressed this question in statistical analyses of all 503 detailed occupations (Reskin and Roos 1985).

The case studies support two empirical generalizations both of which are consistent with the operation of queuing processes. First, in most of the occupations we studied, after they had become less attractive to men, employers hired disproportionate numbers of women. Second, within these nominally desegregating occupations, women tended to be relegated to female enclaves, while men retained the most desirable jobs.[9] These findings confirm Bielby and Baron's (1986) contention that greater balance in the sex composition of *occupations* does not necessarily imply decreased segregation of *jobs* and also establish the fallacy of inferring declines in sex segregation from occupational-level data. Yet social analysts cannot ignore such data, because policymakers and the media use them to assess change, and, as W. I. Thomas said, situations men define as real are real in their consequences. Exaggerated conclusions about women's progress in male occupations support claims that governmental agencies no longer need to intervene in the workplace to ensure equal treatment. Thus it is incumbent on researchers to determine whether or not the trends that superficial comparisons imply are genuine.

Notes

I am grateful to Ross Boylan, Lowell L. Hargens, Heidi Hartmann, and Patricia A. Roos for their comments on earlier drafts of this chapter and to James N. Baron and Ronnie Steinberg for helpful discussions of the issues it addresses. The larger study that gave rise to the ideas in this chapter is a collaborative project with Patricia A. Roos. The case studies on which this chapter is based appears in our book, *Job Queues, Gender Queues: Explaining Women's Inroads into Male Occupations* (1990).

1. I conducted the last two unpublished studies. Unless otherwise noted, assertions about these occupations are based on the case studies whose full citations are in the references. For a description of the case study method, see Reskin and Roos (1990).

2. This analysis takes for granted the existence of multiple labor markets, each composed of a labor queue of potential workers and a job queue of available jobs.

3. Incumbent workers can affect the ordering of the labor queue, for example, through seniority rules that restrict employers' hiring prerogatives.

4. Of course, through labor queues, "supply-side" factors influenced which of the almost 45 million women in the labor force in 1980 moved into formerly male jobs that had become more open to women during the 1970s and which ones were consigned to female occupations.

5. This should be especially common among bosses who share a similar background with male workers, previously held the jobs in question, and currently work with or remain friendly with their former coworkers. Two examples are blue-collar supervisors or sales managers.

6. Unless it is backed by threats from regulatory agencies, pressure from women rarely suffices to persuade employers to assign women to male jobs, partly because it elicits opposition from male workers.

7. Employers can rarely forestall resistance by feminizing entire work teams. Seniority rules may prevent their replacing men, they may doubt whether enough qualified women are available, and they may be unable to train women because male unions control training or because training is too long and expensive.

8. Kessler-Harris (1986) and Strober and Arnold (1987) also recounted how banks exploited sex stereotypes to justify hiring women for banking jobs as well as to exclude them from the same jobs.

9. For further evidence on this point, see Chapter 3 in Reskin and Roos (1990).

References

Astrachan, Anthony. 1986. *How Men Feel*. New York: Anchor.

Baker, Ross. 1964. "Entry of Women into Federal Job World—At a Price." *Smithsonian* 8:82–91.

Becker, Gary. 1957. *The Economics of Discrimination*. Chicago: University of Chicago Press.

Beechey, Veronica and Tessa Perkins. 1987. *A Matter of Hours: Women, Part-Time Work and the Labour Market*. Cambridge, MA: Polity.

Beller, Andrea. 1984. "Trends in Occupational Segregation by Sex, 1960–1981." Pp. 11–26 in *Sex Segregation in the Workplace: Trends, Explanations, Remedies,* edited by B. Reskin. Washington, DC: National Academy Press.

Bergmann, Barbara R. and William Darity. 1981. "Social Relations, Productivity, and Employer Discrimination." *Monthly Labor Review* 104:47–49.

Bielby, William T. and James N. Baron. 1984. "A Woman's Place Is with Other Women: Sex Segregation Within Organizations." Pp. 27–55 in *Sex Segregation in the Workplace: Trends, Explanations, Remedies,* edited by B. Reskin. Washington, DC: National Academy Press.

———. 1986. "Men and Women at Work: Sex Segregation and Statistical Discrimination." *American Journal of Sociology* 91:759–99.

Bird, Chloe. 1990. "High Finance, Small Change: Women's Increased Representation in Bank Management." Pp. 145–66 in B. F. Reskin and P. A. Roos, *Job Queues, Gender Queues: Explaining Women's Inroads into Male Occupations,* Philadelphia: Temple University Press.

Blau, Francine D. 1989. "Occupational Segregation by Gender: A Look at the 1980s." Revised version of a paper presented at the meetings of the American Economics Association, New York.

Carter, Michael J. and Susan Boslego Carter. 1981. "Women's Recent Progress in the Professions or, Women Get a Ticket to Ride After the Gravy Train Has Left the Station." *Feminist Studies* 7:476–504.

Cobble, Dorothy Sue. Forthcoming. "'Drawing the Line': The Construction of a Gendered Workforce in the Food Service Industry." In *Work Engendered,* edited by Ava Baron. Ithaca: Cornell University Press.

Cockburn, Cynthia. 1988. "The Gendering of Jobs: Workplace Relations and the Reproduction of Sex Segregation." Pp. 29–42 in *Gender Segregation at Work,* edited by S. Walby. Milton Keynes: Open University Press.

Cohn, Samuel. 1985. *The Process of Occupational Sex-Typing: The Feminization of Clerical Labor in Great Britain*. Philadelphia: Temple University Press.

Collins, Sharon. 1983. "The Making of the Black Middle Class." *Social Problems* 30:369–82.

Davies, Margery W. 1975. "Women's Place Is at the Typewriter: The Feminization of the Clerical Labor Force." Pp. 279–96 in *Labor Market Segmentation,* edited by R. Edwards, M. Reich, and D. Gordon. Lexington, MA: D. C. Heath.

Detman, Linda. 1990. "Women Behind Bars: The Feminization of Bartending." Pp. 241–56 in B. F. Reskin and P. A. Roos, *Job Queues, Gender Queues: Explaining Women's Inroads into Male Occupations*. Philadelphia: Temple University Press.

Doeringer, Peter B. and Michael J. Piore. 1971. *Internal Labor Markets and Manpower Analysis*. Lexington, MA: D. C. Heath.

Donato, Katharine M. 1990a. "Programming for Change? The Growing Demand for Women Systems Analysts." Pp. 167–82 in B. F. Reskin and P. A. Roos, *Job Queues, Gender Queues: Explaining Women's Inroads into Male Occupations*. Philadelphia: Temple University Press.

———. 1990b. "Keepers of the Corporate Image: Women in Public Relations." Pp. 129–44 in B. F. Reskin and P. A. Roos, *Job Queues, Gender Queues: Explaining Women's Inroads into Male Occupations*. Philadelphia: Temple University Press.

Fields, Judith and Edward Wolff. 1989. "The Decline of Sex Segregation and the Wage Gap." Economic Research Report #89–04. New York: New York University, Starr Center for Applied Economics.

Figart, Deborah M. and Barbara Bergmann. 1989. "Facilitating Women's Occupational Integration." Paper prepared for the U.S. Department of Labor, Commission on Workforce Quality and Labor Market Efficiency, American University.

Gross, Edward. 1968. "*Plus ça Change. . . .* The Sexual Segregation of Occupations over Time." *Social Problems* 16:198–208.

Hacker, Sally L. 1979. "Sex Stratification, Technology and Organizational Change: A Longitudinal Analysis." *Social Problems* 26:539–57.

Hartmann, Heidi I. 1976. "Capitalism, Patriarchy, and Segregation by Sex." *Signs* 1:137–70.

———. 1989. "Comments." Paper presented at the meetings of the American Sociological Association, San Francisco.

Hirsch, Susan E. 1986. "Rethinking the Sexual Division of Labor: Pullman Repair Shops, 1900–1969." *Radical History Review* 3:26–48.

Hodge, Robert W. 1973. "Toward a Theory of Racial Differences in Employment." *Social Forces* 52:16–31.

Kessler-Harris, Alice. 1982. *Out to Work*. New York: Oxford University Press.

———. 1986. "Women's History Goes to Trial: EEOC vs. Sears, Roebuck and Co." *Signs* 1:767–79.

Lewis, Cherie Sue. 1986. "Television License Renewal Challenges by Women's Groups." Ph.D. dissertation, University of Minnesota.

Lieberson, Stanley. 1980. *A Piece of the Pie*. Berkeley: University of California Press.

Milkman, Ruth. 1987. *Gender at Work*. Urbana: University of Illinois Press.

Oppenheimer, Valerie. 1970. *The Female Labor Force in the United States*. Population Monograph Series, no. 5. Berkeley: University of California.

Osterman, Paul. 1979. "Sex Discrimination in Professional Employment: A Case Study." *Industrial and Labor Relations Review* 32:451–64.

Phillips, Anne and Barbara Taylor. 1980. "Sex and Skill." *Feminist Review* 6:79–88.

Phipps, Polly A. 1990a. "Occupational and Industrial Change: Prescription for Feminization." Pp. 111–28 in B. F. Reskin and P. A. Roos, *Job Queues, Gender Queues: Explaining Women's Inroads into Male Occupations*. Philadelphia: Temple University Press.

———. 1990b. "Occupational Resegregation: A Case Study of Insurance Adjusters and Examiners." Pp. 224–40 in B. F. Reskin and P. A. Roos, *Job Queues, Gender Queues: Explaining Women's Inroads into Male Occupations*. Philadelphia: Temple University Press.

Reskin, Barbara F. 1988. "Bringing the Men Back In: Sex Differentiation and the Devaluation of Women's Work." *Gender & Society* 2:58–81.

Reskin, Barbara F. and Patricia A. Roos. 1985. "Collaborative Research on the Determinants of Changes in Occupations' Sex Composition Between 1970 and 1980." National Science Foundation Grant no. 85-NSF-SES–85–12452. Manuscript.

———. 1990. *Job Queues, Gender Queues: Explaining Women's Inroads into Male Occupations*. Philadelphia: Temple University Press.

Roos, Patricia A. 1986. "Women in the Composing Room: Technology and Organization as Determinants of Social Change." Paper presented at the annual meetings of the American Sociological Association, New York.

———. 1990. "Hot Metal to Electronic Composition: Gender, Technology, and Social Change." Pp. 275–98 in B. F. Reskin and P. A. Roos, *Job Queues, Gender Queues: Explaining Women's Inroads into Male Occupations*. Philadelphia: Temple University Press.

Rose, Sonya O. 1988. "Gender Antagonism and Class Conflict." *Social History* 13:191–208.

Rotella, Elyce. 1977. *From Home to Office: U.S. Women at Work, 1870–1930*. Ann Arbor: UMI Research Press.

Sanders, Marlene and Marcia Rock. 1988. *Waiting for Prime Time*. Urbana: University of Illinois Press.

Smith, Joan. 1989. "The Impact of the Reagan Years." Paper presented at the first Annual Women's Policy Research Conference, Washington, DC, May 19.

Steiger, Thomas and Barbara F. Reskin. 1990. "Baking and Baking off: Deskilling and the Changing Sex Make Up of Bakers." Pp. 257–74 in B. F. Reskin and P. A. Roos, *Job Queues, Gender Queues: Explaining Women's Inroads into Male Occupations.* Philadelphia: Temple University Press.

Stolzenberg, Ross. 1982. "Industrial Profits and the Propensity to Employ Women Workers." Paper presented at the Workshop on Job Segregation by Sex, Committee on Women's Employment and Related Social Issues, National Research Council, Washington, DC.

Strober, Myra. 1984. "Toward a General Theory of Occupational Sex Segregation." Pp. 144–56 in *Sex Segregation in the Workplace: Trends, Explanations, Remedies,* edited by B. Reskin. Washington, DC: National Academy Press.

———. 1988. "The Processes of Occupational Segregation: Relative Attractiveness and Patriarchy." Paper presented at the meetings of the American Educational Research Association, New Orleans.

Strober, Myra and Carolyn Arnold. 1987. "The Dynamics of Occupational Segregation Among Bank Tellers." Pp. 107–48 in *Gender in the Workplace,* edited by C. Brown and J. Pechman. Washington, DC: Brookings Institute.

Strom, Sharon Hartman. 1987. "'Machines Instead of Clerks': Technology and the Feminization of Bookkeeping, 1910–1950." Pp. 63–97 in *Computer Chips and Paper Clips.* Vol. 2, edited by H. Hartmann. Washington, DC: National Academy Press.

Thomas, Barbara J. 1990. "Women's Gains in Insurance Sales: Increased Supply, Uncertain Demand." Pp. 183–204 in B. F. Reskin and P. A. Roos, *Job Queues, Gender Queues: Explaining Women's Inroads into Male Occupations.* Philadelphia: Temple University Press.

Thomas, Barbara J. and Barbara F. Reskin. 1990. "A Woman's Place Is Selling Homes: Women's Movement into Real Estate Sales." Pp. 205–24 in B. F. Reskin and P. A. Roos, *Job Queues, Gender Queues: Explaining Women's Inroads into Male Occupations.* Philadelphia: Temple University Press.

Thurow, Lester. 1969. *Poverty and Discrimination.* Washington, DC: Brookings Institute.

———. 1972. "Education and Economic Equality." *The Public Interest* 28:66–81.

Walsh, John P. 1989. "Technological Change and the Division of Labor: The Case of Retail Meatcutters." *Work & Occupations* 16:165–83.

TROND PETERSEN AND LAURIE A. MORGAN

The Within-Job Gender Wage Gap

There are three types of discrimination that can produce wage differences between men and women. (1) Women are differentially allocated to occupations and establishments that pay lower wages. This may involve discrimination partly through differential access to occupations and establishments—that is, the matching process at the point of hire—and partly through subsequent promotions. We call this process *allocative discrimination*. (2) Occupations held primarily by women are paid lower wages than those held primarily by men, although skill requirements and other wage relevant factors are the same. This process, which we call *valuative discrimination,* is addressed by comparable worth initiatives. (3) Women receive lower wages than men within a given occupation and establishment. We call this process *within-job wage discrimination.* Allocative and valuative discrimination involve the segregation of men and women into different occupations, establishments, or both, and may occur without within-job wage discrimination. Thus, although it may be the case that where men and women share the same jobs they receive the same pay, they simply do not share the same jobs all that often.

One conjecture currently accepted by many researchers is that wage differences are less an issue of within-job wage discrimination and more a matter of allocative and valuative processes. That is, the segregation of women into lower paying occupations, establishments, or both, and lower pay in occupations held primarily by women are more important than pay differences within the same job in explaining the gender wage gap. Treiman and Hartmann (1981, 92–93) write, "Although the committee recognizes that instances of unequal pay for the same work have not been entirely eliminated, we believe that they are probably not now the major source of differences in earnings."

This conjecture is drawn primarily from a large literature that focuses on pay differences across and within occupations. One pattern of findings is that the wage gap between men and women becomes smaller as occupational controls become finer, suggesting that a large proportion of the wage gap is explained by occupational distribution (Treiman and Hartmann 1981; Reskin and Roos 1990). For example, Treiman and Hartmann (1981, 33–39) explained 10 to 20 percent of the raw gap using 222 occupational categories and 35 to 40 percent using 479 categories. These studies usually draw on data from the Census or national probability samples that allow no analysis of practices in specific establishments. Additional evidence suggests that, within occupations, the distribution of women across firms or establishments also accounts for some portion of the

Originally published in 1995. Please see complete source information beginning on page 891.

wage gap. For example, Blau (1977) found that in 11 clerical occupations, differences in men's and women's wages were larger between than within establishments.

Yet the prevailing conjecture remains a conjecture. It has not been shown that men and women receive equal pay within given occupations in given establishments. What has been shown is that sex segregation is extensive and pervasive (Bielby and Baron 1984; Petersen and Morgan 1995), but not the extent to which sex segregation accounts for the wage gap or that, when sex segregation is absent, the sexes receive more or less equal treatment. To confirm such a claim, one needs data on wages of men and women in the same detailed occupational group or position within the same establishment. Such data are not widely available except for isolated establishments.

This article reports a large-scale empirical investigation of wage differences between men and women within the same detailed occupational position within the same establishment. We use establishment-level data from a wide variety of industries. In each establishment, individual-level wage data for a large array of detailed occupational groups were collected, providing more accurate wage as well as occupational data than probably any other surveys available, except in some case studies of single establishments (e.g., Hartmann 1987). We focus first on production and clerical employees in 16 U.S. industries in the 1974 to 1983 period, primarily 1974 to 1978, analyzing data on 787,577 employees, 705 industry-specific occupations, 6,057 establishments, and 71,214 occupation-establishment pairs. Second, we focus on seven professional and three administrative occupations across a broad range of industries in 1981, analyzing data on about 740,000 employees distributed across 2,162 establishments and 16,433 occupation-establishment pairs.

We make no attempt to settle the important conceptual issues that go along with the empirical patterns we address, namely the sources of observed patterns, neither from the demand side—that is, discriminatory behavior by employers—or the supply side—that is, behaviors by employees and prospective employees (see England 1992, chap. 2). Nevertheless, our results have implications for the kinds of theoretical issues that are most in need of being addressed and for the type of data that need to be collected and analyzed.

Data

We use two large-scale data sets. The first data set comes from 16 Industry Wage Surveys (IWS) conducted by the U.S. Bureau of Labor Statistics (BLS) in the period 1974 to 1983 (see, e.g., U.S. Department of Labor 1976), corresponding to industry codes at three and more digits as defined in the *Standard Industrial Classification Manual* (see U.S. Executive Office of the President 1987). Eleven industries were surveyed in 1974 to 1978, whereas 5 were surveyed in 1980 to 1983. The populations for the surveys and the sampling from the populations are described in several U.S. Department of Labor publications (see Petersen and Morgan 1995, table 1). Of the 16, 11 are manufacturing industries, and 5 are service industries.

In each industry, the BLS drew a sample of several hundred establishments, often covering a large proportion of the establishments in the industry. For each establishment, information was obtained from establishment records both on establishment characteristics and on a large number of the production and/or clerical workers in the establishment. Within each industry, only a selection of occupations were surveyed—on average 42 occupations per industry. The occupations were selected by the BLS in order to provide a wide representation of production or clerical occupations in an industry. The individual-level data provide information on each individual in the relevant occupation and establishment. Excluded from the data collection were professional and managerial employees. Because these occupations may have exhibited wider variations in wages, even at the occupation-establishment level, there may have been less occupation-establishment level variation in wages here than in samples including professionals and managers.

For each employee surveyed, information was obtained on sex, occupation (an industry-specific code), method of wage payment (incentive- or time-rated), and hourly earnings. No information was collected on race, age, experience, or education. The occupational classification is unusually detailed, corresponding in many cases to nine digits in the *Dictionary of Occupational Titles* (see U.S. Department of Labor 1977). In other cases, the titles are specific to the BLS data, based on industry-specific codes, but are usually as detailed as the nine-digit titles in the *Dictionary of Occupational Titles*.

Wage data are straight-time hourly wages in 13 industries and full-time weekly earnings in the other 3, excluding premium pay for overtime and work on weekends, holidays, and late shifts. Thus, we do not conflate pay earned on regular hours with pay earned on overtime and irregular hours, making the wage data less prone to bias than virtually any other study used for assessing wage discrimination. Men work more overtime hours than women, due either to preference for or better access to overtime hours, and overtime hours are usually paid at a higher rate. Nonproduction bonuses, such as year-end bonuses, are also excluded, whereas incentive pay is included.

The second data set we use is the National Survey of Professional, Administrative, Technical, and Clerical (PATC) employees in 1981, also conducted by the BLS (U.S. Department of Labor 1981). The sampling and data collection design for this survey is similar to that in the IWS data. We use the data on weekly pay for full-time employees in seven professional and three administrative occupations. Each occupation is divided into a set of ranks, corresponding to a hierarchy in terms of authority, responsibility, and qualifications required, yielding for the professional and administrative occupations altogether 51 occupation-by-rank groups, with some man-

agerial positions included among the higher ranks. For example, rank I for chemists is an entry-level job requiring a bachelor's degree in chemistry and no job experience, whereas rank VIII is a job where the incumbent "makes decisions and recommendations that are authoritative and have far-reaching impact on extensive chemical and related activities of the company" (U.S. Department of Labor 1981, 54). The data were collected from broad industries: mining, construction, manufacturing, transportation, communication, electric, gas, sanitary services, retail trade, finance, insurance, and selected services (U.S. Department of Labor 1981, 31).

We have somewhat limited access to the PATC data. We have information on all of the 10 professional and administrative occupations and the 51 occupation-by-rank groups, from 2,162 establishments, covering probably all of the approximately 740,000 employees for which data were collected (see U.S. Department of Labor 1981, table 11). However, unlike the IWS data, we do not have access to the individual-level wage data. We only know the average wages by sex within each of 16,433 occupation-by-rank–establishment pairs. Thus, where a pair is sex integrated, which is the case for 4,036 of the 16,433 pairs, we can compute the wage gap at the occupation-by-rank–establishment level, the level of greatest interest here. Unfortunately, we cannot compute the overall wage gap in an occupation because we do not know the number of men and women employed in the occupation-by-rank–establishment pairs.

Methods

The discussion of methods focuses on the procedures for analyzing the IWS data. Only one of the four central quantities reported can also be computed in the PATC data.

We report all statistics separately for each of the 16 industries in the IWS data.[1] The raw (average) wages, either hourly or full-time weekly earnings, for women and men in an industry are given by $\overline{w}_f$ and $\overline{w}_m$, and the raw proportional wage between women and men is $w_{r,r} = \overline{w}_f / \overline{w}_m$. The average wages for women and men in occupation o are $\overline{w}_{o,f}$, and $\overline{w}_{o,m}$, and the proportional wage is $w_{o,r} = \overline{w}_{o,f} / \overline{w}_{o,m}$. The average wages for women and men in establishment e are $\overline{w}_{e,f}$, and $\overline{w}_{e,m}$, and the proportional wage is $w_{e,r} = \overline{w}_{e,f} / \overline{w}_{e,m}$. The average wages for women and men in occupation-establishment pair oe are $\overline{w}_{oe,f}$ and $\overline{w}_{oe,m}$, and the proportional wage is $w_{oe,r} = \overline{w}_{oe,f} / \overline{w}_{oe,m}$. These computations can only be done for units that are integrated by sex. We multiply each proportional wage by 100 in order to get the average female wage as percent of average male wage at the relevant level. This percentage is referred to as the relative wage in what follows.

We make three computations with relative wages. Each computation answers the following question: suppose sex segregation—by occupation, establishment, or occupation-establishment—were abolished, what then would the remaining relative wage be? These computations are defined in the appendix.

At the occupation level, we report the average of the relative wage across all sex-integrated occupations. We do the same at the establishment level. At the occupation-establishment level, we likewise report the average of the relative wage ($w_{oe,r} \cdot 100$) across all sex-integrated occupation-establishment units (oe). The female wage gap at each of these levels is then given as 100 minus the average of the relative wage at each level. This equals the percent by which women are paid less than men.

The remaining wage gap at the occupation-establishment level can reasonably be interpreted as an estimate of the upper bound on the amount of within-job wage discrimination, the gap one would observe in absence of occupation-establishment sex segregation. It is an upper bound because the remaining gap at that level could have been caused by other factors, such as differences in experience and human capital between men and women in a given category. The difference between the raw wage gap and the wage gap at the occu-

pation-establishment level can thus be interpreted as being attributable to occupation-establishment sex segregation. This part of course need not be caused by discrimination alone.

Results: Wage Differences in IWS Data

We begin with IWS data. Table 1 gives first in column 2 the raw relative wage and then in columns 3 to 5 the relative wages controlling for occupation, for establishment, and for occupation-establishment, computed from equations (1) to (4) in the appendix. Column 1 shows the percentage female in each industry. Column 2 shows that the average of the industry-specific raw relative wages between men and women was 81 percent. Thus the average of the industry-specific female wage gaps was 19 percent, where the wage gap is the percentage by which women earned less than men, computed as 100 minus the relative wage.

Column 3 shows that the female wage gap is reduced to an average, across the 16 industries, of 8 percent when we control for occupation, using equation (2). Column 4 shows that the female wage gap is reduced, across the 16 industries, to an average of 15 percent when we control for establishment, using equation (3). Column 5 shows that the female wage gap is reduced to about 0 to 4 percent when we control for the occupation-establishment pair, using equation (4). The average of the industry-specific female wage gaps is 1.7 percent, after controlling for the occupation-establishment pair.

These results are striking. Controlling for occupation or establishment alone reduces the wage gap somewhat, but not drastically. However, controlling for the occupation-establishment pair reduces the wage gap to a point of virtually no difference between men and women. The remaining female wage gap is on average 1.7 percent across the 16 industries, even without controlling for any individual-level characteristics such as educa-

TABLE 1
Women's Wages Relative to Men's with and without Occupation, Establishment, and
Occupation-Establishment Controls

	Women's Wages as a Percentage of Men's					Percent of Raw Wage Gap Explained by:		
	%F	Raw	Occ	Est	Occ-Est	Occ	Est	Occ-Est
Industry	1	2	3	4	5	6	7	8
Men's and Boys' Shirts	92.5	84.0	92.7	83.1	98.0	54.5	−5.4	87.5
Hospitals	84.8	105.3	95.8	103.7	101.0	178.7	30.7	81.3
Banking*	82.8	64.7	97.3	65.5	98.1	92.4	2.3	94.6
Life Insurance*	75.9	61.5	98.0	61.4	98.9	94.8	−0.3	97.1
Wool Textiles	55.4	87.3	93.8	91.7	98.6	51.3	34.8	89.0
Cotton Man-Made Fiber Textiles	54.6	89.2	96.5	90.5	99.7	67.5	11.8	97.2
Miscellaneous Plastics Products	51.9	77.5	87.4	80.6	97.8	44.1	14.0	90.2
Hotels and Motels	51.5	87.0	91.9	89.1	99.7	37.9	16.4	97.7
Computer and Data Processing*	44.5	67.5	98.4	81.4	98.9	95.1	42.8	96.6
Wood Household Furniture	35.9	85.4	91.3	90.4	95.7	40.3	34.2	70.5
Textile Dyeing and Finishing	19.8	82.7	92.2	90.2	99.0	55.0	43.4	94.2
Machinery	15.5	74.3	88.8	89.0	99.6	56.4	57.2	98.4
Nonferrous Foundries	9.4	81.3	84.1	84.4	97.5	15.1	16.7	86.7
Paints and Varnishes	5.6	85.1	92.6	91.8	96.6	50.2	44.8	77.1
Industrial Chemicals	2.5	83.2	93.2	90.1	97.1	59.6	41.2	82.8
Fabricated Structural Steel	0.6	80.7	86.0	81.5	96.9	27.4	4.1	83.9
Average Across Industries**	42.7	81.0	92.5	85.3	98.3	63.8	24.3	89.1

Note: Column 1, %F, gives the percent female in the industry. Column 2 gives the raw relative wage, from equation (1) in the Appendix. Columns 3–5 give the average of the within occupation within establishment, and within occupation-establishment relative wages, computed from equations (2)–(4). Columns 6–8 give the percent of the raw wage gap, defined as 100 minus the number in column 2, that can be attributed to occupation, establishment, and occupation-establishment segregation, computed from equations (5)–(7).

*This is based on weekly wages for full-time employees.

**Each column gives the unweighted average across industries of the percentages in the respective column.

tion, age, seniority, and race. Occupation-establishment segregation accounts better for wage differences between men and women than any other set of variables studied in the literature on wage differences.[2]

Columns 6 to 8 give a decomposition of the raw wage gap, calculated as 100 minus the relative wage from column 2, into the percentage that is due to occupation, to establishment, and to occupation-establishment segregation, when each dimension is considered alone. These results are based on equations (5) to (7) in the appendix. Column 6 shows that occupational sex segregation

alone accounts for about 64 percent of the wage gap, somewhat more than other studies have shown (e.g., Treiman and Hartmann 1981; Reskin and Roos 1990). Column 7 shows that establishment sex segregation alone accounts for about 24 percent of the wage gap. This is a new result. To date, occupational segregation has been the primary focus of gender wage gap studies. Column 8 shows that occupation-establishment sex segregation alone accounts for a large percentage of the wage gap, ranging from a low of 70.5 percent to a high of 98.4 percent. In 14 of 16 industries, more than 80 percent of the wage gap is explained by occupation-establishment segregation, and among seven of those more than 90 percent is explained, whereas in two industries only 70 percent and 77 percent of the gap is explained.

Again, we have the striking result that the interaction of occupation and establishment segregation not only explains dramatically more of the wage gap than either establishment or occupational segregation alone, it also explains most of the wage differences between men and women. Had men and women been equally distributed on occupation-establishment pairs, on the average 89 percent of the wage gap would have disappeared, assuming that other forms of discrimination would not have emerged.

One point requires discussion here. The female wage gap for the workers in our sample is about 20 percent. This is substantially less than the about 40 percent gap for all full-time workers during the period of the surveys (e.g., Goldin 1990, 61). There are several reasons for this discrepancy. One is that prior studies look at median or average annual earnings for full-time employees. It is probable that men on the average work more hours per year than women and that they also work more overtime hours. Therefore, differences between men and women are likely overstated. Another reason for this difference is that the occupations covered here comprise a relatively narrow range of the overall spectrum. In particular, professional and managerial occupations are excluded from the sample. The excluded occupations are expected to be on average higher paid than those included and to be occupied primarily by men. As a result, we have, when computing the raw wage gap of 19 percent, some degree of de facto control for occupation.

Results: Wage Differences in the PATC Data

The results in the preceding section were based on data mostly for blue-collar, clerical, and some technical employees. It might be suspected that the wage gap among professional, administrative, and managerial employees is greater. In this section we turn our attention to analysis of wage differences among these employees using PATC data.

Table 2 gives the average of the occupation-by-rank–establishment level relative wage, first for seven professional occupations and next for the three administrative ones. The entries in the table correspond to those in column 5 of Table 1. Column 1, titled "overall," gives the average occupation-by-rank–establishment level relative wage across all the ranks in the occupation. Columns 2 to 8 (marked I to VII) give the relative wage by rank within the occupation and establishment, from I (low) to VII (high). The numbers of occupation-by-rank–establishment units used to compute each of the relative wages are in parentheses.

Across the 10 occupations, the average wage gap at the occupation-by-rank–establishment level is 3.1 percent. This gap increases with the rank within the occupations, from 1 percent at the lowest to about 5 percent at the highest ranks, which include some managerial positions. Note that the highest ranks within an occupation vary between the occupations. Of course, the extent to which the gap of about 5 percent at the highest ranks is due to within-job wage discrimination or due to other factors such as experience cannot be addressed with these data.

Conclusion and Discussion

The findings of this article are simple to summarize. First, wage differences within given occupation-establishment pairs were relatively small: on average 1.7 percent among blue-collar and clerical as well as some technical employees, and on average 3.1 percent in seven professional and three administrative occupations, ranging from 1 percent in the lower to 5 percent in the higher ranks in an occupation. Thus, occupation-establishment segregation, not within-job wage discrimination was the driving force for observed wage

TABLE 2

Women's Wages Relative to Men's at the Occupation-by-Rank-Establishment Level, by Occupation,
by Rank within Occupation, and across Occupations for Professional and Administrative Employees,
PATC Data (1981)

| Occupation | Overall | By Rank | | | | | | |
| | | I | II | III | IV | V | VI | VII |
	1	2	3	4	5	6	7	8
Accountants	97.3	99.4	98.5	96.4	96.1	92.9	93.7	
	(1319)	(260)	(338)	(417)	(220)	(75)	(9)	
Chief Accountants	94.7		94.7					
	(1)		(1)					
Auditors	97.8	100.8	98.8	96.5	94.9			
	(294)	(58)	(91)	(104)	(41)			
Public Accountants	99.3	100.4	99.0	99.1	98.2			
	(142)	(42)	(41)	(37)	(22)			
Attorneys	96.4	98.1	97.9	96.1	93.5	95.8	93.6	
	(243)	(44)	(67)	(68)	(44)	(15)	(5)	
Chemists	96.9	98.2	97.9	96.7	95.6	96.2	94.9	96.5
	(366)	(51)	(92)	(93)	(71)	(41)	(14)	(4)
Engineers	96.9	98.9	98.9	96.4	95.3	93.0	96.3	94.1
	(1007)	(192)	(232)	(243)	(167)	(104)	(50)	(19)
Job Analysts	96.9	94.3	99.0	93.9	99.3			
	(67)	(4)	(8)	(26)	(29)			
Directors of Personnel	92.2	101.2	84.8	94.6				
	(8)	(3)	(4)	(1)				
Buyers	95.6	98.2	96.5	93.4	92.1			
	(589)	(104)	(264)	(183)	(38)			
All Occupations	96.9	99.1	98.0	96.0	95.6	93.7	95.6	94.5
	(4036)	(758)	(1138)	(1172)	(632)	(235)	(78)	(23)

Note: The results in columns 1–8 were obtained as follows. The relative wage was first computed for each integrated occupation-by-rank-establishment pair. Then the average of these relative wages was computed for each occupation using equation (4). Next, in columns 2–8, the average of these relative wages was computed for each rank within an occupation, again using equation (4).

differences.[3] Second, establishment segregation was important for wage differences between men and women, although not as important as occupational segregation, a result we could compute only for the blue-collar, clerical, and some technical employees in the IWS data.

The first finding is important. It shows that occupation-establishment segregation accounted for more of the gender wage gap than any other variable or set of variables currently used in studying the gender wage gap. Occupational segregation alone tends to account for about 40 percent of the wage gap, and human capital and other variables also account for about 40 percent (e.g., Treiman and Hartmann 1981, chap. 2). But no set of variables, either individual or structural, accounts for as much as 89 percent, as occupation-establishment segregation did here in the case of blue-collar, clerical, and some technical employees in the IWS data.

This first finding establishes the conjecture already made in the literature, but not yet documented: wage differences are to a larger extent generated by occupation-establishment segregation than by within-job wage discrimination. Along with the first, the second finding shows the need to study establishment as well as occupational segregation.

The implications of the findings are straightforward. In terms of policy, allocative and valuative processes should be given the most attention, and within-job wage discrimination, which is covered by the Equal Pay Act of 1963 and which has been the implicit or explicit focus of much discussion and research, should receive less. Future research on differential wage attainment between men and women should be refocused as follows. The emphasis should be less on within-job wage discrimination and more on three prior processes: (1) the entry of employees into occupations and establishments, that is, the differential access of men and women to positions during the initial hiring or matching process, an allocative mechanism that is not easy to research; (2) career advancement within establishments, that is, the differential rates of promotion for men and women, also an allocative mechanism, but one which is more easily studied (Spilerman 1986); (3) how jobs occupied primarily by women tend to be paid less than those occupied by men—the comparable worth issue, or what we refer to as valuative discrimination, also a line of research well under way (see England 1992).

Two issues arise in the identification of allocative processes as responsible for the gender wage gap. The first is whether segregation patterns are due primarily to discrimination or to differences in productive capacities. The meaning of our results for theory and policy depends on which mechanism operated here. This cannot be settled with our data and is obviously a task for future research. It requires information about productive capacities and would require an analysis of the matching between these and particular jobs.

The second issue concerns the role of supply-side sources of differential attainment between men and women. Of particular interest are the constraints put on women's career attainment from family obligations and household choices. Although these constraints may result most proximally from a traditional household division of labor, not directly from discriminatory behaviors by employers, household decisions are made in light of labor market opportunities, so the two are interdependent. The role of supply-side behaviors and their interrelationship with employer behaviors in generating the observed occupation-establishment segregation is in need of research.

Appendix

The *raw* relative wage between women and men is given as

$$w_{(r,r)} = \frac{\overline{w}_f}{\overline{w}_m} \times 100. \tag{1}$$

The relative wage controlling for occupation obtains as

$$w_{(o,r)} = \frac{1}{N_{o(I)}} \left[\sum_{o=1}^{N_{o(I)}} (w_{o,r}) \right] \times 100. \tag{2}$$

Here, $N_{o(I)}$ is the number of occupations in which both men and women are present.

The establishment-level relative wage obtains as

$$w_{(e,r)} = \frac{1}{N_{e(I)}} \left[\sum_{e=1}^{N_{e(I)}} (w_{e,r}) \right] \times 100. \tag{3}$$

Here, $N_{e(I)}$ is the number of establishments where both men and women are present.

The occupation-establishment-level relative wage obtains as

$$w_{(oe,r)} = \frac{1}{N_{oe(I)}} \left[\sum_{oe=1}^{N_{oe(I)}} (w_{oe,r}) \right] \times 100. \tag{4}$$

Here, $N_{oe(I)}$ is the number of occupation-establishment pairs in which both men and women are present.

The raw wage gap obtains as 100 minus the number in (1). The percentage of the raw wage gap due to occupational segregation alone is given by

$$\%w_{(o,r)} = \frac{w_{(o,r)} - w_{(r,r)}}{100 - w_{(r,r)}} \times 100. \tag{5}$$

The percentage of the raw wage gap due to establishment segregation alone is given by

$$\%w_{(e,r)} = \frac{w_{(e,r)} - w_{(r,r)}}{100 - w_{(r,r)}} \times 100. \tag{6}$$

The percentage of the raw wage gap due to occupation-establishment segregation alone is given by

$$\%w_{(oe,r)} = \frac{w_{(oe,r)} - w_{(r,r)}}{100 - w_{(r,r)}} \times 100. \tag{7}$$

Notes

The article is a version of Petersen and Morgan (1995) that was excerpted and partially rewritten for this volume by Petersen and Morgan with the help of David Grusky.

1. Unfortunately, we cannot compare wages across industries, because the industry data come from different years and hence reflect inflation as well as general wage increases.

2. Although Groshen (1991) and Tomaskovic-Devey (1993) report similar results on wage differences, neither author reported the wage gap at the occupation-establishment level.

3. Similar results are shown in Petersen et al. (1997) for Norway in 1984 and 1990.

References

Bielby, William T., and James N. Baron. 1984. "A Woman's Place is with Other Women: Sex Segregation Within Organizations." Pages 27–55 in *Sex Segregation in the Workplace: Trends, Explanations, Remedies,* edited by Barbara F. Reskin. Washington, D.C.: National Academy Press.

Blau, Francine D. 1977. *Equal Pay in the Office.* Lexington, MA: Lexington Books.

England, Paula. 1992. *Comparable Worth: Theories and Evidence.* Hawthorne, NY: Aldine de Gruyter.

Goldin, Claudia. 1990. *Understanding the Gender Gap: An Economic History of American Women.* New York: Oxford University Press.

Groshen, Erica L. 1991. "The Structure of the Female/Male Wage Differential: Is It Who You Are, What You Do, or Where You Work?" *Journal of Human Resources* 26(3):457–72.

Hartmann, Heidi I. 1987. "Internal Labor Markets and Gender: A Case Study of Promotion." Pages 59–92 in *Gender in the Workplace,* edited by Clair Brown and Joseph Pechman. Washington, D.C.: Brookings Institution.

Petersen, Trond, and Laurie A. Morgan. 1995. "Separate and Unequal: Occupation-Establishment Sex Segregation and the Gender Wage Gap." *American Journal of Sociology* 101(2): 329–61.

Petersen, Trond, Vemund Snartland, Lars-Erik Becken, and Karen Modesta Olsen. 1997. "Within-Job Wage Discrimination and the Gender Wage Gap, The Case of Norway." *European Sociological Review* 13(2):199–215.

Reskin, Barbara F., and Patricia Roos (Eds.). 1990. *Job Queues, Gender Queues: Explaining Women's Inroads into Male Occupations.* Philadelphia: Temple University Press.

Spilerman, Seymour. 1986. "Organizational Rules and the Features of Work Careers." *Research in Social Stratification and Mobility* 5:41–102.

Tomaskovic-Devey, Donald. 1993. *Gender and Race Inequality at Work: The Sources and Consequences of Job Segregation.* Ithaca, NY: ILR Press.

Treiman, Donald J., and Heidi I. Hartmann (Eds.). 1981. *Women, Work, and Wages: Equal Pay for Jobs of Equal Value.* Washington, D.C.: National Academy Press.

U.S. Department of Labor. 1976. *Industry Wage Survey: Miscellaneous Plastics, September 1974.* Bureau of Labor Statistics, Bulletin 1914. Washington, D.C.: U.S. Government Printing Office.

———. 1977. *Dictionary of Occupational Titles.* 4th ed. Bureau of Employment Security. Washington, D.C.: U.S. Government Printing Office.

———. 1981. *National Survey of Professional, Administrative, Technical, and Clerical Pay, March 1981.* Bureau of Labor Statistics, Bulletin 2108. Washington, D.C.: U.S. Government Printing Office.

U.S. Executive Office of the President. 1987. *Standard Industrial Classification Manual. 1987.* Office of Management and Budget. Washington, D.C.: U.S. Government Printing Office.

MARGARET MOONEY MARINI AND PI-LING FAN

The Gender Gap in Earnings at Career Entry

It is well established that in the United States, on average, women's wages are lower than those of men. Data on the 1992 annual earnings of full-time, year-round workers ages 16 and older indicate that, on average, women earned 71 cents for every dollar earned by men (U.S. Bureau of the Census 1993). We analyze gender differences in wages at career entry when market constraints on competition and gender differences in human capital are at their lowest. With rare exceptions, workers at career entry enter jobs from outside employing organizations rather than via internal job ladders, and gender differences in on-the-job training and full-time labor market experience have not yet emerged. Gender differences in earnings are therefore at their lowest at career entry.

We propose a new approach to the analysis of gender differences in wages that identifies several alternative explanatory mechanisms to account for the sorting of women and men into different types of jobs offering different levels of reward. Because labor market rewards derive from the labor market positions occupied, we argue that wage differences among workers, including those between women and men, can be explained by processes that match individuals to jobs. Our

concern is not with explaining the origin of the gender-segregated U.S. labor market and its associated wage structure, but rather with explaining how individual women and men are sorted into different positions in that structure and thereby obtain different levels of reward. Thus, we take the structure of jobs and wages as a characteristic of the economy that is given (predetermined) at the time individuals enter the labor market, and seek to determine how individuals are sorted, or matched, to different jobs. The matching processes we study operate at the *micro level* to sort individuals into existing slots, or job openings, in a given *macro-level* structure. We are particularly interested in distinguishing the extent to which gender differences in wages can be attributed to choices and investments by workers as compared to social influences externally imposed at career entry.

Prior sociological research has not provided an adequate theoretical rationale for analyzing the micro-level associations between measures of occupational and industrial placement and wages. Specifically, research has not identified and distinguished the mechanisms that produce an association between occupational and industrial *placement* and wages *at the micro level* from those that produce an association between occupational and industrial *sectors* and wages *at the macro level*. The association of occupational and industrial sectors and wages is a characteristic of the macro-level wage structure that has evolved via a combination of macro-level and micro-level processes operating over an extended period of time. Based on prior theory and re-

Originally published in 1997. Please see complete source information beginning on page 891.

search, we assume the existence of a wage structure in which relative wage rates reflect the nature of product and labor markets and are influenced by unions and government policies (Marini 1989). Much of the variation in wages is associated with extra-individual factors (e.g., characteristics of the job and employer) that affect prices for the firm's output and the costs of production—not with the characteristics of individual job-holders. Although the wage structure changes over time, the historical evolution of well-defined systems of jobs and firms has created relatively stable segmentation by occupation or job type, industry, and geographical location. Differential wage rates persist long after the market conditions creating them have changed because they become institutionalized in the administrative rules and procedures of organizations and take on normative elements that shape the preferences and relative ratings workers give to jobs.

In the United States, the sex composition of jobs has become a basis of economic segmentation (Treiman and Hartmann 1981; England 1992). With the coming of industrialization, women became "secondary workers" in the labor market; they entered the labor market in smaller numbers and for shorter periods than did men. Initially, occupations and industries were highly segregated by sex, partly because employers developed explicit policies to segregate the workplace and bar married women from employment (Goldin 1990). Societal consensus that differentiation on the basis of sex was appropriate made it possible to employ women and men in different jobs at different wage rates. Although this consensus on gender-role differentiation has eroded and gender discrimination in employment is now illegal, the labor market remains segregated by sex, exhibiting substantial differences in pay between predominantly female jobs and predominantly male jobs. Just as many other wage differentials have persisted long after the conditions creating them have changed, wage differentials between sex-typed jobs have persisted.

Micro-Level Mechanisms of the Gender Wage Gap

Given the existence of a sex-segregated labor market and its associated wage structure, we focus on the micro-level mechanisms by which individual women and men are sorted into positions in the labor market offering different levels of reward. We argue that at least five such mechanisms are potentially at work: (1) Women and men enter the labor market with somewhat different skills and credentials, or different amounts and kinds of human capital. (2) Because of gender differentiation in adult family roles, women and men are in different family situations at career entry, and family structure has different implications for the earnings of the two sexes. (3) As a result of gender-role socialization and gender discrimination prior to labor market entry, women and men have different work and family aspirations, which cause them to aspire to different occupations in the labor market. (4) Upon entry into the labor market, women and men are allocated by employers to jobs with different wage rates, primarily because they are allocated to sex-typed jobs. (5) Because women and men have different social networks, receive different information, and have different access to influence through those social networks, women and men learn of and apply for jobs with different wage rates. Each of these five explanatory mechanisms is discussed briefly below.

Skills and Credentials

The most frequently hypothesized and studied explanation of the gender gap in wages is that women and men acquire different labor market skills and credentials, or different amounts and kinds of human capital. In the human capital theory of economics, workers are seen as rational actors who seek to maximize their lifetime income (utility) by investing in their own productive capacities. Earnings differences among workers arise from workers' different initial and continuing investments in their productivity-related skills. Although economists using the human capital model do not examine the process of socialization, it is assumed that because women and men anticipate engaging in different adulthood activities, women develop better nonmarket skills, whereas men develop better market skills (Becker 1981). Sociologists have also argued that labor market skills and credentials play a role in the determination of wage differences among workers, although they have not argued that market skills result only from rational investment or that the relationship between skills and wages is attributable only to an effect of skills on worker productivity. Sociologists as well as some economists have argued that the effects of worker characteristics such as formal education and labor market experience may reflect other influences.

Previous studies on the effects of worker skills and credentials on earnings have indicated that some but not all of the gender gap in earnings is explained by gender differences in measures of human capital (Mincer and Polachek 1974, 1978; Sandell and Shapiro 1978; Corcoran and Duncan 1979; Mincer and Ofek 1982; U.S. Bureau of the Census 1987). In studies based on samples of individuals of diverse ages, at most about half of the gender gap in wages is associated with mean differences in human capital between the sexes—and in some studies it is considerably less.

Family Roles

A second explanation advanced to account for the wage gap between women and men focuses on the compatibility of employment with gender-differentiated adult family roles. Women continue to do at least two-thirds of household work and are usually responsible for household management and child care, whereas men usually have primary responsibility for financially supporting the family (Juster 1985; Gershuny and Robinson 1988; Robinson 1988; Marini and Shelton 1993).

Because of this longstanding pattern, the adult family role expectations and behavior of women and men may have implications for their labor market outcomes. Previous research has indicated that for women and men, the ages at entry into adult family roles bear opposite relationships to earnings: Early entry into adult family roles is associated with lower earnings among women but with higher earnings among men (Marini et al. 1989). Similarly, being married bears a negative relationship to the earnings of women, but a positive relationship to the earnings of men (Blum 1972; Treiman and Terrell 1975; Ornstein 1976:151, 156; Korenman and Neumark 1992a). Also, the presence and number of children in the home are negatively associated with the earnings of women, but positively associated with the earnings of men (Duncan, Featherman, and Duncan 1972; 236–44; Cramer 1980; Korenman and Neumark 1992b). Because much of the effect of these characteristics of family structure on wages is exerted indirectly via their effect on human capital, particularly on educational attainment and labor market experience, the effects of family structure on women's earnings are usually indirect (Corcoran and Duncan 1979; Hill 1979; Korenman and Neumark 1992b). In contrast, there is evidence that marital status has a direct and positive effect on men's earnings, even after the effects of other influences on wages are considered (Goldin 1990:102). Several explanations have been offered. One is that marriage makes men better workers (more productive), either because the division of labor within the household allows them to invest more in developing their labor market skills or because marriage itself provides an incentive for them to invest more. A second explanation is that men who possess unmeasured characteristics that are highly valued in the labor market are more likely to be married. And a third explanation is that employers show favoritism toward married men, viewing marriage as an indicator of responsibility and stability or of a greater need for income.

Work and Family Aspirations

In a society characterized by marked gender-role differentiation inside and outside the labor market, gender-role socialization and gender discrimination prior to career entry cause women and men to aspire to different types of jobs and to pursue different types of education (Jacobs 1989). Even women and men who have the same amount and types of education choose different jobs. Although gender differences in occupational aspirations are smaller than observed differences in the actual occupational placements of adults, occupational aspirations are highly sex-typed. Among youth ages 14 to 22 in 1979, it was estimated that 61 percent of one sex would have to change occupational aspirations (as measured by the 1970 census detailed occupational classification) to equalize the distributions of aspirations of the two sexes (Marini and Brinton 1984).

A serious problem in economic and sociological analyses of gender differences in wages has been a failure to consider the effects of gender-role socialization on gender differences in occupational orientation. In economics, neoclassical theory treats interindividual variation in preferences as exogenous inputs. Not only has there been no attempt to explain the origin of the values and beliefs on which individuals act, but in the absence of the formal consideration of values and beliefs it is often assumed that individuals simply seek to maximize their earnings. This assumption is problematic because individuals do not value income equally relative to other sources of utility. In the case of job choice, evidence shows that variables other than income affect occupational preferences (Marini et al. 1996). Thus, when the values and beliefs reflected in occupational preferences are ignored and only measures of human capital are considered in models of wage determination, it is impossible to distinguish the effect of worker preferences from other sources of influence, such as the direct experience of discrimination in the labor market.

In sociology, the failure to consider the effects of gender-role socialization on gender differences in occupational orientation arises largely from the mistaken view that the consideration of gender-role socialization locates the explanation for the wage gap in characteristics of individuals rather than the social structure. This view is mistaken because socialization, by definition, has social origins. Socialization is a *life-long, dynamic process* whereby individuals learn about the society in which they live and come to understand what is considered appropriate and desirable behavior. It is also a process by which prevailing ideas and existing behavioral practices, including those resulting from discrimination in earlier historical periods, are passed on to new generations. Thus, like the direct experience of discrimination by employers, socialization is an influence originating outside the individual. Because it begins at birth, however, socialization shapes an individual's values and beliefs prior to labor market entry—and this can affect behavior at entry.

Discrimination

Family structure and work/family aspirations are potential influences on the gender gap in earnings at career entry because values and beliefs (including normative beliefs) internalized prior to labor market entry affect labor market behavior at entry. In contrast, other explanations of the gender gap in earnings recognize that women and men also experience different *external* influences or constraints upon labor market entry. These constraints are usually referred to as labor market discrimination (for detailed reviews, see Blau 1984; Madden 1985; Blau and Ferber 1986; England 1992). Discrimination is most widely recognized to occur when different opportunities and rewards are given to equally qualified women and men by employing organizations. Less widely recognized is the discrimination that occurs through institutionalized personnel procedures governing the recruitment, allocation, and retention of workers (Roos and Reskin 1984). For example, because jobs in most organizations are highly sex-typed, women and men with the same formal employment credentials may be triaged by personnel officers into different jobs, and these different job placements may have important implications for earnings and future career mobility. Due to the evolution of a wage structure in which the sex type and earnings level of a job are related, the recruitment and allocation of workers to jobs perceived as "sex-appropriate" has negative implications for the earnings of women relative to men.

Social Networks

A final mechanism affecting the sorting of individuals to jobs is differential access to information and influence through social networks. This mechanism focuses on neither voluntary choices by workers nor constraints placed on opportunities by employers, but on informal processes of social contact and interaction. The social networks of women and men may provide access to different job-related information and knowledge, and this access may affect entry into different jobs. Previous research has found that personal contact is an important source of information and influence in job searches and that under some circumstances personal contacts result in better jobs and higher incomes than other search methods, at least in the short term (Granovetter 1974; Corcoran, Datcher, and Duncan 1980). Women, however, are considerably less likely than men to use informal information and influence channels in obtaining jobs (Corcoran et al. 1980; Campbell 1988). Moreover, because nonkin networks are disproportionately comprised of members of the same sex and men are more likely to occupy positions with higher pay and authority, women's networks are less able than men's to provide access to information and influence helpful in getting higher paying jobs. As yet, however, there have been no studies on whether using informal information and influence in getting a job affects the gender gap in wages or whether social network effects vary for different types of occupations.

Model

In summary, the gender gap in wages at career entry can be seen as resulting from several influences that affect the sorting of workers into jobs offering different levels of reward: (1) gender differences in job-related skills and credentials, (2) gender differences in adult family roles, (3) gender differences in work and family aspirations, (4) gender discrimination in hiring and job placement by employers, and (5) gender differences in the availability and use of information and influence via social networks. We therefore assume the following model for the determination of wages at career entry:

$$W = f(H, F, A, D, N),$$

where W represents the wage rate, H represents human capital,[1] F represents family roles, A represents aspirations, D represents discrimination, and N represents networks. Because wages are a function of five types of influences that sort incoming cohorts of workers to available jobs within an existing market structure, gender differences in wages at career entry are viewed as a function of gender differences in these five types of influences.

Data and Measures

Our empirical analysis of the micro-level process of wage determination at career entry uses data from the National Longitudinal Survey of Youth (NLSY), a survey of U.S. youth ages 14 to 22 in 1979, who have been surveyed annually in subsequent years. We analyze data for 1979 through 1991, focusing on a sample of 6,111 youth that is representative of the noninstitutionalized civilian population in the sampled age cohorts.[2] Virtually all those in the sample (97 percent of males and 94 percent of females) had entered the full-time labor force prior to the 1991 survey.

To identify the relative influence of the five explanatory mechanisms on the gender gap in wages at career entry, we sought to develop appropriate measures. The operation of three mechanisms could be analyzed directly by measuring and estimating the effects of three categories of worker characteristics: human capital at career entry, family structure at career entry, and work and family aspirations prior to career entry.

We examine more detailed measures of human capital than those usually considered: the interaction of the amount and type of education, a test of developed mental aptitude, part-time labor market experience prior to career entry, knowledge of work, high school grade-point average, parents' education, and self-esteem. To measure the amount and type of *education* we created a set of categorical variables based on the highest level of education completed and the major field of study. *Part-time labor force experience* was measured by the total number of hours (in hundreds) worked during the 4-year period prior to career entry. *Developed mental aptitude* was assessed by the Armed Forces Qualifications Test (AFQT), a test of verbal and mathematical skills. We measured *knowledge of work* by a nine-item test of occupational knowledge that focused on the duties of nine jobs. *High school grade-point average* (GPA) was assessed by the mean of final grades for courses available in data from high school transcripts. We measured *parents' education* by the mean of the mother's and the father's highest levels of education completed because of the high collinearity between mother's education and father's education. If information on education was available for only one parent, the data available for that parent were used instead of the mean. *Self-esteem* was measured by the Rosenberg Self-Esteem Scale. Respondents were asked to indicate their level of agreement with a list of 10 items that yielded a unidimensional factor scale on

which high scores indicated a high level of self-esteem.[3]

Family structure was measured by whether the respondent was married at career entry and by the number of dependents at career entry. *Marital status* was a dichotomous variable coded 1 if married and 0 if single, divorced, or widowed at career entry. *Number of dependents* equalled the total number of persons not counting the respondent and a possible spouse who were dependent on the respondent for at least half of their support at career entry.

Work and family aspirations were measured by the occupation the respondent wanted to have at age 35, the number of children desired, and gender-role attitudes. In prior studies, occupational aspirations have rarely been measured at all, and when they have, unidimensional measures focusing on either the prestige or sex type of the occupation aspired to have been used. We measured *occupational aspiration* as immediately prior to career entry as possible. Respondents' stated aspirations for the occupation they wanted to have at age 35 were coded using 415 categories defined by the 1970 census detailed occupational classification. To measure the earning potential of each occupation aspired to, we calculated the natural log of the median annual earnings of workers ages 18 to 34 in the occupation in 1969 using a special tabulation of data from the 1970 census.[4] We then converted the variable to a z-score to reduce multicollinearity with other independent variables.

Fertility aspiration was measured by the number of children the respondent desired, as stated prior to career entry. *Gender-role attitudes* were also measured prior to career entry based on responses to six statements about the employment of wives.[5] Respondents indicated their level of agreement with each statement on an ordinal scale. We created a scale measuring gender-role attitudes, following the procedures used to create the scale measuring self-esteem. High scores on the factor scale indicated more egalitarian gender-role attitudes.

The data contained no direct measures of discrimination in hiring or job placement or of the operation of social networks. With measures of the other explanatory mechanisms held constant, however, we can infer that the measured effect of gender on job placement is attributable to the combined operation of discrimination and social networks. Similarly, we can infer that gender differences in wages associated with job placement are attributable to the combined effects of discrimination and social networks on gender differences in job placement. Job placement was measured by the occupation and industry in which the respondent worked at career entry. Although there is also job segregation by sex within occupations and industries (Bielby and Baron 1984; Tomaskovic-Devey 1993), this refined level of measurement is not possible in a population sample employed in highly diverse occupations and industries.

Occupational placement at career entry, like occupational aspiration, was measured in 415 categories using the 1970 census detailed occupational classification. The earning level of the occupation was measured by the natural log of the median annual earnings of workers ages 18 to 34 in the occupation in 1969, again using a special tabulation of data from the 1970 census; this variable was then converted to a z-score. *Industrial placement* at career entry was measured in 213 industrial categories according to the 1970 census detailed industrial classification. The earning level of the industry was measured by the natural log of the median annual earnings of all workers in the industry in 1969 based on published data from the 1970 census (U.S. Bureau of the Census 1973). Data on the earnings of workers in different age categories in each industry were unavailable. Like the measures of occupational aspiration and occupational placement, the measure of industrial placement was converted to a z-score.

To study gender differences in wages at career entry, we sought a measure of entry into the adult labor force that would exclude short-term and partial attachments, such as summer and part-time jobs held during schooling. Analyzing event-history data from a study of Illinois high school students in 1957 and 1958 and a 15-year follow-up survey of the same individuals in 1973 and 1974, Marini (1987) examined the implications of alternative operational definitions of labor force entry. Her analysis indicated that entry into the adult labor force is measured most appropriately by either entry into the first full-time job held for at least six months or entry into the first full-time job held after leaving full-time education the first time. These two measures are equivalent for practical purposes, but they are not equivalent to entry into the first full-time job ever held (which includes jobs of short duration that bear little relationship to jobs held after leaving school, such as full-time summer jobs held while in school) or entry into the first full-time job after last leaving full-time education (which occurs at slightly later ages since for some individuals it occurs after some full-time employment and a return to schooling). In the present study, we measure career entry as entry into the first full-time civilian job held after leaving full-time education the first time, where a full-time civilian job was defined by three conditions: working at least 35 hours per week, not being enrolled in full-time schooling, and not being in the military. Wages at career entry are measured by the natural logarithm of the hourly wage rate. Wages are adjusted for inflation using the Consumer Price Index (CPI-U) and are measured in constant dollars with reference to the base period 1982 to 1984 (U.S. Bureau of Labor Statistics 1993:68–69).

Hypotheses

Effects of Worker Characteristics

We use measures of three categories of worker characteristics to analyze the extent to which gender differences in wages at career entry are attributable to gender differences in human capital, family structure, and work and family aspirations. Gender differences in each of these three types of influences could arise either because the mean levels (or amounts) of these variables differ for the two sexes or because the effects of these variables on earnings differ. Based on the results of earlier research, we hypothesize that men have more human capital or more *lucrative* human capital than women, but that no gender difference in the effect of human capital on earnings will occur (Corcoran and Duncan 1979). Because of gender differences in the timing of entry into marriage and parenthood and the sequencing of familial with nonfamilial role changes (Marini 1987), gender differences in family structure at career entry are also expected. Men are expected to be less likely to have married and to have dependents at career entry than are women. In addition, we expect family structure to have different effects on the earnings of the two sexes. Marriage and the number of dependents are expected to have positive effects on the earnings of men, but either no effects or negative effects on the earnings of women. We also hypothesize that men aspire to higher-paid occupations than women and that aspirations have a stronger effect on earnings for men than for women because men are more likely to realize their aspirations (Marini 1980; Sewell, Hauser, and Wolf 1980). We expect no gender difference in fertility aspirations, and controlling for the effects of other variables, we expect neither fertility aspirations nor gender-role attitudes to affect the earnings of either sex.

Role of Job Placement

We view wages as attached to jobs and the associations between job characteristics and wages as an integral part of a wage structure that exists at the macro level and emerges over time through both macro- and micro-level processes. We view individual wages as determined by the five explanatory mechanisms defined above, which match individuals to jobs as they enter the adult labor market

within an existing labor market structure of jobs and associated wages. Because we could directly observe the operation of three of the five hypothesized mechanisms by estimating the effects of measured worker characteristics on wages at career entry, we hypothesize that three categories of worker characteristics—human capital, family structure, and work and family aspirations—have causal effects on wages. However, the operation of two of the five hypothesized mechanisms, discrimination and social networks, could not be observed directly because measures were unavailable. To measure the combined operation of these two mechanisms indirectly, we estimate the extent to which gender differences in occupational and industrial placement help to account for gender differences in wages after the causal effects of gender differences in human capital, family structure, and work and family aspirations are taken into consideration. In doing so, we take as given the associations between occupational and industrial placement and wages, and we do not assume causal effects of occupational and industrial placement on wages.

Results

Table 1 presents the means and standard deviations for all variables for the total sample and by gender. The difference in mean wages by gender indicates that the wage gap at career entry is 16 percent: The women in our sample earn 84 cents for every dollar men earn.

Overall, men have somewhat more human capital and different types of human capital at career entry than do women, since they are somewhat more likely to obtain education in fields offering higher earnings, have more part-time labor force experience, and have higher self-esteem. Women out-perform men in high school, however, as indicated by their higher grade-point averages. Because women marry and become parents earlier than do men, the two sexes also differ in family cir-

TABLE 1
Means and Standard Deviations for Variables in the Analysis: Youth Ages 14 to 22 in 1979:
NLSY, Data Collected from 1979 to 1991

Variable	Total Sample (N = 5,119)		Women (N = 2,588)		Men (N = 2,531)	
	Mean	S.D.	Mean	S.D.	Mean	S.D.
Gender (woman = 1)	.506	.50	—	—	—	—
Race (non-White = 1)	.195	.40	.204	.40	.187	.39
Human Capital						
Years of Education / Major Field of Study						
< 12	.144	.35	.119	.32	.170	.37
12 / general, vocational	.305	.46	.315	.46	.295	.46
12 / college preparatory	.140	.35	.139	.35	.140	.35
13 / business, commerce	.020	.14	.025	.15	.015	.12
13 / natural science, engineering, computing	.015	.12	.008	.09	.023	.15
13 / social science, education, humanities	.021	.14	.025	.16	.018	.13
13 / law, medicine	.007	.08	.012	.11	.002	.05
13 / general, other	.014	.12	.013	.11	.016	.12
14–15 / business, commerce	.031	.17	.037	.19	.024	.15
14–15 / natural science, engineering, computing	.018	.13	.011	.10	.026	.16
14–15 / social science, education, humanities	.033	.18	.037	.19	.029	.17
14–15 / law, medicine	.015	.12	.026	.16	.004	.06
14–15 / general, other	.014	.12	.013	.11	.015	.25
16–17 / business, commerce	.053	.22	.047	.21	.058	.23
16–17 / natural science, engineering, computing	.037	.19	.022	.15	.052	.22
16–17 / social science, education, humanities	.080	.27	.096	.29	.065	.25
16–17 / law, medicine	.013	.11	.023	.15	.003	.05
≥ 16 / general, other	.011	.10	.011	.11	.011	.10
≥ 18 / business, commerce	.003	.06	.002	.04	.005	.07
≥ 18 / natural science, engineering, computing	.005	.07	.002	.04	.007	.09
≥ 18 / social science, education, humanities	.009	.09	.008	.09	.011	.10
≥ 18 / law, medicine	.009	.09	.007	.09	.011	.10
Part-time labor force experience	2.998	1.98	2.793	1.86	3.209	2.07
Developed mental aptitude	.481	.29	.474	.28	.489	.30
Knowledge of work	.671	.23	.667	.22	.676	.23
High school GPA	2.596	.68	2.713	.68	2.479	.67
Parents' education (mean)	11.746	2.91	11.641	2.94	11.853	2.89
Self-esteem	.033	.83	.004	.83	.062	.84
Family Structure						
Marital status (married = 1)	.218	.41	.284	.45	.151	.36
Number of dependents	.224	.62	.318	.72	.128	.47
Work and Family Aspirations						
Occupational aspiration	.018	1.00	−.299	1.07	.334	.81
Fertility aspiration	2.375	1.17	2.384	1.18	2.366	1.16
Gender-role attitudes	.066	.87	.283	.84	−.158	.84
Occupational/Industrial Placement						
Occupational placement	−.003	1.01	−.237	1.05	.236	.92
Industrial placement	−.018	1.03	−.202	1.15	.170	.84
Hourly Wage						
In dollars	5.270	2.52	4.827	2.23	5.726	2.72
Natural log	1.551	.50	1.465	.51	1.640	.48

cumstances at career entry: Women are more likely to be married and more likely to have dependents than are men. In addition, there are differences in the occupational aspirations and gender-role attitudes of the two sexes. Men aspire to higher-earning occupations and have more traditional gender-role attitudes than women. In contrast, the two sexes have similar fertility aspirations. And the occupations and industries in which men are employed pay higher wages than those in which women are employed.

Men's aspirations to enter higher-earning occupations than those aspired to by women reflect to a large degree the association between the sex type and earnings levels of occupations. Recent research indicates that young women value the extrinsic rewards of work as much as young men. Young men attach only slightly more importance than do young women to "a job which provides you with a chance to earn a good deal of money," and young women attach slightly more importance than young men to "a job that most people look up to and respect" (Marini et al. 1996). It is because both sexes to some degree demonstrate a preference for occupations held predominantly by members of their own sex that a consequential difference emerges between the earnings levels of occupations aspired to by the two sexes. It has been argued that if women prefer female-type jobs at lower wages to male-type jobs at higher wages, female-type jobs must have other advantages over male-type jobs (Filer 1985, 1989; Killingsworth 1985). Consideration of the skill requirements, working conditions, and other characteristics of occupations, however, has usually not accounted for the relationship between the sex composition of an occupation and its earnings level (Treiman and Hartmann 1981; Jacobs and Steinberg 1990; England 1992). It is therefore reasonable to infer that the sex type of the occupation itself is an important influence on occupational choice.

Table 2 presents parameter estimates from the regression of log wages at career entry on measures of three categories of worker char-

acteristics for the total sample and by gender. Because respondents in the sample were between the ages of 14 and 22 at the time of the first survey, 9.5 percent of women and 11.5 percent of men began careers prior to the year for which data were collected in that survey. Wages at career entry were therefore not measured for these respondents. To correct for possible bias resulting from censoring this sample, we used the procedure developed by Heckman (1979), which treats the bias resulting from sample censoring as a specification error or omitted variable problem. There was a small, statistically significant effect of sample selection for men and for the total sample, but not for women; however, the correction for sample censoring had no important consequences for the substantive results of our analysis. We therefore present the uncorrected results here.

We include a measure of gender in the analysis for the total sample and a measure of race in the analyses for both the total sample and the gender subgroups. With other measures of worker characteristics in the equation, race has no significant effect on wages in any of our analyses. We did not oversample members of racial minorities here because our objective was to generalize to the U.S. population as a whole. Elsewhere, we have oversampled African Americans and Hispanics in making racial comparisons (Fan and Marini 1995).

The results in Table 2 indicate an effect of gender on wages at career entry, even when the effects of gender differences in human capital, family structure, and work and family aspirations are held constant. This effect can be seen as attributable largely to *extra-individual* factors that produce wage differences between women and men. All the measures of human capital we examined have statistically significant effects on the wages of at least one sex, except for high school grade-point average. The effects of education, part-time labor force experience, and developed mental aptitude are slightly greater for women than for men, whereas the effects of

TABLE 2
Coefficients from the Regression of ln(Wages) at Career Entry on Gender, Race, Human Capital, Family Structure, and Work and Family Aspirations: Youth Ages 14 to 22 in 1979, NLSY, Data Collected from 1979 to 1991

Independent Variable	Total Sample (N = 5,119)		Women (N = 2,588)		Men (N = 2,531)	
	Coef.	t-value	Coef.	t-value	Coef.	t-value
Gender (woman = 1)	−.125	−7.72***	—	—	—	—
Race (non-White = 1)	.018	.90	.016	.55	.020	.71
Human Capital						
Years of Education / Major Field of Study						
12 / general, vocational	−.034	−1.47	.003	.08	−.051	−1.68*
12 / college preparatory	.025	.91	.043	1.06	.029	.74
13 / business, commerce	−.004	−.07	.044	.63	−.046	−.55
13 / natural science, engineering, computing	.148	2.48**	.201	1.80*	.119	1.68*
13 / social science, education, humanities	.071	1.37	.072	1.02	.099	1.27
13 / law, medicine	.036	.43	.098	1.03	−.093	−.47
13 / general, other	−.050	−.81	.049	.52	−.106	−1.29
14–15 / business, commerce	.078	1.70*	.159	2.59**	.004	.05
14–15 / natural science, engineering, computing	.001	.02	.070	.69	−.029	−.41
14–15 / social science, education, humanities	.054	1.21	.096	1.56	.037	.57
14–15 / law, medicine	.282	4.60***	.316	4.46***	.231	1.49
14–15 / general, other	−.011	−.17	.043	.47	−.061	−.72
16–17 / business, commerce	.267	6.54***	.312	5.09***	.245	4.44***
16–17 / natural science, engineering, computing	.400	8.63***	.419	5.31***	.400	6.80***
16–17 / social science, education, humanities	.153	4.20***	.208	4.05***	.107	2.02*
16–17 / law, medicine	.557	8.34***	.611	7.98***	.213	1.15
≥ 16 / general, other	.126	1.77*	.246	2.46**	.019	.19
≥ 18 / business, commerce	.593	4.89***	.681	2.75**	.578	4.14***
≥ 18 / natural science, engineering, computing	.427	4.03***	.489	2.19*	.419	3.45**
≥ 18 / social science, education, humanities	.280	3.59**	.350	2.99**	.248	2.37**
≥ 18 / law, medicine	.450	5.71***	.696	5.74***	.276	2.65**
Part-time labor force experience	.038	10.03***	.049	8.39***	.027	5.42***
Developed mental aptitude	.143	3.27***	.213	3.25**	.078	1.31
Knowledge of work	.097	2.46**	.043	.77	.151	2.72**
High school GPA	.005	.35	.022	1.11	−.021	−1.07
Parents' education (mean)	.004	1.39	.000	.09	.007	1.81*
Self-esteem	.043	4.73***	.035	2.69**	.057	4.37***
Family Structure						
Marital status (married = 1)	.008	.43	−.030	−1.28	.067	2.28*
Number of dependents	−.020	−1.60	−.011	−.75	−.015	−.68
Work and Family Aspirations						
Occupational aspiration	.043	5.60***	.031	3.08**	.056	4.39***
Fertility aspiration	.005	.84	.001	.19	.008	.94
Gender-role attitudes	.003	.29	.002	.17	.003	.26
Intercept	1.227		1.048		1.280	
R^2	.259		.281		.207	

Note: All correlations between the independent variables in Table 2 are less than .65 (data available from the authors).

*p < .05   **p < .01   ***p < .001 (one-tailed tests)

knowledge of work, parents' education, and self-esteem are slightly greater for men than for women. In keeping with the findings of most prior research (e.g., Corcoran and Duncan 1979; Hill 1979; Korenman and Neumark 1992b), our measures of family structure have no direct effect on women's wages. As repeatedly documented (e.g., Goldin 1990; Blackburn and Korenman 1994), however, marital status has a small positive effect on men's wages. Neither fertility aspiration nor gender-role attitudes has a direct effect on the wages of either sex. Occupational aspiration, in contrast, has a significant effect on the wages of both sexes. This effect is somewhat larger for men than for women, indicating that men's aspirations have more important consequences for earnings than do those of women, perhaps because men are more likely than women to realize their aspirations for high-earning occupations. As shown in Table 2, all measures of worker characteristics, including gender, account for less than 30 percent of the variance in earnings at career entry.

Because we view wages as attached to jobs, we do not enter measures of occupational and industrial placement as regressors in the equations in Table 2. Nevertheless, it is of interest to consider how much of the variation in wages at career entry is associated with differences in the occupations and industries in which individuals are employed. With the causal effects of relevant worker characteristics held constant, this association can be assumed to arise largely from the causal influences of employing organizations and networks on job placement, and therefore on individual wages. In Table 3, we report the proportions of variance in wages accounted for by each of six models, as well as the estimated direct effect of gender in these models. Model A considers the effect of gender alone. In subsequent models, additional variables are added. Model D is the equation for the total sample reported in Table 2. This model explains 25.9 percent of the variance in wages. As additional variables are added in Models C and D, the estimated direct effect of gender on wages declines. Whereas in Model A,

where the effect of gender alone is considered, the estimated effect of gender is −.174, in Model D, where other measures of worker characteristics are also considered, the estimated effect of gender is −.125. Thus, 28 percent ([−.174 + .125] / −.174) of the overall effect of gender on wages is attributable to the effect of gender on other measures of worker characteristics.

To consider the relationships of occupational and industrial placement to wages, we add measures of occupation and industry in Models E and F. The addition of occupational placement to the model increases the percent of variance in wages accounted for to 34.8 percent, and the addition of industrial placement increases the percent of variance in earnings accounted for to 40.0 percent. Of particular importance is our finding that much of the effect of gender on wages that is not attributable to gender differences in worker characteristics is associated with gender differences in occupational and industrial placement at career entry. Gender continues to have a statistically significant direct effect on wages, but it is small. Thus, much of the effect of gender on wages that is not attributable to the effect of gender differences in human capital, family structure, and aspirations is attributable to influences that produce gender differences in occupational and industrial placement within the labor market. This net association of occupational and industrial placement with gender differences in wages can be seen as resulting largely from the external influences of employing organizations and network processes. In Model F, the estimated direct effect of gender is −.051. The inclusion of measures of occupational and industrial placement therefore reduces the estimated direct effect of gender by an additional 42 percent ([−.125 + .051]/−.174). This change is attributable to the effect of gender on occupational and industrial placement, which in turn bears a relationship to wages. Together, the inclusion of measures of worker characteristics and occupational and industrial placement reduces the estimated direct effect of gender on wages by 70 percent.

TABLE 3
Direct Effects of Gender on ln(Wages) at Career Entry Estimated under Alternative Models:[a]
Youth Ages 14 to 22 in 1979, NLSY, Data Collected from 1979 to 1991

Model	Gender Effect	t-value	Model R^2
Model A: Gender	−.174	−11.12	.030
Model B: Gender, race	−.172	−11.04	.039
Model C: Gender, race, human capital, family structure	−.148	−9.91	.253
Model D: Gender, race, human capital, family structure, aspirations	−.125	−7.72	.259
Model E: Gender, race, human capital, family structure, aspirations, occupation	−.061	−3.97	.348
Model F: Gender, race, human capital, family structure, aspirations, occupation, industry	−.051	−3.45	.400

[a] These models estimate the additive effect of gender, ignoring interactions between gender and other variables.

More information on the effects of human capital, family structure, aspirations, and occupational and industrial placement on the gender gap in wages is presented in Table 4. Here, we decompose the gender gap in wages using estimates of the means and the effects of variables for each gender (Jones and Kelley 1984). The difference in average wages between men and women is expressed in terms of a component due to gender differences in the means of the explanatory variables and a residual (unexplained) component. Because it is arbitrary whether we use regression coefficients for women or men as the standard for evaluating the amount of the wage gap attributable to gender differences in means of the explanatory variables, we partition the wage gap using each as a standard. This procedure indicates the extent to which the choice of standard affects the estimates obtained. The results of the two two-fold decompositions are shown by:

$$(\ln W_m - \ln W_f) = \Sigma b_f (X_m - X_f)$$
$$+ \text{ unexplained differences;}$$

$$(\ln W_m - \ln W_f) = \Sigma b_m (X_m - X_f)$$
$$+ \text{ unexplained differences;}$$

where $\ln W$ is the mean of the natural logarithm of the hourly wage at career entry, X is the mean of an explanatory variable in the estimated wage equation, and b is the coefficient of an explanatory variable in the estimated wage equation. The subscript m represents males, and f represents females. We also summarize the results of the two decompositions by taking the average of the two estimates.

We use this approach to examine two models. In Model A, we consider only gender differences in worker characteristics. On average, differences in the means of these variables account for 29.7 percent of the gender gap in wages. Gender differences in occupational aspirations account for 16.0 percent of the gender gap in wages. Gender differences in either amount or type of human capital account for 14.3 percent of the wage gap,[6] and gender differences in family structure account for virtually none of the gap.

In Model B, we consider the effects of gender differences in worker characteristics and the effects of gender differences in occupational and industrial placement, which derive from the external influences of employing organizations and network processes. Because we view wages as being attached to jobs, we

TABLE 4
Contributions of Gender Differences on Independent Variables to the Gender Gap in ln(Wages)
at Career Entry: Youth Ages 14 to 22, NLSY, Data Collected from 1979 to 1991

	Model A				Model B			
	Slope			% Based on Average	Slope			% Based on Average
Source of Influence	Women[a]	Men[b]	Average		Women[a]	Men[b]	Average	
Difference (total) in levels on independent variables	.043	.061	.052	29.7	.129	.122	.126	72.0
Race	.000	.000	.000	0.0	.000	.000	.000	0.0
Human capital	.018	.033	.025	14.3	.022	.027	.025	14.3
Family structure	.006	−.006	.000	0.0	.000	−.003	−.001	−0.6
Occupational aspiration	.020	.035	.028	16.0	.007	.027	.017	9.7
Fertility aspiration	−.001	−.001	−.001	−0.6	.000	−.005	−.003	−1.7
Occupation	—	—	—	—	.045	.032	.039	22.3
Industry	—	—	—	—	.055	.044	.049	28.0
Unexplained differences (total)	.132	.114	.123	70.3	.046	.053	.049	28.0
Total gender difference in ln wages (men minus women)	.175	.175	.175	100.0	.175	.175	.175	100.0

[a]$\Sigma b_f (X_m - X_f)$

[b]$\Sigma b_m (X_m - X_f)$

did not enter measures of occupational and industrial placement as regressors in the equations in Table 2; nor did we consider their effect on the gender gap in wages in Model A. Nevertheless, it is of interest to investigate how much of the variation in wages at career entry is associated with differences in the occupations and industries in which individuals are employed, because when the causal effects of relevant worker characteristics are held constant, this association can be assumed to arise largely from the causal influences of employer discrimination and networks on job placement and, therefore, on individual wages as well.

After controlling for the effect of gender differences in worker characteristics, then, gender differences in occupational and industrial placement account, on average, for an additional 42.3 percent ([.126 − .052]/.175) of the gender gap in wages at career entry, bringing to 72.0 percent the total amount of the gap accounted for by differences in the levels of measured variables. Because we hold constant the effects of worker characteristics, including occupational aspirations, gender differences in wages associated with occupational and industrial placement largely reflect the external influences of employing organizations and of network processes. Occupational and industrial placement *uniquely* accounts for 42 percent of the gender gap in wages, and gender differences in measured worker characteristics account for 30 percent of the gender gap in wages. Since gender differences in occupational and industrial placement to some degree underestimate gender differences in job placement, this finding indicates that the gender gap in wages at career entry arises much more from external influences that place women and men in different jobs than from differences in individual characteristics such as career preparation, family structure, and aspirations.

Conclusions

We have proposed a new theoretical approach to the analysis of micro-level processes that produce gender differences in wages. We have argued that because a wage structure has evolved over time that is linked to well-defined systems of jobs and firms, it is important to distinguish between macro-level processes that have produced and continue to produce associations between occupational and industrial sectors and wages and micro-level processes that match individuals to jobs within an existing structure of jobs and associated wages at the time individuals enter the labor market. We identified five explanatory mechanisms operating at the micro level by which women and men can be sorted into different positions in the labor market that offer different levels of reward. We applied this framework to the analysis of gender differences in wages at career entry when women's wages are, on average, 84 percent of men's. Using better measures of job-related skills and credentials than have been used in most previous analyses, and including measures of family structure and detailed measures of work and family aspirations, we found that explanatory mechanisms focusing on the characteristics of workers explained only 30 percent of the gender difference in wages at career entry. Of three categories of worker characteristics studied, gender differences in aspirations were the most important in accounting for the gender wage gap, and gender differences in job-related skills and credentials were almost as important. Gender differences in family structure had no significant direct effect when the effects of worker qualifications and aspirations were considered.

Much of the wage gap between women and men that was not attributable to gender differences in worker characteristics was linked to occupational and industrial placement at career entry. This association suggests that extra-individual influences play an important role in wage determination at career entry. These influences include the alloca-tion of women and men to different jobs by employers, and informal processes of social contact and interaction via networks that provide access to job-related information and influence. Because the labor market is highly segregated by sex and this segregation is linked to wage differences, social influences external to the worker channel the two sexes into different entry-level jobs to which different wage rates are attached: Women are channeled into female-type jobs and men are channeled into male-type jobs. Our analysis indicates that even when the effects of worker qualifications and choices on job placement are effectively controlled by detailed measures, gender differences in job placement bear a strong and significant relationship to gender differences in wages. These findings on the micro-level processes that match individuals to jobs indicate (1) that the association between the sex composition of a job and its wage rate within the organizational structure of the labor market is perpetuated to some degree by micro-level processes that produce gender differences in the aspirations and qualifications with which workers enter the labor market, but (2) that this association is perpetuated even more by micro-level processes that operate at the point of career entry to channel women and men with the same aspirations and qualifications into different, sex-typed jobs.

Notes

An early version of this paper was presented at the World Congress of Sociology, Bielefeld, Germany, July 1994. Our work was supported by Grant R01-HD27598 from the National Institute of Child Health and Human Development and by funding from the College of Liberal Arts and the Graduate School of the University of Minnesota. We gratefully acknowledge the comments of the former *ASR* Editor (Paula England) and Robert M. Hauser, and the assistance of Velda Graham and Lisa Nguyen in typing the paper. Opinions expressed in the paper are ours and not necessarily those of the individuals who generously provided us with comments.

1. Our use of the term "human capital" refers broadly to individual characteristics that have a value in the labor market because of their actual or assumed effect on performance. We use the terms "human capital" and "skills and credentials" interchangeably.

2. To obtain a sample representative of the non-institutionalized civilian population of the United States in the sampled age cohorts, we excluded NLSY respondents in the oversamples of Blacks, Hispanics, and poor Whites.

3. Because responses to the Rosenberg Scale were measured on an ordinal scale, we assumed that each ordinal variable represented a latent continuous variable that was distributed normally with a mean of 0 and a variance of 1. We used PRELIS II, a preprocessor for LISREL, to compute the normal scores and estimate a matrix of polychoric correlations and an accompanying matrix of asymptotic variances and covariances. The polychoric correlations are estimates of the correlations between latent variables calculated from the observed pairwise contingency tables of the ordinal variables. The latent variables were assumed to have a bivariate normal distribution. With these matrices as input, we estimated a measurement model using the weighted least-squares fitting function in LISREL 8.

4. The analysis was done using the special tabulation that Charles B. Nam and Mary G. Powers made for the 1970 census, which we obtained from Robert M. Hauser and John Robert Warren. We also performed the analysis by calculating the natural log of the median annual earnings of all workers in the occupation in 1969 using published data from the 1970 census (U.S. Bureau of the Census 1973b). The results of this analysis were virtually identical to the results of the analysis based on the earnings of workers ages 18 to 34. To approximate the median hourly wage rate, we also tried dividing the median annual earnings of all workers by the product of the mean number of hours worked per week and the mean number of weeks worked per year. This measure of the median hourly wage rate of workers in the occupation did not perform as well as the measure of median annual earnings. Data on median annual earnings from the 1980 census would have provided a measure taken somewhat closer in time to the period when respondents in the NLSY sample first entered the full-time civilian labor force. However, we did not consider it necessary to use data from the 1980 rather than the 1970 census because differences in earnings across occupations (and industries) have been quite stable over time (Duncan 1968; Sobek 1996).

5. The six statements used to measure gender-role attitudes were: (1) A woman's place is in the home, not in the office or shop; (2) A wife who carries out her full family responsibilities doesn't have time for outside employment; (3) The employment of wives leads to more juvenile delinquency; (4) It is much better for everyone concerned if the man is the achiever outside the home and the woman takes care of the home and family; (5) Men should share the work around the house with women, such as doing dishes, cleaning, and so forth; (6) Women are much happier if they stay at home and take care of their family.

6. Of the gender differences in human capital examined, the gender difference in part-time work experience has the greatest effect, accounting for 8.8 percent of the wage gap. Gender differences in the amount and type of education have the next largest effect, but account for only 2.8 percent of the wage gap. Gender differences in the other measures of human capital have more negligible effects.

References

Becker, Gary S. 1981. *A Treatise on the Family.* Cambridge, MA: Harvard University Press.

Bielby, William T. and James N. Baron. 1984. "A Woman's Place Is with Other Women: Sex Segregation within Firms." Pp. 27–55 in *Sex Segregation in the Workplace: Trends, Explanations, Remedies,* edited by B. F. Reskin. Washington, DC: National Academy Press.

Blackburn, McKinley and Sanders Korenman. 1994. "The Declining Marital-Status Earnings Differential." *Journal of Population Economics* 7:247–70.

Blau, Francine D. 1984. "Discrimination against Women: Theory and Evidence." Pp. 53–89 in *Labor Economics: Modern Views,* edited by W. Darity, Jr. Boston, MA: Kluwer-Nijhoff.

Blau, Francine D. and Marianne A. Ferber. 1986. *The Economics of Women, Men and Work.* Englewood Cliffs, NJ: Prentice-Hall.

Blum, Zahava D. 1972. "White and Black Careers During the First Decade of Labor Force Experience. Part II: Income Differences." *Social Science Research* 1:271–92.

Campbell, Karen E. 1988. "Gender Differences in Job-Related Networks." *Work and Occupations* 15:179–200.

Corcoran, Mary, Linda Datcher, and Greg J. Duncan. 1980. "Information and Influence Networks in Labor Markets." Pp. 1–37 in *Five Thousand American Families—Patterns of Economic Progress,* vol. 8, edited by G. J. Duncan and J. N. Morgan. Ann Arbor, MI: University of Michigan.

Corcoran, Mary and Greg J. Duncan. 1979. "Work History, Labor Force Attachment, and

Earnings Differences between the Races and Sexes." *Journal of Human Resources* 14:3–20.

Cramer, James C. 1980. "The Effects of Fertility on Husband's Economic Activity: Evidence from Static, Dynamic, and Nonrecursive Models." *Research in Population Economics* 2:151–82.

Duncan, Otis Dudley. 1968. "Social Stratification and Mobility: Problems in the Measurement of Trend." Pp. 675–719 in *Indicators of Social Change: Concepts and Measurements,* edited by E. B. Sheldon and W. E. Moore. New York: Russell Sage Foundation.

Duncan, Otis Dudley, David L. Featherman, and Beverly Duncan. 1972. *Socioeconomic Background and Achievement.* New York: Seminar Press.

England, Paula. 1992. *Comparable Worth: Theories and Evidence.* New York: Aldine De Gruyter.

Fan, Pi-Ling and Margaret Mooney Marini. 1995. "Gender and Earnings at Career Entry: Racial and Ethnic Variation." Paper presented at the Population Association of America Annual Meeting, April, San Francisco, CA.

Filer, Randall K. 1985. "Male-Female Wage Differences: The Importance of Compensating Differentials." *Industrial and Labor Relations Review* 38:426–37.

———. 1989. "Occupational Segregation, Compensating Differentials, and Comparable Worth." Pp. 153–70 in *Pay Equity: Empirical Inquiries,* edited by R. T. Michael, H. I. Hartmann, and B. O'Farrell. Washington, DC: National Academy Press.

Gershuny, Jonathan and John P. Robinson. 1988. "Historical Changes in the Household Division of Labor." *Demography* 25:537–52.

Goldin, Claudia. 1990. *Understanding the Gender Gap: An Economic History of American Women.* New York: Oxford.

Granovetter, Mark. 1974. *Getting a Job: A Study of Contacts and Careers.* Cambridge, MA: Harvard University Press.

Heckman, James. 1979. "Sample Selection Bias As a Specification Error." *Econometrica* 47:153–61.

Hill, Martha S. 1979. "The Wage Effects of Marital Status and Children." *Journal of Human Resources* 14:579–94.

Jacobs, Jerry A. 1989. *Revolving Doors: Sex Segregation and Women's Careers.* Stanford, CA: Stanford University Press.

Jacobs, Jerry A. and Ronnie J. Steinberg. 1990. "Compensating Differentials and the Male-Female Wage Gap: Evidence from the New York Comparable Worth Study." *Social Forces* 69: 439–68.

Jones, F. L. and Jonathan Kelley. 1984. "Decomposing Differences between Groups: A Cautionary Note on Measuring Discrimination." *Sociological Methods and Research* 12:323–43.

Juster, F. Thomas. 1985. "A Note on Recent Changes in Time Use." Pp. 313–32 in *Time, Goods, and Well-Being,* edited by F. T. Juster and F. P. Stafford. Ann Arbor, MI: Institute for Social Research, University of Michigan.

Killingsworth, Mark. 1985. "The Economics of Comparable Worth: Analytical, Empirical, and Policy Questions." Pp. 86–115 in *Comparable Worth: New Directions for Research,* edited by H. Hartmann. Washington, DC: National Academy Press.

Korenman, Sanders and David Neumark. 1992a. "Does Marriage Really Make Men More Productive?" *Journal of Human Resources* 26:282–307.

———. 1992b. "Marriage, Motherhood, and Wages." *Journal of Human Resources* 27: 233–55.

Madden, Janice F. 1985. "The Persistence of Pay Differentials." *Women and Work* 1:76–114.

Marini, Margaret Mooney. 1980. "Sex Differences in the Process of Occupational Attainment: A Closer Look." *Social Science Research* 9:307–61.

———. 1987. "Measuring the Process of Role Change During the Transition to Adulthood." *Social Science Research* 16:1–38.

———. 1989. "Sex Differences in Earnings in the United States," *Annual Review of Sociology* 15:343–80.

Marini, Margaret Mooney and Mary C. Brinton. 1984. "Sex Typing in Occupational Socialization." Pp. 191–232 in *Sex Segregation in the Workplace: Trends, Explanations, Remedies,* edited by B.F. Reskin. Washington, DC: National Academy Press.

Marini, Margaret Mooney, Pi-Ling Fan, Erica Finley, and Ann M. Beutel. 1996. "Gender and Job Values." *Sociology of Education* 69:49–65.

Marini, Margaret Mooney and Beth Anne Shelton. 1993. "Measuring Household Work: Recent Experience in the United States." *Social Science Research* 22:361–82.

Marini, Margaret Mooney, Hee-Choon Shin, and Jennie Raymond. 1989. "Socioeconomic Consequences of the Process of Transition to Adulthood." *Social Science Research* 18:89–135.

Mincer, Jacob and Soloman W. Polachek. 1974. "Family Investments in Human Capital: Earnings of Women." *Journal of Political Economy* 82(supp.):S76–S108.

———. 1978. "Women's Earnings Reexamined." *Journal of Human Resources* 13:118–34.

Mincer, Jacob and H. Ofek. 1982. "Interrupted Work Careers: Depreciation and Restoration of Human Capital." *Journal of Human Resources* 17:3–24.

Ornstein, Michael D. 1976. *Entry into the American Labor Force.* New York: Academic Press.

Robinson, John P. 1988. "Who's Doing the Housework?" *American Demographics* 10: 24–28, 63.

Roos, Patricia A. and Barbara F. Reskin. 1984. "Institutional Factors Contributing to Sex Segregation in the Workplace." Pp. 235–60 in *Sex Segregation in the Workplace: Trends, Explanations, Remedies.* Washington, DC: National Academy Press.

Sandell, Steven H. and David Shapiro. 1978. "An Exchange: The Theory of Human Capital and Earnings of Women: A Reexamination of the Evidence." *Journal of Human Resources* 13:103–17.

Sewell, William H., Robert M. Hauser, and Wendy C. Wolf. 1980. "Sex, Schooling, and Occupational Status." *American Journal of Sociology* 86:551–83.

Sobak, Matthew. 1996. "Work, Status, and Income: Men in the American Occupational Structure since the Late Nineteenth Century." *Social Science History* 20:169–207.

Tomaskovic-Devey, Donald. 1993. "The Gender and Race Composition of Jobs and the Male/Female, White/Black Pay Gaps." *Social Forces* 72:45–76.

Treiman, Donald J. and Heidi I. Hartmann. 1981. *Women, Work, and Wages: Equal Pay for Jobs of Equal Value.* Washington, DC: National Academy Press.

Treiman, Donald J. and Kermit Terrell. 1975. "Sex and the Process of Status Attainment: A Comparison of Working Women and Men." *American Sociological Review* 40:174–200.

U.S. Bureau of the Census. 1973. *Census of Population: 1970. Subject Reports: Industrial Characteristics,* PC (2)–7B. Washington, DC: U.S. Government Printing Office.

———. 1973b. *Census of Population: 1970. Subject Reports: Occupational Characteristics* PC(2)-7A. Washington, DC: U.S. Government Printing Office.

———. 1987. *Male-Female Differences in Work Experience, Occupation, and Earnings: 1984.* Current Population Reports, Series P–70, No. 10. Washington, DC: U.S. Government Printing Office.

———. 1993. *Money Income of Households, Families, and Persons in the United States: 1992.* Current Population Reports Consumer Income Series P60–184. U.S. Department of Commerce. Washington, DC: U.S. Government Printing Office.

U.S. Bureau of Labor Statistics. 1993. Historical Consumer Price Index for All Urban Consumers (CPI-U): U.S. City Average, All Items, Annual Average. Washington. DC: U.S. Government Printing Office.

BARBARA STANEK KILBOURNE, PAULA ENGLAND,
GEORGE FARKAS, KURT BERON, AND DOROTHEA WEIR

Returns to Skill, Compensating Differentials, and Gender Bias: Effects of Occupational Characteristics on the Wages of White Women and Men[1]

Do employers pay both men and women in one occupation less than those in another occupation with equivalent demands for skill and equally onerous working conditions when a higher percentage of the workers in the second occupation are women or when the job requires skills, such as nurturant social skill, associated with women? These two kinds of gender bias are at issue in policy debates over comparable worth, often called "pay equity." We sketch and test a cultural feminist theory that predicts these two gendered processes of valuation. Is the sex gap in pay affected by women's and men's differential placement across occupations that vary in demands for cognitive, social, and physical skills and physically onerous working conditions? Neoclassical theories of human capital and compensating differentials suggest that these factors are important. Our findings below support some but not all the predictions from neoclassical theory and support our two predictions from cultural feminist theory.

Past Theorizing and Research

For an occupational characteristic to contribute to the sex gap in pay, two things must be true. First, women and men must be differentially distributed across occupations such that the jobs occupied by men and women have different average levels of this characteristic. Second, the characteristic must affect pay. We concentrate the review below on how occupational characteristics affect wages and which characteristics differentiate the jobs held by men and women.

The Neoclassical Theory of Human Capital

The neoclassical economic theory of human capital states that pay differences between individuals are explained by human capital, the stock of skills a person possesses (Becker 1971; Mincer 1974). In this view, employers have to pay more for skilled workers if gain-

Originally published in 1994. Please see complete source information beginning on page 891.

ing these skills was an "investment" (i.e., involved a present cost for a potential future benefit) that the marginal worker would not make without compensation. Marginalism is best understood by imagining workers lined up in order of how much compensation they would require to invest in this human capital, with those requiring no wage premium first. If we go down this line until the jobs are filled, the marginal worker is the last worker hired. The supply side of human capital theory contends that the marginal worker requires a return to be induced to invest in many kinds of human capital. The demand side of human capital theory states that profit-maximizing employers will hire more expensive skilled workers only in jobs where these extra skills increase productivity, and hence profits, enough to cover the higher labor cost (Lang and Dickens 1988).

Most studies operationalize human capital with years of schooling or job experience (which is a proxy for on-the-job learning). However, the theory should apply to all kinds of skills (cognitive, social, or physical) and to learning that takes place in any setting (in school, vocational training programs, and on-the-job training, or through informal socialization). It should also apply whether the prospective worker makes the investment or someone makes it on his or her behalf. All these types of learning involve either out-of-pocket costs (e.g., tuition) or opportunity costs (e.g., wages or leisure foregone while learning).

Human capital theory has implications for pay differences within and between occupations. Our interest is in the latter, so we review studies with occupational characteristics as independent variables. Occupations that require higher levels of cognitive skills and education pay higher wages (England and McLaughlin 1979; England, Chassie, and McCormick 1982; Steinberg et al. 1986; Parcel and Mueller 1989; Parcel 1989; England 1992). Some (Kohn and Schooler 1969; Cain and Treiman 1981; Parcel and Mueller 1989) refer to this as "substantive complexity." De-

spite its positive return for both men and women, this occupational dimension contributes little to the sex gap in pay, because the occupations in which women work require only slightly less of such skill (England et al. 1982; England 1992). Compared to men, women are in occupations requiring about the same level of education but offering less on-the-job training (Corcoran 1979; England 1992).

Findings regarding the effects of occupations' demands for physical skills on wages conflict. With few controls for working conditions, physical strength and other physical skills often show negative or no effects (England and McLaughlin 1979; England et al. 1982; Sorensen 1989b). Even with working conditions controlled, Parcel (1989) found the factor "physical dexterity/perceptual ability" to have no significant effects on 1980 wages of men or women. Parcel and Mueller (1989) found a similar factor to have a positive effect on men's 1970 wages but no significant effect on their 1980 wages or on women's 1970 or 1980 wages. With more elaborate controls for working conditions, England (1992, chap. 3) found net wage premiums for some physical skills, but they explain only a tiny percentage of the sex gap in pay.

How do demands for social skills affect wages? England and McLaughlin (1979) found that men, but not women, gain from working in jobs requiring social skills. However, their measure did not differentiate between the nurturant social skill involved in helping a customer or client and the authoritative social skill involved in managing or supervising other workers. To refine this, England (1992) distinguished two types of social skill, nurturance and authority. For both men and women, she found occupational demand for nurturant social skills to be penalized but for authority to be rewarded, and women's greater concentration in occupations requiring nurturance and men's in those requiring authority explains about 6% of the 1980 sex gap in pay. The New York State pay equity study also found that being in a supervisory position enhances pay and that demands for social skills such as communication with the public and group facilitation have net negative effects on wages (Steinberg et al. 1986; Jacobs and Steinberg 1990a). The positive return to supervisory social skill found in these studies is consistent but the negative return to nurturant social skill is inconsistent with human capital theory.

The Neoclassical Theory of Compensating Differentials

Sometimes occupations differ in pay even after adjustments for human capital requirements. If the differences endure, they cannot be explained by temporary disequilibria from shortages or gluts. Neoclassical theory explains these long-term disparities by the notion of compensating differentials (Smith 1979; Rosen 1986). In this view, the full pay of a job consists of both pecuniary (wage) and nonpecuniary compensation, the latter being the (dis)utility experienced while doing the work. This might include the interest, boredom, discomfort, or danger of the work. According to the theory, jobs with more comfortable, less hazardous working conditions can be filled with lower wages, ceteris paribus. How much higher the wage needs to be in onerous jobs depends on the tastes of the marginal worker (not the average worker). According to the theory, market forces require that the wage paid to the marginal worker in a job also be paid to all otherwise equivalent workers in the job (Smith 1979). A single analysis cannot both test the theory of compensating differentials and ascertain which working conditions are amenities and which are disamenities to the marginal worker. If the theory is assumed to be true, empirical tests of which working conditions have net positive (negative) returns tell us what conditions are perceived by the marginal worker as disamenities (amenities). Alternatively, if we assume that a given work-

ing condition is perceived by the marginal worker as a disamenity (amenity), then the test of the theory is whether it has a net positive (negative) effect on wages. We adopt the latter strategy, making our test subject to assumptions about what is a disamenity.

Our test of compensating differentials focuses on the physical discomfort and hazards associated with occupations (rather than on nonphysical disamenities). Smith's (1979) and Brown's (1980) reviews conclude that a compensating differential is found for the risk of death, but that findings for unpleasant and hazardous working conditions are inconsistent. Barry (1985) and Filer (1985) found that men, but not women, receive a premium for hazardous work. Sorensen (1989b) found that hazardous working conditions lower women's wages in predominantly female occupations. England (1992) found no penalties or premiums for hazards or other physical disamenities for either men or women. No significant effects of "undesirable working conditions" were found in 1970 or 1980 by Parcel and Mueller (1989) or Parcel (1989). Parcel and Mueller (1989) did find a factor that combined physical activities and physically onerous working conditions to yield wage premiums for women in 1970 and for both sexes in 1980. Jacobs and Steinberg's (1990a, p. 452; 1990b) analysis of New York State government jobs showed only one of 14 measures of onerous working conditions to have a statistically positive effect on pay (working with sick patients), while five such variables had significant negative effects (cleaning others' dirt, loud noise, strenuous physical activity, repetition, and being told what to do). Jacobs and Steinberg (1990a) also reviewed comparable worth studies from six other states and one county in New York and reported that onerous working conditions far more commonly had negative rather than positive effects on earnings.

Only one study has investigated compensating differentials with longitudinal data and a model with fixed effects similar to the method that we employ here (Duncan and

Holmlund 1983). Premiums were found for both men and women working in dangerous or physically taxing jobs. Overall, findings are mixed on whether job characteristics that we might assume to be physical disamenities lead to wage premiums.

Neoclassical Theory and Discrimination

Most neoclassical economists doubt the existence of the sort of gender bias in wage setting that we address here (Filer 1989; Killingsworth 1985). They do not believe that market forces will allow employers to pay a discriminatory wage (one lower than that predicted by human capital and compensating differentials) in certain occupations simply because those in the job are predominantly female or because the skills required are stereotypically associated with women. Some economists do posit "crowding," a situation in which predominantly female occupations pay less as a result of hiring discrimination against women who seek to enter predominantly male occupations (Bergmann 1986). The reasoning is that, because employers will not hire women in desirable "male" occupations, the supply of labor for "female" occupations is artificially increased, and thus wages in the female occupations are lowered. But the hiring discrimination in male jobs to which the crowding thesis traces the low wages in female jobs is itself an anomaly within neoclassical theory. Hiring discrimination, particularly that based on the tastes or biases of employers, should eventually be eradicated by competitive market processes (Arrow 1972; England 1992, chap. 2). The idea is that employers who will not hire women are paying a premium for male labor, making their profits lower, and making the probability higher that they will go out of business or lose product market share. Thus, economists generally doubt that gender bias lowers the wages of female occupations.

A Cultural Feminist Theory of Gendered Valuation

We label as "feminist" any perspective that denies the necessity of current levels of gender inequality in rewards, seeing such inequality to be socially constructed, at least in part. The normative portion of feminist theories argues that such inequality *should* be eradicated, while positive portions of feminist theory focus on the mechanisms that create and sustain such inequality. We offer a model of "gendered valuation" to provide part of the explanation for the sex gap in pay and other forms of gender inequality. The central proposition is that cultural processes of valuation are gendered; because women are devalued, social roles (including occupations) and skills that are associated with women are culturally devalued relative to those associated with men. This perspective is consistent with "cultural feminism," the label we use for feminist theories that see the devaluation of women and things associated with them as an important cause of gender inequality.[2]

If cultural values affect what jobs employers value more, and such valuation includes a bias against any job or skill associated with women, then we can predict that predominantly female occupations will pay less than predominantly male occupations, ceteris paribus. We can also predict that nurturant skill will be badly rewarded because of its association with women. Although we will test implications of this view for how occupational characteristics affect rewards, it has relevance to nonoccupational roles as well. Examples include the low level of economic security attached to child rearing and household work, whether done for pay or as a homemaker. Many societies devalue whatever tasks they assign to women, as this perspective would predict (Shepela and Viviano 1984).

Our choice of the terms "cultural" and "valuation" does not imply that we see an exogenous variable that is ideal rather than material. Materially based male power is undoubtedly one reason men succeed in getting their roles defined as more valuable and rewarded. We believe that material and ideal phenomena affect each other reciprocally, so that men's material resources are, at least in part, a product of men's roles being socially defined as more valuable. Our point in labeling the perspective "cultural" is to emphasize the role of the devaluation of typically women's activities in generating gender inequality. Such devaluation affects either men or women who do "women's work."

Sociological work on comparable worth provides evidence for this perspective. It documents a form of sex discrimination in which occupations are paid less than others with equivalent job content because they contain mostly women or involve skills associated with women. Studies have shown that the percentage female in an occupation has a net negative effect on pay, after controlling for occupations' demands for education, other measures of cognitive skill, physical skill, social skill, and onerous working conditions (England et al. 1982; Steinberg et al. 1986; England et al. 1988; Baron and Newman 1989; Parcel 1989; Sorensen 1989*a*; England 1992; see Sorensen [1989*c*] for a review). One mechanism of such devaluation may be the cognitive error of not seeing how much female occupations contribute to the "bottom line" of profit or other organizational goals. Or women's jobs may be devalued because they are erroneously believed to require less effort than men's jobs, because typically female types of effort are culturally invisible. Once interoccupational wage differences are in place, institutional inertia keeps gender-biased interjob wage difference in force.

Another gendered form of devaluation relevant to occupational wage setting is the devaluation of a skill because it is usually (or has historically been) exercised by women (Steinberg and Haignere 1987; Steinberg 1990). Because of these gendered associations, such skills may be devalued across occupations with a range of sex compositions; thus, this is not the same thing as devaluation due to the current sex composition of an occupation. A good example of a skill type associated with women is nurturant skill, the sort of social skill involved in providing a face-to-face service to clients or customers of an organization. Such activity is seen as female because of its relationship to the nurturant behavior entailed in parenting, done primarily by women, and because nurturant paid jobs are usually filled by women.

Our review (above) of research on returns to social skills supported our perspective on gendered devaluation more than it supported human capital theory. Human capital theory suggests that all skills should have positive returns if they require investment. Yet, in those few studies that measured nurturant social skills, occupations requiring such skill were found to pay less than occupations with no such requirement, controlling for other skill demands, working conditions, and the current sex composition of the occupations (Steinberg et al. 1986; England 1992, chap. 3; England et al. 1994). Our analysis will take nurturant skills to be the exemplar of a skill associated with women and will test whether it is devalued. We will consider it to be devalued relative to other skill types if it has either no returns or negative returns.

Sociologists' findings about the devaluation of female occupations and nurturant work are consistent with broader interdisciplinary feminist literature criticizing the devaluation of emotional work in Western culture. The contributions made by emotional nurturance and intimacy have been downplayed in developmental and clinical psychology—seen as natural, original states to be overcome rather than skills to be developed to help oneself and others have a full life (Gilligan 1982; Kittay and Meyers 1987; Keller 1986). The devaluation of emotions is also seen when philosophers of science regard emotional connection as a contaminating distorter rather than a possible route to knowledge (Keller 1985; Schott 1988). The disinclination to use words denoting work for emotional work in sociological theories is also evidence of such devaluation.

This is seen in the words Parsons (1954) chose for the "instrumental/expressive" distinction. He chose the term "expressive" to describe the traditionally female tasks of child rearing and household work, a term that connotes self-indulgence rather than work.

Specific Research Hypotheses

On the basis of the review above, we test predictions from neoclassical and cultural feminist theory. Table 1 summarizes the testable predictions. All are for net effects. No differences in returns for men and women are predicted. The neoclassical theory of human capital predicts positive returns to individual-level skill, measured here by experience and education, and to occupational demands for any kind of skill—cognitive, physical, authoritative, or nurturant. It predicts no effect of occupational sex composition, since discrimination of any form is believed to erode in competitive markets. The neoclassical theory of compensating differentials predicts positive returns to physical disamenities since employers will be unable to fill more onerous jobs without paying a premium. The cultural feminist theory of gendered valuation generates two predictions—that the percentage female in one's occupation has a negative effect on wages and that nurturant social skills are devalued because of their association with women, and thus have either no return or a negative return. (A return of zero would constitute devaluation if other skill types received positive returns.)

Data, Model, Variables, and Hypotheses

Data

We analyze data from the young women's and the young men's cohorts of the National Longitudinal Survey (NLS). The data are from a national probability sample of women aged 14–24 in 1968 and of men aged 14–24 in 1966. We use 1968, 1969, 1970, 1971, 1972, 1973, 1975, 1977, 1978, and 1980 female waves and 1966, 1967, 1968, 1969, 1970, 1971, 1973, 1975, 1976, 1978, 1980, and 1981 male waves, pooling the male and female data together. Each of the male and female panels contains approximately 5,000 individuals. (The data are described in Center for Human Resource Research, Ohio State University [1983].) We confine analysis to whites. We have arranged the longitudinal data into a pooled cross-section time series in which the unit of analysis is an individual in a particular year. We deleted person-years in which the individual was not employed or was employed part-time (less than 35 hours per week).

Fixed-Effects Regression Model and Decomposition

We use a model with fixed effects (Judge et al. 1982) to control for otherwise unmeasured year-specific (period) and person-specific effects. The model is

$$Y_{it} = b_0 + \Sigma b_k X_{kit} + e_{it}, \qquad (1)$$

where

$$e_{it} = u_i + v_t + w_{it}. \qquad (2)$$

Regression coefficients are denoted by b, k indexes measured independent variables (X's), i indexes individuals, t indexes time periods, e is error terms, u is the cross-sectional (individual) component of error, v is the timewise component of error, w is the purely random component of error, and b_0 is the intercept. The dependent variable, Y, is the natural logarithm of hourly earnings. Because period effects on earning are controlled, it is not necessary to change earnings to constant dollars. The resulting coefficients are those that would be obtained if dummy variables for year and person had been included in OLS regression equations. We obtain these coefficients from this OLS model:

$$Y_{it}^* = b_0 + \Sigma b_k X_{kit}^*, \qquad (3)$$

TABLE 1
Predicted Signs and Coefficients from Models Predicting ln Hourly Wage

Variable	Coefficients	Coefficients for Interaction with Sex	Sign Predicted by Theories	
			Neoclassical	Cultural Feminist
Individual characteristics:				
Experience	.0018*/*	.0001*	+	NP
	(114.4)	(5.5)		
Education	.1134*/*	−.0117*	+	NP
	(47.4)	(6.4)		
Married	.1123*/	−.1162*	NP	NP
	(18.5)	(11.8)		
Occupational skill demands:				
Cognitive skill	.0237*/*	.0632*	+	NP
	(5.4)	(7.9)		
Physical skill	.0367*/*	NS[a]	+	NP
	(7.7)			
Authoritative skill	.0057*/	−.0117*	+	NP
	(2.6)	(2.2)		
Nurturant skill	−.0252*/*	−.0210*	+	− or 0
	(5.6)	(3.1)		
% female	−.0004*/*	−.0006*	0	−
	(2.4)	(2.5)		
Physical disamenities:				
Hazards	−.0247*/*	.0628*	+	NP
	(5.3)	(6.7)		
Hot and wet	−.0080*/*	.0362*	+	NP
	(2.4)	(3.7)		
Cold	.0070*/*	−.0303*	+	NP
	(2.5)	(2.4)		

Note. —Asterisk before slash denotes significance ($P < .05$, two tailed test) for men; asterisk after slash denotes significance for women. See text. All interaction terms are the variable in the row multiplied by sex (female = 1); asterisk without slash denotes a significantly different return for men and women. Regression also included industry dummies. Where interactions with sex are included, the coefficient on the main effect (the individual or occupational characteristic) is the effect for men (because, since men were "0," the interaction is "0" times some number, and thus equals "0" for men). The coefficient on the interaction reveals how different the effect of the variable is for women than men. Thus, the effect for women is the main effect plus the coefficient on the interaction. NP = no prediction. $N = 29,810$. Figures in parentheses are t-statistics.

[a] Interaction of sex and physical skill demand not included in this model because it was not significant when a model that included it was run.

where

$$Y_{it}^{\star} = Y_{it} - \overline{Y}_i - \overline{Y}_t + \overline{Y}, \qquad (4)$$

and

$$X_{it}^{\star} = X_{it} - \overline{X}_i - \overline{X}_t + \overline{X}. \qquad (5)$$

That is, an OLS regression is fitted after subtracting from each variable its person mean and year mean and adding the grand mean (across person-years).[3]

The fixed-effects model yields estimates of the effects of occupational characteristics that are free from the sort of selection bias that results from misspecification due to omitted variables. The estimators are not contaminated with spurious effects of any stable, unmeasured individual characteristics that affect both earnings and the occupations into which individuals are selected. Such characteristics include sex, cohort, socioeconomic background, and unchanging aspects of skill, motivation, work habits, preferences, plans, and any other unmeasured human capital. Effects of these variables are controlled for by subtracting the person-mean from each observation; that is, persons serve "as their own controls." Thus, the model ensures that effects we attribute to occupational characteristics are not spurious results of the kinds of workers who enter such occupations. (Of studies reviewed above, only England et al. [1988] and Duncan and Holmlund [1983] used fixed effects.)

We use the regression results to decompose the sex gap in pay. A common technique is to decompose group differences in a dependent variable into proportions due to (1) different means on the independent variables, (2) different slopes, (3) different intercepts, and (4) an interaction between differences in slopes and intercepts. We can distinguish between (2) and (3) only when all independent variables have a nonarbitrary zero point (Jones and Kelley 1984; Aldrich and Buchele 1986), which is not true for our scales, which are based on the *Dictionary of Occupational*

Titles (*DOT*). Moreover, sex differences in men's and women's rates of return to occupational characteristics may reflect within-occupation differences. We are not interested in these here, but rather in differences in pay created by men and women's different distribution across occupations. Thus, we focus on how differences between men and women in their means on variables measuring occupational placement explain differences in their earnings. We ascertain this by multiplying the sex difference in mean for each variable by the slope that indicates its rate of return. Since we include interactions of all variables with sex, yielding information on the size of effect for men and women separately in cases of significant interactions, we face the problem of whether to use male or female coefficients. We provide both estimates, thus providing upper- and lower-bound estimates.

Variables from the NLS

The natural logarithm (ln) of current hourly earnings is our dependent variable. Thus, coefficients, when multiplied by 100, reveal the percentage increase in wages for each one-unit increase in the independent variable.[4] Independent variables include marital status (presently married or not), hours usually worked per week on the current job, the percentage female (in 1970) in one's detailed census occupation,[5] education, employment experience, and industry. Education is the number of years of schooling completed by the survey year. Experience is the total number of weeks of employment (whether full- or part-time) since one year prior to the first survey wave.[6] Industry is measured by collapsing the 1960 detailed census industry categories into dummy variables: (1) agriculture, forestry, fisheries, mining, and construction, (2) manufacture of durable goods, (3) manufacture of nondurable goods, (4) transportation, communication, and other public utilities, (5) wholesale trade, (6) retail trade, (7) finance, insurance, and real estate,

(8) business services, (9) personal services, (10) professional services, (11) entertainment and recreational services, and (12) government. These variables are included to control for the possibility that occupations with a high percentage of women are concentrated in marginal industries. Some analyses have found women overrepresented in such industries (Beck, Horan, and Tolbert 1980; Hodson and England 1986; Coverdill 1988). Controlling for industry is based on the assumption that industries with low wages do not have low wages because of the sex composition of occupations in the industry, but because of factors such as low profits, lack of oligopoly, and labor-intensive production. However, we also report on models (results not shown) that exclude industry. These are the preferred models if we assume that industries' overall wage levels are affected by a preponderance of heavily female occupations. Our basic conclusions hold with either model.

Measurement of the Skill Demands and Working Conditions of Occupations

Regressions include factor-guided scales measuring the demands of one's occupation for cognitive skill, physical skill, and nurturant social skill and measuring three physical working conditions assumed to be disamenities—exposure to hazards, exposure to hot and wet conditions, and exposure to cold. The scales were constructed from manipulations involving a set of occupational characteristics from the fourth edition of the *DOT* (U.S. Department of Labor 1977) and are described in Kilbourne, England, Farkas, Beron, and Weir (1994). We also computed a dummy variable for whether the occupation requires the exercise of authority, measured by coding as "1" occupations with "supervisor" or "manager" in their title. The normalized score for this variable enters the regressions.

Findings

Table 1 presents unstandardized coefficients from regression models with fixed effects. Since the occupational scales were formed by computing unweighted averages of Z (standardized) scores for several DOT (or other) items, with the Z scores standardized across all black and white men and women, the coefficients (times 100) reveal the percentage change in wage associated with one of these units on the scale. We included the interaction of each independent variable with sex, coding females as "1" on the dummy variable for sex; after ascertaining which interactions were significant, we reestimated the equation including only significant interaction effects; table 1 presents this final model. When interaction effects are significant, this means that the return on this independent variable is significantly different for men and women and that the women's slope differs from the men's by the amount of the coefficient on the interaction effect. The coefficients other than interactions can be interpreted as the returns for men, since males are coded "0" and hence the interaction term of sex times the independent variable is zero for men. The significance of the slope for men is given by the significance of these coefficients. We tested separately for the significance of the female coefficients (by running a model in which sex was coded so males were "1," so that coefficients on noninteractive independent variables reveal effects for women); table 1 reports significance levels for both men and women (before and after the slash, respectively) separately.

Table 1 shows positive and significant effects of education and experience, consistent with individual-level predictions from human capital theory, with significant but trivial differences between men's and women's returns. The unusually large returns to education seen here reflect the fact that our measure of education is only time varying across person-year observations that occur after the first full-time job during survey years. Since fixed-effects wage models base coefficients on how individuals' changes on predictors relate to changes in wages, the education coefficients measure rates of return to years of education after first job, which are larger than returns for earlier years of education. Being married has significantly positive effects on men's wages, but nonsignificant effects on women's.

Human capital theory predicts positive returns to cognitive skill demands. A positive and significant effect is found for both men and women (table 1), and the return is significantly larger for women ($.0237 + .0632 = .0869$). Women gain over 8% for every one-unit increase on the cognitive skill demand scale; men gain over 2%. If we exclude education from the equation, and let any returns to the greater average education of those in jobs requiring more cognitive skill be included in the coefficients for cognitive skill, the effects (not shown) become slightly larger ($.0654$ for men and $.1074$ for women), but still significantly larger for women.

Human capital theory also predicts that occupations requiring more physical skill will pay more. Table 1 shows a significant coefficient on physical skill of $.0367$, which does not vary significantly by sex; it indicates that moving to a job requiring one more unit of physical skill increases earnings by over 3%.

Human capital theory also predicts that occupations requiring more authoritative social skill will pay more. Table 1 shows a significant positive return for men, such that those one unit higher on the authority scale make $.57\%$ more. Yet the significant negative interaction effect shows returns to be significantly lower for women than for men; returns for women are nonsignificant.

The last kind of occupational skill demand considered is nurturant social skill, for which human capital theory predicts a positive return while the cultural feminist theory of gendered valuation predicts a negative or zero return. We find a significantly negative return for both men and women. The significant coefficient $-.0252$ shows that each one unit increase in occupations' demand for nurturant social skill lowers men's wages by over 2% (table 1). Women's return is significantly more negative; the significant coefficient for the interaction term shows that the effect for women is $-.0462$ ($-.0252 + [-.0210] = -.0462$), indicating a loss in pay of over 4% for each one unit of increase in nurturant social skill. This is evidence of a devaluation of nurturance, which we believe results from the association of nurturance with women. It is contrary to the positive return predicted by human capital theory and is also contrary to the contention of neoclassical theory that all forms of gender bias should erode in competitive markets.

The cultural feminist theory of gendered valuation predicts a negative effect of occupations' percentage female on wages, while neoclassical theory predicts no effect. The significant coefficient of $-.0004$ tells us that men's wages decrease $.04\%$ for each one-point increase in occupational percentage female (table 1). Thus, if a man moved 100 units of percentage female, from an all-male to an all-female occupation, his pay would go down by about 4%. This effect is significantly larger for women ($-.0004 + [-.0006] = -.0010$), indicating that women would lose 10% of their pay from such a move from a male to a female occupation, assuming the occupations are equivalent in their skill demands and disamenities. This negative effect on wages of being in a predominantly female occupation indicates a gendered process whereby occupations are devalued if they contain more women. Insofar as our scales adequately control for occupations' demands for skills and working conditions, our findings contravene the neoclassical view that gender discrimination cannot persist in competitive labor markets and that any earnings differences between male and female occupations are explained by differing requirements for human capital or (dis)amenities leading to compensating differentials.

Physical disamenities are predicted by the neoclassical theory of compensating differentials to have positive effects on wages. Table 1 shows that being in an occupation involving one extra unit of hazards significantly depresses men's wages by over 2% but signifi-

TABLE 2
Univariate Statistics and Decomposition of ln Wage Gap between Men and Women:
Percentage of Gap Explained by Mean Differences on Independent Variables

Variable	Pooled Mean	Pooled SD	Range	Male Mean	Female Mean	Percentage Explained	
						Male Slope*	Female Slope*
Indiv. characteristics:							
Experience (weeks)	302.04	207.65	0–1,198	319.37	270.50	21	24
Education (years)	12.99	2.40	0–18	13.04	12.89	4	4
Married	.62	.49	0–1	.65	.55	3	0
Occ. skill demands:							
Cognitive skill	.11	.90	−2.00–2.76	.15	.05	1	2
Physical skill	.05	.73	−1.16–2.25	.07	.02	0	0
Authoritative skill	.13	1.22	−.32–3.41	.29	−.15	1	−1
Nurturant skill	.06	.90	−1.05–1.64	−.10	.36	3	5
% female	37.76	34.36	.40–99.00	19.51	70.97	5	12
Physical disamenities:							
Hazards	−.03	.88	−.65–3.66	.20	−.46	−4	6
Hot and wet	−.02	.80	−.24–7.84	.05	−.15	0	1
Cold	−.04	.87	−.13–14.89	0	−.11	0	−1
Industry dummies**						2	2
Wage ($/hr)	4.55	3.14	.03–57.80	5.26	3.24		
ln Wage (ln ¢/hr.)	5.92	.64	1.10–8.66	6.06	5.65		

* Percentage of gap explained is $(\overline{X}_m - \overline{X}_f)\, b/.413$, where $\overline{X}_m$ is male mean, $\overline{X}_f$ is female mean, b is slope (taken or computed from table 1), and .413 is difference between male and female ln wage.

** Results from computing percentage explained for each industrial dummy and summing across them.

cantly increases women's wages by over 3% (−.0247 + .0628 = .0381). Working in an occupation with hot or wet conditions depresses men's wages by a trivial but significant amount and increases women's wages by a significant amount—over 2% for a one-unit change (−.0080 + .0362 = .0282). Exposure to cold conditions provides men with a positive compensating differential, although its magnitude is trivial—an increase of .7% for a one-unit change in cold; however, women receive a significant wage penalty of about 2% (.0070 + [−.0303] = −.0233). Thus, of the six tests for compensating differentials for physical disamenities (three variables × two genders), all are significant, but only three show

the predicted positive returns, and all are very modest in size. If these constructs do indeed measure disamenities for the marginal worker, the theory's prediction of compensating differentials for physical disamenities receives quite limited support.

We next use the regression results, together with sex differences in means on each of the variables, to perform a decomposition of the sex gap in pay. Our goal is to ascertain how much women's and men's placement into occupations differing in their skill demands, working conditions, and sex composition affects the sex gap in the log of pay. Table 2 presents various descriptive statistics, including sex-specific means. Its rightmost two columns present the percentage of the logged wage gap explained by sex differences in means for each independent variable. If this percentage is computed by multiplying the sex difference in mean by the male slopes, and dividing by the total gap in log of pay, we answer the question of what percentage of the gap would be closed if men moved to the female mean, but retained their own rate of return. With female slopes, we assess what would happen if women moved to the male mean but retained their own rate of return. We present both; they can be considered lower- and upper-bound estimates of the contribution of sex differences in means to the pay gap.

Table 2 shows that the sex gap in pay in these data was $2.02, with full-time young women workers earning 62% of the male average. (Recall that wages are in dollars current to the year in question, from 1966 to 1981, so dollar amounts would be much larger in 1981 or in present dollars.) The gap in logged cents per hour, .413, is what is formally decomposed here. Starting with the individual-level variables, table 2 shows that men, on average, have almost one year (48 more weeks) more experience than women. This explains 21%–24% of the sex gap in pay, depending on whether female or male slopes are used. Men's tiny edge over women in education (about .1 year) explains 4% of the pay gap.[7] Thus, individual-level human capital, in the form of employment experience, is one major component of the sex gap in pay, as other studies have also shown (Corcoran and Duncan 1979), but the role of education in the sex gap in pay is very minor.

Table 2 shows that men are in occupations that require, on average, one-tenth (.10) of a unit more cognitive skill. Thus, despite fairly large returns to cognitive skill, this variable explains only 1%–2% of the sex gap in pay. Physical skills contribute less than .5%. This small contribution results from the relatively small mean sex difference in combination with the relatively low returns. Although men, on average, tend to work in occupations

that require them to exercise more authority, the returns to authority are small for men and insignificant for women. Thus, at least among these young workers, authority explains virtually none of the sex gap in pay.

None of the three working conditions make contributions of more than 1% to the pay gap, with the exception of hazards, which explain 6% if female slopes are used. However, hazards contribute negatively if men's negative returns are used, since men are in occupations that score higher on hazards and they face a net penalty for being in such jobs. Overall, then, even though men are more likely than women to be in occupations with those types of physical disamenities we measured, the lack of consistent compensating differentials for physical disamenities for either sex makes these conditions unimportant in explaining the sex gap in pay.

How much of the sex gap in pay is explained by gendered devaluation of occupations because they contain women or require skills associated with women? With respect to effects of occupational sex composition, the average man was in an occupation that was 20% female and the average woman in an occupation that was 71% female, which gives a mean sex difference for this variable of 51%. This explains between 5% and 12% of the sex gap in pay. We took the net negative effect of requirement for nurturant social skills to be evidence of a gendered process by which skill types associated with women are devalued. Women and men differ by .46 units in the mean level of required nurturant social skill of their occupations, with women in occupations requiring more. This difference explains between 3% and 5% of the pay gap, depending on the slope used. If we add the contributions of the devaluation based on occupational sex composition and on nurturant social skill demands, they explain between 8% (if male slopes are used) and 17% (if female slopes are used) of the sex gap in pay. This is evidence that gendered processes of valuation of occupations and skills have an appreciable effect on the sex gap in pay.

Conclusions

Overall, our findings regarding the individual characteristic of experience confirms the importance of human capital theory in explaining between a fifth and a quarter of the sex gap in pay. However, neither occupation-level demands for cognitive or physical skill nor physical disamenities explain much of the sex gap in pay. Thus, the mechanism through which occupational sex segregation produces a sex gap in pay is not that women are in occupations with low skill demands and less onerous working conditions. Rather, in accordance with the cultural feminist theory of gendered valuation, the processes determining which occupations pay well are gendered, such that occupations lose pay if they have a higher percentage of female workers or require nurturant skill.

What do our conclusions contribute to theory? We found some support for both the neoclassical theory of human capital and for the cultural feminist theory of gendered valuation. We found little support for the neoclassical prediction that occupations involving physical disamenities will provide wage premiums as compensating differentials or for the neoclassical contention that discrimination disappears from unaided market forces. Our interpretations hinge on certain assumptions, which we reiterate here.

We interpret the coefficient on occupational percentage female to indicate gender bias in wage setting that devalues female occupations. This interpretation is not vulnerable to the criticism that female occupations contain individuals lower on unmeasured human capital or on motivation to maximize pay, because our use of a fixed-effects model controls for all unchanging, unmeasured differences between individuals. The conclusion does, however, depend on the assumption that our model adequately controls for pay-relevant occupational characteristics. A neoclassical economist might argue that the effect is the spurious result of some unmeasured occupational characteristics, correlated with percent-

age female, that are amenities to the marginal worker and thus lead to lower pay according to the theory of compensating differentials. Alternatively, a neoclassical economist willing to admit that gender bias of some sort is at issue, but not willing to admit that occupations are devalued because of their sex composition, might argue that female occupations pay less because they are more crowded than male occupations and see this crowding in female occupations to result from hiring discrimination against women seeking entry into male occupations.

We claim that the negative return to nurturant social skill indicates bias, the gendered devaluation of these skills because of their association with women. A neoclassical interpretation would be that there is no needed return to human capital of this type because the marginal worker likes nurturant work so much that he or she is willing to learn these skills without compensation and is even willing to take a lower wage for the nonpecuniary pleasure of doing such work. We find this interpretation implausible, but cannot categorically reject it.

We take the lack of consistently positive effects of working conditions that we presume the marginal worker would find onerous as evidence against the theory of compensating differentials. Our interpretation hinges on the assumption that these are disamenities to the marginal worker. An alternative interpretation is that these are not disamenities to the marginal worker, and that other occupational characteristics that are disamenities to the marginal worker do show compensating differentials. While this is possible, we are at least confident that we have demonstrated the lack of consistent compensating differentials for hazards, and for working conditions that are unusually wet, hot, or cold.[8]

If the reader is willing to make the assumptions we have made, our findings suggest a role for both human capital theory and the cultural feminist theory of gendered valuation in explaining between-occupation wage differences and the sex gap in pay.

Notes

1. This research was supported by grants from the National Science Foundation and the Rockefeller Foundation to Paula England and George Farkas. We thank Mark Hayward for providing machine-readable data from the *Dictionary of Occupational Titles* for 1960 categories. The data were assembled by Thomas Daymont and Ronald D'Amico.

2. Echols (1983) and Alcoff (1988) use the term "cultural feminism" to refer to feminism that revalorizes traditionally female activities that have been devalued because of sexism *and* sees women's nurturing as innate or essential to being a woman. We include the former valuation but not the latter essentialism in our definition of cultural feminism.

3. Without correction, t statistics from the model in equation (3) would be inflated because degrees of freedom are not reduced to take account of the implicit variables for persons and time periods. To correct for this, we multiplied standard errors by $\sqrt{NT - K} / \sqrt{NT - N - T - K + 1}$ (where N is the number of individuals, $T = 12$, the number of time periods, and K is the number of independent variables in the model).

4. This is true only for small changes in the independent variable. This is because of an analogue to compound interest and is particularly acute with dummy variables. However, for the coefficients here, making a correction (Halvorsen and Palmquist 1980) changes the results little and thus is not reported.

5. NLS data code respondents' occupation in 1960 census categories. We merged the percentage female in 1970 categories in each 1960 category onto the file from documentation in the codebook for the National Longitudinal Survey of Mature Women.

6. NLS data provide no measure of employment experience prior to a year before the survey. However, given our fixed-effects model, any additive effects of unmeasured prior experience are controlled. Our model includes experience since one year before the first survey wave. In each wave, respondents were asked how many weeks they were employed in the prior year. We added these entries to compute work experience accumulated by any given year. For the years in which no survey was conducted (1974 and 1979 for women and 1972, 1974, 1977, and 1979 for men), we averaged the experience reported for the preceding year and the following years and used this average as an estimate for the missing year. We have not included the square of years of experience to capture diminishing returns to experience in the later life cycle because of the youth of our sample.

7. This is undoubtedly an overestimate of education's role in the sex gap in pay. The fixed-effects model captures the returns to education obtained after the first full-time job. They are about double those found in most other studies, which suggests that returns to "adult" schooling are greater than returns to earlier schooling. However, the decomposition takes the mean differences between men and women for education obtained at any time and multiplies them by education coefficients that pertain only to postjob education. This is an unfortunate side effect of fixed-effects modeling, but one we think is outweighed by the other benefits of such modeling.

8. England (1992) finds evidence of compensating differentials, but only on nonphysical (dis)amenities, and they make no contribution to the sex gap in pay.

References

Alcoff, Linda. 1988. "Cultural Feminism versus Post-structuralism: The Identity Crisis in Feminist Theory." *Signs* 13:405–36.

Aldrich, Mark, and Robert Buchele. 1986. *The Economics of Comparable Worth*. Boston: Ballinger.

Arrow, Kenneth. 1972. "Models of Job Discrimination." Pp. 83–102 in *Racial Discrimination in Economic Life,* edited by A. Pascal. Lexington, Mass.: Lexington, Heath.

Baron, James N., and Andrew E. Newman. 1989. "Pay the Man: Effects of Demographic Composition on Wage Rates in the California Civil Service." Pp. 107–30 in *Pay Equity: Empirical Inquiries,* edited by H. I. Hartmann and R. Michael. Washington, D.C.: National Academy.

Barry, J. 1985. "Women Production Workers: Low Pay and Hazardous Work." *American Economic Review* 75:262–65.

Beck, E. M., Patrick H. Horan, and Charles M. Tolbert II. 1980. "Industrial Segmentation and Labor Market Discrimination." *Social Problems* 28:113–30.

Becker, Gary S. 1971. *Human Capital: A Theoretical and Empirical Analysis with Special Reference to Education,* 2d ed. New York: Columbia University Press.

Bergmann, Barbara. 1986. *The Economic Emergence of Women.* New York: Basic.

Brown, Charles. 1980. "Equalizing Differences in the Labor Market." *Quarterly Journal of Economics* 94:113–34.

Cain, Pamela S., and Donald J. Treiman. 1981. "The *DOT* as a Source of Occupational Data." *American Sociological Review* 46:253–78.

Center for Human Resource Research, Ohio State University. 1983. *National Longitudinal Sur-*

veys Handbook. Columbus, Ohio: Center for Human Resource Research.

Corcoran, Mary, and Greg J. Duncan. 1979. "Work History, Labor Force Attachments, and Earnings Differences between the Races and Sexes." *Journal of Human Resources* 14:3–20.

Coverdill, James E. 1988. "The Dual Economy and Sex Differences in Earnings." *Social Forces* 66 (4): 970–93.

Duncan, Greg J., and Bertil Holmlund. 1983. "Was Adam Smith Right After All? Another Test of the Theory of Compensating Wage Differentials." *Journal of Labor Economics* 1: 366–79.

Echols, Alice. 1983. "The New Feminism of Yin and Yang." Pp. 439–59 in *Powers of Desire: The Politics of Sexuality,* edited by Ann Snitow, Christine Stansell, and Sharon Thompson. New York: Monthly Review.

England, Paula. 1992. *Comparable Worth: Theories and Evidence*. Hawthorne, N.Y.: Aldine de Gruyter.

England, Paula, Marilyn Chassie, and Linda Mc-Cormick. 1982. "Skill Demands and Earnings in Female and Male Occupations." *Sociology and Social Research* 66:147–68.

England, Paula, George Farkas, Barbara Stanek Kilbourne, and Thomas Dou. 1988. "Explaining Occupational Sex Segregation and Wages: Findings from a Model with Fixed Effects." *American Sociological Review* 53:544–58.

England, Paula, Melissa S. Herbert, Barbara Stanek Kilbourne, Lori L. Reid, and Lori Mc-Creary Megdal. 1994. "The Gendered Valuation of Occupations and Skills: Earnings in 1980 Census Occupations." *Social Forces,* in press.

England, Paula, and Steven McLaughlin. 1979. "Sex Segregation of Jobs and Male-Female Income Differentials." Pp. 189–213 in *Discrimination in Organizations,* edited by R. Alvarez, K. Lutterman, and associates. San Francisco: Jossey-Bass.

Filer, Randall K. 1985. "Male-Female Wage Differences: The Importance of Compensating Differentials." *Industrial and Labor Relations Review* 38 (3): 426–37.

———. 1989. "Occupational Segregation, Compensating Differentials and Comparable Worth." Pp. 153–70 in *Pay Equity: Empirical Inquiries,* edited by Robert T. Michael, Heidi I. Hartmann, and Brigid O'Farrell. Washington, D.C.: National Academy.

Gilligan, Carol. 1982. *In a Different Voice: Psychological Theory and Women's Development.* Cambridge, Mass.: Harvard University Press.

Halvorsen, Robert, and Raymond Palmquist. 1980. "The Interpretation of Dummy Variables in Semilogarithmic Equations." *American Economic Review* 70:474–75.

Hodson, Randy, and Paula England. 1986. "Industrial Structure and Sex Differences in Earnings." *Industrial Relations* 25:16–32.

Jacobs, Jerry A., and Ronnie J. Steinberg. 1990a. "Compensating Differentials and the Male-Female Wage Gap: Evidence from the New York State Comparable Worth Study." *Social Forces* 69 (2): 439–68.

———. 1990b. "Compensating Differentials and the Male-Female Wage Gap: A Reply." *Social Forces* 69 (2): 475–78.

Jones, F. L., and Jonathan Kelley. 1984. "Decomposing Differences between Groups: A Cautionary Note on Measuring Discrimination." *Sociological Methods and Research* 12:323–43.

Judge, George, R. C. Hill, W. E. Griffith, H. Lutkepohl, and T. Lee. 1982. *An Introduction to the Theory and Practice of Econometrics.* New York: Wiley.

Keller, Catherine. 1986. *From a Broken Web: Separation, Sexism, and Self.* Boston: Beacon.

Keller, Evelyn Fox. 1985. *Reflections on Gender and Science.* New Haven, Conn.: Yale University Press.

Kilbourne, Barbara Stanek, Paula England, George Farkas, Kurt Beron, and Dorothea Weir. 1994. "Returns to Skill, Compensating Differentials, and Gender Bias: Effects of Occupational Characteristics on the Wages of White Women and Men." *American Journal of Sociology* 100 (3): 689–719.

Killingsworth, Mark. 1985. "The Economics of Comparable Worth: Analytical, Empirical, and Policy Questions." Pp. 86–115 in *Comparable Worth: New Directions for Research,* edited by Heidi Hartmann. Washington, D.C.: National Academy.

Kittay, Eva Feder, and Diane T. Meyers. 1987. *Women and Moral Theory.* Totowa, N.J.: Rowan & Littlefield.

Kohn, Melvin L., and Carmi Schooler. 1969. "Class, Occupation and Orientation." *American Sociological Review* 34:659–78.

Lang, Kevin, and William Dickens. 1988. "Neoclassical Perspectives on Segmented Labor Markets." Pp. 65–88 in *Industries, Firms and Jobs: Sociological and Economic Approaches,* edited by George Farkas and Paula England. New York: Plenum.

Mincer, Jacob. 1974. *Schooling, Experience and Earnings.* New York: National Bureau of Economic Research.

Parcel, Toby. 1989. "Comparable Worth, Occupational Labor Markets and Occupational Earnings: Results from the 1980 Census." Pp. 134–52 in *Pay Equity: Empirical Inquiries,* edited by Robert T. Michael, Heidi I. Hartmann, and Brigid O'Farrell. Washington, D.C.: National Academy.

Parcel, Toby, and Charles W. Mueller. 1989. "Temporal Change in Occupational Earnings Attainment, 1970–1980." *American Sociological Review* 54:622–34.

Parsons, Talcott. 1954. *Essays in Sociological Theory.* New York: Free Press.

Rosen, Sherwin. 1986. "The Theory of Equalizing Differences." Pp. 641–92 in *Handbook of Labor Economics,* vol. 1. Edited by O. Ashenfelter and R. Layard. New York: Elsevier.

Schott, Robin May. 1988. *Cognition and Eros: A Critique of the Kantian Paradigm.* Boston: Beacon.

Shepela, S. T., and A. T. Viviano. 1984. "Some Psychological Factors Affecting Job Segregation and Wages." Pp. 47–58 in *Comparable Worth and Wage Discrimination,* edited by Helen Remick. Philadelphia: Temple University Press.

Smith, Robert S. 1979. "Compensating Wage Differentials and Public Policy: A Review." *Industrial Labor Relations Review* 32 (3): 339–52.

Sorensen, Elaine. 1989a. "Measuring the Effect of Occupational Sex and Race Composition on Earnings." Pp. 49–69 in *Pay Equity: Empirical Inquiries,* edited by Robert T. Michael, Heidi I. Hartmann, and Brigid O'Farrell. Washington, D.C.: National Academy.

———. 1989b. "Measuring the Pay Disparity between Typical Female Occupations and Other Jobs: A Bivariate Selectivity Approach." *Industrial Labor Relations Review* 42:624–39.

———. 1989c. "The Wage Effects of Occupational Sex Composition: A Review and New Findings." Pp. 57–79 in *Comparable Worth: Analyses and Evidence,* edited by M. Anne Hill and Mark Killingsworth. Ithaca, N.Y.: ILR Press.

Steinberg, Ronnie J. 1990. "Social Construction of Skill: Gender, Power, and Comparable Worth." *Work and Occupations* 17:449–82.

Steinberg, Ronnie J., and Lois Haignere. 1987. "Equitable Compensation: Methodological Criteria for Comparable Worth." Pp. 157–82 in *Ingredients for Women's Employment Policy,* edited by C. Bose and G. Spitze. Albany: State University of New York Press.

Steinberg, Ronnie J., Lois Haignere, C. Possin, C. H. Chertos, and K. Treiman. 1986. *The New York State Pay Equity Study: A Research Report.* Albany: State University of New York, Center for Women in Government.

U.S. Department of Labor. 1977. *Dictionary of Occupational Titles,* 4th ed. Washington, D.C.: Government Printing Office.

TONY TAM

Why Do Female Occupations Pay Less?

Background

For the past two decades, scholars of gender inequality in the labor market have sought to understand why occupations with more female workers tend to pay less. This question addresses a robust finding about occupational sex composition and wages: studies based on different samples, units of analysis, and statistical techniques almost always find significant wage effects of occupational sex composition even after accounting for a wide range of personal attributes and occupational characteristics. The evidence of lower wages in "female occupations" (i.e., occupations that are disproportionately female) may reflect subtle gender discrimination. Instead of wage discrimination against *female workers*, gender discrimination may take the form of wage discrimination against *female work*.

The finding of persistent wage effects of occupational sex composition is socially important because it offers crucial support for comparable worth policies. The comparable

Originally published in 1997. Please see complete source information beginning on page 891.

worth movement has long identified occupational wage inequality as a major source of gender inequity in the labor market. The movement claims that there is widespread valuative discrimination against female work, as suggested by research in the laboratory and by surveys of prestige ratings of occupations. Thus the typical comparable worth policy in the United States seeks to equalize wages for occupations (within a firm) that differ mainly in sex composition.

Human Capital and Specialization

The main competing interpretations in the literature on occupational sex composition effects are (a) the devaluation hypothesis that female work is deemed less important and thereby *culturally devalued* (England et al. 1988), and (b) the specialized human capital hypothesis that female occupations require, on average, less substantial investments in *specialized skills* (Tam 1997). The devaluation hypothesis simply refers to a general cultural devaluation of women's labor — a special case of discrimination against women. In a female occupation, *all* workers in the occupation are subject to the devaluation effect. By contrast, the specialized human capital hypothesis claims that the apparent wage penalties against female occupations arise mainly from occupational differences in specialized training. In essence, the same worker is expected to receive different wages for occupations associated with different training requirements for specialized human capital, which may be occupation specific, industry specific, or firm specific.

Human capital may be general (e.g., reading skills and health) or specialized (e.g., knowledge of computer science). Although any investment in human capital is costly, an investor in specialized human capital faces an additional opportunity cost because specialized skills by definition have restricted applicability. For instance, a medical doctor cannot expect to recoup the training cost of attending medical school by becoming a high school

teacher, even if s/he may one day find teaching in high school the most personally gratifying occupation. But a specialized skill also tends to earn higher returns than does a general skill that requires the same amount of training time. The lower pay attached, on average, to female occupations may thus arise because such occupations require less substantial investments in specialized human capital. The sources of sex segregation by specialized training requirement are outside the purview of this paper, but one might hypothesize that (a) employers for occupations requiring specialized human capital may avoid hiring women, (b) specialized occupations discourage potential female recruits because the work environment is often hostile (by virtue of employer or coworker behavior), and (c) women have relatively stronger incentive than men to make training investments that can pay off in many lines of work.

The devaluation hypothesis of course does not deny the existence of market forces in wage determination. The key point of contention is whether gendered cultural bias has sufficiently distorted the market's wage-setting process to generate substantial, unexplained sex composition effects. The specialized human capital hypothesis claims that it does not and that the apparent sex composition effects can be explained by taking account of occupational differences in specialized human capital. This hypothesis is a plausible application of human capital theory but, unfortunately, has never been properly tested in the literature.

Weak Old Tests and Strong New Evidence

The empirical tests necessary for adjudicating between the two hypotheses are surprisingly difficult to achieve, as is the measurement of the extent and degree of discrimination in general (Heckman 1998). There are many traps that would invalidate a test or misguide the interpretation of a finding.[1] Recently I have reexamined the evidence for the devalua-

TABLE 1
Description of Variables

Variable	Description	Mean	SD
Wage	Hourly wage is the ratio of weekly earnings and usual weekly hours.	9.679	5.497
SMSA	1 = residing in a standard metropolitan statistical area, 0 = otherwise.	.725	.446
South	1 = residing in the South, 0 = otherwise.	.303	.459
West	1 = residing in the West, 0 = otherwise.	.181	.385
Midwest	1 = residing in the Midwest, 0 = otherwise.	.272	.445
Veteran	1 = ever in the armed forces, 0 = otherwise.	.160	.366
Union	1 = union member or under union contract, 0 = otherwise.	.187	.390
School	Years of schooling completed.	14.028	2.632
Experience	Potential work experiences, estimated by age – school – 5.[1]	17.702	12.177
Tenure	Years with current employer.	6.779	7.721
Full-time	1 = usually work at least 35 hours a week, 0 = otherwise.	.829	.376
PWOM	Women as a proportion of workers in respondent's occupation.	.465	.324
SVP	Years of specific vocational training for an occupation.[2]	1.977	1.611

Note: The data are for whites in the expanded May 1988 CPS. Most of the valid Ns are 23,019 or slightly less. Valid Ns for experience and tenure are 19,666.

1. For consistency, negative values of experience are recoded "0."

2. From England and Kilbourne's (1988) match of SVP (*DOT*, 4th ed.) with three-digit 1980 census occupations.

---

tion hypothesis and showed that there are strong reasons to question its validity (Tam 1997).

The first reason is a crucial bias in the evidential strategy. The establishment of general empirical support for the devaluation hypothesis essentially follows a "residual" approach because of the difficulty in developing any direct measure of devaluation in survey data. That is, the empirical support for the hypothesis crucially hinges on the existence of substantial and unexplained (i.e., residual) wage penalties against female occupations. The more comprehensive are the theoretically relevant control variables and the larger are the residual effects among workers with comparable characteristics, the stronger is the evidence in favor of the devaluation hypothesis. Virtually all quantitative tests of the devaluation hypothesis adopt this strategy. Nevertheless, this evidential strategy is biased in favor of the devaluation hypothesis because of the potential for omitted-variable bias and, most important, measurement errors in correlated control variables (Tam 2000). Past tests and evidence have been produced and interpreted without taking any account of measurement error and thus fail to provide critical support for devaluation.

The second reason for skepticism is new counter-evidence that simultaneously contradicts the devaluation hypothesis and confirms the specialized human capital hypothesis (Tam 1997, 2000). This evidence uses the May 1988 Current Population Survey (CPS) as the main source of data. Appended to the CPS are two constructed variables: the sex composition (PWOM) of three-digit census occupations, and occupation-specific training time (SVP, measured in years) derived from the fourth edition of the Dictionary of Occupational Titles (DOT). Table 1 describes the key variables used in the analysis.

Table 2 presents the core results that show the extent to which occupation-specific (SVP) and/or industry-specific (INDUSTRY) training can explain PWOM effects. The first major finding pertains to white female workers.

TABLE 2
Regressions of Log Hourly Wages on Demographic, Human Capital, and Industry Variables

	White Women				White Men			
	(1)	(2)	(3)	(4)	(5)	(6)	(7)	(8)
PWOM	−.158	−.187	.011#	−.007#	−.224	−.094	−.141	.002#
	(.016)	(.016)	(.017)	(.018)	(.018)	(.019)	(.018)	(.019)
SVP			.088	.078			.065	.069
			(.004)	(.004)			(.003)	(.003)
INDUSTRY		Yes		Yes		Yes		Yes
		(56.792)		(50.145)		(51.883)		(54.429)
Adjusted R^2	.403	.470	.440	.496	.452	.503	.482	.532

Note: Variables included in all models are South, West, Midwest, SMSA, veteran, union, school, experience and its square, tenure and its square, and full-time. INDUSTRY denotes the control for 22 industries: construction, education, financial/insurance/real estate, wholesale, retail trade, medical (except hospital), hospital, agriculture, mining, manufacturing of durable goods, manufacturing of nondurable goods, postal, other transportation, other utilities, private household service, business/repair, personal services (except private household), entertainment/ recreation, welfare/religious, other professional services, forestry/fisheries, and public administration/armed forces. Nos. in parentheses are standard errors, except that F-statistics are reported for industry effects. N = 9,269 for (1) and (2), 9,265 for (3) and (4), 10,383 for (5) and (6), 10,372 for (7) and (8). Data are for whites in the May 1988 CPS.

Not significant at the .05 level; other presented coefficients are significant at the .05 level.

The gross PWOM effect (−.255, not shown in the table) is substantially reduced (−.158) after controlling for a set of basic variables. This PWOM effect is still negative and substantial, apparently confirming a wage disadvantage against female occupations. However, after adding occupational differences in two measures of specialized human capital, column 4 of table 2 shows that there is virtually no occupational sex composition effect left to be explained. Comparing the coefficients of PWOM across columns 1–4 of table 2 reveals that SVP is the key explanatory variable. After controlling for SVP, the PWOM effects are dramatically reduced to .011 and −.007 without and with control for industry effects, respectively. This finding therefore contradicts the devaluation hypothesis at any reasonable level of statistical significance.

The devaluation hypothesis implies that women's work is devalued for all incumbents (i.e., men and women alike) and via the same cultural process. Columns 5-8 of table 2 examine this implication. After controlling for specialized human capital (SVP and INDUS-

TRY), the PWOM effect among white men becomes practically zero (.002), as was the case for white women (−.007). Equally significant, the model with INDUSTRY alone (column 6) or SVP alone (column 7) fails to fully account for the PWOM effect (−.094 and −.141, respectively) among white men. These results therefore suggest that the sex composition effects among men and women are attributable to gender-specific occupational differences in specialized human capital.

These two results strongly suggest that the PWOM effects are mediated by specialized human capital differences and that the sources of the wage effects of sex composition are gender specific. Both findings contradict the devaluation hypothesis. Moreover, both findings are remarkably robust across racial groups, as shown in Tam (1997, p. 1674). There is absolutely no wage penalty against female occupations: not among women or men, not among whites or blacks.[2]

These striking results are hard to reconcile with a devaluation story but are consistent with the specialized human capital hypothesis. Occupational sex composition is just a handy proxy for unobserved specialized human capital investment. In a related article (Tam 2000), I have further demonstrated that even seemingly supportive findings for the devaluation hypothesis can be accurately predicted (i.e., numerically reproduced) under the specialized human capital hypothesis by assuming a modest level of measurement errors. In sum, the accumulated evidence to date is remarkably strong for the specialized human capital hypothesis.

Positional Capital and Allocative Inequality

Jobs are highly differentiated, interconnected, and form a social structure. Some jobs are more conducive to further opportunities for specialized training, and only certain jobs will generate returns to the specialized skills of a worker. Not surprisingly, jobs are often the focus of career investment, just as human capital is. The capital value of a job is high if it provides the necessary gateway to the accumulation of specialized human capital or the unique promotion path to other jobs that can make the most use of the skills of a worker. The "positional capital" of a worker is made up of the worker's portfolio of ever-occupied jobs that can provide long-term returns in addition to income (Tam 1998). To the extent that male and female occupations offer different positional capital, any discriminatory job allocation by sex could have profound long-term impacts on women's labor market outcomes even in the absence of devaluation of female occupations.

Notes

This essay draws on analyses and arguments that are presented in more detail elsewhere (Tam 1997,

2000). The research presented here was supported by Academia Sinica through the Organization-Centered Society Project and the Institute of European and American Studies.

1. For instance, it is poorly understood that market prices are not determined by the preferences of the average or majority of buyers and sellers, but set at the margin by the final set of exchanges that align supply and demand. The result is that discriminatory intentions, attitudes, and behavior can be pervasive while market wages remain competitive (nondiscriminatory) under a wide variety of scenarios.

2. As Tam (1997) has further demonstrated, these results are reinforced by the fact that there is a large wage advantage, instead of disadvantage, for female occupations among women working part-time. Also, see Tam (1997) for a discussion of various fallback defenses of the devaluation hypothesis, all of which can be shown to be untenable.

References

England, Paula, George Farkas, Barbara S. Kilbourne, and Thomas Dou. 1988. "Explaining Occupational Sex Segregation and Wages: Findings from a Model with Fixed Effects." *American Sociological Review* 53:544-558.

England, Paula, and Barbara S. Kilbourne. 1988. *Occupational Measures from the Dictionaries of Occupational Titles for 1980 Census Detailed Occupations* (MRDF). ICPSR no. 8942. Ann Arbor, Mich.: Inter-University Consortium for Political and Social Research.

Heckman, James J. 1998. "Detecting Discrimination." *Journal of Economic Perspectives* 12 (2):101-116.

Tam, Tony. 1997. "Sex Segregation and Occupational Gender Inequality in the United States: Devaluation or Specialized Training?" *American Journal of Sociology* 102:1652-1692.

———. 1998. "Getting Ahead in the Labor Market: The Positional Capital Approach." Paper presented at the 14th World Congress of Sociology, Montreal, Canada, July 26-August 1.

———. 2000. "Occupational Wage Inequality and Devaluation: A Cautionary Tale of Measurement Error." *American Journal of Sociology* 105:1741-1760.

STANLEY LIEBERSON

Understanding Ascriptive Stratification: Some Issues and Principles

Ascriptive stratification based on gender and age is virtually universal, and ethnic-racial stratification is almost as widespread.[1] However, the specific issues in ascriptive stratification that capture public attention vary widely over time and place, often shifting in dramatic and sometimes unanticipated ways. For example, at different times prominent black-white issues in the United States have included slavery, lynching, discrimination in college fraternities, voting rights, membership in labor unions, de jure school segregation, affirmative action, the underclass, assimilation, Jim Crow laws, residential segregation, and race riots.[2]

The reader will notice that many of the issues confronted in the articles about gender stratification are similar to those discussed in the readings addressing ethnic-racial stratification. These include a variety of work-related problems: inter-group competition for desirable jobs; gaps in income; segregation in occupations; and the disadvantage groups face from the discriminatory behavior of employers, supervisors, and other workers. In both forms of stratification, this focus in turn leads to an understandable interest in whether the magnitude of the gaps and disadvantages are declining through the years. In each case, there is recognition that a variety of "universalistic" factors may be contributing to group disadvantages, such as differences in skills,

This is an original article prepared for this book.

education, and work patterns. Moreover, there is the question of whether these universalistic factors are becoming more or less important relative to the operation of racial or gender discrimination. This question motivates the use of various control variables as a way of evaluating all of the possible influences that may be responsible for an observed gap, as well as determining their relative importance for the outcome. The reader will also note that a number of the papers on both gender and ethnic groups find it helpful to use the notion of queuing to analyze the job market. Queuing refers to a preferential hiring of applicants based on their gender and/or race. (Although not discussed in any of the readings, queuing is almost certainly a valuable tool for thinking about age discrimination in employment as well.) Another common consideration is political and economic power, and the role of group differences in power as a product of disadvantage and simultaneously a cause of disadvantage.

Some other issues, such as comparable worth, are more of a problem for one type of stratification than the other. There are grounds for considering whether the evaluation of the monetary "worth" of a job is influenced by the predominant gender or racial makeup of the incumbents. But it appears to be a stronger consideration for the jobs that have high concentrations of women. Likewise, a central problem is the search for the factors causing women and various ethnic-racial groups to have less attractive jobs or lower incomes. But some of the causes that are investigated are specific to one form of inequality. For example, the location of many blacks in the inner city creates transportation problems that make it difficult to seek employment opportunities in distant suburbs. On the other hand, the difficulty in obtaining (and affording) suitable daytime childcare is an issue faced by many women—regardless of race or ethnic origin.

Whether or not all of the possible causes are the same for each ascriptive group, there is a common analytical problem. Namely, if one finds causes that are not directly a function of discrimination, a separate matter is how far do these causes go in explaining the gaps? In other words, how relevant are they? If they account for only a small part of the total gap, it would be a mistake to overstate their importance in explaining the gender or racial gaps observed. We see this confronted in a number of studies in this section which recognize the possibility of multiple causes and, in turn, attempt to determine the relative importance of each. Racial residential segregation provides a very nice illustration of this sort of question. On the one hand, we know that housing costs vary between neighborhoods, and we also know that whites and blacks differ in their incomes and their wealth. Can one say that these facts account for the very high levels of residential segregation between races? The answer is in the negative since excellent techniques make it clear that only a small part of the high level of segregation is attributable to racial differences in income coupled with the uneven spatial distribution of housing costs.

There are, of course, yet other considerations that are wholly distinctive to each type of stratification. In the case of racial and ethnic issues, a number of the papers touch on questions of generational change. As we compare the immigrant generation to the second generation (i.e., the American-born offspring of immigrants), and so on through the generations, to what degree do the groups experience socioeconomic progress over time in the United States? And, if the groups differ in their progress over time in the United States, what accounts for these gaps? Do they reflect something about the groups? Their timing of arrival? The situation encountered here? The host society? These questions are difficult to answer because not only does American society change through the years, but also changing are the major groups migrating to the United States. If the experience of new immigrant groups in the United States changes over the decades, it is difficult to sort out the relative role of the society's change and the group differences. Several papers attempt to tease out the answers.

Housing is also an issue that is uniquely important for race-ethnic relations. This issue involves matters of residential segregation, the nature of neighborhoods in which groups live, and the enormous handicap that blacks face in wealth accumulation due to discrimination in the operation of the housing market in America.

The readings included here on ascriptive processes are largely directed at issues in the United States, particularly those of a contemporary nature. The reading by Bonacich, on labor markets and ethnic conflict, is the only one to also directly analyze problems of ethnic relations in both the United States and elsewhere. And most of the readings on gender are directed at the United States, although there are three exceptions: the international comparison of sex segregation by Grusky and Charles, and the readings by Firestone and by Hartmann examine the broader contours of gender relations. This emphasis on American issues is understandable, but there is a danger of thereby ignoring broad considerations that operate in a wide variety of specific situations. These general principles of ascriptive stratification remain relatively stable and are applicable to a range of settings; they will remain so even as the specific content changes in the years ahead. Specific contemporary events can be understood as reflecting these broader underlying issues.

As a supplement to the readings offered on these topics, I address here three issues:

(1) some important differences among types of ascribed stratification that are *not* adequately drawn out in the readings for this section; (2) the macrosocietal issues that are common to all forms of ascriptive stratification (but, again, are not adequately drawn out in the readings); (3) the special difficulties in studying ascriptive stratification. Space limitations prevent an extensive treatment in this brief essay, but the lines of thought suggest further consideration for researchers, theorists, and students.

Differences

Observing both similarities and differences in the questions asked by scholars of gender and racial-ethnic stratification, it is appropriate to first consider the more fundamental, structural differences and similarities between these two forms of stratification. All forms of ascribed stratification have certain common features: By definition, they provide differential opportunities, rewards, privileges, and power to individuals based exclusively on criteria fixed at birth that the individual is normally unable to alter. At issue here is whether there are any inherent differences among these types of stratification. This inquiry is different from asking if the disadvantages are of an equal magnitude in a given society—for example, whether the gender gap in income is of the same magnitude as the racial gap, or whether the stereotypes about older people are more unfavorable than those about some other ascribed population. Rather, there are two separate theoretical questions: First, how do age, gender, and ethnic subordination differ in their impact on individuals? Secondly, how do these forms of stratification differ in their impact on societal maintenance?

From the perspective of a given individual, each form of stratification has different consequences. For those experiencing a full life cycle, age stratification is "equitable" under conditions of societal stability—the ascribed disadvantages at one age compensate for the ascribed advantages of another. If seniority provides older persons certain advantages at work, for example, then younger workers will expect similar privileges as they age. Likewise, if young adults aid their aging parents, then they will in turn expect similar support from their own children. In periods of change or societal instability, or for those who cannot expect a full life cycle, the interchange of age-based advantages and disadvantages may disappear or is at least not assured. Under such circumstances, clashes may occur between the interests of different age cohorts. These problems are particularly likely in complex advanced societies where the obligations and duties with each age can change and thereby disrupt the system. Consider, for example, the situation facing young workers who may never benefit from a seniority system because the factory or the jobs may not be there for them in the years ahead. Nevertheless, in a stable system, the benefits and losses from age-based forms of ascriptive stratification are potentially neutral for a given individual. There are compensations at one age for disadvantages at another.[3]

The compensation system operates differently for gender-based forms of stratification; any compensation occurs for the family unit rather than the individual. In a stable family, with an equal number of males and females, gender discrimination creates no net loss for the unit per se, since what one member loses another member gains. There are two forces operating to undermine this pattern. First, the tolerance of unit-based compensation declines radically as the family system becomes unstable, and this then becomes an incentive for women to resist gender-based stratification: They are less assured of spending their life in a stable family with the compensations due them. Second, and probably more important, even without divorce and desertion, there are costs for those members of the disadvantaged sex because their *personal* opportunities, potential roles, restrictions, notions of self, and other imposed handicaps are *not* compensated on an individual basis. The movement toward individuation—that is, a sense of self-interest separate from the larger family entity—makes gender stratification more of an issue for women because they are, as individuals, disadvantaged even if the males in their family receive compensating privileges. The system provides no compensation for them as individuals.

In ethnic stratification, there is no compensation for members of the disadvantaged group per se, either within the life span of the individual or within the family unit. Only members of the society who belong to another ethnic-racial group benefit from the privileges denied through their subordination.[4] In the absence of extraordinarily high levels of intermarriage or some other exceptional situation such as an identification with the larger corporate entity that includes the groups who gain, there are *no* personal compensations.

Ethnic groups are also distinctive in their potential impact on the maintenance of the nation-state. To be sure, all three forms of ascribed stratification may generate reform movements seeking to reduce or eliminate disadvantages in the existing system. However, only ethnic-racial groups have the potential not only to seek reform or revolution but also to separate from the existing nation-state. This is more than hypothetical but is an actuality: Separatism is a threat in many societies (witness Russia, Canada, Cyprus, and Sri Lanka at present) and has occurred in many other settings throughout the decades. Not only can an ethnic-racial group maintain its own society indefinitely, but members often are spatially concentrated in a small number of regions—which makes a cleavage even more feasible. A disadvantaged sex or age group does not have the same potential for separatism, if only because members' spatial concentrations are insignificant (nil for gender and relatively minor for age). More critical, simple biological restrictions make it difficult for one age group or one sex to continue its own society indefinitely.[5]

As a consequence, the nation-state must deal with the potential threat of its disintegration or splintering along ethnic-racial lines. There is a certain tension when the nation-state seeks to maintain the political allegiance of subordinated ethnic-racial groups, since the same political system inevitably helps to maintain ethnic-racial forms of stratification (see the next section). The latter force sometimes leads to extreme oppression. At other times, there is a continuous interplay among groups seeking to alter the system that oppresses them and a nation that modifies its stratification no more than is necessary to maintain itself. (For a more detailed discussion of the distinctive quality of ethnic-racial stratification, see Lieberson [1970]; for an analysis of the types of ethnic-racial contact particularly likely to generate separatist movements, see Lieberson [1961].)

Common Features: Some Political Examples

In this brief essay, it is impossible to discuss all of the general principles influencing the conditions faced by ascribed groups. In most instances of ascriptive stratification, it is probably the case that efforts are made to socialize subordinate groups to their roles. Nevertheless, it is difficult to visualize ascriptive stratification without a coercive dimension that depends—directly or indirectly—on the operation of political institutions. Political processes are therefore a battleground, real or potential, as the advantaged strata maintain their favorable situation and the subordinates seek to alter it. The four political principles that follow illustrate ways of thinking that help us understand more than specific contemporary issues in gender and ethnic-racial relations.

1. The nature and forms of opposition to ascriptive stratification are affected by the way the dominant group responds to reform leaders.
2. All political events alter the relative positions of the dominant and subordinate groups. In the strict sense, there are no neutral political decisions. This accounts, at least in part, for the high de-

gree of political mobilization among subordinate groups.

3. There is a two-way causal interaction between the political position of a group and its economic and social positions. Political power affects economic and social positions, and these positions affect political power.

4. Political power is a "real good" for a group, as suggested previously. But it is also a symbolic good, having a value to each group in and of itself.

Leadership

From the perspective of most contemporary societies, it is startling to realize that ascriptive subordination has not always been considered "illegitimate" by the subordinates themselves, let alone subject to challenge. Indeed, it would be a valuable exercise to consider the broad sweep of social events leading to the rejection of such belief systems. Under any circumstance, it is important to recognize certain principles that operate to affect the nature of leadership when subordination is under challenge. At any given time, many different ideas are circulating within a subordinate group about both the causes of its difficulties and the appropriate actions for correcting them. These ideas and their advocates are implicitly in competition for supporters. The efforts to introduce change typically start in a relatively conservative fashion with leaders who try to ameliorate their group's position by working within the existing system (witness the history of the black protest movement). The leaders—and the ideologies underlying their proposals for change—ultimately stand or fall on the response of the dominant group. Leaders successful in introducing changes will not only retain their following but will probably expand it, and their interpretation of both the group's problems and the appropriate solutions are reinforced. If the dominant group fails to respond positively to these movements, a new set of leaders will emerge who espouse a more aggressive ideol-

ogy based on a different interpretation of the group's problems. Sometimes this trend is not immediately obvious because all leaders and ideologies are temporarily silenced through oppressive measures. However, in the present era, it is only a matter of time before more aggressive ideologies and leaders surface. Indeed, if extreme oppression has occurred, it is almost certain that the new ideologies and leaders will be extreme as well. The net effect, in either case, is that actions of the dominant group affect the competition of ideologies and leaders within the subordinate group.

No Political Decisions Are Neutral

All political decisions differentially affect social groups, whether the group is delineated by ascribed or achieved characteristics. Why is this? In essence, no matter what the basis of a group's formation, members will differ with respect to a wide range of other attributes that can be directly affected by political decisions. Consider how coin collectors, widowers, postal workers, tobacco farmers, joggers, residents of Idaho, gays, and the rural poor will—in the aggregate—each differ on a variety of other attributes such as income, occupation, political affiliation, values, health concerns, civil and social attitudes, and environmental concerns. As a result, political actions that affect the latter attributes will perforce affect these groups, albeit often in relatively minor ways. For example, one could analyze the differential effects of farm support policies, environmental policies, pay raises for employees of the U.S. Postal Service, and Supreme Court appointments on the well-being of the population of joggers. Since joggers are a nonrandom subset of the nation's population, they will differ on other attributes and therefore are differentially affected by these political events. This means that governmental policies and actions cannot be neutral in their impact on these groups, although the impact often is trivial and sometimes is not obvious at the time it occurs.[6] However, no interest group—ascriptive or otherwise—would attempt to address every political event that in some conceivable way affects it; rather, the group will concentrate on those events of greatest real or symbolic consequence (see Lieberson 1971).

There are several factors that make the non-neutral nature of political decisions especially significant for ascriptive groups and motivate them to respond through political means. Let us ignore political issues that have obvious relevance—for example, suffrage for women, elimination of slavery, antidiscrimination legislation, or acts designed to protect or benefit children or the elderly. The direct significance of such issues for specific ascriptive groups are obvious and no different than would be tobacco price supports for tobacco farmers or the funding of AIDS research for gays. Beyond this, however, ascriptive groups are likely to share a broader range of common interests than are most other groupings in the society. Since ascriptive groups are relatively more homogeneous on a larger number of characteristics, a commonality of responses will occur for a far greater array of political events. The differential impact of a wider array of political actions will be more sharply delineated if a group is more distinctive (in quantitative terms) on a larger number of attributes.

Also, since ascriptive disadvantages are usually imposed or at least maintained by political institutions, a high degree of political mobilization occurs as these groups attempt to eliminate their subordination. Keep in mind the key feature of ascriptive group membership: It is involuntary, imposed from the outside, and one cannot escape from it. Not only do disadvantaged ascriptive groups often have stronger bonds for action, but there is a greater likelihood that these nonneutral acts of government will have symbolic overtones insofar as they represent the disposition of government toward the group. When government is the linchpin of ascriptive stratification, more diverse actions are considered of importance because they are taken to represent the disposition of government toward the group, a matter of relatively stronger general concern to them. The members of the Na-

tional Rifle Association (NRA), by contrast, probably have a less generalized and less intensive view of governmental actions beyond those that would impact on their concerns as members of the organization.[7]

Political Power: Its Interaction with the Economic and Social

A two-way interaction exists between political power and the economic and social position of a group. On the one hand, groups use political power to advance their positions in the economic and social spheres. On the other hand, economic and social power is often convertible into political power. It is, as it were, a situation in which the "rich get richer and the poor get poorer." However, there are social factors that alter a group's situation over time. Many exogenous variables can impact on the social order and thereby upset the existing ascriptive stratification system; examples include wars, new labor-force needs, alliances with other groups, demographic shifts, international politics, the clash of ascriptive stratification with other beliefs in the society, and economic changes. Also, as a group gains in one area (say, educational attainment, voting strength, or economic position), the gain changes the balance in other domains, and these changes in turn have additional feedback effects (for an incisive description of early changes in the black population, see Ogburn [1961]). We must recognize not only the feedback nature of these linkages but also that the groups are in competition in what is often a zero-sum situation. With a constant number of senators, for example, the electoral gain of one group is at the expense of other groups. Likewise, there is competition for social and economic positions. An analytical understanding of the ascriptive processes is incomplete if this inherent competition is not understood or is ignored.

This two-way interaction is especially important for ascriptive groups because economically successful members frequently retain considerable identification with their groups and use their economic power in the political realm to advance the position of other members. Usually this identification is retained in part because the larger society still imposes restrictions and subtle prejudices on economically successful members of ascribed groups. By contrast, individuals who are upwardly mobile within the class system are less likely to apply their newfound economic power against class-based advantages because the residue of prejudice and discrimination they experience by virtue of their *class* origins is relatively minor. This suggests that potential members of anticlass movements might be "bought off" more readily than potential members of antiascription movements.

Symbolism

Above and beyond the impact of governmental activities on a group's material well-being and institutional position, government also has a symbolic dimension for these subordinated populations. The election of ethnic or gender compatriots—as well as their participation in the judiciary or appointment to political office—matters not only because such people are believed to better understand ascriptive stratification, are thought to be more committed to reducing it, and may be better able to convey the group perspective to others, but also because holding these offices symbolizes the group position in the society. A group's political position is taken as a *representation* of its members' place in the nation—particularly when in the past such positions were difficult to attain through formal or informal prohibitions. The value is all the more enhanced when requiring the support (through appointments or election) of "others." One must never lose sight of the bread-and-butter importance of these positions, but an added value is in their symbolic meaning, pure and simple. This line of reasoning accounts for the tendency of subordinated populations to monitor their level of political representation so closely.

Caution: Special Difficulties

All forms of ascriptive stratification are emotionally tinged—and for good reason. Since one's gender, ethnicity, age, and other ascribed features are permanent (short of such procedures as passing as a member of another race or ethnic group, undergoing radical surgery, or alteration of appearance through face-lifts or hair transplants), disadvantages stemming from membership in subordinated strata are of great significance. One's own life is deeply affected by these stratification systems, as are other family members, friends, acquaintances, neighbors, and the like (depending on the particular type of stratification). As a consequence, comments about one's group, the interpretation of members' subordination, portrayals in the media, and actual or proposed policies are all significant issues. Particularly important are the perspectives held by the dominant ascriptive group because, by definition, its members hold power and advantage over the subordinate strata. Persons holding a subordinate status often wish to convey the disadvantages experienced, if only because the dominant group does not fully understand and appreciate these difficulties. Moreover, beliefs held among the dominant population affect the subordinate group.

Also, as part of the larger society, members learn many disparaging notions about their group, and it is unsettling to hear them repeated. Women, ethnic groups, and the elderly are intensely aware of the stereotypes held about them by others and of the potential influence of these notions on group position (Lieberson 1982). In addition, the impact of these stereotypes within the ascribed subordinate group itself is important insofar as it affects self-conceptions, patterns of behavior, and the development of strategies for improving the group's position. Conversely, members of the dominant group often interpret their favorable position as deserved rather than as the product of oppressive or discriminatory behavior.

Given these considerations, it is vital to distinguish between two potentially contradictory goals. One goal is the effort to demonstrate that a group is treated unjustly and therefore changes are needed or, obversely, that the group is treated fairly and no change is needed. The second goal is to determine the evidence about a given situation and evaluate stratification theories by the criterion of how closely they account for the data. In the first approach, one is an advocate or attorney for the group, presenting the group's case or argument in a particular light. In the latter approach, all possibilities are on the table, subject to scientific investigation, regardless of the empirical outcome. In a democratic society, it is acceptable and appropriate that groups with given interests attempt to present their case in a convincing manner to achieve a certain outcome. Conversely, it is acceptable and appropriate in a scientific endeavor that evidence and theories be evaluated without regard to their polemical utility or outcome. If these two distinct roles and goals are confused, the result can be ineffective political action (a scientist makes a poor advocate) or disastrous social science (an advocate makes a poor scientist).

When the advocate-scientist distinction is confused or glossed over, it is all too easy to judge scientific work by its impact on the group's position and image in the society rather than to use the same scientific criteria that would have been applied to problems and issues less deeply felt. Ironically, the very intense personal feelings that motivate and stimulate research and theorizing about a topic can undercut the goals of scientific analysis. As already noted, members of the favored group can have difficulties in approaching these topics too. One group is no more intrinsically objective than another. Critical for both social scientists and readers of social science is that theories of ascription and empirical data be evaluated in terms of their scientific validity—in the same way as one evaluates statements about, say, the factors affecting maple syrup production. Data and theories must not be evaluated in terms of either a subordinate group's effort to improve

its situation or the dominant group's eagerness to justify maintenance of the existing advantages. These goals and criteria should not be confused. *The scientific goal should not be evaluated in terms of its impact on advocacy; in turn, the advocacy goal is ultimately a statement of values and norms—scientific evidence may be relevant, but it is not the critical issue.*

It is particularly important to be careful about the terms used to analyze ascriptive stratification. Obviously, special concepts help us understand the processes and provide easy ways to summarize complex matters. Nevertheless, there is a danger in using these terms in a polemical rather than an analytical way. In particular, we must keep in mind that the terms "racist" and "sexist" are increasingly used not only to describe a set of behaviors and attitudes that have been measured and evaluated in a rigorous and objective way but are also used as polemical terms. Social scientists have to consider whether a clear definition of racist or sexist exists such that criteria are applicable in a rigorous manner for a given setting. Otherwise, this is no different from the disposition of some conservatives to label every political proposal that they oppose as "communist." If a woman applies for a job and is not hired, for example, the reason could be sexist or it could not be. Rigorous research and sharply defined criteria are necessary before the assertion is appropriate.

Social-science analyses of ascriptive stratification are also distinctive from popular discussions because there is an effort to verify empirical assertions rather than assume they are true without any evidence. Assertions about the causes of group differences are empirical problems; they are not automatically viewed as true or false in accordance with one's polemical position. In addition, social science at its best does not take a simplistic good-bad approach to these forms of stratification (although the practitioners may personally feel that way as private citizens). Social science does not automatically view the disadvantaged group as largely "deserving" its subordination for reasons such as culture, physical features, or biological origins or in some other fashion such that it is a "fair" outcome. Likewise, all claims about a group's current characteristics are not automatically denied such that the only emphasis is on reform of either the larger social structure and/or on the dispositions of groups enjoying ascriptive advantages at the time.

This means, then, that caution is needed to avoid drawing premature conclusions without sufficient evidence simply because they fit into various polemical positions. The fact is that major macrosocietal questions about gender and ethnic-racial stratification are presently unresolved. This is itself not inherently worrisome; uncertainty and incomplete knowledge are common to any scientific endeavor. What is important, however, is to recognize existing limitations, turning them into research problems rather than claiming more knowledge than is justifiable now.

Consider, by way of illustration, some of the current theorizing on the effects of capitalism on ethnic or gender oppression; these types of macrosocietal effects are often assumed to be present when, in fact, much more rigorous investigation is called for. Although Marxists and others often observe the presence of severe ascriptive stratification in many capitalist societies, this observation, which is unquestionably true, does not itself imply that capitalism is a simple explanation of oppressive ethnic or gender relations. To focus only on stratification in capitalist societies is to execute a logical error. In other words, in order to determine if X_1 causes Y more often (or increases the severity of Y) than does X_2, it is insufficient to look only at Y when X_1 is present. Rather, we must compare the levels of Y in the two conditions, X_1 and X_2. Similarly, to gauge the influence of one type of political economy on gender or ethnic-racial stratification, one must also compare stratification found in other economic settings. The logic of this is, I would hope, fairly obvious. The reader is well-advised, however, to keep it in mind when the influence of capitalism on ascriptive stratification is asserted without presentation of rigorous comparative data. It is one issue to decide

if such ascription is present in capitalist countries; it is another to conclude that capitalism per se causes such forms of stratification. If the latter is true, then one should find lower levels in other types of societies. And this is an empirical question.

The cautions discussed in this last section are familiar to those espousing a rigorous social science that attempts to minimize the impact of personal values on the evaluation of theories and research. However, since one's personal feelings are sometimes at odds with one's intellectual perspective, with the latter overpowered by the former, it is important that the reader keep in mind the especially strong tension that can exist between the two spheres in the analysis of ascriptive stratification.

Notes

1. Henceforth in this essay the terms *ethnic* and *ethnic-racial* are used interchangeably in referring to both racial and ethnic forms.

2. Some of these issues may come and go as fashionable research topics. For example, race riots were a central concern during and immediately after each world war and again in the late 1960s.

3. This premise ignores inequities that can occur for someone who is exceptional and would fare quite favorably at a wide range of ages. Conversely, a highly incompetent person may gain more from the period when age protects him or her than is lost at the disadvantaged age. This is an individual problem—not trivial, to be sure—but not a problem intrinsic to one birth cohort versus another.

4. To be sure, there are some members of the subordinated group who occupy advantageous positions because of their group's situation, but they are inevitably a relatively small number.

5. However, it is now at least possible for women to maintain a society indefinitely through the use of sperm banks and the elimination of male babies.

6. Acts can have unintended consequences, and even social policies developed with a specific group in mind can have unforeseen side effects.

7. This would occur even if members of the organization tend to share other concerns and dispositions regarding events of no consequence to the issue of gun control.

References

Lieberson, Stanley. 1961. "A Societal Theory of Race and Ethnic Relations." *American Sociological Review* 26 (December): 902–910.

———. 1970. "Stratification and Ethnic Groups." *Sociological Inquiry* 40 (Spring): 172–181.

———. 1971. "An Empirical Study of Military-Industrial Linkages." *American Journal of Sociology* 76 (January): 562–584.

———. 1982. "Stereotypes: Their Consequences for Race and Ethnic Interaction." Pp. 47–68 in Robert M. Hauser, David Mechanic, Archibald O. Haller, and Taissa S. Hauser, eds., *Social Structure and Behavior: Essays in Honor of William H. Sewell*. New York: Academic Press.

Ogburn, William Fielding. 1961. "Social Change and Race Relations." Pp. 200–207 in Jitsuichi Masuoka and Preston Valien, eds., *Race Relations: Problems and Theory*. Chapel Hill: University of North Carolina Press.

Part VII
The Future of Stratification

Theories of Industrialism and Modernity

Theories of Post-Industrialism, Post-Socialism, and Post-Modernity
    Post-Industrialism and the New Class
    Post-Socialism
    Post-Modernity

Trends in Income Inequality

Theories of Industrialism and Modernity

CLARK KERR, JOHN T. DUNLOP, FREDERICK H. HARBISON, AND CHARLES A. MYERS

Industrialism and Industrial Man

The Logic of Industrialization

Although industrialization follows widely differing patterns in different countries, some characteristics of the industrialization process are common to all. These "universals" arise from the imperatives intrinsic to the process. They are the prerequisites and the concomitants of industrial evolution. Once under way, the logic of industrialization sets in motion many trends which do more or less violence to the traditional pre-industrial society.

In the actual course of history, the inherent tendencies of the industrial process are never likely to be fully realized. The pre-existing societies and conditions shape and constrain these inherent features. The leaders of economic development influence the directions and the rate of industrial growth; and the existing resources and the contemporaneous developments in other countries are also likely to affect actual events. These influences will be important in every case of industrialization. They do not, however, deny the validity of searching for some of the fundamental directions in which industrialization will haul and pull. Indeed, an under-

standing of these tendencies is requisite to a full appreciation of the influence of historical, cultural, and economic factors on the actual course of industrialization.

What, then, are some of the imperatives of the industrialization process? Given the character of science and technology and the requirements inherent in modern methods of production and distribution, what may be deduced as to the necessary or the likely characteristics of workers and managers and their interrelations? What are the inherent implications of industrialization for the work place and the larger community? What, in sum do the actual histories of those societies with either brief or more extensive industrializing experience suggest about the principal forces implicit in an "industrial revolution"?

The Industrial Work Force

[The workman] becomes an appendage of the machine, and it is only the most simple, most monotonous, and most easily acquired knack, that is required of him. (*Manifesto,* p. 65). . . . Hence, in the place of the hierarchy of specialized workmen that characterizes manufacture, there steps, in the automatic factory, a tendency to equalise and reduce to one and the same level every kind of work that has to be done by the minders of the machines . . . (*Capital,* p. 420). The more modern industry becomes developed, the more is the labour of men superseded by that of women (*Manifesto,*

Originally published in 1960. Please see complete source information beginning on page 891.

p. 66) . . . The various interests and conditions of life within the ranks of the proletariat are more and more equalised, in proportion as machinery obliterates all distinctions of labour, and nearly everywhere reduces wages to the same low level (*Manifesto*, p. 69). . . . The essential division is, into workmen who are actually employed on the machines (among whom are included a few who look after the engine), and into mere attendants (almost exclusively children) of these workmen. . . . In addition to these two principal classes, there is a numerically unimportant class of persons, whose occupation is to look after the whole of the machinery and repair it from time to time such as engineers, mechanics, joiners, etc. (*Capital*, p. 420).[1]

These quotations from the *Manifesto* and *Capital* envisage as the consequence of capitalist production the destruction of the hierarchy of specialized workmen in pre-industrial society and the subsequent leveling of skill, a minor number of skilled labor, engineers, and managers, and the use of women and children for a growing number of unskilled tending and feeding jobs. The historical evidence of the past century, however, suggests a quite different pattern of evolution for the industrial work force.

Industrialization in fact develops and depends upon a concentrated, disciplined industrial work force—a work force with new skills and a wide variety of skills, with high skill levels and constantly changing skill requirements.

The industrialization process utilizes a level of technology far in advance of that of earlier societies. Moreover, the associated scientific revolution generates continual and rapid changes in technology which have decisive consequences for workers, managers, the state, and their interrelations.

The industrial system requires a wide range of skills and professional competency broadly distributed throughout the work force. These specialized human resources are indispensable to the science and technology of industrialism, and their development is one of the major problems of a society engaged in industrializa-

tion. The absence of a highly qualified labor force is as serious an impediment as a shortage of capital goods. The professional, technical, and managerial component of the labor force is particularly strategic since it largely carries the responsibility of developing and ordering the manual and clerical components.

Mobility and the Open Society. The dynamic science and technology of the industrial society creates frequent changes in the skills, responsibilities, and occupations of the work force. Some are made redundant and new ones are created. The work force is confronted with repeated object lessons of the general futility of fighting these changes, and comes to be reconciled, by and large, to repeated changes in ways of earning a living. But there may be continuing conflict over the timing of change and the division of the gains. The industrial society requires continual training and retraining of the work force; the content of an occupation or job classification is seldom set for life, as in the traditional society. Occupational mobility is associated with a high degree of geographical movement in a work force and with social mobility in the larger community both upwards and downwards.

One indication of the extent of occupational shifts which occur in the course of industrialization is reflected in Table 1 for the United States in the period 1900–1960.

Industrialization tends to produce an open society, inconsistent with the assignment of managers or workers to occupations or to jobs by traditional caste, by racial groups, by sex, or by family status. There is no place for the extended family; it is on balance an impediment to requisite mobility. The primary family provides a larger and more mobile labor force. The function of the family under industrialism is constricted: it engages in very little production; it provides little, if any, formal education and occupational training; the family business is substantially displaced by professional management. ". . . economic growth and a transference of women's work from the household to the market go closely hand in hand."[2] In the industrial society the

TABLE 1

Occupational Distribution of Employment, United States, 1900–1960 (thousands of people,
14 years of age and older)

Occupational Group	1960	1900	Change 1900–1960	Per Cent Increase 1900–1960
Total	66,159	29,030	+37,129	128
Total Farm Employment	5,037	10,888	−5,851	−54
Total Non-Farm Employment	61,122	18,142	+42,980	237
White Collar Workers	28,507	5,115	+23,392	457
Professional, Technical, and Kindred Workers	7,418	1,234	+6,184	501
Managers, Officials, and Proprietors	7,032	1,697	+5,335	314
Clerical and Kindred Workers	9,710	877	+8,833	1,007
Sales Workers	4,347	1,306	+3,041	233
Blue Collar Workers	24,280	10,401	+13,879	133
Craftsmen, Foremen, and Kindred Workers	8,606	3,062	+5,544	181
Operatives and Kindred Workers	11,988	3,720	+8,268	222
Laborers	3,686	3,620	+66	2
Service Workers	8,335	2,626	+5,709	217
Service Workers Excluding Household Workers	6,134	1,047	+5,087	486
Private Household Workers	2,201	1,579	+622	39

Source: U.S. Department of Labor, Bureau of Labor Statistics, *Employment and Earnings, 1960;* and U.S. Department of Commerce, "Occupational Trends in the United States," Bureau of the Census Working Paper No. 5 (Washington, 1958), pp. 6–7.

primary family is largely a source of labor supply, a unit of decision-making for household expenditures and savings, and a unit of cultural activity.

This society is always in flux and in motion. As a result of its science and technology, it is continuously rearranging what people do for a living, where they work and where they live, and on what they spend their incomes. Their children come to expect to live different lives from their parents. But mobility in the industrial society is not random; it comes to be organized and governed by a complex of rules of the work community.

Education—The Handmaiden of Industrialism. Industrialization requires an educational system functionally related to the skills and professions imperative to its technology. Such an educational system is not primarily concerned with conserving traditional values or perpetuating the classics; it does not adopt a static view of society, and it does not place great emphasis on training in the traditional law. The higher educational system of the industrial society stresses the natural sciences, engineering, medicine, managerial training—whether private or public—and administrative law. It must steadily adapt to new disciplines and fields of specialization. There is a relatively smaller place for the humanities and arts, while the social sciences are strongly related to the training of managerial groups and technicians for the enterprise and the government. The increased leisure time of industrialism, however, can afford a broader public appreciation of the humanities and the arts.

As in all societies, there is debate over what the youth is to be taught. The largest part of the higher educational system tends to be specialized and designed to produce the very large volume of professionals, technicians, and managers required in the industrial society. There is a case for some degree of generality in the educational system because of the rapidity of change and growth of knowledge during the course of a career. A technically trained work force needs to be able to follow and to adapt to changes in its specialties and to learn to shift to new fields. Generality is also requisite for those coordinating and leading the specialists.

The industrial society tends to create an increasing level of general education for all citizens, not only because it facilitates training and flexibility in the work force, but also because, as incomes rise, natural curiosity increases the demand for formal education, and education becomes one of the principal means of vertical social mobility. It will be observed that the industrial society tends to transform drastically the educational system of the pre-industrial society. Further, the high level of technical and general education requisite to the industrial society cannot but have significant consequences for political life. The means of mass communication play a significant role both in raising standards of general education and in conditioning political activity and shaping political control.

The Structure of the Labor Force. The labor force of the industrial society is highly differentiated by occupations and job classifications, by rates of compensation, and by a variety of relative rights and duties in the work place community. It has form and structure vastly different from the more homogeneous labor force of the traditional society.

The variety of skills, responsibilities, and working conditions at the work place requires an ordering or a hierarchy. There are successive levels of authority of managers and the managed, as well as considerable specialization of function at each level of the hierarchy. Job evaluation and salary plans symbolize the ordering of the industrial work force by function and compensation.[3]

The work force in the industrial society is also structured in the sense that movement within the work community is subjected to a set of rules; hiring, temporary layoffs, permanent redundance, promotions, shift changes, transfers, and retirement are applied to individual workers and managers according to their position, station, seniority, technical competency, or some other measure of status in a group rather than in random fashion. Not all jobs are open at all times to all bidders. The ports of entry into an enterprise are limited, and priorities in selection are established. Movement tends to be relatively easier

within than among job families in an enterprise. Delineation of job families may also vary and will often depend upon whether movement involves promotion, layoff, or transfer.

The industrial system changes the hours of work that prevail in predominantly agricultural societies. The silent night of pre-industrial society yields to the sometimes insistent requirements of continuous operations. The work force is geared to shift operations and the community to a changed attitude toward working at night. Even the holidays and religious days of the traditional society do not escape transformation.

Scale of Society

The technology and specialization of the industrial society are necessarily and distinctively associated with large-scale organizations. Great metropolitan areas arise in the course of industrialization. The national government machinery expands significantly. Economic activity is carried on by large-scale enterprises which require extensive coordination of managers and the managed. A wide variety of rules and norms are essential to secure this coordination.

Urban Dominance. The industrial society is an urban society, concentrated in metropolitan areas with their suburbs and satellite communities. While substantial cities have arisen in pre-industrial societies as commercial and religious centers,[4] urban ways come to permeate the whole of industrial society. Rapid means of transportation and mass communication reduce the variance of subcultures, particularly those based on geography and the contrast between farm and city.

In the industrial society agriculture is simply another industry; it is not a "way of life" to be preserved for its own value or because it constituted a traditional and antecedent form of society. Agricultural units of production (farms) tend to be specialized according to products, and the general farm, substantially self-sufficient, has little place. Indeed, the pro-

TABLE 2
Agricultural Population

Country	Per Cent of Active Population in Agriculture
United Kingdom (1951)	5
United States (1950)	12
Sweden (1950)	20
W. Germany (1950)	23
France (1957)	26
Italy (1957)	31
Japan (1957)	39
U.S.S.R. (1950)	50
Brazil (1950)	58
Egypt (1947)	65
India	71
Iran (ca. 1953)	80
Afghanistan (1954)	85
Nyasaland (1949)	90
Nepal (1952/54)	93

Source: Norton Ginsburg, *Atlas of Economic Development*, Research Paper No. 68, Department of Geography (Chicago: The University of Chicago Press, 1961), pp. 32–33.

portion of the work force engaged in agriculture is a rough index of the degree of industrialization of a society.[5] "To the economic eye a community which needs to have the majority of its people working on the land is merely demonstrating its inefficiency."[6]

Table 2 shows the relative role of agriculture in a number of countries; it reflects the low proportion of agriculture in the economically advanced countries and the high percentage of agricultural population in the less economically advanced societies.

Industrialization tends to promote the values, folkways, and heroes of the city and to weaken those of the farm. Even the art and music of the highly industrialized society can be expected to be substantially different from that of the pre-industrial society.

Large Role for Government. The industrial society is necessarily characterized by a substantial range and scale of activities by the government. In a society of advanced technology there are a larger number of activities for government; for instance, roads and highways, airports, the regulation of traffic, radio and television. Urban development has the same consequences. Technology also creates a more complex military establishment, extending in many directions the activities of government. The more integrated character of the world increases governmental activities in the area of international relations. The scale of some scientific applications and the capital needs of new technologies, such as atomic energy development or space exploration, increase the scope of public agencies. As income rises, the demand of consumers may be for services largely provided by governments, such as education, parks, roads, and health services.

The role of government in countries entering upon industrialization, regardless of political form, may therefore be expected to be greater than before. There is wisdom in the observation: ". . . it is extremely unlikely that the highly modernized systems of the world today could have developed indigenously on the basis of any system other than ones that relied very heavily indeed on private individual operations, and it is extremely unlikely that latecomers can carry out such development without relying very heavily on public operations."[7]

The industrial society and individual freedom, however, are not necessarily to be regarded as antagonists. A high degree of discipline in the work place and a large range of governmental activities is fully consistent with a larger freedom for the individual in greater leisure, a greater range of choice in occupations and place of residence, a greater range of alternatives in goods and services on which to use income, and a very wide range of subgroups or associations in which to choose participation. It is a mistake to regard the industrial society as antithetical to individual freedom by citing ways in which the scope of public and private governments has increased without also noting ways in which industrialization expands individual freedom.

The Web of Rules. The production of goods and services in the industrial society is largely in the hands of large-scale organizations. They consist of hierarchies composed of relatively few managers and staff advisers and a great many to be managed. The managers and the managed are necessarily connected by an elaborate web of rules that is made the more intricate and complex by technology, specialization, and the large scale of operations.

At any one time, the rights and duties of all those in the hierarchy must be established and understood by all.

The web of rules of the work place concerns compensation, discipline, layoffs, transfers and promotions, grievances, and a vast array of matters, some common to all work places and others specialized for the type of activity—factory, airline, railroad, mine, or office—and to the specific establishment. The rules also establish norms of output, pace, and performance. Moreover, the web of rules is never static, and procedures arise for the orderly change of these rules. The industrial system creates an elaborate "government" at the work place and in the work community. It is often observed that primitive societies have extensive rules, customs, and taboos, but a study of the industrial society reflects an even greater complex and a quite different set of detailed rules.

The web of rules depends partially on those technological features and market or budgetary constraints of the work place which are generally common to all types of industrializing countries, and partially on the particular resources and the political and economic forms of the country. The relative strength of these factors, and their mode of interaction, is important to an understanding of any particular industrial society. Cultural and national differences are less significant to the substantive web of rules, the more a country has industrialized. The impact of cultural and national heritage is more clearly discerned in the differences to be found in the process for formulating and promulgating the rules affecting men at work than in the content of the rules themselves.

The tug of industrialization—whatever these initial differences—is toward a greater role for the state in an eventual pluralistic rule-making system. The state does not evolve simply as a class apparatus and instrument for the oppression of another class, as Marx

asserted.[8] Nor does it "wither away" in the ultimate "good society."[9] Governments have a significant role in determining the substantive rules of the work community or in establishing the procedures and responsibilities of those with this power. In the highly industrialized society, enterprise managers, workers, and the government tend to share in the establishment and administration of the rules. The industrial relations system of the industrial society is genuinely tripartite.

Consensus in Society

The industrial society, like any established society, develops a distinctive consensus which relates individuals and groups to each other and provides an integrated body of ideas, beliefs, and value judgments. Various forms of the industrial society may create some distinctive ideological features, but all industrialized societies have some common values.

In the industrial society science and technical knowledge have high values, and scientists and technologists enjoy high prestige and rewards.

Taboos against technical change are eliminated, and high values are placed on being "modern" and "up-to-date," and in "progress" for their own sake.

Education also has a high value because of the fundamental importance of science and the utility of education as a means of social mobility.

The industrial society is an open community encouraging occupational and geographic mobility and social mobility. Industrialization calls for flexibility and competition; it is against tradition and status based upon family, class, religion, race, or caste.

It is pluralistic, with a great variety of associations and groups and of large-scale operations; the individual is attached to a variety of such groups and organizations.

Goods and services have a high value in the industrial society, and the "demonstration effect" is very strong on the part of individuals and groups seeking to imitate the standards of those with higher income levels.

The work force is dedicated to hard work, a high pace of work, and a keen sense of individual responsibility for performance of assigned norms and tasks. Industrial countries may differ with respect to the ideals and drives which underlie devotion to duty and responsibility for performance, but industrialization requires an ideology and an ethic which motivate individual workers. Strict supervision imposed on a lethargic work force will not suffice; personal responsibility for performance must be implanted within workers, front-line supervisors, and top managers.[10]

It is not by accident that the leaders of industrializing countries today exhort their peoples to hard work. "This generation is sentenced to hard labor" (Nehru). "We shall march forward as one people who have vowed to work and to proceed on a holy march of industrializing . . . " (Nasser). "The chief preoccupation of every Communist regime between the Elbe and the China Sea is how to make people work; how to induce them to sow, harvest, mine, build, manufacture and so forth. It is the most vital problem which confronts them day in, day out, and it shapes their domestic policies and to a considerable extent their attitude toward the outside world."[11] There are many counterparts for the Protestant ethic.

The Western tradition has been to harness the drive of individual self-interest; the communist method combines in varying proportions at varying times money incentives, devotion to a revolutionary creed, and the compulsion of terror. Regardless of means, industrialization entails a pace of work and an exercise of personal responsibility seldom known in economic activity in traditional societies.

The function of making explicit a consensus and of combining discrete beliefs and convictions into a reasonably consistent body of ideas is the task of intellectuals in every society. There are probably more intellectuals in the industrial society because of the higher levels of general education, income, and leisure. There are also new patrons to the intellectuals—the university, enterprise, labor organization, voluntary association and government—in place of the old aristocratic patrons. The function of formulating and restating the major values, premises, and consensus of a society from time to time, of reconciling the new industrial processes with the old order, plays a significant role in industrialization. The intellectuals accordingly are an influential group in the creation and molding of industrial society. . . .

The Road Ahead: Pluralistic Industrialism

Men attempt to peer ahead, to understand the structure of history, to alter the process of history, if possible, in accord with their preferences. The history of industrialization to date has not been a smoothly unilinear one; it has been uneven and multilinear. It is likely that in the future it will continue to be both somewhat uneven and multilinear; and there will continue to be some latitude for choice and for chance. Chance may elude man, but choice need not; and the choice of men, within fairly broad limits, can shape history. To predict the future with any accuracy, men must choose their future. The future they appear to be choosing and pressing for is what might be called "pluralistic industrialism."

This term is used to refer to an industrial society which is governed neither by one all-powerful elite (the monistic model) nor by the impersonal interaction of innumerable small groups with relatively equal and fractionalized power (the atomistic model in economic theory). The complexity of the fully developed industrial society requires, in the name of efficiency and initiative, a degree of decentralization of control, particularly in the consumer goods and service trades industries; but it also requires a large measure of central control by the state and conduct of many operations by large-scale organizations.

As the skill level rises and jobs become more responsible, any regime must be more interested in consent, in drawing forth relatively full cooperation. For the sake of real efficiency, this must be freely given. The discipline of the labor gang no longer suffices. With skill and responsibility goes the need for consent, and with consent goes influence and even authority. Occupational and professional groups, of necessity, achieve some prestige and authority as against both the central organs of society and the individual members of the occupation or profession.

Education brings in its wake a new economic equality and a new community of political outlook. This in turn, along with many other developments, helps bring consensus to society. The harsh use of power by the state is no longer so necessary to hold society together at the seams. Education also opens the mind to curiosity and to inquiry, and the individual seeks more freedom to think and to act. It brings a demand for liberty, and can help create conditions in which liberty can safely be assumed. It leads to comparisons among nations with respect to progress and participation.

Industrialism is so complex and subject to such contrary internal pressures that it never can assume a single uniform unchanging structure; but it *can* vary around a general central theme, and that theme is pluralism. While it will take generations before this theme will become universal in societies around the world, the direction of the movement already seems sufficiently clear:

The State that Does Not Wither Away. The state will be powerful. It will, at the minimum, have the responsibility for the economic growth rate; the over-all distribution of income among uses and among individuals; the basic security of individuals (the family formerly was the basic security unit); the stability of the system; providing the essential public services of education, transportation, recreational areas, cultural facilities, and the like; and the responsibility of providing a favorable physical environment for urban man.

In addition, any pluralistic society is subject to three great potential internal problems, and the state is responsible for handling each. One is the conflict among the various power ele-

ments in a pluralistic society. The state must set the rules of the game within which such conflict will occur, enforce these rules, and act as mediator; conflicts between managers and the managed are the most noticeable, but by no means the only ones. Another is the control of collusion by producers against consumers, by any profession against its clients, and by labor and management against the public. Undue aggrandizement of sectional interests is always endemic if not epidemic in a pluralistic society; in fact, one of the arguments for monism and atomism alike is the avoidance of sectionalism. Additionally, the state will come generally, under pluralistic industrialism, to set the rules relating members to their organizations—who may get in, who may stay in, what rights and obligations the members have, what the boundaries are for the activities of the organization, and so on. It will, almost of necessity, be against too much conflict among, or collusion between, or domination of the members by the subsidiary organizations in society.

All these responsibilities mean the state will never "wither away"; that Marx was more utopian than the despised utopians. The state will be the dominant organization in any industrial society. But it may itself be less than fully unitary. It may itself be subject to checks and balances, including the check of public acceptance of its current leadership and its policies.

The Crucial Role of the Enterprise—The Middle Class and the Middle Bureaucracy. The productive enterprise, whether private or public, will be a dominant position under pluralistic industrialism. It will often be large and it must always have substantial authority in order to produce efficiently. This authority will not be complete, for it will be checked by the state, by the occupational association, by the individual employee; but it will be substantial.

The distinction between the private and the public manager will decrease just as the distinction between the private and the public enterprise will diminish; and the distinction among managers will be more according to the size, the product, and the nature of their enterprises. The controlled market and the controlled budget will bring more nearly the same pressures on them. The private enterprise, however, will usually have more freedom of action than the public enterprise; but the middle class and the middle bureaucracy will look much alike.

Associated Man. The occupational or professional association will range alongside the state and the enterprise as a locus of power in pluralistic industrialism; and there will be more occupations and particularly more professions seeking association. Group organizations around skill and position in the productive mechanism will be well-nigh universal. These organizations will affect output norms, comparative incomes, access to employment, and codes of ethics in nearly every occupational walk of life. Their containment within reasonable limits will be a continuing problem; and some of the groups will always seek to invade and infiltrate the government mechanisms which are intended to supervise them.

The Web of Rules. Uniting the state, the enterprise, and the association will be a great web of rules set by the efforts of all the elements, but particularly by the state. This web of rules will also relate the individual to each of these elements. In the contest over who should make the web of rules, the end solution will be that they will be made or influenced by more than one element; they will not be set by the state alone or by the enterprise alone or by the association alone. The web of rules will not equally cover all aspects of life.

From Class War to Bureaucratic Gamesmanship. Conflict will take place in a system of pluralistic industrialism, but it will take less the form of the open strife or the revolt and more the form of the bureaucratic contest. Groups will jockey for position over the placement of individuals, the setting of jurisdictions, the location of authority to make decisions, the forming of alliances, the establish-

ment of formulas, the half-evident withdrawal of support and of effort, the use of precedents and arguments and statistics. Persuasion, pressure, and manipulation will take the place of the face-to-face combat of an earlier age. The battles will be in the corridors instead of the streets, and memos will flow instead of blood. The conflict also will be, by and large, over narrower issues than in earlier times when there was real disagreement over the nature of and the arrangements within industrial society. It will be less between the broad programs of capital and labor, and of agriculture and industry; and more over budgets, rates of compensation, work norms, job assignments. The great battles over conflicting manifestos will be replaced by a myriad of minor contests over comparative details.

From Class Movement to Special Interest Group. Labor-management relations will conform to this new context. Labor organizations will not be component parts of class movements urging programs of total reform, for the consensus of a pluralistic society will have settled over the scene. Nor may they be very heavily identified by industry, particularly with the increasing multiplication and fractionalization of industries. Rather, they may tend to take more the craft, or perhaps better, the occupational form. With skills more diverse, at a generally higher level, and obtained more through formal education, and with geographical mobility greatly increased, professional-type interests should mean more to workers than industry or class ties.

The purpose of these occupational and professional associations will be relatively narrow, mostly the improvement of the status of the occupation in terms of income, prestige, and specification of the rights and duties that accompany it. Generally these organizations will be a conservative force in society, opposed to new ways of doing things, resistant to increased efforts by members of the occupation. The enterprise managers will be the more progressive elements in the society, although they too may become heavily weighted down by checks and balances and rules.

The techniques of the professional associations for achieving their ends will be those of the bureaucratic organization everywhere; a far cry from the individual withdrawal, or the guerilla warfare, or the strike or the political reform movement of earlier times. They will constitute the quarrels between the semi-managed and the semi-managers.

Individuals will identify themselves more closely with their occupation, particularly if it involves a formal training period for entry, and mobility will follow more the lines of the occupation than the lines of the industry or the job possibilities of the immediate geographical area. In terms of identification, the orientation will be more nearly that of the member of a guild than of a class or of a plant community. Mayo will turn out to be as wrong as Marx. Just as the class will lose its meaning, so also will the plant community fail to become the modern counterpart of the primitive tribe. The occupational interest group will represent the employee in his occupational concerns and the occupation will draw his allegiance. Status in the tribe will not give way to status in the plant; nor will status have given way to the individual contract through the march of civilization; rather interest identification will take the place of both status and individual contract in ordering the productive arrangements of men.

Education, occupation, occupational organization will all be drawn together to structure the life-line and the economic interests of many if not most employees.

The New Bohemianism. The individual will be in a mixed situation far removed either from that of the independent farmer organizing most aspects of his own life or from that of the Chinese peasant in the commune under total surveillance. In his working life he will be subject to great conformity imposed not only by the enterprise manager but also by the state and by his own occupational association. For most people, any complete scope for the independent spirit on the job will be missing. However, the skilled worker, while under rules, does get some control over his job,

some chance to organize it as he sees fit, some possession of it. Within the narrow limits of this kind of "job control," the worker will have some freedom. But the productive process tends to regiment. People must perform as expected or it breaks down. This is now and will be increasingly accepted as an immutable fact. The state, the manager, the occupational association are all disciplinary agents. But discipline is often achieved by a measure of persuasion and incentive. The worker will be semi-independent with some choice among jobs, some control of the job, and some scope for the effects of morale; but he will also be confined by labor organizations, pensions, and seniority rules, and all sorts of rules governing the conduct of the job.

Outside his working life the individual may have more freedom under pluralistic industrialism than in most earlier forms of society. Politically he can have some influence. Society has achieved consensus and the state need not exercise rigid political control. Nor in this "Brave New World" need genetic and chemical means be employed to avoid revolt. There will not be any rebellion, anyway, except little bureaucratic revolts that can be settled piecemeal. An educated population will want political choice and can effectively use it. There will also be a reasonable amount of choice in the controlled labor market, subject to the confining limits of one's occupation, and in the controlled product market.

The great new freedom may come in the leisure-time life of individuals. Higher standards of living, more free time, and more education make this not only possible but almost inevitable. Leisure will be the happy hunting ground for the independent spirit. Along with the bureaucratic conservatism of economic and political life may well go a New Bohemianism in the other aspects of life—partly as a reaction to the confining nature of the productive side of society. There may well come a new search for individuality and a new meaning to liberty. The economic system may be highly ordered and the political system barren ideologically; but the social and recreational and cultural aspects of life should be quite diverse and quite changing.

The world will be for the first time a totally literate world. It will be an organization society, but it need not be peopled by "organization men" whose total lives are ruled by their occupational roles.

The areas closest to technology will be the most conformist; those farthest from the requirements of its service, the most free. The rule of technology need not, as Marx thought it would, reach into every corner of society. In fact, there may come a new emphasis on diversity, on the preservation of national and group traits that runs quite counter to the predictions of uniform mass consumption. The new slavery to technology may bring a new dedication to diversity and individuality. This is the two-sided face of pluralistic industrialism that makes it forever a split personality looking in two directions at the same time. The new slavery and the new freedom go hand in hand.

Utopia never arrives, but men may well settle for the benefits of a greater scope for freedom in their personal lives at the cost of considerable conformity in their working lives. If pluralistic industrialism can be said to have a split personality, then the individual in this society will lead a split life too; he will be a pluralistic individual with more than one pattern of behavior and one dominant allegiance.

Social systems will be reasonably uniform around the world as compared with today's situation; but there may be substantial diversity within geographical and cultural areas as men and groups seek to establish and maintain their identity. The differences will be between and among individuals and groups and subcultures rather than primarily between and among the major geographical areas of the world. Society at large may become more like the great metropolitan complexes of Paris or London or New York or Tokyo, urbanized and committed to the industrial way of life, but marked by infinite variety in its details.

Pluralistic industrialism will never reach a final equilibrium. The contest between the forces for uniformity and for diversity will give it life and movement and change. This is a contest which will never reach an ultimate solution. Manager and managed also will struggle all up and down the line of hierarchies all around the world; quiet but often desperate little battles will be fought all over the social landscape.

The uniformity that draws on technology, and the diversity that draws on individuality; the authority that stems from the managers, and the rebellion, however muted, that stems from the managed—these are destined to be the everlasting threads of the future. They will continue in force when class war, and the contest over private versus public initiative, and the battle between the monistic and atomistic ideologies all have been left far behind in the sedimentary layers of history.

Notes

1. The page citations in the *Manifesto* are to K. Marx and F. Engels, *Manifesto of the Communist Party* (Moscow: Foreign Languages Publishing House, 1955); page citations in *Capital* are to Karl Marx, *Capital*, First edition (Moscow: Foreign Languages Publishing House, 1954), English edition. Chapter XV in this first volume of *Capital* is entitled, "Machinery and Modern Industry," pp. 371–507.

2. W. Arthur Lewis, *The Theory of Economic Growth* (London: George Allen and Unwin Ltd., 1955), p. 116.

3. The 32 labor grades in the basic steel industry and the many thousands of jobs described and rated in the manual in use in the United States are eloquent testimony to the way in which an industrial work force is structured. While the details of the ordering vary among countries, the steel industry of all countries reflects a highly differentiated and ordered work force. See Jack Stieber, *The Steel Industry Wage Structure* (Cambridge, Massachusetts: Harvard University Press, 1959). Compare American Iron and Steel Institute, *Steel in the Soviet Union* (New York: 1959), pp. 287–376.

4. Bert F. Hoselitz, "The City, The Factory, and Economic Growth," *American Economic Review* (May 1955), pp. 166–184.

5. If industrializing countries are arrayed in groups according to product per capita, the proportion of the labor force in agriculture and related industries varies from 61.2 per cent in the least developed group to 14.4 per cent in the group with

the highest product per capita. See Simon Kuznets, *Six Lectures on Economic Growth* (Glencoe, Illinois: The Free Press, 1959), pp. 44–45.

6. W. Arthur Lewis, *The Theory of Economic Growth*, p. 92.

7. Marion J. Levy, Jr., "Some Social Obstacles to 'Capital Formation' in 'Underdeveloped Areas,'" in *Capital Formation and Economic Growth*, A Conference of the Universities—National Bureau Committee for Economic Research (New Jersey: Princeton University Press, 1955), p. 461.

8. "Political power, properly so called, is merely the organized power of one class for oppressing another." K. Marx and F. Engels, *Manifesto of the Communist Party* (Moscow: Foreign Languages Publishing House, 1955), p. 95. The highest purpose of the state is the protection of private property; it is an instrument of class domination. See also F. Engels, *Origin of the Family, Private Property and the State*, translated by Ernest Untermann (Chicago: C. H. Kerr & Co., 1902), p. 130, and Paul H. Sweezy, *The Theory of Capitalist Development, Principles of Marxian Political Economy*

(New York: Oxford University Press, 1942), pp. 243–244.

9. In the good society which Marx believed to be the final and inevitable result of the dialectical process, there would no longer be a division of society into economic classes. Since he held the state to be merely an instrument of class coercion, with the disappearance of classes, there would follow a concomitant "withering away" of the state. "The society that is to reorganize production on the basis of free and equal association of the producers, will transfer the machinery of state where it will then belong—into the Museum of Antiquities by the side of the spinning wheel and the bronze age." F. Engels, *Origin of the Family, Private Property and the State*, p. 211.

10. Daniel Bell, *Work and Its Discontents* (Boston: Beacon Press, 1956). "Although religion declined, the significance of work was that it could still mobilize emotional energies into creative challenges" (p. 56).

11. Eric Hoffer, "Readiness to Work" (unpublished manuscript).

DANIEL BELL

The Coming of Post-Industrial Society

The concept of the post-industrial society deals primarily with changes *in the social structure*, the way in which the economy is being transformed and the occupational system reworked, and with the new relations between theory and empiricism, particularly science and technology. These changes can be charted, as I seek to do in this [chapter]. But I do not claim that these changes in social structure *determine* corresponding changes in the polity or the culture. Rather, the changes in social structure pose *questions* for the rest of society in three ways. First, the social structure—especially the social structure—is a structure of roles, designed to coordinate the actions of individuals to achieve specific ends. Roles segment individuals by defining limited modes of behavior appropriate to a particular position, but individuals do not always willingly accept the requirements of a role. One aspect of the post-industrial society, for example, is the increasing bureaucratization of science and the increasing specialization of intellectual work into minute parts. Yet it is not

clear that individuals entering science will accept this segmentation, as did the individuals who entered the factory system a hundred and fifty years ago.

Second, changes in social structure pose "management" problems for the political system. In a society which becomes increasingly conscious of its fate, and seeks to control its own fortunes, the political order necessarily becomes paramount. Since the post-industrial society increases the importance of the technical component of knowledge, it forces the hierophants of the new society—the scientists, engineers, and technocrats—either to compete with politicians or become their allies. The relationship between the social structure and the political order thus becomes one of the chief problems of power in a post-industrial society. And, third, the new modes of life, which depend strongly on the primacy of cognitive and theoretical knowledge, inevitably challenge the tendencies of the culture, which strives for the enhancement of the self and turns increasingly antinomian and anti-institutional.

In this [chapter], I am concerned chiefly with the social structural and political consequences of the post-industrial society. In a later work I shall deal with its relation to culture. But the heart of the endeavor is to trace

---

Originally published in 1973. Please see complete source information beginning on page 891.

the societal changes primarily within the social structure.

"Too large a generalization," Alfred North Whitehead wrote, "leads to mere barrenness. It is the large generalization, limited by a happy particularity, which is the fruitful conception."[1] It is easy—and particularly so today—to set forth an extravagant theory which, in its historical sweep, makes a striking claim to originality. But when tested eventually by reality, it turns into a caricature—viz. James Burnham's theory of the managerial revolution thirty years ago, or C. Wright Mills's conception of the power elite, or W. W. Rostow's stages of economic growth. I have tried to resist that impulse. Instead, I am dealing here with *tendencies,* and have sought to explore the meaning and consequences of those tendencies if the changes in social structure that I describe were to work themselves to their logical limits. But there is no guarantee that they will. Social tensions and social conflicts may modify a society considerably; wars and recriminations can destroy it; the tendencies may provoke a set of reactions that inhibit change. Thus I am writing what Hans Vahinger called an "as if," a fiction, a logical construction of what *could* be, against which the future social reality can be compared in order to see what intervened to change society in the direction it did take.

The concept of the post-industrial society is a large generalization. Its meaning can be more easily understood if one specifies [eleven] dimensions, or components, of the term:

1. *The centrality of theoretical knowledge.* Every society has always existed on the basis of knowledge, but only now has there been a change whereby the codification of theoretical knowledge and materials science becomes the basis of innovations in technology. One sees this primarily in the new science-based industries—computers, electronics, optics, polymers—that mark the last third of the century.

2. *The creation of a new intellectual technology.* Through new mathematical and economic techniques—based on the computer linear programming, Markov chains, stochastic processes and the like—we can utilize modeling, simulation and other tools of system analysis and decision theory in order to chart more efficient, "rational" solutions to economic and engineering, if not social, problems.

3. *The spread of a knowledge class.* The fastest growing group in society is the technical and professional class. In the United States this group, together with managers, made up 25 percent of a labor force of eight million persons in 1975. By the year 2000, the technical and professional class will be the largest single group in the society.

4. *The change from goods to services.* In the United States today more than 65 out of every 100 persons are engaged in services. By 1980, the figure will be about 70 in every 100. A large service sector exists in every society. In a pre-industrial society this is mainly a household and domestic class. (In England, it was the single largest class in the society until about 1870.) In an industrial society, the services are transportation, utilities, and finance, which are auxiliary to the production of goods, and personal service (beauticians, restaurant employees, and so forth). But in a post-industrial society, the new services are primarily human services (principally in health, education and social services) and professional and technical services (e.g., research, evaluation, computers, and systems analysis). The expansion of these services becomes a constraint on economic growth and a source of persistent inflation.

5. *A change in the character of work.* In a pre-industrial world, life is a game against nature in which men wrest their living from the soil, the waters, or the forests, working usually in small groups, subject to the vicissitudes of nature. In an industrial society, work is a game against fabricated nature, in which men become dwarfed by machines as they turn out goods and things. But in a post-industrial world, work is primarily a "game between persons" (between bureaucrat and client, doc-

tor and patient, teacher and student, or within research groups, office groups, service groups). Thus in the experience of work and the daily routine, nature is excluded, artifacts are excluded, and persons have to learn how to live with one another. In the history of human society, this is a completely new and unparalleled state of affairs.

6. *The role of women.* Work in the industrial sector (e.g., the factory) has largely been men's work, from which women have been usually excluded. Work in the post-industrial sector (e.g., human services) provides expanded employment opportunities for women. For the first time, one can say that women have a secure base for economic independence. One sees this in the steadily rising curve of women's participation in the labor force, in the number of families (now 60 percent of the total) that have more than one regular wage earner, and in the rising incidence of divorce as women increasingly feel less dependent, economically, on men.

7. *Science as the imago.* The scientific community, going back to the seventeenth century, has been a unique institution in human society. It has been charismatic, in that it has been revolutionary in its quest for truth and open in its methods and procedures; it derives its legitimacy from the credo that knowledge itself, not any specific instrumental ends, is the goal of science. Unlike other charismatic communities (principally religious groups and messianic political movements), it has not "routinized" its creeds and enforced official dogmas. Yet until recently, science did not have to deal with the bureaucratization of research, the subordination of its inquiries to state-directed goals, and the "test" of its results on the basis of some instrumental payoff. Now science has become inextricably intertwined not only with technology but with the military and with social technologies and societal needs. In all this—a central feature of the post-industrial society—the character of the new scientific institutions—will be crucial for the future of free inquiry and knowledge.

8. *Situses as political units.* Most of sociological analysis has focused its attention on classes or strata, horizontal units of society that exist in superior-subordinate relation to each other. Yet for the post-industrial sectors, it may well be that *situses* (from the Latin *situ,* location), a set of vertical orders, will be the more important loci of political attachment. On page 812, I sketch the possible situses of the post-industrial order. There are four *functional* situses—scientific, technological (i.e., applied skills: engineering, economics, medicine), administrative and cultural—and five *institutional* situses—economic enterprises, government bureaus, universities and research complexes, social complexes (e.g., hospitals, social-service centers), and the military. My argument is that the major interest conflicts will be between the situs groups, and that the attachments to these situses might be sufficiently strong to prevent the organization of the new professional groups into a coherent class in society.[2]

9. *Meritocracy.* A post-industrial society, being primarily a technical society, awards place less on the basis of inheritance or property (though these can command wealth or cultural advantage) than on education and skill. Inevitably the question of a meritocracy becomes a crucial normative question. In this [chapter] I attempt to define the character of meritocracy and defend the idea of a "just meritocracy," or of place based on achievement, through the respect of peers.

10. *The end of scarcity?* Most socialist and utopian theories of the nineteenth century ascribed almost all the ills of society to the scarcity of goods and the competition of men for these scarce goods. In fact, one of the most common definitions of economics characterized it as the art of efficient allocation of scarce goods among competing ends. Marx and other socialists argued that abundance was the precondition for socialism and claimed, in fact, that under socialism there would be no need to adopt normative rules of just distribution, since there would be enough for everyone's needs. In that sense, the defini-

TABLE 1
Stratification and Power

	PRE-INDUSTRIAL	INDUSTRIAL	POST-INDUSTRIAL
Resource	Land	Machinery	Knowledge
Social locus	Farm Plantation	Business firm	University Research institute
Dominant figures	Landowner Military	Businessmen	Scientists Research men
Means of power	Direct control of force	Indirect influence on politics	Balance of technical-political forces Franchises and rights
Class base	Property Military force	Property Political organization Technical skill	Technical skill Political organization
Access	Inheritance Seizure by armies	Inheritance Patronage Education	Education Mobilization Co-optation

tion of communism was the abolition of economics, or the "material embodiment" of philosophy. Yet it is quite clear that scarcity will always be with us. I mean not just the question of scarce resources (for this is still a moot point) but that a post-industrial society, by its nature, brings new scarcities which nineteenth- and early-twentieth-century writers had never thought of. The socialists and liberals had talked of the scarcities of goods; but in the post-industrial society there will be scarcities of information and of time. And the problems of allocation inevitably remain, in the crueler form, even, of man becoming *homo economicus* in the disposition of his leisure time.

11. *The economics of information.* Information is by its nature a collective, not a private, good (i.e., a property). In the marketing of individual goods, it is clear that a "competitive" strategy between producers is to be preferred lest enterprise become slothful or monopolistic. Yet for the optimal social investment in knowledge, we have to follow a "cooperative" strategy in order to increase the spread and use of knowledge in society. This new problem regarding information poses the most fascinating challenges to economists and decision makers in respect to both theory and policy in the post-industrial society. . . .

Who Holds Power?

Decisions are a matter of power, and the crucial questions in any society are: *Who* holds power? And *how* is power held? How power is held is a *system* concept; who holds power is a *group* concept. How one comes to power defines the base and route; who identifies the persons. Clearly, when there is a change in the nature of the system, new groups come to power. (In the tableau of pre-industrial, industrial, and post-industrial societies, the major differences can be shown schematically—see Table 1 on Stratification and Power.)

In the post-industrial society, technical skill becomes the base of and education the mode of access to power; those (or the elite of the group) who come to the fore in this fashion are the scientists. But this does not mean that the scientists are monolithic and act as a corporate group. In actual political situations scientists may divide ideologically (as they have in the recent ABM debate), and different groups of scientists will align themselves with different segments of other elites. In the nature of politics, few groups are monolithic ("the" military, "the" scientists, "the" business class), and any group contending for power will seek allies from different groups. (Thus, in the Soviet Union, for example, where the interest groups are more clear-cut in functional terms—factory managers, central planners, army officers, party officials—and the power struggle more naked, any faction in the Politburo *seeking* power will make alliances *across* group lines. Yet once *in* power, the victors will have to make decisions *between* groups and affect the relative distribution of power of the functional units and shift the weights of the *system*.) In the change of the system in the post-industrial society, two propositions become evident:

1. As a *stratum*, scientists, or more widely the technical intelligentsia, now have to be taken into account in the political process, though they may not have been before.
2. Science itself is ruled by an ethos which is different from the ethos of other major social groups (e.g. business, the military), and this ethos will *predispose* scientists to act in a different fashion, politically, from other groups.

Forty-five years ago Thorstein Veblen, in his *Engineers and the Price System,* foresaw a new society based on technical organization and industrial management, a "soviet of technicians," as he put it in the striking language he loved to use in order to scare and mystify the academic world. In making this prediction, Veblen shared the illusion of that earlier technocrat, Henri de Saint-Simon, that the complexity of the industrial system and the indispensability of the technician made military and political revolutions a thing of the past. "Revolutions in the eighteenth century," Veblen wrote, "were military and political; and the Elder Statesmen who now believe themselves to be making history still believe that revolutions can be made and unmade by the same ways and means in the twentieth century. But any substantial or effectual overturn in the twentieth century will necessarily be an industrial overturn, and by the same token, any twentieth-century revolution can be combatted or neutralized only by industrial ways and means."

If a revolution were to come about in the United States—as a practiced skeptic Veblen was highly dubious of that prospect—it would not be led by a minority political party, as in Soviet Russia, which was a loose-knit and backward industrial region, nor would it come from the trade-union "votaries of the dinner pail," who, as a vested interest themselves, simply sought to keep prices up and labor supply down. It would occur, he said, along the lines "already laid down by the material conditions of its productive industry." And, turning this Marxist prism to his own perceptions, Veblen continued: "These main lines of revolutionary strategy are lines of technical organization and industrial management; essentially lines of industrial engineering; such as will fit the organization to take care of the highly technical industrial system that constitutes the indispensable material foundation of any modern civilized community."

The heart of Veblen's assessment of the revolutionary class is thus summed up in his identification of the "production engineers" as the indispensable "General Staff of the industrial system." "Without their immediate and unremitting guidance and correction the industrial system will not work. It is a mechanically organized structure of the technical processes designed, installed, and conducted by the production engineers. Without them and their constant attention to the industrial equipment, the mechanical appliances of industry will foot up to just so much junk."

This syndicalist idea that revolution in the twentieth century could only be an "industrial overturn" exemplifies the fallacy in so much of Veblen's thought. For as we have learned, no matter how technical social processes may be, the crucial turning points in a society occur in a political form. It is not the technocrat who ultimately holds power, but the politician.

The major changes that have reshaped American society over the past thirty years—the creation of a managed economy, a welfare society, and a mobilized polity—grew out of political responses: in the first instances to ac-

TABLE 2
Reduced Model

Base of Power:	Property	Political Position	Skill
Mode of Access:	Inheritance Entrepreneurial Ability	Machine Membership Co-optation	Education
Social Unit:	Family	Group Party	Individual

commodate the demands of economically insecure and disadvantaged groups—the farmers, workers, blacks and the poor—for protection from the hazards of the market; and later because of the concentration of resources and political objectives following the mobilized postures of the cold war and the space race.

All of this opens up a broader and more theoretical perspective about the changing nature of class and social position in contemporary society. *Class, in the final sense, denotes not a specific group of persons but a system that has institutionalized the ground rules for acquiring, holding, and transferring differential power and its attendant privileges.* In Western society, the dominant system has been property, guaranteed and safeguarded by the legal order, and transmitted through a system of marriage and family. But over the past twenty-five to fifty years, the property system has been breaking up. In American society today, there are three modes of power and social mobility, and this baffles students of society who seek to tease out the contradictory sources of class positions. There is the historic mode of property as the basis of wealth and power, with inheritance as the major route of access. There is technical skill as the basis of power and position, with education as the necessary route of access to skill. And finally there is political office as a base of power, with organization of a machine as the route of access.

One can, in a simplified way, present these modes in Table 2.

The difficulty in the analysis of power in modern Western societies is that these three systems [in Table 2] co-exist, overlap, and interpenetrate. While the family loses its importance as an economic unit, particularly with the decline of family-firms and the break-up of family capitalism, family background is still advantageous in providing impetus (financial, cultural and personal connections) for the family member. Ethnic groups, often blocked in the economic access to position, have resorted to the political route to gain privilege and wealth. And, increasingly, in the post-industrial society, technical skill becomes an overriding condition of competence for place and position. A son may succeed a father as head of a firm, but without the managerial skill to run the enterprise, the firm may lose out in competition with other, professionally managed corporations. To some extent, the owner of a firm and the politician may hire technicians and experts; yet, unless the owner or politician themselves know enough about the technical issues, their judgments may falter.

The rise of the new elites based on skill derives from the simple fact that knowledge and planning—military planning, economic planning, social planning—have become the basic requisites for all organized action in a modern society. The members of this new technocratic elite, with their new techniques of decision-making (systems analysis, linear programming, and program budgeting), have now become essential to the formulation and analysis of decisions on which political judgments have to be made, if not to the wielding of power. It is in this broad sense that the spread of education, research, and administration has created a new constituency—the technical and professional intelligentsia.

While these technologists are not bound by a sufficient common interest to make them a political class, they do have common characteristics. They are, first, the products of a new system in the recruitment for power (just as property and inheritance were the essence of the old system). The norms of the new intelligentsia—the norms of professionalism—are a departure from the hitherto prevailing norms of economic self-interest which have guided a business civilization. In the upper reaches of this new elite—that is, in the scientific community—men hold significantly different values, which could become the foundation of the new ethos for such a class.

Actually, the institution of property itself is undergoing a fundamental revision, in a significant way. In Western society for the past several hundred years, property, as the protection of private rights to wealth, has been the economic basis of individualism. Traditionally the institution of property, as Charles Reich of the Yale Law School has put it, "guards the troubled boundary between individual man and the state." In modern life property has changed in two distinctive ways. One of these is elementary: Individual property has become corporate, and property is no longer controlled by owners but by managers. In a more subtle and diffuse way, however, a new kind of property has emerged, and with it a different kind of legal relationship. To put it more baldly, property today consists not only of visible things (land, possessions, titles) but also of claims, grants, and contracts. The property relationship is not only between persons but between the individual and the government. As Reich points out, "The valuables dispensed by government take many forms, but they all share one characteristic. They are steadily taking the place of the traditional forms of wealth—forms which are held as private property. Social insurance substitutes for savings, a government contract replaces a businessman's customers and goodwill. . . . Increasingly, Americans live on government largess—allocated by government on its own terms, and held by recipients subject to conditions which express 'the public interest.'"[3]

While many forms of this "new property" represent direct grants (subsidies to farmers, corporations, and universities) or are contracts for services or goods (to industry and universities), the most pervasive form is claims held by individuals (social security, medical care, housing allowances) which derive from a new definition of social rights: claims on the community to ensure equality of treatment, claims legitimately due a person so that he will be able to share in the social heritage. And the most important claim of all is full access to education, within the limits of one's talent and potential.

The result of all this is to enlarge the arena of power, and at the same time to complicate the modes of decision-making. The domestic political process initiated by the New Deal was in effect a broadening of the "brokerage" system—the system of political deals between constituencies—although there are now many participants in the game. But there is also a new dimension in the political process, which has given the technocrats a new role. Matters of foreign policy have not been a reflex of internal political forces, but a judgment about the national interest, involving strategy decisions based on the calculation of an opponent's strength and intentions. Once the fundamental policy decision was made to oppose the communist power, many technical decisions, based on military technology and strategic assessments, took on the highest importance in the shaping of subsequent policy. Even a reworking of the economic map of the United States followed as well, with Texas and California gaining great importance because of the electronics and aerospace industries. In these instances technology and strategy laid down the requirements, and only then could business and local political groups seek to modify, or take advantage of, these decisions so as to protect their own economic interests.

In all this, the technical intelligentsia holds a double position. To the extent that it has interests in research, and positions in the universities, it becomes a new constituency—just as the military is a distinct new constituency,

since this country has never before had a permanent military establishment seeking money
and support for science, for research and development. Thus the intelligentsia becomes a
claimant, like other groups, for public support (though its influence is felt in the bureaucratic and administrative labyrinth,
rather than in the electoral system or mass
pressure). At the same time, the technicians
represent an indispensable administrative
staff for the political office holder with his
public following. . . .

If one turns, then, to the societal structure
of the post-industrial society considered along
these two historical axes [of class and power],
two conclusions are evident. First, the major
class of the emerging new society is primarily
a professional class, based on knowledge
rather than property. But second, the control system of the society is lodged not in a
successor-occupational class but in the political order, and the question of who manages
the political order is an open one. (See
"Schema: The Societal Structure of the Post-
Industrial Society.")

In terms of status (esteem and recognition,
and possibly income), the knowledge class
may be the highest class in the new society,

Schema: The Societal Structure of the Post-Industrial Society (U.S. Model)

I.   *Statuses: Axis of Stratification—Based on Knowledge*
     (Horizontal Structures)
     A. The professional class: the four estates
         1. Scientific
         2. Technological (applied skills: engineering,
             economics, medicine)
         3. Administrative
         4. Cultural (artistic and religious)
     B. Technicians and semi-professional
     C. Clerical and sales
     D. Craftsmen and semi-skilled (blue-collar)
II. *Situses: Locations of Occupational Activities*
     (Vertical Structures)
     A. Economic enterprises and business firms
     B. Government (bureaucratic: judicial and
         administrative)
     C. Universities and research institutions
     D. Social complexes (hospitals, social-service
         centers, etc.)
     E. The military
III. *Control System: The Political Order*
     A. The directorate
         1. Office of the President
         2. Legislative leaders
         3. Bureaucratic chiefs
         4. Military chiefs
     B. The polities: constituencies and claimants
         1. Parties
         2. Elites (scientific, academic, business, military)
         3. Mobilized groups
             a) Functional groups (business,
                 professional, labor)
             b) Ethnic groups
             c) Special-focus groups
                 (1) Functional (mayors of cities,
                      poor, etc.)
                 (2) Expressive (youth, women,
                      homosexual, etc.)

but in the nature of that structure there is no intrinsic reason for this class, on the basis of some coherent or corporate identity, to become a new economic interest class, or a new political class which would bid for power. The reasons for this are evident from an inspection of the Schema.

The professional class as I define it is made up of four estates: the scientific, the technological, the administrative, and the cultural.[4] While the estates, as a whole, are bound by a common ethos, there is no intrinsic interest that binds one to the other, except for a common defense of the idea of learning; in fact there are large disjunctions between them. The scientific estate is concerned with the pursuit of basic knowledge and seeks, legitimately, to defend the conditions of such pursuit, untrammeled by political or extraneous influence. The technologists, whether engineers, economists, or physicians, base their work on a codified body of knowledge, but in the application of that knowledge to social or economic purposes they are constrained by the policies of the different situses they are obedient to. The administrative estate is concerned with the management of organizations and is bound by the self-interest of the organization itself (its perpetuation and aggrandizement) as well as the implementation of social purposes, and may come into conflict with one or another of the estates. The cultural estate—artistic and religious—is involved with the expressive symbolism (plastic or ideational) of forms and meanings, but to the extent that it is more intensively concerned with meanings, it may find itself increasingly hostile to the technological and administrative estates. As I noted in the introduction, the axial principle of modern culture, in its concern with the self, is antinomian and anti-institutional, and thus hostile to the functional rationality which tends to dominate the application of knowledge by the technological and administrative estates. Thus in the post-industrial society one finds increasingly a disjunction between social structure and culture which inevitably affects the cohe-

siveness if not the corporate consciousness of the four estates.[5]

While the classes may be represented, horizontally, by *statuses* (headed by the four estates), the society is organized, vertically, by *situses*, which are the actual loci of occupational activities and interests. I use this unfamiliar sociological word *situses* to emphasize the fact that in day-to-day activities the actual play and conflict of interests exist between the organizations to which men belong, rather than between the more diffuse class or status identities. In a capitalist society, the property owner or businessman, as a class, is located exclusively in the business firm or corporation, so that status and situs are joined. In the post-industrial society, however, the four estates are distributed among many different situses. Scientists can work for economic enterprises, government, universities, social complexes, or the military (though the bulk of the "pure" scientists are to be found in the university). And the same distributions hold for the technologists and the managers. Because of this "cross-cutting," the likelihood of a pure "estate" consciousness for political purposes tends to diminish.

Finally, if the major historical turn in the last quarter-century has been the subordination of the economic function to societal goals, the political order necessarily becomes the control system of the society. But who runs it, and for whose (or what) ends? In one respect, what the change may mean is that traditional social conflicts have simply shifted from one arena to another, so that what the traditional classes fought out in the economic realm, where men sought comparative advantage in place, privilege and domination, is now transferred to the political realm, and as that arena widens, the special foci and ethnic groups (the poor and the blacks) now seek to gain through politics the privileges and advantages they could not obtain in the economic order. This is what has been taking place in recent years, and it will continue. The second, and structurally more pervasive, shift is that in the post-industrial society the *situses* rather than the *statuses* would be the major political-interest units in the society. To some extent this is evident in the familiar phenomenon of pressure groups. But in the post-industrial society it is more likely that the *situses* will achieve greater corporate cohesiveness vis-à-vis one another and become the major claimants for public support and the major constituencies in the determination of public policy.[6] And yet the very forces which have re-emphasized the primacy of the political order in a technical world make it imperative to define some coherent goals for the society as a whole and, in the process, to articulate a public philosophy which is more than the sum of what particular situses or social groups may want. In the efforts to forge some such coherence one may find the seeds of the cohesiveness of the professional class in the post-industrial society.

A new social system, contrary to Marx, does not always arise necessarily within the shell of an old one but sometimes outside of it. The framework of feudal society was made up of noblemen, lords, soldiers, and priests whose wealth was based on land. The bourgeois society that took hold in the thirteenth century was made up of artisans, merchants, and free professionals whose property lay in their skills or their willingness to take risks, and whose mundane values were far removed from the fading theatrics of the chivalric style of life. It arose, however, outside the feudal landed structure, in the free communes, or towns, that were no longer seignorial dependencies. And these self-ruling small communes became the cornerstones of the future European mercantile and industrial society.[7]

So, too, the process today. The roots of post-industrial society lie in the inexorable influence of science on productive methods, particularly in the transformation of the electrical and chemical industries at the beginning of the twentieth century. But as Robert Heilbroner has observed: "Science, as we know it, began well before capitalism existed and did not experience its full growth until well after capitalism was solidly entrenched." And science, as a quasi-autonomous force, would extend beyond capitalism. By this token, one can say that the scientific estate—its ethos and its organization—is the monad that contains within itself the imago of the future society.[8] . . .

Meritocracy and Equality

In 1958, the English sociologist Michael Young wrote a fable, *The Rise of the Meritocracy*.[9] It purports to be a "manuscript," written in the year 2033, which breaks off inconclusively for reasons the "narrator" failed to comprehend. The theme is the transformation of English society, by the turn of the twenty-first century, owing to the victory of the principle of achievement over that of ascription (i.e., the gaining of place by assignment or inheritance). For centuries, the elite positions in the society had been held by the children of the nobility on the hereditary principle of succession. But in the nature of modern society, "the rate of social progress depend[ed] on the degree to which power is matched with intelligence." Britain could no longer afford a ruling class without the necessary technical skills. Through the successive school-reform acts, the principle of merit slowly became established. Each man had his place in the society on the basis of "IQ and Effort." By 1990 or thereabouts, all adults with IQs over 125 belonged to the meritocracy.

But with that transformation came an unexpected reaction. Previously, talent had been distributed throughout the society, and each class or social group had its own natural leaders. Now all men of talent were raised into a common elite, and those below had no excuses for their failures; they bore the stigma of rejection, they were known inferiors.

By the year 2034 the Populists had revolted. Though the majority of the rebels were members of the lower classes, the leaders were high-status women, often the wives of leading scientists. Relegated during the early married years to the household because of the need to nurture high-IQ children, the activist women had demanded equality between the sexes, a movement that was then generalized into the demand for equality for all, and for a classless society. Life was not to be ruled by "a mathematical measure" but each person would develop his own diverse capacities for leading his own life.[10] The Populists won. After little more than half a century, the Meritocracy had come to an end.

Is this, too, the fate of the post-industrial society? The post-industrial society, in its initial logic, is a meritocracy. Differential status and differential income are based on technical skills and higher education. Without those achievements one cannot fulfill the requirements of the new social division of labor which is a feature of that society. And there are few high places open without those skills. To that extent, the post-industrial society differs from society at the turn of the twentieth century. The initial change, of course, came in the professions. Seventy years or so ago, one could still "read" law in a lawyer's office and take the bar examination without a college degree. Today, in medicine, law, accounting, and a dozen other professions, one needs a college degree and accrediting, through examination, by legally sanctioned committees of the profession, before one can practice one's art. For many years, until after World War II, business was the chief route open to an ambitious and aggressive person who wanted to strike out for himself. And the rags-to-riches ascent (or, more accurately, clerk-to-capitalist, if one follows the career of a Rockefeller, Harriman, or Carnegie) required drive and ruthlessness rather than education and skills. One can still start various kinds of small businesses (usually, now, by franchise from a larger corporation), but the expansion of such enterprises takes vastly different skills than in the past. Within the corporation, as managerial positions have become professionalized, individuals are rarely promoted from shop jobs below but are chosen from the outside, with a college degree as the passport of recognition. Only in politics, where position may be achieved through the ability to recruit a following, or through patronage, is there a relatively open ladder without formal credentials.

Technical skill, in the post-industrial society, is what the economists call "human capital." An "investment" in four years of college, according to initial estimates of Gary Becker, yields, over the average working life of the male graduate, an annual return of about 13 percent.[11] Graduation from an elite college (or elite law school or business school) gives one a further differential advantage over graduates from "mass" or state schools. Thus, the university, which once reflected the status system of the society, has now become the arbiter of class position. As the gate-keeper, it has gained a quasi-monopoly in determining the future stratification of the society.[12]

Any institution which gains a quasi-monopoly power over the fate of individuals is likely, in a free society, to be subject to quick attack. Thus, it is striking that the populist revolt, which Michael Young foresaw several decades hence, has already begun, at the very onset of the post-industrial society. One sees this in the derogation of the IQ and the denunciation of theories espousing a genetic basis of intelligence; the demand for "open admission" to universities on the part of minority groups in the large urban centers; the pressure for increased numbers of blacks, women, and specific minority groups such as Puerto Ricans and Chicanos in the faculties of universities, by quotas if necessary; and the attack on "credentials" and even schooling itself as the determinant of a man's position in the society. A post-industrial society reshapes the class structure of society by creating new technical elites. The populist reaction, which has begun in the 1970s, raises the demand for greater "equality" as a defense against being excluded from that society. Thus the issue of meritocracy versus equality. . . .

The claim for group rights stands in forma contradiction to the principle of individualism, with its emphasis on achievement and universalism. But in reality it is no more than the extension, to hitherto excluded social units, of the group principle which has undergirded American politics from the start. The group process—which was the vaunted discovery of the "realists" of American political science—consisted largely of economic bargaining between functional or pressure groups operating outside the formal structure of the party system. What we now find are ethnic and ascriptive groups claiming formal representation both in the formal political structure and in all other institutions of the society as well.

These claims are legitimated, further, by the fact that America has been a pluralist society, or has come to accept a new definition of pluralism rather than the homogeneity of Americanism. Pluralism, in its classic conceptions,[13] made a claim for the continuing cultural identity of ethnic and religious groups and for the institutional autonomy of cultural institutions (e.g., universities) from politics. Pluralism was based on the separation of realms. But what we have today is a thoroughgoing politicizing of society in which not only the market is subordinated to political decision but all institutions have to bend to the demands of a political center and politicize themselves in group representational terms. Here, too, there has been another change. In functional group politics, membership was not fixed, and one could find cross-cutting allegiances or shifting coalitions. Today the groups that claim representation—in the political parties, in the universities, in the hospitals and the community—are formed by primordial or biological ties, and one cannot erase the ascriptive nature of sex or color.

And yet, once one accepts the principle of redress and representation of the disadvantaged in the group terms that were initially formulated, it is difficult for the polity to deny those later claims. That is the logic of democracy which has always been present in the ambiguous legacy of the principle of equality.

Notes

1. Alfred North Whitehead, *Science and the Modern World* (New York, 1960; original edition, 1925), p. 46.

2. What is striking is that in the communist world, it is quite clear that *situses* play the major role in politics. One analyzes the play of power, not in class terms, but on the basis of the rivalries among the party, the military, the planning ministries, the industrial enterprises, the collective farms, the cultural institutions—all of which are *situses*.

3. Charles Reich, "The New Property," *The Public Interest,* no. 3 (Spring 1966), p. 57.

4. The suggestion of four estates is derived, of course, from Don K. Price's fruitful book *The Scientific Estate* (Cambridge, Mass., 1965). Price defines four functions in government—the scientific, professional, administrative, and political—and converts each function, as an ideal type, into an estate. My differences with Price are twofold: I think the estates can be represented more accurately as social groups, rather than functions; more importantly, I do not consider the *political* function coeval logically with the others, for I see the political as the control system of the entire societal structure. Terminologically, I have substituted the word "technological" (for the applied skills) where Price uses "professional," since I would reserve "professional" for the larger meaning of the entire class, and I have added a cultural estate, where Price has none. Nonetheless, my indebtedness to Price is great.

5. One might note that the more extreme forms of the "new consciousness" such as Theodore Rozsak's *The Making of a Counter-Culture* and Charles Reich's *The Greening of America* manifest a distinct hostility not only to scientism, but to science as well.

6. The limitation of this analysis is that while the post-industrial society, in its societal structure, increasingly becomes a *functional* society, the political order is not organized in functional terms. Thus the continuing existence of the traditional geographical districts and the dispersal of persons in this fashion means that the political issues at any one time are much more diffuse than the interests of the particular statuses or situses. It would also indicate that the situses would, like the pressure groups, operate primarily through the lobbying of the legislative and executive branches, rather than work directly through the electoral process. Reality complicates immeasurably any ideal-type schemas.

7. Paradoxically, the growth of that society came about only after the self-contained economic life of the commune—its roots—was broken by the rise of larger-scale industry which, in branching out, could buy its raw materials in one town and sell in another, and which made its way, against both the older feudal society and the regulative restrictions

of the commune, in alliance with the monarchical centralization of the newly emerging national state.

8. This is, indeed, Heilbroner's suggestion. See Robert Heilbroner, *The Limits of American Capitalism* (New York, 1966), p. 115.

9. Michael Young, *The Rise of the Meritocracy, 1870–2033* (London, 1958).

10. A theoretician of the Technicians party, Professor Eagle, had argued that marriage partners, in the national interest, should consult the intelligence register, for a high-IQ man who mates with a low-IQ woman is wasting his genes. The activist women, on the other hand, took romance as their banner and beauty as their flag, arguing that marriage should be based on attraction. Their favorite slogan was "Beauty is achievable by all."

11. Gary S. Becker, *Human Capital* (New York, 1964), p. 112. Later writers have suggested this figure may be too high; the point remains that a college degree does provide an investment "yield."

12. For a comprehensive discussion of this major social change, see Jencks and Riesman, *The Academic Revolution* (New York, 1968). For a survey of the reaction, see Stephen Graubard and Geno Ballotti, eds., *The Embattled University* (New York, 1970).

13. See, for example, the work of R. M. MacIver, *The More Perfect Union: A Program for the Control of Inter-group Discrimination* (New York, 1948), and on the religious side, John Courtney Murray, *We Hold These Truths: Reflections on the American Proposition* (New York, 1960).

ALVIN W. GOULDNER

The Future of Intellectuals and the Rise of the New Class

Originally published in 1979. Please see complete source information beginning on page 891.

In all countries that have in the twentieth century become part of the emerging world socioeconomic order, a New Class composed of intellectuals and technical intelligentsia—not the same—enter into contention with the groups already in control of the society's economy, whether these are businessmen or party leaders. A new contest of classes and a new class system is slowly arising in the third world of developing nations, in the second world of the USSR and its client states, and in the first world of late capitalism of North America, Western Europe, and Japan.

The early historical evolution of the New Class in Western Europe, its emergence into the public sphere as a structurally differentiated and (relatively) autonomous social stratum, may be defined in terms of certain critical episodes. What follows is only a synoptic inventory of some episodes decisive in the formation of the New Class.

1. A process of secularization in which most intelligentsia are no longer trained by, living within, and subject to close supervision by a churchly organization, and thus separated from the everyday life of society.[1]

Secularization is important because it desacralizes authority-claims and facilitates challenges to definitions of social reality made by traditional authorities linked to the church. Secularization is important also because it is an infrastructure on which there develops the modern grammar of rationality, or culture of critical discourse, with its characteristic stress on self-groundedness—in Martin Heidegger's sense of the "mathematical project."[2]

2. A second episode in the emergence of the New Class is the rise of diverse vernacular languages, the corresponding decline of Latin as the language of intellectuals, and especially of their scholarly production. Latin becomes a ritual, rather than a technical language. This development further dissolves the membrane between everyday life and the intellectuals—whether clerical or secular.

3. There is a breakdown of the feudal and old regime system of personalized *patronage* relations between the old hegemonic elite and individual members of the New Class as cultural producers; and

4. A corresponding growth of an anonymous *market* for the products and services of the New Class, thus allowing them to make an independent living apart from close supervision and *personalized controls by patrons*. Along with secularization, this means that the residence and work of intellectuals are both now less closely supervised by others.

They may now more readily take personal initiatives in the public, political sphere, while also having a "private" life.

5. The character and development of the emerging New Class also depended importantly on the multi-national structure of European polities. That Europe was not a single empire with a central authority able to impose a single set of norms throughout its territory, but a system of competing and autonomous states with diverse cultures and religions, meant that dissenting intellectuals, scientists, and divines could and did protect their own intellectual innovations by migrating from their home country when conditions there grew insupportable and sojourning in foreign lands. Even the enforced travel of exiled intellectuals also enabled them to enter into a European-wide communication network. In an article (as yet unpublished), Robert Wuthnow has suggested that their often extensive travel led many intellectuals to share a cosmopolitan identity transcending national limits and enhancing their autonomy from local elites.

6. A sixth episode in the formation of the New Class is the waning of the extended, patriarchical family system and its replacement by the smaller, nuclear family. As middle class women become educated and emancipated, they may increasingly challenge paternal authority and side with their children in resisting it. With declining paternal authority and growing maternal influence, the autonomy strivings of children are now more difficult to repress; hostility and rebellion against paternal authority can become more overt. There is, correspondingly, increasing difficulty experienced by paternal authority in imposing and reproducing its social values and political ideologies in their children.

7. Following the French Revolution, there is in many parts of Europe, especially France and Germany, a profound reformation and extension of *public, non*-church controlled, (relatively more) *multi-class* education, at the lower levels as well as at the college, polytechnical, and university levels. On the one hand, higher education in the public school becomes the institutional basis for the *mass* production of the New Class of intelligentsia and intellectuals. On the other hand, the expansion of primary and secondary public school teachers greatly increases the jobs available to the New Class.

As teachers, intellectuals come to be defined, and to define themselves, as responsible for and "representative" of society as a *whole*,[3] rather than as having allegiance to the class interests of their students or their parents. As teachers, they are not defined as having an *obligation* to reproduce parental values in their children. Public teachers supersede private tutors.

8. The new structurally differentiated educational system is increasingly insulated from the family system, becoming an important source of values among students divergent from those of their families. The socialization of the young by their families is now mediated by a *semi*-autonomous group of teachers.

9. While growing public education limits family influence on education, it also increases the influence of the state on education. The public educational system thus becomes a major *cosmopolitanizing* influence on its students, with a corresponding distancing from *localistic* interests and values.

10. Again, the new school system becomes a major setting for the intensive linguistic conversion of students from casual to reflexive speech, or (in Basil Bernstein's terms) from "restricted" linguistic codes to "elaborated" linguistic codes,[4] to a culture of discourse in which claims and assertions may *not* be justified by reference to the speaker's social status. This has the profound consequence of making all *authority-referring* claims potentially problematic.

11. This new culture of discourse often diverges from assumptions fundamental to everyday life, tending to put them into question even when they are linked to the upper classes. These school-inculcated modes of speech are, also, (relatively) situation-free language variants. Their situation-freeness is further heightened by the "communications revolution" in general, and by the development of printing technology, in particular. With the spread of printed materials, definitions of social reality available to intellectuals may now derive increasingly from *distant* persons, from groups geographically, culturally, and historically distant and even from dead persons, and may therefore diverge greatly from any local environment in which they are received. Definitions of social reality made by local elites may now be invidiously contrasted (by intellectuals) with definitions made in other places and times.

12. With the spread of public schools, literacy spreads; humanistic intellectuals lose their exclusiveness and privileged market position, and now experience a status disparity between their "high" culture, as they see it, and their lower deference, repute, income and social power. The social position of humanistic intellectuals, *particularly in a technocratic and industrial society,* becomes more marginal and alienated than that of the technical intelligentsia. The New Class becomes internally differentiated.

13. Finally, a major episode in the emergence of the modern intelligentsia is the changing form of the revolutionary *organization*. Revolution itself becomes a technology to be pursued with "instrumental rationality." The revolutionary organization evolves from a ritualistic, oath-bound secret society into the modern "vanguard" party. When the *Communist Manifesto* remarks that Communists have nothing to hide,[5] it is exactly a proposed emergence into *public* life which is implied. The *Communist Manifesto* was written by Marx and Engels for the "League of Communists," which was born of the "League of the Just" which, in turn, was descended from the "League of Outlaws." This latter group of German emigrants in Paris had a pyramidal structure, made a sharp distinction between upper and lower members, blindfolded members during initiation ceremonies, used recognition signs and passwords, and bound members by an oath.[6] The vanguard organization, however, de-ritualizes participation and entails elements of both the "secret society" and of the public political party. In the vanguard organization, public refers to the public availability of the *doctrine* rather than the availability of the organization or its membership to public scrutiny. Here, to be "public" entails the organization's rejection of "secret doctrines" known only to an elite in the organization—as, for instance, Bakunin's doctrine of an elite dictatorship of anarchists.[7] The *modern* vanguard structure is first clearly encoded in Lenin's *What Is to Be Done?* Here it is plainly held that the proletariat cannot develop a *socialist* consciousness by itself, but must secure this from a scientific theory developed by the intelligentsia.[8] The "vanguard" party expresses the *modernizing* and elite ambitions of the New Class as well as an effort to overcome its political limitations. Lenin's call for the development of "professional" revolutionaries, as the core of the vanguard, is a rhetoric carrying the tacit

promise of a *career*-like life which invites young members of the New Class to "normalize" the revolutionary existence.

I shall return to and enlarge upon *some* of the critical episodes inventoried above. Above all, the attempt is to formulate a frame of reference within which the New Class can be situated, giving some indication of the intellectual work—theoretical and empirical—that needs to be done to understand the New Class as a world historical phenomenon. Rather than viewing the New Class as if it were composed just of technicians or engineers, the effort that follows moves toward a *general* theory of the New Class as encompassing *both* technical intelligentsia *and* intellectuals. Rather than focusing in a parochial way on the United States alone, my interest is in the New Class in *both* late capitalism and in the authoritarian state socialism of the USSR, without arguing or implying any more general "convergence" thesis. I shall suggest that the two most important theoretical foundations needed for a general theory of the New Class will be, first, a theory of its distinctive language behavior, its distinctive culture of discourse and, secondly, a general theory of capital within which the New Class's "human capital" or the old class's moneyed capital will be special cases.

The analysis to follow is grounded in what I can only call my own version of a "neo-Hegelian" sociology, a neo-Hegelianism which is a "left" but certainly not a "young" Hegelianism. It is *left* Hegelianism in that it holds that knowledge and knowledge systems are important in shaping social outcomes, but, far from seeing these as disembodied eternal essences, views them as the ideology of special social classes; and while ready to believe that knowledge is one of the best hopes we have for a humane social reconstruction, also sees our knowledge systems as historically shaped forces that embody limits and, indeed, pathologies.

Like any social object, the New Class can be defined in terms of both its imputed value or goodness and its imputed power.[9] In most

cultural grammars, a "normal" social world is supposed to be one in which the powerful are good and the bad, weak. The temptation to see the world in this manner, to *normalize* it, is difficult to resist and one sees it at work in conceptions of the New Class. Thus Noam Chomsky sees the New Class as cynically corrupt *and* as weak, pliable tools of others. Conversely, John Galbraith views the technical intelligentsia as productively benign *and* as already dominant. Such judgments bear the impress (albeit in different directions) of normalizing tendencies and ought to be routinely suspect.

In contrast to such normalizing tendencies, a left Hegelian sociology accepts dissonance as part of reality. It does not assume that the strong are good or the bad, weak. It accepts the possibility that those who are becoming stronger—such as the New Class—and to whom the future *may* belong, are not always the better and may, indeed, be morally ambiguous.

There are, then, several distinguishable conceptions of the New Class:

1. *New Class as Benign Technocrats:* Here the New Class is viewed as a new historical elite already entrenched in institutional influence which it uses in benign ways for society; it is more or less inevitable and trustworthy: e.g., Galbraith,[10] Bell,[11] Berle and Means.[12]

(*Sed contra:* This obscures the manner in which the New Class egoistically pursues its own special vested interests. Moreover, the power of the New Class today is scarcely entrenched. This view also ignores the limits on the rationality of the New Class.)

2. *New Class as Master Class:* Here the New Class is seen as another moment in a long-continuing circulation of historical elites, as a socialist intelligentsia that brings little new to the world and continues to exploit the rest of society as the old class had, but now uses education rather than money to exploit others: Bakunin,[13] Machajski.[14]

(*Sed contra:* The New Class is more historically unique and discontinuous than this sees; while protecting its own special interests, it is not bound by the same *limits* as the old class and, at least transiently, contributes to collective needs.)

3. *New Class as Old Class Ally:* The New Class is here seen as a benign group of dedicated "professionals" who will uplift the old (moneyed) class from a venal group to a collectivity-oriented elite and who, fusing with it, will forge a new, genteel elite continuous with but better than the past: Talcott Parsons.[15]

(*Sed contra:* Neither group is an especially morally bound agent; the old class is constrained to protect its profits, the New Class is cashing in on its education. Immersed in the present, this view misses the fact that each is ready to exploit the other, if need be, and shows little understanding of the profound (if different) limits imposed on the rationality and morality of each of these groups, and of the important tensions between them.)

4. *New Class as Servants of Power:* Here the New Class is viewed as subservient to the old (moneyed) class which is held to retain power much as it always did, and is simply using the New Class to maintain its domination of society: Noam Chomsky[16] and Maurice Zeitlin.[17]

(*Sed contra:* This ignores the revolutionary history of the twentieth century in which radicalized elements of the New Class played a major leadership role in the key revolutions of our time. It greatly overemphasizes the common interests binding the New and old class, systematically missing the tensions between them; it ignores the fact that elimination of the old class is an historical option open to the New Class. This static conception underestimates the growth in the numbers and influence of the New Class. The view is also unexpectedly Marcusean in overstressing the prospects of old class continuity; it really sees the old class as having no effective opponents, either in the New Class or in the old adversary class, the proletariat. It thus ends as seeing even less social change in prospect than the Parsonian view [#3 above].)

5. *New Class as Flawed Universal Class (my own view):* The New Class is elitist and self-seeking and uses its special knowledge to advance its own interests and power, and to control its own work situation. Yet the New Class may also be the best card that history has presently given us to play. The power of the New Class is growing. It is substantially more powerful and independent than Chomsky suggests, while still much less powerful than is suggested by Galbraith who seems to conflate present reality with future possibility. The power of this morally ambiguous New Class is on the ascendent and it holds a mortgage on at least *one* historical future.

In my own left Hegelian sociology, the New Class bearers of knowledge are seen as an embryonic new "universal class"—as the prefigured embodiment of such future as the working class still has. It is that part of the working class which will survive cybernation. At the same time, a left Hegelian sociology also insists that the New Class is profoundly flawed as a universal class. Moreover, the New Class is not some unified subject or a seamless whole; it, too, has its own internal contradictions. It is a class internally divided with tensions between (technical) intelligentsia and (humanistic) intellectuals. No celebration, mine is a critique of the New Class which does not view its growing power as inevitable, which sees it as morally ambivalent, embodying the collective interest but partially and transiently, while simultaneously cultivating its own guild advantage. . . .

The New Class as a Cultural Bourgeoisie

1. The New Class and the old class are at first undifferentiated; the New Class commonly originates in classes with property advantages, that is, in the old class, or is sponsored by them. The New Class of intellectuals and intelligentsia are the relatively more *educated* counterpart—often the brothers, sisters, or children—of the old moneyed class. Thus the New Class contest sometimes has the character of a *civil war within the upper*

classes. It is the differentiation of the old class into contentious factions. To understand the New Class contest it is vital to understand how the *privileged* and advantaged, not simply the suffering, come to be alienated from the very system that privileges them.

2. The "non-negotiable" objectives of the old moneyed class are to reproduce their capital, at a minimum, but, preferably, to make it accumulate and to appropriate profit: M-C-M′, as Marx said. This is done within a structure in which all of them must compete with one another. This unrelenting competition exerts pressure to rationalize their productive and administrative efforts and unceasingly to heighten efficiency. (Marx called it, "revolutionizing" production.) But this rationalization is dependent increasingly on the efforts of the New Class intelligentsia and its expert skills. It is inherent in its structural situation, then, that the old class must bring the New Class into existence.

3. Much of the New Class is at first trained under the direct control of the old class's firms or enterprises. Soon, however, the old class is separated from the reproduction of the New Class by the emergence and development of a public system of education whose costs are "socialized."[18]

4. The more that the New Class's reproduction derives from specialized systems of public education, the more the New Class develops an ideology that stresses its *autonomy,* its separation from and presumable independence of "business" or political interests. This autonomy is said to be grounded in the specialized knowledge or cultural capital transmitted by the educational system, along with an emphasis on the obligation of educated persons to attend to the welfare of the collectivity. In other words, the *ideology* of "professionalism" emerges.

5. Professionalism is one of the public *ideologies* of the New Class, and is the genteel subversion of the old class by the new. Professionalism is a phase in the historical development of the "collective consciousness" of the New Class. While not overtly a critique of the old class, professionalism is a tacit claim by the New Class to *technical and moral superiority* over the old class, implying that the latter lack technical credentials and are guided by motives of commercial venality. Professionalism silently installs the New Class as the paradigm of virtuous and legitimate authority, performing with technical skill and with dedicated concern for the society-at-large. Professionalism makes a focal claim for the legitimacy of the New Class which tacitly deauthorizes the old class.

On the one side, this is a bid for prestige *within* the established society; on the other, it tacitly presents the New Class as an *alternative* to the old. In asserting its own claims to authority, professionalism in effect *devalues the authority of the old class.*

6. The special privileges and powers of the New Class are grounded in their *individual* control of special cultures, languages, techniques, and of the skills resulting from these. The New Class is a cultural bourgeoisie who appropriates privately the advantages of an historically and collectively produced cultural capital. Let us be clear, then: the New Class is not just *like* the old class; its special culture is not just *like* capital. No metaphor is intended. The special culture of the New Class *is* a stock of capital that generates a stream of income (some of) which it appropriates privately.

7. The fundamental objectives of the New Class are: to increase its own share of the national product; to produce and reproduce the special social conditions enabling them to appropriate privately larger shares of the incomes produced by the special cultures they possess; to control their work and their work settings; and to increase their political power partly in order to achieve the foregoing. The struggle of the New Class is, therefore, to *institutionalize a wage system,* i.e., a social system with a distinct principle of distributive justice: "from each according to his ability, to each according to his work," which is also the norm of "socialism." Correspondingly, the New Class may oppose other social systems and their different systems of privilege, for example, systems that allocate privileges and in-

comes on the basis of controlling stocks of money (i.e., old capital). The New Class, then, is prepared to be egalitarian so far as the privileges of the *old* class are concerned. That is, under certain conditions it is prepared to remove or restrict the special incomes of the old class: profits, rents, interest. The New Class is anti-egalitarian, however, in that it seeks special guild advantages—political powers and incomes—on the basis of its possession of cultural capital. . . .

The New Class as a Speech Community

1. The culture of critical discourse (CCD)[19] is an historically evolved set of rules, a grammar of discourse, which (1) is concerned to *justify* its assertions, but (2) whose *mode* of justification does not proceed by invoking authorities, and (3) prefers to elicit the *voluntary* consent of those addressed solely on the basis of arguments adduced. CCD is centered on a specific speech act: justification. It is a culture of discourse in which there is nothing that speakers will on principle permanently refuse to discuss or make problematic; indeed, they are even willing to talk about the value of talk itself and its possible inferiority to silence or to practice. This grammar is the deep structure of the common ideology shared by the New Class. *The shared ideology of the intellectuals and intelligentsia is thus an ideology about discourse.* Apart from and underlying the various technical languages (or sociolects) spoken by specialized professions, intellectuals and intelligentsia are commonly committed to a culture of critical discourse (CCD). CCD is the latent but mobilizable infrastructure of modern "technical" languages.

2. The culture of critical discourse is characterized by speech that is *relatively* more *situation-free,* more context or field "independent." This speech culture thus values expressly legislated meanings and devalues tacit, context-limited meanings. Its ideal is: "one

word, one meaning," for everyone and forever.

The New Class's special speech variant also stresses the importance of particular modes of *justification,* using especially explicit and articulate rules, rather than diffuse precedents or tacit features of the speech context. The culture of critical speech requires that the validity of claims be justified without reference to the speaker's *societal position or authority.* Here, good speech is speech that can make its own principles *explicit* and is oriented to conforming with them, rather than stressing context-sensitivity and context-variability. Good speech here thus has *theoreticity.*[20]

Being pattern-and-principle-oriented, CCD implies that that which is said may *not* be correct, and may be *wrong.* It recognizes that "What Is" may be mistaken or inadequate and is therefore open to alternatives. CCD is also relatively more *reflexive,* self-monitoring, capable of more metacommunication, that is, of talk about talk; it is able to make its own speech problematic, and to edit it with respect to its lexical and grammatical features, as well as making problematic the validity of its assertions. CCD thus requires considerable "expressive discipline," not to speak of "instinctual renunciation."

3. Most importantly, the culture of critical speech forbids reliance upon the speaker's person, authority, or status in society to justify his claims. As a result, CCD de-authorizes all speech grounded in traditional societal authority, while it authorizes itself, the elaborated speech variant of the culture of critical discourse, as the standard of *all* "serious" speech. From now on, persons and their social positions must not be visible in their speech. Speech becomes impersonal. Speakers hide behind their speech. Speech seems to be dis-embodied, de-contextualized and self-grounded. (This is especially so for the speech of intellectuals and somewhat less so for technical intelligentsia who may not invoke CCD except when their paradigms break down.) The New Class becomes the guild masters of an invisible pedagogy.

4. The culture of critical discourse is the common ideology shared by the New Class, although technical intelligentsia sometimes keep it in latency. The skills and the social conditions required to reproduce it are among the common *interests* of the New Class. Correspondingly, it is in the common interest of the New Class to prevent or oppose all censorship of its speech variety and to install it as the standard of good speech. *The New Class thus has both a common ideology in CCD and common interests in its cultural capital....*

Intelligentsia and Intellectuals

1. There are at least two elites within the New Class: (1) *intelligentsia* whose intellectual interests are fundamentally "technical" and (2) *intellectuals* whose interests are primarily critical, emancipatory, hermeneutic and hence often political. Both elites utilize an elaborated linguistic variant and both are committed to the CCD. Both therefore resist the old class, although doing so in different ways in different settings and to different degrees.

While intellectuals often contribute to revolutionary leadership, they also serve to accommodate the future to the past and to reproduce the past in the future. That's what comes of the love of books. While the technical intelligentsia often wish nothing more than to be allowed to enjoy their opiate obsessions with technical puzzles, it is their social mission to revolutionize technology continually and hence disrupt established social solidarities and cultural values by never contenting themselves with the *status quo*. Revolutionary intellectuals are the medium of an ancient morality; accommodative intelligentsia are the medium of a new amorality. Which is more revolutionary?

2. The sociology and the social psychology of the occupational life of intellectuals and technical intelligentsia differ considerably, as do their cognitive procedures. Thomas Kuhn's notion of "normal science"[21] is a key to the cognitive life of technical intelligentsia and of their differences from intellectuals. A "normal science" is one whose members concentrate their efforts on solving the "puzzles" of "paradigms" on which normal science centers. Technical intelligentsia concentrate on operations within the paradigm(s) of their discipline, exploring its inner symbolic space, extending its principles to new fields, fine-tuning it. Intellectuals, in contrast, are those whose fields of activity more commonly lack consensually validated paradigms, may have several competing paradigms, and they therefore do not take normal science with its single dominating paradigm as the usual case. Intellectuals often transgress the boundaries of the conventional division of labor in intellectual life; they do not reject scholarship, however, but only the *normalization* of scholarship.

3. It would be tempting but far too simple to say, intellectuals produce the "lions" of the New Class, while the intelligentsia produce its "foxes." Who is a lion and who a fox depends on whose way upward is being blocked. Where recruitment of college teachers is under the close control of the national ministry, as for example in Israel, members of the Israeli Communist Party and any who seem well disposed toward it have little chance of being hired.[22] In parts of the Mid-East, then, it is often the case that teachers and other intellectuals are relatively prudent politically, while doctors, engineers, and lawyers—being "independent"—may be more openly radical. Ché Guevara, it will be remembered, was a doctor, as is George Habash; Yasir Arafat was trained as an engineer.

Old Line Bureaucrats, New Staff Intelligentsia

1. With the growth of the technical intelligentsia, the functional autonomy of the old class wanes. The intelligentsia of the New Class manage the new means of production and administration; they also acquire at-hand

control over the new means of communication and of *violence*. If we think of the state's repressive apparatus within the framework of Marxism there is no way to explain the recent revolutions in Ethiopia and Portugal, where the military played a singular role. In less developed countries, military intelligentsia are often the vanguard of the New Class.

Marxism misses the paradox that the old class can influence the state, or any other administrative system for that matter, only with the mediation of the New Class. It is not simply a matter of the split between "management and ownership" within capitalism, first, because that split is no less true of "socialism," and secondly, because the split is not confined to the production of commodities, but also includes the production of *violence*. As the organizational units of the economy and state become larger and more bureaucratic, the survival and control of the old class becomes more attenuated, more indirect, ever more dependent on the intelligentsia of the New Class.

2. The fundamental organizational instrument of our time, the bureaucratic organization, becomes increasingly scientized. The old bureaucratic officials at first provide a protective cover for the growth of the New Class. But as the number and importance of technical experts operating with CCD increases, there is a growing split between the old line bureaucrats and the technical intelligentsia. It becomes ever more difficult even for those *managing* the organization simply to understand the skills of the New Class, let alone to exert an ongoing, close control over them. The bureaucratic organization, as the dominant organizational type of the modern era, is controlled by an uneasy coalition of three elements: (i) top managing directors appointed from outside the bureaucracy and who do not usually control the technical expertise of the New Class or the complex details known to bureaucratic officials, (ii) New Class experts, and (iii) bureaucratic "line" officials whose modes of rationality differ.[23]

3. The cadre of the *old* bureaucratic structure are an officialdom, "bureaucrats," who ground their orders in terms of their legal *authority*: "do this because *I* say so, and I am authorized to say so." They are the *older* elite of the bureaucracy, the "bureaucrats" of legendary stigma, the "line" officials whose position depends simply on their rigorous conformity with organizational rules, obedience to their superiors' orders, the legality of their appointment, and sheer seniority. Their principal function is *control* over the behavior of those beneath them and those outside the organization. They are rooted in the elemental impulse of domination. In short, they are the organization's old "snake brain."

Having no reasons he can speak, the bureaucratic official does not justify his actions by arguing that they contribute to some desirable goal. He simply says he is conforming with the rules which, as Max Weber noted, he treats as "a basis of action for their own sake"; in the sinister phrase, he is "following orders." Either way, he serves as a transmission belt. He is passing on orders or policies that he is expected to obey whatever his personal feeling and whether or not he agrees with them.

These orders or policies are, then, placed beyond the domain of the culture of critical discourse. The old bureaucratic official was designed to be an "agent," uncritically obedient to the organization's top *managers* who, in turn, transmit the ideological and economic interests of social groups outside of the bureaucracy, and who are appointed because they can be relied upon to do just that. Bureaucratic officials are the agents of an internal colonialism, the instruments of an Indirect Rule. The bureaucratic officialdom are the brute part of bureaucracy, the barriers by which the technical intelligentsia are caged, and at the same time they are the protective covering for the New Class's first growth within the bureaucracy.

4. Unlike the older bureaucrats, the new intelligentsia have extensive cultural capital which increases their mobility. The old bureaucrat's skills are often little more than being able to read, write, file, and are limited to their employing bureaucracy. The new intelli-

gentsia's greater cultural capital is, indeed, *more productive of goods and services* and they are, therefore, less concerned to vaunt their personal superiority or to extract deference from those below them. As a result, the old bureaucrats and the new intelligentsia develop and reproduce different systems of social control. Bureaucrats employ a control apparatus based on "ordering and forbidding," threatening and punishing the disobedient or resistant. The intelligentsia of the New Class, capable of increasing services and production, typically seek to control by *rewarding* persons for conformity to their expectations, by providing more material incentives and, also, by educational indoctrination. The intelligentsia of the New Class is a task-centered and work-centered elite having considerable confidence in its own worth and its future and, correspondingly, has less status anxiety that they irrationally impose on others. They are less overbearing and less punishment-prone. They need not, moreover, seek status solely within their own organization and from its staff or clients. Rather, they also seek status in professional associations; they wish the good regard of the knowledgeable.

5. The technical intelligentsia of the New Class is controlled by those incompetent to judge its performances and whose control, therefore, is experienced as irrational.[24] The New Class intelligentsia, then, feel a certain contempt for their superiors; for they are not competent participants in the careful discourse concerning which technical decisions are made. The New Class's intelligentsia are controlled by two echelons above them: one, the *bureaucratic officialdom,* the "line officials," *directly* above them; two, the *political* appointees managing the bureaucracy at its pinnacle, who are not appointed on the basis of their technical competence, but because they represent money capital or politically reliable "commissars." The fundamental structure within which most technical intelligentsia work, then, systematically generates tensions between them, on the one side, and the bureaucratic officials and managers, on the other. It is within the bureaucratic structure

that much of the technical intelligentsia of the New Class begins its struggle to rise. It has one of its first muffled confrontations with the old class within the precincts of a specific organizational structure, the bureaucracy.

6. By comparison with line bureaucrats, the technical intelligentsia of the New Class are veritable philosophers. By comparison with the intellectuals, the intelligentsia may seem *idiots savants.* In contrast to the bureaucrats, however, the intelligentsia seeks nothing for its own sake, gives reasons without invoking authority, and regards nothing as settled once for all. To them, nothing is exempt from reexamination. Unlike the bureaucrats, intelligentsia are not "ritualists" pursuing something without regard to its effectiveness.

7. At the same time, however, nothing is sacred to them; their primary concern is with the technical effectiveness of their means rather than its moral propriety. They are pragmatic nihilists. They are capable of emancipating men from old shibboleths, but they are emancipators who know no limits. Their emancipation has a side effect: cultural destructiveness, *anomie.* The cultural dissolution they bring is precisely that always entailed by the culture of critical discourse, which commonly alienates persons from tradition.[25] In short, *like intellectuals, the intelligentsia, too, are a revolutionary force.* But the revolutionary power of the technical intelligentsia of the New Class is dammed-up by the bureaucratic barrier and the old form of property.

8. If the technical sub-elite of the New Class have the makings of a "benign" elite, they nonetheless remain an *elite.* They have no intention of instituting a social order in which all are *equal* regardless of their cultural capital. They do not think of themselves as an "intellectual proletariat," let alone as an ordinary proletariat. Contributing to the increase of the social surplus by the increased productivity of their cultural capital, they will benignly increase the funds available for welfare, may even accept worker participation in setting incentives, increase consumerism, even increasing job security. Although seeking it

for themselves, they do not tolerate "workers' control" and they do not believe in equality.[26] Talk of "workers' control" is for the most part produced by a different sector of the New Class, by radicalized *intellectuals,* and not the technical intelligentsia.

9. Maoism was essentially an effort to avoid the resurgence of the old line bureaucratic officials and of the technical intelligentsia of the New Class. But the intelligentsia is the more rational elite, increasing both social productivity and social understanding, and now China is liquidating the "cultural revolution" and opting for the New Class.[27] Distilled to essentials, Maoism was an effort to strengthen the bargaining position of the working class (including the peasantry) in its inescapable, forthcoming negotiations with the New Class. For its part, and unlike Maoism, Stalinism was a profoundly regressive force because it sought to subordinate the technical intelligentsia to the most archaic sector, the old bureaucratic officialdom.[28]

As the old class deteriorates and loses control, especially with the rise of state socialism, the real choices are between the new technical intelligentsia and the old line bureaucrats. And it *is* a real choice. The rule of the bureaucratic officialdom is callous and authoritarian, while the rule of the new cultural elite, able to increase the level of productivity, can rely more on rewards than punishment and on the demystified performance of tasks without the mystique of authority or the extortion of personal deference. . . .

The Flawed Universal Class

1. The New Class is the most progressive force in modern society and is a center of whatever human emancipation is possible in the foreseeable future. It has no motives to curtail the forces of production and no wish to develop them solely in terms of their profitability. The New Class possesses the scientific knowledge and technical skills on which the future of modern forces of production depend. At the same time, members of the New Class also manifest increasing sensitivity to the ecological "side effects" or distant diseconomies of continuing technical development. The New Class, further, is a center of opposition to almost all forms of censorship, thus embodying a universal societal interest in a kind of rationality broader than that invested in technology. Although the New Class is at the center of nationalist movements throughout the world, after that phase is secured, the New Class is also the most internationalist and most universalist of all social strata; it is the most cosmopolitan of all elites. Its control over ordinary "foreign" languages, as well as of technical sociolects, enable it to communicate with other nationalities and it is often a member of a technical guild of international scope.

2. For all that, however, the New Class is hardly the end of domination. While its ultimate significance is the end of the old moneyed class's domination, the New Class is also the nucleus of a *new* hierarchy and the elite of a new form of cultural capital.

The historical limits of the New Class are inherent in both the nature of its own characteristic rationality, and in its ambitions as a cultural bourgeoisie. Its culture of critical discourse fosters a purely "theoretical" attitude toward the world. Speakers are held competent to the degree that they know and can *say* the rules, rather than just happening to follow them. The culture of critical discourse thus values the very theoreticity that the "common sense" long suspected was characteristic of intellectuals.

Intellectuals have long believed that those who know the rule, who know the theory by which they act, are superior because they lead an "examined" life. They thus exalt theory over practice, and are concerned less with the success of a practice than that the practice should have submitted itself to a reasonable rule. Since intellectuals and intelligentsia are concerned with doing things in the right way and for the right reason—in other words, since they value doctrinal conformity for its own sake—they (we) have a native tendency toward ritualism and *sectarianism*.

3. The culture of the New Class exacts still other costs: since its discourse emphasizes the importance of carefully edited speech, this has the vices of its virtues: in its *virtuous* aspect, self-editing implies a commendable circumspection, carefulness, self-discipline and "seriousness." In its negative modality, however, self-editing also disposes toward an unhealthy self-consciousness, toward stilted convoluted speech, an inhibition of play, imagination and passion, and continual pressure for expressive discipline. The new rationality thus becomes the source of a new alienation.

Calling for watchfulness and self-discipline, CCD is productive of intellectual reflexivity *and* the loss of warmth and spontaneity. Moreover, that very reflexivity stresses the importance of adjusting action to some pattern of propriety. There is, therefore, a structured inflexibility when facing changing situations; there is a certain disregard of the differences in situations, and an insistence on hewing to the required rule.

This inflexibility and insensitivity to the force of differing contexts, this inclination to impose one set of rules on different cases also goes by the ancient name of "dogmatism." Set in the context of human relationships, the vulnerability of the New Class to dogmatism along with its very *task*-centeredness, imply a certain insensitivity to *persons*, to their feelings and reactions, and open the way to the disruption of human solidarity. Political brutality, then, finds a grounding in the culture of critical discourse; the new rationality may paradoxically allow a new darkness at noon.

4. The paradox of the New Class is that it is both emancipatory *and* elitist. It subverts all establishments, social limits, and privileges, including its own. The New Class bears a culture of critical and careful discourse which is an historically emancipatory rationality. The new discourse (CCD) is the grounding for a critique of established forms of domination and provides an escape from tradition, but it also bears the seeds of a new domination. Its discourse is a lumbering machinery of argumentation that can wither imagination, discourage play, and curb expressivity. The culture of discourse of the New Class seeks to *control* everything, its topic and itself, believing that such domination is the only road to truth. The New Class begins by monopolizing truth and by making itself its guardian. It thereby makes even the claims of the old class dependent on it. The New Class sets itself above others, holding that its speech is better than theirs; that the examined life (*their* examination) is better than the unexamined life which, it says, is sleep and no better than death. Even as it subverts old inequities, the New Class silently inaugurates a new hierarchy of the knowing, the knowledgeable, the reflexive and insightful. Those who talk well, it is held, excel those who talk poorly or not at all. It is now no longer enough simply to be good. Now, one has to explain it. The New Class is the universal class in embryo, but badly flawed.

Notes

1. It is not my intention to suggest that modern intellectuals are merely the secular counterpart of clericals. Indeed, my own stress (as distinct, say, from Edward Shils who does appear to view intellectuals as priests *manqués*) is on the discontinuity of the two.

2. For full development of this, see chapter 2, especially p. 42, of my *Dialectic of Ideology and Technology* (New York, 1976).

3. Doubtless some will insist this is a "false consciousness." But this misses the point. My concern here is with their own definitions of their social role, precisely because these influence the manner in which they perform their roles. As W. I. Thomas and Florian Znaniecki long ago (and correctly) insisted, a thing defined as real is real in its consequences. Moreover, the state who employs most of these teachers is itself interested in having teachers consolidate the tie between students and it itself, rather than with the students' parents.

4. See Basil Bernstein, *Class, Codes and Control,* vol. 1, *Theoretical Studies Towards a Sociology of Language* (London, 1971), vol. 2, *Applied Studies Towards a Sociology of Language* (London, 1973), vol. 3, *Towards a Theory of Educational Transmission* (London, 1975). Bernstein's theory is used here in a critical appropriation facilitated by the work of Dell Hymes and William Labov. My own

critique of Bernstein emerges, at least tacitly, in the discussion of [the "Flawed Universal Class"] in the text. It is developed explicitly in my *Dialectic of Ideology and Technology,* pp. 58–66. While Labov has sharply criticized Bernstein, he himself also stresses the general importance of self-monitored speech and of speech *reflexivity* in general (i.e., not only of careful pronunciation) thus converging with Bernstein's focus on reflexivity as characterizing the elaborated linguistic variant and distinguishing it from the restricted variant. See William Labov, *Sociolinguistic Patterns* (Philadelphia, 1972), p. 208.

5. For example: "The Communists disdain to conceal their views and aims. They openly declare . . ." (*Communist Manifesto* [Chicago, 1888], authorized English edition edited by Engels, p. 58).

6. See E. Hobsbawm, *Primitive Rebels* (Manchester, 1959), p. 167 ff.

7. A secret doctrine is one which, because it is reserved only for the organization elite, can be made known only after persons join organizations and reach a certain membership position in it. A secret doctrine thus is never one which can have been a *motive* for joining the organization in the first instance.

8. Lenin's *What Is to Be Done?* was originally published in 1902.

9. I am grounding myself here in the analysis of dimensions of meaning common to social objects in the pioneering work of Charles Osgood and his collaborators. Their researches have recurrently found three dimensions: goodness/badness, weakness/strength, and activity/passivity. In the *Coming Crisis* I proposed an *equilibrium* condition for the first two dimensions, speaking there of social worlds that were culturally permitted and those unpermitted, defining the latter in terms of a dissonance between imputed goodness/badness and weakness/strength. To "normalize" is to contrive to see an unpermitted world as if it were a permitted one, i.e., to remove the dissonance. See A. W. Gouldner, *The Coming Crisis of Western Sociology* (New York, 1970), especially pp. 484–88. For Osgood's first researches see Charles E. Osgood, George Suci, and Percy Tannenbaum, *The Measurement of Meaning* (Urbana, 1957).

10. *The New Industrial State* (Boston, 1967).

11. *The Coming of Post-Industrial Society* (New York, 1973).

12. *The Modern Corporation and Private Property* (New York, 1932).

13. "It stands to reason that the one who knows more will dominate the one who knows less," M. Bakouinine, *Oeuvres,* Vol. 5 (Paris, 1911), p. 106.

14. See V. F. Calverton, *The Making of Society* (New York, 1937).

15. Talcott Parsons, *The Social System* (Glencoe, 1951), chapter 10; *Essays in Sociological Theory* (Glencoe, 1954), chapter 18; "The Professions," *International Encyclopedia of Social Sciences* (New York, 1968).

16. While Chomsky's position is exhibited in various of his writings, I shall rely here on his most recent statement in his Huizinga lecture, "Intellectuals and the State," delivered at Leiden, 9 October 1977. Citations will be from the manuscript copy. Cf. N. Chomsky, *American Power and the New Mandarins* (New York, 1969).

17. Maurice Zeitlin, "Corporate Ownership and Control: The Large Corporations and the Capitalist Class," *American Journal of Sociology* (March 1974), pp. 1073–1119.

18. Cf. James O'Connor, *Corporations and the State* (New York, 1974), pp. 126–28 for the argument that government financing of R & D and advanced education constitute a socialization of part of the costs of production whose net surplus is privately appropriated.

19. This section is indebted to Basil Bernstein and is based on a critical appropriation of his "elaborated and restricted linguistic codes," which have gone through various re-workings. That controversial classic was published in J. J. Gumperz and D. Hymes, *Directions in Sociolinguistics* (New York, 1972). A recent re-working is to be found in Bernstein's, "Social Class, Language, and Socialization," in T. A. Sebeok, ed., *Current Trends in Linguistics* (The Hague, 1974). For full bibliographic and other details see note 4 above.

20. Cf. Peter McHugh, "A Common-Sense Perception of Deviance," in H. P. Dreitzel, ed., *Recent Sociology, Number 2* (London, 1970), p. 165 ff. For good speech as "serious" speech see David Silverman, "Speaking Seriously," *Theory and Society* (Spring, 1974).

21. Thomas S. Kuhn, *The Structure of Scientific Revolutions* (Chicago, 1970) second edition, enlarged.

22. See Khalil Nakhleh, "Palestinian Dilemma: Nationalist Consciousness and University Education" (ms., 1976).

23. For fuller discussion of the differences and contradictions between bureaucrats and technical intelligentsia, see my *Dialectic of Ideology and Technology,* p. 266 ff.

24. As a consequence, when technical intelligentsia are monitored by organizational superiors, "it is results that count" for it is often only these that *can* be judged.

25. The testimony on this is venerable: in Plato's *Republic,* Socrates proposes to defer training in the dialectic until students are in their thirties and have passed other tests. And then, he warns, great caution is needed: "Why great caution?" "Do you not remark," I said, "how great is the evil which dialectic has introduced?" "What evil?" he said. "The students of the art are filled with lawlessness" (*Re-*

public, 437 DE). For fuller discussion see my *Enter Plato* (New York, 1965), p. 279. In short, the dialectic, like CCD, has certain inherent costs which Nietzsche was among the first to notice. Thus CCD cannot simply be equated with "good" speech.

26. This is no less true for the Marxist contingent of the New Class than of others. Equality has never been a high priority value for Marxism.

27. While editing this, a recent people's congress in Peking eliminated the cultural revolution's "revolutionary committees" in factories and schools, began to refurbish wage differentials, and recharged higher education, the essential reproductive mechanism of the New Class.

28. Louis Althusser's argument, that Stalinism was a fumbled attack on the New Class, has many difficulties. Not least is the fact that among the delegates to the 18th Congress of the CPSU in 1939, two years after the purges, about 26% had higher education, compared to the 10% with higher education among delegates of the 17th Congress in 1934, who were a central target of Stalin's terror. For further discussion, see A. W. Gouldner, "Stalinism," *Telos* (Winter 1977–78).

GØSTA ESPING-ANDERSEN

Social Foundations of Postindustrial Economies

A social trend is basically a projection from the past. Many of the early postindustrial theorists, such as Daniel Bell (1976), predicted a future in which most of what they deemed positive in the era of the 'democratic class struggle' would come to full fruition. Bell's vision was a coming society of professionals and technicians, one where 'situs' rather than class conflict would reign. This was a radical reinterpretation in so far as postindustrial society would do away with class altogether. Also Lipset has now embraced this position (Clark and Lipset, 1991; Clark, Lipset, and Rempel, 1993).

Today's visionaries find much less cause for optimism; their projections are most likely to range from the sombre to the outright gloomy. The sombre view insists that little of substance has changed (Wright, 1989; Erikson and Goldthorpe, 1992; and Hout *et al.*, 1993); that the cleavages of the past remain pretty much intact. The gloom comes from those who see a new era of polarization. American or British observers see a world with a 'declining middle', job polarization, and a new underclass (Harrison and Bluestone, 1988; Jencks and Peterson, 1991; Levy, 1988; Burtless, 1990). Europeans, in contrast, see a two-thirds society with social exclusion, marginalization, and outsider classes (Van Parijs, 1987; Offe, 1985; Esping-Andersen, 1993; Brown and Crompton, 1994).

What the new pessimists see, in brief, is the possibility of a resurgent proletarian underclass and, in its wake, a menacing set of new 'class correlates'. The transAtlantic difference of accent is clearly related to job performance: in North America labour market exclusion is less dramatic than is growing pay inequality, declining real wages, and a swelling army of the working poor. Europe's social safety net manages to stem the tide of inequality but its inferior job performance induces mass exclusion.

How do we understand the postindustrial employment problem? Is there indeed any

Originally published in 1999. Please see complete source information beginning on page 891.

problem? And, if new class configurations are emerging, what is driving them? Besides the radical optimists, such as Lipset *et al.*, who basically deny that there is any problem worthy of discussion, the reigning answers all fall back on the great 'equality-jobs' trade-off. According to mainstream analysis, exclusion in Europe and inequality in America are two sides of the same coin, namely the inevitable consequence of technology and the new global economy. . . .

The Dilemmas of Globalization and Technological Change

Global trade and capital mobility are often seen as the culprits of de-industrialization. The Asian tigers can produce steel, scooters, stereos, or shoes much cheaper than Europe or North America. Even if their regimes are not authoritarian, unionism is weak and labour discipline arguably high. Regardless, they hold a massive competitive edge in terms of wage costs in mass-production industries as well as in many services. Less-skilled workers in advanced economies are no longer cushioned by Keynesianism or import protection. They must now compete in a global labour market.

The special vulnerability of the low-skilled is highlighted in Wood's (1995) study on the impact of imports from the 'South' on labour markets in the 'North'. He paints a fairly dramatic picture of worker displacement and downward wage pressures, in particular for the low-skilled. His findings are, however, widely contested. For one, the lion's share of European trade is *intra-European*. The share of total European Union trade with the outside world is, according to all estimates, less than 10 per cent of total—of which a large proportion is with North America, the Antipodes, or Eastern Europe. Hence, if there is any 'Third World' effect, it must be at the margin. This is more or less what the mainstream view concludes (OECD, 1994).

It is, in the first place, questionable whether globalization really is something new, and if it indeed is altering our capacity to harmonize

equality and full employment. Bairoch (1996) shows that the level of internationalization of trade, finance, and capital today is hardly greater than it was 80 years ago. In fact, it was the period of protectionism and mounting tariffs following World War One and the Great Depression which was anomalous. Moreover, the spurt in globalization over the past few decades has hardly altered the trade dependency of those small, open economies (like the Benelux or Nordic countries) that were *always* open.

With these qualifiers in mind, we might ask ourselves what has *de facto* changed to make equality and social protection problematic now, when once a strong welfare state was viewed as the precondition for successful international performance? It was precisely due to their extreme degree of international vulnerability that the small European economies spearheaded strong worker protection and welfare guarantees after World War Two. Global trade competition is not novel to Belgium or Denmark; it is to the large economies, such as the American or British, or the erstwhile protected ones, such as Australia. Perhaps the real problem is that the late-comers to globalization have chosen the 'low road-low wage' strategy of competition, thus forcing the hand of the vanguards?

Regardless, the facts point to technological change as the more potent source of falling demand for less-qualified workers. Employment lost due to trade competition from the 'South' (i.e. Asia or the Third World) is rather trivial in comparison with the volume of job loss due to 'structural change'. In a few countries (France and Japan), jobs gained from exporting to the 'South' actually outnumber those lost to import penetration. Only the UK and the USA, two countries traditionally dominated by comparatively low-skilled, mass-production industry, exhibit a substantial loss of domestic employment due to competition from Asia or elsewhere.[1]

The really powerful impulse, then, may come from rapid structural and technological change whether or not this was initially propelled by global trade. Whatever the root cause, the employment effect ends up being fairly similar: it raises the returns to education and reduces demand for lower-skilled and less-experienced workers. Hence the unfavourable labour market position of the unskilled in general, but also of youth and women to the extent that they lack experience and practical skills. In either case, therefore, we seem unable to dodge the evil choice between heightened pay and job inequalities, on one hand, or unemployment and exclusion, on the other hand.

Golden Age capitalism could absorb masses of low-skilled workers on simple assembly-line production, churning out mass-production goods for which there was massive demand. It is these kinds of jobs that are rapidly disappearing within the advanced economies and, as we know, virtually all *net* new job growth will have to come from services.

That simple, routine industrial jobs are vanishing must be considered a 'Paretian' welfare gain: the 'South' benefits from taking over simple mass production manufacturing, thus creating domestic jobs and wealth and paving the way for its own process of de-ruralization and, eventually, post-industrialization; the 'North' gains by eliminating its most unpleasant jobs, but only in so far as these are being substituted by more pleasant and better-paid jobs. The optimistic postindustrial theorists believed this to be the case. Current opinion is sceptical, and the data seem to confirm it. We must therefore examine more closely the workings of the service economy.

Dilemmas of the New Service Economy

The decline of industrial employment began in earnest in the 1980s. Between 1979 and 1993, the OECD countries lost an (unweighted) average of 22 per cent of their manufacturing jobs. Some countries (Belgium, France, Norway, Sweden, Spain, and the UK) have been hit especially hard, with a net loss between one-third and one-half.[2] Such magnitudes echo post-war de-ruralization. But to-

day's equivalent to the assembly lines, namely low-end tertiary employment, has greater difficulty absorbing the joint impact of industrial job losses, women's rising labour supply, and the baby-boom cohorts. Why should this be so? In this chapter, I focus on three dilemmas. The first derives from a rarely recognized, inherent characteristic of services themselves: the more we expand the tertiary labour market, the larger is the share of low-skilled services. The second comes from the well-known 'Baumol cost-disease' problem in services (Baumol, 1967). And the third derives from households' economic choices and, in particular, from women's choice to work for pay.

Today, almost all net job creation occurs in services but even with bouyant growth, their ability to absorb masses of redundant industrial workers cannot be taken for granted. Many, like business and health services, are skill-intensive, and the more routine and labour-intensive services (such as social care, waiting, or personal services generally) often require a modicum of social or cultural skills that a redundant steel worker is unlikely to possess. Labour-intensive services, be they in the public or private sector, are very female-dominated; not merely because they are easy-entry jobs, but also because they typically represent a marketized version of conventional domestic tasks. In any case, services and female participation have grown in tandem. To better understand contemporary employment dilemmas, we need to come to grips with the logic of services. First, what precisely is the service economy? Second, what drives it?

Service Occupations

Apart from the pioneering work of Renner (1953) and, more recently, Bell (1976) and Goldthorpe (1982), little attention has been paid to occupational hierarchies in services. Since they were primarily concerned with the new knowledge class, the lower orders have been largely ignored. As in Braverman (1974) and Erikson and Goldthorpe (1992), they are

TABLE 1
Industrial and Postindustrial Occupational Hierarchies

The Industrial Hierarchy	The Service Hierarchy
Managers and executives	Professionals
Administrators, supervisors	Semi-professionals, technicians
Skilled manuals	Skilled service
Unskilled manuals	Unskilled service

TABLE 2
Service Growth and the Professional-Technical Bias of Job Growth, 1980–1990[a]

	Annual Service Growth	Ratio of Professional to Total Growth
Australia	3.3	1.8
Canada	2.8	1.7
UK	2.1	2.8
USA	2.7	1.9
Denmark	0.8	2.0
Sweden	1.2	4.3
Austria	1.9	2.5
Belgium	1.4	3.8
France	1.6	7.3
Germany	1.8	3.1
Japan	1.2	3.8

[a] Years vary according to data availability.

Source: ILO, *Yearbook of Labour Statistics* (various years).

simply lumped together with manual, industrial workers.

Such superimposition is not necessarily warranted. Even low-end service work is in typically less strict command hierarchies, it is less difficult to monitor, and orders will come more from customers than from bosses. Most servicing work is quite individualized. For heuristic reasons, it may therefore be useful to distinguish between the traditional skill and authority hierarchy of 'industrial society' and that of the servicing society.[3] In Table 1, I propose one such classification.

The two hierarchies exclude agricultural occupations and, more importantly, also the self-employed and entrepreneurs. Omitting self-employment may actually be problematic because it is becoming one means of gaining access to the labour market when the supply of 'regular' employment contracts is scarce. This classificatory exercise must be seen as an heuristic device.[4]

Lousy Jobs or Outsiders?

Our present preoccupation with the equality-jobs trade-off may have blinded us to a second dilemma, i.e. professionalization with exclusion or full employment with job polarization. The highly professionalized scenario depicted by postindustrial optimists can be attained only at the price of massive exclusion, while a massive growth of services is likely to produce a mass of 'lousy' jobs. We need therefore to gain a better picture of postindustrial job trends.

The postindustrial pessimists, like Braverman (1974), err on one count: tertiarization undoubtedly implies occupational upgrading. Over the 1980s, professional-technical jobs rose 3–4 times as fast as employment overall in Belgium, Germany, Sweden, and Japan, and an astounding 7 times as fast in France. Their relative growth was less spectacular in Canada and the United States (1.7 and 1.9, respectively), two nations with unusually strong aggregate service expansion.[5] Indications are that the professional bias is inversely related to service economy growth. This comes out in Table 2.

The statistical relationship is in fact quite strong: for each additional percentage point of service job growth, the professional ratio declines by 1.2 points.[6]

Since we must rely almost exclusively on services to furnish new jobs and thus reduce unemployment, the contours of postindustrial employment pose an unpleasant trade-off: we will come close to the professionalized world of Daniel Bell, but only when services are relatively stagnant. And this entails unemploy-

TABLE 3

The Distribution of Occupations and the Size of the Outsider Population (Percentage Change, 1960–1980s, in Parentheses)

	Germany 1985	Sweden 1985	United States 1988
'Industrial' society			
Unskilled manual	16.5 (–0)	12.4 (–42)	14.4 (–33)
Skilled manual	17.3 (–32)	15.2 (–18)	8.7 (–34)
Clerical and sales	29.6 (+30)	18.6 (+16)	28.3 (+21)
Managers[a]	4.5 (+36)	4.0 (–15)	9.1 (+17)
Total	67.9 (–0)	50.2 (–18)	60.4 (–8)
'Servicing' society			
Unskilled service	4.5 (–48)	16.9 (+78)	11.7 (–0)
Skilled service	5.0 (+194)	4.4 (–0)	6.6 (+57)
Professional-technical	17.3 (+121)	21.9 (+89)	18.1 (+56)
Total	26.8 (+47)	43.2 (+70)	36.4 (+31)
'Outsider' society			
Not employed	35.2	16.7	29.5
Long-term unemployment[b]	46.3	5.0	5.6

[a]Includes also self-employed (non-professional).

[b]As a percentage of all unemployed (1990).

Note: The table excludes primary sector occupations.

Sources: Recomputations from Esping-Andersen (1993: Tables 2.3 and 2.4); and OECD (1992; 1994).

ment and labour market exclusion. Vice versa, we can minimize exclusion but here we must pay the price of accepting a less favourable, more 'proletarian' mix of service occupations. This comes out quite clearly when we examine the occupational hierarchies in greater detail.

Table 3 divides the active population, c. mid–1980s, into our 'industrial' and 'postindustrial' hierarchy and, as somewhat of a residual, it provides an estimate of the excluded, 'outsider' population (here measured as a percentage of the working-age population). The three-way comparison between Germany, Sweden, and the United States is chosen because these nations are prototypical examples of three types of welfare regimes— conservative, social democratic, and liberal, respectively. But they also represent three distinct employment trajectories: Germany stands as a best-case version of European jobless growth; Sweden is the epitome of the Nordic welfare state-led model of service expansion; and the United States is, par excellence, the leading example of unregulated, market-driven employment.

On some counts there is convergence. Manual workers decline, and the occupations that constituted the major source of post-war 'middle-class growth', such as managers, clerical, and sales jobs, are now stagnant. Today's growth is undisputably dominated by professionals and semi-professionals. This is all more or less consistent with the prognosis of Bell (1976). Accordingly, chances of upward class mobility in postindustrial societies will depend primarily on how much the skilled and professional service occupations grow. On the other hand, if the objective is full employment there will also be substantial growth of less-qualified service jobs, something that Daniel Bell did not envisage.

A postindustrial paradise would combine full employment with a slim but highly skilled industrial labour force in unison with a professionally dominated service economy. No country comes even close to this. In Germany, which often epitomizes skill-upgrading (see, for example, Kern and Schumann, 1984), skilled manual workers have actually disappeared faster than the unskilled—although from the 1980s onwards, this has reversed. None the less, Germany's services are heavily professional and 'non-proletarian'. High labour costs crowd out private social services; low levels of female participation make them less demanded. One reason for Germany's lower female employment rates is the absence of public care services. And, besides costs, one reason for Germany's stagnant personal services is that families engage in more self-servicing.

As a consequence, German postindustrialization provides no substantial employment outlet for either laid-off manual workers or less-qualified women. Instead, both these groups have been managed primarily through labour reduction strategies: early retirement or unemployment insurance for industrial workers, and discouragement of female careers. Germany may come closest to the postindustrial ideal as regards job structure, but this comes at the expense of employment exclusion.

Sweden does conform to the industrial skill-upgrading thesis but suffers from strong polarization in the service occupations. The phenomenally high levels of female employment go hand-in-hand with huge numbers of (often low-skilled) public-sector jobs. And Sweden's formidable investment in retraining and active manpower programmes has, until the crash in the 1990s, helped recycle redundant industrial workers into alternative jobs. The combination of these two factors implies few labour market outsiders, be it in the form of early retirees, mass unemployment, or discouraged women.

The United States, finally, exhibits skill polarization in both industry and services. It is an economy biased towards unqualified jobs.

De-industrialization has reduced manual employment equally between the skilled and unskilled; declining wages have helped maintain their relative share in industry and services. Of course, our data disguise the fact that, in absolute terms, the number of net new jobs has risen phenomenally. Hence, the absorption of immigrant masses, the huge growth in women's employment, and the relocation of redundant industrial workers were all made possible by the sheer volume of job growth.

The juxtaposition between Germany's more favourable skill mix, and the large share of unskilled servicing jobs in both Sweden and the United States highlights the basic dilemma: today, substantial employment expansion requires heavy growth in consumer and social services, both characteristic of a large unskilled quotient the more they grow—hence an apparent trade-off between either joblessness or a mass of inferior jobs.

The real issue lies in the correlates of class. It makes a notable difference whether inferior jobs provide inferior welfare. In Sweden, they are relatively well-paid and secure welfare state jobs; indeed, private sector 'Mcjobs' hardly exist. While relative pay in Swedish welfare service jobs has been in modest decline, job security has not. A notable aspect of Sweden's gargantuan welfare spending cutbacks in the 1990s is that public employment is safeguarded. In the United States, the low-end service workers are mainly in the private sector, typically poorly paid and excluded from occupational welfare entitlements and basic job security. In Sweden, the concentration of women in low-end servicing jobs is extreme (women account for roughly 80 per cent of the total), while in America the bias is tendentially ethnic—Hispanics—rather than gender-based (Esping-Andersen, 1990; ch. 8).

In summary, there are undisputably forces that pull economies away from job homogeneity and wage equality, and towards polarization. It is therefore doubtful whether the great 'equality-jobs' trade-off overshadows everything else. It is, as we shall now see, more likely that trade-offs overlap.

TABLE 4

The Growing Productivity Gap. Percentage Change in the Ratio of Service-to-Manufacturing Productivity, 1983–1995, for Select Countries[a]

	Ratio of Restaurants to Manufacture	Ratio of Personal Services to Manufacture	Ratio of Business Services to Manufacture	Ratio of Social Services to Manufacture
United States	−7	−47	−55	−62
Denmark	−35	−30	−11	−2
Sweden	−82	−60	−71	−54
France	−56	−41	−38	+4
Netherlands	−40	−19	−38	−28

[a]Productivity is measured as GDP (in constant prices) per person employed.

Source: OECD Data File on Services Statistics on Value Added and Employment.

The Cost-Disease and Service Expansion

Globalization, new technologies, and tertiarization all seem to produce heightened labour market polarization. The productivity lag within many services only helps reinforce this problem. As originally argued by Fourastiér, and subsequently formalized by Baumol (1967), services face a long-run 'cost-disease' problem. This will come about because, in the long haul, productivity grows on average much faster in manufacturing than in (most) services. As shown in Table 4, most services lag—sometimes dramatically—behind manufacturing.

There are three possible responses to the productivity gap. One would be to allow labour costs to adjust to productivity differentials—the market-clearing approach. The downside of unregulated wage adjustment is that this would push earnings in the more stagnant services towards zero. Many services, such as music concerts, psychotherapy, or aged care, are capable of almost no productivity enhancement (at least not without a quality loss), and they would therefore most likely disappear, simply because no one would be willing to perform them at earnings that correspond to relative productivity. The potential limits to the market-clearing strategy is poverty: aggregate service consumption may,

on the one hand, be stimulated by low prices but if, on the other hand, this means that a large population mass is employed at poverty-level wages, aggregate demand will suffer. Low wages can of course be offset by income supplements, as now Canada, Australia, and the United States do with various forms of negative income tax programmes.

The second and, in most countries, typical response has been to allow service earnings to follow general wage developments in the economy. This may matter little for engineering, product design, or financial consultancy, but it risks pricing out of the market labour-intensive, low value-added activities such as personal services, entertainment, or private daycare. Both the Nordic countries and Continental Europe have in common an institutional framework which has this effect: high wage costs across the board and a more compressed earnings distribution. Hence, personal services grow very sluggishly, if at all, and many services become almost extinct. To illustrate the problem, let us examine a prototypical labour-intensive service: laundries.

As we see in Table 5, time-saving household goods (washing-machines) are almost universal everywhere. What varies is the cost of out-servicing and, therefore, laundry jobs. Laundries literally clutter American streets because they are cheap. They are almost impossible to

TABLE 5

The Cost-Disease Illustrated by Laundry Servicing. The Comparative Cost of Washing and Ironing
One Man's Shirt, Employment, and Self-Service Equipment, mid–1990s

	Cost ($US) 1996	Working-Age Population per Laundry Worker[a]	Washing-Machines[b]
Denmark	5.20	3,500	74
Sweden	4.25	727	87
France	4.50		
Germany (West)	3.70	667	88
Italy	3.25	n.a.	96
Spain	3.90	905	87
UK	2.20	750	87
USA	1.50	391	75

[a]Data for the UK are 1993; for the USA, Spain, and Sweden, 1990; for Germany, 1987.

[b]Percentage households equipped with a washing-machine, 1991.

Sources: Employment: United States Statistical Abstract, 1995, Table 668; *Sveriges Statistiska Aarsbok*, 1993, Table 204; German Census of 1987, Part 2, Fachserie 1, Haft 10; Government Statistical Office, *Employment Gazette, Historical Supplement*, no. 4, October 1994; Ministero de Economia y Hacienda, *Prospectiva de las Occupaciones y la Formacion en la Espana de los Noventa*, 1991, App. Table 2. Washing-machines: United States Statistical Abstract, 1995, Table 1376. Prices: own data collection in Italy, Spain, and the United States, and special thanks to Francis Castles, Kevin Farnsworth, Joakim Palme, Jon Kvist, Karl Ulrich Mayer, John Myles, Kari Salminen, and Lucy Roberts for help on price and employment figures.

find in Copenhagen and Stockholm because they are priced out of the market.

In a service-led economy, this kind of cost-disease translates easily into jobless growth. But there is, of course, a third possible solution, namely to subsidize services—either directly via government production, or indirectly via subsidies to consumers. All advanced nations have to a greater or lesser degree adopted the subsidy strategy, especially for vital collective goods such as health and education, or for culturally valued goods such as opera and theatre. The European nations stress direct public provision, the United States favours tax-subsidized private provision. The uniqueness of Scandinavia lies in government's huge role in furnishing labour-intensive, and otherwise unaffordable, care services to families. Hence, Scandinavian tertiarization is uniquely biased towards welfare state jobs and away from market services. In the United States, the lion's share of caring services is marketized while, in Continental Europe, it is basically

familialized. The limits of subsidization are a question of political economy: of the balance of political power and citizens' willingness to be taxed.

The cost-disease problem and the tension between professionalized or more polarized employment growth are clearly closely related. Where the cost-disease in services is severe, and public servicing is scarce, the size of the 'outsider classes' is likely to be large; where it is countered by low-wage labour markets or by public-service provision, exclusion will be less of a problem than growing occupational polarization. It is this nexus which defines the varying employment scenarios within the three principal welfare regimes.

The Micro-Foundations of Postindustrial Employment

As we leave behind us the era of mass production, there is one thing that has not changed. The household still remains the *sine qua non* of how much, and what kind of, employment will grow. How much families save, consume, or produce affects the probability that their members will find themselves employed or unemployed.

Household market purchase is subordinate to three principal factors: levels of income, relative prices, and time constraints.[7] As we know from Engel's Law, our propensity to buy non-essentials, like services, will rise with disposable income. The phenomenal rise in real incomes in the post-war decades allowed us initially to satisfy demand for manufactured household goods, like cars and washing-machines. Subsequently, an increasing share went to servicing less essential needs like entertainment or foreign travel. One obstacle to tertiary sector growth today is that real incomes rise much slower. In the United States, real earnings have been stagnant—even declining for many—since the late 1970s.

But also the distribution of riches matters greatly. A very skewed income distribution may result in a 'Latin American' consumption scenario: a narrow, hyper-serviced élite being waited upon by a mass of impoverished servants. At the other extreme, a very egalitarian income distribution, as in Sweden, may very well impede mass consumption of market services because equal wages mean that service costs will be high.

Rising incomes might also push demand in the direction of 'positional' services, that is, services that are bought for their status value. Following the argument of Hirsh (1976), the 'democratization' of consumption means that traditional status-enhancing goods, like automobiles or cellular phones, eventually lose their prestige value. Hence, as mass consumption spreads so will demand for 'positional' goods (Armani suits or Porsches) and services (haircuts from 'Chez Pierre', rather than the local barbershop).

Secondly, household demand is sensitive to price relativities (the Baumol cost-disease problem). Often the lure of Third-World travel lies in the amazing amount of servicing that our 'tourist dollar' can buy. Price relativities in services are intimately linked to wage differentials and, as we have seen, high wages in low-productivity services might price them out of the market.

Of course, where a service is consumed for its 'positional' value the logic of relative prices is altered, and may even operate in reverse. It is possible that status-seeking clients choose 'Chez Pierre' precisely because he is expensive. The status-hungry may follow outrageous pricing practices as their main signal.

Aside from the more esoteric world of positional goods, the cost-disease problem should be most acute in low-skilled, labour-intensive services that compete head-on with household self-servicing. And herein lies a fundamental misunderstanding in much contemporary economics. It is too often assumed that, since they are largely protected from international competition, services can provide a safe haven of employment—service workers do not compete with, say, Malaysians (except in the case of mass-immigration). True, in most economies the lion's share of services are sheltered from global competition. However, they face an even more ferocious competitor, namely family self-servicing. And, as Gershuny (1978) has stressed, this competition stiffens as households acquire time-saving household machinery (washing-machines, dishwashers, or microwave ovens). Yet, as we saw, Americans are massive consumers of laundries, Europeans wash and iron at home.

The problem is that the marginal cost of services such as laundry, daycare, or home-help services to the elderly affects not only women's ability to pursue careers, but also society's welfare-employment nexus. As women's educational attainment increasingly matches (and surpasses) males', the social cost of housewifery is lost human capital, productive potential, *and* jobs. The high costs of out-servicing in Europe compels families to self-servicing which translates into fewer market services.

Here we come to the third, fundamental condition, namely households' time constraints. The emerging 'postindustrial' household types, be they single person, single parent, or dual-earner households, have one thing in common: a scarcity of time, great difficulties in harmonizing paid employment with family obligations, domestic duties, and leisure.

The trade-off between the burden of domestic unpaid work and paid employment can be quite severe. Since it is unrealistic to expect a major relaxation of this trade-off through male substitution (husbands do not generally compensate significantly with more unpaid work to offset wives' declining hours), the solution must come from outside the household itself. This means either the market or the state.

The employment potential of new household forms comes out in consumer expenditure data. In a pioneering study, Stigler (1956: 88) suggested that restaurant employment should rise with the rate of women's labour force participation. Today, the dual-earner family norm is much stronger and, in some countries, almost universal. This should show up not only in family consumption behaviour, but ultimately also in service-sector job growth. . . .

Job growth in services is, accordingly, caught between rival forces. There are, on the one hand, the constraints that come from the inherent features of tertiarization or globalization and, on the other hand, the potential catalyst that comes from changing family life. If changing household forms can have positive employment effects, our focus should logically turn to which conditions would help maximize just such an effect. Women with careers are likely to reduce fertility, unless the tension between job and children is eased. If, then, access to child care is one constraint, society may find itself locked into a low-fertility equilibrium as seems to be the case in Southern Europe. And this will affect long-term job and growth prospects because, after all, aggregate demand depends on the size and growth of our population. Hence an ample social service infrastructure is one precondition for service-job growth.

The alternative scenario is that women are discouraged from economic activity. In this case, of course, a beneficial job spiral is blunted. The service economy may flourish with more inequality but also with two-earner households. In either case, we face institutional constraints. Some welfare regimes, and some modes of regulating labour markets and the distribution of welfare constrain or ease more than others. It is to this that we turn in the next section.

Recasting Welfare Regimes for a Postindustrial Era

If there is one great question that unites all welfare state researchers, it is this: why is it that nations respond so differently to a set of social risks that, all told, is pretty similar whether you are an American, a Spaniard, or a Swede?

Why is it that Scandinavia responds with social democracy and comprehensive welfare states, Continental Europe and East Asia with familialism and corporatist social insurance, and the Anglo-Saxon world with targeted assistance and maximum markets? There is certainly no want of answers. Some point to nation-building traditions and church–state conflicts, some to etatiste initiative, and some to the configuration of class power. These are all compelling explanations but they beg the question of why, in the first place, did state building move in one or another direction? Why was working-class unity and mobilization so thorough in Sweden and not in America? And why, once formed and forged, did the institutions they built last and then reproduce themselves so successfully? The popular answer in latter-day social science is that institutions, once forged, are overpowering and rarely permit the kind of sweeping change that would be observable to the human eye. We may live in a world of path dependencies where social creations, once cemented, are incomparably tougher than the city of Troy. Very well, but who creates and sustains the hegemony of whatever path dependency that obtains?

Economists often draw large benefits from basic simplicity. Their *homo oeconomicus* is certainly not believable, but he can be a convenient tool with which to proceed and eventually make things more complicated. I shall, for the moment, strive for similar minimalism. Sociologists, of course, crave more complexity, and one *Homo* will therefore not do. Let us allow for three ideal typical *homines: Homo liberalismus, Homo familius,* and *Homo socialdemocraticus.*[8]

Homo liberalismus resembles Mister Economics because he follows no loftier ideal than his own personal welfare calculus. The well-being of others is their affair, not his. A belief in noble self-reliance does not necessarily imply indifference to others. *Homo liberalismus* may be generous, even altruistic. But kindness towards others is a personal affair, not something dictated from above. His ethics tell him that a free lunch is amoral, that collectivism jeopardizes freedom, that individual liberty is a fragile good, easily sabotaged by sinister socialists or paternalistic authoritarians. *Homo liberalismus* prefers a welfare regime where those who can play the market do so, whereas those who cannot must merit charity.

Homo familius inhabits an altogether different planet. He abhors atomism and impersonality and, hence, markets and individualism. His worst enemy is the Hobbesian world of elbows, because self-interest is amoral; a person will find his equilibrium when he puts himself at the service of his family. Freedom, to *Homo familius,* means that he and his kin are immunized from the ceaseless threats that the greater world around him produce. He is not a go-getter with an irresistible urge to challenge the world around him. He is a satisficer, not maximizer, because what really counts is stability and security; a job for life in the postal service is heaven on earth; it will guarantee him and his kin a good life, security and, incidentally, also the means to land a postal job for his daughters and sons. Both *Homo familius* and *femina familia* see patriarchy as a good thing. The family would be unruly without authority and, in any case, respect and status is due to the father, on whose shoulders so much responsibility weighs. To

them, the family is the unrivalled source of solidarity and community because it alone knows what its members need. Alas, the family is fragile since so many individuals must depend on the *pater familias. Homo familius* is therefore quite happy with the idea that the state—or some higher body—eliminates whatever risk of misfortune may arise. Yet, higher bodies are there to service the family, not to command his loyalties. *Homo familius* wants a welfare regime that tames the market and exalts the virtues of close-knit solidarities.

Homo socialdemocraticus is, like a boy scout or good Christian, inclined to believe that he will do better when everybody does better. Doing good to others is not an act of charity and can, indeed, be coolly calculative. *Homo socialdemocraticus* plans his life around the one basic idea that he, and everybody else, will be better off in a world without want but also without free-riders. Society is something that we all are compelled to share, and so we had better share it well. *Homo socialdemocraticus* is, none the less, also a believer in individual, personal empowerment. Collectivism is not pursued for its own sake, but in order to bring out the utmost in each and every individual soul. That is why collective solutions are always the best. But his individualism is cautionary because no one should be granted favours, advantages, special recognition. *Homo socialdemocraticus* must constantly live with a moral clash between individualism and conformity. He loves the idea that we all be equally endowed; he hates the idea that someone may rise above others, particularly above himself. Solidarity is therefore fragile if someone desires to move beyond the common denominator. *Homo socialdemocraticus* is fully convinced that the more we invest in the public good, the better it will become. And this will trickle down to all, himself especially, in the form of a good life. Collective solutions are therefore the single best assurance of a good, if perhaps dull, individual life.

We all combine the instincts of these ideal typical *homines;* we all have moral conflicts. And all societies combine them in one mix or another. Sweden has its *Homines liberalismi* (although many emigrate to Monte Carlo), and America its *Homines socialdemocratici* (many of which show up regularly in Sweden). But how did a sufficient mass manage to profile itself in collective expression, and thereby sway society towards its preferred welfare regime?

Genetics clearly do not create preferences and beliefs. What might account for this is society itself with all its institutions, incentive systems, and inscribed norms of proper conduct. Society's 'median *Homo*' is created, and this is obviously where labour movements or other collective actors have played a key role. If, originally, a labour movement garnered its strength (or failed to do so) from the available raw material, so it also played a constant historical role in reactivating that very same raw material. Institutional path dependency means that one society is likely to reproduce itself in the image of *Homo socialdemocraticus,* another in the image of *Homo familius,* generation after generation. . . .

If core institutional traits are so unyielding to change, it remains unlikely today—as always—that the contemporary welfare state crisis will produce an avalanche of revolutionary change, no matter how urgent such change is claimed to be. Any blueprint for reform is bound to be naïve if it calls for a radical departure from existing welfare regime practice. The IMF is naïve when it asks that European welfare states adopt, lock, stock, and barrel, the Chilean pension system; American leftists, or emergent democratic governments in ex-communist countries, are equally naïve when they call for the importation of the 'Swedish model'. One thing is to redesign or reform the ways in which the *state* delivers welfare, another to recast the entire welfare regime. Academically speaking, there may exist a blueprint for a 'win-win' strategy, for an ideal postindustrial welfare regime. But unless it is compatible with existing welfare regime practice, it may not be practicable. As I shall argue below, optimizing welfare in a postindustrial setting will, none the less, require radical departures. . . .

A Third Way?

Up to a point, but not further, a 'social democratic' approach might furnish the basis for a new, positive equilibrium. A politics of collectivizing families' needs (de-familialization) frees women from unpaid labour, and thereby nurtures the dual-earner household. And this reduces child poverty, and makes households better equipped to weather the storms of flexibilization, since they will usually have one member's earnings to fall back on if the other is made redundant, needs temporary retraining, or suffers wage decline. Two-earner households have stronger social networks, and are less likely to run them down if one partner becomes unemployed.

A social democratic de-familialization strategy can reverse fertility decline if it helps employed mothers square the caring-work circle (mainly via daycare), and if it is willing to cover a good part of the opportunity costs of having children (which means expensive maternity and parental leave as well as generous child allowances). Working mothers may have 'negative productivity' in the sense that their earnings (plus public subsidies) exceed their output. But these costs are potentially recovered via their higher lifelong earnings, the smaller depreciation of their human capital, *and* the resulting fertility dividend.

A fundamental 'postindustrial' dilemma—generally overlooked in contemporary debates—is that families seem no longer inclined to assume the costs of bearing children. As a comparison between fertility in Southern Europe (with Japan) and Scandinavia suggests, the social price of children may be high indeed. Immigration is certainly an alternative, and herein lies a major reason behind North America's (and Australia's) younger age profile. Yet, besides being a rather unrealistic scenario for Europe today, the immigration option poses hard dilemmas of its own. If one of our chief problems is how to absorb masses of low-skilled workers, this would only be compounded by Third World immigration. The advanced economies would clearly prefer highly educated immigrants, yet encouraging such a flow can hardly be considered solidaristic towards Third World nations.

Universalizing the double-earner household (with lots of children) holds yet another promise of welfare improvement. When we add its greater purchasing power to its desperate search for free time, it is a truly promising source of service consumption, from restaurants and leisure parks to child care and home-help services for their aged parents. Thereby families create jobs for waiters, park-keepers, child-minders, and home-helpers. Of course, access to child care is a pre-condition for dual-income families in the first place. This is exactly the point: services beget services; the double-earner household plays the role of employment multiplier. The employment multiplier of working mothers can be quite substantial, especially in those kinds of services that are labour intensive.

Encouraging families to consume more external services is therefore part of a potential 'win-win' strategy. Yet, as we know, relative costs can be a major constraint. This is why, despite the virtual universalization of two-earner households, lower-end personal services in Scandinavia grow very little. They would doubtlessly grow if costs were lower, but this implies greater wage inequality.

This is where *Homo socialdemocraticus* must yield to *Homo liberalismus*. Substantial service employment growth outside the public sector depends on flexibility and low wages, something that social democracy cannot easily accept. The social democratic strategy, as I have outlined it so far, will therefore not escape the fundamental 'equality-jobs' trade-off. We need therefore to resolve one last problem: the very same 'equality-jobs' trade-off with which we started. . . .

There is in truth only one way out of the impasse, namely to redefine what kind of equality we desire. *Homo socialdemocraticus* must be convinced that we cannot aspire for all kinds of equality at once; that some inequalities can be made compatible with some equalities.

The principle of equality that must go is exactly the same that emerged—most forcefully in Scandinavian social democracy—when welfare states sought to respond to the equality-crisis of the 1960s, namely the promise of equality for all 'here-and-now'. In practice, this may not be so difficult a task. *Homo socialdemocraticus,* like many of his rivals, has surely held any number of lousy jobs in his youth. Like all Scandinavians, he left the parental home very early and lived for years on bread and water (this is what he tells his children). Yet, he is now a respectable citizen with a respectable career. Temporary deprivation is unimportant if it does not affect our life chances.

We can return to Schumpeter's omnibus: always full, but always with different people. Everybody gets off at the next stop, or at least where desired. If, like *Homo socialdemocraticus,* we cling to a notion of equality for all, here and now, we shall never resolve the fundamental dilemma of our times. The kinds of inequalities that are inevitable in the world of *Homo liberalismus* can become acceptable, even welcomed, if they coincide with a welfare regime capable of guaranteeing all citizens against entrapment: no one should find him- or herself in an omnibus with locked doors.

Our search for a postindustrial welfare optimum requires, therefore, some kind of a mobility guarantee. What this will look like depends, in turn, on what are the chief causes of social exclusion and inferior life chances. A room full of academics and experts would, no doubt, draft an endlessly long list of causes. Many standard reasons, such as physical or mental handicaps, do not concern us here because they are not inherently part of the equality–jobs trade-off. Two sources of substantial life chance problems stand out: one, the risks associated with marital instability and poverty in childhood; two, inadequate skills.

Diminishing family-induced risks calls for a standard 'social democratic' package of what the feminists call women-friendly policy: child-care services, incentives for mothers to work, and adequate income maintenance to take into account mothers' reduced labour supply and the cost of children. Diminishing labour market induced risks calls for a re-thinking of education, training, and marketable skills.

This is not the place to explore the broad issues of education. But there are a number of basic facts that all can agree upon: the returns to skills are rising, as we would expect in a world increasingly dominated by complex technology; the low-skilled are in rapidly declining demand. To exemplify the importance of skills, Bjorn (1995) shows that the probability of exiting from 'marginality' (basically unemployment or low pay) jumps by 30 points with vocational training, and 50 points with some theoretical training. Closing the skill gap is therefore an extremely effective way of catapulting people out of entrapment, of assuring good life chances. And it also pays off to society in the form of a more productive workforce.

There is clearly nothing earth-shatteringly novel about a call for more education. There is virtually no government or international organization today that does not advocate 'active labour market policy' or 'life-long learning'. But there is widespread scepticism about their effectiveness. Active labour market policy with its 'activation' and training programmes does not always appear to pay off if by this we mean that the unemployed eventually find a stable, promising career. Too often, activation looks more like a temporary parking-lot, or one interlude in a never-ending roundabout of unemployment, training, occasional jobs, and then unemployment again.

Effective or not, many believe that training is useless since there are no jobs for the newly trained. In a static sense this is undeniably often true. But they miss the basic point of the omnibus analogy: for any given individual, skills are the single best source of escape from underprivilege. What we are trying to resolve is a dynamic, life-course issue and not where to place everybody today. A new welfare optimum is, in fact, compatible with the possibility that many of us will experience a spell of unpleasantness.

What we really need to understand better is what kinds of skills and what kind of educa-tion to promote? We are generally aware of the rising demand for multi-skilling, flexible adaptation, and capacity for life-long learning. A worker with a good theoretical base in his vocational training is much easier to upgrade than someone with a high-school diploma unable to understand instructions on an aspirin bottle. This is why German employers use their skilled workers to run computerized production systems while in England they import engineers. We also face a reality where 'social skills' are more fundamental than muscle because of the direct face-to-face mode of service production. What these are is not easy to define, but they undoubtedly include more than the routine 'have a nice day'. A major problem in the contemporary unemployment structure is that laid-off miners and steel workers are unlikely to possess the kinds of social skills that sell a service.

We know from the OECD literacy studies (OECD, 1997) that education—even completed secondary education—may guarantee very little if it ends up producing 15 or 20 per cent Americans incapable of even rudimentary reading, writing, and arithmetic. These do not even possess the minimal level of qualifications needed to be trainable. They are a *de facto* human capital waste, a stratum only too obviously condemned to lifelong low-wage employment or, possibly, crime.

It is this kind of result that must be eliminated from any kind of society if we seriously desire an optimal welfare regime. I therefore close this chapter inviting education experts to design a workable system of skilling entitlements, one that would befit an ideal postindustrial welfare regime. And I invite our political leaders to forge a new coalition of our assorted *homines,* one capable of breaking the deadlock of median-voter support for anachronistic modes of welfare production.

Notes

1. The ratio of jobs lost to competition from the 'South' to jobs lost due to structural change is, for

the period 1970–85: .07 in Denmark; .04 in France; .06 in Germany; .01 in Japan and the Netherlands; .05 in the UK; and .08 in the USA (calculated from OECD, 1994, i, Table 3.10).

2. In the more 'distribution-dominated' economies of Canada, the Netherlands, and the United States, manufacturing decline has been much more modest. Japan (and Denmark) actually experienced net manufacturing job growth. (*Source:* recalculations from OECD, *Historical Statistics,* 1995, Table 1.10).

3. The 'classes' in the industrial order are relatively unproblematic, but those in the servicing hierarchy need some clarification. Professionals are straightforward; semi-professionals refer to occupations such as social workers, nurses, technicians, and teachers. Skilled service workers embrace occupations for which a skill certification is required (hairdressers or nursing assistants, for example). Unskilled service workers are defined as those occupying jobs for which there are no particular skill requirements, tasks that, in principle, anyone could perform (cleaning, waiting, bell-hopping, car-parking, and so forth). For a detailed exposé, see Esping-Andersen (1993).

4. There is none the less evidence that this classification scheme has validity. Salido (1996, ch. 3) has tested it both in terms of construct and criterion validity against the Treiman prestige scale, and also against a battery of hierarchy criteria such as autonomy, decision-making, and supervision, and the results are quite comforting.

5. The job-growth calculations are based on data from ILO, *Yearbook of Labour Statistics* (various years).

6. Estimating the regression equation (using robust regression): Professional ratio = $5.377 - 1.235$ (service growth). T-statistics for the constant = 14.87, and for service growth = -6.93. R-squared = .212 with F = 48.07.

7. The following argumentation lies close to the work of Gershuny (1978).

8. The ideas for this section of the chapter came from a week-end seminar with Jose Maria Maravall and Adam Przeworski (whom I thank for the idea and to whom I apologize for the result).

Bibliography

Bairoch, P. (1996), 'Globalization, Myths and Realities: One Century of External Trade and Foreign Investment', in R. Boyer and D. Drache (eds.), *States Against Markets*. London: Routledge, 173–93.

Baumol, W. (1967), 'The Macroeconomics of Unbalanced Growth', *American Economic Review,* 57: 415–26.

Bell, D. (1976), *The Coming of Postindustrial Society*. New York: Basic Books.

Bjorn, N. H. (1995), 'Causes and Consequences of Persistent Unemployment', Ph.D. diss., Department of Economics, Copenhagen University.

Braverman, H. (1974), *Labor and Monopoly Capital: The Degradation of Work in the Twentieth Century*. New York: Monthly Review Press.

Brown, P. and Crompton, R. (1994), *Economic Restructuring and Social Exclusion*. London: UCL Press.

Burtless, G. (1990) (ed.), *A Future of Lousy Jobs? The Changing Structure of U.S. Wages*. Washington: Brookings Institute.

Clark, T. and Lipset, S. M. (1991), 'Are Social Classes Dying?', *International Sociology,* 4: 397–410.

———. Lipset, S. M., and Rempel, M. (1993), 'The Declining Political Significance of Class', *International Sociology,* 3: 293–316.

Erikson, R. and Goldthorpe, John H. (1992), *The Constant Flux: Class Mobility in Industrial Societies*. Oxford: Clarendon Press.

Esping-Andersen, G. (1990), *The Three Worlds of Welfare Capitalism*. Cambridge: Polity Press.

———. (1993) (ed.), *Changing Classes: Stratification and Mobility in Postindustrial Societies*. London: Sage.

Gershuny, J. (1978), *After Industrial Society: The Emerging Self-service Economy*. London: Macmillan.

Goldthorpe, J. (1982), 'The Service Class, its Formation and Future', in A. Giddens and G. Mackenzie (eds.), *Social Class and the Division of Labour*. Cambridge: Cambridge University Press, 162–87.

Harrison, B. and Bluestone, B. (1988), *The Great U-Turn*, 2nd edn. New York: Basic Books.

Hirsh, F. (1976), *Social Limits to Growth*. Cambridge, Mass.: Harvard University Press.

Hout, M., Brooks, C., and Manza, J. (1993), 'The Persistence of Classes in Postindustrial Societies', *International Sociology,* 3: 259–78.

ILO (1943), *Yearbook of Labour Force Statistics*. Geneva: International Labour Office.

Jencks, C. and Peterson, P. E. (1991) (eds.), *The Urban Underclass*. Washington: Brookings Institute.

Kern, H. and Schumann, M. (1984), *Das Ende der Arbeitsteilung?* Munich: C. H. Beck.

Levy, Frank (1988), *Dollars and Dreams: The Changing American Income Distribution*. New York: W. W. Norton.

OECD (1992), *Employment Outlook*. Paris: OECD.

———. (1994a), *The OECD Jobs Study: Part I and II*. Paris: OECD.

————. (1995*e*), *Historical Statistics*. Paris: OECD.

————. (1997*c*), *Literacy, Skills and the Knowledge Society*. Paris: OECD.

Offe, C. (1985), *Disorganized Capitalism*. Cambridge, Mass.: MIT Press.

Renner, K. (1953), *Nachgelassene Werke,* iii. *Wandlungen der Modernen Gesellschaft*. Wien: Wiener Volksbuchhandlung.

Salido, O. (1996), 'La Movilidad Ocupacional Femenina en Espana: Una Comparacion por Sexo', Ph.D. diss., Universidad Complutense de Madrid, Facultad de Ciencias Politicas y Sociologia (June).

Stigler, G. (1956), *Trends in Employment in the Service Industries*. Princeton: Princeton University Press.

van Parijs, P. (1987), 'A Revolution in Class Theory', *Politics and Society,* 15/4: 453–82.

Wood, A. (1995), *North-South Trade, Employment and Inequality*. Oxford: Clarendon Press.

Wright, E. O. (1989), *The Debate on Classes*. London: Verso.

VICTOR NEE

Postsocialist Stratification

The transitions from state socialism in China, Russia and Eastern Europe provide natural experiments involving change in the stratification order on a scale reminiscent of that experienced in the West during the rise of capitalism. Comparative stratification research builds on modernization theory in assuming that industrial development, whether socialist or capitalist, leads to convergence (Lipset and Zetterberg 1959; Treiman 1970; Grusky and Hauser 1984; Hauser and Grusky 1984). Institutional theorists, however, are skeptical about theories of convergence driven by industrialism. If convergence pointed the way to state socialism's future, the sweeping measures to institute a market economy in industrially developed Eastern Europe and Russia would not have been necessary. Rather than focusing on the effects of industrial growth, institutionalists insist that research on state socialism needs also to take into account underlying differences in institutional forms. Such a focus on alternative institutional forms that provide a deep structure for economic action underlies my argument that the shift from redistribution to markets gives rise to different mechanisms of stratification.

Originally published in 1996. Please see complete source information beginning on page 891.

New institutionalist theory in sociology maintains that institutions shape the structure of incentives and thereby establish the constraints within which rational actors identify and pursue their interests (Nee and Ingram 1998; Cook and Levi 1990). It builds on Polanyi's (1944; North 1977, 1981) insight that economies are embedded in definite institutional arrangements. In Polanyi's view, the problem with neoclassical economics is that its formal models assume the existence of a market economy. Yet comparative studies of human societies, past and present, have demonstrated a variety of institutional forms giving rise to economies organized around fundamentally different operating principles (Polanyi 1957). Hence, the movement of goods and services in an economy is not simply a product of the aggregation of individual maximizing behavior, as assumed in neoclassical economics. In societies integrated by redistribution, goods and services are collected and distributed from a center in accordance with the customs, regulation, ideology, and ad hoc decisions of those social groups that hold redistributive power. Producers pass on a larger share of the economic surplus to the state precisely because they have less bargaining power over the terms of exchange than they would in a market economy. Instead, the state requisitions their products and compels them to work for prices and wages fixed by central bureaus (I. Szelényi 1978). As a consequence, the institutional logic of redistributive economies differs substantively from market economies where goods and services are exchanged directly between buyer and seller (Polanyi 1957; Kornai 1980), and from economies based on reciprocity where trust and cooperation in local social orders allow for balanced exchange (Homans 1950; Sahlins 1972). Redistribution, market, and reciprocity, as alternative institutional forms, incorporate different structures of incentives and constraints and therefore distinct parameters of choice. Elements of each coexist in every society, at various levels, but Polanyi claimed that only one can constitute the dominant integrative mechanism of an economy. In this sense, the "economy" is not narrowly economic but is embedded in customs, social norms, laws, regulations, and the state. Fundamentally, differences in institutional framework are reflected in contrasting structures of property rights (Pryor 1973).

The transition from one dominant institutional form to another entails remaking the fundamental rules that shape economies, from formal regulations and laws to informal conventions and norms. The shift to markets—well underway but far from complete in postsocialist societies—involves changing structures of opportunity (Merton 1949). Whereas opportunities for advancement were previously centered solely on decisions made by the redistributive bureaucracy and within the economy controlled by it, markets open up alternative avenues for mobility through emergent entrepreneurship and the selling of labor power. Under conditions of expanding markets, economic actors strive to institute new rules of competition and cooperation that serve their interests, both through informal arrangements and through formal institutional channels. This entails efforts to change the structure of property rights in a manner that enables entrepreneurs and producers to capture a greater proportion of the economic surplus, previously transferred to the state by administrative fiat. Political actors contribute to instituting change in the formal rules of the game insofar as gains

in productivity increase revenues to the state (North 1981; Nee 1992). Such action at the margins is cumulative and gradually results in transformation of the institutional environment.

Market transition theory (Nee 1989, 1991, 1996) maintains that as power—control over resources—shifts progressively from political disposition to market institutions, there will be a change in the distribution of rewards favoring those who hold market rather than redistributive power. Compared to nonmarket allocation, market exchange enhances the bargaining power of producers. Incentives are improved as producers retain a greater share of the economic surplus. Opportunities for gain depend less on the personal discretion of cadres in positional power. Consequently, the growth of market institutions (i.e., labor markets, subcontracting arrangements, capital markets, and business groups) causes a decline in the significance of socialist redistributive power even in the absence of fundamental change in the political order. In sectors of the socialist economy where a decisive shift to markets has occurred, officials are less likely to gain a dominant advantage from positional power in the state socialist redistributive bureaucracy. Contingent on continuing allocative control over key factor resources, their relative advantage declines as a function of the extent to which markets replace redistribution as the coordinating mechanism of the economy.

In the state socialist redistributive economy, officials act as monopolists who specify and enforce the rules of exchange by administrative fiat and exclude private entrepreneurs from taking part in legitimate economic activities. Because economic actors depend on resources allocated from above, they strive to secure favorable access to these decision makers in order to maximize their access to scarce resources (Walder 1986). By contrast, the shift to the market mechanism reduces dependence on superordinate bureaucratic agencies, as producers and consumers increasingly get needed goods and services through markets. Market-based exchanges stimulate the development of horizontal ties between buyers and sellers, in labor and production markets, resulting in an incremental decline in the relative value of vertical connections—political capital—and an increasing importance of network ties between economic actors in society.[1] In sum, changes in the mechanisms of stratification stem from the expansion of opportunities for gain and profit centering on market institutions. Opportunities are more broadly based and diverse when markets replace and augment the opportunity structure controlled by the state. Moreover, markets provide powerful incentives for direct producers and entrepreneurs, whereas state socialist redistributive economies depress incentives because administratively set prices for labor lack sensitivity to differential performance.

The foregoing line of reasoning may be represented as four closely related hypotheses. These are as follows:

1. *Political capital hypothesis:* In market transactions, economic actors have the right to withhold their labor power or product in emergent markets until a mutually agreed upon price is set, and a greater share of the economic surplus is therefore retained by producers than in a redistributive economy. The relative returns to political capital accordingly decline.

2. *Human capital hypothesis:* There are also stronger incentives for individual effort because rewards are more closely related to individual productivity. This is likely to be reflected in higher returns to human capital, which is among the best indicators of human productivity.

3. *Sector mobility hypothesis:* Producers who shift into the marketized sectors of the transition economy are likely to experience higher returns to their labor and productivity than those who remain in the sectors of the transition economy still controlled by redistribution.

4. *Entrepreneurship hypothesis:* Finally, expanding markets open up alternative avenues of socioeconomic mobility, giving rise to enterpreneurship as a mechanism for upward mobility into the postsocialist elite.

Critics of the theory advance the claim that departures from a centrally planned economy are likely to proceed without fundamental changes in the mechanism of stratification. According to proponents of this perspective, the initial advantages of the redistributive elite are such that this elite will come to dominate the postsocialist stratification order (Rona-Tas 1995; Walder 1996). The old redistributive elite, they argue, occupy strategic positions in political markets, which enable them to adapt flexibly to emerging markets and capture a disproportionate share of the rewards (Parish and Michelson 1996). In Russia, for example, officials and their cronies gained, by means of state-sponsored privatization, ownership rights over public assets—oilfields, mines, utility companies, state-owned enterprises, and so forth. The key issue here is the extensiveness of such power conversion relative to the frequency with which new elites emerge in the market economy. Market transition theory maintains that because an expanding market economy activates a substantially broader base of economic and social participation, even though a substantial element of the political elite succeed in converting political capital to economic capital, cadres as a social group still experience a relative decline. A recent study of the Hungarian elite confirms a very substantial decline in the representation of the nomenklatura in the composition of the postsocialist elite (S. Szelényi 1998). In urban China, where the communist party remains firmly in power, increasing relative returns to human capital are revealed not only in regressions on income (Zhou 2000), but in the

TABLE 1
Summary of Empirical Studies Relevant to Market Transition Theory

Study	Data				Findings			
	Nation	Population	Year	Dependent Variable	Political Capital	Human Capital	Sector Mobility	Entrepreneurship
Szelenyi 1988	Hungary	Rural, whole nation	1982–83	Agricultural goods	Mixed	Yes	—	—
Nee 1989	China	Rural, Fujian Province	1985	Income	Yes	Yes	—	Yes
Nee 1991	China	Rural, Fujian Province	1985	Income	Yes	—	—	Yes
Peng 1992	China	Urban & rural, selected areas	1986	Income	—	Yes	Yes	—
Rona-Tas 1994	Hungary	Urban & rural, whole nation	1989,91	Employment	Inconclusive*	Yes	—	Yes
				Income	Inconclusive*	Yes	—	—
Damanski and Heyns 1995	Poland	Urban & rural, whole nation	1987,91	Income	Yes	Yes	Inconclusive	—
Parish, Zhe, and Li 1995	China	Rural, eastern two-thirds of China	1993	Employment	Mixed	Yes	—	—
				Income	Yes	Yes	Yes	—
Nee 1996	China	Rural, whole nation	1989–90	Employment	Mixed	Yes	—	—
				Income	Yes	No	—	Yes
Parish and Michelson 1996	China	Rural, whole nation	1988	Employment	Inconclusive#	—	—	—
				Income	Inconclusive#	—	—	—
Xie and Hannum 1996	China	Urban, whole nation	1988	Income	Inconclusive#	Inconclusive#	—	—
Bian and Logan 1996	China	Urban, Tianjin	1988,93	Income	Yes*	Yes	Yes	—
Gerber and Hout 1998	Russia	Urban & rural, whole nation	1991–95	Income	—	No	—	Yes
S. Szelenyi (1998)	Hungary	Whole nation	1993	Elite membership	Yes	No	—	—
Brainerd 1998	Russia	Urban & rural, whole nation	1991–94	Income	—	Yes	—	—
Cao and Nee 1999	China	Urban, two southern cities	1994–95	Income	Yes	Yes	Yes	Yes
Zhou 2000	China	Urban, selected areas	1995	Income	Yes*	Yes*	Yes	—

Note: "Yes" means that the finding is consistent with market transition theory, "No" means inconsistent and "—" means inapplicable.
"*" indicates that the finding reported here is based on our own interpretation of the results, which differs from the author's.
"#" indicates that we disagree with the study's research design and hence regard the results as inconclusive.
Source: Nee and Cao (1999, pp. 10–11).

lower chances of promotion for party members even in state-owned enterprises oriented to market action (Cao 1999).

Table 1 provides a meta-analysis of results reported in empirical studies testing market transition theory. The findings confirm the theory's predictions of increasing relative returns to human capital, and its claim that emergent market economies open alternative pathways for upward mobility through entrepreneurship and labor markets in the private/hybrid sectors of the transition economy. However, empirical tests of the prediction of declining relative significance of political capital show mixed results, suggesting that elites in some postsocialist stratification orders have circulated more successfully than in others. Overall, the cumulative evidence from empirical studies points to path-dependent changes in the mechanisms of stratification largely in line with predictions proffered by market transition theory (Nee and Cao 1999).

The institutional changes that accompany the shift from a redistributive to a market economy comprise the causal mechanisms that cumulatively transform the stratification order. Although the transition entails hybrid stratification orders in which elements of the old elite retain and even augment their advantages, the secular trends of increasing returns to human capital and declining relative returns to political capital signal the decline of the redistributive elite. The more developed the market economy, the greater the breadth and diversity of opportunities that develop outside the boundaries of the old redistributive economy. Groups and individuals who were formerly barred from advancement in the state socialist bureaucracy and economy gain chances for social mobility through emergent labor markets and private entrepreneurship. To the extent that new bases of opportunity expand, resources become embedded in alternative networks and institutions, dependence on the established elite declines, and excluded groups gain in power relative to the established elite. Importantly,

such shifts in power need not entail a direct transfer of power as in a regime change but occur as an unintended by-product of institutional change. As in the rise of capitalism in the West, such change in the stratification order occurs gradually over time.

Note

1. This argument is consistent with power dependence theories (Emerson 1962; Hechter 1987) and social resource theory (Lin 1982). As China shifts to market coordination, family firms and social networks will grow in importance in economic transactions (Hamilton 1991).

References

Bian, Yanjie, and John Logan. 1996. "Market Transition and the Persistence of Power: The Changing Stratification in China." *American Sociological Review* 61:739–58.

Brainerd, Elizabeth. 1998. "Winners and Losers in Russia's Economic Transition." *American Economic Review* 88:1094–116.

Cao, Yang. 1999. "Careers Inside Organizations: Comparative Study of Promotion Determination in Urban China." Unpublished manuscript, Department of Sociology, Cornell University.

Cao, Yang, and Victor Nee. 1999. "Remaking Inequality: Market Dependency and Organizational Adaptation in Urban China." Working paper (Ithaca: Department of Sociology, Cornell University).

———. 2000. "Comment: Controversies and Evidence in the Market Transition Debate." *American Journal of Sociology* 105:1175–95.

Cook, Karen Schweers, and Margaret Levi, eds. 1990. *The Limits of Rationality.* Chicago: University of Chicago Press.

Damanski, Henrik, and Barbara Heyns. 1995. "Toward a Theory of the Role of the State in Market Transition: From Bargaining to Markets in Post-Communism." *European Journal of Sociology* 36:317–51.

Emerson, Richard A. 1962. "Power-Dependence Relations." *American Sociological Review* 27:31–41.

Gerber, Theodore, and Michael Hout. 1998. "More Shock than Therapy: Market Transition, Employment, and Income in Russia, 1991–1995." *American Journal of Sociology* 104:1–50.

Grusky, David B., and Robert M. Hauser. 1984. "Comparative Social Mobility Revisited: Models of Convergence and Divergence in 16 Countries." *American Sociological Review* 49: 19–38.

Hamilton, Gary G., ed. 1991. *Business Networks and Economic Development in East and Southeast Asia.* Hong Kong: University of Hong Kong, Centre of Asian Study.

Hechter, Michael. 1987. *Principles of Group Solidarity.* Berkeley: University of California Press.

Homans, George C. 1950. *The Human Group.* New York: Harcourt Brace Jovanovich.

Kornai, János. 1980. *The Economics of Shortage.* Amsterdam: North-Holland.

Lin, Nan. 1982. "Social Resources and Instrumental Action." Pages 131–46 in *Social Structure and Network Analysis,* edited by P. Marsden and N. Lin. Beverly Hills, CA: Sage.

Lipset, Seymour Martin, and Hans L. Zetterberg. 1959. "Social Mobility in Industrial Societies." Pp. 11–75 in *Social Mobility in Industrial Society,* edited by S. M. Lipset and R. Bendix. Berkeley: University of California Press.

Merton, Robert K. 1949. *Social Theory and Social Structure.* New York: Free Press.

Nee, Victor. 1989. "A Theory of Market Transition: From Redistribution to Markets in State Socialism." *American Sociological Review* 54: 663–81.

Nee, Victor. 1991. "Social Inequalities in Reforming State Socialism: Between Redistribution and Markets in China." *American Sociological Review* 56:267–82.

Nee, Victor. 1992. "Organizational Dynamics of Market Transition: Hybrid Forms, Property Rights, and Mixed Economy in China." *Administrative Science Quarterly* 37:1–27.

Nee, Victor. 1996. "The Emergence of a Market Society: Changing Mechanism of Stratification in China." *American Journal of Sociology* 100:908–949.

Nee, Victor, and Paul Ingram. 1998. "Embeddedness and Beyond: Institutions, Exchange, and Social Structure." Pages 19–45 in *The New Institutionalism in Economic Sociology,* edited by M. Brinton and V. Nee. New York: Russell Sage Foundation.

Nee, Victor, and Yang Cao. 1999. "Path Dependent Societal Transformation: Stratification in Hybrid Mixed Economies." *Theory and Society* 28:1–37.

North, Douglass C. 1977. "Markets and Other Allocation Systems in History: The Challenge of Karl Polanyi." *Journal of European Economic History* 6:703–16.

North, Douglass C. 1981. *Structure and Change in Economic History.* New York: Norton.

Parish, William L., Xiaoye Zhe, and Fang Li. 1995. "Nonfarm Work and Marketization of the Chinese Countryside." *China Quarterly* 143:697–730.

Parish, William L., and Ethan Michelson. 1996. "Politics and Markets: Dual Transformations." *American Journal of Sociology* 101:1042–59.

Peng, Yusheng. 1992. "Wage Determination in Rural and Urban China: A Comparison of Public and Private Industrial Sectors." *American Sociological Review* 57:198–213.

Polanyi, Karl. 1944. *The Great Transformation: The Political and Economic Origins of Our Time.* New York: Rinehart.

Polanyi, Karl. 1957. "The Economy as Instituted Process." Pages 243–69 in *Trade and Market in Early Empires,* edited by K. Polanyi, C. Arensberg, and H. Pearson. Glencoe, IL: Free Press.

Pryor, Frederick L. 1973. *Property and Industrial Organization in Communist and Capitalist Nations.* Bloomington: Indiana University Press.

Rona-Tas, Akos. 1994. "The First Shall Be Last? Entrepreneurship and Communist Cadres in the Transition from State Socialism." *American Journal of Sociology* 100:40–69.

Sahlins, Marshall. 1972. *Stone Age Economics.* New York: Aldine.

Szelényi, Iván. 1978. "Social Inequalities in State Socialist Redistributive Economies." *International Journal of Comparative Sociology* 19: 63–87.

———. 1988. *Socialist Entrepreneurs.* Madison, WI: University of Madison Press.

Szelényi, Szonja. 1998. *Equality by Design: The Grand Experiment in Destratification in Socialist Hungary.* Stanford, CA: Stanford University Press.

Treiman, Donald J. 1970. "Industrialization and Social Stratification." Pages 207–34 in *Social Stratification: Research and Theory for the 1970s,* edited by E. O. Laumann. Indianapolis: Bobbs-Merrill.

Walder, Andrew G. 1986. *Communist Neo-Traditionalism: Work and Authority in Chinese Industry.* Berkeley and Los Angeles: University of California Press.

Walder, Andrew G. 1996. "Markets and Inequality in Transitional Economies: Toward Testable Theories." *American Journal of Sociology* 101: 1060–73.

Xie, Yu, and Emily Hannum. 1996. "Regional Variation in Earnings Inequality in Reform-Era Urban China." *American Journal of Sociology* 101:950–992.

Zhou, Xueguang. 2000. "Economic Transformation and Income Inequality in Urban China." *American Journal of Sociology* 2000: 1135–74.

GIL EYAL, IVÁN SZELÉNYI, AND ELEANOR TOWNSLEY

Making Capitalism without Capitalists

There have been a number of schools of thought about which social groups would be best placed to take advantage of market reform after the fall of communism. Market transition theory[1] and research on socialist entrepreneurs[2] suggested that those who had been successful in the second economy during the late communist period would benefit most from the transition to capitalism. In contrast, theorists of political capitalism argued that former cadres were best placed to convert state-socialist privilege into economic capital.[3] Against both these theories we contend that cultural capital became the dominant form of capital in post-communism. The coalition that governs post-communist societies is comprised of technocrats and managers—many of whom held senior positions in communist institutions—and former dissident intellectuals who contributed to the fall of communist regimes at the end of the 1980s.

This [chapter] offers a new theory of the transition to capitalism, by telling the story of how capitalism is being built without capitalists in post-communist Central Europe. We theorize *capitalism without capitalists* as a distinctive new strategy of transition adopted by technocratic–intellectual elites in societies where no class of private owners existed prior to the introduction of market mechanisms. Note, however, that capitalism without capitalists is not necessarily capitalism *without a bourgeoisie*. If one thinks of the bourgeoisie as plural—thus, if one conceives *bourgeoisies* as a social group composed of both possessors of material property (the economic bourgeoisie) and possessors of culture or knowledge (the cultural bourgeoisie)— then one can claim—and we do so in this [chapter]—that post-communist capitalism is being promoted by a broadly defined intelligentsia which is committed to the cause of bourgeois society and capitalist economic institutions.

This approach to analyzing the transition to capitalism in Central Europe necessarily differs both from the classical social and economic theories of Adam Smith and Karl Marx and from twentieth-century visions of corporate, managerial, or other kinds of post-capitalist societies, such as those proposed by Ralf Dahrendorf, Berle and Means, or Daniel Bell. On one hand, classical theorists assumed that there must have been *capitalists before capitalism*. For this reason, these theorists expended much scholarly effort in-

Originally published in 1998. Please see complete source information beginning on page 891.

vestigating the process of the 'original' or 'primitive accumulation' of capital. The rationale was that both logically and historically, private capital accumulation must have occurred before market institutions could operate.[4] On the other hand, a recurrent theme in the study of existing capitalist systems, particularly since the 1930s, has been that the importance of individual private owners is waning. Observing the growth of large corporate organizations, the increasing role of financial institutions, or the growing importance of science/knowledge, varied theorists of 'late' capitalism have argued that the role of capital as the main source of economic growth is ending.[5] There is little doubt within this group that the capitalist system itself remains robust; what is in contention is the shape of *capitalism after capitalists*. Our theory of the transition to capitalism in Central Europe borrows from both these theoretical traditions, but differs from and builds upon them by imagining the historical possibility of *capitalism without capitalists*.

First, like 'capitalists *before* capitalism', ours is primarily a theory of transition. Our central aim is to understand and explain how capitalism can emerge in an economic system with no propertied bourgeoisie. We want to know what agents are building post-communist capitalism, and on whose behalf and for what purposes they act. One possibility is that the technocratic elite of former state-socialist societies may turn itself into a new propertied bourgeoisie and thereby fulfil the classical condition for capitalist development. Indeed, some analysts claim—rather prematurely, in our view—that such a transformation has already occurred. Another possibility is that the liberal intelligentsia will act as an 'intellectual vanguard of the economic bourgeoisie', creating a new class of proprietors from agents other than itself. Having fulfilled its historic mission, the intelligentsia may then return to creative writing, research, or teaching, or it may keep managing capitalist enterprises owned by others.

Within this field of possibilities, however, it is not inconceivable that capitalism will be built without a class of individual proprietors. In this case, we would expect an economic system which looks like those envisioned by twentieth-century theorists of 'capitalism *after* capitalists'. If it is true that the future of capitalist economies will be systems in which individual proprietors do not play a major role (and this proposition has been forcefully challenged by Zeitlin, Domhoff and others[6]), it is possible that Central European societies will emerge as corporate or post-capitalist societies without the historical intervention of a *grande bourgeoisie*. In other words, it is conceivable that post-communist elites will take a historic short cut and move directly to the most 'advanced' stage of corporate capitalism, never sharing their managerial power (even temporarily) with a class of individual owners. . . .

Cultural Capital and Class in Post-Communism

Post-communist society can be described as a unique social structure in which cultural capital is the main source of power, prestige, and privilege. Possession of economic capital places actors only in the middle of the social hierarchy, and the conversion of former political capital into private wealth is more the exception than the rule. Indeed, the conversion of former communist privilege into a post-communist equivalent happens only when social actors possess the right kinds of capital to make the transition. Thus, those who were at the top of the social hierarchy under state socialism can stay there only if they are capable of 'trajectory adjustment', which at the current juncture means if they are well endowed with cultural capital. By contrast, those who relied exclusively on now devalued political capital from the communist era are not able to convert this capital into anything valuable, and are likely to be downwardly mobile. . . .

Our point of departure is Bourdieu's theory of social structure, which we reconstruct using Weber's distinction between rank and class societies.[7] In this way, we hope to bring a comparative-historical dimension into Bourdieu's framework, which was designed initially to explain reproduction rather than social change. (No criticism is implied here: Bourdieu's research site is contemporary French society, where reproduction is the overwhelming trend; we study the recent social history of Central Europe where turbulence and large-scale social change have predominated.) From Bourdieu we borrow the ideas of three forms of capital, social space, and habitus. On this basis, we distinguish between social, economic, and cultural capital, and we conceptualize social structures as 'spaces' which are differentially stratified by various distributions of these types of capital. Individuals 'travel' in these spaces, and if changes in the relative importance of one or another type of capital occurs in their lifetimes, they try to reshuffle their portfolio of different types of capital and convert devalued forms of capital into revalued forms in order to stay 'on trajectory'. On this basis, there are several specific innovations we propose to explain the nature of social change in Central Europe.

1. *We conceptualize pre-communism, communism, and post-communism as three different stratification regimes defined by the dominance of different types of capital.* While Bourdieu used the three types of capital to describe contemporary French society, where economic capital is dominant and the other forms of capital are subordinate, in the ever-changing landscape of Central Europe during the past fifty years we distinguish three qualitatively different social spaces, each of which is defined by the dominance of a different form of capital.

2. *We claim that post-communism is a historically unique system of stratification in which cultural capital is dominant.* This enables us to develop a new theory of post-communist social structure which is consistent with our argument about the crucial roles played by the technocracy and former dissident intellectuals in the transition from social-ism to post-communism. We define capitalism as a class-stratified system in which economic capital is dominant, and communism as a system in which social capital—institutionalized as political capital—was the major source of power and privilege. With the decay of state socialism and the rise of post-communism, the importance of political capital is declining, the role of cultural capital is increasing, and economic capital is sufficient only to locate its possessors in the middle of the social hierarchy.

3. *The transition to post-communism is a shift from socialist rank order to capitalist class stratification.* Drawing on Weber, we conceptualize communism as a society based on rank order. Social capital was dominant, and resulted in a socialist form of patron-client relations. Compared to societies where economic capital was dominant—which we understand, with Weber, to be class-stratified societies—communist societies were examples of modern rank order. With this understanding, we can argue that the transition from communism to capitalism is, in principle, a transition from rank order to class society, and thereby introduce the dynamism of Weber's historical sociology into Bourdieu's structural analysis. Actually existing post-communism, however, as a system of 'capitalism *without* capitalists', occupies a middle position on this scale from rank to class. The *Bildungsbürgertum* [i.e., the educated middle classes] is neither a rank nor a class. Rather, it combines the characteristics and contains the possibilities of both logics of social stratification. . . .

The 'New Class' Project for the Fourth Time?

We have been careful not to call Central European post-capitalism a class society, and in particular we have explicitly avoided referring to technocrats and managers, or the intelligentsia as a whole, as a dominant class.

Rather, the key to our theory of post-communist managerialism and the conception of 'capitalism without capitalists' is that the formation of a propertied bourgeoisie has been relatively slow: market institutions have developed much more rapidly in Central Europe than a capitalist class. It is precisely this weakness of a domestic propertied bourgeoisie which has made it possible for a power bloc, composed of different fractions of intellectual elites, to retain a hegemonic position. At the same time, our answer to the 'Whodunit'? question—that is to say, 'Whose project is post-communism'?—is that it has been the project of the intelligentsia, or at least certain fractions of the intelligentsia. So it seems that the idea of the 'New Class' haunts us—the post-communist power bloc is neither a new nor an old class, but it is composed of intellectuals, and these intellectuals are pursuing a power project.

During the last century—starting with Bakunin in the early 1870s, and stretching to Gouldner in the late 1970s—the idea of a 'New Class' of intellectuals dominating and leading society has haunted the social sciences. In the West, it was thought that intellectuals would replace the propertied bourgeoisie. In Central Europe, it was believed that they would replace the old-guard bureaucracy of communist regimes. And while successive predictions of the imminent rise of the intelligentsia to power proved false, social scientists never seemed to learn their lesson. They kept creating new theories about societies in which intellectuals would dominate. Such theorizing came in waves, was fashionable for a few years, and then discredited for a while, only to be reborn in a somewhat altered form some years later. In an essay published a few years ago, one of us suggested that the stubborn return of the idea of the New Class requires explanation.[8] We argued that while neither the intelligentsia as a whole, nor any of its strata, ever succeeded in establishing itself as a new dominant class, it was probably historically true that intellectuals formulated such 'projects' for power. On

this basis, we interpreted the different waves of New Class theorizing as critical or apologetic—albeit premature—generalizations of such power projects. It may be instructive to think about post-communist managerialism from this perspective, and to contrast it with earlier intellectual class projects.

Between 1870 and 1970 we can identify at least three distinct waves of New Class theorizing, and possibly three intellectual power projects.

We identify the first wave as the 'intellectual class' theory advanced by anarchists of the late nineteenth and early twentieth centuries. This theory contended that Marxism was really the ideology of an intellectual elite, which was trying to use the working-class movement to smuggle itself into a position of class power. When a Marxism-inspired social order was established in the post-revolutionary Soviet Union—taking form as a dictatorship of the Stalinist bureaucracy rather than class rule by 'socialist scholars'—this theory died a peaceful death. However, this does not mean that the anarchist analysis of Marxism as an intellectual ideology was completely without insight. From our perspective, it helps to explain why Central European intellectuals abandoned their *Bildungsbürgertum* project at the turn of the century, and why so many of them were attracted to left-wing radicalism.

The second wave of New Class theories—fashionable in a period roughly from 1930 to the 1950s—consisted of 'bureaucratic-technocratic class' theories. In the version which addressed the social conditions of advanced Western capitalism, New Class theorists argued that the technocratic and/or managerial stratum would fill the gap created by the decline of family capitalism and individual private property.[9] We think these theorists were probably correct in identifying 'New Class' aspirations among managers and technocrats at this time, but they erred in taking the ideologues of managerialism at their word, and underestimating the power of the old moneyed class. Critics of managerialist New Class theories, like Zeitlin and Domhoff,

were correct when they observed that managerialism in the United States and Western
Europe failed because it confronted a strong
propertied bourgeoisie.[10] We tend to side with
the critics in this debate, since there is strong
evidence that the old propertied bourgeoisie is
alive and well. Indeed, it seems that today the
concentration of wealth in the United States
and Western Europe is even more marked,
and fewer people own more of the productive
assets than ever before.

The third wave of New Class theories, created in the 1960s and 1970s, was comprised
of theories of 'the knowledge class'. In their
right-wing version, these theories of the new
class interpreted the radical movements of the
1960s as a power plot by the counter-cultural
intelligentsia to dominate society. By contrast,
social scientists on the political Left emphasized that as science became an increasingly
important factor of production, scientists
would begin replacing property owners as the
dominant group in advanced Western societies.[11] Some of these theorists, most notably
Gouldner, were not thrilled by the prospect of
a society ruled by a new class coalition of the
technical intelligentsia and humanistic intellectuals merged together by the 'culture of
critical discourse', but given the alternatives,
they believed that it might be 'our best card in
history'. As the left radicalism of the 1960s
faded away, however, and as counter-cultural
intellectuals were replaced by Yuppies preach-
ing neo-liberalism, this wave of theorizing
also withered away.

What about post-communist managerialism? Is it possible that we are witnessing a
fourth New Class project this century? Is it
possible that intellectuals are indeed in power,
even though it is 'by default' this time, since
managers have no enemies able to resist their
newly found dominance? Have the prophecies of Berle and Means actually turned out
to be correct—not for the advanced West
but ironically, for Central Europe? Or is post-
communism, as we have analyzed it, simply a
step in the transition to market capitalism as
we know it from the advanced West? Or are

we witnessing the transformation of existing
elements into a new *Gestalt*, of which we
have no adequate conception? We know that
we are shooting at a rapidly moving target,
and social scientists are poor snipers even
when the target does not move.

In this context, it is difficult to answer the
question of whether or not managerialism
will last. It is difficult to predict the chances
that the post-communist power bloc will reproduce itself and the social and economic order it governs. It is unclear whether or not the
post-communist elite will resist the encroach-
ments of international capital, and the attempts of propertied middle classes to accumulate capital and take hold of the command
posts of the economy. Reproduction is a possibility, however. It is conceivable that managers will consolidate their powerful institutional base by allying with national and
international fiscal institutions and, with
monetarism as their ideology, continue to
govern post-communist capitalism as managers. The appropriate positions are ready,
the adequate consciousness has been prepared, and the actors feel comfortable in
their positions and are deeply committed to
their ideology. Furthermore, in post-communist societies the alternatives seem to be difficult. The nationalization of property has
been a process with far-reaching implications, and is possibly irreversible. As the old
joke puts it: we know how to make fish soup
from an aquarium, but how can we build an
aquarium from a bowl of fish soup? East European economists enjoyed citing this joke
before 1989, but they quickly forgot it after
1989. Indeed, one major underpinning of
managers' power is their claim to be the only
ones with the knowledge of how to conduct
the complex task of privatization. And the
more complex the task, the more it is practically impossible to convert former public
property into identifiable individual private
property; thus the more power managers
have. Thinking about post-communist managerialism as the 'fourth wave' of an intellectual project for power is useful, then, since it

helps us to ask these intriguing questions. Moreover, thinking in this way means that we do not simply assume that managerial power is a transitional phenomenon; it allows us to ask: what will society be like if managerialism reproduces itself?

To push our luck even further, we may even wonder whether or not Central European post-communist developments have any relevance for the rest of the world. To put it differently: is Central Europe the future of the West? After all, Central European managerialism may not be all that different from the way Western capitalism operates today: property rights are diffuse, managers exercise a lot of power, and monetarist ideologies are powerful and widespread. As we have already noted, however, these questions about the future are tricky ones, and social scientists are notoriously bad at answering them. Perhaps it would be best to pose the question in a different way and ask: 'If managerialism was a project during the interwar years, as Berle and Means suggested, and if it failed, why did it fail'? Approaching the issue in this way is likely to make us skeptical about the spread of managerialism around the world. Since we argued that managerialism was successful in Central Europe because it did not face powerful enemies like a large propertied bourgeoisie, we would predict that the chances for managerialism in the rest of the world, and especially in the countries of advanced Western capitalism, are slim indeed.

Notes

1. Victor Nee (1989) 'A Theory of Market Transition: From Redistribution to Markets in State Socialism'. *American Sociological Review* 54(5): 663–81.
2. Iván Szelényi (1988) *Socialist Entrepreneurs.* Madison: University of Wisconsin Press.
3. Ákos Rona-Tas (1994) 'The First Shall Be The Last? Entrepreneurship and Communist Cadres in the Transition from Socialism'. *American Journal of Sociology* 100(1): 40–69.
4. Karl Marx (1919) *Das Kapital: Kritik der politischen Ökonomie.* Hamburg: Meissner; Adam

Smith ([1779] 1976). *An Enquiry into the Nature and Causes of the Wealth of Nations.* Oxford: Oxford University Press.
5. For the classic statements on the growth of the large corporation and its consequences, see Adolf Berle and Gardiner Means ([1931] 1968) *The Modern Corporation and Private Property.* New York: Harcourt Brace Jovanovich; and Ralf Dahrendorf (1959) *Class and Class Conflict in Industrial Society.* Stanford, CA: Stanford University Press. For a discussion of the increasingly important role of financial institutions, see Neil Fligstein (1990) *The Transformation of Corporate Control.* Cambridge, MA: Harvard University Press; and for arguments which suggest that the role of capital is ending as the primary motor of economic growth in modern capitalism, see, for example, Daniel Bell ([1973] 1976) *The Coming of Post-industrial Society.* New York: Basic Books.
6. See, for example, Maurice Zeitlin (1974) 'Corporate Ownership and Control: The Large Corporation and the Capitalist Class'. *American Journal of Sociology* 79(5): 1073–1119; G. William Domhoff (1967) *Who Rules America?* Englewood Cliffs, NJ: Prentice Hall; G. William Domhoff (1970) *The Higher Circles: The Governing Class in America.* New York: Random House; and G. William Domhoff (1986) *Who Rules America Now? A View from the 1980s.* New York: Simon & Schuster.
7. Pierre Bourdieu ([1983] 1986) 'The Forms of Capital'. pp. 241–58 in *Handbook of Theory and Research for the Sociology of Education,* ed. John G. Richardson. New York: Greenwood Press; Pierre Bourdieu (1984) *Distinction: A Sociological Critique of the Judgement of Taste.* Cambridge, MA: Harvard University Press; Max Weber ([1915–21] 1978) *Economy and Society.* Berkeley: University of California Press, pp. 926–38.
8. Iván Szelényi and Bill Martin (1988) 'The Three Waves of New Class Theories'. *Theory and Society* 17(4): 645–67.
9. See, for example, Thornstein Veblen ([1919] 1963) *The Engineers and the Price System.* New York: Harcourt & Brace; Adolf Berle and Gardiner Means ([1931] 1968) *The Modern Corporation and Private Property.* New York: Harcourt Brace Jovanovich; James Burnham ([1941] 1962) *The Managerial Revolution.* Bloomington: Indiana University Press; Ralf Dahrendorf (1972) *Class and Class Conflict in Industrial Society.* Stanford, CA: Stanford University Press; John K. Galbraith (1967) *The New Industrial State.* New York: Houghton Mifflin.
10. Maurice Zeitlin (1974) 'Corporate Ownership and Control: The Large Corporation and the Capitalist Class'. *American Journal of Sociology* 79(5):1073–1119; G. William Domhoff (1967)

Who Rules America? Englewood Cliffs, NJ: Prentice Hall; G. William Domhoff (1970) *The Higher Circles: The Governing Class in America.* New York: Random House.

11. Galbraith, in *The New Industrial State,* took this position, and to some extent, so did Daniel Bell ([1973] 1976) *The Coming of Post-Industrial Society.* New York: Basic Books. See also Alvin Gouldner (1979) *The Future of Intellectuals and the Rise of the New Class.* New York: The Continuum Publishing Corporation.

S T U A R T   H A L L

The Meaning of New Times

How new are these 'new times'? Are they the dawn of a New Age or only the whisper of an old one? What is 'new' about them? How do we assess their contradictory tendencies—are they progressive or regressive? These are some of the questions which the ambiguous discourse of 'new times' poses. . . .

If we take the 'new times' idea apart, we find that it is an attempt to capture, within the confines of a single metaphor, a number of different facets of social change, none of which has any necessary connection with the other. In the current debates, a variety of different terms jostle with one another for pride of place, in the attempt to describe these different dimensions of change. They include 'post-industrial', 'post-Fordist', 'revolution of the subject', 'postmodernism'. None of these is wholly satisfactory. Each expresses a clearer sense of what we are leaving behind ('post' everything?) than of where we are heading. Each, however, signifies something important about the 'new times' debate.

'Post-industrial' writers, like Alain Touraine and André Gorz, start from shifts in the technical organisation of industrial capitalist production, with its 'classic' economies of scale, integrated labour processes, advanced division of labour and industrial class

conflicts. They foresee an increasing shift to new productive regimes—with inevitable consequences for social structure and politics. Thus Touraine has written of the replacement of older forms of class struggle by the new social movements; and Gorz's most provocative title is *Farewell To The Working Class*. In these forms, 'new times' touches debates which have already seriously divided the Left. There is certainly an important point about the shifting social and technical landscapes of modern industrial production regimes being made in some of these arguments, though they are open to the criticism that they fall for a sort of technological determinism.

'Post-Fordism' is a broader term, suggesting a whole new epoch distinct from the era of mass production, with its standardised products, concentrations of capital and its 'Taylorist' forms of work organisation and discipline. The debate still rages as to whether 'post-Fordism' actually exists, and if it does, what exactly it is and how extensive it is, either within any single economy or across the advanced industrial economies of the West as a whole. Nevertheless, most commentators would agree that the term covers at least some of the following characteristics of change. A shift is taking place to new 'information technologies' from the chemical and electronic-based technologies which drove the 'second' industrial revolution from the turn of the century onwards—the one which signalled the advance of the American, German and Japanese economies to a leading position, and the relative 'backwardness' and incipient de-

Originally published in 1989. Please see complete source information beginning on page 891.

cline of the British economy. Secondly, there is a shift towards a more flexible specialised and decentralised form of labour process and work organisation, and, as a consequence, a decline of the old manufacturing base (and the regions and cultures associated with it) and the growth of the 'sunrise', computer-based, hi-tech industries and their regions. Thirdly, there is the hiving-off or a contracting-out of functions and services hitherto provided 'in house' on a corporate basis. Fourthly, there is a leading role for consumption, reflected in such things as greater emphasis on choice and product differentiation, on marketing, packaging and design, on the 'targeting' of consumers by lifestyle, taste and culture rather than by the Registrar General's categories of social class.

Fifthly, there has been a decline in the proportion of the skilled, male, manual working class and the corresponding rise of the service and white collar classes. In the domain of paid work itself, there is more flexi-time and part-time working, coupled with the 'feminisation' and 'ethnicisation' of the workforce. Sixthly, there is an economy dominated by the multi-nationals, with their new international division of labour and their greater autonomy of nation state control. Seventhly, there is the 'globalisation' of the new financial markets. Finally, there is the emergence of new patterns of social divisions—especially those between 'public' and 'private' sectors and between the two-thirds who have rising expectations and the 'new poor' and underclasses of the one-third that is left behind on every significant dimension of social opportunity.

It is clear that 'post-Fordism', though having a significant reference to questions of economic organisation and structure, has a much broader social and cultural significance. Thus, for example, it also signals greater social fragmentation and pluralism, the weakening of older collective solidarities and block identities and the emergence of new identities as well as the maximisation of individual choices through personal consumption, as equally significant dimensions of the shift towards 'post-Fordism'.

Some critics have suggested that 'post-Fordism' as a concept marks a return to the old, discredited base-superstructure or economic-determinist model according to which the economy determines everything and all other aspects can be 'read off' as simply reflecting that 'base'. However, the metaphor of 'post-Fordism' does not necessarily carry any such implication. Indeed, it is modelled on Gramsci's earlier use of the term, 'Fordism', at the turn of the century to connote a whole shift in capitalist civilization (which Gramsci certainly did not reduce to a mere phenomenon of the economic base). 'Post-Fordism' should also be read in a much broader way. Indeed, it could just as easily be taken in the opposite way—as signalling the *constitutive* role which social and cultural relations play in relation to any economic system. Post-Fordism as I understand it is not committed to any prior determining position for the economy. But it does insist—as all but the most extreme discourse theorists and culturalists must recognise—that shifts of this order in economic life must be taken seriously in any analysis of our present circumstances.

A recent writer on the subject of contemporary cultural change, Marshall Berman, notes that 'modern environments and experiences cut across all boundaries of geography and ethnicity, of class and nationality, of religion and ideology'—not destroying them entirely, but weakening and subverting them, eroding the lines of continuity which hitherto stabilised our social identities.

The Return of the Subject

One boundary which 'new times' has certainly displaced is that between the 'objective' and subjective dimensions of change. This is the so-called 'revolution of the subject' aspect. The individual subject has become more important, as collective social subjects—like that of class or nation or ethnic group—become more segmented and 'pluralised'. As social theorists have become more concerned with how ideologies actually function, and how political mobilisation really takes place in complex societies, so they have been obliged to take the *'subject'* of these processes more seriously. As Gramsci remarked about ideologies, 'To the extent that ideologies are historically necessary they have a validity which is "psychological"' (*Prison Notebooks* p. 377). At the same time, our models of 'the subject' have altered. We can no longer conceive of 'the individual' in terms of a whole, centred, stable and completed Ego or autonomous, rational 'self'. The 'self' is conceptualised as more fragmented and incomplete, composed of multiple 'selves' or identities in relation to the different social worlds we inhabit, something with a history, 'produced', in process. The 'subject' is differently placed or *positioned* by different discourses and practices.

This is novel conceptual or theoretical terrain. But these vicissitudes of 'the subject' also have their own histories which are key episodes in the passage to 'new times'. They include the cultural revolution of the 1960s; '1968' itself, with its strong sense of politics as 'theatre' and its talk of 'will' and 'consciousness'; feminism, with its insistence that 'the personal is political'; the renewed interest in psychoanalysis, with its rediscovery of the unconscious roots of subjectivity; the theoretical revolutions of the 1960s and 1970s— semiotics, structuralism, 'post-structuralism'—with their concern for language, discourse and representation.

This 'return of the subjective' aspect suggests that we cannot settle for a language in which to describe 'new times' which respects the old distinction between the objective and subjective dimensions of change. 'New times' are both 'out there', changing our conditions of life, and 'in here', working on us. In part, it is *us* who are being 're-made'. But such a conceptual shift presents particular problems for the Left. The conventional culture and discourses of the Left, with its stress on 'objective contradictions', 'impersonal structures' and processes that work 'behind men's (*sic*) backs', have disabled us from confronting the subjective dimension in politics in any very coherent way.

In part, the difficulty lies in the very words and concepts we use. For a long time, being a socialist was synonymous with the ability to translate everything into the language of 'structures'. But it is not only a question of language. In part, the difficulty lies in the fact that men so often provide the categories within which *everybody* experiences things, even on the Left. Men have always found the spectacle of the 'return' of the subjective dimension deeply unnerving. The problem is also theoretical. Classical marxism depended on an assumed correspondence between 'the economic' and 'the political': one could read off political attitudes and objective social interests and motivations from economic class position. For a long time, these correspondences held the theoretical analyses and perspectives of the Left in place. However, any simple correspondence between 'the political' and 'the economic' is exactly what has now disintegrated—practically and theoretically. This has had the effect of throwing the language of politics more over to the cultural side of the equation.

'Postmodernism' is the preferred term which signals this more *cultural* character of 'new times'. 'Modernism', it argues, which dominated the art and architecture, the cultural imagination, of the early decades of the 20th century, and came to represent the look and experience of 'modernity' itself, is at an end. It has declined into the International Style characteristics of the freeway, the wall-of-glass skyscraper and international airports. Modernism's revolutionary impulse—which could be seen in surrealism, Dada, constructivism, the move to an abstract and non-figurative visual culture—has been tamed and contained by the museum. It has become the preserve of an avant-garde élite, betraying its revolutionary and 'populist' impulses.

'Postmodernism', by contrast, celebrates the penetration of aesthetics into everyday life and the ascendancy of popular culture over the High Arts. Theorists like Fredric Jameson and Jean-François Lyotard agree on many of the characteristics of 'the postmodern condition'. They remark on the dominance of image, appearance, surface-effect over depth (was Ronald Reagan a president or just a B-movie actor, real or cardboard cut-out, alive or Spitting Image?). They point to the blurring of image and reality in our media-saturated world (is the Contra war real or only happening on TV?). They note the preference for parody, nostalgia, kitsch and pastiche—the continual re-working and quotation of past styles—over more positive modes of artistic representation, like realism or naturalism. They note, also, a preference for the popular and the decorative over the brutalist or the functional in architecture and design. 'Postmodernism' also has a more philosophical aspect. Lyotard, Baudrillard and Derrida cite the erasure of a strong sense of history, the slippage of hitherto stable meanings, the proliferation of difference, and the end of what Lyotard calls the 'grand narratives' of progress, development, Enlightenment, Rationality, and Truth which, until recently, were the foundations of Western philosophy and politics.

Jameson, however, argues very persuasively that postmodernism is also 'the new cultural logic of capital'—'the purest form of capital yet to have emerged, a prodigious expansion into hitherto uncommodified areas' (Jameson p. 78). His formulations remind us that the changing cultural dynamic we are trying to characterise is clearly connected with the revolutionary energy of modern capital—capital *after* what we used to call its 'highest stages' (Imperialism, Organised or Corporate capitalism), even *later* than 'late capitalism'.

'Post-industrialism', 'post-Fordism', 'Postmodernism' are all different ways of trying to characterise or explain this dramatic, even brutal, resumption of the link between modernity and capitalism. Some theorists argue that, though Marx may have been wrong in his predictions about class as the motor of revolution, he was right—with a vengeance—about capital. Its 'global' expansion continues, with renewed energy in the 1980s, to transform everything in its wake, subordinating every society and social relationship to the

law of commodification and exchange value. Others argue that, with the failures of the stalinist and social-democratic alternatives, and the transformations and upheavals now taking place throughout the communist world, capital has acquired a new lease of life.

Some economists argue that we are simply in the early, up-beat half of the new Kondratiev 'long wave' of capitalist expansion (after which the inevitable downturn or recession will follow). The American social critic whom we quoted earlier, Marshall Berman, relates 'new times' to 'the ever-expanding drastically fluctuating capitalist world markets' (Berman p. 16). Others, with their eye more firmly fixed on the limits and uneven development of capital on a global scale, emphasise more the ceaseless rhythm of the international division of labour, redistributing poverty and wealth, dependency and overdevelopment in new ways across the face of the earth. One casualty of this process is the old idea of some homogeneous 'Third World'. Nowadays, Formosa and Taiwan are integrated into the advanced capitalist economies, as Hong Kong is with the new financial markets. Ethiopia or the Sudan or Bangladesh, on the other hand, belong to a different 'world' altogether. It is the new forms and dynamic of capital as a global force which is marking out these new divisions across the globe.

However, it seems to be the case that, whichever explanation we finally settle for, the really startling fact is that *these* new times clearly belong to a time-zone marked by the march of capital simultaneously across the globe and through the Maginot Lines of our subjectivities.

The title of Berman's book *All That is Solid Melts Into Air*—a quotation from *The Communist Manifesto*—reminds us that Marx was one of the earliest people to grasp the revolutionary connection between capitalism and modernity. In the *Manifesto*, he spoke of the 'constant revolutionising of production, uninterrupted disturbance of all social relations, everlasting uncertainty and agitation' which distinguished 'the bourgeois epoch from all earlier times'. 'All fixed, fast-frozen relationships, with their train of venerable ideas and opinions, are swept away, all new-formed ones become obsolete before they can ossify. All That is Solid Melts Into Air'.

Indeed, as Berman points out, Marx considered the revolution of modern industry and production the necessary precondition for that Promethean or Romantic conception of the social individual which towers over his early writings, with its prospect of the many-sided development of human capacities. In this context, it was not the commodities which the bourgeoisie created which impressed Marx, so much as 'the processes, the powers, the expressions of human life and energy; men (*sic*) working, moving, cultivating, communicating, organising and reorganising nature and themselves' (Berman p. 93). Of course, Marx also understood the one-sided and distorted character of the modernity and type of modern individual produced by this development—how the forms of bourgeois appropriation destroyed the human possibilities it created. But he did not, on this count, refuse it. What he argued was that *only socialism* could complete the revolution of modernity which capitalism had initiated. As Berman puts it, he hoped 'to heal the wounds of modernity through a fuller and deeper modernity'.

Now here exactly is the rub about 'new times' for the Left. The 'promise' of modernity has become, at the end of the 20th century, considerably more ambiguous, its links with socialism and the Left much more tenuous. We have become more aware of the double-edged and problematic character of modernity: what Theodore Adorno called the 'negative dialectic' of enlightenment. Of course, to be 'modern' has *always* meant 'to live a life of paradox and contradiction . . . alive to new possibilities for experience and adventure, frightened by the nihilistic depths to which so many modern adventures lead (e.g., the line from Nietzsche and Wagner to the death camps), longing to create and hold onto something real even as everything melts'.

Some theorists argue—the German philosopher, Jurgen Habermas is one—that this is too pessimistic a reading of 'Enlightenment' and that the project of modernity is not yet completed. But it is difficult to deny that, at the end of the 20th century, the paradoxes of modernity seem even more extreme. 'Modernity' has acquired a relentlessly uneven and contradictory character: material abundance here, producing poverty and immiseration there; greater diversity and choice—but often at the cost of commodification, fragmentation and isolation. More opportunities for participation—but only at the expense of subordinating oneself to the laws of the market. Novelty and innovation—but driven by what often appear to be false needs. The rich 'West'—and the famine-stricken South. Forms of 'development' which destroy faster than they create. The city—privileged scenario of the modern experience for Baudelaire or Walter Benjamin—transformed into the anonymous city, the sprawling city, the inner city, the abandoned city. . . .

These stark paradoxes project uncertainty into any secure judgement or assessment of the trends and tendencies of new times especially on the Left. Are new times to be welcomed for the new possibilities they open? Or rejected for the threat of horrendous disasters (the ecological ones are uppermost in our minds just now) and final closures which they bring in their wake? Terry Eagleton has recently posed the dilemma in comparable terms, when discussing the 'true aporia, impasse or undecidability of a transitional epoch, struggling out as it is from beneath an increasingly clapped-out, discreditable, historically superannuated ideology of Autonomous Man (first cousin to Socialist Man), with no very clear sense as yet of which path out from this pile of ruins is likely to lead us towards an enriched human life and which to the unthinkable terminus of some fashionable new irrationalist barbarism' (Eagleton p. 47). We seem, especially on the Left, permanently impaled on the horns of these extreme and irreconcilable alternatives. . . .

The Cultural Dimension

Another major requirement for trying to think through the complexities and ambiguities of new times is simply to open our minds to the deeply *cultural* character of the revolution of our times. If 'post-Fordism' exists, then it is as much a description of cultural as of economic change. Indeed, that distinction is now quite useless. Culture has ceased (if ever it was—which I doubt) to be a decorative addendum to the 'hard world' of production and things, the icing on the cake of the material world. The word is now as 'material' as the world. Through design, technology and styling, 'aesthetics' has already penetrated the world of modern production. Through marketing, layout and style, the 'image' provides the mode of representation and fictional narrativisation of the body on which so much of modern consumption depends. Modern culture is relentlessly material in its practices and modes of production. And the material world of commodities and technologies is profoundly cultural. Young people, black and white, who can't even spell 'postmodernism' but have grown up in the age of computer technology, rock-video and electronic music, already inhabit such a universe in their heads.

Is this merely the culture of commodified consumption? Are these necessarily Trivial Pursuits? (Or, to bring it right home, a trendy 'designer addiction' to the detritus of capitalism which serious Left magazines like *Marxism Today* should renounce—or even better denounce—forever?) Yes, much—perhaps, even most—of the time. But underlying that, have we missed the opening up of the individual to the transforming rhythms and forces of modern *material* life? Have we become bewitched by who, in the short run, reaps the profit from these transactions (there are vast amounts of it being made), and missed the democratisation of culture which is *also* potentially part of their hidden agenda? Can a socialism of the 21st century revive, or even survive, which is wholly cut off from the landscapes of popular pleasures, however contra-

dictory and 'commodified' a terrain they represent? Are we thinking dialectically enough?

One strategy for getting at the more cultural and subjective dimensions of new times would be to start from the objective characteristics of post-Fordism and simply turn them inside out. Take the new technologies. They not only introduce new skills and practices. They also require new ways of thinking. Technology, which used to be 'hard-nosed' is now 'soft'. And it no longer operates along one, singular line or path of development. Modern technology, far from having a fixed path, is open to constant renegotiation and re-articulation. 'Planning', in this new technological environment, has less to do with absolute predictability and everything to do with instituting a 'regime' out of which a plurality of outcomes will emerge. One, so to speak, plans for contingency. This mode of thinking signals the end of a certain kind of deterministic rationality.

Or consider the proliferation of models and styles, the increased product differentiation, which characterises 'post-Fordist' production. We can see mirrored there wider processes of cultural diversity and differentiation, related to the multiplication of social worlds and social 'logics' typical of modern life in the West.

There has been an enormous expansion of 'civil society', related to the diversification of social worlds in which men and women now operate. At present, most people only relate to these worlds through the medium of consumption. But, increasingly we are coming to understand that to maintain these worlds at an advanced level requires forms of collective consumption far beyond the restricted logic of the market. Furthermore, each of these worlds also has its own codes of behaviour, its 'scenes' and 'economies', and (don't knock it) its 'pleasures'. These already allow those individuals who have some access to them some space in which to reassert a measure of choice and control over everyday life, and to 'play' with its more expressive dimensions. This 'pluralisation' of social life expands the positionalities and identities available to ordinary people (at least in the industrialised world) in their everyday working, social, familial and sexual lives. Such opportunities need to be more, not less, widely available across the globe, and in ways not limited by private appropriation.

This shift of time and activity towards 'civil society' has implications for our thinking about the individual's rights and responsibilities, about new forms of citizenship and about ways of ordering and regulating society other than through the all-encompassing state. They imply a 'socialism' committed to, rather than scared of, diversity and difference.

Of course, 'civil society' is no ideal realm of pure freedom. Its micro-worlds include the multiplication of points of power and conflict—and thus exploitation, oppression and marginalisation. More and more of our everyday lives are caught up in these forms of power, and their lines of intersection. Far from there being no resistance to the system, there has been a proliferation of new points of antagonism, new social movements of resistance organised around them—and, consequently, a generalisation of 'politics' to spheres which hitherto the Left assumed to be apolitical: a politics of the family, of health, of food, of sexuality, of the body. What we lack is any overall map of how these power relations connect and of their resistances. Perhaps there isn't, in that sense, one 'power game' at all, more a network of strategies and powers and their articulations—and thus a politics which is always positional. . . .

By 'ethnicity' we mean the astonishing return to the political agenda of all those points of attachment which give the individual some sense of 'place' and position in the world, whether these be in relation to particular communities, localities, territories, languages, religions or cultures. These days, black writers and film-makers refuse to be restricted to only addressing black subjects. But they insist that others recognise that what they have to say comes out of particular histories and cultures and that everyone speaks from positions within the global distribution of power. Be-

cause these positions change and alter, there is always an engagement with politics as a 'war of position'.

This insistence on 'positioning' provides people with co-ordinates, which are specially important in face of the enormous globalization and transnational character of many of the processes which now shape their lives. The new times seem to have gone 'global' and 'local' at the same moment. And the question of ethnicity reminds us that everybody comes from some place—even if it is only an 'imagined community'—and needs some sense of identification and belonging. A politics which neglects that moment of identity and identification—without, of course, thinking of it as something permanent, fixed or essential—is not likely to be able to command the new times.

Could there be new times without new subjects? Could the world be transformed while its subjects stay exactly the same? Have the forces remaking the modern world left the subjects of that process untouched? Is change possible while *we* remain untransformed? It was always unlikely and is certainly an untenable proposition now. This is another one of those many 'fixed and fast-frozen relationships, venerable ideas and opinions' which, as Marx accurately predicted, new times are quietly melting into thin air.

References

Jean Baudrillard, *The Mirror of Production*, Telos 1979.

Marshall Berman, *All That is Solid Melts Into Air,* Simon and Schuster 1983.

Terry Eagleton, 'Identity', ICA 6, 1987.

André Gorz, *Farewell to the Working Class*, Pluto 1982.

Antonio Gramsci, *Selections from the Prison Notebooks,* Lawrence and Wishart 1971.

Fredric Jameson, 'The Cultural Logic of Capital', *New Left Review* 146, July/August 1984.

Jean-François Lyotard, *The Post-Modern Condition: A Report of Knowledge,* Manchester University Press 1984.

JAN PAKULSKI AND MALCOLM WATERS

The Death of Class

'Class' has always been a contentious concept. In its most famous Marxian version, it is an explanatory term linking the economic sphere of production with the political and ideological superstructure. Here it is also a label for collective social actors, especially for that new historical subject, the proletariat, whose destiny was to transform social consciousness and to turn class society into a classless one. This mixture of sociology and eschatology proved exceptionally potent in propelling the concept to celebrity status. Class became a master term for both sociology and political analysis. With the formation of class parties of the left, the concept was further implicated within the global and national, political and ideological confrontations that became particularly acute during the hot and cold wars of the first three-quarters of the twentieth century. This was especially true in Europe where class became an ideological icon, a battle standard for the left and a bogey for the right. The intellectual left became preoccupied in identifying class divisions and condemning class inequalities, providing the central dogma of radicalized social science throughout the 1960s and 1970s. By contrast, denying the centrality of class became the hallmark of 'bourgeois' sociology. Even if the term was used in an ideologically neutral context, the semantic-ideological halo it acquired made it inherently contentious and prone to political appropriation.

The degree of political appropriation has reduced in recent years. With the declining commitment to Marxism, the collapse of Soviet communism and the waning appeal of socialist ideologies in the West, class is losing its ideological significance and its political centrality. Both the right and the left are abandoning their preoccupation with class issues. The right is turning its attention to morality and ethnicity while the critical left is becoming increasingly concerned about issues of gender, ecology, citizenship and human rights. This rearrangement of political concerns coincides with a shift in intellectual fashion and a growing scepticism about the compatibility of class models with contemporary social reality. Class divisions are losing their self-evident and pervasive character. Class identities are challenged by 'new associations' and new social movements. Class radicalism is no longer the flavour of the month in the intellectual salons and on university campuses. Like beads and Che Guevara berets, class is *passé*, especially among advocates of the postmodernist avant-garde and practitioners of the new gender-, eco- and ethno-centred politics.

Naturally, these shifts in public attention and intellectual fashion cannot be decisive in debates about the objective significance of class. However, they are important because they create an auspicious climate for reaching conclusions on its relevance. For the first time in over half a century, such a debate can be conducted outside the trenches of the Cold War and in a spirit of impartiality and mutual

Originally published in 1996. Please see complete source information beginning on page 891.

respect. In this new climate, arguments about the declining salience of class can no longer be dismissed as symptoms of ideological bias, intellectual weakness or moral corruption. . . .

The debate about classes combines issues of semantics and substance. Although our focus is firmly on the latter we must also pay some attention to the former. This is quite natural in a situation where a concept has been so stretched that it can be used to mean almost any identifiable collectivity ranging from occupational position to political association, and any theoretical object from structural location to collective actor. It is impossible simultaneously to give justice to this semantic diversity and to present a consistent argument against the class paradigm. We therefore focus on analytic usages of 'class' rather than the confused and vague applications of the term in popular discourse. In the context of the latter, 'class' is bound to remain a routinized and vague classificatory term because it is a useful shorthand for a wide range of social entities and divisions. We respect this popular usage but refuse to accept it as evidence of, or an argument for, the relevance of class. We will also avoid defining class in such a restrictive way that it becomes a straw person, on one hand, or can be used to designate any structured inequality or conflict, on the other. The latter strategy transforms the class thesis into a virtual tautology because no known society is egalitarian and free of conflict. However, we do admit that there is a range of legitimate meanings of the term, each of which can be examined independently in terms of its theoretical utility and empirical relevance.

In the analytic vocabulary of contemporary sociology, 'class' refers to a specific social location and causality, a specific pattern of groupness, and a specific form of identification. In the hands of some authors, as in classical Marxism, these aspects are combined, while for others, mainly those who subscribe to Weberian and action approaches, they are separated. However, we subscribe to the broad consensus that class is primarily about *economic-productive* location and determination; that is, it is based on property and/or market relations. People participate in class as producers rather than, say, as consumers, members of gender categories or organizational position-holders, although the impact of class may extend far beyond production roles. When stripped of this economic connotation and detached from its classical Marxist and Weberian roots, 'class' loses most of its explanatory power.

It is equally untenable to treat class as a mere substructure or as a statistical category, without at least drawing some implications for social relationships, social distance, patterns of interaction and patterns of association. Class is sociologically important as a social entity, as *social* class, and as such must transpire in detectable patterns of exploitation, struggle, domination and subordination, or closure. The number of classes, the extent of polarization, the clarity of class boundaries and the extent of conflict between classes may vary because they are not definitional elements. However, a minimum level of detectable clustering or groupness is essential if we are to say that classes exist. A society in which such economically caused social clustering occurs, and where these clusters are the backbone of the social structure, is a *class society*.

Lastly, a fully formed class involves a measure of self-recognition and self-identification on the part of participants, although this identification need not involve explicit class terminology or imply a consciousness of antagonism and struggle. Minimally, the members of a class have to be aware of their commonality and employ some recognized terms for collective self-description. A sense of difference between 'them' and 'us' is a necessary condition for the formation of *class actors* that marks the most developed examples of class articulation.

All of this implies that the articulation of class is a matter of degree. Its strength, and the extent to which it structures society, can vary from a minimal level, where economically based social clustering is weak but still predominant, to an advanced level. Here classes are well articulated in the social, cultural, and political-ideological domains, class identifications predominate, class consciousness is acute, and politics is dominated by struggles between class-based groups and organizations. Few historical instances of whole societies approximate a fully fledged class configuration. More typically only a degree of 'classness' can be observed. Moreover, the strength and the pattern of classness can vary historically and between contemporaneous societies.

The issue of the degree of classness of a society is linked to the issue of the relevance of 'class analysis', a type of social analysis that seeks to identify classes and to trace their social, cultural and political-ideological consequences. Class analysis makes sense only when applied to a class society. Its utility is proportional to the degree of classness. At one extreme, in a fully fledged class society, class analysis can be a legitimate substitute for social analysis. However, if classes are dissolving, a form of analysis that privileges class as an explanatory category has to give way to a more open-ended social analysis.

Historically there have been numerous examples of non-class societies. We embrace the convention that societies based on slave labour, such as ancient Rome and Greece, the estate societies of feudal Europe and modern state-socialist societies are non-class societies. In none of these societies are property and market relations the skeleton of the social structure or the predominant grid of social power. They are all unequal, stratified and conflictual but not made so predominantly by class. Class and class society are, in our vocabulary, distinctly modern phenomena inseparably linked to the market and its institutionalization within the early and mature forms of industrial capitalism.

This leads us to the central argument of this chapter, that classes are dissolving and that the most advanced societies are no longer class societies. The most important aspect is an attenuation of the class identities, class ideologies, and class organizations that framed

West European corporatist politics in the middle of this century. Equally, the communal aspects of class, class subcultures and milieux, have long since disappeared. The issue of the decomposition of economic class mechanisms is more controversial. We cite the following developments: a wide redistribution of property; the proliferation of indirect and small ownership; the credentialization of skills and the professionalization of occupations; the multiple segmentation and globalization of markets; and an increasing role for consumption as a status and lifestyle generator.

We must stress our concentration on the advanced societies of the capitalist West and, to a lesser extent, on the 'newly industrializing countries' (NICs) of East and South East Asia and the rapidly democratizing and marketizing societies of Russia and Eastern Europe. Quite clearly, class remains salient in the 'less developed countries' (LDCs) of Asia, Africa and Latin America that have not reached an advanced social, political and economic stage. In so far as such societies are structured by productive industrial property they clearly remain class societies.

The historical side of the argument charts the process of class decomposition in the industrialized West over the last century and a half. We argue that class societies are specific historical entities. They were born with industrial capitalism, changed their form under the impact of organized or corporate capitalism, and are disappearing in the face of post-industrialization and postmodernization. The early forms of class were chronicled in England by generations of social observers from Engels (1892) to Thompson (1980). They arose in parallel with a gradual decline of such pre-industrial collectivities as village communities and estates and the strengthening of nation-states. From the early twentieth century onward the fate of classes, nation-states and parties became intimately linked. While localized communities of fate were gradually marginalized, politically organized national classes were gradually institutionalized mainly as class parties and trade unions. These national classes were quite different from their predecessors. They were politically generated rather than spontaneous, occupationally heterogeneous, and reconstructed as imagined communities on a national level. Participation in these national classes involved little by way of interaction and communication. Their constitutive common interests were abstract political constructs developed by elites. What such classes lacked in social bonding and cultural cohesion, they compensated for in political organization and strategic coherence. It was these politically organized national classes, the power of which peaked with the establishment of corporatist structures, that became the most powerful social actors and agents of social transformation of the twentieth century. . . .

In summary, the stratification order of capitalist societies can be traced as a succession of three periods roughly demarcated by the nineteenth century, the first three-quarters of the twentieth century, and the contemporary period. In highly formalized and abstracted terms they are as follows.

Economic-class Society. This is a society arranged into patterns of domination and struggle between interest groups that emerge from the economic realm. In the familiar terms of Marx, the classes will be property owners and sellers of labour power, but they can be conceptualized as employers and employees. The dominant class can control the state and maintain itself as a ruling class either by capturing its apparatuses, or by rendering them weak. In so far as the subordinate class undertakes collective action, it will be rebellious or revolutionary in character, aimed at dislodging this ruling class by the abolition of private property. Culture is divided to match class divisions, into dominant and subordinate ideologies and into high and low cultures.

Organized-class Society. This type of society is dominated by a political or state sphere. The state is typically ruled by a single unified bloc, a political-bureaucratic elite, that exercises power over subordinated masses. The bloc may be factionalized horizontally into

formally opposed parties. The elite will comprise either a party leadership or a corporatized leadership integrating party leaders with the leaders of other organized interest groups including economic and cultural ones. The elite uses the coercive power of the state to regulate economics and culture. The state can dominate the economy by redistribution or by the conversion of private into public property, although this need not be a complete accomplishment. Masses, in turn, reorganize themselves in national-political classes rather than in industrial terms by establishing links with milieu parties. Meanwhile, the cultural realm can be unified under the state umbrella or under the aegis of state-sponsored monopolies. It can thus be turned into an industrialized or mass culture.

Status-conventional Society. In this type of society stratification emerges from the cultural sphere. The strata are lifestyle- and/or value-based status configurations. They can form around differentiated patterns of value commitment, identity, belief, symbolic meaning, taste, opinion or consumption. Because of the ephemeral and fragile nature of these resources, a stratification system based on conventional status communities appears as a shifting mosaic which can destabilize the other two spheres. The state is weakened because it cannot rely on mass support, and the economy is weakened (in its capacity for social structuring) because of the critical importance of symbolic values. Each order is deconcentrated by a prevailing orientation to values and utilities that are established conventionally rather than by reference to collective interests.

In failing to recognize these developments the class paradigm has made two errors that have seriously damaged the capacity of sociology to generate public debate about social and economic inequality. First, it has offered continued credence and legitimacy to class theory as a vehicle for the analysis of twentieth-century developments. In an important but not absolutely critical sense, class died somewhere between the beginning of the twentieth century and the end of the Great Depression. It died with the absorption of class struggle into the democratic arena, with the emergence of the fascist and socialist states that so dominated civil society, with the institutionalization of corporatist deals that linked government, capital and labour into common projects, with the mitigation of the effects of the market through such institutions as citizenship and welfare, and with the domination of the planet by superpower politics. The development was not entirely critical because the effects of what we can call 'organized class', the successor to true economic class, could still be analysed sociologically. As a successor to class theory, class analysis is indeed therefore an appropriate and impressive intellectual development in which sociology can take just pride. However, we are now contemplating a second and more critical error. Sociology is continuing to offer class analysis as its main vehicle for the discovery of social inequality and struggle in the trans-millennial period. It is failing to recognize that oppression, exploitation, and conflict are being socially constructed around transcendent conceptions of individual human rights and global values that identify and empower struggles around such diverse focuses as postcolonial racism, sexual preferences, gender discrimination, environmental degradation, citizen participation, religious commitments and ethnic self-determination. These issues have little or nothing to do with class. In the contemporary period of history, the class paradigm is intellectually and morally bankrupt. . . .

Figure 1 is a kind of master diagram that summarizes the substantive argument of this chapter. It shows that the historical transformation from economic-class society to organized-class society to status-conventional society is not merely an issue of stratification but one of wide-ranging societal transformation. The argument offered here is therefore part of the general theoretical effort that focuses on post-industrialization (Bell 1976), detraditionalization (Beck 1992; Giddens 1991), postmodernization (Crook et al. 1992;

Harvey 1989; Lyotard 1984) societal disorganization (Lash and Urry 1987; 1994; Offe 1985) and globalization (Featherstone 1990; Robertson 1992; Waters 1995).

The emerging stratificational picture is represented in such work as that of Kornblum (1974) on Chicago steelworkers that reveals anything but structural and cultural homogeneity. He shows that dense social networks of primary groups cross-cut old class boundaries and establish salient non-class divisions along regional-residential, ethnic, racial and status lines. These are the main focuses for identity formation and local politics. A similar picture is emerging from British studies of communities (e.g. Pahl and Wallace 1985; Williams 1975), political behaviour (e.g. Rose and McAllister 1985; Dunleavy and Husbands 1985) and consumption (Saunders 1990; Featherstone 1991). Here, gender divisions, market fragmentation, housing and consumption-sector cleavages, and state dependency are the main influences on political identities and voting patterns.

Equally Phizacklea's study (1990) of the fashion industry in Britain reveals deep divisions created by combinations of economic inequality, race, gender and locality. She argues that a dual labour market is generated in the garment industry by an intersection between organizational factors (relations between large corporations and small subcontractors), racial and ethnic divisions and a gendered-labour pattern exerted by domestic norms and relations. Recession and cheap imports have pushed 'ethnic entrepreneurs', mainly of Asian extraction, into family businesses that rely on low-paid female labour. These women workers are vulnerable to exploitative conditions by dint of gendered social norms, i.e. notions of 'women's work', modes of migration that often subject female dependants to indebtedness, and social discrimination that restricts their employment options. Such studies of multiple segmentation at the local level are becoming increasingly common.

This multiple socioeconomic and sociocultural fragmentation is very distant from the

FIGURE 1

The registration of stratification orders through system levels

System level

Axial principle	World	Society	Politics	Economy	Community	Domesticity	Gender	Individual
Economic class	Colonialism	*Laissez-faire* state	Plutocratic and revolutionary parties	Owner capitalism	Property order	Reproduction site	Patriarchy	Worker
Organized class	Imperialism	Corporatism	Mass parties	Fordism	Occupational order	Consumer sphere	Reorganized patriarchy (viriarchy)	Citizen
Conventional status	Globalization	Nation	Niche parties	Flexible specialization	Value order	Significant lifeworld	Hyperdifferentiation	Human

kind of class differentiation identified by Lockwood (1958) or Goldthorpe et al. (1969) a generation earlier. They proposed differentiated sub-types of working-class and lower-middle-class orientation that created locally concentrated and culturally homogeneous class communities. By contrast contemporary studies emphasize cultural diversity, especially among younger people. According to Willis (1990), this is the consequence not only of the decline in class-communal ties, but also of a drift away from the institutions that have engendered class identities in the past including community associations, trade unions, and schools. The mass unemployment of the 1980s that placed many young people beyond the class-formational impact of work situation and increasingly under the individualizing effects of commercialized consumer culture also contributed to the process.

We can now theorize this transformation more formally. The four propositions that class theory makes are: economism; groupness; behavioural linkage; and transformative capacity. A status-conventional theory would offer the following parallel propositions:

- The proposition of *culturalism*. Status-conventional stratification is primarily a cultural phenomenon. It is based on subscription to lifestyles that form around consumption patterns, information flows, cognitive agreements, aesthetic preferences and value commitments. Material and power phenomena are reducible to these symbolically manifested lifestyle and value phenomena.
- The proposition of *fragmentation*. Conventional statuses, like classes, are real phenomena. However they consist of a virtually infinite overlap of associations and identifications that are shifting and unstable. Status-conventional society is a fluid matrix of fragile formations that cycle and multiply within a globalized field.
- The proposition of *autonomization*. The subjective orientation and behaviour of any individual or aggregate of individuals are very difficult to predict by virtue of stratificational location. There is no central cleavage or single dimension along which preferences can be ordered. Such attributes as political preference, access to educational opportunity, patterns of marriage and income are self-referential rather than externally constrained.
- The proposition of *resignification* based on subjective interests. The stratification process is continuously fluid. Its openness allows a constant respecification and invention of preferences and symbolic dimensions that provide for continuous regeneration. The source of novelty is a process of restless subjective choice that seeks to gratify churning and unrepressed emotions that include anxiety and aggression as well as desire.

The proposition of culturalism specifies that symbolic dimensions will compete with each other in the field of social structure. This will produce the phenomenon of multiple status cleavages. The stratificational categories of status-conventional society constitute a complex mosaic of taste subcultures, 'new associations', civic initiatives, ethnic and religious revolutionary groups, generational cohorts, community action groups, new social movements, gangs, alternative lifestyle colonies, alternative production organizations, educational alumni, racial brotherhoods, gender sisterhoods, tax rebels, fundamentalist and revivalist religious movements, internet discussion groups, purchasing co-ops, professional associations, and so on. Many are ephemeral, some are continuous and stable.

A key feature of these multiple status cleavages is that because they are specialized and intersecting, membership in any one does not necessarily contradict membership in any other. From the subjective point of view the proposition of fragmentation ensures that individuals apprehend the stratification system as a status bazaar. Individuals can operate simultaneously as members of several status groups and have the potential to be members of any others. Their identities are reflexively self-composed as they move between status adherences. However, the fact of a status market does not imply an absolute voluntarism, and indeed the freedoms in most cases are relevant to exit from status groups rather than entry. Closure processes remain effective in status-conventional society.

The proposition of autonomization nevertheless allows individuals to be profligate in their behaviour. They will tend to spend their resources of time, energy, money, influence, and power in the pursuit of symbolic attachments that tend to advance the interests, identities, values and commitments to which they subscribe and aspire. The very act of doing this will, by the proposition of resignification, tend to redefine and reorder the symbolic dimensions that reference the system. Indeed, a particular effect is the redefinition of some traditional status-membership dimensions, especially education, religion, and ethnicity, into a more ephemeral and conventional regime. So education becomes a marketplace for credentials, religion becomes a vehicle for handling this week's anxieties as one is born again and again and again, and ethnicity is something one rediscovers through community action and involvement.

We must stress that we are not arguing for a decline in inequality and conflict but for a decline in *class* inequality and conflict. One last illustration can confirm the point. The available research shows that, even allowing for recent reversals, during the twentieth century household wealth has become more widely distributed. This is an indicator of the decomposition of class, as normally defined in relation to property. However, at the present time there is also an increasing inequality of income (*The Economist* 5 November 1994). This is not evidence of increasing class inequality but it is evidence of increasing inequality of sumptuary capacity and this links directly with the kind of status-conventional stratification that is theorized here. The income-poor so-called 'underclass' is not class defined but is rather status defined by the symbolizations attached to postcolonial mi-gration, race, ethnicity, gender, age and pattern of family support. Exclusionary closure based on these status attributes consigns people to an 'underclass'. The stigmatization that attaches to the 'underclass' is a function not of its members' exploitation but of their incapacity to consume. An earlier generation of social scientists wrote of poverty as a culture (Lewis 1961; 1966; Valentine 1968). Perhaps it is time to do so once again.

All of this means that complexity is likely to increase. This calls for a theoretical stance that rejects any notion that there is a single conceptual or theoretical crowbar or even a magic word that can open the treasure cave of stratification, inequality and conflict. Contemporary sociology needs to be sensitive to and appreciative of diversity. It must be humble in the face of complexity and ready to accept contingency in relation to social attitudes and behaviours. It must not force a lively, engaging and ethically fraught reality into an inherited and stultifying conceptual straitjacket. If it continues on its procrustean path it will lose its audience.

References

Beck, U (1992) *Risk Society*. London: Sage.

Bell, D (1976) *The Coming of Post-Industrial Society*. New York: Basic/Harper Torchbook (first published 1973).

Crook, S, J Pakulski and M Waters (1992) *Postmodernization*. London: Sage.

Dunleavy, P and C Husbands (1985) *British Democracy at the Crossroads*. London: Allen & Unwin.

Engels, F (1892) *The Condition of the Working Class in England in 1844*. London: Hamden.

Featherstone, M (1990) *Global Culture*. London: Sage.

Featherstone, M (ed) (1991) *Consumer Culture and Postmodernism*. London: Sage.

Giddens, A (1991) *Modernity and Self-Identity*. Cambridge: Polity.

Goldthorpe, J, D Lockwood, F Bechhofer and J Platt (1969) *The Affluent Worker in the Class Structure*. Cambridge: CUP.

Harvey, D (1989) *The Condition of Postmodernity*. Oxford: Blackwell.

Kornblum, W (1974) *Blue Collar Community.* Chicago: Chicago UP.

Lash, S and J Urry (1987) *The End of Organised Capitalism.* Cambridge: Polity.

Lash, S and J Urry (1994) *Economies of Signs and Space.* London: Sage.

Lewis, O (1961) *The Children of Sanchez.* New York: Random House.

Lewis, O (1966) *La Vida: A Puerto Rican Family in the Culture of Poverty.* New York: Random House.

Lockwood, D (1958) *The Blackcoated Worker.* London: Allen & Unwin.

Lyotard, J (1984) *The Postmodern Condition.* Manchester: Manchester UP.

Offe, C (1985) "New Social Movements: Challenging the Boundaries of Institutional Politics." *Social Research* 52(4): 817–68.

Ossowski, S (1963) *Class Structure in the Social Consciousness.* London: Routledge (first published 1958).

Pahl, R and C Wallace (1985) "Household Work Strategies in Economic Recession" in N Redclift and E Mingione (eds) *Beyond Employment.* Oxford: Blackwell.

Phizacklea, A (1990) *Unpacking the Fashion Industry: Gender, Racism and Class in Production.* London: Routledge.

Robertson, R (1992) *Globalization.* London: Sage.

Rose, R and I McAllister (1985) *Voters Begin to Choose.* London: Sage.

Saunders P (1990) *A Nation of Home Owners.* London: Unwin Hyman.

Thompson, E (1980) *The Making of the English Working Class* (2nd edn). Harmondsworth: Penguin (first edn 1968).

Valentine, C (1968) *Culture and Poverty.* Chicago: Chicago UP.

Waters, M (1995) *Globalization.* London: Routledge.

Williams, R (1975) *The Country and the City.* London: Paladin.

Willis, P (1990) *Common Culture.* Milton Keynes: Open UP.

MARTINA MORRIS AND BRUCE WESTERN

Inequality in Earnings: Trends and Implications

Ironically, as some sociologists were debating whether social classes had finally withered away (e.g., Clark and Lipset 1991), earnings inequality in the United States quietly started to grow again. Median income declined and the distribution of income grew markedly more unequal during the last three decades of the twentieth century, reversing a long trend of earnings growth and equalization. Writers in economics and the popular press described, analyzed, and debated this new trend. Sociologists, on the other hand, were, and to a large extent remain, remarkably silent about it. We have continued to address trends in the earnings "gaps" (by gender and race) or focus on poverty alone, leaving the broader trends—stagnation in earnings levels and growing polarization in earnings distributions—to others. We have continued to study how people are allocated to positions in the earnings distribution, rather than the structure of those positions. If the structure had been stable, a narrow focus on allocation might be justifiable. But this has been a period of pervasive economic restructuring, and the impact on earnings distributions both within and be-

tween groups has been profound. Sociological theory provides a rich framework for understanding the broad changes now underway, and we offer this essay as a challenge to the field to critically evaluate the evidence and provide a sociologically informed response.

According to Simon Kuznets (1955), inequality should not be rising in late twentieth-century United States. The Kuznets curve predicts that economic development has an inverted U-shaped relationship to inequality. Inequality first rises as capital is concentrated in the hands of investors, then falls as economic development generates widespread prosperity. For much of this century, in fact, inequality followed the Kuznets path. Earnings inequality peaked on the eve of the Great Depression, then began a long secular decline.[1] Postwar prosperity was marked by a rise in median earnings and stability in earnings inequality. The annual income of the median worker more than doubled from 1950 to 1970, with those at the bottom of the earnings scale making even greater progress. It was, as many observed in chastened hindsight, a rising tide that lifted all boats. These trends reversed in the early 1970s. Median earnings stabilized in 1973 and then began to decline. In 1980 earnings inequality began to rise rapidly. The net result of these two trends was that by the early 1990s, nearly 80 percent of workers earned less than their counterparts

---

Originally published in 1999. Please see complete source information beginning on page 891.

FIGURE 1

The lines trace the real value of wages at each decile relative to its value in 1973. Sample is all workers, from the CPS Outgoing Rotation Group file. The data can be obtained online at http//www.epinet.org/datazone/data/orghourlyxoffs_all.xls. For more analysis of these data see Bernstein and Mishel (1997).

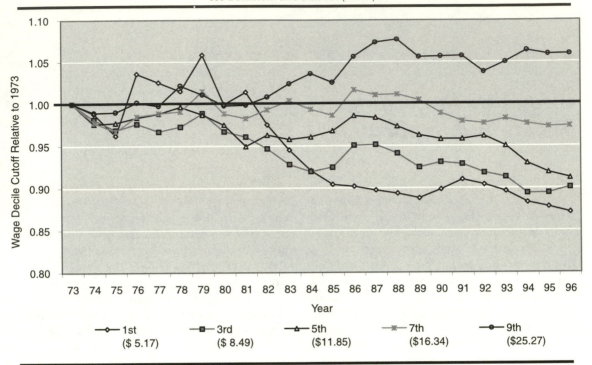

in the 1960s.[2] Although there appeared to be a small uptick in median wages in the last years of the 1990s, it will take decades to make up the losses.

Data from the Current Population Survey (CPS) show these trends in terms of hourly wages (Figure 1).[3] Each line in the figure represents the dollar value of the wage decile cutoff indexed to its value in 1973. The line for decile 1, for example, represents the relative wage earned by the worker at the tenth percentile of the wage distribution over time. If we follow it across the graph, we can see that workers in this decile saw their real wages rise slightly from the mid-1970s to the beginning of the 1980s, fall precipitously during the 1980s, and continue to decline at a lower rate during the 1990s. By 1996, wages for these workers had fallen about 13 percent in real terms (and by 20 percent if the sample is re-

stricted to men). Wages at the median (fifth decile) stagnated through most of the 1970s and 1980s, then fell sharply in the 1990s, losing a total of about 10 percent over the two decades. Only those at the top (ninth decile) experienced some wage gains, a rise of about 5 percent, with most of the increase coming in the late 1980s.

Comparative data suggest that among industrialized countries, only the United Kingdom experienced a similar growth in wage inequality. In France, Germany, and Italy, the earnings ratio of the first to the fifth decile among men declined or remained stable. And while British wage inequality grew, it was driven by gains at the top, not losses at the bottom.[4] The broad stagnation of living standards coupled with a collapse of wages at the bottom is thus a peculiarly American disease, at least in the industrialized democracies.

So the American story since the 1970s is not that the rich got richer and the poor got poorer, but that virtually everyone lost ground, and those at the bottom lost the most. Although mean trends differ by race and sex, all groups experienced a rise in within-group inequality. This leads to a set of research questions that breaks out of the usual "wage-gap" framework and begins to address the general issue of changes in labor market dynamics. We review below supply side, demand side, and institutional accounts of change.

Supply Side Accounts

On the supply side, the labor force expanded by more than 44 million workers from 1950 to 1980, a 70 percent increase. The baby boom, rising women's labor force participation, and growing immigration all increased the share of workers with little work experience, tenure or education. Although a rising supply of "unskilled" workers seems like a natural explanation for falling wages at the bottom of the distribution, the evidence suggests little role for most of these supply side changes:

1. The baby boom generation, born between 1946 and 1964, entered the workforce from 1964 to 1982, a period when earnings of low-wage workers held relatively steady. The dramatic decline in wages at the bottom occurred during the entry of the subsequent "baby bust" cohort, which should instead have benefited from the shrinking labor supply.
2. From 1950 to 1994, the fraction of women working for pay increased from 34 percent to 59 percent. Despite this increase in supply, women's wages rose at every decile of the distribution. Occupational segregation also remained high, indicating the persistence of largely separate labor markets for men and women and suggesting that the impact of women's entry on men's wages was probably small.
3. Immigration, and in particular the rapid influx of Asians and Latin Americans following the 1965 Amendments to the Immigration and Nationality Act, is the one supply side effect that finds some support in the data. Studies find a substantial impact of immigration on the rise in the wage differential between high school dropouts and graduates.

On the boundary between supply and demand explanations lies the debate over the role of education and "skill." Despite a rising supply of workers with a college education,[5] their relative wages began to rise in the mid-1980s. This came to be called a "rise" in the college premium, but it was almost entirely driven by the *collapse* in the earnings of high school graduates and dropouts. Initially, the growth in the education wage gap was attributed to a trade-induced decline in domestic demand for high-school educated workers driven by the relocation of manufacturing to less-developed countries. However, conflicting findings led to the rise of an alternative hypothesis: a rising demand for skill driven by "skill-biased technological change." The proponents of this argument claim that computerization of the workplace and other technological advances increased the demand for high-skill workers well beyond the increase in supply. One study reported that computer use at work raised earnings by as much as 19 percent. Critics countered with an analysis showing that the use of pencils and "sitting while working" had similarly strong effects. Despite the continuing weakness of the empirical evidence, skill-biased technological change remains the dominant explanation among labor economists for the increase in earnings inequality.

Demand Side Accounts

The structure of the labor market also changed substantially during the postwar boom years. Restructuring took two forms: continuing decline in manufacturing employment leading to the rise of a "service economy" and an increase in market-mediated employment relations that featured outsourcing, subcontracting, and temporary, contingent, and part-time work contracts. The trend toward growing employment in the service sector and shrinking employment in manufacturing has continued almost linearly since the 1940s, and by the mid-1990s the service sector accounted for more than 80 percent of total employment. Service sector jobs have traditionally paid less, offered fewer benefits, and relied more on part-time employment. Still, there was no sharp increase in deindustrialization in the 1970s or 1980s that would account for the sharp changes in earnings during these decades. In addition, inequality is growing within the sectors, not simply between them, and declines in manufacturing wages were also substantial. So the simpler versions of the deindustrialization thesis have been discarded.

The "good jobs-bad jobs" debate has therefore been refocused in recent years, noting that high- and low-road employment strategies are being used together, not only within industries, but even within firms. This shifts attention to the trends in the system of employment relations often referred to as the "internal labor market." Cost reduction became an important basis of competition during the 1970s, and internal labor markets became a prime target because they are inflexible and expensive to maintain. The wave of "downsizing" that took place during the late 1980s and 1990s heralded this change. Still, the size of the shift to market-mediated employment is unclear. One study finds that contingent work rose from about 25 percent of employment in 1980 to 35 percent by the end of the decade. Other estimates have been more conservative, ranging from 5 percent to 17 percent of the labor force by the end of decade. Although the shift to market-mediated employment may not be as rapid or revolutionary as some scholars have suggested, the rise in job instability is well documented now, and it has been linked to the declining wages of workers who are not college educated.

Institutional Accounts

Market explanations have dominated research on rising inequality, but supply and demand are clearly mediated by institutional constraints. Relatively fewer studies have examined the role of institutional changes, and those that have focus chiefly on the minimum wage and unions. Both appear to explain part of the decline in wages at the bottom of the distribution. The federal minimum wage was frozen at $3.35/hour from 1980 to 1990. Although less than 10 percent of the working population typically makes the minimum wage, one estimate attributes about 17 percent of the growth in the gap between the wages of college graduates and high-school dropouts to the freeze. The 1990 increase is estimated to have reduced the previous decade's growth in wage inequality by about 30 percent. The decline in unionization may also have played a role. In 1970 unions represented about 27 percent of all wage and salary earners in the United States; by 1993 only 15 percent. When a job change is accompanied by the loss of union status, the wage penalty is on the order of 20 percent after controlling for other worker characteristics. Some studies suggest that the decline in union density may account for about 20 percent of the overall rise in male wage inequality and as much as 50 percent of the rise for male blue-collar workers. As with other potential explanatory factors, however, there is also evidence of increasing earnings inequality among union members.

An increasingly "globalized" economy provides the context in which all of these trends have emerged. Imports from less developed countries (LDCs) are typically produced by low-skill labor, and LDC imports increased by 75 percent between 1978 and 1990. Low-wage imports may be an important cause of declining demand for low-skill U.S. workers, but here again the empirical evidence is mixed. Capital mobility may also raise inequality by diverting investment to countries with low-wage labor, thus reducing labor demand in higher wage countries. In contrast to the theory, however, spending on new plants and equipment overseas by U.S. multinationals has been a declining proportion of total U.S. economic activity.

The Future of Inequality

What does the future hold for earnings inequality in America? That will depend in part on the underlying causal factors and in part on the public response to the current trends. As the review above suggests, the trends are at least now well-documented, but there is little consensus on the causal forces. What is clear is that the simplistic Kuznets curve cannot adequately represent the trends in contemporary inequality, if, indeed, it ever was adequate. Local earnings dynamics increasingly reflect the intersection of national political forces and the growing global reach of capital. At the most basic level, it is a question of whether markets or politics will have the upper hand in earnings determination. If market forces dominate, we would expect that the lower and middle classes will continue to lose the benefits of unionization, internal labor markets, and minimum wage laws, thus producing an increasingly bipolar society as the inequality-reducing institutional reforms of New Deal capitalism erode. Under this scenario, the United States is not becoming like Western Europe, which is likely to bear the continuing imprint of its more deeply institutionalized welfare capitalism, but rather like South America and Eastern Europe, with their (sometimes militarily enforced) laissez-faire systems.

The relocation of manufacturing jobs to less industrialized and lower wage countries has led some to predict that the United States and other highly industrialized countries will evolve into homogeneously high-skill (and, presumably, low inequality) labor markets.

However, this view could only be seen from an ivory tower. Over 80 percent of the U.S. labor force is already employed in the service sector. If this sector holds the clues to our future, then wage stagnation and polarization will clearly continue. Many of the lowest paid, least challenging jobs—cashiers, sales persons, truck drivers, receptionists, and information clerks—are in the service sector. They will never be exported. These particular jobs are also in the top 10 in terms of projected employment growth, led, at number one, by cashiers.

Cross-national variation in earnings inequality, however, makes it clear that distributional trends are not driven by a single logic of, say, capitalist development or post-industrialism. Other countries face similar pressures from global markets and structural change, but have maintained a level of equality that is unknown in the United States. The difference is in politics, not markets. It is possible, therefore, to use political institutions to reverse the trends in wage decline and polarization. To the extent that rising inequality in U.S. earnings can be traced to institutional change, and these are the explanations with the most consistent empirical support, inequality is likely to persist. Institutional change tends to be slow, and trends in institutional change are reversed even more slowly. The prospects for a reversal in declining union organization, for example, are dim. Job growth in the nonunion sector of the economy is so rapid that the maintenance of current levels of private sector unionization would require organizing efforts unprecedented in the postwar period. Despite the massive redistribution of income and wealth to those at the top, there seems to be little political support for institutional changes that would reverse these trends.

Why is it, then, that the decline and polarization of earnings has occasioned so little political response among the population at large? There are many possible reasons. One is that most people now rely on two incomes to support a family, so that individual earnings losses are masked by income pooling.

Another is the explosion of consumer credit, which makes it possible for many to buy what they can no longer afford. Finally, political apathy may be one of the by-products of a high level of inequality. As those at the bottom of the income distribution feel increasingly remote from the mainstream, alienation from politics grows, election turnout declines, and the public sphere shrinks to include just the affluent. The consistuency for redistribution vanishes. In this scenario, graphically detailed by Massey in his provocative 1996 presidential address to the Population Association of America, the persistence of high inequality seems especially likely. The analysis may seem bleak, but it is supported by research that shows that political participation, political information, membership in voluntary associations, and a host of other indicators of political efficacy depend closely on income. The rise in inequality could thus become self-sustaining.

Sociology clearly has an important role to play in understanding the recent trends in economic inequality. It is not just a question of earnings, but of fundamental changes in politics, markets, and life chances. The current earnings trends challenge us to rethink our disciplinary perspective and reintegrate our theoretical and empirical agenda, or else lose the heart of our field to other disciplines.

Notes

1. Here and throughout, detailed keys to the literature are provided by Morris and Western (1999). Other summaries of the literature include Levy and Murnane (1992) and Danziger and Gottschalk (1993; 1995). Comparative trends in earnings inequality are described in OECD (1996, ch. 6).

2. The precise figure depends on the measure used to adjust for inflation, and this is a hotly contested issue.

3. There are at least four different measures of economic well-being that can be examined here: hourly wages, annual earnings, household total earnings, and wealth. All show the same basic pattern, with pronounced rises in inequality. We show hourly wages here because they do not confound labor supply components, such as hours worked and income pooling, with labor pricing. Wages thus better represent the job structure.

4. Inequality does appear to be on the rise in post-socialist economies, although the quantitative evidence here is less reliable. The forces making for such change are, at least on the surface, very different than those at work in the United States, except insofar as one understands them as proceeding from "marketization" in its várious forms (e.g., deunionization, deregulation of wages).

5. About 25 percent of the 25–34-year-old population had a four-year college degree in 1995.

References

Bernstein, Jared, and Lawrence Mishel. 1997. "Has Wage Inequality Stopped Growing?" *Monthly Labor Review* 120:3–16.

Clark, Terry N., and Seymour M. Lipset. 1991. "Are Social Classes Dying?" *International Sociology* 6:397-410.

Danziger, Sheldon, and Peter Gottschalk, eds. 1993. *Uneven Tides: Rising Inequality in America.* New York.

Danziger, Sheldon, and Peter Gottschalk. 1995. *America Unequal.* Cambridge: Harvard University Press.

Kuznets, Simon. 1955. "Economic Growth and Income Inequality (Presidential Address)." *American Economic Review* 45:1–28.

Levy, Frank, and Robert Murnane. 1992. "U.S. Earnings Levels and Earnings Inequality: A Review of Recent Trends and Proposed Explanations." *Journal of Economic Literature* 30: 1333–81.

Massey, Douglas S. 1996. "The Age of Extremes: Concentrated Affluence and Poverty in the Twenty-First Century." *Demography* 33: 395–412.

Morris, Martina, and Bruce Western. 1999. "Inequality in Earnings at the Close of the Twentieth Century." *Annual Review of Sociology* 25:623–57.

Organisation for Economic Cooperation and Development (OECD). 1996. *Employment Outlook.* Paris: OECD.

JOHN W. MEYER

The Evolution of Modern Stratification Systems

The sociological tendency, well represented in the chapters in this volume on "The Future of Social Stratification," has been to see modern stratification systems in a realist vein. Real component individuals and groups, competing and cooperating in real interdependencies, create and change a system of inequalities. Real systems—and thus some sort of functionalism, broadly defined—are involved: To be sure, some theories may place particular stress on competitive interdependence (as in class-conflict models), and others may emphasize economic over other interdependencies, but nearly all share a vision of society as a system made up of interdependent parts.

For example, Kerr and his colleagues see the modern economy as evolving toward greater complexity and thus as functionally requiring changing forms of inequality (including emphases on education and merit). The core themes here are picked up and amplified by the other authors. Bell sees both economic and social complexity as creating (1) functional requirements for new levels of knowledge and competence and (2) a new set of strata linked to education. Although Gouldner has a similar vision, it is generated by class conflict as well as by differentiation, thus producing a recognizably similar, if darker, story. Likewise, this vision again appears in the work of Nee and of Eyal and his colleagues, but now it plays

This is an original article prepared for this book.

out as communist regimes break down rather than as post-industrialism proceeds. Hall, and Pakulski and Waters, have similarly functional visions, but see the postmodern stratification system as built much more around the subjective and cultural than the realist model of industrial society. Culture, here, means taste, lifestyle, status, and subjective preferences. It is broadly linked to the expanding importance of education and the rise of the service sector, emphasized in all the chapters.

More critical writers, often on the left, use exactly the same lines of argument, but for them the functional requirements are those of some economic elites or political forces rather than society as a whole. Esping-Andersen, and Western and Morris, see these basic functional processes as operating to generate actual or potential increases in inequality and breakdowns in social welfare.

Despite their disagreements and conflicts, the authors of these lines of thought all share a general description and analysis of the evolution of modern stratification, a view rooted in a realist vision of modern society as a functioning system. Hall and Pakulski and Waters see realist modernity as having evolved in more subjective and cultural ways, but retain the strong sense of an integrated functioning system. In all the arguments here, expansion produces differentiation and complexity— these require more reliance on education and ultimately new professional strata. Every story told in these chapters amounts, in essence, to either emphasizing or explaining the rising stratificational importance of education and its credentials. As the system expands around the world, modern forms of stratification rooted in education are found everywhere. The story is a standard sociological one, told with varying emphases on conflict and consensus; it is also very similar to the stories modern societies tell about themselves. We emphasize the latter point as of substantive importance in understanding modern societies, not so much as a criticism of stratification theories. If stratification theories function as cultural ideologies, this may help explain the spreading dominance of education.

The conventional story, conveyed repeatedly in these chapters, has some pronounced weaknesses: If expansion is the driving force, why does so much differentiation occur (e.g., in the modern Third World) even without expansion? If education and the new class are relied upon for technically efficient solutions, why can we not find better evidence for their actual efficiency (e.g., Berg 1971)? Above all, if stratification reflects real social requirements, why are the forms of stratification and mobility so strikingly similar across all the extreme variations of modern society?

There is a strong sociological tendency to leave cultural matters out of the equation, aside from some notions that individuals in society may have some socialized tastes in common. When culture is brought in, as in Hall or Pakulski and Waters, it is seen as subjective and individual in character—matters of taste and status—rather than institutionalized collective rules and models. Indeed, in a strain to see education as functional, these authors almost all deemphasize it as a carrier of cultural content. The modern stratification theorist talks about education as human or cultural or social capital, not as culture per se. The idea that modern societies may with some collective self-consciousness be, through direct collective action, creating and changing their stratification system and rooting it more deeply in education, is not given much emphasis. "Class consciousness" is of interest as a dependent variable or as an intervening variable helping to account for various outcomes such as political mobilization. But this is class consciousness in the sense of Marx or Mannheim, who assume an underlying sociological reality and see some form of consciousness as its product. In research terms, it is class consciousness as a property of individuals and groups within society, not a property of the collective itself. More respect than imitation is given to Ossowski (1963), for whom the cultural aspects of stratification can be (1) independent variables and (2) collective or institutional models.

Inattention to collective and cultural aspects of stratification has been a substantial limitation in the field. It has led to extraordinarily mistaken theoretical analyses and predictions (as with the families of theories that have overemphasized the causal and descriptive role of economic dimensions in stratification). In addition, it has led to inattention to some obviously cultural aspects of stratification. In this chapter, corrective reflections are suggested. We offer cultural interpretations of modern differentiation, the rise of education and the service sector, and the overall homogeneity of modern stratification systems.

The cultural perspective we emphasize is an alternative to what we are calling *sociological realism* on several dimensions that in a broader discussion could be distinguished. We may note two of them here. First, modern sociological realists see society as made up of individuals and groups that have prior and natural properties (e.g., motives and interests). Their strivings for equality and their inequality result from these properties and their interaction in social life. A more cultural view treats the existence and standing (and motives and interests) of these entities as highly collectively constructed—as the product of meaning and interpretation in modern schemes and scripts. The construction of modern citizens as formally equal, for example, is seen as an evolution in culture and theory rather than as either natural equalities or a result of interests in interaction (e.g., mystifying tactics or compromises of dominant elites or functionally necessary responses to social complexity).

Second, sociological realism tends to emphasize social systems as affected by high levels of interactive interdependence among their components—as really social systems of interdependent parts. A more collective and cultural view calls attention to the impact of cultural theories and ideologies on this putative interdependence: The high status and importance of many groups, such as the schooled professions, in modern stratification systems arise from cultural ideologies (which in the modern world commonly take the form of functional theories) as much as from "real" interactive dominance and dependence.

Conceptions of Culture

Part of the problem lies with a very limited conception of culture as individual attitudes or vague collective sentiments. In fact, most sociology deeply shares the contemporary bias that modern systems (unlike the traditional ones that anthropologists study) are so overwhelmingly articulated and real that they do not have very much culture: In other words, the rationalism and functionalism of the cultures of modern society are taken as true by the analysts. Hall, and Pakulski and Waters, see the postmodern system as having greatly increased scope for cultural expression and stratification. They see culture as playing a more independent and autonomous role in the future, although the culture they envision tends to be individual and subjective rather than a system of collective rules.

Another way to put this is to note that social-scientific stratification theories are themselves core cultural elements of modern society. They are institutionalized as constitutional principles, but they also may provide cultural bases for criticism and opposition. Although this is obvious with Marxist theories, it is also the case with most others, which provide normative bases with which to defend, attack, or ignore inequalities of various sorts. Stratification theorists may understate

the importance of the cultures of modern systems because stratification theories (though not necessarily only narrowly academic ones) are the central cultural elements involved. Recognizing the cultural character of stratification would weaken the realist vision of society as a real system. It would also undercut some of the scientific claims of stratification theorists: If stratification is cultural theory, the theorists (as classic phenomenological critics have had it) are studying themselves.

Our point here is not to support the often-noted special importance of some intellectuals and scientific professions in modern society. It is to note that explicit theories and ideologies about licit and illicit inequalities are deeply ingrained in the public discussions of the modern system. Most great political conflicts in this system are explicitly and articulately about equality and inequality: Contemporary opinion surveys suggest that even ordinary persons are able to go on at length about inequalities and the conditions under which they are legitimate. Indeed, it is for this reason that the system tends to pick out for great attention some of the ideas of intellectuals (e.g., Smith or Marx) who might be quite obscure in other traditions. The culture of the system tends to make stratification theories important (rather than the theorists simply having some sort of mysterious dominance over the culture); carriers include everyone from ordinary members to political and economic elites and specialized intellectuals.

Our emphasis on a cultural reinterpretation of stratification can be pursued in either a strong or weak form; the difference between the two is immaterial here, for the most part. The strong form (Meyer 1989; Mann 1986; Hall 1986) treats the modern (Western and now worldwide) stratification system as having distinctive cultural roots in such themes as equality and progress. A weak form might argue that more narrowly "real" social forces produced such Western structures as high capitalism or political democracy, after which institutionalization turned such arrangements into cultural recipes to be repeated throughout the world. Either form is good enough for present arguments.

We briefly review the cultural postures built into the stratification theories of modern societies. That is, in discussing what seem to be the most prominent substantive themes in stratification theories, we recognize that modern systems are much affected by their cultures and conceive of stratification theories as prominent parts of these cultures. One important theme is that persons are formally and ultimately equal; another is that inequalities can be justified only by contributions to collective progress. Many lines of sociological thought incorporate such matters as aspects of social reality; we treat them as the cultural rules of modern collective actors. We go on to consider the consequences these cultural postures may have—the things that can be better explained when we recognize the cultural character of stratification theory in the modern system.

Sociological thinking routinely recognizes that stratification systems in the premodern past were cultural constructions. Further, there is a tendency to imagine that in some future utopia (or dystopia) where inequalities are put right (or wrong), cultural principles could again hold sway. This is, obviously, a dramatic counterpoint to the aggressive realism about the present that is characteristic of Marxian theory. We apply the same perspective to contemporary modern society, seeing its stratification system as in part the realization of its cultural visions.

Stratification Principles

Clearly a first cultural principle built into the stratification models of modern theories and societies is the functional one. Society is a system—a rationally analyzable set of components organized as a purposive project—and inequalities among its parts are justified by inequalities in their contributions to collective goods and goals. For example, one can defend or criticize enhanced inequalities mainly by functional arguments. The chapters cited above (particularly those by Bell, Gouldner, Nee, Eyal, Kerr, and their colleagues) do just that: A greater return to private capital is required to promote more investment, or more pay and status are needed for teachers if we wish to select better ones and improve the performance of all, or the complex society requires more educated intellectuals at its center. The idea of social progress is obviously involved in the principle.

The idea that inequality is justified only or mainly by functional considerations is so firmly established (e.g., Rawls 1971) that sociological critics of particular inequalities must argue that they are not really functional but are rather products of tradition or power (as seen in Western and Morris or Esping-Andersen). In such analyses, socially useful achievement is set in opposition to two defective sources of inequality; discussing the issues involved is a modern (and a sociological) obsession. One opposition is mainly with the past and with tradition; achievement is set against ascription in a drama that combines issues of social efficiency with those of social justice. Thus there is great attention to whether favorable evaluations or opportunities are provided to students or workers on merit or whether there is a direct effect of status background. Even if the analyses suggest merit is mainly involved, analysts go further—perhaps the standards of merit are status-biased, or perhaps the resources of those higher in status permit easier or more achievement. A second opposition is to set socially useful and legitimate achievement against power that may pervert goals or means (as when hegemonic capitalism is thought to substitute the requirements of capital for the good of society).

The issues involved here infuse the stratification literature as well as modern social discussion with much normative excitement. Minor details of the distribution of income or education become salient, and analyses of mobility give great attention to causal pathways distinguishable according to their justice and efficiency. On the one hand, there are many conflicts about what is really functional: Radical differences in the interpretation of the functions of private capital or of education can produce very different assessments. On the other hand, broad bands of agreement can be found: There are few defenders of extreme inequalities, of high levels of status consistency, or of high levels of status inheritance. No such defenses occur in the chapters here.

All this takes on more momentum given the second crucial principle of modern stratification (and theory): moral individualism. Individuals are to be ultimately morally equal, and justice is to be assessed in terms of inequality among individuals. The notion goes unquestioned in these chapters, and little reference is made to any possibility of natural inequalities between persons. There is considerable tension, naturally, between this principle and the legitimation of inequality on functional grounds; we later suggest that this tension is a source of a good deal of modern social change.

The individualism of modern stratification theory and research is striking. The important inequality is, for instance, individual income inequality. We do not much care if the genders (or races or families or ethnic groups or groups of differing class origins) have equal incomes. In fact, calculations of the income of a gender, race, ethnic group, or family as a group are very rare, in contrast to stratificational thinking in societies in which corporate groups (e.g., clans or villages) are more real than individuals. We care only, on a per capita basis, if individuals of each gender (or class background or race or ethnicity) have equal incomes. When we attend to cross-national comparisons, we calculate not income differences among countries but income differences per capita. On some questions, other units have moral standing (as when each country has certain rights in international relations, or as when each family or town may be represented in certain activities), but the utterly dominant unit is the individual: Justice is assessed in terms of the equality or inequality of individuals.

The Impact of Stratification Ideology on the Development of the Modern System

Imagine, thus, that the social changes of the modern period are going on under the continuing scrutiny of collective actors and the intellectual advisors of those actors (such as the authors of the chapters in this book). Both actors and advisors, of course, are concerned about the principles of functionality for the collective good and the ultimate equality of individuals. This is not so unrealistic an image: Most modern stratification theorists, including the authors here, work with just these standards, and most (including most of the authors here) aspire to affect public policy; more to the point, decision-making elites in modern systems operate in about the same way.

Theory of Progress

Some effects of the legitimation of inequality in terms of the rational pursuit of progress are noteworthy. First, it seems obvious that rationalistic and progressive ideas of the sort developed in the chapters here have played a role in supporting a great deal of modern social differentiation. Activities can be pulled out of social life and bundled into rationalized elements or roles; their inequalities thus are legitimated. The modern system has been profligate in its creation of new occupations, tasks, organizational forms, and so forth. Not all of this is easy to explain in terms of standard arguments about the real functional requirements of modern development: It is still utterly unclear what actual (as opposed to culturally defined) functional requirements call for such occupations as sociologist or such organizations as therapeutic ones. Rationalistic models not only helped justify the evolution of these minor institutions but also played a role in the historically crucial early Western institutionalization of the capitalist class. Thus, the modern tendency toward extreme differentiation of roles may reflect cultural legitimating pressures as much as instrumental functional requirements; this might help explain the exceptional differentiation characteristic of egalitarian U.S. society in contrast to some other modern systems.

Second, strong and highly culturally theorized notions of progress and the collective good help explain the homogeneity of modern stratification regimes (across country and time) despite great heterogeneity in immediate circumstances. The finding that occupational prestige systems and mobility regimes are relatively homogeneous has been an overpowering surprise in the research literature. One explanation has been a very broad functional image, but this makes little sense in light of the extreme variations in any plausible functional requirements among modern societies. A more realistic explanation is to see the cultural (functional) theories of modernity as widespread and as generating a good deal of stratificational isomorphism: National communities vary enormously, but modern stratification is legitimated in terms of ideal pictures of society, and these models are highly homogeneous (e.g., Anderson 1991 calls most modern societies "imagined communities"). This would also help explain why stratificational change (e.g., in the status of women or ethnic minorities, in the welfare correctives for the class structure, or in educational opportunity) tends to be global in character (Thomas et al. 1987).

Third, the institutionalization of ideas of rationality and progress can help explain the surprising worldwide rise of education as the critical dimension in all modern stratification systems. Education provides a clear legitimating account of sources of improved capacity and also locates this capacity in specific persons and groups (Meyer 1977). Thus, ascriptive and income/power considerations and even some of the functional ones of occupation tend to be replaced by education as the main dimension of status: Education tends to correlate more highly with more outcomes than the other dimensions do, and intergenerational educational correlations are usually higher than the others. Empirical researchers routinely build education into their measures, but both researchers and theorists are slow to let go of their nineteenth-century (cultureless) models of society and continue to use terms like *class* or *socioeconomic status* when education is the main phenomenon at issue in their measures. This peculiarity of labeling variables in modern stratification research is quite revealing of its ideological base in modern culture.

The worldwide rise in educational certification for all sorts of social positions has been discussed as resulting from functional requirements; this is the approach taken in the chapters above (especially those by Bell, Gouldner, Nee, and Kerr and his colleagues). However, critics have noted the utter absence of evidence of such requirements and have seen the expansion as resulting instead from conflict processes (Collins 1979). The conflict explanation is incomplete. Why would so many forces make education, as opposed to other institutional settings, the new arena of competition and conflict? Education becomes the competitive arena in part because myths of rational progress have made educational institutions culturally central.

Finally, we may note the extraordinary—and in the main, unpredicted—rise of the service sector and its new classes: This, along with the rise of education, is the main theme of the chapters above, and in fact integrates them all. By and large, the essays attribute the expansion of the service sector to the functional requirements of the complex society. This is unconvincing because of the absence of empirical evidence that expanded service sectors are indeed functional in this sense. It becomes yet more unconvincing when one realizes that the expansion of the service sector is worldwide—little predicted by the evolutionary development of complexity. Some social theories attribute great feats of power and manipulation to the professions and the state but give no real explanation about where the power and capacity come from. The cultural commitments to rational progress previously noted may provide some explanation for why societies supposedly dominated by their economies (Marx) or their state bureaucracies (Weber) in fact turn out to have the professions (analogous to, of all things, a priesthood) as their leading groups.

Effects of Individualism

There have been several effects of the institutionalization of individualism and equality on stratification. A first consequence is the expansion of social citizenship and of the dimensions of social life it comprehends. Stratification theorists have been so engrossed in the normative search for illicit inequality as to have avoided noticing the rise and expansion of a most important social status in terms of which all are formally equal. For example, Parsons (1970), until his last discussion of stratification, essentially omitted citizenship as an element. With the exception of Esping-Andersen and Pakulski and Waters (who treat the standard of equality as culturally constructed), the scholars represented here simply take for granted that persons are or should be naturally equal, and that inequalities are problematic and require justification. The chapters are written as if this point of view is special to the authors, rather than one of the most widespread cultural principles in the whole modern world, in which the banner of human rights has the highest standing.

Clearly, citizenship is now one of the more important dimensions of status throughout the world—and on such dependent variables as income perhaps the most important one. Obviously, claims for its expansion (in more welfare arenas) have been continuous throughout the modern period (and have tended to increase inequality among citizens of different countries and thus to redefine world stratification). Second, the importance of individual equality has tended to expand education. Not only is education the crucial certifier of inequality, but mass education is a most important constructor of equality as well. Third,

the importance of individual equality has produced considerable expansion of protection of young and old persons (including extensions of personhood to prenatal periods). In this area, as in others, the rise of professional protectors and the growth of organizations with some type of protective agenda have been the most prominent developments.

Equal Persons, Unequal Roles

We next consider the impact of simultaneous emphases on equal individuals and unequal contributions to rational progress. Many observers have noted that the dualistic Western (and now worldwide) emphasis on both individual and collective good has been a mobilizing dynamic in modern history. We consider a few ways in which this works out for stratification.

Role Differentiation. The simultaneous stress on the inequality of activities (i.e., societywide coordination) and the equality of persons generates a great deal of role differentiation. As already noted, theorists such as the authors of the chapters included here have tended to understate the cultural bases of such differentiation. However, differentiation clearly has served to protect central myths in the modern system in two ways: (1) Elaborate role differentiation and the tight organization of activity systems (e.g., in such arrangements as modern formal organizations) help to sustain functional myths and to define activity as primarily linked to social tasks rather than personal status, and (2) more important, the modern system notoriously differentiates activities and roles from persons.

The second point is critical because all sorts of functional roots of this in efficiency pressures (for the most part, unproven) are alleged by the theorists. It is more important to note how much such individual/activity differentiations help sustain the principle of individual equality. In a modern system, we can have a societywide coordination of activity (e.g., public tax policy or other political and economic decision making) implying the utter domination of the activities of millions or billions of people by the activities of a few, without any serious violation of the normative stratificational principle of equality. In a system of this kind, the activities control each other but not the persons: Differentiation is crucial to sustaining the principle of individual equality.

Consider how this works out in terms of measures of income inequality. As Lenski (1966) noted, agrarian societies (e.g., medieval states) had very high levels of income inequality; the disparity is greatly lowered by the modern system. However, in the medieval world all the income of the state was attributed to the king personally, so that the king appeared to be very rich. In the modern world, a differentiation is established: A president gets only a modestly high salary (higher than the best sociologists but lower than the best economists) personally but may control a monumental budget as a property of the presidential role. If this budget were attributed to the president personally, as in medieval accounting, the modern system would show enormously high levels of inequality (a typical head of a modern state would be recorded as having up to half the national income). Neither the medieval accounting nor the modern differentiated one is wrong: The point is that because a great change in organizational accounting has occurred, enormous societywide political control can result with only modest levels of accounted interpersonal inequality.

As a result of the modern differentiation between person and role, decreasing proportions of monetary flows are recorded as individual income, and the well-known growth in all sorts of corporate actors occurs. Our point is that one pressure in this direction arises from the modern demand for individual equality, combined with the modern pressures for rationalization and progress. Differentiation permits increasingly equal individuals in a system of increasingly unequal and ordered activities: It involves, of course, an elaborate modern differentiation between the tastes and motives attributed to persons and those attributed to organizations (Meyer 1986).

Consider how both forms of differentiation—between persons and roles and between different roles—help sustain equality in a modern organization like a university. Some equalities in status and salary among professors are maintained, but some professors may control huge research grants, hiring many servants and much equipment; in both social custom and in tax law, this is not attributed to their persons but to their roles. Further, if the inequalities among professorial roles become too great, a further differentiation occurs, such that the wealth of one professor is located in a specialized institute and controlled by the professor as director of the institute. This control can produce social accountings reflecting great equality of income and power among the professors as persons but great inequality among their roles or activities.

The role differentiation of the modern system (between roles and between roles and persons) solves cultural problems related to stratification theory and can be seen as having cultural or legitimating significance. A sociologically realist perspective treats all this differentiation as arising step-by-step out of the pressures of organizational life. Such a perspective has great difficulty explaining why similar differentiation occurs in many different places (regardless of variation in local problems or needs), is hard pressed to explain the fact that much of the differentiation seems only symbolic in character, and must resort to unsubstantiated arguments about the presumed efficiencies involved in differentiation. The idea employed here—that the functional theory involved is acting as a cultural principle—simplifies the problem.

What are the mechanisms by which cultural commitments produce this sort of differentiation? In our argument, they occur through the relatively articulate and explicit activity of collective actors: public political elites, intellectual and professional theorists, and the like. Modern systems are constantly under scrutiny by cultural theorists looking for precisely such illicit inequalities. Both tax laws and common opinion may penalize the insufficient differentiation of personal and organizational resources and reward instances of clear and "rational" differentiation.

The Rise of Educational Credentialism. The tension between equal individuals and unequal roles can be seen as one of the sources of ever-expanding educational credentialism and its related institutions. More and more social boundaries and mechanisms are installed to keep the structural inconsistency involved maintained. There are the educational credentials themselves, which can be used to legitimate the allocation of formally equal individuals to unequal roles. The legitimation problem then reduces to accounting for inter-individual variations in the "investment" in education. There is no shortage of ancillary social theories with this orientation. Moreover, there are also theories of variations in abilities as well as in tastes that treat role differentiation as a matter of individual choice. Such effects work through the mechanism of relatively articulate collective consciousness and action. Clearly, many groups advocate, and states often require, the replacement of less legitimated and more ascriptive criteria of role entry by educational credentials. This is argued to indicate merit, to deserve public respect and trust, and thus to enhance legitimate status.

The Personnel Society. All of these characteristics are institutionalized in an expanding modern personnel bureaucracy. A surprising feature of modern organizational development, from the point of view of most theories, has been the elaboration of the citizenship of persons within organizations. Many individual rights have expanded to provide organizational protection of individuals from potentially threatening inequalities. Such bureaucracy is seen as both more progressive and more just.

Conclusions

Two closely related themes arise from our discussion. One conclusion is about modern societies: Many aspects of their stratification systems reflect cultural properties of the modern system, as with the expansion of education, the service sector, the personnel bureaucracy, and so forth. This was mostly unexpected by theorists emphasizing the economic or political realism of the modern system: From their point of view, much of the modern social structure reflects distortion, false consciousness, or mystification. The theories tend to be mistaken, precisely in their inattention to the modern system's sensitivity to and cultural analysis of its own stratification system.

A second conclusion is that the underlying culture of the modern stratification system is closely tied to the social-scientific analyses we call stratification theory. The obsessions of theory (e.g., with individual inequality and with the distinction between just and functional inequalities and unjust or power and ascription-ridden ones) are the main cultural themes of modern stratification.

These cultural commitments in fact drive social change. This can help explain many of the puzzling aspects of modern stratification regimes: their homogeneity across time and space, their constant shifts toward education and the service sector, their high levels of differentiation among roles (and especially between roles and persons), and the worldwide expansion in citizenship statuses.

We can illustrate these points by noting that in recent decades, the world itself has come to be conceptualized as a unitary social system or society. The shift to such a conception is rapidly changing public and scientific stratification analyses: Distinctions among individuals in different countries now require rectification (from the point of view of both dependency and human rights ideologies), and a differentiated set of world institutions is rapidly developing. The ultimate goal of stratification theories—both lay and scientific—is no longer the articulation of equal individual personhood combined with social progress at the nation-state level; a bigger arena will presumably undercut some of the structures of the older one. For example, it may delegitimate some efforts to produce equality within

developed nation-states at the cost of enhanced international inequality.

Note

This paper benefited from useful comments on earlier drafts by David Grusky, Ron Jepperson, David
Strang, Marc Ventresca, and members of the Stanford Stratification Seminar.

References

Anderson, Benedict. 1991. *Imagined Communities.* 2nd ed. London:Verso.

Berg, Ivar. 1971. *Education and Jobs: The Great
Training Robbery.* Boston: Beacon.

Collins, Randall. 1979. *The Credential Society: A
Historical Sociology of Education and Stratification.* New York: Academic Press.

Hall, John. 1986. *Powers and Liberties.* New
York: Penguin.

Lenski, Gerhard. 1966. *Power and Privilege.* New
York: McGraw-Hill.

Mann, Michael. 1986. *The Sources of Social
Power.* Cambridge: Cambridge University
Press.

Meyer, John. 1977. "The Effects of Education as
an Institution." *American Journal of Sociology*
83(July):55–77.

———.1986. "The Self and the Life Course."
Pages 199–216 in *Human Development and the
Life Course,* edited by A. B. Sørensen, F. E.
Weinert, and L. R. Sherrod. Hillside, NJ: Erl-
baum.

———.1989. "Conceptions of Christendom."
Pages 395–413 in *Cross-National Research in
Sociology,* edited by M. Kohn. Newbury Park:
Sage.

Ossowski, Stanislaw. 1963. *Class Structure in the
Social Consciousness.* New York: Free Press.

Parsons, Talcott. 1970. "Equality and Inequality
in Modern Society, or Social Stratification Revisited." Pages 13–72 in *Social Stratification*
edited by Edward Laumann. Indianapolis:
Bobbs-Merrill.

Rawls, John. 1971. *A Theory of Justice.* Cambridge: Belknap.

Thomas, George, John Meyer, Francisco Ramirez,
and John Boli. 1987. *Institutional Structure.*
Newbury Park: Sage.

Credits

PART I

1. This is an original article prepared for this book.

PART II

2. Kingsley Davis and Wilbert E. Moore, "Some Principles of Stratification," *American Sociological Review* 10 (April 1945), pp. 242–49.

3. Melvin M. Tumin, "Some Principles of Stratification: A Critical Analysis," *American Sociological Review* 18 (August 1953), pp. 387–94.

4. Claude S. Fischer, Michael Hout, Martín Sánchez Jankowski, Samuel R. Lucas, Ann Swidler, and Kim Voss, *Inequality by Design*, pp. 7–10, 126–28, 241, 260–61, 279–80, 284, 286, 290, 292, 295, 299, 301. Copyright © 1996 by Princeton University Press. Reprinted by permission of Princeton University Press.

5. This is an original article prepared for this book.

PART III

6. Karl Marx, "The Economic and Philosophical Manuscripts," in *Karl Marx: Early Writings*, edited and translated by T. B. Bottomore, pp. 121–31. Copyright © 1963 by McGraw-Hill. Reprinted by permission of McGraw-Hill. "The Holy Family: A Critique of Critical Criticism," in *The Marx-Engels Reader*, edited and translated by Robert C. Tucker, pp. 133–35. Copyright © 1978, 1972 by W. W. Norton & Company, Inc. Used by permission of W. W. Norton & Company.

7. Karl Marx, "The Communist Manifesto," in *Selected Works*, Vol. I (Moscow: Progress Publishers, 1964), pp. 108–119. Reprinted by permission of Progress Publishers. *The Poverty of Philosophy* (New York: International Publishers, 1963), pp. 172–75. Reprinted by permission of International Publishers. "The Eighteenth Brumaire of Louis Bonaparte," in *Selected Works*, Vol. I (Moscow: Progress Publishers, 1963), pp. 478–79. Reprinted by permission of Progress Publishers. *Capital*, Vol. III (Moscow: Progress Publishers, 1967), pp. 885–86. Reprinted by permission of Progress Publishers.

8. C. J. Arthur, ed., *The German Ideology* (New York: International Publishers, 1970), pp. 64–66. Reprinted by permission of International Publishers.

9. Karl Marx, "Wages, Price, and Profit," in *Selected Works*, Vol. II (Moscow: Progress Publishers, 1969), pp. 49, 56–59. Reprinted by permission of Progress Publishers.

10. Ralf Dahrendorf, *Class and Class Conflict in Industrial Society*, pp. 41–43, 47–48, 50–51, 64–67, 165–67, 170–73. Copyright © 1959 by the Board of Trustees of the Leland Stanford Junior University. Reprinted with the permission of Stanford University Press.

11. Eric Olin Wright, "Varieties of Marxist Conceptions of Class Structure," *Politics and Society* 9 (1980), pp. 328–33. Copyright © 1980 by Sage Publications, Inc. Reprinted by permission of Sage Publications, Inc.

12. Eric Olin Wright, "A General Framework for the Analysis of Class Structure," *Politics and Society* 13 (1984), pp. 383–97, 399–402, 417–22. Copyright © 1984 by Sage Publications, Inc. Reprinted by permission of Sage Publications, Inc.

13. Immanuel Wallerstein, "Class Conflict in the Capitalist World-Economy" in *The Capitalist World-Economy* (Cambridge: Cambridge University Press, 1979), pp. 285–86, 291–93. Copyright © 1979 by Immanuel Wallerstein. Reprinted by permission of the author.

14. Max Weber, "Class, Status, Party," in *From Max Weber: Essays in Sociology*, edited by H. H. Gerth & C. Wright Mills, and translated by H. H. Gerth & C. Wright Mills, pp. 180–95. Translation copyright © 1946, 1958 by H. H. Gerth and C. Wright Mills. Used by permission of Oxford University Press, Inc.

15. Max Weber, *The Theory of Social and Economic Organization*, translated by A. M. Henderson and Talcott Parsons, pp. 424–29. Copyright © 1947 by Talcott Parsons; copyright renewed in 1975 by Talcott Parsons. Reprinted with the permission of the Free Press, a Division of Simon and Schuster, Inc.

16. Guenther Roth and Claus Wittich, eds., *Economy and Society, Vol. 1*, pp. 43–46, 341–42, 344. Copyright © 1968 by Taylor & Francis Books, Ltd. Used by permission of Routledge Ltd.

17. Max Weber, *From Max Weber: Essays in Sociology*, edited by H. H. Gerth & C. Wright Mills, and translated by H. H. Gerth & C. Wright Mills, pp. 240–43. Translation copyright © 1946, 1958 by H. H. Gerth and C. Wright Mills. Used by permission of Oxford University Press, Inc.

18. Anthony Giddens, *The Class Structure of the Advanced Societies*, pp. 41–44, 47–49, 102–12. Copyright © 1973 by Anthony Giddens. Reprinted by permission of HarperCollins Publishers, Inc.

19. Frank Parkin, *Marxism and Class Theory: A Bourgeois Critique*, pp. 11–13, 23–25, 27–28, 44–50, 53–58, 62–64, 67–73, 112–13. Copyright © 1979 by Taylor & Francis Books, Ltd. Used by permission of Taylor and Francis Books, Ltd., and Columbia University Press.

20. Emile Durkheim, *The Division of Labor in Society*, with an introduction by Lewis A. Coser, and translated by W. D. Halls, pp. xxxi, xxxii, xxxv, xxxix-xl, xlii-xlv, l-lv, lviii-lix. Introduction copyright © 1984 by Lewis A. Coser. Translation copyright © 1984 by The Higher & Further Education Division, MacMillan Publishers, Ltd. Reprinted with the permission of The Free Press, a Division of Simon and Schuster, Inc.

21. David B. Grusky and Jesper B. Sørensen, "Can Class Analysis Be Salvaged?" *American Journal of Sociology* 103 (1998), pp. 1187–234. Copyright © 1998 by The University of Chicago Press. Used by permission of The University of Chicago Press.

22. Arthur Livingston, ed., *The Ruling Class*, translated by Hannah D. Kahn (New York: McGraw-Hill, 1939), pp. 50–54, 56–62, 65–66. Copyright © by Elizabeth Abbott.

23. C. Wright Mills, *The Power Elite*, pp. 3–18, 20–23, 365–67. Copyright © 1956 by C. Wright Mills. Renewed 1984 by Yaraslave Mills. Used by permission of Oxford University Press.

24. Anthony Giddens, *The Class Structure of the Advanced Societies*, pp. 118–24. Copyright © 1973 by Anthony Giddens. Reprinted by permission of HarperCollins Publishers, Inc.

25. Edward A. Shils, "The Political Class in the Age of Mass Society: Collectivistic Liberalism and Social Democracy," in *Does Who Governs Matter? Elite Circulation in Contemporary Societies*, edited by Moshe Czudnowski, pp. 16–18, 20–22, 27–32. Copyright © 1982 by Northern Illinois University Press.

26. Michael Useem, *The Inner Circle: Large Corporations and the Rise of Business Political Activity in the U.S. and U.K.*, pp. 3–6, 9–16, 59–61, 74–75, 201–2, 206–7. Copyright © 1984 by Oxford University Press, Inc. Used by permission of Oxford University Press, Inc.

27. Gil Eyal, Iván Szelényi, and Eleanor Townsley, *Making Capitalism without Capitalists: The New Ruling Elites in Eastern Europe*, pp. 14–15, 113–15, 117, 119–21, 151–52, 230, 243. Copyright © 1998 by Verso Press. Used by permission of Verso Press.

28. W. Lloyd Warner, *Social Class in America*, p. 5, 11–21, 23–24. Copyright © 1960 by Harper & Row Publishers. Reprinted with permission of HarperCollins Publishers, Inc.

29. Edward A. Shils, "Deference," in *Social Stratification*, edited by J. A. Jackson, pp. 104–8, 115–17, 119–22, 126–29. Copyright © 1968 by Cambridge University Press. Used by permission of Cambridge University Press.

30. Peter M. Blau and Otis Dudley Duncan, *The American Occupational Structure*, pp. 118–24. Copyright © 1967 by Peter M. Blau and Otis Dudley Duncan. Reprinted with the permission of The Free Press, a Division of Simon & Schuster, Inc.

31. Donald J. Treiman, "A Standard Occupational Prestige Scale for Use with Historical Data," *The Journal of Interdisciplinary History* VII (1976), pp. 285–90. Copyright © 1976 by the editors of *The Journal of Interdisciplinary History* and the Massachusetts Institute of Technology. Reprinted with the permission of the editors of *The Journal of Interdisciplinary History* and The MIT Press, Cambridge, Massachusetts.

Part IV

48. Jay MacLeod, *Ain't No Makin' It: Leveled Aspirations in a Low-Income Neighborhood* (Boulder: Westview Press, 1987), pp. 1–2, 4–5, 8, 60–63, 69–75, 78–79, 81, 137–41, 162. Copyright © 1987 by Westview Press, Inc. Reprinted by permission of Westview Press, Inc., a member of the Perseus Books Group.

49. Michael J. Piore, "The Dual Labor Market: Theory and Implications," in *The State and the Poor* (Cambridge, Mass.: Winthrop Publishers, 1970), edited by Samuel H. Beer and Richard E. Barringer, pp. 55–59.

50. Aage B. Sørensen and Arne L. Kalleberg, "An Outline of a Theory of the Matching of Persons to Jobs," in *Sociological Perspectives on Labor Markets,* edited by Ivar Berg, pp. 49–57, 65–69, 72–74. Copyright © 1981 by Academic Press. Reprinted by permission of the publisher. All rights of reproduction in any form reserved.

51. Mark S. Granovetter, "The Strength of Weak Ties," *American Journal of Sociology* 78 (May 1973), pp. 1361–66, 1371–73, 1378–80. Copyright © 1973 by The University of Chicago Press. Used by permission of the University of Chicago Press and the author.

52. Nan Lin, "Social Networks and Status Attainment," *Annual Review of Sociology* 25 (1999), pp. 467–70, 485–87. Copyright © 1999 by Annual Review of Sociology. Used by permission.

53. Ronald S. Burt, "The Contingent Value of Social Capital," *Administrative Science Quarterly* 42 (June 1997), pp. 339–43, 363–65. Copyright © 1997 by *Administrative Science Quarterly.* Used by permission.

54. Richard Breen and John H. Goldthorpe, "Explaining Educational Differentials: Towards a Formal Rational Action Theory," *Rationality and Society* 9 (August 1997), pp. 275–87, 293–300, 302–5. Copyright © 1997 by Sage Publications, Ltd. Used by permission of Sage Publications, Ltd., and the authors.

55. John Allen Logan, "Rational Choice and the TSL Model of Occupational Opportunity," *Rationality and Society* 8 (May 1996), pp. 207–15, 229–30. Copyright © 1996 by Sage Publications, Ltd. Used by permission of Sage Publications, Ltd.

56. This is an original article prepared for this book.

PART V

57. Thorstein Veblen, *The Theory of the Leisure Class* (Boston: Houghton Mifflin Company, 1973), pp. 35–36, 38–43, 61, 65–72, 94, 98. Copyright © 1973 by Houghton Mifflin Company. Used by permission of Houghton Mifflin.

58. Pierre Bourdieu, *Distinction: A Social Critique of the Judgement of Taste* (Cambridge, Mass: Harvard University Press, 1984), pp. 114–15, 128–29, 169–80, 183–97, 199–202, 206–9, 503, 519–21, 523, 572–76. Copyright © 1984 by the President and Fellows of Harvard University Press and Routledge and Kegan Paul, Ltd. Reprinted by permission of the publishers and of Routledge and Kegan Paul, Ltd.

59. Michael Hout, Jeff Manza, and Clem Brooks, "Classes, Unions, and the Realignment of U.S. Presidential Voting, 1952–1992," in *The End of Class Politics? Class Voting in Comparative Perspective,* edited by Geoffrey Evans, pp. 83–90, 95. Copyright © 1999 by Oxford University Press. Used by permission of Oxford University Press.

60. Melvin L. Kohn, "Job Complexity and Adult Personality," in *Themes of Work and Love in Adulthood* (Cambridge, Mass.: Harvard University Press, 1980), edited by Neil J. Smelser and Erik H. Erikson, pp. 193–210. Copyright © 1980 by the President and Fellows of Harvard University Press. Reprinted by permission of the publisher.

61. This is an original article prepared for this book.

PART VI

62. Edna Bonacich, "A Theory of Ethnic Antagonism: The Split Labor Market," *American Sociological Review* (October 1972), pp. 547–59. Copyright © 1972 by the American Sociological Association. Used by permission of the American Sociological Association and the author.

63. Alejandro Portes and Robert D. Manning, "The Immigrant Enclave: Theory and Empirical Exam-

81. Trond Petersen and Laurie A. Morgan, "Separate and Unequal: Occupation-Establishment Sex Segregation and the Gender Wage Gap," *American Journal of Sociology* 101 (September 1995), pp. 329–61. Copyright © 1995 by the University of Chicago Press. Reprinted by permission of the University of Chicago Press and the authors.

82. Margaret Mooney Marini and Pi-Ling Fan, "The Gender Gap in Earnings at Career Entry," *American Sociological Review* 62 (August 1997), pp. 588–604. Copyright © 1997 by the American Sociological Association. Reprinted by permission of the American Sociological Association.

83. Barbara Stanek Kilbourne, Paula England, George Farkas, Kurt Beron, and Dorothea Weir, "Returns to Skill, Compensating Differentials, and Gender Bias: Effects of Occupational Characteristics on the Wages of White Women and Men," *American Journal of Sociology* 100 (November 1994), pp. 689–706, 708–9, 717–19. Copyright © 1994 by the University of Chicago Press. Reprinted by permission of the University of Chicago Press and the authors.

84. Tony Tam, "Sex Segregation and Occupational Gender Inequality in the United States: Devaluation or Specialized Training?" *American Journal of Sociology* 102 (May 1997), pp. 1652–92. Copyright © 1997 by the University of Chicago Press. Reprinted by permission of the University of Chicago Press and the author.

85. This is an original article prepared for this book.

PART VII

86. Clark Kerr, John T. Dunlop, Frederick H. Harbison, and Charles A. Myers, *Industrialism and Industrial Man* (Cambridge, Mass.: Harvard University Press, 1960), pp. 15–27, 232–39, 251–52. Copyright © 1960 by the President and Fellows of Harvard University Press. Copyright © renewed 1988 by the President and Fellows of Harvard University Press. Reprinted by permission of the publisher and Clark Kerr.

87. Daniel Bell, *The Coming of Post-Industrial Society*, pp. xvi-xix, 13–14, 358–64, 374–78, 408–10, 445–46. Copyright © 1973 by Daniel Bell. Foreword copyright © 1976 by Daniel Bell. Reprinted by permission of Basic Books, a member of the Perseus Books Group.

88. Alvin W. Gouldner, *The Future of Intellectuals and the Rise of the New Class* (New York: Continuum Publishing Service, 1979), pp. 1–8, 18–20, 28–29, 48–53, 83–85, 102–4, 106, 110, 112–13. Reprinted by permission of Continuum International Publishing Group.

89. Gøsta Esping-Andersen, *Social Foundations of Postindustrial Economies*, pp. 95–96, 101–4, 106–16, 119, 170–73, 178–80, 182–93, 195–200. Copyright © 1999 by Oxford University Press. Reprinted by permission of Oxford University Press.

90. Victor Nee, "The Emergence of a Market Society: Changing Mechanisms of Stratification in China," *American Journal of Sociology* 101 (January 1996), pp. 908–49. Copyright © 1996 by the University of Chicago Press. Reprinted by permission of the University of Chicago Press.

91. Gil Eyal, Iván Szelényi, and Eleanor Townsley, *Making Capitalism without Capitalists: The New Ruling Elites in Eastern Europe*, pp. 1–2, 6–7, 32–33, 160–63, 229–31, 247–48. Copyright © 1998 by Verso Press. Reprinted by permission of Verso Press.

92. Stuart Hall, "The Meaning of New Times," in *New Times: The Changing Face of Politics in the 1990s*, edited by Stuart Hall and Martin Jacques, pp. 116–25, 128–30, 133–34. Copyright © 1989 by Lawrence & Wishart. Reprinted by permission of Lawrence & Wishart.

93. Jan Pakulski and Malcolm Waters, *The Death of Class*, pp. 1–5, 24–26, 153–58, 160–64, 166–68. Copyright © 1996 by Sage Publications, Ltd. Reprinted with the permission of Sage Publications, Ltd., and the authors.

94. Martina Morris and Bruce Western, "Inequality in Earnings at the Close of the Twentieth Century," *Annual Review of Sociology* 25, pp. 623–57. Copyright © 1999 by Annual Reviews, www.AnnualReviews.org. Reprinted by permission of Annual Reviews.

95. This is an original article prepared for this book.

Supplementary Information on Sources and Excerpting

Emile Durkheim, "The Division of Labor in Society." The text excerpted here was altered in minor ways to make the transition between sections smoother.

David B. Grusky and Jesper B. Sørensen, "Are There Big Social Classes?" This is a commissioned chapter that draws heavily on material in a previously published article ("Can Class Analysis be Salvaged?" *American Journal of Sociology* 103, pp. 1187–234, 1998).

Michael Useem, "The Inner Circle." The excerpts included here are not presented in the same order as they appear in the original.

Gil Eyal, Iván Szelényi, and Eleanor Townsley, "Post-Communist Managerialism." The excerpts included here are not presented in the same order as they appear in the original.

Robert M. Hauser and John Robert Warren, "Socioeconomic Indexes for Occupations: A Review, Update, and Critique." This is a commissioned chapter that draws heavily on material in a previously published article ("Socioeconomic Indexes of Occupational Status: A Review, Update, and Critique," *Sociological Methodology, 1997,* pp. 177–298, 1997).

Aage B. Sørensen, "The Basic Concepts of Stratification Research: Class, Status, and Power." This chapter is a slightly revised version of the same-titled chapter appearing in the first edition of *Social Stratification: Class, Race, and Gender in Sociological Perspective*. The revisions were drafted by the editor (in consultation with Jesper B. Sørensen) because the author, Aage B. Sørensen, was still unwell at the time of the writing of the second edition.

Pitirim A. Sorokin, "Social and Cultural Mobility." For the purpose of conserving space, all discussion of quantitative results were omitted from this selection, and some of the section headings were relocated as well.

David B. Grusky and Robert M. Hauser, "Comparative Social Mobility Revisited."
The excerpts included here are not presented in the same order as they appear in the original.

Robert Erikson and John H. Goldthorpe, "Trends in Class Mobility: The Post-War European Experience." This chapter, although closely related to material appearing in *The Constant Flux*, was originally prepared as a paper for the European Research Conference, "European Society or European Societies," Gausdal, Norway, November 24–27, 1991.

Jay MacLeod, "Ain't No Makin' It: Leveled Aspirations in a Low-Income Neighborhood." The postcript to this selection is taken from *Ain't No Makin' It: Leveled Aspirations in a Low-Income Neighborhood* (Boulder: Westview Press, 1995), pp. 155, 169–70, 196, 240–41. Copyright © 1995 by Westview Press, Inc. Reprinted by permission of Westview Press, a member of the Perseus Books Group.

Aage B. Sørensen and Arne L. Kalleberg, "An Outline of a Theory of the Matching of Persons to Jobs." The excerpts included here are not presented in the same order as they appear in the original.

Pierre Bourdieu, "Distinction: A Social Critique of the Judgement of Taste." This chapter is based on survey data collected by Pierre Bourdieu and on additional complementary data sources (denoted in the text by C.S. I – C.S. V). The passages reproduced in sans serif type, set off by rules, contain "illustrative examples or discussion of ancillary issues" (Bourdieu, *Distinction*, p. xiii). For the purpose of conserving space, many of these passages were excised, as were some of the more detailed tables.

Melvin L. Oliver and Thomas M. Shapiro, "Black Wealth/White Wealth: A New Perspective on Racial Inequality." The excerpts included here are not presented in the same order as they appear in the original.

Herbert J. Gans, "The Possibility of a New Racial Hierarchy in the Twenty-first-century United States." The excerpts included here are not presented in the same order as they appear in the original.

Trond Petersen and Laurie A. Morgan, "The Within-Job Gender Wage Gap." This is a commissioned chapter that draws heavily on material in a previously published article ("Separate and Unequal: Occupation-Establishment Sex Segregation and the Gender Wage Gap," *American Journal of Sociology* 101, pp. 329–61, 1995).

Tony Tam, "Why Do Female Occupations Pay Less?" This is a commissioned chapter that draws heavily on material in a previously published article ("Sex Segregation and Occupational Gender Inequality in the United States: Devaluation or Specialized Training?" *American Journal of Sociology* 102, pp. 1652–92, 1997).

Victor Nee, "Postsocialist Stratification." This is a commissioned chapter that draws heavily on material in a previously published article ("The Emergence of a Market Society: Changing Mechanisms of Stratification in China," *American Journal of Sociology* 101, pp. 908–49, 1996).

Gil Eyal, Iván Szelényi, and Eleanor Townsley, "Making Capitalism Without Capitalists." The excerpts included here are not presented in the same order as they appear in the original.

Martina Morris and Bruce Western, "Inequality in Earnings: Trends and Implications." This is a commissioned chapter that draws heavily on material in a previously published article ("Inequality in Earnings at the Close of the Twentieth Century," *Annual Review of Sociology* 25, pp. 623–57, 1999).

Index

Page numbers in followed by "f" indicate illustrations; page numbers followed by "t" indicate tabular material.

About the Editor

David B. Grusky is Director of the Center for the Study of Inequality, Professor of Sociology at Cornell University, and former National Science Foundation Presidential Young Investigator. He is currently studying the rise and fall of social classes under advanced industrialism, the underlying structure of occupational segregation by sex, race, and ethnicity, the sources of modern and postmodern attitudes toward gender inequality, and long-term trends in patterns of occupational and geographic mobility. He is coeditor (with James Baron and Don Treiman) of *Social Differentiation and Social Inequality* and coauthor (with Maria Charles) of the forthcoming book, *Sex Segregation in Comparative Perspective*.